International
Business

Competing in the Global Marketplace

13e

Charles W.L. Hill

UNIVERSITY OF WASHINGTON

INTERNATIONAL BUSINESS

Published by McGraw-Hill Education, 2 Penn Plaza, New York, NY 10121. Copyright © 2021 by McGraw-Hill Education. All rights reserved. Printed in Singapore. No part of this publication may be reproduced or distributed in any form or by any means, or stored in a database or retrieval system, without the prior written consent of McGraw-Hill Education, including, but not limited to, in any network or other electronic storage or transmission, or broadcast for distance learning.

Some ancillaries, including electronic and print components, may not be available to customers outside the United States.

This book is printed on acid-free paper.

6 7 8 9 MPM 21

ISBN 978-1-260-57586-6
MHID 1-260-57586-1

Cover Image: *Buslik/Shutterstock*

Printed in Singapore

mheducation.com/highered

For my children, **Elizabeth, Charlotte,** and **Michelle**

—Charles W. L. Hill

about the AUTHOR

Charles W. L. Hill
University of Washington

Charles W. L. Hill is the Hughes M. and Katherine Blake Professor of Strategy and International Business in the Foster School of Business at the University of Washington. Professor Hill has taught in the Management, MBA, Executive MBA, Technology Management MBA, and PhD programs at the University of Washington. During his time at the University of Washington, he has received over 25 awards for teaching excellence, including the Charles E. Summer Outstanding Teaching Award.

A native of the United Kingdom, Professor Hill received his PhD from the University of Manchester, UK. In addition to the University of Washington, he has served on the faculties of the University of Manchester, Texas A&M University, and Michigan State University.

Professor Hill has published over 50 articles in top academic journals, including the *Academy of Management Journal, Academy of Management Review, Strategic Management Journal*, and *Organization Science.* Professor Hill has also published several textbooks, including *International Business* (McGraw-Hill) and *Global Business Today* (McGraw-Hill). His work is among the most widely cited in international business and strategic management.

Professor Hill works on a private basis with a number of organizations. His clients have included Microsoft, where he taught in-house executive education courses for two decades. He has also consulted for a variety of other large companies (e.g., AT&T Wireless, Boeing, BF Goodrich, Group Health, Hexcel, Philips Healthcare, Philips Medical Systems, Seattle City Light, Swedish Health Services, Tacoma City Light, Thompson Financial Services, WRQ, and Wizards of the Coast). Additionally, Dr. Hill has served on the advisory board of several start-up companies.

For recreation, Professor Hill enjoys skiing and competitive sailing!

brief CONTENTS

THE PROVEN CHOICE FOR INTERNATIONAL BUSINESS

RELEVANT. PRACTICAL. INTEGRATED.

It is now more than a quarter of a century since work began on the first edition of *International Business: Competing in the Global Marketplace.* By the third edition the book was the most widely used international business text in the world. Since then its market share has only increased. The success of the book can be attributed to a number of unique features. Specifically, for the thirteenth edition we have developed a learning program that

- Is comprehensive, state of the art, and timely.
- Is theoretically sound and practically relevant.
- Focuses on applications of international business concepts.
- Tightly integrates the chapter topics throughout.
- Is fully integrated with results-driven technology.
- Takes full and integrative advantage of globalEDGE. msu.edu–the Google-ranked #1 web resource for "international business resources."

International Business, now in its thirteenth edition, authored by Charles W. L. Hill, is a comprehensive and case-oriented version of our text that lends itself to the core course in international business for those courses that want a deeper focus on the global monetary system, structure of international business, international accounting, and international finance. We cover more and integrated cases in *International Business 13e* and we provide a deeper treatment of the global capital market, the organization of an international business, international accounting, and international finance–topics that are allocated chapters in *International Business 13e* but are not attended to in the shorter treatment of IB in *Global Business Today 11e.*

Like our shorter text, *Global Business Today 11e* (2019), *International Business 13e* focuses on being current, relevant, application rich, accessible, and student focused. Our goal has always been to cover macro and micro issues equally and in a relevant, practical, accessible, and student focused approach. We believe that anything short of such

a breadth and depth of coverage is a serious deficiency. Many of the students in these international business courses will soon be working in global businesses, and they will be expected to understand the implications of international business for their organization's strategy, structure, and functions in the context of the global marketplace. We are proud and delighted to have put together this international business learning experience for the leaders of tomorrow.

Over the years, and through now 13 editions, Dr. Charles Hill has worked hard to adhere to these goals. Since *Global Business Today 9e* (2015), and *International Business 11e* (2017), Charles has been guided not only by his own reading, teaching, and research but also by the invaluable feedback he receives from professors and students around the world, from reviewers, and from the editorial staff at McGraw-Hill Education. His thanks goes out to all of them.

COMPREHENSIVE AND UP-TO-DATE

To be relevant and comprehensive, an international business package must

- Explain how and why the world's cultures, countries, and regions differ.
- Cover economics and politics of international trade and investment.
- Tackle international issues related to ethics, corporate social responsibility, and sustainability.
- Explain the functions and form of the global monetary system.
- Examine the strategies and structures of international businesses.
- Assess the special roles of the various functions of an international business.

Relevance and comprehensiveness also require coverage of the major theories. It has always been a goal to incorporate the insights gleaned from recent academic scholarship into the book. Consistent with this goal, insights from the following research, as a sample of theoretical streams used in the book, have been incorporated:

- New trade theory and strategic trade policy.
- The work of Nobel Prize–winning economist Amartya Sen on economic development.
- Samuel Huntington's influential thesis on the "clash of civilizations."
- Growth theory of economic development championed by Paul Romer and Gene Grossman.
- Empirical work by Jeffrey Sachs and others on the relationship between international trade and economic growth.
- Michael Porter's theory of the competitive advantage of nations.
- Robert Reich's work on national competitive advantage.
- The work of Nobel Prize–winner Douglass North and others on national institutional structures and the protection of property rights.
- The market imperfections approach to foreign direct investment that has grown out of Ronald Coase and Oliver Williamson's work on transaction cost economics.
- Bartlett and Ghoshal's research on the transnational corporation.
- The writings of C. K. Prahalad and Gary Hamel on core competencies, global competition, and global strategic alliances.
- Insights for international business strategy that can be derived from the resource-based view of the firm and complementary theories.
- Paul Samuelson's critique of free trade theory.
- Conceptual and empirical work on global supply chain management—logistics, purchasing (sourcing), operations, and marketing channels.

In addition to including leading-edge theory, in light of the fast-changing nature of the international business environment, we have made every effort to ensure that this product is as up-to-date as possible. A significant amount has happened in the world since we began revisions of this book. By 2019, almost $4 trillion per day were flowing across national borders. The size of such flows fueled concern about the ability of short-term speculative shifts in global capital markets to destabilize the world economy.

The world continued to become more global. As you can see in Chapter 1 on Globalization, trade across country borders has almost exponentially escalated in the last few years. Several Asian economies, most notably China and India, continued to grow their economies at a rapid rate. New multinationals continued to emerge from developing nations in addition to the world's established industrial powers.

Increasingly, the globalization of the world economy affected a wide range of firms of all sizes, from the very large to the very small. We take great pride in covering international business for small- and medium-sized enterprises (SMEs), as well as larger multinational corporations. We also take great pride in covering firms from all around the world. Some sixty SMEs and multinational corporations from all six core continents are covered in the chapters' opening cases, closing cases, and/or Management Focus boxes.

And unfortunately, global terrorism and the attendant geopolitical risks keep emerging in various places globally, many new and inconceivable just a decade ago. These represent a threat to global economic integration and activity. Plus, with the United Kingdom opting to leave the European Union (Brexit), which has implications past 2019, the election of President Donald Trump in the United States (who espouses views on international trade that break with the long established consensus), and several elections around the world, the globe—in many ways—has paid more attention to nationalistic issues over trade. These topics and many more are integrated into this text for maximum learning opportunities.

What's New in the 13th Edition

The success of the first twelve editions of *International Business* was based in part on the incorporation of leading-edge research into the text, the use of the up-to-date examples and statistics to illustrate global trends and enterprise strategy, and the discussion of current events within the context of the appropriate theory. Building on these strengths, our goals for the twelfth edition have focused on the following:

1. Incorporate new insights from scholarly research.
2. Make sure the content covers all appropriate issues.
3. Make sure the text is up-to-date with current events, statistics, and examples.
4. Add new and insightful opening and closing cases in most chapters.
5. Incorporate value-added globalEDGE™ features in every chapter.
6. Connect every chapter to a focus on managerial implications.
7. Provide 20 new integrated cases that can be used as additional cases for specific chapters but, more importantly, as learning vehicles across multiple chapters.

As part of the overall revision process, changes have been made to every chapter in the book. All statistics have been updated to incorporate the most recently available data. As before, we are the only text in International Business that ensures that all material is up-to-date on virtually a daily basis. The copyright for the book is 2021 but you are likely using the text in 2020, 2021, or 2022–we keep it updated to each semester you use the text in your course! We are able to do this by integrating globalEDGE features in every chapter. Specifically, the Google number-one-ranked globaledge.msu.edu site (for "international business resources") is used in each chapter to add value to the chapter material and provide up-to-date data and information. This keeps chapter material constantly and dynamically updated for teachers who want to infuse globalEDGE material into the chapter topics, and it keeps students abreast of current developments in international business.

In addition to updating all statistics, figures, and maps to incorporate most recently published data, a chapter-by-chapter selection of changes for the 13th edition include the following:

Chapter 1: Globalization

- New opening case: How the iPhone is made: Apple's Global Production System
- Updated statistics and figures to incorporate the most recent data on global trade flows and foreign direct investment
- Discussion of the implications of recent political trends (Brexit and the Trump Presidency) and what this might mean for cross border trade and investment
- New closing case: General Motors in China

Chapter 2: National Differences In Political, Economic, and Legal Systems

- New opening case: Kenya: An African Lion
- Updated data on corruption
- New closing case: Transformation in Saudi Arabia

Chapter 3: National Differences In Economic Development

- New opening case: Poland: Eastern Europe's Economic Miracle
- Updated maps, figures, and in-text statistics to reflect most recently available data
- Addition of demographic trends to the discussion of Political Economy and Economic Progress

- Updated discussion of the spread of democracy to reflect recent countertrends toward greater authoritarianism in several nations (e.g., Turkey)
- New closing case: Brazil's Struggling Economy

Chapter 4: Differences In Culture

- New opening case: Singapore: One of the World's Most Multicultural Places
- Inclusion of a discussion of patience across cultures
- Revised the foundation that most religions are now pro-business
- New Country Focus: Determining Your Social Class by Birth
- New Country Focus: Turkey, Its Religion, and Politics
- New closing case: China, Hong Kong, Macau, and Taiwan

Chapter 5: Ethics, Corporate Social Responsibility, and Sustainability

- New opening case: Ericsson, Sweden, and Sustainability
- Deepened focus related to United Nations' Sustainable Development Goals
- Core focus on ethics as a lead-in to corporate social responsibility and sustainability issues (e.g., UN's Sustainable Development Goals).
- New closing case: Sustainability Initiatives at Natura, the Bodyshop, and Aesop

Chapter 6: International Trade Theory

- New opening case: A Tale of Two Nations: Ghana and South Korea
- Updated Country Focus on China and currency manipulation
- Reference to Donal Trump's trade policies under section on mercantilism
- New closing case: Trade Wars are Good and Easy to Win
- Updated balance of payments data in the Appendix to reflect 2018 data

Chapter 7: Government Policy and International Trade

- New opening case: American Steel Tariffs
- Updated discussion of the world trading system to reflect recent developments, including Brexit and the trade policies of President Trump

- New Management Focus: Exporting Desserts by a Hispanic Entrepreneur
- New Management Focus: Two Men and a Truck
- New closing case: Spotify and SoundCloud

Chapter 17: Global Production and Supply Chain Management

- New opening case: Blockchain Technology and Global Supply Chains
- New material on blockchain technology
- New Management Focus: IKEA Production in China
- New Management Focus: Amazon's Global Supply Chains
- New closing case: Procter & Gamble Remakes Its Global Supply Chains

Chapter 18: Global Marketing and Business Analytics

- New chapter title to signal significant new material on Business Analytics
- New opening case: Marketing Sneakers
- New section on Business Analytics
- Revised section: International Marketing Research
- Inclusion of more social media topics throughout
- New Management Focus: Global Branding, Marvel Studios, and Walt Disney Company
- New Management Focus: Burberry's Social Media Marketing
- New closing case: Fake News and Alternative Facts

Chapter 19: Global Human Resource Management

- New opening case: Evolution of the Kraft Heinz Company
- New section: Building a Diverse Global Workforce
- New Management Focus: AstraZeneca and Global Staffing Policy
- New closing case: Global Mobility at Shell

Chapter 20: Accounting and Finance in the International Business

- New opening case: Pfizer, Novartis, Bayer, and GlaxoSmithKline
- New material on the U.S. corporate tax rate and implications

- New Management Focus: Microsoft and Its Foreign Cash Holdings
- New closing case: Shoprite—Financial Success of a Food Retailer in Africa

Integrated Cases

All of the 20 integrated cases are new for *International Business 13e*. Many of these cases build on previous opening and closing chapter cases that have been revised, updated, and oftentimes adopted a new angle or focus. A unique feature of the opening and closing cases for the chapters as well as the integrated cases at the back-end of the text is that we cover all continents of the world and we do so with regional or country issues and large, medium, and small company scenarios. This makes the 60 total cases we have included in *International Business 13e* remarkably wealthy as a learning program.

- Globalization of BMW, Rolls-Royce, and the MINI
- The Decline of Zimbabwe
- Economic Development in Bangladesh
- The Swatch Group and Cultural Uniqueness
- Woolworths' Corporate Responsibility Strategy
- The Trans Pacific Partnership (TPP) is Dead: Long Live the CTPP!
- Boeing and Airbus Are in a Dogfight over Illegal Subsidies
- FDI in the Indian Retail Sector
- Free Trade in Africa
- The Mexican Peso, the Japanese Yen, and Pokemon Go
- Egypt and the IMF
- Alibaba's Record-Setting IPO
- Sony Corporation: Still a Leader Globally?
- Organizational Architecture at P&G
- Cutco Corporation–Sharpening Your Market Entry
- Tata Motors and Exporting
- Alibaba and Global Supply Chains
- Best Buy Doing a Turnaround Again
- Sodexo: Building a Diverse Global Workforce
- Tesla, Inc.–Subsidizing Tesla Automobiles Globally

BEYOND UNCRITICAL PRESENTATION AND SHALLOW EXPLANATION

Many issues in international business are complex and thus necessitate considerations of pros and cons. To demonstrate this to students, we have adopted a critical approach that presents the arguments for and against economic theories, government policies, business strategies, organizational structures, and so on.

Related to this, we have attempted to explain the complexities of the many theories and phenomena unique to international business so the student might fully comprehend the statements of a theory or the reasons a phenomenon is the way it is. We believe that these theories and phenomena are explained in more depth in this work than they are in the competition, which seem to use the rationale that a shallow explanation is little better than no explanation. In international business, a little knowledge is indeed a dangerous thing.

PRACTICAL AND RICH APPLICATIONS

We have always believed that it is important to show students how the material covered in the text is relevant to the actual practice of international business. This is explicit in the later chapters of the book, which focus on the practice of international business, but it is not always obvious in the first half of the book, which considers macro topics. Accordingly, at the end of each chapter in Parts Two, Three, and Four—where the focus is on the environment of international business, as opposed to particular firms—there is a section titled **Focus on Managerial Implications**. In this section, the managerial implications of the material discussed in the chapter are clearly explained. Additionally, most chapters have at least one **Management Focus** box. The purpose of these boxes is to illustrate the relevance of chapter material for the practice of international business.

A **Did You Know?** feature challenges students to view the world around them through the lens of international business (e.g., Did you know that sugar prices in the United States are much higher than sugar prices in the rest of the world?). The author recorded short videos explaining the phenomenon.

In addition, each chapter begins with an **opening case** that sets the stage for the chapter and ends with a **closing case** that illustrates the relevance of chapter material for the practice of international business.

To help students go a step further in expanding their application-level understanding of international business, each chapter incorporates two **globalEDGE**™ **research tasks**. The exercises dovetail with the content just covered.

INTEGRATED PROGRESSION OF TOPICS

A weakness of many texts is that they lack a tight, integrated flow of topics from chapter to chapter. This book explains to students in Chapter 1 how the book's topics are related to each other. Integration has been achieved by organizing the material so that each chapter builds on the material of the previous ones in a logical fashion.

Part One

Chapter 1 provides an overview of the key issues to be addressed and explains the plan of the book. Globalization of markets and globalization of production is the core focus.

Part Two

Chapters 2 through 4 focus on country differences in political economy and culture, and Chapter 5 on ethics, corporate social responsibility, and sustainability issues in international business. Most international business textbooks place this material at a later point, but we believe it is vital to discuss national differences first. After all, many of the central issues in international trade and investment, the global monetary system, international business strategy and structure, and international business functions arise out of national differences in political economy and culture.

Part Three

Chapters 6 through 9 investigate the political economy of global trade and investment. The purpose of this part is to describe and explain the trade and investment environment in which international business occurs.

Part Four

Chapters 10 and 11 describe and explain the global monetary system, laying out in detail the monetary framework in which international business transactions are conducted.

Part Five

In Chapters 12 and 13, attention shifts from the environment to the firm. In other words, we move from a macro focus to a micro focus at this stage of the book. We examine strategies that firms adopt to compete effectively in the international business environment.

Part Six

In Chapters 14 through 17, the focus narrows further to investigate business functions and related operations. These chapters explain how firms can perform their key functions—exporting, importing, and countertrade; global production; global supply chain management; global marketing; global research and development (R&D); human resource management—to compete and succeed in the international business environment.

Throughout the book, the relationship of new material to topics discussed in earlier chapters is pointed out to the students to reinforce their understanding of how the material comprises an integrated whole. We deliberately bring a management focus to the macro chapters (Chapters 1 through 12). We also integrate macro themes in covering the micro chapters (Chapters 13 through 20).

ACCESSIBLE AND INTERESTING

The international business arena is fascinating and exciting, and we have tried to communicate our enthusiasm for it to the student. Learning is easier and better if the subject matter is communicated in an interesting, informative, and accessible manner. One technique we have used to achieve this is weaving interesting anecdotes into the narrative of the text, that is, stories that illustrate theory.

Most chapters also have a **Country Focus** box that provides background on the political, economic, social, or cultural aspects of countries grappling with an international business issue.

ACKNOWLEDGMENTS

Numerous people deserve to be thanked for their assistance in preparing this book. First, thank you to all the people at McGraw-Hill Education who have worked with us on this project:

Peter Jurmu, Portfolio Manager
Haley Burmeister, Product Developer
Nicole Young, Senior Marketing Manager
Julia Blankenship, Marketing Coordinator
Harvey Yep, Content Project Manager (Core)
Keri Johnson, Content Project Manager (Assessment)
Sandy Ludovissy, Senior Buyer
Egzon Shaqiri, Designer
Carrie Burger, Content Licensing Specialist

Second, our thanks go to the reviewers who provided good feedback that helped shape this book:

Yimai Lewis, Georgia State University
Long S. Le, Santa Clara University
Clare R. Greenlaw, Jr., Southern New Hampshire University – COCE
Richard Ajayi, University of Central Florida
Hussain Ahmad, Hofstra University
Erica Kovacs, Indiana University
Marta Szabo White, Georgia State University
C. Jayachandran, Montclair State University, NJ
T.S. Gardner, UNC Wilmington
Marcel Zondag, Western Michigan University
Mamoun Benmamoun, Saint Louis University
Manveer Mann, Montclair State University
Jose Luis Daniel, Saint Xavier University
Walter C. van Hoof, San Jose State University, San Jose, CA
Riikka M. Sarala, UNC Greensboro
Samuel Okoroafo, University of Toledo, Toledo, Ohio
Pamela S. Evers, University of North Carolina Wilmington

A special thanks to David Closs and David Frayer for allowing us to borrow elements of the sections on Strategic Roles for Production Facilities; Make-or-Buy Decisions; Global Supply Chain Functions; Coordination in Global Supply Chains; and Interorganizational Relationships for Chapter 15 of this text from Tomas Hult, David Closs, and David Frayer (2014), *Global Supply Chain Management,* New York: McGraw-Hill.

McGraw Hill **connect**®

FOR INSTRUCTORS

You're in the driver's seat.

Want to build your own course? No problem. Prefer to use our turnkey, prebuilt course? Easy. Want to make changes throughout the semester? Sure. And you'll save time with Connect's auto-grading too.

65%
Less Time Grading

Laptop: McGraw-Hill; Woman/dog: George Doyle/Getty Images

They'll thank you for it.

Adaptive study resources like SmartBook® 2.0 help your students be better prepared in less time. You can transform your class time from dull definitions to dynamic debates. Find out more about the powerful personalized learning experience available in SmartBook 2.0 at **www.mheducation.com/highered/ connect/smartbook**

Make it simple, make it affordable.

Connect makes it easy with seamless integration using any of the major Learning Management Systems— Blackboard®, Canvas, and D2L, among others—to let you organize your course in one convenient location. Give your students access to digital materials at a discount with our inclusive access program. Ask your McGraw-Hill representative for more information.

Padlock: Jobalou/Getty Images

Solutions for your challenges.

A product isn't a solution. Real solutions are affordable, reliable, and come with training and ongoing support when you need it and how you want it. Our Customer Experience Group can also help you troubleshoot tech problems— although Connect's 99% uptime means you might not need to call them. See for yourself at **status. mheducation.com**

Checkmark: Jobalou/Getty Images

SUPPORT AT
every step

Effective, efficient studying.

Connect helps you be more productive with your study time and get better grades using tools like SmartBook 2.0, which highlights key concepts and creates a personalized study plan. Connect sets you up for success, so you walk into class with confidence and walk out with better grades.

Study anytime, anywhere.

Download the free ReadAnywhere app and access your online eBook or SmartBook 2.0 assignments when it's convenient, even if you're offline. And since the app automatically syncs with your eBook and SmartBook 2.0 assignments in Connect, all of your work is available every time you open it. Find out more at **www.mheducation.com/readanywhere**

"I really liked this app—it made it easy to study when you don't have your text-book in front of you."

- Jordan Cunningham,
Eastern Washington University

No surprises.

The Connect Calendar and Reports tools keep you on track with the work you need to get done and your assignment scores. Life gets busy; Connect tools help you keep learning through it all.

Calendar: owattaphotos/Getty Images

Learning for everyone.

McGraw-Hill works directly with Accessibility Services Departments and faculty to meet the learning needs of all students. Please contact your Accessibility Services office and ask them to email accessibility@mheducation.com, or visit **www.mheducation.com/about/accessibility** for more information.

CONTENTS

part four
The Global Monetary System

part five
The Strategy and Structure of International Business

part seven
Integrative Cases

International
Business

Competing in the Global Marketplace

13e

Globalization

1

LEARNING OBJECTIVES

After reading this chapter, you will be able to:

LO1-1 Understand what is meant by the term *globalization*.

LO1-2 Recognize the main drivers of globalization.

LO1-3 Describe the changing nature of the global economy.

LO1-4 Explain the main arguments in the debate over the impact of globalization.

LO1-5 Understand how the process of globalization is creating opportunities and challenges for management practice.

Qilai Shen/In Pictures Ltd./Corbis/Getty Images

How the iPhone Is Made: Apple's Global Production System

OPENING CASE

In its early days, Apple usually didn't look beyond its own backyard to manufacture its devices. A few years after Apple started making its Macintosh computer back in 1983, Steve Jobs bragged that it was "a machine that was made in America." As late as the early 2000s, Apple still manufactured many of its computers at the company's iMac plant in Elk Grove, California. Jobs often said that he was as proud of the Apple's manufacturing plants as he was of the devices themselves.

By 2004, however, Apple had largely turned to foreign manufacturing. The shift to offshore production and assembly reached its peak with the iconic iPhone, which Apple first introduced in 2007. The iPhone contains hundreds of parts, an estimated 90 percent of which are manufactured abroad. Advanced semiconductors come from Germany and Taiwan, memory from Korea and Japan, display panels and circuitry from Korea and Taiwan, rare metals from Africa and Asia, and the gyroscope used for tracking the iPhone's orientation comes from Switzerland. Apple's major subcontractor, the Taiwanese multinational firm, Foxconn, assembles half of all the iPhones sold in the world today at a huge factory in China. Foxconn also has factories devoted to iPhone assembly at several other locations, including Brazil and India. Another Taiwanese-based company, Pegatron, also assembles iPhones for Apple at a factory in China.

Apple still employs some 80,000 people in the United States, and it has kept important activities at home, including product design, software engineering, and marketing. Furthermore, Apple claims that its business supports another 450,000 jobs at U.S.-based suppliers. For example, the glass for the iPhone is manufactured at Corning's U.S. plants in Kentucky, Analog Devices in Massachusetts produces chips that enable the iPhone's touch display, and a Texas Instruments plant in Maine makes electronic components that go in the iPhone. However, over 1.5 million people are involved in the engineering, building, and final assembly of its products *outside* of the United States, many of them working at subcontractors like Foxconn.

When explaining its decision to assemble the iPhone in China, Apple cites a number of factors. While it is true that labor costs are lower in China, Apple executives point out that labor costs only account for a small portion of the total value of its products and are not the main driver of location decisions. Far more important, according to Apple, is the ability of its Chinese subcontractors to respond very quickly to requests from Apple to scale production up and down. In a famous illustration of this capability, back in 2007 Steve Jobs demanded that a glass screen replace the plastic screen on his prototype iPhone. Jobs didn't like the look and feel of plastic screens, which at the time were standard in the industry, nor did he like the way they scratched easily. This last-minute change in the design of the iPhone put Apple's market introduction date at risk. Apple had selected Corning to manufacture large panes of strengthened glass, but finding a manufacturer that could cut those panes into millions of iPhone screens wasn't easy. Then, a bid arrived from a Chinese factory. When the Apple team visited the factory, they found that the plant's owners were already constructing a new wing to cut the glass and were installing equipment. "This is in case you give us the contract," the manager said. The plant also had a warehouse full of glass samples for Apple, and a team of engineers available to work with Apple. They had built onsite dormitories so the factory could run three shifts seven days a week to meet Apple's demanding production schedule. The Chinese company got the bid.

Another critical advantage of China for Apple was that it was much easier to hire engineers there. Apple calculated that about 8,700 industrial engineers were needed to oversee and guide the 200,000 assembly-line workers involved in manufacturing the original iPhone. The company had estimated it would take as long as nine months to find that many engineers in the United States. In China, it took 15 days.

Also important is the clustering together of factories in China. Many of the factories providing components for the iPhone are located close to Foxconn's assembly plant. As one executive noted, "The entire supply chain is in China. You need a thousand rubber gaskets? That's the factory next door. You need a million screws? That factory is a block away. You need a screw made a little bit different? That will take three hours."[*]

All this being said, there are drawbacks to outsourcing to China. Several of Apple's subcontractors have been targeted for their poor working conditions. Criticisms include low pay of line workers, long hours, mandatory overtime for little or no additional pay, and poor safety records. Some former Apple executives say there is an unresolved tension within the company: Executives want to improve working conditions within the factories of subcontractors, such as Foxconn, but that dedication falters when it conflicts with crucial supplier relationships or the fast delivery of new products. In addition, Apple's outsourcing decisions have been criticized by President Trump, who argues that the company is guilty of moving U.S. jobs overseas. While Apple disagrees with this assessment, it has responded by increasing its investment in U.S. facilities. In 2018, for example, the company announced it would invest $30 billion over five years to create 20,000 new Apple jobs in the United States. Most of these jobs, however, are expected to be in software development and data center operations, not manufacturing and assembly.

*C. Duhigg and K. Bradsher, "How U.S. Lost Out on iPhone Work." *The New York Times*, January 22, 2012.

Sources: Sam Costello, "Where Is the iPhone Made?" *Lifewire*, July 14, 2018; David Barboza, "How China Built iPhone City with Billions in Perks for Apple's Partner," *The New York Times*, December 29, 2016; Gu Huini, "Human Costs Are Built into iPad in China," *The New York Times*, January 26, 2012; Chuck Jones, "Apple's $350 Billion US Contribution Was Already on the Cards," *Forbes*, January 19, 2018.

Introduction

Over the past five decades, a fundamental shift has been occurring in the world economy. We have been moving away from a world in which national economies were relatively self-contained entities, isolated from each other by barriers to cross-border trade and investment; by distance, time zones, and language; and by national differences in government regulation, culture, and business systems. We have moved toward a world in which barriers to cross-border trade and investment have declined; perceived distance is shrinking due to advances in transportation and telecommunications technology; material culture is starting to look similar the world over; and national economies are merging into an interdependent, integrated global economic system. The process by which this transformation is occurring is commonly referred to as *globalization*.

At the same time, recent political events have raised some questions about the inevitability of the globalization process. The exit of the United Kingdom from the European Union (Brexit), the renegotiation of the North American Free Trade Agreement (NAFTA) by the Trump Administration, and trade disputes between the United States and many of its trading partners, including most notably China, have all contributed to uncertainty about the future of globalization. While the world seems unlikely to pull back significantly from globalization, there is no doubt that the benefits of globalization are more in dispute now than at any time in the last half century. This is a new reality, albeit perhaps a temporary one, but it is one the international business community will have to adjust to.

The opening case illustrates how one company, Apple, has taken advantage of globalization. Apple has created a global supply chain to efficiently produce its icon iPhone. While product design and software development are undertaken in California, component parts are manufactured all over the world, and the final product is assembled for Apple by Foxconn in factories in China, Brazil, India, and elsewhere. In configuring the production system of the iPhone in this manner, Apple is trying to partner with the most efficient subcontractors, wherever in the world they might reside. Apple could not have configured its production system in this manner had it not been for the systematic reductions in barriers to cross-border trade and investment that have occurred over the last half century.

At the same time, Apple has been criticized by President Trump for placing too much productive activity outside of the United States. Moreover, trade disputes between the United States and China have raised the possibility that China may at some point not be the optimal location for assembling the iPhone. Apple has started to adjust its strategy to account for the potential risks here, establishing assembly operations outside of China (in India, for example), increasing its investment in the United States (in 2018, Apple announced it would invest $30 billion over five years in U.S. facilities, creating 20,000 new jobs in the process), and working with U.S.-based suppliers to help them become efficient Apple partners (Apple has established a $5 billion fund to help those suppliers upgrade their capabilities). Thus, Apple is taking advantage of globalization, and simultaneously hedging against any possible pullback from the level of globalization that existed in 2016, which for now at least may have been a high-water mark, albeit a temporary one.

Proponents of increased global trade argue that cross-cultural engagement and trade across country borders is the future and that returning back to a nationalistic perspective is the past. On the other hand, the nationalistic argument rests in citizens wanting their country to be sovereign, self-sufficient as much as possible, and basically in charge of their own economy and country environment. We will touch on many aspects of this debate throughout this text's 20 integrated chapters.

Globalization now has an impact on almost everything we do. For example, an American medical doctor—let's call her Laurie—might drive to work at her pediatric office in a sports utility vehicle (SUV) that was designed in Stuttgart, Germany, and assembled in Leipzig, Germany, and Bratislava, Slovakia, by Porsche from components from parts suppliers worldwide, which in turn were fabricated from Korean steel and Malaysian rubber. Laurie may have filled her car with gasoline at a Shell service station owned by a

British-Dutch multinational company. The gasoline could have been made from oil pumped out of a well off the coast of Africa by a French oil company that transported it to the United States in a ship owned by a Greek shipping line. While driving to work, Laurie might talk to her stockbroker (using a hands-free, in-car speaker) on an Apple iPhone that was designed in California and assembled in China using chip sets produced in Japan and Europe, glass made by Corning in Kentucky, and memory chips from South Korea. Perhaps on her way, Laurie might tell the stockbroker to purchase shares in Lenovo, a multinational Chinese PC manufacturer whose operational headquarters is in North Carolina and whose shares are listed on the New York Stock Exchange.

This is the world in which we live. In many cases, we simply do not know, or perhaps even care, where a product was designed and where it was made. Just a couple of decades ago, "Made in the USA" or "Made in Germany" had strong meaning and referred to something. The U.S. often stood for quality, and Germany often stood for sophisticated engineering. Now the country of origin for a product has given way to, for example, "Made by BMW," and the company is the quality assurance platform, not the country. In many cases, it goes even beyond the company to the personal relationship a customer has developed with a representative of the company, and so we focus on what has become known as CRM (Customer Relationship Management).

Whether it is still the quality associated with the country of origin of a product, or the assurance given by a specific company regardless of where they manufacture their product, we live in a world where the volume of goods, services, and investments crossing national borders has expanded faster than world output for more than half a century. It is a world in which international institutions such as the World Trade Organization and gatherings of leaders from the world's most powerful economies continue to work for even lower barriers to cross-border trade and investment. The symbols of material culture and popular culture are increasingly global, from Coca-Cola and Starbucks, to Sony PlayStation, Facebook, Netflix video streaming service, IKEA stores, and Apple iPads and iPhones. Vigorous and vocal groups protest against globalization, which they blame for a list of ills from unemployment in developed nations to environmental degradation and the Westernization or Americanization of local cultures. These protesters come from environmental groups, which have been around for some time, but more recently also from nationalistic groups focused on their countries being more sovereign.

For businesses, the globalization process has many opportunities. Firms can expand their revenues by selling around the world and/or reduce their costs by producing in nations where key inputs, including labor, are cheap. The global expansion of enterprises has been facilitated by generally favorable political and economic trends. This has allowed businesses both large and small, from both advanced nations and developing nations, to expand internationally. As globalization unfolds, it is transforming industries and creating anxiety among those who believed their jobs were protected from foreign competition. Advances in technology, lower transportation costs, and the rise of skilled workers in developing countries imply that many services no longer need to be performed where they are delivered. As best-selling author Thomas Friedman has argued, the world is becoming "flat."[1] People living in developed nations no longer have the playing field tilted in their favor. Increasingly, enterprising individuals based in India, China, or Brazil have the same opportunities to better themselves as those living in Western Europe, the United States, or Canada.

In this text, we will take a close look at these issues and many more. We will explore how changes in regulations governing international trade and investment, when coupled with changes in political systems and technology, have dramatically altered the competitive playing field confronting many businesses. We will discuss the resulting opportunities and threats and review the strategies that managers can pursue to exploit the opportunities and counter the threats. We will consider whether globalization benefits or harms national economies. We will look at what economic theory has to say about the outsourcing of manufacturing and service jobs to places such as India and China and look at the benefits and costs of outsourcing, not just to business firms and their employees but to entire economies. First, though, we need to get a better overview of the nature and process of globalization, and that is the function of this first chapter.

LO1-1

Understand what is meant by the term *globalization*.

What Is Globalization?

As used in this text, **globalization** refers to the shift toward a more integrated and interdependent world economy. Globalization has several facets, including the globalization of markets and the globalization of production.

THE GLOBALIZATION OF MARKETS

The **globalization of markets** refers to the merging of historically distinct and separate national markets into one huge global marketplace. Falling barriers to cross-border trade and investment have made it easier to sell internationally. It has been argued for some time that the tastes and preferences of consumers in different nations are beginning to converge on some global norm, thereby helping create a global market.[2] Consumer products such as Citigroup credit cards, Coca-Cola soft drinks, Sony video games, McDonald's hamburgers, Starbucks coffee, IKEA furniture, and Apple iPhones are frequently held up as prototypical examples of this trend. The firms that produce these products are more than just benefactors of this trend; they are also facilitators of it. By offering the same basic product worldwide, they help create a global market.

A company does not have to be the size of these multinational giants to facilitate, and benefit from, the globalization of markets. In the United States, for example, according to the International Trade Administration, more than 300,000 small and medium-sized firms with fewer than 500 employees account for 98 percent of the companies that export. More generally, exports from small and medium-sized companies account for 33 percent of the value of U.S. exports of manufactured goods.[3] Typical of these is B&S Aircraft Alloys, a New York company whose exports account for 40 percent of its $8 million annual revenues.[4] The situation is similar in several other nations. For example, in Germany, a staggering 98 percent of small and midsize companies have exposure to international markets, via either exports or international production. Since 2009, China has been the world's largest exporter, sending more than $2 trillion worth of products and services last year to the rest of the world.

globalEDGE INTERNATIONAL BUSINESS RESOURCES

globalEDGE™ has been the world's go-to site online for global business knowledge since 2001. Google typically ranks the site number 1 for "international business resources" from anywhere in the world you access it. Created by a 30-member team in the International Business Center in the Broad College of Business at Michigan State University under the supervision of Dr. Tomas Hult and Dr. Tunga Kiyak, globalEDGE™ is a knowledge resource that connects international business professionals worldwide to a wealth of information, insights, and learning resources on global business activities.

The site offers the latest and most comprehensive international business and trade content for a wide range of topics. Whether conducting extensive market research, looking to improve your international knowledge, or simply browsing, you're sure to find what you need to sharpen your competitive edge in today's rapidly changing global marketplace. The easy, convenient, and free globalEDGE™ website's tagline is "Your Source for Global Business Knowledge." Take a look at the site at **globaledge.msu.edu**. We will use globalEDGE throughout this text for exercises, information, data, and to keep every facet of the text up-to-date on a daily basis!

Despite the global prevalence of Citigroup credit cards, McDonald's hamburgers, Starbucks coffee, and IKEA stores, for example, it is important not to push too far the view that national markets are giving way to the global market. As we shall see in later chapters, significant differences still exist among national markets along many relevant dimensions, including consumer tastes and preferences, distribution channels, culturally embedded value systems, business systems, and legal regulations. Uber, for example, the fast-growing ride-for-hire service, is finding it needs to refine its entry strategy in many foreign cities in order to take differences in the regulatory regime into account. Such differences frequently require companies to customize marketing strategies, product features, and operating practices to best match conditions in a particular country.

The most global of markets are not typically markets for consumer products—where national differences in tastes and preferences can still be important enough to act as a brake on globalization. They are markets for industrial goods and materials that serve universal needs the world over. These include markets for commodities such as aluminum, oil, and wheat; for industrial products such as microprocessors, DRAMs (computer memory chips), and commercial jet aircraft; for computer software; and for financial assets, from U.S. Treasury bills to Eurobonds, and futures on the Nikkei index or the euro. That being said, it is increasingly evident that many newer high-technology consumer products, such as Apple's iPhone, are being successfully sold the same way the world over.

In many global markets, the same firms frequently confront each other as competitors in nation after nation. Coca-Cola's rivalry with PepsiCo is a global one, as are the rivalries between Ford and Toyota; Boeing and Airbus; Caterpillar and Komatsu in earthmoving equipment; General Electric and Rolls-Royce in aero engines; Sony, Nintendo, and Microsoft in video-game consoles; and Samsung and Apple in smartphones. If a firm moves into a nation not currently served by its rivals, many of those rivals are sure to follow to prevent their competitor from gaining an advantage.[5] As firms follow each other around the world, they bring with them many of the assets that served them well in other national markets—their products, operating strategies, marketing strategies, and brand names—creating some homogeneity across markets. Thus, greater uniformity replaces diversity. In an increasing number of industries, it is no longer meaningful to talk about "the German market," "the American market," "the Brazilian market," or "the Japanese market"; for many firms, there is only the global market.

THE GLOBALIZATION OF PRODUCTION

The **globalization of production** refers to the sourcing of goods and services from locations around the globe to take advantage of national differences in the cost and quality of **factors of production** (such as labor, energy, land, and capital). By doing this, companies hope to lower their overall cost structure or improve the quality or functionality of their product offering, thereby allowing them to compete more effectively. For example, Boeing has made extensive use of outsourcing to foreign suppliers. Consider Boeing's 777 first introduced in 1995: Eight Japanese suppliers make parts for the fuselage, doors, and wings; a supplier in Singapore makes the doors for the nose landing gear; three suppliers in Italy manufacture wing flaps; and so on.[6] In total, some 30 percent of the 777, by value, is built by foreign companies. And for its most recent jet airliner, the 787, Boeing has pushed this trend even further; some 65 percent of the total value of the aircraft is outsourced to foreign companies, 35 percent of which goes to three major Japanese companies.

Part of Boeing's rationale for outsourcing so much production to foreign suppliers is that these suppliers are the best in the world at their particular activity. A global web of suppliers yields a better final product, which enhances the chances of Boeing winning a greater share of total orders for aircraft than its global rival, Airbus. Boeing also outsources some production to foreign countries to increase the chance it will win significant orders from airlines based in that country. For a more detailed look at the globalization of production at Boeing, see the accompanying Management Focus.

Boeing's Global Production System

Executives at the Boeing Corporation, America's largest exporter, say that building a large commercial jet aircraft like the 787 Dreamliner involves bringing together more than a million parts in flying formation. Half a century ago, when the early models of Boeing's venerable 737 and 747 jets were rolling off the company's Seattle-area production lines, foreign suppliers accounted for only 5 percent of those parts, on average. Boeing was vertically integrated and manufactured many of the major components that went into the planes. The largest parts produced by outside suppliers were the jet engines, where two of the three suppliers were American companies. The lone foreign engine manufacturer was the British company Rolls-Royce.

Fast-forward to the modern era, and things look very different. In the case of Boeing's super-efficient 787 Dreamliner, 50 outside suppliers spread around the world account for 65 percent of the value of the aircraft. Italian firm Alenia Aeronautica makes the center fuselage and horizontal stabilizer. Kawasaki of Japan makes part of the forward fuselage and the fixed trailing edge of the wing. French firm Messier-Dowty makes the aircraft's landing gear. German firm Diehl Luftahrt Elektronik supplies the main cabin lighting. Sweden's Saab Aerostructures makes the access doors. Japanese company Jamco makes parts for the lavatories, flight deck interiors, and galleys. Mitsubishi Heavy Industries of Japan makes the wings. KAA of Korea makes the wing tips. And so on.

Why the change? One reason is that 80 percent of Boeing's customers are foreign airlines, and to sell into those nations, it often helps to be giving business to those nations. The trend started in 1974 when Mitsubishi of Japan was given contracts to produce inboard wing flaps for the 747. The Japanese reciprocated by placing big orders for Boeing jets. A second rationale was to disperse component part production to those suppliers who are the best in the world at their particular activity. Over the years, for example, Mitsubishi has acquired considerable expertise in the manufacture of wings, so it was logical for Boeing to use Mitsubishi to make the wings for the 787. Similarly, the 787 is the first commercial jet aircraft to be made almost entirely out of carbon fiber, so Boeing tapped Japan's Toray Industries, a world-class expert in sturdy but light carbon-fiber composites, to supply materials for the fuselage. A third reason for the extensive outsourcing on the 787 was that Boeing wanted to unburden itself of some of the risks and costs associated with developing production facilities for the 787. By outsourcing, it pushed some of those risks and costs onto suppliers, who had to undertake major investments in capacity to ramp up to produce for the 787.

So what did Boeing retain for itself? Engineering design, marketing and sales, and final assembly are done at its Everett plant north of Seattle, all activities where Boeing maintains it is the best in the world. Of major component parts, Boeing made only the tail fin and wing to body fairing (which attaches the wings to the fuselage of the plane). Everything else was outsourced.

As the 787 moved through development, it became clear that Boeing had pushed the outsourcing paradigm too far. Coordinating a globally dispersed production system this extensive turned out to be very challenging. Parts turned up late, some parts didn't "snap together" the way Boeing had envisioned, and several suppliers ran into engineering problems that slowed down the entire production process. As a consequence, the date for delivery of the first jet was pushed back more than four years, and Boeing had to take millions of dollars in penalties for late deliveries. The problems at one supplier, Vought Aircraft in North Carolina, were so severe that Boeing ultimately agreed to acquire the company and bring its production in-house. Vought was co-owned by Alenia of Italy and made parts of the main fuselage.

There are now signs that Boeing is rethinking some of its global outsourcing policy. For its next jet, a new version of its popular wide-bodied 777 jet, the 777X, which will use the same carbon-fiber technology as the 787, Boeing will bring wing production back in-house. Mitsubishi and Kawasaki of Japan produce much of the wing structure for the 787 and for the original version of the 777. However, recently Japan's airlines have been placing large orders with Airbus, breaking with their traditional allegiance to Boeing. This seems to have given Boeing an opening to bring wing production back in-house. Boeing executives also note that Boeing has lost much of its expertise in wing production over the last 20 years due to outsourcing, and bringing it back in-house for new carbon-fiber wings might enable Boeing to regain these important core skills and strengthen the company's competitive position.

Sources: M. Ehrenfreund, "The Economic Reality Behind the Boeing Plane Trump Showed Off," *The Washington Post*, February 17, 2017; K. Epstein and J. Crown, "Globalization Bites Boeing," *Bloomberg Businessweek*, March 12, 2008; H. Mallick, "Out of Control Outsourcing Ruined Boeing's Beautiful Dreamliner," *The Star*, February 25, 2013; P. Kavilanz, "Dreamliner: Where in the World Its Parts Come From," *CNN Money*, January 18, 2013; S. Dubois, "Boeing's Dreamliner Mess: Simply Inevitable?" *CNN Money*, January 22, 2013; and A. Scott and T. Kelly, "Boeing's Loss of a $9.5 Billion Deal Could Bring Jobs Back to the U.S.," *Business Insider*, October 14, 2013.

Early outsourcing efforts were primarily confined to manufacturing activities, such as those undertaken by Boeing and Apple. Increasingly, however, companies are taking advantage of modern communications technology, particularly the Internet, to outsource service activities to low-cost producers in other nations. The Internet has allowed hospitals to outsource some radiology work to India, where images from MRI scans and the like are read at night while U.S. physicians sleep; the results are ready for them in the morning. Many software companies, including Microsoft, now use Indian engineers to perform test functions on software designed in the United States. The time difference allows Indian engineers to run debugging tests on software written in the United States when U.S. engineers sleep, transmitting the corrected code back to the United States over secure Internet connections so it is ready for U.S. engineers to work on the following day. Dispersing value-creation activities in this way can compress the time and lower the costs required to develop new software programs. Other companies, from computer makers to banks, are outsourcing customer service functions, such as customer call centers, to developing nations where labor is cheaper. In another example from health care, workers in the Philippines transcribe American medical files (such as audio files from doctors seeking approval from insurance companies for performing a procedure). Some estimates suggest the outsourcing of many administrative procedures in health care, such as customer service and claims processing, could reduce health care costs in America by more than $100 billion.

The economist Robert Reich has argued that as a consequence of the trend exemplified by companies such as Boeing, Apple, and Microsoft, in many cases it is becoming irrelevant to talk about American products, Japanese products, German products, or Korean products. Increasingly, according to Reich, the outsourcing of productive activities to different suppliers results in the creation of products that are global in nature—that is, "global products."[7] But as with the globalization of markets, companies must be careful not to push the globalization of production too far. As we will see in later chapters, substantial impediments still make it difficult for firms to achieve the optimal dispersion of their productive activities to locations around the globe. These impediments include formal and informal barriers to trade between countries, barriers to foreign direct investment, transportation costs, issues associated with economic and political risk, and the sheer managerial challenge of coordinating a globally dispersed supply chain (an issue for Boeing with the 787 Dreamliner, as discussed in the Management Focus). For example, government regulations ultimately limit the ability of hospitals to outsource the process of interpreting MRI scans to developing nations where radiologists are cheaper.

Nevertheless, the globalization of markets and production will probably continue. Modern firms are important actors in this trend, their actions fostering increased globalization. These firms, however, are merely responding in an efficient manner to changing conditions in their operating environment—as well they should.

The Emergence of Global Institutions

As markets globalize and an increasing proportion of business activity transcends national borders, institutions are needed to help manage, regulate, and police the global marketplace and to promote the establishment of multinational treaties to govern the global business system. Over the past 75 years, a number of important global institutions have been created to help perform these functions, including the **General Agreement on Tariffs and Trade (GATT)** and its successor, the World Trade Organization; the International Monetary Fund and its sister institution, the World Bank; and the United Nations. All these institutions were created by voluntary agreement between individual nation-states, and their functions are enshrined in international treaties.

The **World Trade Organization (WTO)** (like the GATT before it) is primarily responsible for policing the world trading system and making sure nation-states adhere to the rules laid down in trade treaties signed by WTO member states. As of 2019, 164 nations

▶ **Did You Know?**

Did you know that trade as a percentage of GDP for the U.S. has nearly tripled since 1960?

Visit your instructor's Connect® course and click on your eBook or SmartBook® to view a short video explanation from the author.

✓ **TEST PREP**

Use SmartBook to help retain what you have learned. Access your Instructor's Connect course to check out SmartBook or go to **learnsmartadvantage.com** for help.

that collectively accounted for 98 percent of world trade were WTO members, thereby giving the organization enormous scope and influence. The WTO is also responsible for facilitating the establishment of additional multinational agreements among WTO member states. Over its entire history, and that of the GATT before it, the WTO has promoted the lowering of barriers to cross-border trade and investment. In doing so, the WTO has been the instrument of its member states, which have sought to create a more open global business system unencumbered by barriers to trade and investment between countries. Without an institution such as the WTO, the globalization of markets and production is unlikely to have proceeded as far as it has. However, as we shall see in this chapter and in Chapter 7 when we look closely at the WTO, critics charge that the organization is usurping the national sovereignty of individual nation-states.

The **International Monetary Fund (IMF)** and the **World Bank** were both created in 1944 by 44 nations that met at Bretton Woods, New Hampshire. The IMF was established to maintain order in the international monetary system; the World Bank was set up to promote economic development. In the more than seven decades since their creation, both institutions have emerged as significant players in the global economy. The World Bank is the less controversial of the two sister institutions. It has focused on making low-interest loans to cash-strapped governments in poor nations that wish to undertake significant infrastructure investments (such as building dams or roads).

The IMF is often seen as the lender of last resort to nation-states whose economies are in turmoil and whose currencies are losing value against those of other nations. During the past two decades, for example, the IMF has lent money to the governments of troubled states including Argentina, Indonesia, Mexico, Russia, South Korea, Thailand, and Turkey. More recently, the IMF took a proactive role in helping countries cope with some of the effects of the 2008–2009 global financial crisis. IMF loans come with strings attached, however; in return for loans, the IMF requires nation-states to adopt specific economic policies aimed at returning their troubled economies to stability and growth. These requirements have sparked controversy. Some critics charge that the IMF's policy recommendations are often inappropriate; others maintain that by telling national governments what economic policies they must adopt, the IMF, like the WTO, is usurping the sovereignty of nation-states. We will look at the debate over the role of the IMF in Chapter 11.

The **United Nations (UN)** was established October 24, 1945, by 51 countries committed to preserving peace through international cooperation and collective security. Today, nearly every nation in the world belongs to the United Nations; membership now totals 193 countries. When states become members of the United Nations, they agree to accept the obligations of the UN Charter, an international treaty that establishes basic principles of international relations. According to the charter, the UN has four purposes: to maintain international peace and security, to develop friendly relations among nations, to cooperate in solving international problems and in promoting respect for human rights, and to be a center for harmonizing the actions of nations. Although the UN is perhaps best known for its peacekeeping role, one of the organization's central mandates is the promotion of higher standards of living, full employment, and conditions of economic and social progress and development—all issues that are central to the creation of a vibrant global economy. As much as 70 percent of the work of the UN system is devoted to accomplishing this mandate. To do so, the UN works closely with other international institutions such as the World Bank. Guiding the work is the belief that eradicating poverty and improving the well-being of people everywhere are necessary steps in creating conditions for lasting world peace.[8]

Another institution in the news is the **Group of Twenty (G20)**. Established in 1999, the G20 comprises the finance ministers and central bank governors of the 19 largest economies in the world, plus representatives from the European Union and the European Central Bank. Collectively, the G20 represents 90 percent of global GDP and 80 percent of international global trade. Originally established to formulate a coordinated policy response to financial crises in developing nations, in 2008 and 2009 it became the forum through which major nations attempted to launch a coordinated policy response to the global financial crisis that started in America and then rapidly spread around the world, ushering in the first serious global economic recession since 1981.

Drivers of Globalization

Two macro factors underlie the trend toward greater globalization.[9] The first is the decline in barriers to the free flow of goods, services, and capital that has occurred in recent decades. The second factor is technological change, particularly the dramatic developments in communication, information processing, and transportation technologies.

DECLINING TRADE AND INVESTMENT BARRIERS

During the 1920s and 1930s, many of the world's nation-states erected formidable barriers to international trade and foreign direct investment. **International trade** occurs when a firm exports goods or services to consumers in another country. **Foreign direct investment (FDI)** occurs when a firm invests resources in business activities outside its home country. Many of the barriers to international trade took the form of high tariffs on imports of manufactured goods. The typical aim of such tariffs was to protect domestic industries from foreign competition. One consequence, however, was "beggar thy neighbor" retaliatory trade policies, with countries progressively raising trade barriers against each other. Ultimately, this depressed world demand and contributed to the Great Depression of the 1930s.

Having learned from this experience, the advanced industrial nations of the West committed themselves after World War II to progressively reducing barriers to the free flow of goods, services, and capital among nations.[10] This goal was enshrined in the General Agreement on Tariffs and Trade. Under the umbrella of GATT, eight rounds of negotiations among member states worked to lower barriers to the free flow of goods and services. The first round of negotiations went into effect in 1948. The most recent negotiations to be completed, known as the Uruguay Round, were finalized in December 1993. The Uruguay Round further reduced trade barriers; extended GATT to cover services as well as manufactured goods; provided enhanced protection for patents, trademarks, and copyrights; and established the World Trade Organization to police the international trading system.[11] Table 1.1 summarizes the impact of GATT agreements on average tariff rates for *manufactured* goods among several developed nations. As can be seen, average tariff rates have fallen significantly since 1950 and now stand at about 2.0–3.0 percent. Comparable tariff rates in 2017 for China and India were about 8 percent. This represents a sharp decline from 16.2 percent for China in 2000, and 33.6 percent for India in 2000. It's also important to note that in addition to the global efforts of the GATT and WTO, trade barriers have also been reduced by bilateral and regional agreements between two or more

LO1-2

Recognize the main drivers of globalization.

	1913	1950	1990	2018
France	21%	18%	5.9%	1.9%
Germany	20	26	5.9	1.9
Italy	18	25	5.9	1.9
Japan	30	—	3.3	2.1
Netherlands	5	11	5.9	1.9
Sweden	20	9	5.9	1.9
United Kingdom	—	23	5.9	1.9
United States	44	14	5.7	3.0

TABLE 1.1

Average Tariff Rates on Manufactured Products as Percentage of Value

Sources: The 1913–1990 data are from "Who Wants to Be a Giant?" *The Economist: A Survey of the Multinationals*, June 24, 1995, pp. 3–4. The 2018 data are from the *World Development Indicators*, World Bank.

nations. For example, the European Union has reduced trade barriers between its member states, the North American Free Trade Agreement reduced trade barriers between the United States, Mexico, and Canada, and a free trade agreement between the United States and South Korea has reduced trade barriers between those two nations. In the early 1990s, there were less than 50 such agreements in place. Today, there are around 300 such agreements.

Figure 1.1 charts the growth in the value of world merchandised trade and world production between 1960 and 2018 (the most recent year for which data are available). The data are adjusted to take out the effect of inflation and is indexed at a value of 100 in 1960 to allow for an "apples to apples" comparison. What you can see from the chart is that between 1960 and 2018 the value of the world economy (adjusted for inflation) increased 9.4 times, while the value of international trade in merchandised goods increased 22.4 times. This actually underestimates the growth in trade, because trade in services has also been growing rapidly in recent decades. By 2018, the value of world trade in merchandised goods was 19.5 trillion, while the value of trade in services was $5.8 trillion.

Not only has trade in goods and services been growing faster than world output for decades, so has the value of foreign direct investment, in part due to reductions in barriers limiting FDI between countries. According to UN data, some 80 percent of the more than 1,500 changes made to national laws governing foreign direct investment since 2000 have created a more favorable environment. Partly due to such liberalization, the value of FDI has grown significantly over the last 30 years. In 1990, about $244 billion in foreign investment was made by enterprises. By 2018, that figure had increased to $1.3 trillion. As a result of sustained cross-border investment, by 2018 the sales of foreign affiliates of multinational corporations reached $27 trillion, almost $8 trillion more than the value of international trade in 2018, and these affiliates employed some 76 million people.[12]

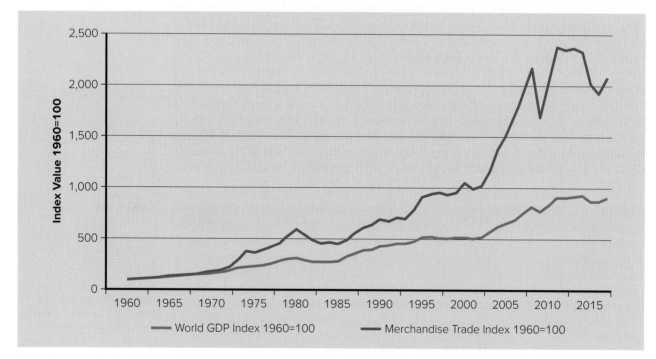

FIGURE 1.1

Value of world merchandised trade and world production 1960–2019.

Sources: World Bank, 2019; World Trade Organization, 2019; United Nations, 2019.

The fact that the volume of world trade has been growing faster than world GDP implies several things. First, more firms are doing what Boeing does with the 777 and 787: dispersing parts of their production process to different locations around the globe to drive down production costs and increase product quality. Second, the economies of the world's nation-states are becoming ever more intertwined. As trade expands, nations are becoming increasingly dependent on each other for important goods and services. Third, the world has become significantly wealthier in the last two decades. The implication is that rising trade is the engine that has helped pull the global economy along.

The globalization of markets and production and the resulting growth of world trade, foreign direct investment, and imports all imply that firms are finding their home markets under attack from foreign competitors. This is true in China, where U.S. companies such as Apple,

BCFC/Shutterstock

General Motors, and Starbucks are expanding their presence. It is true in the United States, where Japanese automobile firms have taken market share away from General Motors and Ford over the past three decades, and it is true in Europe, where the once-dominant Dutch company Philips has seen its market share in the consumer electronics industry taken by Japan's Panasonic and Sony and Korea's Samsung and LG. The growing integration of the world economy into a single, huge marketplace is increasing the intensity of competition in a range of manufacturing and service industries.

However, declining barriers to cross-border trade and investment cannot be taken for granted. As we shall see in subsequent chapters, demands for "protection" from foreign competitors are still often heard in countries around the world, including the United States. Although a return to the restrictive trade policies of the 1920s and 1930s is unlikely, it is not clear whether the political majority in the industrialized world favors further reductions in trade barriers. Indeed, the global financial crisis of 2008–2009 and the associated drop in global output that occurred led to more calls for trade barriers to protect jobs at home. The election of Donald Trump to the Presidency of the United States in 2017 can be seen as a continuation of this counter trend, because Trump ran on a platform advocating higher trade barriers to protect American companies from unfair foreign competition. If trade barriers decline no further, this may slow the rate of globalization of both markets and production.

ROLE OF TECHNOLOGICAL CHANGE

The lowering of trade barriers made globalization of markets and production a theoretical possibility. Technological change has made it a tangible reality. Every year that goes by comes with unique and oftentimes major advances in communication, information processing, and transportation technology, including the explosive emergence of the "Internet of Things."

Communications

Perhaps the single most important innovation since World War II has been the development of the microprocessor, which enabled the explosive growth of high-power, low-cost computing, vastly increasing the amount of information that can be processed by individuals and firms. The microprocessor also underlies many recent advances in telecommunications technology. Over the past 30 years, global communications have been revolutionized by developments in satellite, optical fiber, wireless technologies, and of course the Internet. These technologies rely on the microprocessor to encode, transmit, and decode the vast amount of information that flows along these electronic highways. The cost of microprocessors continues to fall, while their power increases (a phenomenon known as **Moore's law**, which predicts that the power of microprocessor technology doubles and its cost of production falls in half every 18 months).[13]

The Internet

The explosive growth of the Internet since 1994, when the first web browser was introduced, has revolutionized communications and commerce. In 1990, fewer than 1 million users were connected to the Internet. By 1995, the figure had risen to 50 million. By 2018, the Internet had 4 billion users, or 52 percent of the global population.[14] It is no surprise that the Internet has developed into the information backbone of the global economy.

In North America alone, e-commerce retail sales were $517 billion in 2018 (up from almost nothing in 1998), while global e-commerce sales reached $2.5 trillion.[15] Viewed globally, the Internet has emerged as an equalizer. It rolls back some of the constraints of location, scale, and time zones.[16] The Internet makes it much easier for buyers and sellers to find each other, wherever they may be located and whatever their size. It allows businesses, both small and large, to expand their global presence at a lower cost than ever before. Just as important, it enables enterprises to coordinate and control a globally dispersed production system in a way that was not possible 25 years ago.

Transportation Technology

In addition to developments in communications technology, several major innovations in transportation technology have occurred since the 1950s. In economic terms, the most important are probably the development of commercial jet aircraft and superfreighters and the introduction of *containerization*, which simplifies transshipment from one mode of transport to another. The advent of commercial jet travel, by reducing the time needed to get from one location to another, has effectively shrunk the globe. In terms of travel time, New York is now "closer" to Tokyo than it was to Philadelphia in the colonial days.

Containerization has revolutionized the transportation business, significantly lowering the costs of shipping goods over long distances. Because the international shipping industry is responsible for carrying about 90 percent of the *volume* of world trade in goods, this has been an extremely important development.[17] Before the advent of containerization, moving goods from one mode of transport to another was very labor intensive, lengthy, and costly. It could take days and several hundred longshore workers to unload a ship and reload goods onto trucks and trains. With the advent of widespread containerization in the 1970s and 1980s, the whole process can now be executed by a handful of longshore workers in a couple of days. As a result of the efficiency gains associated with containerization, transportation costs have plummeted, making it much more economical to ship goods around the globe, thereby helping drive the globalization of markets and production. Between 1920 and 1990, the average ocean freight and port charges per ton of U.S. export and import cargo fell from $95 to $29 (in 1990 dollars).[18] Today, the typical cost of transporting a 20-foot container from Asia to Europe carrying more than 20 tons of cargo is about the same as the economy airfare for a single passenger on the same journey.

Implications for the Globalization of Production

As transportation costs associated with the globalization of production have declined, dispersal of production to geographically separate locations has become more economical. As a result of the technological innovations discussed earlier, the real costs of information processing and communication have fallen dramatically in the past two decades. These developments make it possible for a firm to create and then manage a globally dispersed production system, further facilitating the globalization of production. A worldwide communications network has become essential for many international businesses. For example, Dell uses the

Internet to coordinate and control a globally dispersed production system to such an extent that it holds only three days' worth of inventory at its assembly locations. Dell's Internet-based system records orders for computer equipment as they are submitted by customers via the company's website and then immediately transmits the resulting orders for components to various suppliers around the world, which have a real-time look at Dell's order flow and can adjust their production schedules accordingly. Given the low cost of airfreight, Dell can use air transportation to speed up the delivery of critical components to meet unanticipated demand shifts without delaying the shipment of final product to consumers. Dell has also used modern communications technology to outsource its customer service operations to India. When U.S. customers call Dell with a service inquiry, they are routed to Bangalore in India, where English-speaking service personnel handle the call.

Implications for the Globalization of Markets

In addition to the globalization of production, technological innovations have facilitated the globalization of markets. Low-cost global communications networks, including those built on top of the Internet, are helping create electronic global marketplaces. As noted earlier, low-cost transportation has made it more economical to ship products around the world, thereby helping create global markets. In addition, low-cost jet travel has resulted in the mass movement of people between countries. This has reduced the cultural distance between countries and is bringing about some convergence of consumer tastes and preferences. At the same time, global communications networks and global media are creating a worldwide culture. U.S. television networks such as CNN and HBO are now received in many countries, Hollywood films are shown the world over, while non-U.S. news networks such as the BBC and Al Jazeera also have a global footprint. In any society, the media are primary conveyors of culture; as global media develop, we must expect the evolution of something akin to a global culture. A logical result of this evolution is the emergence of global markets for consumer products. Clear signs of this are apparent. It is now as easy to find a McDonald's restaurant in Tokyo as it is in New York, to buy an iPad in Rio as it is in Berlin, and to buy Gap jeans in Paris as it is in San Francisco.

Despite these trends, we must be careful not to overemphasize their importance. While modern communications and transportation technologies are ushering in the "global village," significant national differences remain in culture, consumer preferences, and business practices. A firm that ignores differences among countries does so at its peril. We shall stress this point repeatedly throughout this text and elaborate on it in later chapters.

The Changing Demographics of the Global Economy

Hand in hand with the trend toward globalization has been a fairly dramatic change in the demographics of the global economy over the past decades. Half a century ago, four facts described the demographics of the global economy. The first was U.S. dominance in the world economy and world trade picture. The second was U.S. dominance in world foreign direct investment. Related to this, the third fact was the dominance of large, multinational U.S. firms on the international business scene. The fourth was that roughly half the globe—the centrally planned economies of the communist world—was off-limits to Western international businesses. All four of these facts have changed rapidly.

THE CHANGING WORLD OUTPUT AND WORLD TRADE PICTURE

In the early 1960s, the United States was still, by far, the world's dominant industrial power. In 1960, the United States accounted for 38.3 percent of world output, measured by gross domestic product (GDP). By 2018, the United States accounted for 24 percent of world output, with China now at 15.2 percent of world output and the global leader in this category (see Table 1.2). The United States was not the only developed nation to see its relative standing slip. The same occurred to Germany, France, Italy, the United Kingdom, and Canada—these are just a few examples. All were nations that were among the first to industrialize globally.

TEST PREP

Use SmartBook to help retain what you have learned. Access your Instructor's Connect course to check out SmartBook or go to **learnsmartadvantage.com** for help.

LO1-3
Describe the changing nature of the global economy.

TABLE 1.2

Changing Demographics of World Output and World Exports

Sources: Output data from World Bank database, 2019. Trade data from WTO Statistical Database, 2019.

Country	Share of World Output in 1960 (%)	Share of World Output Today (%)	Share of World Exports Today (%)
United States	38.3%	24.0%	8.2%
Germany	8.7	4.6	7.1
France	4.6	3.2	2.8
Italy	3.0	2.4	2.4
United Kingdom	5.3	3.3	2.3
Canada	3.0	2.0	2.2
Japan	3.3	6.0	3.6
China	NA	15.2	11.1

Of course, the change in the U.S. position was not an absolute decline because the U.S. economy grew significantly between 1960 and 2018 (the economies of Germany, France, Italy, the United Kingdom, and Canada also grew during this time). Rather, it was a relative decline, reflecting the faster economic growth of several other economies, particularly China, and several other nations in Asia. For example, as can be seen from Table 1.2, from 1960 to today, China's share of world output increased from a trivial amount to 15.2 percent, making it the world's second-largest economy in terms of its share in world output (the U.S. is still the largest economy overall). Other countries that markedly increased their share of world output included Japan, Thailand, Malaysia, Taiwan, Brazil, and South Korea.

By the end of the 1980s, the U.S.'s position as the world's leading trading nation was being challenged. Over the past 30 years, U.S. dominance in export markets has waned as Japan, Germany, and a number of newly industrialized countries such as South Korea and China have taken a larger share of world exports. During the 1960s, the United States routinely accounted for 20 percent of world exports of manufactured goods. But as Table 1.2 shows, the U.S. share of world exports of goods and services has slipped to 8.2 percent, significantly behind that of China.

As emerging economies such as Brazil, Russia, India, and China—coined the BRIC countries—continue to grow, a further relative decline in the share of world output and world exports accounted for by the United States and other long-established developed nations seems likely. By itself, this is not bad. The relative decline of the United States reflects the growing economic development and industrialization of the world economy, as opposed to any absolute decline in the health of the U.S. economy.

Most forecasts now predict a continued rise in the share of world output accounted for by developing nations such as China, India, Russia, Indonesia, Thailand, South Korea, Mexico, and Brazil, and a commensurate decline in the share enjoyed by rich industrialized countries such as the United Kingdom, Germany, Japan, and the United States. Perhaps more important, if current trends continue, the Chinese economy could be larger than that of the United States within a decade, while the economy of India could become the third largest by 2030.[19]

Overall, the World Bank has estimated that today's developing nations may account for more than 60 percent of world economic activity by 2030, while today's rich nations, which currently account for more than 55 percent of world economic activity, may account for only about 38 percent. Forecasts are not always correct, but these suggest that a shift in the economic geography of the world is now under way, although the magnitude of that shift is not totally evident. For international businesses, the implications of this changing economic geography are clear: Many of tomorrow's economic opportunities may be found in the developing nations of the world, and many of tomorrow's most capable competitors will probably also emerge from these regions. A case in point has been the dramatic expansion of India's software sector, which is profiled in the accompanying Country Focus.

India's Software Sector

Some 30 years ago, a number of small software enterprises were established in Bangalore, India. Typical of these enterprises was Infosys Technologies, which was started by seven Indian entrepreneurs with about $1,000 among them. Infosys now has annual revenues of $10.2 billion and some 200,000 employees, but it is just one of more than 100 software companies clustered around Bangalore, which has become the epicenter of India's fast-growing information technology sector. From a standing start in the mid-1980s, this sector is now generating export sales of more than $100 billion.

The growth of the Indian software sector has been based on four factors. First, the country has an abundant supply of engineering talent. Every year, Indian universities graduate some 400,000 engineers. Second, labor costs in the Indian software sector have historically been low. As recently as 2008, the cost to hire an Indian graduate was roughly 12 percent of the cost of hiring an American graduate (however, this gap is narrowing fast with pay in the sector now only 30–40 percent less than in the United States). Third, many Indians are fluent in English, which makes coordination between Western firms and India easier. Fourth, due to time differences, Indians can work while Americans sleep, creating unique time efficiencies and an around-the-clock work environment.

Initially, Indian software enterprises focused on the low end of the software industry, supplying basic software development and testing services to Western firms. But as the industry has grown in size and sophistication, Indian firms have moved up the market. Today, the leading Indian companies compete directly with the likes of IBM and EDS for large software development projects, business process outsourcing contracts, and information technology consulting services. Over the past 15 years, these markets have boomed, with Indian enterprises capturing a large slice of the pie. One response of Western firms to this emerging competitive threat has been to invest in India to garner the same kind of economic advantages that Indian firms enjoy. IBM, for example, has invested $2 billion in its Indian operations and now has 150,000 employees located there, more than in any other country. Microsoft, too, has made major investments in India, including a research and development (R&D) center in Hyderabad that employs 4,000 people and was located there specifically to tap into talented Indian engineers who did not want to move to the United States.

Sources: "Ameerpet, India's Unofficial IT Training Hub," *The Economist*, March 30, 2017; "America's Pain, India's Gain: Outsourcing," *The Economist*, January 11, 2003, p. 59; "The World Is Our Oyster," *The Economist*, October 7, 2006, pp. 9–10; "IBM and Globalization: Hungry Tiger, Dancing Elephant," *The Economist*, April 7, 2007, pp. 67–69; P. Mishra, "New Billing Model May Hit India's Software Exports," *Live Mint*, February 14, 2013; and "India's Outsourcing Business: On the Turn," *The Economist*, January 19, 2013.

THE CHANGING FOREIGN DIRECT INVESTMENT PICTURE

Reflecting the dominance of the United States in the global economy, U.S. firms accounted for 66.3 percent of worldwide foreign direct investment flows in the 1960s. British firms were second, accounting for 10.5 percent, while Japanese firms were a distant eighth, with only 2 percent. The dominance of U.S. firms was so great that books were written about the economic threat posed to Europe by U.S. corporations.[20] Several European governments, most notably France, talked of limiting inward investment by U.S. firms.

However, as the barriers to the free flow of goods, services, and capital fell, and as other countries increased their shares of world output, non-U.S. firms increasingly began to invest across national borders. The motivation for much of this foreign direct investment by non-U.S. firms was the desire to disperse production activities to optimal locations and to build a direct presence in major foreign markets. Thus, beginning in the 1970s, European and Japanese firms began to shift labor-intensive manufacturing operations from their home markets to developing nations where labor costs were lower. In addition, many Japanese firms invested in North America and Europe—often as a hedge against unfavorable currency movements and the possible imposition of trade barriers. For example, Toyota, the Japanese automobile company, rapidly increased its investment in automobile production facilities in the United States and Europe during the late 1980s and 1990s. Toyota executives believed that an increasingly strong Japanese yen would price Japanese

FIGURE 1.2

FDI outward stock as a percentage of GDP.

Sources: OECD data 2019, World Development Indicators 2019, UNCTAD data base, 2019.

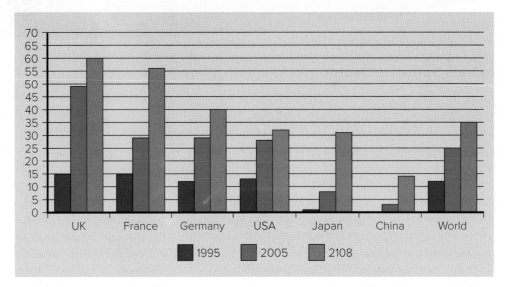

automobile exports out of foreign markets; therefore, production in the most important foreign markets, as opposed to exports from Japan, made sense. Toyota also undertook these investments to head off growing political pressures in the United States and Europe to restrict Japanese automobile exports into those markets.

One consequence of these developments is illustrated in Figure 1.2, which shows the change in the outward stock of foreign direct investment as a percentage of GDP for a selection of countries and the world as a whole. (The **outward stock of foreign direct investment (FDI)** refers to the total cumulative value of foreign investments by firms domiciled in a nation outside of that nation's borders.) Figure 1.2 illustrates a striking increase in the outward stock of FDI over time. For example, in 1995 the outward stock of FDI held by U.S. firms was equivalent to 13 percent of U.S. GDP; by 2018, that figure was 35 percent. For the world as a whole, the outward stock of FDI increased from 12 percent to 35 percent over the same time period. The clear implication is that, increasingly, firms based in a nation depend for their revenues and profits on investments and productive activities in other nations. We live in an increasingly interconnected world.

Figure 1.3 illustrates two other important trends—the sustained growth in cross-border flows of foreign direct investment that has occurred since 1990, and the increasing importance of developing nations as the destination of foreign direct investment. Throughout the 1990s, the amount of investment directed at both developed and developing nations

FIGURE 1.3

FDI inflows (in millions of dollars).

Source: United Nations Conference on Trade and Development, World Investment Report 2019. (Data for 2019–2020 are forecast.)

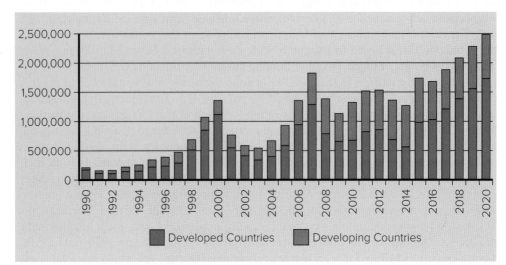

increased dramatically, a trend that reflects the increasing internationalization of business corporations. A surge in foreign direct investment from 1998 to 2000 was followed by a slump from 2001 to 2004, associated with a slowdown in global economic activity after the collapse of the financial bubble of the late 1990s and 2000. The growth of foreign direct investment resumed at "normal" levels for that time in 2005 and continued upward through 2007, when it hit record levels, only to slow again in 2008 and 2009 as the global financial crisis took hold. However, throughout this period, the growth of foreign direct investment into developing nations remained robust. Among developing nations, the largest recipient has been China, which received about $250 billion in inflows last year. As we shall see later in this text, the sustained flow of foreign investment into developing nations is an important stimulus for economic growth in those countries, which bodes well for the future of countries such as China, Mexico, and Brazil—all leading beneficiaries of this trend.

THE CHANGING NATURE OF THE MULTINATIONAL ENTERPRISE

A **multinational enterprise (MNE)** is any business that has productive activities in two or more countries. In the last 50 years, two notable trends in the demographics of the multinational enterprise have been (1) the rise of non-U.S. multinationals and (2) the growth of mini-multinationals.

Non-U.S. Multinationals

In the 1960s, global business activity was dominated by large U.S. multinational corporations. With U.S. firms accounting for about two-thirds of foreign direct investment during the 1960s, one would expect most multinationals to be U.S. enterprises. In addition, British, Dutch, and French enterprises figured prominently on lists of the world's largest multinational enterprises. By 2003, when *Forbes* magazine started to compile its annual ranking of the world's top 2,000 multinational enterprises, 776 of the 2,000 firms, or 38.8 percent, were U.S. enterprises. The second-largest source country was Japan with 16.6 percent of the largest multinationals. The United Kingdom accounted for another 6.6 percent of the world's largest multinationals at the time. As shown in Figure 1.4, by 2019 the U.S. share had fallen to 28.8 percent, or 575 firms, and the Japanese share had declined to 11.1 percent, while Chinese enterprises had emerged to comprise 309 of the total, or 15.5 percent. There has also been a notable increase in multinationals from Taiwan, India, and South Korea.

These shifts in representation of powerful multinational corporations and their home bases can be expected to continue. Specifically, we expect that even more firms from developing nations will emerge as important competitors in global markets, further

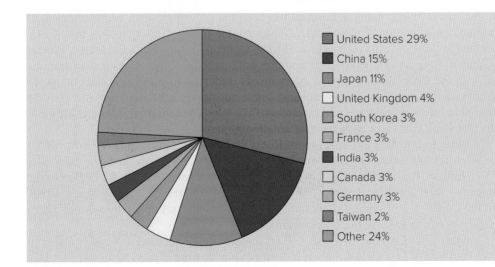

FIGURE 1.4

National share of the largest 2,000 multinational corporations in 2019.

Source: *Forbes* Global 2000 in 2019.

- United States 29%
- China 15%
- Japan 11%
- United Kingdom 4%
- South Korea 3%
- France 3%
- India 3%
- Canada 3%
- Germany 3%
- Taiwan 2%
- Other 24%

The Dalian Wanda Group

The Dalian Wanda Group is perhaps the world's largest real estate company, but is little known outside China. Established in 1988, the Dalian Wanda Group is the largest owner of five-star hotels in the world. The company's real estate portfolio includes 133 Wanda shopping malls and 84 hotels. It also has extensive holdings in the film industry, in sports companies, tourism, and children's entertainment. Dalian Wanda's stated ambition is to become a world-class multinational, a goal it may already have achieved.

In 2012, Dalian Wanda significantly expanded its international footprint when it acquired the U.S. cinema chain AMC Entertainment Holdings for $2.6 billion. At the time, the acquisition was the largest ever of a U.S. company by a Chinese enterprise, surpassing the $1.8 billion takeover of IBM's PC business by Lenovo in 2005. AMC is the second-largest cinema operator in North America, where moviegoers spend more than $10 billion a year on tickets. After the acquisition was completed, the headquarters of AMC remained in Kansas City. Dalian, however, indicated it would inject capital into AMC to upgrade its theaters to show more IMAX and 3D movies.

In 2015, Wanda followed its AMC acquisition with the purchase of Hoyts Group, an Australian cinema operator with more than 150 cinemas. By combining AMC movie theaters with Hoyts and its already extensive movie properties in China, Dalian Wanda has become the largest cinema operator in the world, with more than 500 cinemas. This puts Wanda in a strong position when negotiating distribution terms with movie studios.

Wanda is also expanding its international real estate operations. In 2014, it announced it won a bid for a prime plot of land in Beverly Hills, California. Wanda plans to invest $1.2 billion to construct a mixed-use development. The company also has a sizable project in Chicago, where it is investing $900 million to build the third-tallest building in the city. In addition, Wanda has real estate projects in Spain, Australia, and London.

Today, the Wanda Group is already among the top 400 companies in the world, with some 130,000 employees, $90 billion in assets, and about $45 billion in revenue.

Sources: Keith Weir, "China's Dalian Wanda to Acquire Australia's Hoyts for $365.7 Million," *Reuters*, June 24, 2015; Zachary Mider, "China's Wanda to Buy AMC Cinema Chain for $2.6 Billion," *Bloomberg Businessweek*, May 21, 2012; and Wanda Group Corporate, www.wanda-group.com. Corporate Profile, Official Website of Wanda Group, retrieved March 2019.

shifting the axis of the world economy away from North America and Western Europe and challenging the long dominance of companies from the so-called developed world. One such rising competitor, the Dalian Wanda Group, is profiled in the accompanying Management Focus.

The Rise of Mini-Multinationals

Another trend in international business has been the growth of small and medium-sized multinationals (mini-multinationals).[21] When people think of international businesses, they tend to think of firms such as ExxonMobil, General Motors, Ford, Panasonic, Procter & Gamble, Sony, and Unilever—large, complex multinational corporations with operations that span the globe. Although most international trade and investment is still conducted by large firms, many medium-sized and small businesses are becoming increasingly involved in international trade and investment. The rise of the Internet is lowering the barriers that small firms face in building international sales.

Consider Lubricating Systems Inc. of Kent, Washington. Lubricating Systems, which manufactures lubricating fluids for machine tools, employs 25 people, and generates sales of $6.5 million. It's hardly a large, complex multinational, yet more than $2 million of the company's sales are generated by exports to a score of countries, including Japan, Israel, and the United Arab Emirates. Lubricating Systems has also set up a joint venture with a German company to serve the European market.[22]

Consider also Lixi Inc., a small U.S. manufacturer of industrial X-ray equipment: More than half of Lixi's $24.4 million in revenues comes from exports to Japan.[23] Or take

G. W. Barth, a manufacturer of cocoa-bean roasting machinery based in Ludwigsburg, Germany. Employing just 65 people, this small company has captured 70 percent of the global market for cocoa-bean roasting machines.[24] International business is conducted not just by large firms but also by medium-sized and small enterprises.

THE CHANGING WORLD ORDER

In 1989 and 1991, a series of democratic revolutions swept the communist world. For reasons that are explored in more detail in Chapter 3, in country after country throughout eastern Europe and eventually in the Soviet Union itself, Communist Party governments collapsed. The Soviet Union receded into history, replaced by 15 independent republics. Czechoslovakia divided itself into two states, while Yugoslavia dissolved into a bloody civil war among its five successor states.

Since then, many of the former communist nations of Europe and Asia have seemed to share a commitment to democratic politics and free market economics. For half a century, these countries were essentially closed to Western international businesses. Now, they present a host of export and investment opportunities. Three decades later, the economies of many of the former communist states are still relatively undeveloped, however, and their continued commitment to democracy and market-based economic systems cannot be taken for granted. Disturbing signs of growing unrest and totalitarian tendencies are seen in several eastern European and central Asian states, including Russia, which has shifted back toward greater state involvement in economic activity and authoritarian government.[25] Thus, the risks involved in doing business in such countries are high, but so may be the returns.

In addition to these changes, quieter revolutions have been occurring in China, other countries in Southeast Asia, and Latin America. Their implications for international businesses may be just as profound as the collapse of communism in eastern Europe and Russia some time ago. China suppressed its pro-democracy movement in the bloody Tiananmen Square massacre of 1989. On the other hand, China continues to move progressively toward greater free market reforms. If what is occurring in China continues for two more decades, China may evolve from a third-world business giant into an industrial superpower even more rapidly than Japan did. If China's GDP per capita grows by an average of 6 to 7 percent, which is slower than the 8 to 10 percent growth rate achieved during the past decade, then by 2030 this nation of 1.4 billion people could boast an average GDP per capita of about $23,000, roughly the same as that of Chile or Poland today.

The potential consequences for international business are enormous. On the one hand, China represents a huge and largely untapped market. Reflecting this, between 1983 and today, annual foreign direct investment in China increased from less than $2 billion to $250 billion annually. On the other hand, China's new firms are proving to be very capable competitors, and they could take global market share away from Western and Japanese enterprises (see the Management Focus on the Dalian Wanda Group). Thus, the changes in China are creating both opportunities and threats for established international businesses.

As for Latin America, both democracy and free market reforms have been evident there, too. For decades, most Latin American countries were ruled by dictators, many of whom seemed to view Western international businesses as instruments of imperialist domination. Accordingly, they restricted direct investment by foreign firms. In addition, the poorly managed economies of Latin America were characterized by low growth, high debt, and hyperinflation—all of which discouraged investment by international businesses. In the past two decades, much of this has changed. Throughout much of Latin America, debt and inflation are down, governments have sold state-owned enterprises to private investors, foreign investment is welcomed, and the region's economies have expanded. Brazil, Mexico, and Chile have led the way. These changes have increased the attractiveness of Latin America, both as a market for exports and as a site for foreign direct investment. At the same time, given the long history of economic mismanagement in Latin America, there is no guarantee that these favorable trends will continue. Indeed, Bolivia, Ecuador, and most notably Venezuela have seen shifts back toward greater state involvement in industry in the past few years, and foreign investment is now less welcome than it was during the 1990s. In these nations, the government has seized control of oil and gas fields from foreign investors and has limited the rights of foreign energy companies to extract oil and gas from their nations. Thus, as in the case of eastern Europe, substantial opportunities are accompanied by substantial risks.

GLOBAL ECONOMY OF THE TWENTY-FIRST CENTURY

The past quarter century has seen rapid changes in the global economy. Not withstanding recent developments such as the higher tariffs introduced by the Trump Administration in the United States, barriers to the free flow of goods, services, and capital have been coming down. As their economies advance, more nations are joining the ranks of the developed world. A generation ago, South Korea and Taiwan were viewed as second-tier developing nations. Now they boast large economies, and firms based there are major players in many global industries, from shipbuilding and steel to electronics and chemicals. The move toward a global economy has been further strengthened by the widespread adoption of liberal economic policies by countries that had firmly opposed them for two generations or more. In short, current trends indicate the world is moving toward an economic system that is more favorable for international business.

But it is always hazardous to use established trends to predict the future. The world may be moving toward a more global economic system, but globalization is not inevitable. Countries may pull back from the recent commitment to liberal economic ideology if their experiences do not match their expectations. There are clear signs, for example, of a retreat from liberal economic ideology in Russia. If Russia's hesitation were to become more permanent and widespread, the liberal vision of a more prosperous global economy based on free market principles might not occur as quickly as many hope. Clearly, this would be a tougher world for international businesses.

Also, greater globalization brings with it risks of its own. This was starkly demonstrated in 1997 and 1998, when a financial crisis in Thailand spread first to other East Asian nations and then to Russia and Brazil. Ultimately, the crisis threatened to plunge the economies of the developed world, including the United States, into a recession. We explore the causes and consequences of this and other similar global financial crises in Chapter 11. Even from a purely economic perspective, globalization is not all good. The opportunities for doing business in a global economy may be significantly enhanced, but as we saw in 1997–1998, the risks associated with global financial contagion are also greater. Indeed, during 2008–2009, a crisis that started in the financial sector of America, where banks had been too liberal in their lending policies to homeowners, swept around the world and plunged the global economy into its deepest recession since the early 1980s, illustrating once more that in an interconnected world a severe crisis in one region can affect the entire globe. Still, as explained later in this text, firms can exploit the opportunities associated with globalization while reducing the risks through appropriate hedging strategies. These hedging strategies may also become more and more important as the world balances globalization efforts with a potential increase in nationalistic tendencies by some countries (e.g., recently in the United States and United Kingdom).

✓ **TEST PREP**

Use SmartBook to help retain what you have learned. Access your Instructor's Connect course to check out SmartBook or go to **learnsmartadvantage.com** for help.

LO1-4

Explain the main arguments in the debate over the impact of globalization.

The Globalization Debate

Is the shift toward a more integrated and interdependent global economy a good thing? Many influential economists, politicians, and business leaders seem to think so.[26] They argue that falling barriers to international trade and investment are the twin engines driving the global economy toward greater prosperity. They say increased international trade and cross-border investment will result in lower prices for goods and services.

They believe that globalization stimulates economic growth, raises the incomes of consumers, and helps create jobs in all countries that participate in the global trading system. The arguments of those who support globalization are covered in detail in Chapters 6, 7, and 8. As we shall see, there are good theoretical reasons for believing that declining barriers to international trade and investment do stimulate economic growth, create jobs, and raise income levels. Moreover, as described in Chapters 6, 7, and 8, empirical evidence lends support to the predictions of this theory. However, despite the existence of a compelling body of theory and evidence, globalization has its critics.[27] Some of these critics are vocal and active, taking to the streets to demonstrate their opposition to globalization. Here, we look at the nature of protests against globalization and briefly review the main themes of the debate concerning the merits of globalization. In later chapters, we elaborate on many of these points.

ANTIGLOBALIZATION PROTESTS

Popular demonstrations against globalization date back to December 1999, when more than 40,000 protesters blocked the streets of Seattle in an attempt to shut down a World Trade Organization meeting being held in the city. The demonstrators were protesting against a wide range of issues, including job losses in industries under attack from foreign competitors, downward pressure on the wage rates of unskilled workers, environmental degradation, and the cultural imperialism of global media and multinational enterprises, which was seen as being dominated by what some protesters called the "culturally impoverished" interests and values of the United States. All of these ills, the demonstrators claimed, could be laid at the feet of globalization. The World Trade Organization was meeting to try to launch a new round of talks to cut barriers to cross-border trade and investment. As such, it was seen as a promoter of globalization and a target for the protesters. The protests turned violent, transforming the normally placid streets of Seattle into a running battle between "anarchists" and Seattle's bemused and poorly prepared police department. Pictures of brick-throwing protesters and armored police wielding their batons were duly recorded by the global media, which then circulated the images around the world. Meanwhile, the WTO meeting failed to reach an agreement, and although the protests outside the meeting halls had little to do with that failure, the impression took hold that the demonstrators had succeeded in derailing the meetings.

Emboldened by the experience in Seattle, antiglobalization protesters have made a habit of turning up at major meetings of global institutions. Smaller-scale protests have periodically occurred in several countries, such as France, where antiglobalization activists destroyed a McDonald's restaurant in 1999 to protest the impoverishment of French culture by American imperialism (see the accompanying Country Focus for details). While violent protests may give the antiglobalization effort a bad name, it is clear from the scale of the demonstrations that support for the cause goes beyond a core of anarchists. Large segments of the population in many countries believe that globalization has detrimental effects on living standards, wage rates, and the environment. Indeed, the strong support for President Donald Trump in the 2016 U.S. election was primarily based on his repeated assertions that trade deals had exported U.S. jobs overseas and created unemployment and low wages in America.

Both theory and evidence suggest that many of these fears are exaggerated. Many protests against globalization are tapping into a general sense of loss at the passing of a world in which barriers of time and distance, and significant differences in economic institutions, political institutions, and the level of development of different nations produced a world rich in the diversity of human cultures. However, while the rich citizens of the developed world may have the luxury of mourning the fact that they can now see McDonald's restaurants and Starbucks coffeehouses on their vacations to exotic locations such as Thailand, fewer complaints are heard from the citizens of those countries, who welcome the higher living standards that progress brings.

Protesting Globalization in France

It all started one night in August 1999, but it might as well have been today. Back in 1999, 10 men under the leadership of local sheep farmer and rural activist José Bové crept into the town of Millau in central France and vandalized a McDonald's restaurant under construction, causing an estimated $150,000 in damage. These were no ordinary vandals, however, at least according to their supporters, for the "symbolic dismantling" of the McDonald's outlet had noble aims, or so it was claimed. The attack was initially presented as a protest against unfair American trade policies. The European Union (EU) had banned imports of hormone-treated beef from the United States, primarily because of fears that it might lead to health problems (although EU scientists had concluded there was no evidence of this). After a careful review, the World Trade Organization stated the EU ban was not allowed under trading rules that the EU and United States were party to and that the EU would have to lift it or face retaliation. The EU refused to comply, so the U.S. government imposed a 100 percent tariff on imports of certain EU products, including French staples such as foie gras, mustard, and Roquefort cheese. On farms near Millau, Bové and others raised sheep whose milk was used to make Roquefort. They felt incensed by the American tariff and decided to vent their frustrations on McDonald's.

Bové and his compatriots were arrested and charged. About the same time in the Languedoc region of France, California winemaker Robert Mondavi had reached an agreement with the mayor and council of the village of Aniane and regional authorities to turn 125 acres of wooded hillside belonging to the village into a vineyard. Mondavi planned to invest $7 million in the project and hoped to produce top-quality wine that would sell in Europe and the United States for $60 a bottle. However, local environmentalists objected to the plan, which they claimed would destroy the area's unique ecological heritage. José Bové, basking in sudden fame, offered his support to the opponents, and the protests started. In May 2001, the socialist

mayor who had approved the project was defeated in local elections in which the Mondavi project had become the major issue. He was replaced by a communist, Manuel Diaz, who denounced the project as a capitalist plot designed to enrich wealthy U.S. shareholders at the cost of his villagers and the environment. Following Diaz's victory, Mondavi announced he would pull out of the project. A spokesperson noted, "It's a huge waste, but there are clearly personal and political interests at play here that go way beyond us."*

So, are the French opposed to foreign investment? The experience of McDonald's and Mondavi seems to suggest so, as does the associated news coverage, but look closer and a different reality seems to emerge. Today, McDonald's has more than 1,200 restaurants in France. McDonald's employs 69,000 workers in the country. France is the most profitable market for McDonald's after the United States. In short, 20 years after the protests, France is a major success story for McDonald's. Moreover, France has long been one of the most favored locations for inward foreign direct investment, receiving more than $700 billion of foreign investment between 2000 and 2017, which makes it one of the top destinations for foreign investment in Europe. American companies have always accounted for a significant percentage of this investment. French enterprises have also been significant foreign investors; some 1,100 French multinationals have about $1.1 trillion of assets in other nations. For all of the populist opposition to globalization, French corporations and consumers appear to be embracing it.

*Henley, Jon. "Grapes of Wrath Scares Off US Firm." *Guardian News & Media Limited*, May 18, 2001. https://www.theguardian.com/world/2001/may/18/jonhenley.

Sources: "Behind the Bluster," *The Economist*, May 26, 2001; "The French Farmers' Anti-Global Hero," *The Economist*, July 8, 2000; C. Trueheart, "France's Golden Arch Enemy?" *Toronto Star*, July 1, 2000; United Nations, *World Investment Report*, 2014 (New York & Geneva: United Nations, 2011); and Rob Wile, "The True Story of How McDonald's Conquered France," *Business Insider*, August 22, 2014.

GLOBALIZATION, JOBS, AND INCOME

One concern frequently voiced by globalization opponents is that falling barriers to international trade destroy manufacturing jobs in wealthy advanced economies such as the United States and Western Europe. Critics argue that falling trade barriers allow firms to move manufacturing activities to countries where wage rates are much lower.[28] Indeed, due to the entry of China, India, and countries from eastern Europe into the global trading system, along with global population growth, the pool of global labor has increased more than fivefold between 1990 and today. Other things being equal, we might conclude that this enormous expansion in the global labor force, when coupled with expanding international trade, would have depressed wages in developed nations.

This fear is often supported by anecdotes. For example, D. L. Bartlett and J. B. Steele, two journalists for the *Philadelphia Inquirer* who gained notoriety for their attacks on free trade, cite the case of Harwood Industries, a U.S. clothing manufacturer that closed its U.S. operations, where it paid workers $9 per hour, and shifted manufacturing to Honduras, where textile workers received 48 cents per hour.[29] Because of moves such as this, argue Bartlett and Steele, the wage rates of poorer Americans have fallen significantly over the past quarter of a century.

In the past few years, the same fears have been applied to services, which have increasingly been outsourced to nations with lower labor costs. The popular feeling is that when corporations such as Dell, IBM, or Citigroup outsource service activities to lower-cost foreign suppliers—as all three have done—they are "exporting jobs" to low-wage nations and contributing to higher unemployment and lower living standards in their home nations (in this case, the United States). Some U.S. lawmakers have responded by calling for legal barriers to job outsourcing.

Supporters of globalization reply that critics of these trends miss the essential point about free trade agreements—the benefits outweigh the costs.[30] They argue that free trade will result in countries specializing in the production of those goods and services that they can produce most efficiently, while importing goods and services that they cannot produce as efficiently. When a country embraces free trade, there is always some dislocation—lost textile jobs at Harwood Industries or lost call-center jobs at Dell—but the whole economy is better off as a result. According to this view, it makes little sense for the United States to produce textiles at home when they can be produced at a lower cost in Honduras or China. Importing textiles from China leads to lower prices for clothes in the United States, which enables consumers to spend more of their money on other items. At the same time, the increased income generated in China from textile exports increases income levels in that country, which helps the Chinese purchase more products produced in the United States, such as pharmaceuticals from Amgen, Boeing jets, microprocessors made by Intel, Microsoft software, and Cisco routers.

The same argument can be made to support the outsourcing of services to low-wage countries. By outsourcing its customer service call centers to India, Dell can reduce its cost structure and thereby its prices for computers. U.S. consumers benefit from this development. As prices for computers fall, Americans can spend more of their money on other goods and services. Moreover, the increase in income levels in India allows Indians to purchase more U.S. goods and services, which helps create jobs in the United States. In this manner, supporters of globalization argue that free trade benefits *all* countries that adhere to a free-trade regime.

If the critics of globalization are correct, three things must be shown. First, the share of national income received by labor, as opposed to the share received by the owners of capital (e.g., stockholders and bondholders), should have declined in advanced nations as a result of downward pressure on wage rates. Second, even though labor's share of the economic pie may have declined, this does not mean lower living standards if the size of the total pie has increased sufficiently to offset the decline in labor's share—in other words, if economic growth and rising living standards in advanced economies have offset declines in labor's share (this is the position argued by supporters of globalization). Third, the decline in labor's share of national income must be due to moving production to low-wage countries, as opposed to improvement in production technology and productivity.

Several studies shed light on these issues.[31] First, the data suggest that over the past two decades, the share of labor in national income has declined. However, detailed analysis suggests the share of national income enjoyed by *skilled labor* has actually *increased*, suggesting that the fall in labor's share has been due to a fall in the share taken by *unskilled labor*. A study by the IMF suggested the earnings gap between workers in skilled and unskilled sectors has widened by 25 percent over the past two decades.[32] Another study that focused on U.S. data found that exposure to competition from imports led to a decline in real wages for workers who performed *unskilled* tasks, while having no discernible impact on wages in skilled occupations. The same study found that skilled and unskilled workers in sectors where exports grew saw an increase in their real wages.[33] These figures suggest that *unskilled labor* in sectors that have been exposed to more efficient foreign competition probably has seen its share of national income decline over the past three decades.

However, this does not mean that the *living standards* of unskilled workers in developed nations have declined. It is possible that economic growth in developed nations has offset the fall in the share of national income enjoyed by unskilled workers, raising their living standards. Evidence suggests that real labor compensation has expanded in most developed nations since the 1980s, including the United States. Several studies by the Organisation for Economic Co-operation and Development (OECD), whose members include the 34 richest economies in the world, conclude that while the gap between the poorest and richest segments of society in OECD countries has widened, in *most* countries real income levels have increased for all, including the poorest segment. In one study, the OECD found that real household income (adjusted for inflation) increased by 1.7 percent annually among its member states. The real income level of the poorest 10 percent of the population increased at 1.4 percent on average, while that of the richest 10 percent increased by 2 percent annually (i.e., while everyone got richer, the gap between the most affluent and the poorest sectors of society widened). The differential in growth rates was more extreme in the United States than most other countries. The study found that the real income of the poorest 10 percent of the population grew by just 0.5 percent a year in the United States, while that of the richest 10 percent grew by 1.9 percent annually.[34]

As noted earlier, globalization critics argue that the decline in unskilled wage rates is due to the migration of low-wage manufacturing jobs offshore and a corresponding reduction in demand for unskilled workers. However, supporters of globalization see a more complex picture. They maintain that the weak growth rate in real wage rates for unskilled workers owes far more to a technology-induced shift within advanced economies away from jobs where the only qualification was a willingness to turn up for work every day and toward jobs that require significant education and skills. They point out that many advanced economies report a shortage of highly skilled workers and an excess supply of unskilled workers. Thus, growing income inequality is a result of the wages for skilled workers being bid up by the labor market and the wages for unskilled workers being discounted. In fact, evidence suggests that technological change has had a bigger impact than globalization on the declining share of national income enjoyed by labor.[35] This suggests that a solution to the problem of slow real income growth among the unskilled is to be found not in limiting free trade and globalization but in increasing society's investment in education to reduce the supply of unskilled workers.[36]

Finally, it is worth noting that the wage gap between developing and developed nations is closing as developing nations experience rapid economic growth. For example, one estimate suggests that wages in China will approach Western levels in two decades.[37] To the extent that this is the case, any migration of unskilled jobs to low-wage countries is a temporary phenomenon representing a structural adjustment on the way to a more tightly integrated global economy.

GLOBALIZATION, LABOR POLICIES, AND THE ENVIRONMENT

A second source of concern is that free trade encourages firms from advanced nations to move manufacturing facilities to less developed countries that lack adequate regulations to protect labor and the environment from abuse by the unscrupulous.[38] Globalization critics often argue that adhering to labor and environmental regulations significantly increases the costs of manufacturing enterprises and puts them at a competitive disadvantage in the global marketplace vis-à-vis firms based in developing nations that do not have to comply with such regulations. Firms deal with this cost disadvantage, the theory goes, by moving their production facilities to nations that do not have such burdensome regulations or that fail to enforce the regulations they have.

If this were the case, we might expect free trade to lead to an increase in pollution and result in firms from advanced nations exploiting the labor of less developed nations.[39] This argument was made by those who opposed the 1994 formation of the North American Free Trade Agreement (NAFTA) among Canada, Mexico, and the United States. They painted a picture of U.S. manufacturing firms moving to Mexico so that they would be free to pollute the environment, employ child labor, and ignore workplace safety and health issues, all in the name of higher profits.[40]

Supporters of free trade and greater globalization express doubts about this scenario. They argue that tougher environmental regulations and stricter labor standards go hand in hand with economic progress.[41] In general, as countries get richer, they enact tougher environmental and labor regulations.[42] Because free trade enables developing countries to increase their economic growth rates and become richer, this should lead to tougher environmental and labor laws. In this view, the critics of free trade have got it backward: Free trade does not lead to more pollution and labor exploitation; it leads to less. By creating wealth and incentives for enterprises to produce technological innovations, the free market system and free trade could make it easier for the world to cope with pollution and population growth. Indeed, while pollution levels are rising in the world's poorer countries, they have been falling in developed nations. In the United States, for example, the concentration of carbon monoxide and sulfur dioxide pollutants in the atmosphere has decreased by 60 percent since 1978, while lead concentrations have decreased by 98 percent—and these reductions have occurred against a background of sustained economic expansion.[43]

A number of econometric studies have found consistent evidence of a hump-shaped relationship between income levels and pollution levels (see Figure 1.5).[44] As an economy grows and income levels rise, initially pollution levels also rise. However, past some point, rising income levels lead to demands for greater environmental protection, and pollution levels then fall. A seminal study by Grossman and Krueger found that the turning point generally occurred before per capita income levels reached $8,000.[45]

While the hump-shaped relationship depicted in Figure 1.5 seems to hold across a wide range of pollutants—from sulfur dioxide to lead concentrations and water quality—carbon dioxide emissions are an important exception, rising steadily with higher-income levels. Given that carbon dioxide is a heat-trapping gas and given that there is good evidence that increased atmospheric carbon dioxide concentrations are a cause of global warming, this

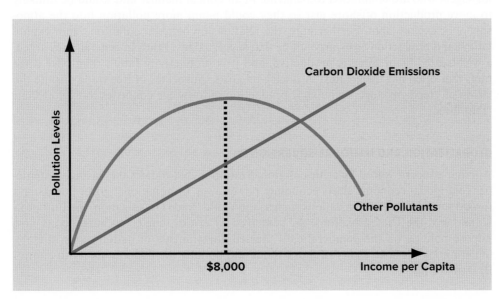

FIGURE 1.5

Income levels and environmental pollution.

Source: C. W. L. Hill and G. T. M. Hult, *Global Business Today* (New York: McGraw-Hill Education, 2018).

should be of serious concern. The solution to the problem, however, is probably not to roll back the trade liberalization efforts that have fostered economic growth and globalization, and raised living standards worldwide, but to get the nations of the world to agree to policies designed to limit carbon emissions. In the view of most economists, the most effective way to do this would be to put a price on carbon-intensive energy generation through a carbon tax. To ensure that this tax does not harm economic growth, economists argue that it should be revenue neutral, with increases in carbon taxes offset by reductions in income or consumption taxes.[46]

Although UN-sponsored talks have had reduction in carbon dioxide emissions as a central aim since the 1992 Earth Summit in Rio de Janeiro, until recently there has been little success in moving toward the ambitious goals for reducing carbon emissions laid down in the Earth Summit and subsequent talks in Kyoto, Japan, in 1997, Copenhagen in 2009, and Paris in 2015, for example. In part, this is because the largest emitters of carbon dioxide, the United States and China, failed to reach agreements about how to proceed. China, a country whose carbon emissions are increasing at a rapid rate, has until recently shown little appetite for tighter pollution controls. As for the United States, political divisions in Congress and a culture of denial have made it difficult for the country to even acknowledge, never mind move forward with, legislation designed to tackle climate change. In late 2014, the United States and China did strike a deal under which both countries agreed to potentially significant reductions in carbon emissions. This was followed by a broadly based multilateral agreement reached in Paris in 2015 that committed the nations of the world to ambitious goals for reducing CO_2 emissions and limiting future increases in global temperatures. However, President Donald Trump pulled the United States out of the Paris agreement in 2017. Trump, who disputes the theory and evidence that rising CO_2 levels are causing climate change, argued that the Paris Accord disadvantaged the United States to the exclusive benefits of other countries. Without the participation of the United States, it is difficult to see the world making significant progress on this issue.

Many supporters of free trade point out that it is possible to tie free trade agreements to the implementation of tougher environmental and labor laws in less developed countries. NAFTA, for example, was passed only after side agreements had been negotiated that committed Mexico to tougher enforcement of environmental protection regulations. Thus, supporters of free trade argue that factories based in Mexico are now cleaner than they would have been without the passage of NAFTA.[47]

They also argue that business firms are not the amoral organizations that critics suggest. While there may be some rotten apples, most business enterprises are staffed by managers who are committed to behaving in an ethical manner and would be unlikely to move production offshore just so they could pump more pollution into the atmosphere or exploit labor. Furthermore, the relationship between pollution, labor exploitation, and production costs may not be that suggested by critics. In general, they argue, a well-treated labor force is productive, and it is productivity rather than base wage rates that often has the greatest influence on costs. Advocates of free trade dispute the vision of greedy managers who shift production to low-wage countries to exploit their labor force.

GLOBALIZATION AND NATIONAL SOVEREIGNTY

Another concern voiced by critics of globalization is that today's increasingly interdependent global economy shifts economic power away from national governments and toward supranational organizations such as the World Trade Organization, the European Union, and the United Nations. As perceived by critics, unelected bureaucrats now impose policies on the democratically elected governments of nation-states, thereby undermining the sovereignty of those states and limiting the nation's ability to control its own destiny.[48]

The World Trade Organization is a favorite target of those who attack the headlong rush toward a global economy. As noted earlier, the WTO was founded in 1995 to police the world trading system established by the General Agreement on Tariffs and Trade. The WTO arbitrates trade disputes among its 164 member states. The arbitration panel can issue a ruling instructing a member state to change trade policies that violate GATT regulations. If the violator refuses to comply with the ruling, the WTO allows other states to impose appropriate trade sanctions on the transgressor. As a result, according to one prominent critic, U.S. environmentalist, consumer rights advocate, and sometime presidential candidate Ralph Nader:

> Under the new system, many decisions that affect billions of people are no longer made by local or national governments but instead, if challenged by any WTO member nation, would be deferred to a group of unelected bureaucrats sitting behind closed doors in Geneva (which is where the headquarters of the WTO are located). The bureaucrats can decide whether or not people in California can prevent the destruction of the last virgin forests or determine if carcinogenic pesticides can be banned from their foods; or whether European countries have the right to ban dangerous biotech hormones in meat. . . . At risk is the very basis of democracy and accountable decision making.[49]

In contrast to Nader, many economists and politicians maintain that the power of supranational organizations such as the WTO is limited to what nation-states collectively agree to grant. They argue that bodies such as the United Nations and the WTO exist to serve the collective interests of member states, not to subvert those interests. Supporters of supranational organizations point out that the power of these bodies rests largely on their ability to persuade member states to follow a certain action. If these bodies fail to serve the collective interests of member states, those states will withdraw their support and the supranational organization will quickly collapse. In this view, real power still resides with individual nation-states, not supranational organizations.

GLOBALIZATION AND THE WORLD'S POOR

Critics of globalization argue that despite the supposed benefits associated with free trade and investment, over the past 100 years or so the gap between the rich and poor nations of the world has gotten wider. In 1870, the average income per capita in the world's 17 richest nations was 2.4 times that of all other countries. In 1990, the same group was 4.5 times as rich as the rest. In 2019, the 34 member states of the Organisation for Economic Co-operation and Development (OECD), which includes most of the world's rich economies, had an average gross national income (GNI) per person of more than $40,000, whereas the world's 40 least developed countries had a GNI of under $1,000 per capita—implying that income per capita in the world's 34 richest nations was 40 times that in the world's 40 poorest.[50]

While recent history has shown that some of the world's poorer nations are capable of rapid periods of economic growth—witness the transformation that has occurred in some Southeast Asian nations such as South Korea, Thailand, and Malaysia—there appear to be strong forces for stagnation among the world's poorest nations. A quarter of the countries with a GDP per capita of less than $1,000 in 1960 had growth rates of less than zero, and a third had growth rates of less than 0.05 percent.[51] Critics argue that if globalization is such a positive development, this divergence between the rich and poor should not have occurred.

Although the reasons for economic stagnation vary, several factors stand out, none of which has anything to do with free trade or globalization.[52] Many of the world's poorest countries have suffered from totalitarian governments, economic policies that destroyed wealth rather than facilitated its creation, endemic corruption, scant protection for property rights, and prolonged civil war. A combination of such factors helps explain why countries such as Afghanistan, Cuba, Haiti, Iraq, Libya, Nigeria, Sudan, Syria, North Korea, and Zimbabwe have failed to improve the economic lot of their citizens during recent decades. A complicating factor is the rapidly expanding populations in many of these countries. Without a major change in government, population growth may exacerbate their problems. Promoters of free trade argue that the best way for these countries to improve their lot is to lower their barriers to free trade and investment and to implement economic policies based on free market economics.[53]

Many of the world's poorer nations are being held back by large debt burdens. Of particular concern are the 40 or so "highly indebted poorer countries" (HIPCs), which are home to some 700 million people. Among these countries, the average government debt burden has been as high as 85 percent of the value of the economy, as measured by gross domestic product, and the annual costs of serving government debt have consumed 15 percent of the country's export earnings.[54] Servicing such a heavy debt load leaves the governments of these countries with little left to invest in important public infrastructure projects, such as education, health care, roads, and power. The result is the HIPCs are trapped in a cycle of poverty and debt that inhibits economic development. Free trade alone, some argue, is a necessary but not sufficient prerequisite to help these countries bootstrap themselves out of poverty. Instead, large-scale debt relief is needed for the world's poorest nations to give them the opportunity to restructure their economies and start the long climb toward prosperity. Supporters of debt relief also argue that new democratic governments in poor nations should not be forced to honor debts that were incurred and mismanaged long ago by their corrupt and dictatorial predecessors.

In the late 1990s, a debt relief movement began to gain ground among the political establishment in the world's richer nations.[55] Fueled by high-profile endorsements from Irish rock star Bono (who has been a tireless and increasingly effective advocate for debt relief), the Dalai Lama, and influential Harvard economist Jeffrey Sachs, the debt relief movement was instrumental in persuading the United States to enact legislation in 2000 that provided $435 million in debt relief for HIPCs. More important perhaps, the United States also backed an IMF plan to sell some of its gold reserves and use the proceeds to help with debt relief. The IMF and World Bank have now picked up the banner and have embarked on a systematic debt relief program.

For such programs to have a lasting effect, however, debt relief must be matched by wise investment in public projects that boost economic growth (such as education) and by the adoption of economic policies that facilitate investment and trade.

Economists argue that the richest nations of the world can help by reducing barriers to the importation of products from the world's poorest nations, particularly tariffs on imports of agricultural products and textiles. High-tariff barriers and other impediments to trade make it difficult for poor countries to export more of their agricultural production. The World Trade Organization has estimated that if the developed nations of the world eradicated subsidies to their agricultural producers and removed tariff barriers to trade in agriculture, this would raise global economic welfare by $128 billion, with $30 billion of that going to poor nations, many of which are highly indebted. The faster growth associated with expanded trade in agriculture could significantly reduce the number of people living in poverty according to the WTO.[56]

Despite the large gap between rich and poor nations, there is evidence of substantial progress. According to data from the World Bank, the percentage of the world's population living in poverty has declined substantially over the last three decades (see Figure 1.6). In 1981, 42.2 percent of the world's population lived in extreme poverty, classified as living on less than $1.90 a day, and 66.4 percent lived on less than $5.50 per day. By 2015, these figures were 10 percent and 46 percent, respectively. Put differently, between 1981 and 2015 the number of people living in extreme poverty fell from 1.9 billion to 736 million, despite the fact that the world's population increased by around 2.5 billion over the same period. The world is getting better, and many economists would argue that globalization, and the opportunities it offers to the world's poorer nations to improve their lot, has much to do with this. On the other hand, by 2015 there were still 3.4 billion people living on less than $5.50 a day, which suggests there is still a considerable way to go.

TEST PREP

Use SmartBook to help retain what you have learned. Access your Instructor's Connect course to check out SmartBook or go to **learnsmartadvantage.com** for help.

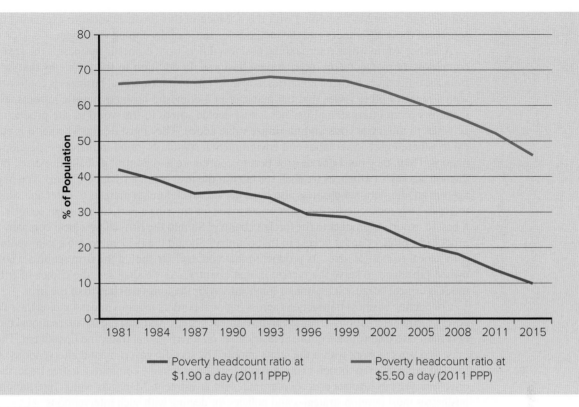

FIGURE 1.6

Percentage of the world's population living in poverty during 1981–2015.

Source: World Bank Data Base on Poverty and Equity, World Development Indicators, 2019.

Managing in the Global Marketplace

Much of this text is concerned with the challenges of managing an international business. An **international business** is any firm that engages in international trade or investment. A firm does not have to become a multinational enterprise, investing directly in operations in other countries, to engage in international business, although multinational enterprises are international businesses. All a firm has to do is export or import products from other countries. As the world shifts toward a truly integrated global economy, more firms—both large and small—are becoming international businesses. What does this shift toward a global economy mean for managers within an international business?

As their organizations increasingly engage in cross-border trade and investment, managers need to recognize that the task of managing an international business differs from that of managing a purely domestic business in many ways. At the most fundamental level, the differences arise from the simple fact that countries are different. Countries differ in their cultures, political systems, economic systems, legal systems, and levels of economic development. Despite all the talk about the emerging global village, and despite the trend toward globalization of markets and production, as we shall see in this text, many of these differences are very profound and enduring.

Differences among countries require that an international business vary its practices country by country. Marketing a product in Brazil may require a different approach from marketing the product in Germany; managing U.S. workers might require different skills from managing Japanese workers; maintaining close relations with a particular level of government may be very important in Mexico and irrelevant in Great Britain; a business strategy pursued in Canada might not work in South Korea; and so on. Managers in an international business must not only be sensitive to these differences but also adopt the appropriate

LO1-5

Understand how the process of globalization is creating opportunities and challenges for management practice.

policies and strategies for coping with them. Much of this text is devoted to explaining the sources of these differences and the methods for successfully coping with them.

A further way in which international business differs from domestic business is the greater complexity of managing an international business. In addition to the problems that arise from the differences between countries, a manager in an international business is confronted with a range of other issues that the manager in a domestic business never confronts. The managers of an international business must decide where in the world to site production activities to minimize costs and maximize value added. They must decide whether it is ethical to adhere to the lower labor and environmental standards found in many less-developed nations. Then, they must decide how best to coordinate and control globally dispersed production activities (which, as we shall see later in the text, is not a trivial problem). The managers in an international business also must decide which foreign markets to enter and which to avoid. They must choose the appropriate mode for entering a particular foreign country. Is it best to export its product to the foreign country? Should the firm allow a local company to produce its product under license in that country? Should the firm enter into a joint venture with a local firm to produce its product in that country? Or should the firm set up a wholly owned subsidiary to serve the market in that country? As we shall see, the choice of entry mode is critical because it has major implications for the long-term health of the firm.

Conducting business transactions across national borders requires understanding the rules governing the international trading and investment system. Managers in an international business must also deal with government restrictions on international trade and investment. They must find ways to work within the limits imposed by specific governmental interventions. As this text explains, even though many governments are nominally committed to free trade, they often intervene to regulate cross-border trade and investment. Managers within international businesses must develop strategies and policies for dealing with such interventions.

Cross-border transactions also require that money be converted from the firm's home currency into a foreign currency and vice versa. Because currency exchange rates vary in response to changing economic conditions, managers in an international business must develop policies for dealing with exchange rate movements. A firm that adopts the wrong policy can lose large amounts of money, whereas one that adopts the right policy can increase the profitability of its international transactions.

In sum, managing an international business is different from managing a purely domestic business for at least four reasons: (1) countries are different, (2) the range of problems confronted by a manager in an international business is wider and the problems themselves more complex than those confronted by a manager in a domestic business, (3) an international business must find ways to work within the limits imposed by government intervention in the international trade and investment system, and (4) international transactions involve converting money into different currencies.

In this text, we examine all these issues in depth, paying close attention to the different strategies and policies that managers pursue to deal with the various challenges created when a firm becomes an international business. Chapters 2, 3, and 4 explore how countries differ from each other with regard to their political, economic, legal, and cultural institutions. Chapter 5 takes a detailed look at the ethical issues, corporate social responsibility, and sustainability issues that arise in international business. Chapters 6, 7, 8, and 9 look at the global trade and investment environment within which international businesses must operate. Chapters 10, 11, and 12 review the global monetary system. These chapters focus on the nature of the foreign exchange market and the emerging global monetary system. Chapters 13 and 14 explore the strategy, organization, and market entry choices of an international business. Chapters 15 through 20 look at the management of various functional operations within an international business, including exporting, importing, countertrade, production, supply chain management, marketing, R&D, finance, and human resources. By the time you complete this text, you should have a good grasp of the issues that managers working in international business have to grapple with on a daily basis, and you should be familiar with the range of strategies and operating policies available to compete more effectively in today's rapidly emerging global economy.

TEST PREP

Use SmartBook to help retain what you have learned. Access your Instructor's Connect course to check out SmartBook or go to **learnsmartadvantage.com** for help.

Key Terms

globalization, p. 6
globalization of markets, p. 6
globalization of production, p. 7
factors of production, p. 7
General Agreement on Tariffs and
    Trade (GATT), p. 9
World Trade Organization
    (WTO), p. 9

International Monetary
    Fund (IMF), p. 10
World Bank, p. 10
United Nations (UN), p. 10
Group of Twenty (G20), p. 10
international trade, p. 11
foreign direct investment
    (FDI), p. 11

Moore's law, p. 14
outward stock of foreign direct
    investment (FDI), p. 18
multinational enterprise
    (MNE), p. 19
international business, p. 31

⊙ SUMMARY

This chapter has shown how the world economy is becoming more global and has reviewed the main drivers of globalization, arguing that they seem to be thrusting nation-states toward a more tightly integrated global economy. It looked at how the nature of international business is changing in response to the changing global economy, discussed concerns raised by rapid globalization, and reviewed implications of rapid globalization for individual managers. The chapter made the following points:

1. Over the past three decades, we have witnessed the globalization of markets and production.

2. The globalization of markets implies that national markets are merging into one huge marketplace. However, it is important not to push this view too far.

3. The globalization of production implies that firms are basing individual productive activities at the optimal world locations for their particular activities. As a consequence, it is increasingly irrelevant to talk about American products, Japanese products, or German products, because these are being replaced by "global" products. Or, in some cases, they are simply replaced by products made by specific companies, such as Apple, Sony, or Microsoft.

4. Two factors seem to underlie the trend toward globalization: declining trade barriers and changes in communication, information, and transportation technologies.

5. Since the end of World War II, barriers to the free flow of goods, services, and capital have been lowered significantly. More than anything else, this has facilitated the trend toward the globalization of production and has enabled firms to view the world as a single market.

6. As a consequence of the globalization of production and markets, in the last decade, world trade has grown faster than world output, foreign direct investment has surged, imports have penetrated more deeply into the world's industrial nations, and competitive pressures have increased in industry after industry.

7. The development of the microprocessor and related developments in communication and information processing technology have helped firms link their worldwide operations into sophisticated information networks. Jet air travel, by shrinking travel time, has also helped link the worldwide operations of international businesses. These changes have enabled firms to achieve tight coordination of their worldwide operations and to view the world as a single market.

8. In the 1960s, the U.S. economy was dominant in the world, U.S. firms accounted for most of the foreign direct investment in the world economy, U.S. firms dominated the list of large multinationals, and roughly half the world—the centrally planned economies of the communist world—was closed to Western businesses.

9. By the 2020s, the U.S. share of world output will have been cut in half, with major shares now being accounted for by European and Southeast Asian economies. The U.S. share of worldwide foreign direct investment will have fallen by about two-thirds. U.S. multinationals will be facing competition from a large number of multinationals. In addition, the emergence of mini-multinationals was noted.

10. One of the most dramatic developments of the past 30 years has been the collapse of communism in eastern Europe, which has created enormous opportunities for international businesses. In addition, the move toward free market economies in China and Latin America is

creating opportunities (and threats) for Western international businesses.

11. The benefits and costs of the emerging global economy are being hotly debated among businesspeople, economists, and politicians. The debate focuses on the impact of globalization on jobs, wages, the environment, working conditions, national sovereignty, and extreme poverty in the world's poorest nations.

12. Managing an international business is different from managing a domestic business for at least

four reasons: (1) countries are different, (2) the range of problems confronted by a manager in an international business is wider and the problems themselves are more complex than those confronted by a manager in a domestic business, (3) managers in an international business must find ways to work within the limits imposed by governments' intervention in the international trade and investment system, and (4) international transactions involve converting money into different currencies.

Critical Thinking and Discussion Questions

1. Describe the shifts in the world economy over the past 30 years. What are the implications of these shifts for international businesses based in the United Kingdom? North America? Hong Kong?

2. "The study of international business is fine if you are going to work in a large multinational enterprise, but it has no relevance for individuals who are going to work in small firms." Evaluate this statement.

3. How have changes in technology contributed to the globalization of markets and production? Would the globalization of production and markets have been possible without these technological changes?

4. "Ultimately, the study of international business is no different from the study of domestic business. Thus, there is no point in having a separate course on international business." Evaluate this statement.

5. How does the Internet affect international business activity and the globalization of the world economy?

6. If current trends continue, China may be the world's largest economy by 2035. Discuss the possible implications of such a development for
   a. the world trading system.
   b. the world monetary system.

   c. the business strategy of today's European and U.S.-based global corporations.
   d. global commodity prices.

7. Reread the Management Focus "Boeing's Global Production System" and answer the following questions:
   a. What are the benefits to Boeing of outsourcing manufacturing of components of the Boeing 787 to firms based in other countries?
   b. What are the potential costs and risks to Boeing of outsourcing?
   c. In addition to foreign subcontractors and Boeing, who else benefits from Boeing's decision to outsource component part manufacturing assembly to other nations? Who are the potential losers?
   d. If Boeing's management decided to keep all production in America, what do you think the effect would be on the company, its employees, and the communities that depend on it?
   e. On balance, do you think that the kind of outsourcing undertaken by Boeing is a good thing or a bad thing for the American economy? Explain your reasoning.

globalEDGE research task globaledge.msu.edu

Use the globalEDGE™ website (**globaledge.msu.edu**) to complete the following exercises:

1. As the drivers of globalization continue to pressure both the globalization of markets and the globalization of production, we continue to see the impact of greater globalization on worldwide trade patterns. HSBC, a large global bank,

analyzes these pressures and trends to identify opportunities across markets and sectors through its *trade forecasts*. Visit the HSBC Global Connections site and use the trade forecast tool to identify which export routes are forecast to see the greatest growth over the next 15 to 20 years. What patterns do you see? What types of countries dominate these routes?

2. You are working for a company that is considering investing in a foreign country. Investing in countries with different traditions is an important element of your company's long-term strategic goals. Management has requested a report regarding the attractiveness of alternative countries based on the potential return of FDI. Accordingly, the ranking of the top 25 countries in terms of FDI attractiveness is a crucial ingredient for your report. A colleague mentioned a potentially useful tool called the Foreign Direct Investment (FDI) Confidence Index. The FDI Confidence Index is a regular survey of global executives conducted by A.T. Kearney. Find this index and provide additional information regarding how the index is constructed.

CLOSING CASE

General Motors in China

In November 2018, General Motors, America's largest home-grown automobile manufacturer, announced it would close three assembly plants in the United States, laying off about 5,600 employees. All of these plants made passenger cars that had fallen out of favor with U.S. consumers, who preferred to purchase sports utility vehicles and pick-up trucks.

Jvdwolf/123RF

President Donald Trump, who has made the revival of traditional U.S. manufacturing industries one of his major goals, quickly tweeted that he was "*Very disappointed with General Motors and their CEO, Mary Barra, for closing plants in Ohio, Michigan and Maryland. Nothing being closed in Mexico & China. The U.S. saved General Motors, and this is the THANKS we get! We are now looking at cutting all @GM subsidies including for electric cars. General Motors made a big China bet years ago when they built plants there (and in Mexico)—don't think that bet is going to pay off. I am here to protect American Workers!*"* In an interview with the *Wall Street Journal,* Trump offered the observation that "*I think GM ought to stop making cars in China and make them here.*"

Trump was right that GM had made a major bet on China. GM has been operating in China since 1997 when it established a joint venture with SAIC Motor, a Chinese state-owned automotive design and manufacturing company. GM has a 50 percent ownership stake in the joint venture, which is known as SAIC-GM. In 2018, GM and its joint venture partner built and sold some 3.64 million vehicles in China, up from 1.2 million in 2011 and 0.4 million in 2006. By comparison, in 2018 GM sold 2.95 million vehicles in the United States. China is now the world's largest automobile market. It's been the largest market for GM since 2012. Despite the size of the Chinese market, there is still lots of room for growth. There are around 173 vehicles per capita in China, compared to 833 per capita in the United States.

GM sells models in China under the Chevrolet, Buick, GMC, Cadillac, Holden, Baojun, Wuling, and Jiefang brands. GM exports almost nothing from the U.S. to China, although it does export one China-built model, the Buick Envision, to the American market. GM says it cannot build the Buick Envision economically in the U.S., because the Chinese market accounts for 80 percent of the model's global sales.

Like many automakers, GM believes it needs factories close to its customers in order to reduce supply chain costs and design vehicles that best suit local market demands. GM also wants to be in China because the country is leading the shift away from gasoline engines toward battery-powered electric motors. Sales of electric vehicles in China are four times higher than in the United States and growing faster. To foster the growth in electric vehicle production, China has been providing generous subsidies to local producers (including SAIC-GM) and consumers. GM has pledged to invest heavily in electric vehicles and plans to launch 20 electric models in China by 2023.

In addition, there have long been tariffs on imports of motor vehicles into China. Local production avoids these. In 2018, China increased tariffs on imports of

*Donald John Trump. *Twitter,* November 27, 2018. **https://twitter.com/ realdonaldtrump**.

American made cars into China from 15 percent to 40 percent in retaliation for wide-ranging tariffs Trump had placed on imports of Chinese products into the United States. These tariff increases had little impact on GM, which produced all of its Chinese sales locally. However, they did impact another American manufacturer, Tesla, which had been doing what Trump wanted GM to do: export production from the United States to China. Tesla's Chinese sales fell in half in the months after the tariffs were raised. In response, Tesla slashed prices in China and stated it would accelerate plans to build production facilities there, opening a factory in 2021 or 2022.

Sources: Trefor Moss, "Why GM Is Likely to Keep Producing in China Despite Trump's Pleas," *The Wall Street Journal*, November 27, 2018; Anjani Trivedi, "GM Needs China more than It Fears Trump," *Bloomberg*, November 27, 2018; Wolf Richter, "GM's Business Is Booming in China," *Business Insider*, December 6, 2018; Jack Perkowski, "What China's Shifting Subsidies Could Mean for Its Electric Vehicle Industry," *Forbes*, July 13, 2018.

Case Discussion Questions

1. What are the long-term prospects for the Chinese market?
2. Does it make sense for GM to produce automobiles for the Chinese market in China? Why?
3. What do you think would happen if GM tried to serve the Chinese market by exporting production from the United States?
4. Why do you think GM went into partnership with a state-owned company to produce automobiles in China? What are the possible benefits of such a venture? What might be the downside?
5. What does this case teach you about benefits and costs of import tariffs?

Design elements: Modern textured halftone: ©VIPRESIONA/ Shutterstock; globalEDGE icon: ©globalEDGE; All others: ©McGraw-Hill Education

Endnotes

1. Thomas L. Friedman, *The World Is Flat* (New York: Farrar, Straus and Giroux, 2005).

2. T. Levitt, "The Globalization of Markets," *Harvard Business Review*, May–June 1983, pp. 92–102.

3. U.S. Department of Commerce, Internal Trade Administration, "Profile of U.S. Exporting and Importing Companies, 2012-2013," April 2015.

4. C. M. Draffen, "Going Global: Export Market Proves Profitable for Region's Small Businesses," *Newsday*, March 19, 2001, p. C18.

5. See F. T. Knickerbocker, *Oligopolistic Reaction and Multinational Enterprise* (Boston: Harvard Business School Press, 1973); R. E. Caves, "Japanese Investment in the U.S.: Lessons for the Economic Analysis of Foreign Investment," *The World Economy* 16 (1993), pp. 279–300.

6. I. Metthee, "Playing a Large Part," *Seattle Post-Intelligencer*, April 9, 1994, p. 13.

7. R. B. Reich, *The Work of Nations* (New York: Knopf, 1991).

8. United Nations, "About the United Nations," www.un.org/en/about-un.

9. J. A. Frankel, "Globalization of the Economy," National Bureau of Economic Research, working paper no. 7858, 2000.

10. J. Bhagwati, *Protectionism* (Cambridge, MA: MIT Press, 1989).

11. F. Williams, "Trade Round Like This May Never Be Seen Again," *Financial Times*, April 15, 1994, p. 8.

12. Data are from UNCTAD, *World Investment Report 2019*, United Nations, 2019.

13. Moore's law is named after Intel founder Gordon Moore.

14. Data compiled from various sources and listed at www.internetworldstats.com/stats.htm.

15. From www.census.gov/mrts/www/ecomm.html. See also S. Fiegerman, "Ecommerce Is Now a Trillion Dollar Industry," *Mashable Business*, February 5, 2013.

16. For a counterpoint, see "Geography and the Net: Putting It in Its Place," *The Economist*, August 11, 2001, pp. 18–20.

17. International Chamber of Shipping, Key Facts, www.ics-shipping.org/shipping-facts/key-facts.

18. Frankel, "Globalization of the Economy."

19. Raj Kumar Ray, "India's Economy to Become 3rd Largest, Surpass Japan, Germany by 2030," *Hindustan Times*, April 28, 2017.

20. N. Hood and J. Young, *The Economics of the Multinational Enterprise* (New York: Longman, 1973).

21. S. Chetty, "Explosive International Growth and Problems of Success Among Small and Medium Sized Firms," *International Small Business Journal*, February 2003, pp. 5–28.

22. R. A. Mosbacher, "Opening Up Export Doors for Smaller Firms," *Seattle Times*, July 24, 1991, p. A7.

23. "Small Companies Learn How to Sell to the Japanese," *Seattle Times*, March 19, 1992.

24. W. J. Holstein, "Why Johann Can Export, but Johnny Can't," *BusinessWeek*, November 3, 1991. Archived at www.businessweek.com/stories/1991-11-03/why-johann-can-export-but-johnny-cant.

25. N. Buckley and A. Ostrovsky, "Back to Business—How Putin's Allies Are Turning Russia into a Corporate State," *Financial Times*, June 19, 2006, p. 11.

26. J. E. Stiglitz, *Globalization and Its Discontents* (New York: W. W. Norton, 2003); J. Bhagwati, *In Defense of Globalization* (New York: Oxford University Press, 2004); Friedman, *The World Is Flat.*

27. See, for example, Ravi Batra, *The Myth of Free Trade* (New York: Touchstone Books, 1993); William Greider, *One World, Ready or Not: The Manic Logic of Global Capitalism* (New York: Simon & Schuster, 1997); D. Radrik, *Has Globalization Gone Too Far?* (Washington, DC: Institution for International Economics, 1997).

28. E. Goldsmith, "The Winners and the Losers," in *The Case Against the Global Economy*, ed. J. Mander and E. Goldsmith (San Francisco: Sierra Club, 1996); Lou Dobbs, *Exporting America* (New York: Time Warner Books, 2004).

29. D. L. Bartlett and J. B. Steele, "America: Who Stole the Dream," *Philadelphia Inquirer*, September 9, 1996.

30. For example, see Paul Krugman, *Pop Internationalism* (Cambridge, MA: MIT Press, 1996).

31. For example, see B. Milanovic and L. Squire, "Does Tariff Liberalization Increase Wage Inequality?" National Bureau of Economic Research, working paper no. 11046, January 2005; B. Milanovic, "Can We Discern the Effect of Globalization on Income Distribution?" *World Bank Economic Review* 19 (2005), pp. 21–44. Also see the summary in Thomas Piketty, "The Globalization of Labor," in *Capital in the Twenty First Century* (Cambridge, MA: Harvard University Press, 2014).

32. See Piketty, "The Globalization of Labor."

33. A. Ebenstein, A. Harrison, M. McMillam, and S. Phillips, "Estimating the Impact of Trade and Offshoring on American Workers Using the Current Population Survey," *Review of Economics and Statistics* 67 (October 2014), pp. 581–95.

34. M. Forster and M. Pearson, "Income Distribution and Poverty in the OECD Area," *OECD Economic Studies* 34 (2002); OECD, "Growing Income Inequality in OECD Countries," *OECD Forum*, May 2, 2011.

35. See Piketty, "The Globalization of Labor."

36. See Krugman, *Pop Internationalism*; D. Belman and T. M. Lee, "International Trade and the Performance of U.S. Labor Markets," in *U.S. Trade Policy and Global Growth*, ed. R. A. Blecker (New York: Economic Policy Institute, 1996).

37. R. B. Freeman, "Labor Market Imbalances: Shortages, Surpluses, or What?" Volume 51, Conference Series, *Federal Reserve Bank of Boston*, 2006.

38. E. Goldsmith, "Global Trade and the Environment," in *The Case Against the Global Economy*, eds. J. Mander and E. Goldsmith (San Francisco: Sierra Club, 1996).

39. P. Choate, *Jobs at Risk: Vulnerable U.S. Industries and Jobs Under NAFTA* (Washington, DC: Manufacturing Policy Project, 1993).

40. P. Choate, *Jobs at Risk: Vulnerable U.S. Industries and Jobs Under NAFTA* (Washington, DC: Manufacturing Policy Project, 1993).

41. B. Lomborg, *The Skeptical Environmentalist* (Cambridge, UK: Cambridge University Press, 2001).

42. H. Nordstrom and S. Vaughan, *Trade and the Environment, World Trade Organization Special Studies No. 4* (Geneva: WTO, 1999).

43. Figures are from "Freedom's Journey: A Survey of the 20th Century. Our Durable Planet," *The Economist*, September 11, 1999, p. 30.

44. For an exhaustive review of the empirical literature, see B. R. Copeland and M. Scott Taylor, "Trade, Growth and the Environment," *Journal of Economic Literature*, March 2004, pp. 7–77.

45. G. M. Grossman and A. B. Krueger, "Economic Growth and the Environment," *Quarterly Journal of Economics* 110 (1995), pp. 353–78.

46. For an economic perspective on climate change, see William Nordhouse, *The Climate Casino* (Princeton, NJ: Yale University Press, 2013).

47. Krugman, *Pop Internationalism.*

48. R. Kuttner, "Managed Trade and Economic Sovereignty," in *U.S. Trade Policy and Global Growth*, ed. R. A. Blecker (New York: Economic Policy Institute, 1996).

49. Nader, Ralph, and Lori Wallach. "GATT, NAFTA, and the subversion of the Democratic Process." U.S. Trade Policy and Global Growth, ed. The Case Against the Global Economy. Sierra Club Books.

50. Lant Pritchett, "Divergence, Big Time," *Journal of Economic Perspectives* 11, no. 3 (Summer 1997), pp. 3–18. The data are from the World Bank's *World Development Indicators*, 2015.

51. Lant Pritchett, "Divergence, Big Time," *Journal of Economic Perspectives* 11, no. 3 (Summer 1997), pp. 3–18. The data are from the World Bank's *World Development Indicators*, 2015.

52. W. Easterly, "How Did Heavily Indebted Poor Countries Become Heavily Indebted?" *World Development*, October 2002, pp. 1677–96; J. Sachs, *The End of Poverty* (New York: Penguin Books, 2006).

53. See D. Ben-David, H. Nordstrom, and L. A. Winters, *Trade, Income Disparity and Poverty.* World Trade Organization Special Studies No. 5 (Geneva: WTO, 1999).

54. William Easterly, "Debt Relief," *Foreign Policy*, November-December 2001, pp. 20–26.

55. Jeffrey Sachs, "Sachs on Development: Helping the World's Poorest," *The Economist*, August 14, 1999, pp. 17–20.

56. World Trade Organization, *Annual Report 2003* (Geneva: WTO, 2004).

National Differences in Political, Economic, and Legal Systems

2

LEARNING OBJECTIVES

After reading this chapter, you will be able to:

LO2-1   Understand how the political systems of countries differ.

LO2-2   Understand how the economic systems of countries differ.

LO2-3   Understand how the legal systems of countries differ.

LO2-4   Explain the implications for management practice of national differences in political economy.

Bartosz Hadyniak/E+/Getty Images

Kenya: An African Lion

OPENING CASE

The East African nation of Kenya has emerged as one of the economic growth stories of sub-Saharan Africa. Real Gross Domestic Product grew at 4.9 percent in 2017 and 5.9 percent in 2018. Growth for 2019 and 2020 is expected to be in the 6 percent range. Kenya is East Africa's economic, financial, and transportation hub. Major industries include agriculture, mining, manufacturing, tourism, communications, and financial services.

When Kenya won its independence from Britain in 1963, the country embraced what was known at the time as "African Socialism." The principles of African Socialism included social development guided by a large public sector, emphasis on the African identity and what it means to be African, and the avoidance of social classes within society. Practically, this meant significant public investment in infrastructure by state-owned companies, coupled with the encouragement of smallholder agricultural production. The country also embraced a policy of import substitution, applying high tariffs to foreign manufactured goods in an attempt to foster domestic production.

While these policies initially produced some gains, particularly in the agricultural sector, by the early 1990s the economy was stagnating. In 1993, Kenya embarked on a program of economic reform and liberalization that included removing price controls, lowering barriers to cross-border trade, privatizing state-owned enterprises, and the adoption of conservative fiscal and monetary macroeconomic policies. Today, the economy of the country is primarily market-based, with relatively low barriers to cross-border trade and investment, and a vibrant private sector.

Paralleling economic reforms there have been political reforms. Like many sub-Saharan Africa nations whose boundaries were drawn by colonial powers, the country was left divided between multiple ethnic groups. Political parties reflected these ethnic divides. Tension between ethnic groups often marred Kenyan politics. The largest ethnic group is the Kikuyu, who, while only comprising 22 percent of the population, have held a disproportionate influence over Kenyan politics since independence. Kenya was effectively a one-party state until the early 1990s. Ethnic conflict has continued since then, often spilling over into the political arena. A new constitution introduced in 2010 has offered the promise of solving some of these long-standing problems. The constitution placed limits on the power of the central government, devolved political power into 47 semi-autonomous regions, and helped create an electoral framework capable of facilitating regular, free, and fair elections. These political reforms have allowed for more democracy, increased business confidence, and helped drive great economic growth in this nation of 50 million people.

Looking forward, one of Kenya's great strengths is the relative youth of its population and an educated workforce. Kenya has universal primary education and a respectable secondary and higher-education system. The country also has a growing urban middle class, which will likely drive the demand for goods and services going forward. That being said, the country still faces some significant headwinds. On the economic front, property rights are not strong, with legal title over land often poorly established. This makes it difficult for Kenyans to raise money for business ventures using their land as collateral. More generally, according to the World Bank, Kenyans face multiple problems starting a business due to bureaucratic procedures and corruption. On average, starting a business in Kenya can take 126 days and involves seven separate procedures. By comparison, in South Korea it takes 11 days and involves two procedures. The World Bank ranks Kenya 61 out of 190 nations on the ease of doing business. Corruption and ethnic conflict remain persistent problems. Transparency International ranked Kenya 144 out of 180 nations on its 2018 corruption index. Terrorism is also a problem with Al-Shabab (a militant group based in neighboring Somalia that has links to Al-Qaeda), which launched violent attacks in the capital of Nairobi in 2013 and 2019. Al-Shabab's goal is to avenge Kenyan interventions in Somalia against Al-Shabab. Despite these problems, however, Kenya shows promise in emerging from its post-colonial past and in becoming a dynamic multi-ethnic state with a thriving economy and a more stable democracy.

Sources: Leighann Spencer, "Kenya's History of Political Violence: Colonialism, Vigilantes and Militias," *The Conversation*, September 28, 2017; Amy Copley, "Figures of the Week: Kenya's Growth Trends and Prospects in Africa's Lions," *Brookings*, November 2, 2016; "Another Terrorist Outrage in Nairobi," *The Economist*, January 16, 2019; X. N. Iraki, "Why Kenya's Economic Prospects Look Promising," *Standard Digital*, January 1, 2019.

Introduction

International business is much more complicated than domestic business because countries differ in many ways. Countries have different political, economic, and legal systems. They vary significantly in their level of economic development and future economic growth trajectory. Cultural practices can vary dramatically, as can the education and skill levels of the population. All these differences can and do have major implications for the practice of international business. They have a profound impact on the benefits, costs, and risks associated with doing business in different countries; the way in which operations in different countries should be managed; and the strategy international firms should pursue in different countries. The main function of this chapter and the next two is to develop an awareness of and appreciation for the significance of country differences in political systems, economic systems, legal systems, economic development, and societal culture. Another function of the three chapters is to describe how the political, economic, legal, and cultural systems of many of the world's nation-states are evolving and to draw out the implications of these changes for the practice of international business.

This chapter focuses on how the political, economic, and legal systems of countries differ. Collectively, we refer to these systems as constituting the political economy of a country. We use the term **political economy** to stress that the political, economic, and legal systems of a country are interdependent; they interact with and influence each other, and in doing so, they affect the level of economic well-being. In Chapter 3, we build on the concepts discussed here to explore in detail how differences in political, economic, and legal systems influence the economic development of a nation-state and its likely future growth trajectory. In Chapter 4, we look at differences in societal culture and at how these differences influence the practice of international business. Moreover, as we will see in Chapter 4, societal culture has an influence on the political, economic, and legal systems in a nation and thus its level of economic well-being. We also discuss how the converse may occur: how political, economic, and legal systems may also shape societal culture.

The opening case illustrates some of the issues discussed in this chapter. Following independence from Britain in 1963, Kenya became a de facto one-party state that embraced socialist ideals, albeit with a distinct "African" hew. By the 1990s, the post-independence political economy of Kenya had resulted in economic stagnation. Things started to change in the early 1990s when opposition political parties were allowed to participate in elections, and the Government embraced economic reforms that included the privatization of public enterprises, liberalization of cross-border trade, and the removal of price controls. Further political reforms took place in 2010 when Kenya adopted a new constitution that devolved significant political power to autonomous regions, a development that many observers believe will help moderate ethnic tensions in the country. Helped by a young and

globalEDGE GET INSIGHTS BY COUNTRY

The "Get Insights by Country" section of globalEDGE™ (**globaledge.msu.edu/global-insights/by/country**) is your source for information and statistical data for nearly every country around the world (more than 200 countries). As related to Chapter 2 of the text, globalEDGE™ has a wealth of information and data on national differences in political economy. These differences are available across a dozen menu categories in the country sections (e.g., economy, history, government, culture, risk). The "Executive Memos" on each country page are also great for abbreviated fingertip access to current information.

well-educated growing urban population, since then the Kenyan economy has performed well and seems on track to achieve growth rates of around 6 percent per annum. The implication is that political and economic reforms have helped boost economic growth in the country, making it a more desirable location for international business. Nevertheless, risks remain for international businesses, including endemic corruption, weak property rights, smoldering ethnic tensions, and terrorism.

Political Systems

LO2-1
Understand how the political systems of countries differ.

The political system of a country shapes its economic and legal systems.[1] Thus, we need to understand the nature of different political systems before discussing economic and legal systems. By **political system**, we mean the system of government in a nation. Political systems can be assessed according to two dimensions. The first is the degree to which they emphasize collectivism as opposed to individualism. The second is the degree to which they are democratic or totalitarian. These dimensions are interrelated; systems that emphasize collectivism tend to lean toward totalitarianism, whereas those that place a high value on individualism tend to be democratic. However, a large gray area exists in the middle. It is possible to have democratic societies that emphasize a mix of collectivism and individualism. Similarly, it is possible to have totalitarian societies that are not collectivist.

COLLECTIVISM AND INDIVIDUALISM

Collectivism refers to a political system that stresses the primacy of collective goals over individual goals.[2] When collectivism is emphasized, the needs of society as a whole are generally viewed as being more important than individual freedoms. In such circumstances, an individual's right to do something may be restricted on the grounds that it runs counter to "the good of society" or to "the common good." Advocacy of collectivism can be traced to the ancient Greek philosopher Plato (427–347 B.C.), who, in *The Republic*, argued that individual rights should be sacrificed for the good of the majority and that property should be owned in common. Plato did not equate collectivism with equality; he believed that society should be stratified into classes, with those best suited to rule (which for Plato, naturally, were philosophers and soldiers) administering society for the benefit of all. In modern times, the collectivist mantle has been picked up by socialists.

Socialism

Modern **socialists** trace their intellectual roots to Karl Marx (1818–1883), although socialist thought clearly predates Marx (elements of it can be traced to Plato). Marx argued that the few benefit at the expense of the many in a capitalist society where individual freedoms are not restricted. While successful capitalists accumulate considerable wealth, Marx postulated that the wages earned by the majority of workers in a capitalist society would be forced down to subsistence levels. He argued that capitalists expropriate for their own use the value created by workers, while paying workers only subsistence wages in return. According to Marx, the pay of workers does not reflect the full value of their labor. To correct this perceived wrong, Marx advocated state ownership of the basic means of production, distribution, and exchange (i.e., businesses). His logic was that if the state owned the means of production, the state could ensure that workers were fully compensated for their labor. Thus, the idea is to manage state-owned enterprise to benefit society as a whole, rather than individual capitalists.[3]

In the early twentieth century, the socialist ideology split into two broad camps. The **communists** believed that socialism could be achieved only through violent revolution and totalitarian dictatorship, whereas the **social democrats** committed themselves to achieving socialism by democratic means, turning their backs on violent revolution and dictatorship. Both versions of socialism waxed and waned during the twentieth century.

The communist version of socialism reached its high point in the late 1970s, when the majority of the world's population lived in communist states. The countries under Communist Party rule at that time included the former Soviet Union; its eastern European client nations (e.g., Poland, Czechoslovakia, Hungary); China; the southeast Asian nations of Cambodia, Laos, and Vietnam; various African nations (e.g., Angola and Mozambique); and the Latin American nations of Cuba and Nicaragua. By the mid-1990s, however, communism was in retreat worldwide. The Soviet Union had collapsed and had been replaced by a collection of 15 republics, many of which were at least nominally structured as democracies. Communism was swept out of eastern Europe by the largely bloodless revolutions of 1989. Although China is still nominally a communist state with substantial limits to individual political freedom, in the economic sphere, the country has moved sharply away from strict adherence to communist ideology. Old-style communism, with state control over all economic activity, hangs on in only a handful of small fringe states, most notably North Korea.

Social democracy also seems to have passed a high-water mark, although the ideology may prove to be more enduring than communism. Social democracy has had perhaps its greatest influence in a number of democratic Western nations, including Australia, Denmark, Finland, France, Germany, Great Britain, Norway, Spain, and Sweden, where social democratic parties have often held political power. Other countries where social democracy has had an important influence include India and Brazil. Consistent with their Marxist roots, after World War II social democratic government in some nations nationalized some private companies, transforming them into state-owned enterprises to be run for the "public good rather than private profit." This trend was most marked in Great Britain where by the end of the 1970s state-owned companies had a monopoly in the telecommunications, electricity, gas, coal, railway, and shipbuilding industries, as well as substantial interests in the oil, airline, auto, and steel industries.

However, experience demonstrated that state ownership of the means of production ran counter to the public interest. In many countries, state-owned companies performed poorly. Protected from competition by their monopoly position and guaranteed government financial support, many became increasingly inefficient. Individuals paid for the luxury of state ownership through higher prices and higher taxes. As a consequence, a number of Western democracies voted many social democratic parties out of office in the late 1970s and early 1980s. They were succeeded by political parties, such as Britain's Conservative Party and Germany's Christian Democratic Party, that were more committed to free market economics. These parties sold state-owned enterprises to private investors (a process referred to as **privatization**). Even where social democratic parties regained the levers of power, as in Great Britain in 1997 when the left-leaning Labor Party won control of the government, they too were now committed to continued private ownership.

Individualism

The opposite of collectivism, **individualism** refers to a philosophy that an individual should have freedom in his or her economic and political pursuits. In contrast to collectivism, individualism stresses that the interests of the individual should take precedence over the interests of the state. Like collectivism, individualism can be traced to an ancient Greek philosopher, in this case Plato's disciple Aristotle (384–322 B.C.). In contrast to Plato, Aristotle argued that individual diversity and private ownership are desirable. In a passage that might have been taken from a speech by contemporary politicians who adhere to a free market ideology, he argued that private property is more highly productive than communal property and will thus stimulate progress. According to Aristotle, communal property receives little care, whereas property that is owned by an individual will receive the greatest care and therefore be most productive.

Individualism was reborn as an influential political philosophy in the Protestant trading nations of England and the Netherlands during the sixteenth century. The philosophy was refined in the work of a number of British philosophers, including David Hume

(1711–1776), Adam Smith (1723–1790), and John Stuart Mill (1806–1873). Individualism exercised a profound influence on those in the American colonies that sought independence from Great Britain. Indeed, the concept underlies the ideas expressed in the Declaration of Independence. In the twentieth century, several Nobel Prize–winning economists—including Milton Friedman, Friedrich von Hayek, and James Buchanan—championed the philosophy.

Individualism is built on two central tenets. The first is an emphasis on the importance of guaranteeing individual freedom and self-expression. The second tenet of individualism is that the welfare of society is best served by letting people pursue their own economic self-interest, as opposed to some collective body (such as government) dictating what is in society's best interest. Or, as Adam Smith put it in a famous passage from *The Wealth of Nations*, "an individual who intends his own gain is led by an invisible hand to promote an end that was no part of his intention. Nor is it always worse for the society that it was no part of it. By pursuing his own interest, he frequently promotes that of the society more effectually than when he really intends to promote it. This author has never known much good done by those who effect to trade for the public good."[4]

The central message of individualism, therefore, is that individual economic and political freedoms are the ground rules on which a society should be based. This puts individualism in conflict with collectivism. Collectivism asserts the primacy of the collective over the individual; individualism asserts the opposite. This underlying ideological conflict shaped much of the recent history of the world. The Cold War, for example, was in many respects a war between collectivism, championed by the former Soviet Union, and individualism, championed by the United States. From the late 1980s until about 2005, the waning of collectivism was matched by the ascendancy of individualism. Democratic ideals and market economics replaced socialism and communism in many states. Since 2005, there have been some signs of a swing back toward left-leaning socialist ideas in several countries, including several Latin America nations such as Venezuela, Bolivia, and Paraguay, along with Russia (see the Country Focus for details). Also, the global financial crisis of 2008–2009 caused some reevaluation of the trends toward individualism, and it remains possible that the pendulum might tilt back the other way.

DEMOCRACY AND TOTALITARIANISM

Democracy and totalitarianism are at different ends of a political dimension. **Democracy** refers to a political system in which government is by the people, exercised either directly or through elected representatives. **Totalitarianism** is a form of government in which one person or political party exercises absolute control over all spheres of human life and prohibits opposing political parties. The democratic–totalitarian dimension is not independent of the individualism–collectivism dimension. Democracy and individualism go hand in hand, as do the communist version of collectivism and totalitarianism. However, gray areas exist; it is possible to have a democratic state in which collective values predominate, and it is possible to have a totalitarian state that is hostile to collectivism and in which some degree of individualism—particularly in the economic sphere—is encouraged. For example, China and Vietnam have seen a move toward greater individual freedom in the economic sphere, but those countries are stilled ruled by parties that have a monopoly on political power and constrain political freedom.

Democracy

The pure form of democracy, as originally practiced by several city-states in ancient Greece, is based on a belief that citizens should be directly involved in decision making. In complex, advanced societies with populations in the tens or hundreds of millions, this is impractical. Most modern democratic states practice **representative democracy**. The United States, for example, is a constitutional republic that operates as a representative democracy. In a representative democracy, citizens periodically elect individuals to represent them. These elected representatives then form a government whose function is to make decisions on

Putin's Russia

The modern Russian state was born in 1991 after the dramatic collapse of the Soviet Union. Early in the post-Soviet era, Russia embraced ambitious policies designed to transform a communist dictatorship with a centrally planned economy into a democratic state with a market-based economic system. The policies, however, were imperfectly implemented. Political reform left Russia with a strong presidency that—in hindsight—had the ability to subvert the democratic process. On the economic front, the privatization of many state-owned enterprises was done in such a way as to leave large shareholdings in the hands of the politically connected, many of whom were party officials and factory managers under the old Soviet system. Corruption was also endemic, and organized crime was able to seize control of some newly privatized enterprises. In 1998, the poorly managed Russian economy went through a financial crisis that nearly bought the country to its knees.

Fast-forward to 2020, and Russia still is a long way from being a modern democracy with a functioning free market–based economic system. On the positive side, the economy grew at a healthy clip during the early 2000s, helped in large part by high prices for oil and gas, Russia's largest exports (in 2013 oil and gas accounted for 75 percent of all Russian exports). Between 2000 and 2013, Russia's gross domestic product (GDP) per capita more than doubled when measured by purchasing power parity. As of 2018, the country boasts the world's 12th-largest economy, just behind that of South Korea and ahead of Spain. Thanks to government oil revenues, public debt is also low by international standards—at just 16 percent of GDP in 2018 (in the United States, by comparison, public debt amounts to 80 percent of GDP). Indeed, Russia has run a healthy trade surplus on the back of strong oil and gas exports for the last decade.

The Russian economy is overly dependent on commodities, particularly oil and gas. This was exposed in mid-2014 when the price of oil started to tumble as a result of rapidly increasing supply from the United States. Between mid-2014 and early 2016, the price of oil fell from $110 a barrel to a low of around $27 before rebounding to $50. This drove a freight train through Russia's public finances. Much of Russia's oil and gas production remains in the hands of enterprises in which the state still has a significant ownership stake. The government has a controlling ownership position in Gazprom and Rosneft, two of the country's largest oil and gas companies. The government used the rise in oil and gas revenues between 2004 and 2014 to increase public spending through state-led investment projects and increases in wages and pensions for government workers. While this boosted private consumption, there has been a dearth of private investment, and productivity growth remains low. This is particularly true among many state-owned enterprises that collectively still account for about half of the Russian economy. Now with

behalf of the electorate. In a representative democracy, elected representatives who fail to perform this job adequately will be voted out of office at the next election.

To guarantee that elected representatives can be held accountable for their actions by the electorate, an ideal representative democracy has a number of safeguards that are typically enshrined in constitutional law. These include (1) an individual's right to freedom of expression, opinion, and organization; (2) a free media; (3) regular elections in which all eligible citizens are allowed to vote; (4) universal adult suffrage; (5) limited terms for elected representatives; (6) a fair court system that is independent from the political system; (7) a nonpolitical state bureaucracy; (8) a nonpolitical police force and armed service; and (9) relatively free access to state information.[5]

Totalitarianism

In a totalitarian country, all the constitutional guarantees on which representative democracies are built—an individual's right to freedom of expression and organization, a free media, and regular elections—are denied to the citizens. In most totalitarian states, political repression is widespread, free and fair elections are lacking, media are heavily censored, basic civil liberties are denied, and those who question the right of the rulers to rule find themselves imprisoned or worse.

lower oil prices, Russia is having to issue more debt to finance public spending.

Russian private enterprises are also hamstrung by bureaucratic red tape and endemic corruption. Transparency International, which ranks countries by the extent of corruption, ranked Russia 138 out of 180 nations in 2018. The state and state-owned enterprises are famous for pushing work to private enterprises that are owned by political allies, which further subverts market-based processes.

On the political front, Russia is becoming less democratic with every passing year. Since 1999, Vladimir Putin has exerted increasingly tight control over Russian politics, either as president or as prime minister. Under Putin, potential opponents have been sidelined, civil liberties have been progressively reduced, and the freedom of the press has been diminished. For example, in response to opposition protests in 2011 and 2012, the Russian government passed laws increasing its control over the Internet, dramatically raising fines for participating in "unsanctioned" street protests, and expanded the definition of treason to further limit opposition activities. Vocal opponents of the régime—from business executives who do not toe the state line to protest groups such as the punk rock protest band Pussy Riot—have found themselves jailed on dubious charges. To make matters worse, Putin has tightened his grip on the legal system. In late 2013, Russia's parliament, which is dominated by Putin supporters, gave the president more power to appoint and fire prosecutors, thereby diminishing the independence of the legal system.

Freedom House, which produces an annual ranking tracking freedom in the world, classifies Russia as "not free" and gives it very low scores for political and civil liberties. Freedom House notes that in the March 2012 presidential elections, Putin benefited from preferential treatment by state-owned media, numerous abuses of incumbency, and procedural "irregularities" during the vote count. Putin won 63.6 percent of the vote against a field of weak, hand-chosen opponents, led by Communist Party leader Gennadiy Zyuganove, with 17.2 percent of the vote. Under a Putin-inspired 2008 constitutional amendment, the term of the presidency was expanded from four years to six. Putin was elected to another six-year term in 2018 in an election that many observers thought was a sham.

In 2014, Putin burnished his growing reputation for authoritarianism when he took advantage of unrest in the neighboring country of Ukraine to annex the Crimea region and to support armed revolt by Russian-speaking separatists in eastern Ukraine. Western powers responded to this aggression by imposing economic sanctions on Russia. Taken together with the rapid fall in oil prices, this pushed the once-booming Russian economy into a recession. Despite economic weaknesses, there is no sign that Putin's hold on power has been diminished; in fact, quite the opposite seems to have occurred.

Sources: "Putin's Russia: Sochi or Bust," *The Economist*, February 1, 2014; "Russia's Economy: The S Word," *The Economist*, November 9, 2013; Freedom House, "Freedom in the World 2019: Russia," www. freedomhouse.org; K. Hille, "Putin Tightens Grip on Legal System," *Financial Times*, November 27, 2013; "A Fourth Term for Russia's Perpetual President," *The Economist*, March 19, 2018.

Four major forms of totalitarianism exist in the world today. Until recently, the most widespread was **communist totalitarianism**. Communism, however, is in decline worldwide, and most of the Communist Party dictatorships have collapsed since 1989. Exceptions to this trend (so far) are China, Vietnam, Laos, North Korea, and Cuba, although most of these states exhibit clear signs that the Communist Party's monopoly on political power is eroding. In many respects, the governments of China, Vietnam, and Laos are communist in name only because those nations have adopted wide-ranging, market-based economic reforms. They remain, however, totalitarian states that deny many basic civil liberties to their populations. On the other hand, there are signs of a swing back toward communist totalitarian ideas in some states, such as Venezuela, where the government of the late Hugo Chávez displayed totalitarian tendencies. The same is true in Russia, where the government of Vladimir Putin has become increasingly totalitarian over time (see the Country Focus).

A second form of totalitarianism might be labeled **theocratic totalitarianism**. Theocratic totalitarianism is found in states where political power is monopolized by a party, group, or individual that governs according to religious principles. The most common form of theocratic totalitarianism is based on Islam and is exemplified by states such as Iran and Saudi Arabia. These states limit freedom of political and religious expression with laws based on Islamic principles.

A third form of totalitarianism might be referred to as **tribal totalitarianism**. Tribal totalitarianism has arisen from time to time in African countries such as Zimbabwe, Tanzania, Uganda, and Kenya. The borders of most African states reflect the administrative boundaries drawn by the old European colonial powers rather than tribal realities. Consequently, the typical African country contains a number of tribes (e.g., in Kenya there are more than 40 tribes). Tribal totalitarianism occurs when a political party that represents the interests of a particular tribe (and not always the majority tribe) monopolizes power. In Kenya, for example, politicians from the Kikuyu tribe have long dominated the political system (see the Opening Case).

A fourth major form of totalitarianism might be described as **right-wing totalitarianism**. Right-wing totalitarianism generally permits some individual economic freedom but restricts individual political freedom, frequently on the grounds that it would lead to the rise of communism. A common feature of many right-wing dictatorships is an overt hostility to socialist or communist ideas. Many right-wing totalitarian governments are backed by the military, and in some cases, the government may be made up of military officers. The fascist regimes that ruled Germany and Italy in the 1930s and 1940s were right-wing totalitarian states. Until the early 1980s, right-wing dictatorships, many of which were military dictatorships, were common throughout Latin America (e.g., Brazil was ruled by a military dictatorship between 1964 and 1985). They were also found in several Asian countries, particularly South Korea, Taiwan, Singapore, Indonesia, and the Philippines. Since the early 1980s, however, this form of government has been in retreat. Most Latin American countries are now genuine multiparty democracies. Similarly, South Korea, Taiwan, and the Philippines have all become functioning democracies, as has Indonesia.

Pseudo-Democracies

Many of the world's nations are neither pure democracies nor iron-clad totalitarian states. Rather they lie between pure democracies and complete totalitarian systems of government. They might be described as imperfect or pseudo-democracies, where authoritarian elements have captured some or much of the machinery of state and use this in an attempt to deny basic political and civil liberties. In the Russia of Vladimir Putin, for example, elections are still held, people compete through the ballot box for political office, and the independent press does not always toe the official line. However, Putin has used his position to systematically limit the political and civil liberties of opposition groups. His control is not yet perfect, though. Voices opposing Putin are still heard in Russia, and in theory, elections are still contested. But in practice, it is becoming increasingly difficult to challenge a man and régime that have systematically extended their political, legal, and economic power over the past two decades (see the Country Focus).

Economic Systems

It should be clear from the previous section that political ideology and economic systems are connected. In countries where individual goals are given primacy over collective goals, we are more likely to find market-based economic systems. In contrast, in countries where collective goals are given preeminence, the state may have taken control over many enterprises; markets in such countries are likely to be restricted rather than free. We can identify three broad types of economic systems: a market economy, a command economy, and a mixed economy.

MARKET ECONOMY

In the archetypal pure **market economy**, all productive activities are privately owned, as opposed to being owned by the state. The goods and services that a country

---

✓ TEST PREP

Use SmartBook to help retain what you have learned. Access your Instructor's Connect course to check out SmartBook or go to **learnsmartadvantage.com** for help.

LO2-2

Understand how the economic systems of countries differ.

produces are not planned by anyone. Production is determined by the interaction of supply and demand and signaled to producers through the price system. If demand for a product exceeds supply, prices will rise, signaling producers to produce more. If supply exceeds demand, prices will fall, signaling producers to produce less. In this system, consumers are sovereign. The purchasing patterns of consumers, as signaled to producers through the mechanism of the price system, determine what is produced and in what quantity.

For a market to work in this manner, supply must not be restricted. A supply restriction occurs when a single firm monopolizes a market. In such circumstances, rather than increase output in response to increased demand, a monopolist might restrict output and let prices rise. This allows the monopolist to take a greater profit margin on each unit it sells. Although this is good for the monopolist, it is bad for the consumer, who has to pay higher prices. It also is probably bad for the welfare of society. Because a monopolist has no competitors, it has no incentive to search for ways to lower production costs. Rather, it can simply pass on cost increases to consumers in the form of higher prices. The net result is that the monopolist is likely to become increasingly inefficient, producing high-priced, low-quality goods, and society suffers as a consequence.

Given the dangers inherent in monopoly, one role of government in a market economy is to encourage vigorous free and fair competition between private producers. Governments do this by banning restrictive business practices designed to monopolize a market (antitrust laws serve this function in the United States and European Union). Private ownership also encourages vigorous competition and economic efficiency. Private ownership ensures that entrepreneurs have a right to the profits generated by their own efforts. This gives entrepreneurs an incentive to search for better ways of serving consumer needs. That may be through introducing new products, by developing more efficient production processes, by pursuing better marketing and after-sale service, or simply through managing their businesses more efficiently than their competitors. In turn, the constant improvement in product and process that results from such an incentive has been argued to have a major positive impact on economic growth and development.[6]

COMMAND ECONOMY

In a pure **command economy**, the government plans the goods and services that a country produces, the quantity in which they are produced, and the prices at which they are sold. Consistent with the collectivist ideology, the objective of a command economy is for government to allocate resources for "the good of society." In addition, in a pure command economy, all businesses are state owned, the rationale being that the government can then direct them to make investments that are in the best interests of the nation as a whole rather than in the interests of private individuals. Historically, command economies were found in communist countries where collectivist goals were given priority over individual goals. Since the demise of communism in the late 1980s, the number of command economies has fallen dramatically. Some elements of a command economy were also evident in a number of democratic nations led by socialist-inclined governments. France and India both experimented with extensive government planning and state ownership, although government planning has fallen into disfavor in both countries.

While the objective of a command economy is to mobilize economic resources for the public good, the opposite often seems to have occurred. In a command economy, state-owned enterprises have little incentive to control costs and be efficient because they cannot go out of business. Also, the abolition of private ownership means there is no incentive for individuals to look for better ways to serve consumer needs; hence, dynamism and innovation are absent from command economies. Instead of growing and becoming more prosperous, such economies tend to stagnate.

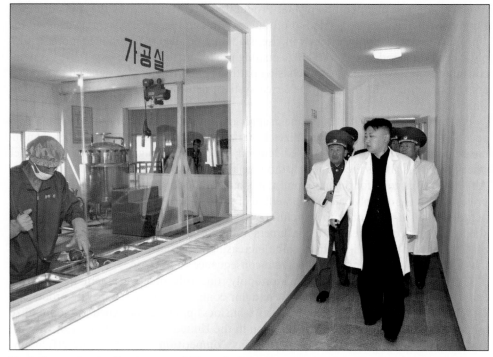

North Korean leader Kim Jong-un visiting a factory.

AFP/Getty Images

MIXED ECONOMY

Mixed economies can be found between market and command economies. In a mixed economy, certain sectors of the economy are left to private ownership and free market mechanisms, while other sectors have significant state ownership and government planning. Mixed economies were once common throughout much of the developed world, although they are becoming less so. Until the 1980s, Great Britain, France, and Sweden were mixed economies, but extensive privatization has reduced state ownership of businesses in all three nations. A similar trend occurred in many other countries where there was once a large state-owned sector, such as Brazil, Italy, and India (although there are still state-owned enterprises in all of these nations). As a counterpoint, the involvement of the state in economic activity has been on the rise again in countries such as Russia and Venezuela, where authoritarian regimes have seized control of the political structure, typically by first winning power through democratic means and then subverting those same structures to maintain their grip on power.

In mixed economies, governments also tend to take into state ownership troubled firms whose continued operation is thought to be vital to national interests. For example, in 2008 the U.S. government took an 80 percent stake in AIG to stop that financial institution from collapsing, the theory being that if AIG did collapse, it would have very serious consequences for the entire financial system. The U.S. government usually prefers market-oriented solutions to economic problems, and in the AIG case, the intention was to sell the institution back to private investors as soon as possible. The United States also took similar action with respect to a number of other troubled private enterprises, including Citigroup and General Motors. In all these cases, the government stake was seen as nothing more than a short-term action designed to stave off economic collapse by injecting capital into troubled enterprises in highly unusually circumstances. As soon as it was able to, the government sold these stakes. In early 2010, for example, the U.S. government sold its stake in Citigroup. The government stake in AIG was sold off in 2012, and by 2014, it had also disposed of its stake in GM.

TEST PREP

Use SmartBook to help retain what you have learned. Access your Instructor's Connect course to check out SmartBook or go to **learnsmartadvantage.com** for help.

Legal Systems

The **legal system** of a country refers to the rules, or laws, that regulate behavior along with the processes by which the laws are enforced and through which redress for grievances is obtained. The legal system of a country is of immense importance to international business. A country's laws regulate business practice, define the manner in which business transactions are to be executed, and set down the rights and obligations of those involved in business transactions. The legal environments of countries differ in significant ways. As we shall see, differences in legal systems can affect the attractiveness of a country as an investment site or market.

Like the economic system of a country, the legal system is influenced by the prevailing political system (although it is also strongly influenced by historical tradition). The government of a country defines the legal framework within which firms do business, and often the laws that regulate business reflect the rulers' dominant political ideology. For example, collectivist-inclined totalitarian states tend to enact laws that severely restrict private enterprise, whereas the laws enacted by governments in democratic states where individualism is the dominant political philosophy tend to be pro-private enterprise and pro-consumer.

Here, we focus on several issues that illustrate how legal systems can vary—and how such variations can affect international business. First, we look at some basic differences in legal systems. Next we look at contract law. Third, we look at the laws governing property rights with particular reference to patents, copyrights, and trademarks. Then we discuss protection of intellectual property. Finally, we look at laws covering product safety and product liability.

DIFFERENT LEGAL SYSTEMS

There are three main types of legal systems—or legal traditions—in use around the world: common law, civil law, and theocratic law.

Common Law

The common law system evolved in England over hundreds of years. It is now found in most of Great Britain's former colonies, including the United States. **Common law** is based on tradition, precedent, and custom. *Tradition* refers to a country's legal history, *precedent* to cases that have come before the courts in the past, and *custom* to the ways in which laws are applied in specific situations. When law courts interpret common law, they do so with regard to these characteristics. This gives a common law system a degree of flexibility that other systems lack. Judges in a common law system have the power to interpret the law so that it applies to the unique circumstances of an individual case. In turn, each new interpretation sets a precedent that may be followed in future cases. As new precedents arise, laws may be altered, clarified, or amended to deal with new situations.

Civil Law

A **civil law system** is based on a detailed set of laws organized into codes. When law courts interpret civil law, they do so with regard to these codes. More than 80 countries—including Germany, France, Japan, and Russia—operate with a civil law system. A civil law system tends to be less adversarial than a common law system because the judges rely on detailed legal codes rather than interpreting tradition, precedent, and custom. Judges under a civil law system have less flexibility than those under a common law system. Judges in a common law system have the power to interpret the law, whereas judges in a civil law system have the power only to apply the law.

Theocratic Law

A **theocratic law system** is one in which the law is based on religious teachings. Islamic law is the most widely practiced theocratic legal system in the modern world, although usage of both Hindu and Jewish law persisted into the twentieth century. Islamic law is primarily a moral rather than a commercial law and is intended to govern all aspects of life.[7] The foundation for Islamic law is the holy book of Islam, the Koran, along with the Sunnah, or decisions and sayings of the Prophet Muhammad, and the writings of Islamic scholars who have derived rules by analogy from the principles established in the Koran and the Sunnah. Because the Koran and Sunnah are holy documents, the basic foundations of Islamic law cannot be changed. However, in practice, Islamic jurists and scholars are constantly debating the application of Islamic law to the modern world. In reality, many Muslim countries have legal systems that are a blend of Islamic law and a common or civil law system.

Although Islamic law is primarily concerned with moral behavior, it has been extended to cover certain commercial activities. An example is the payment or receipt of interest, which is considered usury and outlawed by the Koran. To the devout Muslim, acceptance of interest payments is seen as a grave sin; the giver and the taker are equally damned. This is not just a matter of theology; in several Islamic states, it has also become a matter of law. In the 1990s, for example, Pakistan's Federal Shariat Court, the highest Islamic lawmaking body in the country, pronounced interest to be un-Islamic and therefore illegal and demanded that the government amend all financial laws accordingly. In 1999, Pakistan's Supreme Court ruled that Islamic banking methods should be used in the country after July 1, 2001.[8] By the late 2000s, there were some 500 Islamic financial institutions in the world, and as of 2014, they collectively managed more than $1 trillion in assets. In addition to Pakistan, Islamic financial institutions are found in many of the Gulf states, Egypt, Malaysia, and Iran.[9]

DIFFERENCES IN CONTRACT LAW

The difference between common law and civil law systems can be illustrated by the approach of each to contract law (remember, most theocratic legal systems also have elements of common or civil law). A **contract** is a document that specifies the conditions under which an exchange is to occur and details the rights and obligations of the parties involved. Some form of contract regulates many business transactions. **Contract law** is the body of law that governs contract enforcement. The parties to an agreement normally resort to contract law when one party feels the other has violated either the letter or the spirit of an agreement.

Because common law tends to be relatively ill specified, contracts drafted under a common law framework tend to be very detailed with all contingencies spelled out. In civil law systems, however, contracts tend to be much shorter and less specific because many of the issues are already covered in a civil code. Thus, it is more expensive to draw up contracts in a common law jurisdiction, and resolving contract disputes can be very adversarial in common law systems. But common law systems have the advantage of greater flexibility and allow judges to interpret a contract dispute in light of the prevailing situation. International businesses need to be sensitive to these differences; approaching a contract dispute in a state with a civil law system as if it had a common law system may backfire, and vice versa.

When contract disputes arise in international trade, there is always the question of which country's laws to apply. To resolve this issue, a number of countries, including the United States, have ratified the **United Nations Convention on Contracts for the International Sale of Goods (CISG)**. The CISG establishes a uniform set of rules governing certain aspects of the making and performance of everyday commercial contracts between sellers and buyers who have their places of business in different nations. By adopting the CISG, a nation signals to other adopters that it will treat the convention's rules as part of its law. The CISG applies automatically to all contracts for the sale of goods between different firms based in countries that have ratified the convention, unless the parties to the contract explicitly opt out. One problem with the CISG, however, is that as of 2018, only 89 nations had ratified the convention (the CISG went into effect in 1988).[10] Some of the world's important trading nations, including India and the United Kingdom, have not ratified the CISG.

When firms do not wish to accept the CISG, they often opt for arbitration by a recognized arbitration court to settle contract disputes. The most well known of these courts is the International Court of Arbitration of the International Chamber of Commerce in Paris, which handles more than 500 requests per year from more than 100 countries.[11]

PROPERTY RIGHTS AND CORRUPTION

In a legal sense, the term *property* refers to a resource over which an individual or business holds a legal title, that is, a resource that it owns. Resources include land, buildings, equipment, capital, mineral rights, businesses, and intellectual property (ideas, which are protected by patents, copyrights, and trademarks). **Property rights** refer to the legal rights over the use to which a resource is put and over the use made of any income that may be derived from that resource.[12] Countries differ in the extent to which their legal systems define and protect property rights. Almost all countries now have laws on their books that protect property rights. Even China, still nominally a communist state despite its booming market economy, finally enacted a law to protect the rights of private property holders in 2007 (the law gives individuals the same legal protection for their property as the state has).[13] However, in many countries these laws are not enforced by the authorities, and property rights are violated. Property rights can be violated in two ways: through private action and through public action.

Private Action

In terms of violating property rights, **private action** refers to theft, piracy, blackmail, and the like by private individuals or groups. Although theft occurs in all countries, a weak legal system allows a much higher level of criminal action. For example, in the chaotic period following the collapse of communism in Russia, an outdated legal system, coupled with a weak police force and judicial system, offered both domestic and foreign businesses scant protection from blackmail by the "Russian Mafia." Successful business owners in Russia often had to pay "protection money" to the Mafia or face violent retribution, including bombings and assassinations (about 500 contract killings of businessmen occurred per year in the 1990s).[14]

Russia is not alone in having organized crime problems (and the situation in Russia has improved since the 1990s). The Mafia has a long history in the United States (Chicago in the 1930s was similar to Moscow in the 1990s). In Japan, the local version of the Mafia, known as the *yakuza*, runs protection rackets, particularly in the food and entertainment industries.[15] However, there was a big difference between the magnitude of such activity in Russia in the 1990s and its limited impact in Japan and the United States. The difference arose because the legal enforcement apparatus, such as the police and court system, was weak in Russia following the collapse of communism. Many other countries from time to time have had problems similar to or even greater than those experienced by Russia.

Public Action and Corruption

Public action to violate property rights occurs when public officials, such as politicians and government bureaucrats, extort income, resources, or the property itself from property holders. This can be done through legal mechanisms such as levying excessive taxation, requiring expensive licenses or permits from property holders, taking assets into state ownership without compensating the owners, or redistributing assets without compensating the prior owners. It can also be done through illegal means, or corruption, by demanding bribes from businesses in return for the rights to operate in a country, industry, or location.[16]

Corruption has been well documented in every society, from the banks of the Congo River to the palace of the Dutch royal family, from Japanese politicians to Brazilian bankers, and from government officials in Zimbabwe to the New York City Police Department. The government of the late Ferdinand Marcos in the Philippines was famous for demanding bribes from foreign businesses wishing to set up operations in that country. The same was true of government officials in Indonesia under the rule of former President Suharto. No society is immune to corruption. However, there are systematic differences in the extent of corruption. In some countries, the rule of law minimizes corruption. Corruption is seen and treated as illegal, and when discovered, violators are punished by the full force of the law. In other countries, the rule of law is weak and corruption by bureaucrats and politicians is rife. Corruption is so endemic in some countries that politicians and bureaucrats regard it as a perk of office and openly flout laws against corruption. This seems to have been the case in Brazil until recently; the situation there may be evolving in a more positive direction.

According to Transparency International, an independent nonprofit organization dedicated to exposing and fighting corruption, businesses and individuals spend some $400 billion a year worldwide on bribes related to government procurement contracts alone.[17] Transparency International has also measured the level of corruption among public officials in different countries.[18] As can be seen in Figure 2.1, the organization rated countries such as New Zealand and Sweden as clean; it rated others, such as Russia, Zimbabwe, and Venezuela, as corrupt. Somalia ranked last out of all 180 countries in the survey (the country is often described as a "failed state").

Economic evidence suggests that high levels of corruption significantly reduce the foreign direct investment, level of international trade, and economic growth rate in a country.[19] By siphoning off profits, corrupt politicians and bureaucrats reduce the returns to business investment and, hence, reduce the incentive of both domestic and foreign businesses to invest in that country. The lower level of investment that results hurts economic growth. Thus, we would expect countries with high levels of corruption such as Indonesia, Nigeria, and Russia to have a lower rate of economic growth than might otherwise have been the case. A detailed example of the negative effect that corruption can have on economic development is given in the accompanying Country Focus, which looks at the impact of corruption on economic growth in Brazil.

FIGURE 2.1

Rankings of corruption by country, 2018.

Source: Constructed by the author from raw data from Transparency International, Corruption Perceptions Index 2018.

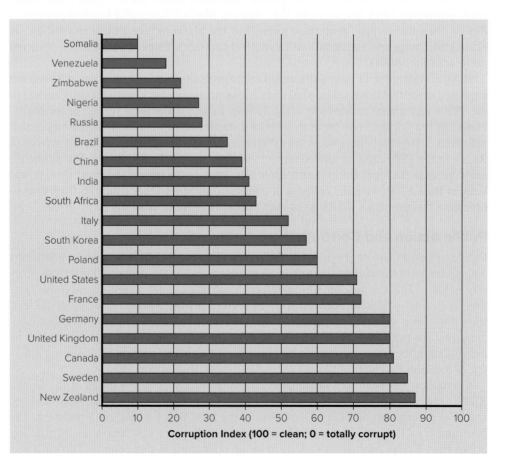

Corruption in Brazil

Brazil is the seventh-largest economy in the world with a gross domestic product of $2 trillion. The country has a democratic government and an economy characterized by moderately free markets, although the country's largest oil producer (Petrobras) and one of its top banks (Banco do Brazil) are both state owned. Many economists, however, have long felt that the country has never quite lived up to its considerable economic potential. A major reason for this has been an endemically high level of corruption that favors those with political connections and discourages investment by more ethical businesses.

Transparency International, a nongovernmental organization that evaluates countries based on perceptions of how corrupt they are, ranked Brazil 105th out of the 180 countries it looked at in its 2018 report. The problems it identifies in Brazil include public officials who demand bribes in return for awarding government contracts and "influence peddling," in which elected officials use their position in government to obtain favors or preferential treatment. Consistent with this, according to a study by the World Economic Forum, Brazil ranks 135th out of 144 countries in the proper use of public funds.

Over the last decade, several corruption scandals have come to light that serve to emphasize Brazil's corruption problem. In 2005, a scandal known as the *mensalao* (the monthly payoff scandal) broke. The scandal started when a midlevel postal official was caught on film pocketing a modest bribe in exchange for promises to favor certain businesses in landing government contracts. Further investigation uncovered a web of influence peddling in which fat monthly payments were given to lawmakers willing to back government initiatives in National Congress. After a lengthy investigation, in late 2012 some 25 politicians and business executives were found guilty of crimes that included bribery, money laundering, and corruption.

The public uproar surrounding the *mensalao* scandal was just starting to die down when in March 2014 another corruption scandal captured the attention of Brazilians. This time it involved the state-owned oil company, Petrobras. Under a scheme that seems to have been operating since 1997, construction firms wanting to do business with Petrobras agreed to pay bribes to the company's executives. Many of these executives were themselves political appointees. The executives would inflate the

value of contracts they awarded, adding a 3 percent "fee," which was effectively a kickback. The 3 percent fee was shared among Petrobras executives, construction industry executives, and politicians. The construction companies established shell companies to make payments and launder the money. According to prosecutors investigating the case, the total value of bribes may have exceeded $3.7 billion.

Four former Petrobras officials and at least 23 construction company executives have been charged with crimes that include corruption and money laundering. In addition, Brazil's Supreme Court has given prosecutors the go-ahead to investigate 48 current or former members of Congress, including the former Brazilian President Fernando Collor de Mello. The Brazilian president, Dilma Rousseff, was also tainted by the scandal. In June 2016, she was suspended from the presidency pending an impeachment trial. She was chair of Petrobras during the time this was occurring. She is also a member of the governing Workers' Party, several members of which seem to have been among the major beneficiaries of the kickback scandal. Although there is no evidence that Rousseff knew of the bribes or profited from them, her ability to govern effectively was severely damaged by association. The scandal so rocked Brazil that it pushed the country close to a recession. In August 2016, Rousseff was impeached and removed from the presidency. Then in 2018 the former Brazilian President, Lula da Silva, was found guilty of corruption. Among the charges against Lula were that, when President, he was given a beach-front apartment by an engineering firm in return for his help in winning lucrative contracts for Petrobras. Lula was sentenced to 12 years in prison.

If there is a bright spot in all of this, it is that the scandals are coming to light. Backed by Supreme Court rulings and public outrage, corrupted politicians, government officials, and business executives are being prosecuted. In the past, that was far less likely to occur.

Sources: Will Conners and Luciana Magalhaes, "Brazil Cracks Open Vast Bribery Scandal," *The Wall Street Journal*, April 7, 2015; Marc Margolis, "In Brazil's Trial of the Century, Lula's Reputation Is at Stake," *Newsweek*, July 27, 2012; "The Big Oily," *The Economist*, January 3, 2015; Donna Bowater, "Brazil's Continuing Corruption Problem," *BBC News*, September 18, 2015; Simon Romero, "Dilma Rousseff Is Ousted as Brazil's President in Impeachment Vote," *The New York Times*, August 31, 2016; "Brazilian Corruption Scandals: All You Need to Know," BBC News, April 8, 2018.

Did Walmart Violate the Foreign Corrupt Practices Act?

In the early 2000s, Walmart wanted to build a new store in San Juan Teotihuacan, Mexico, barely a mile from ancient pyramids that drew tourists from around the world. The owner of the land was happy to sell to Walmart, but one thing stood in the way of a deal: the city's new zoning laws. These prohibited commercial development in the historic area. Not to be denied, executives at the headquarters of Walmart de Mexico found a way around the problem: They paid a $52,000 bribe to a local official to redraw the zoning area so that the property Walmart wanted to purchase was placed *outside* the commercial-free zone. Walmart then went ahead and built the store, despite vigorous local opposition, opening it in late 2004.

A former lawyer for Walmart de Mexico subsequently contacted Walmart executives at the company's corporate headquarters in Bentonville, Arkansas. He told them that Walmart de Mexico routinely resorted to bribery, citing the altered zoning map as just one example. Alarmed, executives at Walmart started their own investigation. Faced with growing evidence of corruption in Mexico, top Walmart executives decided to engage in damage control, rather than coming clean. Walmart's top lawyer shipped the case files back to Mexico and handed over responsibility for the investigation to the general council of Walmart de Mexico. This was an interesting choice as the very same general council was alleged to have authorized bribes. The general council quickly exonerated fellow Mexican executives, and the internal investigation was closed in 2006.

For several years nothing more happened; then, in April 2012, *The New York Times* published an article detailing bribery by Walmart. The *Times* cited the changed zoning map and several other examples of bribery by Walmart: for example, eight bribes totaling $341,000 enabled Walmart to build a Sam's Club in one of Mexico City's most densely populated neighborhoods without a construction license, an environmental permit, an urban impact assessment, or even a traffic permit. Similarly, thanks to nine bribe payments totaling $765,000, Walmart built a vast refrigerated distribution center in an environmentally fragile flood basin north of Mexico City, in an area where electricity was so scarce that many smaller developers were turned away.

Walmart responded to *The New York Times* article by ramping up a second internal investigation into bribery that it had initiated in 2011. By mid-2015, there were reportedly more than 300 outside lawyers working on the investigation, and it had cost more than $612 million in fees. In addition, the U.S. Department of Justice and the Securities and Exchange Commission both announced that they had started investigations into Walmart's practices. In November 2012, Walmart reported that its own investigation into violations had extended beyond Mexico to include China and India. Among other things, it was looking into the allegations by the *Times* that top executives at Walmart, including former CEO Lee Scott Jr., had deliberately squashed earlier investigations. In late 2016 people familiar with the matter stated that the federal investigation had not uncovered evidence of widespread bribery. In November 2017 it was reported that Walmart had settled with the Justice Department and paid a $283 million fine, significantly less than had been expected.

Sources: David Barstow, "Vast Mexican Bribery Case Hushed Up by Wal-Mart after Top Level Struggle," *The New York Times*, April 21, 2012; Stephanie Clifford and David Barstow, "Wal-Mart Inquiry Reflects Alarm on Corruption," *The New York Times*, November 15, 2012; Nathan Vardi, "Why Justice Department Could Hit Wal-Mart Hard over Mexican Bribery Allegations," *Forbes*, April 22, 2012; Phil Wahba,"Walmart Bribery Probe by Feds Finds No Major Misconduct in Mexico," *Fortune*, October 18, 2015; T. Schoenberg and M. Robinson, "Wal-Mart Balks at Paying $600 Million in Bribery Case," *Bloomberg*, October 6, 2016; and Sue Reisinger, "Wal-Mart Reserves $283 million to Settle Mexico FCPA Case," *Corporate Counsel*, November 17, 2017.

Foreign Corrupt Practices Act

In the 1970s, the United States passed the **Foreign Corrupt Practices Act (FCPA)** following revelations that U.S. companies had bribed government officials in foreign countries in an attempt to win lucrative contracts. This law makes it illegal to bribe a foreign government official to obtain or maintain business over which that foreign official has authority, and it requires all publicly traded companies (whether or not they are involved in international trade) to keep detailed records that would reveal whether a violation of the act has occurred. In 2012, evidence emerged that in its eagerness to expand in Mexico, Walmart may have run afoul of the FCPA (for details, see the Management Focus feature).

In 1997, trade and finance ministers from the member states of the Organisation for Economic Co-operation and Development (OECD), an association of 34 major economies including most Western economies (but not Russia, India or China), adopted the Convention on Combating Bribery of Foreign Public Officials in International Business Transactions.[20] The convention obliges member states to make the bribery of foreign public officials a criminal offense.

Both the U.S. law and OECD convention include language that allows exceptions known as facilitating or expediting payments (also called *grease payments* or *speed money*), the purpose of which is to expedite or to secure the performance of a routine governmental action.[21] For example, they allow small payments made to speed up the issuance of permits or licenses, process paperwork, or just get vegetables off the dock and on their way to market. The explanation for this exception to general antibribery provisions is that while grease payments are, technically, bribes, they are distinguishable from (and, apparently, less offensive than) bribes used to obtain or maintain business because they merely facilitate performance of duties that the recipients are already obligated to perform.

THE PROTECTION OF INTELLECTUAL PROPERTY

Intellectual property refers to property that is the product of intellectual activity, such as computer software, a screenplay, a music score, or the chemical formula for a new drug. Patents, copyrights, and trademarks establish ownership rights over intellectual property. A **patent** grants the inventor of a new product or process exclusive rights for a defined period to the manufacture, use, or sale of that invention. **Copyrights** are the exclusive legal rights of authors, composers, playwrights, artists, and publishers to publish and disperse their work as they see fit. **Trademarks** are designs and names, officially registered, by which merchants or manufacturers can differentiate their products (e.g., Christian Dior clothes). In the high-technology "knowledge" economy of the twenty-first century, intellectual property has become an increasingly important source of economic value for businesses. Protecting intellectual property has also become increasingly problematic, particularly if it can be rendered in a digital form and then copied and distributed at very low cost via pirated DVDs or over the Internet (e.g., computer software, music, and video recordings).[22]

The philosophy behind intellectual property laws is to reward the originator of a new invention, book, musical record, clothes design, restaurant chain, and the like for his or her idea and effort. Such laws stimulate innovation and creative work. They provide an incentive for people to search for novel ways of doing things, and they reward creativity. For example, consider innovation in the pharmaceutical industry. A patent will grant the inventor of a new drug a 20-year monopoly in production of that drug. This gives pharmaceutical firms an incentive to undertake the expensive, difficult, and time-consuming basic research required to generate new drugs (it can cost $1 billion in R&D and take 12 years to get a new drug on the market). Without the guarantees provided by patents, companies would be unlikely to commit themselves to extensive basic research.[23]

The protection of intellectual property rights differs greatly from country to country. Although many countries have stringent intellectual property regulations on their books, the enforcement of these regulations has often been lax. This has been the case even among many of the 192 countries that are now members of the **World Intellectual Property Organization**, all of which have signed international treaties designed to protect intellectual property, including the oldest such treaty, the **Paris Convention for the Protection of Industrial Property**, which dates to 1883 and has been signed by more than 170 nations. Weak enforcement encourages the piracy (theft) of intellectual property. China and Thailand have often been among the worst offenders in Asia. Pirated computer software is widely available in China. Similarly, the streets of Bangkok, Thailand's capital, are lined with stands selling pirated copies of Rolex watches, Levi's jeans, DVDs, and computer software.

The computer software industry is an example of an industry that suffers from lax enforcement of intellectual property rights. A study published in 2012 suggested that violations of intellectual property rights cost personal computer software firms revenues equal to $63 billion a year.[24] According to the study's sponsor, the Business Software Alliance, a

Starbucks Wins Key Trademark Case in China

Starbucks has big plans for China. It believes the fast-growing nation will become the company's second-largest market after the United States. Starbucks entered the country in 1999, and by the end of 2016 it had opened more than 1,300 stores. But in China, copycats of well-established Western brands are common. Starbucks faced competition from a look-alike, Shanghai Xing Ba Ke Coffee Shop, whose stores closely matched the Starbucks format, right down to a green-and-white Xing Ba Ke circular logo that mimics Starbucks' ubiquitous logo. The name also mimics the standard Chinese translation for Starbucks. *Xing* means "star," and *Ba Ke* sounds like "bucks."

In 2003, Starbucks decided to sue Xing Ba Ke in Chinese court for trademark violations. Xing Ba Ke's general manager responded by claiming it was just an accident that the logo and name were so similar to that of Starbucks. He claimed the right to use the logo and name because Xing Ba Ke had registered as a company in Shanghai in 1999, before Starbucks entered the city.

"I hadn't heard of Starbucks at the time," claimed the manager, "so how could I imitate its brand and logo?"

However, in January 2006, a Shanghai court ruled that Starbucks had precedence, in part because it had registered its Chinese name in 1998. The court stated that Xing Ba Ke's use of the name and similar logo was "clearly malicious" and constituted improper competition. The court ordered Xing Ba Ke to stop using the name and to pay Starbucks $62,000 in compensation. While the money involved here may be small, the precedent is not. In a country where violation of trademarks has been common, the courts seem to be signaling a shift toward greater protection of intellectual property rights. This is perhaps not surprising because foreign governments and the World Trade Organization have been pushing China hard recently to start respecting intellectual property rights.

Sources: M. Dickie, "Starbucks Wins Case against Chinese Copycat," *Financial Times*, January 3, 2006, p. 1; "Starbucks: Chinese Court Backs Company over Trademark Infringement," *The Wall Street Journal*, January 2, 2006, p. A11; and "Starbucks Calls China Its Top Growth Focus," *The Wall Street Journal*, February 14, 2006, p. 1.

software industry association, some 42 percent of all software applications used in the world were pirated. One of the worst large countries was China, where the piracy rate ran at 77 percent and cost the industry more than $9.8 billion in lost sales, up from $444 million in 1995. The piracy rate in the United States was much lower at 19 percent; however, the value of sales lost was significant because of the size of the U.S. market.[25]

International businesses have a number of possible responses to violations of their intellectual property. They can lobby their respective governments to push for international agreements to ensure that intellectual property rights are protected and that the law is enforced. Partly as a result of such actions, international laws are being strengthened. As we shall see in Chapter 7, the most recent world trade agreement, signed in 1994, for the first time extends the scope of the General Agreement on Tariffs and Trade to cover intellectual property. Under the new agreement, known as the Trade-Related Aspects of Intellectual Property Rights (TRIPS), as of 1995 a council of the World Trade Organization is overseeing enforcement of much stricter intellectual property regulations. These regulations oblige WTO members to grant and enforce patents lasting at least 20 years and copyrights lasting 50 years after the death of the author. Rich countries had to comply with the rules within a year. Poor countries, in which such protection generally was much weaker, had five years of grace, and the very poorest have 10 years.[26] (For further details of the TRIPS agreement, see Chapter 7.)

In addition to lobbying governments, firms can file lawsuits on their own behalf. For example, Starbucks won a landmark trademark copyright case in China against a copycat that signaled a change in the approach in China (see the accompanying Management Focus for details). Firms may also choose to stay out of countries where intellectual property laws are lax, rather than risk having their ideas stolen by local entrepreneurs. Firms also need to be on the alert to ensure that pirated copies of their products produced in countries with weak intellectual property laws don't turn up in their home market or in third countries. U.S. computer software giant Microsoft, for example, discovered that pirated Microsoft software, produced illegally in Thailand, was being sold worldwide as the real thing.

PRODUCT SAFETY AND PRODUCT LIABILITY

Product safety laws set certain safety standards to which a product must adhere. **Product liability** involves holding a firm and its officers responsible when a product causes injury, death, or damage. Product liability can be much greater if a product does not conform to required safety standards. Both civil and criminal product liability laws exist. Civil laws call for payment and monetary damages. Criminal liability laws result in fines or imprisonment. Both civil and criminal liability laws are probably more extensive in the United States than in any other country, although many other Western nations also have comprehensive liability laws. Liability laws are typically the least extensive in less developed nations. A boom in product liability suits and awards in the United States resulted in a dramatic increase in the cost of liability insurance. Many business executives argue that the high costs of liability insurance make American businesses less competitive in the global marketplace.

In addition to the competitiveness issue, country differences in product safety and liability laws raise an important ethical issue for firms doing business abroad. When product safety laws are tougher in a firm's home country than in a foreign country or when liability laws are more lax, should a firm doing business in that foreign country follow the more relaxed local standards or should it adhere to the standards of its home country? While the ethical thing to do is undoubtedly to adhere to home-country standards, firms have been known to take advantage of lax safety and liability laws to do business in a manner that would not be allowed at home.

FOCUS ON MANAGERIAL IMPLICATIONS

THE MACRO ENVIRONMENT INFLUENCES MARKET ATTRACTIVENESS

The material discussed in this chapter has two broad implications for international business. First, the political, economic, and legal systems of a country raise important ethical issues that have implications for the practice of international business. For example, what ethical implications are associated with doing business in totalitarian countries where citizens are denied basic human rights, corruption is rampant, and bribes are necessary to gain permission to do business? Is it right to operate in such a setting? A full discussion of the ethical implications of country differences in political economy is reserved for Chapter 5, where we explore ethics in international business in much greater depth.

Second, the political, economic, and legal environments of a country clearly influence the attractiveness of that country as a market or investment site. The benefits, costs, and risks associated with doing business in a country are a function of that country's political, economic, and legal systems. The overall attractiveness of a country as a market or investment site depends on balancing the likely long-term benefits of doing business in that country against the likely costs and risks. Because this chapter is the first of two dealing with issues of political economy, we will delay a detailed discussion of how political economy impacts the benefits, costs, and risks of doing business in different nation-states until the end of the next chapter, when we have a full grasp of all the relevant variables that are important for assessing benefits, costs, and risks.

For now, other things being equal, a nation with democratic political institutions, a market-based economic system, and strong legal system that protects property rights and limits corruption is clearly more attractive as a place in which to do business than a nation that lacks democratic institutions, where economic activity is heavily regulated by the state, and where corruption is rampant and the rule of law is not respected. On this basis, for example, a country like Canada is a better place in which to do business than the Russia of Vladimir Putin (see the Country Focus: Putin's Russia). That being said, the reality is often more nuanced and complex. For example, China lacks democratic institutions; corruption is widespread; property rights are not always respected; and even though the country has embraced many market-based economic reforms, there are still large numbers of state-owned enterprises—yet many Western businesses feel that they must invest in China. They do so

✓ TEST PREP

Use SmartBook to help retain what you have learned. Access your Instructor's Connect course to check out SmartBook or go to **learnsmartadvantage.com** for help.

LO2-4

Explain the implications for management practice of national differences in political economy.

despite the risks because the market is large, the nation is moving toward a market-based system, economic growth has been strong (although growth rates there have slowed down significantly since 2015), legal protection of property rights has been improving, and China is already the second-largest economy in the world and could ultimately replace the United States as the world's largest. Thus, China is becoming increasingly attractive as a place in which to do business, and given the future growth trajectory, significant opportunities may be lost by not investing in the country. We will explore how changes in political economy affect the attractiveness of a nation as a place in which to do business in Chapter 3.

Key Terms

political economy, p. 40
political system, p. 41
collectivism, p. 41
socialists, p. 41
communists, p. 41
social democrats, p. 41
privatization, p. 42
individualism, p. 42
democracy, p. 43
totalitarianism, p. 43
representative democracy, p. 43
communist totalitarianism, p. 45
theocratic totalitarianism, p. 45
tribal totalitarianism, p. 46

right-wing totalitarianism, p. 46
market economy, p. 46
command economy, p. 47
legal system, p. 49
common law, p. 49
civil law system, p. 49
theocratic law system, p. 49
contract, p. 50
contract law, p. 50
United Nations Convention on
    Contracts for the International
    Sale of Goods (CISG), p. 50
property rights, p. 51
private action, p. 51

public action, p. 51
Foreign Corrupt Practices Act
    (FCPA), p. 54
intellectual property, p. 55
patent, p. 55
copyrights, p. 55
trademarks, p. 55
World Intellectual Property
    Organization, p. 55
Paris Convention for the Protection
    of Industrial Property, p. 55
product safety laws, p. 57
product liability, p. 57

SUMMARY

This chapter has reviewed how the political, economic, and legal systems of countries vary. The potential benefits, costs, and risks of doing business in a country are a function of its political, economic, and legal systems. The chapter made the following points:

1. Political systems can be assessed according to two dimensions: the degree to which they emphasize collectivism as opposed to individualism and the degree to which they are democratic or totalitarian.

2. Collectivism is an ideology that views the needs of society as being more important than the needs of the individual. Collectivism translates into an advocacy for state intervention in economic activity and, in the case of communism, a totalitarian dictatorship.

3. Individualism is an ideology that is built on an emphasis of the primacy of the individual's freedoms in the political, economic, and cultural realms. Individualism translates into an advocacy for democratic ideals and free market economics.

4. Democracy and totalitarianism are at different ends of the political spectrum. In a representative democracy, citizens periodically elect individuals to represent them, and political freedoms are guaranteed by a constitution. In a totalitarian state, political power is monopolized by a party, group, or individual, and basic political freedoms are denied to citizens of the state.

5. There are three broad types of economic systems: a market economy, a command economy, and a mixed economy. In a market economy, prices are free of controls, and private ownership is predominant. In a command economy, prices are set by central planners, productive assets are owned by the state, and private ownership is forbidden. A mixed economy has elements of both a market economy and a command economy.

6. Differences in the structure of law between countries can have important implications for the practice of international business. The degree to which property rights are protected can vary dramatically from country to country, as can product safety and product liability legislation and the nature of contract law.

Critical Thinking and Discussion Questions

1. Free market economies stimulate greater economic growth, whereas state-directed economies stifle growth. Discuss.

2. A democratic political system is an essential condition for sustained economic progress. Discuss.

3. What is the relationship between corruption in a country (i.e., government officials taking bribes) and economic growth? Is corruption always bad?

4. You are the CEO of a company that has to choose between making a $100 million investment in Russia or Poland. Both investments promise the same long-run return, so your choice is driven by risk considerations. Assess the various risks of doing business in each of these nations. Which investment would you favor and why?

5. Read the Management Focus "Did Walmart Violate the Foreign Corrupt Practices Act?" What is your opinion? If you think it did, what do you think the consequences will be for Walmart?

globalEDGE research task globaledge.msu.edu

Use the globalEDGE™ website (**globaledge.msu.edu**) to complete the following exercises:

1. The definition of words and political ideas can have different meanings in different contexts worldwide. In fact, the *Freedom in the World* survey published by Freedom House evaluates the state of political rights and civil liberties around the world. Provide a description of this survey and a ranking (in terms of "freedom") of the world's country leaders and laggards. What factors are taken into consideration in this survey?

2. As the chapter discusses, differences in political, economic, and legal systems have considerable impact on the benefits, costs, and risks of doing business in various countries. The World Bank's "Doing Business Indicators" measure the extent of business regulations in countries around the world. Compare Brazil, Ghana, India, New Zealand, the United States, Sweden, and Turkey in terms of how easily contracts are enforced, how property can be registered, and how investors can be protected. Identify in which area you see the greatest variation from one country to the next.

CLOSING CASE

Transformation in Saudi Arabia

The desert kingdom of Saudi Arabia is a rarity in the modern world, an absolute monarchy whose laws are based upon interpretations of a religious text, the Qur'an, the holy book of Islam. Despite Saudi Arabia's adherence to an archaic form of government, the Saudi economy has historically performed well, primarily due to the country's position as the world's largest oil exporter. In 2017, the country's GDP per capita on a purchasing power parity basis was $54,500, not far behind the $59,800 GDP per capita of the United States.

The oil sector accounts for around 87 percent of government revenues, 42 percent of GDP, and 90 percent of export earnings. In times of high oil prices, the Saudi government has used oil revenues to finance a sprawling government apparatus and to subsidize energy prices, which are among the lowest in the world. In 2014, however, oil prices collapsed, wiping out an annual government surplus. In 2014, the government deficit ballooned to 15 percent of GDP, and it hit 20 percent of GDP in 2016, forcing the country to issue more debt and draw down its foreign exchange reserves. Higher oil prices improved the situation in 2017 and 2018, but the crisis exposed the vulnerability of Saudi Arabia to a fall in oil prices.

To compound matters, Saudi Arabia has a young population—some 70 percent of the population is under the age of 30—and unemployment is high at 12 percent, a combination of factors that many see as a recipe for social unrest. The high unemployment reflects the fact that while there are jobs available outside of the government sector, most of them are taken by low-paid foreign workers, who account for 80 percent of the labor force.

Following the death of his brother, in January 2015 Salman bin Abd al-Aziz Al Saud became King. Breaking with tradition, the aging King quickly devolved substantial power to his son, crown prince Muhammad bin Salman (commonly known as "MBS"). The young crown prince articulated a different vision for Saudi Arabia. Known as Vision 2030, this calls for reducing the kingdom's dependence on oil revenues, privatizing the state-owned oil company Saudi Aramco, cutting energy and water subsidies, growing the private sector, investing $500 billion in a new city called NEOM that will serve as a hub for private and foreign investment, and introducing a value-added tax in order to close the government deficit. At the same time, the crown prince is seeking to loosen the stifling moral codes that have limited cultural life and to promote a "moderate Islam open to the world and all religions."

Not surprisingly, this vision has met with resistance, particularly from members of the sprawling royal family and conservative clergy who have benefited from the status quo. To counter this, the crown prince consolidated his power, removing members of the royal family that disagreed with him and putting his allies in positions of power. This culminated in an unprecedented shake-up in November 2017 when scores of people, including some of the most powerful princes in the kingdom, were arrested in a massive anticorruption sweep and jailed in, of all places, Riyadh's opulent Ritz Carlton.

Whether this power grab will help the crown prince achieve his goals for Saudi Arabia remains to be seen. The government has had to backtrack on plans to reduce subsidies after strong resistance from the population, but it did introduce a 5 percent value-added tax in January 2018.

Plans for the privatization of Saudi Aramco are under way, and the government budget deficit has been cut in half since 2015—although stronger oil prices have had a lot to do with that. Some of the stricter laws have also been relaxed. Women are now allowed to drive, and some banned cultural entertainments once seen as decadent, including going to the cinema, are now allowed. In the long run though, transforming the Saudi economy will require growth in the non-oil private sector, and that is a challenging task.

Moreover, a scandal surrounding the murder of *Washington Post* journalist Jamal Khoshoggi by Saudi operatives in Turkey in October 2018 has at the very least potentially weakened the power of the crown prince. Khoshoggi, a Saudi citizen and U.S. resident, was a critic of the Saudi regime. Although the Saudi government has claimed that his killing was the result of a rogue operation gone wrong, few believe that narrative. Many critics suspect that Muhammad bin Salman was aware of plans to arrest Khoshoggi. Indeed, there is growing evidence that, back in 2017, MBS authorized a secret campaign to silence dissenters, which included the surveillance, kidnapping, detention, and torture of Saudi citizens. Khoshoggi was just the highest-profile case in that operation.

Bandar Algaloud/Saudi Kingdom Council/Handout/Anadolu Agency/ Getty Images

In the wake of Khoshoggi's murder, some foreign investors have reconsidered their ties with the kingdom, and there is little doubt that the fallout from the scandal has made it more difficult for the Saudis to attract foreign investment.

Sources: Asa Fitch, "Saudi Arabia Plans Record Spending in New Budget," *The Wall Street Journal*, December 19, 2017; Brittany De Lea, "Saudi Citizens Plagued by New Taxes, High Unemployment after Oil Price Collapse," *Fox Business*, October 26, 2017; "Saudi Arabia's Unprecedented Shake-up," *The Economist*, November 5, 2017; Mark Mazzetti and Ben Hubbard, "It Wasn't Just Khashoggi: A Saudi Prince's Brutal Drive to Crush Dissent," *The New York Times*, March 17, 2019.

Case Discussion Questions

1. What long-term economic and political problems does Saudi Arabia face?

2. How might the reforms proposed by Muhammad bin Salman potentially address these problems? Who will gain from these reforms? Who might object and push back against them?

3. Current plans for Saudi Aramco call for the state-owned oil company to be privatized. An initial public offering (IPO) is tentatively scheduled for 2021. What are the potential benefits to Saudi Arabia of privatizing Saudi Aramco? Is there a downside?

4. Is it morally correct for international businesses to invest in a country that denies basic rights to women?

5. Is it morally correct for international businesses to invest in an autocratic country where the current leader has been implicated in ordering the murder of one of his critics?

Endnotes

1. As we shall see, there is not a strict one-to-one correspondence between political systems and economic systems. A. O. Hirschman, "The On-and-Off Again Connection between Political and Economic Progress," *American Economic Review* 84, no. 2 (1994), pp. 343–48.

2. For a discussion of the roots of collectivism and individualism, see H. W. Spiegel, *The Growth of Economic Thought* (Durham, NC: Duke University Press, 1991). A discussion of collectivism and individualism can be found in M. Friedman and R. Friedman, *Free to Choose* (London: Penguin Books, 1980).

3. For a classic summary of the tenets of Marxism, see A. Giddens, *Capitalism and Modern Social Theory* (Cambridge, UK: Cambridge University Press, 1971).

4. Smith, Adam. *The Wealth of Nations. The Modern Library.* Random House, Inc., 1937.

5. R. Wesson, *Modern Government–Democracy and Authoritarianism,* 2nd ed. (Englewood Cliffs, NJ: Prentice Hall, 1990).

6. For a detailed but accessible elaboration of this argument, see Friedman and Friedman, *Free to Choose.* Also see P. M. Romer, "The Origins of Endogenous Growth," *Journal of Economic Perspectives* 8, no. 1 (1994), pp. 2–32.

7. T. W. Lippman, *Understanding Islam* (New York: Meridian Books, 1995).

8. "Islam's Interest," *The Economist,* January 18, 1992, pp. 33–34.

9. M. El Qorchi, "Islamic Finance Gears Up," *Finance and Development,* December 2005, pp. 46–50; S. Timewell, "Islamic Finance–Virtual Concept to Critical Mass," *The Banker,* March 1, 2008, pp. 10–16; Lydia Yueh, "Islamic Finance Growing Fast, But Can It Be More Than a Niche Market?" *BBC News,* April 14, 2014.

10. This information can be found on the UN's treaty website at www.uncitral.org/uncitral/en/uncitral_texts/sale_goods/1980CISG.html.

11. International Court of Arbitration, www.iccwbo.org/index_court.asp.

12. D. North, *Institutions, Institutional Change, and Economic Performance* (Cambridge, UK: Cambridge University Press, 1991).

13. "China's Next Revolution," *The Economist,* March 10, 2007, p. 9.

14. P. Klebnikov, "Russia's Robber Barons," *Forbes,* November 21, 1994, pp. 74–84; C. Mellow, "Russia: Making Cash from Chaos," *Fortune,* April 17, 1995, pp. 145–51; "Mr. Tatum Checks Out," *The Economist,* November 9, 1996, p. 78.

15. K. van Wolferen, *The Enigma of Japanese Power* (New York: Vintage Books, 1990), pp. 100–105.

16. P. Bardhan, "Corruption and Development: A Review of the Issues," *Journal of Economic Literature,* September 1997, pp. 1320–46.

17. Transparency International, "Global Corruption Report, 2014," www.transparency.org, 2014.

18. Transparency International, Corruption Perceptions Index 2016, www.transparency.org.

19. J. Coolidge and S. Rose Ackerman, "High Level Rent Seeking and Corruption in African Regimes," World Bank policy research working paper no. 1780, June 1997; K. Murphy, A. Shleifer, and R. Vishny, "Why Is Rent-Seeking So Costly to Growth?" *AEA Papers and Proceedings*, May 1993, pp. 409–14; M. Habib and L. Zurawicki, "Corruption and Foreign Direct Investment," *Journal of International Business Studies* 33 (2002), pp. 291–307; J. E. Anderson and D. Marcouiller, "Insecurity and the Pattern of International Trade," *Review of Economics and Statistics* 84 (2002), pp. 342–52; T. S. Aidt, "Economic Analysis of Corruption: A Survey," *The Economic Journal* 113 (November 2003), pp. 632–53; D. A. Houston, "Can Corruption Ever Improve an Economy?" *Cato Institute* 27 (2007), pp. 325–43; S. Rose Ackerman and B.J. Palifka, *Corruption and Government,* 2nd ed. (Cambridge, UK: Cambridge University Press, 2016).

20. Details can be found at www.oecd.org/corruption/oecdantibriberyconvention.htm.

21. D. Stackhouse and K. Ungar, "The Foreign Corrupt Practices Act: Bribery, Corruption, Record Keeping and More," *Indiana Lawyer,* April 21, 1993.

22. For an interesting discussion of strategies for dealing with the low cost of copying and distributing digital information, see the chapter on rights management in C. Shapiro and H. R. Varian, *Information Rules* (Boston: Harvard Business School Press, 1999). Also see C. W. L. Hill, "Digital Piracy," *Asian Pacific Journal of Management,* 2007, pp. 9–25.

23. Douglass North has argued that the correct specification of intellectual property rights is one factor that lowers the cost of doing business and, thereby, stimulates economic growth and development. See North, *Institutions, Institutional Change, and Economic Performance.*

24. Business Software Alliance, "Ninth Annual BSA Global Software Piracy Study," May 2012, www.bsa.org.

25. Business Software Alliance, "Ninth Annual BSA Global Software Piracy Study," May 2012, www.bsa.org.

26. "Trade Tripwires," *The Economist,* August 27, 1994, p. 61.

National Differences in Economic Development

3

LEARNING OBJECTIVES

After reading this chapter, you will be able to:

LO3-1   Explain what determines the level of economic development of a nation.

LO3-2   Identify the macropolitical and macroeconomic changes occurring worldwide.

LO3-3   Describe how transition economies are moving toward market-based systems.

LO3-4   Explain the implications for management practice of national difference in political economy.

Poland: Eastern Europe's Economic Miracle

OPENING CASE

As the great financial crisis of 2008 and 2009 unfolded, countries across Europe were hit hard. A notable exception was Poland, whose economy grew by 1.5 percent during 2009, while every other economy in the European Union contracted, as did the United States'. Poland's impressive economic performance continued after the crisis. Between 2010 and 2018, Poland's growth rate averaged 3.5 percent per annum, the best in Europe. This country of 38 million now has the largest economy among the post-Communist states of Eastern Europe. How did Poland achieve this?

In 1989, Poland elected its first democratic government after more than four decades of Communist rule. The Government moved quickly to shift the economy away from the centrally planned Soviet model it had been operating under since 1945. Poland embraced market-based economic policies and quickly implemented them through a "shock therapy" program. The country opened its markets to international trade and foreign investment, privatized many state-owned businesses, and made it much easier for entrepreneurs to start their own businesses. In 2004, the country joined the European Union and subsequently adopted the euro, giving it easy access to the large consumer markets of Western Europe. All this helped transform Poland into an export powerhouse. Exports now account for 54 percent of GDP, compared to 34 percent in 2004. By way of comparison, exports account for 30 percent of GDP in the United Kingdom, and just 12 percent in the United States. Poland's exports include machinery and transportation equipment, intermediate manufactured goods, furniture, hardwood products, food, and casual clothing. As a consequence of these changes, between 1989 and 2018 Poland recorded the highest sustained growth in the region. Living standards, measured by GDP per capita at purchasing power parity increased 2.7 times, compared to 1.7 times in the neighboring Czech Republic.

Poland's government has also been fiscally conservative, keeping public debt in check, not allowing it to expand during the recession as many other countries did. This led to investor confidence in the country. Consequently, there was no large outflow of funds during the 2008–2009 economic turmoil. This stands in stark contrast to what happened in the Baltic states, where investors pulled money out of those economies during 2008 and 2009, driving their currencies down, raising the cost of government debt, and precipitating a full-blown economic crisis that required the IMF and EU to step in with financial assistance.

A tight monetary squeeze in the early 2000s, which was designed to curb inflation and ease Poland's entry into the European Union, headed off the asset price bubble, particularly surging home prices that hurt so many other economies around the world. Ironically, the Polish government had been criticized for its tight monetary policy earlier in the decade, but in 2008 and 2009 it served the country well. Post 2009, the Government has continued to adhere to a fairly conservative management of the economy. In 2018, the Government deficit as a percentage of GDP was 1.6 percent, safely below the 3 percent European Union requirement for members of the euro zone. As of 2018, economic growth remains strong, inflation is low at under 2 percent, and the unemployment rate of 3.7 percent is the lowest since 1989.

None of this is to say that Poland is a model state. Looking forward, the country faces several significant economic challenges. First, the work force is aging. Poland faces a shortage of labor in the coming years. For Poland to continue to expand economically, it needs more immigration. Despite some anti-immigration sentiment in the country, the Polish government has been issuing substantially more work permits to immigrants, the majority of whom have come from the Ukraine. Second, the Government recently lowered the retirement age (which exacerbates the labor shortage) and raised social security payments, moves which could create fiscal problems down the road. Third, despite substantial privatization after 1990, Poland still has a mixed economy with several major state-owned enterprises. The government controls the two largest banks, the biggest insurer, and two defense groups, as well as important energy, mining, and petrochemical companies. Political constraints and ongoing interference mean that these enterprises are not always as well managed as they might be and begs the question of whether further privatization is warranted.

Sources: Daniel Tilles, "Poland's Anti-Immigration Government Is Overseeing one of Europe's Biggest Waves of Immigration," *Notes From Poland*, October 3, 2018; J. Rostowski, "The Secret of Poland's Success," *The Wall Street Journal*, February 1, 2010, p. 15; "Not Like the Neighbors," *The Economist*, April 25, 2009, p. 55; "Ahead of Elections, Poland's Ruling Party Offers Huge Handouts," *The Economist*, February 28, 2019; "Poland's State Owned Giants Cope with Unprecedented Turnover," *The Economist*, November 29, 2018; World Bank, *World Development Indicators Online*, Accessed March 22, 2019.

Introduction

In Chapter 2, we described how countries differ with regard to their political systems, economic systems, and legal systems. In this chapter, we build on this material to explain how these differences influence the level of economic development of a nation and, thus, how attractive it is as a place for doing business. We also look at how economic, political, and legal systems are changing around the world and what the implications of this are for the future rate of economic development of nations and regions. The past three decades have seen a general move toward more democratic forms of government, market-based economic reforms, and adoption of legal systems that better enforce property rights. Taken together, these trends have helped foster greater economic development around the world and have created a more favorable environment for international business. In the final section of this chapter, we pull all this material together to explore how differences in political, economic, and legal institutions affect the benefits, costs, and risks of doing business in different nations.

The opening case, which looks at the performance of the Polish economy since 1990, highlights some of these issues. Over the last 30 years Poland has had one of the best performing economies in Europe. This achievement was due to a number of positive factors, including the adoption of a democratic political system, market-based economic reforms, privatization of state-owned enterprises, the reduction of barriers to private enterprise formation, and pro-trade policies, including joining the World Trade Organization and the European Union. As a consequence of these changes, today Poland has a dynamic export-led economy that has substantially raised real living standards for its population. However, Poland now faces labor shortages, which could constrain its economic growth going forward. To continue to grow, it may have to expand its labor force through higher immigration. In recognition of this, its government has recently issued more work permits to immigrants from its troubled neighbor, the Ukraine.

LO3-1

Explain what determines the level of economic development of a nation.

Differences in Economic Development

Different countries have dramatically different levels of economic development. One common measure of economic development is a country's **gross national income (GNI)** per head of population. GNI is regarded as a yardstick for the economic activity of a country; it measures the total annual income received by residents of a nation. Map 3.1 summarizes the GNI per capita of the world's nations in 2018. As can be seen, countries such as Japan, Sweden, Switzerland, the United States, and Australia are among the richest on this measure, whereas the large developing countries of China and India are significantly poorer. Japan, for example, had a 2018 GNI per capita of $41,340, but China achieved only $9,470 and India just $2,020.[1]

GNI per person figures can be misleading because they don't consider differences in the cost of living. For example, although the 2018 GNI per capita of Switzerland at $83,580 exceeded that of the United States by a wide margin, the higher cost of living in Switzerland meant that U.S. citizens could actually afford almost as many goods and services as the average Swiss citizen. To account for differences in the cost of living, one can adjust GNI per capita by purchasing power. Referred to as a **purchasing power parity (PPP)** adjustment, it allows a more direct comparison of living standards in different countries. The base for the adjustment is the cost of living in the United States. The PPP for different countries is then adjusted (up or down) depending on whether the cost of living is lower or higher than in the United States. For example, in 2018 the GNI per capita for China was $9,470 but the PPP per capita was $18,140, suggesting that the cost of living was lower in China and that $9,470 in China would buy as much as $18,140 in the United States. Table 3.1 gives the GNI per capita measured at PPP in 2018 for a selection of countries, along with their GNI per capita, their average annual growth rate in gross domestic product (GDP) from 2009 to 2018, and the overall size of their economy

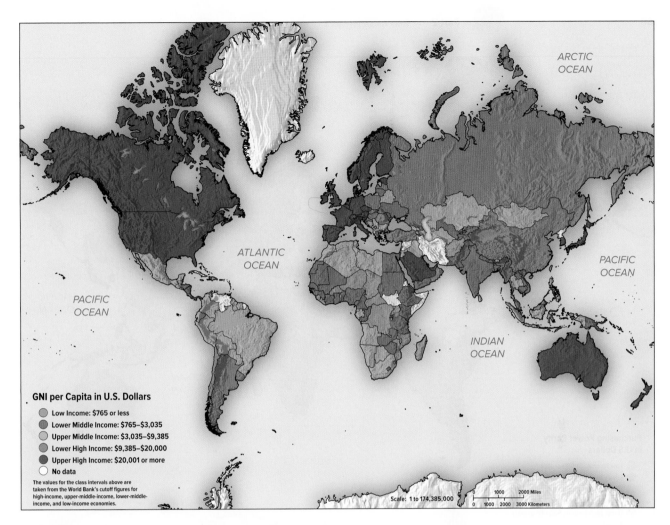

MAP 3.1

GNI per capita, 2018.

GNI per Capita in U.S. Dollars

- Low Income: $765 or less
- Lower Middle Income: $765–$3,035
- Upper Middle Income: $3,035–$9,385
- Lower High Income: $9,385–$20,000
- Upper High Income: $20,001 or more
- No data

The values for the class intervals above are taken from the World Bank's cutoff figures for high-income, upper-middle-income, lower-middle-income, and low-income economies.

Scale: 1 to 174,385,000

TABLE 3.1

Economic Data for Select Countries

Source: World Development Indicators Online, 2018.

Country	GNI per Capita, 2018 ($)	GNI PPP per Capita, 2018 ($)	Annual GDP Growth Rate, 2009–2018 (%)	Size of Economy GDP, 2018 ($ billions)
Brazil	$ 9,140	$15,820	1.2	$ 1,868
China	9,470	18,140	8.0	13,608
Germany	47,450	55,800	1.3	3,998
India	2,020	7,680	7.1	2,726
Japan	41,340	45,000	0.7	4,970
Nigeria	1,960	5,700	4.2	397
Poland	14,150	31,110	3.5	586
Russia	10,230	26,470	0.9	1,658
Switzerland	83,580	69,220	1.5	706
United Kingdom	41,330	45,660	1.3	2,825
United States	62,850	63,390	1.8	20,494

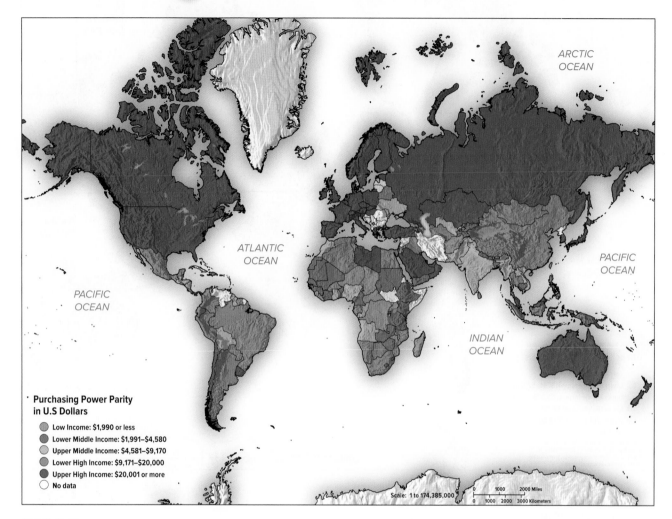

MAP 3.2

GNI PPP per capita, 2018.

 Did You Know?

Did you know that by 2050 India may be the second largest economy in the world and Indonesia the fourth?

Visit your instructor's Connect® course and click on your eBook or SmartBook® to view a short video explanation from the authors.

(measured by GDP). Map 3.2 summarizes the GNI PPP per capita in 2018 for the nations of the world.

As can be seen, there are striking differences in the standards of living among countries. Table 3.1 suggests the average Indian citizen can afford to consume only about 12 percent of the goods and services consumed by the average U.S. citizen on a PPP basis. Given this, we might conclude that despite having a population of 1.2 billion, India is unlikely to be a very lucrative market for the consumer products produced by many Western international businesses. However, this would be incorrect because India has a fairly wealthy middle class of close to 250 million people, despite its large number of poor citizens. In absolute terms, the Indian economy now rivals that of Russia.

To complicate matters, in many countries the "official" figures do not tell the entire story. Large amounts of economic activity may be in the form of unrecorded cash transactions or barter agreements. People engage in such transactions to avoid paying taxes, and although the share of total economic activity accounted for by such transactions may be small in developed economies such as the United States, in some countries (India being an example), they are reportedly very significant. Known as the *black economy* or *shadow economy*, estimates suggest that in India it has been as high as 50 percent of GDP, which

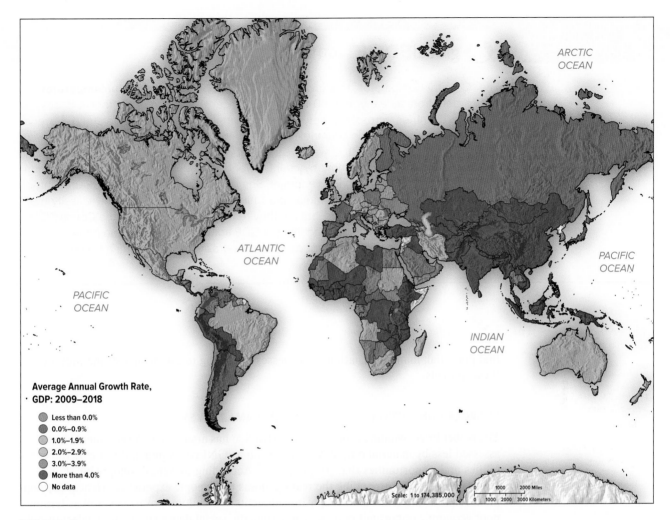

MAP 3.3

Average annual growth rate in GDP (%), 2009–2018.

implies that the Indian economy may be half as big again as the figures reported in Table 3.1. Estimates produced by the European Union suggest that the shadow economy accounted for between 10 and 12 percent of GDP in the United Kingdom and France but 21 percent in Italy and as much as 23 percent in Greece.[2]

The GNI and PPP data give a static picture of development. They tell us, for example, that China is poorer than the United States, but they do not tell us if China is closing the gap. To assess this, we have to look at the economic growth rates achieved by countries. Table 3.1 gives the rate of growth in gross domestic product (GDP) per capita achieved by a number of countries between 2009 and 2018. Map 3.3 summarizes the annual average percentage growth rate in GDP from 2009 to 2018. Although countries such as China and India are currently relatively poor, their economies are already large in absolute terms and growing far more rapidly than those of many advanced nations. They are already huge markets for the products of international businesses. In 2010, China overtook Japan to become the second-largest economy in the world after the United States. Indeed, if both China and the United States maintain their current economic growth rates, China will become the world's largest economy sometime during the next decade. On current trends, India too will be among the largest economies in the world. Given that potential, many international businesses are trying to establish a strong presence in these markets.

BROADER CONCEPTIONS OF DEVELOPMENT: AMARTYA SEN

The Nobel Prize–winning economist Amartya Sen has argued that development should be assessed less by material output measures such as GNI per capita and more by the capa-bilities and opportunities that people enjoy.[3] According to Sen, development should be seen as a process of expanding the real freedoms that people experience. Hence, develop-ment requires the removal of major impediments to freedom: poverty as well as tyranny, poor economic opportunities as well as systematic social deprivation, and neglect of pub-lic facilities as well as the intolerance of repressive states. In Sen's view, development is not just an economic process but a political one too, and to succeed requires the "democratiza-tion" of political communities to give citizens a voice in the important decisions made for the community. This perspective leads Sen to emphasize basic health care, especially for children, and basic education, especially for women. Not only are these factors desirable for their instrumental value in helping achieve higher income levels, but they are also ben-eficial in their own right. People cannot develop their capabilities if they are chronically ill or woefully ignorant.

Sen's influential thesis has been picked up by the United Nations, which has devel-oped the **Human Development Index (HDI)** to measure the quality of human life in different nations. The HDI is based on three measures: life expectancy at birth (a func-tion of health care); educational attainment (measured by a combination of the adult literacy rate and enrollment in primary, secondary, and tertiary education); and whether average incomes, based on PPP estimates, are sufficient to meet the basic needs of life in a country (adequate food, shelter, and health care). As such, the HDI comes much closer to Sen's conception of how development should be measured than narrow eco-nomic measures such as GNI per capita—although Sen's thesis suggests that political freedoms should also be included in the index, and they are not. The HDI is scaled from 0 to 1. Countries scoring less than 0.5 are classified as having low human development (the quality of life is poor), those scoring from 0.5 to 0.8 are classified as having me-dium human development, and those that score above 0.8 are classified as having high human development. Map 3.4 summarizes the HDI scores for 2017, the most recent year for which data are available.

TEST PREP

Use SmartBook to help retain what you have learned. Access your Instructor's Connect course to check out SmartBook or go to **learnsmartadvantage.com** for help.

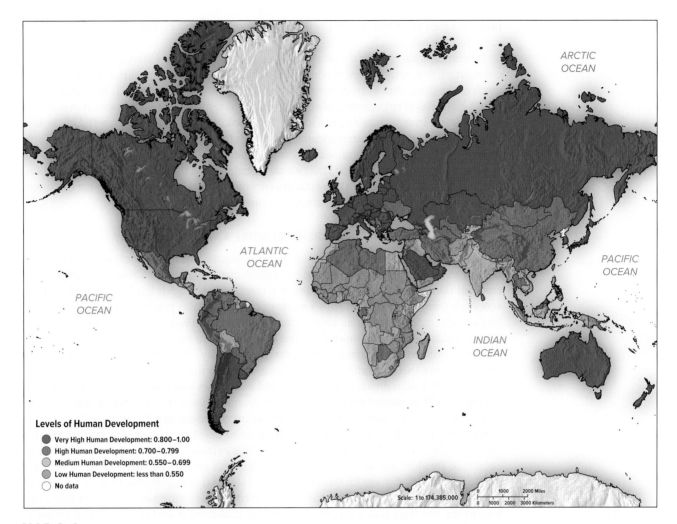

MAP 3.4

Human Development Index, 2017.

 Political Economy and Economic Progress

It is often argued that a country's economic development is a function of its economic and political systems. What then is the nature of the relationship between political economy and economic progress? Despite the long debate over this question among academics and policymakers, it is not possible to give an unambiguous answer. However, it is possible to untangle the main threads of the arguments and make a few generalizations as to the nature of the relationship between political economy and economic progress.

INNOVATION AND ENTREPRENEURSHIP ARE THE ENGINES OF GROWTH

There is substantial agreement among economists that innovation and entrepreneurial activity are the engines of long-run economic growth.[4] Those who make this argument define **innovation** broadly to include not just new products, but also new processes, new organizations, new management practices, and new strategies. Thus, Uber's strategy of letting riders hail a cab using a smartphone application can be seen as an innovation because it was the first company to pursue this strategy in its industry. Similarly, the development of mass-market online retailing by Amazon.com can be seen as an innovation. Innovation and entrepreneurial activity help increase economic activity by creating new products and markets that did not previously exist. Moreover, innovations in production and business processes lead to an increase in the productivity of labor and capital, which further boosts economic growth rates.[5]

Innovation is also seen as the product of entrepreneurial activity. Often, **entrepreneurs** first commercialize innovative new products and processes, and entrepreneurial activity provides much of the dynamism in an economy. For example, the U.S. economy has benefited greatly from a high level of entrepreneurial activity, which has resulted in rapid innovation in products and process. Firms such as Apple, Google, Facebook, Amazon, Dell, Microsoft, Oracle, and Uber were all founded by entrepreneurial individuals to exploit new technology. All these firms created significant economic value and boosted productivity by helping commercialize innovations in products and processes. Thus, we can conclude that if a country's economy is to sustain long-run economic growth, the business environment must be conducive to the consistent production of product and process innovations and to entrepreneurial activity.

INNOVATION AND ENTREPRENEURSHIP REQUIRE A MARKET ECONOMY

This leads logically to a further question: What is required for the business environment of a country to be conducive to innovation and entrepreneurial activity? Those who have considered this issue highlight the advantages of a market economy.[6] It has been argued that the economic freedom associated with a market economy creates greater incentives for innovation and entrepreneurship than either a planned or a mixed economy. In a market economy, any individual who has an innovative idea is free to try to make money out of that idea by starting a business (by engaging in entrepreneurial activity). Similarly, existing businesses are free to improve their operations through innovation. To the extent that they are successful, both individual entrepreneurs and established businesses can reap rewards in the form of high profits. Thus, market economies contain enormous incentives to develop innovations.

In a planned economy, the state owns all means of production. Consequently, entrepreneurial individuals have few economic incentives to develop valuable new innovations because it is the state, rather than the individual, that captures most of the gains. The lack of economic freedom and incentives for innovation was probably a main factor in the economic stagnation of many former communist states and led ultimately to their collapse at the end of the 1980s. Similar stagnation occurred in many mixed economies in those sectors where the state had a monopoly (such as coal mining and telecommunications in Great Britain). This stagnation provided the impetus for the widespread privatization of state-owned enterprises that we witnessed in many mixed economies during the mid-1980s and that is still going on today (*privatization* refers to the process of selling state-owned enterprises to private investors; see Chapter 2 for details).

A study of 102 countries over a 20-year period provided evidence of a strong relationship between economic freedom (as provided by a market economy) and economic growth.[7] The study found that the more economic freedom a country had between 1975 and 1995, the more economic growth it achieved and the richer its citizens became. The six countries that had persistently high ratings of economic freedom from 1975 to 1995 (Hong Kong, Switzerland, Singapore, the United States, Canada, and Germany) were also all in the top 10 in terms of economic growth rates. In contrast, no country with persistently low economic freedom achieved a respectable growth rate. In the 16 countries for which the index of economic freedom declined the most during 1975 to 1995, gross domestic product fell at an annual rate of 0.6 percent. Other studies have reached broadly similar conclusions.

INNOVATION AND ENTREPRENEURSHIP REQUIRE STRONG PROPERTY RIGHTS

Strong legal protection of property rights is another requirement for a business environment to be conducive to innovation, entrepreneurial activity, and hence economic growth.[8] Both individuals and businesses must be given the opportunity to profit from innovative ideas. Without strong property rights protection, businesses and individuals run the risk that the profits from their innovative efforts will be expropriated, either by criminal elements or by the state. The state can expropriate the profits from innovation through legal means, such as excessive taxation, or through illegal means, such as demands from state bureaucrats for kickbacks in return for granting an individual or firm a license to do business in a certain area (i.e., corruption). According to the Nobel Prize–winning economist Douglass North, throughout history many governments have displayed a tendency to engage in such behavior.[9] Inadequately enforced property rights reduce the incentives for innovation and entrepreneurial activity—because the profits from such activity are "stolen"—and hence reduce the rate of economic growth.

The influential Peruvian development economist Hernando de Soto has argued that much of the developing world will fail to reap the benefits of capitalism until property rights are better defined and protected.[10] De Soto's arguments are interesting because he says the key problem is not the risk of expropriation but the chronic inability of property owners to establish legal title to the property they own. As an example of the scale of the problem, he cites the situation in Haiti, where individuals must take 176 steps over 19 years to own land legally. Because most property in poor countries is informally "owned," the absence of legal proof of ownership means that property holders cannot convert their assets into capital, which could then be used to finance business ventures. Banks will not lend money to the poor to start businesses because the poor possess no proof that they own property, such as farmland, that can be used as collateral for a loan. By de Soto's calculations, the total value of real estate held by the poor in third-world and former communist states amounted to more than $9.3 trillion in 2000. If those assets could be converted into capital, the result could be an economic revolution that would allow the poor to bootstrap their way out of poverty. Interestingly enough, the Chinese seem to have taken de Soto's arguments to heart. Despite still being nominally a communist country, in October 2007 the government passed a law that gave private property owners the same rights as the state, which significantly improved the rights of urban and rural landowners to the land that they use (see the accompanying Country Focus).

THE REQUIRED POLITICAL SYSTEM

Much debate surrounds which kind of political system best achieves a functioning market economy with strong protection for property rights.[11] People in the West tend to associate a representative democracy with a market economic system, strong property rights protection, and economic progress. Building on this, we tend to argue that democracy is good for growth. However, some totalitarian regimes have fostered a market economy and strong property rights protection and have experienced rapid economic growth. Five of the fastest-growing economies of the past 40 years—China, South Korea, Taiwan, Singapore, and Hong Kong—had one thing in common at the start of their economic growth: undemocratic governments. At the same time, countries with stable democratic governments, such as India, experienced sluggish economic growth for long periods. In 1992, Lee Kuan Yew, Singapore's leader for many years, told an audience, "I do not believe that democracy necessarily leads to development. I believe that a country needs to develop discipline more than democracy. The exuberance of democracy leads to undisciplined and disorderly conduct which is inimical to development."[12]

However, those who argue for the value of a totalitarian regime miss an important point: If dictators made countries rich, then much of Africa, Asia, and Latin America should have been growing rapidly during 1960 to 1990, and this was not the case. Only a totalitarian regime that is committed to a market system and strong protection of property rights is capable of promoting economic growth. Also, there is no guarantee that a dictatorship will continue to pursue such progressive policies. Dictators are rarely benevolent. Many are tempted to use the apparatus of the state to further their own private ends, violating property rights and stalling economic growth. Given this, it seems likely that democratic regimes are far more conducive to long-term economic growth than are dictatorships, even benevolent ones. Only in a well-functioning, mature democracy are property rights truly secure.[13] Nor should we forget Amartya Sen's arguments reviewed earlier. Totalitarian states, by limiting human freedom, also suppress human development and therefore are detrimental to progress.

ECONOMIC PROGRESS BEGETS DEMOCRACY

While it is possible to argue that democracy is not a necessary precondition for a market economy in which property rights are protected, subsequent economic growth often leads

Property Rights in China

On October 1, 2007, a new property law took effect in China, granting rural and urban landholders far more secure property rights. The law was a much-needed response to how China's economy has changed over the past 30 years as it transitions from a centrally planned system to a more dynamic market-based economy where two-thirds of economic activity is in the hands of private enterprises.

Although all land in China still technically belongs to the state—an ideological necessity in a country where the government still claims to be guided by Marxism—urban landholders had been granted 40- to 70-year leases to use the land, while rural farmers had 30-year leases. However, the lack of legal title meant that landholders were at the whim of the state. Large-scale appropriation of rural land for housing and factory construction had rendered millions of farmers landless. Many were given little or no compensation, and they drifted to the cities where they added to a growing underclass. In both urban and rural areas, property and land disputes had become a leading cause of social unrest. According to government sources, in 2006 there were about 23,000 "mass incidents" of social unrest in China, many related to disputes over property rights.

The 2007 law, which was 14 years in gestation due to a rearguard action fought by left-wing Communist Party activists who objected to it on ideological grounds, gives urban and rural land users the right to automatic renewal of their leases after the expiration of the 30- to 70-year terms. In addition, the law requires that land users be fairly compensated if the land is required for other purposes, and it gives individuals the same legal protection for their property as the state. Taken together with a 2004 change in China's constitution, which stated that private property "was not to be encroached upon," the new law significantly strengthens property rights in China.

Nevertheless, the law has its limitations; most notably, it still falls short of giving peasants marketable ownership rights to the land they farm. If they could sell their land, tens of millions of underemployed farmers might find more productive work elsewhere. Those who stayed could acquire bigger landholdings that could be used more efficiently. Also, farmers might be able to use their landholdings as security against which they could borrow funds for investments to boost productivity.

Recognizing such limitations, in 2016 the ruling Communist Party released a set of guidelines for further shoring up property rights protection, including better legal enforcement of property rights. There is no doubt that additional protection is needed. Chinese firms and residents have continued to suffer under poor property protections, facing eviction to make way for new developments and facing fierce competition as patents and copyrights are repeatedly violated. Whether these new guidelines will improve matters, however, remains to be seen.

Sources: "China's Next Revolution—Property Rights in China," *The Economist*, March 10, 2007, p. 11; "Caught between the Right and Left," *The Economist*, March 10, 2007, pp. 25–27; Z. Keliang and L. Ping, "Rural Land Rights under the PRC Property Law," *China Law and Practice*, November 2007, pp. 10–15; and Sara Hsu, "China Is Finally Improving Property Rights Protection," *Forbes*, November 30, 2016.

to establishment of a democratic regime. Several of the fastest-growing Asian economies adopted more democratic governments during the past three decades, including South Korea and Taiwan. Thus, although democracy may not always be the cause of initial economic progress, it seems to be one consequence of that progress.

A strong belief that economic progress leads to adoption of a democratic regime underlies the fairly permissive attitude that many Western governments have adopted toward human rights violations in China. Although China has a totalitarian government in which human rights are violated, many Western countries have been hesitant to criticize the country too much for fear that this might hamper the country's march toward a free market system. The belief is that once China has a free market system, greater individual freedoms and democracy will follow. Whether this optimistic vision comes to pass remains to be seen.

GEOGRAPHY, EDUCATION, DEMOGRAPHICS, AND ECONOMIC DEVELOPMENT

While a country's political and economic systems are probably the big engine driving its rate of economic development, other factors are also important. One that has received attention is geography.[14] But the belief that geography can influence economic policy, and hence economic growth rates, goes back to Adam Smith. The influential economist Jeffrey Sachs argues that

> throughout history, coastal states, with their long engagements in international trade, have been more supportive of market institutions than landlocked states, which have tended to organize themselves as hierarchical (and often militarised) societies. Mountainous states, as a result of physical isolation, have often neglected market-based trade. Temperate climes have generally supported higher densities of population and thus a more extensive division of labour than tropical regions.[15]

Sachs's point is that by virtue of favorable geography, certain societies are more likely to engage in trade than others and are thus more likely to be open to and develop market-based economic systems, which in turn promotes faster economic growth. He also argues that, irrespective of the economic and political institutions a country adopts, adverse geographic conditions—such as the high rate of disease, poor soils, and hostile climate that afflict many tropical countries—can have a negative impact on development. Together with colleagues at Harvard's Institute for International Development, Sachs tested for the impact of geography on a country's economic growth rate between 1965 and 1990. He found that landlocked countries grew more slowly than coastal economies and that being entirely landlocked reduced a country's growth rate by roughly 0.7 percent per year. He also found that tropical countries grew 1.3 percent more slowly each year than countries in the temperate zone.

Education emerges as another important determinant of economic development (a point that Amartya Sen emphasizes). The general assertion is that nations that invest more in education will have higher growth rates because an educated population is a more productive population. Anecdotal comparisons suggest this is true. In 1960, Pakistanis and South Koreans were on equal footing economically. However, just 30 percent of Pakistani children were enrolled in primary schools, while 94 percent of South Koreans were. By the mid-1980s, South Korea's GNP per person was three times that of Pakistan.[16] A survey of 14 statistical studies that looked at the relationship between a country's investment in education and its subsequent growth rates concluded investment in education did have a positive and statistically significant impact on a country's rate of economic growth.[17] Similarly, the work by Sachs discussed earlier suggests that investments in education help explain why some countries in Southeast Asia, such as Indonesia, Malaysia, and Singapore, have been able to overcome the disadvantages associated with their tropical geography and grow far more rapidly than tropical nations in Africa and Latin America.

Economists also argue that demographic forces are an important determinant of a country's economic growth rate. Assuming a country has institutions in place that promote entrepreneurship and innovation, a country with a young and growing population has greater growth potential than one with an aging stagnant population.[18] A growing population increases the supply of labor. Younger workers also tend to consume more than older retirees, which boosts demand for goods and services. Moreover, an aging population implies that fewer workers are supporting more retirees, which can stress government finances. In the 1970s and 1980s, Japan had one of the most dynamic economies in the world, but low birthrates and an aging population have held back economic growth since the turn of the century. More generally, going forward, low birthrates and an aging population could potentially cause labor shortages and slower economic growth in a number of other major economies, including China, Germany, and the United States. One way around this is for countries with an aging population to permit higher immigration. For example, as we saw in the opening case, Poland has allowed for increased immigration from the Ukraine, largely as a strategy for coping with labor shortages due to an aging population. But immigration can bring political problems and is resisted in a number of countries (Japan, for example, has tight restrictions on immigration despite predictions that the population could fall by 30 percent over the next 40 years due to a very low birthrate).

 TEST PREP

Use SmartBook to help retain what you have learned. Access your Instructor's Connect course to check out SmartBook or go to **learnsmartadvantage.com** for help.

LO3-2

Identify the macropolitical and macroeconomic changes occurring worldwide.

States in Transition

The political economy of many of the world's nation-states has changed radically since the late 1980s. Three trends have been evident. First, during the late 1980s and early 1990s, a wave of democratic revolutions swept the world. Totalitarian governments fell and were replaced by democratically elected governments that were typically more committed to free market capitalism than their predecessors had been. Second, over the same period, there has been a move away from centrally planned and mixed economies and toward a more free market economic model. Third, and counter to the two prior trends, since 2005 there has been a shift back toward greater authoritarianism in some nations, and there are some signs that certain nations may be retreating from the free market model, particularly in the area of international trade where protectionism is on the rise again.

THE SPREAD OF DEMOCRACY

One notable development of the last 30 years has been the spread of democratic political institutions (and, by extension, the decline of totalitarianism). Map 3.5 reports on the extent of totalitarianism in the world as determined by Freedom House.[19] This map charts

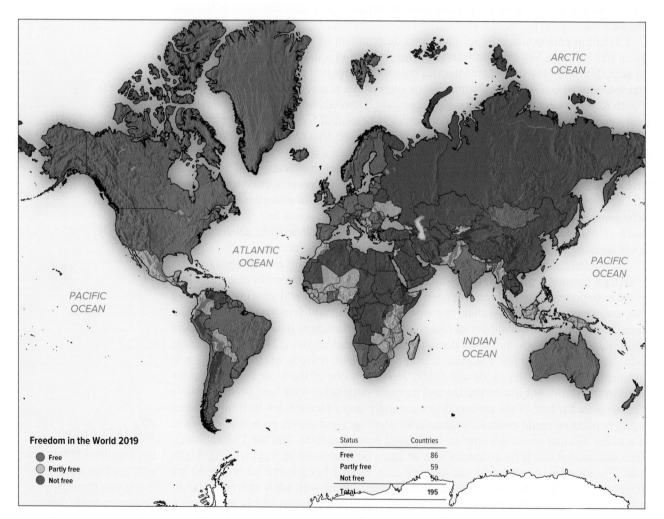

Freedom in the World 2019

- Free
- Partly free
- Not free

Status	Countries
Free	86
Partly free	59
Not free	50
Total	195

MAP 3.5

Freedom in the world, 2019.

political freedom in 2019, grouping countries into three broad groupings: free, partly free, and not free. In "free" countries, citizens enjoy a high degree of political and civil freedoms. "Partly free" countries are characterized by some restrictions on political rights and civil liberties, often in the context of corruption, weak rule of law, ethnic strife, or civil war. In "not free" countries, the political process is tightly controlled and basic freedoms are denied.

Voters wait in a queue in front of the election center in the city of Lagos, Nigeria.

Anadolu Agency/Getty Images

Freedom House classified some 86 countries as free in 2019, accounting for about 44 percent of the world's nations. These countries respect a broad range of political rights. Another 59 countries, accounting for 30 percent of the world's nations, were classified as partly free, while 51 countries representing approximately 26 percent of the world's nations were classified as not free.

Many of the newer democracies are to be found in eastern Europe and Latin America, although there also have been notable gains in Africa during this time, including South Africa and Nigeria. Entrants into the ranks of the world's democracies during the last 30 years include Mexico, which held its first fully free and fair presidential election in 2000 after free and fair parliamentary and state elections in 1997 and 1998; Senegal, where free and fair presidential elections led to a peaceful transfer of power; and Nigeria, where in 2015 for the first time the opposition won an election and there was a peaceful transfer of power.

Three main reasons account for the spread of democracy.[20] First, many totalitarian regimes failed to deliver economic progress to the vast bulk of their populations. The collapse of communism in eastern Europe, for example, was precipitated by the growing gulf between the vibrant and wealthy economies of the West and the stagnant economies of the communist East. In looking for alternatives to the socialist model, the populations of these countries could not have failed to notice that most of the world's strongest economies were governed by representative democracies. Today, the economic success of many of the newer democracies—such as Poland and the Czech Republic in the former communist bloc, the Philippines and Taiwan in Asia, and Chile in Latin America—has strengthened the case for democracy as a key component of successful economic advancement.

Second, new information and communication technologies—including satellite television, desktop publishing, and, most important, the Internet and associated social media—have reduced a state's ability to control access to uncensored information. These technologies have created new conduits for the spread of democratic ideals and information from free societies. Today, the Internet is allowing democratic ideals to penetrate closed societies as never before.[21] Young people who utilized Facebook and Twitter to reach large numbers of people very quickly and coordinate their actions organized the demonstrations in 2011 that led to the overthrow of the Egyptian government.

Third, in many countries, economic advances have led to the emergence of increasingly prosperous middle and working classes that have pushed for democratic reforms. This was certainly a factor in the democratic transformation of South Korea. Entrepreneurs and other business leaders, eager to protect their property rights and ensure the dispassionate enforcement of contracts, are another force pressing for more accountable and open government.

Although democratic institutions became more widespread following the democratic revolutions of the late 1980s, Freedom House notes that, since 2005, there has been a drift back toward more authoritarian modes of government in many nations. Between 1988 and 2005 the share of countries ranked "not free" dropped from 37 percent to 23 percent, and the share of countries ranked as "free" increased from 36 percent to 46 percent. However, from 2005 through to 2019, the share of "not free" countries rose to 26 percent, while the share of countries ranked as "free" dropped to 44 percent. Some 23 countries have suffered a negative status change since 2005. Many of these countries had benefited from the wave of democracy that swept around the world in 1988–1990, but have since backtracked toward a more authoritarian status. In general, in these nations, elections have been compromised, civil liberties including freedom of expression and association have been restricted, the independent press has been attacked or suppressed, and opposition political parties have been restricted.

Consider Turkey, where Recep Tayyip Erdogan was elected president in 2014. Erdogan used a failed coup attempt in 2016 to tighten his control over the country and consolidate power in the presidency. Opposition politicians have been arrested and imprisoned, often on dubious charges. There have been frequent arrests and convictions of journalists and social media users who were critical of the government. There has also been a sharp rise in the number of people charged under a century-old archaic law that makes it a crime to "insult the president." The number of prosecutions for this "crime" increased from almost nothing to over 6,000 in 2017. In 2017, Erdogan called and won a referendum on amending the constitution that extended the power of the President, allowing him to appoint judges and cabinet members, form and regulate ministries, draft budgets, and appoint or remove civil servants, mostly without parliamentary approval. Erdogan won the referendum by a narrow margin: 51.4 percent to 48.6 percent. He can now run for three more terms. While it is true that this extended power was given to Erdogan in a democratic referendum, critics argue that Turkey has now moved toward "one-man rule," and that the Turks have in essence voted away their democracy by a narrow margin, allowing the ruling majority to entrench its position and marginalize any opposition. Freedom House now ranks Turkey as "not free."

As in Turkey, authoritarianism has been gaining ground in several other countries where political and civil liberties have been progressively limited in recent years, including Russia, Ukraine, Indonesia, Ecuador, and Venezuela. An increasingly autocratic Russia annexed the Crimea region from the Ukraine in 2014 and has actively supported pro-Russian rebels in eastern Ukraine. Libya, where there was hope that a democracy might be established, appears to have slipped into anarchy. In Egypt, after a brief flirtation with democracy, the military stepped in, removing the government of Mohamed Morsi, after Morsi and his political movement, the Muslim Brotherhood, exhibited its own authoritarian tendencies. The military-backed government, however, has also acted in an authoritarian manner, effectively reversing much of the progress that occurred after the revolution of 2011. Of note, Freedom House also expressed concerns that under the leadership of Donald Trump, America has stepped back from its traditional role of promoting democracy and human rights around the world, a development that it views with some alarm, because pressure from the United States has historically helped to spread democratic ideals.[22]

THE NEW WORLD ORDER AND GLOBAL TERRORISM

The end of the Cold War and the "new world order" that followed the collapse of communism in eastern Europe and the former Soviet Union, taken together with the demise of many authoritarian regimes in Latin America, gave rise to intense speculation about the future shape of global geopolitics. In an influential book, 25 years ago author Francis Fukuyama argued, "We may be witnessing . . . the end of history as such: that is, the end point of mankind's ideological evolution and the universalization of Western liberal democracy as the final form of human government."[23] Fukuyama went on to argue that the war of ideas may be at an end and that liberal democracy has triumphed.

Many questioned Fukuyama's vision of a more harmonious world dominated by a universal civilization characterized by democratic regimes and free market capitalism. In a controversial book, the late influential political scientist Samuel Huntington argued there is no "universal" civilization based on widespread acceptance of Western liberal democratic ideals.[24] Huntington maintained that while many societies may be modernizing—they are adopting the material paraphernalia of the modern world, from automobiles and

Facebook to Coca-Cola and smartphones—they are not becoming more Western. On the contrary, Huntington theorized that modernization in non-Western societies can result in a retreat toward the traditional, such as the resurgence of Islam in many traditionally Muslim societies. He wrote,

> The Islamic resurgence is both a product of and an effort to come to grips with modernization. Its underlying causes are those generally responsible for indigenization trends in non-Western societies: urbanization, social mobilization, higher levels of literacy and education, intensified communication and media consumption, and expanded interaction with Western and other cultures. These developments undermine traditional village and clan ties and create alienation and an identity crisis. Islamist symbols, commitments, and beliefs meet these psychological needs, and Islamist welfare organizations, the social, cultural, and economic needs of Muslims caught in the process of modernization. Muslims feel a need to return to Islamic ideas, practices, and institutions to provide the compass and the motor of modernization.[25]

Thus, the rise of Islamic fundamentalism is portrayed as a response to the alienation produced by modernization.

In contrast to Fukuyama, Huntington envisioned a world split into different civilizations, each of which has its own value systems and ideology. Huntington predicted conflict between the West and Islam and between the West and China. While some commentators originally dismissed Huntington's thesis, in the aftermath of the terrorist attacks on the United States on September 11, 2001, Huntington's views received new attention. The dramatic rise of the Islamic State (ISIS) in war-torn Syria and neighboring Iraq during 2014–2015 drew further attention to Huntington's thesis, as has the growing penchant for ISIS to engage in terrorist acts outside the Middle East, as in Paris in 2015.

If Huntington's views are even partly correct, they have important implications for international business. They suggest many countries may be difficult places in which to do business, either because they are shot through with violent conflicts or because they are part of a civilization that is in conflict with an enterprise's home country. Huntington's views are speculative and controversial. More likely than his predictions coming to pass is the evolution of a global political system that is positioned somewhere between Fukuyama's universal global civilization based on liberal democratic ideals and Huntington's vision of a fractured world. That would still be a world, however, in which geopolitical forces limit the ability of business enterprises to operate in certain foreign countries.

As for terrorism, in Huntington's thesis, global terrorism is a product of the tension between civilizations and the clash of value systems and ideology. The terror attacks undertaken by al-Qaeda and ISIS are consistent with this view. Others point to terrorism's roots in long-standing conflicts that seem to defy political resolution—the Palestinian, Kashmir, and Northern Ireland conflicts being obvious examples. It is also true that much of the terrorism perpetrated by al-Qaeda affiliates in Iraq during the 2000s and more recently by ISIS in Iraq and Syria can be understood in part as a struggle between radicalized Sunni and Shia factions within Islam. Moreover, a substantial amount of terrorist activity in some parts of the world, such as Colombia, has been interwoven with the illegal drug trade. As former U.S. Secretary of State Colin Powell has maintained, terrorism represents one of the major threats to world peace and economic progress in the twenty-first century.[26]

THE SPREAD OF MARKET-BASED SYSTEMS

Paralleling the spread of democracy since the 1980s has been the transformation from centrally planned command economies to market-based economies. More than 30 countries that were in the former Soviet Union or the eastern European communist bloc have changed their economic systems. A complete list of countries where change is now occurring also would include Asian states such as China and Vietnam, as well as African

ISIS fighters are a visible symbol of the rise of global terrorism in the post Cold War world.

Medyan Dairieh/ZUMA Press, Inc./Alamy Stock Photo

countries such as Angola, Ethiopia, and Mozambique.[27] There has been a similar shift away from a mixed economy. Many states in Asia, Latin America, and Western Europe have sold state-owned businesses to private investors (privatization) and deregulated their economies to promote greater competition.

The rationale for economic transformation has been the same the world over. In general, command and mixed economies failed to deliver the kind of sustained economic performance that was achieved by countries adopting market-based systems, such as the United States, Switzerland, Hong Kong, and Taiwan. As a consequence, even more states have gravitated toward the market-based model.

Map 3.6, based on data from the Heritage Foundation, a politically conservative U.S. research foundation, gives some idea of the degree to which the world has shifted toward market-based economic systems. The Heritage Foundation's index of economic freedom is based on 10 indicators, including the extent to which the government intervenes in the economy, trade policy, the degree to which property rights are protected, foreign investment regulations, taxation rules, freedom from corruption, and labor freedom. A country can score between 100 (freest) and 0 (least free) on each of these indicators. The higher a country's average score across all 10 indicators, the more closely its economy represents the pure market model.

According to the 2019 index, which is summarized in Map 3.6, the world's freest economies are (in rank order) Hong Kong, Singapore, New Zealand, Switzerland, Australia, Ireland, United Kingdom, Canada, and the United Arab Emirates. The United States was ranked 12, Germany came in at 24, Japan at 30, Mexico at 66, France at 71, Russia at 98, China at 100, India at 129, and Brazil at 150. The economies of Zimbabwe, Venezuela, Cuba, and North Korea are to be found at the bottom of the rankings.[28]

Economic freedom does not necessarily equate with political freedom, as detailed in Map 3.6. For example, the two top states in the Heritage Foundation index, Hong Kong and Singapore, cannot be classified as politically free. Hong Kong was reabsorbed into communist China in 1997, and the first thing Beijing did was shut down Hong Kong's freely elected legislature. Singapore is ranked as only partly free on Freedom House's index of political freedom, due to practices such as widespread press censorship.

 TEST PREP

Use SmartBook to help retain what you have learned. Access your Instructor's Connect course to check out SmartBook or go to **learnsmartadvantage.com** for help.

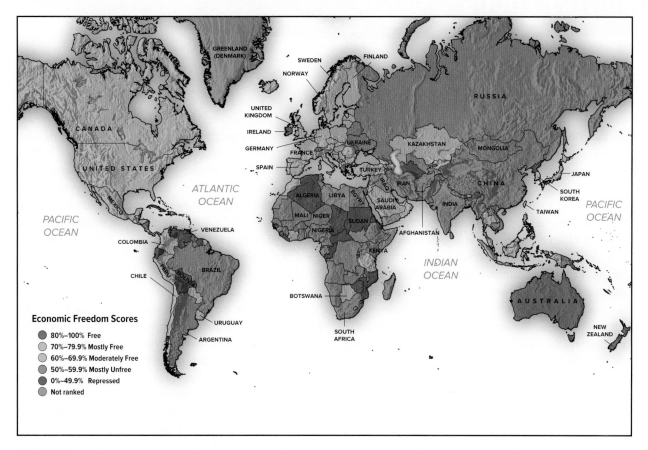

MAP 3.6

Index of economic freedom, 2019.

Source: "Interactive Heat Map." The Heritage Foundation, 2019. www.heritage.org/index/heatmap.

The Nature of Economic Transformation

LO3-3

Describe how transition economies are moving toward market-based systems.

The shift toward a market-based economic system often entails a number of steps: deregulation, privatization, and creation of a legal system to safeguard property rights.[29]

DEREGULATION

Deregulation involves removing legal restrictions to the free play of markets, the establishment of private enterprises, and the manner in which private enterprises operate. Before the collapse of communism, the governments in most command economies exercised tight control over prices and output, setting both through detailed state planning. They also prohibited private enterprises from operating in most sectors of the economy, severely restricted direct investment by foreign enterprises, and limited international trade. Deregulation in these cases involved removing price controls, thereby allowing prices to be set by the interplay between demand and supply; abolishing laws regulating the establishment and operation of private enterprises; and relaxing or removing restrictions on direct investment by foreign enterprises and international trade.

In mixed economies, the role of the state was more limited; but here, too, in certain sectors the state set prices, owned businesses, limited private enterprise, restricted investment by foreigners, and restricted international trade. For these countries, deregulation has involved the same kind of initiatives that we have seen in former command economies, although the transformation has been easier because these countries often had a vibrant private sector. India is an example of a country that has substantially deregulated its economy over the past two decades (see the upcoming Country Focus).

India's Economic Transformation

After gaining independence from Britain in 1947, India adopted a democratic system of government. The economic system that developed in India after 1947 was a mixed economy characterized by a large number of state-owned enterprises, centralized planning, and subsidies. This system constrained the growth of the private sector. Private companies could expand only with government permission. It could take years to get permission to diversify into a new product. Much of heavy industry, such as auto, chemical, and steel production, was reserved for state-owned enterprises. Production quotas and high tariffs on imports also stunted the development of a healthy private sector, as did labor laws that made it difficult to fire employees.

By the early 1990s, it was clear this system was incapable of delivering the kind of economic progress that many Southeast Asian nations had started to enjoy. In 1994, India's economy was still smaller than Belgium's, despite having a population of 950 million. Its GDP per capita was a paltry $310, less than half the population could read, only 6 million had access to telephones, and only 14 percent had access to clean sanitation; the World Bank estimated that some 40 percent of the world's desperately poor lived in India, and only 2.3 percent of the population had an annual household income in excess of $2,484.

The lack of progress led the government to embark on an ambitious economic reform program. Starting in 1991, much of the industrial licensing system was dismantled. Several areas once closed to the private sector were opened, including electricity generation, parts of the oil industry, steelmaking, air transport, and some areas of the telecommunications industry. Investment by foreign enterprises, formerly allowed only grudgingly and subject to arbitrary ceilings, was suddenly welcomed. Approval was made automatic for foreign equity stakes of up to 51 percent in an Indian enterprise, and 100 percent foreign ownership was allowed under certain circumstances. Raw materials and many industrial goods could be freely imported, and the maximum tariff that could be levied on imports was reduced from 400 percent to 65 percent. The top income tax rate was also reduced, and corporate tax fell from 57.5 percent to 46 percent in 1994, and then to 35 percent in 1997. The government also announced plans to start privatizing India's state-owned businesses, some 40 percent of which were losing money in the early 1990s.

Judged by some measures, the response to these economic reforms has been impressive. The Indian economy expanded at an annual rate of about 7 percent from 1997 to 2017. Foreign investment, a key indicator of how attractive foreign companies thought the Indian economy was, jumped from $150 million in 1991 to over $40 billion in 2017. In the information technology sector, India has emerged as a vibrant global center for software development with sales of $150 billion and exports of $117 billion in 2017, up from sales of just $150 million in 1990. In pharmaceuticals, too, Indian companies are emerging as credible players in the global marketplace, primarily by selling low-cost, generic versions of drugs that have come off patent in the developed world.

However, the country still has a long way to go. Attempts to further reduce import tariffs have been stalled by political opposition from employers, employees, and politicians who fear that if barriers come down, a flood of inexpensive Chinese products will enter India. The privatization program continues to hit speed bumps—the latest in September 2003 when the Indian Supreme Court ruled that the government could not privatize two state-owned oil companies without explicit approval from the parliament. State-owned firms still account for 38 percent of national output in the nonfarm sector, yet India's private firms are 30 to 40 percent more productive than state-owned enterprises. There has also been strong resistance to reforming many of India's laws that make it difficult for private business to operate efficiently. For example, labor laws make it almost impossible for firms with more than 100 employees to fire workers, creating a disincentive for entrepreneurs to increase their enterprises beyond 100 employees. Other laws mandate that certain products can be manufactured only by small companies, effectively making it impossible for companies in these industries to attain the scale required to compete internationally.

Sources: "India's Breakthrough Budget?" *The Economist*, March 3, 2001; "America's Pain, India's Gain," *The Economist*, January 11, 2003, p. 57; Joanna Slater, "In Once Socialist India, Privatizations Are Becoming More Like Routine Matters," *The Wall Street Journal*, July 5, 2002, p. A8; "India's Economy: Ready to Roll Again?" *The Economist*, September 20, 2003, pp. 39–40; Joanna Slater, "Indian Pirates Turned Partners," *The Wall Street Journal*, November 13, 2003, p. A14; "The Next Wave: India," *The Economist*, December 17, 2005, p. 67; M. Dell, "The Digital Sector Can Make Poor Nations Prosper," *Financial Times*, May 4, 2006, p. 17; "What's Holding India Back," *The Economist*, March 8, 2008, p. 11; "Battling the Babu Raj," *The Economist*, March 8, 2008, pp. 29–31; Rishi Lyengar, "India Tops Foreign Investment Rankings Ahead of U.S. and China," *Time*, October 11, 2015; and "FDI in India," *Indian Brand Equity Foundation,* March 2018.

PRIVATIZATION

Hand in hand with deregulation has come a sharp increase in privatization. Privatization, as discussed in Chapter 2, transfers the ownership of state property into the hands of private individuals, frequently by the sale of state assets through an auction.[30] Privatization is seen as a way to stimulate gains in economic efficiency by giving new private owners a powerful incentive—the reward of greater profits—to search for increases in productivity, to enter new markets, and to exit losing ones.[31]

The privatization movement started in Great Britain in the early 1980s when then-Prime Minister Margaret Thatcher started to sell state-owned assets such as the British telephone company, British Telecom (BT). In a pattern that has been repeated around the world, this sale was linked with the deregulation of the British telecommunications industry. By allowing other firms to compete head to head with BT, deregulation ensured that privatization did not simply replace a state-owned monopoly with a private monopoly. Since the 1980s, privatization has become a worldwide phenomenon. More than 8,000 acts of privatization were completed around the world between 1995 and 1999.[32] Some of the most dramatic privatization programs occurred in the economies of the former Soviet Union and its eastern European satellite states. In the Czech Republic, for example, three-quarters of all state-owned enterprises were privatized between 1989 and 1996, helping push the share of gross domestic product accounted for by the private sector up from 11 percent in 1989 to 60 percent in 1995.[33]

Privatization is still ongoing today. For example, in 2017 the Brazilian government announced the privatization of a state-owned electric company, airports, highways, ports, and the lottery (see the opening case). In Saudi Arabia, the government has plans to privatize the state-owned oil company, Saudi Aramco. Conversely, in China the privatization of inefficient state-owned enterprises has slowed down somewhat as the state pursues a "mixed ownership" strategy.[34]

Despite this three-decade trend, large amounts of economic activity are still in the hands of state-owned enterprises in many nations. In China, for example, state-owned companies still dominate the banking, energy, telecommunications, health care, and technology sectors. Overall, they account for about 40 percent of the country's GDP. The World Bank cautioned China that unless it reformed these sectors—liberalizing them and privatizing many state-owned enterprises—the country runs the risk of experiencing a serious economic crisis.[35]

As privatization has proceeded, it has become clear that simply selling state-owned assets to private investors is not enough to guarantee economic growth. Studies of privatization have shown that the process often fails to deliver predicted benefits if the newly privatized firms continue to receive subsidies from the state and if they are protected from foreign competition by barriers to international trade and foreign direct investment.[36] In such cases, the newly privatized firms are sheltered from competition and continue acting like state monopolies. When these circumstances prevail, the newly privatized entities often have little incentive to restructure their operations to become more efficient. For privatization to work, it must also be accompanied by a more general deregulation and opening of the economy. Thus, when Brazil decided to privatize the state-owned telephone monopoly, Telebrás Brazil, the government also split the company into four independent units that were to compete with each other and removed barriers to foreign direct investment in telecommunications services. This action ensured that the newly privatized entities would face significant competition and thus would have to improve their operating efficiency to survive.

LEGAL SYSTEMS

As noted in Chapter 2, a well-functioning market economy requires laws protecting private property rights and providing mechanisms for contract enforcement. Without a legal system that protects property rights and without the machinery to enforce that system, the incentive to engage in economic activity can be reduced substantially by private and public entities, including organized crime, that expropriate the profits generated by the efforts of private-sector entrepreneurs. For example, when communism collapsed in eastern Europe, many countries lacked the legal structure required to protect property rights, all property having been held by the state. Although many nations have made big strides toward instituting the required system, it may be years before the legal system is functioning as smoothly as it does in the West. For example, in most eastern European nations, the title to urban and agricultural property is often uncertain because of incomplete and inaccurate records, multiple pledges on the same property, and unsettled claims resulting from demands for restitution from owners in the pre-communist era. Also, although most countries have improved their commercial codes, institutional weaknesses still undermine contract enforcement. Court capacity is often inadequate, and procedures for resolving contract disputes out of court are often lacking or poorly developed.[37] Nevertheless, progress is being made. In 2004, for example, China amended its constitution to state that "private property was not to be encroached upon," and in 2007 it enacted a new law on property rights that gave property holders many of the same protections as those enjoyed by the state (see the Country Focus "Property Rights in China").[38]

Implications of Changing Political Economy

The global changes in political and economic systems discussed earlier have several implications for international business. The long-standing ideological conflict between collectivism and individualism that defined the twentieth century is less in evidence today. The West won the Cold War, and Western ideology is more widespread. Although command economies remain and totalitarian dictatorships can still be found around the world, and although there has been some retreat from democratic institutions, the world remains a more democratic place, with a much greater adherence to a market-based economic system than was the case prior to 1988.

For nearly 50 years, half of the world was off-limits to Western businesses. Since the late 1980s, much of that has changed. Many of the national markets of eastern Europe, Latin America, Africa, and Asia may still be underdeveloped, but they are potentially enormous. With a population of more than 1.3 billion, the Chinese market alone is potentially bigger than that of the United States, the European Union, and Japan combined. Similarly, India, with about 1.2 billion people, is a potentially huge market. Latin America has another 600 million potential consumers. It is unlikely that China, India, Vietnam, or any of the other states now moving toward a market system will attain the living standards of the West soon. Nevertheless, the upside potential is so large that companies need to consider investing there. For example, if China and the United States continue to grow at the rates they did from 1996 through 2018, China will surpass the United States to become the world's largest national economy within the next two decades.

Just as the potential gains are large, so are the risks. There is no guarantee that democracy will thrive in many of the world's newer democratic states, particularly if these states have to grapple with severe economic setbacks. Authoritarianism is on the rise again and totalitarian dictatorships could return, although they are unlikely to be of the communist variety. Though the bipolar world of the Cold War era has vanished, it may be replaced by a multipolar world dominated by a number of civilizations. In such a world, much of the economic promise inherent in the global shift toward market-based economic systems may stall in the face of conflicts between civilizations. While the long-term potential for economic gain from investment in the world's new market economies is large, the risks associated with any such investment are also substantial. It would be foolish to ignore these. The financial system in China, for example, is not transparent, and many suspect that Chinese banks hold a high proportion of nonperforming loans on their books. If true, these bad debts could trigger a significant financial crisis during the next decade in China, which would dramatically lower growth rates.

FOCUS ON MANAGERIAL IMPLICATIONS

BENEFITS, COSTS, RISKS, AND OVERALL ATTRACTIVENESS OF DOING BUSINESS INTERNATIONALLY

LO3-4

Explain the implications for management practice of national difference in political economy.

As noted in Chapter 2, the political, economic, and legal environments of a country clearly influence the attractiveness of that country as a market or investment site. In this chapter, we argued that countries with democratic regimes, market-based economic policies, and strong protection of property rights are more likely to attain high and sustained economic growth rates and are thus a more attractive location for international business. It follows that the benefits, costs, and risks associated with doing business in a country are a function of that country's political, economic, and legal systems. The overall attractiveness of a country as a market or investment site depends on balancing the likely long-term benefits of doing business in that country against the likely costs and risks. Here, we consider the determinants of benefits, costs, and risks.

Benefits

In the most general sense, the long-run monetary benefits of doing business in a country are a function of the size of the market, the present wealth (purchasing power) of consumers in that market, and the likely future wealth of consumers. While some markets are very large when measured by number of consumers (e.g., India), relatively low living standards may imply limited purchasing power and, therefore, a relatively small market when measured in economic terms. International businesses need to be aware of this distinction, but they also need to keep in mind the likely future prospects of a country. In 1960, South Korea was viewed as just another impoverished third-world nation. By 2017, it had the world's 11th-largest economy. International firms that recognized South Korea's potential in 1960 and began to do business in that country may have reaped greater benefits than those that wrote off South Korea.

By identifying and investing early in a potential future economic star, international firms may build brand loyalty and gain experience in that country's business practices. These will pay back substantial dividends if that country achieves sustained high economic growth rates. In contrast, late entrants may find that they lack the brand loyalty and experience necessary to achieve a significant presence in the market. In the language of business strategy, early entrants into potential future economic stars may be able to reap substantial first-mover advantages, while late entrants may fall victim to late-mover disadvantages.[39] (**First-mover advantages** are the advantages that accrue to early entrants into a market. **Late-mover disadvantages** are the handicaps that late entrants might suffer.) This kind of reasoning has been driving significant inward investment into China, which may become the world's largest economy by 2030 if it continues growing at current rates (China is already the world's second-largest national economy). For more than two decades, China has been the largest recipient of foreign direct investment in the developing world as international businesses—including General Motors, Volkswagen, Coca-Cola, and Unilever—try to establish a sustainable advantage in this nation.

A country's economic system and property rights regime are reasonably good predictors of economic prospects. Countries with free market economies in which property rights are protected tend to achieve greater economic growth rates than command economies or economies where property rights are poorly protected. It follows that a country's economic system, property rights regime, and market size (in terms of population) probably constitute reasonably good indicators of the potential long-run benefits of doing business in a country. In contrast, countries where property rights are not well respected and where corruption is rampant tend to have lower levels of economic growth. We must be careful about generalizing too much from this, however, because both China and India have achieved high growth rates despite relatively weak property rights regimes and high levels of corruption. In both countries, the shift toward a market-based

Coca-Cola has been in China for about 40 years, and about 140 million servings of the company's products are enjoyed daily in China.

Testing/Shutterstock

economic system has produced large gains despite weak property rights and endemic corruption.

Costs

A number of political, economic, and legal factors determine the costs of doing business in a country. With regard to political factors, a company may be pushed to pay off politically powerful entities in a country before the government allows it to do business there. The need to pay what are essentially bribes is greater in closed totalitarian states than in open democratic societies where politicians are held accountable by the electorate (although this is not a hard-and-fast distinction). Whether a company should actually pay bribes in return for market access should be determined on the basis of the legal and ethical implications of such action. We discuss this consideration in Chapter 5, when we look closely at the issue of business ethics.

With regard to economic factors, one of the most important variables is the sophistication of a country's economy. It may be more costly to do business in relatively primitive or undeveloped economies because of the lack of infrastructure and supporting businesses. At the extreme, an international firm may have to provide its own infrastructure and supporting business, which obviously raises costs. When McDonald's decided to open its first restaurant in Moscow, it found that to serve food and drink indistinguishable from that served in McDonald's restaurants elsewhere, it had to vertically integrate backward to supply its own needs. The quality of Russian-grown potatoes and meat was too poor. Thus, to protect the quality of its product, McDonald's set up its own dairy farms, cattle ranches, vegetable plots, and food-processing plants within Russia. This raised the cost of doing business in Russia, relative to the cost in more sophisticated economies where high-quality inputs could be purchased on the open market.

As for legal factors, it can be more costly to do business in a country where local laws and regulations set strict standards with regard to product safety, safety in the workplace, environmental pollution, and the like (because adhering to such regulations is costly). It can also be more costly to do business in a country like the United States, where the absence of a cap on damage awards has meant spiraling liability insurance rates. It can be more costly to do business in a country that lacks well-established laws for regulating business practice (as is the case in many of the former communist nations). In the absence of a well-developed body of business contract law, international firms may find no satisfactory way to resolve contract disputes and, consequently, routinely face large losses from contract violations. Similarly, local laws that fail to adequately protect intellectual property can lead to the theft of an international business's intellectual property and lost income.

Risks

As with costs, the risks of doing business in a country are determined by a number of political, economic, and legal factors. **Political risk** has been defined as the likelihood that political forces will cause drastic changes in a country's business environment that adversely affect the profit and other goals of a business enterprise.[40] So defined, political risk tends to be greater in countries experiencing social unrest and disorder or in countries where the underlying nature of a society increases the likelihood of social unrest. Social unrest typically finds expression in strikes, demonstrations, terrorism, and violent conflict. Such unrest is more likely to be found in countries that contain more than one ethnic nationality, in countries where competing ideologies are battling for political control, in countries where economic mismanagement has created high inflation and falling living standards, or in countries that straddle the "fault lines" between civilizations.

Social unrest can result in abrupt changes in government and government policy or, in some cases, in protracted civil strife. Such strife tends to have negative economic implications for the profit goals of business enterprises. For example, in the aftermath of the 1979 Islamic revolution in Iran, the Iranian assets of numerous U.S. companies were seized by the new Iranian government without compensation. Similarly, the violent disintegration of the Yugoslavian federation into warring states, including Bosnia, Croatia, and Serbia, precipitated a collapse in the local economies and in the profitability of investments in those countries.

More generally, a change in political regime can result in the enactment of laws that are less favorable to international business. In Venezuela, for example, the populist socialist politician Hugo Chávez held power from 1998 until his death in 2013. Chávez declared himself to be a "Fidelista," a follower of Cuba's Fidel Castro. He pledged to improve the lot of the poor in Venezuela through government intervention in private business and frequently railed against American imperialism, all of which is of concern to Western enterprises doing business in the country. Among other actions, he increased the royalties that foreign oil companies operating in Venezuela had to pay the government from 1 to 30 percent of sales.

Other risks may arise from a country's mismanagement of its economy. An **economic risk** can be defined as the likelihood that economic mismanagement will cause drastic changes in a country's business environment that hurt the profit and other goals of a particular business enterprise. Economic risks are not independent of political risk. Economic mismanagement may give rise to significant social unrest and, hence, political risk. Nevertheless, economic risks are worth emphasizing as a separate category because there is not always a one-to-one relationship between economic mismanagement and social unrest. One visible indicator of economic mismanagement tends to be a country's inflation rate. Another is the level of business and government debt in the country.

The collapse in oil prices that occurred in 2014–2015 exposed economic mismanagement and increased economic risk in a number countries that had been overly dependent upon oil revenues to finance profligate government spending. In countries such as Russia, Saudi Arabia, and Venezuela, high oil prices had enabled national governments to spend lavishly on social programs and public sector infrastructure. As oil prices collapsed, these countries saw government revenues tumble. Budget deficits began to climb sharply, their currencies fell on foreign exchange markets, price inflation began to accelerate as the price of imports rose, and their economies started to contract, increasing unemployment and creating the potential for social disruption. None of this was good for those countries, nor did it benefit foreign business that had invested in those economies.

On the legal front, risks arise when a country's legal system fails to provide adequate safe-guards in the case of contract violations or to protect property rights. When legal safeguards are weak, firms are more likely to break contracts or steal intellectual property if they perceive it as being in their interests to do so. Thus, a **legal risk** can be defined as the likelihood that a trading partner will opportunistically break a contract or expropriate property rights. When legal risks in a country are high, an international business might hesitate entering into a long-term contract or joint-venture agreement with a firm in that country. For example, in the 1970s when the Indian government passed a law requiring all foreign investors to enter into joint ventures with Indian companies, U.S. companies such as IBM and Coca-Cola closed their investments in India. They believed that the Indian legal system did not provide adequate protection of intellectual property rights, creating the very real danger that their Indian partners might expropriate the intellectual property of the American companies—which for IBM and Coca-Cola amounted to the core of their competitive advantage.

Overall Attractiveness

The overall attractiveness of a country as a potential market or investment site for an international business depends on balancing the benefits, costs, and risks associated with doing business in that country (see Figure 3.1). Generally, the costs and risks associated with doing business in a foreign country are typically lower in economically advanced and politically stable democratic nations and greater in less developed and politically unstable nations. The calculus is complicated, however, because the potential long-run benefits are dependent not only on a nation's current stage of economic development or political stability but also on likely future economic growth rates. Economic growth appears to be a function of a free market system and a country's capacity for growth (which may be greater in less developed nations). This leads us to conclude that, other things being equal, the benefit–cost–risk trade-off is likely to be most favorable in politically stable developed and developing nations that have free market systems and no dramatic upsurge in either inflation rates or private-sector debt. It is likely to be least favorable in politically unstable developing nations that operate with a mixed or command economy or in developing nations where speculative financial bubbles have led to excess borrowing.

FIGURE 3.1

Country attractiveness.

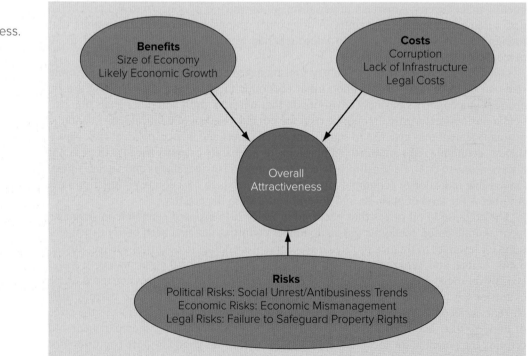

Key Terms

gross national income (GNI), p. 64
purchasing power parity
    (PPP), p. 64
Human Development Index
    (HDI), p. 68

innovation, p. 69
entrepreneurs, p. 70
deregulation, p. 79
first-mover advantages, p. 83
late-mover disadvantages, p. 83

political risk, p. 85
economic risk, p. 85
legal risk, p. 86

SUMMARY

This chapter reviewed how the political, economic, and legal systems of countries vary. The potential benefits, costs, and risks of doing business in a country are a function of its political, economic, and legal systems. The chapter made the following points:

1. The rate of economic progress in a country seems to depend on the extent to which that country has a well-functioning market economy in which property rights are protected.

2. Many countries are now in a state of transition. There is a marked shift away from totalitarian governments and command or mixed economic systems and toward democratic political institutions and free market economic systems.

3. The attractiveness of a country as a market and/or investment site depends on balancing the likely long-run benefits of doing business in that country against the likely costs and risks.

4. The benefits of doing business in a country are a function of the size of the market (population), its present wealth (purchasing power), and its future growth prospects. By investing early in countries that are currently poor but are nevertheless growing rapidly, firms can gain first-mover advantages that will pay back substantial dividends in the future.

5. The costs of doing business in a country tend to be greater where political payoffs are required to gain market access, where supporting infrastructure is lacking or underdeveloped, and where adhering to local laws and regulations is costly.

6. The risks of doing business in a country tend to be greater in countries that are politically unstable, subject to economic mismanagement, and lacking a legal system to provide adequate safeguards in the case of contract or property rights violations.

Critical Thinking and Discussion Questions

1. What is the relationship among property rights, corruption, and economic progress? How important are anticorruption efforts in the effort to improve a country's level of economic development?

2. You are a senior manager in a U.S. automobile company considering investing in production facilities in China, Russia, or Germany. These facilities will serve local market demand. Evaluate the benefits, costs, and risks associated with doing business in each nation. Which country seems the most attractive target for foreign direct investment? Why?

3. Reread the Country Focus "India's Economic Transformation" and answer the following questions.

    a. What kind of economic system did India operate under during 1947–1990? What kind of system is it moving toward today? What are the impediments to completing this transformation?

    b. How might widespread public ownership of businesses and extensive government regulations have affected (*i*) the efficiency of state and private businesses and (*ii*) the rate of new business formation in India during the 1947–1990 time frame? How do you think these factors affected the rate of economic growth in India during this time frame?

c. How would privatization, deregulation, and the removal of barriers to foreign direct investment affect the efficiency of business, new business formation, and the rate of economic growth in India during the post-1990 period?

d. India now has pockets of strengths in key high-technology industries such as software

and pharmaceuticals. Why do you think India is developing strength in these areas? How might success in these industries help generate growth in the other sectors of the Indian economy?

e. Given what is now occurring in the Indian economy, do you think the country represents an attractive target for inward investment by foreign multinationals selling consumer products? Why?

globalEDGE research task globaledge.msu.edu

Use the globalEDGE™ website (**globaledge.msu.edu**) to complete the following exercises:

1. Increased instability in the global marketplace can introduce unanticipated risks in a company's daily transactions. Your company must evaluate these *commercial transaction* risks for its foreign operations in Argentina, China, Egypt, Poland, and South Africa. A risk analyst at your firm said you could evaluate both the political and commercial risk of these countries simultaneously. Provide a commercial transaction risk overview of all five countries for top management. In your evaluation, indicate possible

corrective measures in the countries with considerably high political and/or commercial risk.

2. Managers at your firm are very concerned about the influence of terrorism on its long-term strategy. To counter this issue, the CEO has indicated you must identify the countries where *terrorism threats* and political risk are minimal. This will provide the basis for the development of future company facilities, which need to be built in all major continents in the world. Include recommendations on which countries in each continent would serve as a good candidate for your company to further analyze.

CLOSING CASE

Brazil's Struggling Economy

Between 2000 and 2012, Brazil had one of the fastest-growing economies in the world, expanding by over 5 percent per year. In 2012, the Brazilian economy temporarily surpassed that of the United Kingdom, making it the world's sixth-largest economy. Brazil's economic gains were partly due to booming international demand for commodities and high commodity prices. Brazil is a major exporter of coffee, soybeans, and iron ore. The country also benefited from strong domestic demand, cheap credit in international markets, inflows of foreign capital, tame inflation (important in a country with a

history of hyperinflation), and moderately conservative macro-economic policies. Since 2012, however, Brazil has been beset by a deep economic malaise. Economic growth decelerated in 2013. The economy entered into a serious recession in 2014. Economic activity contracted by over 3.5 percent in both 2015 and 2016 before growing by a sluggish 0.7 percent in 2017 and just 1.1 percent in 2018.

Brazil's economic problems were partly due to weaker demand for exports and a fall in global commodity prices. In 2010, exports grew 11.6 percent, but that growth stalled in 2012, and in 2014 exports contracted by 1 percent. However, the country has other deep structural problems that led to a fall in domestic demand. Under the leadership of President Dilma Rousseff and her left-of-center Workers' Party, between 2011 and 2014 the government spent extravagantly on higher pensions and unproductive tax breaks for favored industries. When the economic slowdown hit, unemployment surged to over 12 percent and tax revenues slumped. As a result of higher outlays and lower tax revenues, the fiscal deficit swelled from 2 percent of GDP in 2010 to 10 percent in 2015. This pushed up total government debt to 70 percent of GDP and required higher interest rates to sell government bonds, which were seen as increasingly risky. The government also raised interest rates to keep inflation in check, which historically has been a problem in Brazil. Because of high interest rates, the cost of servicing government debt expanded to 7 percent of GDP—and, of course, higher interest rates, by raising borrowing costs for consumers and businesses, further depressed economic activity.

Paulo Vilela/Shutterstock

Given high interest rates, the only way for the government to get the fiscal deficit under control is to cut spending and raise taxes. This has not been easy to do. A central problem in Brazil is the country's pension obligations. The pension system entitles Brazilians to retire, on average, at just 54. Pension obligations already account for 13 percent of GDP. Without reform, that figure could balloon to 25 percent by mid-century as the population ages.

In addition, tariff barriers protecting inefficient local enterprises from foreign competition, labor laws, and burdensome tax laws have long been seen as a drag on the Brazilian economy. A typical manufacturing firm spends 2,600 hours a year complying with the country's complex tax code; the Latin American average is 356 hours. Labor laws make it expensive to fire even incompetent workers. And protection from international competition has resulted in manufacturing productivity that is low by international standards. To compound matters, the country has been beset by a massive corruption scandal that has reached into the highest levels of government. This resulted in the impeachment of Rousseff in 2016 and further damaged confidence in the economy (see the Country Focus "Corruption in Brazil" in Chapter 2).

In 2016, Michel Temer replaced Rousseff as President. He made a promising start to reforming the economy. He froze public spending in real terms for the next 20 years. He also overhauled the country's labor laws, making it much easier to fire unproductive workers. Inflation moderated significantly, and a rise in commodity prices helped increase exports. This allowed the central bank to reduce interest rates to 6.75 percent (they were as high as 12 percent), further boosting economic growth. There was also a rash of privatizations—including that of the leading electric utility, Eletrobras—as the government sought to raise capital by selling state assets and tried to increase the efficiency of the economy. What remains is to fix the country's pension problems. This would require raising the retirement age significantly. Temer ran up against strong resistance. His initial proposals failed to garner enough votes in the Brazilian congress to change the law on pensions.

In October 2018, Brazil held elections. Temer's left wing Worker's Party lost the election. The victor, Jair Bolsonaro of the right-wing Social Liberal Party, ran on a law-and-order ticket, promising to fix Brazil's high crime rate. He also stated he would make necessary reforms to the country's pension system.

Sources: Denise Chrispim Marin, "Brazil's Half Glass Economy," *Global Finance*, October 3, 2017; "Michel Temer Is Trying to Fix Brazil's Pension Systems," *The Economist*, February 15, 2018; "Will Brazil's Future Arrive?" *The Economist*, August 17, 2017; "Brazil's Fall," *The Economist*, January 2, 2016; Jeffrey T. Lewis, "Brazil Posted Lackluster Economic Growth in 2018," *The Wall Street Journal*, February 28, 2019.

Case Discussion Questions

1. Brazil was seen as one of the world's fastest-growing developing economies in the 2000–2010 period. What were the foundations of this success?

2. Why did Brazil's economic growth falter after 2012? How much of the damage was self-inflicted, and how much was due to factors outside of the country's control?

3. What do you think of Temer's economic reforms? Were they on the right track?

4. What policies do you think Brazil should adopt going forward to reignite economic growth? How easy would it be to implement these policies in Brazil?

Endnotes

1. World Bank, *World Development Indicators Online,* 2019.

2. Brindusa Mihaela Tudose and Raluca Irina Clipa, "An Analysis of the Shadow Economy in EU Countries," CES Working Papers," Volume 111, Issue 2, pp. 303-312, 2018. www.ceswp.uaic.ro/articles/CESWP2016_VIII2_TUD.pdf.

3. A. Sen, *Development as Freedom* (New York: Knopf, 1999).

4. G. M. Grossman and E. Helpman, "Endogenous Innovation in the Theory of Growth," *Journal of Economic Perspectives* 8, no. 1 (1994), pp. 23-44; P. M. Romer, "The Origins of Endogenous Growth," *Journal of Economic Perspectives* 8, no. 1 (1994), pp. 2-22.

5. W. W. Lewis, *The Power of Productivity* (Chicago: University of Chicago Press, 2004).

6. F. A. Hayek, *The Fatal Conceit: Errors of Socialism* (Chicago: University of Chicago Press, 1989).

7. J. Gwartney, R. Lawson, and W. Block, *Economic Freedom of the World: 1975-1995* (London: Institute of Economic Affairs, 1996); C. Doucouliagos and M. Ali Ulubasoglu, "Economic Freedom and Economic Growth: Does Specification Make a Difference?" *European Journal of Political Economy* 22 (March 2006), pp. 60-81.

8. D. North, *Institutions, Institutional Change, and Economic Performance* (Cambridge, UK: Cambridge University Press, 1991). See also K. M. Murphy, A. Shleifer, and R. Vishney, "Why Is Rent Seeking So Costly to Growth?," *American Economic Review* 83, no. 2 (1993), pp. 409-14; K. E. Maskus, "Intellectual Property Rights in the Global Economy," Institute for International Economics, 2000.

9. North, *Institutions, Institutional Change and Economic Performance.*

10. H. de Soto, *The Mystery of Capital: Why Capitalism Triumphs in the West and Fails Everywhere Else* (New York: Basic Books, 2000).

11. A. O. Hirschman, "The On-and-Off Again Connection between Political and Economic Progress," *American Economic Review* 84, no. 2 (1994), pp. 343-48; A. Przeworski and F. Limongi, "Political Regimes and Economic Growth," *Journal of Economic Perspectives* 7, no. 3 (1993), pp. 51-59.

12. Hirschman, Albert O. "The On-and-off Again Connection between Political and Economic Progress." *The American Economic Review* 84, no. 2, Papers and Proceedings of the Hundred and Sixth Annual Meeting of the American Economic Association (May, 1994): 343--48. https://www.jstor.org/stable/2117856?seq=1#page_scan_tab_contents.

13. For details of this argument, see M. Olson, "Dictatorship, Democracy, and Development," *American Political Science Review,* September 1993.

14. For example, see Jared Diamond's Pulitzer Prize-winning book *Guns, Germs, and Steel* (New York: Norton, 1997). Also see J. Sachs, "Nature, Nurture and Growth," *The Economist,* June 14, 1997, pp. 19-22; J. Sachs, *The End of Poverty* (New York: Penguin Books, 2005).

15. Sachs, Jeffrey. "Nature, Nurture and Growth." *The Economist,* June 12, 1997. https://www.economist.com/special/1997/06/12/nature-nurture-and-growth.

16. "What Can the Rest of the World Learn from the Classrooms of Asia?" *The Economist,* September 21, 1996, p. 24.

17. J. Fagerberg, "Technology and International Differences in Growth Rates," *Journal of Economic Literature* 32 (September 1994), pp. 1147-75.

18. D. Baker, J. B. Delong and P. R. Krugman, "Asset Returns and Economic Growth," *Brookings Papers on Economic Activity,* 2005, 289-330; G. S. Becker, E. L. Laeser, and K. M. Murphy, "Population and Economic Growth," *American Economic Review,* 89(2) pp. 214-228.

19. See The Freedom House Survey Team, "Freedom in the World 2018," and associated materials, www.freedomhouse.org.

20. Freedom House, "Democracies Century: A Survey of Political Change in the Twentieth Century, 1999," www.freedomhouse.org.

21. L. Conners, "Freedom to Connect," *Wired,* August 1997, pp. 105-6.

22. Diego Cupolo, "Turks Have Voted Away Their Democracy," *The Atlantic,* June 25, 2018; "Turkey: End Prosecutions for 'Insulting the President,'" *Human Rights Watch,* October 17, 2018.

23. Fukuyama, Francis. "The End of History?" *The National Interest* (Summer 1989). https://history.msu.edu/hst203/files/2011/02/Fukuyama-The-End-of-History.pdf.

24. S. P. Huntington, *The Clash of Civilizations and the Remaking of World Order* (New York: Simon & Schuster, 1996).

25. Huntington, Samuel. *The Clash of Civilizations And the Remaking of World Order.* New York: Simon & Schuster, 2011.

26. U.S. National Counterterrorism Center, *Reports on Incidents of Terrorism, 2005,* April 11, 2006.

27. S. Fischer, R. Sahay, and C. A. Vegh, "Stabilization and the Growth in Transition Economies: The Early Experience," *Journal of Economic Perspectives* 10 (Spring 1996), pp. 45-66.

28. M. Miles et al., *2018 Index of Economic Freedom* (Washington, DC: Heritage Foundation, 2018).

29. International Monetary Fund, *World Economic Outlook: Focus on Transition Economies* (Geneva: IMF, October 2000). "Transition Economies, an IMF Perspective on Progress and Prospects," IMF, November 3, 2000.

30. J. C. Brada, "Privatization Is Transition—Is It?" *Journal of Economic Perspectives,* Spring 1996, pp. 67–86.

31. See S. Zahra et al., "Privatization and Entrepreneurial Transformation," *Academy of Management Review* 3, no. 25 (2000), pp. 509–24.

32. N. Brune, G. Garrett, and B. Kogut, "The International Monetary Fund and the Global Spread of Privatization," *IMF Staff Papers* 51, no. 2 (2003), pp. 195–219.

33. Fischer et al., "Stabilization and Growth in Transition Economies."

34. Shannon Sims, "Brazil's Privatization Push," *US News and World Reports*, October 11, 2017; Jane Cai, "Forget Privatization, Xi Has Other Big Plans for Bloated State Firms," *South China Morning Post*, September 6, 2017.

35. "China 2030," World Bank, 2012.

36. J. Sachs, C. Zinnes, and Y. Eilat, "The Gains from Privatization in Transition Economies: Is Change of Ownership Enough?" CAER discussion paper no. 63 (Cambridge, MA: Harvard Institute for International Development, 2000).

37. M. S. Borish and M. Noel, "Private Sector Development in the Visegrad Countries," World Bank, March 1997.

38. "Caught between Right and Left," *The Economist*, March 8, 2007.

39. For a discussion of first-mover advantages, see M. Liberman and D. Montgomery, "First-Mover Advantages," *Strategic Management Journal* 9 (Summer Special Issue, 1988), pp. 41–58.

40. S. H. Robock, "Political Risk: Identification and Assessment," *Columbia Journal of World Business*, July–August 1971, pp. 6–20.

Differences in Culture

4

LEARNING OBJECTIVES

After reading this chapter, you will be able to:

LO4-1   Explain what is meant by the culture of a society.

LO4-2   Identify the forces that lead to differences in social culture.

LO4-3   Identify the business and economic implications of differences in culture.

LO4-4   Recognize how differences in social culture influence values in business.

LO4-5   Demonstrate an appreciation for the economic and business implications of cultural change.

George Hammerstein/Corbis/Glow Images

Singapore: One of the World's Most Multicultural Places

OPENING CASE

Singapore (**www.gov.sg**) has a population of roughly 5.7 million people, with 100 percent of its citizens living in urban areas due to its city-state infrastructure. (Athens in Greece, and Rome in Italy, began as city-states, also.) A city-state is often defined as a sovereign state, basically a type of small independent country that usually consists of a single city and smaller peripheral dependent territories. Singapore and Vatican City (the Holy See) are considered the most well-known city-states in the world today. As for Vatican City, it is a city-state surrounded by Rome in Italy, and is of course the headquarters of the Roman Catholic Church, where the Pope resides.

Singapore is in Southeastern Asia, and is an island city between southern Malaysia and Indonesia. The climate is tropical with two distinct monsoon seasons: Northeastern monsoon (December to March) and Southwestern monsoon (June to September). Despite its small size, Singapore ranks 14th globally in exporting, 16th in importing, and has a positive trade balance that places the country 9th in the world on the export-to-import ratio. Among corporations and global travelers, Singapore is favored for many reasons, such as low corruption, global connectedness, ease of doing business, global competitiveness, innovation, opportunities, economic freedom, networked readiness, and reasonable taxes. Some of the negatives include environmental performance, freedom of the press, and political leadership.

One of the most fascinating characteristics of Singapore is its unique multicultural makeup. Not only is it a city-state, it is also very young compared to other places that have become equally multicultural and successful in the global marketplace. It was only about half a century ago that Singapore gained independence from Malaysia (on August 9, 1965). The tiny island nation is proud of the diverse cultures and religions that meld in relative harmony within its borders. While the majority of Singapore's residents are of Chinese origin, other prominent ethnic groups include Malays, Indians, and Eurasians. People from the United States and Canada are also represented, but in smaller numbers. To be culturally inclusive and in an effort to ensure that communication remains smooth among its citizens, Singapore boasts four official languages: English, Malay, Mandarin, and Tamil.

Singapore is a costly destination for tourists, and many of its residents pay hefty sums to live there. Nevertheless, Singapore's melting-pot culture makes the country unique and a bridge between various parts of the world. Companies and people engage with Singapore for these cultural and business reasons. So, how costly is Singapore for multinational corporations? The benefits must outweigh the costs, given the myriad companies in Singapore. Indeed, several cost-based indices exist to rank countries in the world, and these indices provide a picture of how costly, or inexpensive, Singapore is for people and businesses. For example, the Index of Economic Freedom (developed by The Heritage Foundation) focuses on assessing the fundamental right of every human to control his or her own labor and property. Singapore is ranked number 2 on the IEF, meaning the country is very accommodating.

Another index that shows Singapore's cost to companies is The Paying Taxes Indicator. This index, generated by PricewaterhouseCoopers (PwC) and The World Bank, investigates and compares tax regimes across economies worldwide. Again, Singapore scores high, ranking number 7 in the world. This means Singapore's government welcomes and facilitates multinational corporations doing business in the city-state. Because Singapore is small, many companies benefit from the robust infrastructure of its centralized government, as well as its pervasive accommodations for foreign businesses. In the end, businesses thrive in Singapore, even if tourists and citizens find the country costly. (Singapore is usually ranked as one of the most expensive cities to live in.)

For its part, the Singapore Board of Tourism stresses that "Singapore is where cultures, religions, and even passions meet!" The idea is that Singapore's strength in diversity is why people and companies should engage with their city-state. Billed as one of the most harmonious and plural nations on the planet, its ethnic communities are vibrant and diverse, its religions co-exist in harmony, its varied peoples celebrate as one, and as a result of it all, its citizens' passions come alive.

Sources: Marcelina Morfin, "The 10 Most Multicultural Cities in the World," April 16, 2018; Karen Gilchrist, "Singapore Named the World's Most Expensive City," CNBC, March 14, 2018; Amir Yusof, "Principles for Budget 2019 Reflect the Singapore way," Channel NewsAsia, February 28, 2019; "Singapore on globalEDGE," globaledge.msu.edu/countries/singapore, March 1, 2019.

Introduction

In Chapters 2 and 3, we saw how national differences in political, economic, and legal systems influence the benefits, costs, and risks associated with doing business in various countries of the world. In this chapter, we explore how differences in culture—both across and within countries—can have an effect on a company's international business strategies. This includes a focus on the development and implementation of international business strategies for all types of companies—from small to medium to large companies. Large multinational corporations often become the focus in textbooks, but culture affects every size and type of organization.

Several themes run through this chapter. The first is that business success in many, if not most, countries requires cross-cultural literacy. By **cross-cultural literacy** we mean understanding how cultural differences across and within countries can have an effect on the way business is practiced. It is sometimes easy to forget how different cultures across the globe really are even today.[1] Beneath the veneer of globalization, deep cultural differences often remain that can have a marked effect on a number of issues in a company's value chain. These differences are also what create a common bond—a value system—among people in a country, in essence a reason for the country to exist. Culturally based value systems can also reside in families, companies, and world regions. Sometimes even industries have distinct value systems.[2]

Numerous values and norms reside in these cultural systems. Some affect international business, some do not, and with some it is hard to tell if they affect international strategy and implementation. For example, Sweden has been found to be the country where people tend to be most patient among the 195 countries in the world (followed by the Netherlands and the United States). A team of researchers concluded, "Populations of European ancestry tend to be more patient than the world mean. Indeed, all of the 10 most patient countries in the world are either located in the neo-European, English-speaking world, or else in Western Europe, with the Scandinavian countries exhibiting particularly high levels of patience."[3] The country where people tend to be least patient is Nicaragua (followed by Rwanda and Georgia). Patience, risk aversion, reciprocity, altruism, and trust are all culture-related factors that make each country unique.

The opening case shows that Singapore is unique in its multicultural blend of people's backgrounds and characteristics. Contrary to cultural differences that often separate people and create friction, Singaporeans value their multicultural makeup and draw strength from it. Not only is Singapore a city-state, it is also very young compared to other places that have become equally multicultural and economically successful. Singapore gained independence from Malaysia in 1965, and since then the tiny island nation has proudly nurtured diverse cultures and religions that melt together in harmony. The majority of Singapore's residents are of Chinese origin. Other prominent groups include Malays, Indians, and Eurasians (Americans and Canadians are also represented, but in smaller numbers). To be culturally inclusive, Singapore boasts four official languages: English, Malay, Mandarin, and Tamil. Perhaps we can go as far as saying that, as one of the most multicultural places in the world, Singapore creates a unique cultural homogeneity out of its diverse existence.

Skipping ahead to the end of this chapter, the closing case on China, Hong Kong, Macau, and Taiwan highlights some of the traditional deep cultural differences that can exist. However, this occurs in a region that many believe consists of nations and areas with a very similar cultural background—i.e., Greater China. Instead, what we find is that throughout the colonial era, Hong Kong's citizens developed a distinct "Hong Kong identity" that seeks to be recognized as a unique culturally based "national identity." Meanwhile, the Taiwanese culture, a blend of Confucian Han Chinese and Taiwanese aboriginal cultures, is often at odds with mainland China. On the positive side, Macau has had a better experience with mainland China due to the economic difficulties that preceded the handover of Macau from Portugal to China in 1999. China came in as a helping hand economically at the right time, resulting in a much better partnership between China and Macau than between China and Hong Kong and Taiwan, respectively. Macau is also being positioned as a key diplomatic player in China's relations with Portuguese-speaking countries.

While some observers around the world may simply refer to the Greater China Region as "Chinese," the deeply ingrained cultural values of the region's separate entities are very different from each other as a practical matter. Consequently, cultural differences affect doing business in the region differently. This includes the various cost factors at play. As such, another theme we develop in this chapter is that a relationship exists between culture and the cost of doing business in a country or region. Different countries will be either more or less supportive of the market-based mode of production and sales to customers (i.e., where supply and demand set the prices for products and services).

For example, cultural factors were the triggers that lowered the costs of doing business in Japan and helped explain Japan's rapid ascent as an industrialized and competitive nation in the world about half a century ago.[4] Cultural factors can also trigger rising costs in doing business. Historically, class divisions were an important aspect of the British culture, and for a long time, firms operating in the United Kingdom found it difficult to achieve cooperation between management and labor. Class divisions led to a high level of industrial disputes in the UK during the same period that Japan was developing into a global force. This mismatch hurt the United Kingdom but opened up doors for Japan. It also raised the costs of doing business in Britain relative to the costs in countries such as Germany, Japan, Norway, Sweden, and Switzerland, where class conflict was historically less prevalent. Cultural foundations in many ways are also behind the last decade of nationalistic movements around the world (e.g., France, Germany, United Kingdom, United States), often resulting in higher tariffs and overall international trade costs across country borders.

The examples of Japan and the United Kingdom bring us to another theme we explore in this chapter: Culture is not static. Culture is rooted in the values and norms we have as people, and those are generally tied to doing something over a period of time. Think about it. If you do the same thing over and over, it becomes a habit, and then you almost take it for granted. But sometimes you break the habit and start something new or change how you do certain things. Culture is very much the same. Culture can and does evolve, although the rate at which cultures change is a subject of dispute. (From a personal vantage point, how easy or often do we change habits?) Generally, culture evolves as certain behaviors of people become ingrained and coded into people's values and norms. A cultural mindset develops that is consistent with people's behavior over time. Then, at some point again in the future, things may happen that cause people's behavior to once more change, and so culture continues to evolve.

You likely realize that your own personal cultural values and norms are hard to change. The same goes for the culture of a society, which evolves when large population segments in a country or region adopt values based on common ways of behaving. Societal changes are usually very slow moving. Importantly, multinational corporations operating across national cultures typically have unique values and norms as well. Consequently, many individuals have certain values and norms in their personal lives, possibly a (slightly) different set of vales and norms at work, and yet a different way of behaving in society. This is not to say that there are not overlaps, but many people also act differently in each context based on values and norms that pertain to a specific context.

What Is Culture?

LO4-1
Explain what is meant by the culture of a society.

People have a hard time agreeing on a simple definition of *culture*. This makes it difficult to be strategic about what type of culture can be created in small, medium, and large companies operating in some portion of the world's 195 countries. Because culture as a system of values and norms resides in multiple layers of society (people, families, companies, industries, countries, and world regions), we also have to take into account these important layers of culture and how they interact with each other.

If we go back to the 1870s, anthropologist Edward Tylor defined culture as "that complex whole which includes knowledge, belief, art, morals, law, custom, and other capabilities acquired by man as a member of society."[5] Since then, thousands of definitions have been argued over and defended by diverse experts from many cultures—in other words, culture actually affects how different people define *culture* itself!

Look around your college or university. Do you think the students can collectively define culture in a universally acceptable way that fits all geographic areas represented by the students or even among a smaller group of your friends? The answer is probably maybe, but after a few tries. However, we will make it easier by focusing on culture as it relates to international business (instead of everything related to culture).

To start, Florence Kluckhohn and Fred Strodtbeck's values orientation theory of culture states that all definitions of culture must answer a limited number of universal problems, that the value-based solutions are limited in number and universally known, and that different cultures have different preferences among them.[6] Following their work, other prominent specialists have supported the idea of a universal set of human values serving as the basis for culture; see Milton Rokeach's work on "the nature of human values" and Shalom Schwartz's work on the "theory of basic human values."[7] Rokeach and Schwartz are prominent culture experts who have had a significant influence on theorists, including Geert Hofstede.

Also supportive of a finite set of human values, Geert Hofstede, a Dutch expert on cross-cultural differences and international management, defined *culture* as "the collective programming of the mind which distinguishes the members of one human group from another."[8] Hofstede's work is by far the most used culture research in business over the last half a century, and this textbook relies on his scientific approach to understand how, when, and why culture has an impact on multinational corporations. At the basic level, culture includes systems of values, and values are among the building blocks of culture.[9] Another complementary definition of culture comes from sociologists Zvi Namenwirth and Robert Weber, who see culture as a system of ideas and argue that these ideas constitute a design for living.[10]

Discussion in this textbook subscribes to culture as conceptualized by Hofstede and influenced by the team of Namenwirth and Weber. As such, **culture** is a system of values and norms that are shared among a group of people and that when taken together constitute a design for living. **Values** are ideas about what a group believes to be good, right, and desirable. Put differently, values are shared assumptions about how things ought to be.[11] **Norms** are the social rules and guidelines that prescribe appropriate behavior in particular situations. **Society** refers to a group of people sharing a common set of values and norms. While a society may be equivalent to a country, some countries have several societies or subcultures, and some societies embrace more than one country. For example, the Scandinavian countries of Denmark, Finland, Iceland, Norway, and Sweden are often viewed as culturally being one society. The implication is that if one Scandinavian country's people like a product from a company, there is a very good chance customers from the other Scandinavian countries will as well.

Geert Hofstede, often viewed as the top expert on cross-cultural differences in international business, presents his work in Istanbul, Turkey, at the Academy of International Business conference.

Academy of International Business (AIB)

VALUES AND NORMS

Values form the bedrock of a culture. Values provide the context within which a society's norms are established and justified. They may include a society's attitudes toward such concepts as individual freedom, democracy, truth, justice, honesty, loyalty, social obligations, collective responsibility, women, love, sex, marriage, and so on. Values are not just abstract concepts; they are invested with considerable emotional significance. People argue, fight, and even die over values, such as freedom. Freedom and security are often the core reasons the political leadership in many developed nations (e.g., United States) uses when justifying their country engaging in various parts of the world. Values are also reflected in the economic systems of a society. For example, as we saw in Chapter 2, democratic free market capitalism is a reflection of a philosophical value system that emphasizes individual freedom.[12]

Norms are the social rules that govern people's actions toward one another. These norms can be subdivided into two major categories: folkways and mores. Both of these norm-related categories were coined in 1906 by William Graham Sumner, an American sociologist, and they are still applicable and embedded in our societies. **Folkways** are the routine conventions of everyday life. Generally, folkways are actions of little moral significance. Rather, they are social conventions that deal with things like appropriate dress code, good social manners, eating with the correct utensils, neighborly behavior, and so on. Although folkways define the way people are expected to behave, violations of them are not normally a serious matter. People who violate folkways may be thought of as eccentric or ill-mannered, but they are not usually considered to be evil or bad. In many countries, foreigners may initially be excused for violating folkways. However, traveling managers are increasingly expected to know about specific dress codes, social and professional manners, eating with the correct utensils, and business etiquette. The evolution of norms now demands that business partners at least try to behave according to the folkways in the country in which they are doing business.

A good example of a folkway is people's attitude toward time. People are very aware of what time it is, the passage of time, and the importance of time in the United States and northern European cultures such as Germany, Netherlands, and the Scandinavian countries (Denmark, Finland, Iceland, Norway, and Sweden). In these cultures, business people are very conscious about scheduling their time and are quickly irritated when time is wasted because a business associate is late for a meeting or if they are kept waiting for any reason. Time is really money in the minds of these business people.

The opposite of the time-conscious Americans, Germans, Dutch, and Scandinavians, business people in many Arabic, Latin, and African cultures view time as more elastic. Keeping to a schedule is viewed as less important than building a relationship or finishing an interaction with people. For example, an American businessperson might feel slighted if he or she is kept waiting for 30 minutes outside the office of a Latin American executive before a meeting. However, the Latin American person may simply be completing an interaction with another associate and view the information gathered from this as more important than sticking to a rigid schedule. The Latin American executive intends no disrespect, but due to a mutual misunderstanding about the importance of time, the American may see things differently. Similarly, Saudi Arabian attitudes toward time have been shaped by their nomadic Bedouin heritage, in which precise time played no real role and arriving somewhere "tomorrow" might mean next week. Like Latin Americans, many Saudis are unlikely to understand Westerners' obsession with precise times and schedules.

Folkways also include rituals and symbolic behavior. Rituals and symbols are the most visible manifestations of a culture and constitute the outward expression of deeper values. For example, upon meeting a foreign business executive, a Japanese executive will hold his business card in both hands and bow while presenting the card to the foreigner.[13] This ritual behavior is loaded with deep cultural symbolism. The card specifies the rank of the Japanese executive, which is a very important piece of information in a hierarchical society such as Japan. The bow is a sign of respect, and the deeper the angle of the bow, the greater the reverence one person shows for the other. The person receiving the card is expected to examine it carefully (Japanese often have business cards with Japanese printed on one side and English printed on the other), which is a way of returning respect and acknowledging the card giver's position in the hierarchy. The foreigner is also expected to bow when taking the card and to return the greeting by presenting the Japanese executive with his or her own card, similarly bowing in the process. To not do so and to fail to read the card that he or she has been given, instead casually placing it in a jacket, pocket, or purse, violates this important folkway and is considered rude.

Mores refer to norms that are more widely observed, have greater moral significance than folkways, and are central to the functioning of a society and to its social life. Violating mores can bring serious retribution, ill will, and the collapse of any business deal. Mores are often so important that they have been enacted into law. Mores, to use extreme examples, include laws against theft, adultery, incest, and cannibalism. All advanced societies have laws against theft and cannibalism, among other things, but in modern times not necessarily adultery. Many mores (and laws) differ across cultures. In the United States, for example, drinking alcohol is widely accepted, whereas in Saudi Arabia the consumption of alcohol is viewed as violating important social mores and is punishable by imprisonment (as some Western citizens working in Saudi Arabia have discovered to their dismay). That said, countries like Saudi Arabia and the United Arab Emirates are becoming more tolerant of Westerners behaving like Westerners in their countries—such as when their Western comrades drink alcohol, as long as they do not flaunt it. Over time, mores may be implemented differently depending on where you are and who you are, and it pays to know the difference.

CULTURE, SOCIETY, AND THE NATION-STATE

We have defined a society as a group of people who share a common set of values and norms; that is, people who are bound together by a common culture. There is not a strict one-to-one correspondence between a society and a nation-state. Nation-states are political creations. While nation-states are often studied for their "national identity," "national character," and even "competitive advantage of nations," in reality they may contain a single culture or several subcultures.[14] The French nation can be thought of as the political embodiment of French culture. However, the nation of Canada has a French culture too, and at least three core cultures—an Anglo culture, a French-speaking "Quebecois" culture, and a Native American culture. Similarly, many of the 54 African nations have important cultural differences among tribal groups, as horrifically exhibited in the early 1990s when Rwanda dissolved into a bloody civil war between two tribes, the Tutsis and Hutus. Africa is not alone in this regard. India, for example, is composed of many distinct cultural groups with their own rich history and traditions (e.g., Andhras, Gonds, Gujaratis, Marathas, Oriya, Rajputs, Tamils).

Cultures can also embrace several nations, as with the Scandinavian countries of Denmark, Finland, Iceland, Norway, and Sweden. These Scandinavian nations trace their cultural values and norms back centuries, and this cultural mindset still resides in most Scandinavians. Next time you meet some Scandinavians, see if you can pick out which country they are from! There is also a strong case for considering Islamic society a culture that is shared by citizens of many different nations in the Middle East, Asia, and Africa. Of course, there are nuances to the Islamic world—those who adhere to various degrees, or different elements, of Islam. As you will recall from Chapter 3, this view of expansive cultures that embrace several nations underpins Samuel Huntington's view of a world that is fragmented into different civilizations, including Western, Islamic, and Sinic (Chinese) cultures.[15] In fact, many international business scholars make the culture argument as a way of saying that companies should not target countries in a multinational strategic approach today, but instead focus on dividing up the world's 195 countries into like-minded business regions.

To complicate things further, as we mentioned earlier, it is also possible to talk about culture at different levels within a country. It is reasonable to talk about "American society" and "American culture," but there are several societies within America, each with its own culture. For example, in the United States, one can talk about African American culture, Cajun culture, Chinese American culture, Hispanic culture, Indian culture, Irish American culture, Southern culture, and many more cultural groups. In some way, this means that the relationship between culture and country is often ambiguous. Even if a country can be characterized as having a single homogeneous culture, often that national culture is a mosaic of subcultures (e.g., Singapore). To honor these cultural nuances,

FIGURE 4.1

Determinants of culture.

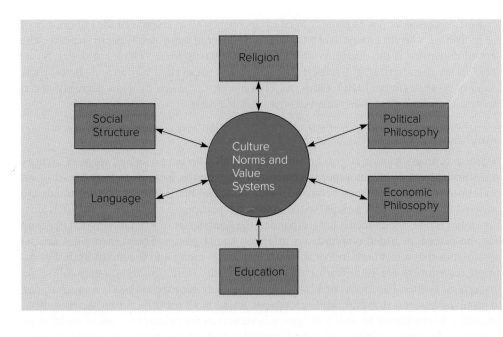

business people need to be aware of the delicate issues that pertain to folkways, and they also need to make sure not to violate mores in the country or culture in which they intend to do business. Increased globalization has meant an increased number of business relationships across countries and cultures, but not necessarily an increased cultural understanding to go with it. Culture is a complex phenomenon with multiple dimensions and multiple levels always worthy of study.[16]

DETERMINANTS OF CULTURE

The values and norms of a culture do not emerge fully formed. As we have explained, values and norms evolve over time in response to a number of factors, including prevailing political and economic philosophies, the social structure of a society, and the dominant religion, language, and education (see Figure 4.1). Ultimately, a culture forms when people's behaviors—as a result of these various influences—become ingrained in people's daily activities, patterns, and ways of doing things.

We discussed political and economic philosophies in Chapter 2. Such philosophies clearly influence the value systems of a society. For example, the values found in communist North Korea toward freedom, justice, and individual achievement are clearly different from the opposite values found in Sweden, precisely because each society operates according to different political and economic philosophies. In the next sections of this chapter, we discuss the influence of social structure, religion, language, and education. The chain of causation runs both ways. While factors such as social structure and religion clearly influence the values and norms of a society, the values and norms of a society can influence social structure and religion. That means that people's behaviors can lead to culture evolving, and the existing culture also affects how people behave.

Social Structure

A society's **social structure** refers to its basic social organization. It indicates how a society is organized in terms of the values, norms, and relationships that are part of its fabric. How society operates and how people, groups, and companies treat each other both emerge from, and are determinants of, the behaviors of individuals in that specific society.

Two dimensions are particularly important when explaining differences across social structures (although many dimensions exist beyond these two). The first is the degree to which the basic unit of a social organization is the individual, as opposed to the group, or even company

LO4-2

Identify the forces that lead to differences in social culture.

TEST PREP

Use SmartBook to help retain what you have learned. Access your Instructor's Connect course to check out SmartBook or go to **learnsmartadvantage.com** for help.

for which a person works. In general, Western societies tend to emphasize the importance of the individual, whereas groups tend to figure much larger in many non-Western societies. The second dimension is the degree to which a society is stratified into classes or castes. Some societies are characterized by a relatively high degree of social stratification and relatively low mobility between strata (India). Other societies are characterized by a low degree of social stratification and high mobility between strata (United States).

INDIVIDUALS AND GROUPS

A **group** is an association of two or more individuals who have a shared sense of identity and who interact with each other in structured ways on the basis of a common set of expectations about each other's behavior.[17] Human social life is group life. Individuals are involved in families, work groups, social groups, recreational groups, and potentially myriad other groups. Social media have expanded the boundaries of what is included in group life and placed an added emphasis on extended social groups. Social media has unique possibilities that affect both individuals within a social group and the group itself. For example, consumers are significantly more likely to buy from the brands they follow on Instagram, Twitter, Facebook, or LinkedIn, or that they get exposed to via Snapchat, due to group influences. However, while groups are found in all societies, some societies differ according to the degree to which the group is viewed as the primary means of social organization.[18] In some societies, individual attributes and achievements are viewed as being more important than group membership; in others, the reverse is true.

LO4-3

Identify the business and economic implications of differences in culture.

The Individual

In Chapter 2, we discussed individualism as a political philosophy. However, individualism is more than just an abstract political philosophy. In many societies, the individual is the basic building block of social organization. This is reflected not just in the political and economic organization of society but also in the way people perceive themselves and relate to each other in social and business settings. The value systems of many Western societies, for example, emphasize individual achievement. The social standing of individuals is not so much a function of whom they work for as of their individual performance in whatever work setting they choose. More and more, individuals are regarded as "independent contractors" even though they belong to and work for a company. These individuals build their personal brands by utilizing the knowledge, skills, and experience they have, which often translates to increased salaries and promotions or another company seeking their employment, if they believe the company can benefit from that person's capabilities. In science, the label "star scientist" has become synonymous with these individual high-producers of innovative products based on their knowledge, skills, and experience.[19]

The emphasis on individual performance has both potential beneficial and harmful aspects. In the United States, the emphasis on individual performance finds expression in an admiration of rugged individualism, entrepreneurship, and innovation. One benefit of this is the high level of entrepreneurial activity in the United States, in Europe, and throughout many of the so-called developed nations. Over time, entrepreneurial individuals in the United States have created lots of new products and new ways of doing business (personal computers, photocopiers, computer software, biotechnology, supermarkets, discount retail stores, social media). One can argue that the dynamism of the U.S. economy owes much to the philosophy of individualism. Highly individualistic societies are often synonymous with those capable of constantly innovating by having a flowing stream of creative ideas for new products and services.

Individualism also finds expression in a high degree of managerial mobility between companies, as our "personal brand" example illustrated earlier, and this is not always a good thing. Although moving from company to company may be good for individual managers who are trying to build impressive résumés and increase their salaries, it is not necessarily a good thing for companies. The lack of loyalty and commitment to a company and the tendency to move on for a better offer can result in managers who have good general skills but lack the knowledge, experience, and network of contacts that come from years of working for the same company. An effective manager draws on company-specific experience, knowledge, and a network of contacts to find solutions to current problems, and companies may suffer if their managers lack these attributes. One positive aspect of high managerial mobility, however, is that executives are exposed to different ways of doing business. The ability to compare business practices helps executives identify how good practices and techniques developed in one firm might be profitably applied to other firms.

The Group

In contrast to the Western emphasis on the individual, the group is the primary unit of social organization in many other societies. For example, in Japan, the social status of an individual has traditionally been determined as much by the standing of the group to which he or she belongs as by his or her individual performance.[20] In traditional Japanese society, the group was the family or village to which an individual belonged. Today, the group has frequently come to be associated with the work team or business organization. In a now-classic study of Japanese society, Nakane noted how this expresses itself in everyday life:

> When a Japanese faces the outside (confronts another person) and affixes some position to himself socially he is inclined to give precedence to institution over kind of occupation. Rather than saying, "I am a typesetter" or "I am a filing clerk," he is likely to say, "I am from B Publishing Group" or "I belong to S company."[21]

Nakane goes on to observe that the primacy of the group often evolves into a deeply emotional attachment in which identification with the group becomes very important in a person's life. For example, as a student, you will often identify yourself as going to a specific university or, soon enough, as a graduate of that university—and the latter identification as an alumnus is something you will carry with you for life. In many cases, we also extend that group thinking beyond a company, organization, or university. For example, we talk about being part of a university-related conference—for example, "I'm going to Michigan State University, and we are part of the Big Ten Conference." Or, "I'm going to the University of Washington, and we are part of the Pac-12 Conference."

At the country level, one central value of Japanese culture is the importance attached to group membership. This may have beneficial implications for business firms. Strong identification with the group is argued to create pressures for mutual self-help and collective action. If the worth of an individual is closely linked to the achievements of the group, as Nakane maintains is the case in Japan, this creates a strong incentive for individual members of the group to work together for the common good. Some argue that the success of Japanese companies in the global economy has been based partly on their ability to achieve close cooperation between individuals within a company and between companies. This has found expression in the widespread diffusion of self-managing work teams within Japanese organizations; the close cooperation among different functions within Japanese companies (e.g., among manufacturing, marketing, and R&D); and the cooperation between a company and its suppliers on issues such as design, quality control, and inventory reduction.[22] In all these cases, cooperation is driven by the need to improve the performance of the group.

The primacy of the value of group identification also discourages managers and other workers from moving from one company to another. Lifetime employment in a particular company was long the norm in certain sectors of the Japanese economy (estimates suggest that between 20 and 40 percent of all Japanese employees have formal or informal lifetime employment guarantees), albeit those norms have changed significantly in recent decades, with much more movement being seen between companies. Over the years, managers and workers build up knowledge, experience, and a network of interpersonal business contacts. All these things can help managers perform their jobs more effectively and achieve cooperation with others.

However, the primacy of the group is not always beneficial. Just as U.S. society is characterized by a great deal of entrepreneurship, reflecting the primacy of values associated with individualism, some argue that Japanese society is characterized by a corresponding lack of entrepreneurship. Although the long-run consequences are unclear, one implication is that the United States could continue to create more new industries than Japan and continue to be more successful at pioneering radically new products and new ways of doing business. By most estimates, the United States has led the world in innovation for some time, especially radically new products and services, and the country's individualism is a strong contributor to this innovative mindset. At the same time, some group-oriented countries, such as Japan, do very well in innovation also, especially non-radical "normal" innovations, according to the GE Global Innovation Barometer.[23] This is an indication that multiple paths to being innovative exist in both individualistic and group-oriented cultures, drawing from the uniqueness of the particular culture and what core competencies are reflected in the culture.[24] Some argue that individualistic societies are great at creating innovative ideas while collectivist, or group-oriented, societies are better at the implementation of those ideas (taking the idea to the market).

LO4-2

Identify the forces that lead to differences in social culture.

SOCIAL STRATIFICATION

All societies are stratified on a hierarchical basis into social categories—that is, into **social strata.** These strata are typically defined on the basis of socioeconomic characteristics such as family background, occupation, and income. Individuals are born into a particular stratum. They become a member of the social category to which their parents belong. Individuals born into a stratum toward the top of the social hierarchy tend to have better life chances than those born into a stratum toward the bottom of the hierarchy. They are likely to have better education, health, standard of living, and work opportunities. Although all societies are stratified to some degree, they differ in two related ways. First, they differ from each other with regard to the degree of mobility between social strata. Second, they differ with regard to the significance attached to social strata in business contexts. Overall, social stratification is based on four basic principles:[25]

1. Social stratification is a trait of society, not a reflection of individual differences.
2. Social stratification carries over a generation to the next generation.
3. Social stratification is generally universal but variable.
4. Social stratification involves not just inequality but also beliefs.

Social Mobility

The term **social mobility** refers to the extent to which individuals can move out of the strata into which they are born. Social mobility varies significantly from society to society. The most rigid system of stratification is a caste system. A **caste system** is a closed system of stratification in which social position is determined by the family into which a person is born, and change in that position is usually not possible during an individual's lifetime. Often, a caste position carries with it a specific occupation. Members of one caste might be shoemakers, members of another might be butchers, and so on. These occupations are embedded in the caste and passed down through the family to succeeding generations. Although the number of societies with caste systems diminished rapidly during the twentieth century, one partial example still remains. India has four main castes and several thousand subcastes. Even though the caste system was officially abolished in 1949, two years after India became independent, it is still a force in rural Indian society where occupation and marital opportunities are still partly related to caste (for more details, see the accompanying Country Focus on the caste system in India today, "Determining Your Social Class by Birth").[26]

A **class system** is a less rigid form of social stratification in which social mobility is possible. It is a form of open stratification in which the position a person has by birth can be changed through his or her own achievements or luck. Individuals born into a class at

Determining Your Social Class by Birth

Modern India is a country of dramatic contrasts. The country's information technology (IT) sector is among the most vibrant in the world, with companies such as Tata Consultancy Services, Cognizant Technology Solutions, Infosys, and Wipro as powerful global players. Cognizant is an interesting company in that it was founded as a technology arm of Dun & Bradstreet (USA), but it is typically considered an Indian IT company because a majority of its employees are based in India. In fact, many IT companies locate or operate in India because of its strong IT knowledge, human capital, and culture.

Traditionally, India has had one of the strongest caste systems in the world. Somewhat sadly, as a British author, this caste system still exists today even though it was officially abolished in 1949, and many Indians actually prefer it this way! At the core, the caste system has no legality in India, and discrimination against lower castes is illegal. India has also enacted numerous new laws and social initiatives to protect and improve living conditions of lower castes in the country.

Prior to 1949, India's caste system was definitely an impediment to social mobility, and some say it remains difficult to move across castes. But the stranglehold on people's socioeconomic conditions is becoming a fading memory among the educated, urban middle-class Indians who make up the majority of employees in the high-tech economy. Unfortunately, the same is not true in rural India, where some 64 percent of the nation's population still resides. In the rural part of the country, the caste remains a pervasive influence.

For example, a young female engineer at Infosys, who grew up in a small rural village and is a *dalit* (sometimes called a "scheduled caste"), recounts how she never entered the house of a *Brahmin*, India's elite priestly caste, even though half of her village were *Brahmins*. And when a *dalit* was hired to cook at the school in her native village, *Brahmins* withdrew their children from the school. The

engineer herself is the beneficiary of a charitable training scheme developed by Infosys. Her caste, making up about 16 percent of the country (or around 212 million people), is among the poorest in India, with some 91 percent making less than $100 a month.

To try to correct this historical inequality, politicians have talked for years about extending the employment quota system to private enterprises. The government has told private companies to hire more *dalits* and members of tribal communities and have been warned that "strong measures" will be taken if companies do not comply. Private employers are resisting attempts to impose quotas, arguing with some justification that people who are guaranteed a job by a quota system are unlikely to work very hard.

At the same time, progressive employers realize they need to do something to correct the inequalities, and unless India taps into the lower castes, it may not be able to find the employees required to staff rapidly growing high-technology enterprises. As a consequence, the Confederation of Indian Industry implemented a package of *dalit*-friendly measures, including scholarships for bright lower-caste children. Building on this, Infosys is leading the way among high-tech enterprises. The company provides special training to low-caste engineering graduates who have failed to get a job in industry after graduation. While the training does not promise employment, so far almost all graduates who completed the seven-month training program have been hired by Infosys and other enterprises. Positively, Infosys programs are a privatized version of the education offered in India to try to break down India's caste system.

Sources: Mari Marcel Thekaekara, "India's Caste System Is Alive and Kicking—and Maiming and Killing," *The Guardian*, August 15, 2016; Noah Feldman, "India's High Court Favors Nationalism over Democracy," *Bloomberg View*, January 8, 2017; "Why Some of India's Castes Demand to Be Reclassified," *The Economist*, February 16, 2016.

the bottom of the hierarchy can work their way up; conversely, individuals born into a class at the top of the hierarchy can slip down.

While many societies have class systems, social mobility within a class system also varies from society to society. For example, some sociologists have argued that the United Kingdom has a more rigid class structure than certain other Western societies, such as the United States.[27] Historically, British society was divided into three main classes: the upper class, which was made up of individuals whose families for generations had wealth, prestige, and

occasionally power; the middle class, whose members were involved in professional, managerial, and clerical occupations; and the working class, whose members earned their living from
manual occupations. The middle class was further subdivided into the upper-middle class,
whose members were involved in important managerial occupations and the prestigious professions (lawyers, accountants, doctors), and the lower-middle class, whose members were involved in clerical work (bank tellers) and the less prestigious professions (school teachers).

The British class system exhibited significant divergence between the life chances of members of different classes. The upper and upper-middle classes typically sent their children to
a select group of private schools, where they would not mix with lower-class children and
where they picked up many of the speech accents and social norms that marked them as being from the higher strata of society. These same private schools also had close ties with the
most prestigious universities, such as Oxford and Cambridge. Until fairly recently, Oxford
and Cambridge guaranteed a certain number of places for the graduates of these private
schools. Having been to a prestigious university, the offspring of the upper and upper-middle
classes then had an excellent chance of being offered a prestigious job in companies, banks,
brokerage firms, and law firms run by members of the upper and upper-middle classes.

Modern British society is now rapidly leaving behind this class structure and moving toward more of a classless society. However, sociologists continue to dispute this finding. For
example, one study reported that state schools in the London Borough (suburb) of Islington,
which now has a population of 230,000, had only 79 candidates for university, while one prestigious private school alone, Eton, sent more than that number to Oxford and Cambridge.[28]
This, according to the study's authors, implies that "money still begets money." They argue
that a good school means a good university, a good university means a good job, and merit
has only a limited chance of elbowing its way into this tight circle. In another survey, a sociologist noted that class differentials in educational achievement have changed surprisingly little
over the last few decades in many societies, despite assumptions to the contrary.[29]

Another society for which class divisions have historically been of some importance has
been China, where there has been a long-standing difference between the life chances of
the rural peasantry and urban dwellers. Ironically, this historic division was strengthened
during the high point of communist rule because of a rigid system of household registration that restricted most Chinese to the place of their birth for their lifetime. Bound to
collective farming, peasants were cut off from many urban privileges—compulsory education, quality schools, health care, public housing, even varieties of food, to name only a
few—and they largely lived in poverty. Social mobility was very limited. This system crum-
bled following the reforms of a few decades ago, and as a consequence, migrant peasant
laborers have flooded into China's cities looking for work. Sociologists now hypothesize
that a new class system is emerging in China based less on the rural–urban divide and
more on urban occupation.[30]

The class system in the United States is less pronounced than in India, the United Kingdom, and China and mobility is greater. Like the UK, the United States has its own upper,
middle, and working classes. However, class membership is determined to a much greater
degree by individual economic achievements, as opposed to background and schooling.
Thus, an individual can, by his or her own economic achievement, move smoothly from
the working class to the upper class in a lifetime. Successful individuals from humble origins are highly respected in American society. Part of the admiration comes from entrepreneurs in the United States who have done exceedingly well creating and marketing their
products, services, and ideas (e.g., Andrew Carnegie, Henry Ford, Oprah Winfrey, Bill
Gates, and Larry Page).

LO4-3

Identify the business and
economic implications of
differences in culture.

Significance

From a business perspective, the stratification of a society is significant if it affects the
operations of companies. In American society, the high degree of social mobility and the
extreme emphasis on individualism limit the impact of class background on business
operations. The same is true in Japan, where most of the population perceives itself to be
middle class. In a country such as the United Kingdom or India, however, the relative lack

of class mobility and the differences between classes have resulted in the emergence of class consciousness. **Class consciousness** refers to a condition by which people tend to perceive themselves in terms of their class background, and this shapes their relationships with members of other classes.

This has been played out in British society in the traditional hostility between upper-middle-class managers and their working-class employees. Mutual antagonism and lack of respect historically made it difficult to achieve cooperation between management and labor in many British companies and resulted in a relatively high level of industrial disputes. However, the past two decades have seen a dramatic reduction in industrial disputes, which bolsters the arguments of those who claim that the country is moving toward a classless society. Interestingly, some argue that the United Kingdom leaving the European Union ("Brexit") has become a class-related negotiation and outcome that may take the Brits decades to solve effectively. Also, as noted earlier, class consciousness may be reemerging in urban China, and may ultimately prove significant in the country.

Overall, an antagonistic relationship between management and labor classes, and the resulting lack of cooperation and high level of industrial disruption, tends to raise the costs of production in countries characterized by significant class divisions. This can make it more difficult for companies based in such countries to establish a competitive advantage in the global economy. China has seen a slowdown in its economy, Britain is engulfed in Brexit repercussions, the United States faces nationalistic tendencies, and India still practices a caste system that limits mobility. These are not historical artifacts; they are here and now and companies need to strategically plan accordingly.

Religious and Ethical Systems

Religion may be defined as a system of shared beliefs and rituals that are concerned with the realm of the sacred.[31] An **ethical system** refers to a set of moral principles, or values, that are used to guide and shape behavior.[32] Most of the world's ethical systems are the product of religions. Thus, we can talk about Christian ethics and Islamic ethics. However, there is a major exception to the principle that ethical systems are grounded in religion. Confucianism and Confucian ethics influence behavior and shape culture in parts of Asia, yet it is incorrect to characterize Confucianism as a religion.

The relationship among religion, ethics, and society is subtle and complex. Of the thousands of religions in the world today, four dominate in terms of numbers of adherents: Christianity with roughly 2.20 billion adherents, Islam with around 1.60 billion adherents, Hinduism with 1.10 billion adherents (primarily in India), and Buddhism with about 535 million adherents (see Map 4.1). Although many other religions have an important influence in certain parts of the modern world (e.g., Shintoism in Japan, with roughly 40 million followers, and Judaism, which has 18 million adherents and accounts for 75 percent of the population of Israel), their numbers pale in comparison with these dominant religions. We review these four religions, along with Confucianism, focusing on their potential business implications.

Some scholars have theorized that the most important business implications of religion center on the extent to which different religions shape attitudes toward work and entrepreneurship and the degree to which religious ethics affect the costs of doing business. However, it is hazardous to make sweeping generalizations about the nature of the relationship among religion, ethical systems, and business practice. Nations with Catholic, Protestant, Muslim, Hindu, and Buddhist majorities all show evidence of entrepreneurial activity and economic growth in various ways.

Interestingly, research by economists Robert Barro and Rachel McCleary suggest that strong religious beliefs, particularly beliefs in heaven, hell, and an afterlife, have a positive impact on economic growth rates, irrespective of the particular religion in question.[33] Barro and McCleary looked at religious beliefs and economic growth rates in 59 countries.

TEST PREP

Use SmartBook to help retain what you have learned. Access your Instructor's Connect course to check out SmartBook or go to **learnsmartadvantage.com** for help.

LO4-2

Identify the forces that lead to differences in social culture.

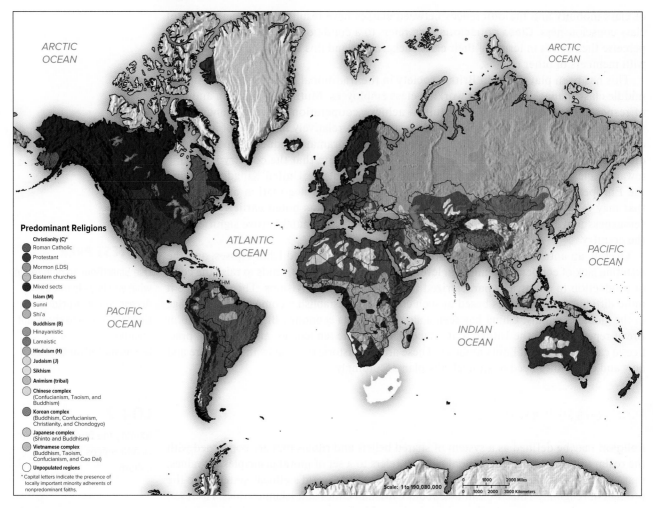

MAP 4.1

World religions.

Source: "Map 14," in Allen, John L., and Sutton, Christopher J., *Student Atlas of World Politics,* 10th ed. New York, NY: McGraw-Hill Companies, Inc., 2013.

Their conclusion was that higher religious beliefs stimulate economic growth because they help sustain aspects of individual behavior that lead to higher productivity. At the same time, other professionals suggest such economic growth is a function of sound economic policy and not necessarily religions or religious ethics.

CHRISTIANITY

Christianity is the most widely practiced religion in the world, with some 2.20 billion followers. The vast majority of Christians live in Europe and the Americas, although their numbers are growing rapidly in Africa. Christianity grew out of Judaism. Like Judaism, it is a monotheistic religion (monotheism is the belief in one God). A religious division in the eleventh century led to the establishment of two major Christian organizations: the Roman Catholic Church and the Orthodox Church. Today, the Roman Catholic Church accounts for more than half of all Christians, most of whom are found in southern Europe and Latin America. The Orthodox Church, while less influential, is still of major importance in several countries (especially Greece and Russia). In the sixteenth century, the Reformation led to a further split with Rome; the result was Protestantism. The nonconformist nature of Protestantism has facilitated the emergence of numerous denominations under the Protestant umbrella (Baptist, Methodist, Calvinist, and so on).

Economic Implications of Christianity

LO4-3

Identify the business and economic implications of differences in culture.

Several sociologists have argued that, of the main branches of Christianity—Catholic, Orthodox, and Protestant—the latter has the most important economic implications. In 1904, prominent German sociologist Max Weber made a connection between Protestant ethics and "the spirit of capitalism" that has since become legendary.[34] Weber noted that capitalism emerged in Western Europe, where

> business leaders and owners of capital, as well as the higher grades of skilled labor, and even more the higher technically and commercially trained personnel of modern enterprises, are overwhelmingly Protestant.[35]

Weber theorized that there was a relationship between Protestantism and the emergence of capitalism. He argued that Protestant ethics emphasizes the importance of hard work and wealth creation (for the glory of God) and frugality (abstinence from worldly pleasures). According to Weber, this kind of value system was needed to facilitate the development of capitalism. Protestants worked hard and systematically to accumulate wealth. Their ascetic beliefs suggested that rather than consuming the wealth by indulging in worldly pleasures, they should invest it in the expansion of capitalist enterprises. Thus, the combination of hard work and the accumulation of capital, which could be used to finance investment and expansion, paved the way for the development of capitalism in Western Europe and subsequently in the United States. In contrast, Weber argued that the Catholic promise of salvation in the next world, rather than this world, did not foster the same kind of work ethic.

Protestantism also may have encouraged capitalism's development in another way. By breaking away from the hierarchical domination of religious and social life that characterized the Catholic Church for much of its history, Protestantism gave individuals more freedom to develop their own relationship with God. The right to freedom of form of worship was central to the nonconformist nature of early Protestantism. This emphasis on individual religious freedom may have paved the way for the subsequent emphasis on individual economic and political freedoms and the development of individualism as an economic and political philosophy. As we saw in Chapter 2, such a philosophy forms the bedrock on which entrepreneurial free market capitalism is based. Building on this, some scholars claim there is a connection between individualism, as inspired by Protestantism, and the extent of entrepreneurial activity in a nation.[36] Again, we must be careful not to generalize too much from this historical sociological view. While nations with a strong Protestant tradition such as Britain, Germany, and the United States were early leaders in the Industrial Revolution, nations with Catholic or Orthodox majorities show significant and sustained entrepreneurial activity and economic growth in the modern world.

ISLAM

LO4-2

Identify the forces that lead to differences in social culture.

With about 1.60 billion adherents, Islam is the second largest of the world's major religions. Islam dates to 610 A.D. when the Prophet Muhammad began spreading the word, although the Muslim calendar begins in 622 A.D. when, to escape growing opposition, Muhammad left Mecca for the oasis settlement of Yathrib, later known as Medina. Adherents of Islam are referred to as Muslims. Muslims constitute a majority in more than 40 countries and inhabit a nearly contiguous stretch of land from the northwest coast of Africa, through the Middle East, to China and Malaysia in the Far East.

Islam has roots in both Judaism and Christianity (Islam views Jesus Christ as one of God's prophets). Like Christianity and Judaism, Islam is a monotheistic religion. The central principle of Islam is that there is but the one true omnipotent God (Allah). Islam requires unconditional acceptance of the uniqueness, power, and authority of God and the understanding that the objective of life is to fulfill the dictates of His will in the hope of admission to paradise. According to Islam, worldly gain and temporal power are an illusion. Those who pursue riches on earth may gain them, but those who forgo worldly ambitions to seek the favor of Allah may gain the greater treasure: entry into paradise. Other major principles of Islam include (1) honoring and respecting parents, (2) respecting the rights of others, (3) being generous but not a squanderer, (4) avoiding killing except for justifiable causes, (5) not committing adultery, (6) dealing justly and equitably with others, (7) being of pure heart and mind, (8) safeguarding the possessions of orphans, and (9) being humble and unpretentious.[37] Parallels exist with central principles of Judaism and Christianity.

Islam is an all-embracing way of life governing the totality of a Muslim's being.[38] As God's surrogate in this world, a Muslim is not a totally free agent, but is circumscribed by religious principles—by a code of conduct for interpersonal relations—in social and economic activities. Religion is paramount in all areas of life. A Muslim lives in a social structure that is shaped by Islamic values and norms of moral conduct. The ritual of everyday life in a Muslim country is striking to a Western visitor. Among other things, orthodox Muslim ritual requires prayer five times a day (business meetings may be put on hold while the Muslim participants engage in their daily prayer ritual), demands that women should be dressed in a certain manner, and forbids the consumption of pork and alcohol.

Islamic Fundamentalism

The past three decades, in particular, have witnessed the growth of a social movement often referred to as Islamic fundamentalism.[39] In the West, Islamic fundamentalism is associated with militants, terrorists, and violent upheavals, such as the bloody conflict in Algeria, the killing of foreign tourists in Egypt, and the September 11, 2001, attacks on the World Trade Center and Pentagon in the United States. For most, this characterization is misleading. Just as Christian fundamentalists are motivated by deeply held religious values that are firmly rooted in their faith, so are Islamic fundamentalists.

A small minority of radical "fundamentalists" who have hijacked the religion to further their own political and violent ends perpetrate the violence that the Western media associates with Islamic fundamentalism. Radical Islamic fundamentalists exist in various forms today, but the most notorious is probably ISIS—an acronym for Islamic State of Iraq and Syria. Now, the violence associated with radical Islamic fundamentalists can be seen across other religions as well. Some Christian "fundamentalists" have incited their own political engagement and violence. The vast majority of Muslims point out that Islam teaches peace, justice, and tolerance, not violence and intolerance. In fact, the foundation is that Islam explicitly repudiates the violence that a radical minority practices.

The rise of Islamic fundamentalism has no one cause. In part, it is a response to the social pressures created in traditional Islamic societies by the move toward modernization and by the influence of Western ideas, such as liberal democracy; materialism; equal rights for women; and attitudes toward sex, marriage, and alcohol. In many Muslim countries, modernization has been accompanied by a growing gap between a rich urban minority and an impoverished urban and rural majority. For the impoverished majority, modernization has offered little in the way of tangible economic progress, while threatening the traditional value system. Thus, for a Muslim who cherishes his or her traditions and feels that their identity is jeopardized by the encroachment of Western values, Islamic fundamentalism is a cultural anchor.

Fundamentalists demand a commitment to strict religious beliefs and rituals. The result has been a marked increase in the use of symbolic gestures that confirm Islamic values. In areas where fundamentalism is strong, women have resumed wearing floor-length, long-sleeved dresses and covering their hair; religious studies have increased in universities; the publication of religious tracts has increased; and public religious orations have risen.[40] Also, the sentiments of some fundamentalist groups are often anti-Western. Rightly or wrongly, Western influence is blamed for a range of social ills, and many fundamentalists' actions are directed against Western governments, cultural symbols, businesses, and individuals.

In several Muslim countries, fundamentalists have gained political power and have used this to try to make Islamic law the law of the land (as set down in the Koran, the bible of Islam). There are grounds for this in Islamic doctrine. Islam makes no distinction between church and state. It is not just a religion; Islam is also the source of law, a guide to statecraft, and an arbiter of social behavior. Muslims believe that every human endeavor is within the purview of their faith—and this includes political activity—because the only purpose of any activity is to do God's will.[41] Muslim fundamentalists have been most successful in Iran, where a fundamentalist party has held power since 1979, but they also have had an influence in many other countries, such as Afghanistan, Algeria, Egypt, Pakistan, Saudi Arabia, and Sudan.

Economic Implications of Islam

LO4-3

Identify the business and economic implications of differences in culture.

The Koran establishes some explicit economic principles, many of which are pro-free enterprise.[42] The Koran speaks approvingly of free enterprise and earning profit through trade and commerce (the Prophet Muhammad himself was once a trader). The protection of the right to private property is also embedded within Islam, although Islam asserts that all property is a favor from Allah (God), who created and so owns everything. Those who hold property are regarded as trustees rather than owners. As trustees, they are entitled to receive profits from the property but are admonished to use it in a righteous, socially beneficial, and prudent manner. This reflects Islam's concern with social justice. Islam is critical of those who earn profit through the exploitation of others. In the Islamic view, humans are part of a collective in which the wealthy have obligations to help the disadvantaged. In Muslim countries, it is fine to earn a profit, so long as that profit is justly earned and not based on the exploitation of others. It also helps if those making profits undertake charitable acts to help the poor. Furthermore, Islam stresses the importance of living up to contractual obligations, keeping one's word, and abstaining from deception. For a closer look at how Islam, capitalism, and globalization can coexist, see the accompanying Country Focus on the region around Kayseri in central Turkey.

Given the Islamic proclivity to favor market-based systems, Muslim countries are likely to be receptive to international businesses as long as those businesses behave in a manner that is consistent with Islamic ethics, customs, and business practices. But, in Islamic countries where fundamentalism is on the rise, general hostility toward Western-owned businesses is also likely to increase. When foreigners are involved in predominantly Muslim countries, one unique economic principle of Islam can come into play. Islam prohibits the payment or receipt of interest, which is considered illegal. This is not just a matter of theology; in several Islamic states, it is also a matter of law. The Koran clearly condemns interest, which is called *riba* in Arabic, as exploitative and unjust. For many years, banks operating in Islamic countries conveniently ignored this condemnation, but starting in the 1970s with the establishment of an Islamic bank in Egypt, Islamic banks opened in predominantly Muslim countries. Now there are hundreds of Islamic banks in more than 50 countries with assets of around $1.6 trillion; plus more than $1 trillion is managed by mutual funds that adhere to Islamic principles.[43] Even conventional banks are entering the market: both Citigroup and HSBC, two of the world's largest financial institutions, now offer Islamic financial services. While only Iran and Sudan enforce Islamic banking conventions, in an increasing number of countries customers can choose between conventional banks and Islamic banks.

Conventional banks make a profit on the spread between the interest rate they have to pay to depositors and the higher interest rate they charge borrowers. Because Islamic banks cannot pay or charge interest, they must find a different way of making money. Islamic banks have experimented with two different banking methods—the *mudarabah* and the *murabaha*.[44]

Turkey, Its Religion, and Politics

For years now, Turkey has been lobbying the European Union to allow it to join the free trade bloc as a member state. Even as grumblings take place in some EU countries about leaving (e.g., Brexit), Turkey is all in to join if it can. If the EU says yes, it will be the first Muslim state in the European Union. But this is unlikely to happen any time soon; after all, it has been half a century in the making!

Many critics in the EU worry that Islam and Western-style capitalism do not mix well and that, as a consequence, allowing Turkey into the EU would be a mistake. However, a close look at what is going on in Turkey suggests this view may be misplaced. Consider the area around the city of Kayseri in central Turkey. Many dismiss this poor, largely agricultural region of Turkey as a non-European backwater, far removed from the secular bustle of Istanbul. It is a region where traditional Islamic values hold sway. And yet it is a region that has produced so many thriving Muslim enterprises that it is sometimes called the "Anatolian Tiger." Businesses based here include large food manufacturers, textile companies, furniture manufacturers, and engineering enterprises, many of which export a substantial percentage of their production.

Local business leaders attribute the success of companies in the region to an entrepreneurial spirit that they say is part of Islam. They point out that the Prophet Muhammad, who was himself a trader, preached merchant honor and commanded that 90 percent of a Muslim's life be devoted to work in order to put food on the table. Outside observers have gone further, arguing that what is occurring around Kayseri is an example of Islamic Calvinism, a fusion of traditional Islamic values and the work ethic often associated with Protestantism in general and Calvinism in particular.

However, not everyone agrees that Islam is the driving force behind the region's success. Saffet Arslan, the managing director of Ipek, the largest furniture producer in the region (which exports to more than 30 countries), says another force is at work: globalization! According to Arslan, over the past three decades, local Muslims who once eschewed making money in favor of focusing on religion are now making business a priority. They see the Western world, and Western capitalism, as a model, not Islam, and because of globalization and the opportunities associated with it, they want to become successful.

If there is a weakness in the Islamic model of business that is emerging in places such as Kayseri, some say it can be found in traditional attitudes toward the role of women in the workplace and the low level of female employment in the region. According to a report by the European Stability Initiative, the same group that holds up the Kayseri region as an example of Islamic Calvinism, the low participation of women in the local workforce is the Achilles' heel of the economy and may stymie the attempts of the region to catch up with the countries of the European Union.

Sources: Marc Champion, "Turkey's President Is Close to Getting What He's Always Wanted," *Bloomberg BusinessWeek*, February 8, 2017; "Dress in a Muslim Country: Turkey Covers Up," *The Economist*, January 26, 2017; "Turkey's Future Forward to the Past: Can Turkey's Past Glories Be Revived by Its Grandiose Islamist President?" *The Economist*, January 3, 2015.

Glow Images

A *mudarabah* contract is similar to a profit-sharing scheme. Under *mudarabah*, when an Islamic bank lends money to a business, rather than charging interest, it takes a share in the profits that are derived from the investment. Similarly, when a business (or individual) deposits money at an Islamic bank, the deposit is treated as an equity in whatever activity the bank uses the capital for to invest. Thus, the depositor receives a share in the profit from the bank's investment (as opposed to interest payments) according to an agreed-upon ratio. Some Muslims claim this is a more efficient system than the Western banking system because it encourages both long-term savings and long-term investment. However, there is no hard evidence of this, and many believe that a *mudarabah* system is less efficient than a conventional Western banking system.

The second Islamic banking method, the *murabaha* contract, is the most widely used among the world's Islamic banks, primarily because it is the easiest to implement. In a *murabaha* contract, when a firm wishes to purchase something using a loan—let's say a piece of equipment that costs $1,000—the firm tells the bank after having negotiated the price with the equipment manufacturer. The bank then buys the equipment for $1,000, and the borrower buys it back from the bank at some later date for, say, $1,100, a price that includes a $100 markup for the bank. A cynic might point out that such a markup is functionally equivalent to an interest payment, and it is the similarity between this method and conventional banking that makes it so much easier to adopt.

HINDUISM

Hinduism has approximately 1.10 billion adherents, most of them on the Indian subcontinent. Hinduism began in the Indus Valley in India more than 4,000 years ago, making it the world's oldest major religion. Unlike Christianity and Islam, its founding is not linked to a particular person. Nor does it have an officially sanctioned sacred book such as the Bible or the Koran. Hindus believe that a moral force in society requires the acceptance of certain responsibilities, called *dharma*. Hindus believe in reincarnation, or rebirth into a different body, after death. Hindus also believe in *karma*, the spiritual progression of each person's soul. A person's karma is affected by the way he or she lives. The moral state of an individual's karma determines the challenges he or she will face in the next life. By perfecting the soul in each new life, Hindus believe that an individual can eventually achieve *nirvana*, a state of complete spiritual perfection that renders reincarnation no longer necessary. Many Hindus believe that the way to achieve nirvana is to lead a severe ascetic lifestyle of material and physical self-denial, devoting life to a spiritual rather than material quest.

LO4-2

Identify the forces that lead to differences in social culture.

Economic Implications of Hinduism

Max Weber, famous for expounding on the Protestant work ethic, also argued that the ascetic principles embedded in Hinduism do not encourage the kind of entrepreneurial activity in pursuit of wealth creation that we find in Protestantism.[45] According to Weber, traditional Hindu values emphasize that individuals should be judged not by their material achievements but by their spiritual achievements. Hindus perceive the pursuit of material well-being as making the attainment of nirvana more difficult. Given the emphasis on an ascetic lifestyle, Weber thought that devout Hindus would be less likely to engage in entrepreneurial activity than devout Protestants.

LO4-3

Identify the business and economic implications of differences in culture.

Mahatma Gandhi, the famous Indian nationalist and spiritual leader, was certainly the embodiment of Hindu asceticism. It has been argued that the values of Hindu asceticism and self-reliance that Gandhi advocated had a negative impact on the economic development of post-independence India.[46] But we must be careful not to read too much into Weber's rather old arguments. Modern India is a very dynamic entrepreneurial society, and millions of hardworking entrepreneurs form the economic backbone of the country's rapidly growing economy, especially in the information technology sector.[47]

Historically, Hinduism also supported India's caste system. The concept of mobility between castes within an individual's lifetime makes no sense to traditional Hindus. Hindus see mobility between castes as something that is achieved through spiritual progression and reincarnation. An individual can be reborn into a higher caste in his or her next life if he or she achieves spiritual development in this life. Although the caste system has been abolished in India, as discussed earlier in the chapter, it still casts a long shadow over Indian life.

LO4-2

Identify the forces that lead to differences in social culture.

BUDDHISM

Buddhism, with some 535 million adherents, was founded in the sixth century B.C. by Siddhartha Gautama in what is now Nepal. Siddhartha renounced his wealth to pursue an ascetic lifestyle and spiritual perfection. His adherents claimed he achieved nirvana but decided to remain on earth to teach his followers how they, too, could achieve this state of spiritual enlightenment. Siddhartha became known as the Buddha (which means "the awakened one"). Today, most Buddhists are found in Central and Southeast Asia, China, Korea, and Japan. According to Buddhism, suffering originates in people's desires for pleasure. Cessation of suffering can be achieved by following a path for transformation. Siddhartha offered the Noble Eightfold Path as a route for transformation. This emphasizes right seeing, thinking, speech, action, living, effort, mindfulness, and meditation. Unlike Hinduism, Buddhism does not support the caste system. Nor does Buddhism advocate the kind of extreme ascetic behavior that is encouraged by Hinduism. Nevertheless, like Hindus, Buddhists stress the afterlife and spiritual achievement rather than involvement in this world.

LO4-3

Identify the business and economic implications of differences in culture.

Economic Implications of Buddhism

The emphasis on wealth creation that is embedded in Protestantism is historically not found in Buddhism. Thus, in Buddhist societies, we do not see the same kind of cultural stress on entrepreneurial behavior that Weber claimed could be found in the Protestant West. But unlike Hinduism, the lack of support for the caste system and extreme ascetic behavior suggests that a Buddhist society may represent a more fertile ground for entrepreneurial activity than a Hindu culture. In effect, innovative ideas and entrepreneurial activities may take hold throughout society independent of which caste a person may belong to, but again, each culture is uniquely oriented toward its own types of entrepreneurial behavior.

In Buddhism, societies were historically more deeply rooted to their local place in the natural world.[48] This means that economies were more localized, with relations between people and also between culture and nature being relatively unmediated. In the modern economy, complex technologies and large-scale social institutions have led to a separation between people and also between people and the natural world. Plus, as the economy grows, it is difficult to understand and appreciate the potential effects people have on the natural world. Both of these separations are antithetical to the Buddha's teachings.

Interestingly, recent trends actually bring in the "Zen" orientation from Buddhism into business in the Western world.[49] Now there are some 700 trademarks containing the word *Zen* in the United States alone, according to the U.S. Patent and Trademark Office. "In business, 'Zen' is often a synonym for ordinary nothingness," blogged Nancy Friedman, a corporate copywriter who consults with businesses on naming and branding. She said that "*Zen* can be combined with *mail* to describe 'an incoming e-mail message with no message or attachments.' *Zen spin* is a verb meaning 'to tell a story without saying anything at all.' And *to zen* a computing problem means to figure it out in an intuitive flash—perhaps while you're plugged into the earphones of your ZEN system available from Creative."[50]

CONFUCIANISM

Confucianism was founded in the fifth century B.C. by K'ung-Fu-tzu, more generally known as Confucius. For more than 2,000 years until the 1949 communist revolution, Confucianism was the official ethical system of China. While observance of Confucian ethics has been weakened in China since 1949, many people still follow the teachings of Confucius, principally in China, Korea, and Japan. Confucianism teaches the importance of attaining personal salvation through right action. Although not a religion, Confucian ideology has become deeply embedded in the culture of these countries over centuries and has an impact on the lives of many millions more.[51] Confucianism is built around a comprehensive ethical code that sets down guidelines for relationships with others. High moral and ethical conduct and loyalty to others are central to Confucianism. Unlike religions, Confucianism is not concerned with the supernatural and has little to say about the concept of a supreme being or an afterlife.

LO4-2

Identify the forces that lead to differences in social culture.

Economic Implications of Confucianism

Some scholars maintain that Confucianism may have economic implications as profound as those Weber argued were found in Protestantism, although they are of a different nature.[52] Their basic thesis is that the influence of Confucian ethics on the culture of China, Japan, South Korea, and Taiwan, by lowering the costs of doing business in those countries, may help explain their economic success. In this regard, three values central to the Confucian system of ethics are of particular interest: loyalty, reciprocal obligations, and honesty in dealings with others.

LO4-3

Identify the business and economic implications of differences in culture.

In Confucian thought, loyalty to one's superiors is regarded as a sacred duty—an absolute obligation. In organizations based in Confucian cultures, the loyalty that binds employees to the heads of their organization can reduce the conflict between management and labor that we find in more class-conscious societies. Cooperation between management and labor can be achieved at a lower cost in a culture where the virtue of loyalty is emphasized in the value systems. However, in a Confucian culture, loyalty to one's superiors, such as a worker's loyalty to management, is not blind loyalty.

The concept of reciprocal obligations is also important. Confucian ethics stresses that superiors are obliged to reward the loyalty of their subordinates by bestowing blessings on them. If these "blessings" are not forthcoming, then neither will be the loyalty. This Confucian ethic is central to the Chinese concept of *guanxi*, which refers to relationship networks supported by reciprocal obligations.[53] *Guanxi* means relationships, although in business settings it can be better understood as connections. Today, Chinese will often cultivate a *guanxiwang*, or "relationship network," for help. Reciprocal obligations are the glue that holds such networks together. If those obligations are not met—if favors done are not paid back or reciprocated—the reputation of the transgressor is tarnished, and the person will be less able to draw on his or her *guanxiwang* for help in the future. Thus, the implicit threat of social sanctions is often sufficient to ensure that favors are repaid, obligations are met, and relationships are honored. In a society that lacks a rule-based legal tradition, and thus legal ways of redressing wrongs such as violations of business agreements, *guanxi* is an important mechanism for building long-term relationships and getting business done in China. For an example of the importance of *guanxi,* read the accompanying Management Focus on China.

A third concept found in Confucian ethics is the importance attached to honesty. Confucian thinkers emphasize that although dishonest behavior may yield short-term benefits

China and Its *Guanxi*

A few years ago, DMG emerged as one of China's fastest-growing advertising agencies with a client list that includes Unilever, Sony, Nabisco, Audi, Volkswagen, China Mobile, and dozens of other Chinese brands. Dan Mintz, the company's founder, said that the success of DMG was connected strongly to what the Chinese call *guanxi*.

Guanxi means relationships or business connections. The concept has its roots in the Confucian philosophy of valuing social hierarchy and reciprocal obligations. Confucian ideology has a 2,000-year-old history in China. Confucianism stresses the importance of relationships, both within the family and between a master and the servant. Confucian ideology also teaches that people are not created equal. In Confucian thought, loyalty and obligations to one's superiors (or to family) are regarded as a sacred duty, but at the same time, this loyalty has its price. Social superiors are obligated to reward the loyalty of their social inferiors by bestowing "blessings" upon them; thus, the obligations are reciprocal. Chinese will often cultivate a *guanxiwang*, or "relationship network," for help. There is a tacit acknowledgment that if you have the right *guanxi*, legal rules can be broken, or at least bent.

Mintz, who is fluent in Mandarin, cultivated his *guanxiwang* by going into business with two young Chinese who had connections, Bing Wu and Peter Xiao. Wu, who works on the production side of the business, was a former national gymnastics champion, which translates into prestige and access to business and government officials. Xiao comes from a military family with major political connections. Together, these three have been able to open doors that long-established Western advertising agencies could not. They have done it in large part by leveraging the contacts of Wu and Xiao and by backing up their connections with what the Chinese call *Shi li*, the ability to do good work.

A case in point was DMG's campaign for Volkswagen, which helped the German company become ubiquitous in China. The ads used traditional Chinese characters, which had been banned by Chairman Mao during the cultural revolution in favor of simplified versions. To get permission to use the characters in film and print ads—a first in modern China—the trio had to draw on high-level government contacts in Beijing. They won over officials by arguing that the old characters should be thought of not as "characters" but as art. Later, they shot TV spots for the ad on Shanghai's famous Bund, a congested boulevard that runs along the waterfront of the old city. Drawing again on government contacts, they were able to shut down the Bund to make the shoot. DMG has also filmed inside Beijing's Forbidden City, even though it is against the law to do so. Using his contacts, Mintz persuaded the government to lift the law for 24 hours. As Mintz has noted, "We don't stop when we come across regulations. There are restrictions everywhere you go. You have to know how get around them and get things done."[*]

Today, DMG Entertainment has expanded into being a Chinese-based production and distribution company. While it began as an advertising agency, the company started distributing non-Chinese movies in the Chinese market in the late 2000s (e.g., *Iron Man 3,* the sixth-highest-grossing film of all time in China) as well as producing Chinese films, the first being *Founding of a Republic,* a movie that marked the 60th anniversary of the People's Republic of China. In these activities, DMG is also enjoying *guanxi* in the country. *Variety* reported that DMG benefited from "strong connections" with Chinese government officials and the state-run China Film Group Corporation.

*Graser, Marc, "Featured Player," *Variety*, October 18, 2004.

Sources: Rob Cain, "Chinese Studio DMG Emerges as Bidder for Major Stake in Paramount Pictures," *Media and Entertainment*, March 15, 2016; Ali Jaafar, "China's DMG Inks Deal with Hasbro to Launch First 'Transformers' Live Action Attraction," *Deadline Hollywood*, January 16, 2016; A. Busch, "China's DMG and Valiant Entertainment Partner to Expand Superhero Universe," *Deadline Hollywood*, March 12, 2015; C. Coonan, "DMG's Dan Mintz: Hollywood's Man in China," *Variety*, June 5, 2013; and Simon Montlake, "Hollywood's Mr China: Dan Mintz, DMG," *Forbes*, August 29, 2012.

for the transgressor, dishonesty does not pay in the long run. The importance attached to honesty has major economic implications. When companies can trust each other not to break contractual obligations, the costs of doing business are lowered. Expensive lawyers are not needed to resolve contract disputes. In a Confucian society, people may be less hesitant to commit substantial resources to cooperative ventures than in a society where honesty is less pervasive. When companies adhere to Confucian ethics, they can trust each other not to violate the terms of cooperative agreements. Thus, the costs of achieving cooperation between companies may be lower in societies such as Japan relative to societies where trust is less pervasive.

For example, it has been argued that the close ties between the automobile companies and their component parts suppliers in Japan are facilitated by a combination of trust and reciprocal obligations. These close ties allow the auto companies and their suppliers to work together on a range of issues, including inventory reduction, quality control, and design. The competitive advantage of Japanese auto companies such as Toyota may in part be explained by such factors.[54] Similarly, the combination of trust and reciprocal obligations is central to the workings and persistence of *guanxi* networks in China.

Language

One obvious way in which many countries differ is the language used by the population. By language, we mean both the spoken and the unspoken means of communication. Language is also one of the defining characteristics of a culture. Oftentimes, learning a language entails learning the culture and vice versa. Some would even argue that a person cannot get entrenched in a culture without knowing its dominant language.

SPOKEN LANGUAGE

Language does far more than just enable people to communicate with each other. The nature of a language also structures the way we perceive the world. The language of a society can direct the attention of its members to certain features of the world rather than others. The classic illustration of this phenomenon is that whereas the English language has but one word for snow, the language of the Inuit (Eskimos) lacks a general term for it. Instead, distinguishing different forms of snow is so important in the lives of the Inuit that they have 24 words that describe different types of snow (e.g., powder snow, falling snow, wet snow, drifting snow).[55]

Because language shapes the way people perceive the world, it also helps define culture. Countries with more than one language often have more than one culture. Canada has an English-speaking culture and a French-speaking culture. Tensions between the two can run quite high, with a substantial proportion of the French-speaking minority demanding independence from a Canada "dominated by English speakers." The same phenomenon can be observed in many other countries. Belgium is divided into Flemish and French speakers, and tensions between the two groups exist. In Spain, a Basque-speaking minority with its own distinctive culture has been agitating for independence from the Spanish-speaking majority for decades. On the Mediterranean island of Cyprus, the culturally diverse Greek- and Turkish-speaking populations of the island continually engage in some level of conflict. The island is now partitioned into two parts as a consequence. While it does not necessarily follow that language differences create differences in culture and, therefore, separatist pressures (witness the harmony in Switzerland, where four languages are spoken), there certainly seems to be a tendency in this direction.[56]

Mandarin (Chinese) is the mother tongue of the largest number of people, followed by English and Hindi, which is spoken mainly in India. However, the most widely spoken language in the world is English, followed by French, Spanish, and Mandarin (many people speak English as a second language). English is increasingly becoming the language of international business, as it has been in much of the developed world for years. When Japanese and German businesspeople get together to do business, it is almost certain they will communicate in English. However, though English is widely used, learning the local language yields considerable advantages. Most people prefer to converse in their own language, and being able to speak the local language can build rapport and goodwill.

International businesses that do not understand the local language often make blunders through improper translation, take longer to negotiate business deals, or may lose a potential deal altogether.

For example, some time ago, the Sunbeam Corporation used the English words for its "Mist-Stick" mist-producing hair-curling iron when it entered the German market, only to discover after an expensive advertising campaign that *mist* means excrement in German. General Motors was troubled by the lack of enthusiasm among Puerto Rican dealers for its Chevrolet Nova. When literally translated into Spanish, *nova* means star. However, when spoken it sounds like "no va," which in Spanish means "it doesn't go." General Motors changed the name of the car to Caribe.[57] Ford made a similar and somewhat embarrassing mistake in Brazil. The Ford Pinto may well have been a good car, but the Brazilians wanted no part of a car called "pinto," which is slang for tiny male genitals in Brazil. Even the world's largest furniture manufacturer, IKEA from Sweden, ran into branding issues when it named a plant pot "Jättebra" (which means great or superbly good in Swedish). Unfortunately, *Jättebra* resembles the Thai slang word for sex. Pepsi's slogan "come alive with the Pepsi Generation" did not quite work in China. People in China took it to mean "bring your ancestors back from the grave."

LO4-2

Identify the forces that lead to differences in social culture.

UNSPOKEN LANGUAGE

Unspoken language refers to nonverbal communication. We all communicate with each other by a host of nonverbal cues. The raising of eyebrows, for example, is a sign of recognition in most cultures, while a smile is a sign of joy. Many nonverbal cues, however, are culturally bound. A failure to understand the nonverbal cues of another culture can lead to a communication failure. For example, making a circle with the thumb and the forefinger is a friendly gesture in the United States, but it is a vulgar sexual invitation in Greece and Turkey. Similarly, while most Americans and Europeans use the thumbs-up gesture to indicate that "it's all right," in Greece the gesture is obscene.

Another aspect of nonverbal communication is personal space, which is the comfortable amount of distance between you and someone you are talking with. In the United States, the customary distance apart in a business discussion is five to eight feet. In Latin America, it is three to five feet. Consequently, many North Americans unconsciously feel that Latin Americans are invading their personal space and can be seen backing away from them during a conversation. Indeed, the American may feel that the Latin is being aggressive and pushy. In turn, the Latin American may interpret such backing away as aloofness. The result can be a regrettable lack of rapport between two businesspeople from different cultures.

 TEST PREP

Use SmartBook to help retain what you have learned. Access your Instructor's Connect course to check out SmartBook or go to **learnsmartadvantage.com** for help.

LO4-2

Identify the forces that lead to differences in social culture.

Education

Formal education plays a key role in a society, and it is usually the medium through which individuals learn many of the languages, knowledge, and skills that are indispensable in a modern society. Formal education supplements the family's role in socializing the young into the values and norms of a society. Values and norms are taught both directly and indirectly. Schools generally teach basic facts about the social and political nature of a society. They also focus on the fundamental obligations of citizenship. In addition, cultural norms are taught indirectly at school. Respect for others, obedience to authority, honesty, neatness, being on time, and so on are all part of the "hidden curriculum" of schools. The use of a grading system teaches children the value of personal achievement and competition.[58]

From an international business perspective, one important aspect of education is its role as a determinant of national competitive advantage.[59] The availability of a pool of skilled and knowledgeable workers is a major determinant of the likely economic success of a country. In analyzing the competitive success of Japan, for example, Harvard Business

School Professor Michael Porter notes that after the last World War, Japan had almost nothing except for a pool of skilled and educated human resources:

> With a long tradition of respect for education that borders on reverence, Japan possessed a large pool of literate, educated, and increasingly skilled human resources. . . . Japan has benefited from a large pool of trained engineers. Japanese universities graduate many more engineers per capita than in the United States. . . . A first-rate primary and secondary education system in Japan operates based on high standards and emphasizes math and science. Primary and secondary education is highly competitive. . . . Japanese education provides most students all over Japan with a sound education for later education and training. A Japanese high school graduate knows as much about math as most American college graduates.[60]

Porter's point is that Japan's excellent education system is an important factor explaining the country's postwar economic success. Not only is a good education system a determinant of national competitive advantage, but it is also an important factor guiding the location choices of international businesses. The trend to outsource information technology jobs to India, for example, is partly due to the presence of significant numbers of trained engineers in India, which in turn is a result of the Indian education system. By the same token, it would make little sense to base production facilities that require highly skilled labor in a country where the education system was so poor that a skilled labor pool was not available, no matter how attractive the country might seem regarding other dimensions, such as cost.

The general education level of a country is also a good index of the kind of products that might sell in a country, and of the type of promotional materials that should be used. As an example, a country where more than 50 percent of the population is illiterate is unlikely to be a good market for popular books. But perhaps more importantly, promotional materials containing written descriptions of mass-marketed products are unlikely to have an effect in a country where half of the population cannot read. It is far better to use pictorial promotions in such circumstances.

Culture and Business

Of considerable importance for a multinational corporation, or any company—small, medium, or large—with operations in different countries, is how a society's culture affects the values found in the workplace. Management processes and practices may need to vary according to culturally determined work-related values. For example, if the cultures of Brazil and the United Kingdom or the United States and Sweden result in different work-related values, a company with operations in the different countries should vary its management processes and practices to account for these differences.

The most famous study of how culture relates to values in the workplace was undertaken by Geert Hofstede.[61] As part of his job as a psychologist working for IBM, Hofstede collected data on employee attitudes and values for more than 116,000 individuals. Respondents were matched on occupation, age, and gender. The data enabled him to compare dimensions of culture across 50 countries. Hofstede initially isolated four dimensions that he claimed summarized the different cultures[62]—power distance, uncertainty avoidance, individualism versus collectivism, and masculinity versus femininity—and then, later on, he added a fifth dimension inspired by Confucianism that he called long-term versus short-term orientation.[63]

The fifth dimension was added as a function of the data obtained via the Chinese Value Survey (CVS), an instrument developed by Michael Harris Bond based on discussions with Hofstede.[64] Bond used input from "Eastern minds," as Hofstede called it, to develop the Chinese Value Survey. Bond also references Chinese scholars as helping him create the values that exemplify this new long-term versus short-term orientation. In his original research, Bond called the fifth dimension "Confucian work dynamism," but Hofstede said that in practical terms, the dimension refers to a long-term versus short-term orientation.

TEST PREP

Use SmartBook to help retain what you have learned. Access your Instructor's Connect course to check out SmartBook or go to **learnsmartadvantage.com** for help.

LO4-4

Recognize how differences in social culture influence values in business.

Hofstede's **power distance** dimension focused on how a society deals with the fact that people are unequal in physical and intellectual capabilities. According to Hofstede, high power distance cultures were found in countries that let inequalities grow over time into inequalities of power and wealth. Low power distance cultures were found in societies that tried to play down such inequalities as much as possible.

The **individualism versus collectivism** dimension focused on the relationship between the individual and his or her fellows. In individualistic societies, the ties between individuals were loose, and individual achievement and freedom were highly valued. In societies where collectivism was emphasized, the ties between individuals were tight. In such societies, people were born into collectives, such as extended families, and everyone was supposed to look after the interest of his or her collective.

Hofstede's **uncertainty avoidance** dimension measured the extent to which different cultures socialized their members into accepting ambiguous situations and tolerating uncertainty. Members of high uncertainty avoidance cultures placed a premium on job security, career patterns, retirement benefits, and so on. They also had a strong need for rules and regulations; the manager was expected to issue clear instructions, and subordinates' initiatives were tightly controlled. Lower uncertainty cultures are characterized by both a readiness to take risks and less emotional resistance to change.

Hofstede's **masculinity versus femininity** dimension looked at the relationship between gender and work roles. In masculine cultures, gender roles were differentiated, and traditional "masculine values," such as achievement and effective exercise of power, determined cultural ideals. In feminine cultures, gender roles were less distinguished, and little differentiation was made between men and women in the same job.

The **long-term versus short-term orientation** dimension refers to the extent to which a culture programs its citizens to accept delayed gratification of their material, social, and emotional needs. It captures attitudes toward time, persistence, ordering by status, protection of face, respect for tradition, and reciprocation of gifts and favors. The label refers to these "values" being derived from Confucian teachings.

Hofstede created an index score for each of these five dimensions that ranged from 0 to 100 (with 100 being a high score).[65] By using IBM, Hofstede was able to hold company influences as a constant across cultures. Thus, any differences across the country cultures would by design be due to differences in the countries' cultures and not the company's culture. He averaged the scores for all employees from a given country to create the index score for each dimension.

A strong movement is under way to add a sixth dimension to Hofstede's work. Geert Hofstede, working with Michael Minkov's analysis of the World Values Survey, added a promising new dimension called indulgence versus restraint (IND) in 2010.[66] On January 17, 2011, Hofstede delivered a webinar for SIETAR Europe called "New Software of the Mind" to introduce the third edition of *Cultures and Organizations*, in which the results of Minkov's analysis were included to support this sixth dimension. In addition, in a keynote delivered at the annual meeting of the Academy of International Business (http://aib.msu.edu) in Istanbul, Turkey, on July 6, 2013, Hofstede again presented results and theoretical rationale to support the indulgence versus restraint dimension. *Indulgence* refers to a society that allows relatively free gratification of basic and natural human drives related to enjoying life and having fun. *Restraint* refers to a society that suppresses gratification of needs and regulates it by means of strict social norms. Despite years in the making, strong support exists for the original four dimensions of Hofstede's work, and many agree on the fifth dimension as well, but a number of scholars remain skeptical about the latest sixth addition.

Table 4.1 summarizes data for 15 selected countries for the five established dimensions of individualism versus collectivism, power distance, uncertainty avoidance, masculinity versus femininity, and long-term versus short-term orientation (the Hofstede data were collected for 50 countries and the Bond data were collected for 23 countries; numerous other researchers have also added to the country samples). Western nations such as the United States, Canada, and United Kingdom score high on the individualism scale and low on the power distance scale. Latin American and Asian countries emphasize collectivism over individualism and score high on the power distance scale. Table 4.1 also reveals that

	Power Distance	Uncertainty Avoidance	Individualism	Masculinity	Long-Term Orientation
Australia	36	51	90	61	31
Brazil	69	76	38	49	65
Canada	39	48	80	52	23
Germany (F.R.)	35	65	67	66	31
United Kingdom	35	35	89	66	25
India	77	40	48	56	61
Japan	54	92	46	95	80
Netherlands	38	53	80	14	44
New Zealand	22	49	79	58	30
Pakistan	55	70	14	50	00
Philippines	94	44	32	64	19
Singapore	74	8	20	48	48
Sweden	31	29	71	5	33
Thailand	64	64	20	34	56
United States	40	46	91	62	29

TABLE 4.1

Work-Related Values for 15 Selected Countries

Source: Hofstede Insights; www.hofstede-insights.com/product/compare-countries, Accessed March 7, 2019.

Japan's culture has strong uncertainty avoidance and high masculinity. This characterization fits the standard stereotype of Japan as a country that is male dominant and where uncertainty avoidance exhibits itself in the institution of lifetime employment. Sweden and Denmark stand out as countries that have both low uncertainty avoidance and low masculinity (high emphasis on "feminine" values).

Hofstede's results are interesting for what they tell us in a very general way about differences among cultures. Many of Hofstede's findings are consistent with standard stereotypes about cultural differences. For example, many people believe Americans are more individualistic and egalitarian than the Japanese (they have a lower power distance), who in turn are more individualistic and egalitarian than Mexicans. Similarly, many might agree that Latin countries place a higher emphasis on masculine value—they are machismo cultures—than the Scandinavian countries of Denmark and Sweden. As might be expected, East Asian countries such as Japan and Thailand scored high on long-term orientation, while nations such as the United States and Canada scored low.

However, we should be careful about reading too much into Hofstede's research. It has been criticized on a number of points.[67] First, Hofstede assumes there is a one-to-one correspondence between culture and the nation-state, but as we discussed earlier, many countries have more than one culture. Second, Hofstede's research may have been culturally bound. The research team was composed of Europeans and Americans. The questions they asked of IBM employees—and their analysis of the answers—may have been shaped by their own cultural biases and concerns. The later addition of the long-term versus short-term dimension illustrates this point. Third, Hofstede's informants worked not only within a single industry, the computer industry, but also within one company, IBM. At the time, IBM was renowned for its own strong corporate culture and employee selection procedures, making it possible that the employees' values were different in important respects from the values of the cultures from which those employees came, as we also pointed out earlier.

Still, Hofstede's work is the leading research the world has seen on culture. It represents a great starting point for managers trying to figure out how cultures differ and what that might mean for management practices. Also, several other scholars have found strong evidence that differences in culture affect values and practices in the workplace, and Hofstede's basic results have been replicated using more diverse samples of individuals in different settings.[68] Nevertheless, managers should use the results with caution. One reason for caution is the plethora of new cultural values surveys and data points that are starting to become important additions to Hofstede's work. Two additional cultural values frameworks that have been examined and have been related to work and business issues are the Global Leadership and Organizational Behavior Effectiveness instrument and the World Values Survey.

The *Global Leadership and Organizational Behavior Effectiveness (GLOBE)* instrument is designed to address the notion that a leader's effectiveness is contextual.[69] It is embedded in the societal and organizational values and norms of the people being led. The initial GLOBE findings from 62 societies involving 17,300 middle managers from 951 organizations build on findings by Hofstede and other culture researchers. The GLOBE research established nine cultural dimensions: power distance, uncertainty avoidance, humane orientation, institutional collectivism, in-group collectivism, assertiveness, gender egalitarianism, future orientation, and performance orientation.

The *World Values Survey (WVS)* is a research project spanning more than 100 countries that explores people's values and norms, how they change over time, and what impact they have in society and on business.[70] The WVS includes dimensions for support for democracy; tolerance of foreigners and ethnic minorities; support for gender equality; the role of religion and changing levels of religiosity; the impact of globalization; attitudes toward the environment, work, family, politics, national identity, culture, diversity, and insecurity; and subjective well-being.

As a reminder, culture is just one of many factors that might influence the economic success of a nation. While culture's importance should not be ignored, neither should it be overstated. The Hofstede framework is the most significant and studied framework of culture as it relates to work values and business that we have ever seen. But some of the newer culture frameworks (e.g., GLOBE, WVS) are also becoming popular in the literature, and they have potential to complement and perhaps even supplant Hofstede's work with additional validation and connection to work-related values, business, and marketplace issues. At the same time, the factors discussed in Chapters 2 and 3—economic, political, and legal systems—are probably more important than culture in explaining differential economic growth rates over time.

✓ **TEST PREP**

Use SmartBook to help retain what you have learned. Access your Instructor's Connect course to check out SmartBook or go to **learnsmartadvantage.com** for help.

LO4-5

Demonstrate an appreciation for the economic and business implications of cultural change.

Cultural Change

An important point we want to make in this chapter on culture is that culture is not a constant; it evolves over time.[71] Changes in value systems can be slow and painful for a society. Change, however, does occur and can often be quite profound. At the beginning of the 1960s, the idea that women might hold senior management positions in major corporations was not widely accepted. Today, of course, it is a natural and welcomed reality, and most people in the United States could not fathom it any other way. For example, in 2012 Virginia Rometty became the CEO of IBM; Mary Barra became the CEO of General Motors in 2014; and Corie Barry became the CEO of Best Buy in 2019—all companies with more than $40 billion in annual sales (GM $147B, IBM $80B, and Best Buy $40B). GM's Mary Barra has been named to the *Time 100*, and *Forbes* named her one of the World's 100 Most Powerful Women. As another example, 24 of the CEO positions at S&P 500 companies were held by women in 2019; obviously still a large discrepancy compared with the opportunities for men, but an improvement from decades earlier, and one that is likely to continue to improve. In mainstream American society, no one any longer questions the development or capability of women in the business world, and it is amazing to think the country once did.

For another illustration of cultural change, consider Japan. Some business professionals argue that a cultural shift has been occurring in Japan, with a move toward greater individualism.[72] The Japanese office worker, or "salary person," is characterized as being loyal to his or her boss and the organization to the point of giving up evenings, weekends, and vacations to serve the organization. However, a new generation of office workers may not fit this model. An individual from the new generation is likely to be more direct than the traditional Japanese. This new-generation person acts more like a Westerner, a *gaijin*. He or she does not live for the company and will move on if he or she gets an offer of a better job or has to work too much overtime.[73]

Leila Navidi/Minneapolis Star Tribune/ZUMA Wire/Alamy Stock Photo

Several studies have suggested that economic advancement and globalization may be important factors in societal change.[74] There is evidence that economic progress is accompanied by a shift in values away from collectivism and toward individualism.[75] As Japan has become richer, the cultural emphasis on collectivism has declined and greater individualism is being witnessed. One reason for this shift may be that richer societies exhibit less need for social and material support built on collectives, whether the collective is the extended family or the company. People are better able to take care of their own needs. As a result, the importance attached to collectivism declines, while greater economic freedoms lead to an increase in opportunities for expressing individualism.

The culture of societies may also change as they become richer because economic progress affects a number of other factors, which in turn influence culture. For example, increased urbanization and improvements in the quality and availability of education are both a function of economic progress, and both can lead to declining emphasis on the traditional values associated with poor rural societies. The World Values Survey, which we mentioned earlier, has documented how values change. The study linked these changes in values to changes in a country's level of economic development.[76] As countries get richer, a shift occurs away from "traditional values" linked to religion, family, and country, and toward "secular-rational" values. Traditionalists say religion is important in their lives. They have a strong sense of national pride; they also think that children should be taught to obey and that the first duty of a child is to make his or her parents proud.

The merging or convergence of cultures can also be traced to the world today being more globalized than ever. Advances in transportation and communication, technology, and international trade have set the tone for global corporations (e.g., Disney, Microsoft, Google) to be part of bringing diverse cultures together into a form of homogeneity we have not seen before.[77] There are endless examples of global companies helping to foster a ubiquitous, social-media-driven youth culture. Plus, with countries around the world climbing the ladder of economic progress, some argue that the conditions for less cultural variation have been created. There may be a slow but steady convergence occurring across different cultures toward some universally accepted values and norms. This is known as the *convergence* hypothesis, and such convergence at least is happening at younger ages of the population. Older people still appear culturally different, however—their world remains spiky and is not yet flat![78]

At the same time, we should not ignore important countertrends, such as the shift toward Islamic fundamentalism in several countries; the continual separatist movement in Quebec, Canada; ethnic strains and separatist movements in Russia; nationalist movements in the United Kingdom (Brexit); and the election of a populist, nationally oriented Donald Trump as the 45th president of the United States. Such countertrends are a reaction to the pressures for cultural convergence. In an increasingly modern and materialistic world, some societies are trying to reemphasize their cultural roots and uniqueness. It is also important to note that while some elements of culture change quite rapidly—particularly the use of material symbols— other elements change slowly. Thus, just because people the world over wear jeans, eat at McDonald's, use smartphones, watch their national version of *American Idol*, and drive Ford cars to work, we should not assume they have also adopted American (or Western) values. Often they have not.[79] Thus, a distinction must be made between the visible material aspects of culture and its deep structure, particularly its core social values and norms. The deep structure changes only slowly, and differences are often far more persistent.

 TEST PREP

Use SmartBook to help retain what you have learned. Access your Instructor's Connect course to check out SmartBook or go to **learnsmartadvantage.com** for help.

FOCUS ON MANAGERIAL IMPLICATIONS

CULTURAL LITERACY AND COMPETITIVE ADVANTAGE

International business is different from national business because countries and societies are different. Societies differ because their cultures vary. Their cultures vary because of differences in social structure, religion, language, education, economic philosophy, and political philosophy. Three important implications for international business flow from these differences. The first is the need to develop cross-cultural literacy. There is a need not only to appreciate that cultural differences exist but also to appreciate what such differences mean for international business. A second implication centers on the connection between culture and national competitive advantage. A third implication looks at the connection between culture and ethics in decision making. In this section, we explore the first two of these issues in depth. The connection between culture and ethics is explored in Chapter 5.

Cross-Cultural Literacy

One of the biggest dangers confronting a company that goes abroad for the first time is the danger of being ill-informed. International businesses that are ill-informed about another culture are likely to fail. Doing business in different cultures requires adaptation to conform to the value systems and norms of that culture. Adaptation can embrace all aspects of an international firm's operations in a foreign country. The way in which deals are negotiated, appropriate incentive pay systems for salespeople, the structure of the organization, name of a product, tenor of relations between management and labor, the manner in which the product is promoted, and so on, are all sensitive to cultural differences. What works in one culture might not work in another.

To combat the danger of being ill-informed, international businesses should consider employing local citizens to help them do business in a particular culture. They must also ensure that home-country executives are well-versed enough to understand how differences in culture affect the practice of business. Transferring executives globally at regular intervals to expose them to different cultures will help build a cadre of knowledgeable executives. An international business must also be constantly on guard against the dangers of *ethnocentric behavior*. **Ethnocentrism** is a belief in the superiority of one's own ethnic group or culture. Hand in hand with ethnocentrism goes a disregard or contempt for the culture of other countries. Unfortunately, ethnocentrism is all too prevalent; many Americans are guilty of it, as are many French people, Japanese people, British people, and so on.

Anthropologist Edward T. Hall has described how Americans, who tend to be informal in nature, react strongly to being corrected or reprimanded in public.[80] This can cause problems in Germany, where a cultural tendency toward correcting strangers can shock and offend most Americans. For their part, Germans can be a bit taken aback by the tendency of Americans to call people by their first name. This is uncomfortable enough among executives of the same rank, but it can be seen as insulting when a junior American executive addresses a more senior German manager by his or her first name without having been invited to do so. Hall concludes it can take a long time to get on a first-name basis with a German; if you rush the process, you will be perceived as over friendly and rude—and that may not be good for business.

Hall also notes that cultural differences in attitude to time can cause myriad problems. He notes that in the United States, giving a person a deadline is a way of increasing the urgency or relative importance of a task. However, in the Middle East, giving a deadline can have exactly the opposite effect. The American who insists an Arab business associate make his mind up in a hurry is likely to be perceived as overly demanding and exerting undue pressure. The result may be exactly the opposite, with the Arab going slow as a reaction to the American's rudeness. The American may believe that an Arab associate is being rude if he shows up late to a meeting because he met a friend in the street and stopped to talk. The American, of course, is very concerned about time and scheduling. But for the Arab, finishing the discussion with a friend is more important than adhering to a strict schedule. Indeed, the Arab may be puzzled as to why the American attaches so much importance to time and schedule.

Culture and Competitive Advantage

One theme that surfaces in this chapter is the relationship between culture and national competitive advantage.[81] Put simply, the value systems and norms of a country influence the costs of doing business in that country. The costs of doing business in a country influence the ability of firms to establish a competitive advantage. We have seen how attitudes toward cooperation between management and labor, toward work, and toward the payment of interest are influenced by social structure and religion. It can be argued that the class-based conflict between workers and management in class-conscious societies raises the costs of doing business. Similarly, some sociologists have argued that the ascetic "other-worldly" ethics of Hinduism may not be as supportive of capitalism as the ethics embedded in Protestantism and Confucianism. Islamic laws banning interest payments may raise the costs of doing business by constraining a country's banking system.

Some scholars have argued that the culture of modern Japan lowers the costs of doing business relative to the costs in most Western nations. Japan's emphasis on group affiliation, loyalty, reciprocal obligations, honesty, and education all boost the competitiveness of Japanese companies—at least that is the argument. The emphasis on group affiliation and loyalty encourages individuals to identify strongly with the companies in which they work. This tends to foster an ethic of hard work and cooperation between management and labor "for the good of the company." In addition, the availability of a pool of highly skilled labor, particularly engineers, has helped Japanese enterprises develop cost-reducing process innovations that have boosted their productivity.[82] Thus, cultural factors may help explain the success enjoyed by many Japanese businesses. Most notably, it has been argued that the rise of Japan as an economic power during the second half of the twentieth century may be in part attributed to the economic consequences of its culture.[83]

It also has been argued that the Japanese culture is less supportive of entrepreneurial activity than, say, American society. In many ways, entrepreneurial activity is a product of an individualistic mindset, not a classic characteristic of the Japanese. This may explain why American enterprises, rather than Japanese corporations, dominate industries where entrepreneurship and innovation are highly valued, such as computer software and biotechnology. Of course, exceptions to this generalization exist. Masayoshi Son recognized the potential of software far faster than any of Japan's corporate giants. He set up his company, Softbank, in 1981, and over the past 40 years has built it into Japan's top software distributor. Similarly, entrepreneurial individuals established major Japanese companies such as Sony and Matsushita.

For international business, the connection between culture and competitive advantage is important for two reasons. First, the connection suggests which countries are likely to produce the most viable competitors. For example, we might argue that U.S. enterprises are likely to see continued growth in aggressive, cost-efficient competitors from those Pacific Rim nations where a combination of free-market economics, Confucian ideology, group-oriented social structures, and advanced education systems can all be found (e.g., South Korea, Taiwan, Japan, and, increasingly, China). Second, the connection between culture and competitive advantage has important implications for the choice of countries in which to locate production facilities and do business.

Consider a hypothetical case where a company has to choose between two countries, A and B, for locating a production facility. Both countries are characterized by low labor costs and good access to world markets. Both countries are of roughly the same size (in terms of population), and both are at a similar stage of economic development. In country

A, the education system is underdeveloped, the society is characterized by a marked stratification between the upper and lower classes, and there are six major linguistic groups. In country B, the education system is well developed, social stratification is lacking, group identification is valued by the culture, and there is only one linguistic group. Which country makes the best investment site?

Country B probably does. In country A, the conflict between management and labor, and between different language groups, can be expected to lead to social and industrial disruption, thereby raising the costs of doing business.[84] The lack of a good education system also can be expected to work against the attainment of business goals. The same kind of comparison could be made for an international business trying to decide where to push its products, country A or B. Again, country B would be the logical choice because cultural factors suggest that in the long run, country B is the nation most likely to achieve the greatest level of economic growth.

But as important as culture is to people, companies, and society, it is probably less important than economic, political, and legal systems in explaining differential economic growth between nations. Cultural differences are significant, but we should not overemphasize their importance in the economic sphere. For example, earlier we noted that Max Weber argued that the ascetic principles embedded in Hinduism do not encourage entrepreneurial activity. While this is an interesting thesis, recent years have seen an increase in entrepreneurial activity in India, particularly in the information technology sector, where India is an important global player. The ascetic principles of Hinduism and caste-based social stratification have apparently not held back entrepreneurial activity in this sector.

Key Terms

cross-cultural literacy, p. 94
culture, p. 96
values, p. 96
norms, p. 96
society, p. 96
folkways, p. 97
mores, p. 98
social structure, p. 99
group, p. 100

social strata, p. 102
social mobility, p. 102
caste system, p. 102
class system, p. 102
class consciousness, p. 105
religion, p. 105
ethical system, p. 105
power distance, p. 118

individualism versus
    collectivism, p. 118
uncertainty avoidance, p. 118
masculinity versus
    femininity, p. 118
long-term versus short-term
    orientation, p. 118
ethnocentrism, p. 122

 SUMMARY

This chapter has looked at the nature of culture and discussed a number of implications for business practice. The chapter made the following points:

1. Culture is a complex phenomenon that includes knowledge, beliefs, art, morals, law, customs, and other capabilities acquired by people as members of society.

2. Values and norms are the central components of a culture. Values are abstract ideals about what a society believes to be good, right, and desirable.

Norms are social rules and guidelines that prescribe appropriate behavior in particular situations.

3. Values and norms are influenced by political forces, economic philosophy, social structure, religion, language, and education. And, the value systems and norms of a country can affect the costs of doing business in that country.

4. The social structure of society refers to its basic social organization. Two main dimensions along

which social structures differ are the individual–group dimension and the stratification dimension.

5. In some societies, the individual is the basic building block of a social organization. These societies emphasize individual achievements above all else. In other societies, the group is the basic building block of the social organization. These societies emphasize group membership and group achievements above all else.

6. Virtually all societies are stratified into different classes. Class-conscious societies are characterized by low social mobility and a high degree of stratification. Less class-conscious societies are characterized by high social mobility and a low degree of stratification.

7. Religion may be defined as a system of shared beliefs and rituals that is concerned with the realm of the sacred. Ethical systems refer to a set of moral principles, or values, that are used to guide and shape behavior. The world's major religions are Christianity, Islam, Hinduism, and Buddhism. The value systems of different religious and ethical systems have different implications for business practice.

8. Language is one defining characteristic of a culture. It has both spoken and unspoken

dimensions. In countries with more than one spoken language, we tend to find more than one culture.

9. Formal education is the medium through which individuals learn knowledge and skills as well as become socialized into the values and norms of a society. Education plays a role in the determination of national competitive advantage.

10. Geert Hofstede studied how culture relates to values in the workplace. He isolated five dimensions that summarized different cultures: power distance, uncertainty avoidance, individualism versus collectivism, masculinity versus femininity, and long-term versus short-term orientation.

11. Culture is not a constant; it evolves, albeit often slowly. Economic progress and globalization are two important engines of cultural change.

12. One danger confronting a company that goes abroad is being ill-informed. To develop cross-cultural literacy, companies operating globally should consider employing host-country nationals, build a cadre of cosmopolitan executives, and guard against the dangers of ethnocentric behavior.

Critical Thinking and Discussion Questions

1. Discuss why the culture of a country might influence the costs of doing business in that country. Illustrate your answer with country and company examples.

2. Do you think that business practices in an Islamic country are likely to differ from business practices in a Christian country? If so, how? If not, why?

3. Choose two countries that appear to be culturally diverse (e.g., Sweden and Colombia). Compare the cultures of those countries, and then indicate how cultural differences influence (*a*) the costs of doing business in each country, (*b*) the likely future economic development of each country, and (*c*) differences in business practices.

4. Reread the Country Focus "Turkey, Its Religion, and Politics." Then answer the following questions:

   a. Can you see anything in the values and norms of Islam that is hostile to business? Explain.

   b. What does the experience of the region around Kayseri teach about the relationship between Islam and business?

c. What are the implications of Islamic values toward business for the participation of a country such as Turkey in the global economy or becoming a member of the European Union?

5. Reread the Management Focus "China and Its *Guanxi*" and answer the following questions:

   a. Why do you think it is so important to cultivate *guanxi* and *guanxiwang* in China?

   b. What does the experience of DMG tell us about the way things work in China? What would likely happen to a business that obeyed all the rules and regulations, rather than trying to find a way around them like Dan Mintz?

   c. What ethical issues might arise when drawing on *guanxiwang* to get things done in China? What does this suggest about the limits of using *guanxiwang* for a Western business committed to high ethical standards?

globalEDGE research task   globaledge.msu.edu

Use the globalEDGE™ website (**globaledge.msu.edu**) to complete the following exercises:

1. You are preparing for a business trip to Brazil, where you will need to interact extensively with local professionals. As a result, you want to collect information about the local culture and business practices prior to your departure. A colleague from Latin America recommends that you visit the Brazil page on globalEDGE and read through the country insights and data available. Prepare a short description of the most striking cultural characteristics that may affect business interactions in this country.

2. Typically, cultural factors drive the differences in business etiquette encountered during international business travel. In fact, Middle Eastern cultures exhibit significant differences in business etiquette when compared to Western cultures. Prior to leaving for your first business trip to the region, a colleague informed you that globalEDGE can help you (as can a globalEDGE-promoted guide titled *Business Etiquette around the World*). Identify five tips regarding business etiquette in the Middle Eastern country of your choice (e.g., Turkey).

CLOSING CASE

China, Hong Kong, Macau, and Taiwan

Today, a lot of discussion centers on how much economic power, political influence, and international competitiveness the People's Republic of China (PRC) has achieved in the international marketplace in just a few decades. Culturally, such power in the international marketplace also begs the questions of how much influence China is likely to have moving forward, and what this means for China's influence culturally around the world. So far, other powerful countries in the world have focused on China's economic influence, but what about the country's influence on culture?

China, along with India, Brazil, and Russia, form the so-called BRIC countries (an acronym formulated using their initial letters), which have been viewed as the business engines of tomorrow (especially China and India), based on their immense economic potential. The BRICs, which cover a quarter of the world's landmass and contain 40 percent of its population, had a combined GDP of $20 trillion in 2001. Today, these increasingly market-oriented economies boast a GDP of $37 trillion (or 22 percent of global GDP), a figure forecast to reach $120 trillion by 2050. Together, they control more than 43 percent of the world's currency reserves ($4 trillion) and 20 percent of its trade. Is it too simplistic and naïve to think that the BRIC countries–especially China and Russia–only have a focus on economic power? Clearly, Russia has engaged in at least some political activities that have had tremendous global effects (e.g., election meddling). And what about

China? Many reports and investigations suggest the country is likewise engaged in political meddling. Does that affect culture around the world also?

The BRIC countries' economic size and population were the simplistic starting point to group them as powerful marketplaces–to export products to, and to buy products from. These datapoints led former Goldman Sachs chief economist Jim O'Neill to first coin the acronym BRIC to highlight the immense collective economic potential of these four emerging markets. However, despite many countries' and companies' enthusiasm for increased global interaction and economic exchange with the BRIC economies, especially China and India, many have found that cultural differences hinder their ability to conduct business in these countries. Not only is the culture different between each BRIC country and most of the globe's remaining 191 countries, but the business and societal cultures within the BRIC countries are also vastly different from each other.

Plus, the outlook for the BRICs may not be as positive as we have been led to believe anyway. For example, the structural transformation of China (the main driver of the BRICs) from an export-driven economy to one relying more on domestic consumption, has added some woes. The likelihood is that the trend of annual increases of exports to China from much of the developed world will also slow down. We will see trade increases, nevertheless, just not as significantly as in the past decade. China is a gigantic market that we must pay attention to, of course. China is beginning to also influence the world's culture outwardly. Economics still drive China's global operations, albeit with an eye toward also influencing the international marketplace in such a way that it favors China—both in its home market and abroad.

For example, China is still trying to implement the "one country, two systems" approach—a constitutional principle formulated by Deng Xiaoping—which involves how to merge mainland China with Hong Kong and Macau. With Xi Jinping president of China for the foreseeable future as a function of his de facto lifetime appointment when term limits were removed in 2018, China's political infrastructure is unlikely to change much. Consequently, China's culture at home and how it handles business issues abroad is unlikely to change much as well. Beyond Hong Kong and Macau, Taiwan presents an even bigger ongoing structural, legal, and cultural challenge for China. While Hong Kong and Macau mostly fall in line within China's basic parameters, Taiwan does not.

Hong Kong, a business port located off the southeast coast of China in eastern Asia, traces its history to the Old Stone Age, and really became entrenched in today's infrastructure with its inclusion into the Chinese empire during the Qin dynasty (221–206 B.C.). However, Hong Kong was a self-governing British colony from 1841 to 1997, at which time it became a Special Administrative Region (SAR) of the People's Republic of China (on July 1, 1997), pursuant to the 1984 Sino-British Joint Declaration. Throughout this colonial era, Hong Kong's citizens developed a distinctive "Hong Kong identity." To this day, the cultural differences between mainland China and Hong Kong are often pronounced, and whenever mainland China tries to assert its influence, their relationship becomes more contentious. The sentiment in Hong Kong is that it needs to be recognized as having a unique culture and a "national identity." Hong Kong is often, in many ways, at odds with mainland China in this way, and periodic clashes flare.

Prior to 1999, Macau was a Portuguese colony, that became an overseas province under Portuguese administration from 1887 to 1999. Macau was both the first and last European colony in China. Just before its return to China in 1999, Macau experienced a number of economic difficulties. Its biggest revenue items—gaming and tourism—decreased drastically in 1993, followed by the collapse of the property market in 1994, and then the economic crisis in 1997 that affected much of Asia. By the time 1999 came around for a handover from Portugal to China, most locals welcomed the change because of deteriorating public order, rising crime rates, and widespread corruption that had infiltrated the culture during the last years of the Portuguese-Macau government. Today, Macau is being positioned as a key diplomatic player in China's relations with Portuguese-speaking countries.

Taiwan, officially named the Republic of China (ROC), is an island nation (Island of Taiwan, formerly Formosa). It is the most populous country, with the largest economy, that is not a member of the United Nations. Taiwan was ceded by the Qing dynasty to Japan in 1895 after the Sino-Japanese War. The Republic of China was established in 1912 after the fall of the Qing dynasty, while Taiwan was under Japanese rule. However, China has consistently claimed sovereignty over Taiwan and asserted that the Republic of China (ROC) is no longer in legitimate existence. Under its One-China Policy, China even refuses to engage in diplomatic relations with any country that recognizes Taiwan. In this semi-independent state, Taiwan has experienced solid economic growth and industrialization, creating a stable industrial economy. The culture blends Confucianist Han Chinese and Taiwanese aboriginal influences.

When mainland China, Hong Kong, Macau, and Taiwan are combined, we often talk about the larger entity "Greater China" or the "Greater China Region." Obviously, there is no legal entity or sovereignty associated with this "greater region," except in business/economic development terms. Some argue that the "region" can be seen as being culturally homogeneous, but such arguments do not hold up well given the clashes between mainland China on one hand and Hong Kong and Taiwan on the other. Interestingly, Macau has been more positive about its relationship with China, perhaps due to experiencing serious financial difficulties immediately prior to the 1999 handover from Portugal (these financial difficulties were essentially solved by China).

Overall, given the strained relationships between China and its close cultural neighbors, the phrase "sinophone world" ("Chinese-speaking world") is often used instead of Greater China to incorporate mainland China, Hong Kong, Macau, and Taiwan. The "sinophone world" may look like a culturally homogenous region, but is far from it.

Sources: Tomas Hult, "The U.S. Shouldn't Fret over Cheaper Yuan," *Time*, August 14, 2015; Tomas Hult, "Why the Fed Is No Longer the Center of the Financial Universe," *Fortune*, September 17, 2015; Tomas Hult, "Does the Global Stock Market Sell-Off Signal the BRIC Age Is Already Over?" *The Conversation*, August 28, 2015; Tomas Hult, "U.S. Shouldn't Fret over Cheaper Yuan: China's Growing Middle Class Will Keep Buying 'Made In America,'" *The Conversation*, August 13, 2015; Tomas Hult, "The BRIC Countries," *globalEDGE Business Review*, 3 (4), 2009; Mark Esposito, Amit Kapoor, and Deepti Mathur, "What Is the State of the BRICS Economies?" *World Economic Forum*, April 19, 2016.

Case Discussion Questions

1. When Goldman Sachs chief economist Jim O'Neill coined the acronym BRIC in 2001 to refer to Brazil, Russia, India, and China, the focus was to highlight the immense collective economic potential of these countries. Since that time, China and Russia have influenced the international marketplace in political ways as well. How do you think these four countries—or a subset of them—will likely influence the world's cultures in the next 10 years?

2. Anyone who has been to Hong Kong typically says it is different from mainland China, more like Singapore, albeit with a strong connection to China. Do you think Hong Kong will become more like China in the next few years, or will China leverage Hong Kong as an asset to engage more capitalistically in the international marketplace instead?

3. Macau was under Portuguese influence until 1999, which is not that long ago. Many in Macau welcomed the Chinese takeover so that the area could be better taken care of (e.g., infrastructure, economy). But being part of the Portuguese administration from 1887 to 1999 clearly has imbued their cultural values and beliefs in the mindset of Macau's citizens. How are these values and beliefs likely to influence the Macau–China relationship in the years to come?

4. Taiwan maintains diplomatic relations with some 76 member states of the United Nations (19 in an official capacity and 57 in an unofficial capacity). The nation's culture is a blend of Confucianist Han Chinese and Taiwanese aboriginal influences. How would you handle the link between China and Taiwan—culturally, economically, and politically?

Endnotes

1. D. Barry, *Exporters! The Wit and Wisdom of Small Businesspeople Who Sell Globally* (Washington, DC: International Trade Administration, U.S. Department of Commerce, 2013); T. Hult, D. Ketchen, D. Griffith, C. Finnegan, T. Padron-Gonzalez, F. Harmancioglu, Y. Huang, M. Talay, and S. Cavusgil, "Data Equivalence in Cross-Cultural International Business Research: Assessment and Guidelines," *Journal of International Business Studies*, 2008, pp. 1027–44; S. Ronen and O. Shenkar, "Mapping World Cultures: Cluster Formation, Sources, and Implications," *Journal of International Business Studies*, 2013, pp. 867–97.

2. This is a point made effectively by K. Leung, R. S. Bhagat, N. R. Buchan, M. Erez, and C. B. Gibson, "Culture and International Business: Recent Advances and Their Implications for Future Research," *Journal of International Business Studies*, 2005, pp. 357–78. Several research articles and books also support the notion that significant cultural differences still exist in the world; for example, T. Hult, D. Closs, and D. Frayer, *Global Supply Chain Management: Leveraging Processes, Measurements, and Tools for Strategic Corporate Advantage* (New York: McGraw-Hill, 2014).

3. Falk, Armin, Anke Becker, Thomas Dohmen, and Benjamin Enke, "Global Evidence on Economic Preferences," *Quarterly Journal of Economics* 133, no. 4 (November 2018): 1645–692.

4. See R. Dore, *Taking Japan Seriously* (Stanford, CA: Stanford University Press, 1987).

5. Tylor, Edward Burnett. *Primitive Culture: Researches Into the Development of Mythology, Philosophy, Religion, Art, and Custom,* Vol. 1. London: John Murray, 1871.

6. F. Kluckhohn and F. Strodtbeck, *Variations in Value Orientations* (Evanston, IL: Row, Peterson, 1961); C. Kluckhohn, "Values and Value Orientations in the Theory of Action," in T. Parsons and E. A. Shils (Eds.), *Toward a General Theory of Action* (Cambridge, MA: Harvard University Press, 1951).

7. M. Rokeach, *The Nature of Human Values* (New York: Free Press, 1973); S. Schwartz, "Universals in the Content and Structure of Values: Theory and Empirical Tests in 20 Countries," in M. Zanna (Ed.), *Advances in Experimental Social Psychology*, vol. 25 (New York: Academic Press, 1992), pp. 1–65.

8. G. Hofstede, *Culture's Consequences: International Differences in Work-Related Values* (Thousand Oaks CA: Sage, 1984), p. 21.

9. G. Hofstede, *Culture's Consequences: International Differences in Work-Related Values* (Thousand Oaks, CA: Sage, 1984), p. 21.

10. J. Z. Namenwirth and R. B. Weber, *Dynamics of Culture* (Boston: Allen & Unwin, 1987), p. 8.

11. R. Mead, *International Management: Cross-Cultural Dimensions* (Oxford: Blackwell Business, 1994), p. 7.

12. G. Hofstede, *Culture's Consequences: Comparing Values, Beliefs, Behaviors, Institutions and Organizations Across Nations* (Thousand Oaks, CA: Sage, 2001).

13. E. T. Hall and M. R. Hall, *Hidden Differences: Doing Business with the Japanese* (New York: Doubleday, 1987).

14. B. Keillor and T. Hult, "A Five-Country Study of National Identity: Implications for International Marketing Research and Practice," *International Marketing Review*, 1999, pp. 65–82; T. Clark, "International Marketing and National Character: A Review and Proposal for an Integrative Theory," *Journal of Marketing*, 1990, pp. 66–79; M. E. Porter, *The Competitive Advantage of Nations* (New York: Free Press, 1990).

15. S. P. Huntington, *The Clash of Civilizations* (New York: Simon & Schuster, 1996).

16. F. Vijver, D. Hemert, and Y. Poortinga, *Multilevel Analysis of Individuals and Cultures* (New York: Taylor & Francis, 2010).

17. M. Thompson, R. Ellis, and A. Wildavsky, *Cultural Theory* (Boulder, CO: Westview Press, 1990).

18. M. Douglas, *In the Active Voice* (London: Routledge, 1982), pp. 183–254.

19. L. Zucker and M. Darby, "Star-Scientist Linkages to Firms in APEC and European Countries: Indicators of Regional Institutional Differences Affecting Competitive Advantage," *International Journal of Biotechnology*, 1999, pp. 119–31.

20. C. Nakane, *Japanese Society* (Berkeley: University of California Press, 1970).

21. Nakane, Chie. *Japanese Society.* University of California Press, 1972.

22. For details, see M. Aoki, *Information, Incentives, and Bargaining in the Japanese Economy* (Cambridge, UK: Cambridge University Press, 1988); M. L. Dertouzos, R. K. Lester, and R. M. Solow, *Made in America* (Cambridge, MA: MIT Press, 1989).

23. Global Innovation Barometer 2018 is a product by Ideas Lab and is supported by General Electric (GE). The GE Global Innovation Barometer explores how business leaders around the world view innovation and how those perceptions are influencing business strategies in an increasingly complex and globalized environment. It is the largest global survey of business executives dedicated to innovation. GE is now surveying more than 3,000 executives in 25 countries, www.ge.com/reports/innovation-barometer-2018.

24. P. Skarynski and R. Gibson, *Innovation to the Core: A Blueprint for Transforming the Way Your Company Innovates* (Boston, MA: Harvard Business School Press, 2008); L. Edvinsson and M. Malone, *Intellectual Capital: Realizing Your Company's True Value by Finding Its Hidden Brainpower* (New York: Harper Collins, 1997); T. Davenport and L. Prusak, *Working Knowledge: How Organizations Manage What They Know* (Boston, MA: Harvard Business School Press, 1998).

25. G. Macionis and L. John, *Sociology* (Toronto, Ontario: Pearson Canada, Inc., 2010), pp. 224–25.

26. E. Luce, *The Strange Rise of Modern India* (Boston: Little, Brown, 2006); D. Pick and K. Dayaram, "Modernity and Tradition in the Global Era: The Re-invention of Caste in India," *International Journal of Sociology and Social Policy*, 2006, pp. 284–301.

27. For an excellent historical treatment of the evolution of the English class system, see E. P. Thompson, *The Making of the English Working Class* (London: Vintage Books, 1966). See also R. Miliband, *The State in Capitalist Society* (New York: Basic Books, 1969), especially Chapter 2. For more recent studies of class in British societies, see Stephen Brook, *Class: Knowing Your Place in Modern Britain* (London: Victor Gollancz, 1997); A. Adonis and S. Pollard, *A Class Act: The Myth of Britain's Classless Society* (London: Hamish Hamilton, 1997); J. Gerteis and M. Savage, "The Salience of Class in Britain and America: A Comparative Analysis," *British Journal of Sociology*, June 1998.

28. Adonis and Pollard, *A Class Act*.

29. J. H. Goldthorpe, "Class Analysis and the Reorientation of Class Theory: The Case of Persisting Differentials in Education Attainment," *British Journal of Sociology*, 2010, pp. 311–35.

30. Y. Bian, "Chinese Social Stratification and Social Mobility," *Annual Review of Sociology* 28 (2002), pp. 91–117.

31. N. Goodman, *An Introduction to Sociology* (New York: Harper-Collins, 1991).

32. O. C. Ferrell, J. Fraedrich, and L. Ferrell, *Business Ethics: Ethical Decision Making and Cases* (Mason, OH: Cengage Learning, 2012).

33. R. J. Barro and R. McCleary, "Religion and Economic Growth across Countries," *American Sociological Review*, October 2003, pp. 760–82; R. McCleary and R. J. Barro, "Religion and Economy," *Journal of Economic Perspectives*, Spring 2006, pp. 49–72.

34. M. Weber, *The Protestant Ethic and the Spirit of Capitalism* (New York: Scribner's, 1958, original 1904–1905). For an excellent review of Weber's work, see A. Giddens, *Capitalism and Modern Social Theory* (Cambridge, UK: Cambridge University Press, 1971).

35. Weber, Max. *The Protestant Ethic and the Spirit of Capitalism.* Routledge: Taylor & Francis, 1930.

36. A. S. Thomas and S. L. Mueller, "The Case for Comparative Entrepreneurship," *Journal of International Business Studies* 31, no. 2 (2000), pp. 287–302; S. A. Shane, "Why Do Some Societies Invent More than Others?" *Journal of Business Venturing* 7 (1992), pp. 29–46.

37. See S. M. Abbasi, K. W. Hollman, and J. H. Murrey, "Islamic Economics: Foundations and Practices," *International Journal of Social Economics* 16, no. 5 (1990), pp. 5–17; R. H. Dekmejian, *Islam in Revolution: Fundamentalism in the Arab World* (Syracuse, NY: Syracuse University Press, 1995).

38. T. W. Lippman, *Understanding Islam* (New York: Meridian Books, 1995).

39. Dekmejian, *Islam in Revolution*.

40. M. K. Nydell, *Understanding Arabs* (Yarmouth, ME: Intercultural Press, 1987).

41. Lippman, *Understanding Islam*.

42. The material in this section is based largely on Abbasi et al., "Islamic Economics."

43. "Sharia Calling," *The Economist*, November 12, 2010; N. Popper, "Islamic Banks, Stuffed with Cash, Explore Partnerships in West," *The New York Times*, December 26, 2013.

44. "Forced Devotion," *The Economist*, February 17, 2001, pp. 76–77.

45. For details of Weber's work and views, see Giddens, *Capitalism and Modern Social Theory*.

46. See, for example, the views expressed in "A Survey of India: The Tiger Steps Out," *The Economist*, January 21, 1995.

47. "High-Tech Entrepreneurs Flock to India," *PBS News Hour*, February 9, 2014, www.pbs.org/newshour/bb/high-tech-entrepreneurs-flock-india, accessed March 7, 2014.

48. H. Norberg-Hodge, "Buddhism in the Global Economy," International Society for Ecology and Culture, www.localfutures.org/publications/online-articles/buddhism-in-the-global-economy, accessed March 7, 2014.

49. P. Clark, "Zen and the Art of Startup Naming," *Bloomberg Businessweek*, August 30, 2013, www.businessweek.com/articles/2013-08-30/zen-and-the-art-of-startup-naming, accessed March 7, 2014.

50. Clark, Patrick. "Zen and the Art of Startup Naming." *Bloomberg Businessweek,* October 9, 2013.

51. Hofstede, *Culture's Consequences*.

52. See Dore, *Taking Japan Seriously*; C. W. L. Hill, "Transaction Cost Economizing as a Source of Comparative Advantage: The Case of Japan," *Organization Science* 6 (1995).

53. C. C. Chen, Y. R. Chen, and K. Xin, "Guanxi Practices and Trust in Management," *Organization Science* 15, no. 2 (March–April 2004), pp. 200–10.

54. See Aoki, *Information, Incentives, and Bargaining*; J. P. Womack, D. T. Jones, and D. Roos, *The Machine That Changed the World* (New York: Rawson Associates, 1990).

55. This hypothesis dates back to two anthropologists, Edward Sapir and Benjamin Lee Whorf. See E. Sapir, "The Status of Linguistics as a Science," *Language* 5 (1929), pp. 207–14; B. L. Whorf, *Language, Thought, and Reality* (Cambridge, MA: MIT Press, 1956).

56. The tendency has been documented empirically. See A. Annett, "Social Fractionalization, Political Instability, and the Size of Government," *IMF Staff Papers* 48 (2001), pp. 561–92.

57. D. A. Ricks, *Big Business Blunders: Mistakes in Multinational Marketing* (Homewood, IL: Dow Jones-Irwin, 1983).

58. Goodman, *An Introduction to Sociology*.

59. Porter, *The Competitive Advantage of Nations*.

60. Porter, Michael E. *Competitive Advantage of Nations: Creating and Sustaining Superior Performance*. Simon and Schuster, 2011.

61. G. Hofstede, "The Cultural Relativity of Organizational Practices and Theories," *Journal of International Business Studies*, Fall 1983, pp. 75–89; G. Hofstede, *Cultures and Organizations: Software of the Mind* (New York: McGraw-Hill USA, 1997); Hofstede, *Culture's Consequences*.

62. Hofstede, "The Cultural Relativity of Organizational Practices and Theories"; Hofstede, *Cultures and Organizations*.

63. Hofstede, *Culture's Consequences*.

64. G. Hofstede and M. Bond, "Hofstede's Culture Dimensions: An Independent Validation Using Rokeach's Value Survey," *Journal of Cross-Cultural Psychology* 15 (December 1984), pp. 417–33.

65. The factor scores for the long-term versus short-term orientation, using Bond's survey, were brought into a 0–100 range by a linear transformation (LTO = 50 × F + 50, in which F is the factor score). However, the data for China came in after Hofstede and Bond had standardized the scale, and they put China outside the range at LTO = 118 (which indicates a very strong long-term orientation).

66. G. Hofstede, G. J. Hofstede, and M. Minkov, *Cultures and Organizations: Software of the Mind*, 3d ed. (New York: McGraw-Hill, 2010).

67. For a more detailed critique, see Mead, *International Management*, pp. 73–75.

68. For example, see W. J. Bigoness and G. L. Blakely, "A Cross-National Study of Managerial Values," *Journal of International Business Studies*, December 1996, p. 739; D. H. Ralston, D. H. Holt, R. H. Terpstra, and Y. Kai-Cheng, "The Impact of National Culture and Economic Ideology on Managerial Work Values," *Journal of International Business Studies* 28, no. 1 (1997), pp. 177–208; P. B. Smith, M. F. Peterson, and Z. Ming Wang, "The Manager as a Mediator of Alternative Meanings," *Journal of International Business Studies* 27, no. 1 (1996), pp. 115–37; L. Tang and P. E. Koves, "A Framework to Update Hofstede's Cultural Value Indices," *Journal of International Business Studies* 39 (2008), pp. 1045–63.

69. R. House, P. Hanges, M. Javidan, P. Dorfman, and V. Gupta, *Culture, Leadership, and Organizations: The GLOBE Study of 62 Societies* (Thousand Oaks, CA: Sage, 2004); J. Chhokar, F. Brodbeck, and R. House, *Culture and Leadership across the World: The GLOBE Book of In-Depth Studies of 25 Societies* (New York: Routledge, 2012).

70. R. Inglehart, *Modernization and Postmodernization: Cultural, Economic, and Political Change in 43 Societies* (Princeton, NJ: Princeton University Press, 1997). Information and data on the World Values Survey can be found at www.worldvaluessurvey.org.

71. For evidence of this, see R. Inglehart, "Globalization and Postmodern Values," *The Washington Quarterly*, Winter 2000, pp. 215–28.

72. Mead, *International Management*, chap. 17.

73. "Free, Young, and Japanese," *The Economist*, December 21, 1991.

74. Namenwirth and Weber, *Dynamics of Culture*; Inglehart, "Globalization and Postmodern Values."

75. G. Hofstede, "National Cultures in Four Dimensions," *International Studies of Management and Organization* 13, no. 1 (1983), pp. 46–74; Tang and Koves, "A Framework to Update Hofstede's Cultural Value Indices."

76. See Inglehart, "Globalization and Postmodern Values." For updates, see www.isr.umich.edu/cps/project_wvs.html.

77. Hofstede, "National Cultures in Four Dimensions."

78. D. A. Ralston, D. H. Holt, R. H. Terpstra, and Y. Kai-Chung, "The Impact of National Culture and Economic Ideology on Managerial Work Values," *Journal of International Business Studies*, 2007, pp. 1–19.

79. See Leung et al., "Culture and International Business."

80. Hall and Hall, *Understanding Cultural Differences*.

81. Porter, *The Competitive Advantage of Nations*.

82. See Aoki, *Information, Incentives, and Bargaining*; Dertouzos et al., *Made in America*; Porter, *The Competitive Advantage of Nations*, pp. 395–97.

83. See Dore, *Taking Japan Seriously*; Hill, "Transaction Cost Economizing as a Source of Comparative Advantage."

84. For empirical work supporting such a view, see Annett, "Social Fractionalization, Political Instability, and the Size of Government."

Ethics, Corporate Social Responsibility, and Sustainability

5

LEARNING OBJECTIVES

After reading this chapter, you will be able to:

LO5-1   Understand the ethical, corporate social responsibility, and sustainability issues faced by international businesses.

LO5-2   Recognize an ethical, corporate social responsibility, and/or sustainability dilemma.

LO5-3   Identify the causes of unethical behavior by managers as they relate to business, corporate social responsibility, or sustainability.

LO5-4   Describe the different philosophical approaches to business ethics that apply globally.

LO5-5   Explain how global managers can incorporate ethical considerations into their decision making in general, as well as corporate social responsibility and sustainability initiatives.

Atmosphere1/123RF

Ericsson, Sweden, and Sustainability

OPENING CASE

According to Toronto, Canada-based Corporate Knights, which ranks the Top 100 Most Sustainable Corporations, Swedish-based Ericsson is ranked number 21 in the world for its sustainability efforts. That makes Ericsson, headquartered in Sweden, the top-ranked multinational corporation for its sustainability efforts, in a country that is ranked at the top on the United Nations' Sustainable Development Goals (SDG Index). It says a lot to be the best on sustainability in the country that is itself the best among the world's nations when it comes to sustainability. The SDG Index includes 156 of the 195 countries in the world (all countries with reliable data on the 17 SDG dimensions), while the index by Corporate Knights is based on analyses of some 7,500 corporations with annual revenues in excess of $1 billion.

Perhaps it is only logical that Ericsson (**ericsson.com**) would place high in both the world ranking and in Sweden. Ericsson has integrated the United Nations' SDGs as part of its framework for how to describe and measure the company's impact on society. The view of Ericsson is that the Information and Communication Technologies (ICT) that are the core of Ericsson's products and services in the global marketplace can help achieve all 17 SDGs. By applying Ericsson's technology and expertise, the thought is that the company has made a positive impact and supported those SDGs ratified by 193 UN-member nations in 2015. Specifically, ICT in combination with a well-integrated corporate sustainability strategy can help tackle a range of global challenges. This thinking is how Ericsson works with technological advancements to continue being a responsible and relevant driver of positive change on society.

Sweden (**Sweden.se**) has benefited from Ericsson's sustainability influence and efforts. The country is consistently ranked number one in the world regarding sustainability, according to the SDG Index. Sweden is a country of 10 million, with thousands of coastal islands and inland lakes, along with vast boreal forests and glaciated mountains. It is very protective of its environment, and its government and corporations spend a great deal of time protecting that environment. For example, more than half of the energy used in Sweden comes from renewable energy sources. Also, Americans release about four times as much carbon dioxide (CO_2) into the atmosphere as the average Swede.

Sweden is also a data-rich country, reporting on almost every aspect of each citizen's daily life. Somewhat uniquely, in Sweden, which is overflowing with technological advancement, thousands of people have also had microchips inserted into their hands. The chips are designed to speed up people's daily routines and make their lives more convenient, by accessing their homes, offices, gyms, and so on by simply swiping their hands against digital readers. The chips are designed to provide access to almost anything digital readers will allow, including data collection on sustainability efforts. Such sophisticated data collection permeates Swedish society. For example, Ericsson has reported on sustainability performance for over 25 years, evolving with the times from environmental disclosure to the broader "triple bottom line" approach (i.e., environmental, social, and economic development) and, more recently, to the responsible business practices that Ericsson has adopted.

For the country, Sweden is focused on a sustainability agenda called Climate Roadmap, a direct operationalization of Roadmap 2050, which is an initiative of the European Union (**www.roadmap2050.eu**): "The mission of (the) Roadmap 2050 project is to provide a practical, independent and objective analysis of pathways to achieve a low-carbon economy in Europe, in line with the energy security, environmental and economic goals of the European Union. The Roadmap 2050 project is an initiative of the European Climate Foundation (ECF)."[*] To support this initiative, Sweden passed a new climate law that became effective in 2018, which committed the country to reach carbon neutrality by 2045. Guided by a Climate Policy Council, the law also sets out how the goals are to be achieved. The climate action plan must be evaluated on an annual basis to reach intermediary emission reduction targets for 2030 and 2040.

Another unique aspect of Sweden's sustainability effort is the country's recycling "revolution." Swedes recycle 99 percent of their household waste. Weine Wiqvist, CEO of the Swedish Waste Management and Recycling Association (Avfall Sverige), still thinks the country and its citizens can do more, however. He argues that about half of all household waste is burned, meaning it is turned into energy. Wiqvist explains that if the country could instead reuse the materials, the result would be less energy being used to create a new product than burning the waste for energy. "We are trying to 'move up the refuse ladder,' as we say, from burning to material recycling by promoting recycling and working with authorities,"[**] he says. Despite the high ratio of burning waste to reusing it, the positive for Sweden is that waste in landfills is not an issue in the country anymore. All waste is used in some form.

Likewise, when the United Nations launched the SDGs in 2015, Ericsson was there, leading the industry. With expertise in ICT and a sustainability strategy incorporated into the Ericsson's business, the company has a strong platform for making decisive advances. In fact, Ericsson is one of the few organizations in the world that has directly connected each of the 17 SDGs to specific issues that pertain to the company, and especially the ICT industry that Ericsson operates in. For example, SDG goal 11 is focused on sustainable cities and communities. In this area,

*Roadmap 2050. Roadmap.

**Avfall Sverige/Swedish Institute.

Ericsson states that "ICT can reduce administration costs and improve access to key areas such as health care, education and banking, and provide a platform for inclusion."****

****"Global Goals SDG 11," Ericsson, 2019, **https://www.ericsson.com/en/about-us/sustainability-and-corporate-responsibility/sustainable-development-goals/goal-11.**

Sources: Susanne Arvidsson, "Lessons from Sweden in Sustainable Business," *The Conversation*, December 11, 2017; Maddy Savage, "The Swedish Wasteland That Is Now a Sustainability Star," *BBC News*, October 3, 201; Klas Ericson, Martin Bauer, and Andreas Scheibenpflug, "How Sweden Lays the Foundation for Sustainable Manufacturing," *Business Sweden*, February 19, 2019; Ben Wilde, "How Sweden Became the World's Most Sustainable Country: Top 5 Reasons," *Adec Innovations*, January 12, 2016; "Energy Use in Sweden," Sweden.se, February 19, 2019; Dominic Hogg, "The Dark Truth Behind Sweden's Revolutionary Recycling Schemes," *The Independent*, December 13, 2016; "Sweden Turns Goal to Reach Carbon Neutrality in 2045 Into Law," *Climate Policy Observer*, June 16, 2017.

Introduction

Ethics, corporate social responsibility, and sustainability are intertwined issues facing companies, industries, countries, and regional societies worldwide. These "social" issues arise frequently in international business, often because business practices and regulations differ from nation to nation. With regard to lead pollution, for example, what is allowed in Mexico is outlawed in the United States. The tricky part is also that what is ethical, socially responsible, or sustainable often is not a legal obligation that companies and countries face.

Instead, "doing good" is often a self-correcting measure that companies or industries place on themselves and countries adopt as a business model (it may be a legal issue within one country but seldom carries universally to all other countries in the world). Ultimately, differences in "sustainable" practices can create dilemmas for businesses. Understanding the nature of these dilemmas and deciding the course of action to pursue when confronted with them is a central theme in this chapter. We blend a lot of business ethics with corporate social responsibility and sustainability issues to capture a global understanding of the issues around the world.

globalEDGE ONLINE COURSE MODULES

globalEDGE™ has a series of interactive "online course modules"—free educational learning opportunities for business people, policy officials, and students. These modules focus on issues that are important to international business. Each module includes a wealth of content, a case study or anecdotes, glossary of terms, questions to consider, and a list of references. See more at **globaledge.msu.edu/reference-desk/online-course-modules.** The combination of the textbook and the globalEDGE™ online course modules serves as an excellent resource that you can use to prepare for NASBITE's Certified Global Business Professional Credential. Achieving the industry-leading CGBP credential ensures that employees are able to practice global business at the professional level—including ethics, corporate social responsibility, and sustainability—required in today's competitive global environment. View the questions in the modules as a test of your readiness to achieve the CGBP credential.

These are not easy issues to capture, understand, or even buy into at all times. For example, we know that some toy manufacturers have been violating safety regulations for decades, and many companies will likewise continue to do so in the future across all product and industry categories. For the toy industry specifically, time will tell, assuming we can track the ingredients in the materials being used to make toys. What we do know is that about a third of the toys that are exported out of China are often tainted with heavy metals above the norm. Unfortunately, it is not illegal to use lead, for example, in plastics at this time. It is an ethical issue and perhaps also a sustainability issue—and usually a voluntary one—that some companies tackle and others choose to sidestep. The obvious reason some companies take shortcuts is simple math or capitalism—the large size of market opportunities in the toy industry. A basic question then is: Can it be considered unethical to manufacture toys that include heavy metals that are bad for children to ingest and come in contact with when using the toys in their proper way? What about corporate social responsibility among a country's companies or the companies' sustainable business practices?

The sustainability dynamics between a country and a company is illustrated in the opening case on Ericsson and Sweden. Since the ratification by 193 countries in September 2015 of the United Nations' Sustainable Development Goals (SDGs), Sweden has performed the best of all countries on the 17 SDGs and accompanying 169 measures. Meanwhile, Ericsson ranked number 21 in the world in the Top 100 Most Sustainable Corporations, and is the top-ranked company in Sweden on incorporating sustainability into its strategies. Basically, Sweden provides a superb infrastructure and resources for companies like Ericsson to implement sustainability practices. This is a huge difference compared to China and its many toy companies, which operate in less than ideal situations, polluting the environment and also using heavy metals like lead—which are forbidden in the Unites States and many other countries—to produce toys for the international marketplace.

The core starting point for this chapter is ethics. Ethics serves as the foundation for what people do or do not do, and ultimately ethical behavior of employees results in corporate social responsibility and sustainability practices engaged in by the company. Companies' involvement in corporate social responsibility practices and sustainability initiatives can be traced to the ethical foundation of its employees and other stakeholders, such as customers, shareholders, suppliers, regulators, and communities.[1] *Ethics* refers to accepted principles of right or wrong that govern the conduct of a person, the members of a profession, or the actions of an organization. **Business ethics** are the accepted principles of right and wrong governing the conduct of businesspeople, and an **ethical strategy** is a strategy, or course of action, that does not violate these accepted principles.

Broadly, as a start, we look at how ethical issues should be incorporated into decision making in an international business. We also review the reasons for poor ethical decision making and discuss different philosophical approaches to business ethics. Then, using the ethical decision-making process as our platform, we present a series of illustrations via two Management Focus boxes related to Volkswagen and Stora Enso. The chapter closes by reviewing the different processes that managers can adopt to make sure that ethical considerations are incorporated into decision making in international business and how these decisions filter into corporate social responsibility and sustainability efforts.

Ethics and International Business

LO5-1

Understand the ethical, corporate social responsibility, and sustainability issues faced by international businesses

Many of the ethical issues in international business are rooted in differences in political systems, laws, economic development, and culture across countries. What is considered normal practice in one nation may be considered unethical in another. Also, what is illegal in one country may even be normal ethical business practice in another. There are significant reasons why countries and these country-level differences exist—otherwise, we could just have a one-world mentality, as China does with its "One-China Policy" (i.e., a policy stating there is only one country of China, despite the fact there are two governments with

China in its name: the People's Republic of China, what is commonly referred to as China; and the Republic of China, which is commonly referred to as Taiwan). The One-China Policy has not been universally adopted around the world and, likewise, a one-world policy is unlikely to happen. Consequently, we will have differences in political systems, laws, economic development, and culture across the globe's 195 countries.

The unique complexities of legal and ethical differences, in particular, make it incredibly difficult to come up with global standards for ethics, corporate social responsibility, and sustainability. As we discussed in the opening case on Ericsson and Sweden, the United Nations did have its 193-member nations ratify the Sustainable Development Goals in 2015, but they are far from being achieved (although the goal is set to be met by 2030). Instead, managers in multinational corporations need to be particularly sensitive to these systematic country-level differences when they do business throughout the world. Many businesspeople try to advocate or even enforce their home country view on companies in other countries without much thinking about the implications for the relationship. In the international business setting, the most common ethical issues involve employment practices, human rights, environmental regulations, corruption, and the moral obligation of multinational corporations. We will discuss each.

EMPLOYMENT PRACTICES

When work conditions in another country (host nation) are inferior to those in a multinational corporation's home nation, which standards should be applied? Those of the home nation, those of the host nation, or something in between? While few would suggest that pay and work conditions should be the same across nations, how different can they be before we find it to be unacceptable? For example, while 12-hour workdays, extremely low pay, and a failure to protect workers against toxic chemicals may be common in some less developed and so-called emerging nations, does this mean that it is okay for a multinational company to tolerate such working conditions in its subsidiaries or to condone it by using local subcontractors in those countries? Without taking into account the potential financial implications, it would be easy to simply say that every company should be as ethical, socially responsible, and sustainable as its home-country environment dictates. But it's not really that simple.

Some time ago, Nike found itself in the center of a storm of protests when news reports revealed that working conditions at many of its subcontractors were poor. A *48 Hours* report on CBS painted a picture of young women who worked with toxic materials six days a week in poor conditions for only 20 cents an hour at a Vietnamese subcontractor. The report also stated that a living wage in Vietnam was at least $3 a day, an income that could not be achieved at the subcontractor without working substantial overtime. Nike and its subcontractors were not breaking any laws, but questions were raised about the ethics of using "sweatshop labor" to make what were essentially fashion accessories. It may have been legal, but was it ethical to use subcontractors who, by developed-nation standards, clearly exploited their workforce? Nike's critics thought not, and the company found itself the focus of a wave of demonstrations and consumer boycotts. These exposés surrounding Nike's use of subcontractors forced the company to reexamine its policies. Realizing that even though it was breaking no law, its subcontracting policies were perceived as unethical, Nike's management established a code of conduct for its subcontractors and instituted annual monitoring by independent auditors of all subcontractors.[2]

As the Nike case demonstrates, a strong argument can be made that it is not appropriate for a multinational firm to tolerate poor working conditions in its foreign operations or those of subcontractors. However, this still leaves unanswered the question of which standards should be applied. We shall return to and consider this issue in more detail later in the chapter. For now, note that establishing minimal acceptable standards that safeguard the basic rights and dignity of employees, auditing foreign subsidiaries and subcontractors on a regular basis to make sure those standards are met, and taking corrective action if they are not up to standards are a good way to guard against ethical abuses. For another example of problems with working practices among suppliers, read the accompanying Management Focus, which looks at Volkswagen and the company's staggering public debacle regarding software used to unethically, and in many cases illegally, lower the output data for air polluting emissions.

HUMAN RIGHTS

Basic human rights still are not respected in a large number of nations, and several historical and current examples exist to illustrate this point. Rights taken for granted in developed nations, such as freedom of association, freedom of speech, freedom of assembly, freedom of movement, and freedom from political repression, for example, are not universally accepted worldwide (see Chapter 2 for details). One of the most obvious historical examples was South Africa during the days of white rule and apartheid, which did not end until 1994. This may seem like a long time ago, but the effects of the old system still linger to this day. Also, in many countries today we see an increase in authoritarian populists who are attacking human rights principles and fueling distrust of democratic institutions.

South Africa represents an example that most people can relate to, remember, or at least know about, and is relatively easy to understand (compared with authoritarian populist politicians infringing on human rights). The apartheid system denied basic political rights to the majority nonwhite population of South Africa, mandated segregation between whites and nonwhites, reserved certain occupations exclusively for whites, and prohibited blacks from being placed in positions where they would manage whites. Despite the odious nature of this system, businesses from developed nations operated in South Africa for decades before changes started happening. In the decade prior to apartheid's abolishment, however, many questioned the ethics of doing so. They argued that inward investment by foreign multinationals supported the repressive apartheid regime, at least indirectly, by boosting the South African economy. Thankfully, several businesses started to change their policies in the 1990s and 2000s.[3] Gearing up for the 2030s and beyond, the assumption is that most businesses will follow the idea of, for example, the United Nation's all-encompassing Sustainable Development Goals 2030 (established in September 2015). In doing so, more and more companies are now using ethical behavior as a core philosophy when competing for work.

General Motors, which had significant activities in South Africa, was at the forefront of this trend. GM adopted what came to be called the *Sullivan principles*, named after Leon Sullivan, an African American Baptist minister who later became a member of GM's board of directors. Sullivan argued that it was ethically justified for GM to operate in South Africa so long as two conditions were fulfilled. First, the company should not obey the apartheid laws in its own South African operations (a form of passive resistance). Second, the company should do everything within its power to promote the abolition of apartheid laws. As a practical matter, Sullivan's principles ultimately became widely adopted by U.S. firms operating in South Africa. The beginning of the end of apartheid, we think, was when these foreign companies, like GM, violated the South African apartheid laws and the government of South Africa did not take any action against the companies. Clearly, South Africa did not want to antagonize important foreign investors, which then led to more and more foreign companies operating in the country choosing to disobey the apartheid laws.

After 10 years, Leon Sullivan concluded that simply following the two principles was not sufficient to break down the apartheid regime and that American companies, even those adhering to his principles, could not ethically justify their continued presence in South Africa. Over the next few years, numerous companies divested their South African operations, including Exxon, General Motors, IBM, and Xerox. At the same time, many state pension funds signaled they would no longer hold stock in companies that did

"Emissionsgate" at Volkswagen

Volkswagen, often abbreviated as VW, is a German automaker founded by the German Labor Front. The company is headquartered in Wolfsburg. It is the flagship marquee of the Volkswagen Group and, for the first time ever, became the top automaker in the world in 2017 and has maintained that number one position. Volkswagen said it delivered 10.8 million vehicles worldwide, while the nearest competitors Renault Nissan Mitsubishi (10.3 million) and Toyota (10.3 million) had very similar global sales, some 500,000 units below VW (with General Motors following just behind, but with strong sales in China).

To go along with its car numbers, VW had revenue of about $129 billion for these vehicles and an employee workforce of some 630,000 people. These staggering numbers and the ranking as the top automobile manufacturer in the world came at the same time Volkswagen was facing perhaps the biggest challenge in its 80-year history (the company was founded in 1937).

Sometimes referred to as "emissionsgate" or "dieselgate," the Volkswagen emissions scandal began in September 2015 when the U.S. Environmental Protection Agency (EPA) issued a notice of violation of the Clean Air Act to the German automaker. EPA is an agency of the U.S. federal government that was created to protect human health and the environment by writing and enforcing regulations based on laws passed by the U.S. Congress. The EPA has been around since 1970, although the Trump administration has proposed a series of more than 40 cuts to the EPA (slashing the EPA workforce by more than 3,000 people and $2 billion in funding).

In a rather astonishing finding, the EPA determined that Volkswagen had intentionally programmed engines to activate emissions controls only during lab testing. The unethical programming by VW caused the vehicles' nitrogen oxide output—which is the most relevant factor for air pollution standards—to register at lower levels to meet strict U.S. standards during the crucial laboratory regulatory testing. In reality, the vehicles emitted up to 40 times more NO_x on the streets. Volkswagen used this unethical and very sophisticated computer programming in about 11 million cars worldwide, out of which 500,000 vehicles were in use in the United States (for model years 2009–2015).

VW went to great lengths to make this work. The software in the cars sensed when the car was being tested in a regulatory lab, and then the software automatically activated equipment in the vehicle that reduced emissions.

Raymond Boyd/Michael Ochs Archives/Getty Images

Think about that in terms of the decision making that had to go into making this unethical choice! Additionally, the software turned the car's equipment down during regular driving on the streets or highways, resulting in increasing emissions way above legal limits. The only reasoning for doing this is to save fuel or to improve the car's torque and acceleration. Thus, not only were the emissions off, and unethically adjusted, the car's performance statistics were also affected in a positive way—which, obviously, can be seen as another unethical decision or by-product of the emissions software.

The software was modified to adjust components such as catalytic converters or valves that were used to recycle a portion of the exhaust gases. These are the components that are meant to reduce emissions of nitrogen oxide, an air pollutant that can cause emphysema, bronchitis, and several other respiratory diseases. The severity of this air pollution resulted in a $4.3 billion settlement with U.S. regulators. VW also agreed to sweeping reforms, new audits, and oversight by an independent monitor for three years. Internally, VW disciplined dozens of engineers, which is interesting because it at least implies that the top-level managers were not aware of the software installation and unethical use.

Sources: Nathan Bomey, "Volkswagen Passes Toyota as World's Largest Automaker Despite Scandal," *USA Today*, January 30, 2017; Bertel Schmitt, "It's Official: Volkswagen Is World's Largest Automaker in 2016. Or Maybe Toyota," *Forbes*, January 30, 2017; Rob Davis, "Here Are 42 of President Donald Trump's Planned EPA Budget Cuts," *The Oregonian*, March 2, 2017; "VW Expects to Sanction More Employees in Emissions Scandal: Chairman," *CNBC*, March 7, 2017.

business in South Africa, which helped persuade several companies to divest their South African operations. These divestments, coupled with the imposition of economic sanctions from the United States and other governments, contributed to the abandonment of white minority rule and apartheid in South Africa and the introduction of democratic elections in 1994. This is when Nelson Mandela was elected president of South Africa, after having served 27 years in prison for conspiracy and sabotage to overthrow the white government of South Africa (Mandela won the Nobel Peace Prize in 1993 and passed away in 2013). Ultimately, adopting an ethical stance by these large multinational corporations was argued to have helped improve human rights in South Africa.[4]

Although change has come in South Africa, many repressive regimes still exist in the world. In fact, according to the Freedom House, only about 45 percent of the world's population of 7.6 billion people are living in free democratic countries (30 percent are partly free and 25 percent are not free). People in countries that are not considered free by the Freedom House typically face severe consequences if they try to exercise their most basic rights, such as expressing their views, assembling peacefully, and organizing independently of the countries in which they live.

This lack of universal freedom in many countries begs the question: Is it ethical for multinational corporations to do business in these repressive countries? As an answer, it is often argued that inward investment by a multinational can be a force for economic, political, and social progress that ultimately improves the rights of people in repressive regimes. This position was first discussed in Chapter 2, when we noted that economic progress in a nation could create pressure for democratization. In general, this belief suggests that it is ethical for a multinational to do business in nations that lack the democratic structures and human rights records of developed nations. Investment in China, for example, is frequently justified on the grounds that although China's human rights record is often questioned by human rights groups and although the country is not a democracy, continuing inward investment will help boost economic growth and raise living standards. These developments will ultimately create pressures from the Chinese people for more participatory government, political pluralism, and freedom of expression and speech.

There is a limit to this argument. As in the case of South Africa, some regimes are so repressive that investment cannot be justified on ethical grounds. Another example would be Myanmar (formerly known as Burma). Ruled by a military dictatorship since 1962, Myanmar has one of the worst human rights records in the world. Beginning in the mid-1990s, many companies exited Myanmar, judging the human rights violations to be so extreme that doing business there could not be justified on ethical grounds. However, a cynic might note that Myanmar has a small economy and that divestment carries no great economic penalty for firms, unlike, for example, divestment from China. Interestingly, after decades of pressure from the international community, the military government of Myanmar finally acquiesced and allowed limited democratic elections to be held, resulting in the country being rated as "partly free" today according to the Freedom House.

ENVIRONMENTAL POLLUTION

Ethics, social responsibility, and sustainability issues can arise when environmental regulations in host nations are inferior to those in the home nation. Ethics drive what people decide to do, and corporate social responsibility and sustainability drive what companies ultimately decide to do. Many developed nations have substantial regulations governing the emission of pollutants, the dumping of toxic chemicals, the use of toxic materials in the workplace, and so on. Those regulations are often lacking in developing nations, and, according to critics, the result can be higher levels of pollution from the operations of multinationals than would be allowed at home.

From a practical and moneymaking standpoint, we can ask: Should a multinational corporation feel free to pollute in a developing nation? The answer seems simplistic: To do so

People wearing breathing masks at Tian'anmen Square in China's capital city, Beijing.

Kevin Frayer/Getty Images News/Getty Images

hardly seems ethical. Is there a danger that amoral management might move production to a developing nation precisely because costly pollution controls are not required and the company is, therefore, free to despoil the environment and perhaps endanger local people in its quest to lower production costs and gain a competitive advantage? What is the right and moral thing to do in such circumstances: pollute to gain an economic advantage or make sure that foreign subsidiaries adhere to common standards regarding pollution controls?

These questions take on added importance because some parts of the environment are a public good that no one owns but anyone can despoil. Even so, many companies answer illogically and say that some degree of pollution is acceptable. If the issue becomes degree of pollution instead of preventing as much pollution as possible, then the strategic decision has been turned around—everyone will start arguing about the degree that is acceptable instead of what to do to prevent pollution in the first place. The problematic part of this argument and equation for measuring pollution is that no one owns the atmosphere or the oceans, but polluting both, no matter where the pollution originates, harms all.[5] In such cases, a phenomenon known as the *tragedy of the commons* becomes applicable. The tragedy of the commons occurs when a resource held in common by all but owned by no one is overused by individuals, resulting in its degradation. The phenomenon was first named by Garrett Hardin when describing a particular problem in sixteenth-century England. Large open areas, called commons, were free for all to use as pasture. The poor put out livestock on these commons and supplemented their meager incomes. It was advantageous for each to put out more and more livestock, but the social consequence was far more livestock than the commons could handle. The result was overgrazing, degradation of the commons, and the loss of this much-needed supplement.[6]

Corporations can contribute to the *global tragedy of the commons* by moving production to locations where they are free to pump pollutants into the atmosphere or dump them in oceans or rivers, thereby harming these valuable global commons. While such action may be legal, is it ethical? Again, such actions seem to violate basic societal notions of ethics and corporate social responsibility. This issue is taking on greater importance as concerns about human-induced global warming move to center stage. Most climate scientists argue that human industrial and commercial activity is increasing the amount of carbon dioxide in the atmosphere; carbon dioxide is a greenhouse gas, which reflects heat back to the earth's surface, warming the globe; and as a result, the average temperature of the earth is increasing. The accumulated scientific evidence from numerous databases supports this argument.[7] Consequently, societies around the world are starting to restrict the amount of carbon dioxide that can be emitted into the atmosphere as a by-product of industrial and commercial activity. However, regulations differ from nation to nation. Given this, is it ethical for a company to try to escape tight emission limits by moving production to a country with lax regulations, when doing so will contribute to global warming? Again, many would argue that doing so violates basic ethical principles.

CORRUPTION

As noted in Chapter 2, corruption has been a problem in almost every society in history, and it continues to be one today.[8] There always have been and always will be corrupt government officials. International businesses can gain and have gained economic advantages by making payments to those officials. A classic example concerns a well-publicized incident involving Carl Kotchian, then president of Lockheed. He made a $12.6 million payment to Japanese agents and government officials to secure a large order for Lockheed's TriStar jet from Nippon Air. When the payments were discovered, U.S. officials charged Lockheed with falsification of its records and tax violations. Although such payments were supposed to be an accepted business practice in Japan (they might be viewed as an exceptionally lavish form of gift giving), the revelations created a scandal there, too. The government ministers in question were criminally charged, one committed suicide, the government fell in disgrace, and the Japanese people were outraged. Apparently, such a payment was not an accepted way of doing business in Japan! The payment was nothing more than a bribe, paid to corrupt officials, to secure a large order that might otherwise have gone to another manufacturer, such as Boeing. Kotchian clearly engaged in unethical behavior—and to argue that the payment was an "acceptable form of doing business in Japan" was self-serving and incorrect.

The Lockheed case was the impetus for the **Foreign Corrupt Practices Act (FCPA)** in the United States, discussed in Chapter 2. The act outlawed paying of bribes to foreign government officials to gain business, and this was the case even if other countries' companies could do it. Some U.S. businesses immediately objected that the act would put U.S. firms at a competitive disadvantage (there is no evidence that has occurred).[9] The act was subsequently amended to allow for "facilitating payments." Sometimes known as *speed money* or *grease payments*, facilitating payments are *not* payments to secure contracts that would not otherwise be secured, nor are they payments to obtain exclusive preferential treatment. Rather they are payments to ensure receiving the standard treatment that a business ought to receive from a foreign government but might not due to the obstruction of a foreign official.

The trade and finance ministers from the member states of the Organization for Economic Co-operation and Development (OECD) later on followed the U.S. lead and adopted the **Convention on Combating Bribery of Foreign Public Officials in International Business Transactions**.[10] The convention, which went into force in 1999, obliges member states and other signatories to make the bribery of foreign public officials a criminal offense. The convention excludes facilitating payments made to expedite routine government action.

While facilitating payments, or *speed money*, are excluded from both the Foreign Corrupt Practices Act and the OECD convention on bribery, the ethical implications of making such payments are unclear. From a practical standpoint, giving bribes might be the price that must be paid to do a greater good (assuming the investment creates jobs and assuming the practice is not illegal). Several economists advocate this reasoning, suggesting that in the context of pervasive and cumbersome regulations in developing countries, corruption may improve efficiency and help growth! These economists theorize that in a country where preexisting political structures distort or limit the workings of the market mechanism, corruption in the form of black-marketeering, smuggling, and side payments to government bureaucrats to "speed up" approval for business investments may enhance welfare.[11] Arguments such as this persuaded the U.S. Congress to exempt facilitating payments from the FCPA.

In contrast, other economists have argued that corruption reduces the returns on business investment and leads to low economic growth.[12] In a country where corruption is common, unproductive bureaucrats who demand side payments for granting the enterprise permission to operate may siphon off the profits from a business activity. This reduces businesses' incentive to invest and may retard a country's economic growth rate. One study of the connection between corruption and economic growth in 70 countries found that corruption had a significant negative impact on a country's growth rate.[13] Another study found that firms that paid more in bribes are likely to spend more, not less, management time with bureaucrats negotiating regulations and that this tended to raise the costs of the firm.[14]

Consequently, many multinationals have adopted a zero-tolerance policy. For example, the large oil multinational BP has a zero-tolerance approach toward facilitating payments. Other corporations have a more nuanced approach. Dow Corning used to formally state a few years ago in its Code of Conduct that "in countries where local business practice dictates such [facilitating] payments and there is no alternative, facilitating payments are to be for the minimum amount necessary and must be accurately documented and recorded."[15] This statement recognized that business practices and customs differ from country to country. At the same time, Dow Corning allowed for facilitating payments when "there is no alternative," although they were also stated to be strongly discouraged. More recently, the latest version of Dow Corning's Code of Conduct has removed the section on "international business guidelines" altogether, so our assumption has to be that the company is taking a stronger zero-tolerance approach.

At the same time, as with many companies, Dow Corning may have realized that the nuances between a bribe and a facilitating payment are unclear. Many U.S. companies have sustained FCPA violations due to facilitating payments that were made but did not fall within the general rules allowing such payments. For example, global freight forwarder Con-way paid a $300,000 penalty for making hundreds of what could be considered small payments to various customs officials in the Philippines. In total, Con-way distributed some $244,000 to these officials who were induced to violate customs regulations, settle disputes, and not enforce fines for administrative violations.[16]

TEST PREP

Use SmartBook to help retain what you have learned. Access your Instructor's Connect course to check out SmartBook or go to **learnsmartadvantage.com** for help.

LO5-2

Recognize an ethical, corporate social responsibility, and/or sustainability dilemma.

Ethical Dilemmas

The ethical obligations of a multinational corporation toward employment conditions, human rights, corruption, and environmental pollution are not always clear-cut. However, what is becoming clear-cut is that managers and their companies are feeling more of the marketplace pressures from customers and other stakeholders to be transparent in their ethical decision making. At the same time, there is no universal worldwide agreement about what constitutes accepted ethical principles. From an international business perspective, some argue that what is ethical depends on one's cultural perspective.[17] In the United States, it is considered acceptable to execute murderers, but in many cultures, this type of punishment is not acceptable—execution is viewed as an affront to human dignity, and the death penalty is outlawed. Many Americans find this attitude strange, but, for example, many Europeans find the American approach barbaric. For a more business-oriented example, consider the practice of "gift giving" between the parties to a business negotiation. While this is considered right and proper behavior in many Asian cultures, some Westerners view the practice as a form of bribery and therefore unethical, particularly if the gifts are substantial.

International managers often confront very real ethical dilemmas where the appropriate course of action is not clear. For example, imagine that a visiting American executive finds that a foreign subsidiary in a poor nation has hired a 12-year-old girl to work on a factory floor. Appalled to find that the subsidiary is using child labor in direct violation of the company's own ethical code, the American instructs the local manager to replace the child with an adult. The local manager dutifully complies. The girl, an orphan, who is the only breadwinner for herself and her six-year-old brother, is unable to find another job, so in desperation she turns to prostitution. Two years later, she dies of AIDS. Had the visiting American understood the gravity of the girl's situation, would he still have requested her replacement? Would it have been better to stick with the status quo and allow the girl to continue working? Probably not, because that would have violated the reasonable prohibition against child labor found in the company's own ethical code. What then would have been the right thing to do? What was the obligation of the executive given this ethical dilemma?

A young girl making cigarettes in Bagan, Myanmar.
Angela N Perryman/Shutterstock

There are no easy answers to these questions. That is the nature of **ethical dilemmas**—situations in which none of the available alternatives seems ethically acceptable.[18] In this case, employing child labor was not acceptable, but given that she was employed, neither was denying the child her only source of income. What this American executive needs, what all managers need, is a moral compass, or perhaps an ethical algorithm, to guide them through such an ethical dilemma to find an acceptable solution. Later, we will outline what such a moral compass, or ethical algorithm, might look like. For now, it is enough to note that ethical dilemmas exist because many real-world decisions are complex; difficult to frame; and involve first-, second-, and third-order consequences that are hard to quantify. Doing the right thing, or even knowing what the right thing might be, is often far from easy.[19]

Roots of Unethical Behavior

Examples are plentiful of international managers behaving in a manner that might be judged unethical in an international business setting. Why do managers behave in an unethical manner? There is no simple answer to this question because the causes are complex, but some generalizations can be made and these issues are rooted in six determinants of ethical behavior: personal ethics, decision-making processes, organizational culture, unrealistic performance goals, leadership, and societal culture (see Figure 5.1).[20]

PERSONAL ETHICS

Societal business ethics are not divorced from *personal ethics*, which are the generally accepted principles of right and wrong governing the conduct of individuals. Personal ethics have an effect on business ethics, which ultimately, as we will see in the Focus on Managerial Implications section of this chapter, have an effect on a company's socially responsible practices and sustainability activities. As individuals, we are typically taught that it is wrong to lie and cheat—it is unethical—and that it is right to behave with integrity and honor and to stand up for what we believe to be right and true. This is generally true across societies. The personal ethical code that guides our behavior comes from a number of sources, including our parents, our schools, our religion, and the media. Our personal ethical code exerts a profound influence on the way we behave as businesspeople. An individual with a strong sense of personal ethics is less likely to behave in an unethical manner in

TEST PREP

Use SmartBook to help retain what you have learned. Access your Instructor's Connect course to check out SmartBook or go to **learnsmartadvantage.com** for help.

LO5-3

Identify the causes of unethical behavior by managers as they relate to business, corporate social responsibility, or sustainability.

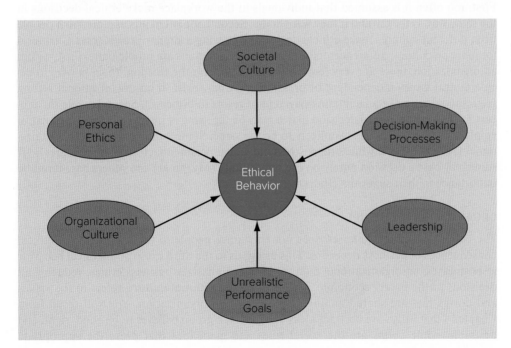

FIGURE 5.1

Determinants of ethical behavior.

a business setting. It follows that the first step to establishing a strong sense of business ethics is for a society to emphasize strong personal ethics.

Home-country managers working abroad in multinational firms (expatriate managers) may experience more than the usual degree of pressure to violate their personal ethics. They are away from their ordinary social context and supporting culture, and they are psychologically and geographically distant from the parent company. They may be based in a culture that does not place the same value on ethical norms important in the manager's home country, and they may be surrounded by local employees who have less rigorous ethical standards. The parent company may pressure expatriate managers to meet unrealistic goals that can only be fulfilled by cutting corners or acting unethically. For example, to meet centrally mandated performance goals, expatriate managers might give bribes to win contracts or might implement working conditions and environmental controls that are below minimally acceptable standards. Local managers might encourage the expatriate to adopt such behavior. Due to its geographic distance, the parent company may be unable to see how expatriate managers are meeting goals or may choose not to see how they are doing so, allowing such behavior to flourish and persist.

DECISION-MAKING PROCESSES

Several studies of unethical behavior in a business setting have concluded that businesspeople sometimes do not realize they are behaving unethically, primarily because they simply fail to ask, "Is this decision or action ethical?"[21] Instead, they apply a straightforward business calculus to what they perceive to be a business decision, forgetting that the decision may also have an important ethical dimension. The fault lies in processes that do not incorporate ethical considerations into business decision making. This may have been the case at Nike when managers originally made subcontracting decisions. Those decisions were probably made based on good economic logic. Subcontractors were probably chosen based on business variables such as cost, delivery, and product quality, but the key managers simply failed to ask, "How does this subcontractor treat its workforce?" If they thought about the question at all, they probably reasoned that it was the subcontractor's concern, not theirs.

To improve ethical decision making in a multinational firm, the best starting point is to better understand how individuals make decisions that can be considered ethical or unethical in an organizational environment.[22] Two assumptions must be taken into account. First, too often it is assumed that individuals in the workplace make ethical decisions in the same way as they would if they were home. Second, too often it is assumed that people from different cultures make ethical decisions following a similar process (see Chapter 4 for more on cultural differences). Both of these assumptions are problematic. First, within an organization, there are very few individuals who have the freedom (e.g., power) to decide ethical issues independent of pressures that may exist in an organizational setting (e.g., should we make a facilitating payment or resort to bribery?). Second, while the process for making an ethical decision may largely be the same in many countries, the relative emphasis on certain issues is unlikely to be the same. Some cultures may stress organizational factors (Japan), while others stress individual personal factors (United States), yet some may base a decision purely on the opportunity (Myanmar) and others base it on the importance to their superiors (India).

ORGANIZATIONAL CULTURE

The culture in some businesses does not encourage people to think through the ethical consequences of business decisions. This brings us to the third cause of unethical behavior in businesses: an organizational culture that deemphasizes business ethics, reducing all decisions to the purely economic. The term **organizational culture** refers to the values and norms that are shared among employees of an organization. You will recall from Chapter 4 that *values* are abstract ideas about what a group believes to be good, right, and desirable, while *norms* are the social rules and guidelines that prescribe appropriate behavior in particular situations. Just as societies have cultures, so do business organizations, as we discussed in Chapter 4. Together, values and norms shape the culture of a business organization, and that culture has an important influence on the ethics of business decision making.

For example, paying bribes to secure business contracts was long viewed as an acceptable way of doing business within certain companies. It was, in the words of an investigator of a case against Daimler, "standard business practice" that permeated much of the organization, including departments such as auditing and finance that were supposed to detect and halt such behavior. It can be argued that such a widespread practice could have persisted only if the values and norms of the organization implicitly approved of paying bribes to secure business.

UNREALISTIC PERFORMANCE GOALS

The fourth cause of unethical behavior has already been hinted at: the pressure from the parent company to meet unrealistic performance goals that can be attained only by cutting corners or acting in an unethical manner. In these cases, bribery may be viewed as a way to hit challenging performance goals. The combination of an organizational culture that legitimizes unethical behavior, or at least turns a blind eye to such behavior, and unrealistic performance goals may be particularly toxic. In such circumstances, there is a greater than average probability that managers will violate their own personal ethics and engage in unethical behavior. Conversely, an organization's culture can do just the opposite and reinforce the need for ethical behavior. At Hewlett-Packard, for example, Bill Hewlett and David Packard, the company's founders, propagated a set of values known as The HP Way. These values, which shape the way business is conducted both within and by the corporation, have an important ethical component. Among other things, they stress the need for confidence in and respect for people, open communication, and concern for the individual employee.

LEADERSHIP

The Hewlett-Packard example suggests a fifth root cause of unethical behavior: leadership. Leaders help establish the culture of an organization, and they set the example, rules, and guidelines that others follow as well as the structure and processes for operating both strategically and in daily operations. Employees often operate and work within a defined structure with a mindset very much similar to the overall culture of the organization that employs them.

Additionally, employees in business often take their cue from business leaders, and if those leaders do not behave in an ethical manner, the employees might not either. It is not just what leaders say that matters but what they do or do not do. What message, then, did the leaders at Daimler send about corrupt practices? Presumably, they did very little to discourage them and may have encouraged such behavior.

SOCIETAL CULTURE

Societal culture may well have an impact on the propensity of people and organizations to behave in an unethical manner. One study of 2,700 firms in 24 countries found that there were significant differences among the ethical policies of firms headquartered in different countries.[23] Using Hofstede's dimensions of social culture (see Chapter 4), the study found that enterprises headquartered in cultures where individualism and uncertainty avoidance are strong were more likely to emphasize the importance of behaving ethically than firms headquartered in cultures where masculinity and power distance are important cultural attributes. Such analysis suggests that enterprises headquartered in a country such as Russia, which scores high on masculinity and power distance measures, and where corruption is endemic, are more likely to engage in unethical behavior than enterprises headquartered in Scandinavia.

 TEST PREP

Use SmartBook to help retain what you have learned. Access your Instructor's Connect course to check out SmartBook or go to **learnsmartadvantage.com** for help.

Philosophical Approaches to Ethics

In this section, we look at several different philosophical approaches to business ethics in the global marketplace. Basically, all individuals adopt a process for making ethical (or unethical) decisions. This process is based on their personal philosophical approach to ethics—that is, the underlying moral fabric of the individual.

We begin with what can best be described as straw men, which either deny the value of business ethics or apply the concept in a very unsatisfactory way. Having discussed and, we hope you agree, dismissed the straw men, we move on to consider approaches that are favored by most moral philosophers and form the basis for current models of ethical behavior in international businesses.

STRAW MEN

The straw men approach to business ethics is raised by scholars primarily to demonstrate that they offer inappropriate guidelines for ethical decision making in a multinational enterprise. Four such approaches to business ethics are commonly discussed in the literature. These approaches can be characterized as the Friedman doctrine, cultural relativism, the righteous moralist, and the naive immoralist. All these approaches have some inherent value, but all are unsatisfactory in important ways. Nevertheless, sometimes companies adopt these approaches.

The Friedman Doctrine

The Nobel Prize–winning economist Milton Friedman wrote an article in *The New York Times* in 1970 that has since become a classic straw man example that business ethics scholars outline only to then tear down.[24] Friedman's basic position is that "the social responsibility of business is to increase profits," so long as the company stays within the rules of law. He explicitly rejects the idea that businesses should undertake social expenditures beyond those mandated by the law and required for the efficient running of a business. For example, his arguments suggest that improving working conditions beyond the level required by the law *and* necessary to maximize employee productivity will reduce profits and is therefore not appropriate. His belief is that a firm should maximize its profits because that is the way to maximize the returns that accrue to the owners of the firm, its shareholders. If the shareholders then wish to use the proceeds to make social investments, that is their right, according to Friedman, but managers of the firm should not make that decision for them.

Although Friedman is talking about social responsibility and "ethical custom," rather than business ethics per se, many business ethics scholars equate social responsibility with ethical behavior and thus believe Friedman is also arguing against business ethics. However, the assumption that Friedman is arguing against ethics is not quite true, for Friedman does argue that there is only one social responsibility of business: to increase the profitability of the enterprise so long as it stays within the law, which is taken to mean that it engages in open and free competition without deception or fraud.[25]

> There is one and only one social responsibility of business—to use its resources and engage in activities designed to increase its profits so long as it stays within the rules of the game, which is to say that it engages in open and free competition without deception or fraud.[26]

In other words, Friedman argues that businesses should behave in a socially responsible manner, according to ethical custom and without deception and fraud.

Critics charge that Friedman's arguments break down under examination. This is particularly true in international business, where the "rules of the game" are not well established and differ from country to country. Consider again the case of sweatshop labor. Child labor may not be against the law in a developing nation, and maximizing productivity may not require that a multinational firm stop using child labor in that country, but it is still immoral to use child labor because the practice conflicts with widely held views about what is the right and proper thing to do. Similarly, there may be no rules against pollution in a less developed nation and spending money on pollution control may reduce the profit rate of the firm, but generalized notions of morality would hold that it is still unethical to dump toxic pollutants into rivers or foul the air with gas releases. In addition to the local consequences of such pollution, which may have serious health effects for the surrounding population, there is also a global consequence as pollutants degrade those two global commons so important to us all: the atmosphere and the oceans.

Cultural Relativism

Another straw man often raised by business ethics scholars is **cultural relativism**, which is the belief that ethics are nothing more than the reflection of a culture—all ethics are culturally determined—and that accordingly, a firm should adopt the ethics of the culture in which it is operating.[27] This approach is often summarized by the maxim *when in Rome, do as the Romans do.* As with Friedman's approach, cultural relativism does not stand up to a closer look. At its extreme, cultural relativism suggests that if a culture supports slavery, it is okay to use slave labor in a country. Clearly, it is not! Cultural relativism implicitly rejects the idea that universal notions of morality transcend different cultures, but as we argue later in the chapter, some universal notions of morality are found across cultures.

While dismissing cultural relativism in its most sweeping form, some ethicists argue there is residual value in this approach.[28] We agree. As we noted in Chapter 3, societal values and norms do vary from culture to culture, and customs do differ, so it might follow that certain business practices are ethical in one country but not another. Indeed, the facilitating payments allowed in the Foreign Corrupt Practices Act can be seen as an acknowledgment that in some countries, the payment of speed money to government officials is necessary to get business done, and, if not ethically desirable, it is at least ethically acceptable.

The Righteous Moralist

A **righteous moralist** claims that a multinational's home-country standards of ethics are the appropriate ones for companies to follow in foreign countries. This approach is typically associated with managers from developed nations. While this seems reasonable at first blush, the approach can create problems. Consider the following example: An American bank manager was sent to Italy and was appalled to learn that the local branch's accounting department recommended grossly underreporting the bank's profits for income tax purposes.[29] The manager insisted that the bank report its earnings accurately, American style. When he was called by the Italian tax department to the firm's tax hearing, he was told the firm owed three times as much tax as it had paid, reflecting the department's standard assumption that each firm underreports its earnings by two-thirds. Despite his protests, the new assessment stood. In this case, the righteous moralist has run into a problem caused by the prevailing cultural norms in the country where he was doing business. How should he respond? The righteous moralist would argue for maintaining the position, while a more pragmatic view might be that in this case, the right thing to do is to follow the prevailing cultural norms because there is a big penalty for not doing so.

The main criticism of the righteous moralist approach is that its proponents go too far. While there are some universal moral principles that should not be violated, it does not always follow that the appropriate thing to do is adopt home-country standards. For example, U.S. laws set down strict guidelines with regard to minimum wage and working conditions. Does this mean it is ethical to apply the same guidelines in a foreign country, paying people the same as they are paid in the United States, providing the same benefits and working conditions? Probably not, because doing so might nullify the reason for investing in that country and therefore deny locals the benefits of inward investment by the multinational. Clearly, a more nuanced approach is needed.

The Naive Immoralist

A **naive immoralist** asserts that if a manager of a multinational sees that firms from other nations are not following ethical norms in a host nation, that manager should not either. The classic example to illustrate the approach is known as the drug lord problem. In one variant of this problem, an American manager in Colombia routinely pays off the local drug lord to guarantee that her plant will not be bombed and that none of her employees will be kidnapped. The manager argues that such payments are ethically defensible because everyone is doing it.

The objection is twofold. First, to say that an action is ethically justified if everyone is doing it is not sufficient. If firms in a country routinely employ 12-year-olds and make them work 10-hour days, is it therefore ethically defensible to do the same? Obviously not, and the company does have a clear choice. It does not have to abide by local practices, and it can decide not to invest in a country where the practices are particularly odious. Second, the multinational must recognize that it does have the ability to change the prevailing practice in a country. It can use its power for a positive moral purpose. This is what BP is doing by adopting a zero-tolerance policy with regard to facilitating payments. BP is stating that the prevailing practice of making facilitating payments is ethically wrong, and it is incumbent upon the company to use its power to try to change the standard. While some might argue that such an approach smells of moral imperialism and a lack of cultural sensitivity, if it is consistent with standards in the global community, it may be ethically justified.

UTILITARIAN AND KANTIAN ETHICS

In contrast to the straw men just discussed, most moral philosophers see value in utilitarian and Kantian approaches to business ethics. These approaches were developed in the eighteenth and nineteenth centuries, and although they have been largely superseded by more modern approaches, they form part of the tradition on which newer approaches have been constructed.

The utilitarian approach to business ethics dates to philosophers such as David Hume (1711–1776), Jeremy Bentham (1748–1832), and John Stuart Mill (1806–1873). The **utilitarian approach to ethics** holds that the moral worth of actions or practices is determined by their consequences.[30] An action is judged desirable if it leads to the best possible balance of good consequences over bad consequences. Utilitarianism is committed to the maximization of good and the minimization of harm. Utilitarianism recognizes that actions have multiple consequences, some of which are good in a social sense and some of which are harmful. As a philosophy for business ethics, it focuses attention on the need to weigh carefully all the social benefits and costs of business activity and to pursue only those actions where the benefits outweigh the costs. The best decisions, from a utilitarian perspective, are those that produce the greatest good for the greatest number of people.

Many businesses have adopted specific tools such as cost-benefit analysis and risk assessment that are firmly rooted in a utilitarian philosophy. Managers often weigh the benefits and costs of an action before deciding whether to pursue it. An oil company considering drilling in the Alaskan wildlife preserve must weigh the economic benefits of increased oil production and the creation of jobs against the costs of environmental degradation in a fragile ecosystem. An agricultural biotechnology company such as Monsanto must decide whether the benefits of genetically modified crops that produce natural pesticides outweigh the risks. The benefits include increased crop yields and reduced need for chemical fertilizers. The risks include the possibility that Monsanto's insect-resistant crops might make matters worse over time if insects evolve a resistance to the natural pesticides engineered into Monsanto's plants, rendering the plants vulnerable to a new generation of superbugs.

The utilitarian philosophy does have some serious drawbacks as an approach to business ethics. One problem is measuring the benefits, costs, and risks of a course of action. In the case of an oil company considering drilling in Alaska, how does one measure the potential harm done to the region's ecosystem? The second problem with utilitarianism is that the philosophy omits the consideration of justice. The action that produces the greatest good for the greatest number of people may result in the unjustified treatment of a minority. Such action cannot be ethical, precisely because it is unjust. For example, suppose that in the interests of keeping down health insurance costs, the government decides to screen people for the HIV virus and deny insurance coverage to those who are HIV positive. By reducing health costs, such action might produce significant benefits for a large number of people, but the action is unjust because it discriminates unfairly against a minority.

Kantian ethics is based on the philosophy of Immanuel Kant (1724–1804). **Kantian ethics** holds that people should be treated as ends and never purely as *means* to the ends of others. People are not instruments, like a machine. People have dignity and need to be respected as such. Employing people in sweatshops, making them work long hours for low pay in poor working conditions, is a violation of ethics, according to Kantian philosophy, because it treats people as mere cogs in a machine and not as conscious moral beings that have dignity. Although contemporary moral philosophers tend to view Kant's ethical philosophy as incomplete—for example, his system has no place for moral emotions or sentiments such as sympathy or caring—the notion that people should be respected and treated with dignity resonates in the modern world.

RIGHTS THEORIES

Developed in the twentieth century, **rights theories** recognize that human beings have fundamental rights and privileges that transcend national boundaries and cultures. Rights establish a minimum level of morally acceptable behavior. One well-known definition of a fundamental right construes it as something that takes precedence over or "trumps" a collective good. Thus, we might say that the right to free speech is a fundamental right that takes precedence over all but the most compelling collective goals and overrides, for example, the interest of the state in civil harmony or moral consensus.[31] Moral theorists argue that fundamental human rights form the basis for the *moral compass* that managers should navigate by when making decisions that have an ethical component. More precisely, they should not pursue actions that violate these rights.

The notion that there are fundamental rights that transcend national borders and cultures was the underlying motivation for the United Nations **Universal Declaration of Human Rights**, adopted in 1948, which has been ratified by almost every country and lays down principles that should be adhered to irrespective of the culture in which one is doing business.[32] Echoing Kantian ethics, Article 1 of this declaration states

> All human beings are born free and equal in dignity and rights. They are endowed with reason and conscience and should act towards one another in a spirit of brotherhood.[33]

Article 23 of this declaration, which relates directly to employment, states:

1. Everyone has the right to work, to free choice of employment, to just and favorable conditions of work, and to protection against unemployment.
2. Everyone, without any discrimination, has the right to equal pay for equal work.
3. Everyone who works has the right to just and favorable remuneration ensuring for himself and his family an existence worthy of human dignity, and supplemented, if necessary, by other means of social protection.
4. Everyone has the right to form and to join trade unions for the protection of his interests.[34]

Clearly, the rights to "just and favorable conditions of work," "equal pay for equal work," and remuneration that ensures an "existence worthy of human dignity" embodied in Article 23 imply that it is unethical to employ child labor in sweatshop settings and pay less than subsistence wages, even if that happens to be common practice in some countries. These are fundamental human rights that transcend national borders.

It is important to note that along with *rights* come *obligations*. Because we have the right to free speech, we are also obligated to make sure that we respect the free speech of others. The notion that people have obligations is stated in Article 29 of the Universal Declaration of Human Rights:

1. Everyone has duties to the community in which alone the free and full development of his personality is possible.[35]

Within the framework of a theory of rights, certain people or institutions are obligated to provide benefits or services that secure the rights of others. Such obligations also fall on more than one class of moral agent (a *moral agent* is any person or institution that is capable of moral action such as a government or corporation).

For example, to escape the high costs of toxic waste disposal in the West, several firms shipped their waste in bulk to African nations, where it was disposed of at a much lower cost. At one time, five European ships unloaded toxic waste containing dangerous poisons in Nigeria. Workers wearing sandals and shorts unloaded the barrels for $2.50 a day and placed them in a dirt lot in a residential area. They were not told about the contents of the barrels.[36] Who bears the obligation for protecting the rights of workers and residents to safety in a case like this? According to rights theorists, the obligation rests not on the shoulders of one moral agent but on the shoulders of all moral agents whose actions might harm or contribute to the harm of the workers and residents. Thus, it was the obligation not just of the Nigerian government but also of the multinational firms that shipped the toxic waste to make sure it did no harm to residents and workers. In this case, both the government and the multinationals apparently failed to recognize their basic obligation to protect the fundamental human rights of others.

JUSTICE THEORIES

Justice theories focus on the attainment of a just distribution of economic goods and services. A **just distribution** is one that is considered fair and equitable. There is no one theory of justice, and several theories of justice conflict with each other in important ways.[37] Here, we focus on one particular theory of justice that is both very influential and has important ethical implications. The theory is attributed to philosopher John Rawls.[38] Rawls argues that all economic goods and services should be distributed equally except when an unequal distribution would work to everyone's advantage.

According to Rawls, valid principles of justice are those with which all persons would agree if they could freely and impartially consider the situation. Impartiality is guaranteed by a conceptual device that Rawls calls the *veil of ignorance*. Under the veil of ignorance, everyone is imagined to be ignorant of all of his or her particular characteristics, for example, race, sex, intelligence, nationality, family background, and special talents. Rawls then asks what system people would design under a veil of ignorance. Under these conditions, people would unanimously agree on two fundamental principles of justice.

The first principle is that each person is permitted the maximum amount of basic liberty compatible with a similar liberty for others. Rawls takes these to be political liberty (e.g., the right to vote), freedom of speech and assembly, liberty of conscience and freedom of thought, the freedom and right to hold personal property, and freedom from arbitrary arrest and seizure.

The second principle is that once equal basic liberty is ensured, inequality in basic social goods—such as income and wealth distribution, and opportunities—is to be allowed *only* if such inequalities benefit everyone. Rawls accepts that inequalities can be justified if the system that produces inequalities is to the advantage of everyone. More precisely, he formulates what he calls the *difference principle*, which is that inequalities are justified if they benefit the position of the least-advantaged person. So, for example, wide variations in income and wealth can be considered just if the market-based system that produces this unequal distribution also benefits the least-advantaged members of society. One can argue that a well-regulated, market-based economy and free trade, by promoting economic growth, benefit the least-advantaged members of society. In principle at least, the inequalities inherent in such systems are therefore just (in other words, the rising tide of wealth created by a market-based economy and free trade lifts all boats, even those of the most disadvantaged).

In the context of international business ethics, Rawls' theory creates an interesting perspective. Managers could ask themselves whether the policies they adopt in foreign operations would be considered just under Rawls' veil of ignorance. Is it just, for example, to pay foreign workers less than workers in the firm's home country? Rawls' theory would suggest it is, so long as the inequality benefits the least-advantaged members of the global society (which is what economic theory suggests). Alternatively, it is difficult to imagine that managers operating under a veil of ignorance would design a system where foreign employees were paid subsistence wages to work long hours in sweatshop conditions and where they were exposed to toxic materials. Such working conditions are clearly unjust in Rawls' framework, and therefore, it is unethical to adopt them. Similarly, operating under a veil of ignorance, most people would probably design a system that imparts some protection from environmental degradation to important global commons, such as the oceans, atmosphere, and tropical rain forests. To the extent that this is the case, it follows that it is unjust, and by extension unethical, for companies to pursue actions that contribute toward extensive degradation of these commons. Thus, Rawls' veil of ignorance is a conceptual tool that contributes to the moral compass that managers can use to help them navigate through difficult ethical dilemmas.

FOCUS ON MANAGERIAL IMPLICATIONS

MAKING ETHICAL DECISIONS INTERNATIONALLY

What, then, is the best way for managers in a multinational corporation to make sure that ethical considerations figure into international business decisions?

How do managers decide on an ethical course of action when confronted with decisions pertaining to working conditions, human rights, corruption, and environmental pollution? From an ethical perspective, how do managers determine the moral obligations that flow from the power of a multinational? In many cases, there are no easy answers to these questions: Many of the most vexing ethical problems arise because there are very real dilemmas inherent in them and no obvious correct action. Nevertheless, managers can and should do many things to make sure that basic ethical principles are adhered to and that ethical issues are routinely inserted into international business decisions.

Here, we focus on seven actions that an international business and its managers can take to make sure ethical issues are considered in business decisions: (1) favor hiring and promoting people with a well-grounded sense of personal ethics; (2) build an organizational culture and exemplify leadership behaviors that place a high value on ethical behavior; (3) put decision-making processes in place that require people to consider the ethical dimension of business decisions; (4) institute ethics officers in the organization; (5) develop moral courage; (6) make corporate social responsibility a cornerstone of enterprise policy; and (7) pursue strategies that are sustainable.

Hiring and Promotion

It seems obvious that businesses should strive to hire people who have a strong sense of personal ethics and would not engage in unethical or illegal behavior. Similarly, you would expect a business to not promote people, and perhaps to fire people, whose behavior does not match generally accepted ethical standards. However, actually doing so is very difficult. How do you know that someone has a poor sense of personal ethics? In our society, we have an incentive to hide a lack of personal ethics from public view. Once people realize that you are unethical, they will no longer trust you.

Is there anything that businesses can do to make sure they do not hire people who subsequently turn out to have poor personal ethics, particularly given that people have an

TEST PREP

Use SmartBook to help retain what you have learned. Access your Instructor's Connect course to check out SmartBook or go to **learnsmartadvantage.com** for help.

LO5-5

Explain how global managers can incorporate ethical considerations into their decision making in general, as well as corporate social responsibility and sustainability initiatives.

incentive to hide this from public view (indeed, the unethical person may lie about his or her nature)? Businesses can give potential employees psychological tests to try to discern their ethical predispositions, and they can check with prior employers or other employees regarding someone's reputation (e.g., by asking for letters of reference and talking to people who have worked with the prospective employee). The latter is common and does influence the hiring process. Promoting people who have displayed poor ethics should not occur in a company where the organizational culture values the need for ethical behavior and where leaders act accordingly.

Not only should businesses strive to identify and hire people with a strong sense of personal ethics, but it also is in the interests of prospective employees to find out as much as they can about the ethical climate in an organization. Who wants to work at a multinational such as Enron, which ultimately entered bankruptcy because unethical executives had established risky partnerships that were hidden from public view and that existed in part to enrich those same executives?

Organizational Culture and Leadership

To foster ethical behavior, businesses need to build an organizational culture that values ethical behavior. Three things are particularly important in building an organizational culture that emphasizes ethical behavior. First, the businesses must explicitly articulate values that emphasize ethical behavior. Virtually all great companies do this by establishing a **code of ethics**, which is a formal statement of the ethical priorities a business adheres to. Often, the code of ethics draws heavily on documents such as the UN Universal Declaration of Human Rights, which itself is grounded in Kantian and rights-based theories of moral philosophy. Others have incorporated ethical statements into documents that articulate the values or mission of the business. For example, the Academy of International Business (the top professional organization in international business) has a Code of Ethics for its leadership (as well as a COE for its members):[39]

> **AIB's Motivation for the Code of Ethics of the Leadership:** The leadership of an organization is ultimately responsible for the creation of the values, norms and practices that permeate the organization and its membership. A strong ethically grounded organization is only possible when it is governed by a strong ethical committee. The term "committee" is used for succinctness; it includes all organizational structures that have managerial, custodial, decision-making or financial authority within an organization.[*]

Having articulated values in a code of ethics or some other document, leaders in the business must give life and meaning to those words by repeatedly emphasizing their importance *and then acting on them*. This means using every relevant opportunity to stress the importance of business ethics and making sure that key business decisions not only make good economic sense but also are ethical. Many companies have gone a step further by hiring independent auditors to make sure they are behaving in a manner consistent with their ethical codes. Nike, for example, has hired independent auditors to make sure that subcontractors used by the company are living up to Nike's code of conduct.

Finally, building an organizational culture that places a high value on ethical behavior requires incentive and reward systems, including promotions that reward people who engage in ethical behavior and sanction those who do not. At General Electric, for example, former CEO Jack Welch has described how he reviewed the performance of managers, dividing them into several different groups. These included over-performers who displayed the right values and were singled out for advancement and bonuses, as well as over-performers who displayed the wrong values and were let go. Welch was not willing to tolerate leaders within the company who did not act in accordance with the central values of the company, even if they were in all other respects skilled managers.[40]

---

*"Code of Ethics for the Academy of International Business Leadership," Academy of International Business, October 11, 2018, **https://documents.aib.msu.edu/policies/AIB-Leadership-Code-of-Ethics-20181011.pdf.**

Decision-Making Processes

In addition to establishing the right kind of ethical culture in an organization, business-people must be able to think through the ethical implications of decisions in a systematic way. To do this, they need a moral compass, and both rights theories and Rawls' theory of justice help provide such a compass. Beyond these theories, some experts on ethics have proposed a straightforward practical guide—or ethical algorithm—to determine whether a decision is ethical.[41] According to these experts, a decision is acceptable on ethical grounds if a businessperson can answer yes to each of these questions:

- Does my decision fall within the accepted values or standards that typically apply in the organizational environment (as articulated in a code of ethics or some other corporate statement)?

- Am I willing to see the decision communicated to all stakeholders affected by it—for example, by having it reported in newspapers, on television, or via social media?

- Would the people with whom I have a significant personal relationship, such as family members, friends, or even managers in other businesses, approve of the decision?

Others have recommended a five-step process to think through ethical problems (this is another example of an ethical algorithm).[42] In step 1, businesspeople should identify which stakeholders a decision would affect and in what ways. A firm's **stakeholders** are individuals or groups that have an interest, claim, or stake in the company, in what it does, and in how well it performs.[43] They can be divided into internal stakeholders and external stakeholders. **Internal stakeholders** are individuals or groups who work for or own the business. They include primary stakeholders such as employees, the board of directors, and shareholders. **External stakeholders** are all the other individuals and groups that have some direct or indirect claim on the firm. Typically, this group comprises primary stakeholders such as customers, suppliers, governments, and local communities as well as secondary stakeholders such as special-interest groups, competitors, trade associations, mass media, and social media.[44]

All stakeholders are in an exchange relationship with the company.[45] Each stakeholder group supplies the organization with important resources (or contributions), and in exchange each expects its interests to be satisfied (by inducements).[46] For example, employees provide labor, skills, knowledge, and time and in exchange expect commensurate income, job satisfaction, job security, and good working conditions. Customers provide a company with its revenues and in exchange want quality products that represent value for money. Communities provide businesses with local infrastructure and in exchange want businesses that are responsible citizens and seek some assurance that the quality of life will be improved as a result of the business firm's existence.

Stakeholder analysis involves a certain amount of what has been called *moral imagination*.[47] This means standing in the shoes of a stakeholder and asking how a proposed decision might impact that stakeholder. For example, when considering outsourcing to subcontractors, managers might need to ask themselves how it might feel to be working under substandard health conditions for long hours.

Step 2 involves judging the ethics of the proposed strategic decision, given the information gained in step 1. Managers need to determine whether a proposed decision would violate the *fundamental rights* of any stakeholders. For example, we might argue that the right to information about health risks in the workplace is a fundamental entitlement of employees. Similarly, the right to know about potentially dangerous features of a product is a fundamental entitlement of customers (something tobacco companies violated when they did not reveal to their customers what they knew about the health risks of smoking). Managers might also want to ask themselves whether they would allow the proposed strategic decision if they were designing a system under Rawls' veil of ignorance. For example, if the issue under consideration was whether to outsource work to a subcontractor with low pay and poor working conditions, managers might want to ask themselves whether they would allow such action if they were considering it under a veil of ignorance, where they themselves might ultimately be the ones to work for the subcontractor.

The judgment at this stage should be guided by various moral principles that should not be violated. The principles might be those articulated in a corporate code of ethics or other company documents. In addition, certain moral principles that we have adopted as members of society—for instance, the prohibition on stealing—should not be violated. The judgment at this stage will also be guided by the decision rule that is chosen to assess the proposed strategic decision. Although maximizing long-run profitability is the decision rule that most businesses stress, it should be applied subject to the constraint that no moral principles are violated—that the business behaves in an ethical manner.

Step 3 requires managers to establish moral intent. This means the business must resolve to place moral concerns ahead of other concerns in cases where either the fundamental rights of stakeholders or key moral principles have been violated. At this stage, input from top management might be particularly valuable. Without the proactive encouragement of top managers, middle-level managers might tend to place the narrow economic interests of the company before the interests of stakeholders. They might do so in the (usually erroneous) belief that top managers favor such an approach.

Step 4 requires the company to engage in ethical behavior. Step 5 requires the business to audit its decisions, reviewing them to make sure they were consistent with ethical principles, such as those stated in the company's code of ethics. This final step is critical and often overlooked. Without auditing past decisions, businesspeople may not know if their decision process is working and if changes should be made to ensure greater compliance with a code of ethics.

Ethics Officers

To make sure that a business behaves in an ethical manner, firms now must have oversight by a high-ranking person or people known to respect legal and ethical standards. These individuals—often referred to as ethics officers—are responsible for managing their organization's ethics and legal compliance programs. They are typically responsible for (1) assessing the needs and risks that an ethics program must address; (2) developing and distributing a code of ethics; (3) conducting training programs for employees; (4) establishing and maintaining a confidential service to address employees' questions about issues that may be ethical or unethical; (5) making sure that the organization is in compliance with government laws and regulations; (6) monitoring and auditing ethical conduct; (7) taking action, as appropriate, on possible violations; and (8) reviewing and updating the code of ethics periodically.[48] Because of these broad topics covered by the ethics officer, in many businesses ethics officers act as an internal ombudsperson with responsibility for handling confidential inquiries from employees, investigating complaints from employees or others, reporting findings, and making recommendations for change.

For example, United Technologies, a multinational aerospace company with worldwide revenues of more than $60 billion, has had a formal code of ethics since 1990.[49] United Technologies has some 450 business practice officers (the company's name for ethics officers), who are responsible for making sure the code is followed. United Technologies also established an "ombudsperson" program in 1986 that lets employees inquire anonymously about ethics issues. The program has received some 60,000 inquiries since 1986, and more than 10,000 cases have been handled by the ombudsperson. These very early initiatives by United Technologies have led to a robust, ethical, and responsible corporate infrastructure.

Moral Courage

It is important to recognize that employees in an international business may need significant *moral courage*. Moral courage enables managers to walk away from a decision that is profitable but unethical. Moral courage gives an employee the strength to say no to a superior who instructs her to pursue actions that are unethical. Moral courage gives employees the integrity to go public to the media and blow the whistle on persistent unethical behavior in a company. Moral courage does not come easily; there are well-known cases where individuals have lost their jobs because they blew the whistle on corporate behaviors they thought unethical, telling the media about what was occurring.[50]

However, companies can strengthen the moral courage of employees by committing themselves to not retaliate against employees who exercise moral courage, say no to superiors, or otherwise complain about unethical actions. For example, consider the following excerpt from the Academy of International Business Code of Ethics:

> **AIB Statement of Commitment by Its Leadership:** In establishing policy for and on behalf of the Academy of International Business's members, I am a custodian in trust of the assets of this organization. The AIB's members recognize the need for competent and committed elected committee members to serve their organization and have put their trust in my sincerity and abilities. In return, the members deserve my utmost effort, dedication, and support. Therefore, as a committee member of the AIB, I acknowledge and commit that I will observe a high standard of ethics and conduct as I devote my best efforts, skills and resources in the interest of the AIB and its members. I will perform my duties as a committee member in such a manner that the members' confidence and trust in the integrity, objectivity and impartiality of the AIB are conserved and enhanced. To do otherwise would be a breach of the trust which the membership has bestowed upon me.[51]

This statement ensures that all members serving in leadership positions within the Academy of International Business adhere to and uphold the highest commitment and responsibility to be ethical in their AIB leadership activities. A freestanding and independent AIB Ombuds Committee handles all ethical issues and violations to ensure independence and the highest moral code.

Corporate Social Responsibility

Multinational corporations have power that comes from their control over resources and their ability to move production from country to country. Although that power is constrained not only by laws and regulations but also by the discipline of the market and the competitive process, it is substantial. Some moral philosophers argue that with power comes the social responsibility for multinationals to give something back to the societies that enable them to prosper and grow.

The concept of **corporate social responsibility (CSR)** refers to the idea that businesspeople should consider the social consequences of economic actions when making business decisions and that there should be a presumption in favor of decisions that have both good economic and social consequences.[52] In its purest form, corporate social responsibility can be supported for its own sake simply because it is the right way for a business to behave. Advocates of this approach argue that businesses, particularly large successful businesses, need to recognize their *noblesse oblige* and give something back to the societies that have made their success possible. *Noblesse oblige* is a French term that refers to honorable and benevolent behavior considered the responsibility of people of high (noble) birth. In a business setting, it is taken to mean benevolent behavior that is the responsibility of *successful* enterprises. This has long been recognized by many businesspeople, resulting in a substantial and venerable history of corporate giving to society, with businesses making social investments designed to enhance the welfare of the communities in which they operate.

Power itself is morally neutral; how power is used is what matters. It can be used in a positive way to increase social welfare, which is ethical, or it can be used in a manner that is ethically and morally suspect. Managers at some multinationals have acknowledged a moral obligation to use their power to enhance social welfare in the communities where they do business. BP, one of the world's largest oil companies, has made it part of the company policy to undertake "social investments" in the countries where it does business.[53] In Algeria, BP has been investing in a major project to develop gas fields near the desert town of Salah. When the company noticed the lack of clean water in Salah, it built two desalination plants to provide drinking water for the local community and distributed containers to residents so they could take water from the plants to their homes. There was no economic reason for BP to make this social investment, but the company believes it is morally obligated to use its power in constructive ways. The action, while a small thing for BP, is a very important thing for the local community. For another example of corporate social responsibility in practice, see the accompanying Management Focus feature on the Finnish company Stora Enso.

Corporate Social Responsibility at Stora Enso

Stora Enso is a Finnish pulp and paper manufacturer that was formed by the merger of Swedish mining and forestry products company Stora and Finnish forestry products company Enso-Gutzeit Oy in 1998. The company is headquartered in Helsinki, the capital of Finland, and it has approximately 25,000 employees. In 2000, the company bought Consolidated Papers in North America. Stora Enso also expanded into South America, Asia, and Russia. By 2005, Stora Enso had become the world's largest pulp and paper manufacturer as measured by production capacity. However, the North American operations were sold in 2007 to NewPage Corporation.

To this day, Stora Enso has a long-standing tradition of corporate social responsibility on a global scale. As part of the company's section "Global Responsibility in Stora Enso," the company states that "for Stora Enso, Global Responsibility means realizing concrete actions that will help us fulfil [sic] our Purpose, which is to do good for the people and the planet." Stora Enso continues to state:

Our purpose "do good for the people and the planet" is the ultimate reason why we run our business. It is the overriding rule that guides us in all that we do: producing and selling our renewable products, buying trees from a local forest-owner in Finland, selling electricity generated at Stora Enso Skoghall Mill, or managing our logistics on a global scale.[54]

Interestingly, Stora Enso also asserts that it realizes that this statement is rather bold and perhaps not even fully believable. But the company suggests that it makes the company accountable for its actions; that is, setting its purpose boldly in writing. At the same time, Stora Enso positions the company as though it has always been attending to the "socially responsible" needs of doing good for the people and the planet. It illustrates this by maintaining that it has created and enhanced communities around its mills, developed innovative systems to reduce the use of scarce resources, and maintained good relationships with key stakeholders such as forest owners, their own employees, governments, and local communities near its mills.

Tracing its past and reflecting on its future, Stora Enso has adopted three lead areas for its global responsibility strategy: people and ethics, forests and land use, and environment and efficiency. For people and ethics, the company focuses on conducting business in a socially responsible manner throughout its global value chain. For forests and land use, it focuses on an innovative and responsible approach on forestry and land use to make it a preferred partner and a good local community citizen. For the environment and efficiency, the focus is on resource-efficient operations that help the company achieve superior environmental performance related to its products.

While a number of companies have corporate social responsibility statements incorporated as part of their websites, annual reports, and talking points, Stora Enso also presents clear targets and performance goals that are assessed by established metrics. Its overall operations are guided by corporate-level targets for environmental and social performance, aptly named Stora Enso's Global Responsibility Key Performance Indicators (KPIs). Targets are publicly listed in a document titled "Targets and Performance" and include two to five basic categories of measures for each of the three lead areas. For people and ethics, the dimensions cover health and safety, human rights, ethics and compliance, sustainable leadership, and responsible sourcing. For forests and land use, the dimensions cover efficiency of land use and sustainable forestry. For environment and efficiency, the dimensions cover climate and energy, material efficiency, and process water discharges. The "Targets and Performance" document also lists performance in the prior year, targets in the current year, and strategic objectives related to each dimension.

Sources: "Global Responsibility in Stora Enso," www.storaenso.com; K. Vita, "Stora Enso Falls as UBS Plays Down Merger Talk: Helsinki Mover," *Bloomberg Businessweek*, September 30, 2013; M. Huuhtanen, "Paper Maker Stora Enso Selling North American Mills," *USA Today*, September 21, 2007.

Sustainability

As managers in international businesses strive to translate ideas about corporate social responsibility into strategic actions, many are gravitating toward strategies that are viewed as *sustainable*. By **sustainable strategies**, we refer to strategies that not only help the multinational firm make good profits, but that also do so without harming the environment while simultaneously ensuring that the corporation acts in a socially responsible manner with regard to its stakeholders.[55] The core idea of *sustainability* is that the organization—through its actions—does not exert a negative impact on the ability of future generations to meet their own economic needs and that its actions impart long-run economic *and* social benefits on stakeholders.[56]

A company pursuing a sustainable strategy would not adopt business practices that deplete the environment for short-term economic gain because doing so would impose a cost on future generations. In other words, international businesses that pursue sustainable strategies try to ensure that they do not precipitate or participate in a situation that results in a tragedy of the commons Thus, for example, a company pursuing a sustainable strategy would try to reduce its carbon footprint (CO_2 emissions) so that it does not contribute to global warming.

Nor would a company pursuing a sustainable strategy adopt policies that negatively affect the well-being of key stakeholders such as employees and suppliers because managers would recognize that in the long run, this would harm the company. The company that pays its employees so little that it forces them into poverty, for example, may find it hard to recruit employees in the future and may have to deal with high employee turnover, which imposes its own costs on an enterprise. Similarly, a company that drives down the prices it pays to its suppliers so far that the suppliers cannot make enough money to invest in upgrading their operations may find that in the long run, its business suffers poor-quality inputs and a lack of innovation among its supplier base.

Starbucks has a goal of ensuring that 100 percent of its coffee is ethically sourced. By this, it means that the farmers who grow the coffee beans it purchases use sustainable farming methods that do not harm the environment and that they treat their employees well and pay them fairly. Starbucks agronomists work directly with farmers in places such as Costa Rica and Rwanda to make sure that they use environmentally responsible farming methods. The company also provides loans to farmers to help them upgrade their production methods. As a result of these policies, some 9 percent of Starbucks coffee beans are "fair trade" sourced and the remaining 91 percent are ethically sourced.

Key Terms

business ethics, p. 135
ethical strategy, p. 135
Foreign Corrupt Practices Act (FCPA), p. 141
Convention on Combating Bribery of Foreign Public Officials in International Business Transactions, p. 141
ethical dilemma, p. 142

organizational culture, p. 144
cultural relativism, p. 147
righteous moralist, p. 147
naive immoralist, p. 148
utilitarian approach to ethics, p. 148
Kantian ethics, p. 149
rights theories, p. 149
Universal Declaration of Human Rights, p. 149

just distribution, p. 150
code of ethics, p. 152
stakeholders, p. 153
internal stakeholders, p. 153
external stakeholders, p. 153
corporate social responsibility (CSR), p. 155
sustainable strategies, p. 157

◯ SUMMARY

This chapter discussed the source and nature of ethical issues in international businesses, the different philosophical approaches to business ethics, the steps managers can take to ensure that ethical issues are respected in international business decisions, and the roles of corporate social responsibility and sustainability in practice. The chapter made the following points:

1. The term *ethics* refers to accepted principles of right or wrong that govern the conduct of a person, the members of a profession, or the actions of an organization. Business ethics are the accepted principles of right or wrong governing the conduct of businesspeople. An ethical strategy is one that does not violate these accepted principles.

2. Ethical issues and dilemmas in international business are rooted in the variations among political systems, law, economic development, and culture from country to country.

3. The most common ethical issues in international business involve employment practices, human rights, environmental regulations, corruption, and social responsibility of multinational corporations.

4. Ethical dilemmas are situations in which none of the available alternatives seems ethically acceptable.

5. Unethical behavior is rooted in personal ethics, societal culture, psychological and geographic distances of a foreign subsidiary from the home office, a failure to incorporate ethical issues into strategic and operational decision making, a dysfunctional culture, and failure of leaders to act in an ethical manner.

6. Moral philosophers contend that approaches to business ethics such as the Friedman doctrine, cultural relativism, the righteous moralist, and the naive immoralist are unsatisfactory in important ways.

7. The Friedman doctrine states that the only social responsibility of business is to increase profits, as long as the company stays within the rules of law. Cultural relativism contends that one should adopt the ethics of the culture in which one is doing business. The righteous moralist monolithically applies home-country ethics to a foreign situation, while the naive immoralist believes that if a manager of a multinational sees that firms from other nations are not following ethical norms in a host nation, that manager should not either.

8. Utilitarian approaches to ethics hold that the moral worth of actions or practices is determined by their consequences, and the best decisions are those that produce the greatest good for the greatest number of people.

9. Kantian ethics state that people should be treated as ends and never purely as *means* to the ends of others. People are not instruments, like a machine. People have dignity and need to be respected as such.

10. Rights theories recognize that human beings have fundamental rights and privileges that transcend national boundaries and cultures. These rights establish a minimum level of morally acceptable behavior.

11. The concept of justice developed by John Rawls suggests that a decision is just and ethical if people would allow it when designing a social system under a veil of ignorance.

12. To make sure that ethical issues are considered in international business decisions, managers should (*a*) favor hiring and promoting people with a well-grounded sense of personal ethics, (*b*) build an organizational culture and exemplify leadership behaviors that place a high value on ethical behavior, (*c*) put decision-making processes in place that require people to consider the ethical dimension of business decisions, (*d*) establish ethics officers in the organization with responsibility for ethical decision making, (*e*) be morally courageous and encourage others to do the same, (*f*) make corporate social responsibility a cornerstone of enterprise policy, and (*g*) pursue strategies that are sustainable.

13. Multinational corporations that are practicing business-focused sustainability integrate a focus on market orientation, addressing the needs of multiple stakeholders, and adhering to corporate social responsibility principles.

Critical Thinking and Discussion Questions

1. A visiting American executive finds that a foreign subsidiary in a less developed country has hired a 12-year-old girl to work on a factory floor, in violation of the company's prohibition on child labor. He tells the local manager to replace the child and tell her to go back to school. The local manager tells the American executive that the child is an orphan with no other means of support, and she will probably become a street child if she is denied work. What should the American executive do?

2. Drawing on John Rawls's concept of the veil of ignorance, develop an ethical code that will (*a*) guide the decisions of a large oil multinational toward environmental protection and (*b*) influence the policies of a clothing company in their potential decision of outsourcing their manufacturing operations.

3. Under what conditions is it ethically defensible to outsource production to the developing world where labor costs are lower when such actions also involve laying off long-term employees in the firm's home country?

4. Do you think facilitating payments (*speed payments*) should be ethical? Does it matter in which country, or part of the world, such payments are made?

5. A manager from a developing country is overseeing a multinational's operations in a country where drug trafficking and lawlessness are rife. One day, a representative of a local "big man" approaches the manager and asks for a "donation" to help the big man provide housing for the poor. The representative tells the manager that in return for the donation, the big man will make sure that the manager has a productive stay in his country. No threats are made, but the manager is well aware that the big man heads a criminal organization that is engaged in drug trafficking. He also knows that the big man does indeed help the poor in the rundown neighborhood of the city where he was born. What should the manager do?

6. Milton Friedman stated in his famous article in *The New York Times* in 1970 that "the social responsibility of business is to increase profits."[*] Do you agree? If not, do you prefer that multinational corporations adopt a focus on corporate social responsibility or sustainability practices?

7. Can a company be good at corporate social responsibility but not be sustainability oriented? Is it possible to focus on sustainability but not corporate social responsibility? Based on reading the Focus on Managerial Implications section, discuss how much CSR and sustainability are related and how much the concepts differ from each other.

---

*M. Friedman, "The Social Responsibility of Business Is to Increase Profits," *The New York Times Magazine*, September 13, 1970.

globalEDGE research task globaledge.msu.edu

Use the globalEDGE™ website (**globaledge.msu.edu**) to complete the following exercises:

1. Promoting respect for universal human rights is a central dimension of many countries' foreign policy. As history has shown, human rights abuses are an important concern worldwide. Some countries are more ready to work with other governments and civil society organizations to prevent abuses of power. The annual *Country Reports on Human Rights Practices* are designed to assess the state of democracy and human rights around the world, call attention to violations, and—where needed—prompt needed changes in U.S. policies toward particular countries. Find the latest annual *Country Reports on Human Right Practices* for the BRIC countries (Brazil, Russia, India, and China), and create a table to compare the findings under the "Worker Rights" sections. What commonalities do you see? What differences are there?

2. The use of bribery in the business setting is an important ethical dilemma many companies face both domestically and abroad. The Bribe Payers Index is a study published every three years to assess the likelihood of firms from leading economies to win business overseas by offering bribes. It also ranks industry sectors based on the prevalence of bribery. Compare the five industries thought to have the largest problems with bribery with those five that have the least problems. What patterns do you see? What factors make some industries more conducive to bribery than others?

CLOSING CASE

Sustainability Initiatives at Natura, The Body Shop, and Aesop

Corporate Knights, a research firm from Toronto, Canada, puts together the Global 100, a ranking of the world's most sustainable companies, based on annual data analytics. Using data available publicly, Corporate Knights rates large firms on 17 key measures, evaluating their management of resources, finances, and employees (e.g., energy, carbon footprint, water use, waste productivity, clean air). They consider about 4,000 companies worldwide with market values of at least $2 billion.

For several years, Natura & Co SA from Brazil has been among the world's leaders, regularly ranking in the Top 20 each year. This is an incredibly admirable feat, because Natura is also the world's largest cosmetics company. Cosmetics has a lot of potential to be less than sustainable in manufacturing and operations, but Natura has bucked that trend. Natura (**naturaeco.com**), headquartered in São Paulo, Brazil, was founded in 1969. The company has more than 18,000 employees and revenue of about $4.4 billion. Natura has three prominent subsidiaries that strive to be as sustainable in their operations as possible: Natura Cosmetics, The Body Shop, and Aesop. The latter two brands are often viewed as standalone organizations by customers.

Natura Cosmetics develops, produces, distributes, and sells cosmetics, fragrances, and hygiene products. Natura's products include creams, deodorants, lipsticks, lotions, makeup accessories, perfumes, shampoos, shaving creams, soaps, and sunscreens, among others. Its portfolio is made up of brand names such as Amo, Ekos, Tododia, Aguas, Chronos, Erva Doce, Homem, Horus, Seve, and Luna. The company employs more than 7,000 people in seven countries: Brazil, Argentina, Chile, Mexico, Peru, Colombia, and France. Sustainable development has been Natura's guiding principle since it was founded. Sustainability, along with a passion for Customer Relationship Management (CRM), led the company to adopt direct sales as its main commercial strategy. To support its direct sales model, more than 1,421,000 consultants around the world promote the company's values and products directly to customers. To be sustainable, innovation is at the heart of Natura's development policy. For example, last year the company spent about $75 million on product development, launching 164 products and achieving an innovation index of 64.8 percent (the percentage of revenue from products launched in the last two years).

The Body Shop is a well-known, formerly British cosmetics, skin care, and perfume company that was founded in 1976 by Anita and Gordon Roddick. The company offers more than 1,000 products, which it sells in some 3,100 owned and franchised stores in 66 countries. The Body Shop is still based in East Croydon and Littlehampton in the United Kingdom, but was bought from French cosmetics company L'Oréal (which owned The Body Shop from 2006 to 2017) by Natura in June 2017 for $1.2 billion (£880 million). Famously, The Body Shop has been a leader in banning animal testing of cosmetics products worldwide since the 1980s and is tirelessly working to ban animal testing in the cosmetics industry. This position also feeds into its sustainability initiatives. Anita Roddick said that "My hope for the future of The Body Shop is primarily vested in those people who will be the custodians of our culture and values."* This custodianship includes the pledge of being the world's most ethical, sustainable company. For example, The Body Shop has unveiled an "Enrich Not Exploit" slogan that will underpin all aspects of its operations. This pioneering commitment reaffirmed the global cosmetics brand's positioning as a leader in ethical and sustainable business practices.

Aesop was founded by hairdresser Dennis Paphitis in 1987 in Melbourne, Australia. Suzanne Santos, as Aesop's first employee, was also instrumental in the foundation and growth of the company. Aesop is viewed as an Australian skin care brand, owned fully by Natura since 2016 (although Natura had part ownership since 2012). The brand has been identified as unique in the way it markets itself in today's social media world. In a somewhat unorthodox way, this includes not using traditional advertisements or discount sales to promote its products. Instead, Aesop gets its promotional communication mostly by word-of-mouth for the design of its products, stores, and events, which are a singular mix of indulgent product experiences, thoughtful language, and modern minimalist design (compare this with the Swedish furniture giant IKEA that often receives similar reviews of minimalist but superb design in the furniture business).

With its core subsidiaries (Natura Cosmetics, The Body Shop, and Aesop), Natura & Co SA has redefined

*Roddick, Anita Dame, "Building For The Future. Our Values Performance 2014/2015 & Our New Commitment," The Body Shop, 2016.

success in business on a global scale. It was the first publicly traded company to become a "Certified B Corporation." A Certified B Corporation is a company that focuses on two specific sustainability issues. First, it has reached a threshold standard for its impact on society and the environment. Second, the company must have committed to consider the impact of its business decisions on its wider stakeholders, not just its shareholders. Currently, only 2,200 B Corps exist worldwide, and their core sustainability focus is on the interdependence between society, environment, and economy. Importantly, Natura's actions show that it is possible to make a positive difference for the environment while also ensuring the financial viability of the company through profit making. This mindset also drove Natura's purchase of The Body Shop in 2017, the first billion-dollar B Corp acquisition by another B Corp.

Sources: Deanna Utroske, "The Body Shop Launches New Campaign for UN Animal Testing Ban," *Cosmetics Design*, March 22, 2018; Andres Schipani, "Body Shop Owner Natura Targets Global Growth," *Financial Times*, February 4, 2018; Corporate Knights, "2018 Global 100 Results," www.corporateknights.com/reports/2018-global-100; "The Body Shop Marks 40th Year with Pledge to Be World's Most Ethical, Sustainable Global Company," *Sustainable Brands*, February 12, 2016; Charmain Love, Katie Hill, and Marcel Fukayama, "Building Bridges: Natura, Aesop and The Body Shop Join Their Businesses as Forces for Good," *B the Change*, September 13, 2017.

CASE DISCUSSION QUESTIONS

1. With its three core companies (Natura Cosmetics, The Body Shop, and Aesop), Natura & Co SA blends three different business models for interacting with the customer. In the end, all three models are focused on sustainable business practices. What can other companies learn from Natura & Co SA on how to be sustainable?

2. The Body Shop has been a leader in banning animal testing of cosmetics products worldwide since the 1980s and is tirelessly working to ban animal testing in the cosmetics industry. Is this part of being sustainable or is animal testing a different focus?

3. Aesop is not using traditional advertisements or discount sales to promote its products. Instead, Aesop gets its promotional communication mostly by word-of-mouth for the design of its products, stores, and events, which are a singular mix of indulgent product experiences, thoughtful language, and modern minimalist design. If you had to interact with Natura & Co SA, which customer engagement model—Natura's, The Body Shop's, or Aesop's—would be the best for you and why?

4. How much would it mean to you that a company operated in a sustainable way? Would you pay 5 percent, 10 percent, or 25 percent more for a product if the quality was the same as nonsustainable alternatives? What if the quality of the product was lower but the price the same?

Design elements: Modern textured halftone: ©VIPRESIONA/ Shutterstock; globalEDGE icon: ©globalEDGE; All others: ©McGraw-Hill Education

Endnotes

1. T. Hult, "Market-Focused Sustainability: Market Orientation Plus!" *Journal of the Academy of Marketing Science* 39 (2011), pp. 1–6; T. Hult, J. Mena, O. C. Ferrell, and L. Ferrell, "Stakeholder Marketing: A Definition and Conceptual Framework," *AMS Review* 1 (2011), pp. 44–65.

2. S. Greenhouse, "Nike Shoe Plant in Vietnam Is Called Unsafe for Workers," *The New York Times*, November 8, 1997; V. Dobnik, "Chinese Workers Abused Making Nikes, Reeboks," *Seattle Times*, September 21, 1997, p. A4.

3. R. K. Massie, *Loosing the Bonds: The United States and South Africa in the Apartheid Years* (New York: Doubleday, 1997).

4. Not everyone agrees that the divestment trend had much influence on the South African economy. For a counterview, see S. H. Teoh, I. Welch, and C. P. Wazzan, "The Effect of Socially Activist Investing on the Financial Markets: Evidence from South Africa," *The Journal of Business* 72, no. 1 (January 1999), pp. 35–60.

5. Peter Singer, *One World: The Ethics of Globalization* (New Haven, CT: Yale University Press, 2002).

6. Garrett Hardin, "The Tragedy of the Commons," *Science* 162, no. 1 (1968), pp. 243–48.

7. For a summary of the evidence, see S. Solomon, D. Qin, M. Manning, Z. Chen, M. Marquis, K. B. Averyt, M. Tignor, and H. L. Miller, eds., *Contribution of Working Group I to the Fourth Assessment Report of the Intergovernmental Panel on Climate Change* (Cambridge, UK: Cambridge University Press, 2007).

8. J. Everett, D. Neu, and A. S. Rahaman, "The Global Fight against Corruption," *Journal of Business Ethics* 65 (2006), pp. 1–18.

9. R. T. De George, *Competing with Integrity in International Business* (Oxford, UK: Oxford University Press, 1993).

10. Details can be found at www.oecd.org/corruption/ oecdantibriberyconvention.htm.

11. B. Pranab, "Corruption and Development," *Journal of Economic Literature* 36 (September 1997), pp. 1320–46.

12. A. Shleifer and R. W. Vishny, "Corruption," *Quarterly Journal of Economics* 108 (1993), pp. 599–617; I. Ehrlich and F. Lui, "Bureaucratic Corruption and Endogenous Economic Growth," *Journal of Political Economy* 107 (December 1999), pp. 270–92.

13. P. Mauro, "Corruption and Growth," *Quarterly Journal of Economics* 110 (1995), pp. 681–712.

14. D. Kaufman and S. J. Wei, "Does Grease Money Speed up the Wheels of Commerce?" World Bank policy research working paper, January 11, 2000.

15. Center for the Study of Ethics in the Professions, http://ethics. iit.edu.

16. B. Vitou, R. Kovalevsky, and T. Fox, "Time to Call a Spade a Spade. Facilitation Payments and Why Neither Bans Nor Exemption Work," http://thebriberyact.com/2011/02/03/time-to-call-a-spade-a-spade-facilitation-payments-why-neither-bans-nor-exemptions-work, accessed March 8, 2014.

17. This is known as the "when in Rome perspective." T. Donaldson, "Values in Tension: Ethics Away from Home," *Harvard Business Review*, September–October 1996.

18. De George, *Competing with Integrity in International Business*.

19. For a discussion of the ethics of using child labor, see J. Isern, "Bittersweet Chocolate: The Legacy of Child Labor in Cocoa Production in Cote d'Ivoire," *Journal of Applied Management and Entrepreneurship* 11 (2006), pp. 115–32.

20. S. W. Gellerman, "Why Good Managers Make Bad Ethical Choices," in *Ethics in Practice: Managing the Moral Corporation*, ed. K. R. Andrews (Cambridge, MA: Harvard Business School Press, 1989).

21. D. Messick and M. H. Bazerman, "Ethical Leadership and the Psychology of Decision Making," *Sloan Management Review* 37 (Winter 1996), pp. 9–20.

22. O. C. Ferrell, J. Fraedrich, and L. Ferrell, *Business Ethics*, 9th ed. (Mason, OH: Cengage, 2013).

23. B. Scholtens and L. Dam, "Cultural Values and International Differences in Business Ethics," *Journal of Business Ethics*, 2007.

24. M. Friedman, "The Social Responsibility of Business Is to Increase Profits," *The New York Times Magazine*, September 13, 1970. Reprinted in T. L. Beauchamp and N. E. Bowie, *Ethical Theory and Business*, 7th ed. (Englewood Cliffs, NJ: Prentice Hall, 2001).

25. Friedman, "The Social Responsibility of Business Is to Increase Profits."

26. Friedman, Milton. "The Social Responsibility of Business Is to Increase Profits." *The New York Times*, September 13, 1970.

27. For example, see Donaldson, "Values in Tension: Ethics Away from Home." See also N. Bowie, "Relativism and the Moral Obligations of Multinational Corporations," in T. L. Beauchamp and N. E. Bowie, *Ethical Theory and Business*, 7th ed. (Englewood Cliffs, NJ: Prentice Hall, 2001).

28. For example, see De George, *Competing with Integrity in International Business*.

29. This example is often repeated in the literature on international business ethics. It was first outlined by A. Kelly in "Case Study—Italian Style Mores," in T. Donaldson and P. Werhane, *Ethical Issues in Business* (Englewood Cliffs, NJ: Prentice Hall, 1979).

30. See Beauchamp and Bowie, *Ethical Theory and Business*.

31. T. Donaldson, *The Ethics of International Business* (Oxford: Oxford University Press, 1989).

32. Found at www.un.org/Overview/rights.html.

33. The Universal Declaration of Human Rights." Article 1, United Nations, 1948. https://www.un.org/en/universal-declaration-human-rights.

34. The Universal Declaration of Human Rights." Article 23, United Nations, 1948. https://www.un.org/en/universal-declaration-human-rights.

35. UN Universal Declaration of Human Rights, Article 29.

36. Donaldson, *The Ethics of International Business*.

37. See Chapter 10 in Beauchamp and Bowie, *Ethical Theory and Business*.

38. J. Rawls, *A Theory of Justice*, rev. ed. (Cambridge, MA: Belknap Press, 1999).

39. https://aib.msu.edu/aboutleadership.asp.

40. J. Bower and J. Dial, "Jack Welch: General Electric's Revolutionary," Harvard Business School Case 9-394-065, April 1994.

41. For example, see R. E. Freeman and D. Gilbert, *Corporate Strategy and the Search for Ethics* (Englewood Cliffs, NJ: Prentice Hall, 1988); T. Jones, "Ethical Decision Making by Individuals in Organizations," *Academy of Management Review* 16 (1991), pp. 366–95; J. R. Rest, *Moral Development: Advances in Research and Theory* (New York: Praeger, 1986).

42. Freeman and Gilbert, *Corporate Strategy and the Search for Ethics*; Jones, "Ethical Decision Making by Individuals in Organizations"; Rest, *Moral Development*.

43. See E. Freeman, *Strategic Management: A Stakeholder Approach* (Boston: Pitman Press, 1984); C. W. L. Hill and T. M. Jones, "Stakeholder-Agency Theory," *Journal of Management Studies* 29 (1992), pp. 131–54; J. G. March and H. A. Simon, *Organizations* (New York: Wiley, 1958).

44. Hult et al., "Stakeholder Marketing."

45. Hult, "Market-Focused Sustainability: Market Orientation Plus!"; Hult et al., "Stakeholder Marketing."

46. Hill and Jones, "Stakeholder-Agency Theory"; March and Simon, *Organizations*.

47. De George, *Competing with Integrity in International Business*.

48. "Our Principles," Unilever, www.unilever.com.

49. The code can be accessed at the United Technologies website, www.utc.com.

50. C. Grant, "Whistle Blowers: Saints of Secular Culture," *Journal of Business Ethics*, September 2002, pp. 391–400.

51. "Code of Ethics for the Academy of International Business Leadership," Academy of International Business, October 11, 2018, https://documents.aib.msu.edu/policies/AIB-Leadership-Code-of-Ethics-20181011.pdf.

52. S. A. Waddock and S. B. Graves, "The Corporate Social Performance–Financial Performance Link," *Strategic Management Journal* 8 (1997), pp. 303–19; I. Maignan, O. C. Ferrell, and T. Hult, "Corporate Citizenship: Cultural Antecedents and Business Benefits," *Journal of the Academy of Marketing Science* 27 (1999), pp. 455–69.

53. Details can be found at BP's website, www.bp.com.

54. Hult, G. Tomas M. "Market-Focused Sustainability: Market Orientation Plus!" *Journal of the Academy of Marketing Science* 39, no. 1 (2011). https://ssrn.com/abstract=1671794 or http://dx.doi.org/10.2139/ssrn.1671794.

55. T. Hult, "Market-Focused Sustainability: Market Orientation Plus!"

56. M. Clarkson, "A Stakeholder Framework for Analyzing and Evaluating Corporate Social Performance," *Academy of Management Review* 20 (1995), pp. 92–117; R. Freeman, *Strategic Management: A Stakeholder Approach*(Marshfield, MA: Pitman, 1984); T. Hult, J. Mena, O. Ferrell, and L. Ferrell, "Stakeholder Marketing: A Definition and Conceptual Framework," *AMS Review* 1 (2011), pp. 44–65.

International Trade Theory

6

LEARNING OBJECTIVES

After reading this chapter, you will be able to:

LO6-1   Understand why nations trade with each other.

LO6-2   Summarize the different theories explaining trade flows between nations.

LO6-3   Recognize why many economists believe that unrestricted free trade between nations will raise the economic welfare of countries that participate in a free trade system.

LO6-4   Explain the arguments of those who maintain that government can play a proactive role in promoting national competitive advantage in certain industries.

LO6-5   Understand the important implications that international trade theory holds for management practice.

Nick Haslam/Alamy Stock Photo

A Tale of Two Nations: Ghana and South Korea

OPENING CASE

In 1970, South Korea and the West African nation of Ghana had similar living standards. South Korea's GDP per capita was $260, and Ghana's was $250. Nearly 50 years later, South Korea boasts the world's 11th-largest economy and has a GDP per capita of $32,000, while Ghana's GDP per capita is just $1,786. Clearly, South Korea has grown much faster than Ghana over the last half century. According to a World Bank study, part of the explanation can be found in the different attitudes of both countries toward international trade during the second half of the twentieth century.

Ghana gained its independence from Great Britain in 1957. The country's first President, Kwame Nkrumah, was an early advocate of pan-African socialism. His policies included high tariffs on many imported goods in an effort to foster self-sufficiency in certain manufactured goods, and the adoption of policies that discouraged exports. The results of these inward-oriented policies were a disaster for Ghana. Between 1970 and 1983, living standards in Ghana fell by 35 percent.

For example, when Ghana gained independence, it was a major producer and exporter of cocoa. A combination of favorable climate, good soils, and ready access to world shipping routes made Ghana an ideal place to produce cocoa. Following independence, the government created a state-controlled cocoa marketing board. The board set prices for cocoa and was the sole buyer of cocoa in the country. The board held down the prices it paid farmers for cocoa, while selling their produce on the world market at world prices. Thus, the board might pay farmers 25 cents a pound, and then resell the cocoa on the world market at 50 cents a pound. In effect, the board was taxing exports by paying cocoa producers considerably less than they would get for their product on the world market. The proceeds were then used by the government to fund a policy of nationalization and industrialization to promote self-sufficiency.

Over time, the price that farmers got paid for their cocoa increased by far less than the rate of inflation and the price of cocoa on the world market. As returns to growing cocoa declined, farmers started to switch from producing cocoa to producing subsistence foodstuffs that could be sold profitably within Ghana. The country's production of cocoa and its cocoa exports plummeted. At the same time, the government's attempts to build an industrial base through investments in state-run enterprises failed to yield the anticipated gains. By the 1980s, Ghana was a country in economic crisis, with falling exports and a lack of foreign currency earnings to pay for imports.

In contrast, South Korea embraced a policy of low import barriers on manufactured goods and the creation of incentives to promote exports. Import tariffs and quotas were progressively reduced from the late 1950s onward. In the late 1950s, import tariffs stood at 60 percent. By the 1980s, they were reduced to nearly zero on most manufactured goods. The number of goods subjected to restrictive import quotas was also reduced from more than 90 percent in the 1950s to zero by the early 1980s. Export incentives included lower tax rates on export earnings and low-interest financing for investments in export-oriented industries.

Faced with competition from imports, Korean enterprises had to be efficient to survive. Given the incentives to engage in export activity, in the 1960s Korean producers took advantage of the country's abundant supply of low-cost labor to produce labor-intensive manufactured goods, such as textiles and clothing for the world market. This led to a shift in Korea away from agriculture, toward manufacturing. As labor costs rose, Korean enterprises progressively moved into more capital-intensive goods, including steel, shipbuilding, automobiles, electronics, and telecommunications. In making these shifts, Korean firms were able to draw upon the country's well-educated labor force. The result was export-led growth that dramatically raised living standards for the average Korean.

By the 1990s, Ghana recognized that its economic policies had failed. In 1992, the government started to liberalize the economy, removing price controls, privatizing state-owned enterprises, instituting market-based reforms, and opening Ghana up to foreign investors. Over the next decade, more than 300 state-owned enterprises were privatized, and the new, largely privately held economy was booming, enabling Ghana to achieve one of the highest growth rates in sub-Saharan Africa. The country was helped by the discovery of oil in 2007. Ghana is now a significant exporter of oil. In addition, Ghana remains a major producer and exporter of cocoa, as well as gold. Although the state-run cocoa marketing board still exists, it has been reformed to ensure that farmers get a fair share of their export earnings. Today, one of its stated functions is to promote exports and protect farmers from the adverse impact of volatile commodity prices. In short, Ghana has shifted away from its inward-oriented trade policy.

Sources: "Poor Man's Burden: A Survey of the Third World," *The Economist*, September 23, 1980; J. S. Mah, "Export Promotion Policies, Export Composition and Economic Development in Korea," *Law and Development Review*, 2011; D. M. Quaye, "Export Promotion Programs and Export Performance," *Review of International Business and Strategy*, 2016; T. Williams, "An African Success Story: Ghana's Cocoa Marketing System," *IDS Working Papers*, January 2009.

Introduction

The opening case illustrates the gains that can come from international trade. The economic policies of the Ghanaian government after its independence from Great Britain discouraged trade with other nations. The result was a shift in Ghana's resources away from productive uses (growing cocoa) and toward unproductive uses (subsistence agriculture). In contrast, the economic policies of the South Korean government strongly encouraged trade with other nations. The result was a shift in South Korean resources away from uses where it had no comparative advantage (agriculture) and toward more productive uses (manufacturing). Partly as a consequence of their divergent policies toward international trade, South Korea has grown significantly faster than Ghana over the last half century.

To understand why different approaches to international trade yield different results, we need to take a close look at the intellectual foundations for trade policy; at the impact of trade policy on jobs, income, and economic growth; and at how global trade policy has evolved over the last 70 years. We should also consider the reasons for foreign direct investment (FDI) by corporations because FDI may be a substitute for trade (i.e., exports), or it may support greater global trade. For example, many car companies invest in production facilities in Mexico because that is a good base from which to export finished cars to many other countries.

This is the first of four chapters that deal with the global trade and investment environment. In this chapter, we focus on the theoretical foundations of trade policy. We will also look at what the economic evidence tells us about the relationship between trade policies and economic growth. In Chapter 7, we chart the development of the world trading system, discuss different aspects of trade policy, and look at how trade policy is managed by national and global institutions. In Chapter 8, we discuss the reasons for foreign direct investment and the government policies adopted to manage foreign investment. In Chapter 9, we look at the reasons for creating trading blocks such as the European Union and NAFTA, and we discuss how these transnational agreements have worked out in practice. By the time you have finished these four chapters, you should have a very solid understanding of the international trade and investment environment, and you will understand the extremely important impact that trade and investment policies have upon the practice of international business.

An Overview of Trade Theory

We open this chapter with a discussion of mercantilism. Propagated in the sixteenth and seventeenth centuries, mercantilism advocated that countries should simultaneously encourage exports and discourage imports. Although mercantilism is an old and largely discredited doctrine, its echoes remain in modern political debate and in the trade policies of many countries. Indeed, some have argued that Donald Trump espouses mercantilist views. Next, we look at Adam Smith's theory of absolute advantage. Proposed in 1776, Smith's theory was the first to explain why unrestricted free trade is beneficial to a country. **Free trade** refers to a situation in which a government does not attempt to influence through quotas or duties what its citizens can buy from another country or what they can produce and sell to another country. Smith argued that the invisible hand of the market mechanism, rather than government policy, should determine what a country imports and what it exports. His arguments imply that such a laissez-faire stance toward trade was in the best interests of a country. Building on Smith's work are two additional theories that we review. One is the theory of comparative advantage, advanced by the nineteenth-century English economist David Ricardo. This theory is the intellectual basis of the modern argument for unrestricted free trade. In the twentieth century, Ricardo's work was refined by two Swedish economists, Eli Heckscher and Bertil Ohlin, whose theory is known as the Heckscher–Ohlin theory.

THE BENEFITS OF TRADE

The great strength of the theories of Smith, Ricardo, and Heckscher-Ohlin is that they identify with precision the specific benefits of international trade. Common sense suggests that some international trade is beneficial. For example, nobody would suggest that Iceland should grow its own oranges. Iceland can benefit from trade by exchanging some of the products that it can produce at a low cost (fish) for some products that it cannot produce at all (oranges). Thus, by engaging in international trade, Icelanders are able to add oranges to their diet of fish.

The theories of Smith, Ricardo, and Heckscher-Ohlin go beyond this commonsense notion, however, to show why it is beneficial for a country to engage in international trade *even for products it is able to produce for itself.* This is a difficult concept for people to grasp. For example, many people in the United States believe that American consumers should buy products made in the United States by American companies whenever possible to help save American jobs from foreign competition. The same kind of nationalistic sentiments can be observed in many other countries.

However, the theories of Smith, Ricardo, and Heckscher-Ohlin tell us that a country's economy may gain if its citizens buy certain products from other nations that could be produced at home. The gains arise because international trade allows a country to *specialize* in the manufacture and export of products that can be produced most efficiently in that country, while importing products that can be produced more efficiently in other countries.

LO6-1
Understand why nations trade with each other.

▶ **Did You Know?**

Did you know that the last time the United States imposed tariffs on imports of steel it led to job losses?

Visit your instructor's Connect® course and click on your eBook or SmartBook® to view a short video explanation from the author.

globalEDGE TRADE TUTORIALS

In this chapter, we discuss benefits and costs associated with free trade, discuss the benefits of international trade, and explain the pattern of international trade in today's world economy. The general idea is that international trade theories explain why it can be beneficial for a country to engage in trade across country borders, even though countries are at different stages of development, have different product needs, and produce different types of products. International trade theory assumes that countries—through their governments, laws, and regulations—engage in more or less trade across borders. In reality, the vast majority of trade happens across borders by companies from different countries. As related to this chapter, check out globalEDGE™'s "trade tutorials" section, where lots of information, data, and tools are compiled related to trading internationally (**globaledge.msu.edu/global-resources/trade-tutorials**). The potpourri of trade resources includes export tutorials, online course modules, a glossary, a free trade agreement tariff tool, and much more. The glossary includes lots of terms related to trade. For example, "trade surplus" is defined as a situation in which a country's exports exceeds its imports (i.e., it represents a net inflow of domestic currency from foreign markets). The opposite is called trade deficit and is considered a net outflow, but how is it really defined? The globalEDGE™ glossary can help.

Thus, it may make sense for the United States to specialize in the production and export of commercial jet aircraft because the efficient production of commercial jet aircraft requires resources that are abundant in the United States, such as a highly skilled labor force and cutting-edge technological know-how. On the other hand, it may make sense for the United States to import textiles from Bangladesh because the efficient production of textiles requires a relatively cheap labor force—and cheap labor is not abundant in the United States.

Of course, this economic argument is often difficult for segments of a country's population to accept. With their future threatened by imports, U.S. textile companies and their

A Rolex Group logo sits on display above a luxury wristwatch store in Vienna, Austria.

Bloomberg/Getty Images

employees have tried hard to persuade the government to limit the importation of textiles by demanding quotas and tariffs. Although such import controls may benefit particular groups, such as textile businesses and their employees, the theories of Smith, Ricardo, and Heckscher–Ohlin suggest that the economy as a whole is hurt by such action. One of the key insights of international trade theory is that limits on imports are often in the interests of domestic producers but not domestic consumers.

THE PATTERN OF INTERNATIONAL TRADE

The theories of Smith, Ricardo, and Heckscher–Ohlin help explain the pattern of international trade that we observe in the world economy. Some aspects of the pattern are easy to understand. Climate and natural resource endowments explain why Ghana exports cocoa, Brazil exports coffee, Saudi Arabia exports oil, and China exports crawfish. However, much of the observed pattern of international trade is more difficult to explain. For example, why does Japan export automobiles, consumer electronics, and machine tools? Why does Switzerland export chemicals, pharmaceuticals, watches, and jewelry? Why does Bangladesh export garments? David Ricardo's theory of comparative advantage offers an explanation in terms of international differences in labor productivity. The more sophisticated Heckscher–Ohlin theory emphasizes the interplay between the proportions in which the factors of production (such as land, labor, and capital) are available in different countries and the proportions in which they are needed for producing particular goods. This explanation rests on the assumption that countries have varying endowments of the various factors of production. Tests of this theory, however, suggest that it is a less powerful explanation of real-world trade patterns than once thought.

One early response to the failure of the Heckscher–Ohlin theory to explain the observed pattern of international trade was the product life-cycle theory. Proposed by Raymond Vernon, this theory suggests that early in their life cycle, most new products are produced in and exported from the country in which they were developed. As a new product becomes widely accepted internationally, however, production starts in other countries. As a result, the theory suggests, the product may ultimately be exported back to the country of its original innovation.

In a similar vein, during the 1980s, economists such as Paul Krugman developed what has come to be known as the new trade theory. **New trade theory** (for which Krugman won the Nobel Prize in economics in 2008) stresses that in some cases, countries specialize in the production and export of particular products not because of underlying differences in factor endowments but because in certain industries the world market can support only a limited number of firms. (This is argued to be the case for the commercial aircraft industry.) In such industries, firms that enter the market first are able to build a competitive advantage that is subsequently difficult to challenge. Thus, the observed pattern of trade between nations may be due in part to the ability of firms within a given nation to capture first-mover advantages. The United States is a major exporter of commercial jet aircraft because American firms such as Boeing were first movers in the world market. Boeing built a competitive advantage that has subsequently been difficult for firms from countries with equally favorable factor endowments to challenge (although Europe's Airbus has succeeded in doing that). In a work related to the new trade theory, Michael Porter developed a theory referred to as the theory of national competitive advantage. This attempts to explain why particular nations achieve international success in particular industries. In addition to factor endowments, Porter points out the importance of country factors such as domestic demand and domestic rivalry in explaining a nation's dominance in the production and export of particular products.

TRADE THEORY AND GOVERNMENT POLICY

Although all these theories agree that international trade is beneficial to a country, they lack agreement in their recommendations for government policy. Mercantilism makes a case for government involvement in promoting exports and limiting imports. The theories of Smith, Ricardo, and Heckscher–Ohlin form part of the case for unrestricted free trade. The argument for unrestricted free trade is that both import controls and export incentives (such as subsidies) are self-defeating and result in wasted resources. Both the new trade theory and Porter's theory of national competitive advantage can be interpreted as justifying some limited government intervention to support the development of certain export-oriented industries. We discuss the pros and cons of this argument, known as strategic trade policy, as well as the pros and cons of the argument for unrestricted free trade, in Chapter 7.

Mercantilism

The first theory of international trade, mercantilism, emerged in England in the mid-sixteenth century. The principle assertion of mercantilism was that gold and silver were the mainstays of national wealth and essential to vigorous commerce. At that time, gold and silver were the currency of trade between countries; a country could earn gold and silver by exporting goods. Conversely, importing goods from other countries would result in an outflow of gold and silver from those countries. The main tenet of **mercantilism** was that it was in a country's best interests to maintain a trade surplus, to export more than it imported. By doing so, a country would accumulate gold and silver and, consequently, increase its national wealth, prestige, and power. As the English mercantilist writer Thomas Mun put it in 1630:

> The ordinary means therefore to increase our wealth and treasure is by foreign trade, wherein we must ever observe this rule: to sell more to strangers yearly than we consume of theirs in value.[1]

Consistent with this belief, the mercantilist doctrine advocated government intervention to achieve a surplus in the balance of trade. The mercantilists saw no virtue in a large volume of trade. Rather, they recommended policies to maximize exports and minimize imports. To achieve this, imports were limited by tariffs and quotas, while exports were subsidized.

The classical economist David Hume pointed out an inherent inconsistency in the mercantilist doctrine in 1752. According to Hume, if England had a balance-of-trade surplus with France (it exported more than it imported), the resulting inflow of gold and silver would swell the domestic money supply and generate inflation in England. In France, however, the outflow of gold and silver would have the opposite effect. France's money supply would contract, and its prices would fall. This change in relative prices between France and England would encourage the French to buy fewer English goods (because they were becoming more expensive) and the English to buy more French goods (because they were becoming cheaper). The result would be a deterioration in the English balance of trade and an improvement in France's trade balance, until the English surplus was eliminated. Hence, according to Hume, in the long run, no country could sustain a surplus on the balance of trade and so accumulate gold and silver as the mercantilists had envisaged.

The flaw with mercantilism was that it viewed trade as a zero-sum game. (A **zero-sum game** is one in which a gain by one country results in a loss by another.) It was left to Adam Smith and David Ricardo to show the limitations of this approach and to demonstrate that trade is a positive-sum game, or a situation in which all countries can benefit. Despite this, the mercantilist doctrine is by no means dead. For example, the U.S. President Donald Trump appears to advocate neo-mercantilist policies.[2] Neo-mercantilists equate political power with economic power and economic power with a balance-of-trade surplus. Critics argue that several nations have adopted a neo-mercantilist strategy that is designed to simultaneously boost exports and limit imports.[3] For example, they charge that China long pursued a neo-mercantilist policy, deliberately keeping its currency value low against the U.S. dollar in order to sell more goods to the United States and other developed nations, and thus amass a trade surplus and foreign exchange reserves (see the accompanying Country Focus).

LO6-2

Summarize the different theories explaining trade flows between nations.

Is China Manipulating Its Currency in Pursuit of a Neo-Mercantilist Policy?

China's rapid rise in economic power has been built on export-led growth. For decades, the country's exports have been growing faster than its imports. This has led some critics to claim that China is pursuing a neo-mercantilist policy, trying to amass record trade surpluses and foreign currency that will give it economic power over developed nations. By the end of 2014, its foreign exchange reserves exceeded $3.8 trillion, some 60 percent of which were held in U.S.-denominated assets such as U.S. Treasury bills. Observers worried that if China ever decided to sell its holdings of U.S. currency, that would depress the value of the dollar against other currencies and increase the price of imports into America.

America's trade deficit with China has been a particular cause for concern. In 2017, this reached a record $375 billion. At the same time, China has long resisted attempts to let its currency float freely against the U.S. dollar. Many have claimed that China's currency has been too cheap and that this keeps the prices of China's goods artificially low, which fuels the country's exports. China, the critics charge, is guilty of currency manipulation.

So is China manipulating the value of its currency to keep exports artificially cheap? The facts of the matter are less clear than the rhetoric. China actually started to allow the value of the *yuan* (China's currency) to appreciate against the dollar in July 2005, albeit at a slow pace. In July 2005, one U.S. dollar purchased 8.11 yuan. By January 2014 one U.S. dollar purchased 6.05 yuan, which implied a 25 percent increase in the price of Chinese exports, not what one would expect from a country that was trying to keep the price of its exports low through currency manipulation.

Moreover, in 2015 and 2016, the rate of growth in China started to slow significantly. China's stock market fell sharply, and capital started to leave the country, with investors selling yuan and buying U.S. dollars. To stop the yuan from *declining* in value against the U.S. dollar, China began to spend about $100 billion of its foreign exchange reserves *every month* to buy yuan on the open market. Far from allowing its currency to decline against the U.S. dollar, thereby giving a boost to its exports, China was trying to prop up its value, running down its foreign exchange reserves by $2 trillion in the process. This action seems inconsistent with the charges that the country is pursuing a neo-mercantilist policy by artificially depressing the value of its currency. In recognition of these developments, in late 2017 the U.S. Treasury Department declined to name China a currency manipulator and moderated its criticism of the country's foreign exchange policies. On the other hand, The Treasury said that it remained concerned by the lack of progress in reducing China's bilateral trade surplus with the United States.

Sources: S. H. Hanke, "Stop the Mercantilists," *Forbes*, June 20, 2005, p. 164; G. Dyer and A. Balls, "Dollar Threat as China Signals Shift," *Financial Times*, January 6, 2006; Richard Silk, "China's Foreign Exchange Reserves Jump Again," *The Wall Street Journal*, October 15, 2013; Terence Jeffrey, "U.S. Merchandise Trade Deficit with China Hit Record in 2015," cnsnews.com, February 9, 2016; "Trump's Chinese Currency Manipulation," *The Wall Street Journal*, December 7, 2016; Elena Holodny, "The Treasury Department Backs Down on Some of Its Criticisms of China's Currency Policies," *Business Insider*, October 18, 2017; and Ana Swanson,"U.S.-China Trade Deficit Hits Record, Fueling Trade Fight," *The New York Times*, February 6, 2018.

LO6-2

Summarize the different theories explaining trade flows between nations.

Absolute Advantage

In his 1776 landmark book *The Wealth of Nations*, Adam Smith attacked the mercantilist assumption that trade is a zero-sum game. Smith argued that countries differ in their ability to produce goods efficiently. In his time, the English, by virtue of their superior manufacturing processes, were the world's most efficient textile manufacturers. Due to the combination of favorable climate, good soils, and accumulated expertise, the French had the world's most efficient wine industry. The English had an *absolute advantage* in the production of textiles, while the French had an *absolute advantage* in the production of wine. Thus, a country has an **absolute advantage** in the production of a product when it is more efficient than any other country at producing it.

According to Smith, countries should specialize in the production of goods for which they have an absolute advantage and then trade these goods for those produced by other countries. In Smith's time, this suggested the English should specialize in the production of textiles, while the French should specialize in the production of wine. England could get all the wine it needed by selling its textiles to France and buying wine in exchange. Similarly, France could get all the textiles it needed by selling wine to England and buying textiles in exchange. Smith's basic argument, therefore, is that a country should never produce goods at home that it can buy at a lower cost from other countries. Smith demonstrates that by specializing in the production of goods in which each has an absolute advantage, both countries benefit by engaging in trade.

Consider the effects of trade between two countries, Ghana and South Korea. The production of any good (output) requires resources (inputs) such as land, labor, and capital. Assume that Ghana and South Korea both have the same amount of resources and that these resources can be used to produce either rice or cocoa. Assume further that 200 units of resources are available in each country. Imagine that in Ghana it takes 10 resources to produce 1 ton of cocoa and 20 resources to produce 1 ton of rice. Thus, Ghana could produce 20 tons of cocoa and no rice, 10 tons of rice and no cocoa, or some combination of rice and cocoa between these two extremes. The different combinations that Ghana could produce are represented by the line GG' in Figure 6.1. This is referred to as Ghana's *production possibility frontier (PPF)*. Similarly, imagine that in South Korea it takes 40 resources to produce 1 ton of cocoa and 10 resources to produce 1 ton of rice. Thus, South Korea could produce 5 tons of cocoa and no rice, 20 tons of rice and no cocoa, or some combination between these two extremes. The different combinations available to South Korea are represented by the line KK' in Figure 6.1, which is South Korea's PPF. Clearly, Ghana has an absolute advantage in the production of cocoa. (More resources are needed to produce a ton of cocoa in South Korea than in Ghana.) By the same token, South Korea has an absolute advantage in the production of rice.

Now consider a situation in which neither country trades with any other. Each country devotes half its resources to the production of rice and half to the production of cocoa. Each country must also consume what it produces. Ghana would be able to produce 10 tons of cocoa and 5 tons of rice (point A in Figure 6.1), while South Korea would be able to produce 10 tons of rice and 2.5 tons of cocoa (point B in Figure 6.1). Without trade, the combined production of both countries would be 12.5 tons of cocoa (10 tons in Ghana plus 2.5 tons in South Korea) and 15 tons of rice (5 tons in Ghana and 10 tons in South Korea). If each country were to specialize in producing the good for which it had an absolute advantage and then trade with the other for the good it lacks, Ghana could produce 20 tons of cocoa, and South Korea could produce 20 tons of rice. Thus, by specializing, the production of both goods could be increased. Production of cocoa would increase from 12.5 tons to 20 tons, while production of rice would

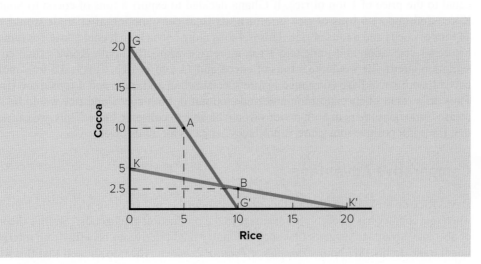

FIGURE 6.1

The theory of absolute advantage.

TABLE 6.1

Absolute Advantage and
the Gains from Trade

Resources Required to Produce 1 Ton of Cocoa and Rice		
	Cocoa	**Rice**
Ghana	10	20
South Korea	40	10
Production and Consumption without Trade		
Ghana	10.0	5.0
South Korea	2.5	10.0
Total production	12.5	15.0
Production with Specialization		
Ghana	20.0	0.0
South Korea	0.0	20.0
Total production	20.0	20.0
Consumption after Ghana Trades 6 Tons of Cocoa for 6 Tons of South Korean Rice		
Ghana	14.0	6.0
South Korea	6.0	14.0
Increase in Consumption as a Result of Specialization and Trade		
Ghana	4.0	1.0
South Korea	3.5	4.0

increase from 15 tons to 20 tons. The increase in production that would result from specialization is therefore 7.5 tons of cocoa and 5 tons of rice. Table 6.1 summarizes these figures.

By engaging in trade and swapping 1 ton of cocoa for 1 ton of rice, producers in both countries could consume more of both cocoa and rice. Imagine that Ghana and South Korea swap cocoa and rice on a one-to-one basis; that is, the price of 1 ton of cocoa is equal to the price of 1 ton of rice. If Ghana decided to export 6 tons of cocoa to South Korea and import 6 tons of rice in return, its final consumption after trade would be 14 tons of cocoa and 6 tons of rice. This is 4 tons more cocoa than it could have consumed before specialization and trade and 1 ton more rice. Similarly, South Korea's final consumption after trade would be 6 tons of cocoa and 14 tons of rice. This is 3.5 tons more cocoa than it could have consumed before specialization and trade and 4 tons more rice. Thus, as a result of specialization and trade, output of both cocoa and rice would be increased, and consumers in both nations would be able to consume more. Thus, we can see that trade is a positive-sum game; it produces net gains for all involved.

LO6-2

Summarize the different theories explaining trade flows between nations.

Comparative Advantage

David Ricardo took Adam Smith's theory one step further by exploring what might happen when one country has an absolute advantage in the production of all goods.[4] Smith's theory of absolute advantage suggests that such a country might derive no benefits from international trade. In his 1817 book *Principles of Political Economy*, Ricardo showed that this was

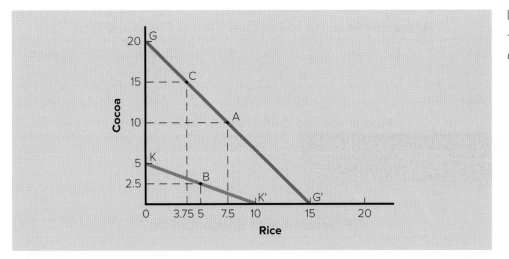

FIGURE 6.2

The theory of comparative advantage.

not the case. According to Ricardo's theory of comparative advantage, it makes sense for a country to specialize in the production of those goods that it produces most efficiently and to buy the goods that it produces less efficiently from other countries, even if this means buying goods from other countries that it could produce more efficiently itself.[5] While this may seem counterintuitive, the logic can be explained with a simple example.

Assume that Ghana is more efficient in the production of both cocoa and rice; that is, Ghana has an absolute advantage in the production of both products. In Ghana it takes 10 resources to produce 1 ton of cocoa and 13.33 resources to produce 1 ton of rice. Thus, given its 200 units of resources, Ghana can produce 20 tons of cocoa and no rice, 15 tons of rice and no cocoa, or any combination in between on its PPF (the line GG' in Figure 6.2). In South Korea, it takes 40 resources to produce 1 ton of cocoa and 20 re-sources to produce 1 ton of rice. Thus, South Korea can produce 5 tons of cocoa and no rice, 10 tons of rice and no cocoa, or any combination on its PPF (the line KK' in Figure 6.2). Again assume that without trade, each country uses half its resources to produce rice and half to produce cocoa. Thus, without trade, Ghana will produce 10 tons of cocoa and 7.5 tons of rice (point A in Figure 6.2), while South Korea will produce 2.5 tons of cocoa and 5 tons of rice (point B in Figure 6.2).

In light of Ghana's absolute advantage in the production of both goods, why should it trade with South Korea? Although Ghana has an absolute advantage in the production of both cocoa and rice, it has a comparative advantage only in the production of cocoa: Ghana can produce 4 times as much cocoa as South Korea, but only 1.5 times as much rice. Ghana is *comparatively* more efficient at producing cocoa than it is at producing rice.

Without trade the combined production of cocoa will be 12.5 tons (10 tons in Ghana and 2.5 in South Korea), and the combined production of rice will also be 12.5 tons (7.5 tons in Ghana and 5 tons in South Korea). Without trade each country must consume what it produces. By engaging in trade, the two countries can increase their combined pro-duction of rice and cocoa, and consumers in both nations can consume more of both goods.

THE GAINS FROM TRADE

Imagine that Ghana exploits its comparative advantage in the production of cocoa to increase its output from 10 tons to 15 tons. This uses up 150 units of resources, leaving the remaining 50 units of resources to use in producing 3.75 tons of rice (point C in Figure 6.2). Meanwhile, South Korea specializes in the production of rice, producing 10 tons. The combined output of both cocoa and rice has now increased. Before special-ization, the combined output was 12.5 tons of cocoa and 12.5 tons of rice. Now it is 15 tons of cocoa and 13.75 tons of rice (3.75 tons in Ghana and 10 tons in South Korea). The source of the increase in production is summarized in Table 6.2.

TABLE 6.2

Comparative Advantage and the Gains from Trade

Resources Required to Produce 1 Ton of Cocoa and Rice		
	Cocoa	**Rice**
Ghana	10	13.33
South Korea	40	20
Production and Consumption without Trade		
Ghana	10.0	7.5
South Korea	2.5	5.0
Total production	12.5	12.5
Production with Specialization		
Ghana	15.0	3.75
South Korea	0.0	10.0
Total production	15.0	13.75
Consumption after Ghana Trades 4 Tons of Cocoa for 4 Tons of South Korean Rice		
Ghana	11.0	7.75
South Korea	4.0	6.0
Increase in Consumption as a Result of Specialization and Trade		
Ghana	1.0	0.25
South Korea	1.5	1.0

Not only is output higher, but both countries also can now benefit from trade. If Ghana and South Korea swap cocoa and rice on a one-to-one basis, with both countries choosing to exchange 4 tons of their export for 4 tons of the import, both countries are able to consume more cocoa and rice than they could before specialization and trade (see Table 6.2). Thus, if Ghana exchanges 4 tons of cocoa with South Korea for 4 tons of rice, it is still left with 11 tons of cocoa, which is 1 ton more than it had before trade. The 4 tons of rice it gets from South Korea in exchange for its 4 tons of cocoa, when added to the 3.75 tons it now produces domestically, leave it with a total of 7.75 tons of rice, which is 0.25 ton more than it had before specialization. Similarly, after swapping 4 tons of rice with Ghana, South Korea still ends up with 6 tons of rice, which is more than it had before specialization. In addition, the 4 tons of cocoa it receives in exchange is 1.5 tons more than it produced before trade. Thus, consumption of cocoa and rice can increase in both countries as a result of specialization and trade.

The basic message of the theory of comparative advantage is that *potential world production is greater with unrestricted free trade than it is with restricted trade*. Ricardo's theory suggests that consumers in all nations can consume more if there are no restrictions on trade. This occurs even in countries that lack an absolute advantage in the production of any good. In other words, to an even greater degree than the theory of absolute advantage, *the theory of comparative advantage suggests that trade is a positive-sum game in which all countries that participate realize economic gains*. This theory provides a strong rationale for encouraging free trade. So powerful is Ricardo's theory that it remains a major intellectual weapon for those who argue for free trade.

QUALIFICATIONS AND ASSUMPTIONS

The conclusion that free trade is universally beneficial is a rather bold one to draw from such a simple model. Our simple model includes many unrealistic assumptions:

1. We have assumed a simple world in which there are only two countries and two goods. In the real world, there are many countries and many goods.

2. We have assumed away transportation costs between countries.

3. We have assumed away differences in the prices of resources in different countries. We have said nothing about exchange rates, simply assuming that cocoa and rice could be swapped on a one-to-one basis.

4. We have assumed that resources can move freely from the production of one good to another within a country. In reality, this is not always the case.

5. We have assumed constant returns to scale; that is, that specialization by Ghana or South Korea has no effect on the amount of resources required to produce one ton of cocoa or rice. In reality, both diminishing and increasing returns to specialization exist. The amount of resources required to produce a good might decrease or increase as a nation specializes in production of that good.

6. We have assumed that each country has a fixed stock of resources and that free trade does not change the efficiency with which a country uses its resources. This static assumption makes no allowances for the dynamic changes in a country's stock of resources and in the efficiency with which the country uses its resources that might result from free trade.

7. We have assumed away the effects of trade on income distribution within a country.

Given these assumptions, can the conclusion that free trade is mutually beneficial be extended to the real world of many countries, many goods, positive transportation costs, volatile exchange rates, immobile domestic resources, nonconstant returns to specialization, and dynamic changes? Although a detailed extension of the theory of comparative advantage is beyond the scope of this book, economists have shown that the basic result derived from our simple model can be generalized to a world composed of many countries producing many different goods.[6] Despite the shortcomings of the Ricardian model, research suggests that the basic proposition that countries will export the goods that they are most efficient at producing is borne out by the data.[7]

However, once all the assumptions are dropped, the case for unrestricted free trade, while still positive, has been argued by some economists associated with the "new trade theory" to lose some of its strength.[8] We return to this issue later in this chapter and in the next when we discuss the new trade theory. In a recent and widely discussed analysis, the Nobel Prize–winning economist Paul Samuelson argued that contrary to the standard interpretation, in certain circumstances the theory of comparative advantage predicts that a rich country might actually be *worse* off by switching to a free trade regime with a poor nation.[9] We consider Samuelson's critique in the next section.

EXTENSIONS OF THE RICARDIAN MODEL

Let us explore the effect of relaxing three of the assumptions identified earlier in the simple comparative advantage model. Next, we relax the assumptions that resources move freely from the production of one good to another within a country, that there are constant returns to scale, and that trade does not change a country's stock of resources or the efficiency with which those resources are utilized.

Immobile Resources

In our simple comparative model of Ghana and South Korea, we assumed that producers (farmers) could easily convert land from the production of cocoa to rice and vice versa. While this assumption may hold for some agricultural products, resources do not always shift quite so easily from producing one good to another. A certain amount of friction is involved. For example, embracing a free trade regime for an advanced economy such as the United States often implies that the country will produce less of some labor-intensive goods, such as textiles, and more of some knowledge-intensive goods, such as computer software or biotechnology products. Although the country as a whole will gain from such a shift, textile producers will lose. A textile worker in South Carolina is probably not qualified to write software for Microsoft. Thus, the shift to free trade may mean that she becomes unemployed or has to accept another less attractive job, such as working at a fast-food restaurant.

Resources do not always move easily from one economic activity to another. The process creates friction and human suffering, too. While the theory predicts that the benefits of free trade outweigh the costs by a significant margin, this is of cold comfort to those who bear the costs. Accordingly, political opposition to the adoption of a free trade regime typically comes from those whose jobs are most at risk. In the United States, for example, textile workers and their unions have long opposed the move toward free trade precisely because this group has much to lose from free trade. Governments often ease the transition toward free trade by helping retrain those who lose their jobs as a result. The pain caused by the movement toward a free trade regime is a short-term phenomenon, while the gains from trade once the transition has been made are both significant and enduring.

Diminishing Returns

The simple comparative advantage model developed above assumes constant returns to specialization. By **constant returns to specialization** we mean the units of resources required to produce a good (cocoa or rice) are assumed to remain constant no matter where one is on a country's production possibility frontier (PPF). Thus, we assumed that it always took Ghana 10 units of resources to produce 1 ton of cocoa. However, it is more realistic to assume diminishing returns to specialization. Diminishing returns to specialization occur when more units of resources are required to produce each additional unit. While 10 units of resources may be sufficient to increase Ghana's output of cocoa from 12 tons to 13 tons, 11 units of resources may be needed to increase output from 13 to 14 tons, 12 units of resources to increase output from 14 tons to 15 tons, and so on. Diminishing returns imply a convex PPF for Ghana (see Figure 6.3), rather than the straight line depicted in Figure 6.2.

It is more realistic to assume diminishing returns for two reasons. First, not all resources are of the same quality. As a country tries to increase its output of a certain good, it is increasingly likely to draw on more marginal resources whose productivity is not as great as

FIGURE 6.3

Ghana's PPF under diminishing returns.

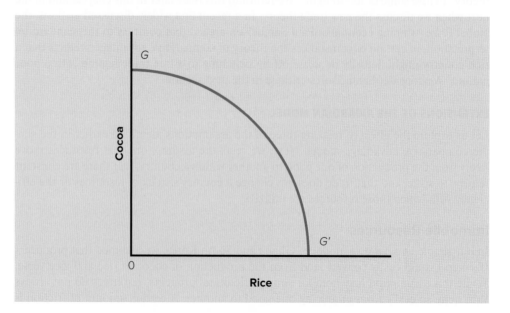

those initially employed. The result is that it requires ever more resources to produce an equal increase in output. For example, some land is more productive than other land. As Ghana tries to expand its output of cocoa, it might have to utilize increasingly marginal land that is less fertile than the land it originally used. As yields per acre decline, Ghana must use more land to produce 1 ton of cocoa.

A second reason for diminishing returns is that different goods use resources in different proportions. For example, imagine that growing cocoa uses more land and less labor than growing rice and that Ghana tries to transfer resources from rice production to cocoa production. The rice industry will release proportionately too much labor and too little land for efficient cocoa production. To absorb the additional resources of labor and land, the cocoa industry will have to shift toward more labor-intensive methods of production. The effect is that the efficiency with which the cocoa industry uses labor will decline, and returns will diminish.

Diminishing returns show that it is not feasible for a country to specialize to the degree suggested by the simple Ricardian model outlined earlier. Diminishing returns to specialization suggest that the gains from specialization are likely to be exhausted before specialization is complete. In reality, most countries do not specialize, but instead produce a range of goods. However, the theory predicts that it is worthwhile to specialize until that point where the resulting gains from trade are outweighed by diminishing returns. Thus, the basic conclusion that unrestricted free trade is beneficial still holds, although because of diminishing returns, the gains may not be as great as suggested in the constant returns case.

Dynamic Effects and Economic Growth

LO6-3

Recognize why many economists believe that unrestricted free trade between nations will raise the economic welfare of countries that participate in a free trade system.

The simple comparative advantage model assumed that trade does not change a country's stock of resources or the efficiency with which it utilizes those resources. This static assumption makes no allowances for the dynamic changes that might result from trade. If we relax this assumption, it becomes apparent that opening an economy to trade is likely to generate dynamic gains of two sorts.[10] First, free trade might increase a country's stock of resources as increased supplies of labor and capital from abroad become available for use within the country. For example, this has been occurring in eastern Europe since the early 1990s, with many western businesses investing significant capital in the former communist countries.

Second, free trade might also increase the efficiency with which a country uses its resources. Gains in the efficiency of resource utilization could arise from a number of factors. For example, economies of large-scale production might become available as trade expands the size of the total market available to domestic firms. Trade might make better technology from abroad available to domestic firms; better technology can increase labor productivity or the productivity of land. (The so-called green revolution had this effect on agricultural outputs in developing countries.) Also, opening an economy to foreign competition might stimulate domestic producers to look for ways to increase their efficiency. Again, this phenomenon has arguably been occurring in the once-protected markets of eastern Europe, where many former state monopolies have had to increase the efficiency of their operations to survive in the competitive world market.

Dynamic gains in both the stock of a country's resources and the efficiency with which resources are utilized will cause a country's PPF to shift outward. This is illustrated in Figure 6.4, where the shift from PPF^1 to PPF^2 results from the dynamic gains that arise from free trade. As a consequence of this outward shift, the country in Figure 6.4 can produce more of both goods than it did before introduction of free trade. The theory suggests that opening an economy to free trade not only results in static gains of the type discussed earlier but also results in dynamic gains that stimulate economic growth. If this is so, then one might think that the case for free trade becomes stronger still, and in general it does. However, as noted, one of the leading economic theorists of the twentieth century, Paul Samuelson, argued that in some circumstances, dynamic gains can lead to an outcome that is not so beneficial.

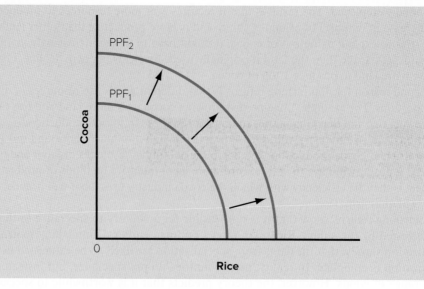

Trade, Jobs, and Wages: The Samuelson Critique

Paul Samuelson's critique looks at what happens when a rich country—the United States—enters into a free trade agreement with a poor country—China—that rapidly improves its productivity after the introduction of a free trade regime (i.e., there is a dynamic gain in the efficiency with which resources are used in the poor country). Samuelson's model suggests that in such cases, the lower prices that U.S. consumers pay for goods imported from China following the introduction of a free trade regime *may* not be enough to produce a net gain for the U.S. economy if the dynamic effect of free trade is to lower real wage rates in the United States. As he stated in a *New York Times* interview, "Being able to purchase groceries 20 percent cheaper at Wal-Mart (due to international trade) does not necessarily make up for the wage losses (in America)."[11]

Samuelson was particularly concerned about the ability to offshore service jobs that traditionally were not internationally mobile, such as software debugging, call-center jobs, accounting jobs, and even medical diagnosis of MRI scans (see the accompanying Country Focus for details). Advances in communications technology since the development of the World Wide Web in the early 1990s have made this possible, effectively expanding the labor market for these jobs to include educated people in places such as India, the Philippines, and China. When coupled with rapid advances in the productivity of foreign labor due to better education, the effect on middle-class wages in the United States, according to Samuelson, may be similar to mass inward migration into the country: It will lower the market clearing wage rate, *perhaps* by enough to outweigh the positive benefits of international trade.

Having said this, it should be noted that Samuelson concedes that free trade has historically benefited rich countries (as data discussed later seem to confirm). Moreover, he notes that introducing protectionist measures (e.g., trade barriers) to guard against the theoretical possibility that free trade may harm the United States in the future may produce a situation that is worse than the disease they are trying to prevent. To quote Samuelson: "Free trade may turn out pragmatically to be still best for each region in comparison to lobbyist-induced tariffs and quotas which involve both a perversion of democracy and non-subtle deadweight distortion losses."[12]

One notable recent study by MIT economist David Autor and his associates found evidence in support of Samuelson's thesis. The study has been widely quoted in the media and cited by politicians. Autor and his associates looked at every county in the United States for its manufacturers' exposure to competition from China.[13] The researchers found that regions most exposed to China tended not only to lose more manufacturing jobs, but

Moving U.S. White-Collar Jobs Offshore

Economists have long argued that free trade produces gains for all countries that participate in a free trading system. As globalization continues to sweep through the U.S. economy, many people are wondering if this is true. During the 1980s and 1990s, free trade was associated with the movement of low-skill, blue-collar manufacturing jobs out of rich countries such as the United States and toward low-wage countries—textiles to Costa Rica, athletic shoes to the Philippines, steel to Brazil, electronic products to Thailand, and so on. While many observers bemoaned the "hollowing out" of U.S. manufacturing, economists stated that high-skill and high-wage white-collar jobs associated with the knowledge-based economy would stay in the United States. Computers might be assembled in Thailand, so the argument went, but they would continue to be designed in Silicon Valley by highly skilled U.S. engineers, and software applications would be written in the United States by programmers at Apple, Microsoft, Adobe, Oracle, and the like.

Developments over the past several decades have people questioning this assumption. Many American companies have been moving white-collar, knowledge-based jobs to developing nations where they can be performed for a fraction of the cost. For example, a few years ago Bank of America cut nearly 5,000 jobs from its 25,000-strong, U.S.-based information technology workforce. Some of these jobs were transferred to India, where work that costs $100 an hour in the United States could be done for $20 an hour. One beneficiary of Bank of America's downsizing is Infosys Technologies Ltd., a Bangalore, India, information technology firm where 250 engineers now develop information technology applications for the bank. Other Infosys employees are busy processing home loan applications for U.S. mortgage companies. Nearby in

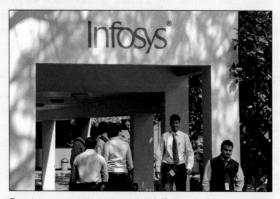

Employees walk below the Infosys Ltd. logo at the company's campus in Electronics City in Bangalore, India.

Vivek Prakash/Bloomberg/Getty Images

the offices of another Indian firm, Wipro Ltd., radiologists interpret 30 CT scans a day for Massachusetts General Hospital that are sent over the internet. At yet another Bangalore business, engineers earn $10,000 a year designing leading-edge semiconductor chips for Texas Instruments. Nor is India the only beneficiary of these changes.

Some architectural work also is being outsourced to lower-cost locations. Flour Corp., a Texas-based construction company, employs engineers and drafters in the Philippines, Poland, and India to turn layouts of industrial facilities into detailed specifications. For a Saudi Arabian chemical plant Flour designed, 200 young engineers based in the Philippines earning less than $3,000 a year collaborated in real time over the internet with elite U.S. and British engineers who make up to $100,000 a year. Why did Flour do this? According to the company, the answer was simple. Doing so reduces the prices of a project by 15 percent, giving the company a cost-based competitive advantage in the global market for construction design. Also troubling for future job growth in the United States, some high-tech start-ups are outsourcing significant work right from inception. For example, Zoho Corporation, a California-based start-up offering online web applications for small businesses, has about 20 employees in the United States and more than 1,000 in India!

Sources: P. Engardio, A. Bernstein, and M. Kripalani, "Is Your Job Next?" *BusinessWeek*, February 3, 2003, pp. 50–60; "America's Pain, India's Gain," *The Economist*, January 11, 2003, p. 57; M. Schroeder and T. Aeppel, "Skilled Workers Mount Opposition to Free Trade, Swaying Politicians," *The Wall Street Journal*, October 10, 2003, pp. A1, A11; D. Clark,"New U.S. Fees on Visas Irk Outsources," *The Wall Street Journal*, August 16, 2010, p. 6; and J. R. Hagerty, "U.S. Loses High Tech Jobs as R&D Shifts to Asia," *The Wall Street Journal*, January 18, 2012, p. B1.

also to see overall employment decline. Areas with higher exposure to China also had larger increases in workers receiving unemployment insurance, food stamps, and disability payments. The costs to the economy from the increased government payments amounted to two-thirds of the gains from trade with China. In other words, many of the ways trade with China has helped the United States—such as providing inexpensive goods to U.S. consumers—have been wiped out. Even so, like Samuelson the authors of this study argued that in the long run, free trade is a good thing. They note, however, that the rapid rise of China has resulted in some large adjustment costs that, in the short run, significantly reduce the gains from trade.

Other economists have dismissed Samuelson's fears.[14] While not questioning his analysis, they note that as a practical matter, developing nations are unlikely to be able to upgrade the skill level of their workforce rapidly enough to give rise to the situation in Samuelson's model. In other words, they will quickly run into diminishing returns. However, such rebuttals are at odds with data suggesting that Asian countries are rapidly upgrading their educational systems. For example, about 56 percent of the world's engineering degrees awarded in 2008 were in Asia, compared with 4 percent in the United States![15]

Evidence for the Link between Trade and Growth

Many economic studies have looked at the relationship between trade and economic growth.[16] In general, these studies suggest that as predicted by the standard theory of comparative advantage, countries that adopt a more open stance toward international trade enjoy higher growth rates than those that close their economies to trade. Jeffrey Sachs and Andrew Warner created a measure of how "open" to international trade an economy was and then looked at the relationship between "openness" and economic growth for a sample of more than 100 countries from 1970 to 1990.[17] Among other findings, they reported

> We find a strong association between openness and growth, both within the group of developing and the group of developed countries. Within the group of developing countries, the open economies grew at 4.49 percent per year, and the closed economies grew at 0.69 percent per year. Within the group of developed economies, the open economies grew at 2.29 percent per year, and the closed economies grew at 0.74 percent per year.[18]

A study by Wacziarg and Welch updated the Sachs and Warner data through the late 1990s. They found that over the period 1950–1998, countries that liberalized their trade regimes experienced, on average, increases in their annual growth rates of 1.5–2.0 percent compared to preliberalization times.[19] An exhaustive survey of 61 studies published between 1967 and 2009 concluded: "The macroeconomic evidence provides dominant support for the positive and significant effects of trade on output and growth."[20]

The message seems clear: Adopt an open economy and embrace free trade, and your nation will be rewarded with higher economic growth rates. Higher growth will raise income levels and living standards. This last point has been confirmed by a study that looked at the relationship between trade and growth in incomes. The study, undertaken by Jeffrey Frankel and David Romer, found that on average, a 1 percentage point increase in the ratio of a country's trade to its gross domestic product increases income per person by at least 0.5 percent.[21] For every 10 percent increase in the importance of international trade in an economy, average income levels will rise by at least 5 percent. Despite the short-term adjustment costs associated with adopting a free trade regime, which can be significant, trade would seem to produce greater economic growth and higher living standards in the long run, just as the theory of Ricardo would lead us to expect.[22]

 TEST PREP

Use SmartBook to help retain what you have learned. Access your Instructor's Connect course to check out SmartBook or go to **learnsmartadvantage.com** for help.

LO6-2

Summarize the different theories explaining trade flows between nations.

Heckscher–Ohlin Theory

Ricardo's theory stresses that comparative advantage arises from differences in productivity. Thus, whether Ghana is more efficient than South Korea in the production of cocoa depends on how productively it uses its resources. Ricardo stressed labor productivity and argued that differences in labor productivity between nations underlie the notion of comparative advantage. Swedish economists Eli Heckscher (in 1919) and Bertil Ohlin (in 1933) put forward a different explanation of comparative advantage. They argued that comparative advantage arises from differences in national factor endowments.[23] By **factor endowments**, they meant the extent to which a country is endowed with such resources as land, labor, and capital. Nations have varying factor endowments, and different factor endowments explain differences in factor costs; specifically, the more abundant a factor, the lower its cost. The Heckscher–Ohlin theory predicts that countries will export those goods that make intensive use of factors that are locally abundant, while importing goods that make intensive use of factors that are locally scarce. Thus, the Heckscher–Ohlin theory attempts to explain the pattern of international trade that we observe in the world economy. Like Ricardo's theory, the Heckscher–Ohlin theory argues that free trade is beneficial. Unlike Ricardo's theory, however, the Heckscher–Ohlin theory argues that the pattern of international trade is determined by differences in factor endowments, rather than differences in productivity.

The Heckscher–Ohlin theory has commonsense appeal. For example, the United States has long been a substantial exporter of agricultural goods, reflecting in part its unusual abundance of arable land. In contrast, China has excelled in the export of goods produced in labor-intensive manufacturing industries. This reflects China's relative abundance of low-cost labor. The United States, which lacks abundant low-cost labor, has been a primary importer of these goods. Note that it is relative, not absolute, endowments that are important; a country may have larger absolute amounts of land and labor than another country but be relatively abundant in one of them.

THE LEONTIEF PARADOX

The Heckscher–Ohlin theory has been one of the most influential theoretical ideas in international economics. Most economists prefer the Heckscher–Ohlin theory to Ricardo's theory because it makes fewer simplifying assumptions. Because of its influence, the theory has been subjected to many empirical tests. Beginning with a famous study published in 1953 by Wassily Leontief (winner of the Nobel Prize in economics in 1973), many of these tests have raised questions about the validity of the Heckscher–Ohlin theory.[24] Using the Heckscher–Ohlin theory, Leontief postulated that because the United States was relatively abundant in capital compared to other nations, the United States would be an exporter of capital-intensive goods and an importer of labor-intensive goods. To his surprise, however, he found that U.S. exports were less capital intensive than U.S. imports. Because this result was at variance with the predictions of the theory, it has become known as the *Leontief paradox.*

No one is quite sure why we observe the Leontief paradox. One possible explanation is that the United States has a special advantage in producing new products or goods made with innovative technologies. Such products may be less capital intensive than products whose technology has had time to mature and become suitable for mass production. Thus, the United States may be exporting goods that heavily use skilled labor and innovative entrepreneurship, such as computer software, while importing heavy manufacturing products that use large amounts of capital. Some empirical studies tend to confirm this.[25] Still, tests of the Heckscher–Ohlin theory using data for a large number of countries tend to confirm the existence of the Leontief paradox.[26]

This leaves economists with a difficult dilemma. They prefer the Heckscher–Ohlin theory on theoretical grounds, but it is a relatively poor predictor of real-world international trade patterns. On the other hand, the theory they regard as being too limited, Ricardo's theory of comparative advantage, actually predicts trade patterns with greater accuracy. The best solution to this dilemma may be to return to the Ricardian idea that trade patterns are largely driven by international differences in productivity. Thus, one might argue that the United States exports commercial aircraft and imports textiles not because its factor endowments are especially suited to aircraft manufacture and not suited to textile manufacture, but because the United States is relatively more efficient at producing air-craft than textiles. A key assumption in the Heckscher–Ohlin theory is that technologies are the same across countries. This may not be the case. Differences in technology may lead to differences in productivity, which in turn, drives international trade patterns.[27] Thus, Japan's success in exporting automobiles from the 1970s onward has been based not only on the relative abundance of capital but also on its development of innovative manu-facturing technology that enabled it to achieve higher productivity levels in automobile production than other countries that also had abundant capital. Empirical work suggests that this theoretical explanation may be correct.[28] The new research shows that once dif-ferences in technology across countries are controlled for, countries do indeed export those goods that make intensive use of factors that are locally abundant, while importing goods that make intensive use of factors that are locally scarce. In other words, once the impact of differences of technology on productivity is controlled for, the Heckscher–Ohlin theory seems to gain predictive power.

TEST PREP

Use SmartBook to help retain what you have learned. Access your Instructor's Connect course to check out SmartBook or go to **learnsmartadvantage.com** for help.

LO6-2

Summarize the different theories explaining trade flows between nations.

The Product Life-Cycle Theory

Raymond Vernon initially proposed the product life-cycle theory in the mid-1960s.[29] Vernon's theory was based on the observation that, for most of the twentieth century, a very large proportion of the world's new products had been developed by U.S. firms and sold first in the U.S. market (e.g., mass-produced automobiles, televisions, instant cameras, photocopiers, personal computers, and semiconductor chips). To explain this, Vernon argued that the wealth and size of the U.S. market gave U.S. firms a strong incentive to develop new consumer products. In addition, the high cost of U.S. labor gave U.S. firms an incentive to develop cost-saving process innovations.

Just because a new product is developed by a U.S. firm and first sold in the U.S. market, it does not follow that the product must be produced in the United States. It could be produced abroad at some low-cost location and then exported back into the United States. However, Vernon argued that most new products were initially produced in America. Apparently, the pioneering firms believed it was better to keep production facilities close to the market and to the firm's center of decision making, given the uncertainty and risks inherent in introducing new products. Also, the demand for most new products tends to be based on nonprice factors. Consequently, firms can charge relatively high prices for new products, which obviates the need to look for low-cost production sites in other countries.

Vernon went on to argue that early in the life cycle of a typical new product, while de-mand is starting to grow rapidly in the United States, demand in other advanced countries is limited to high-income groups. The limited initial demand in other advanced countries does not make it worthwhile for firms in those countries to start producing the new prod-uct, but it does necessitate some exports from the United States to those countries.

Over time, demand for the new product starts to grow in other advanced countries (e.g., Great Britain, France, Germany, and Japan). As it does, it becomes worthwhile for foreign producers to begin producing for their home markets. In addition, U.S. firms might set up production facilities in those advanced countries where demand is growing. Consequently, production within other advanced countries begins to limit the potential for exports from the United States.

As the market in the United States and other advanced nations matures, the product becomes more standardized, and price becomes the main competitive weapon. As this oc-curs, cost considerations start to play a greater role in the competitive process. Producers based in advanced countries where labor costs are lower than in the United States (e.g., Italy and Spain) might now be able to export to the United States. If cost pressures be-come intense, the process might not stop there. The cycle by which the United States lost its advantage to other advanced countries might be repeated once more, as developing countries (e.g., Thailand) begin to acquire a production advantage over advanced countries. Thus, the locus of global production initially switches from the United States to other advanced nations and then from those nations to developing countries.

The consequence of these trends for the pattern of world trade is that over time, the United States switches from being an exporter of the product to an importer of the product as production becomes concentrated in lower-cost foreign locations.

PRODUCT LIFE-CYCLE THEORY IN THE TWENTY-FIRST CENTURY

Historically, the product life-cycle theory seems to be an accurate explanation of international trade patterns. Consider photocopiers: The product was first developed in the early 1960s by Xerox in the United States and sold initially to U.S. users. Originally, Xerox exported photocopiers from the United States, primarily to Japan and the advanced countries of Western Europe. As demand began to grow in those countries, Xerox entered into joint ventures to set up production in Japan (Fuji-Xerox) and Great Britain (Rank-Xerox). In addition, once Xerox's patents on the photocopier process expired, other foreign competitors began to enter the market (e.g., Canon in Japan and Olivetti in Italy). As a consequence, exports from the United States declined, and U.S. users began to buy some photocopiers from lower-cost foreign sources, particularly Japan. More recently, Japanese companies found that manufacturing costs are too high in their own country, so they have begun to switch production to developing countries such as Thailand. Thus, initially the United States and now other advanced countries (e.g., Japan and Great Britain) have switched from being exporters of photocopiers to importers. This evolution in the pattern of international trade in photocopiers is consistent with the predictions of the product life-cycle theory that mature industries tend to go out of the United States and into low-cost assembly locations.

However, the product life-cycle theory is not without weaknesses. Viewed from an Asian or European perspective, Vernon's argument that most new products are developed and introduced in the United States seems ethnocentric and dated. Although it may be true that during U.S. dominance of the global economy (from 1945 to 1975), most new products were introduced in the United States, there have always been important exceptions. These exceptions appear to have become more common in recent years. Many new products are now first introduced in Japan (e.g., video-game consoles) or South Korea (e.g., Samsung smartphones). Moreover, with the increased globalization and integration of the world economy discussed in Chapter 1, an increasing number of new products (e.g., tablet computers, smartphones, and digital cameras) are now introduced simultaneously in the United States and many European and Asian nations. This may be accompanied by globally dispersed production, with particular components of a new product being produced in those locations around the globe where the mix of factor costs and skills is most favorable (as predicted by the theory of comparative advantage). In sum, although Vernon's theory may be useful for explaining the pattern of international trade during the period of American global dominance, its relevance in the modern world seems more limited.

New Trade Theory

The new trade theory began to emerge in the 1970s when a number of economists pointed out that the ability of firms to attain economies of scale might have important implications for international trade.[30] **Economies of scale** are unit cost reductions associated with a large scale of output. Economies of scale have a number of sources, including the ability to spread fixed costs over a large volume and the ability of large-volume producers to utilize specialized employees and equipment that are more productive than less specialized employees and equipment. Economies of scale are a major source of cost reductions in many industries, from computer software to automobiles and from pharmaceuticals to aerospace. For example, Microsoft realizes economies of scale by spreading the fixed costs of developing new versions of its Windows operating system, which runs to about $10 billion, over the 2 billion or so personal computers on which each new system is ultimately

TEST PREP

Use SmartBook to help retain what you have learned. Access your Instructor's Connect course to check out SmartBook or go to **learnsmartadvantage.com** for help.

LO6-2

Summarize the different theories explaining trade flows between nations.

installed. Similarly, automobile companies realize economies of scale by producing a high volume of automobiles from an assembly line where each employee has a specialized task.

New trade theory makes two important points: First, through its impact on economies of scale, trade can increase the variety of goods available to consumers and decrease the average cost of those goods. Second, in those industries in which the output required to attain economies of scale represents a significant proportion of total world demand, the global market may be able to support only a small number of enterprises. Thus, world trade in certain products may be dominated by countries whose firms were first movers in their production.

LO6-3

Recognize why many economists believe that unrestricted free trade between nations will raise the economic welfare of countries that participate in a free trade system.

INCREASING PRODUCT VARIETY AND REDUCING COSTS

Imagine first a world without trade. In industries where economies of scale are important, both the variety of goods that a country can produce and the scale of production are limited by the size of the market. If a national market is small, there may not be enough demand to enable producers to realize economies of scale for certain products. Accordingly, those products may not be produced, thereby limiting the variety of products available to consumers. Alternatively, they may be produced but at such low volumes that unit costs and prices are considerably higher than they might be if economies of scale could be realized.

Now consider what happens when nations trade with each other. Individual national markets are combined into a larger world market. As the size of the market expands due to trade, individual firms may be able to better attain economies of scale. The implication, according to new trade theory, is that each nation may be able to specialize in producing a narrower range of products than it would in the absence of trade, yet by buying goods that it does not make from other countries, each nation can simultaneously increase the *variety* of goods available to its consumers and *lower the costs* of those goods; thus, trade offers an opportunity for mutual gain even when countries do not differ in their resource endowments or technology.

Suppose there are two countries, each with an annual market for 1 million automobiles. By trading with each other, these countries can create a combined market for 2 million cars. In this combined market, due to the ability to better realize economies of scale, more varieties (models) of cars can be produced, and cars can be produced at a lower average cost, than in either market alone. For example, demand for a sports car may be limited to 55,000 units in each national market, while a total output of at least 100,000 per year may be required to realize significant scale economies. Similarly, demand for a minivan may be 80,000 units in each national market, and again a total output of at least 100,000 per year may be required to realize significant scale economies. Faced with limited domestic market demand, firms in each nation may decide not to produce a sports car, because the costs of doing so at such low volume are too great. Although they may produce minivans, the cost of doing so will be higher, as will prices, than if significant economies of scale had been attained. Once the two countries decide to trade, however, a firm in one nation may specialize in producing sports cars, while a firm in the other nation may produce minivans. The combined demand for 110,000 sports cars and 160,000 minivans allows each firm to realize scale economies. Consumers in this case benefit from having access to a product (sports cars) that was not available before international trade and from the lower price for a product (minivans) that could not be produced at the most efficient scale before international trade. Trade is thus mutually beneficial because it allows the specialization of production, the realization of scale economies, the production of a greater variety of products, and lower prices.

ECONOMIES OF SCALE, FIRST-MOVER ADVANTAGES, AND THE PATTERN OF TRADE

A second theme in new trade theory is that the pattern of trade we observe in the world economy may be the result of economies of scale and first-mover advantages. **First-mover advantages** are the economic and strategic advantages that accrue to early entrants into an industry.[31] The ability to capture scale economies ahead of later entrants, and thus benefit from a lower cost structure, is an important first-mover advantage. New trade theory argues that for those products where economies of scale are significant and represent a substantial proportion of world demand, the first movers in an industry can gain a scale-based cost advantage that later entrants find almost impossible to match. Thus, the pattern of trade that we observe for such products may reflect first-mover advantages. Countries may dominate in the export of certain goods because economies of scale are important in their production and because firms located in those countries were the first to capture scale economies, giving them a first-mover advantage.

For example, consider the commercial aerospace industry. In aerospace, there are substantial scale economies that come from the ability to spread the fixed costs of developing a new jet aircraft over a large number of sales. It cost Airbus some $25 billion to develop its superjumbo jet, the 550-seat A380, which entered service in 2007. To recoup those costs and break even, Airbus will have to sell at least 250 A380 planes. By 2018, it had sold some 240 aircraft. If Airbus can sell more than 350 A380 planes, it will apparently be a profitable venture. Total demand over the first 20 years of service for this class of aircraft was estimated to be between 400 and 600 units. Thus, at best, the global market could probably profitably support only one producer of jet aircraft in the superjumbo category. It follows that the European Union might come to dominate in the export of very large jet aircraft, primarily because a European-based firm, Airbus, was the first to produce a superjumbo jet aircraft and realize scale economies. Other potential producers, such as Boeing, might have been shut out of the market because they lack the scale economies that Airbus enjoys. Because it pioneered this market category, Airbus captured a *first-mover advantage* based on *scale economies* that was difficult for rivals to match, and that resulted in the European Union becoming the *leading exporter* of very large jet aircraft. (As it turns out, however, the super-jumbo market may not be big enough to support even one producer. In early 2019, Airbus announced that it will stop producing the A380 in 2021 due to weak demand.)

IMPLICATIONS OF NEW TRADE THEORY

New trade theory has important implications. The theory suggests that nations may benefit from trade even when they do not differ in resource endowments or technology. Trade allows a nation to specialize in the production of certain products, attaining scale economies and lowering the costs of producing those products, while buying products that it does not produce from other nations that specialize in the production of other products. By this mechanism, the variety of products available to consumers in each nation is increased, while the average costs of those products should fall, as should their price, freeing resources to produce other goods and services.

The theory also suggests that a country may predominate in the export of a good simply because it was lucky enough to have one or more firms among the first to produce that good. Because they are able to gain economies of scale, the first movers in an industry may get a lock on the world market that discourages subsequent entry. First-movers' ability to benefit from increasing returns creates a barrier to entry. In the commercial aircraft industry, the fact that Boeing and Airbus are already in the industry and have the benefits of economies of scale discourages new entry and reinforces the dominance of America and Europe in the trade of midsize and large jet aircraft. This dominance is further reinforced because global demand may not be sufficient to profitably support another producer of midsize and large jet aircraft in the industry. So although Japanese firms might be able to compete in the market, they have decided not to enter the industry but to ally themselves as major subcontractors with primary producers (e.g., Mitsubishi Heavy Industries is a major subcontractor for Boeing on the 777 and 787 programs).

New trade theory is at variance with the Heckscher–Ohlin theory, which suggests a country will predominate in the export of a product when it is particularly well endowed with those factors used intensively in its manufacture. New trade theorists argue that the United States is a major exporter of commercial jet aircraft not because it is better endowed with the factors of production required to manufacture aircraft, but because one of the first movers in the industry, Boeing, was a U.S. firm. The new trade theory is not at variance with the theory of comparative advantage. Economies of scale increase productivity. Thus, the new trade theory identifies an important source of comparative advantage.

This theory is quite useful in explaining trade patterns. Empirical studies seem to support the predictions of the theory that trade increases the specialization of production within an industry, increases the variety of products available to consumers, and results in lower average prices.[32] With regard to first-mover advantages and international trade, a study by Harvard business historian Alfred Chandler suggests the existence of first-mover advantages is an important factor in explaining the dominance of firms from certain nations in specific industries.[33] The number of firms is very limited in many global industries, including the chemical industry, the heavy construction-equipment industry, the heavy truck industry, the tire industry, the consumer electronics industry, the jet engine industry, and the computer software industry.

Perhaps the most contentious implication of the new trade theory is the argument that it generates for government intervention and strategic trade policy.[34] New trade theorists stress the role of luck, entrepreneurship, and innovation in giving a firm first-mover advantages. According to this argument, the reason Boeing was the first mover in commercial jet aircraft manufacture—rather than firms such as Great Britain's De Havilland and Hawker Siddeley or Holland's Fokker, all of which could have been—was that Boeing was both lucky and innovative. One way Boeing was lucky is that De Havilland shot itself in the foot when its Comet jet airliner, introduced two years earlier than Boeing's first jet airliner, the 707, was found to be full of serious technological flaws. Had De Havilland not made some serious technological mistakes, Great Britain might have become the world's leading exporter of commercial jet aircraft. Boeing's innovativeness was demonstrated by its independent development of the technological know-how required to build a commercial jet airliner. Several new trade theorists have pointed out, however, that Boeing's research and development (R&D) was largely paid for by the U.S. government; the 707 was a spin-off from a government-funded military program (the entry of Airbus into the industry was also supported by significant government subsidies). Herein is a rationale for government intervention: By the sophisticated and judicious use of subsidies, could a government increase the chances of its domestic firms becoming first movers in newly emerging industries, as the U.S. government apparently did with Boeing (and the European Union did with Airbus)? If this is possible, and the new trade theory suggests it might be, we have an economic rationale for a proactive trade policy that is at variance with the free trade prescriptions of the trade theories we have reviewed so far. We consider the policy implications of this issue in Chapter 7.

TEST PREP

Use SmartBook to help retain what you have learned. Access your Instructor's Connect course to check out SmartBook or go to **learnsmartadvantage.com** for help.

LO6-2

Summarize the different theories explaining trade flows between nations.

National Competitive Advantage: Porter's Diamond

Michael Porter, the famous Harvard strategy professor, has also written extensively on international trade.[35] Porter and his team looked at 100 industries in 10 nations. Like the work of the new trade theorists, Porter's work was driven by a belief that existing theories of international trade told only part of the story. For Porter, the essential task was to explain why a nation achieves international success in a particular industry. Why does Japan do so well in the automobile industry? Why does Switzerland excel in the production and export of precision instruments and pharmaceuticals? Why do Germany and the United States do so well in the chemical industry? These questions cannot be answered easily by the Heckscher–Ohlin theory, and the theory of comparative advantage offers only a partial explanation. The theory of comparative advantage would say that Switzerland excels in the production and export of precision instruments because it uses its resources very productively in these industries. Although this may be correct, this does not explain why Switzerland is more productive in this industry than Great Britain, Germany, or Spain. Porter tries to solve this puzzle.

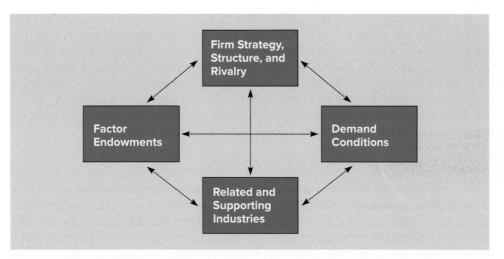

FIGURE 6.5

The determinants of national competitive advantage: Porter's diamond.

Source: Michael E. Porter, *The Competitive Advantage of Nations* (New York: Free Press, 1990; republished with a new introduction, 1998), p. 72.

Porter theorizes that four broad attributes of a nation shape the environment in which local firms compete, and these attributes promote or impede the creation of competitive advantage (see Figure 6.5). These attributes are

- *Factor endowments*—a nation's position in factors of production, such as skilled labor or the infrastructure necessary to compete in a given industry.
- *Demand conditions*—the nature of home-country demand for the industry's product or service.
- *Related and supporting industries*—the presence or absence of supplier industries and related industries that are internationally competitive.
- *Firm strategy, structure, and rivalry*—the conditions governing how companies are created, organized, and managed and the nature of domestic rivalry.

Porter speaks of these four attributes as constituting the *diamond*. He argues that firms are most likely to succeed in industries or industry segments where the diamond is most favorable. He also argues that the diamond is a mutually reinforcing system. The effect of one attribute is contingent on the state of others. For example, Porter argues favorable demand conditions will not result in competitive advantage unless the state of rivalry is sufficient to cause firms to respond to them.

Porter maintains that two additional variables can influence the national diamond in important ways: chance and government. Chance events, such as major innovations, can reshape industry structure and provide the opportunity for one nation's firms to supplant another's. Government, by its choice of policies, can detract from or improve national advantage. For example, regulation can alter home demand conditions, antitrust policies can influence the intensity of rivalry within an industry, and government investments in education can change factor endowments.

FACTOR ENDOWMENTS

Factor endowments lie at the center of the Heckscher–Ohlin theory. While Porter does not propose anything radically new, he does analyze the characteristics of factors of production. He recognizes hierarchies among factors, distinguishing between *basic factors* (e.g., natural resources, climate, location, and demographics) and *advanced factors* (e.g., communication infrastructure, sophisticated and skilled labor, research facilities, and technological know-how). He argues that advanced factors are the most significant for competitive advantage. Unlike the naturally endowed basic factors, advanced factors are a product of investment by individuals, companies, and governments. Thus, government investments in basic and higher education, by improving the general skill and knowledge level of the population and by stimulating advanced research at higher education institutions, can upgrade a nation's advanced factors.

The relationship between advanced and basic factors is complex. Basic factors can provide an initial advantage that is subsequently reinforced and extended by investment in advanced factors. Conversely, disadvantages in basic factors can create pressures to invest in advanced factors. An obvious example of this phenomenon is Japan, a country that lacks arable land and mineral deposits and yet through investment has built a substantial endowment of advanced factors. Porter notes that Japan's large pool of engineers (reflecting a much higher number of engineering graduates per capita than almost any other nation) has been vital to Japan's success in many manufacturing industries.

DEMAND CONDITIONS

Porter emphasizes the role home demand plays in upgrading competitive advantage. Firms are typically most sensitive to the needs of their closest customers. Thus, the characteristics of home demand are particularly important in shaping the attributes of domestically made products and in creating pressures for innovation and quality. Porter argues that a nation's firms gain competitive advantage if their domestic consumers are sophisticated and demanding. Such consumers pressure local firms to meet high standards of product quality and to produce innovative products. For example, Porter notes that Japan's sophisticated and knowledgeable buyers of cameras helped stimulate the Japanese camera industry to improve product quality and to introduce innovative models.

RELATED AND SUPPORTING INDUSTRIES

The third broad attribute of national advantage in an industry is the presence of suppliers or related industries that are internationally competitive. The benefits of investments in advanced factors of production by related and supporting industries can spill over into an industry, thereby helping it achieve a strong competitive position internationally. Swedish strength in fabricated steel products (e.g., ball bearings and cutting tools) has drawn on strengths in Sweden's specialty steel industry. Technological leadership in the U.S. semiconductor industry provided the basis for U.S. success in personal computers and several other technically advanced electronic products. Similarly, Switzerland's success in pharmaceuticals is closely related to its previous international success in the technologically related dye industry.

One consequence of this process is that successful industries within a country tend to be grouped into clusters of related industries. This was one of the most pervasive findings of Porter's study. One such cluster Porter identified was in the German textile and apparel sector, which included high-quality cotton, wool, synthetic fibers, sewing machine needles, and a wide range of textile machinery. Such clusters are important because valuable knowledge can flow between the firms within a geographic cluster, benefiting all within that cluster. Knowledge flows occur when employees move between firms within a region and when national industry associations bring employees from different companies together for regular conferences or workshops.[36]

FIRM STRATEGY, STRUCTURE, AND RIVALRY

The fourth broad attribute of national competitive advantage in Porter's model is the strategy, structure, and rivalry of firms within a nation. Porter makes two important points here. First, different nations are characterized by different management ideologies, which either help them or do not help them build national competitive advantage. For example, Porter noted the predominance of engineers in top management at German and Japanese firms. He attributed this to these firms' emphasis on improving manufacturing processes and product design. In contrast, Porter noted a predominance of people with finance backgrounds leading many U.S. firms. He linked this to U.S. firms' lack of attention to improving manufacturing processes and product design. He argued that the dominance of finance led to an overemphasis on maximizing short-term financial returns. According to Porter, one consequence of these different management ideologies was a relative loss of U.S.

competitiveness in those engineering-based industries where manufacturing processes and product design issues are all-important (e.g., the automobile industry).

Porter's second point is that there is a strong association between vigorous domestic rivalry and the creation and persistence of competitive advantage in an industry. Vigorous domestic rivalry induces firms to look for ways to improve efficiency, which makes them better international competitors. Domestic rivalry creates pressures to innovate, to improve quality, to reduce costs, and to invest in upgrading advanced factors. All this helps create world-class competitors. Porter cites the case of Japan:

> Nowhere is the role of domestic rivalry more evident than in Japan, where it is all-out warfare in which many companies fail to achieve profitability. With goals that stress market share, Japanese companies engage in a continuing struggle to outdo each other. Shares fluctuate markedly. The process is prominently covered in the business press. Elaborate rankings measure which companies are most popular with university graduates. The rate of new product and process development is breathtaking.[37]

EVALUATING PORTER'S THEORY

Porter contends that the degree to which a nation is likely to achieve international success in a certain industry is a function of the combined impact of factor endowments, domestic demand conditions, related and supporting industries, and domestic rivalry. He argues that the presence of all four components is usually required for this diamond to boost competitive performance (although there are exceptions). Porter also contends that government can influence each of the four components of the diamond—either positively or negatively. Factor endowments can be affected by subsidies, policies toward capital markets, policies toward education, and so on. Government can shape domestic demand through local product standards or with regulations that mandate or influence buyer needs. Government policy can influence supporting and related industries through regulation and influence firm rivalry through such devices as capital market regulation, tax policy, and antitrust laws.

If Porter is correct, we would expect his model to predict the pattern of international trade that we observe in the real world. Countries should be exporting products from those industries where all four components of the diamond are favorable, while importing in those areas where the components are not favorable. Is he correct? We simply do not know. Porter's theory has not been subjected to detailed empirical testing. Much about the theory rings true, but the same can be said for the new trade theory, the theory of comparative advantage, and the Heckscher–Ohlin theory. It may be that each of these theories, which complement each other, explains something about the pattern of international trade.

FOCUS ON MANAGERIAL IMPLICATIONS

LOCATION, FIRST-MOVER ADVANTAGES, AND GOVERNMENT POLICY

Why does all this matter for business? There are at least three main implications for international businesses of the material discussed in this chapter: location implications, first-mover implications, and government policy implications.

Location

Underlying most of the theories we have discussed is the notion that different countries have particular advantages in different productive activities. Thus, from a profit perspective, it makes sense for a firm to disperse its productive activities to those countries where, according to the theory of international trade, they can be performed most efficiently. If design can be performed most efficiently in France, that is where design facilities should be located; if the manufacture of basic components can be performed most efficiently in Singapore, that is where they should be manufactured; and if final assembly can be

LO6-4

Explain the arguments of those who maintain that government can play a proactive role in promoting national competitive advantage in certain industries.

 TEST PREP

Use SmartBook to help retain what you have learned. Access your Instructor's Connect course to check out SmartBook or go to **learnsmartadvantage.com** for help.

LO6-5

Understand the important implications that international trade theory holds for management practice.

performed most efficiently in China, that is where final assembly should be performed. The result is a global web of productive activities, with different activities being performed in different locations around the globe depending on considerations of comparative advantage, factor endowments, and the like. If the firm does not do this, it may find itself at a competitive disadvantage relative to firms that do.

First-Mover Advantages

According to the new trade theory, firms that establish a first-mover advantage with regard to the production of a particular new product may subsequently dominate global trade in that product. This is particularly true in industries where the global market can profitably support only a limited number of firms, such as the aerospace market, but early commitments may also seem to be important in less concentrated industries. For the individual firm, the clear message is that it pays to invest substantial financial resources in trying to build a first-mover, or early mover, advantage, even if that means several years of losses before a new venture becomes profitable. The idea is to preempt the available demand, gain cost advantages related to volume, build an enduring brand ahead of later competitors, and, consequently, establish a long-term sustainable competitive advantage. Although the details of how to achieve this are beyond the scope of this book, many publications offer strategies for exploiting first-mover advantages and for avoiding the traps associated with pioneering a market (first-mover disadvantages).[38]

Government Policy

The theories of international trade also matter to international businesses because firms are major players on the international trade scene. Business firms produce exports, and business firms import the products of other countries. Because of their pivotal role in international trade, businesses can exert a strong influence on government trade policy, lobbying to promote free trade or trade restrictions. The theories of international trade claim that promoting free trade is generally in the best interests of a country, although it may not always be in the best interest of an individual firm. Many firms recognize this and lobby for open markets.

For example, when the U.S. government announced its intention to place a tariff on Japanese imports of liquid crystal display (LCD) screens in the 1990s, IBM and Apple Computer protested strongly. Both IBM and Apple pointed out that (1) Japan was the lowest-cost source of LCD screens; (2) they used these screens in their own laptop computers; and (3) the proposed tariff, by increasing the cost of LCD screens, would increase the cost of laptop computers produced by IBM and Apple, thus making them less competitive in the world market. In other words, the tariff, designed to protect U.S. firms, would be self-defeating. In response to these pressures, the U.S. government reversed its posture.

Unlike IBM and Apple, however, businesses do not always lobby for free trade. In the United States, for example, restrictions on imports of steel have periodically been put into place in response to direct pressure by U.S. firms on the government (the latest example being in March 2018 when the Trump administration placed a 25 percent tariff on imports of foreign steel). In some cases, the government has responded to pressure from domestic companies seeking protection by getting foreign companies to agree to "voluntary" restrictions on their imports, using the implicit threat of more comprehensive formal trade barriers to get them to adhere to these agreements (historically, this has occurred in the automobile industry). In other cases, the government used what are called "antidumping" actions to justify tariffs on imports from other nations (these mechanisms will be discussed in detail in Chapter 7).

As predicted by international trade theory, many of these agreements have been self-defeating, such as the voluntary restriction on machine tool imports agreed to in 1985. Shielded from international competition by import barriers, the U.S. machine tool industry had no incentive to increase its efficiency. Consequently, it lost many of its export markets to more efficient foreign competitors. Because of this misguided action, the U.S.

machine tool industry shrunk during the period when the agreement was in force. For anyone schooled in international trade theory, this was not surprising.[39]

Finally, Porter's theory of national competitive advantage also contains policy implications. Porter's theory suggests that it is in the best interest of business for a firm to invest in upgrading advanced factors of production (for example, to invest in better training for its employees) and to increase its commitment to research and development. It is also in the best interests of business to lobby the government to adopt policies that have a favorable impact on each component of the national diamond. Thus, according to Porter, businesses should urge government to increase investment in education, infrastructure, and basic research (because all these enhance advanced factors) and to adopt policies that promote strong competition within domestic markets (because this makes firms stronger international competitors, according to Porter's findings).

Key Terms

free trade, p. 166
new trade theory, p. 168
mercantilism, p. 169
zero-sum game, p. 169
absolute advantage, p. 170
constant returns to
   specialization, p. 176

factor endowments, p. 181
economies of scale, p. 183
first-mover advantages, p. 184
balance-of-payments
   accounts, p. 195
current account, p. 196
current account deficit, p. 196

current account surplus, p. 196
capital account, p. 196
financial account, p. 196

SUMMARY

This chapter reviewed a number of theories that explain why it is beneficial for a country to engage in international trade and explained the pattern of international trade observed in the world economy. The theories of Smith, Ricardo, and Heckscher–Ohlin all make strong cases for unrestricted free trade. In contrast, the mercantilist doctrine and, to a lesser extent, the new trade theory can be interpreted to support government intervention to promote exports through subsidies and to limit imports through tariffs and quotas.

In explaining the pattern of international trade, this chapter shows that, with the exception of mercantilism, which is silent on this issue, the different theories offer largely complementary explanations. Although no one theory may explain the apparent pattern of international trade, taken together, the theory of comparative advantage, the Heckscher–Ohlin theory, the product life-cycle theory, the new trade theory, and Porter's theory of national competitive advantage do suggest which factors are important. Comparative advantage tells us that productivity differences are important; Heckscher–Ohlin tells us that factor endowments matter; the product life-cycle theory tells us that where a new product is introduced is important; the new trade theory tells us that increasing returns to specialization and first-mover advantages

matter; Porter tells us that all these factors may be important insofar as they affect the four components of the national diamond. The chapter made the following points:

1. Mercantilists argued that it was in a country's best interests to run a balance-of-trade surplus. They viewed trade as a zero-sum game, in which one country's gains cause losses for other countries.

2. The theory of absolute advantage suggests that countries differ in their ability to produce goods efficiently. The theory suggests that a country should specialize in producing goods in areas where it has an absolute advantage and import goods in areas where other countries have absolute advantages.

3. The theory of comparative advantage suggests that it makes sense for a country to specialize in producing those goods that it can produce most efficiently, while buying goods that it can produce relatively less efficiently from other countries—even if that means buying goods from other countries that it could produce more efficiently itself.

4. The theory of comparative advantage suggests that unrestricted free trade brings about

increased world production—that is, that trade is a positive-sum game.

5. The theory of comparative advantage also suggests that opening a country to free trade stimulates economic growth, which creates dynamic gains from trade. The empirical evidence seems to be consistent with this claim.

6. The Heckscher–Ohlin theory argues that the pattern of international trade is determined by differences in factor endowments. It predicts that countries will export those goods that make intensive use of locally abundant factors and will import goods that make intensive use of factors that are locally scarce.

7. The product life-cycle theory suggests that trade patterns are influenced by where a new product is introduced. In an increasingly integrated global economy, the product life-cycle theory seems to be less predictive than it once was.

8. New trade theory states that trade allows a nation to specialize in the production of certain goods, attaining scale economies and lowering the costs of producing those goods, while buying goods that it does not produce from other nations that are similarly specialized. By this mechanism, the variety of goods available to consumers in each nation is increased, while the average costs of those goods should fall.

9. New trade theory also states that in those industries where substantial economies of scale imply that the world market will profitably support only a few firms, countries may predominate in the export of certain products simply because they had a firm that was a first mover in that industry.

10. Some new trade theorists have promoted the idea of strategic trade policy. The argument is that government, by the sophisticated and judicious use of subsidies, might be able to increase the chances of domestic firms becoming first movers in newly emerging industries.

11. Porter's theory of national competitive advantage suggests that the pattern of trade is influenced by four attributes of a nation: (*a*) factor endowments, (*b*) domestic demand conditions, (*c*) related and supporting industries, and (*d*) firm strategy, structure, and rivalry.

12. Theories of international trade are important to an individual business firm primarily because they can help the firm decide where to locate its various production activities.

13. Firms involved in international trade can and do exert a strong influence on government policy toward trade. By lobbying government, business firms can promote free trade or trade restrictions.

Critical Thinking and Discussion Questions

1. Mercantilism is a bankrupt theory that has no place in the modern world. Discuss.

2. Is free trade fair? Discuss.

3. Unions in developed nations often oppose imports from low-wage countries and advocate trade barriers to protect jobs from what they often characterize as "unfair" import competition. Is such competition "unfair"? Do you think that this argument is in the best interests of (*a*) the unions, (*b*) the people they represent, and/or (*c*) the country as a whole?

4. What are the potential costs of adopting a free trade regime? Do you think governments should do anything to reduce these costs? Why?

5. Reread the Country Focus "Is China Manipulating Its Currency in Pursuit of a Neo-Mercantilist Policy?"
   a. Do you think China is pursuing a currency policy that can be characterized as neo-mercantilist?
   b. What should the United States, and other countries, do about this?

6. Reread the Country Focus "Moving U.S. White-Collar Jobs Offshore."
   a. Who benefits from the outsourcing of skilled white-collar jobs to developing nations? Who are the losers?
   b. Will developed nations like the United States suffer from the loss of high-skilled and high-paying jobs?

7. Is there a difference between the transference of high-paying white-collar jobs, such as computer programming and accounting, to developing nations, and low-paying blue-collar jobs? If so, what is the difference, and should government do anything to stop the flow of white-collar jobs out of the country to countries such as India?

8. Drawing upon the new trade theory and Porter's theory of national competitive advantage, outline the case for government policies that would build national competitive advantage in biotechnology. What kinds of policies would you recommend that the government adopt?

Are these policies at variance with the basic free trade philosophy?

9. The world's poorest countries are at a competitive disadvantage in every sector of their economies. They have little to export; they have no capital; their land is of poor quality; they often have too many people given available work opportunities; and they are poorly educated. Free trade cannot possibly be in the interests of such nations. Discuss.

globalEDGE research task globaledge.msu.edu

Use the globalEDGE™ website (**globaledge.msu.edu**) to complete the following exercises:

1. The *World Trade Organization International Trade Statistics* is an annual report that provides comprehensive, comparable, and updated statistics on trade in merchandise and commercial services. The report is an assessment of world trade flows by country, region, and main product or service categories. Using the most recent statistics available, identify the top 10 countries that lead in the export and import of merchandise trade, respectively. Which countries appear in the top 10 in both exports and imports? Can you explain why these countries appear at the top of both lists?

2. Food is an integral part of understanding different countries, cultures, and lifestyles. You run a chain of high-end premium restaurants in the United States, and you are looking for unique Australian wines you can import. However, you must first identify which *Australian suppliers* can provide you with premium wines. After searching through the Australian supplier directory, identify three to four companies that can be potential suppliers. Then, develop a list of criteria you would need to ask these companies about to select which one to work with.

CLOSING CASE

"Trade Wars Are Good and Easy to Win"

At 3:50 a.m. on March 2, 2018, Donald Trump, the 45th President of the United States, took to his favorite medium, Twitter, to espouse his views on an important policy issue: international trade. He tweeted "When a country (USA) is losing many billions of dollars on trade with virtually every country it does business with, trade wars are good and easy to win. When we are down $100 billion with a certain country and they get cute, don't trade anymore – we win big. It's easy!"*

Trump's tweet was a response to backlash over his decision to impose a 25 percent tariff on imports of steel, and a 10 percent tariff on imports of aluminum. The

Ron Sachs, Pool/Getty Images News/Getty Images

Trump administration claimed these tariffs were necessary to protect two industries that were important for national security. His critics had a different take. They argued that the tariffs would raise input costs for consumers of steel and aluminum, which included construction companies, manufacturers of construction equipment, appliance makers, auto manufacturers, makers of containers and packaging (e.g., beer cans), and aerospace companies. Among those hit by higher costs due to these tariffs would be two of the U.S.'s largest exporters: Boeing and Caterpillar Tractor. The critics also noted that there are only 140,000 people employed in the steel and aluminum industries, whereas 6.5 million Americans are employed in industries that *use* steel and aluminum, where input prices have just gone up.

*Donald John Trump, Twitter, March 2, 2018, **https://twitter.com/realdonaldtrump**.

Trump's actions should not have been a surprise. In contrast to all U.S. presidents since World War II, Donald Trump has long voiced strong opposition to trade deals designed to lower tariff barriers and foster the free flow of goods and services between the United States and its trading partners. During the presidential election campaign, he called the North American Free Trade Agreement (NAFTA) "the worst trade deal maybe ever signed anywhere." Upon taking office, his administration launched a renegotiation of NAFTA, with the aim of making the treaty more favorable to the U.S. As a candidate, he vowed to "kill" the Trans Pacific Partnership (TPP), a free trade deal among 12 Pacific Rim countries, including the United States (but excluding China), negotiated by the Obama administration. In his first week in office, he signed an executive order formally withdrawing the United States from the TPP. He has even threatened to pull the United States out of the World Trade Organization (WTO) if the global trade body interferes with his plans to impose tariffs.

Trump's position seems to be based on a belief that trade is a game that the United States needs to win. He appears to equate winning with running a trade surplus, and sees the persistent U.S. trade deficit as a sign of American weakness. In his words, "you only have to look at our trade deficit to see that we are being taken to the cleaners by our trading partners."** He believes that other countries have taken advantage of the United States in trade deals, and the result has been a sharp decline in manufacturing jobs in the United States. China and Mexico have been frequent targets of his criticisms, and he has argued that China's trade surplus with the United States is a result of that country's currency manipulation, which he believes has made Chinese exports artificially cheap. He seems to think that the U.S. can win at the trade game by becoming a tougher negotiator and extracting favorable terms from foreign nations that want access to the U.S. market. He has even characterized previous American trade negotiators as "stupid people," "political hacks and diplomats," and "saps," and has suggested that he should become "negotiator in chief."

In contrast to Donald Trump's espoused position, the pro-trade policies of the last 70 years were based upon a substantial body of economic theory and evidence that suggests free trade has a positive impact on the economic growth rate of *all* nations that participate in a free trade system. According to this work, free trade doesn't destroy jobs; it creates jobs and raises national income. To be sure, some sectors will lose jobs when a nation moves to a free trade regime, but the argument is that jobs created

elsewhere in the economy will more than compensate for such losses, and in aggregate, the nation will be better off.

The United States has long been the world's largest economy, largest foreign investor, and one of the three largest exporters (along with China and Germany). Due to exports and foreign direct investments in other countries, 43 percent of the sales of all American firms in the S&P 500 stock market index are made outside of U.S. borders. As a result of the U.S.'s economic power, Americans' long adherence to free trade policies has helped to set the tone for the world trading system. In large part, the post–World War II international trading system, with its emphasis on lowering barriers to international trade and investment, was only possible because of vigorous American leadership. Now with the ascendancy of Donald Trump to the presidency, that seems to be changing. Pro-free traders argue that if Trump continues to push for more protectionist trade policies—and his rhetoric and cabinet picks suggest he will—the unintended consequences could include retaliation from the U.S.'s trading partners, a trade war characterized by higher tariffs, a decline in the volume of world trade, job losses in the United States, and lower economic growth around the world. As evidence, they point to the last time such protectionist policies were implemented. That was in the early 1930s, when a trade war between nations deepened the Great Depression.

Sources: "Donald Trump on Free Trade," *On the Issues*, www.ontheissues.org/2016/Donald_Trump_Free_Trade.htm; Keith Bradsher, "Trump's Pick on Trade Could Put China in a Difficult Spot," *The New York Times*, January 13, 2017; William Mauldin, "Trump Threatens to Pull U.S. Out of World Trade Organization," *The Wall Street Journal*, July 24, 2016; "Trump's Antitrade Warriors," *The Wall Street Journal*, January 16, 2017; "Donald Trump's Trade Bluster," *The Economist*, December 10, 2016; and Chad Brown, "Trump's Steel and Aluminum Tariffs Are Counterproductive," Peterson Institute for International Economics, March 7, 2018.

Case Discussion Questions

1. What economic theory of trade do Donald Trump's views seem most closely aligned with?
2. What are the possible benefits of Donald Trump's position on international trade? What are the potential costs and risks of his position?
3. Do you think Trump is correct? Are trade wars good and easy to win? What does it mean to "win" a trade war? What does it mean to "lose"?

**Donald J. Trump and Dave Shiflett, *The America We Deserve: on Free Trade*, Renaissance Books, 2000.

Appendix: International Trade and the Balance of Payments

International trade involves the sale of goods and services to residents in other countries (exports) and the purchase of goods and services from residents in other countries (imports). A country's **balance-of-payments accounts** keep track of the payments to and receipts from other countries for a particular time period. These include payments to foreigners for imports of goods and services, and receipts from foreigners for goods and services exported to them. A summary copy of the U.S. balance-of-

payments accounts for 2018 is given in Table A.1. In this appendix, we briefly describe the form of the balance-of-payments accounts, and we discuss whether a current account deficit, often a cause of much concern in the popular press, is something to worry about.

BALANCE-OF-PAYMENTS ACCOUNTS

Balance-of-payments accounts are divided into three main sections: the current account, the capital account, and

TABLE A.1

U.S. Balance-of-Payments Accounts, 2018

Source: Bureau of Economic Analysis.

Current Account	$ Millions
Exports of goods, services, and income receipts (credits)	$3,701,694
Goods	1,672,331
Services	828,425
Primary income receipts	1,060,362
Secondary income receipts	140,576
Imports of goods, services, and income (debits)	4,190,166
Goods	2,563,651
Services	559,211
Primary income payments	816,066
Secondary income payments	251,237
Capital Account	
Capital transfer receipts	9,418
Capital transfer debits	10
Financial Account	
Net U.S. acquisition of financial assets	301,618
Net U.S. incurrence of liabilities	800,913
Net financial derivatives	−20,261
Statistical discrepancy	−40,491
Balances	
Balance on current account	−488,472
Balance on capital account	9,409
Balance on primary income	244,295
Balance on secondary income	−110,661

the financial account (to confuse matters, what is now called the capital account until recently was part of the current account, and the financial account used to be called the capital account). The **current account** records transactions that pertain to four categories, all of which can be seen in Table A.1. The first category, goods, refers to the export or import of physical goods (e.g., agricultural foodstuffs, autos, computers, chemicals). The second category is the export or import of services (e.g., intangible products such as banking and insurance services, royalty payments on intellectual property, and earnings from foreign tourists who visit the U.S.). The third category, primary income receipts or payments, refers to income from foreign investments or payments to foreign investors (e.g., interest and dividend receipts or payments). The third category also includes payments that foreigners have made to U.S. residents for work performed outside the United States and payments that U.S. entities make to foreign residents. The fourth category, secondary income receipts or payments, refers to the transfer of a good, service, or asset to the U.S. government or U.S. private entities, or the transfer to a foreign government or entity in the case of payments (this includes tax payments, foreign pension payments, cash transfers, etc.).

A **current account deficit** occurs when a country imports more goods, services, and income than it exports. A **current account surplus** occurs when a country exports more goods, services, and income than it imports. Table A.1 shows that in 2018 the United States ran a current account deficit of $488.472 billion. This is often a headline-grabbing figure and is widely reported in the news media. The U.S. current account deficit reflects the fact that America imports far more physical goods than it exports. (The United States typically runs a surplus on trade in services and on income payments.)

The 2006 current account deficit of $803 billion was the largest on record and was equivalent to about 6.5 percent of the country's GDP. The deficit has shrunk since then. The 2018 current account deficit represented just 2.4 percent of GDP. Many people find the fact that the United States runs a persistent deficit on its current account to be disturbing, the common assumption being that high import of goods displaces domestic production, causes unemployment, and reduces the growth of the U.S. economy. However, the issue is more complex than this. Fully understanding the implications of a large and persistent deficit requires that we look at the rest of the balance-of-payments accounts.

The **capital account** records one-time changes in the stock of assets. As noted earlier, until recently this item was included in the current account. The capital account includes capital transfers, such as debt forgiveness and migrants' transfers (the goods and financial assets that accompany migrants as they enter or leave the country).

In the big scheme of things, this is a relatively small figure amounting to $9.4 billion in 2018.

The **financial account** (formerly the capital account) records transactions that involve the purchase or sale of assets. Thus, when a German firm purchases stock in a U.S. company or buys a U.S. bond, the transaction enters the U.S. balance of payments as a credit on the financial account. This is because capital is flowing into the country. When capital flows out of the United States, it enters the financial account as a debit.

The financial account is comprised of a number of elements. The net U.S. acquisition of financial assets includes the change in foreign assets owned by the U.S. government (e.g., U.S. official reserve assets) and the change in foreign assets owned by private individuals and corporations (including changes in assets owned through foreign direct investment). As can be seen from Table A.1, in 2018 there was a $301.6 billion increase in U.S. ownership of foreign assets, which tells us that the U.S. government and U.S. private entities were purchasing more foreign assets than they were selling. The net U.S. incurrence of liabilities refers to the change in U.S. assets owned by foreigners. In 2018, foreigners increased their holdings of U.S. assets by $800 billion, signifying that foreigners were net acquirers of U.S. stocks, bonds (including Treasury bills), and physical assets such as real estate.

A basic principle of balance-of-payments accounting is double-entry bookkeeping. Every international transaction automatically enters the balance of payments twice—once as a credit and once as a debit. Imagine that you purchase a car produced in Japan by Toyota for $20,000.

Because your purchase represents a payment to another country for goods, it will enter the balance of payments as a debit on the current account. Toyota now has the $20,000 and must do something with it. If Toyota deposits the money at a U.S. bank, Toyota has purchased a U.S. asset—a bank deposit worth $20,000—and the transaction will show up as a $20,000 credit on the financial account. Or Toyota might deposit the cash in a Japanese bank in return for Japanese yen. Now the Japanese bank must decide what to do with the $20,000. Any action that it takes will ultimately result in a credit for the U.S. balance of payments. For example, if the bank lends the $20,000 to a Japanese firm that uses it to import personal computers from the United States, then the $20,000 must be credited to the U.S. balance-of-payments current account. Or the Japanese bank might use the $20,000 to purchase U.S. government bonds, in which case it will show up as a credit on the U.S. balance-of-payments financial account.

Thus, any international transaction automatically gives rise to two offsetting entries in the balance of payments. Because of this, the sum of the current account balance, the capital account, and the financial account balance should always add up to zero. In practice, this does not always occur due to the existence of "statistical discrepancies," the source of which need not concern us here (note that in 2018, the statistical discrepancy amounted to $40.5 billion).

DOES THE CURRENT ACCOUNT DEFICIT MATTER?

As discussed earlier, there is some concern when a country is running a deficit on the current account of its balance of payments.[40] In recent years, a number of rich countries, including most notably the United States, have run persistent current account deficits. When a country runs a current account deficit, the money that flows to other countries can then be used by those countries to purchase assets in the deficit country. Thus, when the United States runs a trade deficit with China, the Chinese use the money that they receive from U.S. consumers to purchase U.S. assets such as stocks, bonds, and the like. Put another way, a deficit on the current account is financed by selling assets to other countries—that is, by increasing liabilities on the financial account. Thus, the persistent U.S. current account deficit is being financed by a steady sale of U.S. assets (stocks, bonds, real estate, and whole corporations) to other countries. In short, countries that run current account deficits become net debtors.

For example, as a result of financing its current account deficit through asset sales, the United States must deliver a stream of interest payments to foreign bondholders, rents to foreign landowners, and dividends to foreign stockholders. One might argue that such payments to foreigners drain resources from a country and limit the funds available for investment within the country. Because investment within a country is necessary to stimulate economic growth, a persistent current account deficit can choke off a country's future economic growth. This is the basis of the argument that persistent deficits are bad for an economy. However, things are not this simple. For one thing, in an era of global capital markets, money is efficiently directed toward its highest value uses, and over the past quarter of a century, many of the highest value uses of capital have been in the United States. So even though capital is flowing out of the United States in the form of payments to foreigners, much of that capital finds its way right back into the country to fund productive investments in the United States. In short, it is not clear that the current account deficit chokes off U.S. economic growth. In fact, notwithstanding the 2008–2009 recession, the U.S. economy has grown substantially over the past 30 years, despite running a persistent current account deficit and despite financing that deficit by selling U.S. assets to foreigners. This is precisely because foreigners reinvest much of the income earned from U.S. assets and from exports to the United States right back into the United States. This revisionist view, which has gained in popularity in recent years, suggests that a persistent current account deficit might not be the drag on economic growth it was once thought to be.[41]

Having said this, there is still a nagging fear that at some point, the appetite that foreigners have for U.S. assets might decline. If foreigners suddenly reduced their investments in the United States, what would happen? In short, instead of reinvesting the dollars that they earn from exports and investment in the United States back into the country, they would sell those dollars for another currency, European euros, Japanese yen, or Chinese yuan, for example, and invest in euro-, yen-, and yuan-denominated assets instead. This would lead to a fall in the value of the dollar on foreign exchange markets, and that in turn would increase the price of imports and lower the price of U.S. exports, making them more competitive, which should reduce the overall level of the current account deficit. Thus, in the long run, the persistent U.S. current account deficit could be corrected via a reduction in the value of the U.S. dollar. The concern is that such adjustments may not be smooth. Rather than a controlled decline in the value of the dollar, the dollar might suddenly lose a significant amount of its value in a very short time, precipitating a "dollar crisis."[42] Because the U.S. dollar is the world's major reserve currency and is held by many foreign governments and banks, any dollar crisis could deliver a body blow to the world economy and at the very least trigger a global economic slowdown. That would not be a good thing.

Endnotes

1. Spiegel, W. Henry. *The Growth of Economics Thought*. NC: Duke University Press, 1991.

2. Binyamin Applebaum, "On Trade, Donald Trump Breaks with 200 Years of Economic Orthodoxy," *The New York Times*, March 10, 2016.

3. M. Solis, "The Politics of Self-Restraint: FDI Subsidies and Japanese Mercantilism," *The World Economy* 26 (February 2003), pp. 153–70; Kevin Hamlin, "China Is a Growing Threat to Global Competitors, Kroeber Says," *Bloomberg News*, June 28, 2016.

4. S. Hollander, *The Economics of David Ricardo* (Buffalo: University of Toronto Press, 1979).

5. D. Ricardo, *The Principles of Political Economy and Taxation* (Homewood, IL: Irwin, 1967, first published in 1817).

6. For example, R. Dornbusch, S. Fischer, and P. Samuelson, "Comparative Advantage: Trade and Payments in a Ricardian Model with a Continuum of Goods," *American Economic Review* 67 (December 1977), pp. 823–39.

7. B. Balassa, "An Empirical Demonstration of Classic Comparative Cost Theory," *Review of Economics and Statistics*, 1963, pp. 231–38.

8. See P. R. Krugman, "Is Free Trade Passé?" *Journal of Economic Perspectives* 1 (Fall 1987), pp. 131–44.

9. P. Samuelson, "Where Ricardo and Mill Rebut and Confirm Arguments of Mainstream Economists Supporting Globalization," *Journal of Economic Perspectives* 18, no. 3 (Summer 2004), pp. 135–46.

10. P. Samuelson, "The Gains from International Trade Once Again," *Economic Journal* 72 (1962), pp. 820–29.

11. Lohr, Steve. "An Elder Challenges Outsourcing's Orthodoxy." *The New York Times*, September 9, 2004. https://www.nytimes.com/2004/09/09/business/worldbusiness/an-elder-challenges-outsourcings-orthodoxy.html.

12. Samuelson, A. Paul. "Where Ricardo and Mill Rebut and Confirm Arguments of Mainstream Economists Supporting Globalization." *Journal of Economic Perspective* 18, no. 3 (Summer 2004): 143.

13. D. H. Autor, D. Dorn, and Gordon H. Hanson, "The China Syndrome: Local Labor Market Effects of Import Competition in the United States," *American Economic Review* 103, no. 6 (October 2013).

14. See A. Dixit and G. Grossman, "Samuelson Says Nothing about Trade Policy," Princeton University, 2004, accessed from http://depts.washington.edu/teclass/ThinkEcon/readings/Kalles/Dixit%20and%20Grossman%20on%20Samuelson.pdf.

15. J. R. Hagerty, "U.S. Loses High Tech Jobs as R&D Shifts to Asia," *The Wall Street Journal*, January 18, 2012, p. B1.

16. For example, J. D. Sachs and A. Warner, "Economic Reform and the Process of Global Integration," *Brookings Papers on Economic Activity*, 1995, pp. 1–96; J. A. Frankel and D. Romer, "Does Trade Cause Growth?" *American Economic Review* 89, no. 3 (June 1999), pp. 379–99; D. Dollar and A. Kraay, "Trade, Growth and Poverty," working paper, Development Research Group, World Bank, June 2001. Also, for an accessible discussion of the relationship between free trade and economic growth, see T. Taylor, "The Truth about Globalization," *Public Interest, Spring 2002, pp. 24–44; D. Acemoglu, S. Johnson, and J. Robinson, "The Rise of Europe: Atlantic Trade, Institutional Change and Economic Growth," American Economic Review 95, no. 3 (2005), pp. 547–79; T. Singh, "Does International Trade Cause Economic Growth?" The World Economy 33, no. 11 (2010), pp. 1517–64.*

17. Sachs and Warner, "Economic Reform and the Process of Global Integration."

18. Warner, Andrew, and Jeffrey D. Sachs. "Economics Reform and the Process of Global Integration." Brookings Papers on Economic Activity, 1995. https://www.brookings.edu/wp-content/uploads/1995/01/1995a_bpea_sachs_warner_aslund_fischer.pdf.

19. R. Wacziarg and K. H. Welch, "Trade Liberalization and Growth: New Evidence," *World Bank Economic Review* 22, no. 2 (June 2008).

20. T. Singh, "Does International Trade Cause Economic Growth?" *The World Economy* 33, no. 11 (November 2010), pp. 1517–64.

21. J. A. Frankel and D. H. Romer, "Does Trade Cause Growth?" *American Economic Review* 89, no. 3 (June 1999), pp. 370–99.

22. A recent skeptical review of the empirical work on the relationship between trade and growth questions these results. See F. Rodriguez and D. Rodrik, "Trade Policy and Economic Growth: A Skeptic's Guide to the Cross-National Evidence," *National Bureau of Economic Research Working Paper Series*, working paper no. 7081 (April 1999). Even these authors, however, cannot find any evidence that trade hurts economic growth or income levels.

23. B. Ohlin, *Interregional and International Trade* (Cambridge, MA: Harvard University Press, 1933). For a summary, see R. W. Jones and J. P. Neary, "The Positive Theory of International Trade," in *Handbook of International Economics*, R. W. Jones and P. B. Kenen, eds. (Amsterdam: North Holland, 1984).

24. W. Leontief, "Domestic Production and Foreign Trade: The American Capital Position Re-examined," *Proceedings of the American Philosophical Society* 97 (1953), pp. 331–49.

25. R. M. Stern and K. Maskus, "Determinants of the Structure of U.S. Foreign Trade," *Journal of International Economics* 11 (1981), pp. 207–44.

26. See H. P. Bowen, E. E. Leamer, and L. Sveikayskas, "Multicountry, Multifactor Tests of the Factor Abundance Theory," *American Economic Review* 77 (1987), pp. 791–809.

27. D. Trefler, "The Case of the Missing Trade and Other Mysteries," *American Economic Review* 85 (December 1995), pp. 1029–46.

28. D. R. Davis and D. E. Weinstein, "An Account of Global Factor Trade," *American Economic Review* 91, no. 5 (December 2001), pp. 1423–52.

29. R. Vernon, "International Investments and International Trade in the Product Life Cycle," *Quarterly Journal of Economics, May 1966, pp. 190–207; R. Vernon and L. T. Wells, The Economic Environment of International Business, 4th ed. (Englewood Cliffs, NJ: Prentice Hall, 1986).*

30. For a good summary of this literature, see E. Helpman and P. Krugman, *Market Structure and Foreign Trade: Increasing Returns, Imperfect Competition, and the International Economy* (Boston: MIT Press, 1985). Also see P. Krugman, "Does the New Trade Theory Require a New Trade Policy?" *World Economy* 15, no. 4 (1992), pp. 423–41.

31. M. B. Lieberman and D. B. Montgomery, "First-Mover Advantages," *Strategic Management Journal* 9 (Summer 1988), pp. 41–58; W. T. Robinson and Sungwook Min, "Is the First to Market the First to Fail?" *Journal of Marketing Research* 29 (2002), pp. 120–28.

32. J. R. Tybout, "Plant and Firm Level Evidence on New Trade Theories," *National Bureau of Economic Research Working Paper Series*, working paper no. 8418 (August 2001), www.nber.org; S. Deraniyagala and B. Fine, "New Trade Theory versus Old Trade Policy: A Continuing Enigma," *Cambridge Journal of Economics* 25 (November 2001), pp. 809–25.

33. A. D. Chandler, *Scale and Scope* (New York: Free Press, 1990).

34. Krugman, "Does the New Trade Theory Require a New Trade Policy?"

35. M. E. Porter, *The Competitive Advantage of Nations* (New York: Free Press, 1990). For a good review of this book, see R. M. Grant, "Porter's Competitive Advantage of Nations: An Assessment," *Strategic Management Journal* 12 (1991), pp. 535–48.

36. B. Kogut, ed., *Country Competitiveness: Technology and the Organizing of Work* (New York: Oxford University Press, 1993).

37. Agrawal, Raj. *International Trade*. Excel Books India, 2001.

38. Lieberman and Montgomery, "First-Mover Advantages." See also Robinson and Min, "Is the First to Market the First to Fail?"; W. Boulding and M. Christen, "First-Mover Disadvantage," *Harvard Business Review, October 2001, pp. 20–21; R. Agarwal and M. Gort, "First-Mover Advantage and the Speed of Competitive Entry," Journal of Law and Economics 44 (2001), pp. 131-59.*

39. C. A. Hamilton, "Building Better Machine Tools," *Journal of Commerce*, October 30, 1991, p. 8; "Manufacturing Trouble," *The Economist*, October 12, 1991, p. 71.

40. P. Krugman, *The Age of Diminished Expectations* (Cambridge, MA: MIT Press, 1990); J. Bernstein and Dean Baker, "Why Trade Deficits Matter," *The Atlantic*, December 8, 2016.

41. D. Griswold, "Are Trade Deficits a Drag on U.S. Economic Growth?" *Free Trade Bulletin*, March 12, 2007; O. Blanchard, "Current Account Deficits in Rich Countries," *National Bureau of Economic Research Working Paper Series*, working paper no. 12925, February 2007.

42. S. Edwards, "The U.S. Current Account Deficit: Gradual Correction or Abrupt Adjustment?" *National Bureau of Economic Research Working Paper Series*, working paper no. 12154, April 2006.

Government Policy and International Trade

7

LEARNING OBJECTIVES
After reading this chapter, you will be able to:

LO7-1   Identify the policy instruments used by governments to influence international trade flows.

LO7-2   Understand why governments sometimes intervene in international trade.

LO7-3   Summarize and explain the arguments against strategic trade policy.

LO7-4   Describe the development of the world trading system and the current trade issue.

LO7-5   Explain the implications for managers of developments in the world trading system.

American Steel Tariffs

OPENING CASE

In March 2018, President Trump imposed a 25 percent tariff on imports of foreign steel into the United States (and a 10 percent tariff on aluminum imports). In justifying the steel tariff, Trump argued that a strong domestic steel industry was necessary for the national security of the United States. In 2017, some 36 million tons of steel were imported into the U.S., while 81.6 million tons were produced domestically. Import penetration into the U.S. had increased from about 23 percent of total steel consumption in 2007 to 31 percent in 2017. The U.S. exports about 2 million tons of steel per year. There were roughly 140,000 people employed in the U.S. steel industry in 2018, and around 6.5 million employed in industries that consumed steel, including construction, machinery, and automobiles.

This was not the first time the U.S. steel industry had been the beneficiary of import tariffs. The industry has a long history of tariff protection. Some critics complain that this is linked to the importance of steel producing states such as Indiana, Pennsylvania, and Ohio in U.S. Presidential elections. In 2002, the Bush administration placed tariffs ranging from 8 percent to 30 percent on imports of foreign steel. The U.S. exempted its NAFTA partners Canada and Mexico from these tariffs. The Bush tariffs were lifted nine months later after significant opposition from businesses in steel consuming industries, who claimed that higher steel prices were resulting in significant job losses. In 2016, the Obama administration imposed punitive tariffs as high as 500 percent on imports of some steel products from China, arguing that Chinese producers were dumping excess steel production in the United States at below the costs of production. Due to the Obama tariffs (which remain in place), by the time of Trump's announcement, China accounted for only 2 percent of U.S. steel imports. The largest steel exporters to the U.S. in 2017 were Canada, South Korea, Mexico, and Brazil.

The Trump administration argued that this round of steel tariffs would help revitalize the struggling U.S. steel industry. Critics countered that the result would be higher prices for steel consumers and job losses in those industries. The early evidence is mixed. Domestic steel production in the U.S. increased by around 7 percent in the first year after the tariffs were imposed, while imports fell around 10 percent. The prices of U.S. steel products increased by around 20 percent in 2018 and profits for U.S. steel producers improved. Flush with cash, there have been several announcements regarding planned expansions in capacity from domestic steel producers, including Nucor, Steel Dynamics Inc., and U.S. Steel Corp. These plans would add about 8.3 million tons of production to the U.S. steel industry, increasing its capacity by 14 percent.

On the other hand, some steel consumers have pushed back, pointing out that higher steel prices are hurting their businesses. General Motors, a major steel consumer, announced in November 2018 that Trump's tariffs on steel (and aluminum) would cost it over $1 billion a year. The company announced plans to shut several plants and eliminate 15,000 jobs (although higher steel prices were not the only factor here). Similarly, the iconic American motorcycle manufacturer Harley Davidson announced that its 2018 profits were wiped out by higher metal costs due to Trump's tariffs. The company has announced plans to move some production overseas as a way of avoiding the high costs of metals in the United States and supporting foreign sales. Only time will tell if the announcements from GM and Harley Davidson are indicative of the impact that higher steel prices will have on many American businesses. If these are the first salvo, Trump's steel tariffs may ultimately be judged to be no more successful than those imposed by George Bush in 2002. Analysis of the Bush tariffs suggested that the gains to steel producers were outweighed by the losses to U.S. steel consumers.

Sources: Bob Tita and Alistair MacDonald, "Foreign Steel Keeps Flowing into the U.S. despite Tariffs," *The Wall Street Journal*, December 5, 2018; International Trade Administration, *Steel Imports Report: United States*, June 2018; Alistair MacDonald, "Tariffs Roil Global Steel Trade, Creating Winners and Losers," *The Wall Street Journal*, November 29, 2018; Doug Mataconis, "After Trump's Tariffs, American Steel Industry Faces Downturn," Outside the Beltway, January 19, 2019; Ruth Simon, "A Tale of Two Steel Firms and Their Diverging Paths Under Trump's Tariffs," *The Wall Street Journal*, February 10, 2019; "Tariffs on Steel and Aluminum are Creating Some Winners," *The Economist*, August 9, 2018; G. C. Hufbauer and B. Goodrich, "Steel Policy: The Good, the Bad, and the Ugly," *Peterson Institute: International Economics Policy Briefs*, January 2003.

Introduction

The review of the classical trade theories of Smith, Ricardo, and Heckscher–Ohlin in Chapter 6 showed that in a world without trade barriers, trade patterns are determined by the relative productivity of different factors of production in different countries. Countries will specialize in products they can make most efficiently, while importing products they can produce less efficiently. Chapter 6 also laid out the intellectual case for free trade. Remember, **free trade** refers to a situation in which a government does not attempt to restrict what its citizens can buy from or sell to another country. As we saw in Chapter 6, the theories of Smith, Ricardo, and Heckscher–Ohlin predict that the consequences of free trade include both static economic gains (because free trade supports a higher level of domestic consumption and more efficient utilization of resources) and dynamic economic gains (because free trade stimulates economic growth and the creation of wealth).

This chapter looks at the political reality of international trade. Although many nations are nominally committed to free trade, they tend to intervene in international trade to protect the interests of politically important groups or promote the interests of key domestic producers. For example, there is a long history of the U.S. government intervening in the steel industry, imposing import tariffs to protect domestic producers from market share losses due to the importation of less expensive foreign steel. The last three U.S. presidents, Bush, Obama, and Trump, have all authorized tariffs on foreign steel imports. Motivations for doing so include national security concerns, a belief that certain foreign steel producers were dumping production of steel on the U.S. market at below the costs of production, and a desire to boost U.S. steel production and steel-making jobs. In every case, however, these potential benefits must be weighed against the impact of higher steel prices for U.S. consumers of steel, which include firms in the automobile, construction, machinery, and appliance industries. By raising input costs, steel tariffs may have reduced profitability, led to job losses, and reduced competitiveness among firms that consume steel products.

This chapter starts by describing the range of policy instruments that governments use to intervene in international trade. A detailed review of governments' various political and economic motives for intervention follows. In the third section of this chapter, we consider how the case for free trade stands up in view of the various justifications given for government intervention in international trade. Then we look at the emergence of the modern international trading system, which is based on the **General Agreement on Tariffs and Trade (GATT)** and its successor, the World Trade Organization (WTO). The GATT and WTO are the creations of a series of multinational treaties. The final section of this chapter discusses the implications of this material for management practice.

LO7-1

Identify the policy instruments used by governments to influence international trade flows.

▶ **Did You Know?**

Did you know that one of the first arguments for protectionist trade policies was proposed by Alexander Hamilton in 1792?

Visit your instructor's Connect® course and click on your eBook or SmartBook® to view a short video explanation from the author.

Instruments of Trade Policy

Trade policy uses seven main instruments: tariffs, subsidies, import quotas, voluntary export restraints, local content requirements, administrative policies, and antidumping duties. Tariffs are the oldest and simplest instrument of trade policy. As we shall see later in this chapter, they are also the instrument that the GATT and WTO have been most successful in limiting. A fall in tariff barriers in recent decades has been accompanied by a rise in non-tariff barriers, such as subsidies, quotas, voluntary export restraints, and antidumping duties.

TARIFFS

A **tariff** is a tax levied on imports (or exports). Tariffs fall into two categories. **Specific tariffs** are levied as a fixed charge for each unit of a good imported (e.g., $3 per barrel of oil). **Ad valorem tariffs** are levied as a proportion of the value of the imported good. In most cases, tariffs are placed on imports to protect domestic producers from foreign competition by raising the price of imported goods. However, tariffs also produce revenue for the government. Until the income tax was introduced, for example, the U.S. government received most of its revenues from tariffs.

Import tariffs are paid by the importer (and export tariffs by the exporter). Thus, the 25 percent ad valorem tariff placed on imports of foreign steel by President Trump in 2017 are paid for not by foreign steel producers, but by the American importers. These import tariffs are in effect a tax on American consumers. The important thing to understand about an import tariff is who suffers and who gains. The government gains because the tariff increases government revenues. Domestic producers gain because the tariff affords them some protection against foreign competitors by increasing the cost of imported foreign goods. Consumers lose because they must pay more for certain imports. For example, as noted in the opening case, in 2002 the U.S. government placed an ad valorem tariff of 8 to 30 percent on imports of foreign steel. The idea was to protect domestic steel producers from cheap imports of foreign steel. In this case, however, the effect was to raise the price of steel products in the United States between 30 and 50 percent. A number of U.S. steel consumers, ranging from appliance makers to automobile companies, objected that the steel tariffs would raise their costs of production and make it more difficult for them to compete in the global marketplace. Whether the gains to the government and domestic producers exceed the loss to consumers depends on various factors, such as the amount of the tariff, the importance of the imported good to domestic consumers, the number of jobs saved in the protected industry, and so on. In the steel case, many argued that the losses to steel consumers apparently outweighed the gains to steel producers. In November 2003, the World Trade Organization declared that the tariffs represented a violation of the WTO treaty, and the United States removed them in December of that year. Interestingly, this ruling did not stop Donald Trump from imposing a 25 percent tariff on imports of foreign steel in March 2018. If the tariffs are challenged, as seems likely, the WTO will in all probability reach a similar conclusion.

In general, two conclusions can be derived from economic analysis of the effect of import tariffs.[1] First, tariffs are generally pro-producer and anticonsumer. While they protect producers from foreign competitors, this restriction of supply also raises domestic prices. For example, a study by Japanese economists calculated that tariffs on imports of foodstuffs, cosmetics, and chemicals into Japan cost the average Japanese consumer about $890 per year in the form of higher prices. Almost all studies find that import tariffs impose significant costs on domestic consumers in the form of higher prices. Second, import tariffs reduce the overall efficiency of the world economy. They reduce efficiency because a protective tariff encourages domestic firms to produce products at home that could be produced more efficiently abroad. The consequence is an inefficient utilization of resources.[2]

Sometimes tariffs are levied on exports of a product from a country. Export tariffs are less common than import tariffs. In general, export tariffs have two objectives: first, to raise revenue for the government, and second, to reduce exports from a sector, often for political reasons. For example, in 2004 China imposed a tariff on textile exports. The primary objective was to moderate the growth in exports of textiles from China, thereby alleviating tensions with other trading partners. China also had tariffs on steel exports but removed many of those in late 2015.

SUBSIDIES

A **subsidy** is a government payment to a domestic producer. Subsidies take many forms, including cash grants, low-interest loans, tax breaks, and government equity participation in domestic firms. By lowering production costs, subsidies help domestic producers in two ways: (1) competing against foreign imports and (2) gaining export markets. Agriculture tends to be one of the largest beneficiaries of subsidies in most countries. The European Union has been paying out about €44 billion annually ($55 billion) in farm subsidies. The farm bill that passed the U.S. Congress in 2018 contained subsidies to producers of roughly $25 billion a year for the next 10 years. The Japanese also have a long history of supporting inefficient domestic producers with farm subsidies. According to the World Trade Organization, in mid-2000 countries spent some $300 billion on subsidies, $250 billion of which was spent by 21 developed nations.[3] In response to a severe sales slump following

Are the Chinese Illegally Subsidizing Auto Exports?

In late 2012, during that year's presidential election campaign, the Obama administration filed a complaint against China with the World Trade Organization. The complaint claimed that China was providing export subsidies to its auto and auto parts industries. The subsidies included cash grants for exporting, grants for R&D, subsidies to pay interest on loans, and preferential tax treatment.

The United States estimated the value of the subsidies to be at least $1 billion between 2009 and 2011. The complaint also pointed out that in the years 2002 through 2011, the value of China's exports of autos and auto parts increased more than ninefold from $7.4 billion to $69.1 billion. The United States was China's largest market for exports of auto parts during this period. The United States asserted that, to some degree, this growth may have been helped by subsidies. The complaint went on to claim that these subsidies hurt producers of automobiles and auto parts in the United States. This is a large industry in the United States, employing more than 800,000 people and generating some $350 billion in sales.

While some in the labor movement applauded the move, the response from U.S. auto companies and auto parts producers was muted. One reason for this is that many U.S. producers do business in China and, in all probability, want to avoid retaliation from the Chinese government. GM, for example, has a joint venture and two wholly owned subsidiaries in China and is doing very well there.

In addition, some U.S. producers benefit by purchasing cheap Chinese auto parts, so any retaliatory tariffs imposed on those imports might actually raise their costs.

More cynical observers saw the move as nothing more than political theater. The week before the complaint was filed, the Republican presidential candidate, Mitt Romney, had accused the Obama administration of "failing American workers" by not labeling China a currency manipulator. So perhaps the complaint was in part simply another move on the presidential campaign chessboard.

In February 2014, the United States expanded its complaint with the WTO against China, arguing that the country had an illegal export subsidy program that includes not only auto parts, but also textiles, apparel and footwear, advanced materials and metals, speciality chemicals, medical products and agriculture. In 2016, after pressure from the WTO and U.S., China agreed to eliminate a wide range of subsidies for its exporters. Michael Froman, the U.S. Trade Representative, announced the deal, calling it "a win for Americans employed in seven diverse sectors that run the gamut from agriculture to textiles."

Sources: James Healey, "U.S. Alleges Unfair China Auto Subsidies in WTO Action," *USA Today*, September 17, 2012; M. A. Memoli, "Obama to Tell WTO That China Illegally Subsidizes Auto Imports," *Los Angeles Times*, September 17, 2012; Vicki Needham, "US Launches Trade Case against China's Export Subsidy Program," *The Hill*, February 11, 2014; and David J. Lynch, "China Eliminates Subsidies for Its Exporters," *Financial Times*, April 14, 2016.

the global financial crisis, between mid-2008 and mid-2009, some developed nations gave $45 billion in subsidies to their automobile makers. While the purpose of the subsidies was to help them survive a very difficult economic climate, one of the consequences was to give subsidized companies an unfair competitive advantage in the global auto industry. Somewhat ironically, given the government bailouts of U.S. auto companies during the global financial crisis, in 2012 the Obama administration filed a complaint with the WTO arguing that the Chinese were illegally subsidizing exports of autos and auto parts. Details are given in the accompanying Country Focus feature.

The main gains from subsidies accrue to domestic producers, whose international competitiveness is increased as a result. Advocates of strategic trade policy (which, as you will recall from Chapter 6, is an outgrowth of the new trade theory) favor subsidies to help domestic firms achieve a dominant position in those industries in which economies of scale are important and the world market is not large enough to profitably support more than a few firms (aerospace and semiconductors are two such industries). According to this argument, subsidies can help a firm achieve a first-mover advantage in an emerging industry. If this is achieved, further gains to the domestic economy arise from the employment and tax revenues that a major global company can generate. However, government subsidies must be paid for, typically by taxing individuals and corporations.

Whether subsidies generate national benefits that exceed their national costs is debatable. In practice, many subsidies are not that successful at increasing the international competitiveness of domestic producers. Rather, they tend to protect the inefficient and promote excess production. One study estimated that if advanced countries abandoned subsidies to farmers, global trade in agricultural products would be 50 percent higher and the world as a whole would be better off by $160 billion.[4] Another study estimated that removing all barriers to trade in agriculture (both subsidies and tariffs) would raise world income by $182 billion.[5] This increase in wealth arises from the more efficient use of agricultural land.

IMPORT QUOTAS AND VOLUNTARY EXPORT RESTRAINTS

An **import quota** is a direct restriction on the quantity of some good that may be imported into a country. The restriction is usually enforced by issuing import licenses to a group of individuals or firms. For example, the United States has a quota on cheese imports. The only firms allowed to import cheese are certain trading companies, each of which is allocated the right to import a maximum number of pounds of cheese each year. In some cases, the right to sell is given directly to the governments of exporting countries.

A common hybrid of a quota and a tariff is known as a tariff rate quota. Under a **tariff rate quota**, a lower tariff rate is applied to imports within the quota than those over the quota. For example, as illustrated in Figure 7.1, an ad valorem tariff rate of 10 percent might be levied on 1 million tons of rice imports into South Korea, after which an out-of-quota rate of 80 percent might be applied. Thus, South Korea might import 2 million tons of rice, 1 million at a 10 percent tariff rate and another 1 million at an 80 percent tariff. Tariff rate quotas are common in agriculture, where their goal is to limit imports over quota.

A variant on the import quota is the voluntary export restraint. A **voluntary export restraint (VER)** is a quota on trade imposed by the exporting country, typically at the request of the importing country's government. For example, in 2012 Brazil imposed what amounts to voluntary export restraints on shipments of vehicles from Mexico to Brazil. The two countries have a decade-old free trade agreement, but a surge in vehicles heading to Brazil from Mexico prompted Brazil to raise its protectionist walls. Mexico agreed to quotas on Brazil-bound vehicle exports for three years.[6] Foreign producers agree to VERs because they fear more damaging punitive tariffs or import quotas might follow if they do not. Agreeing to a VER is seen as a way to make the best of a bad situation by appeasing protectionist pressures in a country.

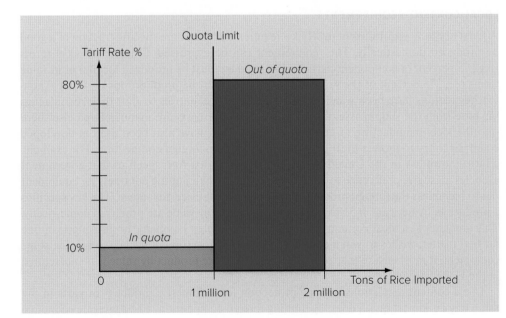

FIGURE 7.1

Hypothetical tariff rate quota.

As with tariffs and subsidies, both import quotas and VERs benefit domestic producers by limiting import competition. As with all restrictions on trade, quotas do not benefit consumers. An import quota or VER always raises the domestic price of an imported good. When imports are limited to a low percentage of the market by a quota or VER, the price is bid up for that limited foreign supply. The extra profit that producers make when supply is artificially limited by an import quota is referred to as a **quota rent**.

If a domestic industry lacks the capacity to meet demand, an import quota can raise prices for *both* the domestically produced and the imported good. This happened in the U.S. sugar industry, in which a tariff rate quota system has long limited the amount foreign producers can sell in the U.S. market. According to one study, import quotas have caused the price of sugar in the United States to be as much as 40 percent greater than the world price.[7] These higher prices have translated into greater profits for U.S. sugar producers, which have lobbied politicians to keep the lucrative agreement. They argue U.S. jobs in the sugar industry will be lost to foreign producers if the quota system is scrapped.

EXPORT TARIFFS AND BANS

An **export tariff** is a tax placed on the export of a good. The goal behind an export tariff is to discriminate *against* exporting in order to ensure that there is sufficient supply of a good within a country. For example, in the past, China has placed an export tariff on the export of grain to ensure that there is sufficient supply in China. Similarly, during its infrastructure building boom, China had an export tariff in place on certain kinds of steel products to ensure that there was sufficient supply of steel within the country. The steel tariffs were removed in late 2015. Because most countries try to encourage exports, export tariffs are relatively rare.

An **export ban** is a policy that partially or entirely restricts the export of a good. One well-known example was the ban on exports of U.S. crude oil production that was enacted by Congress in 1975. At the time, Organization of the Petroleum Exporting Countries (OPEC) was restricting the supply of oil in order to drive up prices and punish Western nations for their support of Israel during conflicts between Arab nations and Israel. The export ban in the United States was seen as a way of ensuring a sufficient supply of domestic oil at home, thereby helping to keep the domestic price down and boosting national security. The ban was lifted in 2015 after lobbying from American oil producers, who believed that they could get higher prices for some of their output if they were allowed to sell on world markets.

LOCAL CONTENT REQUIREMENTS

A **local content requirement (LCR)** is a requirement that some specific fraction of a good be produced domestically. The requirement can be expressed either in physical terms (e.g., 75 percent of component parts for this product must be produced locally) or in value terms (e.g., 75 percent of the value of this product must be produced locally). Local content regulations have been widely used by developing countries to shift their manufacturing base from the simple assembly of products whose parts are manufactured elsewhere into the local manufacture of component parts. They have also been used in developed countries to try to protect local jobs and industry from foreign competition. For example, a little-known law in the United States, the Buy America Act, specifies that government agencies must give preference to American products when putting contracts for equipment out to bid unless the foreign products have a significant price advantage. The law specifies a product as "American" if 51 percent of the materials by value are produced domestically. This amounts to a local content requirement. If a foreign company, or an American one for that matter, wishes to win a contract from a U.S. government agency to provide some equipment, it must ensure that at least 51 percent of the product by value is manufactured in the United States.

Local content regulations provide protection for a domestic producer of parts in the same way an import quota does: by limiting foreign competition. The aggregate economic effects are also the same; domestic producers benefit, but the restrictions on imports raise the prices of imported components. In turn, higher prices for imported components are passed on to consumers of the final product in the form of higher final prices. So as with all trade policies, local content regulations tend to benefit producers and not consumers.

ADMINISTRATIVE POLICIES

In addition to the formal instruments of trade policy, governments of all types sometimes use informal or administrative policies to restrict imports and boost exports. **Administrative trade policies** are bureaucratic rules designed to make it difficult for imports to enter a country. It has been argued that the Japanese are the masters of this trade barrier. In recent decades, Japan's formal tariff and nontariff barriers have been among the lowest in the world. However, critics charge that the country's informal administrative barriers to imports more than compensate for this. For example, Japan's car market has been hard for foreigners to crack. In 2016, only 6 percent of the 4.9 million cars sold in Japan were foreign, and only 1 percent were U.S. cars. American car makers have argued for decades that Japan makes it difficult to compete by setting up regulatory hurdles, such as vehicle parts standards, that don't exist anywhere else in the world. Ironically, the Trans Pacific Partnership (TPP) addressed this issue. America would have reduced tariffs on imports of Japanese light trucks in return for Japan adopting U.S. standards on auto parts, which would have made it easier to import and sell American cars in Japan. However, President Donald Trump pulled America out of the TPP in January 2017.[8]

ANTIDUMPING POLICIES

In the context of international trade, **dumping** is variously defined as selling goods in a foreign market at below their costs of production or as selling goods in a foreign market at below their "fair" market value. There is a difference between these two definitions; the fair market value of a good is normally judged to be greater than the costs of producing that good because the former includes a "fair" profit margin. Dumping is viewed as a method by which firms unload excess production in foreign markets. Some dumping may be the result of predatory behavior, with producers using substantial profits from their home markets to subsidize prices in a foreign market with a view to driving indigenous competitors out of that market. Once this has been achieved, so the argument goes, the predatory firm can raise prices and earn substantial profits.

Antidumping policies are designed to punish foreign firms that engage in dumping. The ultimate objective is to protect domestic producers from unfair foreign competition. Although antidumping policies vary from country to country, the majority are similar to those used in the United States. If a domestic producer believes that a foreign firm is dumping production in the U.S. market, it can file a petition with two government agencies, the Commerce Department and the International Trade Commission (ITC). If a complaint has merit, the Commerce Department may impose an antidumping duty on the offending foreign imports (antidumping duties are often called **countervailing duties**). These duties, which represent a special tariff, can be fairly substantial and stay in place for up to five years. The accompanying Management Focus discusses how a firm, U.S. Magnesium, used antidumping legislation to gain protection from unfair foreign competitors.

 TEST PREP

Use SmartBook to help retain what you have learned. Access your instructor's Connect course to check out SmartBook or go to **learnsmartadvantage.com** for help.

The Case for Government Intervention

LO7-2

Understand why governments sometimes intervene in international trade.

Now that we have reviewed the various instruments of trade policy that governments can use, it is time to look at the case for government intervention in international trade. Arguments for government intervention take two paths: political and economic. Political arguments for intervention are concerned with protecting the interests of certain groups within a nation (normally producers), often at the expense of other groups (normally consumers), or with achieving some political objective that lies outside the sphere of

Protecting U.S. Magnesium

In February 2004, U.S. Magnesium, the sole surviving U.S. producer of magnesium, a metal that is primarily used in the manufacture of certain automobile parts and aluminum cans, filed a petition with the U.S. International Trade Commission (ITC) contending that a surge in imports had caused material damage to the U.S. industry's employment, sales, market share, and profitability. According to U.S. Magnesium, Russian and Chinese producers had been selling the metal at prices significantly below market value. During 2002 and 2003, imports of magnesium into the United States rose 70 percent, while prices fell by 40 percent, and the market share accounted for by imports jumped to 50 percent from 25 percent.

"The United States used to be the largest producer of magnesium in the world," a U.S. Magnesium spokesperson said at the time of the filing. "What's really sad is that you can be state of the art and have modern technology, and if the Chinese, who pay people less than 90 cents an hour, want to run you out of business, they can do it. And that's why we are seeking relief."[*]

During a yearlong investigation, the ITC solicited input from various sides in the dispute. Foreign producers and consumers of magnesium in the United States argued that falling prices for magnesium during 2002 and 2003 simply reflected an imbalance between supply and demand due to additional capacity coming on stream not from Russia or China but from a new Canadian plant that opened in 2001 and from a planned Australian plant. The Canadian plant shut down in 2003, the Australian plant never came on stream, and prices for magnesium rose again in 2004.

Magnesium consumers in the United States also argued to the ITC that imposing antidumping duties on foreign imports of magnesium would raise prices in the United States significantly above world levels. A spokesperson for Alcoa, which mixes magnesium with aluminum to make alloys for cans, predicted that if antidumping duties were imposed, high magnesium prices in the United States would force Alcoa to move some production out of the United States. Alcoa also noted that in 2003, U.S. Magnesium was unable to supply all of Alcoa's needs, forcing the company to turn to imports. Consumers of magnesium in the automobile industry asserted that high

prices in the United States would drive engineers to design magnesium out of automobiles or force manufacturing elsewhere, which would ultimately hurt everyone.

The six members of the ITC were not convinced by these arguments. In March 2005, the ITC ruled that both China and Russia had been dumping magnesium in the United States. The government decided to impose duties ranging from 50 percent to more than 140 percent on imports of magnesium from China. Russian producers faced duties ranging from 19 percent to 22 percent. The duties were to be levied for five years, after which the ITC would revisit the situation. The ITC revoked the antidumping order on Russia in February 2011 but decided to continue placing the duties on Chinese producers. They were finally removed by the ITC in 2014.

According to U.S. Magnesium, the initial favorable ruling allowed the company to reap the benefits of nearly $50 million in investments made in its manufacturing plant and enabled the company to boost its capacity by 28 percent by the end of 2005. Commenting on the favorable ruling, a U.S. Magnesium spokesperson noted, "Once unfair trade is removed from the marketplace we'll be able to compete with anyone."

U.S. Magnesium's customers and competitors, however, did not view the situation as one of unfair trade. While the imposition of antidumping duties no doubt helped to protect U.S. Magnesium and the 400 people it employed from foreign competition, magnesium consumers in the United States felt they were the ultimate losers, a view that seemed to be confirmed by price data. In early 2010, the price for magnesium alloy in the United States was $2.30 per pound, compared to $1.54 in Mexico, $1.49 in Europe, and $1.36 in China.

[*]Dave Anderton, "U.S. Magnesium Lands Ruling on Unfair Imports," *Deseret News*, October 1, 2004, **https://www.deseretnews.com/article/595095137/US-Magnesium-lauds-ruling-on-unfair-imports.html**.

Sources: Dave Anderton, "U.S. Magnesium Lands Ruling on Unfair Imports," *Deseret News*, October 1, 2004, p. D10; "U.S. Magnesium and Its Largest Consumers Debate before U.S. ITC," *Platt's Metals Week*, February 28, 2005, p. 2; S. Oberbeck, "U.S. Magnesium Plans Big Utah Production Expansion," *Salt Lake Tribune*, March 30, 2005; "US to Keep Anti-dumping Duty on China Pure Magnesium," *Chinadaily.com*, September 13, 2012; Lance Duronl, "No Duties for Chinese Magnesium Exporter, CIT Affirms," *Law360*, June 2, 2015; and Dan Ikenson, "Death by Antidumping," *Forbes*, January 3, 2011.

economic relationships, such as protecting the environment or human rights. Economic arguments for intervention are typically concerned with boosting the overall wealth of a nation (to the benefit of all, both producers and consumers).

POLITICAL ARGUMENTS FOR INTERVENTION

Political arguments for government intervention cover a range of issues, including preserving jobs, protecting industries deemed important for national security, retaliating against unfair foreign competition, protecting consumers from "dangerous" products, furthering the goals of foreign policy, and advancing the human rights of individuals in exporting countries.

Protecting Jobs and Industries

Perhaps the most common political argument for government intervention is that it is necessary for protecting jobs and industries from unfair foreign competition. Competition is most often viewed as unfair when producers in an exporting country are subsidized in some way by their government. For example, it has been repeatedly claimed that Chinese enterprises in several industries, including aluminum, steel, and auto parts, have benefited from extensive government subsidies. Such logic was behind the complaint that the Obama administration filed with the WTO against Chinese auto parts producers in 2012 (see the Country Focus "Are the Chinese Illegally Subsidizing Auto Exports?" in this chapter). More generally, Robert Scott of the Economic Policy Institute has claimed that the growth in the U.S.–China trade deficit between 2001 and 2015 was, to a significant degree, the result of unfair competition, including direct subsidies to Chinese producers and currency manipulations. Scott estimated that as many as 3.4 million U.S. jobs were lost as a consequence.[9] Donald Trump tapped into anxiety about job losses due to unfair trade from China during his successful 2016 presidential run.

On the other hand, critics charge that claims of unfair competition are often overstated for political reasons. For example, as noted in the opening case, President George W. Bush placed tariffs on imports of foreign steel in 2002 as a response to "unfair competition," but critics were quick to point out that many of the U.S. steel producers that benefited from these tariffs were located in states that Bush needed to win reelection in 2004. A political motive also underlay establishment of the Common Agricultural Policy (CAP) by the European Union. The CAP was designed to protect the jobs of Europe's politically powerful farmers by restricting imports and guaranteeing prices. However, the higher prices that resulted from the CAP have cost Europe's consumers dearly. This is true of many attempts to protect jobs and industries through government intervention. For example, the imposition of steel tariffs in 2002 raised steel prices for American consumers, such as automobile companies, making them less competitive in the global marketplace.

Protecting National Security

Countries sometimes argue that it is necessary to protect certain industries because they are important for national security. Defense-related industries often get this kind of attention (e.g., aerospace, advanced electronics, and semiconductors). Although now uncommon, this argument is still made sometimes. When the Trump administration announced tariffs on imports of foreign steel and aluminum on March 1, 2018, national security issues were cited as a primary justification. This was the first time since 1986 that a national security threat was used to justify tariffs imposed by the United States. In 2017, the United States was importing about 30 percent of steel used in the country, with the largest source of imports being Canada and Mexico. Interestingly, and counter to the argument of the Trump administration, critics argued that by raising input prices for many U.S. defense contractors, who tend to be big consumers of steel and aluminum, the tariffs would actually harm the U.S. defense industry and have a negative impact on national security.[10]

globalEDGE   TRADE LAW

Government policy and international trade is the core focus of this chapter. This topic area has far-ranging implications, such as trade policy, free trade, and the world's international trading system. Basically, we are talking about a lot of legalistic aspects starting at the government level and moving all the way to what organizations and even individuals can and cannot do globally when trading. The globalEDGE™ section "Trade Law" **(globaledge.msu. edu/global-resources/trade-law)** is a unique compilation of globalEDGE™ partner-designed "compendiums of trade laws," country- and region-specific trade law, free online learning modules created for globalEDGE™ on various aspects of trade law, and much more. One fascinating resource related to trade law is the Anti-Counterfeiting and Product Protection Program (A-CAPPP). A-CAPPP includes counterfeiting-related webinars, presentations, and research-related materials and working papers. Do you know what counterfeiting is? Take a look at the "Trade Law" section of globalEDGE™ and especially the A-CAPPP site to become more familiar with the topic. (Is China really as bad as many in the international community think?)

Retaliating

Some argue that governments should use the threat to intervene in trade policy as a bargaining tool to help open foreign markets and force trading partners to "play by the rules of the game." The U.S. government has used the threat of punitive trade sanctions to try to get the Chinese government to enforce its intellectual property laws. Lax enforcement of these laws had given rise to massive copyright infringements in China that had been costing U.S. companies such as Microsoft hundreds of millions of dollars per year in lost sales revenues. After the United States threatened to impose 100 percent tariffs on a range of Chinese imports and after harsh words between officials from the two countries, the Chinese agreed to tighter enforcement of intellectual property regulations.[11]

If it works, such a politically motivated rationale for government intervention may liberalize trade and bring with it resulting economic gains. It is a risky strategy, however. A country that is being pressured may not back down and instead may respond to the imposition of punitive tariffs by raising trade barriers of its own. This is exactly what the Chinese government threatened to do when pressured by the United States, although it ultimately did back down. If a government does not back down, the results could be higher trade barriers all around and an economic loss to all involved.

Protecting Consumers

Many governments have long had regulations to protect consumers from unsafe products. The indirect effect of such regulations often is to limit or ban the importation of such products. For example, in 2003 several countries, including Japan and South Korea, decided to ban imports of American beef after a single case of mad cow disease was found in Washington State. The ban was designed to protect consumers from what was seen to be an unsafe product. Together, Japan and South Korea accounted for about $2 billion of U.S. beef sales, so the ban had a significant impact on U.S. beef producers. After two years, both countries lifted the ban, although they placed stringent requirements on U.S. beef imports to reduce the risk of importing beef that might be tainted by mad cow disease (e.g., Japan required that all beef must come from cattle under 21 months of age).

Furthering Foreign Policy Objectives

Governments sometimes use trade policy to support their foreign policy objectives.[12] A government may grant preferential trade terms to a country with which it wants to build strong relations. Trade policy has also been used several times to pressure or punish "rogue states" that do not abide by international law or norms. Iraq labored under extensive trade sanctions after the UN coalition defeated the country in the 1991 Gulf War until the 2003 invasion of Iraq by U.S.-led forces. The theory is that such pressure might persuade the rogue state to mend its ways, or it might hasten a change of government. In the case of Iraq, the sanctions were seen as a way of forcing that country to comply with several UN resolutions. The United States has maintained long-running trade sanctions against Cuba (despite the move by the Obama administration to "normalize" relations with Cuba, these sanctions are still in place). Their principal function is to impoverish Cuba in the hope that the resulting economic hardship will lead to the downfall of Cuba's communist government and its replacement with a more democratically inclined (and pro-U.S.) regime. The United States has also had trade sanctions in place against Libya and Iran, both of which were accused of supporting terrorist action against U.S. interests and building weapons of mass destruction. In late 2003, the sanctions against Libya seemed to yield some returns when that country announced it would terminate a program to build nuclear weapons. The U.S. government responded by relaxing those sanctions. Similarly, the U.S. government used trade sanctions to pressure the Iranian government to halt its alleged nuclear weapons program. Following a 2015 agreement to limit Iran's nuclear program, it relaxed some of those sanctions. However, the Trump administration has since reimposed significant sanctions, arguing that Iran was not adhering to the 2015 agreement.

Other countries can undermine unilateral trade sanctions. The U.S. sanctions against Cuba, for example, did not stop other Western countries from trading with Cuba. The U.S. sanctions have done little more than help create a vacuum into which other trading nations, such as Canada and Germany, have stepped.

Protecting Human Rights

Protecting and promoting human rights in other countries is an important element of foreign policy for many democracies. Governments sometimes use trade policy to try to improve the human rights policies of trading partners. For example, as discussed in Chapter 5, the U.S. government long had trade sanctions in place against the nation of Myanmar, in no small part due to the poor human rights practices in that nation. In late 2012, the United States said that it would ease trade sanctions against Myanmar in response to democratic reforms in that country. Similarly, in the 1980s and 1990s, Western governments used trade sanctions against South Africa as a way of pressuring that nation to drop its apartheid policies, which were seen as a violation of basic human rights.

ECONOMIC ARGUMENTS FOR INTERVENTION

With the development of the new trade theory and strategic trade policy (see Chapter 6), the economic arguments for government intervention have undergone a renaissance in recent years. Until the early 1980s, most economists saw little benefit in government intervention and strongly advocated a free trade policy. This position has changed at the margins with the development of strategic trade policy, although as we will see in the next section, there are still strong economic arguments for sticking to a free trade stance.

The Infant Industry Argument

The **infant industry argument** is by far the oldest economic argument for government intervention. Alexander Hamilton proposed it in 1792. According to this argument, many developing countries have a potential comparative advantage in manufacturing, but new manufacturing industries cannot initially compete with established industries in developed countries. To allow manufacturing to get a toehold, the argument is that governments should temporarily support new industries (with tariffs, import quotas, and subsidies) until they have grown strong enough to meet international competition.

This argument has had substantial appeal for the governments of developing nations during the past 50 years, and the GATT has recognized the infant industry argument as a

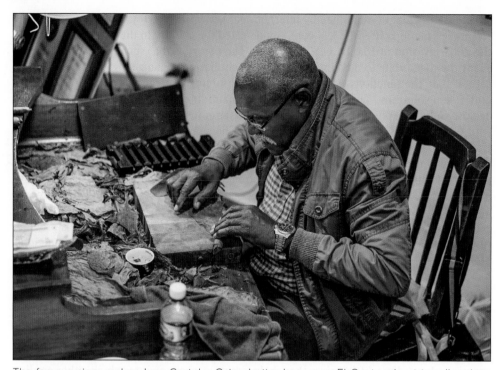

The famous cigar maker Jose Castelar Cairo, better known as El Cueto, about to roll a cigar, in Havana, Cuba.

Esben Hansen/123RF

legitimate reason for protectionism. Nevertheless, many economists remain critical of this argument for two main reasons. First, protection of manufacturing from foreign competition does no good unless the protection helps make the industry efficient. In case after case, however, protection seems to have done little more than foster the development of inefficient industries that have little hope of ever competing in the world market. Brazil, for example, built the world's 10th-largest auto industry behind tariff barriers and quotas. Once those barriers were removed in the late 1980s, however, foreign imports soared, and the industry was forced to face up to the fact that after 30 years of protection, the Brazilian auto industry was one of the world's most inefficient.[13]

Second, the infant industry argument relies on an assumption that firms are unable to make efficient long-term investments by borrowing money from the domestic or international capital market. Consequently, governments have been required to subsidize long-term investments. Given the development of global capital markets over the past 20 years, this assumption no longer looks as valid as it once did. Today, if a developing country has a potential comparative advantage in a manufacturing industry, firms in that country should be able to borrow money from the capital markets to finance the required investments. Given financial support, firms based in countries with a potential comparative advantage have an incentive to endure the necessary initial losses in order to make long-run gains without requiring government protection. Many Taiwanese and South Korean firms did this in industries such as textiles, semiconductors, machine tools, steel, and shipping. Thus, given efficient global capital markets, the only industries that would require government protection would be those that are not worthwhile.

Strategic Trade Policy

Some new trade theorists have proposed the strategic trade policy argument.[14] We reviewed the basic argument in Chapter 6 when we considered the new trade theory. The new trade theory argues that in industries in which the existence of substantial economies of scale implies that the world market will profitably support only a few firms, countries may predominate in the export of certain products simply because they have firms that were able to capture first-mover advantages. The long-term dominance of Boeing in the commercial aircraft industry has been attributed to such factors.

The **strategic trade policy** argument has two components. First, it is argued that by appropriate actions, a government can help raise national income if it can somehow ensure that the firm or firms that gain first-mover advantages in an industry are domestic rather than foreign enterprises. Thus, according to the strategic trade policy argument, a government should use subsidies to support promising firms that are active in newly emerging industries. Advocates of this argument point out that the substantial R&D grants that the U.S. government gave Boeing in the 1950s and 1960s probably helped tilt the field of competition in the newly emerging market for passenger jets in Boeing's favor. (Boeing's first commercial jet airliner, the 707, was derived from a military plane.) Similar arguments have been made with regard to Japan's rise to dominance in the production of liquid crystal display screens (used in computers). Although these screens were invented in the United States, the Japanese government, in cooperation with major electronics companies, targeted this industry for research support in the late 1970s and early 1980s. The result was that Japanese firms, not U.S. firms, subsequently captured first-mover advantages in this market.

The second component of the strategic trade policy argument is that it might pay a government to intervene in an industry by helping domestic firms overcome the barriers to entry created by foreign firms that have already reaped first-mover advantages. This argument underlies government support of Airbus, Boeing's major competitor (see the opening case). Formed in 1966 as a consortium of four companies from Great Britain, France, Germany, and Spain, Airbus had less than 5 percent of the world commercial aircraft market when it began production in the mid-1970s. By 2017, it was splitting the market with Boeing. How did Airbus achieve this? According to the U.S. government, the answer is an $18 billion subsidy from the governments of Great Britain, France, Germany, and Spain.[15] Without this subsidy, Airbus would never have been able to break into the world market.

If these arguments are correct, they support a rationale for government intervention in international trade. Governments should target technologies that may be important in the future and use subsidies to support development work aimed at commercializing those technologies. Furthermore, government should provide export subsidies until the domestic firms have established first-mover advantages in the world market. Government support may also be justified if it can help domestic firms overcome the first-mover advantages enjoyed by foreign competitors and emerge as viable competitors in the world market (as in the Airbus and semiconductor examples). In this case, a combination of home-market protection and export-promoting subsidies may be needed.

The Revised Case for Free Trade

The strategic trade policy arguments of the new trade theorists suggest an economic justification for government intervention in international trade. This justification challenges the rationale for unrestricted free trade found in the work of classic trade theorists such as Adam Smith and David Ricardo. In response to this challenge to economic orthodoxy, a number of economists—including some of those responsible for the development of the new trade theory, such as Paul Krugman—point out that although strategic trade policy looks appealing in theory, in practice it may be unworkable. This response to the strategic trade policy argument constitutes the revised case for free trade.[16]

RETALIATION AND TRADE WAR

Krugman argues that a strategic trade policy aimed at establishing domestic firms in a dominant position in a global industry is a beggar-thy-neighbor policy that boosts national income at the expense of other countries. A country that attempts to use such policies will probably provoke retaliation. In many cases, the resulting trade war between two or more

 TEST PREP

Use SmartBook to help retain what you have learned. Access your instructor's Connect course to check out SmartBook or go to **learnsmartadvantage.com** for help.

LO7-3

Summarize and explain the arguments against strategic trade policy.

interventionist governments will leave all countries involved worse off than if a hands-off approach had been adopted in the first place. If the U.S. government were to respond to the Airbus subsidy by increasing its own subsidies to Boeing, for example, the result might be that the subsidies would cancel each other out. In the process, both European and U.S. taxpayers would end up supporting an expensive and pointless trade war, and both Europe and the United States would be worse off.

Krugman may be right about the danger of a strategic trade policy leading to a trade war. The problem, however, is how to respond when one's competitors are already being supported by government subsidies; that is, how should Boeing and the United States respond to the subsidization of Airbus? According to Krugman, the answer is probably not to engage in retaliatory action but to help establish rules of the game that minimize the use of trade-distorting subsidies. This is what the World Trade Organization seeks to do. It should also be noted that antidumping policies can be used to target competitors supported by subsidies who are selling goods at prices that are below their costs of production.

DOMESTIC POLICIES

Governments do not always act in the national interest when they intervene in the economy; politically important interest groups often influence them. The European Union's support for the Common Agricultural Policy (CAP), which arose because of the political power of French and German farmers, is an example. The CAP benefits inefficient farmers and the politicians who rely on the farm vote but not consumers in the EU, who end up paying more for their foodstuffs. Thus, a further reason for not embracing strategic trade policy, according to Krugman, is that such a policy is almost certain to be captured by special-interest groups within the economy, which will distort it to their own ends. Krugman concludes that in the United States,

> To ask the Commerce Department to ignore special-interest politics while formulating detailed policy for many industries is not realistic; to establish a blanket policy of free trade, with exceptions granted only under extreme pressure, may not be the optimal policy according to the theory but may be the best policy that the country is likely to get.[17]

LO7-4

Describe the development of the world trading system and the current trade issue.

Development of the World Trading System

Economic arguments support unrestricted free trade. While many governments have recognized the value of these arguments, they have been unwilling to unilaterally lower their trade barriers for fear that other nations might not follow suit. Consider the problem that two neighboring countries, say, Brazil and Argentina, face when deciding whether to lower trade barriers between them. In principle, the government of Brazil might favor lowering trade barriers, but it might be unwilling to do so for fear that Argentina will not do the same. Instead, the government might fear that the Argentineans will take advantage of Brazil's low barriers to enter the Brazilian market while continuing to shut Brazilian products out of their market through high trade barriers. The Argentinean government might believe that it faces the same dilemma. The essence of the problem is a lack of trust. Both governments recognize that their respective nations will benefit from lower trade barriers between them, but neither government is willing to lower barriers for fear that the other might not follow.[18]

Such a deadlock can be resolved if both countries negotiate a set of rules to govern cross-border trade and lower trade barriers. But who is to monitor the governments to make sure they are playing by the trade rules? And who is to impose sanctions on a government that cheats? Both governments could set up an independent body to act as a referee. This referee could monitor trade between the countries, make sure that no side cheats, and impose sanctions on a country if it does cheat in the trade game.

While it might sound unlikely that any government would compromise its national sovereignty by submitting to such an arrangement, since World War II an international trading framework has evolved that has exactly these features. For its first 50 years, this framework was known as the General Agreement on Tariffs and Trade (GATT). Since 1995, it has been known as the World Trade Organization (WTO). Here, we look at the evolution and workings of the GATT and WTO.

FROM SMITH TO THE GREAT DEPRESSION

As noted in Chapter 5, the theoretical case for free trade dates to the late eighteenth century and the work of Adam Smith and David Ricardo. Free trade as a government policy was first officially embraced by Great Britain in 1846, when the British Parliament repealed the Corn Laws. The Corn Laws placed a high tariff on imports of foreign corn. The objectives of the Corn Laws tariff were to raise government revenues and to protect British corn producers. There had been annual motions in Parliament in favor of free trade since the 1820s, when David Ricardo was a member. However, agricultural protection was withdrawn only as a result of a protracted debate when the effects of a harvest failure in Great Britain were compounded by the imminent threat of famine in Ireland. Faced with considerable hardship and suffering among the populace, Parliament narrowly reversed its long-held position.

During the next 80 years or so, Great Britain, as one of the world's dominant trading powers, pushed the case for trade liberalization, but the British government was a voice in the wilderness. Its major trading partners did not reciprocate the British policy of unilateral free trade. The only reason Britain kept this policy for so long was that as the world's largest exporting nation, it had far more to lose from a trade war than did any other country.

By the 1930s, the British attempt to stimulate free trade was buried under the economic rubble of the Great Depression. Economic problems were compounded in 1930, when the U.S. Congress passed the Smoot–Hawley tariff. Aimed at avoiding rising unemployment by protecting domestic industries and diverting consumer demand away from foreign products, the **Smoot–Hawley Act** erected an enormous wall of tariff barriers. Almost every industry was rewarded with its "made-to-order" tariff. The Smoot–Hawley Act had a damaging effect on employment abroad. Other countries reacted by raising their own tariff barriers. U.S. exports tumbled in response, and the world slid further into the Great Depression.[19]

1947–1979: GATT, TRADE LIBERALIZATION, AND ECONOMIC GROWTH

Economic damage caused by the beggar-thy-neighbor trade policies that the Smoot–Hawley Act ushered in exerted a profound influence on the economic institutions and ideology of the post–World War II world. The United States emerged from the war both victorious and economically dominant. After the debacle of the Great Depression, opinion in the U.S. Congress had swung strongly in favor of free trade. Under U.S. leadership, the GATT was established in 1947.

The GATT was a multilateral agreement whose objective was to liberalize trade by eliminating tariffs, subsidies, import quotas, and the like. From its foundation in 1947 until it was superseded by the WTO, the GATT's membership grew from 19 to more than 120 nations. The GATT did not attempt to liberalize trade restrictions in one fell swoop; that would have been impossible. Rather, tariff reduction was spread over eight rounds.

In its early years, the GATT was by most measures very successful. For example, the average tariff declined by nearly 92 percent in the United States between the Geneva Round of 1947 and the Tokyo Round of 1973–1979. Consistent with the theoretical arguments first advanced by Ricardo and reviewed in Chapter 5, the move toward free trade under the GATT appeared to stimulate economic growth.

1980–1993: PROTECTIONIST TRENDS

During the 1980s and early 1990s, the trading system erected by the GATT came under strain as pressures for greater protectionism increased around the world. There were three reasons for the rise in such pressures during the 1980s. First, the economic success of Japan during that time strained the world trading system (much as the success of China has created strains today). Japan was in ruins when the GATT was created. By the early

1980s, however, it had become the world's second-largest economy and its largest exporter. Japan's success in such industries as automobiles and semiconductors might have been enough to strain the world trading system. Things were made worse by the widespread perception in the West that despite low tariff rates and subsidies, Japanese markets were closed to imports and foreign investment by administrative trade barriers.

Second, the world trading system was strained by the persistent trade deficit in the world's largest economy, the United States. The consequences of the U.S. deficit included painful adjustments in industries such as automobiles, machine tools, semiconductors, steel, and textiles, where domestic producers steadily lost market share to foreign competitors. The resulting unemployment gave rise to renewed demands in the U.S. Congress for protection against imports.

A third reason for the trend toward greater protectionism was that many countries found ways to get around GATT regulations. Bilateral voluntary export restraints (VERs) circumvented GATT agreements, because neither the importing country nor the exporting country complained to the GATT bureaucracy in Geneva—and without a complaint, the GATT bureaucracy could do nothing. Exporting countries agreed to VERs to avoid more damaging punitive tariffs. One of the best-known examples was the automobile VER between Japan and the United States, under which Japanese producers promised to limit their auto imports into the United States as a way of defusing growing trade tensions. According to a World Bank study, 16 percent of the imports of industrialized countries in 1986 were subjected to nontariff trade barriers such as VERs.[20]

THE URUGUAY ROUND AND THE WORLD TRADE ORGANIZATION

Against the background of rising pressures for protectionism, in 1986, GATT members embarked on their eighth round of negotiations to reduce tariffs, the Uruguay Round (so named because it occurred in Uruguay). This was the most ambitious round of negotiations yet. Until then, GATT rules had applied only to trade in manufactured goods and commodities. In the Uruguay Round, member countries sought to extend GATT rules to cover trade in services. They also sought to write rules governing the protection of intellectual property, to reduce agricultural subsidies, and to strengthen the GATT's monitoring and enforcement mechanisms.

The Uruguay Round dragged on for seven years before an agreement was reached on December 15, 1993. It went into effect July 1, 1995. The Uruguay Round contained the following provisions:

1. Tariffs on industrial goods were to be reduced by more than one-third, and tariffs were to be scrapped on more than 40 percent of manufactured goods.
2. Average tariff rates imposed by developed nations on manufactured goods were to be reduced to less than 4 percent of value, the lowest level in modern history.
3. Agricultural subsidies were to be substantially reduced.
4. GATT fair trade and market access rules were to be extended to cover a wide range of services.
5. GATT rules also were to be extended to provide enhanced protection for patents, copyrights, and trademarks (intellectual property).
6. Barriers on trade in textiles were to be significantly reduced over 10 years.
7. The World Trade Organization was to be created to implement the GATT agreement.

The World Trade Organization

The WTO acts as an umbrella organization that encompasses the GATT along with two new sister bodies, one on services and the other on intellectual property. The WTO's General Agreement on Trade in Services (GATS) has taken the lead in extending free trade agreements to services. The WTO's Agreement on Trade-Related Aspects of Intellectual Property Rights (TRIPS) is an attempt to narrow the gaps in the way intellectual property rights are protected around the world and to bring them under common international rules. WTO has taken over responsibility for arbitrating trade disputes and monitoring the trade policies of member countries. While the WTO operates on the basis of consensus as the GATT did, in the area of dispute settlement, member countries are no longer able to block adoption of arbitration reports. Arbitration panel reports on trade disputes between member countries are automatically adopted by the WTO unless there is a consensus to reject them. Countries that have been found by the arbitration panel to violate GATT rules may appeal to a permanent appellate body, but its verdict is binding. If offenders fail to comply with the recommendations of the arbitration panel, trading partners have the right to compensation or, in the last resort, to impose (commensurate) trade sanctions. Every stage of the procedure is subject to strict time limits. Thus, the WTO has something that the GATT never had—teeth.[21]

WTO: EXPERIENCE TO DATE

By 2019, the WTO had 164 members, including China, which joined at the end of 2001, and Russia, which joined in 2012. WTO members collectively account for 98 percent of world trade. Since its formation, the WTO has remained at the forefront of efforts to promote global free trade. Its creators expressed the belief that the enforcement mechanisms granted to the WTO would make it more effective at policing global trade rules than the GATT had been. The great hope was that the WTO might emerge as an effective advocate and facilitator of future trade deals, particularly in areas such as services. The experience so far has been mixed. After a strong early start, since the late 1990s the WTO has been unable to get agreements to further reduce barriers to international trade and trade and investment. There has been very slow progress with the current round of trade talks (the Doha Round). There was also a shift back toward some limited protectionism following the global financial crisis of 2008–2009. More recently, the 2016 vote by the British to leave the European Union (Brexit) and the election of Donald Trump to the presidency in the United States have suggested that the world may be shifting back toward greater protectionism. These developments have raised a number of questions about the future direction of the WTO. Donald Trump, in particular, has expressed ambivalence about the value of the WTO, and under his leadership the United States has stepped back from supporting the institution.

WTO as Global Police

The first two decades in the life of the WTO suggest that its policing and enforcement mechanisms are having a positive effect.[22] Between 1995 and 2018, more than 500 trade disputes between member countries were brought to the WTO.[23] This record compares with a total of 196 cases handled by the GATT over almost half a century. Of the cases brought to the WTO, three-fourths have been resolved by informal consultations between the disputing countries. Resolving the remainder has involved more formal procedures, but these have been largely successful. In general, countries involved have adopted the WTO's recommendations. The fact that countries are using the WTO represents an important vote of confidence in the organization's dispute resolution procedures.

Expanded Trade Agreements

As explained earlier, the Uruguay Round of GATT negotiations extended global trading rules to cover trade in services. The WTO was given the role of brokering future agreements to open up global trade in services. The WTO was also encouraged to extend its reach to encompass regulations governing foreign direct investment, something the GATT had never done. Two of the first industries targeted for reform were the global telecommunication and financial services industries.

In February 1997, the WTO brokered a deal to get countries to agree to open their telecommunication markets to competition, allowing foreign operators to purchase ownership stakes in domestic telecommunication providers and establishing a set of common rules for fair competition. Most of the world's biggest markets—including the United States, European Union, and Japan—were fully liberalized by January 1, 1998, when the pact went into effect. All forms of basic telecommunication service are covered, including voice telephone, data, and satellite and radio communications. Many telecommunication companies responded positively to the deal, pointing out that it would give them a much greater ability to offer their business customers one-stop shopping—a global, seamless service for all their corporate needs and a single bill.

This was followed in December 1997 with an agreement to liberalize cross-border trade in financial services. The deal covered more than 95 percent of the world's financial services market. Under the agreement, which took effect at the beginning of March 1999, 102 countries pledged to open (to varying degrees) their banking, securities, and insurance sectors to foreign competition. In common with the telecommunication deal, the accord covers not just cross-border trade but also foreign direct investment. Seventy countries agreed to dramatically lower or eradicate barriers to foreign direct investment in their financial services sector. The United States and the European Union (with minor exceptions) are fully open to inward investment by foreign banks, insurance, and securities companies. As part of the deal, many Asian countries made important concessions that allow significant foreign participation in their financial services sectors for the first time.

THE FUTURE OF THE WTO: UNRESOLVED ISSUES AND THE DOHA ROUND

Since the successes of the 1990s, the World Trade Organization has struggled to make progress on the international trade front. Confronted by a slower growing world economy after 2001, many national governments have been reluctant to agree to a fresh round of policies designed to reduce trade barriers. Political opposition to the WTO has been growing in many nations. As the public face of globalization, some politicians and nongovernmental organizations blame the WTO for a variety of ills, including high unemployment, environmental degradation, poor working conditions in developing nations, falling real wage rates among the lower paid in developed nations, and rising income inequality. The rapid rise of China as a dominant trading nation has also played a role here. Reflecting sentiments like those toward Japan 25 years ago, many perceive China as failing to play by the international trading rules, even as it embraces the WTO.

Against this difficult political backdrop, much remains to be done on the international trade front. Four issues at the forefront of the agenda of the WTO are antidumping policies, the high level of protectionism in agriculture, the lack of strong protection for intellectual property rights in many nations, and continued high tariff rates on nonagricultural goods and services in many nations. We shall look at each in turn before discussing the latest round of talks between WTO members aimed at reducing trade barriers, the Doha Round, which began in 2001 and now seem to be stalled.

Antidumping Actions

Antidumping actions proliferated during the 1990s and 2000s. WTO rules allow countries to impose antidumping duties on foreign goods that are being sold cheaper than at home or below their cost of production when domestic producers can show that they are being harmed. Unfortunately, the rather vague definition of what constitutes "dumping" has proved to be a loophole that many countries are exploiting to pursue protectionism.

Between 1995 and December 2017, WTO members had reported implementation of some 5,529 antidumping actions to the WTO. India initiated the largest number of antidumping actions, some 888; the EU initiated 502 over the same period, and the United States, 659. China accounted for 1,269 complaints, South Korea for 417, the United States for 283, Taipei (China) for 296, and Japan for 202. Antidumping actions seem to be concentrated in certain sectors of the economy, such as basic metal industries (e.g., aluminum and steel), chemicals, plastics, and machinery and electrical equipment.[24] These sectors account for approximately 70 percent of all antidumping actions reported to the WTO. Since 1995, these four sectors have been characterized by periods of intense competition and excess productive capacity, which have led to low prices and profits (or losses) for firms in those industries. It is not unreasonable, therefore, to hypothesize that the high level of antidumping actions in these industries represents an attempt by beleaguered manufacturers to use the political process in their nations to seek protection from foreign competitors, which they claim are engaging in unfair competition. While some of these claims may have merit, the process can become very politicized as representatives of businesses and their employees lobby government officials to "protect domestic jobs from unfair foreign competition," and government officials, mindful of the need to get votes in future elections, oblige by pushing for antidumping actions. The WTO is clearly worried by the use of antidumping policies, suggesting that it reflects persistent protectionist tendencies and pushing members to strengthen the regulations governing the imposition of antidumping duties.

Protectionism in Agriculture

Another focus of the WTO has been the high level of tariffs and subsidies in the agricultural sector of many economies. Tariff rates on agricultural products are generally much higher than tariff rates on manufactured products or services. For example, the average tariff rates on nonagricultural products among developed nations are around 2 percent. On agricultural products, however, the average tariff rates are 15.4 percent for Canada, 11.9 percent for the European Union, 17.4 percent for Japan, and 4.8 percent for the United States.[25] The implication is that consumers in countries with high tariffs are paying significantly higher prices than necessary for agricultural products imported from abroad, which leaves them with less money to spend on other goods and services.

The historically high tariff rates on agricultural products reflect a desire to protect domestic agriculture and traditional farming communities from foreign competition. In addition to high tariffs, agricultural producers also benefit from substantial subsidies. According to estimates from the Organisation for Economic Co-operation and Development (OECD), government subsidies on average account for about 17 percent of the cost of agricultural production in Canada, 21 percent in the United States, 35 percent in the European Union, and 59 percent in Japan.[26] OECD countries spend more than $300 billion a year in agricultural subsidies.

Not surprisingly, the combination of high tariff barriers and subsidies introduces significant distortions into the production of agricultural products and international trade

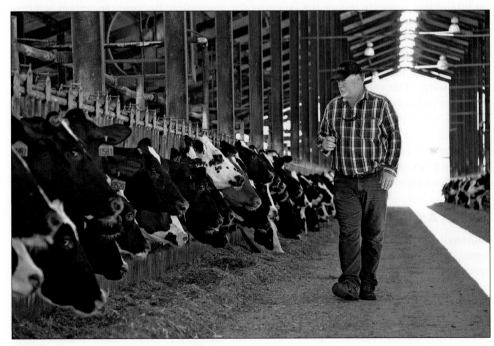

Production operations at J.M. Larson Dairy.

of those products. The net effect is to raise prices to consumers, reduce the volume of agricultural trade, and encourage the overproduction of products that are heavily subsidized (with the government typically buying the surplus). Because global trade in agriculture currently amounts to around 10 percent of total merchandized trade, the WTO argues that removing tariff barriers and subsidies could significantly boost the overall level of trade, lower prices to consumers, and raise global economic growth by freeing consumption and investment resources for more productive uses. According to estimates from the International Monetary Fund, removal of tariffs and subsidies on agricultural products would raise global economic welfare by $128 billion annually.[27] Others suggest gains as high as $182 billion.[28]

The biggest defenders of the existing system have been the advanced nations of the world, which want to protect their agricultural sectors from competition by low-cost producers in developing nations. In contrast, developing nations have been pushing hard for reforms that would allow their producers greater access to the protected markets of the developed nations. Estimates suggest that removing all subsidies on agricultural production alone in OECD countries could return to the developing nations of the world three times more than all the foreign aid they currently receive from the OECD nations.[29] In other words, free trade in agriculture could help jump-start economic growth among the world's poorer nations and alleviate global poverty.

Protection of Intellectual Property

Another issue that has become increasingly important to the WTO has been protecting intellectual property. The 1995 Uruguay agreement that established the WTO also contained an agreement to protect intellectual property (the Trade-Related Aspects of Intellectual Property Rights, or TRIPS, agreement). The TRIPS regulations oblige WTO members to grant and enforce patents lasting at least 20 years and copyrights lasting 50 years. Rich countries had to comply with the rules within a year. Poor countries, in which such protection was generally much weaker, had five years' grace, and the very poorest had 10 years.' The basis for this agreement was a strong belief among signatory nations that the protection of intellectual property through patents, trademarks, and copyrights must be an essential element of the international trading system. Inadequate protections for intellectual property reduce the incentive for innovation. Because innovation is a central engine of economic growth and rising living standards, the argument has been that a multilateral agreement is needed to protect intellectual property.

Without such an agreement, it is feared that producers in a country—let's say, India—might market imitations of patented innovations pioneered in a different country—say, the United States. This can affect international trade in two ways. First, it reduces the export opportunities in India for the original innovator in the United States. Second, to the extent that the Indian producer is able to export its pirated imitation to additional countries, it also reduces the export opportunities in those countries for the U.S. inventor. Also, one can argue that because the size of the total world market for the innovator is reduced, its incentive to pursue risky and expensive innovations is also reduced. The net effect would be less innovation in the world economy and less economic growth.

Market Access for Nonagricultural Goods and Services

Although the WTO and the GATT have made big strides in reducing the tariff rates on nonagricultural products, much work remains. Although most developed nations have brought their tariff rates on industrial products down to under 4 percent of value, exceptions still remain. In particular, while average tariffs are low, high tariff rates persist on certain imports into developed nations, which limit market access and economic growth. For example, Australia and South Korea, both OECD countries, still have bound tariff rates of 15.1 percent and 24.6 percent, respectively, on imports of transportation equipment (*bound tariff rates* are the highest rate that can be charged, which is often, but not always, the rate that is charged). In contrast, the bound tariff rates on imports of

Estimating the Gains from Trade for the United States

A study published by the Institute for International Economics tried to estimate the gains to the American economy from free trade. According to the study, due to reductions in tariff barriers under the GATT and WTO since 1947, by 2003 the gross domestic product (GDP) of the United States was 7.3 percent higher than would otherwise be the case. The benefits of that amounted to roughly $1 trillion a year, or $9,000 extra income for each American household per year.

The same study tried to estimate what would happen if America concluded free trade deals with all its trading partners, reducing tariff barriers on all goods and services to zero. Using several methods to estimate the impact, the study concluded that additional annual gains of between $450 billion and $1.3 trillion could be realized. This final march to free trade, according to the authors of the study, could safely be expected to raise incomes of the average American household by an additional $4,500 per year.

The authors also tried to estimate the scale and cost of employment disruption that would be caused by a move to universal free trade. Jobs would be lost in certain sectors and gained in others if the country abolished all tariff barriers. Using historical data as a guide, they estimated that 226,000 jobs would be lost every year due to expanded trade, although some two-thirds of those losing jobs would find reemployment after a year. Reemployment, however, would be at a wage that was 13 to 14 percent lower. The study concluded that the disruption costs would total some $54 billion annually, primarily in the form of lower lifetime wages to those whose jobs were disrupted as a result of free trade. Offset against this, however, must be the higher economic growth resulting from free trade, which creates many new jobs and raises household incomes, creating another $450 billion to $1.3 trillion annually in *net* gains to the economy. In other words, the estimated annual gains from trade are far greater than the estimated annual costs associated with job disruption, and more people benefit than lose as a result of a shift to a universal free trade regime.

Source: S. C. Bradford, P. L. E. Grieco, and G. C. Hufbauer, "The Payoff to America from Global Integration," in *The United States and the World Economy: Foreign Policy for the Next Decade*, C. F. Bergsten, ed. (Washington, DC: Institute for International Economics, 2005).

transportation equipment into the United States, European Union, and Japan are 2.7 percent, 4.8 percent, and 0 percent, respectively. A particular area for concern is high tariff rates on imports of selected goods from developing nations into developed nations.

In addition, tariffs on services remain higher than on industrial goods. The average tariff on business and financial services imported into the United States, for example, is 8.2 percent, into the EU it is 8.5 percent, and into Japan it is 19.7 percent.[30] Given the rising value of cross-border trade in services, reducing these figures can be expected to yield substantial gains.

The WTO would like to bring down tariff rates still further and reduce the scope for the selective use of high tariff rates. The ultimate aim is to reduce tariff rates to zero. Although this might sound ambitious, 40 nations have already moved to zero tariffs on information technology goods, so a precedent exists. Empirical work suggests that further reductions in average tariff rates toward zero would yield substantial gains. One estimate by economists at the World Bank suggests that a broad global trade agreement coming out of the Doha negotiations could increase world income by $263 billion annually, of which $109 billion would go to poor countries.[31] Another estimate from the OECD suggests a figure closer to $300 billion annually.[32] See the accompanying Country Focus for estimates of the benefits to the American economy from free trade.

Looking farther out, the WTO would like to bring down tariff rates on imports of nonagricultural goods into developing nations. Many of these nations use the infant industry argument to justify the continued imposition of high tariff rates; however, ultimately these rates need to come down for these nations to reap the full benefits of international trade. For example, the bound tariff rates of 53.9 percent on imports of transportation equipment into India and 33.6 percent on imports into Brazil, by raising domestic prices, help protect inefficient domestic producers and limit economic growth by reducing the real income of consumers who must pay more for transportation equipment and related services.

A New Round of Talks: Doha

In 2001, the WTO launched a new round of talks between member states aimed at further liberalizing the global trade and investment framework. For this meeting, it picked the remote location of Doha in the Persian Gulf state of Qatar. The talks were originally scheduled to last three years, although they have already gone on for 17 years and are currently stalled.

The Doha agenda includes cutting tariffs on industrial goods and services, phasing out subsidies to agricultural producers, reducing barriers to cross-border investment, and limiting the use of antidumping laws. The talks are currently ongoing. They have been characterized by halting progress punctuated by significant setbacks and missed deadlines. A September 2003 meeting in Cancún, Mexico, broke down, primarily because there was no agreement on how to proceed with reducing agricultural subsidies and tariffs; the EU, United States, and India, among others, proved less than willing to reduce tariffs and subsidies to their politically important farmers, while countries such as Brazil and certain West African nations wanted free trade as quickly as possible. In 2004, both the United States and the EU made a determined push to start the talks again. Since then, however, no progress has been made, and the talks are in deadlock, primarily because of disagreements over how deep the cuts in subsidies to agricultural producers should be. As of 2018, the goal was to reduce tariffs for manufactured and agricultural goods by 60 to 70 percent and to cut subsidies to half of their current level—but getting nations to agree to these goals was proving exceedingly difficult.

MULTILATERAL AND BILATERAL TRADE AGREEMENTS

In response to the apparent failure of the Doha Round to progress, many nations have pushed forward with **multilateral or bilateral trade agreements**, which are reciprocal trade agreements between two or more partners. For example, in 2014 Australia and China entered into a bilateral free trade agreement. Similarly, in March 2012 the United States entered into a bilateral free trade agreement with South Korea. Under this agreement, 80 percent of U.S. exports of consumer and industrial products became duty free, and 95 percent of bilateral trade in industrial and consumer products will be duty free by 2017 (this agreement was revised in 2018; see the Closing Case). The agreement was estimated to boost U.S. GDP by some $10 to $12 billion. Under the Obama administration, the United States pursued two major multilateral trade agreements, one with 11 other Pacific Rim countries including Australia, New Zealand, Japan, Malaysia, and Chile (the TPP), and another with the European Union. However, following the accession of Donald Trump to the presidency in the United States, the U.S. withdrew from the TPP (although the remaining 11 nations went ahead with a revised agreement) and the trade agreement being negotiated with the EU was put on ice.

Multilateral and bilateral trade agreements are designed to capture gain from trade beyond those agreements currently attainable under WTO treaties. Multilateral and bilateral trade agreements are allowed under WTO rules, and countries entering into these agreements are required to notify the WTO. As of 2019, more than 470 regional or bilateral trade agreements were in force. Reflecting the lack of progress on the Doha Round, the number of such agreements has increased significantly since 2000 when only 94 were in force.

THE WORLD TRADING SYSTEM UNDER THREAT

In 2016, two events challenged the long-held belief that there was a global consensus behind the 70-year push to embrace free trade and lower barriers to the cross-border flow of goods and services. The first was the decision by the British to withdraw from the European Union following a national referendum (Brexit). We discuss Brexit in more detail in Chapter 9, but it is worth noting that the British intention to withdraw from what is arguably one of the most successful free trade zones in the world is a big setback for those who argue that free trade is a good thing. The second event was the victory of Donald Trump in the 2016 U.S. presidential election. As discussed in Chapter 6, Trump appears to hold mercantilist views on trade. He seems opposed to many free trade deals. Indeed, one of his first actions was to pull the United States out of the Trans Pacific Partnership, a 12-nation free trade zone that was close to ratification. In early 2018, he placed tariffs on imports of solar panels, washing machines, steel, and aluminum into the United States, in all probability in violation of WTO rules. Trump also renegotiated NAFTA and has expressed hostility to the WTO. Most notably, Trump sidestepped the WTO's rules-based arbitration mechanisms in his trade dispute with China. In late 2019, the Trump administration also blocked replacements for two judges on the WTO's appellate body, which hears appeals in trade disputes. With just one judge remaining, it will no longer be able to hear new cases, which effectively undermines the WTO's enforcement mechanism. The significance of these developments is that heretofore both Britain and America have been leaders in the global push toward greater free trade. While Britain still seems committed to free trade, despite the Brexit decision, the position of the United States, the world's largest economy, is less clear. If the U.S. continues to turn its back on new free trade deals (such as the TPP) dismantles existing ones (as Trump threatened to do with NAFTA), and sidesteps the WTO, other nations could follow. If this happens, the impact on the world economy will almost certainly be negative, resulting in greater protectionism, slower economic growth, and higher unemployment around the globe.

FOCUS ON MANAGERIAL IMPLICATIONS

TRADE BARRIERS, FIRM STRATEGY, AND POLICY IMPLICATIONS

What are the implications for business practice? Why should the international manager care about the political economy of free trade or about the relative merits of arguments for free trade and protectionism? There are two answers to this question. The first concerns the impact of trade barriers on a firm's strategy. The second concerns the role that business firms can play in promoting free trade or trade barriers.

Trade Barriers and Firm Strategy

To understand how trade barriers affect a firm's strategy, consider first the material in Chapter 6. Drawing on the theories of international trade, we discussed how it makes sense for the firm to disperse its various production activities to those countries around the globe where they can be performed most efficiently. Thus, it may make sense for a firm to design and engineer its product in one country, to manufacture components in another, to perform final assembly operations in yet another country, and then export the finished product to the rest of the world.

Clearly, trade barriers constrain a firm's ability to disperse its productive activities in such a manner. First and most obvious, tariff barriers raise the costs of exporting products to a country (or of exporting partly finished products between countries). This may put the firm at a competitive disadvantage relative to indigenous competitors in that country. In response, the firm may then find it economical to locate production facilities in that country so that it can compete on even footing. Second, quotas may limit a firm's ability to serve a country from locations outside that country. Again, the response by the firm might be to set up production facilities in that country—even though it may result in higher production costs.

Such reasoning was one of the factors behind the rapid expansion of Japanese automaking capacity in the United States during the 1980s and 1990s. This followed the establishment of a VER agreement between the United States and Japan that limited U.S. imports of Japanese automobiles. Today, Donald Trump's threat to impose high tariffs on companies that shift their production to other nations in order to reduce costs—and then export goods back to the United States—is forcing some enterprises to rethink their outsourcing strategy. In particular, a number of automobile companies, including Ford and General Motors, have

TEST PREP

Use SmartBook to help retain what you have learned. Access your instructor's Connect course to check out SmartBook or go to **learnsmartadvantage.com** for help.

LO7-5

Explain the implications for managers of developments in the world trading system.

modified their plans to shift some production to factories in Mexico and have announced plans to expand U.S. production in order to appease the Trump administration.[33]

Third, to conform to local content regulations, a firm may have to locate more production activities in a given market than it would otherwise. Again, from the firm's perspective, the consequence might be to raise costs above the level that could be achieved if each production activity were dispersed to the optimal location for that activity. And finally, even when trade barriers do not exist, the firm may still want to locate some production activities in a given country to reduce the threat of trade barriers being imposed in the future.

All these effects are likely to raise the firm's costs above the level that could be achieved in a world without trade barriers. The higher costs that result need not translate into a significant competitive disadvantage relative to other foreign firms, however, if the countries imposing trade barriers do so to the imported products of all foreign firms, irrespective of their national origin. But when trade barriers are targeted at exports from a particular nation, firms based in that nation are at a competitive disadvantage to firms of other nations. The firm may deal with such targeted trade barriers by moving production into the country imposing barriers. Another strategy may be to move production to countries whose exports are not targeted by the specific trade barrier.

Finally, the threat of antidumping action limits the ability of a firm to use aggressive pricing to gain market share in a country. Firms in a country also can make strategic use of antidumping measures to limit aggressive competition from low-cost foreign producers. For example, the U.S. steel industry has been very aggressive in bringing antidumping actions against foreign steelmakers, particularly in times of weak global demand for steel and excess capacity. In 1998 and 1999, the United States faced a surge in low-cost steel imports as a severe recession in Asia left producers there with excess capacity. The U.S. producers filed several complaints with the International Trade Commission. One argued that Japanese producers of hot rolled steel were selling it at below cost in the United States. The ITC agreed and levied tariffs ranging from 18 to 67 percent on imports of certain steel products from Japan (these tariffs are separate from the steel tariffs discussed earlier).[34]

Policy Implications

As noted in Chapter 6, business firms are major players on the international trade scene. Because of their pivotal role in international trade, firms can and do exert a strong influence on government policy toward trade. This influence can encourage protectionism, or it can encourage the government to support the WTO and push for open markets and freer trade among all nations. Government policies with regard to international trade can have a direct impact on business.

Consistent with strategic trade policy, examples can be found of government intervention in the form of tariffs, quotas, antidumping actions, and subsidies helping firms and industries establish a competitive advantage in the world economy. In general, however, the arguments contained in this chapter and in Chapter 6 suggest that government intervention has three drawbacks. Intervention can be self-defeating because it tends to protect the inefficient rather than help firms become efficient global competitors. Intervention is dangerous; it may invite retaliation and trigger a trade war. Finally, intervention is unlikely to be well executed, given the opportunity for such a policy to be captured by special-interest groups. Does this mean that business should simply encourage government to adopt a laissez-faire free trade policy?

Most economists would probably argue that the best interests of international business are served by a free trade stance but not a laissez-faire stance. It is probably in the best long-run interests of the business community to encourage the government to aggressively promote greater free trade by, for example, strengthening the WTO. Business probably has much more to gain from government efforts to open protected markets to imports and foreign direct investment than from government efforts to support certain domestic industries in a manner consistent with the recommendations of strategic trade policy.

This conclusion is reinforced by a phenomenon we touched on in Chapter 1—the increasing integration of the world economy and internationalization of production that has occurred over the past two decades. We live in a world where many firms of all national origins increasingly depend on globally dispersed production systems for their competitive advantage. Such systems are the result of freer trade. Freer trade has brought great advantages to firms that have exploited it and to consumers who benefit from the resulting lower prices. Given the danger of retaliatory action, business firms that lobby their governments to engage in protectionism must realize that by doing so, they may be denying themselves the opportunity to build a competitive advantage by constructing a globally dispersed production system. By encouraging their governments to engage in protectionism, their own activities and sales overseas may be jeopardized if other governments retaliate. This does not mean a firm should never seek protection in the form of antidumping actions and the like, but it should review its options carefully and think through the larger consequences.

Key Terms

free trade, p. 202
General Agreement on Tariffs and Trade (GATT), p. 202
tariff, p. 202
specific tariff, p. 202
ad valorem tariff, p. 202
subsidy, p. 203
import quota, p. 205
tariff rate quota, p. 205

voluntary export restraint (VER), p. 205
quota rent, p. 206
export tariff, p. 206
export ban, p. 206
local content requirement (LCR), p. 206
administrative trade policies, p. 207

dumping, p. 207
antidumping policies, p. 207
countervailing duties, p. 207
infant industry argument, p. 211
strategic trade policy, p. 213
Smoot–Hawley Act, p. 215
multilateral or bilateral trade agreements, p. 222

SUMMARY

This chapter described how the reality of international trade deviates from the theoretical ideal of unrestricted free trade reviewed in Chapter 6. In this chapter, we reported the various instruments of trade policy, reviewed the political and economic arguments for government intervention in international trade, reexamined the economic case for free trade in light of the strategic trade policy argument, and looked at the evolution of the world trading framework. While a policy of free trade may not always be the theoretically optimal policy (given the arguments of the new trade theorists), in practice it is probably the best policy for a government to pursue. In particular, the long-run interests of business and consumers may be best served by strengthening international institutions such as the WTO. Given the danger that isolated protectionism might escalate into a trade war, business probably has far more to gain from government efforts to open protected markets to imports and foreign direct investment (through the WTO) than from government efforts to protect domestic industries from foreign competition. The chapter made the following points:

1. Trade policies such as tariffs, subsidies, antidumping regulations, and local content requirements tend to be pro-producer and anticonsumer. Gains accrue to producers (who are protected from foreign competitors), but consumers lose because they must pay more for imports.

2. There are two types of arguments for government intervention in international trade:

political and economic. Political arguments for intervention are concerned with protecting the interests of certain groups, often at the expense of other groups, or with promoting goals with regard to foreign policy, human rights, consumer protection, and the like. Economic arguments for intervention are about boosting the overall wealth of a nation.

3. A common political argument for intervention is that it is necessary to protect jobs. However, political intervention often hurts consumers, and it can be self-defeating. Countries sometimes argue that it is important to protect certain industries for reasons of national security. Some argue that government should use the threat to intervene in trade policy as a bargaining tool to open foreign markets. This can be a risky policy; if it fails, the result can be higher trade barriers.

4. The infant industry argument for government intervention contends that to let manufacturing get a toehold, governments should temporarily support new industries. In practice, however, governments often end up protecting the inefficient.

5. Strategic trade policy suggests that, with subsidies, government can help domestic firms gain first-mover advantages in global industries where economies of scale are important. Government subsidies may also help domestic firms overcome barriers to entry into such industries.

6. The problems with strategic trade policy are twofold: (*a*) Such a policy may invite retaliation, in which case all will lose, and (*b*) strategic trade policy may be captured by special-interest groups, which will distort it to their own ends.

7. The GATT was a product of the postwar free trade movement. The GATT was successful in lowering trade barriers on manufactured goods and commodities. The move toward greater free trade under the GATT appeared to stimulate economic growth.

8. The completion of the Uruguay Round of GATT talks and the establishment of the World Trade Organization have strengthened the world trading system by extending GATT rules to services, increasing protection for intellectual property, reducing agricultural subsidies, and enhancing monitoring and enforcement mechanisms.

9. Trade barriers act as a constraint on a firm's ability to disperse its various production activities to optimal locations around the globe. One response to trade barriers is to establish more production activities in the protected country.

10. Business may have more to gain from government efforts to open protected markets to imports and foreign direct investment than from government efforts to protect domestic industries from foreign competition.

Critical Thinking and Discussion Questions

1. Do you think governments should consider human rights when granting preferential trading rights to countries? What are the arguments for and against taking such a position?

2. Whose interests should be the paramount concern of government trade policy: the interests of producers (businesses and their employees) or those of consumers?

3. Given the arguments relating to the new trade theory and strategic trade policy, what kind of trade policy should business be pressuring government to adopt?

4. You are an employee of a U.S. firm that produces personal computers in Thailand and then exports them to the United States and other countries for sale. The personal computers were originally produced in Thailand to take advantage of relatively low labor costs and a skilled workforce. Other possible locations considered at the time were Malaysia and Hong Kong. The U.S. government decides to impose punitive 100 percent ad valorem tariffs on imports of computers from Thailand to punish the country for administrative trade barriers that restrict U.S. exports to Thailand. How should your firm respond? What does this tell you about the use of targeted trade barriers?

5. Reread the Management Focus "Protecting U.S. Magnesium." Who gains most from the antidumping duties levied by the United States on imports of magnesium from China and Russia? Who are the losers? Are these duties in the best national interests of the United States?

⬤ global**EDGE** research task globaledge.msu.edu

Use the globalEDGE™ website (**globaledge.msu.edu**) to complete the following exercises:

1. You work for a pharmaceutical company that hopes to provide products and services in New Zealand. Yet management's current knowledge of this country's trade policies and barriers is limited. After searching a resource that summarizes the *import and export regulations*, outline the most important foreign trade barriers your firm's managers must keep in mind while developing a strategy for entry into New Zealand's pharmaceutical market.

2. The number of member nations of the World Trade Organization has increased considerably in recent years. In addition, some nonmember countries have observer status in the WTO. Such status requires accession negotiations to begin within five years of attaining this preliminary position. Visit the WTO's website to identify a list of current members and observers. Identify the last five countries that joined the WTO as members. Also, examine the list of current observer countries. Do you notice anything in particular about the countries that have recently joined or have observer status?

CLOSING CASE

The United States and South Korea Strike a Revised Trade Deal

In 2012, a free trade deal between the United States and South Korea went into effect. In 2016, the United States exported $63.8 billion in goods and services to South Korea, and imported $80.8 billion, resulting in a trade deficit of $17 billion. During the U.S. election campaign in 2016, Donald Trump, who became President in 2017, called the deal "horrible" and a "job killer."

Given Trump's opposition to the free trade deal, it was no surprise when, in January 2018, the U.S. announced it was entering into negotiations with South Korea to revise the terms of the agreement. Complicating matters were two factors. First, in early March 2018, the Trump administration placed a 25 percent tariff on imports of steel. As the third-largest supplier of foreign steel to the United States, these tariffs threatened to harm the South Korean steel industry. Moreover, the global tariffs were technically in violation of the World Trade Organization treaty, to which both the United States and South Korea were signatories. Second, South Korea is an important U.S. ally. The country's support was crucial in putting pressure on North Korea to halt its nuclear weapons program. Given this, many observers wondered why the Trump administration was pressuring South Korea at a time when it needed to work together with the nation to keep North Korea in check.

Perhaps because of geopolitical considerations, the negotiations proceeded very quickly. Trade in automobiles was central to the negotiations, because the Trump administration saw it as a primary cause of the trade deficit. In 2017, the United States imported nearly $16 billion worth of South Korean passenger cars, but exported only $1.5 billion worth to South Korea. Significant automobile production in the U.S. is concentrated in swing states such as Michigan and Ohio, which helped elect Trump to the presidency.

In late March, the two countries announced they had reached a revised deal. Under the terms of this deal, South Korea would be exempt from the 25 percent tariff on steel imports into the United States. Instead, South Korea agreed to a quota that would limit its steel exports to the U.S. to about 70 percent of what they had been in 2017.

In return, South Korea made two concessions. First, the deal extended for 20 years a 25 percent tariff on exports of South Korean light trucks to the United States (under the original agreement, the 25 percent tariff was set to expire in 2021). This will likely be a significant boon to U.S. auto manufactures, because the light truck segment is one that they dominate. Second, the Koreans agreed to lift their

Kim Jae-Hwan/AFP/Getty Images

annual quota on imports of U.S. cars into the country from 25,000 per manufacturer to 50,000 per manufacturer. Beyond that, U.S. cars sold in South Korea would have to adhere to Korea's stringent safety and environmental standards, which the Trump administration has characterized as "burdensome regulations" designed to make it difficult for U.S. companies to sell vehicles in Korea. That being said, the reality is that U.S. auto companies were not even close to reaching the old quota limit of 25,000 cars a year, so lifting the cap may be primarily symbolic.

The deal will also establish a side agreement between the United States and South Korea that is intended to deter "competitive devaluation" of both countries' currencies—which can artificially lower the cost of imports bought by consumers—and to create more transparency on issues of monetary policy. Administration officials suggested that this new type of arrangement was likely to be replicated in other trade deals, though they acknowledged it was not enforceable.

The deal allows President Trump to claim that his "get tough" approach to trade negotiations works. For their part, the South Koreans were reportedly pleased that they didn't have to give ground on opening up their agricultural industry to U.S. imports, where administrative tariff barriers have limited importation of some low-priced American foodstuffs such as rice and potatoes.

Sources: Michael Shear and Alan Rappeport, "Trump Secures Trade Deal with South Korea Ahead of Nuclear Talks," *The New York Times*, March 27, 2018; Scott Horsley, "Trump Administration Strikes Trade Deal with South Korea," *NPR Politics*, March 27, 2018; Patrick Gillespie, "New US Deal with South Korea: What You Need to Know," *CNN Money*, March 28, 2018.

Case Discussion Questions

1. Why do you think the Obama administration pursued a trade deal with Korea in 2012? What were the potential economic and political benefits? What were the potential costs?

2. Is there any evidence that the 2012 free trade deal between the United States and South Korea was a "job killer" as claimed by President Trump?

3. What were the motivations of the Trump administration in renegotiating the 2012 deal?

4. Who benefits from the revised (2018) deal? Who might lose? Does the 2018 deal represent an improvement over that ratified in 2012?

Design elements: Modern textured halftone: ©VIPRESIONA/ Shutterstock; globalEDGE icon: ©globalEDGE; All others: ©McGraw-Hill Education

Endnotes

1. For a detailed welfare analysis of the effect of a tariff, see P. R. Krugman and M. Obstfeld, *International Economics: Theory and Policy* (New York: HarperCollins, 2000), Ch. 8.

2. Christian Henn and Brad McDonald, "Crisis Protectionism: The Observed Trade Impact," *IMF Economic Review* 62, no. 1 (April 2014), pp. 77–118.

3. World Trade Organization, *World Trade Report 2006* (Geneva: WTO, 2006).

4. The study was undertaken by Kym Anderson of the University of Adelaide. See "A Not So Perfect Market," *The Economist: Survey of Agriculture and Technology*, March 25, 2000, pp. 8–10.

5. K. Anderson, W. Martin, and D. van der Mensbrugghe, "Distortions to World Trade: Impact on Agricultural Markets and Farm Incomes," *Review of Agricultural Economics* 28 (Summer 2006), pp. 168–94.

6. J. B. Teece, "Voluntary Export Restraints Are Back; They Didn't Work the Last Time," *Automotive News*, April 23, 2012.

7. G. Hufbauer and Z. A. Elliott, *Measuring the Costs of Protectionism in the United States* (Washington, DC: Institute for International Economics, 1993).

8. Sean McLain, "American Cars in Japan: Lost in Translation," *The Wall Street Journal*, January 26, 2017.

9. Robert E. Scott. "Growth in US-China Trade Deficit Between 2001–2015 Cost 3.4 Million Jobs," Economic Policy Institute, January 31, 2017.

10. Alan Goldstein, "Sematech Members Facing Dues Increase; 30% Jump to Make Up for Loss of Federal Funding," *Dallas Morning News*, July 27, 1996, p. 2F.

11. N. Dunne and R. Waters, "U.S. Waves a Big Stick at Chinese Pirates," *Financial Times*, January 6, 1995, p. 4.

12. Peter S. Jordan, "Country Sanctions and the International Business Community," *American Society of International Law Proceedings of the Annual Meeting* 20, no. 9 (1997), pp. 333–42.

13. "Brazil's Auto Industry Struggles to Boost Global Competitiveness," *Journal of Commerce*, October 10, 1991, p. 6A.

14. For reviews, see J. A. Brander, "Rationales for Strategic Trade and Industrial Policy," in *Strategic Trade Policy and the New International Economics*, P. R. Krugman, ed. (Cambridge, MA: MIT Press, 1986); P. R. Krugman, "Is Free Trade Passé?" *Journal of Economic Perspectives* 1 (1987), pp. 131–44; P. R. Krugman, "Does the New Trade Theory Require a New Trade Policy?" *World Economy* 15, no. 4 (1992), pp. 423–41.

15. "Airbus and Boeing: The Jumbo War," *The Economist*, June 15, 1991, pp. 65–66.

16. For details, see Krugman, "Is Free Trade Passé?"; Brander, "Rationales for Strategic Trade and Industrial Policy."

17. Krugman, R. Paul. "Is Free Trade Passé?" *The Journal of Economic Perspectives* 1, no. 2 (Autumn 1987), 131–44. https:// www.jstor.org/stable/1942985?seq=1#page_scan_tab_contents.

18. This dilemma is a variant of the famous prisoner's dilemma, which has become a classic metaphor for the difficulty of achieving cooperation between self-interested and mutually suspicious entities. For a good general introduction, see A. Dixit and B. Nalebuff, *Thinking Strategically: The Competitive Edge in Business, Politics, and Everyday Life* (New York: Norton, 1991).

19. Note that the Smoot-Hawley Act did not cause the Great Depression. However, the beggar-thy-neighbor trade policies that it ushered in certainly made things worse. See J. Bhagwati, *Protectionism* (Cambridge, MA: MIT Press, 1988).

20. World Bank, *World Development Report* (New York: Oxford University Press, 1987).

21. Frances Williams, "WTO—New Name Heralds New Powers," *Financial Times*, December 16, 1993, p. 5; Frances Williams, "GATT's Successor to Be Given Real Clout," *Financial Times*, April 4, 1994, p. 6.

22. W. J. Davey, "The WTO Dispute Settlement System: The First Ten Years," *Journal of International Economic Law*, March 2005, pp. 17-28; WTO Annual Report, 2016, archived at www.wto.org/english/res_e/publications_e/anrep16_e.htm.

23. Information provided on WTO website, www.wto.org/english/tratop_e/dispu_e/dispu_status_e.htm.

24. Data at www.wto.org/english/tratop_e/adp_e/adp_e.htm.

25. World Trade Organization, *World Tariff Profiles 2017* (Geneva: WTO, 2017).

26. OECD (2018), *Agricultural Policy Monitoring and Evaluation 2018*, OECD Publishing, Paris, https://doi.org/10.1787/agr_pol-2018-en.

27. World Trade Organization, *Annual Report by the Director General 2003* (Geneva: WTO, 2003).

28. Anderson et al., "Distortions to World Trade."

29. World Trade Organization, *Annual Report 2002* (Geneva: WTO, 2002).

30. S. C. Bradford, P. L. E. Grieco, and G. C. Hufbauer, "The Payoff to America from Global Integration," in *The United States and the World Economy: Foreign Policy for the Next Decade*, C. F. Bergsten, ed. (Washington, DC: Institute for International Economics, 2005).

31. World Bank, *Global Economic Prospects 2005* (Washington, DC: World Bank, 2005).

32. "Doha Development Agenda," *OECD Observer*, September 2006, pp. 64–67.

33. Peter Nicholas, "Trump Warns Auto Executive on Moving Business Overseas," *The Wall Street Journal*, January 24, 2017.

34. "Punitive Tariffs Are Approved on Imports of Japanese Steel," *The New York Times*, June 12, 1999, p. A3.

part three The Global Trade and Investment Environment

Foreign Direct Investment

8

LEARNING OBJECTIVES
After reading this chapter, you will be able to:

LO8-1   Recognize current trends regarding foreign direct investment (FDI) in the world economy.

LO8-2   Explain the different theories of FDI.

LO8-3   Understand how political ideology shapes a government's attitudes toward FDI.

LO8-4   Describe the benefits and costs of FDI to home and host countries.

LO8-5   Explain the range of policy instruments that governments use to influence FDI.

LO8-6   Identify the implications for managers of the theory and government policies associated with FDI.

Shen Chunchen/VCG/Getty Images

Starbucks' Foreign Direct Investment

OPENING CASE

Forty years ago, Starbucks was a single store in Seattle's Pike Place Market selling premium-roasted coffee. Today, it is a global roaster and retailer of coffee, with more than 28,000 stores in 76 countries. Starbucks set out on its current course in the 1980s when the company's director of marketing, Howard Schultz, came back from a trip to Italy enchanted with the Italian coffeehouse experience. Schultz, who later became CEO, persuaded the company's owners to experiment with the coffee-house format—and the Starbucks experience was born. The strategy was to sell the company's own premium roasted coffee and freshly brewed espresso-style coffee beverages, along with a variety of pastries, coffee accessories, teas, and other products, in a tastefully designed coffeehouse setting. From the outset, the company focused on selling "a third-place experience," rather than just the coffee. The formula led to spectacular success in the United States, where Starbucks went from obscurity to one of the best-known brands in the country in a decade. Thanks to Starbucks, coffee stores became places for relaxation, chatting with friends, reading the newspaper, holding business meetings, or (more recently) browsing the web.

In 1995, with 700 stores across the United States, Starbucks began exploring foreign opportunities. The first target market was Japan. The company established a joint venture with a local retailer, Sazaby Inc. Each company held a 50 percent stake in the venture: Starbucks Coffee of Japan. Starbucks initially invested $10 million in this venture, its first foreign direct investment. The Starbucks format was then licensed to the venture, which was charged with taking over responsibility for growing Starbucks' presence in Japan.

To make sure the Japanese operations replicated the "Starbucks experience" in North America, Starbucks transferred some employees to the Japanese operation. The joint venture agreement required all Japanese store managers and employees to attend training classes similar to those given to U.S. employees. The agreement also required that stores adhere to the design parameters established in the United States. In 2001, the company introduced a stock option plan for all Japanese employees, making it the first company in Japan to do so. Skeptics doubted that Starbucks would be able to replicate its North American success overseas, but by the end of 2018 Starbucks' had some 1,286 stores and a profitable business in Japan. Along the way, in 2015, Starbucks acquired Starbucks Coffee of Japan, making the stores wholly owned as opposed to licensed.

After Japan, the company embarked on an aggressive foreign investment program. In 1998, it purchased Seattle Coffee, a British coffee chain with 60 retail stores, for $84 million. An American couple, originally from Seattle, had started Seattle Coffee with the intention of establishing a Starbucks-like chain in Britain. By 2018, Starbucks had almost 1,000 stores in the UK.

In the late 1990s, Starbucks also opened stores in Taiwan, China, Singapore, Thailand, New Zealand, South Korea, and Malaysia. In Asia, Starbucks' most common strategy was to license its format to a local operator or joint venture partner in return for initial licensing fees and royalties on store revenues. As in Japan, Starbucks insisted on an intensive employee-training program and strict specifications regarding the format and layout of the store.

China has developed into Starbucks' fastest-growing market and is now second only to the United States in terms of store count and revenues. Although China has historically been a nation of tea drinkers, the third-place coffee culture pioneered by Starbucks has gained significant traction in the nation's large cities where wealthy and middle-class customers will pay $5 for a cup of coffee. As with many other nations, Starbucks originally entered China by setting up a joint venture with a local company and licensing its format to that entity. That changed in 2018 when Starbucks bought out its East China venture partner in order to attain greater control over its growth strategy. According to Belinda Wong, CEO of Starbucks' China operations, "Full ownership will give us the opportunity to fully leverage the company's robust business infrastructure to deliver an elevated coffee, in-store third place experience and digital innovation to our customers, and further strengthen the career development opportunities for our people".[*] The company now aims to have 6,000 wholly owned stores in China by the end of 2022, up from 3,500 at the end of fiscal 2018.

[*]Belinda Wong, "Starbucks Acquires Remaining Shares of East China Business; Move Accelerates Company's Long-term Commitment to China," Starbucks, 2017.

Sources: Starbucks 2018 10K; J. Ordonez, "Starbucks to Start Major Expansion in Overseas Market," *The Wall Street Journal*, October 27, 2000, p. B10; S. Homes and D. Bennett, "Planet Starbucks," *BusinessWeek*, September 9, 2002, pp. 99–110; "Starbucks Outlines International Growth Strategy," *Business Wire*, October 14, 2004; A. Yeh, "Starbucks Aims for New Tier in China," *Financial Times*, February 14, 2006, p. 17; Laurie Burkitt, "Starbucks to Add Thousands of Stores in China," *The Wall Street Journal*, January 12, 2016; "Starbucks to Acquire remaining Shares of East China JV," Starbucks press release, July 27, 2017; Jon Bird, "Roasted: How China Is Showing the Way for Starbucks in the US," *Forbes*, January 15, 2019; Eric Sylvers, "After 25,000 Stores in 78 Countries, Starbucks Turns to Italy," *The Wall Street Journal*, September 6, 2018.

Introduction

Foreign direct investment (FDI) occurs when a firm invests directly in facilities to produce or market a good or service in a foreign country. According to the U.S. Department of Commerce, FDI occurs whenever a U.S. citizen, organization, or affiliated group takes an interest of 10 percent or more in a foreign business entity. Once a firm undertakes FDI, it becomes a multinational enterprise. The investments made by Starbucks in stores in countries such as Japan, the UK, and China are all examples of FDI (see the opening case). While much FDI takes the form of greenfield ventures—building up subsidiaries from scratch—acquisitions and joint ventures with well-established foreign entities are also important vehicles for foreign direct investment. Starbucks has used both of these.

This chapter begins by looking at the importance of FDI in the world economy. Next, we review the theories that have been used to explain why enterprises undertake foreign direct investment. These theories can explain why Starbucks entered into joint venture partnerships with local producers in order to license its store format in countries such as Japan and China. These countries are so different from the U.S. in terms of their business systems, laws, and culture that Starbucks needed the expertise of a foreign partner to help navigate the problems associated with doing business in a foreign country. After discussing theories of FDI, this chapter then looks at U.S. government policy toward foreign direct investment. The chapter closes with a section on the implications of the material discussed here, as they relate to management practice.

LO8-1

Recognize current trends regarding foreign direct investment (FDI) in the world economy.

Foreign Direct Investment in the World Economy

When discussing foreign direct investment, it is important to distinguish between the flow of FDI and the stock of FDI. The **flow of FDI** refers to the amount of FDI undertaken over a given time period (normally a year). The **stock of FDI** refers to the total accumulated value of foreign-owned assets at a given time. We also talk of **outflows of FDI**, meaning the flow of FDI out of a country, and **inflows of FDI**, the flow of FDI into a country.

TRENDS IN FDI

The past 25 years have seen a marked increase in both the flow and stock of FDI in the world economy. The average yearly *outflow* of FDI increased from $250 billion in 1990 to a peak of $2.2 trillion in 2007, before slipping back to around $1 trillion by 2018 (see Figure 8.1).[1] Despite the pullback since 2007, since 1990 the flow of FDI has accelerated faster than the growth in world trade and world output. For example, between 1990 and 2017, the total flow of FDI from all countries increased around sixfold, while world trade by value grew fourfold and world output by around 60 percent.[2] As a result of the strong FDI flows, by 2018 the global stock of FDI was about $31 trillion. The foreign affiliates of multinationals had $27 trillion in global sales in 2018, compared to $23 trillion in global exports of goods and services, and accounted for more than one-third of all cross-border trade in goods and services.[3] Clearly, by any measure, FDI is a very important phenomenon in the global economy.

FDI has grown rapidly for several reasons. First, despite the general decline in trade barriers over the past 30 years, firms still fear protectionist pressures. Executives see FDI as a way of circumventing future trade barriers. Given the rising pressures for protectionism associated with the election of Donald Trump as President in the United States and the decision by the British to leave the European Union, this seems likely to continue for some time. Second, much of the increase in FDI has been driven by the political and economic changes that have been occurring in many of the world's developing nations. The general shift toward democratic political institutions and free market economies that we discussed in Chapter 3 has encouraged FDI. Across much of Asia, eastern Europe, and Latin America, economic growth, economic deregulation, privatization programs that are open to foreign investors, and removal of many restrictions on FDI have made these countries more

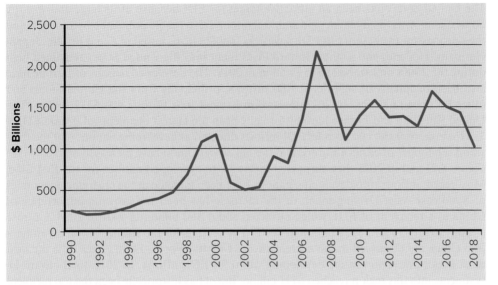

FIGURE 8.1

FDI outflows, 1990–2018 ($ billions).

Source: UNCTAD statistical data set, http://unctadstat.unctad.org.

attractive to foreign multinationals. According to the United Nations, According to UN data, some 80 percent of the more that 1,500 changes made to national laws governing foreign direct investment since 2000 have created a more favorable environment.[4]

The globalization of the world economy has also had a positive effect on the volume of FDI. Many firms see the whole world as their market, and they are undertaking FDI in an attempt to make sure they have a significant presence in many regions of the world. For example, around 43 percent of the sales of American firms in the S&P 500 index are generated abroad.[5] For reasons that we explore later in this book, many firms now believe it is important to have production facilities close to their major customers. This too creates pressure for greater FDI.

THE DIRECTION OF FDI

Historically, most FDI has been directed at the developed nations of the world as firms based in advanced countries invested in the others' markets (see Figure 8.2). During the 1980s and 1990s, the United States was often the favorite target for FDI inflows.

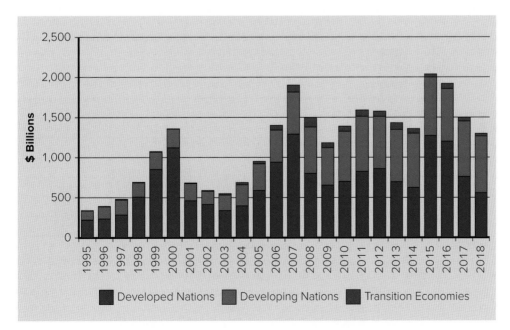

FIGURE 8.2

FDI inflows by region, 1995–2018 ($ billions).

Source: UNCTAD statistical data set, http://unctadstat.unctad.org.

The United States has been an attractive target for FDI because of its large and wealthy domestic markets, its dynamic and stable economy, a favorable political environment, and the openness of the country to FDI. Investors include firms based in Great Britain, Japan, Germany, Holland, and France. Inward investment into the United States remained high during the 2000s and stood at $252 billion in 2018. The developed nations of Europe have also been recipients of significant FDI inflows, principally from the United States and other European nations. In 2017, inward investment into Europe was $172 billion. The United Kingdom and France have historically been the largest recipients of inward FDI.[6]

However, over the last decade, FDI inflows directed at developing nations and the transition economies of eastern Europe and the old Soviet Union have increased markedly (see Figure 8.2) and in 2018 they surpassed inflows into developed nations for the first time. Most recent inflows into developing nations have been targeted at the emerging economies of Southeast Asia. Driving much of the increase has been the growing importance of China as a recipient of FDI, which attracted about $60 billion of FDI in 2004 and rose steadily to hit a record $139 billion in 2018.[7] The reasons for the strong flow of investment into China are discussed in the accompanying Country Focus. Latin America is the next most important region in the developing world for FDI inflows. In 2017, total inward investments into this region reached $147 billion. Brazil has historically been the top recipient of inward FDI in Latin America. In Central America, Mexico has been a big recipient of inward investment thanks to its proximity to the United States and to NAFTA. In 2018, some $32 billion of investments were made by foreigners in Mexico. At the other end of the scale, Africa has long received the smallest amount of inward investment, $46 billion in 2018. In recent years, Chinese enterprises have emerged as major investors in Africa, particularly in extraction industries, where they seem to be trying to ensure future supplies of valuable raw materials. The inability of Africa to attract greater investment is in part a reflection of the political unrest, armed conflict, and frequent changes in economic policy in the region.[8]

THE SOURCE OF FDI

Since World War II, the United States has consistently been the largest source country for FDI. Other important source countries include the United Kingdom, France, Germany, the Netherlands, and Japan. Collectively, these six countries accounted for 60 percent of all FDI outflows for 1998–2018 (see Figure 8.3). As might be expected, these countries have long predominated in rankings of the world's largest multinationals, although as noted in Chapter 1, mainland China is now rising fast in the rankings.[9] Excluding China,

Did You Know?

Did you know that the value of Foreign Direct Investment has been growing faster than world trade and world output?

Visit your instructor's Connect® course and click on your eBook or Smartbook® to view a short video explanation from the author.

FIGURE 8.3

Cumulative FDI outflows, 1998–2018 ($ billions).

Source: UNCTAD statistical data set, http://unctadstat.unctad.org.

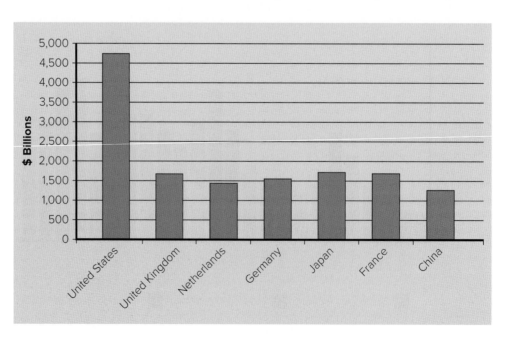

Foreign Direct Investment in China

Beginning in late 1978, China's leadership decided to move the economy away from a centrally planned socialist system to one that was more market driven. The result has been 40 years of sustained high economic growth rates of between 6–10 percent, compounded annually. This growth attracted substantial foreign investment. Starting from a tiny base, foreign investment increased to an annual average rate of $2.7 billion between 1985 and 1990 and then surged to $40 billion annually in the late 1990s, making China the second-biggest recipient of FDI inflows in the world after the United States. The growth has continued, with inward investments into China hitting $136 billion in 2017 (with another $104 billion going into Hong Kong). Over the past 20 years, this inflow has resulted in the establishment of more than 300,000 foreign-funded enterprises in China. The total stock of FDI in mainland China grew from almost nothing in 1978 to $1.49 trillion in 2017 (another $1.97 trillion of FDI stock was in Hong Kong).

The reasons for this investment are fairly obvious. With a population of more than 1.3 billion people, China represents the world's largest market. Historically, import tariffs made it difficult to serve this market via exports, so FDI was required if a company wanted to tap into the country's huge potential. China joined the World Trade Organization in 2001. As a result, average tariff rates on imports have fallen from 15.4 percent to about 8 percent today. Even so, avoiding the tariff on imports is still a motive for investing in China (at 8 percent, tariffs are still significantly above the average of 1.9 percent found in many developed nations). Notwithstanding tariff rates, many foreign firms believe that doing business in China requires a substantial presence in the country to build *guanxi*, the crucial relationship networks (see Chapter 4 for details). Furthermore, a combination of relatively inexpensive labor and tax incentives, particularly for enterprises that establish themselves in special economic zones, makes China an attractive base from which to serve Asian or world markets with exports (although rising labor costs in China are now making this less important).

Less obvious, at least to begin with, was how difficult it would be for foreign firms to do business in China. For one thing, despite decades of growth, China still lags behind developed nations in the wealth and sophistication of its consumer market. This limits opportunities for Western firms. For example, real GDP per capita in China was only $7,329 in 2017, compared to $53,129 in the United States. Moreover, income and wealth in China is skewed towards a few areas, notably around Beijing and Shanghai, where real household income per capita is about four times the level in the country's poorest provinces.

Other problems include a highly regulated environment, which can make it problematic to conduct business transactions, and shifting tax and regulatory regimes. Then there are problems with local joint-venture partners that are inexperienced, opportunistic, or simply operate according to different goals. One U.S. manager explained that when he laid off 200 people to reduce costs, his Chinese partner hired them all back the next day. When he inquired why they had been hired back, the Chinese partner, which was government owned, explained that as an agency of the government, it had an "obligation" to reduce unemployment. Western firms also need to be concerned about protecting their intellectual property because there is a history of intellectual property not being respected in China, although this may now be starting to change.

Sources: Interviews by the author while in China; United Nations, *World Investment Report*, 2017; Linda Ng and C. Tuan, "Building a Favorable Investment Environment: Evidence for the Facilitation of FDI in China," *The World Economy*, 2002, pp. 1095–114; S. Chan and G. Qingyang, "Investment in China Migrates Inland," *Far Eastern Economic Review*, May 2006, pp. 52–57; Rachel Chang, "Here's What China's Middle Classes Really Earn—and Spend," *Bloomberg*, March 9, 2016; Yi Wen, Income and Living Standards Across China," *On the Economy Blog*, Federal Reserve Bank of St Louis, January 8, 2018; Gordon Orr, "A Pocket Guide to Doing Business in China," *McKinsey*, October 2014, archived at www.mckinsey.com/business-functions/strategy-and-corporate-finance/our-insights/a-pocket-guide-to-doing-business-in-china.

these nations dominate primarily because they were the most developed nations with the largest economies during much of the postwar period and therefore home to many of the largest and best-capitalized enterprises. Many of these countries also had a long history as trading nations and naturally looked to foreign markets to fuel their economic expansion. Thus, it is no surprise that enterprises based there have been at the forefront of foreign investment trends.

The dramatic rise of China, particularly since 2010 when outward investment by Chinese multinationals started to surge, may soon upset this long established narrative. In 2005, Chinese firms invested some $12 billion internationally. Since then, the figure has risen steadily, reaching a record $196 billion in 2016 before slipping back to $130 billion in 2018. Firms based in Hong Kong accounted for another $87 billion of outward FDI in 2017 and $85 billion in 2018. Much of the outward investment by Chinese firms has been directed at extractive industries in less developed nations (e.g., China has been a major investor in African countries). A major motive for these investments has been to gain access to raw materials, of which China is one of the world's largest consumers. There are signs, however, that Chinese firms are starting to turn their attention to more advanced nations. In 2017, Chinese firms invested $25 billion in the United States, up from $146 million in 2003.[10]

THE FORM OF FDI: ACQUISITIONS VERSUS GREENFIELD INVESTMENTS

FDI takes two main forms. The first is a **greenfield investment**, which involves the establishment of a new operation in a foreign country. The second involves acquiring or merging with an existing firm in the foreign country. UN estimates indicate that some 40 to 80 percent of all FDI inflows were in the form of mergers and acquisitions between 1998 and 2018.[11] However, FDI flows into developed nations differ markedly from those into developing nations. In the case of developing nations, only about one-third or less of FDI is in the form of cross-border mergers and acquisitions. The lower percentage of mergers and acquisitions may simply reflect the fact that there are fewer target firms to acquire in developing nations.

When contemplating FDI, when do firms prefer to acquire existing assets rather than undertake greenfield investments? We consider this question in depth in Chapter 15. For now, we can make a few basic observations. First, mergers and acquisitions are quicker to execute than greenfield investments. This is an important consideration in the modern business world where markets evolve very rapidly. Many firms apparently believe that if they do not acquire a desirable target firm, then their global rivals will. Second, foreign firms are acquired because those firms have valuable strategic assets, such as brand loyalty, customer relationships, trademarks or patents, distribution systems, production systems, and the like. It is easier and perhaps less risky for a firm to acquire those assets than to build them from the ground up through a greenfield investment. Third, firms make acquisitions because they believe they can increase the efficiency of the acquired unit by transferring capital, technology, or management skills. However, as we discuss in Chapter 15, there is evidence that many mergers and acquisitions fail to realize their anticipated gains.[12]

LO8-2

Explain the different theories of FDI.

Theories of Foreign Direct Investment

In this section, we review several theories of foreign direct investment. These theories approach the various phenomena of foreign direct investment from three complementary perspectives. One set of theories seeks to explain why a firm will favor direct investment as a means of entering a foreign market when two other alternatives, exporting and licensing, are open to it. Another set of theories seeks to explain why firms in the same industry often undertake foreign direct investment at the same time and why they favor certain locations over others as targets for foreign direct investment. Put differently, these theories attempt to explain the observed *pattern* of foreign direct investment flows. A third theoretical perspective, known as the **eclectic paradigm**, attempts to combine the two other perspectives into a single holistic explanation of foreign direct investment (this theoretical perspective is *eclectic* because the best aspects of other theories are taken and combined into a single explanation).

WHY FOREIGN DIRECT INVESTMENT?

Why do firms go to the trouble of establishing operations abroad through foreign direct investment when two alternatives, exporting and licensing, are available to them for exploiting the profit opportunities in a foreign market? **Exporting** involves producing goods at home

Burberry Shifts Its Entry Strategy in Japan

Burberry, the icon British luxury apparel company best known for its high-fashion outerwear, has been operating in Japan for nearly half a century. Until recently, its branded products were sold under a licensing agreement with Sanyo Shokai. The Japanese company had considerable discretion as to how it utilized the Burberry brand. It sold everything from golf bags to miniskirts and Burberry-clad Barbie dolls in its 400 stores around the country, typically at prices significantly below those Burberry charged for its high-end products in the United Kingdom.

For a long time, it looked like a good deal for Burberry. Sanyo Shokai did all of the market development in Japan, generating revenues of around $800 million a year and paying Burberry $80 million in annual royalty payments. However, by 2007, Burberry's CEO, Angela Ahrendts, was becoming increasingly dissatisfied with the Japanese licensing deal and 22 others like it in countries around the world. In Ahrendts's view, the licensing deals were diluting Burberry's core brand image. Licensees such as Sanyo Shokai were selling a wide range of products at a much lower price point than Burberry charged for products in its own stores. "In luxury," Ahrendts once remarked, "ubiquity will kill you—it means that you're not really luxury anymore." Moreover, with an increasing number of customers buying Burberry products online and on trips to Britain, where the brand was considered very upmarket, Ahrendts felt that it was crucial for Burberry to tightly control its global brand image.

Ahrendts was determined to rein in licensees and regain control of Burberry's sales in foreign markets, even if it meant taking a short-term hit to sales. She started off the process of terminating licensees before leaving Burberry to run Apple's retail division in 2014. Her hand-picked successor as CEO, Christopher Bailey, who rose through the design function at Burberry, has continued to pursue this strategy.

In Japan, the license was terminated in 2015. Sanyo Shokai was required to close nearly 400 licensed Burberry stores. Burberry is not giving up on Japan, however. After all, Japan is the world's second-largest market for luxury goods. Instead, the company will now sell products through a limited number of wholly owned stores. The goal is to have 35 to 50 stores in the most exclusive locations in Japan by 2018. They will offer only high-end products, such as Burberry's classic $1,800 trench coat. In general, the price point will be 10 times higher than was common for most Burberry products in Japan. The company realizes the move is risky and fully expects sales to initially fall before rising again as it rebuilds its brand, but CEO Bailey argues that the move is absolutely necessary if Burberry is to have a coherent global brand image for its luxury products.

Sources: Kathy Chu and Megumi Fujikawa, "Burberry Gets a Grip on Brand in Japan," *The Wall Street Journal*, August 15–16, 2015; Angela Ahrendts, "Burberry's CEO on Turning an Aging British Icon into a Global Luxury Brand," *Harvard Business Review*, January–February 2013; Tim Blanks, "The Designer Who Would be CEO," *The Wall Street Journal Magazine*, June 18, 2015; and G. Fasol, "Burberry Solves Its 'Japan Problem,' at Least for Now," *Japan Strategy*, August 19, 2015.

and then shipping them to the receiving country for sale. **Licensing** involves granting a foreign entity (the licensee) the right to produce and sell the firm's product in return for a royalty fee on every unit sold. The question is important, given that a cursory examination of the topic suggests that foreign direct investment may be both expensive and risky compared with exporting and licensing. FDI is expensive because a firm must bear the costs of establishing production facilities in a foreign country or of acquiring a foreign enterprise. FDI is risky because of the problems associated with doing business in a different culture where the rules of the game may be very different. Relative to indigenous firms, there is a greater probability that a foreign firm undertaking FDI in a country for the first time will make costly mistakes due to its ignorance. When a firm exports, it need not bear the costs associated with FDI, and it can reduce the risks associated with selling abroad by using a native sales agent. Similarly, when a firm allows another enterprise to produce its products under license, the licensee bears the costs or risks (e.g., fashion retailer Burberry originally entered Japan via a licensing contract with a Japanese retailer—see the accompanying Management Focus). So why do so many firms apparently prefer FDI over either exporting or licensing? The answer can be found by examining the limitations of exporting and licensing as means for capitalizing on foreign market opportunities.

Limitations of Exporting

The viability of exporting physical goods is often constrained by transportation costs and trade barriers. When transportation costs are added to production costs, it becomes unprofitable to ship some products over a large distance. This is particularly true of products that have a low value-to-weight ratio and that can be produced in almost any location. For such products, the attractiveness of exporting decreases, relative to either FDI or licensing. This is the case, for example, with cement. Thus, Cemex, the large Mexican cement maker, has expanded internationally by pursuing FDI, rather than exporting. For products with a high value-to-weight ratio, however, transportation costs are normally a minor component of total landed cost (e.g., electronic components, personal computers, medical equipment, computer software, etc.) and have little impact on the relative attractiveness of exporting, licensing, and FDI.

Transportation costs aside, some firms undertake foreign direct investment as a response to actual or threatened trade barriers such as import tariffs or quotas. By placing tariffs on imported goods, governments can increase the cost of exporting relative to foreign direct investment and licensing. Similarly, by limiting imports through quotas, governments increase the attractiveness of FDI and licensing. For example, the wave of FDI by Japanese auto companies in the United States that started in the mid-1980s and continues to this day has been partly driven by protectionist threats from Congress and by tariffs on the importation of Japanese vehicles, particularly light trucks (SUVs), which still face a 25 percent import tariff into the United States. For Japanese auto companies, these factors decreased the profitability of exporting and increased that of foreign direct investment. In this context, it is important to understand that trade barriers do not have to be physically in place for FDI to be favored over exporting. Often, the desire to reduce the threat that trade barriers might be imposed is enough to justify foreign direct investment as an alternative to exporting.

globalEDGE RANKINGS

Cross-border investments have been ramped up to a relatively large degree in the last decade. Even with the economic downturn that started in 2008, the world continued to see a great deal of foreign direct investment by companies in the last decade. Now, when the economic prosperity is likely to be better, given that we are removed from those downturn days, the expectation is that more foreign direct investment will be considered by companies. On globalEDGE™, there are myriad opportunities to gain more knowledge about foreign direct investment (FDI). The "Rankings" section is a great starting point (**globaledge. msu.edu/global-resources/rankings**). In this section, globalEDGE™ features several reports by A.T. Kearney—with one of them squarely centered on foreign direct investment and a "confidence index" for FDI. The companies that participate in the regular study account for more than $2 trillion in annual global revenue! Which countries are in the top three in the investment confidence index, and do you agree that the three countries are the best ones to invest in if you were running a company?

Limitations of Licensing

A branch of economic theory known as **internalization theory** seeks to explain why firms often prefer foreign direct investment over licensing as a strategy for entering foreign markets (this approach is also known as the **market imperfections** approach).[13] According to internalization theory, licensing has three major drawbacks as a strategy for exploiting foreign market opportunities. First, *licensing may result in a firm's giving away valuable technological know-how to a potential foreign competitor.* In a classic example, in the 1960s,

RCA licensed its leading-edge color television technology to a number of Japanese companies, including Matsushita and Sony. At the time, RCA saw licensing as a way to earn a good return from its technological know-how in the Japanese market without the costs and risks associated with foreign direct investment. However, Matsushita and Sony quickly assimilated RCA's technology and used it to enter the U.S. market to compete directly against RCA. As a result, RCA was relegated to being a minor player in its home market, while Matsushita and Sony went on to have a much bigger market share.

A second problem is that *licensing does not give a firm the tight control over production, marketing, and strategy in a foreign country that may be required to maximize its profitability.* With licensing, control over production (of a good or a service), marketing, and strategy are granted to a licensee in return for a royalty fee. However, for both strategic and operational reasons, a firm may want to retain control over these functions. One reason for wanting control over the *strategy* of a foreign entity is that a firm might want its foreign subsidiary to price and market very aggressively as a way of keeping a foreign competitor in check. Unlike a wholly owned subsidiary, a licensee would probably not accept such an imposition because it would likely reduce the licensee's profit, or it might even cause the licensee to take a loss. Another reason for wanting control over the *strategy* of a foreign entity is to make sure that the entity does not damage the firm's brand. This was the primary reason fashion retailer Burberry recently terminated its licensing agreement in Japan and switched to a strategy of direct ownership of its own retail stores in the Japanese market (see the Management Focus about Burberry for details).

One reason for wanting control over the *operations* of a foreign entity is that the firm might wish to take advantage of differences in factor costs across countries, producing only part of its final product in a given country, while importing other parts from where they can be produced at lower cost. Again, a licensee would be unlikely to accept such an arrangement because it would limit the licensee's autonomy. For reasons such as these, when tight control over a foreign entity is desirable, foreign direct investment is preferable to licensing.

A third problem with licensing arises when the firm's competitive advantage is based not as much on its products as on the management, marketing, and manufacturing capabilities that produce those products. The problem here is that *such capabilities are often not amenable to licensing.* While a foreign licensee may be able to physically reproduce the firm's product under license, it often may not be able to do so as efficiently as the firm could itself. As a result, the licensee may not be able to fully exploit the profit potential inherent in a foreign market.

For example, consider Toyota, a company whose competitive advantage in the global auto industry is acknowledged to come from its superior ability to manage the overall process of designing, engineering, manufacturing, and selling automobiles—that is, from its management and organizational capabilities. Indeed, Toyota is credited with pioneering the development of a new production process, known as *lean production*, that enables it to produce higher-quality automobiles at a lower cost than its global rivals.[14] Although Toyota could license certain products, its real competitive advantage comes from its management and process capabilities. These kinds of skills are difficult to articulate or codify; they certainly cannot be written down in a simple licensing contract. They are organizationwide and have been developed over the years. They are not embodied in any one individual but instead are widely dispersed throughout the company. Put another way, Toyota's skills are embedded in its organizational culture, and culture is something that cannot be licensed. Thus, if Toyota were to allow a foreign entity to produce its cars under license, the chances are that the entity could not do so as efficiently as could Toyota. In turn, this would limit the ability of the foreign entity to fully develop the market potential of that product. Such reasoning underlies Toyota's preference for direct investment in foreign markets, as opposed to allowing foreign automobile companies to produce its cars under license.

All of this suggests that when one or more of the following conditions holds, markets fail as a mechanism for selling know-how and FDI is more profitable than licensing: (1) when the firm has valuable know-how that cannot be adequately protected by a licensing contract, (2) when the firm needs tight control over a foreign entity to maximize its market share and earnings in that country, and (3) when a firm's skills and know-how are not amenable to licensing.

Advantages of Foreign Direct Investment

It follows that a firm will favor foreign direct investment over exporting as an entry strategy when transportation costs or trade barriers make exporting unattractive. Furthermore, the firm will favor foreign direct investment over licensing (or franchising) when it wishes to maintain control over its technological know-how, or over its operations and business strategy, or when the firm's capabilities are simply not amenable to licensing, as may often be the case. Moreover, gaining technology, productive assets, market share, brand equity, distribution systems, and the like through FDI by purchasing the assets of an established company can all speed up market entry, improve production in the firm's home base, and facilitate the transfer of technology from the acquired company to the acquiring company. We return to this topic in Chapter 13 when we discuss different entry strategies.

THE PATTERN OF FOREIGN DIRECT INVESTMENT

Observation suggests that firms in the same industry often undertake foreign direct investment at about the same time. Also, firms tend to direct their investment activities toward the same target markets. The two theories we consider in this section attempt to explain the patterns that we observe in FDI flows.

Strategic Behavior

One theory is based on the idea that FDI flows are a reflection of strategic rivalry between firms in the global marketplace. An early variant of this argument was expounded by F. T. Knickerbocker, who looked at the relationship between FDI and rivalry in oligopolistic industries.[15] An **oligopoly** is an industry composed of a limited number of large firms (e.g., an industry in which four firms control 80 percent of a domestic market would be defined as an oligopoly). A critical competitive feature of such industries is interdependence of the major players: What one firm does can have an immediate impact on the major competitors, forcing a response in kind. By cutting prices, one firm in an oligopoly can take market share away from its competitors, forcing them to respond with similar price cuts to retain their market share. Thus, the interdependence between firms in an oligopoly leads to imitative behavior; rivals often quickly imitate what a firm does in an oligopoly.

Imitative behavior can take many forms in an oligopoly. One firm raises prices, and the others follow; one expands capacity, and the rivals imitate lest they be left at a disadvantage in the future. Knickerbocker argued that the same kind of imitative behavior characterizes FDI. Consider an oligopoly in the United States in which three firms—A, B, and C—dominate the market. Firm A establishes a subsidiary in France. Firms B and C decide that if successful, this new subsidiary may knock out their export business to France and give a first-mover advantage to firm A. Furthermore, firm A might discover some competitive asset in France that it could repatriate to the United States to torment firms B and C on their native soil. Given these possibilities, firms B and C decide to follow firm A and establish operations in France.

Studies that have looked at FDI by U.S. firms show that firms based in oligopolistic industries tended to imitate each other's FDI.[16] The same phenomenon has been observed with regard to FDI undertaken by Japanese firms.[17] For example, Toyota and Nissan responded to investments by Honda in the United States and Europe by undertaking their own FDI in the United States and Europe. Research has also shown that models of strategic behavior in a global oligopoly can explain the pattern of FDI in the global tire industry.[18]

Knickerbocker's theory can be extended to embrace the concept of multipoint competition. **Multipoint competition** arises when two or more enterprises encounter each other in different regional markets, national markets, or industries.[19] Economic theory suggests that rather like chess players jockeying for advantage, firms will try to match each other's moves in different markets to try to hold each other in check. The idea is to ensure that a rival does not gain a commanding position in one market and then use the profits generated there to subsidize competitive attacks in other markets.

Although Knickerbocker's theory and its extensions can help explain imitative FDI behavior by firms in oligopolistic industries, it does not explain why the first firm in an oligopoly decides to undertake FDI rather than to export or license. Internalization theory addresses this phenomenon. The imitative theory also does not address the issue of whether FDI is more efficient than exporting or licensing for expanding abroad. Again, internalization theory addresses the efficiency issue. For these reasons, many economists favor internalization theory as an explanation for FDI, although most would agree that the imitative explanation tells an important part of the story.

THE ECLECTIC PARADIGM

The eclectic paradigm has been championed by the late British economist John Dunning.[20] Dunning argues that in addition to the various factors discussed earlier, location-specific advantages are also of considerable importance in explaining both the rationale for and the direction of foreign direct investment. By **location-specific advantages**, Dunning means the advantages that arise from utilizing resource endowments or assets that are tied to a particular foreign location and that a firm finds valuable to combine with its own unique assets (such as the firm's technological, marketing, or management capabilities). Dunning accepts the argument of internalization theory that it is difficult for a firm to license its own unique capabilities and know-how. Therefore, he argues that combining location-specific assets or resource endowments with the firm's own unique capabilities often requires foreign direct investment. That is, it requires the firm to establish production facilities where those foreign assets or resource endowments are located.

An obvious example of Dunning's arguments are natural resources, such as oil and other minerals, which are—by their character—specific to certain locations. Dunning suggests that to exploit such foreign resources, a firm must undertake FDI. Clearly, this explains the FDI undertaken by many of the world's oil companies, which have to invest where oil is located in order to combine their technological and managerial capabilities with this valuable location-specific resource. Another obvious example is valuable human resources, such as low-cost, highly skilled labor. The cost and skill of labor varies from country to country. Because labor is not internationally mobile, according to Dunning it makes sense for a firm to locate production facilities in those countries where the cost and skills of local labor are most suited to its particular production processes.

However, Dunning's theory has implications that go beyond basic resources such as minerals and labor. Consider Silicon Valley, which is the world center for the computer and semiconductor industry. Many of the world's major computer and semiconductor companies—such as Apple Computer, Hewlett-Packard, Oracle, Google, and Intel—are located close to each other in the Silicon Valley region of California. As a result, much of the cutting-edge research and product development in computers and semiconductors occurs there. According to Dunning's arguments, knowledge being generated in Silicon Valley with regard to the design and manufacture of computers and semiconductors is available nowhere else in the world. To be sure, that knowledge is commercialized as it diffuses throughout the world, but the leading edge of knowledge generation in the computer and semiconductor industries is to be found in Silicon Valley. In Dunning's language, this means that Silicon Valley has a *location-specific advantage* in the generation of knowledge related to the computer and semiconductor industries. In part, this advantage comes from the sheer concentration of intellectual talent in this area, and in part, it arises

Google Headquarters in Mountain View, California, USA.

Phillip Bond/Alamy Stock Photo

from a network of informal contacts that allows firms to benefit from each other's knowledge generation. Economists refer to such knowledge "spillovers" as **externalities**, and there is a well-established theory suggesting that firms can benefit from such externalities by locating close to their source.[21]

Insofar as this is the case, it makes sense for foreign computer and semiconductor firms to invest in research and, perhaps, production facilities so they too can learn about and utilize valuable new knowledge before those based elsewhere, thereby giving them a competitive advantage in the global marketplace.[22] Evidence suggests that European, Japanese, South Korean, and Taiwanese computer and semiconductor firms are investing in the Silicon Valley region precisely because they wish to benefit from the externalities that arise there.[23] Others have argued that direct investment by foreign firms in the U.S. biotechnology industry has been motivated by desire to gain access to the unique location-specific technological knowledge of U.S. biotechnology firms.[24] Dunning's theory, therefore, seems to be a useful addition to those outlined previously because it helps explain how location factors affect the direction of FDI.[25]

Political Ideology and Foreign Direct Investment

Historically, political ideology toward FDI within a nation has ranged from a dogmatic radical stance that is hostile to all inward FDI at one extreme to an adherence to the noninterventionist principle of free market economics at the other. Between these two extremes is an approach that might be called *pragmatic nationalism*.

THE RADICAL VIEW

The radical view traces its roots to Marxist political and economic theory. Radical writers argue that the multinational enterprise (MNE) is an instrument of imperialist domination. They see the MNE as a tool for exploiting host countries to the exclusive benefit of their capitalist–imperialist home countries. They argue that MNEs extract profits from the host country and take them to their home country, giving nothing of value to the host country in exchange. They note, for example, that key technology is tightly controlled by the MNE and that important jobs in the foreign subsidiaries of MNEs go to home-country nationals rather than to citizens of the host country. Because of this, according to the radical view, FDI by the MNEs of advanced capitalist nations keeps the less developed countries of the world relatively backward and dependent on advanced capitalist nations for investment, jobs, and technology. Thus, according to the extreme version of this view, no country should ever permit foreign corporations to undertake FDI because they can never be instruments of economic development, only of economic domination. Where MNEs already exist in a country, they should be immediately nationalized.[26]

From 1945 until the 1980s, the radical view was very influential in the world economy. Until the collapse of communism between 1989 and 1991, the countries of eastern Europe were opposed to FDI. Similarly, communist countries elsewhere—such as China, Cambodia, and Cuba—were all opposed in principle to FDI (although, in practice, the Chinese started to allow FDI in mainland China in the 1970s). Many socialist countries—particularly in Africa, where one of the first actions of many newly independent states was to nationalize foreign-owned enterprises—also embraced the radical position. Countries whose political ideology was more nationalistic than socialistic further embraced the radical position. This was true in Iran and India, for example, both of which adopted tough policies restricting FDI and nationalized many foreign-owned enterprises. Iran is a particularly interesting case because its Islamic government, while rejecting Marxist theory, essentially embraced the radical view that FDI by MNEs is an instrument of imperialism.

By the early 1990s, the radical position was in retreat. There seem to be three reasons for this: (1) the collapse of communism in eastern Europe; (2) the generally abysmal economic performance of those countries that embraced the radical position, in addition to a

TEST PREP

Use SmartBook to help retain what you have learned. Access your instructor's Connect course to check out SmartBook or go to **learnsmartadvantage.com** for help.

LO8-3

Understand how political ideology shapes a government's attitudes toward FDI.

growing belief by many of these countries that FDI can be an important source of technology and jobs and can stimulate economic growth; and (3) the strong economic performance of those developing countries that embraced capitalism rather than radical ideology (e.g., Singapore, Hong Kong, and Taiwan). Despite this, the radical view lingers on in some countries, such as Venezuela, where the government of Hugo Chavez, and that of his successor Nicolas Maduro, have both viewed foreign multinationals as an instrument of domination.

THE FREE MARKET VIEW

The free market view traces its roots to classical economics and the international trade theories of Adam Smith and David Ricardo (see Chapter 6). The intellectual case for this view has been strengthened by the internalization explanation of FDI. The free market view argues that international production should be distributed among countries according to the theory of comparative advantage. Countries should specialize in the production of those goods and services that they can produce most efficiently. Within this framework, the MNE is an instrument for dispersing the production of goods and services to the most efficient locations around the globe. Viewed this way, FDI by the MNE increases the overall efficiency of the world economy.

Imagine that Dell decided to move assembly operations for many of its personal computers from the United States to Mexico to take advantage of lower labor costs in Mexico. According to the free market view, moves such as this can be seen as increasing the overall efficiency of resource utilization in the world economy. Mexico, due to its lower labor costs, has a comparative advantage in the assembly of PCs. By moving the production of PCs from the United States to Mexico, Dell frees U.S. resources for use in activities in which the United States has a comparative advantage (e.g., the design of computer software, the manufacture of high value-added components such as microprocessors, or basic R&D). Also, consumers benefit because the PCs cost less than they would if they were produced domestically. In addition, Mexico gains from the technology, skills, and capital that the computer company transfers with its FDI. Contrary to the radical view, the free market view stresses that such resource transfers benefit the host country and stimulate its economic growth. Thus, the free market view argues that FDI is a benefit to both the source country and the host country.

PRAGMATIC NATIONALISM

In practice, many countries have adopted neither a radical policy nor a free market policy toward FDI but, instead, a policy that can best be described as pragmatic nationalism.[27] The pragmatic nationalist view is that FDI has both benefits and costs. FDI can benefit a host country by bringing capital, skills, technology, and jobs, but those benefits come at a cost. When a foreign company rather than a domestic company produces products, the profits from that investment go abroad. Many countries are also concerned that a foreign-owned manufacturing plant may import many components from its home country, which has negative implications for the host country's balance-of-payments position.

Recognizing this, countries adopting a pragmatic stance pursue policies designed to maximize the national benefits and minimize the national costs. According to this view, FDI should be allowed so long as the benefits outweigh the costs. Japan offers an example of pragmatic nationalism. Until the 1980s, Japan's policy was probably one of the most restrictive among countries adopting a pragmatic nationalist stance. This was due to Japan's perception that direct entry of foreign (especially U.S.) firms with ample managerial resources into the Japanese markets could hamper the development and growth of its own industry and technology.[28] This belief led Japan to block the majority of applications to invest in Japan. However, there were always exceptions to this policy. Firms that had important technology were often permitted to undertake FDI if they insisted that they would neither license their technology to a Japanese firm nor enter into a joint venture with a Japanese enterprise. IBM and Texas Instruments were able to set up wholly owned subsidiaries in Japan by adopting this negotiating position. From the perspective of the Japanese government, the benefits of FDI in such cases—the stimulus that these firms might impart to the Japanese economy—outweighed the perceived costs.

Another aspect of pragmatic nationalism is the tendency to aggressively court FDI believed to be in the national interest by, for example, offering subsidies to foreign MNEs in the form of tax breaks or grants. The countries of the European Union often seem to be competing with each other to attract U.S. and Japanese FDI by offering large tax breaks and subsidies. Historically, Britain has been the most successful at attracting Japanese investment in the automobile industry. Nissan, Toyota, and Honda now have major assembly plants in Britain and use the country as their base for serving the rest of Europe—with obvious employment and balance-of-payments benefits for Britain (what happens to these investments if and when Britain exits from the EU remains to be seen). At the time of writing, Britain is scheduled to leave the EU on January 31st, 2020. Similarly, within the United States, individual states often compete with each other to attract FDI, offering generous financial incentives in the form of tax breaks to foreign companies looking to set up operations in the country.

SHIFTING IDEOLOGY

Recent years have seen a marked decline in the number of countries that adhere to a radical ideology. Although few countries have adopted a pure free market policy stance, an increasing number of countries are gravitating toward the free market end of the spectrum and have liberalized their foreign investment regime. This includes many countries that 30 years ago were firmly in the radical camp (e.g., the former communist countries of eastern Europe, many of the socialist countries of Africa, and India) and several countries that until recently could best be described as pragmatic nationalists with regard to FDI (e.g., Japan, South Korea, Italy, Spain, and most Latin American countries). One result has been the surge in the volume of FDI worldwide, which, as we noted earlier, has been growing faster than world trade. Another result has been an increase in the volume of FDI directed at countries that have liberalized their FDI regimes in the last 20 years, such as China, India, and Vietnam.

As a counterpoint, there is some evidence of a shift to a more hostile approach to foreign direct investment in some nations. Venezuela and Bolivia have become increasingly hostile to foreign direct investment. In 2005 and 2006, the governments of both nations unilaterally rewrote contracts for oil and gas exploration, raising the royalty rate that foreign enterprises had to pay the government for oil and gas extracted in their territories. Following his election victory in 2006, Bolivian president Evo Morales nationalized the nation's gas fields and stated that he would evict foreign firms unless they agreed to pay about 80 percent of their revenues to the state and relinquish production oversight. In some developed nations, there is increasing evidence of hostile reactions to inward FDI as well. In Europe in 2006, there was a hostile political reaction to the attempted takeover of Europe's largest steel company, Arcelor, by Mittal Steel, a global company controlled by the Indian entrepreneur Lakshmi Mittal. In mid-2005, China National Offshore Oil Company withdrew a takeover bid for Unocal of the United States after highly negative reaction in Congress about the proposed takeover of a "strategic asset" by a Chinese company.

LO8-4

Describe the benefits and costs of FDI to home and host countries.

Benefits and Costs of FDI

To a greater or lesser degree, many governments can be considered pragmatic nationalists when it comes to FDI. Accordingly, their policy is shaped by a consideration of the costs and benefits of FDI. Here, we explore the benefits and costs of FDI, first from the perspective of a host (receiving) country and then from the perspective of the home (source) country. In the next section, we look at the policy instruments governments use to manage FDI.

HOST-COUNTRY BENEFITS

The main benefits of inward FDI for a host country arise from resource-transfer effects, employment effects, balance-of-payments effects, and effects on competition and economic growth.

Resource-Transfer Effects

Foreign direct investment can make a positive contribution to a host economy by supplying capital, technology, and management resources that would otherwise not be available and thus boost that country's economic growth rate.

With regard to capital, many MNEs, by virtue of their large size and financial strength, have access to financial resources not available to host-country firms. These funds may be available from internal company sources, or, because of their reputation, large MNEs may find it easier to borrow money from capital markets than host-country firms would.

As for technology, you will recall from Chapter 3 that technology can stimulate economic development and industrialization. Technology can take two forms, both of which are valuable. Technology can be incorporated in a production process (e.g., the technology for discovering, extracting, and refining oil), or it can be incorporated in a product (e.g., personal computers). However, many countries lack the research and development resources and skills required to develop their own indigenous product and process technology. This is particularly true in less developed nations. Such countries must rely on advanced industrialized nations for much of the technology required to stimulate economic growth, and FDI can provide it.

Research supports the view that multinational firms often transfer significant technology when they invest in a foreign country.[29] For example, a study of FDI in Sweden found that foreign firms increased both the labor and total factor productivity of Swedish firms that they acquired, suggesting that significant technology transfers had occurred (technology typically boosts productivity).[30] Also, a study of FDI by the Organisation for Economic Co-operation and Development (OECD) found that foreign investors invested significant amounts of capital in R&D in the countries in which they had invested, suggesting that not only were they transferring technology to those countries but they may also have been upgrading existing technology or creating new technology in those countries.[31]

An employee uses a robotic arm to fit a wheel onto a Volkswagen AG Vento automobile on the production line at the Volkswagen India Pvt. plant in Chakan, Maharashtra, India.

Udit Kulshrestha/Bloomberg/Getty Images

Foreign management skills acquired through FDI may also produce important benefits for the host country. Foreign managers trained in the latest management techniques can often help improve the efficiency of operations in the host country, whether those operations are acquired or greenfield developments. Beneficial spin-off effects may also arise when local personnel who are trained to occupy managerial, financial, and technical posts in the subsidiary of a foreign MNE leave the firm and help establish indigenous firms. Similar benefits may arise if the superior management skills of a foreign MNE stimulate local suppliers, distributors, and competitors to improve their own management skills.

Employment Effects

Another beneficial employment effect claimed for FDI is that it brings jobs to a host country that would otherwise not be created there. The effects of FDI on employment are both direct and indirect. Direct effects arise when a foreign MNE employs a number of host-country citizens. Indirect effects arise when jobs are created in local suppliers as a result of the investment and when jobs are created because of increased local spending by employees of the MNE. The indirect employment effects are often as large as, if not larger than, the direct effects. For example, when Toyota decided to open a new auto plant in France, estimates suggested the plant would create 2,000 direct jobs and perhaps another 2,000 jobs in support industries.[32]

Cynics argue that not all the "new jobs" created by FDI represent net additions in employment. In the case of FDI by Japanese auto companies in the United States, some argue that the jobs created by this investment have been more than offset by the jobs lost in U.S.-owned auto companies, which have lost market share to their Japanese competitors. As a consequence of such substitution effects, the net number of new jobs created by FDI may not be as great as initially claimed by an MNE. The issue of the likely net gain in employment may be a major negotiating point between an MNE wishing to undertake FDI and the host government.

When FDI takes the form of an acquisition of an established enterprise in the host economy as opposed to a greenfield investment, the immediate effect may be to reduce employment as the multinational tries to restructure the operations of the acquired unit to improve its operating efficiency. However, even in such cases, research suggests that once the initial period of restructuring is over, enterprises acquired by foreign firms tend to increase their employment base at a faster rate than domestic rivals. An OECD study found that foreign firms created new jobs at a faster rate than their domestic counterparts.[33]

Balance-of-Payments Effects

FDI's effect on a country's balance-of-payments accounts is an important policy issue for most host governments. A country's **balance-of-payments accounts** track both its payments to and its receipts from other countries. Governments normally are concerned when their country is running a deficit on the current account of their balance of payments. The **current account** tracks the export and import of goods and services. A current account deficit, or *trade deficit* as it is often called, arises when a country is importing more goods and services than it is exporting. Governments typically prefer to see a current account surplus rather than a deficit. The only way in which a current account deficit can be supported in the long run is by selling off assets to foreigners (for a detailed explanation of why this is the case, see the appendix to Chapter 6). For example, the persistent U.S. current account deficit since the 1980s has been financed by a steady sale of U.S. assets (stocks, bonds, real estate, and whole corporations) to foreigners. Because national governments invariably dislike seeing the assets of their country fall into foreign hands, they prefer their nation to run a current account surplus. There are two ways in which FDI can help a country achieve this goal.

First, if the FDI is a substitute for imports of goods or services, the effect can be to improve the current account of the host country's balance of payments. Much of the FDI by Japanese automobile companies in the United States and Europe, for example, can be seen as substituting for imports from Japan. Thus, the current account of the U.S. balance of payments has improved somewhat because many Japanese companies are now supplying the U.S. market from production facilities in the United States, as opposed to facilities in Japan. Insofar as this has reduced the need to finance a current account deficit by asset sales to foreigners, the United States has clearly benefited.

A second potential benefit arises when the MNE uses a foreign subsidiary to export goods and services to other countries. According to a UN report, inward FDI by foreign multinationals has been a major driver of export-led economic growth in a number of developing and developed nations.[34] For example, in China, exports increased from $26 billion in 1985 to over $2 trillion in 2018. Much of this dramatic export growth was due to the presence of foreign multinationals that invested heavily in China.

Effect on Competition and Economic Growth

Economic theory tells us that the efficient functioning of markets depends on an adequate level of competition between producers. When FDI takes the form of a greenfield investment, the result is to establish a new enterprise, increasing the number of players in a market and thus consumer choice. In turn, this can increase the level of competition in a national market, thereby driving down prices and increasing the economic welfare of consumers. Increased competition tends to stimulate capital investments by firms in plant, equipment, and R&D as they struggle to gain an edge over their rivals. The long-term results may include increased productivity growth, product and process innovations, and greater economic growth.[35] Such beneficial effects seem to have occurred in the South Korean retail sector following the liberalization of FDI regulations in 1996. FDI by large Western discount stores—including Walmart, Costco, Carrefour, and Tesco—seems to have encouraged indigenous discounters such as E-Mart to improve the efficiency of their own operations. The results have included more competition and lower prices, which benefit South Korean consumers. In a similar vein, the Indian government has been opening up that country's retail sector to FDI, partly because it believes that inward investment by efficient global retailers such as Walmart, Carrefour, and IKEA will provide the competitive stimulus that is necessary to improve the efficiency of India's fragmented retail system.

FDI's impact on competition in domestic markets may be particularly important in the case of services, such as telecommunications, retailing, and many financial services, where exporting is often not an option because the service has to be produced where it is delivered.[36] For example, under a 1997 agreement sponsored by the World Trade Organization, 68 countries accounting for more than 90 percent of world telecommunications revenues pledged to start opening their markets to foreign investment and competition and to abide by common rules for fair competition in telecommunications. Before this agreement, most of the world's telecommunications markets were closed to foreign competitors, and in most countries, the market was monopolized by a single carrier, which was often a state-owned enterprise. The agreement has dramatically increased the level of competition in many national telecommunications markets, producing two major benefits. First, inward investment has increased competition and stimulated investment in the modernization of telephone networks around the world, leading to better service. Second, the increased competition has resulted in lower prices.

HOST-COUNTRY COSTS

Three costs of FDI concern host countries. They arise from possible adverse effects on competition within the host nation, adverse effects on the balance of payments, and the perceived loss of national sovereignty and autonomy.

Adverse Effects on Competition

Host governments sometimes worry that the subsidiaries of foreign MNEs may have greater economic power than indigenous competitors. If it is part of a larger international organization, the foreign MNE may be able to draw on funds generated elsewhere to subsidize its costs in the host market, which could drive indigenous companies out of business and allow the firm to monopolize the market. Once the market is monopolized, the foreign MNE could raise prices above those that would prevail in competitive markets, with harmful effects on the economic welfare of the host nation. This concern tends to be greater in countries that have few large firms of their own (generally, less developed countries). It tends to be a relatively minor concern in most advanced industrialized nations.

In general, while FDI in the form of greenfield investments should increase competition, it is less clear that this is the case when the FDI takes the form of acquisition of an established enterprise in the host nation. Because an acquisition does not result in a net increase in the number of players in a market, the effect on competition may be neutral. When a foreign investor acquires two or more firms in a host country and subsequently merges them, the effect may be to reduce the level of competition in that market, create monopoly power for the foreign firm, reduce consumer choice, and raise prices. For example, in India, Hindustan Lever Ltd., the Indian subsidiary of Unilever, acquired its main local rival, Tata Oil Mills, to assume a dominant position in the bath soap (75 percent) and detergents (30 percent) markets. Hindustan Lever also acquired several local companies in other markets, such as the ice cream makers Dollops, Kwality, and Milkfood. By combining these companies, Hindustan Lever's share of the Indian ice cream market went from zero to 74 percent.[37] However, although such cases are of obvious concern, there is little evidence that such developments are widespread. In many nations, domestic competition authorities have the right to review and block any mergers or acquisitions that they view as having a detrimental impact on competition. If such institutions are operating effectively, this should be sufficient to make sure that foreign entities do not monopolize a country's markets.

Adverse Effects on the Balance of Payments

The possible adverse effects of FDI on a host country's balance-of-payments position are twofold. First, set against the initial capital inflow that comes with FDI must be the subsequent outflow of earnings from the foreign subsidiary to its parent company. Such outflows show up as capital outflow on balance-of-payments accounts. Some governments have responded to such outflows by restricting earnings that can be repatriated to a foreign subsidiary's home country. A second concern arises when a foreign subsidiary imports a substantial number of its inputs from abroad, which results in a debit on the current account of the host country's balance of payments. One criticism leveled against Japanese-owned auto assembly operations in the United States, for example, is that they tend to import many component parts from Japan. Because of this, the favorable impact of this FDI on the current account of the U.S. balance-of-payments position may not be as great as initially supposed. The Japanese auto companies responded to these criticisms by pledging to purchase 75 percent of their component parts from U.S.-based manufacturers (but not necessarily U.S.-owned manufacturers). When the Japanese auto company Nissan invested in the United Kingdom, Nissan responded to concerns about local content by pledging to increase the proportion of local content to 60 percent and subsequently raising it to more than 80 percent.

Possible Effects on National Sovereignty and Autonomy

Some host governments worry that FDI is accompanied by some loss of economic independence. The concern is that key decisions that can affect the host country's economy will be made by a foreign parent that has no real commitment to the host country and over which the host country's government has no real control. Most economists dismiss such concerns as groundless and irrational. Political scientist Robert Reich has noted that such concerns are the product of outmoded thinking because they fail to account for the growing interdependence of the world economy.[38] In a world in which firms from all advanced nations are increasingly investing in each other's markets, it is not possible for one country to hold another to "economic ransom" without hurting itself.

HOME-COUNTRY BENEFITS

The benefits of FDI to the home (source) country arise from three sources. First, the home country's balance of payments benefits from the inward flow of foreign earnings. FDI can also benefit the home country's balance of payments if the foreign subsidiary creates demands for home-country exports of capital equipment, intermediate goods, complementary products, and the like.

Second, benefits to the home country from outward FDI arise from employment effects. As with the balance of payments, positive employment effects arise when the foreign subsidiary creates demand for home-country exports. Thus, Toyota's investment in auto assembly operations in Europe has benefited both the Japanese balance-of-payments position and employment in Japan, because Toyota imports some component parts for its European-based auto assembly operations directly from Japan.

Third, benefits arise when the home-country MNE learns valuable skills from its exposure to foreign markets that can subsequently be transferred back to the home country. This amounts to a reverse resource-transfer effect. Through its exposure to a foreign market, an MNE can learn about superior management techniques and superior product and process technologies. These resources can then be transferred back to the home country, contributing to the home country's economic growth rate.[39]

HOME-COUNTRY COSTS

Against these benefits must be set the apparent costs of FDI for the home (source) country. The most important concerns center on the balance-of-payments and employment effects of outward FDI. The home country's balance of payments may suffer in three ways. First, the balance of payments suffers from the initial capital outflow required to finance the FDI. This effect, however, is usually more than offset by the subsequent inflow of foreign earnings. Second, the current account of the balance of payments suffers if the purpose of foreign investment is to serve the home market from a low-cost production location. Third, the current account of the balance of payments suffers if the FDI is a substitute for direct exports. Thus, insofar as Toyota's assembly operations in the United States are intended to substitute for direct exports from Japan, the current account position of Japan will deteriorate.

With regard to employment effects, the most serious concerns arise when FDI is seen as a substitute for domestic production. This was the case with Toyota's investments in the United States and Europe. One obvious result of such FDI is reduced home-country employment. If the labor market in the home country is already tight, with little unemployment, this concern may not be that great. However, if the home country is suffering from unemployment, concern about the export of jobs may arise. For example, one objection frequently raised by U.S. labor leaders to the free trade pact among the United States, Mexico, and Canada (see Chapter 9) is that the United States would lose hundreds of thousands of jobs as U.S. firms invest in Mexico to take advantage of cheaper labor and then export back to the United States.[40]

INTERNATIONAL TRADE THEORY AND FDI

When assessing the costs and benefits of FDI to the home country, keep in mind the lessons of international trade theory (see Chapter 6). International trade theory tells us that home-country concerns about the negative economic effects of offshore production may be misplaced. The term **offshore production** refers to FDI undertaken to serve the home market. An example would be U.S. automobile companies investing in auto parts production facilities in Mexico. Far from reducing home-country employment, such FDI may actually stimulate economic growth (and hence employment) in the home country by freeing home-country resources to concentrate on activities where the home country has a comparative advantage. In addition, home-country consumers benefit if the price of the particular product falls as a result of the FDI. Also, if a company were prohibited from making such investments on the grounds of negative employment effects while its international competitors reaped the benefits of low-cost production locations, it would undoubtedly lose market share to its international competitors. Under such a scenario, the adverse long-run economic effects for a country would probably outweigh the relatively minor balance-of-payments and employment effects associated with offshore production.

TEST PREP

Use SmartBook to help retain what you have learned. Access your instructor's Connect course to check out SmartBook or go to **learnsmartadvantage.com** for help.

 Government Policy Instruments and FDI

LO8-5

Explain the range of policy instruments that governments use to influence FDI.

We have reviewed the costs and benefits of FDI from the perspective of both home country and host country. We now turn our attention to the policy instruments that home (source) countries and host countries can use to regulate FDI.

HOME-COUNTRY POLICIES

Through their choice of policies, home countries can both encourage and restrict FDI by local firms. We look at policies designed to encourage outward FDI first. These include foreign risk insurance, capital assistance, tax incentives, and political pressure. Then, we look at policies designed to restrict outward FDI.

Encouraging Outward FDI

Many investor nations now have government-backed insurance programs to cover major types of foreign investment risk. The types of risks insurable through these programs include the risks of expropriation (nationalization), war losses, and the inability to transfer profits back home. Such programs are particularly useful in encouraging firms to undertake investments in politically unstable countries.[41] In addition, several advanced countries also have special funds or banks that make government loans to firms wishing to invest in developing countries. As a further incentive to encourage domestic firms to undertake FDI, many countries have eliminated double taxation of foreign income (i.e., taxation of income in both the host country and the home country). Last, and perhaps most significant, a number of investor countries (including the United States) have used their political influence to persuade host countries to relax their restrictions on inbound FDI. For example, in response to direct U.S. pressure, Japan relaxed many of its formal restrictions on inward FDI. In response to further U.S. pressure, Japan relaxed its informal barriers to inward FDI. One beneficiary of this trend was Toys "R" Us, which, after five years of intensive lobbying by company and U.S. government officials, opened its first retail stores in Japan in December 1991. By 2012, Toys "R" Us had more than 170 stores in Japan, and its Japanese operation, in which Toys "R" Us retained a controlling stake, had a listing on the Japanese stock market. Interestingly, although Toys "R" Us ceased operations in the United States in 2017 due to bankruptcy, it continues to operate in Japan.

Restricting Outward FDI

Virtually all investor countries, including the United States, have exercised some control over outward FDI from time to time. One policy has been to limit capital outflows out of concern for the country's balance of payments. From the early 1960s until 1979, for example, Britain had exchange-control regulations that limited the amount of capital a firm could take out of the country. Although the main intent of such policies was to improve the British balance of payments, an important secondary intent was to make it more difficult for British firms to undertake FDI.

In addition, countries have occasionally manipulated tax rules to try to encourage their firms to invest at home. The objective behind such policies is to create jobs at home rather than in other nations. At one time, Britain adopted such policies. The British advanced corporation tax system taxed British companies' foreign earnings at a higher rate than their domestic earnings. This tax code created an incentive for British companies to invest at home.

Finally, countries sometimes prohibit national firms from investing in certain countries for political reasons. Such restrictions can be formal or informal. For example, formal U.S. rules prohibited U.S. firms from investing in countries such as Cuba and Iran, whose political ideology and actions are judged to be contrary to U.S. interests. Similarly, during the 1980s, informal pressure was applied to dissuade U.S. firms from investing in South Africa. In this case, the objective was to pressure South Africa to change its apartheid laws, which happened during the early 1990s.

HOST-COUNTRY POLICIES

Host countries adopt policies designed both to restrict and to encourage inward FDI. As noted earlier in this chapter, political ideology has determined the type and scope of these policies in the past. In the last decade of the twentieth century, many countries moved quickly away from adhering to some version of the radical stance and prohibiting much FDI toward a situation where a combination of free market objectives and pragmatic nationalism took hold.

Encouraging Inward FDI

It is common for governments to offer incentives to foreign firms to invest in their countries. Such incentives take many forms, but the most common are tax concessions, low-interest loans, and grants or subsidies. Incentives are motivated by a desire to gain from the resource-transfer and employment effects of FDI. They are also motivated by a desire to capture FDI away from other potential host countries. For example, in the mid-1990s, the governments of Britain and France competed with each other on the incentives they offered Toyota to invest in their respective countries. In the United States, state governments often compete with each other to attract FDI. For example, Kentucky offered Toyota an incentive package worth $147 million to persuade it to build its U.S. automobile assembly plants there. The package included tax breaks, new state spending on infrastructure, and low-interest loans.[42]

Restricting Inward FDI

Host governments use a wide range of controls to restrict FDI in one way or another. The two most common are ownership restraints and performance requirements. Ownership restraints can take several forms. In some countries, foreign companies are excluded from specific fields. They are excluded from tobacco and mining in Sweden and from the development of certain natural resources in Brazil, Finland, and Morocco. In other industries, foreign ownership may be permitted although a significant proportion of the equity of the subsidiary must be owned by local investors. Foreign ownership is restricted to 25 percent or less of an airline in the United States. In India, foreign firms were prohibited from owning media businesses until 2001, when the rules were relaxed, allowing foreign firms to purchase up to 26 percent of an Indian newspaper.

The rationale underlying ownership restraints seems to be twofold. First, foreign firms are often excluded from certain sectors on the grounds of national security or competition. Particularly in less developed countries, the feeling seems to be that local firms might not be able to develop unless foreign competition is restricted by a combination of import tariffs and controls on FDI. This is a variant of the infant industry argument discussed in Chapter 7.

Second, ownership restraints seem to be based on a belief that local owners can help maximize the resource-transfer and employment benefits of FDI for the host country. Until the 1980s, the Japanese government prohibited most FDI but allowed joint ventures between Japanese firms and foreign MNEs if the MNE had a valuable technology. The Japanese government clearly believed such an arrangement would speed up the subsequent diffusion of the MNE's valuable technology throughout the Japanese economy.

Performance requirements can also take several forms. Performance requirements are controls over the behavior of the MNE's local subsidiary. The most common performance requirements are related to local content, exports, technology transfer, and local participation in top management. As with certain ownership restrictions, the logic underlying performance requirements is that such rules help maximize the benefits and minimize the costs of FDI for the host country. Many countries employ some form of performance requirements when it suits their objectives. However, performance requirements tend to be more common in less developed countries than in advanced industrialized nations.[43]

INTERNATIONAL INSTITUTIONS AND THE LIBERALIZATION OF FDI

Until the 1990s, there was no consistent involvement by multinational institutions in the governing of FDI. This changed with the formation of the World Trade Organization in 1995. The WTO embraces the promotion of international trade in services. Because many services have to be produced where they are sold, exporting is not an option (e.g., one cannot export McDonald's hamburgers or consumer banking services). Given this, the WTO has become involved in regulations governing FDI. As might be expected for an institution created to promote free trade, the thrust of the WTO's efforts has been to push for the liberalization of regulations governing FDI, particularly in services. Under the auspices of the WTO, two extensive multinational agreements were reached in 1997 to liberalize trade in telecommunications and financial services. Both these agreements contained detailed clauses that require signatories to liberalize their regulations governing inward FDI, essentially opening their markets to foreign telecommunications and financial services companies. The WTO has had less success trying to initiate talks aimed at establishing a universal set of rules designed to promote the liberalization of FDI. Led by Malaysia and India, developing nations have so far rejected efforts by the WTO to start such discussions.

✓ TEST PREP

Use SmartBook to help retain what you have learned. Access your instructor's Connect course to check out SmartBook or go to **learnsmartadvantage.com** for help.

FDI AND GOVERNMENT POLICY

LO8-6

Identify the implications for managers of the theory and government policies associated with FDI.

Several implications for business are inherent in the material discussed in this chapter. In this section, we deal first with the implications of the theory and then turn our attention to the implications of government policy.

The Theory of FDI

The implications of the theories of FDI for business practice are straightforward. First, the location-specific advantages argument associated with John Dunning does help explain the *direction* of FDI. However, the location-specific advantages argument does not explain *why* firms prefer FDI to licensing or to exporting. In this regard, from both an explanatory and a business perspective, perhaps the most useful theories are those that focus on the limitations of exporting and licensing—that is, internalization theories. These theories are useful because they identify with some precision how the relative profitability of foreign direct investment, exporting, and licensing varies with circumstances. The theories suggest that exporting is preferable to licensing and FDI so long as transportation costs are minor and trade barriers are trivial. As transportation costs or trade barriers increase, exporting becomes unprofitable, and the choice is between FDI and licensing. Because FDI is more costly and more risky than licensing, other things being equal, the theories argue that licensing is preferable to FDI. Other things are seldom equal, however. Although licensing may work, it is not an attractive option when one or more of the following conditions exist: (1) the firm has valuable know-how that cannot be adequately protected by a licensing contract, (2) the firm needs tight control over a foreign entity to maximize its market share and earnings in that country, and (3) a firm's skills and capabilities are not amenable to licensing. Figure 8.4 presents these considerations as a decision tree.

Firms for which licensing is not a good option tend to be clustered in three types of industries:

- High-technology industries in which protecting firm-specific expertise is of paramount importance and licensing is hazardous.

- Global oligopolies, in which competitive interdependence requires that multinational firms maintain tight control over foreign operations so that they have the ability to launch coordinated attacks against their global competitors.

- Industries in which intense cost pressures require that multinational firms maintain tight control over foreign operations (so that they can disperse production to locations around the globe where factor costs are most favorable in order to minimize costs and maximize value).

Although empirical evidence is limited, the majority of studies seem to support these conjectures.[44] In addition, licensing is not a good option if the competitive advantage of a firm is based upon managerial or marketing knowledge that is embedded in the routines of the firm or the skills of its managers and that is difficult to codify in a "book of blueprints." This would seem to be the case for firms based in a fairly wide range of industries.

Firms for which licensing is a good option tend to be in industries whose conditions are opposite to those just specified. That is, licensing tends to be more common, and more profitable, in fragmented, low-technology industries in which globally dispersed manufacturing is not an option. A good example is the fast-food industry. McDonald's has expanded globally by using a franchising strategy. Franchising is essentially the service-industry version of licensing, although it normally involves much longer-term commitments than licensing. With franchising, the firm licenses its brand name to a foreign firm in return for a percentage of the franchisee's profits. The franchising contract specifies the conditions that the franchisee must fulfill if it is to use the franchisor's brand name. Thus, McDonald's allows foreign firms to use its brand name so long as they agree to run their restaurants on exactly the same lines as McDonald's restaurants elsewhere in the world. This strategy

FIGURE 8.4

A decision framework.

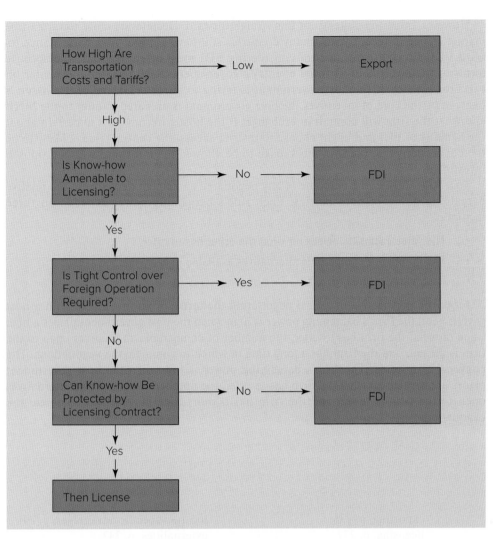

makes sense for McDonald's because (1) like many services, fast food cannot be exported; (2) franchising economizes the costs and risks associated with opening up foreign markets; (3) unlike technological know-how, brand names are relatively easy to protect using a contract; (4) there is no compelling reason for McDonald's to have tight control over franchisees; and (5) McDonald's know-how, in terms of how to run a fast-food restaurant, is amenable to being specified in a written contract (e.g., the contract specifies the details of how to run a McDonald's restaurant).

Finally, it should be noted that the product life-cycle theory and Knickerbocker's theory of FDI tend to be less useful from a business perspective. The problem with these two theories is that they are descriptive rather than analytical. They do a good job of describing the historical evolution of FDI, but they do a relatively poor job of identifying the factors that influence the relative profitability of FDI, licensing, and exporting. Indeed, the issue of licensing as an alternative to FDI is ignored by both these theories.

Government Policy

A host government's attitude toward FDI should be an important variable in decisions about where to locate foreign production facilities and where to make a foreign direct investment. Other things being equal, investing in countries that have permissive policies toward FDI is clearly preferable to investing in countries that restrict FDI.

However, often the issue is not this straightforward. Despite the move toward a free market stance in recent years, many countries still have a rather pragmatic stance toward FDI. In such cases, a firm considering FDI must often negotiate the specific terms of the investment with the country's government. Such negotiations center on two broad issues. If the host government is trying to attract FDI, the central issue is likely to be the kind of incentives the host government is prepared to offer to the MNE and what the firm will commit in exchange. If the host government is uncertain about the benefits of FDI and might choose to restrict access, the central issue is likely to be the concessions that the firm must make to be allowed to go forward with a proposed investment.

To a large degree, the outcome of any negotiated agreement depends on the relative bargaining power of both parties. Each side's bargaining power depends on three factors:

- The value each side places on what the other has to offer.
- The number of comparable alternatives available to each side.
- Each party's time horizon.

From the perspective of a firm negotiating the terms of an investment with a host government, the firm's bargaining power is high when the host government places a high value on what the firm has to offer, the number of comparable alternatives open to the firm is greater, and the firm has a long time in which to complete the negotiations. The converse also holds. The firm's bargaining power is low when the host government places a low value on what the firm has to offer, the number of comparable alternatives open to the firm is fewer, and the firm has a short time in which to complete the negotiations.[45]

Key Terms

flow of FDI, p. 232
stock of FDI, p. 232
outflows of FDI, p. 232
inflows of FDI, p. 232
greenfield investment, p. 236
eclectic paradigm, p. 236

exporting, p. 236
licensing, p. 237
internalization theory, p. 238
market imperfections, p. 238
oligopoly, p. 240
multipoint competition, p. 240

location-specific advantages, p. 241
externalities, p. 242
balance-of-payments
 accounts, p. 246
current account, p. 246
offshore production, p. 249

SUMMARY

This chapter reviewed theories that attempt to explain the pattern of FDI between countries and to examine the influence of governments on firms' decisions to invest in foreign countries. The chapter made the following points:

1. Any theory seeking to explain FDI must explain why firms go to the trouble of acquiring or establishing operations abroad when the alternatives of exporting and licensing are available to them.

2. High transportation costs or tariffs imposed on imports help explain why many firms prefer FDI or licensing over exporting.

3. Firms often prefer FDI to licensing when (*a*) a firm has valuable know-how that cannot be adequately protected by a licensing contract, (*b*) a firm needs tight control over a foreign entity in order to maximize its market share and earnings in that country, and (*c*) a firm's skills and capabilities are not amenable to licensing.

4. Knickerbocker's theory suggests that much FDI is explained by imitative behavior by rival firms in an oligopolistic industry.

5. Dunning has argued that location-specific advantages are of considerable importance in explaining the nature and direction of FDI. According to Dunning, firms undertake FDI to exploit resource endowments or assets that are location-specific.

6. Political ideology is an important determinant of government policy toward FDI. Ideology ranges from a radical stance that is hostile to FDI to a noninterventionist, free market stance. Between the two extremes is an approach best described as pragmatic nationalism.

7. Benefits of FDI to a host country arise from resource-transfer effects, employment effects, and balance-of-payments effects.

8. The costs of FDI to a host country include adverse effects on competition and balance of payments and a perceived loss of national sovereignty.

9. The benefits of FDI to the home (source) country include improvement in the balance of payments as a result of the inward flow of foreign earnings, positive employment effects when the foreign subsidiary creates demand for home-country exports, and benefits from a reverse resource-transfer effect. A reverse resource-transfer effect arises when the foreign subsidiary learns valuable skills abroad that can be transferred back to the home country.

10. The costs of FDI to the home country include adverse balance-of-payments effects that arise from the initial capital outflow and from the export substitution effects of FDI. Costs also arise when FDI exports jobs abroad.

11. Home countries can adopt policies designed to both encourage and restrict FDI. Host countries try to attract FDI by offering incentives and try to restrict FDI by dictating ownership restraints and requiring that foreign MNEs meet specific performance requirements.

Critical Thinking and Discussion Questions

1. In 2008, inward FDI accounted for some 63.7 percent of gross fixed capital formation in Ireland, but only 4.1 percent in Japan. (*Gross fixed capital formation* refers to investments in fixed assets such as factories, warehouses, and retail stores.) What do you think explains this difference in FDI inflows into the two countries?

2. Compare and contrast these explanations of FDI: internalization theory and Knickerbocker's theory of FDI. Which theory do you think offers the best explanation of the historical pattern of FDI? Why?

3. What are the strengths of the eclectic theory of FDI? Can you see any shortcomings? How does the eclectic theory influence management practice?

4. Read the Management Focus titled "Burberry Shifts Its Entry Strategy in Japan" and then answer the following questions:

    a. Why did Burberry initially choose a licensing strategy to expand its presence in Japan?

    b. What limitations of licensing became apparent over time? Should Burberry have expected these drawbacks to arise?

    c. Was terminating the Japanese licensing agreement and opening wholly owned stores the correct strategy for Burberry? What are the risks here?

4. You are the international manager of a U.S. business that has just developed a revolutionary new personal computer that can perform the same functions as existing PCs but costs only half as much to manufacture. Several patents protect the unique design of this computer. Your CEO has asked you to formulate a recommendation for how to expand into Western Europe. Your options are (*a*) to export from the United States, (*b*) to license a European firm to manufacture and market the computer in Europe, or (*c*) to set up a wholly owned subsidiary in Europe. Evaluate the pros and cons of each alternative and suggest a course of action to your CEO.

globalEDGE research task globaledge.msu.edu

Use the globalEDGE™ website (**globaledge.msu.edu**) to complete the following exercises:

1. The *World Investment Report* published annually by UNCTAD provides a summary of recent trends in FDI, as well as quick access to comprehensive investment statistics. Identify the table of *largest transnational corporations* from developing and transition countries. The ranking is based on the foreign assets each corporation owns. Based only on the top 20 companies, provide a summary of the countries and industries represented. Do you notice any common traits from your analysis? Did any industries or countries in the top 20 surprise you? Why?

2. An integral part of successful foreign direct investment is to understand the target market opportunities and the nature of the risk inherent in possible investment projects, particularly in developing countries. You work for a company that builds wastewater and sanitation infrastructure in such countries. *The Multilateral Investment Guarantee Agency (MIGA)* provides insurance for risky projects in these markets. Identify the sector brief for the water and wastewater sector, and prepare a report to identify the major risks that projects in this sector tend to face and how MIGA can assist in such projects.

CLOSING CASE

Geely Goes Global

Zhejiang Geely Holding Group Co., Ltd (**zgh.com**)—or Geely, for short—is a Chinese auto manufacturer that started in 1986 as a manufacturer of refrigerators. Founded by Li Shufu, an energetic entrepreneur and car enthusiast, the Hangzhou-based company did not enter the automobile business until 1997. Today, it is the second-largest private automobile manufacturer in China's booming car market.

Li Shufu reportedly has a great appreciation for design. He scrapped three batches of poorly designed and built models before finally arriving at one that met his expectations: a four-door subcompact sedan introduced in 2002 and known as the Ziyoujian (*Free Cruiser* in English). In a clear sign that Geely had yet to develop its own design and engineering skills, the car was actually designed by the South Korean firm Daewoo Motors.

It was around this time that Li started to think about owning Volvo, his personal favorite carmaker. Based in Sweden, Volvo had been acquired by Ford Motor Company in 1999 for $6.45 billion. In 2009, Li got his chance when Ford, battered by the Great Recession that had hammered the auto market in the United States and Europe, announced it would sell many of its specialty car brands, including Volvo. In 2010, Geely reached an agreement to purchase Volvo for $1.8 billion. At the time, this was the largest overseas acquisition by a Chinese automaker.

Roger Lundsten/AFP/Getty Images

Many observers had low expectations for the acquisition, but they have later been proved wrong. The marriage of Volvo's brand and engineering design skills with Geely's manufacturing capabilities has proved to be a winning combination. Today, Volvo cars are still engineered, designed, and tested in Gothenburg, Sweden, and they still retain their Swedish character, but they are assembled at two new plants in China and a new plant in South Carolina, all built after the acquisition.

Geely has big plans for the South Carolina plant. It is now producing Volvo S60 sedans for sale in the United States, but in a few years the plant is expected to be expanded to produce Volvo SUVs, increasing output to

150,000 units a year and doubling the number of U.S. employees to almost 4,000. According to Katarina Fjording, Volvo's vice president of manufacturing and logistics for the Americas, the U.S. plant required a bigger commitment than those in China, where Geely was already building cars and where it had an established logistics and supplier base. In South Carolina, the company has had to do everything from scratch.

Since the acquisition, China has emerged as a major market for Volvo cars, where the brand is valued for its safety and elegance. The company's aim is to produce the safest car on the road that handles well under any roadside conditions. Geely has pledge to produce a "death-proof" car by 2020, with a commitment that no one should be seriously injured or killed in a new Volvo. The technologies required to achieve this include auto steering, adaptive cruise control, and pedestrian and animal detection for collision warnings and avoidance, all technologies that are being developed in Gothenburg.

The proof of the strategy is in the sales figures. In 2018, sales of Geely's Volvo brand rose 12.4 percent year-on-year to a new record high for the 92-year-old brand. All regions contributed to the 642,000 Volvo cars sold. Sales in China grew by 14 percent, and sales in the U.S. grew by 20 percent. China is now the largest market for the Volvo brand, with 131,000 units sold in 2018, followed by the U.S., where 98,000 units were sold.

Emboldened by its success with Volvo, Geely is now making more foreign investments. In 2017, it acquired a controlling stake in the British sports car manufacturer Lotus Cars, a 49.9 percent stake in Proton, Malaysia's largest car company, and minority stakes in the Swedish Truck Company, the Volvo Group (the one time parent of Volvo Cars), and Daimler-Benz.

Sources: Pamela Ambler, "Volvo and Geely: The Unlikely Marriage of Swedish Tech and Chinese Manufacturing," *Forbes*, January 23, 2018; Sui-Lee Wee, "Geely Buys Stake in Volvo Trucks," *The New York Times*, December 27, 2017; "Volvo Cars Sets New Global Sales Record in 2018", Volvo Car Group, January 4, 2019; B. Gruley and J. Butler, "How China's 36th Best Car Company Saved Volvo," *Bloomberg Businessweek*, May 24, 2018.

Case Discussion Questions

1. Why did Geely acquire Volvo? What are the benefits of acquisition? What are the potential costs and risks?

2. The Volvo acquisition allowed Geely to grow its sales in China. Why might an acquisition have been preferred to simply licensing the brand and know-how from Volvo (assuming that was an option)?

3. Following the Volvo acquisition, Geely built a new, wholly owned factory to produce Volvo cars in the United States. Why was a direct investment strategy preferred to other ways of growing the U.S. market, such as through exporting or licensing the Volvo brand and designs to another producer?

4. What are the benefits of Geely's investment in South Carolina to the U.S. economy? What are the potential costs? Do you think it was in the interests of the United States to let this investment proceed?

Endnotes

1. United Nations, Conference on Trade and Development, Statistical Database, accessed July 2018, http://unctadstat.unctad.org.

2. World Trade Organization, *International Trade Statistics*, 2018 (Geneva: WTO, 2018); United Nations, *World Investment Report*, 2019.

3. United Nations, *World Investment Report, 2019.*

4. United Nations, *World Investment Report*, 2018 (New York and Geneva: United Nations, 2018).

5. Howard Silverblatt, *S&P 500 2017: Global Sales*, S&P Dow Jones Indices.

6. United Nations, Conference on Trade and Development, Statistical Database.

7. United Nations, Conference on Trade and Development, Statistical Database.

8. United Nations, Conference on Trade and Development, Statistical Database.

9. United Nations, *World Investment Report, 2018.*

10. American Enterprise Institute, Chinese Investments in the United States, archived online at http://www.aei.org/feature/china-tracker/.

11. United Nations, *World Investment Report, 2019.*

12. See D. J. Ravenscraft and F. M. Scherer, *Mergers, Selloffs and Economic Efficiency* (Washington, DC: Brookings Institution, 1987); A. Seth, K. P. Song, and R. R. Pettit, "Value Creation

and Destruction in Cross-Border Acquisitions," *Strategic Management Journal* 23 (2002), pp. 921–40; B. Ayber and A. Ficici, "Cross-Border Acquisitions and Firm Value," *Journal of International Business Studies*, 40 (2009), pp. 1317–38.

13. For example, see S. H. Hymer, *The International Operations of National Firms: A Study of Direct Foreign Investment* (Cambridge, MA: MIT Press, 1976); A. M. Rugman, *Inside the Multinationals: The Economics of Internal Markets* (New York: Columbia University Press, 1981); D. J. Teece, "Multinational Enterprise, Internal Governance, and Industrial Organization," *American Economic Review* 75 (May 1983), pp. 233–38; C. W. L. Hill and W. C. Kim, "Searching for a Dynamic Theory of the Multinational Enterprise: A Transaction Cost Model," *Strategic Management Journal* 9 (special issue, 1988), pp. 93–104; A. Verbeke, "The Evolutionary View of the MNE and the Future of Internalization Theory," *Journal of International Business Studies* 34 (2003), pp. 498–501; J. H. Dunning, "Some Antecedents of Internalization Theory," *Journal of International Business Studies* 34 (2003), pp. 108–28; A. H. Kirca, W. D. Fernandez, and S.K. Kundu, "An Empirical Analysis of Internalization Theory in Emerging Markets," *Journal of World Business* 51 (2016), pp. 628–40.

14. J. P. Womack, D. T. Jones, and D. Roos, *The Machine That Changed the World* (New York: Rawson Associates, 1990).

15. The argument is most often associated with F. T. Knickerbocker, *Oligopolistic Reaction and Multinational Enterprise* (Boston: Harvard Business School Press, 1973). See also K. Head, T. Mayer, and J. Ries, "Revisiting Oligopolistic Reaction: Are Decisions on Foreign Direct Investment Strategic Complements?" *Journal of Economics and Management Strategy* 11 (2002), pp. 453–72.

16. The studies are summarized in R. E. Caves, *Multinational Enterprise and Economic Analysis*, 2nd ed. (Cambridge, UK: Cambridge University Press, 1996).

17. See R. E. Caves, "Japanese Investment in the US: Lessons for the Economic Analysis of Foreign Investment," *The World Economy* 16 (1993), pp. 279–300; B. Kogut and S. J. Chang, "Technological Capabilities and Japanese Direct Investment in the United States," *Review of Economics and Statistics* 73 (1991), pp. 401–43; J. Anand and B. Kogut, "Technological Capabilities of Countries, Firm Rivalry, and Foreign Direct Investment," *Journal of International Business Studies*, 1997, pp. 445–65.

18. K. Ito and E. L. Rose, "Foreign Direct Investment Location Strategies in the Tire Industry," *Journal of International Business Studies* 33 (2002), pp. 593–602.

19. H. Haveman and L. Nonnemaker, "Competition in Multiple Geographical Markets," *Administrative Science Quarterly* 45 (2000), pp. 232–67; L. Fuentelsaz and J. Gomez, "Multipoint Competition, Strategic Similarity and Entry into Geographic Markets," *Strategic Management Journal* 27 (2006), pp. 447–57.

20. J. H. Dunning, *Explaining International Production* (London: Unwin Hyman, 1988); J. H. Dunning, "Reappraising the Eclectic Paradigm in an Age of Alliance Capital," in J. H. Dunning, ed., *The Eclectic Paradigm: A Framework for Synthesizing and Comparing Theories of International Business from Different Disciplines or Perspectives* (London: Palgrave McMillian, 2015).

21. P. Krugman, "Increasing Returns and Economic Geography," *Journal of Political Economy* 99, no. 3 (1991), pp. 483–99.

22. J. M. Shaver and F. Flyer, "Agglomeration Economies, Firm Heterogeneity, and Foreign Direct Investment in the United States," *Strategic Management Journal* 21 (2000), pp. 1175–93.

23. J. H. Dunning and R. Narula, "Transpacific Foreign Direct Investment and the Investment Development Path," *South Carolina Essays in International Business*, May 1995.

24. W. Shan and J. Song, "Foreign Direct Investment and the Sourcing of Technological Advantage: Evidence from the Biotechnology Industry," *Journal of International Business Studies*, 1997, pp. 267–84.

25. For some additional evidence, see L. E. Brouthers, K. D. Brouthers, and S. Warner, "Is Dunning's Eclectic Framework Descriptive or Normative?" *Journal of International Business Studies* 30 (1999), pp. 831–44.

26. For elaboration, see S. Hood and S. Young, *The Economics of the Multinational Enterprise* (London: Longman, 1979); P. M. Sweezy and H. Magdoff, "The Dynamics of U.S. Capitalism," *Monthly Review Press*, 1972.

27. For an example of this policy as practiced in China, see L. G. Branstetter and R. C. Freenstra, "Trade and Foreign Direct Investment in China: A Political Economy Approach," *Journal of International Economics* 58 (December 2002), pp. 335–58.

28. M. Itoh and K. Kiyono, "Foreign Trade and Direct Investment," in *Industrial Policy of Japan*, R. Komiya, M. Okuno, and K. Suzumura, eds. (Tokyo: Academic Press, 1988).

29. E. Borensztein and J. De Gregorio, "How Does Foreign Direct Investment Affect Economic Growth?" *Journal of International Economics* 45 (June 1998), pp. 115–35; X. J. Zhan and T. Ozawa, *Business Restructuring in Asia: Cross-Border M&As in Crisis Affected Countries* (Copenhagen: Copenhagen Business School, 2000); I. Costa, S. Robles, and R. de Queiroz, "Foreign Direct Investment and Technological Capabilities," *Research Policy* 31 (2002), pp. 1431–43; B. Potterie and F. Lichtenberg, "Does Foreign Direct Investment Transfer Technology across Borders?" *Review of Economics and Statistics* 83 (2001), pp. 490–97; K. Saggi, "Trade, Foreign Direct Investment and International Technology Transfer," *World Bank Research Observer* 17 (2002), pp. 191–235; W. N. W. Azman-Saini, A. Z. Baharumshah and S. Hook Law, "Foreign Direct Investment, Economic Freedom and Economic Growth: International Evidence," *Economic Modelling* 27 (2010), pp. 1079–89.

30. K. M. Moden, "Foreign Acquisitions of Swedish Companies: Effects on R&D and Productivity," Research Institute of International Economics, 1998, mimeo.

31. "Foreign Friends," *The Economist*, January 8, 2000, pp. 71–72.

32. A. Jack, "French Go into Overdrive to Win Investors," *Financial Times*, December 10, 1997, p. 6.

33. "Foreign Friends."

34. United Nations, *World Investment Report, 2014* (New York and Geneva: United Nations, 2014).

35. R. Ram and K. H. Zang, "Foreign Direct Investment and Economic Growth," *Economic Development and Cultural Change* 51 (2002), pp. 205–25.

36. United Nations, *World Investment Report, 2014.*

37. United Nations, *World Investment Report, 2000* (New York and Geneva: United Nations, 2000).

38. R. B. Reich, *The Work of Nations: Preparing Ourselves for the 21st Century* (New York: Knopf, 1991).

39. This idea has been articulated, although not quite in this form, by C. A. Bartlett and S. Ghoshal, *Managing across Borders: The Transnational Solution* (Boston: Harvard Business School Press, 1989).

40. P. Magnusson, "The Mexico Pact: Worth the Price?" *Business-Week*, May 27, 1991, pp. 32–35.

41. C. Johnston, "Political Risk Insurance," in *Assessing Corporate Political Risk*, D. M. Raddock, ed. (Totowa, NJ: Rowman & Littlefield, 1986).

42. M. Tolchin and S. Tolchin, *Buying into America: How Foreign Money Is Changing the Face of Our Nation* (New York: Times Books, 1988).

43. L. D. Qiu and Z. Tao, "Export, Foreign Direct Investment and Local Content Requirements," *Journal of Development Economics* 66 (October 2001), pp. 101–25.

44. See R. E. Caves, *Multinational Enterprise and Economic Analysis* (Cambridge, UK: Cambridge University Press, 1982); A. H. Kirca et al., "Firm-Specific Assets, Multinationality, and Financial Performance: A Meta-Analytic Review and Theoretical Integration," *Academy of Management Journal* 54 (2011), pp. 47–72.

45. For a good general introduction to negotiation strategy, see M. H. Bazerman and M. A. Neale, *Negotiating Rationally* (New York: Free Press, 1992); A. Dixit and B. Nalebuff, *Thinking Strategically: The Competitive Edge in Business, Politics, and Everyday Life* (New York: Norton, 1991); H. Raiffa, *The Art and Science of Negotiation* (Cambridge, MA: Harvard University Press, 1982).

Regional Economic Integration

9

LEARNING OBJECTIVES

After reading this chapter, you will be able to:

LO9-1   Describe the different levels of regional economic integration.

LO9-2   Understand the economic and political arguments for regional economic integration.

LO9-3   Understand the economic and political arguments against regional economic integration.

LO9-4   Explain the history, current scope, and future prospects of the world's most important regional economic agreements.

LO9-5   Understand the implications for management practice that are inherent in regional economic integration agreements.

The Cost of Brexit

OPENING CASE

On January 1, 1973, the United Kingdom joined the European Economic Community (as the European Union was known then). The belief was that by joining the Community, the UK would be able to strengthen its trading ties with other member states in Europe and enjoy substantial gains from trade, which would result in greater economic growth going forward. However, the decision was politically controversial, with many in the UK fearing that membership would limit the country's national sovereignty. A 1975 referendum reaffirmed Britain's commitment to staying in the Community, with 67 percent of the electorate voting in favor of continued membership.

Fast forward to June 2016, and the UK held another referendum on membership of the European Union. The core issue was the same as that which produced the 1975 referendum; a significant proportion of the country felt that membership of the EU was negatively impacting the country's national sovereignty. Flash points included (1) surging immigration from EU member states in Eastern Europe, such as Poland, and concerns that expansion of the EU to include Turkey would lead to even more immigration, (2) the growing power of the EU bureaucracy in Brussels, and (3) the inability of Britain to make its own trade deals while a member of the EU. Those who wanted to leave argued that Britain would be economically better off in the long run if it exited the EU. Those who wanted to remain argued that, by exiting, Britain would suffer substantial economic harm from the loss of easy access to the EU's large single market. In the end, the "leave" campaign won the referendum over "remain" by 51.89 percent of the vote to 48.11 percent. This narrow victory did little to ease political tensions in the country, but the ruling Conservative government, which itself was deeply split on the issue, now had to negotiate an exit deal with the EU.

Negotiating an exit deal that minimizes the economic dislocation of exit while satisfying those in the leave camp who want to quickly sever ties with the EU proved to be anything but easy. Facing political chaos, the country requested an extension beyond the original March 29, 2019 exit date in order to try and broker a deal that could pass muster in the UK Parliament. The EU agreed to extend the deadline until October 31, 2019, and then January 31st, 2020. Notwithstanding this, it has already become apparent that whatever the long-run impact is of exiting the EU, in the short run the uncertainty surrounding the form and timing of Brexit has already imposed economic harm on the UK economy.

One study from a Bank of England economist suggests that, since the referendum in June 2016, the cost to the UK has been running at £40 billion a year, which implies a loss of about 2 percent of GDP by the end of 2018 compared to where the country would have been. The study suggests that a primary reason for lower economic growth in the UK has been the stagnation of business investment due to the uncertainty surrounding Brexit. Of primary concern to many UK-based businesses is how their access to the EU's single market will be impacted by any Brexit deal, given that tariffs on exports to the EU rates might rise after Brexit.

Another estimate from economists at Standard & Poor's suggests that, by the end of 2018, the UK economy was around 3 percent smaller (a loss of £66 billion) than it would have been had the decision been to remain in the EU. The S&P team suggests that, in addition to lower business investment, a depreciation in the value of the British pound following the referendum contributed to higher inflation in the UK, which put a damper on household spending, depressing demand in the economy. The S&P study also noted that while currency depreciation would normally be expected to boost exports, no such effect was observed in the UK case. One explanation for this may be that businesses in other EU countries were unwilling to increase their purchases of UK goods and services, even at lower prices, given the uncertainty surrounding Brexit.

Looking forward, there is ample anecdotal evidence that many firms with substantial UK assets will move some production out of the country if the final Brexit deal is not to their liking and the country loses preferential access to the EU single market. Among those threatening to relocate facilities to mainland Europe or reduce UK investments are automakers Honda, Nissan, Land Rover, and Ford; the consumer electronics companies Sony and Panasonic; Dyson, the innovative British consumer products company; aircraft-maker Airbus; and banking giant J.P. Morgan.

Sources: R. Partington, "Cost of Brexit to UK Economy Running at £40 Billion a Year," *The Guardian*, February 15, 2019; Felix Todd, "From Dyson to JP Morgan, Here Are the Companies that Could Leave the UK After Brexit," *Compelo*, February 19, 2019; E. Nelson, "In an Alternative Universe Without Brexit, the UK Economy Is 3% Larger," *Quartz*, April 4, 2019; J. Edwards, "The Price of Brexit Has Been £66 Billion So Far, Plus an Impending Recession," *Business Insider*, April 7, 2019.

Introduction

The past two decades have witnessed a proliferation of regional trade blocs that promote **regional economic integration**. World Trade Organization (WTO) members are required to notify the WTO of any regional trade agreements in which they participate. By 2019, all members had notified the WTO of participation in one or more regional trade agreements. As of 2019, there were 294 regional trade agreements in force.[1]

Consistent with the predictions of international trade theory and particularly the theory of comparative advantage (see Chapter 6), agreements designed to promote freer trade within regions are believed by economists to produce gains from trade for all member countries. The General Agreement on Tariffs and Trade (GATT) and its successor, the World Trade Organization, also seek to reduce trade barriers. However, the WTO has a global perspective and 164 members, which can make reaching an agreement extremely difficult. By entering into regional agreements, groups of countries aim to reduce trade barriers more rapidly than can be achieved under the auspices of the WTO, thereby achieving greater gains from trade than allowed for under WTO rules. Establishing regional trade agreements has been an important policy approach in recent years due to the failure of the WTO to make any progress with its latest round of trade talks, the Doha Round, initiated in 2001 but currently in limbo (see Chapter 7). Given the failure of the Doha Round, national governments have felt that they can better advance their trade agenda through multilateral agreements than through the WTO.

Nowhere has the movement toward regional economic integration been more ambitious than in Europe. On January 1, 1993, the European Union formally removed many barriers to doing business across borders within the EU in an attempt to create a single market with 340 million consumers. Today, the EU has a population of more than 500 million and a gross domestic product of $18 trillion, making it second only to the United States in economic terms. That being said, the 2016 vote by the British to negotiate an exit from the EU (Brexit) has cast a cloud over the future of the European project. Moreover, as the opening case documents, some believe that Brexit will result in lower economic growth in the United Kingdom as British firms and consumers lose the benefits of belonging to the EU single market. Ironically, if this does occur, it will provide evidence in support of the gains from trade that are to be had by participating in a well-constructed regional trade agreement.

Similar moves toward regional integration are being pursued elsewhere in the world. Canada, Mexico, and the United States entered into the NAFTA on January 1, 1994. Ultimately, NAFTA aimed to remove all barriers to the free flow of goods and services among the three countries. While the implementation of NAFTA has resulted in job losses in some sectors of the U.S. economy, in aggregate and consistent with the predictions of international trade theory, most economists argue that the benefits of greater regional trade outweigh any costs. However, the administration of President Donald Trump criticized NAFTA, blaming it for significant job losses in the United States, and has negotiated a new agreement, known as the United States–Mexico–Canada Agreement (USMCA).

globalEDGE   REGIONAL TRADE AGREEMENTS

Regional economic integration is the focus of Chapter 9, and the value-added portion of globalEDGE™ that captures the ongoing development of major trade agreements worldwide is called "Regional Trade Agreements" **(globaledge.msu.edu/global-resources/regional-trade-agreements)**. In this section of globalEDGE™, the most critical agreements of the some 300 that exist today are included, with direct access to the home pages for each agreement. The landing page for "Regional Trade Agreements" also includes globalEDGE's own "Trade

Bloc Insights," which takes the user to a wealth of information and data (e.g., an overview of each agreement, its history, the countries included in the membership, related agreements, online resources, statistics, and an executive summary of what the agreement entails). In Chapter 9, we cover several of the trade agreements to provide an overview of the global marketplace. But which agreements are not covered in detail in the book, and which ones are covered on globalEDGE? What do you know, for example, about ECOWAS and SADC? How many members are in ECOWAS and SADC, respectively, and are any of these agreements overlapping? When were the treaties of ECOWAS and SADC started?

South America, too, has moved toward regional integration. For example, in 1991, Argentina, Brazil, Paraguay, and Uruguay implemented an agreement known as Mercosur to start reducing barriers to trade between each other, and although progress within Mercosur has been halting, the institution is still in place. There are also ongoing attempts at regional economic integration in Africa, where 26 countries signed an agreement to try and reduce tariffs and costly customs processes in order to stimulate economic growth in the region.

This chapter explores the economic and political debate surrounding regional economic integration, paying particular attention to the economic and political benefits and costs of integration; reviews progress toward regional economic integration around the world; and maps the important implications of regional economic integration for the practice of international business. We will discuss current developments that threatened the future of the EU, as well as the successor to NAFTA, the USCMA. Before tackling these objectives, we first need to examine the levels of integration that are theoretically possible.

Levels of Economic Integration

Several levels of economic integration are possible in theory (see Figure 9.1). From least integrated to most integrated, they are a free trade area, a customs union, a common market, an economic union, and, finally, a full political union.

LO9-1

Describe the different levels of regional economic integration.

FIGURE 9.1

Levels of economic integration.

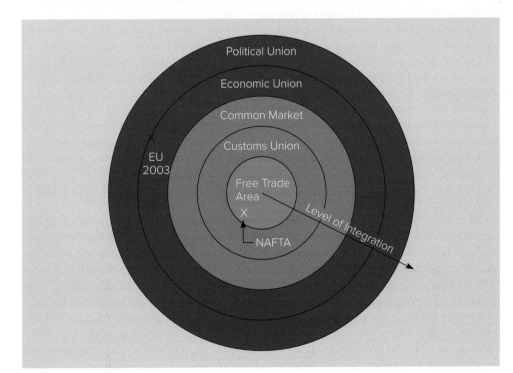

In a **free trade area**, all barriers to the trade of goods and services among member countries are removed. In the theoretically ideal free trade area, no discriminatory tariffs, quotas, subsidies, or administrative impediments are allowed to distort trade between members. Each country, however, is allowed to determine its own trade policies with regard to nonmembers. Thus, for example, the tariffs placed on the products of nonmember countries may vary from member to member. Free trade agreements are the most popular form of regional economic integration, accounting for almost 90 percent of regional agreements.[2]

The most enduring free trade area in the world is the **European Free Trade Association (EFTA)**. Established in January 1960, the EFTA currently joins four countries—Norway, Iceland, Liechtenstein, and Switzerland—down from seven in 1995 (three EFTA members—Austria, Finland, and Sweden—joined the EU on January 1, 1996). The EFTA was founded by those western European countries that initially decided not to be part of the European Community (the forerunner of the EU). Its original members included Austria, Great Britain, Denmark, Finland, and Sweden, all of which are now members of the EU. The emphasis of the EFTA has been on free trade in industrial goods. Agriculture was left out of the arrangement, each member being allowed to determine its own level of support. Members are also free to determine the level of protection applied to goods coming from outside the EFTA. Other free trade areas include the North American Free Trade Agreement (NAFTA) and its successor, the United States-Canada-Mexico Agreement (USCMA), which we discuss in depth later in the chapter.

The customs union is one step farther along the road to full economic and political integration. A **customs union** eliminates trade barriers between member countries and adopts a common external trade policy. Establishment of a common external trade policy necessitates significant administrative machinery to oversee trade relations with nonmembers. Most countries that enter into a customs union desire even greater economic integration down the road. The EU began as a customs union, but it has now moved beyond this stage. The current version of the Andean Community (formerly known as the Andean Pact) is a free trade area that includes Bolivia, Colombia, Ecuador, and Peru, and which aspires to be a customs union, but that so far has been imperfectly implemented. The Andean Community established free trade between member countries, and in theory imposes a common tariff of 5 to 20 percent on products imported from outside.[3]

The next level of economic integration, a **common market**, has no barriers to trade among member countries, includes a common external trade policy, and allows factors of production to move freely among members. Labor and capital are free to move because there are no restrictions on immigration, emigration, or cross-border flows of capital among member countries. Establishing a common market demands a significant degree of harmony and cooperation on fiscal, monetary, and employment policies. Achieving this degree of cooperation has proved very difficult. For years, the European Union functioned as a common market, although it has now moved beyond this stage. Mercosur—the South American grouping of Argentina, Brazil, Paraguay, and Uruguay—hopes to eventually establish itself as a common market. Venezuela was accepted as a full member of Mercosur, but then was indefinitely suspended from the group in December 2016 due to its undemocratic policies.

An economic union entails even closer economic integration and cooperation than a common market. Like the common market, an **economic union** involves the free flow of products and factors of production among member countries and the adoption of a common external trade policy, but it also requires a common currency, harmonization of members' tax rates, and a common monetary and fiscal policy. Such a high degree of integration demands a coordinating bureaucracy and the sacrifice of significant amounts of national sovereignty to that bureaucracy. The EU is an economic union, although an imperfect one because not all members of the EU have adopted the euro, the currency of the EU; differences in tax rates and regulations across countries still remain; and some markets, such as the market for energy, are still not fully deregulated.

The move toward economic union raises the issue of how to make a coordinating bureaucracy accountable to the citizens of member nations. The answer is through **political union** in which a central political apparatus coordinates the economic, social, and foreign policy of the member states. The EU is on the road toward at least partial political union. The European Parliament, which plays an important role in the EU, has been directly elected by citizens of the EU countries since the late 1970s. In addition, the Council of Ministers (the controlling, decision-making body of the EU) is composed of government ministers from each EU member. The United States provides an example of even closer political union; in the United States, independent states are effectively combined into a single nation.

TEST PREP

Use SmartBook to help retain what you have learned. Access your instructor's Connect course to check out SmartBook or go to **learnsmartadvantage.com** for help.

The Case for Regional Integration

LO9-2

Understand the economic and political arguments for regional economic integration.

The case for regional integration is both economic and political, and it is typically not accepted by many groups within a country, which explains why most attempts to achieve regional economic integration have been contentious and halting. In this section, we examine the economic and political cases for integration and discuss two impediments to integration. In the next section, we look at the case against integration.

THE ECONOMIC CASE FOR INTEGRATION

The economic case for regional integration is straightforward. We saw in Chapter 6 how economic theories of international trade predict that unrestricted free trade will allow countries to specialize in the production of goods and services that they can produce most efficiently. The result is greater world production than would be possible with trade restrictions. That chapter also revealed how opening a country to free trade stimulates economic growth, which creates dynamic gains from trade. Chapter 8 detailed how foreign direct investment (FDI) can transfer technological, marketing, and managerial know-how to host nations. Given the central role of knowledge in boosting economic growth, opening a country to FDI also is likely to stimulate economic growth. In sum, economic theories suggest that free trade and investment is a positive-sum game, in which all participating countries stand to gain.

Given this, the theoretical ideal is an absence of barriers to the free flow of goods, services, and factors of production among nations. However, as we saw in Chapters 7 and 8, a case can be made for government intervention in international trade and FDI. Because many governments have accepted part or all of the case for intervention, unrestricted free trade and FDI have proved to be only an ideal. Although international institutions such as the WTO have been moving the world toward a free trade regime, success has been less than total. In a world of many nations and many political ideologies, it is very difficult to get all countries to agree to a common set of rules.

Against this background, regional economic integration can be seen as an attempt to achieve additional gains from the free flow of trade and investment between countries beyond those attainable under global agreements such as the WTO. It is easier to establish a free trade and investment regime among a limited number of adjacent countries than among the world community. Coordination and policy harmonization problems are largely a function of the number of countries that seek agreement. The greater the number of countries involved, the more perspectives that must be reconciled, and the harder it will be to reach agreement. Thus, attempts at regional economic integration are motivated by a desire to exploit the gains from free trade and investment.

THE POLITICAL CASE FOR INTEGRATION

The political case for regional economic integration also has loomed large in several attempts to establish free trade areas, customs unions, and the like. Linking neighboring economies and making them increasingly dependent on each other creates incentives for political cooperation between the neighboring states and reduces the potential for violent conflict. In addition, by grouping their economies, the countries can enhance their political weight in the world.

These considerations underlay the 1957 establishment of the European Community (EC), the forerunner of the EU. Europe had suffered two devastating wars in the first half of the twentieth century, both arising out of the unbridled ambitions of nation-states. Those who have sought a united Europe have always had a desire to make another war in Europe unthinkable. Many Europeans also believed that after World War II, the European nation-states were no longer large enough to hold their own in world markets and politics. The need for a united Europe to deal with the United States and the politically alien Soviet Union loomed large in the minds of many of the EC's founders.[4] A long-standing joke in Europe is that the European Commission should erect a statue to Joseph Stalin, for without the aggressive policies of the former dictator of the old Soviet Union, the countries of western Europe may have lacked the incentive to cooperate and form the EC.

The establishment of NAFTA also had a political aspect to it. Many NAFTA supporters felt that the trade agreement would help promote democracy and economic growth in Mexico. This, they argued, would be good for the United States, since it would reduce the flow of illegal immigration from Mexico. In fact, illegal immigration from Mexico rose from 2.9 million in 1995 to almost 7 million in 2007. However, since then, the strong Mexican economy has indeed led to a reduction in illegal immigration from Mexico. By 2017 the number Mexican illegal immigrants living in the United States had fallen to 5.8 million.[5]

IMPEDIMENTS TO INTEGRATION

Despite the strong economic and political arguments in support, integration has never been easy to achieve or sustain for two main reasons. First, although economic integration aids the majority, it has its costs. While a nation as a whole may benefit significantly from a regional free trade agreement, certain groups will lose, at least in the short to medium term. Moving to a free trade regime can involve painful adjustments. Due to the establishment of NAFTA, some Canadian and U.S. workers in such industries as textiles—which employ low-cost, low-skilled labor—lost their jobs as Canadian and U.S. firms moved production to Mexico. The promise of significant net benefits to the Canadian and U.S. economies as a whole is little comfort to those who lose as a result of NAFTA. Such groups have been at the forefront of opposition to NAFTA and will continue to oppose any widening of the agreement.

A second impediment to integration arises from concerns over national sovereignty. For example, Mexico's concerns about maintaining control of its oil interests resulted in an agreement with Canada and the United States to exempt the Mexican oil industry from any liberalization of foreign investment regulations achieved under NAFTA. Concerns about national sovereignty arise because close economic integration demands that countries give up some degree of control over such key issues as monetary policy, fiscal policy (e.g., tax policy), and trade policy. This has been a major stumbling block in the EU. To achieve full economic union, the EU introduced a common currency, the euro, controlled by a central EU bank. Although most member states have signed on, Great Britain remained an important holdout. A politically important segment of public opinion in that country opposed a common currency on the grounds that it would require relinquishing control of the country's monetary policy to the EU, which many British perceive as a bureaucracy run by foreigners. In 1992, the British won the right to opt out of any single currency agreement. In 2016, the British held a referendum on their continuing membership of the EU and voted to leave the EU (discussed later in the chapter). Concerns over national sovereignty, particularly with regard to immigration policy, were the major factor persuading the British government that a referendum was necessary.

TEST PREP

Use SmartBook to help retain what you have learned. Access your instructor's Connect course to check out SmartBook or go to **learnsmartadvantage.com** for help.

The Case against Regional Integration

Although the tide has been running in favor of regional free trade agreements, some economists have expressed concern that the benefits of regional integration have been oversold, while the costs have often been ignored.[6] They point out that the benefits of regional integration are determined by the extent of trade creation, as opposed to trade diversion. **Trade creation** occurs when high-cost domestic producers are replaced by low-cost producers within the free trade area. It may also occur when higher-cost external producers are replaced by lower-cost external producers within the free trade area. **Trade diversion** occurs when lower-cost external suppliers are replaced by higher-cost suppliers within the free trade area. A regional free trade agreement will benefit the world only if the amount of trade it creates exceeds the amount it diverts.

Suppose the United States and Mexico imposed tariffs on imports from all countries and then set up a free trade area, scrapping all trade barriers between themselves but maintaining tariffs on imports from the rest of the world. If the United States began to import textiles from Mexico, would this change be for the better? If the United States previously produced all its own textiles at a higher cost than Mexico, then the free trade agreement has shifted production to the cheaper source. According to the theory of comparative advantage, trade has been created within the regional grouping, and there would be no decrease in trade with the rest of the world. Clearly, the change would be for the better. If, however, the United States previously imported textiles from Costa Rica, which produced them more cheaply than either Mexico or the United States, then trade has been diverted from a low-cost source—a change for the worse.

In theory, WTO rules should ensure that a free trade agreement does not result in trade diversion. These rules allow free trade areas to be formed only if the members set tariffs that are not higher or more restrictive to outsiders than the ones previously in effect. However, as we saw in Chapter 7, GATT and the WTO do not cover some nontariff barriers. As a result, regional trade blocs could emerge whose markets are protected from outside competition by high nontariff barriers. In such cases, the trade diversion effects might outweigh the trade creation effects. The only way to guard against this possibility, according to those concerned about this potential, is to increase the scope of the WTO so it covers nontariff barriers to trade. There is no sign that this is going to occur any time soon, however, so the risk remains that regional economic integration will result in trade diversion.

Regional Economic Integration in Europe

Europe has two trade blocs—the European Union and the European Free Trade Association. Of the two, the EU is by far the more significant, not just in terms of membership (the EU currently has 28 members, although the British have voted to exit the union; the EFTA has four), but also in terms of economic and political influence in the world economy. The EU has been viewed as an emerging economic and political superpower of the same order as the United States, although the exit of Britain may alter this perception. Accordingly, we will concentrate our attention on the EU.[7]

EVOLUTION OF THE EUROPEAN UNION

The **European Union (EU)** is the product of two political factors: (1) the devastation of western Europe during two world wars and the desire for a lasting peace and (2) the European nations' desire to hold their own on the world's political and economic stage. In addition, many Europeans were aware of the potential economic benefits of closer economic integration of the countries.

The forerunner of the EU, the European Coal and Steel Community, was formed in 1951 by Belgium, France, West Germany, Italy, Luxembourg, and the Netherlands. Its objective was to remove barriers to intragroup shipments of coal, iron, steel, and scrap metal.

LO9-3
Understand the economic and political arguments against regional economic integration.

TEST PREP

Use SmartBook to help retain what you have learned. Access your instructor's Connect course to check out SmartBook or go to **learnsmartadvantage.com** for help.

LO9-4
Explain the history, current scope, and future prospects of the world's most important regional economic agreements.

With the signing of the **Treaty of Rome** in 1957, the European Community (EC) was established. The name changed again in 1993 when the European Community became the European Union following the ratification of the Maastricht Treaty (discussed later).

The Treaty of Rome provided for the creation of a common market. Article 3 of the treaty laid down the key objectives of the new community, calling for the elimination of internal trade barriers and the creation of a common external tariff and requiring member states to abolish obstacles to the free movement of factors of production among the members. To facilitate the free movement of goods, services, and factors of production, the treaty provided for any necessary harmonization of the member states' laws. Furthermore, the treaty committed the EC to establish common policies in agriculture and transportation.

The community grew in 1973, when Great Britain, Ireland, and Denmark joined. These three were followed in 1981 by Greece; in 1986 by Spain and Portugal; and in 1995 by Austria, Finland, and Sweden—bringing the total membership to 15 (East Germany became part of the EC after the reunification of Germany in 1990). Another 10 countries joined the EU on May 1, 2004—eight of them from eastern Europe plus the small Mediterranean nations of Malta and Cyprus. Bulgaria and Romania joined in 2007 and Croatia in 2013, bringing the total number of member states to 28 (see Map 9.1). Through these

MAP 9.1

Member states of the European Union in 2019.

Source: European Union, 1995–2019.

enlargements, the EU has become a global economic power. The number of members will fall to 27 in 2020 assuming Britain exits the EU as planned on January 31, 2020.

POLITICAL STRUCTURE OF THE EUROPEAN UNION

The economic policies of the EU are formulated and implemented by a complex and still-evolving political structure. The four main institutions in this structure are the European Commission, the Council of the European Union, the European Parliament, and the Court of Justice.[8]

The **European Commission** is responsible for proposing EU legislation, implementing it, and monitoring compliance with EU laws by member states. Headquartered in Brussels, Belgium, it is run by a group of commissioners appointed by each member country for five-year renewable terms. There are 28 commissioners, one from each member state (there will be 27 assuming the UK exits). A president of the commission is chosen by member states, and the president then chooses other members in consultation with the states. The entire commission has to be approved by the European Parliament before it can begin work. The commission has a monopoly in proposing European Union legislation. The commission makes a proposal, which goes to the Council of the European Union and then to the European Parliament. The council cannot legislate without a commission proposal in front of it. The commission is also responsible for implementing aspects of EU law, although in practice much of this must be delegated to member states. Another responsibility of the commission is to monitor member states to make sure they are complying with EU laws. In this policing role, the commission will normally ask a state to comply with any EU laws that are being broken. If this persuasion is not sufficient, the commission can refer a case to the Court of Justice.

The European Commission's role in competition policy has become increasingly important to business in recent years. Since 1990, when the office was formally assigned a role in competition policy, the EU's competition commissioner has been steadily gaining influence as the chief regulator of competition policy in the member nations of the EU. As with antitrust authorities in the United States, which include the Federal Trade Commission and the Department of Justice, the role of the competition commissioner is to ensure that no one enterprise uses its market power to drive out competitors and monopolize markets. In 2009, for example, the commission fined Intel a record €1.06 billion for abusing its market power in the computer chip market. The previous record for a similar abuse was €497 million imposed on Microsoft in 2004 for blocking competition in markets for server computers and media software. In 2018, the EU imposed a €4.34 billion fine on Google for anticompetitive behavior. (See the accompanying Management Focus for details.)

The commissioner also reviews proposed mergers and acquisitions to make sure they do not create a dominant enterprise with substantial market power.[9] For example, in 2000 a proposed merger between Time Warner of the United States and EMI of the United Kingdom, both music recording companies, was withdrawn after the commission expressed concerns that the merger would reduce the number of major record companies from five to four and create a dominant player in the $40 billion global music industry.

The **European Council** represents the interests of member states. It is clearly the ultimate controlling authority within the EU because draft legislation from the commission can become EU law only if the council agrees. The council is composed of one representative from the government of each member state. The membership, however, varies depending on the topic being discussed. When agricultural issues are being discussed, the agriculture ministers from each state attend council meetings; when transportation is being discussed, transportation ministers attend; and so on. Before 1987, all council issues had to be decided by unanimous agreement among member states. This often led to marathon council sessions and a failure to make progress or reach agreement on commission proposals. In an attempt to clear the resulting logjams, the Single European Act formalized the use of majority voting rules on issues "which have as their object the establishment and functioning of a single market." Most other issues, however, such as tax regulations

The European Commission and Google

In June 2018, the European Commission announced that it had imposed a record €4.3 billion fine on Google for anti-competitive behavior (just over $5 billion). The antitrust case against Google involved Android, the mobile phone operating system created by Google, and all sorts of related software, including Google Play, its app store, a suite of other apps, and most significantly, Google's internet search engine.

Android is the dominant mobile phone operating system in the EU with a market share of over 70 percent (Apple's iOS operating system has much of the rest). Moreover, the Google search engine completely dominates the EU market with a 97 percent share. For smartphone makers and telecom operators, Android's dominance makes Android a must-have operating system. According to the Commission, Google used its Android dominance to give smartphone makers and telecom operators an all-or-nothing choice: If they want to install any of Google's programs on an Android device, they have to install them all and show the icons in prominent positions. Because these firms have to, at a minimum, install the app store application to make their phone viable, they effectively have no choice but to comply with Google's demands—meaning they have to install Google's internet search engine app in a prominent position, whether they want to or not.

The Commission believes that this bundling practice denies producers of rival programs "the chance to innovate and compete on the merits" and "consumers the benefits of effective competition." Put differently, the aim of the all or nothing choice is to protect Google's programs, and most notably its dominant search engine, from competition.

The Commission has left it to Google to comply with its findings, requiring that the company rectify its infringements by ending the all-or-nothing choice. In theory, this will give rivals a better chance of selling their own apps for Android that might compete with Google's internet search app, Google play, Google Docs, and the like. If Google does not comply, the Commission has indicated it will impose further fines on Google, amounting to up to 5 percent of the daily worldwide revenue of Alphabet, Google's parent.

Sources: "Google Is Fined €4.3bn in the Biggest Ever Antitrust Penalty," *The Economist*, July 21, 2018; "Antitrust: Commission Fines Google €4.3 Billion for Illegal Practices Regarding Android Mobile Devices to Strengthen Dominance of Google's Search Engine," European Commission Press Release, July 18, 2018.

and immigration policy, still require unanimity among council members if they are to become law. The votes that a country gets in the council are related to the size of the country. For example, Germany, a large country, has 29 votes, whereas Denmark, a much smaller state, has seven votes.

As of early 2019, the **European Parliament** has 751 members and is directly elected by the populations of the member states. The parliament, which meets in Strasbourg, France, is primarily a consultative rather than legislative body. It debates legislation proposed by the commission and forwarded to it by the council. It can propose amendments to that legislation, which the commission and ultimately the council are not obliged to take up but often will. The power of the parliament recently has been increasing, although not by as much as parliamentarians would like. The European Parliament now has the right to vote on the appointment of commissioners as well as veto some laws (such as the EU budget and single-market legislation).

One major debate waged in Europe during the past few years is whether the council or the parliament should ultimately be the most powerful body in the EU. Some in Europe expressed concern over the democratic accountability of the EU bureaucracy. One side argued that the answer to this apparent democratic deficit lay in increasing the power of the parliament, while others think that true democratic legitimacy lies with elected governments, acting through the Council of the European Union.[10] After significant debate, in December 2007, the member states signed a new treaty, the **Treaty of Lisbon**, under which the power of the European Parliament was increased. When it took effect in December 2009, for the first time in history the European Parliament was the co-equal legislator for almost all European laws.[11] The Treaty of Lisbon also created a new position, a president of the European Council, who serves a 30-month term and represents the nation-states that make up the EU.

The **Court of Justice**, which is composed of one judge from each country, is the supreme appeals court for EU law. Like commissioners, the judges are required to act as independent officials, rather than as representatives of national interests. The commission or a member country can bring other members to the court for failing to meet treaty obligations. Similarly, member countries, member companies, or member institutions can bring the commission or council to the court for failure to act according to an EU treaty.

THE SINGLE EUROPEAN ACT

The Single European Act was born of a frustration among members that the community was not living up to its promise. By the early 1980s, it was clear that the EC had fallen short of its objectives to remove barriers to the free flow of trade and investment among member countries and to harmonize the wide range of technical and legal standards for doing business. Against this background, many of the EC's prominent businesspeople mounted an energetic campaign in the early 1980s to end the EC's economic divisions. The EC responded by creating the Delors Commission. Under the chairperson Jacques Delors, the commission proposed that all impediments to the formation of a single market be eliminated by December 31, 1992. The result was the Single European Act, which became EC law in 1987.

The Objectives of the Act

The purpose of the Single European Act was to have one market in place by December 31, 1992. The act proposed the following changes:[12]

- Remove all frontier controls among EC countries, thereby abolishing delays and reducing the resources required for complying with trade bureaucracy.

- Apply the principle of "mutual recognition" to product standards. A standard developed in one EC country should be accepted in another, provided it met basic requirements in such matters as health and safety.

- Institute open public procurement to nonnational suppliers, reducing costs directly by allowing lower-cost suppliers into national economies and indirectly by forcing national suppliers to compete.

- Lift barriers to competition in the retail banking and insurance businesses, which should drive down the costs of financial services, including borrowing, throughout the EC.

- Remove all restrictions on foreign exchange transactions between member countries by the end of 1992.

- Abolish restrictions on cabotage—the right of foreign truckers to pick up and deliver goods within another member state's borders—by the end of 1992. Estimates suggested this would reduce the cost of haulage within the EC by 10 to 15 percent.

All those changes were expected to lower the costs of doing business in the EC, but the single-market program was also expected to have more complicated supply-side effects. For example, the expanded market was predicted to give EC firms greater opportunities to exploit economies of scale. In addition, it was thought that the increase in competitive intensity brought about by removing internal barriers to trade and investment would force EC firms to become more efficient. To signify the importance of the Single European Act, the European Community also decided to change its name to the European Union once the act took effect.

Impact

The Single European Act has had an impact on the EU economy.[13] The act provided the impetus for the restructuring of substantial sections of European industry. Many firms have shifted from national to pan-European production and distribution systems in an attempt to realize scale economies and better compete in a single market. The results have included faster economic growth than would otherwise have been the case. According to empirical research, the single market raised GDP by between 2 and 5 percent in its first 15 years (different empirical studies generated different results, although all pointed to a positive impact).[14] However, more than a quarter of a century after the formation of a single market, there is little doubt that the reality still falls short of the ideal. Although the EU is undoubtedly moving toward a single marketplace, long-established legal, cultural, and language differences among nations mean that implementation has been uneven.

THE ESTABLISHMENT OF THE EURO

In February 1992, EC members signed the **Maastricht Treaty**, which committed them to adopting a common currency by January 1, 1999.[15] The euro is now used by 19 of the member states of the European Union; these 19 states are members of what is often referred to as the *euro zone*. It encompasses 330 million EU citizens and includes the powerful economies of Germany and France. Many of the countries that joined the EU on May 1, 2004, and the two that joined in 2007 originally planned to adopt the euro when they fulfilled certain economic criteria—a high degree of price stability, a sound fiscal situation, stable exchange rates, and converged long-term interest rates (the current members had to meet the same criteria). However, the events surrounding the EU sovereign debt crisis of 2010–2012 persuaded many of these countries to put their plans on hold, at least for the time being (further details provided later).

Establishment of the euro was a remarkable political feat with few historical precedents. It required participating national governments to give up their own currencies and national control over monetary policy. Governments do not routinely sacrifice national sovereignty for the greater good, indicating the importance that the Europeans attach to the euro. By adopting the euro, the EU has created the second most widely traded currency in the world after the U.S. dollar. Some believe that the euro could come to rival the dollar as the most important currency in the world.

Three long-term EU members—Great Britain, Denmark, and Sweden—decided to sit on the sidelines. The countries agreeing to the euro locked their exchange rates against each other January 1, 1999. Euro notes and coins were not actually issued until January 1, 2002. In the interim, national currencies circulated in each participating state. However, in each country, the national currency stood for a defined amount of euros. After January 1, 2002, euro notes and coins were issued and the national currencies were taken out of circulation. By mid-2002, all prices and routine economic transactions within the euro zone were in euros.

Benefits of the Euro

Europeans decided to establish a single currency in the EU for a number of reasons. First, they believe that businesses and individuals realize significant savings from having to handle one currency, rather than many. These savings come from lower foreign exchange and hedging costs. For example, people going from Germany to France no longer have to pay a commission to a bank to change German deutsche marks into French francs. Instead, they are able to use euros. According to the European Commission, such savings amount to 0.5 percent of the European Union's GDP.

Second, and perhaps more important, the adoption of a common currency makes it easier to compare prices across Europe. This has been increasing competition because it has become easier for consumers to shop around. For example, if a German finds that cars sell for less in France than Germany, he may be tempted to purchase from a French car dealer rather than his local car dealer. Alternatively, traders may engage in arbitrage to exploit such price differentials, buying cars in France and reselling them in Germany. The only way that German car dealers will be able to hold onto business in the face of such competitive pressures will be to reduce the prices they charge for cars. As a consequence of such pressures, the introduction of a common currency has led to lower prices, which translates into substantial gains for European consumers.

Third, faced with lower prices, European producers have been forced to look for ways to reduce their production costs to maintain their profit margins. The introduction of a common currency, by increasing competition, has produced long-run gains in the economic efficiency of European companies.

Fourth, the introduction of a common currency has given a boost to the development of a highly liquid pan-European capital market. Over time, the development of such a capital market should lower the cost of capital and lead to an increase in both the level of investment and the efficiency with which investment funds are allocated. This could be especially helpful to smaller companies that have historically had difficulty borrowing money from domestic banks. For example, the capital market of Portugal is very small and illiquid, which makes it extremely difficult for bright Portuguese entrepreneurs with a good idea to borrow money at a reasonable price. However, in theory, such companies can now tap a much more liquid pan-European capital market.

Finally, the development of a pan-European, euro-denominated capital market will increase the range of investment options open to both individuals and institutions. For example, it will now be much easier for individuals and institutions based in, let's say, Holland to invest in Italian or French companies. This will enable European investors to better diversify their risk, which again lowers the cost of capital, and should also increase the efficiency with which capital resources are allocated.[16]

Costs of the Euro

The drawback, for some, of a single currency is that national authorities have lost control over monetary policy. Thus, it is crucial to ensure that the EU's monetary policy is well managed. The Maastricht Treaty called for establishment of the independent European Central Bank (ECB), similar in some respects to the U.S. Federal Reserve, with a clear mandate to manage monetary policy so as to ensure price stability. The ECB, based in Frankfurt, is meant to be independent from political pressure—although critics question this. Among other things, the ECB sets interest rates and determines monetary policy across the euro zone.

The implied loss of national sovereignty to the ECB underlies the decision by Great Britain, Denmark, and Sweden to stay out of the euro zone. Many in these countries are suspicious of the ECB's ability to remain free from political pressure and to keep inflation under tight control.

In theory, the design of the ECB should ensure that it remains free of political pressure. The ECB is modeled on the German Bundesbank, which historically has been the most independent and successful central bank in Europe. The Maastricht Treaty prohibits the ECB from taking orders from politicians. The executive board of the bank, which consists of a president, vice president, and four other members, carries out policy by issuing instructions to national central banks. The policy itself is determined by the governing council, which consists of the executive board plus the central bank governors from the euro zone countries. The governing council votes on interest rate changes. Members of the executive board are appointed for eight-year nonrenewable terms, insulating them from political pressures to get reappointed. So far, the ECB has established a solid reputation for political independence.

According to critics, another drawback of the euro is that the EU is not what economists would call an optimal currency area. In an **optimal currency area**, similarities in the underlying structure of economic activity make it feasible to adopt a single currency and use a single exchange rate as an instrument of macroeconomic policy. Many of the European economies in the euro zone, however, are very dissimilar. For example, Finland and Portugal have different wage rates, tax regimes, and business cycles, and they may react very differently to external economic shocks. A change in the euro exchange rate that helps Finland may hurt Portugal. Obviously, such differences complicate macroeconomic policy. For example, when euro economies are not growing in unison, a common monetary policy may mean that interest rates are too high for depressed regions and too low for booming regions.

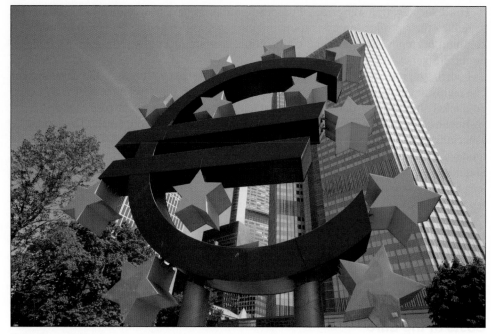

Euro sign sculpture.

Martin Leissl/Bloomberg/Getty Images

One way of dealing with such divergent effects within the euro zone is for the EU to engage in fiscal transfers, taking money from prosperous regions and pumping it into depressed regions. Such a move, however, opens a political can of worms. Would the citizens of Germany forgo their "fair share" of EU funds to create jobs for underemployed Greece workers? Not surprisingly, there is strong political opposition to such practices.

The Euro Experience

Since its establishment January 1, 1999, the euro has had a volatile trading history against the world's major currency, the U.S. dollar. After starting life in 1999 at €1 = $1.17, the euro stood at a robust all-time high of €1 = $1.54 in early March 2008. One reason for the rise in the value of the euro was that the flow of capital into the United States stalled as the U.S. financial markets fell during 2007 and 2008. Many investors took money out of the United States, selling dollar-denominated assets such as U.S. stocks and bonds, and purchasing euro-denominated assets. Falling demand for U.S. dollars and rising demand for euros translated into a fall in the value of the dollar against the euro. Furthermore, in a vote of confidence in both the euro and the ability of the ECB to manage monetary policy within the euro zone, many foreign central banks added more euros to their supply of foreign currencies. In the first three years of its life, the euro never reached the 13 percent of global reserves made up by the deutsche mark and other former euro zone currencies. The euro didn't jump that hurdle until early 2002 and hit 28 percent in 2009. By the end of 2018, the euro accounted for about 20 percent of global foreign exchange reserves.[17]

Since 2008 however, the euro has weakened against a basket of currencies, reflecting persistent concerns over slow economic growth and large budget deficits among several EU member states, particularly Greece, Portugal, Ireland, Italy, and Spain. During the 2000s, all these governments had sharply increased their government debt to finance public spending. Government debt as a percentage of GDP hit record levels in many of these nations. By 2010, private investors became increasingly concerned that these nations would not be able to service their sovereign debt, particularly given the economic slowdown following the 2008–2009 global financial crisis. They sold off government bonds of troubled nations, driving down bond prices and driving up the cost of government borrowing (bond prices and interest rates are inversely related). This led to fears that several national governments, particularly Greece, might default on their sovereign debt, plunging the euro zone into an economic crisis.

To try to stave off such a sovereign debt crisis, in May 2010, the euro zone nations and the International Monetary Fund (IMF) agreed to a €110 billion bailout package to help rescue Greece. In November 2010, the EU and IMF agreed to a bailout package for Ireland of €85 billion; in May 2011, euro zone countries and the IMF instituted a €78 billion bailout plan for Portugal. In return for these loans, all three countries had to agree to sharp reductions in government spending, which meant slower economic growth and high unemployment until government debt was reduced to more sustainable levels. While Italy and Spain did not request bailout packages, both countries were forced by falling bond prices to institute austerity programs that required big reductions in government spending. The euro zone nations also set up a permanent bailout fund—the European Stability Mechanism—worth about €500 billion, which was designed to restore confidence in the euro. As detailed in the accompanying Country Focus, by 2015 Greece had been granted three more bailout packages in an attempt to forestall a full-blown default on payment of its sovereign debt. As might be expected, economic turmoil within the EU led to a decline in the value of the euro. By early 2019, the dollar–euro exchange rate stood at €1 = $1.13, significantly below its 2008 value. The euro also declined against most of the world's other major currencies between late 2008 and early 2019, primary due to relatively slow economic growth in the EU.

Potentially troubling for the long-run success of the euro, many of the newer EU nations that had committed to adopting the euro put their plans on hold. Countries like Poland and the Czech Republic had no desire to join the euro zone and then have their taxpayers help bail out the profligate governments of countries like Italy and Greece. To compound matters, the sovereign debt crisis had exposed a deep flaw in the euro zone: It was difficult for fiscally more conservative nations like Germany to limit profligate spending by the governments of other nations that might subsequently create strains and impose costs on the entire euro zone. The Germans in particular found themselves in the unhappy position of having to underwrite loans to bail out the governments of Greece, Portugal, and Ireland. This started to erode support for the euro in the stronger EU states. To try to correct this flaw, 25 of the then 27 countries in the EU signed a fiscal pact in January 2012 that made it more difficult for member states to break tight new rules on government deficits (the United Kingdom and Czech Republic abstained; Croatia joined in 2013).

ENLARGEMENT OF THE EUROPEAN UNION

Enlargement of the EU into eastern Europe has been discussed since the collapse of communism at the end of the 1980s. By the end of the 1990s, 13 countries had applied to become EU members. To qualify for EU membership, the applicants had to privatize state assets, deregulate markets, restructure industries, and tame inflation. They also had to enshrine complex EU laws into their own systems, establish stable democratic governments, and respect human rights.[18] In December 2002, the EU formally agreed to accept the applications of 10 countries, and they joined May 1, 2004. The new members included the Baltic countries, the Czech Republic, and the larger nations of Hungary and Poland. The only new members not in eastern Europe were the Mediterranean island nations of Malta and Cyprus. Their inclusion in the EU expanded the union to 25 states, stretching from the Atlantic to the borders of Russia; added 23 percent to the landmass of the EU; brought 75 million new citizens into the EU, building an EU with a population of 450 million people; and created a single continental economy with a GDP of close to €11 trillion. In 2007, Bulgaria and Romania joined, and in 2013, Croatia joined, bringing total membership to 28 nations.

Welcome sign to Croatia when the country joined the European Union.

Frederick Florin/AFP/Getty Images

The Greek Sovereign Debt Crisis

When the euro was established, some critics worried that free-spending countries in the euro zone (such as Italy and Greece) might borrow excessively, running up large public-sector deficits that they could not finance. This would then rock the value of the euro, requiring their more sober brethren, such as Germany or France, to step in and bail out the profligate nation. In 2010, this worry became a reality as a financial crisis in Greece hit the value of the euro.

The financial crisis had its roots in a decade of free spending by the Greek government, which ran up a high level of debt to finance extensive spending in the public sector. Much of the spending increase could be characterized as an attempt by the government to buy off powerful interest groups in Greek society, from teachers and farmers to public-sector employees, rewarding them with high pay and extensive benefits. To make matters worse, the government misled the international community about the level of its indebtedness. In October 2009, a new government took power and quickly announced that the 2009 public-sector deficit, which had been projected to be around 5 percent, would actually be 12.7 percent. The previous government had apparently been cooking the books.

This shattered any faith that international investors might have had in the Greek economy. Interest rates on Greek government debt quickly surged to 7.1 percent,

about 4 percentage points higher than the rate on German bonds. Two of the three international rating agencies also cut their ratings on Greek bonds and warned that further downgrades were likely. The main concern now was that the Greek government might not be able to refinance some €20 billion of debt that would mature in April or May 2010. A further concern was that the Greek government might lack the political willpower to make the large cuts in public spending necessary to bring down the deficit and restore investor confidence.

Nor was Greece alone in having large public-sector deficits. Three other euro zone countries—Spain, Portugal, and Ireland—also had large debt loads, and interest rates on their bonds surged as investors sold out. This raised the specter of financial contagion, with large-scale defaults among the weaker members of the euro zone. If this did occur, the EU and IMF would most certainly have to step in and rescue the troubled nations. With this possibility, once considered very remote, investors started to move money out of euros, and the value of the euro started to fall on the foreign exchange market.

Recognizing that the unthinkable might happen—and that without external help, Greece might default on its government debt, pushing the EU and the euro into a major crisis—in May 2010, the euro zone countries, led by Germany, along with the IMF agreed to lend Greece up to

The new members were not able to adopt the euro for several years, and free movement of labor among the new and existing members was prohibited until then. Consistent with theories of free trade, the enlargement should create added benefits for all members. However, given the small size of the eastern European economies (together they amount to only 5 percent of the GDP of current EU members), the initial impact will probably be small. The biggest notable change might be in the EU bureaucracy and decision-making processes, where budget negotiations among 28 nations (27 post Brexit) are more problematic than negotiations among 15 nations.

Left standing at the door is Turkey. Turkey, which has long lobbied to join the union, presents the EU with some difficult issues. The country has had a customs union with the EU since 1995, and about half its international trade is already with the EU. However, full membership has been denied because of concerns over human rights issues (particularly Turkish policies toward its Kurdish minority). In addition, some on the Turkish side suspect the EU is not eager to let a primarily Muslim nation of 74 million people, which has one foot in Asia, join the EU. The EU formally indicated in December 2002 that it would allow the Turkish application to proceed with no further delay in December 2004 if the country improved its human rights record to the satisfaction of the EU. In

€110 billion. These loans were judged sufficient to cover Greece's financing needs for three years. In exchange, the Greek government agreed to implement a series of strict austerity measures. These included tax increases, major cuts in public-sector pay, reductions in benefits enjoyed by public-sector employees (e.g., the retirement age was increased to 65 from 61, and limits were placed on pensions), and reductions in the number of public-sector enterprises from 6,000 to 2,000. However, the Greek economy contracted so fast in 2010 and 2011 that tax revenues plunged. By the end of 2011, the Greek economy was almost 29 percent smaller than it had been in 2005, while unemployment approached 20 percent. The contracting tax base limited the ability of the government to pay down debt. By early 2012, yields on 10-year Greek government debt reached 34 percent, indicating that many investors now expected Greece to default on its sovereign debt. This forced the Greek government to seek further aid from the euro zone countries and the IMF. As a condition for a fresh €130 billion bailout plan, the Greek government had to get holders of Greek government bonds to agree to the biggest sovereign debt restructuring in history, In effect, bondholders agreed to write off 53.5 percent of the debt they held.

While the Greek government did not technically default on its sovereign debt, to many it seemed as if the EU and IMF had orchestrated an orderly partial default. By early 2014, it looked as if the Greek economy had finally turned a corner and was on the way to recovery. Yields on 10-year bonds had fallen below 8 percent, and the government was running a budget surplus before interest payments.

Unfortunately, things took a turn for the worse in 2014, when it became clear that despite economic progress, Greece did not have the funds to repay its creditors on time and would have to issue new bonds in order to do so. Following a decision to call a snap election, in January 2015, a radical left-wing "anti-bailout" party was swept into power. The financial minister of the new government suggested that Greece should default on its scheduled debt repayments to its largest creditor, Germany. This initiated a crisis in the euro zone and helped precipitate a sharp decline in the value of the euro against the U.S. dollar.

Following further negotiations, Greece's creditors agreed to a third bailout in late 2015—but only after Greece agreed to implement further austerity measures and economic reforms. Greece received its final loan from creditors under this bailout in August 2018. The country now owes the EU and the IMF roughly €290 billion. To finance this debt, Greece has agreed to run a budget surplus through 2060, accept continued EU supervision, and impose additional austerity measures. Although the Greek economy is now growing again, unemployment remains the highest in the EU at 20 percent, and the IMF believes that the Greek economy, which has shrunk by 25 percent since the beginning of the crisis, will likely require further debt relief.

Sources: "A Very European Crisis," *The Economist*, February 6, 2010, pp. 75–77; L. Thomas, "Is Debt Trashing the Euro?" *The New York Times*, February 7, 2010, pp. 1, 7; "Bite the Bullet," *The Economist*, January 15, 2011, pp. 77–79; "The Wait Is Over," *The Economist*, March 17, 2012, pp. 83–84; "Aegean Stables," *The Economist*, January 11, 2014; Liz Alderman, "Greece's Debt Crisis Explained," *The New York Times*, November 8, 2015; Liz Alderman, "Europe Says Greece Is a Comeback Story. The IMF Isn't Convinced," *The New York Times*, July 31, 2018.

December 2004, the EU agreed to allow Turkey to start accession talks in October 2005, but in late 2016, the European Parliament voted to suspend negotiations following Turkish government purges of opposition groups and a belief that Turkey was tilting towards authoritarianism.

BRITISH EXIT FROM THE EUROPEAN UNION (BREXIT)

On June 23, 2016, and by a narrow margin, the British electorate voted in a national referendum to leave the EU. In early 2017, the British government formally notified the EU of its intention to exit the EU. Under the Treaty of Lisbon, it had two years to negotiate the terms of exit with the EU, which was scheduled to occur on March 29, 2019. As this date approached, with no clear exit deal on the table and political turmoil in Britain over the terms of exit, the British government asked for an extension. The EU granted an extension until January 31, 2020. Following a December 2019 general election victory by the pro Brexit Conservative Party led by Prime Minister Boris Johnson, Brexit is now a certainty. After exiting on January 31st, 2020, the British will have until December 20, 2020 to negotiate a trade deal with the EU. In the interim, much of the relationship between Britain and the EU will remain the same while Britain and the EU work out specifics on trade, security cooperation, and a range of other details.

While the British have enjoyed the benefits of free trade within Europe, a segment of the population has never been comfortable with the loss of national sovereignty implied by membership within the EU. The British have often railed against regulations imposed by the EU bureaucracy in Brussels, and more recently, immigration has become a key issue. Immigration from within the EU hit record levels in 2015. Much of that immigration has been from eastern Europe. Many of the immigrants have been low skilled and work in restaurants, hotels, and retail stores. The campaign for leaving the EU claimed that exit would allow the British to "take back control" of immigration. In the referendum, London, Scotland, and Northern Ireland voted to stay in the EU, whereas most of the rest of the country voted for exit. The vote was also split by age and education. The younger and more educated voted to stay in the EU, while the older and less educated voted to leave.

The impending exit of Britain creates an existential problem for the EU. Britain is the EU's second-largest national economy. It is seen by many smaller member countries as an important counterweight to the economic power of Germany. In the aftermath of the British vote, right-wing politicians in Holland, Denmark, and France also called for referendums on continuing EU membership, raising fears that the British vote might trigger a "rush for the exits." While this seems unlikely to occur, there is little doubt that an EU without Britain will lose some of its economic and political clout on the world stage, and the EU itself will be diminished. Given the importance of immigration in the British vote, further expansion of the EU now seems unlikely, particularly with regard to Turkey.

As for Britain, most experts predict that the country will bear short- to medium-term costs as a result of this decision (see the opening case for further details).[19] Britain is now less likely to attract inward investment from foreign multinationals, some multinationals may move operations to other EU countries to maintain access to the single market, exports to the EU may fall, London risks losing its position as the financial capital of Europe, and economic growth may be lower than it otherwise might have been. Furthermore, given that the Scots voted by a large margin to stay in the EU, this once again raises the possibility of Scottish independence from the United Kingdom. In the long run, whether Britain benefits from exit depends on its ability to negotiate trade deals with the EU and other major economic powers—including the United States, Japan, and China—to replace the benefits it will lose by exiting from the EU. In a world that is becoming increasingly resistant to free trade deals, there is no guarantee that the British will be able to do this. The British government would certainly like to extract favorable trade terms with the EU as part of its exit negotiations, but the EU is likely to insist that in order to get full access to the single market, the British adopt EU regulations permitting the free movement of labor. This is something that the British are unlikely to accept given how important an issue immigration was in the referendum.

TEST PREP

Use SmartBook to help retain what you have learned. Access your instructor's Connect course to check out SmartBook or go to **learnsmartadvantage.com** for help.

Regional Economic Integration in the Americas

No other attempt at regional economic integration comes close to the EU in its boldness or its potential implications for the world economy, but there have been significant attempts at regional economic integration in the Americas. The most notable is the North American Free Trade Agreement, which at the time of writing is in the process of being superseded by the USMCA. In addition to NAFTA, several other trade blocs are in the offing in the Americas (see Map 9.2), the most significant of which appear to be the Andean Community and Mercosur.

THE NORTH AMERICAN FREE TRADE AGREEMENT

The governments of the United States and Canada in 1988 agreed to enter into a free trade agreement, which took effect January 1, 1989. The goal of the agreement was to eliminate all tariffs on bilateral trade between Canada and the United States by 1998. This was followed in 1991 by talks among the United States, Canada, and Mexico aimed at establishing a **North American Free Trade Agreement (NAFTA)** for the three countries. The talks concluded in August 1992 with an agreement in principle, and the following year, the agreement was ratified by the governments of all three countries. The agreement became law January 1, 1994.[20]

MAP 9.2

Economic integration in the Americas.

Continental Commerce
- NAFTA/UCMCA
- Mercosur
- Andean Community
- Central America
- Caribbean Community

Scale: 1 to 174,385,000

NAFTA'S Contents

The contents of NAFTA include the following:

- Abolition by 2004 of tariffs on 99 percent of the goods traded among Mexico, Canada, and the United States.

- Removal of most barriers on the cross-border flow of services, allowing financial institutions, for example, unrestricted access to the Mexican market by 2000.

- Protection of intellectual property rights.

- Removal of most restrictions on foreign direct investment among the three member countries, although special treatment (protection) will be given to Mexican energy and railway industries, American airline and radio communications industries, and Canadian culture.

- Application of national environmental standards, provided such standards have a scientific basis. Lowering of standards to lure investment is described as being inappropriate.

- Establishment of two commissions with the power to impose fines and remove trade privileges when environmental standards or legislation involving health and safety, minimum wages, or child labor are ignored.

The Case for NAFTA

Proponents of NAFTA have argued that the free trade area should be viewed as an opportunity to create an enlarged and more efficient productive base for the entire region. Advocates acknowledge that one effect of NAFTA would be that some U.S. and Canadian firms would move production to Mexico to take advantage of lower labor costs. (In 2015, the average hourly labor cost in Mexican automobile factories was $8–$10 an hour including benefits, compared to $42–$58 an hour in the United States.[21]) Movement of production to Mexico, they argued, was most likely to occur in lower-skilled, labor-intensive manufacturing industries in which Mexico might have a comparative advantage. Advocates of NAFTA argued that many would benefit from such a trend. Mexico would benefit from much-needed inward investment and employment. The United States and Canada would benefit because the increased incomes of the Mexicans would allow them to import more U.S. and Canadian goods, thereby increasing demand and making up for the jobs lost in industries that moved production to Mexico. U.S. and Canadian consumers would benefit from the lower prices of products made in Mexico. In addition, the international competitiveness of U.S. and Canadian firms that moved production to Mexico to take advantage of lower labor costs would be enhanced, enabling them to better compete with Asian and European rivals.

▶ Did You Know?

Did you know that NAFTA is in the process of being replaced by the USMCA?

Visit your instructor's Connect® course and click on your eBook or SmartBook® to view a short video explanation from the author.

The Case against NAFTA

Those who opposed NAFTA claimed that ratification would be followed by a mass exodus of jobs from the United States and Canada into Mexico as employers sought to profit from Mexico's lower wages and less strict environmental and labor laws. According to one extreme opponent, Ross Perot, up to 5.9 million U.S. jobs would be lost to Mexico after NAFTA in what he famously characterized as a "giant sucking sound." Most economists, however, dismissed these numbers as being absurd and alarmist. They argued that Mexico would have to run a bilateral trade surplus with the United States of close to $300 billion for job loss on such a scale to occur—and $300 billion was the size of Mexico's GDP. In other words, such a scenario seemed implausible.

More sober estimates of the impact of NAFTA ranged from a net creation of 170,000 jobs in the United States (due to increased Mexican demand for U.S. goods and services) and an increase of $15 billion per year to the joint U.S. and Mexican GDP to a net loss of 490,000 U.S. jobs. To put these numbers in perspective, employment in the U.S. economy was predicted to grow by 18 million from 1993 to 2003. As most economists repeatedly stressed, NAFTA would have a small impact on both Canada and the United States. It could hardly be any other way, because the Mexican economy was only 5 percent of the size of the U.S. economy. Signing NAFTA required the largest leap of economic faith from Mexico rather than Canada or the United States. Falling trade barriers would expose Mexican firms to highly efficient U.S. and Canadian competitors that, when compared to the average Mexican firm, had far greater capital resources, access to highly educated and skilled workforces, and much greater technological sophistication. The short-run outcome was likely to be painful economic restructuring and unemployment in Mexico. But advocates of NAFTA claimed there would be long-run dynamic gains in the efficiency of Mexican firms as they adjusted to the rigors of a more competitive marketplace. To the extent that this occurred, they argued, Mexico's economic growth rate would accelerate, and Mexico might become a major market for Canadian and U.S. firms.[22]

Environmentalists also voiced concerns about NAFTA. They pointed to the sludge in the Rio Grande and the smog in the air over Mexico City and warned that Mexico could degrade clean air and toxic waste standards across the continent. They pointed out that the lower Rio Grande was the most polluted river in the United States and that, with NAFTA, chemical waste and sewage would increase along its course from El Paso, Texas, to the Gulf of Mexico.

There was also opposition in Mexico to NAFTA from those who feared a loss of national sovereignty. Mexican critics argued that their country would be dominated by U.S. firms that would not really contribute to Mexico's economic growth but instead would use Mexico as a low-cost assembly site while keeping their high-paying, high-skilled jobs north of the border.

NAFTA: The Results

Studies of NAFTA's impact suggest its initial effects muted, and both advocates and detractors may have been guilty of exaggeration.[23] On average, studies indicate that NAFTA's overall impact has been small but positive.[24] NAFTA was meant to increase trade among the three member states, and it appears to have done so.

In 1990, U.S. trade with Canada and Mexico accounted for about 25 percent of total U.S. trade. By 2017, the figure was over 40 percent. Canada and Mexico are now among the top three trading partners of the United States (the other is China), accounting for $1.3 trillion in cross-border trade in goods and services in 2017, up from $290 billion in 1993.[25] All three countries also experienced strong productivity growth in the first 10 years NAFTA was in place. In Mexico, labor productivity has increased by 50 percent. The passage of NAFTA may well have contributed to this.

Estimates suggest that employment effects of NAFTA have been moderate to small. The most pessimistic estimate of job losses comes from a study published by the left-leaning Economic Policy Institute. This study suggests that the United States lost about 850,000 jobs between 1993 and 2013 due to NAFTA, or 42,500 jobs a year on average. To put this loss in context, between 1992 and 2000, the U.S. economy created 2.86 million jobs *every year* on average. Other studies suggest that NAFTA had a far more moderate job impact in the United States. One recent study concluded that at most, 5 percent of U.S. job losses per year can be traced to NAFTA, and most of those who lose jobs find work elsewhere. Similarly, a review of empirical studies by the OECD concluded that "the net employment effects were relatively small, although there were adjustments across sectors displacing workers."[26]

A study of the welfare effects of NAFTA, which take into account its impact on national income, suggest that Mexico and the United States saw small welfare gains of 1.31 percent and 0.08 percent, respectively, while Canada suffered a welfare loss of 0.06 percent. The same study noted that real wages increased for all NAFTA members, with Mexico registering the largest gain. Similarly, a study by the Peterson Institute for International Economics concluded that the United States was $127 billion richer every year thanks to NAFTA. These studies support the general conclusion that contrary to political rhetoric, the impact of NAFTA has been quite small.[27]

THE UNITED STATES–CANADA–MEXICO AGREEMENT (USCMA)

Despite data suggesting that NAFTA has had a small positive impact on U.S. national income and, at worse, a small negative impact on employment, the trade deal continues to be the target of criticism. Politicians on both the right (Donald Trump) and the left (Bernie Sanders) have taken aim at NAFTA, claiming that the free trade area has been responsible for significant job losses in the United States. While the economic data do not offer much support for these assertions, anecdotal evidence of job layoffs due to NAFTA can be found in some sectors, such as the automobile industry where Mexico has made major gains in recent years.

Notwithstanding the muted impact of NAFTA, following the accession of Donald Trump to the U.S. presidency, NAFTA has been renegotiated. Known as the **United States-Mexico-Canada Agreement**, or **USMCA** for short, this new agreement does make some changes to the 25-year-old NAFTA treaty. Most significantly, NAFTA required automakers to produce 62.5 percent of a vehicle's content in North America to qualify for zero tariffs. The USMCA raises that threshold to 75 percent. The idea is the compel automakers to source fewer parts for a car assembled in North America from Germany, Japan, South Korea or China.

The USMCA agreement also mandates that by 2023, 40 percent of parts for any tariff-free vehicle must come from a so-called "high wage" factory. Those factories must pay a minimum of $16 an hour in average salaries for production workers, which is about triple the average wage in a Mexican factory right now.

The Trump administration clearly hopes these provisions will increase the production of automobiles and component parts in the United States. Critics see the USMCA as likely to result in trade diversion rather than trade creation, and argue that the consequences may include higher costs to North American automobile producers, and higher prices for consumers.

To become law and supersede NAFTA, the USMCA must be ratified by legislators in all three countries, which now seems likely to happen. In the United States as of late December 2019, an amended version of the USMCA treaty which provides greater protections for U.S. workers has been agreed to by the Executive and the House of Representatives, with just the Senate needed to sign off. Canada and Mexico seem almost certain to ratify the amended agreement, since a likely alternative, Donald Trump attempting to pull the US out of NAFTA, would be a far worse outcome for them.

THE ANDEAN COMMUNITY

Bolivia, Chile, Ecuador, Colombia, and Peru signed an agreement in 1969 to create the Andean Pact. The **Andean Community** was largely based on the EU model but was far less successful at achieving its stated goals. The integration steps begun in 1969 included an internal tariff reduction program, a common external tariff, a transportation policy, a common industrial policy, and special concessions for the smallest members, Bolivia and Ecuador.

By the mid-1980s, the Andean Pact had all but collapsed and had failed to achieve any of its stated objectives. There was no tariff-free trade among member countries, no common external tariff, and no harmonization of economic policies. Political and economic problems seem to have hindered cooperation among member countries. The countries of the Andean Pact have had to deal with low economic growth, hyperinflation, high unemployment, political unrest, and crushing debt burdens. In addition, the dominant political ideology in many of the Andean countries during this period tended toward the radical-socialist end of the political spectrum. Because such an ideology is hostile to the free market economic principles on which the Andean Pact was based, progress toward closer integration could not be expected.

The tide began to turn in the late 1980s when, after years of economic decline, the goernments of Latin America began to adopt free market economic policies. In 1990, the heads of the five current members of the Andean Community—Bolivia, Ecuador, Peru, Colombia, and Venezuela—met in the Galápagos Islands. The resulting Galápagos Declaration effectively relaunched the Andean Pact, which was renamed the Andean Community in 1997. The declaration's objectives included the establishment of a free trade area by 1992, a customs union by 1994, and a common market by 1995. This last milestone has not been reached. A customs union of sorts was implemented in 1995—although Peru opted out and Bolivia received preferential treatment until 2003. The Andean Community now operates as a partial customs union. In December 2005, it signed an agreement with Mercosur to restart stalled negotiations on the creation of a free trade area between the two trading blocs. Those negotiations are proceeding at a slow pace. In late 2006, Venezuela withdrew from the Andean Community as part of that country's attempts to join Mercosur.

MERCOSUR

Mercosur originated in 1988 as a free trade pact between Brazil and Argentina. The modest reductions in tariffs and quotas accompanying this pact reportedly helped bring about an 80 percent increase in trade between the two countries in the late 1980s.[28] This success encouraged the expansion of the pact in March 1990 to include Paraguay and Uruguay as full members. In 2012, the pact was further expanded when Venezuela joined Mercosur. However, in 2016 Venezuela was suspended from Mercosur for violating the pact's democratic principles and engaging in widespread human rights violations.

The initial aim of Mercosur was to establish a full free trade area by the end of 1994 and a common market sometime thereafter. In December 1995, Mercosur's members agreed to a five-year program under which they hoped to perfect their free trade area and move toward a full customs union—something that has yet to be achieved.[29] For its first eight years or so, Mercosur seemed to be making a positive contribution to the economic growth rates of its member states. Trade among the four core members quadrupled between 1990 and 1998. The combined GDP of the four member states grew at an annual average rate of 3.5 percent between 1990 and 1996, a performance that is significantly better than the four attained during the 1980s.[30]

However, Mercosur had its critics, including Alexander Yeats, a senior economist at the World Bank, who wrote a stinging critique.[31] According to Yeats, the trade diversion effects of Mercosur outweigh its trade creation effects. Yeats pointed out that the fastest-growing items in intra-Mercosur trade were cars, buses, agricultural equipment, and other capital-intensive goods that are produced relatively inefficiently in the four member countries. In other words, Mercosur countries, insulated from outside competition by tariffs that run as high as 70 percent of value on motor vehicles, are investing in factories that build products that are too expensive to sell to anyone but themselves. The result, according to Yeats, is that Mercosur countries might not be able to compete globally once the group's external trade barriers come down. In the meantime, capital is being drawn away from more efficient enterprises. In the near term, countries with more efficient manufacturing enterprises lose because Mercosur's external trade barriers keep them out of the market.

Mercosur hit a significant roadblock in 1998, when its member states slipped into recession and intrabloc trade slumped. Trade fell further in 1999, following a financial crisis in Brazil that led to the devaluation of the Brazilian real, which immediately made the goods of other Mercosur members 40 percent more expensive in Brazil, their largest export market. At this point, progress toward establishing a full customs union all but stopped. Things deteriorated further in 2001, when Argentina, beset by economic stresses, suggested the customs union be temporarily suspended. Argentina wanted to suspend Mercosur's tariff so that it could abolish duties on imports of capital equipment, while raising those on consumer goods to 35 percent (Mercosur had established a 14 percent import tariff on both sets of goods). Brazil agreed to this request, effectively halting Mercosur's quest to become a fully functioning customs union.[32] Hope for a revival arose in 2003, when new Brazilian President Lula da Silva announced his support for a revitalized and expanded Mercosur modeled after the EU with a larger membership, a common currency, and a democratically elected Mercosur parliament.[33] In 2010, the members of Mercosur did agree on a common customs code to avoid outside goods having to pay tariffs more than once, an important step toward achieving a full customs union. Since 2010, however, Mercosur has made little forward progress, and the jury is still out on whether it will become a fully functioning customs union.

CENTRAL AMERICAN COMMON MARKET, CAFTA, AND CARICOM

Two other trade pacts in the Americas have not made much progress. In the early 1960s, Costa Rica, El Salvador, Guatemala, Honduras, and Nicaragua attempted to set up a **Central American Common Market**. It collapsed in 1969, when war broke out between Honduras and El Salvador after a riot at a soccer match between teams from the two countries. Since then, the member countries have made some progress toward reviving their agreement (the five founding members were joined by the Dominican Republic). The proposed common market was given a boost in 2003, when the United States signaled its intention to enter into bilateral free trade negotiations with the group. These culminated in a 2004 agreement to establish a free trade agreement between the six countries and the United States. Known as the **Central America Free Trade Agreement (CAFTA)**, the aim is to lower trade barriers between the United States and the six countries for most goods and services.

A customs union was to have been created in 1991 among the English-speaking Caribbean countries under the auspices of the Caribbean Community. Referred to as **CARICOM**, it was established in 1973. However, it repeatedly failed to progress toward economic integration. A formal commitment to economic and monetary union was adopted by CARICOM's member states in 1984, but since then, little progress has been made. In October 1991, the CARICOM governments failed, for the third consecutive time, to meet a deadline for establishing a common external tariff. Despite this, CARICOM expanded to 15 members by 2005. In early 2006, six CARICOM members established the **Caribbean Single Market and Economy (CSME)**. Modeled on the EU's single market, CSME's goal is to lower trade barriers and harmonize macroeconomic and monetary policy between member states.[34]

Regional Economic Integration Elsewhere

Numerous attempts at regional economic integration have been tried throughout Asia, Africa, and elsewhere. One of the most significant is the Association of Southeast Asian Nations (ASEAN), although there have been numerous attempts to establish free trade agreements in Africa (see the closing case in this chapter), and there are ongoing efforts to establish free trade agreements between the United States and 11 other nations bordering the Pacific (the Trans Pacific Partnership, or TPP) and the United States and the European Union (the Transatlantic Trade and Investment Partnership, or TTIP).

ASSOCIATION OF SOUTHEAST ASIAN NATIONS

Formed in 1967, the **Association of Southeast Asian Nations (ASEAN)** includes Brunei, Cambodia, Indonesia, Laos, Malaysia, Myanmar, Philippines, Singapore, Thailand, and Vietnam. Laos, Myanmar, Vietnam, and Cambodia have all joined recently, creating a regional grouping of 600 million people with a combined GDP of some $2 trillion (see Map 9.3). The basic objective of ASEAN is to foster freer trade among member countries and to achieve cooperation in their industrial policies. Progress so far has been limited, however.

Until recently, only 5 percent of intra-ASEAN trade consisted of goods whose tariffs had been reduced through an ASEAN preferential trade arrangement. This may be changing. In 2003, an ASEAN Free Trade Area (AFTA) among the six original members of ASEAN came into full effect. The AFTA has cut tariffs on manufacturing and agricultural products to less than 5 percent. However, there are some significant exceptions to this tariff reduction. Malaysia, for example, refused to bring down tariffs on imported cars until 2005 and then agreed to lower the tariff only to 20 percent, not the 5 percent called for under the AFTA. Malaysia wanted to protect Proton, an inefficient local carmaker, from foreign competition. Similarly, the Philippines has refused to lower tariff rates on petrochemicals, and rice, the largest agricultural product in the region, will remain subject to higher tariff rates until at least 2020.[35]

Notwithstanding such issues, ASEAN and AFTA are at least progressing toward establishing a free trade zone. Vietnam joined the AFTA in 2006, Laos and Myanmar in 2008, and Cambodia in 2010. The goal was to reduce import tariffs among the six original members to zero by 2010 and to do so by 2015 for the newer members (although important exceptions to that goal, such as tariffs on rice, will persist).

ASEAN signed a free trade agreement with China that removes tariffs on 90 percent of traded goods. This went into effect January 1, 2010. Trade between China and ASEAN members more than tripled during the first decade of the twenty-first century, and this agreement should spur further growth.[36]

REGIONAL TRADE BLOCS IN AFRICA

African countries have been experimenting with regional trade blocs for half a century. Nominally there are now 19 trade blocs on the African continent. Many countries are members of more than one group. Although the number of trade groups is impressive, progress toward the establishment of meaningful trade blocs has been slow.

MAP 9.3

ASEAN countries.

Many of these groups have been dormant for years. Significant political turmoil in several African nations has persistently impeded any meaningful progress. Also, deep suspicion of free trade exists in several African countries. The argument most frequently heard is that because these countries have less developed and less diversified economies, they need to be "protected" by tariff barriers from unfair foreign competition. Given the prevalence of this argument, it has been hard to establish free trade areas or customs unions.

A meaningful attempt to reenergize the free trade movement in Africa occurred in early 2001, when Kenya, Uganda, and Tanzania, member states of the East African Community (EAC), committed themselves to relaunching their bloc, 24 years after it collapsed. The three countries, with 80 million inhabitants, intend to establish a customs union, regional court, legislative assembly, and, eventually, a political federation.

Their program includes cooperation on immigration, road and telecommunication networks, investment, and capital markets. However, while local business leaders welcomed the relaunch as a positive step, they were critical of the EAC's failure in practice to make progress on free trade. At the EAC treaty's signing in November 1999, members gave themselves four years to negotiate a customs union, with a draft slated for the end of 2001. But that fell far short of earlier plans for an immediate free trade zone, shelved after Tanzania and Uganda, fearful of Kenyan competition, expressed concerns that the zone could create imbalances similar to those that contributed to the breakup of the first community.[37] Nevertheless, in 2005 the EAC did start to implement a customs union. In 2007, Burundi and Rwanda joined the EAC. The EAC established a common market in 2010 and is now striving toward an eventual goal of monetary union.

In 2015, in what is a promising sign, representatives from 26 African nations signed an agreement pledging to work together to establish a free trade area that would remove or reduce many tariffs and eliminate time-consuming customs procedures between them. Known as the Tripartite Free Trade Area (TFTA), this common market would encompass more than 630 million people and link together three existing regional trading blocks in Southern and Eastern Africa with a combined gross domestic product of $1.2 trillion and more than $102 billion in trade among member states (see this chapter's closing case for further details). This was followed up by an even more ambitious free trade pact, known as the Continental Free Trade Area (CAFTA), which 44 countries signed onto in March of 2018. Whether these pacts will be more meaningful than prior attempts to liberalize trade in Africa remains to be seen, but African leaders do seem to be actively embracing free trade like never before so there are reasons for optimism.

OTHER TRADE AGREEMENTS

As noted in Chapter 7, following the failure of the Doha Round of talks to extend the WTO, the United States and many other nations have placed renewed emphasis on bilateral and multilateral trade agreements. Under President Obama, the United States was pursuing two major multilateral trade agreements: the Trans Pacific Partnership (TPP) with 11 other Pacific Rim countries (including Australia, New Zealand, Japan, South Korea, Malaysia, and Chile) and the Transatlantic Trade and Investment Partnership (TTIP) with the European Union. However, President Trump pulled the United States out of the TPP and negotiations on the TTIP have been put on hold.

FOCUS ON MANAGERIAL IMPLICATIONS

REGIONAL ECONOMIC INTEGRATION THREATS

Currently, the most significant developments in regional economic integration are occurring in the EU and NAFTA. Although some of the Latin American trade blocs and ASEAN may have economic significance in the future, developments in the EU and NAFTA currently have more profound implications for business practice. Accordingly, in this section, we concentrate on the business implications of those two groups. Similar conclusions, however, could be drawn with regard to the creation of a single market anywhere in the world.

Opportunities

Regional economic integration has created significant opportunities for businesses to grow the market for their goods and services and lower their factor costs. Markets that were formerly protected from foreign competition have become more open, and the costs of doing business have fallen. The latter is particularly true in the case of the EU's single market and, to a lesser extent, NAFTA (and its successor the USMCA). In these zones, free movement of goods and services across borders, harmonized product standards, simplified tax regimes, and in the case of the euro zone a single currency, have made it increasingly possible for businesses to realize potentially significant cost economies by centralizing production of products, or component parts, in those EU and NAFTA/UMSCA locations where the mix of factor costs and skills is optimal. Rather than producing a product in each of the 28 EU countries (27 after the British exit) or the three NAFTA/USMCA countries, a firm may be able to serve the whole EU or North American market from a single location. This location must be chosen carefully, of course, with an eye on local factor

TEST PREP

Use SmartBook to help retain what you have learned. Access your instructor's Connect course to check out SmartBook or go to **learnsmartadvantage.com** for help.

LO9-5

Understand the implications for management practice that are inherent in regional economic integration agreements.

costs and skills. Pursuit of such gain has led to the establishment of extensive cross border supply chains in both the EU and North America, which in turn implies that the economies of these regions have become more tightly integrated.

That being said, it is important to recognize that even after the removal of barriers to trade and investment, enduring differences in culture and competitive practices might limit the ability of companies to realize cost economies by centralizing production in key locations and producing a standardized product for a single multiple-country market. Consider the case of Atag Holdings NV, a Dutch maker of kitchen appliances.[38] Atag thought it was well placed to benefit from the single market but found it tough going. Atag's plant is just one mile from the German border and near the center of the EU's population. The company thought it could cater to both the "potato" and "spaghetti" belts—marketers' terms for consumers in northern and southern Europe—by producing two main product lines and selling these standardized "euro-products" to "euro-consumers." The main benefit of doing so is the economy of scale derived from mass production of a standardized range of products. Atag quickly discovered that the "euro-consumer" was a myth. Consumer preferences vary much more across nations than Atag had thought. Consider ceramic cooktops: Atag planned to market just two varieties throughout the EU but found it needed 11. Belgians, who cook in huge pots, require extra-large burners. Germans like oval pots and burners to fit. The French need small burners and very low temperatures for simmering sauces and broths. Germans like oven knobs on the top; the French want them on the front. Most Germans and French prefer black and white ranges; the British demand a range of colors, including peach, pigeon blue, and mint green.

Threats

Just as the emergence of single markets creates opportunities for business, it also presents a number of threats. For one thing, the business environment within each grouping has become more competitive. The lowering of barriers to trade and investment among countries has led to increased price competition throughout the EU and NAFTA/USMCA.

Over time, price differentials across nations will decline in a single market. This is a direct threat to any firm doing business in EU or NAFTA/USMCA countries. To survive in the tougher single-market environment, firms must take advantage of the opportunities offered by the creation of a single market to rationalize their production and reduce their costs. Otherwise, they will be at a severe disadvantage.

A further threat to firms outside these trading blocs arises from the likely long-term improvement in the competitive position of many firms within the areas. This is particularly relevant in the EU, where many firms have historically been limited by a high-cost structure in their ability to compete globally with North American and Asian firms. The creation of a single market and the resulting increased competition in the EU produced serious attempts by many EU firms to reduce their cost structure by rationalizing production. This transformed many EU companies into more efficient global competitors. The message for non-EU businesses is that they need to respond to the emergence of more capable European competitors by reducing their own cost structures.

Another threat to firms outside of trading areas is the threat of being shut out of the single market by the creation of a "trade fortress." The charge that regional economic integration might lead to a fortress mentality is most often leveled at the EU. Although the free trade philosophy underpinning the EU theoretically argues against the creation of any fortress in Europe, occasional signs indicate the EU may raise barriers to imports and investment in certain "politically sensitive" areas, such as autos. Non-EU firms might be well advised, therefore, to set up their own EU operations. This could also occur in the NAFTA countries, but it seems less likely.

The emerging role of the European Commission in competition policy suggests the EU is increasingly willing and able to intervene and impose conditions on companies proposing mergers and acquisitions. This is a threat insofar as it limits the ability of firms to pursue the corporate strategy of their choice. The commission may require significant concessions from businesses as a precondition for allowing proposed mergers and acquisitions to proceed. While this constrains the strategic options for firms, it should be remembered that in taking such action, the commission is trying to maintain the level of competition in Europe's single market, which should benefit consumers.

Finally, there is a clear threat to business in the growing opposition to free trade areas. We have seen this in the United States, where President Trump pulled the U.S. out of the TPP and initiated a contentious renegotiation of NAFTA. We have also seen it in the European Union, where the scheduled exit of the British in 2020 (Brexit) might result in the weakening of the EU. If the EU and NAFTA/UMSCA are diminished, some of the gains from trade will be lost, and many of the benefits that businesses enjoyed will disappear as well.

Key Terms

regional economic integration, p. 262
free trade area, p. 264
European Free Trade Association (EFTA), p. 264
customs union, p. 264
common market, p. 264
economic union, p. 264
political union, p. 265
trade creation, p. 267
trade diversion, p. 267
European Union (EU), p. 267

Treaty of Rome, p. 268
European Commission, p. 269
European Council, p. 269
European Parliament, p. 270
Treaty of Lisbon, p. 270
Court of Justice, p. 271
Maastricht Treaty, p. 272
optimal currency area, p. 273
North American Free Trade Agreement (NAFTA), p. 278
United States–Mexico–Canada Agreement (USMCA), p. 281

Andean Community, p. 282
Mercosur, p. 282
Central American Common Market, p. 283
Central America Free Trade Agreement (CAFTA), p. 283
CARICOM, p. 283
Caribbean Single Market and Economy (CSME), p. 284
Association of Southeast Asian Nations (ASEAN), p. 284

SUMMARY

This chapter pursued three main objectives: to examine the economic and political debate surrounding regional economic integration; to review the progress toward regional economic integration in Europe, the Americas, and elsewhere; and to distinguish the important implications of regional economic integration for the practice of international business. The text made the following points:

1. A number of levels of economic integration are possible in theory. In order of increasing integration, they include a free trade area, a customs union, a common market, an economic union, and full political union.

2. In a free trade area, barriers to trade among member countries are removed, but each country determines its own external trade policy. In a customs union, internal barriers to trade are removed, and a common external trade policy is adopted. A common market is similar to a customs union, except that a common market also allows factors of production to move freely among countries. An economic union involves even closer integration, including the establishment of a common currency and the harmonization of tax rates. A political union is the logical culmination of attempts to achieve ever-closer economic integration.

3. Regional economic integration is an attempt to achieve economic gains from the free flow of trade and investment between neighboring countries.

4. Integration is not easily achieved or sustained. Although integration brings benefits to the majority, it is never without costs for the minority. Concerns over national sovereignty often slow or stop integration attempts. In 2016, these concerns resulted in Britain voting for exit from the EU.

5. Regional integration will not increase economic welfare if the trade creation effects in the free trade area are outweighed by the trade diversion effects.

6. The Single European Act sought to create a true single market by abolishing administrative barriers to the free flow of trade and investment among EU countries.

7. Seventeen EU members now use a common currency, the euro. The economic gains from a common currency come from reduced exchange costs, reduced risk associated with currency fluctuations, and increased price competition within the EU.

8. Increasingly, the European Commission is taking an activist stance with regard to competition policy, intervening to restrict mergers and acquisitions that it believes will reduce competition in the EU.

9. Although no other attempt at regional economic integration comes close to the EU in terms of potential economic and political significance, various other attempts are being made in the world. The most notable include NAFTA in North America, the Andean Community and Mercosur in Latin America, and ASEAN in Southeast Asia.

10. The creation of single markets in the EU and North America means that many markets that were formerly protected from foreign competition are now more open. This creates major investment and export opportunities for firms within and outside these regions.

11. The free movement of goods across borders, the harmonization of product standards, and the simplification of tax regimes make it possible for firms based in a free trade area to realize potentially enormous cost economies by centralizing production in those locations within the area where the mix of factor costs and skills is optimal.

12. The lowering of barriers to trade and investment among countries within a trade group will probably be followed by increased price competition.

Critical Thinking and Discussion Questions

1. NAFTA produced significant net benefits for the Canadian, Mexican, and U.S. economies. Discuss.

2. What are the economic and political arguments for regional economic integration? Given these arguments, why don't we see more substantial examples of integration in the world economy?

3. What, in general, was the effect of the creation of a single market and a single currency within the EU on competition within the EU? Why?

4. Do you think it is correct for the European Commission to restrict mergers between American companies that do business in Europe? (For example, the European Commission vetoed the proposed merger between WorldCom and Sprint, both U.S. companies, and it carefully reviewed the merger between AOL and Time Warner, again both U.S. companies.)

5. What were the causes of the 2010–2012 sovereign debt crisis in the EU? What does this crisis tell us about the weaknesses of the euro? Do you think the euro will survive the sovereign debt crisis?

6. How should a U.S. firm that currently exports only to ASEAN countries respond to the creation of a single market in this regional grouping?

7. How should a firm with self-sufficient production facilities in several ASEAN countries respond to the creation of a single market? What are the constraints on its ability to respond in a manner that minimizes production costs?

8. After a promising start, Mercosur, the major Latin American trade agreement, has faltered and made little progress since 2000. What problems are hurting Mercosur? What can be done to solve these problems?

globalEDGE research task globaledge.msu.edu

Use the globalEDGE™ website (**globaledge.msu.edu**) to complete the following exercises:

1. The World Trade Organization maintains a database of *regional trade agreements*. You can search this database to identify all agreements that a specific country participates in. Search the database to identify the trade agreements that Japan currently participates in. What patterns do you see? Which region (or regions) of the world does Japan seem to be focusing on in its trade endeavors?

2. Your company has assigned you the task of investigating the various trade blocs in Africa to see if your company can benefit from these trade agreements while expanding into African markets. The first trade bloc you come across is *COMESA*. Prepare a short executive summary for your company, explaining the level of integration the bloc has currently achieved, the level it aspires to accomplish, and the relationships it has with other African trade blocs.

CLOSING CASE

NAFTA 2.0: The USCMA

In his 2016 presidential campaign, Donald Trump repeatedly criticized the North American Free Trade Agreement (NAFTA) as an unfair deal in which Americans had been taken to the cleaners by Mexico. Trump claimed that NAFTA had cost American manufacturers millions of jobs, even though there is little evidence to suggest this is the case. After becoming president, Trump stuck to his word and initiated a renegotiation of NAFTA.

Trump's anti-NAFTA stance sent shockwaves through industry on both sides of the border. Since NAFTA was signed in 1994, trade between the United States, Canada, and Mexico has tripled to $1.3 trillion. In 2017, the United States exported $342 billion of goods and services to Canada, and $277 billion to Mexico, while importing $339 billion from Canada and $355 billion from Mexico. The U.S. ran a $2.8 billion surplus in trade with Canada, and a $69 billion deficit with Mexico. Canada and Mexico are now the largest export markets for the United States, accounting for a third of all U.S. exports, and the largest sources of imports behind China.

The renegotiation of NAFTA was complicated by the fact that multilayered supply chains now span both sides of the U.S.-Mexico border. Nowhere is this more true than in the automobile industry. Auto parts manufactured in the United States may be shipped to plants in Mexico, where finished cars are assembled and then shipped back to the United States for final sale (the converse also occurs, with parts manufactured in Mexico being shipped to U.S. final assembly plants). In 2017, U.S. producers

exported $21 billion of finished automobiles and automotive parts to Mexico, but imported $84 billion in autos and parts from Mexico. Without that $63 billion trade deficit in autos and auto parts, the United States would be running only a $6 billion trade deficit with Mexico.

Perhaps because he recognizes the lopsided nature of trade in auto and auto parts between the United States and Mexico, President Trump has taken it upon himself to criticize auto producers that have moved production to Mexico or are planning to do so. Following criticism from Trump, Ford canceled plans to build a $1.6 billion auto assembly plant in Mexico. President Trump has also criticized General Motors, Toyota, and BMW for their plans to invest in Mexican assembly operations. Jawboning aside, as part of the NAFTA renegotiations, the Trump administration was looking at different options for restructuring trade with Mexico. These include placing tariffs on imports of autos from Mexico.

In the end, on September 30, 2018, the Trump administration reached an agreement with Mexico and Canada on a revised version of NAFTA. Known as the United States–Mexico–Canada Agreement, or USMCA for short, this agreement must now be ratified by legislators in all three countries. The USMCA does make some changes to the 25-year-old NAFTA agreement. Most significantly, NAFTA required automakers to produce 62.5 percent of a vehicle's content in North America to qualify for zero tariffs. The USMCA raises that threshold to 75 percent. That's meant to force automakers to source fewer parts for a car assembled in North America from Germany, Japan, South Korea, or China. The new agreement also mandates that, by 2023, 40 percent of parts for any tariff-free vehicle must come from a so-called "high wage" factory. Those factories must pay a minimum of $16 an hour in average salaries for production workers, which is about triple the average wage in a Mexican factory right now.

The Trump administration clearly hopes these provisions will increase the production of automobiles and component parts in the United States. That may occur, but critics also note that the consequences may include higher costs to North American automobile producers, and higher prices for consumers. As of late 2019 the USMCA has yet to be ratified by the three countries (although ratification seems imminent). Until that occurs, NAFTA will remain in force.

Sources: U.S. Census Bureau, www.census.gov/foreign-trade/index.html, accessed April 10, 2018; Robbie Whelan, "Gloom Descends on Mexico's NAFTA Capital," *The Wall Street Journal*, January 26, 2017; Dudley Althaus and Christina Rogers, "Donald Trump's NAFTA Plan Would Confront Globalized Auto Industry," *The Wall Street Journal*, November 10, 2016; William Mauldin and David Luhnow, "Donald Trump Posed to Pressure Mexico on Trade," *The Wall Street Journal*, November 21, 2016; and Siobhan Hughes et al., "Trump Tariffs Spark GOP Rift," *The Wall Street Journal*, March 5, 2018.

Case Discussion Questions

1. On balance, do you think that NAFTA has been a net positive or negative for the United States economy? What about for the economies of Mexico and Canada?

2. Why do you think Donald Trump was so focused on renegotiating NAFTA during and after his successful presidential campaign?

3. What is your assessment of the USCMA? What are the potential benefits of this agreement for the United States? What are the costs? On balance, does this agreement represent an improvement over NAFTA?

4. On balance, is the USCMA good for Canada and Mexico?

Design elements: Modern textured halftone: ©VIPRESIONA/ Shutterstock; globalEDGE icon: ©globalEDGE; All others: ©McGraw-Hill Education

Endnotes

1. Information taken from World Trade Organization website and current as of April 2019, www.wto.org.

2. Information taken from World Trade Organization website and current as of April 2019, www.wto.org.

3. The Andean Community has been through a number of changes since its inception. The latest version was established in 1991. See "Free-Trade Free for All," *The Economist*, January 4, 1991, p. 63.

4. D. Swann, *The Economics of the Common Market*, 6th ed. (London: Penguin Books, 1990). Michelle Egan, *Single Markets: Economic Integration in Europe and the United State*s (Oxford: Oxford University Press, 2015).

5. Pew Research Center, "What We Know about Illegal Immigration from Mexico," March 2, 2017.

6. See J. Bhagwati, "Regionalism and Multilateralism: An Overview," Columbia University Discussion Paper 603, Department of Economics, Columbia University, New York; A. de la Torre and M. Kelly, "Regional Trade Arrangements," International Monetary Fund Occasional Paper 93, March 1992; J. Bhagwati, "Fast Track to Nowhere," *The Economist*, October 18, 1997, pp. 21–24; Jagdish Bhagwati, *Free Trade Today* (Princeton and Oxford: Princeton University Press, 2002); B. K. Gordon, "A High Risk Trade Policy," *Foreign Affairs* 82 no. 4 (July–August 2003), pp. 105–15; M. Dai, Y. Votov, and T. Zylkin, "On the Trade Diversion Effects of Free Trade Agreements," *Economic Letters* 122 (2014), pp. 321–25.

7. N. Colchester and D. Buchan, *Europower: The Essential Guide to Europe's Economic Transformation in 1992* (London: The Economist Books, 1990); D. Swann, The *Economics of Europe: From Common Market to European Union* (London, Penguin Books, 2000); Michelle P. Egan, *Single Markets: Economic Integration in Europe and the United States* (Oxford: Oxford University Press, 2015)

8. Swann, *Economics of the Common Market*; Colchester and Buchan, *Europower*; "The European Union: A Survey," *The Economist*, October 22, 1994; "The European Community: A Survey," *The Economist*, July 3, 1993; European Union website at http://europa.eu.

9. E. J. Morgan, "A Decade of EC Merger Control," *International Journal of Economics and Business*, November 2001, pp. 451-73.

10. "The European Community: A Survey," 1993.

11. Tony Barber, "The Lisbon Reform Treaty," *FT.com*, December 13, 2007.

12. "One Europe, One Economy," *The Economist*, November 30, 1991, pp. 53-54; "Market Failure: A Survey of Business in Europe," *The Economist*, June 8, 1991, pp. 6-10. Michelle P. Egan, *Single Markets: Economic Integration in Europe and the United States* (Oxford: Oxford University Press, 2015)

13. Alan Riley, "The Single Market Ten Years On," *European Policy Analyst*, December 2002, pp. 65–72.

14. Deutsche Bank, "The Single European Market 20 Years On," *EU Monitor*, October 31, 2013.

15. See C. Wyploze, "EMU: Why and How It Might Happen," *Journal of Economic Perspectives* 11 (1997), pp. 3–22; M. Feldstein, "The Political Economy of the European Economic and Monetary Union," *Journal of Economic Perspectives* 11 (1997), pp. 23–42.

16. "One Europe, One Economy"; Feldstein, "The Political Economy of the European Economic and Monetary Union."

17. Richard Leong, "US Dollar Share of Global Currency reserves Hits Near 5-Year Low," *Reuters*, December 28, 2018.

18. Details regarding conditions of membership and the progression of enlargement negotiations can be found at http://europa.eu/pol/enlarg/index_en.htm.

19. Chris Giles, "Brexit in Seven Charts—The Economic Impact," *Financial Times*, June 27, 2016.

20. "What Is NAFTA?" *Financial Times*, November 17, 1993, p. 6; S. Garland, "Sweet Victory," *BusinessWeek*, November 29, 1993, pp. 30–31.

21. Bernie Woodall, "U.S. Autoworkers Face Threat as Car Makers Drawn to Mexico," *Reuters*, March 26, 2015.

22. "NAFTA: The Showdown," *The Economist*, November 13, 1993, pp. 23–36.

23. N. C. Lustog, "NAFTA: Setting the Record Straight," *The World Economy*, 1997, pp. 605–14; G. C. Hufbauer and J. J. Schott, *NAFTA Revisited: Achievements and Challenges* (Washington, DC: Institute for International Economics, 2005).

24. W. Thorbecke and C. Eigen-Zucchi, "Did NAFTA Cause a Giant Sucking Sound?" *Journal of Labor Research*, Fall 2002, pp. 647–58; G. Gagne, "North American Free Trade, Canada, and U.S. Trade Remedies: An Assessment after Ten Years," *The World Economy*, 2000, pp. 77–91; Hufbauer and Schott, *NAFTA Revisited*; J. Romalis, "NAFTA's and Custfa's Impact on International Trade," *Review of Economics and Statistics* 98, no. 3 (2007), pp. 416–35; "NAFTA at 20: Ready to Take Off Again?" *The Economist*, January 4, 2014. G. C. Hufbauer, C. Cimno, and T. Moran, "NAFTA at 20: Misleading Charges and Positive Achievements," Peterson Institute for International Economics, May 2014.

25. Data from the U.S. Census Bureau.

26. C. J. O'Leary, R. W. Eberts, and B. M. Pittelko, "Effects of NAFTA on US Employment and Policy Responses: A Product of the International Collaborative Initiative on Trade and Employment (ICITE)," *OECD Trade Policy Papers*, no. 131 (Paris: OECD Publishing, 2012); Hufbauer, Cimno, and Moran, "NAFTA at 20: Misleading Charges and Positive Achievements."

27. L. Caliendo and F. Parro, "Estimates of the Trade and Welfare Effects of NAFTA," *Review of Economic Studies*, July 2014; Hufbauer, Cimno, and Moran, "NAFTA at 20: Misleading Charges and Positive Achievements."

28. "The Business of the American Hemisphere," *The Economist*, August 24, 1991, pp. 37–38.

29. "NAFTA Is Not Alone," *The Economist*, June 18, 1994, pp. 47–48.

30. "Murky Mercosur," *The Economist*, July 26, 1997, pp. 66–67.

31. See M. Philips, "South American Trade Pact under Fire," *The Wall Street Journal*, October 23, 1996, p. A2; A. J. Yeats, *Does Mercosur's Trade Performance Justify Concerns about the Global Welfare-Reducing Effects of Free Trade Arrangements? Yes!* (Washington, DC: World Bank, 1996); D. M. Leipziger et al., "Mercosur: Integration and Industrial Policy," *The World Economy*, 1997, pp. 585–604.

32. "Another Blow to Mercosur," *The Economist*, March 31, 2001, pp. 33–34.

33. "Lula Lays Out Mercosur Rescue Mission," *Latin America Newsletters*, February 4, 2003, p. 7.

34. "CARICOM Single Market Begins," *EIU Views*, February 3, 2006.

35. "Every Man for Himself: Trade in Asia," *The Economist*, November 2, 2002, pp. 43–44.

36. L. Gooch, "Asian Free-Trade Zone Raises Hopes," *The New York Times*, January 1, 2010, p. B3.

37. M. Turner, "Trio Revives East African Union," *Financial Times*, January 16, 2001, p. 4.

38. T. Horwitz, "Europe's Borders Fade," *The Wall Street Journal*, May 18, 1993, pp. A1, A12; "A Singular Market," *The Economist*, October 22, 1994, pp. 10–16; "Something Dodgy in Europe's Single Market," *The Economist*, May 21, 1994, pp. 69–70.

The Foreign Exchange Market

10

LEARNING OBJECTIVES

After reading this chapter, you will be able to:

LO10-1   Describe the functions of the foreign exchange market.

LO10-2   Understand what is meant by spot exchange rates.

LO10-3   Recognize the role that forward exchange rates play in insuring against foreign exchange risk.

LO10-4   Understand the different theories explaining how currency exchange rates are determined and their relative merits.

LO10-5   Identify the merits of different approaches toward exchange rate forecasting.

LO10-6   Compare and contrast the differences among translation, transaction, and economic exposure, and explain the implications for management practice.

Scott Eells/Bloomberg/Getty Images

Managing Foreign Currency Exposure at 3M

OPENING CASE

3M is one of America's oldest and most venerable diversified industrial corporations. The company is known for its strong consumer brands, such as Scotch, Scotchgard, Post-it, Scotch-Brite, and ACE Bandages, but in truth its consumer business only constitutes a small part of its activities. The company also has many product offerings with applications in industrial areas such as automotive, healthcare, electronics, and energy, as well as safety and graphics. 3M has a well-earned reputation for being an innovation machine, plowing 6 percent of its annual revenues back into R&D. A long history of innovation has given 3M a portfolio of 55,000 products, many of which command high margins. Some 30 percent of its sales come from products introduced in the last five years.

In addition to being an innovation machine, 3M is also one of the most international of all U.S. companies. The company generates around 60 percent of its $32 billion in annual revenues from sales outside of the United States. This large global business has sales in 200 countries and operations in 70. The company has 200 plants around the world, manufactures many of its own inputs in addition to final products, and has built up networks of regional supply chains to better manage inventory, improve customer responsiveness, achieve economies of scale, and realize the productivity gains that come from manufacturing products in the optimal location.

Dealing with this vast array of international sales, as well as intra-company transactions, creates a problem for 3M. Specifically, changes in the value of currencies against each other can significantly impact its earnings and revenues when translated back into U.S. dollars, impact the value of intra-company transactions, and alter the attractiveness of different nations as possible locations for manufacturing activities. 3M estimates that adverse movements in currencies decreased the company's pretax profits by $42 million in 2018 and $111 million in 2017. (As an American company, 3M reports its financial results in U.S. dollars.) These estimates include the effect of translating profits from local currencies back into U.S. dollars, the impact of currency fluctuations on the transfer of products between 3M operations located in different nations, and transaction gains and losses including those on derivative instruments designed to reduce foreign currency exchange rate risk. For example, in 2018, an increase in the value of the U.S. dollar against the currencies of many other countries reduced 3M's foreign sales (when they were translated back into U.S. dollars) by some 2.3 percent. Of course, the opposite can also occur.

Foreign currency risk arises because the value of currencies will fluctuate against each other over time, and it is not easy to forecast how they will move against each other. In 2018, for example, the U.S. dollar increased in value by 5.2 percent against a trade weighted basket of other currencies, which included the euro, yen, British pound, Swiss Franc, and Australian dollar. The implication is that foreign sales, when translated back into U.S. dollars, will have fallen, on average, by 5.2 percent over the year.

Like many companies, 3M tries to reduce its exposure to such adverse effects by hedging its foreign exchange risk. The company enters into what are known as foreign exchange forward contracts, in advance of a foreign transaction, to "lock in" the exchange rate. The company may lock in exchange rates as much as 36 months in advance. For example, if 3M is exporting a product to the euro zone with payment in euros expected in three months, and it thinks that the U.S. dollar might appreciate against the euro over the next three months but it's not sure about this, it might purchase a three-month forward contract that locks in a certain dollar–euro exchange rate. By doing this, it knows what revenue it will get from the sale at that time in terms of dollars, and dollar sales are not reduced by a rise in the value of the dollar against the euro over the next three months. Of course, such forward contracts are not free, and nor are they perfect. In the face of uncertainty, the company may bet incorrectly and lose out. If the dollar falls against the euro over the next three months, instead of rising as 3M expected, 3M would have been better off not hedging, because the unhedged dollar value of its euro sales would have increased.

As circumstances warrant, 3M also uses foreign currency forward contracts and foreign currency debt as hedging instruments to protect the value of portions of the company's net investments in foreign operations. For example, in 2018, its European operations were partly financed by €4.1 billion in euro-denominated debt. If that debt were denominated in U.S. dollars, but had to be serviced by 3M's European operations, then the cost of servicing that debt in euros for the European subsidiaries would go up if the euro declined in value against the dollar, thereby reducing 3M's euro-zone profits when denominated in U.S. dollars. It is by actions such as these that 3M reduces its exposure to the unpredictable movements in currency exchange rates over time.

Source: 3M 2018 10k Statement.

Introduction

Like many enterprises in the global economy, the earnings and revenues of the American multinational 3M are impacted by changes in the relative value of currencies over time (see the opening case for details). If the U.S. dollar *appreciates* in value against most foreign currencies, as occurred in 2018, then a global company such as 3M might see the dollar value of its foreign currency revenues decline. Indeed, in 2018, 3M's foreign sales were reduced by 2.3 percent when translated back into dollars. Alternatively, if the dollar *depreciates* in value, the dollar value of its foreign currency revenues might increase. The 3M example illustrates that what happens in the foreign exchange market can have an important impact on the sales and profits of an enterprise. Accordingly, it is very important for managers to understand how the foreign exchange market works and what the impact of changes in currency exchange rates might be for their enterprise and its strategy.

This chapter has three main objectives. The first is to explain how the foreign exchange market works. The second is to examine the forces that determine exchange rates and to discuss the degree to which it is possible to predict future exchange rate movements. The third objective is to map the implications for international business of exchange rate movements. This chapter is the first of three that deal with the international monetary system and its relationship to international business. Chapter 11 explores the institutional structure of the international monetary system. The institutional structure is the context within which the foreign exchange market functions. As we shall see, changes in the institutional structure of the international monetary system can exert a profound influence on the development of foreign exchange markets.

The **foreign exchange market** is a market for converting the currency of one country into that of another country. An **exchange rate** is simply the rate at which one currency is converted into another. For example, Toyota uses the foreign exchange market to convert the dollars it earns from selling cars in the United States into Japanese yen. Without the foreign exchange market, international trade and international investment on the scale that we see today would be impossible; companies would have to resort to barter. The foreign exchange market is the lubricant that enables companies based in countries that use different currencies to trade with each other.

We know from earlier chapters that international trade and investment have their risks. Some of these risks exist because future exchange rates cannot be perfectly predicted. The rate at which one currency is converted into another can change over time. For example, at the start of 2001, 1 U.S. dollar bought 1.065 euros, but by early 2014, 1 U.S. dollar bought only 0.74 euro. The dollar had fallen sharply in value against the euro. This made American goods cheaper in Europe, boosting export sales. At the same time, it made European goods more expensive in the United States, which hurt the sales and profits of European companies that sold goods and services to the United States. The pricing advantage enjoyed by U.S. companies, however, disappeared between 2015 and 2018 as economic weakness in Europe and a stronger U.S. economy resulted in a fall in the value of the euro. By early 2019, 1 U.S. dollar bought 0.88 euro, meaning that American exports to the euro zone had become more expensive. Changes in currency values such as these often take managers by surprise, and if they have not hedged against the possible risk, sales and profits can be significantly affected.

One function of the foreign exchange market is to provide some insurance against the risks that arise from such volatile changes in exchange rates, commonly referred to as *foreign exchange risk*. Although the foreign exchange market offers some insurance against foreign exchange risk, it cannot provide complete insurance. It is not unusual for international businesses to suffer losses (or gains) because of unpredicted changes in exchange rates. Currency fluctuations can make seemingly profitable trade and investment deals unprofitable, and vice versa.

We begin this chapter by looking at the functions and the form of the foreign exchange market. This includes distinguishing among spot exchanges, forward exchanges, and currency swaps. Then we consider the factors that determine exchange rates. We also look at how foreign trade is conducted when a country's currency cannot be exchanged for other currencies, that is, when its currency is not convertible. The chapter closes with a discussion of these things in terms of their implications for business.

globalEDGE DATABASE OF INTERNATIONAL BUSINESS STATISTICS

The "global money system" can have a significant effect on how companies operate globally. Often, companies have to deal with exchange rates, monetary systems, and the capital market on both country and regional levels. But the influences of countries on the regional and global money system are significant (i.e., countries set the tone for the parameters of the foreign exchange market and the international monetary system). The globalEDGE™ Database of International Business Statistics (DIBS) includes time-series data beginning in the 1990s until today and covers more than 200 countries and more than 5,000 data variables. Countries, regions, and the world use these types of data points to drive the global money system, and everyone who is interested in better understanding the global capital market needs to know about them! Register free on globalEDGE™ to gain access to the DIBS database right now; students have free access to DIBS, and DIBS can be found at **globaledge.msu.edu/tools-and-data/dibs**.

The Functions of the Foreign Exchange Market

LO10-1

Describe the functions of the foreign exchange market.

The foreign exchange market serves two main functions. The first is to convert the currency of one country into the currency of another. The second is to provide some insurance against **foreign exchange risk**, or the adverse consequences of unpredictable changes in exchange rates.[1]

CURRENCY CONVERSION

Each country has a currency in which the prices of goods and services are quoted. In the United States, it is the dollar ($); in Great Britain, the pound (£); in France, Germany, and the other 17 members of the euro zone, it is the euro (€); in Japan, the yen (¥); and so on. In general, within the borders of a particular country, one must use the national currency. A U.S. tourist cannot walk into a store in Edinburgh, Scotland, and use U.S. dollars to buy a bottle of Scotch whisky. Dollars are not recognized as legal tender in Scotland; the tourist must use British pounds. Fortunately, the tourist can go to a bank and exchange her dollars for pounds. Then she can buy the whisky.

When a tourist changes one currency into another, she is participating in the foreign exchange market. The exchange rate is the rate at which the market converts one currency into another. For example, an exchange rate of €1 = $1.07 specifies that 1 euro buys 1.07 U.S. dollars. The exchange rate allows us to compare the relative prices of goods and services in different countries. A U.S. tourist wishing to buy a bottle of Scotch whisky in Edinburgh may find that she must pay £30 for the bottle, knowing that the same bottle costs $35 in the United States. Is this a good deal? Imagine the current pound/dollar exchange rate is £1.00 = $1.25 (i.e., 1 British pound buys $1.25). Our intrepid tourist takes out her calculator and converts £30 into dollars. (The calculation is 30 × 1.25.) She finds that the bottle of Scotch costs the equivalent of $37.50. She is surprised that a bottle of Scotch whisky could cost less in the United States than in Scotland despite shipping costs (alcohol is taxed heavily in Great Britain).

Tourists are minor participants in the foreign exchange market; companies engaged in international trade and investment are major ones. International businesses have four main uses of foreign exchange markets. First, the payments a company receives for its exports, the income it receives from foreign investments, or the income it receives from licensing agreements with foreign firms may be in foreign currencies. To use those funds in its home country, the company must convert them to its home country's currency.

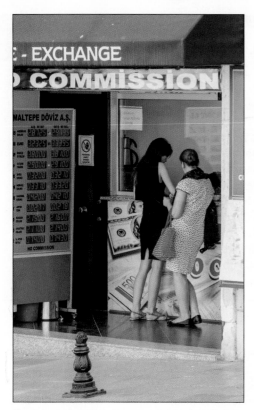

Tourists exchanging currency in Istanbul, Turkey.

Muratart/Shutterstock

Consider the Scotch distillery that exports its whisky to the United States. The distillery is paid in dollars, but because those dollars cannot be spent in Great Britain, they must be converted into British pounds. Similarly, Toyota sells its cars in the United States for dollars; it must convert the U.S. dollars it receives into Japanese yen to use them in Japan.

Second, international businesses use foreign exchange markets when they must pay a foreign company for its products or services in its country's currency. For example, Dell buys many of the components for its computers from Malaysian firms. The Malaysian companies must be paid in Malaysia's currency, the ringgit, so Dell must convert money from dollars into ringgit to pay them.

Third, international businesses also use foreign exchange markets when they have spare cash that they wish to invest for short terms in money markets. For example, consider a U.S. company that has $10 million it wants to invest for three months. The best interest rate it can earn on these funds in the United States may be 2 percent. Investing in a South Korean money market account, however, may earn 6 percent. Thus, the company may change its $10 million into Korean won and invest it in South Korea. Note, however, that the rate of return it earns on this investment depends not only on the Korean interest rate but also on the changes in the value of the Korean won against the dollar in the intervening period.

Currency speculation is the fourth use of foreign exchange markets. **Currency speculation** typically involves the short-term movement of funds from one currency to another in the hopes of profiting from shifts in exchange rates. Consider again a U.S. company with $10 million to invest for three months. Suppose the company suspects that the U.S. dollar is overvalued against the Japanese yen. That is, the company expects the value of the dollar to depreciate (fall) against that of the yen. Imagine the current dollar/yen exchange rate is $1 = ¥120. The company exchanges its $10 million into yen, receiving ¥1.2 billion ($10 million × 120 = ¥1.2 billion). Over the next three months, the value of the dollar depreciates against the yen until $1 = ¥100. Now the company exchanges its ¥1.2 billion back into dollars and finds that it has $12 million. The company has made a $2 million profit on currency speculation in three months on an initial investment of $10 million! In general, however, companies should beware, for speculation by definition is a very risky business. The company cannot know for sure what will happen to exchange rates. While a speculator may profit handsomely if his speculation about future currency movements turns out to be correct, he can also lose vast amounts of money if it turns out to be wrong.

A kind of speculation that has become more common in recent years is known as the **carry trade**. The carry trade involves borrowing in one currency where interest rates are low and then using the proceeds to invest in another currency where interest rates are high.[2] For example, if the interest rate on borrowings in Japan is 1 percent but the interest rate on deposits in American banks is 6 percent, it can make sense to borrow in Japanese yen, convert the money into U.S. dollars, and deposit it in an American bank. The trader can make a 5 percent margin by doing so, minus the transaction costs associated with changing one currency into another. The speculative element of this trade is that its success is based on a belief that there will be no adverse movement in exchange rates (or interest rates for that matter) that will make the trade unprofitable. However, if the yen were to rapidly increase in value against the dollar, then it would take more U.S. dollars to repay the original loan, and the trade could fast become unprofitable. The dollar/yen carry trade was actually very significant during the mid-2000s, peaking at more than $1 trillion in 2007, when some 30 percent of trade on the Tokyo foreign exchange market was related to the carry trade.[3] This carry trade declined in importance during 2008–2009 because interest rate differentials were falling as U.S. rates came down, making the trade less profitable. By late 2016, there were signs that the dollar/yen carry trade was becoming important again as negative interest rates in Japan, coupled with rising interest rates in the United States, were making it profitable to borrow in yen again and convert the money into U.S. dollars.[4]

INSURING AGAINST FOREIGN EXCHANGE RISK

A second function of the foreign exchange market is to provide insurance against foreign exchange risk, which is the possibility that unpredicted changes in future exchange rates will have adverse consequences for the firm. When a firm insures itself against foreign exchange risk, it is engaging in *hedging*. To explain how the market performs this function, we must first distinguish among spot exchange rates, forward exchange rates, and currency swaps.

Spot Exchange Rates

When two parties agree to exchange currency and execute the deal immediately, the transaction is referred to as a spot exchange. Exchange rates governing such "on the spot" trades are referred to as spot exchange rates. The **spot exchange rate** is the rate at which a foreign exchange dealer converts one currency into another currency on a particular day. Thus, when our U.S. tourist in Edinburgh goes to a bank to convert her dollars into pounds, the exchange rate is the spot rate for that day.

Spot exchange rates are reported on a real-time basis on many financial websites. An exchange rate can be quoted in two ways: as the amount of foreign currency one U.S. dollar will buy or as the value of a dollar for one unit of foreign currency. Thus, on April 15, 2019, at 12:30 p.m., Eastern Standard Time, 1 U.S. dollar bought €0.88, and €1 euro bought US$1.13.

Spot rates change continually, often on a minute-by-minute basis (although the magnitude of changes over such short periods is usually small). The value of a currency is determined by the interaction between the demand and supply of that currency relative to the demand and supply of other currencies. For example, if lots of people want U.S. dollars and dollars are in short supply, and few people want British pounds and pounds are in plentiful supply, the spot exchange rate for converting dollars into pounds will change. The dollar is likely to appreciate against the pound (or the pound will depreciate against the dollar). Imagine the spot exchange rate is £1 = $1.25 when the market opens. As the day progresses, dealers demand more dollars and fewer pounds. By the end of the day, the spot exchange rate might be £1 = $1.23. Each pound now buys fewer dollars than at the start of the day. The dollar has appreciated, and the pound has depreciated.

Forward Exchange Rates

Changes in spot exchange rates can be problematic for an international business. For example, a U.S. company that imports high-end cameras from Japan knows that in 30 days it must pay yen to a Japanese supplier when a shipment arrives. The company will pay the Japanese supplier ¥200,000 for each camera, and the current dollar/yen spot exchange rate is $1 = ¥120. At this rate, each camera costs the importer $1,667 (i.e., 1,667 = 200,000/120). The importer knows she can sell the cameras the day they arrive for $2,000 each, which yields a gross profit of $333 on each ($2,000 − $1,667). However, the importer will not have the funds to pay the Japanese supplier until the cameras are sold. If, over the next 30 days, the dollar unexpectedly depreciates against the yen, say, to $1 = ¥95, the importer will still have to pay the Japanese company ¥200,000 per camera but in dollar terms that would be equivalent to $2,105 per camera, which is more than she can sell the cameras for. A depreciation in the value of the dollar against the yen from $1 = ¥120 to $1 = ¥95 would transform a profitable deal into an unprofitable one.

To *insure* or *hedge* against this risk, the U.S. importer might want to engage in a forward exchange. A **forward exchange** occurs when two parties agree to exchange currency and execute the deal at some specific date in the future. Exchange rates governing such future transactions are referred to as **forward exchange rates**. For most major currencies, forward exchange rates are quoted for 30 days, 90 days, and 180 days into the future. In some cases, it is possible to get forward exchange rates for several years into the future.

LO10-2
Understand what is meant by spot exchange rates.

LO10-3
Recognize the role that forward exchange rates play in insuring against foreign exchange risk.

Returning to our camera importer example, let us assume the 30-day forward exchange rate for converting dollars into yen is $1 = ¥110. The importer enters into a 30-day forward exchange transaction with a foreign exchange dealer at this rate and is guaranteed that she will have to pay no more than $1,818 for each camera (1,818 = 200,000/110). This guarantees her a profit of $182 per camera ($2,000 − $1,818). She also insures herself against the possibility that an unanticipated change in the dollar/yen exchange rate will turn a profitable deal into an unprofitable one.

In this example, the spot exchange rate ($1 = ¥120) and the 30-day forward rate ($1 = ¥110) differ. Such differences are normal; they reflect the expectations of the foreign exchange market about future currency movements. In our example, the fact that $1 bought more yen with a spot exchange than with a 30-day forward exchange indicates foreign exchange dealers expected the dollar to depreciate against the yen in the next 30 days. When this occurs, we say the dollar is selling at a discount on the 30-day forward market (i.e., it is worth less than on the spot market). Of course, the opposite can also occur. If the 30-day forward exchange rate were $1 = ¥130, for example, $1 would buy more yen with a forward exchange than with a spot exchange. In such a case, we say the dollar is selling at a premium on the 30-day forward market. This reflects the foreign exchange dealers' expectations that the dollar will appreciate against the yen over the next 30 days.

In sum, when a firm enters into a forward exchange contract, it is taking out insurance against the possibility that future exchange rate movements will make a transaction unprofitable by the time that transaction has been executed. Although many firms routinely enter into forward exchange contracts to hedge their foreign exchange risk, sometimes this can work against the company. An example is given in the accompanying Management Focus, which explains how the hedging strategy adopted by the Brazilian regional jet manufacturer, Embraer, backfired.

Currency Swaps

The preceding discussion of spot and forward exchange rates might lead you to conclude that the option to buy forward is very important to companies engaged in international trade—and you would be right. According to the most recent data, forward instruments account for almost two-thirds of all foreign exchange transactions, while spot exchanges account for about one-third.[5] However, the vast majority of these forward exchanges are not forward exchanges of the type we have been discussing but rather a more sophisticated instrument known as currency swaps.

A **currency swap** is the simultaneous purchase and sale of a given amount of foreign exchange for two different value dates. Swaps are transacted between international businesses and their banks, between banks, and between governments when it is desirable to move out of one currency into another for a limited period without incurring foreign exchange risk. A common kind of swap is spot against forward. Consider a company such as Apple. Imagine Apple assembles laptop computers in the United States, but the screens are made in Japan. Apple also sells some of the finished laptops in Japan. So, like many companies, Apple both buys from and sells to Japan. Imagine Apple needs to change $1 million into yen to pay its supplier of laptop screens today. Apple knows that in 90 days it will be paid ¥120 million by the Japanese importer that buys its finished laptops. It will want to convert these yen into dollars for use in the United States. Let us say today's spot exchange rate is $1 = ¥120 and the 90-day forward exchange rate is $1 = ¥110. Apple sells $1 million to its bank in return for ¥120 million. Now Apple can pay its Japanese supplier. At the same time, Apple enters into a 90-day forward exchange deal with its bank for converting ¥120 million into dollars. Thus, in 90 days Apple will receive $1.09 million (¥120 million/110 = $1.09 million). Because the yen is trading at a premium on the 90-day forward market, Apple ends up with more dollars than it started with (although the opposite could also occur). The swap deal is just like a conventional forward deal in one important respect: It enables Apple to insure itself against foreign exchange risk. By engaging in a swap, Apple knows today that the ¥120 million payment it will receive in 90 days will yield $1.09 million.

TEST PREP

Use SmartBook to help retain what you have learned. Access your instructor's Connect course to check out SmartBook or go to **learnsmartadvantage.com** for help.

Embraer and the Gyrations of the Brazilian Real

For many years, Brazil was a country battered by persistently high inflation. As a result, the value of its currency, the real, depreciated steadily against the U.S. dollar. This changed in the early 2000s, when the Brazilian government was successful in bringing down annual inflation rates into the single digits. Lower inflation, coupled with policies that paved the way for the expansion of the Brazilian economy, resulted in a steady appreciation of the real against the U.S. dollar. In May 2004, 1 real bought $0.3121; by August 2008, 1 real bought $0.65, an appreciation of more than 100 percent.

The appreciation of the real against the dollar was a mixed bag for Embraer, the world's largest manufacturer of regional jets of up to 110 seats and one of Brazil's most prominent industrial companies. Embraer purchases many of the parts that go into its jets, including the engines and electronics, from U.S. manufacturers. As the real appreciated against the dollar, these parts cost less when translated into reals, which benefited Embraer's profit margins. However, the company also prices its aircraft in U.S. dollars, as do all manufacturers in the global market for commercial jet aircraft. So, as the real appreciated against the dollar, Embraer's dollar revenues were compressed when exchanged back into reals.

To try to deal with the impact of currency appreciation on its revenues, in the mid-2000s, Embraer started to hedge against future appreciation of the real by buying forward contracts (forward contracts give the holder the right to exchange one currency—in this case, dollars—for another—in this case, reals—at some point in the future at a predetermined exchange rate). If the real had continued to appreciate, this would have been a great strategy for Embraer because the company could have locked in the rate at which sales made in dollars were exchanged back into reals. Unfortunately for Embraer, as the global financial crisis unfolded in 2008, investors fled to the dollar, which they viewed as a safe haven, and the real *depreciated* against the dollar. Between August 2008 and November 2008, the value of the real fell by almost 40 percent against the dollar. But for the hedging, this depreciation would have actually increased Embraer's revenues in reals. Embraer, however, had locked itself into a much higher real/dollar exchange rate, and the company was forced to take a $121 million loss on what was essentially a bad currency bet.

Since the shock of 2008, Embraer has cut back on currency hedging, and most of its dollar sales and purchases are not hedged. This makes Embraer's sales revenues very sensitive to the real/dollar exchange rate. By 2010, the Brazilian real was once more appreciating against the U.S. dollar, which pressured Embraer's revenues. By 2012, however, the Brazilian economy was stagnating, while inflation was starting to increase again. This led to a sustained fall in the value of the real, which fell from 1 real = $0.644 in July 2011 to 1 real = $0.32 by February 2017, a depreciation of 50 percent. What was bad for the Brazilian currency, however, was good for Embraer, whose stock price surged to the highest price since February 2008 on speculation that the decline on the real would lead to a boost in Embraer's revenues when expressed in reals.

Sources: D. Godoy, "Embraer Rallies as Brazilian Currency Weakens," *Bloomberg*, May 31, 2013; K. Kroll, "Embraer Fourth Quarter Profits Plunge 44% on Currency Woes," *Cleveland.com*, March 27, 2009; "A Fall from Grace: Brazil's Mediocre Economy," *The Economist*, June 8, 2013; and "Brazil's Economy: The Deterioration," *The Economist*, December 7, 2013.

The Nature of the Foreign Exchange Market

The foreign exchange market is not located in any one place. It is a global network of banks, brokers, and foreign exchange dealers connected by electronic communications systems. When companies wish to convert currencies, they typically go through their own banks rather than entering the market directly. The foreign exchange market has been growing at a rapid pace, reflecting a general growth in the volume of cross-border trade and investment (see Chapter 1). In March 1986, the average total value of global foreign exchange trading was about $200 billion per day. By April 2016, the last date for which we have solid data, it had hit $5.1 trillion a day.[6] The most important trading centers are London (37 percent of activity); New York (18 percent of activity); and Zurich, Tokyo, and Singapore (all with around 5 to 6 percent of activity).[7] Major secondary trading centers include Frankfurt, Paris, Hong Kong, and Sydney.

London's dominance in the foreign exchange market is due to both history and geography. As the capital of the world's first major industrial trading nation, London had become the world's largest center for international banking by the end of the nineteenth century, a position it has retained. Today, London's central position between Tokyo and Singapore to the east and New York to the west has made it the critical link between the East Asian and New York markets. Due to the particular differences in time zones, London opens soon after Tokyo closes for the night and is still open for the first few hours of trading in New York. It is an open question, however, as to how the decision to exit from the EU (Brexit) will affect London's position as a global trading center.[8]

Two features of the foreign exchange market are of particular note. The first is that the market never sleeps. Tokyo, London, and New York are all shut for only three hours out of every 24. During these three hours, trading continues in a number of minor centers, particularly San Francisco and Sydney, Australia. The second feature of the market is the integration of the various trading centers. High-speed computer linkages among trading centers around the globe have effectively created a single market. The integration of financial centers implies there can be no significant difference in exchange rates quoted in the trading centers. For example, if the yen/dollar exchange rate quoted in London at 3 p.m. is ¥120 = $1, the yen/dollar exchange rate quoted in New York at the same time (10 a.m. New York time) will be identical. If the New York yen/dollar exchange rate were ¥125 = $1, a dealer could make a profit through **arbitrage**, buying a currency low and selling it high. For example, if the prices differed in London and New York as given, a dealer in New York could take $1 million and use that to purchase ¥125 million. She could then immediately sell the ¥125 million for dollars in London, where the transaction would yield $1.041666 million, allowing the trader to book a profit of $41,666 on the transaction. If all dealers tried to cash in on the opportunity, however, the demand for yen in New York would rise, resulting in an appreciation of the yen against the dollar such that the price differential between New York and London would quickly disappear. Because foreign exchange dealers are always watching their computer screens for arbitrage opportunities, the few that arise tend to be small, and they disappear in minutes.

Another feature of the foreign exchange market is the important role played by the U.S. dollar. Although a foreign exchange transaction can involve any two currencies, most transactions involve dollars on one side. This is true even when a dealer wants to sell a non-dollar currency and buy another. A dealer wishing to sell Mexican pesos for Japanese yen, for example, will usually sell the pesos for dollars and then use the dollars to buy yen. Although this may seem a roundabout way of doing things, it is actually cheaper than trying to find a holder of pesos who wants to buy yen. Because the volume of international transactions involving dollars is so great, it is not hard to find dealers who wish to trade dollars for pesos or yen.

Due to its central role in so many foreign exchange deals, the dollar is a vehicle currency. In 2018, 90 percent of all foreign exchange transactions involved dollars on one side of the transaction. After the dollar, the most important vehicle currencies were the euro (31 percent), the Japanese yen (21 percent), and the British pound (12 percent)—reflecting the historical importance of these trading entities in the world economy.

TEST PREP

Use SmartBook to help retain what you have learned. Access your instructor's Connect course to check out SmartBook or go to **learnsmartadvantage.com** for help.

LO10-4

Understand the different theories explaining how currency exchange rates are determined and their relative merits.

Economic Theories of Exchange Rate Determination

At the most basic level, exchange rates are determined by the demand and supply of one currency relative to the demand and supply of another. For example, if the demand for dollars outstrips the supply of them and if the supply of Japanese yen is greater than the demand for them, the dollar/yen exchange rate will change (see the opening case). The dollar will appreciate against the yen (and the yen will depreciate against the dollar). However, while differences in relative demand and supply explain the determination of exchange rates, they do so only in a superficial sense. This simple explanation does not reveal what factors underlie the demand for and supply of a currency. Nor does it tell us when the demand for dollars will exceed the supply (and vice versa) or when the supply of Japanese yen will exceed demand for them (and vice versa). Neither does it show under what conditions a currency is in demand or under what conditions it is not demanded. In this section, we will review economic theory's answers to these questions. This will give us a deeper understanding of how exchange rates are determined.

If we understand how exchange rates are determined, we may be able to forecast exchange rate movements. Because future exchange rate movements influence export opportunities, the profitability of international trade and investment deals, and the price competitiveness of foreign imports, this is valuable information for an international business. Unfortunately, there is no simple explanation. The forces that determine exchange rates are complex, and no theoretical consensus exists, even among academic economists who study the phenomenon every day. Nonetheless, most economic theories of exchange rate movements seem to agree that three factors have an important impact on future exchange rate movements in a country's currency: the country's price inflation, its interest rate, and market psychology.[9]

PRICES AND EXCHANGE RATES

To understand how prices are related to exchange rate movements, we first need to discuss an economic proposition known as the law of one price. Then we will discuss the theory of purchasing power parity (PPP), which links changes in the exchange rate between two countries' currencies to changes in the countries' price levels.

The Law of One Price

The **law of one price** states that in competitive markets free of transportation costs and barriers to trade (such as tariffs), identical products sold in different countries must sell for the same price when their price is expressed in terms of the same currency.[10] For example, if the exchange rate between the British pound and the dollar is £1 = $2, a jacket that retails for $80 in New York should sell for £40 in London (because $80/$2 = £40). Consider what would happen if the jacket cost £30 in London ($60 in U.S. currency). At this price, it would pay a trader to buy jackets in London and sell them in New York (an example of *arbitrage*). The company initially could make a profit of $20 on each jacket by purchasing it for £30 ($60) in London and selling it for $80 in New York (we are assuming away transportation costs and trade barriers). However, the increased demand for jackets in London would raise their price in London, and the increased supply of jackets in New York would lower their price there. This would continue until prices were equalized. Thus, prices might equalize when the jacket cost £35 ($70) in London and $70 in New York (assuming no change in the exchange rate of £1 = $2).

Purchasing Power Parity

If the law of one price were true for all goods and services, the *purchasing power parity (PPP)* exchange rate could be found from any individual set of prices. By comparing the prices of identical products in different currencies, it would be possible to determine the "real," or PPP, exchange rate that would exist if markets were efficient. (An **efficient market** has no impediments to the free flow of goods and services, such as trade barriers.)

A less extreme version of the PPP theory states that given relatively efficient markets—that is, markets in which few impediments to international trade exist—the price of a "basket of goods" should be roughly equivalent in each country. To express the PPP theory in symbols, let $P_\$$ be the U.S. dollar price of a basket of particular goods and $P_¥$ be the price of the same basket of goods in Japanese yen. The PPP theory predicts that the dollar/yen exchange rate, $E_{\$/¥}$, should be equivalent to

$$E_{\$/¥} = P_\$/P_¥$$

Thus, if a basket of goods costs $200 in the United States and ¥20,000 in Japan, PPP theory predicts that the dollar/yen exchange rate should be $200/¥20,000 or $0.01 per Japanese yen (i.e., $1 = ¥100).

Every year, the news magazine *The Economist* publishes its own version of the PPP theorem, which it refers to as the "Big Mac Index." *The Economist* has selected McDonald's Big Mac as a proxy for a "basket of goods" because it is produced according to more or less the same recipe in about 120 countries. The Big Mac PPP is the exchange rate that would have hamburgers costing the same in each country. According to *The Economist,* comparing a country's actual exchange rate with the one predicted by the PPP theorem based on relative prices of Big Macs is a test of whether a currency is undervalued or not. This is not a totally serious exercise, as *The Economist* admits, but it does provide a useful illustration of the PPP theorem.

To calculate the index, *The Economist* converts the price of a Big Mac in a country into dollars at current exchange rates and divides that by the average price of a Big Mac in America. According to the PPP theorem, the prices should be the same. If they are not, it implies that the currency is either overvalued against the dollar or undervalued. For example, in January 2019, the average price of a Big Mac in the United States was $5.58, while it was 20.9 yuan in China (or $3.05 at the January 2019 exchange rate of $1 = 6.85 yuan). This suggests that the exchange rate should be $1 = 3.75 yuan and that the Chinese yuan is undervalued by 45 percent!

The next step in the PPP theory is to argue that the exchange rate will change if relative prices change. For example, imagine there is no price inflation in the United States, while prices in Japan are increasing by 10 percent a year. At the beginning of the year, a basket of goods costs $200 in the United States and ¥20,000 in Japan, so the dollar/yen exchange rate, according to PPP theory, should be $1 = ¥100. At the end of the year, the basket of goods still costs $200 in the United States, but it costs ¥22,000 in Japan. PPP theory predicts that the exchange rate should change as a result. More precisely, by the end of the year

$$E_{s/¥} = \$200/¥22,000$$

Thus, ¥1 = $0.0091 (or $1 = ¥110). Because of 10 percent price inflation, the Japanese yen has depreciated by 10 percent against the dollar. One dollar will buy 10 percent more yen at the end of the year than at the beginning.

Money Supply and Price Inflation

In essence, PPP theory predicts that changes in relative prices will result in a change in exchange rates. Theoretically, a country in which price inflation is running wild should expect to see its currency depreciate against that of countries in which inflation rates are lower. If we can predict what a country's future inflation rate is likely to be, we can also predict how the value of its currency relative to other currencies—its exchange rate—is likely to change. The growth rate of a country's money supply determines its likely future inflation rate.[11] Thus, in theory at least, we can use information about the growth in money supply to forecast exchange rate movements.

Inflation is a monetary phenomenon. It occurs when the quantity of money in circulation rises faster than the stock of goods and services—that is, when the money supply increases faster than output increases. Imagine what would happen if everyone in the country was suddenly given $10,000 by the government. Many people would rush out to spend their extra money on those things they had always wanted—new cars, new furniture, better clothes, and so on. There would be a surge in demand for goods and services. Car dealers, department stores, and other providers of goods and services would respond to this upsurge in demand by raising prices. The result would be price inflation.

A government increasing the money supply is analogous to giving people more money. An increase in the money supply makes it easier for banks to borrow from the government and for individuals and companies to borrow from banks. The resulting increase in credit causes increases in demand for goods and services. Unless the output of goods and services is growing at a rate similar to that of the money supply, the result will be inflation. This relationship has been observed time after time in country after country.

So now we have a connection between the growth in a country's money supply, price inflation, and exchange rate movements. Put simply, *when the growth in a country's money supply is faster than the growth in its output, price inflation is fueled.* The PPP theory tells us that a country with a high inflation rate will see depreciation in its currency exchange rate. In

TABLE 10.1

Macroeconomic Data for Bolivia, April 1984 to October 1985

Source: Juan-Antonio Morales, "Inflation Stabilization in Bolivia," in *Inflation Stabilization: The Experience of Israel, Argentina, Brazil, Bolivia, and Mexico,* edited by Michael Bruno et al. Cambridge, MA: MIT Press, 1988.

Month	Money Supply (billions of pesos)	Price Level Relative to 1982 (average = 1)	Exchange Rate (pesos per dollar)
1984			
April	270	21.1	3,576
May	330	31.1	3,512
June	440	32.3	3,342
July	599	34.0	3,570
August	718	39.1	7,038
September	889	53.7	13,685
October	1,194	85.5	15,205
November	1,495	112.4	18,469
December	3,296	180.9	24,515
1985			
January	4,630	305.3	73,016
February	6,455	863.3	141,101
March	9,089	1,078.6	128,137
April	12,885	1,205.7	167,428
May	21,309	1,635.7	272,375
June	27,778	2,919.1	481,756
July	47,341	4,854.6	885,476
August	74,306	8,081.0	1,182,300
September	103,272	12,647.6	1,087,440
October	132,550	12,411.8	1,120,210

one of the clearest historical examples, in the mid-1980s, Bolivia experienced *hyperinflation—* an explosive and seemingly uncontrollable price inflation in which money loses value very rapidly. Table 10.1 presents data on Bolivia's money supply, inflation rate, and its peso's exchange rate with the U.S. dollar during the period of hyperinflation. The exchange rate is actually the "black market" exchange rate because the Bolivian government prohibited converting the peso to other currencies during the period. The data show that the growth in money supply, the rate of price inflation, and the depreciation of the peso against the dollar all moved in step with each other. This is just what PPP theory and monetary economics predict. Between April 1984 and July 1985, Bolivia's money supply increased by 17,433 percent, prices increased by 22,908 percent, and the value of the peso against the dollar fell by 24,662 percent! In October 1985, the Bolivian government instituted a dramatic stabilization plan— which included the introduction of a new currency and tight control of the money supply— and by 1987, the country's annual inflation rate was down to 16 percent.[12]

Another way of looking at the same phenomenon is that an increase in a country's money supply, which increases the amount of currency available, changes the relative demand-and-supply conditions in the foreign exchange market. If the U.S. money supply is growing more rapidly than U.S. output, dollars will be relatively more plentiful than the currencies of countries where monetary growth is closer to output growth. As a result of this relative increase in the supply of dollars, the dollar will depreciate on the foreign exchange market against the currencies of countries with slower monetary growth.

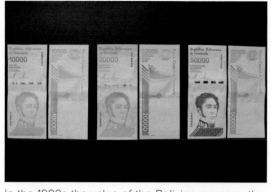

In the 1980s the value of the Bolivian currency, the Bolivian, depreciated rapidly due to hyperinflation.

Carolina Cabral/Getty Images

Government policy determines whether the rate of growth in a country's money supply is greater than the rate of growth in output. A government can increase the money supply simply by telling the country's central bank to issue more money. Governments tend to do this to finance public expenditure (building roads, paying government workers, paying for defense, etc.). A government could finance public expenditure by raising taxes, but because nobody likes paying more taxes and because politicians do not like to be unpopular, they have a natural preference for expanding the money supply. Unfortunately, there is no magic money tree. The result of *excessive* growth in money supply is typically price inflation. However, this has not stopped governments around the world from expanding the money supply, with predictable results. If an international business is attempting to predict future movements in the value of a country's currency on the foreign exchange market, it should examine that country's policy toward monetary growth. If the government seems committed to controlling the rate of growth in money supply, the country's future inflation rate may be low (even if the current rate is high) and its currency should not depreciate too much on the foreign exchange market. If the government seems to lack the political will to control the rate of growth in money supply, the future inflation rate may be high, which is likely to cause its currency to depreciate. Historically, many Latin American governments have fallen into this latter category, including Argentina, Bolivia, Brazil, and most recently, Venezuela, where uncontrolled growth in the money supply led to the inflation rate hitting 1 million percent in 2018 (i.e., the currency was essentially worthless). In late 2010, when the U.S. Federal Reserve decided to promote growth by expanding the U.S. money supply using a technique known as quantitative easing, critics charged that this too would lead to inflation and a decline in the value of the U.S. dollar on foreign exchange markets, but are they right? For a discussion of this, see the accompanying Country Focus.

Empirical Tests of PPP Theory

PPP theory predicts that exchange rates are determined by relative prices and that changes in relative prices will result in a change in exchange rates. A country in which price inflation is running wild should expect to see its currency depreciate against that of countries with lower inflation rates. This is intuitively appealing, but is it true in practice? There are several good examples of the connection between a country's price inflation and exchange rate position (such as Bolivia). However, extensive empirical testing of PPP theory has yielded mixed results.[13] While PPP theory seems to yield relatively accurate predictions in the long run, it does not appear to be a strong predictor of short-run movements in exchange rates covering time spans of five years or less.[14] In addition, the theory seems to best predict exchange rate changes for countries with high rates of inflation and underdeveloped capital markets. The theory is less useful for predicting short-term exchange rate movements between the currencies of advanced industrialized nations that have relatively small differentials in inflation rates.

The failure to find a strong link between relative inflation rates and exchange rate movements has been referred to as the purchasing power parity puzzle. Several factors may explain the failure of PPP theory to predict exchange rates more accurately.[15] PPP theory assumes away transportation costs and barriers to trade. In practice, these factors are significant, and they tend to create significant price differentials between countries. Transportation costs are certainly not trivial for many goods. Moreover, as we saw in Chapter 7, governments routinely intervene in international trade, creating tariff and nontariff barriers to cross-border trade. Barriers to trade limit the ability of traders to use arbitrage to equalize prices for the same product in different countries, which is required for the law of one price to hold. Government intervention in cross-border trade, by violating the assumption of efficient markets, weakens the link between relative price changes and changes in exchange rates predicted by PPP theory.

PPP theory may not hold if many national markets are dominated by a handful of multinational enterprises that have sufficient market power to be able to exercise some influence over prices, control distribution channels, and differentiate their product offerings between

Quantitative Easing, Inflation, and the Value of the U.S. Dollar

In fall 2010, the U.S. Federal Reserve (the Fed) decided to expand the U.S. money supply by entering the open market and purchasing $600 billion in U.S. government bonds from bondholders, a technique known as *quantitative easing*. Where did the $600 billion come from? The Fed simply created new bank reserves and used this cash to pay for the bonds. It had, in effect, printed money. The Fed took this action in an attempt to stimulate the U.S. economy, which, in the aftermath of the 2008–2009 global financial crisis, was struggling with low economic growth and high unemployment rates. The Fed had already tried to stimulate the economy by lowering short-term interest rates, but these were already close to zero, so it decided to lower medium- to longer-term rates; its tool for doing this was to pump $600 billion into the economy, increasing the supply of money and lowering its price, the interest rate. The Fed pursued further rounds of quantitative easing in 2011 through to 2013. In 2014, with the U.S. economy getting stronger and unemployment falling below 6 percent, the Fed progressively reduced its bond buying program. It ended the program in October 2014. By that time, the Fed had effectively pumped more than $3.5 trillion into the U.S. economy.

Critics were quick to attack the Fed's moves. Many claimed that the policy of expanding the money supply would fuel inflation and lead to a decline in the value of the U.S. dollar on the foreign exchange market. Some even called the policy a deliberate attempt by the Fed to debase the value of the U.S. currency, thereby driving down its value and promoting U.S. exports, which, if true, would be a form of mercantilism.

However, these charges may be unfounded for two reasons. First, at the time, the core U.S. inflation rate was the lowest in 50 years. In fact, the Fed actually feared the risk of deflation (a persistent fall in prices), which is a very damaging phenomenon. When prices are falling, people hold off their purchases because they know that goods will be cheaper tomorrow than they are today. This can result in a collapse in aggregate demand and high unemployment. The Fed felt that a little inflation—say, 2 percent per year—might be a good thing. Second, U.S. economic growth had been weak, unemployment was high, and there was excess productive capacity in the economy. Consequently, if the injection of money into the economy did stimulate demand, this would not translate into price inflation because the first response of businesses would be to expand output to utilize their excess capacity. Defenders of the Fed argued that the important point, which the critics seemed to be missing, was that expanding the money supply leads to only higher price inflation when unemployment is relatively low and there is not much excess capacity in the economy, a situation that did not exist in fall 2010. As for the currency market, its reaction was muted. At the beginning of November 2010, just before the Fed announced its policy, a trade-weighted index of the value of the dollar against a basket of other major currencies stood at 72. At the end of January 2014, it stood at 78—a slight appreciation. In short, currency traders did not seem to be selling off the dollar or reflecting worries about high inflation rates.

By March 2016, with the program over, there was no sign of a surge in price inflation in the U.S. economy. Indeed, inflation rates remained near historic lows. Moreover, far from weakening, the U.S. dollar had increased in value against most currencies, and the index value stood at 92. The Fed, it would seem, had been right and the critics were wrong.

Sources: P. Wallsten and S. Reddy, "Fed's Bond Buying Plan Ignites Growing Criticism," *The Wall Street Journal*, November 15, 2010; S. Chan, "Under Attack, the Fed Defends Policy of Buying Bonds," *International Herald Tribune*, November 17, 2010; "What QE Means for the World; Positive Sum Currency Wars," *The Economist*, February 14, 2013.

nations.[16] In fact, this situation seems to prevail in a number of industries. In such cases, dominant enterprises may be able to exercise a degree of pricing power, setting different prices in different markets to reflect varying demand conditions. This is referred to as price discrimination. For price discrimination to work, arbitrage must be limited. According to this argument, enterprises with some market power may be able to control distribution channels and therefore limit the unauthorized resale (arbitrage) of products purchased in another national market. They may also be able to limit resale (arbitrage) by differentiating otherwise identical products among nations along some line, such as design or packaging.

For example, even though the version of Microsoft Office sold in China may be less expensive than the version sold in the United States, the use of arbitrage to equalize prices may be limited because few Americans would want a version that was based on Chinese characters. The design differentiation between Microsoft Office for China and for the United States means that the law of one price would not work for Microsoft Office, even if transportation costs were trivial and tariff barriers between the United States and China did not exist. If the inability to practice arbitrage were widespread enough, it would break the connection between changes in relative prices and exchange rates predicted by the PPP theorem and help explain the limited empirical support for this theory.

Another factor of some importance is that governments also intervene in the foreign exchange market in attempting to influence the value of their currencies. We look at why and how they do this in Chapter 11. For now, the important thing to note is that governments regularly intervene in the foreign exchange market, and this further weakens the link between price changes and changes in exchange rates. One more factor explaining the failure of PPP theory to predict short-term movements in foreign exchange rates is the impact of investor psychology and other factors on currency purchasing decisions and exchange rate movements. We discuss this issue in more detail later in this chapter.

INTEREST RATES AND EXCHANGE RATES

Economic theory tells us that interest rates reflect expectations about likely future inflation rates. In countries where inflation is expected to be high, interest rates also will be high, because investors want compensation for the decline in the value of their money. This relationship was first formalized by economist Irvin Fisher and is referred to as the Fisher effect. The **Fisher effect** states that a country's "nominal" interest rate (i) is the sum of the required "real" rate of interest (r) and the expected rate of inflation over the period for which the funds are to be lent (I). More formally,

$$i = r + I$$

For example, if the real rate of interest in a country is 5 percent and annual inflation is expected to be 10 percent, the nominal interest rate will be 15 percent. As predicted by the Fisher effect, a strong relationship seems to exist between inflation rates and interest rates.[17]

We can take this one step further and consider how it applies in a world of many countries and unrestricted capital flows. When investors are free to transfer capital between countries, real interest rates will be the same in every country. If differences in real interest rates did emerge between countries, arbitrage would soon equalize them. For example, if the real interest rate in Japan was 10 percent and only 6 percent in the United States, it would pay investors to borrow money in the United States and invest it in Japan. The resulting increase in the demand for money in the United States would raise the real interest rate there, while the increase in the supply of foreign money in Japan would lower the real interest rate there. This would continue until the two sets of real interest rates were equalized.

It follows from the Fisher effect that if the real interest rate is the same worldwide, any difference in interest rates between countries reflects differing expectations about inflation rates. Thus, if the expected rate of inflation in the United States is greater than that in Japan, U.S. nominal interest rates will be greater than Japanese nominal interest rates.

Because we know from PPP theory that there is a link (in theory, at least) between inflation and exchange rates and because interest rates reflect expectations about inflation, it follows that there must also be a link between interest rates and exchange rates. This link is known as the international Fisher effect. The **International Fisher effect (IFE)** states that for any two countries, the spot exchange rate should change in an equal amount but in the opposite direction to the difference in nominal interest rates between the two countries. Stated more formally, the change in the spot exchange rate between the United States and Japan, for example, can be modeled as follows:

$$\frac{S_1 - S_2}{S_2} \times 100 = i_\$ - i_¥$$

where $i_\$$ and $i_¥$ are the respective nominal interest rates in the United States and Japan, S_1 is the spot exchange rate at the beginning of the period, and S_2 is the spot exchange rate at the end of the period. If the U.S. nominal interest rate is higher than Japan's, reflecting greater expected inflation rates, the value of the dollar against the yen should fall by that interest rate differential in the future. So if the interest rate in the United States is 10 percent and in Japan it is 6 percent, we would expect the value of the dollar to depreciate by 4 percent against the Japanese yen.

Do interest rate differentials help predict future currency movements? The evidence is mixed; as in the case of PPP theory, in the long run, there seems to be a relationship between interest rate differentials and subsequent changes in spot exchange rates. However, considerable short-run deviations occur. Like PPP, the international Fisher effect is not a good predictor of short-run changes in spot exchange rates.[18]

INVESTOR PSYCHOLOGY AND BANDWAGON EFFECTS

Empirical evidence suggests that neither PPP theory nor the international Fisher effect is particularly good at explaining short-term movements in exchange rates. One reason may be the impact of investor psychology on short-run exchange rate movements. Evidence reveals that various psychological factors play an important role in determining the expectations of market traders as to likely future exchange rates.[19] In turn, expectations have a tendency to become self-fulfilling prophecies.

A particularly famous example of this mechanism occurred in September 1992, when the international financier George Soros made a huge bet against the British pound. Soros borrowed billions of pounds, using the assets of his investment funds as collateral, and immediately sold those pounds for German deutsche marks (this was before the advent of the euro). This technique, known as short selling, can earn the speculator enormous profits if he can subsequently buy back the pounds he sold at a much better exchange rate and then use those pounds, purchased cheaply, to repay his loan. By selling pounds and buying deutsche marks, Soros helped start pushing down the value of the pound on the foreign exchange markets. More importantly, when Soros started shorting the British pound, many foreign exchange traders, knowing Soros's reputation, jumped on the bandwagon and did likewise. This triggered a classic bandwagon effect with traders moving as a herd in the same direction at the same time. As the bandwagon effect gained momentum, with more traders selling British pounds and purchasing deutsche marks in expectation of a decline in the pound, their expectations became a self-fulfilling prophecy. Massive selling forced down the value of the pound against the deutsche mark. In other words, the pound declined in value not so much because of any major shift in macroeconomic fundamentals but because investors followed a bet placed by a major speculator, George Soros.

According to a number of studies, investor psychology and bandwagon effects play an important role in determining short-run exchange rate movements.[20] However, these effects can be hard to predict. Investor psychology can be influenced by political factors and by microeconomic events, such as the investment decisions of individual firms, many of which are only loosely linked to macroeconomic fundamentals, such as relative inflation rates. Also, bandwagon effects can be both triggered and exacerbated by the idiosyncratic behavior of politicians. Something like this seems to have occurred in Southeast Asia during 1997 when, one after another, the currencies of Thailand, Malaysia, South Korea, and Indonesia lost between 50 and 70 percent of their value against the U.S. dollar in a few months.

SUMMARY OF EXCHANGE RATE THEORIES

Relative monetary growth, relative inflation rates, and nominal interest rate differentials are all moderately good predictors of long-run changes in exchange rates. They are poor predictors of short-run changes in exchange rates, however, perhaps because of the impact of psychological factors, investor expectations, and bandwagon effects on short-term currency movements. This information is useful for an international business. Insofar as the long-term profitability of foreign investments, export opportunities, and the price competitiveness of foreign imports are all influenced by long-term movements in exchange rates, international businesses would be advised to pay attention to countries' differing monetary growth, inflation, and interest rates. International businesses that engage in foreign exchange transactions on a day-to-day basis could benefit by knowing some predictor s of short-term foreign exchange rate movements. Unfortunately, short-term exchange rate movements are difficult to predict.

LO10-5

Identify the merits of different approaches toward exchange rate forecasting.

Exchange Rate Forecasting

A company's need to predict future exchange rate variations raises the issue of whether it is worthwhile for the company to invest in exchange rate forecasting services to aid decision making. Two schools of thought address this issue. The efficient market school argues that forward exchange rates do the best possible job of forecasting future spot exchange rates and, therefore, investing in forecasting services would be a waste of money. The other school of thought, the inefficient market school, argues that companies can improve the foreign exchange market's estimate of future exchange rates (as contained in the forward rate) by investing in forecasting services. In other words, this school of thought does not believe the forward exchange rates are the best possible predictors of future spot exchange rates.

THE EFFICIENT MARKET SCHOOL

Forward exchange rates represent market participants' collective predictions of likely spot exchange rates at specified future dates. If forward exchange rates are the best possible predictor of future spot rates, it would make no sense for companies to spend additional money trying to forecast short-run exchange rate movements. Many economists believe the foreign exchange market is efficient at setting forward rates.[21] An efficient market is one in which prices reflect all available public information. (If forward rates reflect all available information about likely future changes in exchange rates, a company cannot beat the market by investing in forecasting services.)

If the foreign exchange market is efficient, forward exchange rates should be unbiased predictors of future spot rates. This does not mean the predictions will be accurate in any specific situation. It means inaccuracies will not be consistently above or below future spot rates; they will be random. Many empirical tests have addressed the efficient market hypothesis. Although most of the early work seems to confirm the hypothesis (suggesting that companies should not waste their money on forecasting services), some studies have challenged it.[22] There is some evidence that forward rates are not unbiased predictors of future spot rates and that more accurate predictions of future spot rates can be calculated from publicly available information.[23]

THE INEFFICIENT MARKET SCHOOL

Citing evidence against the efficient market hypothesis, some economists believe the foreign exchange market is inefficient. An **inefficient market** is one in which prices do not reflect all available information. In an inefficient market, forward exchange rates will not be the best possible predictors of future spot exchange rates.

If this is true, it may be worthwhile for international businesses to invest in forecasting services (as many do). The belief is that professional exchange rate forecasts might provide better predictions of future spot rates than forward exchange rates do. However, the track record of professional forecasting services is not that good.[24] For example, forecasting services did not predict the 1997 currency crisis that swept through Southeast Asia, nor did they predict the rise in the value of the dollar that occurred during late 2008, a period when the United States fell into a deep financial crisis that some thought would lead to a decline in the value of the dollar (it appears that the dollar rose because it was seen as a relatively safe currency in a time when many nations were experiencing economic trouble).

APPROACHES TO FORECASTING

Assuming the inefficient market school is correct that the foreign exchange market's estimate of future spot rates can be improved, on what basis should forecasts be prepared? Here again, there are two schools of thought. One adheres to fundamental analysis, while the other uses technical analysis.

Fundamental Analysis

Fundamental analysis draws on economic theory to construct sophisticated econometric models for predicting exchange rate movements. The variables contained in these models

 Did You Know?

Did you know that the value of the U.S. dollar fluctuates significantly against the value of the euro?

Visit your instructor's Connect® course and click on your eBook or SmartBook® to view a short video explanation from the author.

typically include those we have discussed, such as relative money supply growth rates, inflation rates, and interest rates. In addition, they may include variables related to balance-of-payments positions.

Running a deficit on a balance-of-payments current account (a country is importing more goods and services than it is exporting) creates pressures that may result in the depreciation of the country's currency on the foreign exchange market.[25] Consider what might happen if the United States were running a persistent current account balance-of-payments deficit (as it has been). Because the United States would be importing more than it was exporting, people in other countries would be increasing their holdings of U.S. dollars. If these people were willing to hold their dollars, the dollar's exchange rate would not be influenced. However, if these people converted their dollars into other currencies, the supply of dollars in the foreign exchange market would increase (as would demand for the other currencies). This shift in demand and supply would create pressures that could lead to the depreciation of the dollar against other currencies.

This argument hinges on whether people in other countries are willing to hold dollars. This depends on such factors as U.S. interest rates, the return on holding other dollar-denominated assets such as stocks in U.S. companies, and, most important, inflation rates. So, in a sense, the balance-of-payments situation is not a fundamental predictor of future exchange rate movements. But what makes financial assets such as stocks and bonds attractive? The answer is prevailing interest rates and inflation rates, both of which affect underlying economic growth and the real return to holding U.S. financial assets. Given this, we are back to the argument that the fundamental determinants of exchange rates are monetary growth, inflation rates, and interest rates.

Technical Analysis

Technical analysis uses price and volume data to determine past trends, which are expected to continue into the future. This approach does not rely on a consideration of economic fundamentals. Technical analysis is based on the premise that there are analyzable market trends and waves and that previous trends and waves can be used to predict future trends and waves. Since there is no theoretical rationale for this assumption of predictability, many economists compare technical analysis to fortune-telling. Despite this skepticism, technical analysis has gained favor in recent years.[26]

Currency Convertibility

Until this point, we have assumed that the currencies of various countries are freely convertible into other currencies. Due to government restrictions, a significant number of currencies are not freely convertible into other currencies. A country's currency is said to be **freely convertible** when the country's government allows both residents and nonresidents to purchase unlimited amounts of a foreign currency with it. A currency is said to be **externally convertible** when only nonresidents may convert it into a foreign currency without any limitations. A currency is **nonconvertible** when neither residents nor nonresidents are allowed to convert it into a foreign currency.

Free convertibility is not universal. Many countries place some restrictions on their residents' ability to convert the domestic currency into a foreign currency (a policy of external convertibility). Restrictions range from the relatively minor (such as restricting the amount of foreign currency they may take with them out of the country on trips) to the major (such as restricting domestic businesses' ability to take foreign currency out of the country). External convertibility restrictions can limit domestic companies' ability to invest abroad, but they present few problems for foreign companies wishing to do business in that country. For example, even if the Japanese government tightly controlled the ability of its residents to convert the yen into U.S. dollars, all U.S. businesses with deposits in Japanese banks may at any time convert all their yen into dollars and take them out of the country. Thus, a U.S. company with a subsidiary in Japan is assured that it will be able to convert the profits from its Japanese operation into dollars and take them out of the country.

Serious problems arise, however, under a policy of nonconvertibility. This was the practice of the former Soviet Union, and it continued to be the practice in Russia for several years after the collapse of the Soviet Union. When strictly applied, nonconvertibility means that although a U.S. company doing business in a country such as Russia may be able to generate significant ruble profits, it may not convert those rubles into dollars and take them out of the country. Obviously, this is not desirable for international business.

Governments limit convertibility to preserve their foreign exchange reserves. A country needs an adequate supply of these reserves to service its international debt commitments and to purchase imports. Governments typically impose convertibility restrictions on their currency when they fear that free convertibility will lead to a run on their foreign exchange reserves. This occurs when residents and nonresidents rush to convert their holdings of domestic currency into a foreign currency—a phenomenon generally referred to as **capital flight**. Capital flight is most likely to occur when the value of the domestic currency is depreciating rapidly because of hyperinflation or when a country's economic prospects are shaky in other respects. Under such circumstances, both residents and nonresidents tend to believe that their money is more likely to hold its value if it is converted into a foreign currency and invested abroad. Not only will a run on foreign exchange reserves limit the country's ability to service its international debt and pay for imports, but it will also lead to a precipitous depreciation in the exchange rate as residents and nonresidents unload their holdings of domestic currency on the foreign exchange markets (thereby increasing the market supply of the country's currency). Governments fear that the rise in import prices resulting from currency depreciation will lead to further increases in inflation. This fear provides another rationale for limiting convertibility.

Companies can deal with the nonconvertibility problem by engaging in countertrade. **Countertrade** refers to a range of barter-like agreements by which goods and services can be traded for other goods and services. Countertrade can make sense when a country's currency is nonconvertible. For example, consider the deal that General Electric struck with the Romanian government when that country's currency was nonconvertible. When General Electric won a contract for a $150 million generator project in Romania, it agreed to take payment in the form of Romanian goods that could be sold for $150 million on international markets. In a similar case, the Venezuelan government negotiated a contract with Caterpillar under which Venezuela would trade 350,000 tons of iron ore for Caterpillar heavy construction equipment. Caterpillar subsequently traded the iron ore to Romania in exchange for Romanian farm products, which it then sold on international markets for dollars.[27]

How important is countertrade? Twenty years ago, a large number of nonconvertible currencies existed in the world, and countertrade was quite significant. However, in recent years, many governments have made their currencies freely convertible, and the percentage of world trade that involves countertrade is probably significantly below 5 percent.[28]

TEST PREP

Use SmartBook to help retain what you have learned. Access your instructor's Connect course to check out SmartBook or go to **learnsmartadvantage.com** for help.

LO10-6

Compare and contrast the differences among translation, transaction, and economic exposure, and explain the implications for management practice.

FOCUS ON MANAGERIAL IMPLICATIONS

FOREIGN EXCHANGE RATE RISK

This chapter contains a number of clear implications for business. First, it is critical that international businesses understand the influence of exchange rates on the profitability of trade and investment deals. Adverse changes in exchange rates can make apparently profitable deals unprofitable. As noted, the risk introduced into international business transactions by changes in exchange rates is referred to as foreign exchange risk. Foreign exchange risk is usually divided into three main categories: transaction exposure, translation exposure, and economic exposure.

Transaction Exposure

Transaction exposure is the extent to which the income from individual transactions is affected by fluctuations in foreign exchange values. Such exposure includes obligations for the purchase or sale of goods and services at previously agreed prices and the borrowing or lending of funds in foreign currencies. For example, suppose in 2004, an American airline agreed to purchase 10 Airbus 330 aircraft for €120 million each for a total price of €1.20 billion, with delivery scheduled for 2008 and payment due then. When the contract was signed in 2004, the dollar/euro exchange rate stood at $1 = €1.10, so the American airline anticipated paying $1.09 billion for the 10 aircraft when they were delivered (€1.2 billion/1.1 = $1.09 billion). However, imagine that the value of the dollar depreciates against the euro over the intervening period, so that a dollar buys only €0.80 in 2008 when payment was due ($1 = €0.80). Now the total cost in U.S. dollars is $1.5 billion (€1.2 billion/0.80 = $1.5 billion), an increase of $0.41 billion! The transaction exposure here is $0.41 billion, which is the money lost due to an adverse movement in exchange rates between the time when the deal was signed and when the aircraft were paid for.

Translation Exposure

Translation exposure is the impact of currency exchange rate changes on the reported financial statements of a company. Translation exposure is concerned with the present measurement of past events. The resulting accounting gains or losses are said to be unrealized—they are "paper" gains and losses—but they are still important. Consider a U.S. firm with a subsidiary in Mexico. If the value of the Mexican peso depreciates significantly against the dollar, this would substantially reduce the dollar value of the Mexican subsidiary's equity. In turn, this would reduce the total dollar value of the firm's equity reported in its consolidated balance sheet. This would raise the apparent leverage of the firm (its debt ratio), which could increase the firm's cost of borrowing and potentially limit its access to the capital market. Similarly, if an American firm has a subsidiary in the European Union and the value of the euro depreciates rapidly against that of the dollar over a year, this will reduce the dollar value of the euro profit made by the European subsidiary, resulting in negative translation exposure. In fact, many U.S. firms suffered from significant negative translation exposure in Europe during 2000, precisely because the euro did depreciate rapidly against the dollar. In 2002–2007, the euro rose in value against the dollar. This positive translation exposure boosted the dollar profits of American multinationals with significant operations in Europe. Between mid-2014 and early 2015, the euro slumped in value against the dollar, compressing the dollar profits of American multinationals with significant European exposure.

Economic Exposure

Economic exposure is the extent to which a firm's future international earning power is affected by changes in exchange rates. Economic exposure is concerned with the long-run effect of changes in exchange rates on future prices, sales, and costs. This is distinct from transaction exposure, which is concerned with the effect of exchange rate changes on individual transactions, most of which are short-term affairs that will be executed within a few weeks or months. Consider the effect of wide swings in the value of the dollar on many U.S. firms' international competitiveness. The rapid rise in the value of the dollar on the foreign exchange market in the 1990s hurt the price competitiveness of many U.S. producers in world markets. U.S. manufacturers that relied heavily on exports saw their export volume and world market share decline. The reverse phenomenon occurred in 2000–2009, when the dollar declined against most major currencies. The fall in the value of the dollar helped increase the price competitiveness of U.S. manufacturers in world markets. Between mid-2014 and early 2015, the dollar increased significantly in value against most major currencies, decreasing the price competitiveness of U.S. exporters. In 2017, the opposite occurred, with the dollar falling in value, increasing the price competitiveness of U.S. exporters, but in 2018 the dollar reversed course again, increasing in value and making U.S. exports more expensive.

REDUCING TRANSLATION AND TRANSACTION EXPOSURE

A number of tactics can help firms minimize their transaction and translation exposure. These tactics primarily protect short-term cash flows from adverse changes in exchange rates. We have already discussed two of these tactics at length in the chapter, entering into forward exchange rate contracts and buying swaps. In addition to buying forward and using swaps, firms can minimize their foreign exchange exposure through leading and lagging payables and receivables—that is, paying suppliers and collecting payment from customers early or late depending on expected exchange rate movements. A **lead strategy** involves attempting to collect foreign currency receivables (payments from customers) early when a foreign currency is expected to depreciate and paying foreign currency payables (to suppliers) before they are due when a currency is expected to appreciate. A **lag strategy** involves delaying collection of foreign currency receivables if that currency is expected to appreciate and delaying payables if the currency is expected to depreciate. Leading and lagging involve accelerating payments from weak-currency to strong-currency countries and delaying inflows from strong-currency to weak-currency countries.

Lead and lag strategies can be difficult to implement, however. The firm must be in a position to exercise some control over payment terms. Firms do not always have this kind of bargaining power, particularly when they are dealing with important customers who are in a position to dictate payment terms. Also, because lead and lag strategies can put pressure on a weak currency, many governments limit leads and lags. For example, some countries set 180 days as a limit for receiving payments for exports or making payments for imports.

REDUCING ECONOMIC EXPOSURE

Reducing economic exposure requires strategic choices that go beyond the realm of financial management. The key to reducing economic exposure is to distribute the firm's productive assets to various locations so the firm's long-term financial well-being is not severely affected by adverse changes in exchange rates. This is a strategy that firms both large and small sometimes pursue. For example, during the 2000s, fearing that the euro would continue to strengthen against the U.S. dollar, some European firms that did significant business in the United States set up local production facilities in that market to ensure that a rising euro did not put them at a competitive disadvantage relative to their local rivals. Similarly, Toyota has production plants distributed around the world in part to make sure that a rising yen does not price Toyota cars out of local markets. Caterpillar has also pursued this strategy, setting up factories around the world that can act as a hedge against the possibility that a strong dollar will price Caterpillar's exports out of foreign markets. In 2008, 2009, and 2014–2015, all periods of dollar strength, this real hedge proved to be very useful.

OTHER STEPS FOR MANAGING FOREIGN EXCHANGE RISK

A firm needs to develop a mechanism for ensuring it maintains an appropriate mix of tactics and strategies for minimizing its foreign exchange exposure. Although there is no universal agreement as to the components of this mechanism, a number of common themes stand out.[29] First, central control of exposure is needed to protect resources efficiently and ensure that each subunit adopts the correct mix of tactics and strategies. Many companies have set up in-house foreign exchange centers. Although such centers may not be able to execute all foreign exchange deals—particularly in large, complex multinationals where myriad transactions may be pursued simultaneously—they should at least set guidelines for the firm's subsidiaries to follow.

Second, firms should distinguish between, on one hand, transaction and translation exposure and, on the other, economic exposure. Many companies seem to focus on reducing their transaction and translation exposure and pay scant attention to economic exposure, which may have more profound long-term implications.[30] Firms need to develop strategies for dealing with economic exposure. For example, Stanley Black & Decker, the maker of power tools, has a strategy for actively managing its economic risk. The key to Stanley Black & Decker's strategy is flexible sourcing. In response to foreign exchange movements, Stanley Black & Decker can move production from one location to another to offer the most competitive pricing. Stanley Black & Decker manufactures in more than a dozen locations around the world—in Europe, Australia, Brazil, Mexico, and Japan. More than 50 percent of the company's productive assets are based outside North America. Although each of Stanley Black & Decker's factories focuses on one or two products to achieve economies of scale, there is considerable overlap. On average, the company runs its factories at no more than 80 percent capacity, so most are able to switch rapidly from producing one product to producing another or to add a product. This allows a factory's production to be changed in response to foreign exchange movements. For example, if the dollar depreciates against other currencies, the amount of imports into the United States from overseas subsidiaries can be reduced and the amount of exports from U.S. subsidiaries to other locations can be increased.[31]

Third, the need to forecast future exchange rate movements cannot be overstated, although as we saw earlier in the chapter this is a tricky business. No model comes close to perfectly predicting future movements in foreign exchange rates. The best that can be said is that in the short run, forward exchange rates provide the best predictors of exchange rate movements, and in the long run, fundamental economic factors—particularly relative inflation rates—should be watched because they influence exchange rate movements. Some firms attempt to forecast exchange rate movements in-house; others rely on outside forecasters. However, all such forecasts are imperfect attempts to predict the future.

Fourth, firms need to establish good reporting systems so the central finance function (or in-house foreign exchange center) can regularly monitor the firm's exposure positions. Such reporting systems should enable the firm to identify any exposed accounts, the exposed position by currency of each account, and the time periods covered.

Finally, on the basis of the information it receives from exchange rate forecasts and its own regular reporting systems, the firm should produce monthly foreign exchange exposure reports. These reports should identify how cash flows and balance sheet elements might be affected by forecasted changes in exchange rates. The reports can then be used by management as a basis for adopting tactics and strategies to hedge against undue foreign exchange risks.

Surprisingly, some of the largest and most sophisticated firms don't take such precautionary steps, exposing themselves to very large foreign exchange risks.

Key Terms

 SUMMARY

This chapter explained how the foreign exchange market works, examined the forces that determine exchange rates, and then discussed the implications of these factors for international business. Given that changes in exchange rates can dramatically alter the profitability of foreign trade and investment deals, this is an area of major interest to international business. The chapter made the following points:

1. One function of the foreign exchange market is to convert the currency of one country into the currency of another. A second function of the foreign exchange market is to provide insurance against foreign exchange risk.

2. The spot exchange rate is the exchange rate at which a dealer converts one currency into another currency on a particular day.

3. Foreign exchange risk can be reduced by using forward exchange rates. A forward exchange rate is an exchange rate governing future transactions. Foreign exchange risk can also be reduced by engaging in currency swaps. A swap is the simultaneous purchase and sale of a given amount of foreign exchange for two different value dates.

4. The law of one price holds that in competitive markets that are free of transportation costs and barriers to trade, identical products sold in different countries must sell for the same price when their price is expressed in the same currency.

5. Purchasing power parity (PPP) theory states the price of a basket of particular goods should be roughly equivalent in each country. PPP theory

predicts that the exchange rate will change if relative prices change.

6. The rate of change in countries' relative prices depends on their relative inflation rates. A country's inflation rate seems to be a function of the growth in its money supply.

7. The PPP theory of exchange rate changes yields relatively accurate predictions of long-term trends in exchange rates but not of short-term movements. The failure of PPP theory to predict exchange rate changes more accurately may be due to transportation costs, barriers to trade and investment, and the impact of psychological factors such as bandwagon effects on market movements and short-run exchange rates.

8. Interest rates reflect expectations about inflation. In countries where inflation is expected to be high, interest rates also will be high.

9. The international Fisher effect states that for any two countries, the spot exchange rate should change in an equal amount but in the opposite direction to the difference in nominal interest rates.

10. The most common approach to exchange rate forecasting is fundamental analysis. This relies on variables such as money supply growth,

11. In many countries, the ability of residents and nonresidents to convert local currency into a foreign currency is restricted by government policy. A government restricts the convertibility of its currency to protect the country's foreign exchange reserves and to halt any capital flight.

12. Nonconvertibility of a currency makes it very difficult to engage in international trade and investment in the country. One way of coping with the nonconvertibility problem is to engage in countertrade—to trade goods and services for other goods and services.

13. The three types of exposure to foreign exchange risk are transaction exposure, translation exposure, and economic exposure.

14. Tactics that insure against transaction and translation exposure include buying forward, using currency swaps, and leading and lagging payables and receivables.

15. Reducing a firm's economic exposure requires strategic choices about how the firm's productive assets are distributed around the globe.

Critical Thinking and Discussion Questions

1. The interest rate on South Korean government securities with one-year maturity is 4 percent, and the expected inflation rate for the coming year is 2 percent. The interest rate on U.S. government securities with one-year maturity is 7 percent, and the expected rate of inflation is 5 percent. The current spot exchange rate for Korean won is $1 = W1,200. Forecast the spot exchange rate one year from today. Explain the logic of your answer.

2. Two countries, Great Britain and the United States, produce just one good: beef. Suppose the price of beef in the United States is $2.80 per pound, and in Britain it is £3.70 per pound.

    a. According to PPP theory, what should the dollar/pound spot exchange rate be?

    b. Suppose the price of beef is expected to rise to $3.10 in the United States and to £4.65 in Britain. What should the one-year forward dollar/pound exchange rate be?

    c. Given your answers to parts *a* and *b*, and given that the current interest rate in the United States is 10 percent, what would you expect the current interest rate to be in Britain?

3. Reread the Management Focus "Embraer and the Gyrations of the Brazilian Real," and then answer the following questions:

    a. What does the recent economic history of Brazil tell you about the relationship between price inflation and exchange rates? What other factors might determine exchange rates for the Brazilian real?

    b. Is a decline in value of the real against the U.S. dollar good for Embraer, bad for Embraer, or a mixed bag? Explain your answer.

    c. What kind of foreign exchange rate risks is Embraer exposed to? Can Embraer reduce these risks? How?

    d. Do you think Embraer's decision to try to hedge against further appreciation of the real in the early 2000s was a good decision? What was the alternative?

    e. Since 2008, Embraer has significantly reduced its dollar hedging operations. Is this wise?

    f. Between mid-2014 and early 2015, the real depreciated significantly against the U.S. dollar. What do you think the impact was on Embraer?

4. You manufacture wine goblets. In mid-June, you receive an order for 10,000 goblets from Japan. Payment of ¥400,000 is due in mid-December. You expect the yen to rise from its present rate of $1 = ¥130 to $1 = ¥100 by December. You can borrow yen at 6 percent a year. What should you do?

5. You are the CFO of a U.S. firm whose wholly owned subsidiary in Mexico manufactures component parts for your U.S. assembly operations. The subsidiary has been financed by bank borrowings in the United States. One of your analysts told you that the Mexican peso is expected to depreciate by 30 percent against the dollar on the foreign exchange markets over the next year. What actions, if any, should you take?

globalEDGE research task globaledge.msu.edu

Use the globalEDGE™ website (**globaledge.msu.edu**) to complete the following exercises:

1. One of your company's essential suppliers is located in Japan. Your company needs to make a 1-million Japanese yen payment in six months. Considering that your company primarily operates in U.S. dollars, you are assigned the task of deciding on a strategy to minimize your transaction exposure. Identify the *spot* and *forward exchange rates* between the two currencies. What factors influence your decision to use each? Which one would you choose? How many dollars must you spend to acquire the amount of yen required?

2. Sometimes analysts use the price of specific products in different locations to compare currency valuation and purchasing power. For example, *The Economist*'s Big Mac Index compares the purchasing power parity of many countries based on the price of a Big Mac. Using Google, locate the latest edition of this index that is accessible. Identify the five countries (and their currencies) with the lowest purchasing power parity according to this classification. Which currencies, if any, are overvalued?

CLOSING CASE

The Fluctuating Value of the Yuan Gives Chinese Businesses a Lesson in Foreign Exchange Risk

Between 2015 and early 2018, the Chinese currency, the yuan, fluctuated significantly in value against the U.S. dollar, giving Chinese businesses an object lesson in the importance of managing for foreign exchange risk.

From August 2015 through to December 2016, the value of the yuan in dollars *depreciated* by 12 percent from 6.2 to the dollar to 6.95 to the dollar. This depreciation was triggered by a slowdown in the Chinese economy, which led to an outflow of capital from China. Even though the Chinese government spent heavily to try to prop up the value of the yuan, using $1.5 trillion of dollar-denominated foreign exchange reserves to purchase yuan, they could not halt the decline in its value against the dollar.

While the depreciation in the yuan boosted exports, it also resulted in an unanticipated increase in the yuan price of key imports, which raised costs for a number of Chinese companies. About 980 listed Chinese companies reported combined foreign-exchange losses of 48.7 billion yuan in 2015, almost 13 times higher than 2014, according to data compiled by *Bloomberg*. Hardest hit were Chinese airlines, many of which imported aviation fuel that was paid for in dollars. As the cost of fuel in terms of yuan went up, their profits slumped. In total, the Chinese airline sector registered foreign exchange losses of 17.9 billion yuan for 2015, compared with 951.7 million a year earlier. The big three state-owned airlines—China Southern Airlines Co, China Eastern Airlines Corp, and Air China Ltd—suffered 15.85 billion yuan in foreign-exchange currency losses in 2015.

In 2017, conditions reversed. Between January 2017 and April 2018, the yuan *appreciated* in value by 10 percent against the dollar, increasing from 6.95 to the dollar to 6.27 to the dollar. The appreciation was due to a number of factors, including a return to stronger growth in China and the election of Donald Trump in the United States. The latter event seems initially to have reduced the confidence that foreign investors had in the United States and resulted in an outflow of capital as they sought to diversify their holdings of foreign assets and currency. The dollar also fell after members of the Trump administration made statements suggesting that they were happy to see it decline, because they believed it boosted U.S. exports.

The appreciation in the value of the yuan against the dollar from January 2017 onward reduced the yuan costs for Chinese companies that imported goods priced in dollars, such as aviation fuel. Thus, Air China noted in its 2017 annual report that a 1 percent gain in the yuan against the greenback can boost its net profits by about 280 million yuan, primarily due to reductions in the cost of aviation fuel.

On the other hand, the appreciation of the yuan raised the dollar price of Chinese exports. Many exporters saw their profits squeezed as a result. In early February 2018, Guangdong Goworld, a supplier to Apple, said in a stock exchange filing that it had suffered an estimated foreign exchange loss of 45 million yuan (US$7.2 million) in January 2018 owing to a stronger yuan. The January figure alone was equal to 94 percent of its foreign exchange losses for the first three quarters of 2017. It also translated into 34 percent of its net profits in the first nine months of 2017. The Shenzhen-listed company manufactures and sells printed circuit boards, liquid crystal displays (LCDs), and ultrasonic electronic measuring instruments to developed markets, including the U.S., Europe, Australia, and Japan.

In another example, a spokesperson for Zhejiang NHU Co., a producer of vitamins, said that even as the vitamin export market experienced a boom in 2017, the company suffered millions of yuan in foreign exchange losses. The basic problem was that the company negotiated dollar prices for its vitamins in 2016, but by the end of 2017, each dollar of sales was yielding less revenues when translated back into yuan (thanks to the appreciation of the yuan). To deal with this problem, the company set up a team to discuss the issue and employed means such as hedging and forward exchange transactions to try to minimize foreign exchange risks.

Sources: Maggie Zhang and Daniel Ren, "It Has Dealt Us a Heavy Blow," *South China Morning Post*, April 7, 2018; Xie Yu, "Chinese Companies Foreign

The profitability of Chinese Airlines depends in part upon the yuan–dollar exchange rate.

Paul J. Richards/AFP/Getty Images

Exchange Losses Soared Last Year," *South China Morning Post*, April 6, 2016; and "Exporters Feel the Bite of a Stronger Yuan," *Global Times*, April 2, 2018

Case Discussion Questions

1. Why did the Chinese yuan *depreciate* against the dollar between August 2015 and December 2016? What were the benefits of the depreciation for China? What were the costs?

2. Why do you think the Chinese government tried to limit the depreciation by using dollars to buy yuan? Why did it not stop the fall in the yuan?

3. Why did conditions reverse in 2017, with the yuan *appreciating* against the dollar? What does this tell you about how the foreign exchange market works?

4. What could importers such as the Chinese airlines have done to limit the negative impact of a depreciation in the value of the yuan against the dollar in 2016? Should they have done this?

5. If you were a Chinese exporter, what might you have done if you had anticipated the appreciation in the value of the yuan against the dollar that occurred in 2017?

Design elements: Modern textured halftone: ©VIPRESIONA/ Shutterstock; globalEDGE icon: ©globalEDGE; All others: ©McGraw-Hill Education

Endnotes

1. For a good general introduction to the foreign exchange market, see R. Weisweiller, *How the Foreign Exchange Market Works* (New York: New York Institute of Finance, 1990). A detailed description of the economics of foreign exchange markets can be found in P. R. Krugman and M. Obstfeld, *International Economics: Theory and Policy* (New York: HarperCollins, 1994).

2. Oscar Jorda and Alan Taylor, "The Carry Trade and Fundamentals: Nothing to Fear but FEER Itself," *Journal of International Economics* 88 (2012), pp. 74–90.

3. "The Domino Effect," *The Economist*, July 5, 2008, p. 85.

4. Leo Lewis, "Speculations of a Yen Carry Trade Revival Grow," *Financial Times*, December 22, 2016.

5. Bank for International Settlements, *Tri-annual Central Bank Survey of Foreign Exchange and Derivatives Market Activity, April 2016* (Basle, Switzerland: BIS, December 11, 2016).

6. Bank for International Settlements, *Tri-annual Central Bank Survey of Foreign Exchange and Derivatives Market Activity, April 2016.*

7. Bank for International Settlements, *Tri-annual Central Bank Survey of Foreign Exchange and Derivatives Market Activity, April 2016.*

8. M. Dickson, "Capital Gain: How London Is Thriving as It Takes on the Global Competition," *Financial Times*, March 27, 2006, p. 11; Patrick Jenkins, "The City of London Faces the Future Beyond Brexit," *Financial Times*, October 3, 2016.

9. For a comprehensive review, see M. Taylor, "The Economics of Exchange Rates," *Journal of Economic Literature* 33 (1995), pp. 13–47.

10. Krugman and Obstfeld, *International Economics.*

11. M. Friedman, *Studies in the Quantity Theory of Money* (Chicago: University of Chicago Press, 1956). For an accessible explanation, see M. Friedman and R. Friedman, *Free to Choose* (London: Penguin Books, 1979), chap. 9.

12. Juan-Antonio Morales, "Inflation Stabilization in Bolivia," in *Inflation Stabilization: The Experience of Israel, Argentina, Brazil, Bolivia, and Mexico*, ed. Michael Bruno et al. (Cambridge, MA: MIT Press, 1988); *The Economist, World Book of Vital Statistics* (New York: Random House, 1990).

13. For reviews and various articles, see H. J. Edison, J. E. Gagnon, and W. R. Melick, "Understanding the Empirical Literature on Purchasing Power Parity," *Journal of International Money and Finance* 16 (February 1997), pp. 1–18; J. R. Edison, "Multi-Country Evidence on the Behavior of Purchasing Power Parity under the Current Float," *Journal of International Money and Finance* 16 (February 1997), pp. 19–36; K. Rogoff, "The Purchasing Power Parity Puzzle," *Journal of Economic Literature* 34 (1996), pp. 647–68; D. R. Rapach and M. E. Wohar, "Testing the Monetary Model of Exchange Rate Determination: New Evidence from a Century of Data," *Journal of International Economics,* December 2002, pp. 359–85; M. P. Taylor, "Purchasing Power Parity," *Review of International Economics,* August 2003, pp. 436–56; H. Kim and YK Moh, "A Century of Purchasing Power Parity Confirmed," *Journal of International Money and Finance* 29 (2010), pp. 1398–1405.

14. M. Obstfeld and K. Rogoff, "The Six Major Puzzles in International Economics," *National Bureau of Economic Research Working Paper Series*, paper no. 7777, July 2000.

15. M. Obstfeld and K. Rogoff, "The Six Major Puzzles in International Economics."

16. See M. Devereux and C. Engel, "Monetary Policy in the Open Economy Revisited: Price Setting and Exchange Rate Flexibility," *National Bureau of Economic Research Working Paper Series*, paper no. 7665, April 2000. See also P. Krugman, "Pricing to Market When the Exchange Rate Changes," in *Real Financial Economics*, ed. S. Arndt and J. Richardson (Cambridge, MA: MIT Press, 1987).

17. For a summary of the evidence, see the survey by Taylor, "The Economics of Exchange Rates."

18. R. E. Cumby and M. Obstfeld, "A Note on Exchange Rate Expectations and Nominal Interest Differentials: A Test of the Fisher Hypothesis," *Journal of Finance*, June 1981, pp. 697–703; L. Coppock and M. Poitras, "Evaluating the Fisher Effect in Long Term Cross Country Averages," *International Review of Economics and Finance* 9 (2000), pp. 181–203.

19. Taylor, "The Economics of Exchange Rates." See also R. K. Lyons, *The Microstructure Approach to Exchange Rates* (Cambridge, MA: MIT Press, 2002); P. De Grauwe and M. Grimaldi, *The Exchange Rate in a Behavioral Finance Framework* (Princeton, NJ: Princeton University Press, 2006).

20. See H. L. Allen and M. P. Taylor, "Charts, Noise, and Fundamentals in the Foreign Exchange Market," *Economic Journal* 100 (1990), pp. 49–59; T. Ito, "Foreign Exchange Rate Expectations: Micro Survey Data," *American Economic Review* 80 (1990), pp. 434–49; T. F. Rotheli, "Bandwagon Effects and Run Patterns in Exchange Rates," *Journal of International Financial Markets, Money and Institutions* 12, no. 2 (2002), pp. 157–66.

21. For example, see E. Fama, "Forward Rates as Predictors of Future Spot Rates," *Journal of Financial Economics,* October 1976, pp. 361–77.

22. L. Kilian and M. P. Taylor, "Why Is It So Difficult to Beat the Random Walk Forecast of Exchange Rates?" *Journal of International Economics* 20 (May 2003), pp. 85–103; R. M. Levich, "The Efficiency of Markets for Foreign Exchange," in *International Finance*, ed. G. D. Gay and R. W. Kold (Richmond, VA: Robert F. Dane, 1983).

23. J. Williamson, *The Exchange Rate System* (Washington, DC: Institute for International Economics, 1983); R. H. Clarida, L. Sarno, M. P. Taylor, and G. Valente, "The Out of Sample Success of Term Structure Models as Exchange Rate Predictors," *Journal of International Economics* 60 (May 2003), pp. 61–84.

24. Kilian and Taylor, "Why Is It So Difficult to Beat the Random Walk Forecast of Exchange Rates?"

25. Rogoff, "The Purchasing Power Parity Puzzle."

26. C. Engel and J. D. Hamilton, "Long Swings in the Dollar: Are They in the Data and Do Markets Know It?" *American Economic Review*, September 1990, pp. 689–713.

27. J. R. Carter and J. Gagne, "The Do's and Don'ts of International Countertrade," *Sloan Management Review*, Spring 1988, pp. 31–37.

28. D. S. Levine, "Got a Spare Destroyer Lying Around?" *World Trade* 10 (June 1997), pp. 34–35; Dan West, "Countertrade," *Business Credit,* April 2001, pp. 64–67.

29. For details on how various firms manage their foreign exchange exposure, see the articles contained in the special foreign exchange issue of *Business International Money Report*, December 18, 1989, pp. 401–12.

30. See *Business International Money Report*, December 18, 1989, pp. 401–12.

31. S. Arterian, "How Black & Decker Defines Exposure," *Business International Money Report*, December 18, 1989, pp. 404, 405, 409.

The International Monetary System

11

LEARNING OBJECTIVES

After reading this chapter, you will be able to:

LO11-1   Describe the historical development of the modern global monetary system.

LO11-2   Explain the role played by the World Bank and the IMF in the international monetary system.

LO11-3   Compare and contrast the differences between a fixed and a floating exchange rate system.

LO11-4   Identify exchange rate regimes used in the world today and why countries adopt different exchange rate regimes.

LO11-5   Understand the debate surrounding the role of the IMF in the management of financial crises.

LO11-6   Explain the implications of the global monetary system for management practice.

Chintung Lee/Shutterstock

Pakistan Takes Another IMF Loan

OPENING CASE

In early April 2019, Pakistan announced it would take a $6 to $8 billion loan package from the IMF in order to help deal with a balance-of-payments crisis. The crisis had been triggered by a rise in the country's trade deficit and budget deficits, both of which reached 5 percent of GDP in 2018. The trade deficit required the country to use its foreign exchange reserves to pay for imports, but these shrank rapidly during 2018, falling from $19 billion in January 2018 to under $7 billion by January 2019. Recognizing the economic risks here, currency traders had sold off the Pakistan rupee. With not enough foreign exchange reserves in central bank coffers to protect the value of the currency, pay for imports, and serve existing foreign debt obligations, the government was forced to accept a significant devaluation of the rupee. In April 2017, the official exchange rate was $1 = 103.6 rupees. By April 2019, it was $1 = 142 rupees, a devaluation of around 37 percent. Despite this decline, Pakistan's exports had not picked up, and higher import prices were fueling inflation, which reached an annual rate of 9.4 percent in February 2019, up from 3.65 percent in April 2018. Without an IMF loan, Pakistan would probably run out of foreign exchange reserves sometime in 2019, precipitating a much more serious economic crisis.

This was not Pakistan's first IMF bailout—it had agreed to 12 prior loan packages since the early 1980s. Pakistan had regularly failed to meet conditions attached to its previous IMF loans. These conditions have included cutting government spending, taking steps to eliminate a very high rate of tax evasion in the country, and privatizing bloated and poorly managed state-owned corporations. The nation had only managed to successfully complete one prior IMF program, meaning that it received all the disbursements as planned, on a $6.6 billion three-year facility that ended in 2016. Even then, a number of requirements were relaxed.

The current crisis has been exacerbated by China's Belt and Road initiative. This initiative is designed to upgrade the infrastructure of Asia and Central and Eastern Europe to facilitate greater trade and economic development. It includes investments in railways, roads, ports, and power systems in 65 countries. Pakistan is one of those countries. So far, the country has agreed to over $60 billion of Chinese financing for various road and power plant projects. It all sounds great, but these projects have required imports that have exacerbated Pakistan's trade deficit. Moreover, debt payments to the Chinese have eaten into Pakistan's foreign exchange reserves and widened the budget deficit. Indeed, debt payments now make up the second largest item in the government budget after spending on Pakistan's large military. Military spending and debt payments together now count for half of all government spending in Pakistan.

Prior to going to the IMF for its most recent loan, Pakistan had tried to solve the crisis by raising funds from other external sources. Prime Minister Imran Khan was reluctant to appeal to the IMF. Khan, a former star cricket player with movie star good looks, was elected in July 2018 with the tacit approval of the military, an institution that had ruled Pakistan for half of the time since it gained independence from the British in 1949. Khan had criticized prior administrations for going to the IMF and had promised to break the begging bowl habit. To his credit, he has managed to get financial commitments from Saudi Arabia and the United Arab Emirates, who have offered over $30 billion in investments and loans, including some short-term financing to deal with the ongoing crisis. In addition, China had promised to provide some additional short-term financing. But it became apparent that this was not enough, and some IMF funding would be required.

For Khan, the problem with IMF funding is that it comes with conditions attached, which may not prove too popular among his supporters. Although these conditions have not yet been made public, they are likely to include fixing the tax system, cutting government spending (including that on the military), raising interest rates, and privatization. To be sure, in the past, Pakistan has been able to get such conditions "relaxed," but that may be harder this time around. In recognition of its strategic importance in the war against terror, Pakistan had long been the recipient of financial help from the United States, and the IMF, as a U.S.-backed institution, had tended to go easy on the country. Under President Trump, however, U.S. support of Pakistan's military has been cut, and the mercurial President has been very critical of tacit support among the country's military for the Taliban in neighboring Afghanistan.

Sources: G. Abbas, "Pakistan to Avail $6-8bn IMF Package, Says Asad Umar," *Pakistan Today*, April 15, 2019; S. Shah, "Pakistan Turns to Gulf Countries to Keep Economy Afloat," *The Wall Street Journal*, January 22, 2019; "Pakistan's New Prime Minister Turns to the IMF," *The Economist*, October 11, 2018; K. Haider, F. Mangi, and C. Kay, "For Pakistan's 13th IMF Bailout, Expect Tougher Conditions," *Bloomberg*, October 11, 2018.

Introduction

In this chapter, we look at the international monetary system and its role in determining exchange rates. The **international monetary system** refers to the institutional arrangements that govern exchange rates. In Chapter 10, we assumed the foreign exchange market was the primary institution for determining exchange rates and the impersonal market forces of demand and supply determined the relative value of any two currencies (i.e., their exchange rate). Furthermore, we explained that the demand and supply of currencies are influenced by their respective countries' relative inflation rates and interest rates. When the foreign exchange market determines the relative value of a currency, we say that the country is adhering to a **floating exchange rate** regime. Four of the world's major trading currencies—the U.S. dollar, the European Union's euro, the Japanese yen, and the British pound—are all free to float against each other. Thus, their exchange rates are determined by market forces and fluctuate against each other day to day, if not minute to minute. However, the exchange rates of many currencies are not determined by the free play of market forces; other institutional arrangements are adopted.

Many of the world's developing nations peg their currencies, primarily to the dollar or the euro. A **pegged exchange rate** means the value of the currency is fixed relative to a reference currency, such as the U.S. dollar, and then the exchange rate between that currency and other currencies is determined by the reference currency exchange rate.

Other countries, while not adopting a formal pegged rate, try to hold the value of their currency within some range against an important reference currency such as the U.S. dollar or a "basket" of currencies. This is often referred to as a **managed-float system** or a **dirty-float system**. It is a float because, in theory, the value of the currency is determined by market forces, but it is a managed (or dirty) float (as opposed to a clean float) because the central bank of a country will intervene in the foreign exchange market to try to maintain the value of its currency if it depreciates (or appreciates) too rapidly against an important reference currency. This has been the policy adopted by the Pakistani government since the 1980s (see the opening case). The value of the Pakistani currency, the rupee, has been linked to a basket of other currencies—including the dollar, yen, and euro—and it is allowed to vary in value against individual currencies, but only within limits.

globalEDGE GLOBALEDGE™ BLOG

The international monetary system captures our attention because here we are talking about the institutional arrangements that govern exchange rates, and this is a tricky business in which countries have leverage to influence their country's currency value but do not necessarily always use it. The options for how the value, or "rate," is set for a currency are many: floating exchange rate, pegged exchange rate, dirty float, and fixed exchange rate are the ones covered in Chapter 11. We start the chapter with some history related to the "gold standard," a practice that takes us back to ancient times. Technically, no country uses the gold standard any longer but many, including the United States, hold substantial gold reserves. The international monetary system depends on a lot of variables (see the globalEDGE™ Database of International Business Statistics, which we covered in Chapter 10); today, these variables also include "behavioral" (perception) issues in addition to hard, concrete data. The globalEDGE™ Blog has been a favored "international business" vehicle to stay current on important topics, often related to monetary issues. Check out the globalEDGE™ Blog (**globaledge.msu.edu/blog**), see what is covered on monetary issues, and engage with people from around the world on issues that are of interest to you.

Still other countries have operated with a **fixed exchange rate**, in which the values of a set of currencies are fixed against each other at some mutually agreed-on exchange rate. Before the introduction of the euro in 1999, several member states of the European Union operated with fixed exchange rates within the context of the **European Monetary System (EMS)**. For a quarter of a century after World War II, the world's major industrial nations participated in a fixed exchange rate system. Although this system collapsed in 1973, some still argue that the world should attempt to reestablish it.

Another option is for a country to abandon its own currency and instead adopt another currency (typically the U.S. dollar—a process referred to as **dollarization**). Dollarization is sometimes used when a country is suffering from severe macroeconomic problems, such as high inflation, that are making its own currency worthless. This was the case with Ecuador in 2000, which abandoned its own currency in favor of the U.S. dollar after suffering from hyperinflation. Dollarization is now being considered as an option for Venezuela, a country whose currency has been rendered worthless by hyperinflation.

This chapter explains how the international monetary system works and points out its implications for international business. To understand how the system works, we must review its evolution. We begin with a discussion of the gold standard and its breakup during the 1930s. Then we discuss the 1944 Bretton Woods conference. The Bretton Woods conference created two major international institutions that play a role in the international monetary system—the International Monetary Fund (IMF) and the World Bank. The IMF was given the task of maintaining order in the international monetary system; the World Bank's role was to promote development. The Bretton Woods system of fixed exchange rates collapsed in 1973. Since then, the world has operated with a mixed system in which some currencies are allowed to float freely, but many are either managed by government intervention or pegged to another currency.

Notwithstanding the collapse of the fixed exchange rate system, today both the IMF and the World Bank continue to play major roles in the world economy and in the international monetary system. For example, in 2019, the IMF stepped in to help Pakistan navigate its way through a currency crisis caused by decades of poor economic policies and expanding trade and budget deficits (see the opening case). Pakistan has not been able to generate enough foreign exchange reserves to cover its international obligations, including paying for imports and serving foreign debt. As its foreign reserves have shrunk, the Pakistani rupee has declined in value against major world currencies, boosting import prices and inflation. A loan from the IMF will help the country to serve its international obligations and maintain the value of the rupee, but as in the Pakistani case, such loans come with conditions attached requiring the recipient to take concrete steps to improve its economy.

Finally, we discuss the implications of all this material for international business. We will see how the exchange rate policy adopted by a government can have an important impact on the outlook for business operations in a given country. We also look at how the policies adopted by the IMF can have an impact on the economic outlook for a country and, accordingly, on the costs and benefits of doing business in that country.

The Gold Standard

LO11-1

Describe the historical development of the modern global monetary system.

The gold standard had its origin in the use of gold coins as a medium of exchange, unit of account, and store of value—a practice that dates to ancient times. When international trade was limited in volume, payment for goods purchased from another country was typically made in gold or silver. However, as the volume of international trade expanded in the wake of the Industrial Revolution, a more convenient means of financing international trade was needed. Shipping large quantities of gold and silver around the world to finance international trade seemed impractical. The solution adopted was to arrange for payment in paper currency and for governments to agree to convert the paper currency into gold on demand at a fixed rate.

MECHANICS OF THE GOLD STANDARD

Pegging currencies to gold and guaranteeing convertibility is known as the **gold standard**. By 1880, most of the world's major trading nations, including Great Britain, Germany,

Japan, and the United States, had adopted the gold standard. Given a common gold standard, the value of any currency in units of any other currency (the exchange rate) was easy to determine.

For example, under the gold standard, 1 U.S. dollar was defined as equivalent to 23.22 grains of "fine" (pure) gold. Thus, one could, in theory, demand that the U.S. government convert that one dollar into 23.22 grains of gold. Because there are 480 grains in an ounce, one ounce of gold cost \$20.67 (480/23.22). The amount of a currency needed to purchase one ounce of gold was referred to as the **gold par value**. The British pound was valued at 113 grains of fine gold. In other words, one ounce of gold cost £4.25 (480/113). From the gold par values of pounds and dollars, we can calculate what the exchange rate was for converting pounds into dollars; it was £1 = \$4.87 (i.e., \$20.67/£4.25).

STRENGTH OF THE GOLD STANDARD

The great strength claimed for the gold standard was that it contained a powerful mechanism for achieving balance-of-trade equilibrium by all countries.[1] A country is said to be in **balance-of-trade equilibrium** when the income its residents earn from exports is equal to the money its residents pay to other countries for imports (the current account of its balance of payments is in balance). Suppose there are only two countries in the world, Japan and the United States. Imagine Japan's trade balance is in surplus because it exports more to the United States than it imports from the United States. Japanese exporters are paid in U.S. dollars, which they exchange for Japanese yen at a Japanese bank. The Japanese bank submits the dollars to the U.S. government and demands payment of gold in return. (This is a simplification of what would occur, but it will make our point.)

Under the gold standard, when Japan has a trade surplus, there is a net flow of gold from the United States to Japan. These gold flows automatically reduce the U.S. money supply and swell Japan's money supply. As we saw in Chapter 10, there is a close connection between money supply growth and price inflation. An increase in money supply will raise prices in Japan, while a decrease in the U.S. money supply will push U.S. prices downward. The rise in the price of Japanese goods will decrease demand for these goods, while the fall in the price of U.S. goods will increase demand for these goods. Thus, Japan will start to buy more from the United States, and the United States will buy less from Japan, until a balance-of-trade equilibrium is achieved.

This adjustment mechanism seems so simple and attractive that even today, nearly 80 years after the final collapse of the gold standard, some people believe the world should return to a gold standard.

THE PERIOD BETWEEN THE WARS: 1918–1939

The gold standard worked reasonably well from the 1870s until the start of World War I in 1914, when it was abandoned. During the war, several governments financed part of their massive military expenditures by printing money. This resulted in inflation, and by the war's end in 1918, price levels were higher everywhere. The United States returned to the gold standard in 1919, Great Britain in 1925, and France in 1928.

Great Britain returned to the gold standard by pegging the pound to gold at the prewar gold parity level of £4.25 per ounce, despite substantial inflation between 1914 and 1925. This priced British goods out of foreign markets, which pushed the country into a deep depression. When foreign holders of pounds lost confidence in Great Britain's commitment to maintaining its currency's value, they began converting their holdings of pounds into gold. The British government saw that it could not satisfy the demand for gold without seriously depleting its gold reserves, so it suspended convertibility in 1931.

The United States followed suit and left the gold standard in 1933 but returned to it in 1934, raising the dollar price of gold from \$20.67 per ounce to \$35.00 per ounce. Because more dollars were needed to buy an ounce of gold than before, the implication was that the dollar was worth less. This effectively amounted to a devaluation of the dollar relative to other currencies. Thus, before the devaluation, the pound/dollar exchange rate was

£1 = $4.87, but after the devaluation it was £1 = $8.24. By reducing the price of U.S. exports and increasing the price of imports, the government was trying to create employment in the United States by boosting output (the U.S. government was basically using the exchange rate as an instrument of trade policy—something it now accuses China of doing). However, a number of other countries adopted a similar tactic, and in the cycle of competitive devaluations that soon emerged, no country could win.

The net result was the shattering of any remaining confidence in the system. With countries devaluing their currencies at will, one could no longer be certain how much gold a currency could buy. Instead of holding onto another country's currency, people often tried to change it into gold immediately, lest the country devalue its currency in the intervening period. This put pressure on the gold reserves of various countries, forcing them to suspend gold convertibility. By the start of World War II in 1939, the gold standard was dead.

The Bretton Woods System

In 1944, at the height of World War II, representatives from 44 countries met at Bretton Woods, New Hampshire, to design a new international monetary system. With the collapse of the gold standard and the Great Depression of the 1930s fresh in their minds, these statesmen were determined to build an enduring economic order that would facilitate postwar economic growth. There was consensus that fixed exchange rates were desirable. In addition, the conference participants wanted to avoid the senseless competitive devaluations of the 1930s, and they recognized that the gold standard would not ensure this. The major problem with the gold standard as previously constituted was that no multinational institution could stop countries from engaging in competitive devaluations.

The agreement reached at Bretton Woods established two multinational institutions—the International Monetary Fund (IMF) and the World Bank. The task of the IMF would be to maintain order in the international monetary system and that of the World Bank would be to promote general economic development. The Bretton Woods agreement also called for a system of fixed exchange rates that would be policed by the IMF. Under the agreement, all countries were to fix the value of their currency in terms of gold but were not required to exchange their currencies for gold. Only the dollar remained convertible into gold—at a price of $35 per ounce. Each country decided what it wanted its exchange rate to be vis-à-vis the dollar and then calculated the gold par value of the currency based on that selected dollar exchange rate. All participating countries agreed to try to maintain the value of their currencies within 1 percent of the par value by buying or selling currencies (or gold) as needed. For example, if foreign exchange dealers were selling more of a country's currency than demanded, that country's government would intervene in the foreign exchange markets, buying its currency in an attempt to increase demand and maintain its gold par value.

Another aspect of the Bretton Woods agreement was a commitment not to use devaluation as a weapon of competitive trade policy. However, if a currency became too weak to defend, a devaluation of up to 10 percent would be allowed without any formal approval by the IMF. Larger devaluations required IMF approval.

THE ROLE OF THE IMF

The IMF Articles of Agreement were heavily influenced by the worldwide financial collapse, competitive devaluations, trade wars, high unemployment, hyperinflation in Germany and elsewhere, and general economic disintegration that occurred between the two world wars. The aim of the Bretton Woods agreement, of which the IMF was the main custodian, was to try to avoid a repetition of that chaos through a combination of discipline and flexibility.

Discipline

A fixed exchange rate regime imposes discipline in two ways. First, the need to maintain a fixed exchange rate puts a brake on competitive devaluations and brings stability to the world trade environment. Second, a fixed exchange rate regime imposes monetary discipline on

TEST PREP

Use SmartBook to help retain what you have learned. Access your instructor's Connect course to check out SmartBook or go to **learnsmartadvantage.com** for help.

LO11-2

Explain the role played by the World Bank and the IMF in the international monetary system.

countries, thereby curtailing price inflation. For example, consider what would happen under a fixed exchange rate regime if Great Britain rapidly increased its money supply by printing pounds. As explained in Chapter 10, the increase in money supply would lead to price inflation. Given fixed exchange rates, inflation would make British goods uncompetitive in world markets, while the prices of imports would become more attractive in Great Britain. The result would be a widening trade deficit in Great Britain, with the country importing more than it exports. To correct this trade imbalance under a fixed exchange rate regime, Great Britain would be required to restrict the rate of growth in its money supply to bring price inflation back under control. Thus, fixed exchange rates are seen as a mechanism for controlling inflation and imposing economic discipline on countries.

Flexibility

Although monetary discipline was a central objective of the Bretton Woods agreement, it was recognized that a rigid policy of fixed exchange rates would be too inflexible. It would probably break down just as the gold standard had. In some cases, a country's attempts to reduce its money supply growth and correct a persistent balance-of-payments deficit could force the country into recession and create high unemployment. The architects of the Bretton Woods agreement wanted to avoid high unemployment, so they built limited flexibility into the system. Two major features of the IMF Articles of Agreement fostered this flexibility: IMF lending facilities and adjustable parities.

The IMF stood ready to lend foreign currencies to members to tide them over during short periods of balance-of-payments deficits, when a rapid tightening of monetary or fiscal policy would hurt domestic employment. A pool of gold and currencies contributed by IMF members provided the resources for these lending operations. A persistent balance-of-payments deficit can lead to a depletion of a country's reserves of foreign currency, forcing it to devalue its currency. By providing deficit-laden countries with short-term foreign currency loans, IMF funds would buy time for countries to bring down their inflation rates and reduce their balance-of-payments deficits. The belief was that such loans would reduce pressures for devaluation and allow for a more orderly and less painful adjustment.

Countries were to be allowed to borrow a limited amount from the IMF without adhering to any specific agreements. However, extensive drawings from IMF funds would require a country to agree to increasingly stringent IMF supervision of its macroeconomic policies. Heavy borrowers from the IMF must agree to monetary and fiscal conditions set down by the IMF, which typically included IMF-mandated targets on domestic money supply growth, exchange rate policy, tax policy, government spending, and so on.

The system of adjustable parities allowed for the devaluation of a country's currency by more than 10 percent if the IMF agreed that a country's balance of payments was in "fundamental disequilibrium." The term *fundamental disequilibrium* was not defined in the IMF's Articles of Agreement, but it was intended to apply to countries that had suffered permanent adverse shifts in the demand for their products. Without devaluation, such a country would experience high unemployment and a persistent trade deficit until the domestic price level had fallen far enough to restore a balance-of-payments equilibrium. The belief was that devaluation could help sidestep a painful adjustment process in such circumstances.

THE ROLE OF THE WORLD BANK

The official name for the World Bank is the International Bank for Reconstruction and Development (IBRD). When the Bretton Woods participants established the World Bank, the need to reconstruct the war-torn economies of Europe was foremost in their minds. The bank's initial mission was to help finance the building of Europe's economy by providing low-interest loans. As it turned out, the World Bank was overshadowed in this role by the Marshall Plan, under which the United States lent money directly to European nations to help them rebuild. So the bank turned its attention to development and began lending money to third-world nations. In the 1950s, the bank concentrated on public-sector projects. Power stations, road building, and other transportation investments were much in favor. During the 1960s, the bank also began to lend heavily in support of agriculture, education, population control, and urban development.

The bank lends money under two schemes. Under the IBRD scheme, money is raised through bond sales in the international capital market. Borrowers pay what the bank calls a market rate of interest—the bank's cost of funds plus a margin for expenses. This "market" rate is lower than commercial banks' market rate. Under the IBRD scheme, the bank offers low-interest loans to risky customers whose credit rating is often poor, such as the governments of underdeveloped nations.

A second scheme is overseen by the International Development Association (IDA), an arm of the bank created in 1960. Resources to fund IDA loans are raised through subscriptions from wealthy members such as the United States, Japan, and Germany. IDA loans go only to the poorest countries. Borrowers have up to 50 years to repay at an interest rate of less than 1 percent a year. The world's poorest nations receive grants and interest-free loans.

The Collapse of the Fixed Exchange Rate System

The system of fixed exchange rates established at Bretton Woods worked well until the late 1960s, when it began to show signs of strain. The system finally collapsed in 1973, and since then, we have had a managed-float system. To understand why the system collapsed, one must appreciate the special role of the U.S. dollar in the system. As the only currency that could be converted into gold and as the currency that served as the reference point for all others, the dollar occupied a central place in the system. Any pressure on the dollar to devalue could wreak havoc with the system, and that is what occurred.

Most economists trace the breakup of the fixed exchange rate system to the U.S. macroeconomic policy package of 1965–1968.[2] To finance both the Vietnam conflict and his welfare programs, President Lyndon Johnson backed an increase in U.S. government spending that was not financed by an increase in taxes. Instead, it was financed by an increase in the money supply, which led to a rise in price inflation from less than 4 percent in 1966 to close to 9 percent by 1968. At the same time, the rise in government spending had stimulated the economy. With more money in their pockets, people spent more—particularly on imports—and the U.S. trade balance began to deteriorate.

The increase in inflation and the worsening of the U.S. foreign trade position gave rise to speculation in the foreign exchange market that the dollar would be devalued. Things came to a head in spring 1971, when U.S. trade figures showed that for the first time since 1945, the United States was importing more than it was exporting. This set off massive purchases of German deutsche marks in the foreign exchange market by speculators who guessed that the mark would be revalued against the dollar. On a single day, May 4, 1971, the Bundesbank (Germany's central bank) had to buy $1 billion to hold the dollar/deutsche mark exchange rate at its fixed exchange rate, given the great demand for deutsche marks. On the morning of May 5, the Bundesbank purchased another $1 billion during the first hour of foreign exchange trading! At that point, the Bundesbank faced the inevitable and allowed its currency to float.

In the weeks following the decision to float the deutsche mark, the foreign exchange market became increasingly convinced that the dollar would have to be devalued. However, devaluation of the dollar was no easy matter. Under the Bretton Woods provisions, any other country could change its exchange rates against all currencies simply by fixing its dollar rate at a new level. But as the key currency in the system, the dollar could be devalued only if all countries agreed to simultaneously revalue against the dollar. Many countries did not want this, because it would make their products more expensive relative to U.S. products.

To force the issue, President Richard Nixon announced in August 1971 that the dollar was no longer convertible into gold. He also announced that a new 10 percent tax on imports would remain in effect until U.S. trading partners agreed to revalue their currencies against the dollar. This brought the trading partners to the bargaining table, and in December 1971, an agreement was reached to devalue the dollar by about 8 percent against foreign currencies. The import tax was then removed. The problem was not solved, however. The U.S. balance-of-payments position continued to deteriorate throughout 1973, while the nation's money supply continued to expand at an inflationary rate. Speculation continued to grow

TEST PREP

Use SmartBook to help retain what you have learned. Access your instructor's Connect course to check out SmartBook or go to **learnsmartadvantage.com** for help.

LO11-3

Compare and contrast the differences between a fixed and a floating exchange rate system.

that the dollar was still overvalued and that a second devaluation would be necessary. In anticipation, foreign exchange dealers began converting dollars to deutsche marks and other currencies. After a massive wave of speculation in February 1973, which culminated with European central banks spending $3.6 billion on March 1 to try to prevent their currencies from appreciating against the dollar, the foreign exchange market was closed. When the foreign exchange market reopened March 19, the currencies of Japan and most European countries were floating against the dollar, although many developing countries continued to peg their currency to the dollar, and many do to this day. At that time, the switch to a floating system was viewed as a temporary response to unmanageable speculation in the foreign exchange market. But it is now more than 40 years since the Bretton Woods system of fixed exchange rates collapsed, and the temporary solution looks permanent.

The Bretton Woods system had an Achilles' heel: The system could not work if its key currency, the U.S. dollar, was under speculative attack. The Bretton Woods system could work only as long as the U.S. inflation rate remained low and the United States did not run a balance-of-payments deficit. Once these things occurred, the system soon became strained to the breaking point.

The Floating Exchange Rate Regime

The floating exchange rate regime that followed the collapse of the fixed exchange rate system was formalized in January 1976, when IMF members met in Jamaica and agreed to the rules for the international monetary system that are in place today.

THE JAMAICA AGREEMENT

The Jamaica meeting revised the IMF's Articles of Agreement to reflect the new reality of floating exchange rates. The main elements of the Jamaica agreement include the following:

- Floating rates were declared acceptable. IMF members were permitted to enter the foreign exchange market to even out "unwarranted" speculative fluctuations.
- Gold was abandoned as a reserve asset. The IMF returned its gold reserves to members at the current market price, placing the proceeds in a trust fund to help poor nations. IMF members were permitted to sell their own gold reserves at the market price.
- Total annual IMF quotas—the amount member countries contribute to the IMF—were increased to $41 billion. (Since then, they have been increased to $767 billion, while the membership of the IMF has been expanded to include 188 countries. Non-oil-exporting, less developed countries were given greater access to IMF funds.)

EXCHANGE RATES SINCE 1973

Since March 1973, exchange rates have become much more volatile and less predictable than they were between 1945 and 1973.[3] This volatility has been partly due to a number of unexpected shocks to the world monetary system, including:

- The oil crisis in 1971, when the Organization of the Petroleum Exporting Countries (OPEC) quadrupled the price of oil. The harmful effect of this on the U.S. inflation rate and trade position resulted in a further decline in the value of the dollar.
- The loss of confidence in the dollar that followed a sharp rise in the U.S. inflation rate in 1977–1978.
- The oil crisis of 1979, when OPEC once again increased the price of oil dramatically: this time, it was doubled.
- The unexpected rise in the dollar between 1980 and 1985, despite a deteriorating balance-of-payments picture.
- The rapid fall of the U.S. dollar against the Japanese yen and German deutsche mark between 1985 and 1987, and against the yen between 1993 and 1995.

- The partial collapse of the European Monetary System in 1992.

- The 1997 Asian currency crisis, when the Asian currencies of several countries—including South Korea, Indonesia, Malaysia, and Thailand—lost between 50 and 80 percent of their value against the U.S. dollar in a few months.

- The global financial crisis of 2008–2010 and the sovereign debt crisis in the European Union during 2010–2011.

Figure 11.1 summarizes how the value of the U.S. dollar has fluctuated against an index of trading currencies between January 1973 and January 2019. (The index, which was set equal to 100 in March 1973, is a weighted average of the foreign exchange values of the U.S. dollar against a basket of other currencies.) An interesting phenomenon in Figure 11.1 is the rapid rise in the value of the dollar between 1980 and 1985 and its subsequent fall between 1985 and 1988. A similar, though less pronounced, rise and fall in the value of the dollar occurred between 1995 and 2012. You will also notice an uptick in the value of the dollar between mid-2014 and early 2019. We briefly discuss the rise and fall of the dollar during these periods, because this tells us something about how the international monetary system has operated in recent years.[4]

The rise in the value of the dollar between 1980 and 1985 occurred when the United States was running a large and growing trade deficit, importing substantially more than it exported. Conventional wisdom would suggest that the increased supply of dollars in the foreign exchange market as a result of the trade deficit should lead to a reduction in the value of the dollar, but as shown in Figure 11.1, it increased in value. Why?

A number of favorable factors overcame the unfavorable effect of a trade deficit. Strong economic growth in the United States attracted heavy inflows of capital from foreign investors seeking high returns on capital assets. High real interest rates attracted foreign investors seeking high returns on financial assets. At the same time, political turmoil in other parts of the world, along with relatively slow economic growth in the developed countries of Europe, helped create the view that the United States was a good place to invest. These inflows of capital increased the demand for dollars in the foreign exchange market, which pushed the value of the dollar upward against other currencies.

The fall in the value of the dollar between 1985 and 1988 was caused by a combination of government intervention and market forces. The rise in the dollar, which priced U.S.

FIGURE 11.1

Major currencies dollar index, 1973–2019.

Source: Data from www.federalreserve.gov.

goods out of foreign markets and made imports relatively cheap, had contributed to a dismal trade picture. In 1985, the United States posted a then-record-high trade deficit of more than $160 billion. This led to growth in demands for protectionism in the United States. In September 1985, the finance ministers and central bank governors of the so-called Group of Five major industrial countries (Great Britain, France, Japan, Germany, and the United States) met at the Plaza Hotel in New York City and reached what was later referred to as the Plaza Accord. They announced that it would be desirable for most major currencies to appreciate vis-à-vis the U.S. dollar and pledged to intervene in the foreign exchange markets, selling dollars, to encourage this objective. The dollar had already begun to weaken during summer 1985, and this announcement further accelerated the decline.

The dollar continued to decline until 1987. The governments of the Group of Five began to worry that the dollar might decline too far, so the finance ministers of the Group of Five met in Paris in February 1987 and reached a new agreement known as the Louvre Accord. They agreed that exchange rates had been realigned sufficiently and pledged to support the stability of exchange rates around their current levels by intervening in the foreign exchange markets when necessary to buy and sell currency. Although the dollar continued to decline for a few months after the Louvre Accord, the rate of decline slowed, and by early 1988, the decline had ended.

Except for a brief speculative flurry around the time of the Persian Gulf War in 1991, the dollar was relatively stable for the first half of the 1990s. However, in the late 1990s, the dollar again began to appreciate against most major currencies, including the euro after its introduction, even though the United States was still running a significant balance-of-payments deficit. Once again, the driving force for the appreciation in the value of the dollar was that foreigners continued to invest in U.S. financial assets, primarily stocks and bonds, and the inflow of money drove up the value of the dollar on foreign exchange markets. The inward investment was due to a belief that U.S. financial assets offered a favorable rate of return.

By 2002, foreigners had started to lose their appetite for U.S. stocks and bonds, and the inflow of money into the United States slowed. Instead of reinvesting dollars earned from exports to the United States in U.S. financial assets, they exchanged those dollars for other currencies, particularly euros, to invest them in non-dollar-denominated assets. One reason for this was the continued growth in the U.S. trade deficit, which hit a record $791 billion in 2005 (by 2016, it had fallen to $502 billion). Although the U.S. trade deficits had been setting records for decades, this deficit was the largest ever when measured as a percentage of the country's GDP (6.3 percent of GDP in 2005).

The record deficit meant that even more dollars were flowing out of the United States into foreign hands, and those foreigners were less inclined to reinvest those dollars in the United States at a rate required to keep the dollar stable. This growing reluctance of foreigners to invest in the United States was in turn due to several factors. First, there was a slowdown in U.S. economic activity during 2001–2002. Second, the U.S. government's budget deficit expanded rapidly after 2001. This led to fears that ultimately the budget deficit would be financed by an expansionary monetary policy that could lead to higher price inflation. Third, from 2003 onward, U.S. government officials began to "talk down" the value of the dollar, in part because the administration believed that a cheaper dollar would increase exports and reduce imports, thereby improving the U.S. balance-of-trade position.[5] Foreigners saw this as a signal that the U.S. government would not intervene in the foreign exchange markets to prop up the value of the dollar, which increased their reluctance to reinvest dollars earned from export sales in U.S. financial assets. As a result of these factors, demand for dollars weakened, and the value of the dollar slid on the foreign exchange markets—hitting an index value of 80.5 in June 2011, the lowest value since the index began in 1973. Some believed that the dollar would have fallen even further had not oil-producing states recycled the dollars they were earning from sales of crude oil back into the U.S. economy. At the time, these states were benefiting from high oil prices (oil is priced in U.S. dollars), and they chose to invest the dollars they earned back into the United States, rather than selling them for another currency.

Interestingly, from mid-2008 through early 2009, the dollar staged a moderate rally against major currencies, despite the fact that the American economy was suffering from

▶ Did You Know?

Did you know that the Turkish lira lost 40% of its value against the U.S. dollar during the first nine months of 2018?

Visit your instructor's Connect® course and click on your eBook or SmartBook® to view a short video explanation from the author.

a serious financial crisis. The reason seems to be that despite America's problems, things were even worse in many other countries, and foreign investors saw the dollar as a safe haven and put their money in low-risk U.S. assets, particularly low-yielding U.S. government bonds. This rally faltered in mid-2009 as investors became worried about the level of U.S. indebtedness. However, between 2014 and early 2019, the dollar yet again increased significantly in value, primarily because of the strength of the U.S. economy, which had emerged from the great financial crisis of 2008–2009 in better shape than any other major developed nation, with higher economic growth rates and lower levels of unemployment.

This review tells us that in recent history, both market forces and government intervention have determined the value of the dollar. Under a floating exchange rate regime, market forces have produced a volatile dollar exchange rate. Governments have sometimes responded by intervening in the market—buying and selling dollars—in an attempt to limit the market's volatility and to correct what they see as overvaluation (in 1985) or potential undervaluation (in 1987) of the dollar. In addition to direct intervention, statements from government officials have frequently influenced the value of the dollar. The dollar may not have declined by as much as it did in 2004, for example, had not U.S. government officials publicly ruled out any action to stop the decline. Paradoxically, a signal not to intervene can affect the market. The frequency of government intervention in the foreign exchange market explains why the current system is sometimes thought of as a *managed-float system* or a *dirty-float system*.

TEST PREP

Use SmartBook to help retain what you have learned. Access your instructor's Connect course to check out SmartBook or go to **learnsmartadvantage.com** for help.

Fixed versus Floating Exchange Rates

The breakdown of the Bretton Woods system has not stopped the debate about the relative merits of fixed versus floating exchange rate regimes. Disappointment with the system of floating rates in recent years has led to renewed debate about the merits of fixed exchange rates. This section reviews the arguments for fixed and floating exchange rate regimes.[6] We discuss the case for floating rates before studying why many critics are disappointed with the experience under floating exchange rates and yearn for a system of fixed rates.

THE CASE FOR FLOATING EXCHANGE RATES

The case in support of floating exchange rates has three main elements: monetary policy autonomy, automatic trade balance adjustments, and economic recovery following a severe economic crisis.

Monetary Policy Autonomy

It is argued that under a fixed system, a country's ability to expand or contract its money supply as it sees fit is limited by the need to maintain exchange rate parity. Monetary expansion can lead to inflation, which puts downward pressure on a fixed exchange rate (as predicted by the PPP theory; see Chapter 10). Similarly, monetary contraction requires high interest rates (to reduce the demand for money). Higher interest rates lead to an inflow of money from abroad, which puts upward pressure on a fixed exchange rate. Thus, to maintain exchange rate parity under a fixed system, countries were limited in their ability to use monetary policy to expand or contract their economies.

Advocates of a floating exchange rate regime argue that removal of the obligation to maintain exchange rate parity would restore monetary control to a government. If a government faced with unemployment wanted to increase its money supply to stimulate domestic demand and reduce unemployment, it could do so unencumbered by the need to maintain its exchange rate. While monetary expansion might lead to inflation, this would lead to a depreciation in the country's currency. If PPP theory is correct, the resulting currency depreciation on the foreign exchange markets should offset the effects of inflation. Although under a floating exchange rate regime, domestic inflation would have an impact on the exchange rate, it should have no impact on businesses' international cost competitiveness due to exchange rate depreciation. The rise in domestic costs should be exactly offset by the fall in the value of the country's currency on the foreign exchange markets. Similarly, a government could use monetary policy to contract the economy without worrying about the need to maintain parity.

Trade Balance Adjustments

Under the Bretton Woods system, if a country developed a permanent deficit in its balance of trade (importing more than it exported) that could not be corrected by domestic policy, this would require the IMF to agree to currency devaluation. Critics of this system argue that the adjustment mechanism works much more smoothly under a floating exchange rate regime. They argue that if a country is running a trade deficit, the imbalance between the supply and demand of that country's currency in the foreign exchange markets (supply exceeding demand) will lead to depreciation in its exchange rate. In turn, by making its exports cheaper and its imports more expensive, exchange rate depreciation should correct the trade deficit.

Crisis Recovery

Advocates of floating exchange rates also argue that exchange rate adjustments can help a country to deal with economic crises. When a country is hit by a severe economic crisis, its currency typically declines on foreign exchange markets. The reason for this is that investors respond to the crisis by taking their money out of the country, selling the local currency, and driving down its value. At some point, however, the currency becomes so cheap that it starts to stimulate exports. This is what occurred in Iceland after the krona lost 50 percent of its value against the U.S. dollar and euro following a banking crisis in 2008. By 2009, exports of fish and aluminum from Iceland were booming, which helped pull the Icelandic economy out of a recession. A similar process occurred in South Korean after the 1997 Asian banking crisis. The value of the South Korean won plunged to 1,700 per dollar from around 800. In turn, the cheap won helped South Korea increase its exports and resulted in an export-led economic recovery. On the other hand, in both countries, the declining value of the currency did raise import prices and led to an increase in inflation, so there is a price that has to be paid for an export-led recovery due to falling currency values.

A contrast can be drawn with the recent situation in Greece, where the economy imploded following the 2008–2009 global financial crisis and has struggled to recover. Part of the problem in Greece is that it gave up its own currency to adopt the euro in 2001, and the euro has remained quite strong; thus, Greece cannot rely on a falling local currency to boost exports and stimulate economic recovery.

THE CASE FOR FIXED EXCHANGE RATES

The case for fixed exchange rates rests on arguments about monetary discipline, speculation, uncertainty, and the lack of connection between the trade balance and exchange rates.

Monetary Discipline

We have already discussed the nature of monetary discipline inherent in a fixed exchange rate system when we discussed the Bretton Woods system. The need to maintain fixed exchange rate parity ensures that governments do not expand their money supplies at inflationary rates. While advocates of floating rates argue that each country should be allowed to choose its own inflation rate (the monetary autonomy argument), advocates of fixed rates argue that governments all too often give in to political pressures and expand the monetary supply far too rapidly, causing unacceptably high price inflation. A fixed exchange rate regime would ensure that this does not occur.

Speculation

Critics of a floating exchange rate regime also argue that speculation can cause fluctuations in exchange rates. They point to the dollar's rapid rise and fall during the 1980s, which they claim had nothing to do with comparative inflation rates and the U.S. trade deficit but everything to do with speculation. They argue that when foreign exchange dealers see a currency depreciating, they tend to sell the currency in the expectation of future depreciation, regardless of the currency's longer-term prospects. As more traders jump on the bandwagon, the expectations of depreciation are realized. Such destabilizing speculation tends to accentuate the fluctuations around the exchange rate's long-run value. It can damage a country's economy by distorting export and import prices. Thus, advocates of a fixed exchange rate regime argue that such a system will limit the destabilizing effects of speculation.

Uncertainty

Speculation also adds to the uncertainty surrounding future currency movements that characterizes floating exchange rate regimes. The unpredictability of exchange rate movements in the post–Bretton Woods era has made business planning difficult, and it adds risk to exporting, importing, and foreign investment activities. Given a volatile exchange rate, international businesses do not know how to react to the changes—and often they do not react. Why change plans for exporting, importing, or foreign investment after a 6 percent fall in the dollar this month, when the dollar may rise 6 percent next month? This uncertainty, according to the critics, dampens the growth of international trade and investment. They argue that a fixed exchange rate, by eliminating such uncertainty, promotes the growth of international trade and investment. Advocates of a floating system reply that the forward exchange market ensures against the risks associated with exchange rate fluctuations (see Chapter 10), so the adverse impact of uncertainty on the growth of international trade and investment has been overstated.

Trade Balance Adjustments and Economic Recovery

Those in favor of floating exchange rates argue that floating rates help adjust trade imbalances and can assist with economic recovery after a crisis. Critics question the closeness of the link between the exchange rate, the trade balance, and economic growth. They claim trade deficits are determined by the balance between savings and investment in a country, not by the external value of its currency.[7] They argue that depreciation in a currency will lead to inflation (due to the resulting increase in import prices). This inflation, they state, will wipe out any apparent gains in cost competitiveness that arise from currency depreciation. In other words, a depreciating exchange rate will not boost exports and reduce imports, as advocates of floating rates claim; it will simply boost price inflation. In support of this argument, those who favor fixed rates point out that the 40 percent drop in the value of the dollar between 1985 and 1988 did not correct the U.S. trade deficit. In reply, advocates of a floating exchange rate regime argue that between 1985 and 1992, the U.S. trade deficit fell from more than $160 billion to about $70 billion, and they attribute this in part to the decline in the value of the dollar. Moreover, the experience of countries like South Korea and Iceland seems to suggest that floating rates can help a country recover from a severe economic crisis.

WHO IS RIGHT?

Which side is right in the vigorous debate between those who favor a fixed exchange rate and those who favor a floating exchange rate? Economists cannot agree. Business, as a major player on the international trade and investment scene, has a large stake in the resolution of the debate. Would international business be better off under a fixed regime, or are flexible rates better? The evidence is not clear.

However, a fixed exchange rate regime modeled along the lines of the Bretton Woods system probably will not work. Speculation ultimately broke the system, a phenomenon that advocates of fixed rate regimes claim is associated with floating exchange rates! Nevertheless, a different kind of fixed exchange rate system might be more enduring and might foster the stability that would facilitate more rapid growth in international trade and investment. In the next section, we look at potential models for such a system and the problems with such systems.

Exchange Rate Regimes in Practice

Governments around the world pursue a number of different exchange rate policies. These range from a pure "free float" in which the exchange rate is determined by market forces, to a pegged system that has some aspects of the pre-1973 Bretton Woods system of fixed exchange rates. Some 21 percent of the IMF's members allow their currency to float freely. Another 23 percent intervene in only a limited way (the so-called "managed float" as practiced by China, among other nations—see the accompanying Country Focus for details). A further 5 percent of IMF members now have no separate legal tender of their own (this figure excludes

TEST PREP

Use SmartBook to help retain what you have learned. Access your instructor's Connect course to check out SmartBook or go to **learnsmartadvantage.com** for help.

LO11-4

Identify exchange rate regimes used in the world today and why countries adopt different exchange rate regimes.

China's Exchange Rate Regime

For years, there have been claims from politicians in the United States that the Chinese actively manipulate their currency, the yuan, keeping its value low against the dollar and other major currencies in order to boost Chinese exports. In November 2015, for example, presidential hopeful Donald Trump claimed that "the wanton manipulation of China's currency" is "robbing Americans of billions of dollars in capital and millions of jobs." But is this claim true? Would it even be possible for China to manipulate the foreign exchange markets to artificially depress the value of their currency? To answer these questions, one needs to look at the history of exchange rate determination for China and understand something about how the international monetary system actually works.

For most of its history, the Chinese yuan was pegged to the U.S. dollar at a fixed exchange rate. When China started to open up its economy to foreign trade and investment in the 1980s, the yuan was devalued by the Chinese government in order to improve the competitiveness of Chinese exports. Thus, the official yuan/USD pegged exchange rate was increased from 1.50 yuan per U.S. dollar in 1980 to 8.62 yuan per U.S. dollar in 1994. With China's exports growing and the country running a growing current account trade surplus, pressure began to increase for China to let its currency appreciate. In response, between 1997 and 2005, the exchange rate was fixed at 8.27 yuan per U.S. dollar, which represented a small appreciation. One could argue that during this period, China's currency was indeed undervalued and that this was the result of government policy.

By the 2000s, China's growing importance in the global economy and the rise of its export-led economy led to calls for the country to reevaluate its fixed exchange rate policy. In response, in July 2005, the country adopted a managed floating exchange rate system. Under this system, the exchange rate for the yuan was set with reference to a basket of foreign currencies that included the U.S. dollar, the euro, the Japanese yen, and the British pound. The daily exchange rate was allowed to float within a narrow band of 0.3 percent around the central parity. The daily band was extended to 0.5 percent in 2007, 1 percent in 2012, and 2 percent in 2014.

Over time, this managed-float system allowed for the appreciation of the Chinese yuan. For example, against the U.S. dollar, the exchange rate changed from 8.27 yuan per dollar in mid-2005 to 6.0875 yuan per U.S. dollar on July 20, 2015, representing an appreciation of 26 percent. More generally, the effective exchange rate index of the yuan against a basket of more than 60 other currencies increased from 86.3 in July 2005 to 123.8 by early 2016, representing as appreciation of 43 percent. The yuan has appreciated by less than this against the U.S. dollar primarily because the U.S. dollar has also been relatively strong and appreciated against many other currencies over the same time period.

These data suggest that rather than artificially trying to keep its currency undervalued, since July 2005, the Chinese have allowed the yuan to increase in value against other currencies, albeit within the constraints imposed by the managed float. In late 2015, this commitment was put to the test when a slowdown in the rate of growth of the Chinese economy led to an outflow of capital from China, which put downward pressure on the yuan. The Chinese responded by trying to maintain the value of the yuan, using its foreign exchange reserves, which are primarily held in U.S. dollars, to buy yuan on the open market and shore up its value. Reports suggest that China spent $500 billion in 2015 to shore up the value of the yuan and more than $1 trillion in 2016. These actions reduced China's foreign exchange reserves to $3.011 trillion by January 2017, the lowest level since 2012. China appears to be trying to keep the yuan from depreciating below 7 yuan to the U.S. dollar.

One reason for China to protect the value of the yuan against the dollar: A large number of Chinese companies have dollar-denominated debt. If the yuan falls against the dollar, the price of serving that debt goes up when translated into yuan. This could stress the financials of those companies (possibly pushing some into bankruptcy) and make it more difficult for China to hit the government's economic growth targets. Another reason: China might want to head off charges from the Trump administration that it continues to keep the value of its currency artificially low.

Sources: T. Hult, "The U.S. Shouldn't Fret over Cheaper Yuan," *Time*, August 14, 2015; "The Yuan and the Markets," *The Economist*, January 16, 2016; Madison Gesiotto, "The Negative Effects of China's Currency Manipulation Explained," *Washington Times*, November 13, 2015; Matthew Slaughter, "The Myths of China's Currency Manipulation," *The Wall Street Journal*, January 8, 2016; "The Curious Case of China's Currency," *The Economist*, August 11, 2015; and L. Wei, "China Foreign Exchange Reserves Keep Dropping," *The Wall Street Journal*, January 8, 2017.

the European Union countries that have adopted the euro). These are typically smaller states, mostly in Africa or the Caribbean, that have no domestic currency and have adopted a foreign currency as legal tender within their borders, typically the U.S. dollar or the euro (see the opening case). The remaining countries use more inflexible systems, including a fixed peg arrangement (43 percent) under which they peg their currencies to other currencies, such as the U.S. dollar or the euro, or to a basket of currencies. Other countries have adopted a system under which their exchange rate is allowed to fluctuate against other currencies within a target zone (an adjustable peg system). In this section, we look more closely at the mechanics and implications of exchange rate regimes that rely on a currency peg or target zone.

PEGGED EXCHANGE RATES

Under a pegged exchange rate regime, a country will peg the value of its currency to that of a major currency so that, for example, as the U.S. dollar rises in value, its own currency rises too. Pegged exchange rates are popular among many of the world's smaller nations. As with a full fixed exchange rate regime, the great virtue claimed for a pegged exchange rate is that it imposes monetary discipline on a country and leads to low inflation. For example, if Belize pegs the value of the Belizean dollar to that of the U.S. dollar so that US$1 = B$1.97, then the Belizean government must make sure the inflation rate in Belize is similar to that in the United States. If the Belizean inflation rate is greater than the U.S. inflation rate, this will lead to pressure to devalue the Belizean dollar (i.e., to alter the peg). To maintain the peg, the Belizean government would be required to rein in inflation. Of course, for a pegged exchange rate to impose monetary discipline on a country, the country whose currency is chosen for the peg must also pursue sound monetary policy.

Evidence shows that adopting a pegged exchange rate regime moderates inflationary pressures in a country. An IMF study concluded that countries with pegged exchange rates had an average annual inflation rate of 8 percent, compared with 14 percent for intermediate regimes and 16 percent for floating regimes.[8] However, many countries operate with only a nominal peg and in practice are willing to devalue their currency rather than pursue a tight monetary policy. It can be very difficult for a smaller country to maintain a peg against another currency if capital is flowing out of the country and foreign exchange traders are speculating against the currency. Something like this occurred in 1997, when a combination of adverse capital flows and currency speculation forced several Asian countries, including Thailand and Malaysia, to abandon pegs against the U.S. dollar and let their currencies float freely. Malaysia and Thailand would not have been in this position had they dealt with a number of problems that began to arise in their economies during the 1990s, including excessive private-sector debt and expanding current account trade deficits.

CURRENCY BOARDS

Hong Kong's experience during the 1997 Asian currency crisis added a new dimension to the debate over how to manage a pegged exchange rate. During late 1997, when other Asian currencies were collapsing, Hong Kong maintained the value of its currency against the U.S. dollar at about $1 = HK$7.80 despite several concerted speculative attacks. Hong Kong's currency board has been given credit for this success. A country that introduces a **currency board** commits itself to converting its domestic currency on demand into another currency at a fixed exchange rate. To make this commitment credible, the currency board holds reserves of foreign currency equal at the fixed exchange rate to at least 100 percent of the domestic currency issued. The system used in Hong Kong means its currency must be fully backed by the U.S. dollar at the specified exchange rate. This is still not a true fixed exchange rate regime because the U.S. dollar—and, by extension, the Hong Kong dollar—floats against other currencies, but it has some features of a fixed exchange rate regime.

Under this arrangement, the currency board can issue additional domestic notes and coins only when there are foreign exchange reserves to back it. This limits the ability of the government to print money and, thereby, create inflationary pressures. Under a strict currency board system, interest rates adjust automatically. If investors want to switch out of domestic currency into, for example, U.S. dollars, the supply of domestic currency will shrink. This will cause interest rates to rise until it eventually becomes attractive for investors to hold the local currency again. In the case of Hong Kong, the interest rate on three-month deposits climbed as high as 20 percent in late 1997, as investors switched out of Hong Kong dollars and into U.S. dollars. The dollar peg held, however, and interest rates declined again.

Since its establishment in 1983, the Hong Kong currency board has weathered several storms. This success persuaded several other countries in the developing world to consider a similar system. Argentina introduced a currency board in 1991 (but abandoned it in 2002), and Bulgaria, Estonia, and Lithuania have all gone down this road in recent years. Despite interest in the arrangement, however, critics are quick to point out that currency boards have their drawbacks.[9] If local inflation rates remain higher than the inflation rate in the country to which the currency is pegged, the currencies of countries with currency boards can become noncompetitive and overvalued (this is what happened in the case of Argentina, which had a currency board). Also, under a currency board system, government lacks the ability to set interest rates. Interest rates in Hong Kong, for example, are effectively set by the U.S. Federal Reserve. In addition, economic collapse in Argentina in 2001 and the subsequent decision to abandon its currency board dampened much of the enthusiasm for this mechanism of managing exchange rates.

TEST PREP

Use SmartBook to help retain what you have learned. Access your instructor's Connect course to check out SmartBook or go to **learnsmartadvantage.com** for help.

LO11-5

Understand the debate surrounding the role of the IMF in the management of financial crises.

Crisis Management by the IMF

Many observers initially believed that the collapse of the Bretton Woods system in 1973 would diminish the role of the IMF within the international monetary system. The IMF's original function was to provide a pool of money from which members could borrow, short term, to adjust their balance-of-payments position and maintain their exchange rate. Some believed the demand for short-term loans would be considerably diminished under a floating exchange rate regime. A trade deficit would presumably lead to a decline in a country's exchange rate, which would help reduce imports and boost exports. No temporary IMF adjustment loan would be needed. Consistent with this, after 1973, most industrialized countries tended to let the foreign exchange market determine exchange rates in response to demand and supply. Since the early 1970s, the rapid development of global capital markets has generally allowed developed countries such as Great Britain and the United States to finance their deficits by borrowing private money, as opposed to drawing on IMF funds.

Despite these developments, the activities of the IMF have expanded over the past 30 years. By 2019, the IMF had 189 members, around 40 of which had some kind of IMF program in place. In 1997, the institution implemented its largest rescue packages until that date, committing more than $110 billion in short-term loans to three troubled Asian countries—South Korea, Indonesia, and Thailand. This was followed by additional IMF rescue packages in Turkey, Russia, Argentina, and Brazil. IMF loans increased again in late 2008 as the global financial crisis took hold. Between 2008 and 2010, the IMF made more than $100 billion in loans to troubled economies such as Latvia, Greece, and Ireland. In April 2009, in response to the growing financial crisis, major IMF members agreed to triple the institution's resources from $250 billion to $750 billion, thereby giving the IMF the financial leverage to act aggressively in times of global financial crisis.

The IMF's activities have expanded because periodic financial crises have continued to hit many economies in the post–Bretton Woods era. The IMF has repeatedly lent money to nations experiencing financial crises, requesting in return that the governments enact certain macroeconomic policies. Critics of the IMF claim these policies have not always been as beneficial as the IMF might have hoped and, in some cases, may have made things worse. Following the IMF loans to several Asian economies, these criticisms reached new levels, and a vigorous debate was waged as to the appropriate role of the IMF. In this section, we discuss some of the main challenges the IMF has had to deal with over the past three decades and review the ongoing debate over the role of the IMF.

The IMF and Iceland's Economic Recovery

When the global financial crisis hit in 2008, tiny Iceland suffered more than most. The country's three biggest banks had been expanding at a breakneck pace since 2000, when the government privatized the banking sector. With a population of around 320,000, Iceland was too small for the banking sector's ambitions, so the banks started to expand into other Scandinavian countries and the United Kingdom. They entered local mortgage markets, purchased foreign financial institutions, and opened foreign branches—attracting depositors by offering high interest rates. The expansion was financed by debt, much of it structured as short-term loans that had to be regularly refinanced. By early 2008, the three banks held debts that amounted to almost six times the value of the entire economy of Iceland! So long as they could periodically refinance this debt, it was not a problem. However, in 2008, global financial markets imploded following the bankruptcy of Lehman Brothers and the collapse of the U.S. housing market. In the aftermath, financial markets froze. The Icelandic banks found that they could not refinance their debt, and they faced bankruptcy.

The Icelandic government lacked the funds to bail out the banks, so it decided to let the big three fail. In quick succession, the local stock market plunged 90 percent, and unemployment increased ninefold. The krona, Iceland's currency, plunged on foreign exchange markets, pushing up the price of imports, and inflation soared to 18 percent. Iceland appeared to be in free fall. The economy shrank by almost 7 percent in 2009 and another 4 percent in 2010.

To stem the decline, the government secured $10 billion in loans from the International Monetary Fund (IMF)

and other countries. The Icelandic government stepped in to help local depositors, seizing the domestic assets of the Icelandic banks and using IMF and other loans to backstop deposit guarantees. Far from implementing austerity measures to solve the crisis, the Icelandic government looked for ways to shore up consumer spending. For example, the government provided means-tested subsidies to reduce the mortgage interest expenses of borrowers. The idea was to stop domestic consumer spending from imploding and further depressing the economy.

With the financial system stabilized, thanks to the IMF and other foreign loans, what happened next is an object lesson in the value of having a floating currency. The fall in the value of the krona helped boost Iceland's exports, such as fish and aluminum, while depressing demand for costly imports, such as automobiles. By 2009, the krona was worth half as much against the U.S. dollar and euro as it was in 2007 before the crisis. Iceland's exports surged and imports slumped. While the high cost of imports did stoke inflation, booming exports started to pump money back into the Icelandic economy. In 2011, the economy grew again at a 3.1 percent annual rate. This was followed by 2.7 percent growth in 2012 and 4 percent growth in 2013, while unemployment fell from a high of nearly 10 percent to 4.4 percent at the end of 2013.

Sources: Charles Forelle, "In European Crisis, Iceland Emerges as an Island of Recovery," *The Wall Street Journal*, May 19, 2012, pp. A1, A10; "Coming in from the Cold," *The Economist*, December 16, 2010; Charles Duxbury, "Europe Gets Cold Shoulder in Iceland," *The Wall Street Journal*, April 26, 2012; and "Iceland," *The World Factbook 2013* (Washington, DC: Central Intelligence Agency, 2013).

FINANCIAL CRISES IN THE POST–BRETTON WOODS ERA

A number of broad types of financial crises have occurred over the past 30 years, many of which have required IMF involvement. A **currency crisis** occurs when a speculative attack on the exchange value of a currency results in a sharp depreciation in the value of the currency or forces authorities to expend large volumes of international currency reserves and sharply increase interest rates to defend the prevailing exchange rate. This happened in Pakistan in 2018–2019, and the IMF stepped in to help stabilize the value of the Pakistani currency, the rupee, on foreign exchange markets by lending it foreign currency (see the opening case for details). A **banking crisis** refers to a loss of confidence in the banking system that leads to a run on banks, as individuals and companies withdraw their deposits. This is what happened in Iceland in 2008. The experience of Iceland with the IMF is discussed in depth in the accompanying Country Focus. A **foreign debt crisis** is a situation in which a country cannot service its foreign debt obligations, whether private-sector or government debt. This happened to Greece, Ireland,

and Portugal in 2010, and was also an issue in the most recent IMF intervention in Pakistan (see the opening case).

These crises tend to have common underlying macroeconomic causes: high relative price inflation rates, a widening current account deficit, excessive expansion of domestic borrowing, high government deficits, and asset price inflation (such as sharp increases in stock and property prices).[10] At times, elements of currency, banking, and debt crises may be present simultaneously, as in the 1997 Asian crisis, the 2000–2002 Argentinean crisis, the 2010 crisis in Ireland, and Pakistan's recent 2018–2019 crisis.

To assess the frequency of financial crises, the IMF looked at the macroeconomic performance of a group of 53 countries from 1975 to 1997 (22 of these countries were developed nations, and 31 were developing countries).[11] The IMF found there had been 158 currency crises, including 55 episodes in which a country's currency declined by more than 25 percent. There were also 54 banking crises. The IMF's data suggest that developing nations were more than twice as likely to experience currency and banking crises as developed nations. It is not surprising, therefore, that most of the IMF's loan activities since the mid-1970s have been targeted toward developing nations.

In 1997, several Asian currencies started to fall sharply as international investors came to the realization that there was a speculative investment bubble in the region. They took their money out of local currencies, changing it into U.S. dollars, and those currencies started to fall precipitously. The currency declines started in Thailand and then, in a process of contagion, quickly spread to other countries in the region. Stabilizing those currencies required massive help from the IMF. In the case of South Korea, local enterprises had built up huge debt loads as they invested heavily in new industrial capacity. By 1997, they found they had too much industrial capacity and could not generate the income required to service their debt. South Korean banks and companies had also made the mistake of borrowing in dollars, much of it in the form of short-term loans that would come due within a year. Thus, when the Korean won started to decline in fall 1997 in sympathy with the problems elsewhere in Asia, South Korean companies saw their debt obligations balloon. Several large companies were forced to file for bankruptcy. This triggered a decline in the South Korean currency and stock market that was difficult to halt.

With its economy on the verge of collapse, the South Korean government requested $20 billion in standby loans from the IMF on November 21. As the negotiations progressed, it became apparent that South Korea was going to need far more than $20 billion. On December 3, 1997, the IMF and South Korean government reached a deal to lend $55 billion to the country. The agreement with the IMF called for the South Koreans to open their economy and banking system to foreign investors. South Korea also pledged to restrain Korea's largest enterprises, the *chaebol*, by reducing their share of bank financing and requiring them to publish consolidated financial statements and undergo annual independent external audits. On trade liberalization, the IMF said South Korea would comply with its commitments to the World Trade Organization to eliminate trade-related subsidies and restrictive import licensing and would streamline its import certification procedures, all of which should open the South Korean economy to greater foreign competition.[12]

EVALUATING THE IMF'S POLICY PRESCRIPTIONS

By 2019, the IMF had programs in around 40 countries that were struggling with economic and/or currency problems. All IMF loan packages come with conditions attached. Until very recently, the IMF has always insisted on a combination of tight macroeconomic policies, including cuts in public spending, higher interest rates, and tight monetary policy. It has also often pushed for the deregulation of sectors formerly protected from domestic and foreign competition, privatization of state-owned assets, and better financial reporting from the banking sector. These policies are designed to cool overheated economies by reining in inflation and reducing government spending and debt. This set of policy prescriptions has come in for tough criticisms from many observers, and the IMF itself has started to modify its approach.[13]

The IMF Managing Director Christine Lagarde addresses the Development Committee at the World Bank Headquarters in Washington, DC.

Stephen Jaffe/IMF/Handout/Getty Images News/Getty Images

Inappropriate Policies

One criticism is that the IMF's traditional policy prescriptions represent a "one-size-fits-all" approach to macroeconomic policy that is inappropriate for many countries. In the case of the 1997 Asian crisis, critics argue that the tight macroeconomic policies imposed by the IMF were not well suited to countries that are suffering not from excessive government spending and inflation but from a private-sector debt crisis with deflationary undertones.[14]

In South Korea, for example, the government had been running a budget surplus for years (it was 4 percent of South Korea's GDP in 1994–1996), and inflation was low at about 5 percent. South Korea had the second-strongest financial position of any country in the Organisation for Economic Co-operation and Development. Despite this, critics say, the IMF insisted on applying the same policies that it applies to countries suffering from high inflation. The IMF required South Korea to maintain an inflation rate of 5 percent. However, given the collapse in the value of its currency and the subsequent rise in price for imports such as oil, critics claimed inflationary pressures would inevitably increase in South Korea. So to hit a 5 percent inflation rate, the South Koreans would be forced to apply an unnecessarily tight monetary policy. Short-term interest rates in South Korea did jump from 12.5 to 21 percent immediately after the country signed its initial deal with the IMF. Increasing interest rates made it even more difficult for companies to service their already excessive short-term debt obligations, and critics used this as evidence to argue that the cure prescribed by the IMF might actually increase the probability of widespread corporate defaults, not reduce them.

At the time, the IMF rejected this criticism. According to the IMF, the central task was to rebuild confidence in the won. Once this was achieved, the won would recover from its oversold levels, reducing the size of South Korea's dollar-denominated debt burden when expressed in won and making it easier for companies to service their debt. The IMF also argued that by requiring South Korea to remove restrictions on foreign direct investment, foreign capital would flow into the country to take advantage of cheap assets. This, too, would increase demand for the Korean currency and help improve the dollar/won exchange rate.

South Korea did recover fairly quickly from the crisis, supporting the position of the IMF. While the economy contracted by 7 percent in 1998, by 2000, it had rebounded and grew at a 9 percent rate (measured by growth in GDP). Inflation, which peaked at 8 percent in 1998, fell to 2 percent by 2000, and unemployment fell from 7 to 4 percent over the same period. The won hit a low of $1 = W1,812 in early 1998 but by 2000 was back to an exchange rate of around $1 = W1,200, at which it seems to have stabilized.

Moral Hazard

A second criticism of the IMF is that its rescue efforts are exacerbating a problem known to economists as moral hazard. **Moral hazard** arises when people behave recklessly because they know they will be saved if things go wrong. Critics point out that many Japanese and Western banks were far too willing to lend large amounts of capital to over-leveraged Asian companies during the boom years of the 1990s. These critics argued that the banks should have been forced to pay the price for their rash lending policies, even if that meant some banks would have closed.[15] Only by taking such drastic action, the argument goes, will banks learn the error of their ways and not engage in rash lending in the future. By providing support to these countries, the IMF is reducing the probability of debt default and in effect bailing out the banks whose loans gave rise to this situation.

This argument ignores two critical points. First, if some Japanese or Western banks with heavy exposure to the troubled Asian economies were forced to write off their loans due to widespread debt default, the impact would have been difficult to contain. The failure of large Japanese banks, for example, could have triggered a meltdown in the Japanese financial markets. That would almost inevitably lead to a serious decline in stock markets around the world, which was the very risk the IMF was trying to avoid by stepping in with financial support. Second, it is incorrect to imply that some banks have not had to pay the price for rash lending policies. The IMF insisted on the closure of banks in South Korea, Thailand, and Indonesia after the 1997 Asian financial crisis. Foreign banks with short-term loans outstanding to South Korean enterprises have been forced by circumstances to reschedule those loans at interest rates that do not compensate for the extension of the loan maturity.

Lack of Accountability

The final criticism of the IMF is that it has become too powerful for an institution that lacks any real mechanism for accountability.[16] The IMF has determined macroeconomic policies in those countries, yet according to critics such as noted economist Jeffrey Sachs, the IMF, with a staff of less than 1,000, lacks the expertise required to do a good job. Evidence of this, according to Sachs, can be found in the fact that the IMF was singing the praises of the Thai and South Korean governments only months before both countries lurched into crisis. Then the IMF put together a draconian program for South Korea without having deep knowledge of the country. Sachs's solution to this problem is to reform the IMF so it makes greater use of outside experts and its operations are open to greater outside scrutiny.

Observations

As with many debates about international economics, it is not clear which side is correct about the appropriateness of IMF policies. There are cases where one can argue that IMF policies had been counterproductive or only had limited success. For example, one might question the success of the IMF's involvement in Turkey given that the country has had to implement some 18 IMF programs since 1958! But the IMF can also point to some notable accomplishments, including its success in containing the Asian crisis, which could have rocked the global international monetary system to its core, and its actions in 2008–2010 to contain the global financial crisis, quickly stepping in to rescue Iceland, Ireland, Greece, and Latvia. Similarly, many observers give the IMF credit for its deft handling of politically difficult situations, such as the Mexican peso crisis, and for successfully promoting a free market philosophy.

Several years after the IMF's intervention, the economy of Asia recovered. Certainly, the kind of catastrophic implosion that might have occurred had the IMF not stepped in had been averted, and although some countries still faced considerable problems, it is not clear that the IMF should take much blame for this. The IMF cannot force countries to adopt the policies required to correct economic mismanagement. While a government may commit to taking corrective action in return for an IMF loan, internal political problems may make it difficult for a government to act on that commitment. In such cases, the IMF is caught between a rock and a hard place, because if it decided to withhold money, it might trigger financial collapse and the kind of contagion that it seeks to avoid.

Finally, it is notable that in recent years the IMF has started to change its policies. In response to the global financial crisis of 2008–2009, the IMF began to urge countries to adopt policies that included fiscal stimulus and monetary easing—the direct opposite of what the fund traditionally advocated. Some economists in the fund are also now arguing that higher inflation rates might be a good thing, if the consequence is greater growth in aggregate demand, which would help pull nations out of recessionary conditions. The IMF, in other words, is starting to display the very flexibility in policy responses that its critics claim it lacks. While the traditional policy of tight controls on fiscal policy and tight monetary policy targets might be appropriate for countries suffering from high inflation rates, the Asian economic crisis and the 2008–2009 global financial crisis were caused not by high inflation rates but by excessive debt, and the IMF's "new approach" seems tailored to deal with this.[17]

FOCUS ON MANAGERIAL IMPLICATIONS

CURRENCY MANAGEMENT, BUSINESS STRATEGY, AND GOVERNMENT RELATIONS

The implications for international businesses of the material discussed in this chapter fall into three main areas: currency management, business strategy, and corporate–government relations.

Currency Management

An obvious implication with regard to currency management is that companies must recognize that the foreign exchange market does not work quite as depicted in Chapter 10. The current system is a mixed system in which a combination of government intervention and speculative activity can drive the foreign exchange market. Companies engaged in significant foreign exchange activities need to be aware of this and to adjust their foreign exchange transactions accordingly. For example, the currency management unit of Caterpillar claims it made millions of dollars in the hours following the announcement of the Plaza Accord by selling dollars and buying currencies that it expected to appreciate on the foreign exchange market following government intervention.

Under the present system, speculative buying and selling of currencies can create very volatile movements in exchange rates (as exhibited by the rise and fall of the dollar during the 1980s and the Asian currency crisis of the late 1990s). Contrary to the predictions of the purchasing power parity theory (see Chapter 10), exchange rate movements during the 1980s and 1990s often did not seem to be strongly influenced by relative inflation rates. Insofar as volatile exchange rates increase foreign exchange risk, this is not good news for business. On the other hand, as we saw in Chapter 10, the foreign exchange market has developed a number of instruments, such as the forward market and swaps, that can help ensure against foreign exchange risk. Not surprisingly, use of these instruments has increased markedly since the breakdown of the Bretton Woods system in 1973.

Business Strategy

The volatility of the current global exchange rate regime presents a conundrum for international businesses. Exchange rate movements are difficult to predict, and yet their movement can have a major impact on a business's competitive position. For a detailed example, see the accompanying Management Focus on Airbus. Faced with uncertainty about the future value of currencies, firms can utilize the forward exchange market, which

TEST PREP

Use SmartBook to help retain what you have learned. Access your instructor's Connect course to check out SmartBook or go to **learnsmartadvantage.com** for help.

LO11-6

Explain the implications of the global monetary system for management practice.

Airbus and the Euro

Airbus had reason to celebrate in 2003; for the first time in the company's history, it delivered more commercial jet aircraft than long-time rival Boeing. Airbus delivered 305 planes in 2003, compared to Boeing's 281. The celebration, however, was muted because the strength of the euro against the U.S. dollar was casting a cloud over the company's future. Airbus, which is based in Toulouse, France, prices planes in dollars, just as Boeing has always done. But more than half of Airbus's costs are in euros. So as the dollar drops in value against the euro—and it dropped by more than 50 percent between 2002 and the end of 2009—Airbus's costs rise in proportion to its revenue, squeezing profits in the process.

In the short run, the fall in the value of the dollar against the euro did not hurt Airbus. The company fully hedged its dollar exposure in 2005 and was mostly hedged for 2006. However, anticipating that the dollar would stay weak against the euro, Airbus started to take other steps to reduce its economic exposure to a strong European currency. Recognizing that raising prices is not an option given the strong competition from Boeing, Airbus decided to focus on reducing its costs. As a step toward doing this, Airbus gave U.S. suppliers a greater share of work on new aircraft models, such as the A380 superjumbo and the A350. It also shifted supply work on some of its older models from European to American-based suppliers. This increased the proportion of its costs that were in dollars, making profits less vulnerable to a rise in the value of the euro and reducing the costs of building an aircraft when they were converted back into euros.

In addition, Airbus pushed its European-based suppliers to start pricing in U.S. dollars. Because the costs of many suppliers were in euros, the suppliers found that to comply with Airbus's wishes, they too had to move more work to the United States or to countries whose currency

Aircraft factory assembly line.

Xenotar/E+/Getty Images

is pegged to the U.S. dollar. Thus, one large French-based supplier, Zodiac, announced that it was considering acquisitions in the United States. Not only was Airbus pushing suppliers to price components for commercial jet aircraft in dollars, but the company was also requiring suppliers to its A400M program, a military aircraft that will be sold to European governments and priced in euros, to price components in U.S. dollars. Beyond these steps, the CEO of EADS, Airbus's parent company, publicly stated it might be prepared to assemble aircraft in the United States if that would help win important U.S. contracts. While this strategy made good sense for years, it worked against Airbus between mid-2014 and 2018 as the dollar rose rapidly against the euro.

Sources: D. Michaels, "Airbus Deliveries Top Boeing's; But Several Obstacles Remain," *The Wall Street Journal*, January 16, 2004, p. A9; J. L. Gerondeau, "Airbus Eyes U.S. Suppliers as Euro Gains," *Seattle Times*, February 21, 2004, p. C4; "Euro's Gains Create Worries in Europe," HoustonChronicle.com, January 13, 2004, 3; and K. Done, "Soft Dollar and A380 Hitches Lead to EADS Losses," *Financial Times*, November 9, 2006, p. 32.

Airbus has done. However, the forward exchange market is far from perfect as a predictor of future exchange rates (see Chapter 10). It is also difficult, if not impossible, to get adequate insurance coverage for exchange rate changes that might occur several years in the future. The forward market tends to offer coverage for exchange rate changes a few months—not years—ahead. Given this, it makes sense to pursue strategies that will increase the company's strategic flexibility in the face of unpredictable exchange rate movements—that is, to pursue strategies that reduce the economic exposure of the firm (which we first discussed in Chapter 10).

Maintaining strategic flexibility can take the form of dispersing production to different locations around the globe as a real hedge against currency fluctuations (this seems to be what Airbus has considered). Consider the case of Daimler-Benz, Germany's export-oriented automobile and aerospace company. In June 1995, the company stunned the German business community when it announced it expected to post a severe loss in 1995 of about $720 million. The cause was Germany's strong currency, which had appreciated by 4 percent against a basket of major currencies since the beginning of 1995 and had risen by more than 30 percent against the U.S. dollar since late 1994. By mid-1995, the exchange rate against the dollar stood at $1 = DM1.38. Daimler's management believed it could not make money with an exchange rate under $1 = DM1.60. Daimler's senior managers concluded the appreciation of the mark against the dollar was probably permanent, so they decided to move substantial production outside of Germany and increase purchasing of foreign components. The idea was to reduce the vulnerability of the company to future exchange rate movements. Even before the company's acquisition of Chrysler Corporation in 1998, the Mercedes-Benz division planned to produce 10 percent of its cars outside Germany by 2000, mostly in the United States. Similarly, the move by Japanese automobile companies to expand their productive capacity in the United States and Europe can be seen in the context of the increase in the value of the yen between 1985 and 1995, which raised the price of Japanese exports. For the Japanese companies, building production capacity overseas was a hedge against continued appreciation of the yen (as well as against trade barriers).

Another way of building strategic flexibility and reducing economic exposure involves contracting out manufacturing. This allows a company to shift suppliers from country to country in response to changes in relative costs brought about by exchange rate movements. However, this kind of strategy may work only for low-value-added manufacturing (e.g., textiles), in which the individual manufacturers have few if any firm-specific skills that contribute to the value of the product. It may be less appropriate for high-value-added manufacturing, in which firm-specific technology and skills add significant value to the product (e.g., the heavy equipment industry) and in which switching costs are correspondingly high. For high-value-added manufacturing, switching suppliers will lead to a reduction in the value that is added, which may offset any cost gains arising from exchange rate fluctuations.

The roles of the IMF and the World Bank in the current international monetary system also have implications for business strategy. Increasingly, the IMF has been acting as the macroeconomic police of the world economy, insisting that countries seeking significant borrowings adopt IMF-mandated macroeconomic policies. These policies typically include anti-inflationary monetary policies and reductions in government spending. In the short run, such policies usually result in a sharp contraction of demand. International businesses selling or producing in such countries need to be aware of this and plan accordingly. In the long run, the kind of policies imposed by the IMF can promote economic growth and an expansion of demand, which create opportunities for international business.

Corporate–Government Relations

As major players in the international trade and investment environment, businesses can influence government policy toward the international monetary system. For example, intense government lobbying by U.S. exporters helped convince the U.S. government that intervention in the foreign exchange market was necessary. With this in mind, business can and should use its influence to promote an international monetary system that facilitates the growth of international trade and investment. Whether a fixed or floating regime is optimal is a subject for debate. However, exchange rate volatility such as the world experienced during the 1980s and 1990s creates an environment less conducive to international trade and investment than one with more stable exchange rates. Therefore, it would seem to be in the interests of international business to promote an international monetary system that minimizes volatile exchange rate movements, particularly when those movements are unrelated to long-run economic fundamentals.

Key Terms

international monetary
  system, p. 322
floating exchange rate, p. 322
pegged exchange rate, p. 322
managed-float system, p. 322
dirty-float system, p. 322

fixed exchange rate, p. 323
European Monetary System
  (EMS), p. 323
dollarization, p. 323
gold standard, p. 323
gold par value, p. 324

balance-of-trade equilibrium, p. 324
currency board, p. 335
currency crisis, p. 337
banking crisis, p. 337
foreign debt crisis, p. 337
moral hazard, p. 340

SUMMARY

This chapter explained the workings of the international monetary system and pointed out its implications for international business. The chapter made the following points:

1. The gold standard is a monetary standard that pegs currencies to gold and guarantees convertibility to gold. It was thought that the gold standard contained an automatic mechanism that contributed to the simultaneous achievement of a balance-of-payments equilibrium by all countries. The gold standard broke down during the 1930s as countries engaged in competitive devaluations.

2. The Bretton Woods system of fixed exchange rates was established in 1944. The U.S. dollar was the central currency of this system; the value of every other currency was pegged to its value. Significant exchange rate devaluations were allowed only with the permission of the International Monetary Fund (IMF). The role of the IMF was to maintain order in the international monetary system (a) to avoid a repetition of the competitive devaluations of the 1930s and (b) to control price inflation by imposing monetary discipline on countries.

3. The fixed exchange rate system collapsed in 1973, primarily due to speculative pressure on the dollar following a rise in U.S. inflation and a growing U.S. balance-of-trade deficit.

4. Since 1973, the world has operated with a floating exchange rate regime, and exchange rates have become more volatile and far less predictable. Volatile exchange rate movements have helped reopen the debate over the merits of fixed and floating systems.

5. The case for a floating exchange rate regime claims (a) such a system gives countries autonomy regarding their monetary policy and (b) floating exchange rates facilitate smooth adjustment of trade imbalances.

6. The case for a fixed exchange rate regime claims (a) the need to maintain a fixed exchange rate imposes monetary discipline on a country; (b) floating exchange rate regimes are vulnerable to speculative pressure; (c) the uncertainty that accompanies floating exchange rates dampens the growth of international trade and investment; and (d) far from correcting trade imbalances, depreciating a currency on the foreign exchange market tends to cause price inflation.

7. In today's international monetary system, some countries have adopted floating exchange rates; some have pegged their currency to another currency, such as the U.S. dollar; and some have pegged their currency to a basket of other currencies, allowing their currency to fluctuate within a zone around the basket.

8. In the post–Bretton Woods era, the IMF has continued to play an important role in helping countries navigate their way through financial crises by lending significant capital to embattled governments and by requiring them to adopt certain macroeconomic policies.

9. An important debate is occurring over the appropriateness of IMF-mandated macroeconomic policies. Critics charge that the IMF often imposes inappropriate conditions on developing nations that are the recipients of its loans.

10. The current managed-float system of exchange rate determination has increased the importance of currency management in international businesses.

11. The volatility of exchange rates under the current managed-float system creates both opportunities and threats. One way of responding to this volatility is for companies to build strategic flexibility and limit their economic exposure by dispersing production to different locations around the globe by contracting out manufacturing (in the case of low-value-added manufacturing) and other means.

Critical Thinking and Discussion Questions

1. Why did the gold standard collapse? Is there a case for returning to some type of gold standard? What is it?

2. What opportunities might current IMF lending policies to developing nations create for international businesses? What threats might they create?

3. Do you think the standard IMF policy prescriptions of tight monetary policy and reduced government spending are always appropriate for developing nations experiencing a currency crisis? How might the IMF change its approach? What would the implications be for international businesses?

4. Debate the relative merits of fixed and floating exchange rate regimes. From the perspective of an international business, what are the most important criteria in a choice between the systems? Which system is the more desirable for an international business?

5. Imagine that Canada, the United States, and Mexico decide to adopt a fixed exchange rate system. What would be the likely consequences of such a system for (*a*) international businesses and (*b*) the flow of trade and investment among the three countries?

6. Reread the Country Focus "The IMF and Iceland's Economic Recovery," and then answer the following questions:

   a. What were the main causes of Iceland's economic troubles in 2008?

   b. Was Iceland facing a classic currency crisis, or was this a banking crisis?

   c. How did Iceland recover from its 2008–2009 crisis? What are the important lessons to draw from this case?

   d. Iceland did not implement the austerity policies that are so often associated with IMF loans, and yet the economy recovered. Does this suggest that austerity policies do not work?

7. Reread the Country Focus "China's Exchange Rate Regime," and then answer the following questions:

   a. Why do you think that the Chinese historically pegged the value of the yuan to the U.S. dollar?

   b. Why did the Chinese move to a managed-float system in 2005?

   c. What are the benefits that China might gain by allowing the yuan to float freely against other major currencies such as the U.S. dollar and the euro? What are the risks? What do you think they should do?

   d. Is there any evidence that the Chinese kept the level of their currency artificially low in the past to boost exports? Is China keeping it artificially low today?

   e. What policy stance should the United States and the EU adopt toward China with regard to how it manages the value of its currency?

globalEDGE research task globaledge.msu.edu

Use the globalEDGE™ website (**globaledge.msu.edu**) to complete the following exercises:

1. The *Global Financial Stability Report* is a semiannual report published by the International Capital Markets division of the International Monetary Fund. The report includes an assessment of the risks facing the global financial markets. Locate and download the latest report to get an overview of the most important issues currently under discussion. Also, download a report from five years ago. How do issues from five years ago compare with financial issues identified in the current report?

2. An important element to understanding the international monetary system is keeping updated on current growth trends worldwide. A German colleague told you yesterday that *Deutsche Bank Research* provides an effective way to stay informed on important topics in international finance from a European perspective. One area of focus for the site is emerging markets and economic and financial challenges faced by these markets. Find an emerging market research report for analysis. On which emerging market region did you choose to focus? What are the key takeaways from your chosen report?

CLOSING CASE

Can Dollarization Save Venezuela?

Venezuela is in deep trouble. Although the country boasts the largest oil reserves on the planet, a fact that should make it rich, poor governance has created an economic crisis of historic proportions and turned the country into the poorest in Latin America. The economy contracted by 16.5 percent in 2016, 12 percent in 2017, and another 18 percent in 2018, while unemployment surged to over 34 percent. Due to food shortages, two-thirds of the population have reported significant weight loss. Three million people (about 10 percent of the population) have fled the country. Over 85 percent are now living below the poverty line. It is one of the biggest economic catastrophes in modern history.

The country's economic decline dates back to the rule of Hugo Chavez, who took power in 1999. Chavez significantly raised the royalty rate that foreign oil companies had to pay the government. Oil companies responded by not investing in Venezuela and looking for oil elsewhere. Chavez then compounded the problem by pushing out the professional management of the state-run oil company and replacing them with his own political appointees. The results included underinvestment in exploration and extraction infrastructure, as well as a falling oil output. By 2017, oil output had plunged by 50 percent from its peak in 1998, a major problem for a country where crude oil makes up about 95 percent of exports.

Early in his rule, Chavez spent oil revenues liberally on social programs, including price controls and fuel subsidies. These initially helped the poor and boosted his popularity. However, by 2012, significant strains were showing in the economy, including declining oil production and exports, rising unemployment, high inflation, and ballooning government deficits.

In 2013, Chavez died and was succeeded by Nicolas Maduro. Maduro continued on the trajectory set by Chavez. Unfortunately for him, oil prices and output both fell sharply, reducing government revenue. Rather than abandon social programs and subsidies, Maduro simply expanded the government budget deficit, raising it to a staggering 38 percent of GDP by 2017. He financed that deficit by printing money. Predictably, the result has been hyperinflation. The inflation rate surged to 250 percent in 2016, and then to 2700 percent per year in 2017, and close to a million percent in 2018. This made the country's currency, the *bolivar*, worthless, stifling commerce, which depends upon a stable currency.

On the foreign exchange market, the value of the bolivar collapsed, falling from 64 per U.S. dollar in 2014 to

Janusz Pienkowski/Shutterstock

960 per dollar by early 2016, and around 100,000 per USD by early 2018! It should be noted that this was the exchange rate on the black market. The official exchange rate set by the Venezuelan government, which no one pays attention to, stayed at 10 bolivars per USD. With the bolivar now viewed as worthless, no one wants to trade with Venezuela unless they get paid in U.S. dollars. With not enough dollars in Venezuela to finance international transactions, that means a shortage of many goods.

When a country experiences this kind of currency crisis, the normal response is to call in the International Monetary Fund (IMF). In return for a loan of funds, the IMF will often advocate austerity programs to reduce the government budget deficit, along with high interest rates and tight controls over the growth in money supply to reduce inflation. Other policies advocated by the IMF include the removal of price controls and subsidies and the privatization of state-owned enterprises. However, all of these actions are an anathema to Maduro, who continues to adhere to a hard-line socialist ideology and blame foreign and domestic capitalists for the country's ills.

Opposition figures in Venezuela have suggested another solution to the country's currency problems—dollarization. The process would involve abandoning the bolivar, and the government introducing cash denominated in U.S. dollars to keep commerce moving. In fact, *de facto* dollarization is already under way in Venezuela. Increasingly, merchants are ignoring price controls and pricing goods in U.S. dollars at their free market value. Unfortunately, Venezuela's economic collapse has been so severe that most Venezuelans only earn the equivalent of a few dollars per month, so this doesn't help them. For dollarization to work, the government would have to purchase about $10 billion worth of U.S. notes and coins and put those in circulation.

There are precedents for dollarization. Ecuador adopted the U.S. dollar in 2000 in order to overcome soaring inflation and a collapse in the value of that country's currency, the *sucre*. While the switch was painful—salaries initially fell by 40 percent and savings and pension accounts were ravaged—wages and prices stabilized and the economy recovered and started to grow again. However, Maduro has long vilified the United States, so without a change in government, it is difficult to see a dollarization effort for Venezuela.

Sources: John Otis and Kejal Vyas, "The Dollar Rescued Ecuador: Can It Save Venezuela?" *The Wall Street Journal*, March 27, 2018; Matt O'Brian, "Venezuela Should Be Rich, but Its Government Has Destroyed Its Economy," *The Washington Post*, January 21, 2015; Patricia Laya, "One Dollar Now

Buys 103,000 Bolivars in Venezuela's Black Market," *Bloomberg Markets*, December 1, 2017; Matt O'Brian, "Venezuela is the Biggest Economic Disaster in Modern History," *The Washington Post*, February 1, 2019.

Case Discussion Questions

1. What are the root causes of Venezuela's economic problems?

2. Why won't Venezuela bring in the IMF to help with its economic problems?

3. How might dollarization help solve Venezuela's economic problems? What is required for dollarization to be implemented?

4. In addition to dollarization, what else needs to happen for Venezuela to fix its economic problems?

Design elements: Modern textured halftone: ©VIPRESIONA/ Shutterstock; globalEDGE icon: ©globalEDGE; All others: ©McGraw-Hill Education

Endnotes

1. The argument goes back to eighteenth-century philosopher David Hume. See D. Hume, "On the Balance of Trade," reprinted in *The Gold Standard in Theory and in History,* ed. B. Eichengreen (London: Methuen, 1985).

2. R. Solomon, *The International Monetary System, 1945-1981* (New York: Harper & Row, 1982).

3. International Monetary Fund, *World Economic Outlook, 2005* (Washington, DC: IMF, May 2005).

4. For an extended discussion of the dollar exchange rate in the 1980s, see B. D. Pauls, "US Exchange Rate Policy: Bretton Woods to the Present," *Federal Reserve Bulletin,* November 1990, pp. 891–908.

5. R. Miller, "Why the Dollar Is Giving Way," *BusinessWeek,* December 6, 2004, pp. 36–37.

6. For a feel for the issues contained in this debate, see P. Krugman, *Has the Adjustment Process Worked?* (Washington, DC: Institute for International Economics, 1991); "Time to Tether Currencies," *The Economist,* January 6, 1990, pp. 15–16; P. R. Krugman and M. Obstfeld, *International Economics: Theory and Policy* (New York: HarperCollins, 1994); J. Shelton, *Money Meltdown* (New York: Free Press, 1994); and S. Edwards, "Exchange Rates and the Political Economy of Macroeconomic Discipline," *American Economic Review* 86, no. 2 (May 1996), pp. 159–63.

7. The argument is made by several prominent economists, particularly Stanford University's Robert McKinnon. See R. McKinnon,

"An International Standard for Monetary Stabilization," *Policy Analyses in International Economics* 8 (1984). The details of this argument are beyond the scope of this book. For a relatively accessible exposition, see P. Krugman, *The Age of Diminished Expectations* (Cambridge, MA: MIT Press, 1990).

8. A. R. Ghosh and A. M. Gulde, "Does the Exchange Rate Regime Matter for Inflation and Growth?" *Economic Issues,* no. 2 (1997).

9. "The ABC of Currency Boards," *The Economist,* November 1, 1997, p. 80.

10. International Monetary Fund, *World Economic Outlook, 1998* (Washington, DC: IMF, 1998).

11. International Monetary Fund, *World Economic Outlook, 1998.*

12. T. S. Shorrock, "Korea Starts Overhaul; IMF Aid Hits $55 Billion," *Journal of Commerce*, December 8, 1997, p. 3A.

13. See J. Sachs, "Economic Transition and Exchange Rate Regime," *American Economic Review* 86, no. 92 (May 1996), pp. 147–52; and J. Sachs, "Power unto Itself," *Financial Times,* December 11, 1997, p. 11.

14. Sachs, "Power unto Itself."

15. Martin Wolf, "Same Old IMF Medicine," *Financial Times,* December 9, 1997, p. 12.

16. Sachs, "Power unto Itself."

17. "New Fund, Old Fundamentals," *The Economist,* May 2, 2009, p. 78.

The Global Capital Market

12

LEARNING OBJECTIVES

After reading this chapter, you will be able to:

LO12-1   Describe the benefits of the global capital market.

LO12-2   Identify why the global capital market has grown so rapidly.

LO12-3   Understand the risks associated with the globalization of capital markets.

LO12-4   Compare and contrast the benefits and risks associated with the Eurocurrency market, the global bond market, and the global equity market.

LO12-5   Understand how foreign exchange risks affect the cost of capital.

Qin Lang/Xinhua/Getty Images

Chinese IPOs in the United States

OPENING CASE

In China, the number eight is an omen of good luck and prosperity. Certainly, 2018 was a prosperous year for Chinese firms undertaking Initial Public Offerings (IPOs) in the United States. Some 33 Chinese companies had IPOs on the New York Stock Exchange and NASDAQ, raising $9.17 billion in the process. The number of Chinese IPOs in the United States was well ahead of the 17 IPOs in 2017, which raised $3.8 billion, and was the largest number since 2010, which had 39 listings. The 2018 IPOs were strongly weighted toward technology companies, and included Tencent's video platform, iQiyi (a Chinese rival of Netflix), and electric carmaker Nio (dubbed the Tesla of China).

The vibrant market for Chinese IPOs in the United States was somewhat surprising given escalating trade tensions between the United States and China during 2018. However, for many Chinese tech firms there are compelling reasons for doing an IPO in the United States, as opposed to Hong Kong or Shanghai. For a start, 2018 was a bad year for Chinese stock markets. The Shanghai Stock Exchange ended the year down 25 percent, its worst annual performance since 2008, while the Hong Kong Hang Seng market fell about 14 percent. The drop in the Chinese markets was precipitated both by the simmering trade war with the United States, and slowing economic growth in the country.

Against this background, Chinese investors had a diminished appetite for technology IPOs, which are often seen as more risky than the IPOs for more established enterprises. In the United States, by contrast, there was a strong appetite for investing in Chinese tech IPOs, with many investors seeing this as a way to participate in China's enormous domestic market and vibrant long-term growth prospects, particularly in technology, as the country's living standards continue to rise. The United States is also home to more large institutional investors, some of whom seek to channel a small portion of their funds into risky ventures, with hopes of scoring large gains. Put simply, the supply of capital for high-risk tech IPOs was greater in the United States than China.

Another factor is that stock market regulations make it easier for founders to retain control of their enterprises after IPOs in the United States. American exchanges have long allowed for dual class shares, in which founders maintain control of class A shares that give them super voting rights, while raising capital from the sale of class B shares that have limited or no voting rights. Moreover, American exchanges allow IPOs for enterprises that have yet to generate revenues, such as research-stage biotech companies, while Chinese exchanges have historically not allowed that. In 2018, in response to the advantages enjoyed by American exchanges, Hong Kong changed its listing standards to allow for duel class shares and opened the doors to biotech firms that have yet to generate revenues.

A risk associated with investing in Chinese IPOs offered through American exchanges is that, in addition to duel class shareholdings, they can have complex ownership structures. The typical Chinese IPO uses variable interest entities (VIEs). This is a structure in which the Chinese company creates two entities: one in China that holds the permits and licenses needed to do business there; and the other an offshore entity, often in a tax haven such as the Cayman islands, in which foreign investors can buy shares through an IPO. The Chinese entity, which is usually owned by top executives, pays fees and royalties to the offshore company in contractual arrangements. The risk here is that foreign investors don't actually own stock in the Chinese domicile company, and local management or even the Chinese government could force a split with the listed company, leaving U.S. investors high and dry. As the prospectus for Chinese IPOs often warns investors, "you may face difficulties protecting your interests, and your ability to protect your rights through U.S. courts may be limited, because we are incorporated under Cayman Islands law."* These risks, however, have not deterred U.S. investors.

All this being said, Hong Kong still dominated the market for Chinese IPOs in 2018, with 76 new offerings, a record number, that generated proceeds of $31 billion. This included China Tower, a state-owned company that is the world's largest operator of telecommunications towers. China Tower has 1.9 million tower sites and 2.8 million tenets in China, and rents out capacity on its towers to mobile phone carriers. The company raised $6.9 billion in its Hong Kong IPO, making it the world's largest listing in 2018. It will use the proceeds to build new towers and upgrade existing ones as it accelerates its role out of fifth-generation (5G) network capabilities.

*Ciara Linnane, "Futu Is the First Big Chinese IPO of 2019," *Market Watch*, March 11, 2019.

Sources: "China Tower Raises $6.9 Billion in World's Largest IPO in Two Years," *Reuters*, August 1, 2018; N. Bullock, "Number of Chinese IPOs in US Hits Eight Year High," *Financial Times*, December 26, 2018; T. Poletti, "Chinese IPOs Raked in $9 Billion in U.S. Cash," *Market Watch*, December 31, 2018.

Introduction

Over the last 30 years, we have moved from a world in which national capital markets were segmented from each other by regulatory barriers to capital flows toward a world in which the capital market is becoming increasingly global. This has clear benefits for corporations, but as we shall see, it also comes with some risks. The opening case touches on some of the issues here. Nowadays, it is not unusual for companies located in one country, such as China, to raise capital in another country, such as the United States, by offering its stock for sale there. As described in the opening case, in 2018, 33 Chinese firms raised $9 billion in capital by undertaking Initial Public Offerings (IPOs) not in China, but in the United States. They did this to take advantage of the stronger demand in the U.S. for shares in risky Chinese tech IPOs compared to Hong Kong and Shanghai. Put differently, their cost of capital was lower in the United States than in China. In addition, as the opening case makes clear, regulatory differences can make it more attractive to raise capital in certain markets. Thus, the ability to establish duel ownership structures and variable interest entities makes New York an attractive location for risky tech ventures to raise capital.

This chapter looks at the global market for capital. We begin by studying the benefits associated with the globalization of capital markets. This is followed by a more detailed look at the growth of the international capital market and the macroeconomic risks associated with such growth. Next, we review three important segments of the global capital market: the Eurocurrency market, the international bond market, and the international equity market. As usual, we close the chapter by pointing out some of the implications for the practice of international business.

Benefits of the Global Capital Market

LO12-1

Describe the benefits of the global capital market.

Although this section is about the global capital market, it opens by discussing the functions of a generic capital market. Then, we look at the limitations of domestic capital markets and discuss the benefits of using global capital markets.

THE FUNCTIONS OF A GENERIC CAPITAL MARKET

Capital markets bring together those who want to invest money and those who want to borrow money (see Figure 12.1). Those who want to invest money include corporations with surplus cash, individuals, and nonbank financial institutions (e.g., pension funds, insurance companies). Those who want to borrow money include individuals, companies, and governments. Between these two groups are the market makers. Market makers are the financial service companies that connect investors and borrowers, either directly or indirectly. They include commercial banks (e.g., Citi; Bank of America) and investment banks (e.g., Goldman Sachs; J.P. Morgan).

Commercial banks perform an indirect connection function. They take cash deposits from corporations and individuals and pay them a rate of interest in return. They then lend that money to borrowers at a higher rate of interest, making a profit from the difference in interest rates (commonly referred to as the *interest rate spread*). Investment banks perform a direct connection function. They bring investors and borrowers together and charge commissions for doing so. For example, Goldman Sachs may act as a stockbroker for an individual who wants to invest some money. Its personnel will advise her as to the most attractive purchases and buy stock on her behalf, charging a fee for the service.

FIGURE 12.1

The main players in the generic capital market.

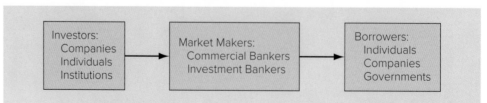

Capital market loans to corporations are either equity loans or debt loans. An equity loan is made when a corporation sells stock to investors. The money the corporation receives in return for its stock can be used to purchase plants and equipment, fund R&D projects, pay wages, and so on. A share of stock gives its holder a claim to a firm's profit stream. Ultimately, the corporation honors this claim by paying dividends to the stockholders (although many fast-growing young corporations do not start to issue dividends until the business has matured and growth rate slows). The amount of the dividends is not fixed in advance. Rather, it is determined by management based on how much profit the corporation is making. Investors purchase stock both for its dividend yield and in anticipation of gains in the price of the stock, which in theory reflects future dividend yields. Stock prices increase when a corporation is projected to have greater earnings in the future, which increases the probability that it will raise future dividend payments.

A debt loan requires the corporation to repay a predetermined portion of the loan amount (the sum of the principal plus the specified interest) at regular intervals regardless of how much profit it is making. Management has no discretion as to the amount it will pay investors. Debt loans include cash loans from banks and funds raised from the sale of corporate bonds to investors. When an investor purchases a corporate bond, he purchases the right to receive a specified fixed stream of income from the corporation for a specified number of years (i.e., until the bond maturity date). The maturity period of debt loans vary from the very long term, such as 20 years, to extremely short-term loans, including those with a maturity of just one day.

globalEDGE GLOSSARY TERMS

This *International Business* textbook covers what is commonly referred to as a "survey" of topics in international business. As such, the book includes a lot of terms, definitions, and technical language associated with international business and worldwide trade. One chapter that covers many important details is the one you are reading currently on global capital markets. While the goal is to provide readers of the textbook with state-of-the-art knowledge, every possible term and definition that may be important when conducting international business around the world cannot be covered in this textbook (due to space and the volume of terms). Instead, globalEDGE provides several hundred relevant terms and definitions. They help in understanding certain scenarios in this book, and more importantly, understanding practical scenarios you may encounter in the workplace. To help with this chapter (and other chapters), check out globalEDGE's glossary section at **globaledge.msu.edu/reference-desk/glossary**. Think of the glossary, definitions, and breadth of terminology as a quick refresher of the main issues in international business.

ATTRACTIONS OF THE GLOBAL CAPITAL MARKET

A global capital market benefits both borrowers and investors. It benefits borrowers by increasing the supply of funds available for borrowing and by lowering the cost of capital. It benefits investors by providing a wider range of investment opportunities, thereby allowing them to build portfolios of international investments that diversify their risks.

The Borrower's Perspective: Lower Cost of Capital

In a purely domestic capital market, the pool of investors is limited to residents of the country. This places an upper limit on the supply of funds available to borrowers. In other words, the liquidity of the market is limited. A global capital market, with its much larger pool of investors, provides a larger supply of funds for borrowers to draw on.

FIGURE 12.2

Market liquidity and the cost of capital.

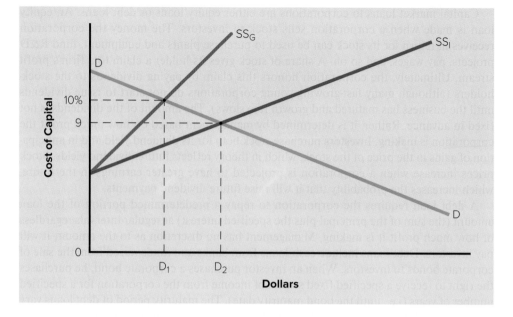

Perhaps the most important drawback of the limited liquidity of a purely domestic capital market is that the cost of capital tends to be higher than it is in a global market. The cost of capital is the price of borrowing money, which is the rate of return that borrowers must pay investors. This is the interest rate on debt loans, and the dividend yield and expected capital gains on equity loans. In a purely domestic market, the limited pool of investors implies that borrowers must pay more to persuade investors to lend them their money. The larger pool of investors in an international market implies that borrowers will be able to pay less.

The argument is illustrated in Figure 12.2, using Deutsche Telekom, the German telecommunications company, as an example. In 1996, in what was one of the first major global offerings, Deutsche Telekom raised more than $13 billion by simultaneously offering shares for sales in Frankfurt, New York, London, and Tokyo. The vertical axis in Figure 12.2 is the cost of capital (the price of borrowing money), and the horizontal axis is the amount of money available at varying interest rates. The Deutsche Telekom demand curve for borrowings is DD. Note that the Deutsche Telekom demand for funds varies with the cost of capital; the lower the cost of capital, the more money Deutsche Telekom will borrow. (Money is just like anything else; the lower its price, the more of it people can afford.) The supply curve of funds available in the German capital market is SS_G, and the funds available in the global capital market is represented by SS_I. Note that Deutsche Telekom can borrow more funds more cheaply on the global capital market. As Figure 12.2 illustrates, the greater pool of resources in the global capital market—the greater liquidity—both lowers the cost of capital and increases the amount Deutsche Telekom can borrow. Thus, the advantage of a global capital market to borrowers is that it lowers the cost of capital.

Problems of limited liquidity are not restricted to less developed nations, which naturally tend to have smaller domestic capital markets. In recent decades, even very large enterprises based in some of the world's largest economies have tapped the international capital markets in their search for greater liquidity and a lower cost of capital. One of the largest offerings of the global capital market era was that of the Industrial and Commercial Bank of Japan, which is discussed in the accompanying Management Focus.[1]

The Investor's Perspective: Portfolio Diversification

By using the global capital market, investors have a much wider range of investment opportunities than in a purely domestic capital market. The most significant consequence of this choice is that investors can diversify their portfolios internationally, thereby

The Industrial and Commercial Bank of China Taps the Global Capital Market

In October 2006, the Industrial and Commercial Bank of China, or ICBC, successfully completed what was then the world's largest ever initial public offering (IPO), raising some $21 billion. It beat Japan's 1998 IPO of NTT DoCoMo by a wide margin to earn a place in the record books (NTT raised $18.4 billion in its IPO).

The ICBC offering followed the IPOs of a number of other Chinese banks and corporations. Indeed, Chinese enterprises had been regularly tapping global capital markets for the prior decade as the Chinese have sought to fortify the balance sheets of the country's largest companies, to improve corporate governance and transparency, and to give China's industry leaders global recognition. Between 2000 and 2006, Chinese companies raised more than $100 billion from the equity markets. About half of that came in 2005 and 2006, largely from the country's biggest banks. Shares sold by Chinese companies are also accounting for a greater share of global equity sales—about 10 percent in 2006 compared to 2.8 percent in 2001, surpassing the total amount raised by companies in the world's then-second-largest economy, Japan.

To raise this amount of capital, Chinese corporations have been aggressively courting international investors. In the case of ICBC, it simultaneously listed its IPO shares on the Shanghai stock exchange and the Hong Kong exchange. The rationale for the Hong Kong listing was that regulations in Hong Kong are in accordance with international standards, while those in Shanghai have some way to go. By listing in Hong Kong, ICBC signaled to potential investors that it would adhere to the strict reporting and governance standards expected of the top global companies.

The ICBC listing attracted considerable interest from foreign investors, who saw it as a way to invest in the Chinese economy. ICBC has a nationwide bank network of more than 18,000 branches, the largest in the nation. It claims 2.5 million corporate customers and 150 million personal accounts. Some 1,000 institutions from across the globe reportedly bid for shares in the IPO. Total orders from these institutions were equivalent to 40 times the amount of stock offered for sale. In other words, the offering was massively oversubscribed. Indeed, the issue generated a total demand of some $430 billion, almost twice the value of Citi, the world's largest bank by market capitalization. The listing on Hong Kong attracted some $350 billion in orders from global investors, more than any other offering in Hong Kong's history. The domestic portion of the stock sales, through the Shanghai exchange, attracted some $80 billion in orders. This massive oversubscription enabled ICBC to raise the issuing price for its shares and reap some $2 billion more than planned.

Sources: K. Linebaugh, "Record IPO Could Have Been Even Bigger," *The Wall Street Journal*, October 21, 2006, p. B3; "Deals That Changed the Market in 2006: ICBC's Initial Public Offering," *Euromoney*, February 7, 2007, p. 1; T. Mitchell, "ICBC Discovers That Good Things Come to Those Who Wait," *Financial Times*, October 26, 2006, p. 40.

reducing their risk to less than what could be achieved in a purely domestic capital market. We consider how this works in the case of stock holdings, although the same argument could be made for bond holdings.

Consider an investor who buys stock in a biotech firm that has not yet produced a new product. Imagine the price of the stock is very volatile—investors are buying and selling the stock in large numbers in response to information about the firm's prospects. Such stocks are risky investments; investors may win big if the firm produces a marketable product; but investors may also lose all their money if the firm fails to come up with a product that sells. Investors can guard against the risk associated with holding this stock by buying other firms' stocks, particularly those weakly or negatively correlated with the biotech stock. By holding a variety of stocks in a diversified portfolio, the losses incurred when some stocks fail to live up to their promise are offset by the gains enjoyed when other stocks exceed their promise.

As an investor increases the number of stocks in her portfolio, the portfolio's risk declines. At first, this decline is rapid. Soon, however, the rate of decline falls off and asymptotically approaches the systematic risk of the market. *Systematic risk* refers to movements in a stock portfolio's value that are attributable to macroeconomic forces affecting all firms in an economy, rather than factors specific to an individual firm. The systematic risk is the level of nondiversifiable risk in an economy. Data from a classic study by Solnik[2] suggested that a fully diversified U.S. portfolio is only about 27 percent as risky as a typical individual stock.

By diversifying a portfolio internationally, an investor can reduce the level of risk even further because the movements of stock market prices across countries are not perfectly correlated. For example, one study looked at the correlation among three stock market indexes. The Standard & Poor's 500 (S&P 500) summarized the movement of large U.S. stocks. The Morgan Stanley Capital International Europe, Australia, and Far East Index (EAFE) summarized stock market movements in other developed nations. The third index, the International Finance Corporation Global Emerging Markets Index (IFC), summarized stock market movements in less developed "emerging economies." From 1981 to 1994, the correlation between the S&P 500 and EAFE indexes was 0.45, suggesting they moved together only about 20 percent of the time (i.e., $0.45 \times 0.45 = 0.2025$). The correlation between the S&P 500 and IFC indexes was even lower at 0.32, suggesting they moved together only a little more than 10 percent of the time.[3] Other studies have confirmed that despite casual observations, different national stock markets appear to be only moderately correlated. One study found that between 1972 and 2000 the average pairwise correlation between the world's four largest equity markets in the United States, United Kingdom, Germany, and Japan was 0.475, suggesting that these markets moved in tandem only about 22 percent of the time ($0.475 \times 0.472 = 0.22$ or 22 percent of shared variance).[4]

The relatively low correlation between the movement of stock markets in different countries reflects two basic factors. First, countries pursue different macroeconomic policies and face different economic conditions, so their stock markets respond to different forces and can move in different ways. For example, in 1997, the stock markets of several Asian countries, including South Korea, Malaysia, Indonesia, and Thailand, lost more than 50 percent of their value in response to the Asian financial crisis, while at the same time the S&P 500 increased in value by more than 20 percent. Second, some stock markets are still somewhat segmented from each other by capital controls—that is, by restrictions on cross-border capital flows (although as noted earlier, such restrictions are declining rapidly). The most common restrictions include limits on the amount of a firm's stock that a foreigner can own and limits on the ability of a country's citizens to invest their money outside that country. For example, until recently it was difficult for foreigners to own more than 30 percent of the equity of South Korean enterprises. Such barriers to cross-border capital flows limit the ability of capital to roam the world freely in search of the highest risk-adjusted return. Consequently, at any one time there may be too much capital invested in some markets and too little in others. This will tend to produce differences in rates of return across stock markets.[5] The implication is that by diversifying a portfolio to include foreign stocks, an investor can reduce the level of risk below that incurred by holding only domestic stocks.

According to the classic study by Bruno Solnik,[6] a fully diversified portfolio that contains stocks from many countries is less than half as risky as a fully diversified portfolio that contains only U.S. stocks. Solnik found that a fully diversified portfolio of international stocks is only about 12 percent as risky as a typical individual stock, whereas a fully diversified portfolio of U.S. stocks is about 27 percent as risky as a typical individual stock.

There is a perception, increasingly common among investment professionals, that the growing integration of the global economy and the emergence of the global capital market have increased the correlation between different stock markets, reducing the benefits of international diversification.[7] Today, it is argued, if the U.S. economy enters a recession, and the U.S. stock market declines rapidly, other markets follow suit. Indeed, this is what seems to have occurred in 2008 and 2009 as the financial crisis that started in the United States swept around the world. Another study by Solnik suggests there may be some truth to this assertion, but the rate of integration is not occurring as rapidly as the popular perception would lead one to believe. Solnik and his associate looked at the correlation between 15 major stock markets in developed countries between 1971 and 1998. They found that on average, the correlation of monthly stock market returns increased from 0.66 in 1971 to 0.75 in 1998, indicating some convergence over time, but that "the regression results were weak," which suggests that this "average" relationship was not strong and that there was considerable variation among countries.[8] Similarly, a more recent study confirmed this basic finding, suggesting that even today, most of the time a portfolio equally diversified across all available markets can reduce portfolio risk to about 35 percent of the volatility associated with a single market (i.e., a 65 percent reduction in risk).[9]

The implication here is that international portfolio diversification can still reduce risk. Moreover, the correlation between stock market movements in developed and emerging markets seems to be lower, and the rise of stock markets in developing nations, such as China, has given international investors many more opportunities for international portfolio diversification.[10]

The risk-reducing effects of international portfolio diversification would be greater were it not for the volatile exchange rates associated with the current floating exchange rate regime. Floating exchange rates introduce an additional element of risk into investing in foreign assets. As we have said repeatedly, adverse exchange rate movements can transform otherwise profitable investments into unprofitable investments. The uncertainty engendered by volatile exchange rates may be acting as a brake on the otherwise rapid growth of the international capital market.

GROWTH OF THE GLOBAL CAPITAL MARKET

According to data from the Bank for International Settlements, the global capital market is growing at a rapid pace. Stocks, bonds, and bank loans currently total over $300 trillion, more than three times the size of the world economy.[11] There seem to be two factors driving this growth—advances in information technology and deregulation by governments.

LO12-2

Identify why the global capital market has grown so rapidly.

Information Technology

Financial services is an information-intensive industry. It draws on large volumes of information about markets, risks, exchange rates, interest rates, creditworthiness, and so on. It uses this information to make decisions about what to invest where, how much to charge borrowers, how much interest to pay to depositors, and the value and riskiness of a range of financial assets including corporate bonds, stocks, government securities, and currencies.

Because of this information intensity, the financial services industry has been revolutionized more than any other industry by advances in information technology since the 1970s. The growth of international communications technology has facilitated instantaneous communication between any two points on the globe. At the same time, rapid advances in data processing capabilities have allowed market makers to absorb and process large volumes of information from around the world. According to one study, because of these technological developments, the real cost of recording, transmitting, and processing information fell by 95 percent between 1964 and 1990.[12] With the rapid rise of the internet and the massive increase in computing power that we have seen since 1990, it seems likely that the cost of recording, transmitting, and processing information has fallen by a similar amount since 1990 and is now trivial.

Such developments have facilitated the emergence of an integrated international capital market. It is now technologically possible for financial services companies to engage in 24-hour-a-day trading, whether it is in stocks, bonds, foreign exchange, or any other financial asset. Due to advances in communications and data processing technology, the international capital market never sleeps. San Francisco closes one hour before Tokyo opens, but during this period trading continues in New Zealand.

The integration facilitated by technology has a dark side.[13] "Shocks" that occur in one financial center now spread around the globe very quickly. For example, the financial crisis that began in the United States in 2008 quickly spread around the globe. However, most market participants would argue that the benefits of an integrated global capital market far outweigh any potential costs. Moreover, despite the fact that shocks in national financial markets do seem to spill over into other markets, on average the correlation between movements in national equity markets remains relatively low, suggesting that such shocks may have a relatively moderate long-term impact outside their home market.[14]

Deregulation

In country after country, financial services has historically been the most tightly regulated of all industries. Governments around the world have traditionally kept other countries' financial service firms from entering their capital markets. In some cases, they have also restricted the overseas expansion of their domestic financial services firms. In many countries, the law has also segmented the domestic financial services industry. In the United States, for example, until the late 1990s commercial banks were prohibited from performing the functions of investment banks, and vice versa. Historically, many countries have limited the ability of foreign investors to purchase significant equity positions in domestic companies. They have also limited the amount of foreign investment that their citizens could undertake. In the 1970s, for example, capital controls made it very difficult for a British investor to purchase American stocks and bonds.

Many of these restrictions have been crumbling since the early 1980s. In part, this has been a response to the development of the Eurocurrency market, which from the beginning was outside national control. (This is explained later in the chapter.) It has also been a response to pressure from financial services companies, which have long wanted to operate in a less regulated environment. Increasing acceptance of the free market ideology associated with an individualistic political philosophy also has a lot to do with the global trend toward the deregulation of financial markets (see Chapter 2). Whatever the reason, deregulation in a number of key countries has undoubtedly facilitated the growth of the international capital market.

The trend began in the United States in the late 1970s and early 1980s with a series of changes that allowed foreign banks to enter the U.S. capital market and domestic banks to expand their operations overseas. In Great Britain, the so-called Big Bang of October 1986 removed barriers that had existed between banks and stockbrokers and allowed foreign financial service companies to enter the British stock market. Restrictions on the entry of foreign securities houses have been relaxed in Japan, and Japanese banks are now allowed to open international banking facilities. In France, the "Little Bang" of 1987 opened the French stock market to outsiders and to foreign and domestic banks. In Germany, foreign banks are now allowed to lend and manage foreign euro issues, subject to reciprocity agreements.[15] All of this has enabled financial services companies to transform themselves from primarily domestic companies into global operations with major offices around the world— a prerequisite for the development of a truly international capital market. As we saw in Chapter 8, in late 1997 the World Trade Organization brokered a deal that removed many of the restrictions on cross-border trade in financial services. This deal facilitated further growth in the size of the global capital market.

In addition to the deregulation of the financial services industry, many countries beginning in the 1970s started to dismantle capital controls, loosening both restrictions on inward investment by foreigners and outward investment by their own citizens and corporations. By the 1980s, this trend spread from developed nations to the emerging economies of the world as countries across Latin America, Asia, and eastern Europe started to dismantle decades-old restrictions on capital flows.

The trends toward deregulation of financial services and removal of capital controls were still firmly in place until 2008. However, the global financial crisis of 2008–2009 prompted many to wonder if deregulation had gone too far, and it focused attention on the need for new regulations to govern certain sectors of the financial services industry, including the hedge funds, which operate largely outside of existing regulatory boundaries.

(**Hedge funds** are private investment funds that position themselves to make "long bets" on assets that they think will increase in value and "short bets" on assets that they think will decline in value.) Given the benefits associated with the globalization of capital, notwithstanding the current contraction, over the long term the growth of the global capital market can be expected to continue. While most commentators see this as a positive development, some believe the globalization of capital holds inherent serious risks.

GLOBAL CAPITAL MARKET RISKS

Some analysts are concerned that due to deregulation and reduced controls on cross-border capital flows, individual nations are becoming more vulnerable to speculative capital flows. They see this as having a destabilizing effect on national economies.[16] Harvard economist Martin Feldstein, for example, has argued that most of the capital that moves internationally is pursuing temporary gains, and it shifts in and out of countries as quickly as conditions change.[17] He distinguishes between this short-term capital, or "hot money," and "patient money" that would support long-term cross-border capital flows. To Feldstein, patient money is still relatively rare, primarily because although capital is free to move internationally, its owners and managers still prefer to keep most of it at home. Feldstein supports his arguments with statistics that demonstrate that although vast amounts of money flows through the foreign exchange markets every day, "when the dust settles, most of the savings done in each country stays in that country."[18] Feldstein argues that the lack of patient money is due to the relative paucity of information that investors have about foreign investments. In his view, if investors had better information about foreign assets, the global capital market would work more efficiently and be less subject to short-term speculative capital flows. Feldstein claims that Mexico's economic problems in the mid-1990s were the result of too much hot money flowing in and out of the country and too little patient money. This example is reviewed in detail in the accompanying Country Focus.

A lack of information about the fundamental quality of foreign investments may encourage speculative flows in the global capital market. Faced with a lack of quality information, investors may react to dramatic news events in foreign nations and pull their money out too quickly. Despite advances in information technology, it is still difficult for investors to get access to the same quantity and quality of information about foreign investment opportunities that they can get about domestic investment opportunities. This information gap is exacerbated by different accounting conventions in different countries, which makes the direct comparison of cross-border investment opportunities difficult for all but the most sophisticated investor (see Chapter 19 for details). For example, historically German accounting principles have been different from those found in the United States and presented quite a different picture of the health of a company. Thus, when the Germany company Daimler-Benz translated its German financial accounts into U.S.-style accounts in 1993, as it had to do to be listed on the New York Stock Exchange, it found that while it had made a profit of $97 million under German rules, under U.S. rules it had lost $548 million![19] However, in the 2000s there has been rapid movement toward harmonization of different national accounting standards, which is certainly improving the quality of information available to investors (see Chapter 20 for details).

Given the problems created by differences in the quantity and quality of information, many investors have yet to venture into the world of cross-border investing, and those who do are prone to reverse their decision on the basis of limited (and perhaps inaccurate) information. However, if the international capital market continues to grow, financial intermediaries likely will increasingly provide quality information about foreign investment opportunities. Better information should increase the sophistication of investment decisions and reduce the frequency and size of speculative capital flows. Although concerns about the volume of "hot money" sloshing around in the global capital market increased as a result of the Asian financial crisis, IMF research suggests there has not been an increase in the volatility of financial markets since the 1970s.[20]

LO12-3

Understand the risks associated with the globalization of capital markets.

TEST PREP

Use SmartBook to help retain what you have learned. Access your instructor's Connect course to check out SmartBook or go to **learnsmartadvantage.com** for help.

Did the Global Capital Markets Fail Mexico?

In early 1994, soon after passage of the North American Free Trade Agreement (NAFTA), Mexico was widely admired among the international community as a shining example of a developing country with a bright economic future. Since the late 1980s, the Mexican government had pursued sound monetary, budget, tax, and trade policies. By historical standards, inflation was low, the country was experiencing solid economic growth, and exports were booming. This robust picture attracted capital from foreign investors; between 1991 and 1993, foreigners invested more than $75 billion in the Mexican economy, more than in any other developing nation.

If there was a blot on Mexico's economic report card, it was the country's growing current account (trade) deficit. Mexican exports were booming but so were its imports. In the 1989–1990 period, the current account deficit was equivalent to about 3 percent of Mexico's gross domestic product. In 1991, it increased to 5 percent, and by 1994, it was running at an annual rate of more than 6 percent. Bad as this might seem, it is not unsustainable and should not bring an economy crashing down. The United States has been running a current account deficit for decades with apparently little in the way of ill effects. A current account deficit will not be a problem for a country as long as foreign investors take the money they earn from trade with that country and reinvest it within the country. This has been the case in the United States for years, and during the early 1990s, it was occurring in Mexico too. Thus, companies such as Ford took the pesos they earned from exports to Mexico and reinvested those funds in productive capacity in Mexico, building auto plants to serve the future needs of the Mexican market and to export elsewhere.

Unfortunately for Mexico, much of the $25 billion annual inflow of capital it received during the early 1990s was not the kind of patient long-term money that Ford was putting into Mexico. Rather, according to economist Martin Feldstein, much of the inflow was short-term capital that could flee if economic conditions changed for the worse. This is what seems to have occurred. In February 1994, the U.S. Federal Reserve began to increase U.S. interest rates. This led to a rapid fall in U.S. bond prices. At the same time, the yen began to appreciate sharply against the U.S. dollar. These events resulted in large losses for many managers of short-term capital, such as hedge fund managers and banks, which had been betting on exactly the opposite happening. Many hedge funds had been betting that interest rates

would fall, bond prices would rise, and the dollar would appreciate against the yen.

Faced with large losses, money managers tried to reduce the riskiness of their portfolios by pulling out of risky situations. About the same time, events took a turn for the worse in Mexico. An armed uprising in the southern state of Chiapas, the assassination of the leading candidate in the presidential election campaign, and an accelerating inflation rate all helped produce a feeling that Mexican investments were riskier than had been assumed. Money managers began to pull many of their short-term investments out of the country.

As hot money flowed out, the Mexican government realized it could not continue to count on capital inflows to finance its current account deficit. The government had assumed the inflow was mainly composed of patient, long-term money. In reality, much of it appeared to be short-term money. As money flowed out of Mexico, the Mexican government had to commit more foreign reserves to defending the value of the peso against the U.S. dollar, which was pegged at 3.5 pesos to the dollar. Currency speculators entered the picture and began to bet against the Mexican government by selling pesos short. Events came to a head in December 1994 when the Mexican government was essentially forced by capital flows to abandon its support for the peso. Over the next month, the peso lost 40 percent of its value against the dollar, the government was forced to introduce an economic austerity program, and the Mexican economic boom came to an abrupt end.

According to Martin Feldstein, the Mexican economy was brought down not by currency speculation on the foreign exchange market, but by a lack of long-term patient money. He argued that Mexico offered, and still offers, many attractive long-term investment opportunities, but because of the lack of information on long-term investment opportunities in Mexico, most of the capital flowing into the country from 1991 to 1993 was short-term, speculative money, the flow of which could quickly be reversed. If foreign investors had better information, Feldstein argued, Mexico should have been able to finance its current account deficit from inward capital flows because patient capital would naturally gravitate toward attractive Mexican investment opportunities.

Sources: Martin Feldstein, "Global Capital Flows: Too Little, Not Too Much," The Economist, June 24, 1995, pp. 72–73; R. Dornbusch, "We Have Salinas to Thank for the Peso Debacle," BusinessWeek, January 16, 1995, p. 20; P. Carroll and C. Torres, "Mexico Unveils Program of Harsh Fiscal Medicine," The Wall Street Journal, March 10, 1995, pp. A1, A6. See also Martin Feldstein and Charles Horioka, "Domestic Savings and International Capital Flows," Economic Journal 90 (1980), pp. 314–29.

The Eurocurrency Market

LO12-4

Compare and contrast the benefits and risks associated with the Eurocurrency market, the global bond market, and the global equity market.

A **Eurocurrency** is any currency banked outside its country of origin. Eurodollars, which account for about two-thirds of all Eurocurrencies, are dollars banked outside the United States. Other important Eurocurrencies include the Euro-yen, the Euro-pound, and the Euro-euro! The term *Eurocurrency* is actually a misnomer, because a Eurocurrency can be created anywhere in the world; the persistent *Euro-* prefix reflects the European origin of the market. The Eurocurrency market has been an important and relatively low-cost source of funds for international businesses.

GENESIS AND GROWTH OF THE MARKET

The Eurocurrency market was born in the mid-1950s when eastern European holders of dollars, including the former Soviet Union, were afraid to deposit their holdings of dollars in the United States lest they be seized by the U.S. government to settle U.S. residents' claims against business losses resulting from the communist takeover of eastern Europe.[21] These countries deposited many of their dollar holdings in Europe, particularly in London. Additional dollar deposits came from various western European central banks and from companies that earned dollars by exporting to the United States. These two groups deposited their dollars in London banks, rather than U.S. banks, because they were able to earn a higher rate of interest (which will be explained).

The Eurocurrency market received a major push in 1957 when the British government prohibited British banks from lending British pounds to finance non-British trade, a business that had been very profitable for British banks. British banks began financing the same trade by attracting dollar deposits and lending dollars to companies engaged in international trade and investment. Because of this historical event, London became, and has remained, the leading center of Eurocurrency trading.

The Eurocurrency market received another push in the 1960s when the U.S. government enacted regulations that discouraged U.S. banks from lending to non-U.S. residents. Would-be dollar borrowers outside the United States found it increasingly difficult to borrow dollars in the United States to finance international trade, so they turned to the Eurodollar market to obtain the necessary dollar funds.

The U.S. government changed its policies after the 1973 collapse of the Bretton Woods system (see Chapter 11), removing an important impetus to the growth of the Eurocurrency market. However, another political event, the oil price increases engineered by OPEC in the 1973–1974 and 1979–1980 periods, gave the market another big shove. As a result of the oil price increases, the Arab members of OPEC accumulated huge amounts of dollars. They were afraid to place their money in U.S. banks or their European branches, lest the U.S. government attempt to confiscate them. (Iranian assets in U.S. banks and their European branches were frozen by President Carter in 1979 after Americans were taken hostage at the U.S. embassy in Tehran; their fear was not unfounded.) Instead, these countries deposited their dollars with banks in London, further increasing the supply of Eurodollars.

Although these various political events contributed to the growth of the Eurocurrency market, they alone were not responsible for it. The market grew because it offered real financial advantages—initially to those who wanted to deposit dollars or borrow dollars and later to those who wanted to deposit and borrow other currencies. We now look at the source of these financial advantages.

ATTRACTIONS OF THE EUROCURRENCY MARKET

The main factor that makes the Eurocurrency market attractive to both depositors and borrowers is its lack of government regulation. This allows banks to offer higher interest rates on Eurocurrency deposits than on deposits made in the home currency, making Eurocurrency deposits attractive to those who have cash to deposit. The lack of regulation also allows banks to charge borrowers a lower interest rate for Eurocurrency borrowings

FIGURE 12.3

Interest rate spreads
in domestic and
Eurocurrency markets.

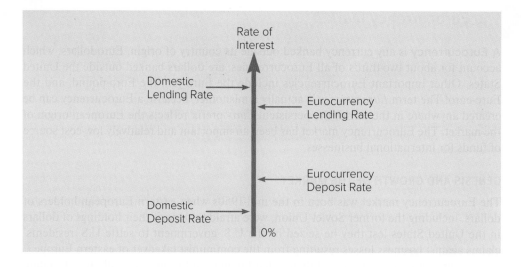

than for borrowings in the home currency, making Eurocurrency loans attractive for those who want to borrow money. In other words, the spread between the Eurocurrency deposit rate and the Eurocurrency lending rate is less than the spread between the domestic deposit and lending rates (see Figure 12.3). To understand why this is so, we must examine how government regulations raise the costs of domestic banking.

Domestic currency deposits are regulated in all industrialized countries. Such regulations ensure that banks have enough liquid funds to satisfy demand if large numbers of domestic depositors should suddenly decide to withdraw their money. All countries operate with certain reserve requirements. For example, each time a U.S. bank accepts a deposit in dollars, it must place some fraction of that deposit in a non-interest-bearing account at a Federal Reserve Bank as part of its required reserves. Similarly, each time a British bank accepts a deposit in pounds sterling, it must place a certain fraction of that deposit with the Bank of England.

Banks are given much more freedom in their dealings in foreign currencies, however. For example, the British government does not impose reserve requirement restrictions on deposits of foreign currencies within its borders. Nor are the London branches of U.S. banks subject to U.S. reserve requirement regulations, provided those deposits are payable only outside the United States. This gives Eurobanks a competitive advantage.

For example, suppose a bank based in New York faces a 10 percent reserve requirement. According to this requirement, if the bank receives a $100 deposit, it can lend out no more than $90 of that, and it must place the remaining $10 in a non-interest-bearing account at a Federal Reserve bank. Suppose the bank has annual operating costs of $1 per $100 of deposits and that it charges 10 percent interest on loans. The highest interest the New York bank can offer its depositors and still cover its costs is 8 percent per year. Thus, the bank pays the owner of the $100 deposit (0.08 × $100 =) $8, earns (0.10 × $90 =) $9 on the fraction of the deposit it is allowed to lend, and just covers its operating costs.

In contrast, a Eurobank can offer a higher interest rate on dollar deposits and still cover its costs. The Eurobank, with no reserve requirements regarding dollar deposits, can lend out all of a $100 deposit. Therefore, it can earn 0.10 × $100 = $10 at a loan rate of 10 percent. If the Eurobank has the same operating costs as the New York bank ($1 per $100 deposit), it can pay its depositors an interest rate of 9 percent, a full percentage point higher than that paid by the New York bank, and still cover its costs. That is, it can pay out 0.09 × $100 = $9 to its depositor, receive $10 from the borrower, and be left with $1 to cover operating costs. Alternatively, the Eurobank might pay the depositor 8.5 percent (which is still above the rate paid by the New York bank), charge borrowers 9.5 percent (still less than the New York bank charges), and cover its operating costs. Thus, the Eurobank has a competitive advantage vis-à-vis the New York bank in both its deposit rate and its loan rate.

Clearly, there are strong financial motivations for companies to use the Eurocurrency market. By doing so, they receive a higher interest rate on deposits and pay less for loans. Given this, the surprising thing is not that the Euromarket has grown rapidly but that it hasn't grown even faster. Why do any depositors hold deposits in their home currency when they could get better yields in the Eurocurrency market?

DRAWBACKS OF THE EUROCURRENCY MARKET

The Eurocurrency market has two drawbacks. First, when depositors use a regulated banking system, they know that the probability of a bank failure that would cause them to lose their deposits is very low. Regulation maintains the liquidity of the banking system. In an unregulated system such as the Eurocurrency market, the probability of a bank failure that would cause depositors to lose their money is greater (although, in absolute terms, still low). Thus, the lower interest rate received on home-country deposits reflects the costs of insuring against bank failure. Some depositors are more comfortable with the security of such a system and are willing to pay the price.

Second, borrowing funds internationally can expose a company to foreign exchange risk. For example, consider a U.S. company that uses the Eurocurrency market to borrow Euro-pounds—perhaps because it can pay a lower interest rate on Euro-pound loans than on dollar loans. Imagine, however, that the British pound subsequently appreciates against the dollar. This would increase the dollar cost of repaying the Euro-pound loan and thus the company's cost of capital. This possibility can be insured against by using the forward exchange market (as we saw in Chapter 10), but the forward exchange market does not offer perfect insurance. Consequently, many companies borrow funds in their domestic currency to avoid foreign exchange risk, even though the Eurocurrency markets may offer more attractive interest rates.

TEST PREP

Use SmartBook to help retain what you have learned. Access your instructor's Connect course to check out SmartBook or go to **learnsmartadvantage.com** for help.

The Global Bond Market

The global bond market has grown rapidly over the last four decades. Bonds are an important means of financing for many companies. The most common kind of bond is a fixed-rate bond. The investor who purchases a fixed-rate bond receives a fixed set of cash payoffs. Each year until the bond matures, the investor gets an interest payment, and then at maturity he gets back the face value of the bond.

International bonds are of two types: foreign bonds and Eurobonds. **Foreign bonds** are sold outside the borrower's country and are denominated in the currency of the country in which they are issued. Thus, when Dow Chemical issues bonds in Japanese yen and sells them in Japan, it is issuing foreign bonds. Many foreign bonds have nicknames; foreign bonds sold in the United States are called Yankee bonds, foreign bonds sold in Japan are Samurai bonds, and foreign bonds sold in Great Britain are bulldogs. Companies will issue international bonds if they believe that it will lower their cost of capital. For example, during the late 1990s and early 2000s, many companies issued Samurai bonds in Japan to take advantage of the very low interest rates in Japan. In early 2001, 10-year Japanese government bonds yielded 1.24 percent, compared with 5 percent for comparable U.S. government bonds. Against this background, companies found that they could raise debt at a cheaper rate in Japan than the United States.

Eurobonds are normally underwritten by an international syndicate of banks and placed in countries other than the one in whose currency the bond is denominated. For example, a bond may be issued by a German corporation, denominated in U.S. dollars, and sold to investors outside the United States by an international syndicate of banks. Eurobonds are routinely issued by multinational corporations, large domestic corporations, sovereign governments, and international institutions. They are usually offered simultaneously in several national capital markets, but not in the capital market of the country, nor to residents of the country, in whose currency they are denominated. Historically, Eurobonds accounted for the lion's share of international bond issues, but increasingly they are being eclipsed by foreign bonds.

ATTRACTIONS OF THE EUROBOND MARKET

Three features of the Eurobond market make it an appealing alternative to most major domestic bond markets, specifically:

- An absence of regulatory interference.
- Less stringent disclosure requirements than in most domestic bond markets.
- A favorable tax status.

Regulatory Interference

National governments often impose controls on domestic and foreign issuers of bonds denominated in the local currency and sold within their national boundaries. These controls tend to raise the cost of issuing bonds. However, government limitations are generally less stringent for securities denominated in foreign currencies and sold to holders of those foreign currencies. Eurobonds fall outside the regulatory domain of any single nation. As such, they can often be issued at a lower cost to the issuer.

Disclosure Requirements

TEST PREP

Use SmartBook to help retain what you have learned. Access your instructor's Connect course to check out SmartBook or go to **learnsmartadvantage.com** for help.

Eurobond market disclosure requirements tend to be less stringent than those of several national governments. For example, if a firm wishes to issue dollar-denominated bonds within the United States, it must first comply with SEC disclosure requirements. The firm must disclose detailed information about its activities, the salaries and other compensation of its senior executives, stock trades by its senior executives, and the like. In addition, the issuing firm must submit financial accounts that conform to U.S. accounting standards. For non-U.S. firms, redoing their accounts to make them consistent with U.S. standards can be very time-consuming and expensive. Therefore, many firms have found it cheaper to issue Eurobonds, including those denominated in dollars, than to issue dollar-denominated bonds within the United States.

Favorable Tax Status

Did You Know?

Did you know that China and Japan are the largest foreign holders of U.S. Treasury Bills?

Visit your instructor's Connect® course and click on your eBook or SmartBook® to view a short video explanation from the author.

Before 1984, U.S. corporations issuing Eurobonds were required to withhold for U.S. income tax up to 30 percent of each interest payment to foreigners. This did not encourage foreigners to hold bonds issued by U.S. corporations. Similar tax laws were operational in many countries at that time, and they limited market demand for Eurobonds. U.S. laws were revised in 1984 to exempt from any withholding tax foreign holders of bonds issued by U.S. corporations. As a result, U.S. corporations found it feasible for the first time to sell Eurobonds directly to foreigners. Repeal of the U.S. laws caused other governments—including those of France, Germany, and Japan—to liberalize their tax laws likewise to avoid outflows of capital from their markets. The consequence was an upsurge in demand for Eurobonds from investors who wanted to take advantage of their tax benefits.

The Global Equity Market

Historically, substantial regulatory barriers separated national equity markets from each other. Not only was it often difficult to take capital out of a country and invest it elsewhere, but corporations also frequently lacked the ability to list their shares on stock markets outside their home nations. These regulatory barriers made it difficult for a corporation to attract significant equity capital from foreign investors. These barriers tumbled fast during the 1980s and 1990s. The global equity market enabled firms to attract capital from international investors, to list their stock on multiple exchanges, and to raise funds by issuing equity or debt around the world. For example, in 1994 Daimler-Benz, Germany's largest industrial company, raised $300 million by issuing new shares not in Germany, but in Singapore.[22] Similarly, in 1996 the German telecommunications provider Deutsche Telekom raised some $13.3 billion by simultaneously listing its shares for sale on stock exchanges in Frankfurt, London, New York, and Tokyo. These German companies elected to raise equity through foreign markets because they reasoned that their domestic capital market was too small to supply the requisite funds at a reasonable cost. To lower their cost of capital, they tapped into the large and highly liquid global capital market.

More recently, many Chinese companies have been raising equity capital through foreign stock issues. In 2010, a record 39 Chinese companies issued stock through the New York Stock Exchange, giving them access to more capital at a lower cost than would have been possible if they had just issued stock in China.[23] In 2014, in what was the largest IPO ever, the Chinese internet company Alibaba raised $25 billion in equity capital on the New York Stock Exchange. Of course, the other side of the coin is that if foreign entities are going to issue stock in New York, London, or another major foreign market, they also have to adhere to the stringent requirements for financial reporting that are common in those markets.

Although we have talked about the growth of the global equity market, strictly speaking there is no international equity market in the sense that there are international currency and bond markets. Rather, many countries have their own domestic equity markets in which corporate stock is traded. The largest of these domestic equity markets are to be found in the United States, Great Britain, Japan, and Hong Kong. Although each domestic equity market is still dominated by investors who are citizens of that country and companies incorporated in that country, developments are internationalizing the world equity market. Investors are investing heavily in foreign equity markets to diversify their portfolios. Facilitated by deregulation and advances in information technology, this trend seems to be here to stay.

An interesting consequence of the trend toward international equity investment is the internationalization of corporate ownership. Today, it is still generally possible to talk about U.S. corporations, British corporations, and Japanese corporations, primarily because the majority of stockholders (owners) of these corporations are of the respective nationality. However, this is changing. Increasingly, U.S. citizens are buying stock in companies incorporated abroad, and foreigners are buying stock in companies incorporated in the United States. Looking into the future, Robert Reich has mused about "the coming irrelevance of corporate nationality."[24]

A second development internationalizing the world equity market is that companies with historic roots in one nation are broadening their stock ownership by listing their stock in the equity markets of other nations. The reasons are primarily financial. Listing stock on a foreign market is often a prelude to issuing stock in that market to raise capital. The idea is to tap into the liquidity of foreign markets, thereby increasing the funds available for investment and lowering the firm's cost of capital. (The relationship between liquidity and the cost of capital was discussed earlier in the chapter.) Firms also often list their stock on foreign equity markets to facilitate future acquisitions of foreign companies. Other reasons for listing a company's stock on a foreign equity market are that the company's stock and stock options can be used to compensate local management and employees, it satisfies the desire for local ownership, and it increases the company's visibility with local employees, customers, suppliers, and bankers. Although firms based in developed nations were the first to start listing their stock on foreign exchanges, increasingly firms from developing countries who find their own growth limited by an illiquid domestic capital market are exploiting this opportunity.

Foreign Exchange Risk and the Cost of Capital

While a firm can borrow funds at a lower cost in the global capital market than in the domestic capital market, foreign exchange risk complicates this picture under a floating exchange rate regime. Adverse movements in foreign exchange rates can substantially increase the cost of foreign currency loans, which is what happened to many Asian companies during the 1997–1998 Asian financial crisis.

Consider a South Korean firm that wants to borrow 1 billion Korean won for one year to fund a capital investment project. The company can borrow this money from a Korean bank at an interest rate of 10 percent and, at the end of the year, pay back the loan plus interest for a total of W1.10 billion. Or the firm could borrow dollars from an international

✓ **TEST PREP**

Use SmartBook to help retain what you have learned. Access your instructor's Connect course to check out SmartBook or go to **learnsmartadvantage.com** for help.

LO12-5

Understand how foreign exchange risks affect the cost of capital.

bank at a 6 percent interest rate. At the prevailing exchange rate of $1 = W1,000, the firm would borrow $1 million and the total loan cost would be $1.06 million, or W1.06 billion. By borrowing dollars, the firm could reduce its cost of capital by 4 percent, or W40 million. However, this saving is predicated on the assumption that during the year of the loan, the dollar/won exchange rate stays constant. Instead, imagine that the won depreciates sharply against the U.S. dollar during the year and ends the year at $1 = W1,500. (This occurred in late 1997 when the won declined in value from $1 = W1,000 to $1 = W1,500 in two months.) The firm still has to pay the international bank $1.06 million at the end of the year, but now this costs the company W1.59 billion (i.e., $1.06 million × 1,500). As a result of the depreciation in the value of the won, the cost of borrowing in U.S. dollars has soared from 6 percent to 59 percent, a huge rise in the firm's cost of capital. Although this may seem like an extreme example, it happened to many South Korean firms in 1997 at the height of the Asian financial crisis. Not surprisingly, many of them were pushed into technical default on their loans.

Unpredictable movements in exchange rates can inject risk into foreign currency borrowing, making something that initially seems less expensive ultimately much more expensive. The borrower can hedge against such a possibility by entering into a forward contract to purchase the required amount of the currency being borrowed at a predetermined exchange rate when the loan comes due (see Chapter 10 for details). Although this will raise the borrower's cost of capital, the added insurance limits the risk involved in such a transaction. Unfortunately, many Asian borrowers did not hedge their dollar-denominated short-term debt, so when their currencies collapsed against the dollar in 1997, many saw a sharp increase in their cost of capital.

When a firm borrows funds from the global capital market, it must weigh the benefits of a lower interest rate against the risks of an increase in the real cost of capital due to adverse exchange rate movements. Although using forward exchange markets may lower foreign exchange risk with short-term borrowings, it cannot remove the risk. Most important, the forward exchange market does not provide adequate coverage for long-term borrowings.

TEST PREP

Use SmartBook to help retain what you have learned. Access your instructor's Connect course to check out SmartBook or go to **learnsmartadvantage.com** for help.

FOCUS ON MANAGERIAL IMPLICATIONS

GROWTH OF THE GLOBAL CAPITAL MARKET

The implications of the material discussed in this chapter for international business are quite straightforward but no less important for being obvious. The growth of the global capital market has created opportunities for international businesses that wish to borrow and/or invest money. On the borrowing side, by using the global capital market, firms can often borrow funds at a lower cost than is possible in a purely domestic capital market. This conclusion holds no matter what form of borrowing a firm uses—equity, bonds, or cash loans. The lower cost of capital on the global market reflects its greater liquidity and the general absence of government regulation. Government regulation tends to raise the cost of capital in most domestic capital markets. The global market, being transnational, escapes regulation. Balanced against this, however, is the foreign exchange risk associated with borrowing in a foreign currency.

On the investment side, the growth of the global capital market is providing opportunities for firms, institutions, and individuals to diversify their investments to limit risk. By holding a diverse portfolio of stocks and bonds in different nations, an investor can reduce total risk to a lower level than can be achieved in a purely domestic setting. Once again, however, foreign exchange risk is a complicating factor.

Key Terms

hedge fund, p. 357
Eurocurrency, p. 359

foreign bonds, p. 361

Eurobonds, p. 361

SUMMARY

This chapter explained the functions and form of the global capital market and defined the implications of these for international business practice. This chapter made the following points:

1. The function of a capital market is to bring those who want to invest money together with those who want to borrow money.

2. Relative to a domestic capital market, the global capital market has a greater supply of funds available for borrowing, and this makes for a lower cost of capital for borrowers.

3. Relative to a domestic capital market, the global capital market allows investors to diversify portfolios of holdings internationally, thereby reducing risk.

4. The growth of the global capital market during recent decades can be attributed to advances in information technology, the widespread deregulation of financial services, and the relaxation of regulations governing cross-border capital flows.

5. A Eurocurrency is any currency banked outside its country of origin. The lack of government regulations makes the Eurocurrency market attractive to both depositors and borrowers. Due to the absence of regulation, the spread between the Eurocurrency deposit and lending rates is less than the spread between the domestic deposit and lending rates. This gives Eurobanks a competitive advantage.

6. The global bond market has two classifications: the foreign bond market and the Eurobond market. Foreign bonds are sold outside of the borrower's country and are denominated in the currency of the country in which they are issued. A Eurobond issue is normally underwritten by an international syndicate of banks and placed in countries other than the one in whose currency the bond is denominated. Eurobonds account for the lion's share of international bond issues.

7. The Eurobond market is an attractive way for companies to raise funds due to the absence of regulatory interference, less stringent disclosure requirements, and Eurobonds' favorable tax status.

8. Foreign investors are investing in other countries' equity markets to reduce risk by diversifying their stock holdings among nations.

9. Many companies are now listing their stock in the equity markets of other nations, primarily as a prelude to issuing stock in those markets to raise additional capital. Other reasons for listing stock in another country's exchange are to facilitate future stock swaps; to enable the company to use its stock and stock options for compensating local management and employees; to satisfy local ownership desires; and to increase the company's visibility among its local employees, customers, suppliers, and bankers.

10. When borrowing funds from the global capital market, companies must weigh the benefits of a lower interest rate against the risks of greater real costs of capital due to adverse exchange rate movements.

11. One major implication of the global capital market for international business is that companies can often borrow funds at a lower cost of capital in the international capital market than they can in the domestic capital market.

12. The global capital market provides greater opportunities for businesses and individuals to build a truly diversified portfolio of international investments in financial assets, which lowers risk.

Critical Thinking and Discussion Questions

1. Why has the global capital market grown so rapidly in recent decades? Do you think this growth will continue throughout the next decade? Why or why not?

2. In 2008–2009, the world economy retrenched in the wake of a global financial crisis. Do you think the globalization of capital markets contribute to this crisis? If so, what can be done to stop global financial contagion in the future?

3. A firm based in Norway has found that its growth is restricted by the limited liquidity of the Norwegian capital market. List the firm's options for raising money on the global capital market. Discuss the pros and cons of each

option, and make a recommendation. How might your recommended options be affected if the Norwegian krona depreciates significantly on the foreign exchange markets over the next two years?

4. Happy Company wants to raise $2 million with debt financing. The funds are needed to finance working capital, and the firm will repay them with interest in one year. Happy Company's treasurer is considering three options:

   a. Borrowing U.S. dollars from Security Pacific Bank at 8 percent.

   b. Borrowing British pounds from Midland Bank at 14 percent.

   c. Borrowing Japanese yen from Sanwa Bank at 5 percent.

If Happy borrows foreign currency, it will not cover it; that is, it will simply change foreign currency for dollars at today's spot rate and buy the same foreign currency a year later at the spot rate then in effect. Happy Company estimates the pound will depreciate by 5 percent relative to the dollar and the yen will appreciate 3 percent relative to the dollar in the next year. From which bank should Happy Company borrow?

globalEDGE research task globaledge.msu.edu

Use the globalEDGE™ website (**globaledge.msu.edu**) to complete the following exercises:

1. The top management team of your not-for-profit organization would like to find out more about investing in environmentally responsible companies in Europe. *FTSE* develops various indexes for the global financial markets. A series of indexes, called ESG, cover social, environmental, and good governance standards. One of these is the Environmental Europe 40 Index. Download the index's factsheet for your analysis. Evaluate the top

10 companies, countries, and industries represented in this index. What patterns do you see?

2. The Bureau of Economic Analysis is an agency of the U.S. Department of Commerce. It lists data about the U.S. economic accounts, including current investment positions and the amount of direct investment by multinational corporations in the United States and abroad. Prepare a brief report regarding the direct investments of other countries in the United States. Include in your report the leading countries in foreign direct investment.

CLOSING CASE

Saudi Aramco

In 2015, the government of Saudi Arabia announced an ambitious plan, known as Vision 2030, to diversify the economy beyond oil. Saudi's plans to modernize its economy will require copious funding, something that will strain the finances of the desert kingdom. The country relies heavily on oil, with 87 percent of the budget, 42 percent of GDP, and 90 percent of export earnings being derived from oil revenues. As a consequence of lower oil prices and higher government outlays, the Saudi government has recently been running large budget deficits. In 2016, the deficit hit $90 billion, or 13 percent of GDP. To raise the funds for Vision 2030, therefore, the government

decided to sell off shares in Saudi Aramco, the state-run oil company that has exclusive control over Saudi Arabia's oil reserves.

Saudi Aramco is one of the largest enterprises on earth. Saudi Arabia possesses about 16 percent of the world's oil reserves, including some of the lowest-cost reserves on the planet. This gives Saudi Aramco 10 times the reserves of the largest private oil company, ExxonMobil. Saudi government estimates suggest that Saudi Aramco is worth $2 trillion. Based on this valuation, the government is proposing to sell 5 percent of the shares of Saudi Aramco to private investors, which would raise $100 billion in capital for the government—enough to fund aggressive investments in non-oil ventures to support Vision 2030. If this comes to pass, the initial public offering (IPO) of Saudi Aramco will be the largest in history by a wide margin.

Raising $100 billion in capital has its challenges, not least of which is that the Saudi stock exchange, or Tadawul, is far too small and illiquid to absorb such a massive stock offering. As it stands, the entire Saudi stock market only lists 170 companies and has a total market capitalization of around $350 billion. Offering 5 percent of Saudi Aramco through the Tadawul will not result in a high price for the stock; there is simply not enough local demand to support that. The only way to raise $100 billion is to offer stock of Saudi Aramco for sale not just on the Tadawul, but also on one or more additional large and highly liquid stock markets. The exchanges being considered include New York, London, and Singapore. For example, with a market capitalization of more than $20 trillion, the New York Stock Exchange is far more able to absorb the offering than the Tadawul. Listing on multiple exchanges will make the IPO available to a much wider pool of investors, thus potentially increasing demand and driving up the price, making it more likely that the Saudi government will hit its target of raising $100 billion.

If Saudi Aramco does list on larger exchanges, which seems highly likely, it will have to abide by the strict accounting regulations and reporting requirements of those markets. Regular financial reporting will increase the transparency of Saudi Aramco, which in turn will increase investor confidence in the IPO and thus increase demand and drive up the market price of the stock. Another benefit of listing on multiple exchanges is that it will make it easier for Saudi Aramco to undertake additional stock offerings down the road and to issue debt securities in those markets.

Initially, the IPO was planned for 2018. However, skepticism from potential foreign investors about the official estimates of Saudi Aramco's oil reserves resulted in the IPO being delayed. To satisfy potential investors, Saudi Arabia commissioned an independent audit from a respected Dallas-based consultancy. The results of this audit, released in early 2019, confirmed that the kingdom controls more than 260 billion barrels in oil reserves.

Other factors have also pushed back the IPO date, including an ongoing dispute over where to list the IPO. Apparently, not all Saudis are happy with the notion of listing the IPO in New York, or any other foreign financial center for that matter. With the date of the IPO still uncertain, Saudi Aramco has decided to issue bonds in the second quarter of 2019. In order to tap into the global

Hassan Ammar/AFP/Getty Images

debt market, Aramco will release additional financial information, offering a deeper glimpse into a private company whose inner workings are very opaque. As for the IPO, currently it is targeted for 2021.

Sources: J. Blas and W. Mahdi, "Saudi Arabia's Oil Wealth Is about to Get a Reality Check," *Bloomberg,* February 23, 2017; M. Farrell and N. Parasie, "Saudi Aramco IPO: The Biggest Fee Event in Wall Street History," *The Wall Street Journal,* June 9, 2016; J. Everington, "Saudi Aims to Double the Size of the Stock Market," *The National,* April 5, 2016; T. DiChristopher, "Saudi Arabia Plots New Path to Long Delayed Aramco IPO," *CNBC,* January 10, 2019.

Case Discussion Questions

1. Why does the government of Saudi Arabia want Saudi Aramco to undertake an IPO? Should the fact that the funds raised will not be used to invest in Saudi Aramco matter to investors?

2. Saudi Aramco is a tightly held state-owned enterprise with a history of secrecy. How might this impact the IPO? What concerns might potential investors have? How might these concerns impact Saudi Aramco's cost of capital? What does Saudi Aramco need to do to reassure investors and deal with these concerns?

3. Could Saudi Aramco raise $100 billion by offering shares for sale on just the local Tadawul stock exchange? Why is it considering other stock exchanges? If it does restrict where it offers shares, what might the potential impact be?

4. If you were advising Saudi Aramco on their IPO strategy, what would your advice be?

Endnotes

1. K. Linebaugh, "Record IPO Could Have Been Even Bigger," *The Wall Street Journal,* October 21, 2006, p. B3.

2. B. Solnik, "Why Not Diversify Internationally Rather Than Domestically?" *Financial Analysts Journal,* July 1974, p. 17.

3. C. G. Luck and R. Choudhury, "International Equity Diversification for Pension Funds," *Journal of Investing* 5, no. 2 (1996), pp. 43–53.

4. W. N. Goetzmann, L. Li, and K. G. Rouwenhorst, "Long-Term Global Market Correlations," *The Journal of Business,* January 2005, pp. 78–126.

5. Ian Domowitz, Jack Glen, and Ananth Madhavan, "Market Segmentation and Stock Prices: Evidence from an Emerging Market," *Journal of Finance* 3, no. 3 (1997), pp. 1059–68.

6. Solnik, "Why Not Diversify Internationally Rather Than Domestically?"

7. A. Lavine, "With Overseas Markets Now Moving in Sync with U.S. Markets, It's Getting Harder to Find True Diversification Abroad," *Financial Planning,* December 1, 2000, pp. 37–40.

8. B. Solnik and J. Roulet, "Dispersion as Cross-Sectional Correlation," *Financial Analysts Journal* 56, no. 1 (2000), pp. 54–61.

9. W. Goetzmann, L. Li, and K. Rouwenhorst, "Long-Term Global Market Correlations," *Journal of Business* 78 (2005), pp. 1–38. See also R. Vermeulen, "International Diversification during the Financial Crisis: A Blessing for Equity Investors?" *Journal of International Money and Finance* 35 (2013), pp. 104–23.

10. W. Goetzmann, L. Li, and K. Rouwenhorst, "Long-Term Global Market Correlations," *Journal of Business* 78 (2005), pp. 1–38. See also R. Vermeulen, "International Diversification during the Financial Crisis: A Blessing for Equity Investors?" *Journal of International Money and Finance* 35 (2013), pp. 104–23.

11. Bank for International Settlements, *BIS Quarterly Review,* March 2013.

12. T. F. Huertas, "U.S. Multinational Banking: History and Prospects," in *Banks as Multinationals,* ed. G. Jones (London: Routledge, 1990).

13. G. J. Millman, *The Vandals' Crown* (New York: Free Press, 1995).

14. Goetzmann et al., "Long-Term Global Market Correlations"; Vermeulen, "International Diversification during the Financial Crisis: A Blessing for Equity Investors?"

15. P. Dicken, *Global Shift: The Internationalization of Economic Activity* (London: Guilford Press, 1992).

16. P. Dicken, *Global Shift: The Internationalization of Economic Activity* (London: Guilford Press, 1992).

17. M. Feldstein, "Global Capital Flows: Too Little, Not Too Much," *The Economist,* June 24, 1995, pp. 72–73.

18. M. Feldstein, "Global Capital Flows: Too Little, Not Too Much," *The Economist,* June 24, 1995, p. 73.

19. D. Duffy and L. Murry, "The Wooing of American Investors," *The Wall Street Journal,* February 25, 1994, p. A14.

20. International Monetary Fund, *World Economic Outlook* (Washington, DC: IMF, 1998).

21. C. Schenk, "The Origins of the Eurodollar Market in London, 1955-1963," *Explorations in Economic History* 35 (1998), pp. 221–39.

22. D. Waller, "Daimler in $250m Singapore Placing," *Financial Times,* May 10, 1994.

23. L. Spears and C. Vannucci, "China's Latest American IPOs Slump as Offerings Increase to Annual Record," *Bloomberg Businessweek,* December 6, 2010.

24. R. Reich, *The Work of Nations* (New York: Knopf, 1991).

The Strategy of International Business

13

LEARNING OBJECTIVES

After reading this chapter, you will be able to:

LO13-1   Explain the concept of global strategy.

LO13-2   Recognize how firms can profit by expanding globally.

LO13-3   Understand how pressures for cost reductions and local responsiveness influence strategic choice.

LO13-4   Identify and choose the different global strategies for competing in the global marketplace.

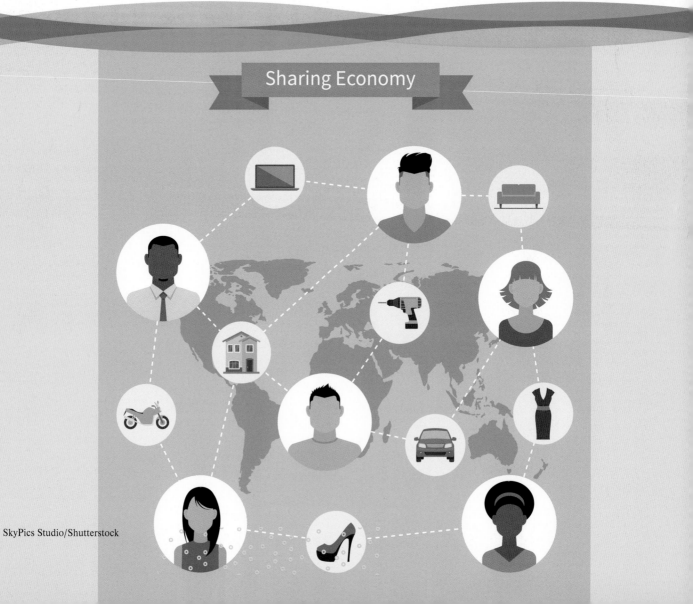

Sharing Economy

SkyPics Studio/Shutterstock

International Strategy in the Sharing Economy

OPENING CASE

Small, medium-sized, and large companies, as well as upstart entrepreneurial ventures, all strategize about the "sharing economy" and how to make it supplant more traditional international commerce. The following are a few relevant dates for this opening case: Airbnb started in 2008, Uber in 2009, Turo in 2010, Lyft in 2012, and Lime and Bird both began in 2017. These are some of the more obvious global success stories that most people have heard of and many readers have also used—whether it be while vacationing in Stockholm (where the entire country of Sweden is listed on Airbnb), in getting to the airport in Toronto, Canada, by enlisting Uber or Lyft, or using scooters like Bird and Lime to conveniently take in the Eiffel Tower and the surrounding Park Champ de Mars in Paris, France. Or, such companies may come in handy when you are looking to fit in with the rich and famous in, say, Dubai, United Arab Emirates, by using Turo's services to get behind the wheel of that Lamborghini you have always wanted to test drive (exciting outings like this would cost you about $800 per day, but it is certainly cheaper than buying the car).

Bird and Lime are covered in the opening case of Chapter 14, so here we will focus on Airbnb, Uber, Turo, and Lyft. First, however, let's trace today's sharing economy and give proper thanks to early-on peer-to-peer businesses like eBay. eBay started in 1995 (a few years after the internet became publicly available in 1991) and allows anyone to become a retailer, almost instantly. More recent sharing businesses, such as Uber, Lyft, Turo, and Airbnb, let individuals act as an ad hoc taxi service, car-hire firm, and boutique hotel when it suits them. This gives entrepreneurial-minded people a chance to enter the global marketplace without the typical startup costs, and it lets customers have more choices and even more decision-making power. Plus, who would have thought of driving a Lamborghini in Dubai—even at a steep cost—just a few years ago. This Lamborghini example symbolizes the sharing economy nicely. A dynamic mix of risk, reward, and trust must be involved for the sharing economy to work, and the players in the global marketplace are building that infrastructure rapidly.

If the sharing-economy infrastructure can be built rapidly and also engage companies across other, traditionally oriented industries and sectors, the options seem endless. A brief look at the evolution of Airbnb, Uber, Turo, and Lyft (followed by organizational issues that we cover for Bird and Lime in the opening case in Chapter 14) can help generate more diverse ideas and opportunities, and highlight international strategy issues. After all, when the author of this textbook went to college, the core focus was on getting a great education, building a network of friends and business links, and starting your career at some large, respectable company. Today, many college students—in business schools, at least—think up creative, entrepreneurial ideas that they can take to market while still in school or shortly thereafter.

Airbnb was founded in 2008 by Brian Chesky, Joe Gebbia, and Nathan Blecharczyk as a way to disrupt the hospitality industry and offer lodging alternatives and tourism experiences worldwide. The initial idea was as cleverly launched as it is simple to understand. Former schoolmates Brian Chesky and Joe Gebbia could not afford rent for their loft apartment in high-priced San Francisco, so they put an air mattress in their living room and turned their living space into a bed and breakfast. In February 2008, Nathan Blecharczyk, Chesky's former roommate, joined AirBed & Breakfast as the third co-founder, and the trio soon shortened the name to Airbnb. From Bamboo Eco Cottages in Indonesia to the Aromatica Treehouse in Italy, Airbnb is everywhere. Sweden took this literally when they announced in 2017 that the whole country was listed on Airbnb. As a collaboration between Airbnb and the "Visit Sweden" campaign, the Scandinavian country's listing is an effort to promote Sweden's "freedom to roam" principle, or *allemansrätten*, which gives people the right to freely explore all public spaces across the country.

Uber was founded in 2009 by Garrett Camp and Travis Kalanick, and was initially called UberCab. In an epiphany, Camp came up with the idea for Uber after spending $800 hiring a private car to transport him and his friends on New Year's Eve. What Camp really wanted to do was figure out a way he could make the transportation service more affordable and easily available to the average customer. In 2011, the name was shortened to Uber, and in 2012, Uber rolled out UberX—a service that allows entrepreneurial people to be part of the Uber family by using their own vehicles to provide customer transportation. Since then, Uber has been on the cutting-edge of transportation services and technologies, from self-driving cars, to a carpooling service, and even a helicopter service. Today, Uber operates across six continents in several hundred locations, but the brand is a household name even in locations that do not yet have Uber. Thanks to the way Uber disrupted the taxi market, partly through its clever marketing, Uber is now known across the globe.

Lyft began in 2012 and was founded by John Zimmer and Logan Green who met through a mutual friend on Facebook. Both Zimmer and Green were thinking about starting a ride-sharing service. Initially called Zimride and focusing on a potential target market of students on college campuses, it was renamed Lyft and soon became Uber's fiercest competitor in the United States and Canada. Like Uber, Lyft is a transportation company also based in San Francisco, California, but with operations primarily in the United States and Canada (compared with Uber, which is on every continent except Antarctica). Lyft develops, markets, and operates the Lyft mobile app for smartphones. Like Uber, Lyft is valued in the billions of dollars; having seen an infusion of $500 million in 2016, for example, from the likes of General Motors. Strangely, as China aggressively tries to grow its own ride-sharing service, Didi Kuaidi, and undermine Uber's existing inroads, China is also investing in Lyft—as is the Chinese firm Alibaba and Tencent, and also Japanese Softbank Capital—all of which are trying to join the anti-Uber alliance.

Turo is a peer-to-peer car sharing company, formerly known as RelayRides, that was founded by Shelby Clark in 2010 in Boston, Massachusetts. He was inspired by similar online marketplaces in other industries, such as Airbnb and eBay. But, like the ideas that created Airbnb, Uber, and Lyft, Shelby Clark first tried car sharing when his car died after a cross-country move from Massachusetts to California. (As you have likely surmised, the seeds of all these enterprises seem to come from trying to solve irritating everyday issues.) Clark loved living a car-free life, but thought car sharing would work better if it was "for the people, by the people," a neighbor-to-neighbor experience. So, he founded Turo, which is now headquartered in San Francisco, California, like Airbnb, Uber, Lyft, and Lime (Bird's headquarters is in Santa Monica, California, a six-hour drive from San Francisco). There is clearly something about San Francisco that makes companies in the sharing economy want to be headquartered in the iconic, technology-oriented metropolitan area.

Turo, so far, is more limited in the international marketplace than Airbnb and Uber, but it seems to be on the same global trajectory as Lyft.

So, whether it is Airbnb, Uber, Lyft, Turo, or any of the numerous choices we have as customers in the international marketplace in the sharing economy, disruptive market forces will continually demand new, innovative products and services. The experience of companies like Apple getting into the phone market in 2007—a market that had been dominated by companies that now either do not exist or are barely hanging on—is a commonplace phenomenon across industry sectors today that are often populated by entrepreneurial upstarts. The name of the game is disruption, with the notion of increasing customer value, solving lifestyle issues, and often creating innovative solutions by facilitating peer-to-peer interactions. International strategy today is built around an "easy-to-do, hard not-to-do" mindset of solving common problems that customers value in uncommon ways.

So, what solutions are you coming up with to help the world in your remaining years in college?

Sources: Alison Millington, Sweden Has Just Listed the Entire Country on Airbnb," *Business Insider*, May 24, 2017; "Lyft-off or Crash-Land?" *The Economist*, March 3, 2019; "The Rise of the Sharing Economy," *The Economist*, March 9, 2013; "50+ World Changing Peer-To-Peer Companies," *Currency Fair*, March 26, 2014; Alyson Shontell and Shana Lebowitz, "Lyft's Cofounders Met on Facebook and Lived on Opposite Coasts," *Business Insider*, October 17, 2018.

 Introduction

Up to this point in the text, we have focused on the worldwide environment in which multinational corporations and so-called SMEs (small and medium-sized enterprises) compete in the global marketplace.[1] These initial 12 "macro" chapters have included content on the different political, economic, and cultural institutions found in nations, the international trade and investment framework, and the international monetary system. Additionally, we have placed a strong emphasis on managerial implications associated with each of these macro topics, with separate sections in each of the 12 chapters on what the macro topics mean for managerial strategy and action globally. This managerial focus has been complemented with Management Focus and Country Focus features throughout the chapters to capture relevant knowledge you need to have in relation to running a global company.

Starting with this "strategy" chapter that we are now beginning, our focus shifts from the macro environment to the firm itself and, in particular, to the actions managers can take to compete more effectively as an international business.[2] To begin the sequence of eight chapters on running a firm, which comprise the remainder of the text, Chapter 13 looks at how organizations can increase revenue (and profits) by expanding their operations in foreign markets.

This is international business strategy—an intersection of strategy, international environment, and the performance of the firm. Importantly, we distinguish between revenue and profit; even nonprofit companies need to make enough revenue to offset costs to stay in business in the long term. Profit-focused companies, on the other hand, often focus on making more revenue than needed to cover costs, which allows them to realize a profit on what they sell. In this context, we discuss the different strategies that firms pursue when competing around the world, consider the pros and cons of the strategies, and elaborate on the various factors that affect a firm's choice of international strategy. Key issues in this chapter are value creation, global value chains (which we also cover more deeply in Chapter 17)[3] and how multinational corporations achieve superior performance.[4]

Value creation is a core focus of the opening case on international strategies in the sharing economy. Instead of highlighting one company or scenario, as we often do in cases, we provide a discussion of several sharing-economy companies. Companies of all sizes and backgrounds strategize about the "sharing economy" and how they can be part of supplanting more traditional international commerce, or at least provide additional services to customers. The examples are plentiful and powerful. We highlight four: Airbnb, Uber, Lyft, and Turo.

Traditional companies (e.g., Coca Cola; Microsoft) still exist, of course, and many are thriving. We will discuss such companies in Chapter 13, because they are still important to many customers.

Consequently, to complement the opening case on international strategies in the sharing economy that we live in, the closing case on Red Bull shows a company that has developed a unique, energetic, and fluid approach to competing. As we discuss in the case, many people around the world think that Red Bull is a local product. They do such a great job of promoting a universal Red Bull brand that customers in all countries soon consider it their own "local" brand that is recognized globally. Did you know that Red Bull is an Austrian–Thai company? To be both locally oriented and sport a global image, Red Bull communicates via their own Red Bull Media House, various social media, and uses content marketing that is customized to diverse audiences around the world. As such, Red Bull also has a relatively unique form of international strategy—it's not the same type of unique spirit displayed by the sharing-economy companies cited in the opening case, but it nevertheless employs a different operations model than traditional brick-and-mortar companies.

To blend tradition with newness in international strategy, the Management Focus sections in this chapter (i.e., AB InBev, IKEA, and Unilever) tackle more time-tested international strategy models and traditional companies as a complement to what we see in the opening and closing cases of the chapter. With more than 200 brands and strong coverage internationally of its different brands, AB InBev is a strategically unique and highly organized global company. Similarly, if you walk into an IKEA store anywhere in the world, you will recognize it instantly. Global strategy standardization is rampant at IKEA. Unilever is a bit different, but is still more traditional than nontraditional. With the company's Dutch–British background, Unilever is a dual-listed company consisting of Unilever NV based in Rotterdam, Netherlands, and Unilever PLC based in London, England. The dual-listed company operates as a single business, with a shared board of directors.

Strategy and the Firm

LO13-1

Explain the concept of global strategy.

When we talk about strategy and the firm, we refer to the firm in the most common way as a method to organize activities. This means that the firm can also be called multinational enterprise, multinational corporation, an international business, international organization, global company, and so on. A unique type of firm, though, is what we call an SME—a small and medium-sized enterprise. SMEs are companies that have fewer than 500 employees (U.S.) or fewer than 250 employees (Europe). Throughout the text, we use a variety of terminologies in largely the same context for the larger firms, but we specify clearly when we talk about SMEs because these companies have global strategies that sometimes differ from their larger counterparts.[5] Importantly, though, whereas most textbooks in business focus on large companies, we take great pride in, and have dedicated much effort to, discussing content as it relates to small and medium-sized firms, as well as to large firms.

FIGURE 13.1

Determinants of
enterprise value.

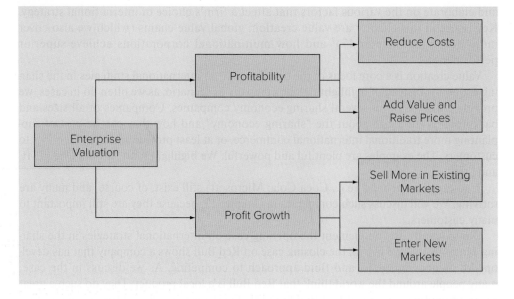

Also, before we discuss the strategies that managers in the multinational enterprise can pursue, we need to review some basic principles of strategy. A firm's **strategy** can be defined as the actions that managers take to attain the goals of the firm. For most firms, the preeminent goal is to maximize the value of the firm for its owners and its shareholders (subject to the very important constraint that the activities undertaken are done in a legal, ethical, and socially responsible manner—see Chapter 5 for details). To maximize the value of a firm, managers must pursue strategies that increase the *profitability* of the enterprise and its rate of *profit growth* over time (see Figure 13.1). **Profitability** can be measured in a number of ways, but for consistency, we define it as the rate of return that the firm makes on its invested capital (ROI), which is calculated by dividing the net profits of the firm by total invested capital.[6] **Profit growth** is measured by the percentage increase in net profits over time. In general, higher profitability and a higher rate of profit growth will increase the value of an enterprise and thus the returns garnered by its owners, the shareholders.[7]

Managers can increase the profitability of the firm by pursuing strategies that lower costs or by pursuing strategies that add value to the firm's products, which enables the firm to raise prices and/or to maintain an existing customer base.[8] Managers can increase the rate at which the firm's profits grow over time by pursuing strategies to sell more products in existing markets or by pursuing strategies to enter new markets. Making a decision to expand internationally can help managers boost the firm's profitability *and* increase the rate of profit growth over time.

VALUE CREATION

The way to increase the profitability of a firm is to create more value.[9] The amount of value a firm creates is generally measured by the difference between its costs of production and the quality that consumers perceive in its products. In general, the more value customers place on a firm's products, the higher the price the firm can charge for those products. However, the price a firm charges for a good or service is typically less than the value placed on that good or service by the customer. This is because the customer captures some of that value in the form of what economists call a consumer surplus.[10] The customer is able to do this because the firm is competing with other firms for the customer's business, so the firm must charge a lower price than it could were it a monopoly supplier. Also, it is normally impossible to segment the market to such a degree that the firm can charge each customer a price that reflects a specific customer's

FIGURE 13.2

Value creation.

assessment of the value of a product, which economists refer to as a customer's reservation price. For these reasons, the price that gets charged tends to be slightly less than the value placed on the product by many customers.

Figure 13.2 illustrates these value concepts. The value of a product to an *average* consumer is V, the average price that the firm can charge a consumer for that product given competitive pressures and its ability to segment the market is P, and the average unit cost of producing that product is C (C comprises all relevant costs, including the firm's cost of capital). The firm's profit per unit sold (p) is equal to $P - C$, while the consumer surplus per unit is equal to $V - P$ (another way of thinking of the consumer surplus is as "value for the money"; the greater the consumer surplus, the greater the value for the money the consumer gets). The firm makes a profit so long as P is greater than C, and its profit will be greater the lower C is *relative* to P. The difference between V and P is in part determined by the intensity of competitive pressure in the marketplace; the lower the intensity of competitive pressure, the higher the price charged relative to V.[11] In general, the higher the firm's profit per unit sold, the greater its profitability, all else being equal.

The firm's **value creation** is measured by the difference between V and C ($V - C$); a company creates value by converting inputs that cost C into a product on which consumers place a value of V. A company can create more value ($V - C$) either by lowering production costs, C, or by making the product more attractive through superior design, styling, functionality, features, reliability, after-sales service, and the like, so that consumers place a greater value on it (V increases) and, consequently, are willing to pay a higher price (P increases). This discussion suggests that *a firm has high profits when it creates more value for its customers and does so at a lower cost*. We refer to a strategy that focuses primarily on lowering production costs as a *low-cost strategy*. We refer to a strategy that focuses primarily on increasing the attractiveness of a product as a *differentiation strategy*.[12]

Michael Porter has argued that *low cost* and *differentiation* are two basic strategies for creating value and attaining a competitive advantage in an industry.[13] According to Porter, superior profitability goes to those firms that can create superior value, and the way to create superior value is to drive down the cost structure of the business and/or differentiate the product in some way so that consumers value it more and are prepared to pay a premium price. Superior value creation relative to rivals does not necessarily require a firm to have the lowest-cost structure in an industry or to create the most valuable product in the eyes of consumers. However, it does require that the gap between value (V) and cost of production (C) be greater than the gap attained by competitors.

STRATEGIC POSITIONING

Porter notes that it is important for a firm to be explicit about its choice of strategic emphasis with regard to value creation (differentiation) and low cost, and to configure its internal operations to support that strategic emphasis.[14] Figure 13.3 illustrates his

FIGURE 13.3

Strategic choice in the
international hotel
industry.

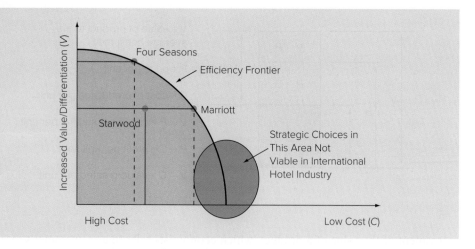

point. The convex curve in Figure 13.3 is what economists refer to as an *efficiency frontier*. The efficiency frontier shows all of the different positions that a firm can adopt with regard to adding value to the product (*V*) and low cost (*C*) assuming that its internal operations are configured efficiently to support a particular position (note that the horizontal axis in Figure 13.3 is reverse scaled—moving along the axis to the right implies lower costs). The efficiency frontier has a convex shape because of diminishing returns. Diminishing returns imply that when a firm already has significant value built into its product offering, increasing value by a relatively small amount requires significant additional costs. The converse also holds, when a firm already has a low-cost structure, it has to give up a lot of value in its product offering to get additional cost reductions.

Figure 13.3 plots three hotel brands with a global presence that cater to international travelers, Four Seasons, Marriott International, and Starwood (the Starwood conglomerate of hotel brands, such as Westin and Sheraton, was bought by Marriott in 2016). Four Seasons positions itself as a luxury chain and emphasizes the value of its product offering, which drives up its costs of operations. The Marriott and Starwood brands are positioned more in the middle of the market. Both emphasize sufficient value to attract international business travelers but are not luxury chains like Four Seasons. In Figure 13.3, Four Seasons and Marriott are shown to be on the efficiency frontier, indicating that their internal operations are well configured to their strategy and run efficiently. Starwood is inside the frontier, indicating that its operations are not running as efficiently as they might be and that its costs are too high. This implies that Starwood is less profitable than Four Seasons and Marriott and that its managers must take steps to improve the company's performance. The purchase by Marriott of the Starwood collection of brands in 2016 was potentially a way to leverage the global strategy across multiple hotel brands.

Porter emphasizes that it is very important for management to decide where the company wants to be positioned with regard to value (*V*) and cost (*C*), to configure operations accordingly, and to manage them efficiently to make sure the firm is operating on the efficiency frontier. However, not all positions on the efficiency frontier are viable. In the international hotel industry, for example, there might not be enough demand to support a chain that emphasizes very low cost and strips all the value out of its product offering (see Figure 13.3). International travelers are relatively affluent and expect a degree of comfort (value) when they travel away from home.

A central tenet of the basic strategy paradigm is that to maximize its profitability, a firm must do three things: (1) pick a position on the efficiency frontier that is viable in the sense that there is enough demand to support that choice; (2) configure its internal operations, such as manufacturing, marketing, logistics, information systems, human

AB InBev, Beer Globally, and Creating Value

The company AB InBev may not sound familiar to everyone, but spelled out, its name likely becomes clearer to most people, especially the beer-loving population of the world. Anheuser-Busch InBev originates from the Den Hoorn brewery in Leuven, Belgium, which dates back to 1366, and the pioneering spirit of the Anheuser & Co. brewery, with origins in St. Louis, Missouri, since 1852. Today, AB InBev is the leading global brewer and one of the world's top consumer products companies.

AB InBev has operations in 25 countries, sales in more than 100 countries, revenue of $44 billion, 155,000 employees, and 7 of the top 10 most valuable beer brands. These seven brands are: Budweiser, Bud Light, Stella Artois, Skol, Corona, Brahma, and Modelo Especial. Budweiser, Corona, and Stella Artois are marketed as "global brands," while Beck's, Leffe, and Hoegaarden are considered "international brands" in AB InBev's brand portfolio. The company also has 15 "local champions," which represent leadership in their respective local markets. These local brands include Jupiler (the most popular beer in Belgium), Quilmes (an original Argentinean lager since 1890), and Harbin (from the oldest brewery in North China). In total, AB InBev's portfolio consists of more than 200 brands.

With so many brands and strong coverage internationally of these different brands, strategically AB InBev is a unique and highly organized global company. Carlos Brito (CEO) and Olivier Goudet (chairman of the board) have stated that the company's ambition is to build a great, enduring company for the next 100 years. The core management team consists of the CEO, nine Executive Board members, and six zone presidents. The six zone presidents are responsible for the following sales areas: Latin America South, Latin America North, Asia Pacific, North America, Mexico, and Europe.

Using this management structure, AB InBev has built leading positions in the important beer profit markets of the world through a combination of organic growth and selected, value-enhancing acquisitions. The company follows a focus brands strategy in which the majority of the resources are devoted to those brands that have the greatest long-term growth potential. Investment behind the brands is fueled by a disciplined approach to cost management and efficiency. AB InBev has a strong track record of industry-leading margins and cash flow generation. In 2015, this led to growth of 12.6 percent of the company's three global brands (Budweiser, Corona, and Stella Artois), for example, and strong earnings in North America and most of Latin America.

The foundation for AB InBev's global strategy is the company's "Dream-People-Culture" approach. The goal is that despite having operations in many countries around the world, with different national cultures, AB InBev operates as one company, with one dream and one culture uniting them. There is also a focus on having the right people in the right place at the right time. This culture is built on ownership, informality, candor, transparency, and meritocracy.

Strategically, AB InBev has 10 principles driving everything it does. At the core, AB InBev is focused on a shared dream that energizes everyone to work in the same direction to be the best beer company in the world, bring people together, and make the world a better place. Additional principles cover people strengths, the quality of teams, striving for increased satisfaction, consumer focus, ownership, common sense and simplicity, cost management, leadership, and hard work and responsibility.

Sources: D. Leonard, "Can Craft Beer Survive AB InBev?" *Bloomberg Business*, June 25, 2015; V. Wong, "Why AB InBev and Big Brewers Are Betting on Hard Cider," *Bloomberg Business*, May 13, 2013; J. Colley, "The Big Beer Merger Won't Bring Down the Price of a Pint," *Newsweek*, October 18, 2015; C. Purdy, "There's a Less Obvious Reason Why AB InBev Is Buying Up Craft Breweries," *Quartz*, December 23, 2015; AB InBev Annual Report 2015, annualreport.ab-inbev.com.

resources, and so on, so that they support that position; and (3) make sure that the firm has the right organization structure in place to execute its strategy. *The strategy, operations, and organization of the firm must all be consistent with each other if it is to attain a competitive advantage and garner superior profitability.* By **operations** we mean the different value creation activities a firm undertakes, which we review next. The accompanying Management Focus provides an illustration of how AB InBev creates value in the beer industry globally by adopting a strategy paradigm that is centered on maximizing profitability.

FIGURE 13.4

The value chain.

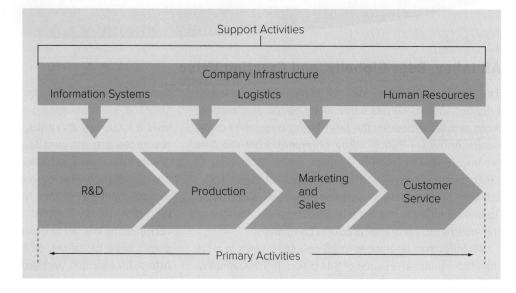

THE FIRM AS A VALUE CHAIN

The operations of a firm can be thought of as a value chain composed of a series of distinct value creation activities,[15] including production, marketing and sales, materials management, R&D, human resources, information systems, and the firm infrastructure. We can categorize these value creation activities, or operations, as primary activities and support activities (see Figure 13.4).[16] As noted, if a firm is to implement its strategy efficiently, and position itself on the efficiency frontier shown in Figure 13.3, it must manage these activities effectively and in a manner that is consistent with its strategy.

Primary Activities

Primary activities have to do with the design, creation, and delivery of the product; its marketing; and its support and after-sale service. Following normal practice, in the value chain illustrated in Figure 13.4, the primary activities are divided into four functions: research and development, production, marketing and sales, and customer service.

Research and development (R&D) is concerned with the design of products and production processes. Although we think of R&D as being associated with the design of physical products and production processes in manufacturing enterprises, many service companies also undertake R&D. For example, banks compete with each other by developing new financial products and new ways of delivering those products to customers. Online banking and smart debit cards are two examples of product development in the banking industry. Earlier examples of innovation in the banking industry included automated teller machines, credit cards, and debit cards. Through superior product design, R&D can increase the functionality of products, which makes them more attractive to consumers (raising V). Alternatively, R&D may result in more efficient production processes, thereby cutting production costs (lowering C). Either way, the R&D function can create value.

Production is concerned with the creation of a good or service. For physical products, when we talk about production, we generally mean manufacturing. Thus, we can talk about the production of an automobile. For services such as banking or health care, "production" typically occurs when the service is delivered to the customer (e.g., when a bank originates a loan for a customer, it is engaged in "production" of the loan). For a retailer such as Walmart, "production" is concerned with selecting the merchandise, stocking the store, and ringing up the sale at the cash register. For MTV, production is concerned with the creation, programming, and broadcasting of content, such as music videos and thematic shows. The production activity of a firm creates value by performing its activities efficiently so lower costs result (lower C) and/or by performing them in such a way that a higher-quality product is produced (which results in higher V).

The marketing and sales functions of a firm can help create value in several ways.[17] Through brand positioning and advertising, the marketing function can increase the value (V) that consumers perceive to be contained in a firm's product. If these create a favorable impression of the firm's product in the minds of consumers, they increase the price that can be charged for the firm's product. For example, Ford produced a high-value version of its Ford Expedition SUV. Sold as the Lincoln Navigator and priced around $10,000 higher, the Navigator has the same body, engine, chassis, and design as the Expedition, but through skilled advertising and marketing, supported by some fairly minor features changes (e.g., more accessories and the addition of a Lincoln-style engine grille and nameplate), Ford has fostered the perception that the Navigator is a "luxury SUV." This marketing strategy has increased the perceived value (V) of the Navigator relative to the Expedition and enables Ford to charge a higher price for the car (P).

Marketing and sales can also create value by discovering consumer needs and communicating them back to the R&D function of the company, which can then design products that better match those needs. For example, the allocation of research budgets at Pfizer, the world's largest pharmaceutical company, is determined by the marketing function's assessment of the potential market size associated with solving unmet medical needs. Thus, Pfizer is currently directing significant monies to R&D efforts aimed at finding treatments for Alzheimer's disease, principally because marketing has identified the treatment of Alzheimer's as a major unmet medical need in nations around the world where the population is aging.

The role of the enterprise's service activity is to provide after-sale service and support. This function can create a perception of superior value (V) in the minds of consumers by solving customer problems and supporting customers after they have purchased the product. Caterpillar, the U.S.-based manufacturer of heavy earthmoving equipment, can get spare parts to any point in the world within 24 hours, thereby minimizing the amount of downtime its customers have to suffer if their Caterpillar equipment malfunctions. This is an extremely valuable capability in an industry where downtime is very expensive. It has helped to increase the value that customers associate with Caterpillar products and thus the price that Caterpillar can charge.

Support Activities

The support activities of the value chain provide inputs that allow the primary activities to occur (see Figure 13.4). In terms of attaining a competitive advantage, support activities can be as important as, if not more important than, the primary activities of the firm.

Consider information systems; these systems refer to the electronic systems for managing inventory, tracking sales, pricing products, selling products, dealing with customer service inquiries, and so on. Information systems, when coupled with the communications features of the internet, can alter the efficiency and effectiveness with which a firm manages its other value creation activities. Dell, for example, has used its information systems to attain a competitive advantage over rivals. When customers place an order for a Dell product over the firm's website, that information is immediately transmitted, via the internet, to suppliers, who then configure their production schedules to produce and ship that product so that it arrives at the right assembly plant at the right time. These systems have reduced the amount of inventory that Dell holds at its factories to under two days, which is a source of cost savings.

The logistics function controls the transmission of physical materials through the value chain, from procurement through production and into distribution. The efficiency with which this is carried out can significantly reduce cost (lower C), thereby creating more value. The combination of logistics systems and information systems is a particularly potent source of cost savings in many enterprises, such as Dell, where information systems tell Dell on a real-time basis where in its global logistics network parts are, when they will arrive at an assembly plant, and thus how production should be scheduled.

The human resource function can help create more value in a number of ways. It ensures that the company has the right mix of skilled people to perform its value creation activities effectively. The human resource function also ensures that people are adequately trained, motivated, and compensated to perform their value creation tasks. In a multinational enterprise, one of the things human resources can do to boost the competitive position of the firm is to take advantage of its transnational reach to identify, recruit, and develop a cadre of skilled managers, regardless of their nationality, who can be groomed to take on senior management positions. They can find the very best, wherever they are in the world. Indeed, the senior management ranks of many multinationals are becoming increasingly diverse, as managers from a variety of national backgrounds have ascended to senior leadership positions. Japan's Sony, for example, is now headed not by a Japanese national, but by Howard Stringer, a Welshman.

The final support activity is the company infrastructure, or the context within which all the other value creation activities occur. The infrastructure includes the organization structure, control systems, and culture of the firm. Because top management can exert considerable influence in shaping these aspects of a firm, top management should also be viewed as part of the firm's infrastructure. Through strong leadership, top management can consciously shape the infrastructure of a firm and through that the performance of all its value creation activities.

 TEST PREP

Use SmartBook to help retain what you have learned. Access your instructor's Connect course to check out SmartBook or go to **learnsmartadvantage.com** for help.

LO13-2
Recognize how firms can profit by expanding globally.

Global Expansion, Profitability, and Profit Growth

Expanding globally gives firms opportunities to increase their profitability and rate of profit growth in ways not available to purely domestic enterprises.[18] Firms that operate internationally are able to:

1. Expand the potential size of the market for their domestic products by selling those products (or services) in the global marketplace.
2. Realize location economies by dispersing value creation activities to those worldwide locations where they can be performed most efficiently and effectively.
3. Realize greater cost economies from experience effects by serving an expanded global market from a geographically central location.
4. Earn a greater return-on-investment by leveraging valuable skills developed in international operations and transferring them to other entities within the firm.

A firm's ability to increase its profitability and profit growth by pursuing these strategies is sometimes constrained by the need to customize some portion of its product offering, marketing strategy, and business strategy to differing national conditions—that is, by the imperative of localization. As the world becomes "flatter" and more homogeneous—at least for the younger-aged population—customization will also decrease. We are not there yet, however. Many of the world's 195 countries have customers with differing needs, wants, purchasing power, and authority to buy products and services. In such cases, a firm's global expansion comes with the potential for increased profitability, as well as increased cost factors, that have to be weighted rationally.

EXPANDING THE MARKET

A company can increase its growth rate by taking goods or services developed at home and selling them internationally. Almost all multinationals started out doing just this. For example, Procter & Gamble developed most of its best-selling products (such as Pampers disposable diapers and Ivory soap) in the United States and subsequently sold them around the world. Likewise, although Microsoft developed its software in the United States, from its earliest days, the company has always focused on selling that software in international markets. Automobile companies such as Volkswagen (Germany) and Toyota (Japan) also grew by developing products at home and then selling them in international markets. The returns from such a strategy are likely to be greater if indigenous competitors in the nations that a company enters lack comparable products (e.g., availability of the product, quality of the product, price of the product). Thus, Toyota increased its profits by entering the large automobile market of North America, offering products that were different from those offered by local rivals (Ford and GM) by their quality, price, and reliability.

The success of many multinational companies that expand in this manner is based not just upon the goods or services that they sell in foreign nations, but also upon the core competencies that underlie the development, production, and marketing of those goods or services. The term **core competence** refers to skills within the firm that competitors cannot easily match or imitate.[19] These skills may exist in any of the firm's value creation activities—production, marketing, R&D, human resources, logistics, general management, and so on. Such skills are typically expressed in product offerings that other firms find difficult to match or imitate. Core competencies are the bedrock of a firm's competitive advantage. They enable a firm to reduce the costs of value creation and/or to create perceived value in such a way that premium pricing is possible (e.g., many believe that Apple uses premium pricing for its line of iPhones).

For example, Toyota has a core competence in the production of cars. It is able to produce high-quality, well-designed cars at a lower delivered cost than any other firm in the world. The competencies that enable Toyota to do this seem to reside primarily in the firm's production and logistics functions.[20] Similarly, IKEA has a core competence in the design of stylish and affordable furniture that can be manufactured at a low cost and flat-packed. McDonald's has a core competence in managing fast-food operations (it is still one of the most skilled firms in the world in this industry). Procter & Gamble has a core competence in developing and marketing name-brand consumer products (it is one of the most skilled firms in the world in this business).

Because core competencies are, by definition, the source of a firm's competitive advantage, the successful global expansions by manufacturing companies such as Toyota, IKEA, and P&G were based not just on leveraging products and selling them in foreign markets, but also on the transfer of core competencies to foreign markets where indigenous competitors lacked comparable competencies. The same can be said of companies engaged in the service sectors of an economy, such as financial institutions, restaurant chains, and hotels. Expanding the market for their services often means replicating their business model in foreign nations (albeit with some changes to account for local differences). Firms like Starbucks and Subway, for example, expanded rapidly outside their home markets in the United States by taking the basic business model that they developed at home and using that as a blueprint for establishing international operations.

LOCATION ECONOMIES

Earlier chapters revealed that countries differ along a range of dimensions—including economic, political, legal, and cultural dimensions—and that these differences can either raise or lower the costs of doing business in a country. The theory of international trade also teaches that due to differences in factor costs, certain countries have a comparative advantage in the production of certain products. Japan might excel in the production of automobiles and consumer electronics; the United States in the production of computer software, pharmaceuticals, biotechnology products, and financial services.[21] For a firm that is trying to survive in a competitive global market (this implies that *trade barriers and transportation costs* are permitting), the firm will benefit by basing each value creation activity it performs at that location where economic, political, legal, and cultural conditions, including relative factor costs, are most conducive to the performance of that activity.

Firms that pursue such a strategy can realize what we refer to as **location economies**, which are the economies that arise from performing a value creation activity in the optimal location for that activity, wherever in the world that might be (transportation costs and trade barriers permitting).[22] Locating a value creation activity in the optimal location for that activity can have one of two effects: *It can lower the costs of value creation and help the firm achieve a low-cost position, and/or it can enable a firm to differentiate its product offering from those of competitors.* In terms of Figure 13.2, it can lower C and/or increase V (which in general supports higher pricing), both of which boost the profitability of the enterprise.

For an example of how this works in an international business, consider ClearVision Optical, a manufacturer and distributor of eyewear. Founded by Fred Friedfeld in 1949, the firm now sells online to customers in the United States, Europe, Asia, North Africa, Latin America, and the Caribbean. ClearVision is now a multinational firm with production facilities on three continents and customers around the world. The company began its move toward becoming a multinational when its sales were still less than $20 million in the United States. At the time, the U.S. dollar was very strong, and this made U.S.-based manufacturing expensive. Low-priced imports were taking an ever-larger share of the U.S. eyewear market, and ClearVision realized it could not survive unless it also began to import. Initially, the firm bought from independent overseas manufacturers, primarily in Hong Kong. However, the firm became dissatisfied with these suppliers' product quality and delivery. As ClearVision's volume of imports increased, the company decided that the best way to guarantee quality and delivery was to set up ClearVision's own manufacturing operation overseas. Accordingly, ClearVision found a Chinese partner, and together they opened a manufacturing facility in Hong Kong, with ClearVision being the majority shareholder.

At the time, the choice of the Hong Kong location was influenced by its combination of low labor costs (which is not true in Hong Kong anymore), a skilled workforce, and tax breaks given by the Hong Kong government. The firm's objective at this point was to lower production costs by locating value creation activities at an appropriate location. After a few years, however, the increasing industrialization of Hong Kong and a growing labor shortage had pushed up wage rates to the extent that it was no longer a low-cost location. In response, ClearVision and its Chinese partner moved part of their manufacturing to a plant in mainland China to take advantage of the lower wage rates. Again, the goal was to lower production costs. The parts for eyewear frames manufactured at this plant were shipped to the Hong Kong factory for final assembly, and then distributed to worldwide markets.

At the same time, ClearVision was looking for opportunities to invest in foreign eyewear firms with reputations for fashionable design and high quality. Its objective was not to reduce production costs but to launch a line of high-quality differentiated, "designer" eyewear. ClearVision did not have the design capability in-house to support such a line, but the company knew that certain foreign manufacturers did. As a result, ClearVision invested in factories in Japan, France, and Italy, holding a minority share in each case. These factories now supply eyewear for ClearVision's Status Eye division, which markets high-priced designer eyewear.

Thus, to deal with a threat from foreign competition, ClearVision adopted a strategy intended to lower its cost structure (lower C): shifting its production from a high-cost location, the United States, to a low-cost location, first Hong Kong and later China. Then ClearVision adopted a strategy intended to increase the perceived value of its product (increase V) so it could charge a premium price (P). Reasoning that premium pricing in eyewear depended on superior design, its strategy involved investing capital in French, Italian, and Japanese factories that had reputations for superior design. In sum, ClearVision's strategies included some actions intended to reduce its costs of creating value and other actions intended to add perceived value to its product through differentiation. The overall goal was to increase the value created by ClearVision and thus the profitability of the enterprise. To the extent that these strategies were successful, the firm attained a higher profit margin and greater profitability than if it had remained a U.S.-based manufacturer of eyewear.

Creating a Global Web

Generalizing from the ClearVision example, one result of this kind of thinking is the creation of a **global web** of value creation activities, with different stages of the value chain being dispersed to those locations around the globe where perceived value is maximized or where the costs of value creation are minimized.[23] Consider Lenovo's ThinkPad laptop computers (Lenovo is the Chinese computer company that purchased IBM's personal computer operations in 2005).[24] This product is designed in the United States by engineers because Lenovo believes that the United States is the best location in the world to do the basic design work. As a generalized example, the case, keyboard, and hard drive are made in Thailand; the display screen and memory in South Korea; the built-in wireless card in Malaysia; and the microprocessor in the United States.

In each case, these components are manufactured and sourced from the optimal location given current factor costs. The components are then shipped to an assembly operation in China, where the product is assembled before being shipped worldwide, including to the United States, for final sale. Lenovo assembles the ThinkPad in Mexico because managers have calculated that due to low labor costs, the costs of assembly can be minimized there while maintaining expected quality. The marketing and sales strategy for North America is developed by Lenovo personnel in the United States, primarily because managers believe that due to their knowledge of the local marketplace, U.S. personnel add more value to the product through their marketing efforts than personnel based elsewhere.

In theory, a firm that realizes location economies by dispersing each of its value creation activities to its optimal location should have a competitive advantage vis-à-vis a firm that bases all of its value creation activities at a single location. It should be able to better differentiate its product offering (thereby raising perceived value, V) and lower its cost structure (C) than its single-location competitor. In a world where competitive pressures are increasing, such a strategy may become an imperative for survival. The wrinkle, though, is if countries start becoming more nationalistic and raise trade barriers. In such a case, there will be less global efficiency, more friction in trade, and the result may be that the dynamics of location economies will change.

Some Caveats

Introducing transportation costs and trade barriers complicates this picture. Due to favorable factor endowments, New Zealand may have a comparative advantage for automobile assembly operations, but high transportation costs of parts that often would be heavy can make it an uneconomical location from which to serve global markets. Another caveat concerns the importance of assessing political and economic risks when making location decisions. Even if a country looks very attractive as a production location when measured against all the standard criteria, if its government is unstable or totalitarian, the firm might be advised not to base production there. (Political risk is discussed in Chapter 2.) Similarly, if the government appears to be pursuing inappropriate economic policies that could lead to foreign exchange risk, that might be another reason for not basing production in that location, even if other factors look favorable. Plus, we already mentioned global efficiency dynamics as a reason to think carefully about location economics (i.e., countries pursuing nationalistic interests, higher trade barriers, and incentives for home-country companies). In such cases, companies may not realize the efficiencies expected by location economics.

EXPERIENCE EFFECTS

The **experience curve** refers to systematic reductions in production costs that have been observed to occur over the life of a product.[25] A number of studies have observed that a product's production costs decline by some quantity about each time cumulative output doubles. The relationship was first observed in the aircraft industry, where each time cumulative output of airframes was doubled, unit costs typically declined to 80 percent of their previous level.[26] Thus, production cost for the fourth airframe would be 80 percent of production cost for the second airframe, the eighth airframe's production costs 80 percent of the fourth's, the sixteenth's 80 percent of the eighth's, and so on. Figure 13.5 illustrates this experience curve relationship between unit production costs and *cumulative* output (the relationship is for *cumulative* output over time and *not* output in any one period, such as a year). Two things explain this: learning effects and economies of scale.

Learning Effects

Learning effects refer to cost savings that come from learning by doing.[27] Labor, for example, learns by repetition how to carry out a task, such as assembling airframes, most efficiently. Labor productivity increases over time as individuals learn the most efficient ways to perform particular tasks. Equally important in new production facilities, management typically learns how to manage the new operation more efficiently over time. Hence, production costs decline due to increasing labor productivity and management efficiency, which increases the firm's profitability.

Learning effects tend to be more significant when a technologically complex task is repeated because there is more that can be learned about the task. Thus, learning effects will be more significant in an assembly process involving 1,000 complex steps than in one of only 100 simple steps. No matter how complex the task, however, learning effects typically disappear after a while. It has been suggested that they are important only during the start-up period of a new process and that they cease after two or three years.[28] Any decline in the experience curve after such a point is due to economies of scale.

FIGURE 13.5

The experience curve.

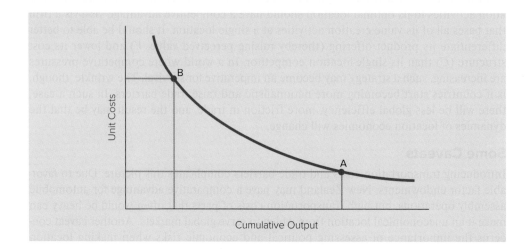

Economies of Scale

Economies of scale refer to the reductions in unit cost achieved by producing a large volume of a product. Attaining economies of scale lowers a firm's unit costs and increases its profitability.[29] Economies of scale have a number of sources. One is the ability to spread fixed costs over a large volume.[30] Fixed costs are the costs required to set up a production facility, develop a new product, and the like. They can be substantial. For example, the fixed cost of establishing a new production line to manufacture semiconductor chips now exceeds $1 billion. Similarly, according to one estimate, developing a new drug and bringing it to market costs about $800 million and takes about 12 years.[31] The only way to recoup such high fixed costs may be to sell the product worldwide, which reduces average unit costs by spreading fixed costs over a larger volume. The more rapidly that cumulative sales volume is built up, the more rapidly fixed costs can be amortized over a large production volume, and the more rapidly unit costs will fall.

Second, a firm may not be able to attain an efficient scale of production unless it serves global markets. In the automobile industry, for example, an efficiently scaled factory is one designed to produce about 200,000 units a year. Automobile firms would prefer to produce a single model from each factory since this eliminates the costs associated with switching production from one model to another. If domestic demand for a particular model is only 100,000 units a year, the inability to attain a 200,000-unit output will drive up average unit costs. By serving international markets as well, however, the firm may be able to push production volume up to 200,000 units a year, thereby reaping greater scale economies, lowering unit costs, and boosting profitability.

Finally, as global sales increase the size of the enterprise, so its bargaining power with suppliers increases, which may allow it to attain economies of scale in purchasing, bargaining down the cost of key inputs and boosting profitability that way. For example, Walmart has used its enormous sales volume as a lever to bargain down the price it pays suppliers for merchandise sold through its stores.

Strategic Significance

The strategic significance of the experience curve is clear. Moving down the experience curve allows a firm to reduce its cost of creating value (to lower C in Figure 13.2) and increase its profitability. The firm that moves down the experience curve most rapidly will have a cost advantage vis-à-vis its competitors. Firm A in Figure 13.5, because it is farther down the experience curve, has a clear cost advantage over firm B.

Many of the underlying sources of experience-based cost economies are plant-based. This is true for most learning effects as well as for the economies of scale derived by spreading the fixed costs of building productive capacity over a large output, attaining an efficient scale of output, and utilizing a plant more intensively. Thus, one key to progressing downward on the experience curve as rapidly as possible is to increase the volume produced by a single plant as rapidly as possible. Because global markets are larger than domestic markets, a firm that serves a global market from a single location is likely to build accumulated volume more quickly than a firm that serves only its home market or that serves multiple markets from multiple production locations. Thus, serving a global market from a single location is consistent with moving down the experience curve and establishing a low-cost position. In addition, to get down the experience curve rapidly, a firm may need to price and market aggressively so demand will expand rapidly. It will also need to build sufficient production capacity for serving a global market. Also, the cost advantages of serving the world market from a single location will be even more significant if that location is the optimal one for performing the particular value creation activity.

Once a firm has established a low-cost position, it can act as a barrier to new competition. Specifically, an established firm that is well down the experience curve, such as firm A in Figure 13.5, can price so that it is still making a profit while new entrants, which are farther up the curve, are suffering losses. Intel is one of the masters of this kind of strategy. The costs of building a state-of-the-art facility to manufacture microprocessors are so large (now around $5 billion) that to make this investment pay Intel must pursue experience curve effects, serving world markets from a limited number of plants to maximize the cost economies that derive from scale and learning effects.

LEVERAGING SUBSIDIARY SKILLS

Implicit in our earlier discussion of core competencies is the idea that valuable skills are developed first at home and then transferred to foreign operations. However, for more mature multinationals that have already established a network of subsidiary operations in foreign markets, the development of valuable skills can just as well occur in foreign subsidiaries.[32] Skills can be created anywhere within a multinational's global network of operations, wherever people have the opportunity and incentive to try new ways of doing things. The creation of skills that help lower the costs of production, or enhance perceived value and support higher product pricing, is not the monopoly of the corporate center.

Leveraging the skills created within subsidiaries and applying them to other operations within the firm's global network may create value. McDonald's increasingly is finding that its foreign franchisees are a source of valuable new ideas. Faced with slow growth in France, its local franchisees have begun to experiment not only with the menu, but also with the layout and theme of restaurants. Gone are the ubiquitous golden arches; gone too are many of the utilitarian chairs and tables and other plastic features of the fast-food giant. Many McDonald's restaurants in France now have hardwood floors, exposed brick walls, and even armchairs. Half of the more than 1,400 outlets in France have been upgraded to a level that would make them unrecognizable to an American. The menu too has been changed to include premier sandwiches, such as chicken on focaccia bread, priced some 30 percent higher than the average hamburger. In France at least, the strategy seems to be working. Following the change, increases in same-store sales rose from 1 percent annually to 3.4 percent. Impressed with the impact, McDonald's executives are considering similar changes at other McDonald's restaurants in markets where same-store sales growth is sluggish, including the United States.[33]

For the managers of the multinational enterprise, this phenomenon creates important new challenges. First, they must have the humility to recognize that valuable skills that lead to competencies can arise anywhere within the firm's global network, not just at the corporate center. Second, they must establish an incentive system that encourages local employees to acquire new skills. This is not as easy as it sounds. Creating new skills involves a degree of risk. Not all new skills add value. For every valuable idea created by a McDonald's subsidiary in a foreign country, there may be several failures. The management of the multinational must install incentives that encourage employees to take the necessary risks. The company must reward people for successes and not sanction them unnecessarily for taking risks that did not pan out. Third, managers must have a process for identifying when valuable new skills have been created in a subsidiary. And finally, they need to act as facilitators, helping transfer valuable skills within the firm.

PROFITABILITY AND PROFIT GROWTH SUMMARY

We have seen how firms that expand globally can increase their profitability and profit growth by entering new markets where indigenous competitors lack similar competencies, by lowering costs and adding value to their product offering through the attainment of location economies, by exploiting experience curve effects, and by transferring valuable skills between their global network of subsidiaries. For completeness, it should be noted that strategies that increase profitability may also expand a firm's business and thus enable it to attain a higher rate of profit growth. For example, by simultaneously realizing location economies and experience effects, a firm may be able to produce a more highly valued product at a lower unit cost, thereby boosting profitability. The increase in the perceived value of the product may also attract more customers, thereby increasing revenues and profits as well.

Rather than raising prices to reflect the higher perceived value of the product, the firm's managers may elect to hold prices low in order to increase global market share and attain greater scale economies (in other words, they may elect to offer consumers better "value for money"). Such a strategy could increase the firm's rate of profit growth even

TEST PREP

Use SmartBook to help retain what you have learned. Access your instructor's Connect course to check out SmartBook or go to **learnsmartadvantage.com** for help.

further since consumers will be attracted by prices that are low relative to value. The strategy might also increase profitability if the scale economies that result from market share gains are substantial. In sum, managers need to keep in mind the complex relationship between profitability and profit growth when making strategic decisions about pricing.

Cost Pressures and Pressures for Local Responsiveness

LO13-3
Understand how pressures for cost reductions and local responsiveness influence strategic choice.

Firms that compete in the global marketplace typically face two types of competitive pressure that affect their ability to realize location economies and experience effects and to leverage products and transfer competencies and skills within the enterprise. They face *pressures for cost reductions* and *pressures to be locally responsive* (see Figure 13.6).[34] These competitive pressures place conflicting demands on a firm. Responding to pressures for cost reductions requires that a firm try to minimize its unit costs. But responding to pressures to be locally responsive requires that a firm differentiates its product offering and marketing strategy from country to country—perhaps also within regions or segments in a country—in an effort to accommodate the diverse demands arising from national differences in consumer needs and wants, business practices, distribution channels, competitive conditions, and government policies. Because differentiation across and within countries can involve significant duplication and a lack of product standardization, it may raise costs in production, component parts, or raw materials.

While some enterprises, such as firm A in Figure 13.6, face high pressures for cost reductions and low pressures for local responsiveness, and others, such as firm B, face low pressures for cost reductions and high pressures for local responsiveness, many companies are in the position of firm C. They face high pressures for *both* cost reductions and local responsiveness. Dealing with these conflicting and contradictory pressures is a difficult strategic challenge, primarily because being locally responsive tends to raise costs.

PRESSURES FOR COST REDUCTIONS

In competitive global markets, international businesses often face pressures for cost reductions. Responding to pressures for cost reduction requires a firm to try to lower the costs of value creation. A manufacturer, for example, might mass-produce a standardized product at the optimal location in the world, wherever that might be, to realize economies of scale, learning effects, and location economies. Alternatively, a firm might outsource certain functions to low-cost foreign suppliers in an attempt to reduce costs. A service business such as a bank might respond to cost pressures by moving some back-office functions, such as information processing, to developing nations where wage rates are lower.

FIGURE 13.6

Pressures for cost reductions and local responsiveness.

IKEA's Global Strategy

Enter an IKEA store anywhere in the world and you recognize it instantly. Global strategy standardization is rampant! Its warehouse-type stores all sell the same broad range of affordable home furnishings, kitchens, accessories, and food. Most of the products are instantly recognizable as IKEA merchandise, with their clean yet tasteful lines and functional design. With its Swedish heritage (IKEA was founded in 1943 as a mail-order company, and the first store opened in Sweden in 1958), the outside of the store is wrapped in blue and yellow: the colors of the Swedish flag. IKEA has annual sales of about $37 billion and employs more than 150,000 workers. Interestingly, IKEA is responsible for about 1 percent of the world's commercial-product wood consumption.

IKEA' name comes from its founder—the acronym consists of the initials of his first and last name (Ingvar Kamprad), along with the first initial of the farm where he grew up (Elmtaryd) and that of his hometown in Sweden (Agunnaryd). Overall, Sweden has 20 IKEA stores, which is fewer than that in Germany (49 stores), the United States (42), France (32), and Italy (21). Spain also has 20 IKEA stores. With 351 stores in 46 countries, IKEA is the largest furniture retailer in the world. Basically, the furniture market is one of the least global

markets, with local tastes, needs, and interests much different than for many other products across industries. The largest IKEA store is in Gwangmyeong, South Korea, at some 640,000 square feet.

The IKEA store itself will be laid out as a maze that requires customers to walk through every department before they reach the checkout stations. The stores are often structured as a one-way layout, leading customers counterclockwise along what IKEA calls "the long natural way." This "way" is designed to encourage customers to see the store in its entirety. Cut-off points and shortcuts exist, but are not easy to figure out. It is even difficult to get back out after having a meal in the famous IKEA restaurant with its Swedish food. (Meatballs anyone?)

Just before the checkout, there is an in-store warehouse where customers can pick up the items they purchased. The furniture is packed flat for ease of transportation and requires assembly by the customer. Value is stressed to a great extent (the price customers pay for the quality furniture they get). If you look at customers in the store, you will see that many are in there 20s and 30s. IKEA sells to the same basic customers worldwide: young, upwardly

Pressures for cost reduction can be particularly intense in industries producing commodity-type products where meaningful differentiation on non-price factors is difficult and price is the main competitive weapon. This tends to be the case for products that serve universal needs. **Universal needs** exist when the tastes and preferences of consumers in different nations are similar if not identical. This is the case for conventional commodity products such as bulk chemicals, petroleum, steel, sugar, and the like. It also tends to be the case for many industrial and consumer products, for example, handheld calculators, semiconductor chips, personal computers, and liquid crystal display screens.

Pressures for cost reductions are also intense in industries where major competitors are based in low-cost locations, where there is persistent excess capacity and where consumers are powerful and face low switching costs. The liberalization of the world trade and investment environment in recent decades, by facilitating greater international competition, has generally increased cost pressures.[35] For an example of a company that has discovered how important the pressures of cost production can be, read the accompanying Management Focus on IKEA's global strategy.

PRESSURES FOR LOCAL RESPONSIVENESS

Pressures for local responsiveness arise from national differences in consumer needs and wants, infrastructure, business practices, distribution channels, and from host-government demands. Responding to pressures to be locally responsive requires a firm to differentiate its products and marketing strategy from country to country to accommodate these factors, all of which tends to raise the firm's cost structure.

mobile people who are looking for tasteful yet inexpensive "disposable" furniture of a certain quality standard for the price they are willing to pay.

A global network of more than 1,000 suppliers based in more than 50 countries manufactures most of the 12,000 or so products that IKEA sells. IKEA itself focuses on the design of products and works closely with suppliers to bring down manufacturing costs. Developing a new product line can be a painstaking process that takes years. IKEA's designers will develop a prototype design (e.g., a small couch), look at the price that rivals charge for a similar piece, and then work with suppliers to figure out a way to cut prices by 40 percent without compromising on quality. IKEA also manufactures about 10 percent of what it sells in-house and uses the knowledge gained to help its suppliers improve their productivity, thereby lowering costs across the entire supply chain.

Look a little closer, however, and you will see subtle differences among the IKEA offerings in North America, Europe, and China. In North America, sizes are different to reflect the American demand for bigger beds, furnishings, and kitchenware. This adaptation to local tastes and preferences was the result of a painful learning experience for IKEA. When the company first entered the United States in the late 1980s, it thought consumers would flock to its stores the same way they had in western Europe. At first, consumers did, but they didn't buy as much, and sales fell short of expectations. IKEA discovered that its European-style sofas were not big enough, their wardrobe drawers were not deep enough, their glasses were too small, and kitchens didn't fit U.S. appliances. So the company set about redesigning its offerings to better match American tastes and was rewarded with accelerating sales growth. Lesson learned.

When IKEA entered China in the 2000s, it made adaptations to the local market. The store layout reflects the layout of many Chinese apartments, where most people live, and because many Chinese apartments have balconies, IKEA's Chinese stores include a balcony section. IKEA has also had to shift its locations in China, where car ownership lags behind that in Europe and North America. In the West, IKEA stores are located in suburban areas and have lots of parking space. In China, stores are located near public transportation, and IKEA offers a delivery service so that Chinese customers can get their purchases home.

Sources: Lindsey Rupp, "Ikea, Dollar General CEOs Lobby Republicans in Tax Showdown," *Bloomberg Businessweek*, March 7, 2017; D. L. Yohn, "How IKEA Designs Its Brand Success," *Forbes*, June 10, 2015; J. Kane, "The 21 Emotional Stages of Shopping at IKEA, From Optimism to Total Defeat," *The Huffington Post*, May 6, 2015; J. Leland, "How the Disposable Sofa Conquered America," *The New York Times Magazine*, October 5, 2005, p. 45; "The Secret of IKEA's Success," *The Economist*, February 24, 2011; B. Torekull, *Leading by Design: The IKEA Story* (New York: HarperCollins, 1998); P. M. Miller, "IKEA with Chinese Characteristics," *Chinese Business Review*, July–August 2004, pp. 36–69.

Differences in Customer Tastes and Preferences

Strong pressures for local responsiveness emerge when customer tastes and preferences differ significantly between countries, as they often do for deeply embedded historic or cultural reasons. In such cases, a multinational's products and marketing message have to be customized to appeal to the tastes and preferences of local customers. This typically creates pressure to delegate production and marketing responsibilities and functions to a firm's overseas subsidiaries.

For example, some time ago the automobile industry moved toward the creation of "world cars." The idea was that global companies such as General Motors, Ford, and Toyota would be able to sell the same basic vehicle the world over, sourcing it from centralized production locations. If successful, the strategy would have enabled automobile companies to reap significant gains from global scale economies. However, this strategy frequently ran aground on the hard rocks of consumer reality. Consumers in different automobile markets seem to have different tastes and preferences and demand different types of vehicles. North American consumers show a strong demand for pickup trucks. This is particularly true in the South and West, where many families have a pickup truck as a second or third car. But in European countries, pickup trucks are seen purely as utility vehicles and are purchased primarily by firms rather than individuals. As a consequence, the product mix and marketing message needs to be tailored to consider the different nature of demand in North America and Europe.

Some have argued that customer demands for local customization are on the decline worldwide.[36] According to this argument, modern communications and transport technologies have created the conditions for a convergence of the tastes and preferences of consumers from different nations. The result is the emergence of enormous global markets for standardized consumer products. The worldwide acceptance of Subway sandwiches, McDonald's hamburgers, Coca-Cola, Gap clothes, Apple iPhones, and Microsoft's Xbox— all of which are sold globally as standardized products—are often cited as evidence of the increasing homogeneity of the global marketplace. In particular, younger customers are becoming more homogeneous around the world in their needs and wants.

However, this argument may not hold in many consumer goods markets. Significant differences in consumer needs, wants, tastes, and preferences still exist across nations and cultures. Managers in international businesses do not yet have the luxury of being able to ignore these differences, and they may not for a long time to come. This is especially true when it comes to customers that are a bit older (e.g., at least 40 years, maybe 50 years old). While younger customers are becoming more and more alike worldwide (e.g., college students in the United States often have similar wants and needs as college students in Europe and Asia), more mature customers still have significant needs and wants for uniquely country-specific products and services. The better marketing question is: When today's younger customers get older, will they maintain their homogeneous needs and wants around the world, or will they also skew their wants and needs toward more country-specific products and services?

Differences in Infrastructure and Traditional Practices

Pressures for local responsiveness arise from differences in infrastructure or traditional practices among countries, creating a need to customize products accordingly. Fulfilling this need may require the delegation of manufacturing and production functions to foreign subsidiaries. For example, in North America, consumer electrical systems are based on 110 volts, whereas in most European countries, 240-volt systems are standard. Thus, domestic electric appliances have to be customized for this difference in infrastructure. Plus, plugs and socket types for electrical outlets differ around the world. By some estimates, there are 15 different types of plugs and outlets used in 195 countries (**www.worldstandards.eu**).

Although many national differences in infrastructure are rooted in history, some are quite recent. For example, different technical standards exist in different parts of the world in the wireless telecommunications industry. A technical standard known as GSM is common in Europe, and an alternative standard, CDMA, is more common in the United States and parts of Asia. Equipment designed for GSM will not work on a CDMA network and vice versa. Thus, companies such as Apple and Samsung need to customize their product offerings according to the technical standards that prevail in a given country. Thankfully, more and more mobile phones and infrastructures are becoming compatible around the world—at least behind the scenes—so that customers don't have to think about it much (e.g., GSM quad-band phones).

Differences in Distribution Channels

A firm's marketing strategies may have to be responsive to differences in distribution channels among countries, which may necessitate the delegation of marketing functions to national subsidiaries. In the pharmaceutical industry, for example, the British and Japanese distribution systems are radically different from the U.S. system. British and Japanese doctors will not accept or respond favorably to a U.S.-style high-pressure sales force. Thus, pharmaceutical companies have to adopt different marketing practices in Britain and Japan compared with the United States—soft sell versus hard sell. Similarly, Poland, Brazil, and Russia all have similar per capita income on a purchasing power parity basis, but there are big differences in distribution systems across the three countries. In Brazil, supermarkets account for 36 percent of food retailing, in Poland for 18 percent, and in Russia for less than 1 percent. These differences in channels require that companies adapt their own distribution and sales strategy. We cover distribution channels more when we talk about global supply chains.

Host-Government Demands

Economic and political demands imposed by host-country governments may require local responsiveness. For example, pharmaceutical companies are subject to local clinical testing, registration procedures, and pricing restrictions, all of which make it necessary that the manufacturing and marketing of a drug should meet local requirements. Because governments and government agencies control a significant proportion of the health care budget in most countries, they are in a powerful position to demand a high level of local responsiveness.

More generally, threats of protectionism, economic nationalism, and local content rules (which require that a certain percentage of a product should be manufactured locally) dictate that international businesses manufacture locally. For example, consider Bombardier, the Canadian-based manufacturer of railcars, aircraft, jet boats, and snowmobiles. Bombardier has 12 railcar factories across Europe. Critics of the company argue that the resulting duplication of manufacturing facilities leads to high costs and helps explain why Bombardier makes lower profit margins on its railcar operations than on its other business lines. In reply, managers at Bombardier argue that in Europe, informal rules with regard to local content favor people who use local workers. To sell railcars in Germany, they claim, you must manufacture in Germany. The same goes for Belgium, Austria, and France. To try to address its cost structure in Europe, Bombardier has centralized its engineering and purchasing functions, but it has no plans to centralize manufacturing.[37]

Rise of Regionalism

Traditionally, we have tended to think of pressures for local responsiveness as being derived from *national* differences in tastes and preferences, infrastructure, and the like. While this is still often the case, there is also a tendency toward the convergence of tastes, preferences, infrastructure, distribution channels, and host-government demands with a broader *region* that is composed of two or more nations.[38] We tend to see this when there are strong pressures for convergence due to, for example, a shared history and culture or the establishment of a trading block where there are deliberate attempts to harmonize trade policies, infrastructure, regulations, and the like.

The most obvious example of a region is the European Union, and particularly the euro zone countries within that trade bloc, where there are institutional forces that are pushing toward convergence (see Chapter 9 for details). The creation of a single EU market—with a single currency, common business regulations, standard infrastructure, and so on—cannot help but result in the reduction of certain national differences among countries within the EU and the creation of one regional rather than several national markets. Indeed, at the economic level at least, that is the explicit intent of the EU.

Another example of regional convergence is North America, which includes the United States, Canada, and to some extent in some product markets, Mexico. Canada and the United States share history, language, and much of their culture, and both are members of NAFTA (and the new United States–Mexico–Canada Agreement, USMCA). Mexico is clearly different in many regards, but its proximity to the United States implies that for some product markets (e.g., automobiles) it might be reasonable to consider Mexico as part of a relatively homogeneous regional market. We might also talk about the Latin America region, where shared Spanish history, cultural heritage, and language (with the exception of Brazil, which was colonized by the Portuguese) means that national differences are somewhat moderated. It can also be argued that Greater China, which includes the city-states of Hong Kong and Singapore along with Taiwan, is a coherent region, as is much of the Middle East, where a strong Arab culture and shared history may limit national differences. Similarly, Russia and some of the former states of the Soviet Union, such as Belarus and Ukraine, might be considered part of a larger regional market, at least for some products, as could the five countries in Scandinavia (Denmark, Finland, Iceland, Norway, Sweden).

Taking a regional perspective is important because it may suggest that localization at the regional rather than the national level is the appropriate strategic response. For example, rather than produce cars for each national market within Europe or North America, it makes far more sense for car manufacturers to build cars for the European or North American regions. The ability to standardize a product offering within a region allows for the attainment of greater scale economies, and hence lower costs, than if each nation had to have its own offering. At the same time, this perspective should not be pushed too far.

 TEST PREP

Use SmartBook to help retain what you have learned. Access your instructor's Connect course to check out SmartBook or go to **learnsmartadvantage.com** for help.

There are still deep and profound cultural differences among France, Germany, and Italy—all members of the EU—that may in turn require some degree of local customization at the *national* level. For example, the United Kingdom is leaving the EU (e.g., Brexit) due to these national differences. Managers must thus make a judgment call about the appropriate level of aggregation given (1) the product market they are looking at and (2) the nature of national differences and trends for regional convergence. What might make sense for automobiles, for example, might not be appropriate for packaged food products.

LO13-4

Identify and choose the different global strategies for competing in the global marketplace.

Choosing a Strategy

Pressures for local responsiveness (e.g., due to customers' needs, wants, tastes, and preferences) imply that it may not be possible for a firm to realize the full benefits from economies of scale, learning effects, and location economies. In fact, it may not be possible or even realistic to think that a firm can serve the global marketplace from a single, low-cost location, producing a globally standardized product and marketing it worldwide to attain the cost reductions associated with experience effects. The need to customize the product to local conditions may work against the implementation of such a strategy.

For example, automobile firms, for roughly the last half century, have found that Japanese, American, and European consumers demand different kinds of cars, and this necessitates producing products that are customized for regional markets. In response, firms such as General Motors, Nissan, Honda, Ford, and Toyota are pursuing a strategy of establishing top-to-bottom design and production facilities in each of these important world regions to better serve local demands.[39] Although such customization brings benefits, it also limits the ability of a firm to realize significant scale economies and location economies.

In addition, pressures for local responsiveness imply that it may not be possible to leverage skills and products associated with a firm's core competencies fully from one nation to another. Concessions often have to be made to local conditions—basically, it's all about getting the sale. The trade-off between obtaining the sale or not by taking a standardized product and customizing it at least to some degree to the local customer needs is rooted in a cost/benefit analysis and opportunity assessment. Despite being depicted as "poster child" for the proliferation of standardized global products, even McDonald's has found that it has to customize its product offerings (i.e., its menu) to account for national differences in tastes and preferences. As we can also see in several cases in this text, companies such as Domino's, Subway, and other McDonald's competitors also customize to local tastes and preferences.

General Motors' supercar, the Chevrolet Corvette Z06, being showcased in Stuttgart, Germany.

Buschmen/123RF

FIGURE 13.7

Four basic strategies.

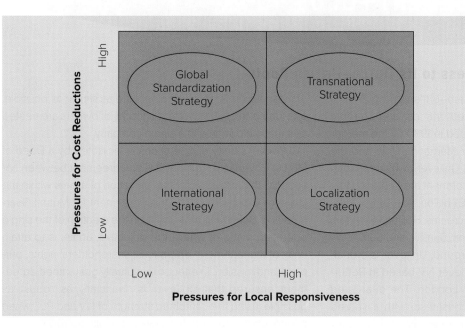

How do differences in the strength of pressures for cost reductions versus those for local responsiveness affect a firm's choice of strategy? Firms typically choose among four main strategic postures when competing internationally. These can be characterized as a global standardization strategy, a localization strategy, a transnational strategy, and an international strategy.[40] The appropriateness of each strategy varies given the extent of pressures for cost reductions and local responsiveness. Figure 13.7 illustrates the conditions under which each of these strategies is most appropriate.

GLOBAL STANDARDIZATION STRATEGY

Firms that pursue a **global standardization strategy** focus on increasing profitability and profit growth by reaping the cost reductions that come from economies of scale, learning effects, and location economies. Their strategic goal is to pursue a low-cost strategy on a global scale. The production, marketing, R&D, and supply chain activities of firms pursuing a global standardization strategy are concentrated in a few favorable locations. Firms pursuing a global standardization strategy try not to customize their product offering and marketing strategy to local conditions because customization involves shorter production runs and the duplication of functions, which tend to raise costs. Instead, they prefer to market a standardized product worldwide so that they can reap the maximum benefits from economies of scale and learning effects. They also tend to use their cost advantage to support aggressive pricing in world markets.

A global standardization strategy makes the most sense when there are strong pressures for cost reductions and demands for local responsiveness are minimal. Increasingly, these conditions prevail in many industrial goods industries, whose products often serve universal needs. In the semiconductor industry, for example, global standards have emerged, creating enormous demands for standardized global products. At times, companies such as Intel and Unilever pursue global standardization strategies. However, these conditions are not always found in many consumer goods markets, where demands for local responsiveness remain high. The strategy is inappropriate when demands for local responsiveness can remain high. To focus on global strategy with local responsiveness, take a look at the accompanying Management Focus on Unilever's Dutch–British roots.

LOCALIZATION STRATEGY

A **localization strategy** focuses on increasing profitability by customizing the firm's goods or services so that they provide a good match to tastes and preferences in different national markets. Localization is most appropriate when there are substantial differences across

Unilever's Responsiveness to Its Dutch–British Roots

Unilever (**unilever.com**) is a Dutch–British company co-headquartered in Rotterdam, Netherlands, and London, England. The company was founded in 1930 by the merger of the Dutch margarine producer Margarine Unie and the British soapmaker Lever Brothers. Unilever owns more than 400 brands, but the core of its assortment are 14 brands that have annual sales of more than €1 billion: Axe/Lynx, Dove, Omo, Becel/Flora, Heartbrand ice creams, Hellmann's, Knorr, Lipton, Lux, Magnum, Rama, Rexona, Sunsilk, and Surf.

With the Dutch–British background, Unilever is a dual-listed company consisting of Unilever NV based in Rotterdam and Unilever PLC based in London. The dual-listed company operates as a single business, with a shared board of directors. However, Unilever NV and Unilever PLC have different shareholder constituencies, and shareholders cannot convert or exchange the shares of one company for shares of the other.

The Unilever Group—integration of Unilever NV (Netherlands) and Unilever PLC (United Kingdom)—is organized and made functional by a number of agreements between the parent companies of NV and PLC. These agreements, together with provisions in their respective articles of association, are jointly known as the Foundation Agreements. These Foundation Agreements enable Unilever to attain unity of management, operations, shareholders' rights, purpose, and mission.

Unilever's Equalization Agreement regulates the common rights of the shareholders of both NV and PLC. The objective of the Equalization Agreement is to ensure that the positions of these two sets of shareholders are as similar as possible. The idea is to ensure that both groups of owners are treated as if they held shares in a single company.

Unilever's unity of operations is facilitated by a Deed of Mutual Covenants. This deed is an agreement between NV and PLC that provides for the allocation of assets within the Unilever Group. Relatedly, the Agreement for Mutual Guarantees of Borrowing also assists in the creation of the single operating platform where the objective, again, is to attain unity of management, operations, shareholders' rights, purpose, and mission. In effect, this mutually guaranteed agreement ensures that Unilever is financially as robust as possible, using the combined strength of NV and PLC when asking lenders for certain significant public borrowings.

To structure its operations and management of the more than 400 brands, Unilever is organized into four main divisions: Foods, Refreshment (beverages and ice cream), Home Care, and Personal Care. These divisions employ about 170,000 people, produce sales of some €55 billion annually (about $60 billion U.S. dollars), and have 57 percent of their business in emerging markets. On a daily basis, 2.5 billion people worldwide, a staggering number, use Unilever products (out of the 7.5 billion people in the world).

Sources: "About Unilever," March 22, 2017 (unilever.com/about/who-we-are/about-Unilever); "Unilever's Legal Structure and Foundation Agreements," March 22, 2017 (unilever.com/investor-relations/agm-and-corporate-governance/legal-structure-and-foundation-agreements); Port Sunlight, "Unilever: In Search of the Good Business," *The Economist*, August 9, 2014; Rob Davies, "Unilever Bids to Heal Shareholder Rift Amid 'Garage Sale' Warnings," *The Guardian*, March 19, 2017.

nations with regard to consumer tastes and preferences and where cost pressures are not too intense. By customizing the product offering to local demands, the firm increases the value of that product in the local market. On the downside, because it involves some duplication of functions and smaller production runs, customization limits the ability of the firm to capture the cost reductions associated with mass-producing a standardized product for global consumption. The strategy may make sense, however, if the added value associated with local customization supports higher pricing, which enables the firm to recoup its higher costs, or if it leads to substantially greater local demand, enabling the firm to reduce costs through the attainment of some scale economies in the local market.

At the same time, firms still have to keep an eye on costs. Firms pursuing a localization strategy still need to be efficient and, whenever possible, to capture some scale economies from their global reach. As noted earlier, many automobile companies have found that they have to customize some of their product offerings to local market demands—for example, producing large pickup trucks for U.S. consumers and small, fuel-efficient cars for Europeans and Japanese. At the same time, these multinationals try to get some scale economies from their global volume by using common vehicle platforms and components across many different models, and manufacturing those platforms and components at efficiently scaled factories that are optimally located. By designing their products in this way, these companies have been able to localize their product offering, yet simultaneously capture some scale economies, learning effects, and location economies.

TRANSNATIONAL STRATEGY

We have argued that a global standardization strategy makes most sense when cost pressures are intense and demands for local responsiveness are limited. Conversely, a localization strategy makes most sense when demands for local responsiveness are high but cost pressures are moderate or low. What happens, however, when the firm simultaneously faces both strong cost pressures and strong pressures for local responsiveness? How can managers balance the competing and inconsistent demands such divergent pressures place on the firm? According to some researchers, the answer is to pursue what has been called a transnational strategy.

Two of these researchers, Christopher Bartlett and Sumantra Ghoshal, argue that competitive conditions are so intense that to survive, firms must do all they can to respond to pressures for cost reductions and local responsiveness. They must try to realize location economies and experience effects, to leverage products internationally, to transfer core competencies and skills within the company, and to simultaneously pay attention to pressures for local responsiveness.[41] Bartlett and Ghoshal note that in the modern multinational enterprise, core competencies and skills do not reside just in the home country, but can develop in any of the firm's worldwide operations. Thus, they maintain that the flow of skills and product offerings should not be all one way, from home country to foreign subsidiary. Rather, the flow should also be from foreign subsidiary to home country and from foreign subsidiary to foreign subsidiary. Transnational enterprises, in other words, must also focus on leveraging subsidiary skills.

In essence, firms that pursue a **transnational strategy** are trying to simultaneously achieve low costs through location economies, economies of scale, and learning effects; differentiate their product offering across geographic markets to account for local differences; and foster a multidirectional flow of skills between different subsidiaries in the firm's global network of operations. As attractive as this may sound in theory, the strategy is not an easy one to pursue since it places conflicting demands on the company. Differentiating the product to respond to local demands in different geographic markets raises costs, which runs counter to the goal of reducing costs. Companies such as 3M and ABB (one of the world's largest engineering conglomerates) have tried to embrace a transnational strategy and found it difficult to implement.

How best to implement a transnational strategy is one of the most complex questions large multinationals are grappling with today. Few if any enterprises have perfected this strategic posture. But some clues as to the right approach can be derived from a number of companies. For an example, consider the case of Caterpillar. The need to compete with low-cost competitors such as Komatsu of Japan forced Caterpillar to look for greater cost economies. However, variations in construction practices and government regulations across countries mean that Caterpillar also has to be responsive to local demands. Therefore, Caterpillar confronted significant pressures for cost reductions *and* for local responsiveness.

To deal with cost pressures, Caterpillar redesigned its products to use many identical components and invested in a few large-scale component manufacturing facilities, sited at favorable locations, to fill global demand and realize scale economies. At the same time, the company augments the centralized manufacturing of components with assembly plants in each of its major global markets. At these plants, Caterpillar adds local product features, tailoring the finished product to local needs. Thus, Caterpillar is able to realize many of the benefits of global manufacturing while reacting to pressures for local responsiveness by differentiating its product among national markets.[42] Caterpillar doubled output per employee, significantly reducing its overall cost structure in the process. Meanwhile, Komatsu and Hitachi, which are still wedded to a Japan-centric global strategy, have seen their cost advantages evaporate and have been steadily losing market share to Caterpillar.

Changing a firm's strategic posture to build an organization capable of supporting a transnational strategy is a complex and challenging task. Some would say it is too complex, because the strategy implementation problems of creating a viable organization structure and control systems to manage this strategy are immense.

INTERNATIONAL STRATEGY

Sometimes it is possible to identify multinational firms that find themselves in the fortunate position of being confronted with low cost pressures and low pressures for local responsiveness. Many of these enterprises have pursued an **international strategy**, taking products first produced for their domestic market and selling them internationally with only minimal local customization. The distinguishing feature of many such firms is that they are selling a product that serves universal needs, but they do not face significant competitors, and thus unlike firms pursuing a global standardization strategy, they are not confronted with pressures to reduce their cost structure.

Xerox found itself in this position after its invention and commercialization of the photocopier. The technology underlying the photocopier was protected by strong patents, so for several years Xerox did not face competitors—it had a monopoly. The product serves universal needs, and it was highly valued in most developed nations. Thus, Xerox was able to sell the same basic product the world over, charging a relatively high price for that product. Because Xerox did not face direct competitors, it did not have to deal with strong pressures to minimize its cost structure. However, that has changed for Xerox, and it now faces stronger competition in the international marketplace.

Enterprises pursuing an international strategy have followed a similar developmental pattern as they expanded into foreign markets. They tend to centralize product development functions such as R&D at home. However, they also tend to establish manufacturing and marketing functions in each major country or geographic region in which they do business. The resulting duplication can raise costs, but this is less of an issue if the firm does not face strong pressures for cost reductions. Although they may undertake some local customization of product offering and marketing strategy, this tends to be rather limited in scope. Ultimately, in most firms that pursue an international strategy, the head office retains fairly tight control over marketing and product strategy.

Other firms that have pursued this strategy include Procter & Gamble and Microsoft. Historically, Procter & Gamble developed innovative new products in Cincinnati and then transferred them wholesale to local markets. Similarly, the bulk of Microsoft's product development work occurs in Redmond, Washington, where the company is headquartered. Although some localization work is undertaken elsewhere, this is limited to producing foreign-language versions of popular Microsoft programs.

THE EVOLUTION OF STRATEGY

The Achilles' heel of the international strategy is that over time, competitors inevitably emerge, and if managers do not take proactive steps to reduce their firm's cost structure, it will be rapidly outflanked by efficient global competitors. This is exactly what happened to Xerox. Japanese companies such as Canon ultimately invented their way around Xerox's patents, produced their own photocopiers in very efficient manufacturing plants, priced them below Xerox's products, and rapidly took global market share from Xerox. In the final analysis, Xerox's reduced sales were not due to the emergence of competitors, for ultimately that was bound to occur, but due to its failure to proactively reduce its cost structure in advance of the emergence of efficient global competitors. The message in this story is that an international strategy may not be viable in the long term, and to survive, firms need to shift toward a global standardization strategy or a transnational strategy in advance of competitors (see Figure 13.8).

The same can be said about a localization strategy. Localization may give a firm a competitive edge, but if it is simultaneously facing aggressive competitors, the company will also have to reduce its cost structure, and the only way to do that may be to shift toward a transnational strategy. This is what Procter & Gamble has been doing. Thus, as competition intensifies, international and localization strategies tend to become less viable, and managers need to direct their companies toward either a global standardization strategy or a transnational strategy.

TEST PREP

Use SmartBook to help retain what you have learned. Access your instructor's Connect course to check out SmartBook or go to **learnsmartadvantage.com** for help.

FIGURE 13.8

Changes in strategy
over time.

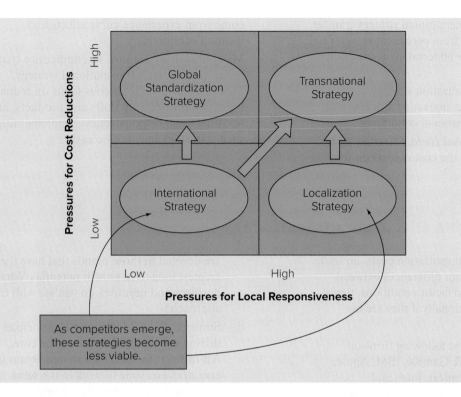

As competitors emerge, these strategies become less viable.

Key Terms

SUMMARY

This chapter reviewed basic principles of strategy and the various ways in which firms can profit from global expansion. It also looked at the strategies that firms competing globally can adopt. The chapter made the following points:

1. A strategy can be defined as the actions that managers take to attain the goals of the firm. For most multinational corporations, especially publicly traded firms, the preeminent goal is to maximize shareholder value. Maximizing shareholder value requires firms to focus on increasing their profitability and the growth rate of profits over time.

2. International expansion may enable a firm to earn greater returns by transferring the product offerings derived from its core competencies to markets where indigenous competitors lack those product offerings and competencies.

3. It may pay a firm to base each value creation activity it performs at that location where factor conditions are most conducive to the performance of that activity. We refer to this strategy as focusing on the attainment of location economies.

4. By rapidly building sales volume for a standardized product, international expansion can assist a firm in moving down the experience curve by realizing learning effects and economies of scale.

5. A multinational firm can create additional value by identifying valuable skills created within its foreign subsidiaries and leveraging those skills within its global network of operations. These leverage issues are part of the firm's global value chains.

6. The best strategy for a firm to pursue often depends on a consideration of the pressures for cost reductions and for local responsiveness.

7. Firms pursuing an international strategy transfer the products derived from core competencies to foreign markets while undertaking some limited local customization.

8. Firms pursuing a localization strategy customize their product offering, marketing strategy, and business strategy to national conditions.

9. Firms pursuing a global standardization strategy focus on reaping the cost reductions that

come from experience curve effects and location economies.

10. Many industries are now so competitive that firms must adopt a transnational strategy. This involves a simultaneous focus on reducing costs, transferring skills and products, and boosting local responsiveness. Implementing such a strategy may not be easy.

Critical Thinking and Discussion Questions

1. In a world of zero transportation costs, no trade barriers, and significant differences between nations with regard to factor conditions, firms must expand internationally if they are to survive. Discuss.

2. Plot the position of the following firms on Figure 13.6: Procter & Gamble, IBM, Apple, Coca-Cola, Dow Chemical, Intel, and McDonald's. In each case justify your answer.

3. In what kind of industries does a localization strategy make sense? When does a global standardization strategy make the most sense?

4. Reread the Management Focus "AB InBev, Beer Globally, and Creating Value," and then answer the following questions:

   a. With more than 200 brands and strong coverage internationally of the different brands, strategically AB InBev is a unique and highly organized global company. Do they have too many brands? Why or why not?

   b. The company follows a focused brands strategy in which the majority of the resources

are devoted to those brands that have the greatest long-term growth potential. What positives and negatives do you see with this approach?

   c. Strategically, AB InBev has 10 principles driving everything they do. At the core, AB InBev is focused on a shared dream that energizes everyone to work in the same direction to be the best beer company in the world, bring people together, and create a better world. Additional principles cover people strengths, quality of teams, striving for increased satisfaction, consumer focus, ownership, common sense and simplicity, cost management, leadership, and hard work and responsibility. Should large multinational corporations really be built on strong principles, or do they need a more flexible structure?

5. What do you see as the main organizational problems that are likely to be associated with the implementation of a transnational strategy?

globalEDGE research task globaledge.msu.edu

Use the globalEDGE™ website (**globaledge.msu.edu**) to complete the following exercises:

1. Your company, a white goods manufacturer (primarily major kitchen appliances) based in the United States, has decided to pursue international expansion opportunities in sub-Saharan Africa. To achieve some economies of scale, your strategy is to minimize local adaptation. Focusing on a comparison of two sub-Saharan African countries of your choice, prepare an executive summary that features aspects of the product where standardization will simply not

be possible and adaptation to local conditions will be essential.

2. A. T. Kearney publishes an annual study to help retailers prioritize their global development strategies by ranking the retail expansion attractiveness of emerging countries based on a particular set of criteria. Find the latest version of this *Global Retail Development Index*. What criteria are used to identify the attractiveness of the retail environment in emerging countries? Categorize the top 10 countries by world region. Are there any of these countries that surprise you? Why or why not?

CLOSING CASE

Red Bull: A Leader in International Strategy

Where was Red Bull founded? Many people in the United States and other countries think Red Bull is a product to their own country because the company does such a fantastic job of marketing the brand. Red Bull also plays up the amazing energy, go-getter attitude, and fun risk taking that the brand symbolizes in most things they do. In almost a literal sense, "Red Bull gives you wings," as their slogan says. To support the company's international strategy, Red Bull hosts a number of extreme sporting events around the world. This includes the Red Bull Indianapolis Grand Prix in the United States, the Red Bull Air Race in the UK, the Red Bull Soapbox Race in Jordan, the Red Bull Cliff Diving World Series, the Red Bull Air Race, Red Bull Crashed Ice, and stand-out stunts such as the Stratos space diving. But there also many other global strategic placements engineered by the Red Bull brand.

The answer to the opening question is that Red Bull is from Austria, although saying it is an Austrian–Thai company is also true. In 1984, Austrian entrepreneur Dietrich Mateschitz and Thai businessperson Chaleo Yoovidhya founded Red Bull GmbH. While working for German manufacturer Blendax (later acquired by Procter & Gamble), Mateschitz traveled to Thailand and met Chaleo, owner of TC Pharmaceutical. The two struck a cord and eventually started Red Bull a couple of years later. Today, Red Bull is viewed as one of the world's top companies because of its international business strategy, in particular its international marketing strategy (keep that in mind for Chapter 18, the Global Marketing and Business Analytics chapter). Worldwide, Red Bull also has the highest market share of all energy drinks, with more than 6 billion cans sold annually (that is almost one can for every person worldwide).

Why is it called Red Bull? The name actually plays up its founders' backgrounds. In Thai, *daeng* means red, and *krating* is the name of a large wild bovine in Southeast Asia, called a gaur in formal English. A gaur, however, is also informally referred to as a bull. Red Bull is sold in a tall and slim blue-silver can, while Krating Daeng is in a shorter gold can. To capture the historical context for this case, Krating Daeng was the instigator and became the basis for the creation of Red Bull. While Red Bull is the bestselling energy drink in most parts of the world, both Red Bull and Krating Daeng are sold worldwide (in about 165 countries). Red Bull is viewed as an Austrian company, and Krating Daeng as a Thai company. Krating Daeng was founded by Chaleo; when Mateschitz met Chaleo, they created Red Bull as a spinoff and modified the ingredients in the drink to suit Western tastes.

In many ways, Red Bull's event marketing strategy is what drives their international business strategy. The events listed in this section's opening paragraph very much exemplify the brand that Red Bull has become and tries to strategically nurture, and displays what has given the company the vibrant reputation it has—essentially its "brand myth"—turning it into something of a legend. Red Bull truly mass markets its products in a unique way! They do not engage in traditional marketing, and their overall international business strategy is somewhat unorthodox. Contrary to most other multinational corporations, the events they dream up and the teams they support drive the company's international business strategy (e.g., soccer/football clubs RB Leipzig, FC Red Bull Salzburg, FC Liefering, Red Bull Brasil, New York Red Bulls, and Formula One teams Red Bull Racing and Scuderia Toro Rosso).

Aside from these extreme events and sports teams, Red Bull's packaging plays a significant role in its global appeal and is at the core of its international business strategy. Some say that Red Bull really looks like a product that fits the idea of a global economy. It's not in a normal can or bottle, and has a much broader appeal to a wider global audience. It's not an American or Asian product in look and content, nor does it have the look and content of any other world area. By lacking a clear geographic focus, customers across the globe feel more connected to Red Bull, associating it with their local products. Plus, Red Bull's consistent packaging worldwide has helped the brand go global with a very consistent international business strategy.

It's fascinating that Red Bull has created an international business strategy by focusing on a universal product concept, unique and standout packaging, and extreme event sponsorship without also tackling the architecture of the company itself. Most other multinational corporations have to balance their focus on strategy and organizational infrastructure to operate a well-functioning international strategy. Red Bull drives certain concepts hard and that works superbly well for them. They communicate their clear and consistent messages via their own Red Bull Media House, using inspirational videos and activities on social media and generating content marketing that is uniquely customized to diverse audiences. They also focus on the freedoms of the individual, and rely on user-generated content, where customers share their own exciting lifestyles.

Sources: Hanna Fleishman, "13 Businesses with Brilliant Global Marketing Strategies," February 9, 2018; Alex Siminoff, "Red Bull Stomps All Over Global Marketing," *Art + Marketing*, April 28, 2017; Nitin Pangarkar and Mohit Agarwal, "The Wind Behind Red Bull's Wings," *Forbes*, June 24, 2013; Celine Cnossen, Yuan Li, Neha Sampath, Whitney Taylor-Maisano, and Viktor Tsonev, "What Gives Red Bull Wings: Creating a Successful Market-Oriented Organization," American Marketing Association, April 24, 2018; "Global Energy Drinks Market Opportunities 2018: Red Bull GmbH, Rockstar, Monster Energy, Amway Global," *Market Watch*, March 14, 2018.

Case Discussion Questions

1. As an Austrian–Thai company, Red Bull has done a remarkable job of positioning itself internationally by coming across as a local company in every country where Red Bull is sold. Would you be more or less likely to buy Red Bull knowing the brand is Austrian but with a strong Thai influence? Does it generally matter to consumers where a product originates from?

2. Worldwide, Red Bull has the highest market share of all energy drinks, with more than 6 billion cans sold annually (that's almost one can for every person worldwide). So, either *you* drink Red Bull, or your friend does! Does the sheer number of Red Bull cans sold—basically its popularity—make you more or less interested in supporting the product with your purchase?

3. Red Bull mass markets its products in a unique way. To support the company's international business strategy, Red Bull hosts a number of extreme sporting events. Personally, how reachable are you as a customer via these extreme sporting events, or does it even matter? Some marketers believe that just knowing the "brand myth" and Red Bull "legend" is enough to make people buy the product. Do you agree or no, and why?

Design elements: Modern textured halftone: ©VIPRESIONA/ Shutterstock; globalEDGE icon: ©globalEDGE; All others: ©McGraw-Hill Education

Endnotes

1. Sui Sui and Matthias Baum, "Internationalization Strategy, Firm Resources and the Survival of SMEs in the Export Market," *Journal of International Business Studies* 45, no. 7 (September 2014), pp. 821–41.

2. Constantine S. Katsikeas, Neil A. Morgan, Leonidas C. Leonidou, and G. Tomas M. Hult, "Assessing Performance Outcomes in Marketing," *Journal of Marketing* 80, no. 2 (2016), pp. 1-20.

3. Tomas Hult, David Closs, and David Frayer, *Global Supply Chain Management: Leveraging Processes, Measurements, and Tools for Strategic Corporate Advantage* (New York: McGraw-Hill Professional, 2014).

4. Katsikeas et al., "Assessing Performance Outcomes in Marketing."

5. Gary A. Knight and Daekwan Kim, "International Business Competence and the Contemporary Firm," *Journal of International Business Studies* 40, 2 (2009), pp. 255-73.

6. More formally, ROIC = Net profit after tax ÷ Capital, where capital includes the sum of the firm's equity and debt. This way of calculating profitability is highly correlated with return on assets.

7. T. Copeland, T. Koller, and J. Murrin, *Valuation: Measuring and Managing the Value of Companies* (New York: Wiley, 2000).

8. Katsikeas et al., "Assessing Performance Outcomes in Marketing."

9. Hult, Closs, and Frayer, *Global Supply Chain Management: Leveraging Processes, Measurements, and Tools for Strategic Corporate Advantage.*

10. The concept of consumer surplus is an important one in economics. For a more detailed exposition, see D. Besanko, D. Dranove, and M. Shanley, *Economics of Strategy* (New York: Wiley, 1996).

11. However, $P = V$ only in the special case where the company has a perfect monopoly and where it can charge each customer a unique price that reflects the value of the product to that customer (i.e., where perfect price discrimination is possible). More generally, except in the limiting case of perfect price discrimination, even a monopolist will see most consumers capture some of the value of a product in the form of a consumer surplus.

12. This point is central to the work of M. E. Porter, *Competitive Advantage* (New York: Free Press, 1985). See also chap. 4 in P. Ghemawat, *Commitment: The Dynamic of Strategy* (New York: Free Press, 1991).

13. M. E. Porter, *Competitive Strategy* (New York: Free Press, 1980).

14. M. E. Porter, "What Is Strategy?" *Harvard Business Review,* On-point Enhanced Edition article, February 1, 2000.

15. G. Tomas M. Hult, Forrest V. Morgeson III, Neil A. Morgan, Sunil Mithas, and Claes Fornell, "Do Firms Know What Their

Customers Think and Why?" *Journal of the Academy of Marketing Science* 45, no. 1 (2017), pp. 37–54.

16. Porter, *Competitive Advantage.*

17. Claes Fornell, Forrest V. Morgeson III, and G. Tomas M. Hult, "Stock Returns on Customer Satisfaction Do Beat the Market: Gauging the Effect of a Marketing Intangible," *Journal of Marketing* 80, no. 5 (2016), pp. 92–107.

18. Empirical evidence does seem to indicate that, on average, international expansion is linked to greater firm profitability. For some examples, see M. A. Hitt, R. E. Hoskisson, and H. Kim, "International Diversification, Effects on Innovation and Firm Performance," *Academy of Management Journal* 40, no. 4 (1997), pp. 767–98; S. Tallman and J. Li, "Effects of International Diversity and Product Diversity on the Performance of Multinational Firms," *Academy of Management Journal* 39, no. 1 (1996), pp. 179–96.

19. This concept has been popularized by G. Hamel and C. K. Prahalad, *Competing for the Future* (Boston: Harvard Business School Press, 1994). The concept is grounded in the resource-based view of the firm; for a summary, see J. B. Barney, "Firm Resources and Sustained Competitive Advantage," *Journal of Management* 17 (1991), pp. 99–120; K. R. Conner, "A Historical Comparison of Resource-Based Theory and Five Schools of Thought within Industrial Organization Economics: Do We Have a New Theory of the Firm?" *Journal of Management* 17 (1991), pp. 121–54.

20. J. P. Womack, D. T. Jones, and D. Roos, *The Machine That Changed the World* (New York: Rawson Associates, 1990).

21. M. E. Porter, *The Competitive Advantage of Nations* (New York: Free Press, 1990).

22. Mark F Peterson, Mikael Søndergaard, Aycan Kara (2017), "Traversing cultural boundaries in IB: The complex relationships between explicit country and implicit cultural group boundaries at multiple levels," *Journal of International Business Studies,* doi:10.1057/s41267-017-0082-z

23. See R. B. Reich, *The Work of Nations* (New York: Knopf, 1991); P. J. Buckley and N. Hashai, "A Global System View of Firm Boundaries," *Journal of International Business Studies,* January 2004, pp. 33–50; Yong Kyu Lew, Rudolf R Sinkovics, Mo YaminZaheer Khan, "Trans-Specialization Understanding in International Technology Alliances: The Influence of Cultural Distance," *Journal of International Business Studies* 47, no. 5 (2016), pp. 577–94.

24. D. Barboza, "An Unknown Giant Flexes Its Muscles," *The New York Times,* December 4, 2004, pp. B1, B3.

25. G. Hall and S. Howell, "The Experience Curve from an Economist's Perspective," *Strategic Management Journal* 6 (1985), pp. 197–212.

26. A. A. Alchain, "Reliability of Progress Curves in Airframe Production," *Econometrica* 31 (1963), pp. 697–98.

27. Eric Fang and Shaoming Zou, "The Effects of Absorptive and Joint Learning on the Instability of International Joint Ventures in Emerging Economies," *Journal of International Business Studies* 41, no. 5 (2010), pp. 906–24.

28. Hall and Howell, "The Experience Curve from an Economist's Perspective."

29. Markus Taussig, "Foreignness as Both a Global Asset and a Local Liability: How Host Country Idiosyncrasies and Business Activities Matter," *Journal of International Business Studies* 48, no. 4 (2016), pp. 498–522.

30. For a full discussion of the source of scale economies, see D. Besanko, D. Dranove, and M. Shanley, *Economics of Strategy* (New York: Wiley, 1996).

31. This estimate was provided by the Pharmaceutical Manufacturers Association.

32. See J. Birkinshaw and N. Hood, "Multinational Subsidiary Evolution: Capability and Charter Change in Foreign Owned Subsidiary Companies," *Academy of Management Review* 23 (October 1998), pp. 773–95; A. K. Gupta and V. J. Govindarajan, "Knowledge Flows within Multinational Corporations," *Strategic Management Journal* 21 (2000), pp. 473–96; V. J. Govindarajan and A. K. Gupta, *The Quest for Global Dominance* (San Francisco: Jossey-Bass, 2001); T. S. Frost, J. M. Birkinshaw, and P. C. Ensign, "Centers of Excellence in Multinational Corporations," *Strategic Management Journal* 23 (2002), pp. 997–1018; U. Andersson, M. Forsgren, and U. Holm, "The Strategic Impact of External Networks," *Strategic Management Journal* 23 (2002), pp. 979–96.

33. S. Leung, "Armchairs, TVs and Espresso: Is It McDonald's?" *The Wall Street Journal,* August 30, 2002, pp. A1, A6.

34. C. K. Prahalad and Yves L. Doz, *The Multinational Mission: Balancing Local Demands and Global Vision* (New York: Free Press, 1987). Also see J. Birkinshaw, A. Morrison, and J. Hulland, "Structural and Competitive Determinants of a Global Integration Strategy," *Strategic Management Journal* 16 (1995), pp. 637–55; P. Ghemawat, *Redefining Global Strategy* (Boston: Harvard Business School Press, 2007).

35. Prahalad and Doz, *The Multinational Mission.* Prahalad and Doz actually talk about local responsiveness rather than local customization.

36. T. Levitt, "The Globalization of Markets," *Harvard Business Review,* May–June 1983, pp. 92–102.

37. C. J. Chipello, "Local Presence Is Key to European Deals," *The Wall Street Journal,* June 30, 1998, p. A15.

38. For an extended discussion see G. S. Yip and G. Tomas M. Hult, *Total Global Strategy* (Boston: Pearson, 2012); A. M. Rugman and A. Verbeke, "A Perspective on Regional and Global Strategies of Multinational Enterprises," *Journal of International Business Studies* 35, no. 1 (2004), pp. 3–18; C. A. Bartlett and S. Ghoshal, *Managing across Borders* (Boston: Harvard Business School Press, 1989).

39. David Hollister, Ray Tadgerson, David Closs, and Tomas Hult, *Second Shift: The Inside Story of the Keep GM Movement* (New York: McGraw-Hill Professional, 2017).

40. Bartlett and Ghoshal, *Managing across Borders.*

41. Bartlett and Ghoshal, *Managing across Borders.* Pankaj Ghemawat makes a similar argument, although he does not use the term *transnational.* See Ghemawat, *Redefining Global Strategy.*

42. T. Hout, M. E. Porter, and E. Rudden, "How Global Companies Win Out," *Harvard Business Review,* September–October 1982, pp. 98–108.

The Organization of International Business

14

LEARNING OBJECTIVES

After reading this chapter, you will be able to:

LO14-1   Explain what is meant by organizational architecture.

LO14-2   Describe the different organizational architecture choices that can be made in an international business.

LO14-3   Explain how the organizational architecture can be matched to global strategy to improve performance.

LO14-4   Discuss what is required for an international business to change its organizational architecture so it better matches its global strategy.

Image of Sport/Newscom

Bird, Lime, and Organizing Globally

OPENING CASE

Bird and Lime, both founded in 2017, are exceptional "sharing economy" companies that serve targeted international customers. On Bird's website, the company's (and the industry's) concept is explained nicely: "As cities across the globe continue to grow, so too does our need for greater mobility. We're facing more pollution, congestion, and gridlock than ever before. The near-term solution is in partnering with cities to rebalance our existing streets and improve the way we all get around, not in adding more cars to our roads or redesigning the entire transit landscape"* (**www.bird.co/about**).

Similarly, Lime states that the company focuses on smart mobility for the modern world: "Lime is founded on a simple idea that all communities deserve access to smart, affordable mobility. Through the equitable distribution of shared scooters, bikes and transit vehicles, we aim to reduce dependence on personal automobiles for short distance transportation and leave future generations with a cleaner, healthier planet"** (**www.li.me/about-us**).

Bird was founded by Travis VanderZanden in September 2017. He was formerly an executive at Lyft and Uber, so his background was front-and-center in the sharing economy already. Bird is a dockless scooter-sharing company headquartered in Santa Monica, California. The company operates electric scooters in over 100 cities throughout North America, Europe, and Asia, with some 10 million rides in its first year of operation. The Chinese manufacturers Ninebot and Xiaomi provide most of the scooters to Bird. Internationally, Bird expanded initially into France and Israel in August 2018—roughly 11 months after its founding—and then continued with Belgium and Austria the following month. It is now in more than a dozen countries. As illustrated in the company's concept earlier, Bird is passionate about vibrant communities that have less traffic, cleaner air, and safer streets. The company is working actively with cities and universities across the world to provide new transportation options, complement public transit systems, and invest in safety infrastructure that benefits everyone.

Lime was founded by Toby Sun and Brad Bao in January 2017 and is headquartered in San Francisco, California. The company name is really Neutron Holdings, Inc., but does its business under the Lime branding, formerly known as LimeBike. As a transportation-rental company, the core services offered include bicycle, scooter, and car-sharing systems in various cities worldwide. The systems offer dockless transportation devices which users find and unlock via a mobile app. University campuses and large cities worldwide are the main target populations for Lime. Lime is in more than 20 countries—only a couple of years after its founding—and is valued at $2.4 billion, with operating funds contributed so far from investors of $765 million. The company's backing is strong,

*About: Bird, **www.bird.co/about**.
Our Mission: Lime, **www.li.me/about.

and so is its commitment to international business. To capitalize on its global engagement, Lime recently hired its first Global Community Director. This person's responsibility is to design and develop a world-class grassroots brand-building strategy through which Lime's vision resonates in local communities around the world.

Both Bird and Lime have targeted a unique market niche. Some 40 percent of all trips using vehicles are under three miles, a perfect segment of the transportation market for companies like Bird and Lime. Since 8 in 10 people also believe that car traffic and pollution are problems in their cities and on campuses, some 70 percent of the people want new transportation options. While Bird and Lime have received flack from citizens and government representatives for obstructing walkways and cluttering the landscape on campuses and in cities, Bird and Lime scooters also cut down vehicle use and reduce the volume of traffic in high-density areas. Plus, their scooters are small compared to any other vehicle. One traditional parking spot for a car can fit 10 scooters. Collectively, these features mean that scooters help reduce pollution and improve air quality compared to other modes of transportation.

Both Bird and Lime have also created a structure whereby they work with communities to offer their service. Communities and organizations can request their service to provide access to constituents. However, so far, the Bird and Lime services started very similarly to Uber and Lyft—with limited regulations, if any, in the communities they serve. In essence, neighborhoods are now trying to catch up when it comes to regulation and oversight, if they think it is needed (some communities feel it is needed; some do not). For example, Los Angeles was overrun with scooters that caused traffic jams and other nuisances. City officials banned the companies until city leaders could develop policies to control the services. Higher fees to obtain operating permits and a cap on the total number of scooters that can operate around the city are two of the usual options. So, the evolution of the community-company organizational partnership for Bird and Lime follows the pattern of what Uber and Lyft have been facing.

On the operational side, both Bird and Lime use virtual organizations to make sure their scooters run, that they can be easily found in populous areas where customers want them, and that their scooters follow all existing community regulations or those that are currently in the making. For example, powered by electricity, the scooters are recharged by "Bird Chargers" and "Lime Juicers" at night. This virtual network of people is important. Because the scooters are electric, they need to be charged every day. To do this, Bird and Lime both utilize independent contractors (i.e., regular people to pick up these scooters at night, charge them in their homes, and put them back out on the street for the public to use by early morning the next day).

So, whether it is the gadgets themselves (scooters), the technology used to connect people in the sharing economy (smartphone apps; GPS), or the network of independent contractors that these companies depend on, the future for the scooter world is interesting. Bird and Lime rule the international marketplace right now, but U.S. companies such as Spin, Goat, and Skip, and European firms such as Tier, Voi, and Flash, or even Uber and Lyft, are now in the scooter business and may chip away at the market share of Bird and Lime.

Sources: Eric Newcomer, "Lime and Bird Raise Millions, But at Far Lower Valuations Than Hoped," *Bloomberg BusinessWeek*, January 17, 2019; Ethan May, "Here's Everything You Need to Know About Bird and Lime Electric Scooters," *IndyStar*, June 21, 2018; Don Reisinger, "Why Bird and Lime Scooters Are Invading US Cities Everywhere," *Tom's Guide*, August 13, 2018; Megan Rose Dickey, "Electric Scooters Are Going Worldwide," *TechCrunch*, April 11, 2019; Nate Lanxon, "Europe's Scooter Firms Said to Talk Mergers as Lime Expands," *Bloomberg BusinessWeek*, February 7, 2019.

Introduction

Oftentimes, when we talk about how internationally oriented companies are organized, we think of large multinational corporations like AB InBev, IKEA, and Unilever (discussed in the Management Focus features in Chapter 13 on The Strategy of International Business) or Walmart and P&G (covered in the closing and integrated cases, respectively, of this chapter). The two Management Focus boxes in this chapter discuss these companies, as well as others that are more traditional (Dow and Lincoln Electric).

However, it is also important to cover newer firms and organizing scenarios, as with the "sharing economy" examples in the opening case of Chapter 13 (Airbnb, Uber, Lyft, and Turo). The sharing economy continues to give rise to a number of companies that are based on peer-to-peer products and services or some form of sharing. As an economic model, the sharing economy has had a significant impact on companies and how they organize their activities. There has to be more flexibility and openness in organizational structures (such as with open access software). The defining characteristic of a **sharing economy** is in the economic model that we often define as a peer-to-peer based activity of acquiring, providing, or sharing access to products and services facilitated among providers and customers via a community based on-line platform (e.g., a smartphone app).

As suggested by the strategy examples of AB InBev, IKEA, Unilever (Chapter 13) and organizational examples of Walmart, P&G, Dow, and Lincoln (Chapter 14), this chapter is concerned with identifying the organizational architecture that international businesses use to manage and direct their global operations. As also suggested by the coverage of Airbnb, Uber, Lyft, and Turo (Chapter 13) and Bird and Lime (Chapter 14), today's organizational architectures are, in some cases, more flexible, fluid, and virtual than what we have seen for decades. The peer-to-peer business model is becoming increasingly popular for larger companies and at least some of their architectures.

Consequently, both types of organizational architectures—traditional and sharing-economy architectures—are important to discuss in a chapter on organizations. By **organizational architecture**, we mean the totality of a firm's organization, including formal organizational structure, control systems and incentives, processes, organizational culture, and people. The core argument outlined in this chapter is that superior enterprise profitability requires that three conditions be fulfilled.

First, the different elements of a firm's organizational architecture must be internally consistent. For example, the control and incentive systems used in the firm must be consistent with the structure of the enterprise. This includes the virtual team that some companies draw on to make their business models and organizational architecture work (e.g., Uber and Lyft).

Second, the organizational architecture must match or fit the strategy of the firm—strategy and architecture must be consistent.[1] For example, if a firm is pursuing a global standardization strategy but has the wrong kind of organizational architecture in place, it is unlikely that it will be able to execute that strategy effectively and so poor performance may result. Large companies (e.g., Microsoft) strategically changing to be more nimble and innovative face this fit issue all the time (e.g., IBM).

Third, the strategy and architecture of the firm must not only be consistent with each other but also make sense given the competitive conditions prevailing in the firm's markets—strategy, architecture, and competitive environment must all be consistent.[2] For example, a firm pursuing a localization strategy might have the right kind of organizational architecture in place for that strategy. However, if it competes in markets where cost pressures are intense and demands for local responsiveness are low, it will still have inferior performance because a global standardization strategy is more appropriate in such an environment.

To explore the issues illustrated by examples such as Walmart and Procter & Gamble, but also Bird and Lime, this chapter opens by discussing in more detail the concepts of organizational architecture and fit. Next, it turns to a more detailed exploration of various components of architecture—structure, control systems and incentives, organizational culture, and processes—and explains how these components must be internally consistent. (We look at the "people" component of architecture in Chapter 19, where we discuss human resource strategy in the multinational firm.) After reviewing the various components of architecture, we look at ways in which architecture can be matched to strategy and the environment to achieve superior performance. The chapter closes with a discussion of organizational change. Periodically, firms have to change or adapt their organization so that it matches new strategic and competitive realities (e.g., Uber and Lyft entering the scooter business led by Bird and Lime).

Organizational Architecture

As noted in the introduction, the term *organizational architecture* refers to the totality of a firm's organization, including formal organizational structure, control systems and incentives, organizational culture, processes, and people.[3] Figure 14.1 illustrates these different elements.

Organizational structure refers to three things: First, the formal division of the organization into subunits such as product divisions, national operations, and functions (most organizational charts display this aspect of structure); second, the location of decision-making responsibilities within that structure (e.g., centralized/ formalized/flexible, and/or specialized); and third, the establishment of integrating mechanisms to coordinate the activities of subunits, including cross-functional and pan-regional teams.

Control systems refers to the metrics used to measure the performance of subunits and to make judgments about how well managers are running those subunits. For example, Unilever has historically measured the performance of national operating subsidiary companies according to profitability. Meanwhile, Lime measures the performance of its

LO14-1

Explain what is meant by organizational architecture.

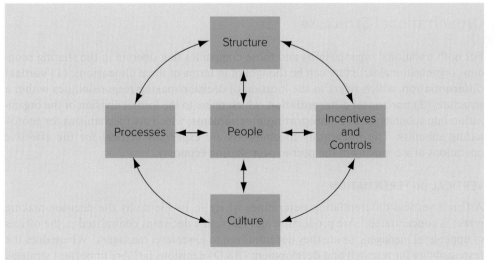

FIGURE 14.1

Organizational architecture.

independent contractors of Lime Juicers by the number of scooters picked up, charged, and placed back in service at certain spots by early morning.

Incentives are the devices used to reward appropriate managerial behavior. Incentives are very closely tied to performance metrics. For example, the incentives of a manager in charge of a national operating subsidiary might be linked to the performance of that company. Specifically, he or she might receive a bonus if her subsidiary exceeds its performance targets. Lime Juicers do not receive full payment if they have the scooters back after 7 a.m. in the morning.

Processes are the manner in which decisions are made and work is performed within the organization. Examples are the processes for formulating strategy, for deciding how to allocate resources within a firm, or for evaluating the performance of managers and giving feedback.[4] Processes are distinct from the location of decision-making responsibilities within an organization, although both involve decisions. While the CEO might have ultimate responsibility for deciding the strategy of the firm (i.e., the decision-making responsibility is centralized), the process he or she uses to make that decision might include the solicitation of feedback from lower-level managers.

Organizational culture refers to the norms and value systems that are shared among the employees of an organization. Just as societies have cultures (see Chapter 4 for details), so do organizations. Organizations can be viewed as societies of individuals who come together to perform collective tasks. They have their own distinctive patterns of culture and subculture.[5] As we shall see, organizational culture can have a profound impact on how a firm performs. Finally, by **people** we mean not only the employees of the organization, but also the strategy used to recruit, compensate, and retain those individuals and the type of people that they are in terms of their skills, values, and orientation (discussed in depth in Chapter 19).

As illustrated by the arrows in Figure 14.1, the various components of an organization's architecture are not independent of each other: Each component shapes, and is shaped by, other components of the architecture. An obvious example is a strategy regarding people. This can be used proactively to hire individuals whose internal values are consistent with those that the firm wishes to emphasize in its organizational culture. Thus, the people component of architecture can be used to reinforce (or not) the prevailing culture of the organization. For example, Unilever has historically made an effort to hire managers who were sociable and placed a high value on consensus and cooperation, values that the enterprise wished to emphasize in its own culture.[6] P&G has made a concerted effort to hire people from countries in which it has operations; some 140 nationalities are represented in P&G's workforce compared with the 180 countries in which it sells products. If a firm is going to maximize its profitability, it must pay close attention to achieving internal consistency between the various components of its architecture.

LO14-2

Describe the different organizational architecture choices that can be made in an international business.

Organizational Structure

For both traditional organizations and those companies that operate in the sharing economy, organizational structure can be thought of in terms of three dimensions: (1) **vertical differentiation**, which refers to the location of decision-making responsibilities within a structure; (2) **horizontal differentiation**, which refers to the formal division of the organization into subunits; and (3) **integrating mechanisms**, which are mechanisms for coordinating subunits. The integrating mechanisms are especially critical for the effective operations of a company in the peer-to-peer sharing economy.

VERTICAL DIFFERENTIATION

A firm's vertical differentiation determines where in its hierarchy the decision-making power is concentrated.[7] Are production and marketing decisions centralized in the offices of upper-level managers, or are they decentralized to lower-level managers? Where does the responsibility for research and development (R&D) decisions lie? Are important strategic and financial decisions pushed down to operating units, or are they concentrated in the hands of top management, often referred to as the C-suite executives? And so on. There are arguments for both centralization and decentralization (and certain specialization in cases that are unique—e.g., new startups in the sharing economy).

Arguments for Centralization

There are four main arguments for centralization. First, centralization can facilitate coordination and integration of operations. For example, consider a firm that has a component manufacturing operation in Taiwan and an assembly operation in Mexico. The activities of these two operations may need to be coordinated to ensure a smooth flow of products from the component operation to the assembly operation. This might be achieved by centralizing production scheduling at the firm's head office. Second, centralization can help ensure that decisions are consistent with organizational objectives. When decisions are decentralized to lower-level managers, those managers may make decisions at variance with top management's goals. Centralization of important decisions minimizes the chance of this occurring.

Third, by concentrating power and authority in one individual or a management team, centralization can give top-level managers the means to bring about needed major organizational changes. Fourth, centralization can avoid the duplication of activities that occurs when similar activities are carried on by various subunits within the organization. For example, many international firms centralize their R&D functions at one or two locations to ensure that R&D work is not duplicated. Production activities may be centralized at key locations for the same reason.

globalEDGE BUSINESS BEAT

globalEDGE has partnered with the Michigan Business Network to offer a radio show called globalEDGE Business Beat (gBB). gBB is available worldwide to more than 200 countries and territories via **globalEDGE.msu.edu**. Charles W. L. Hill is a regular guest on the radio show. globalEDGE Business Beat covers interviews and discussions with a wide range of global leaders in business, government, and academe to spread the word about the latest thoughts, tools, and markets to succeed globally. Oftentimes, these interviews focus on the best organizational architecture for companies to develop to succeed globally. For example, top leaders from large organizations such as Domino's, Saatchi and Saatchi X, and the U.S. Department of Commerce have been featured. But focus is also placed on small and medium-sized companies and their globalization efforts. The podcasts are available on globalEDGE (see **globaledge.msu.edu/get-connected/globaledge-business-beat** for podcasts and air times).

Arguments for Decentralization

There are five main arguments for decentralization. First, top management can become overburdened when decision-making authority is centralized, and this can result in poor decisions, slow decision-making, and not the best decision being made. Decentralization gives top management time to focus on critical issues by delegating more routine issues to lower-level managers. Second, motivational research favors decentralization. Behavioral scientists have long argued that people are willing to give more to their jobs when they have a greater degree of individual freedom and control over their work.

Third, decentralization permits greater flexibility—more rapid response to competitive markets and environmental changes—because decisions do not have to be "referred up the hierarchy" unless they are exceptional in nature. Fourth, decentralization can result in better decisions. In a decentralized structure, managers who are located closer to the customers—or at least closer to where the products and services are developed—often have a better grasp of what decisions need to be made than top-level executives (although they clearly have a better picture of the overall company). Fifth, decentralization can increase control. Decentralization can be used to establish relatively autonomous, self-contained subunits within an organization. Subunit managers can then be held accountable for subunit performance. The more responsibility subunit managers have for decisions that impact subunit performance, the fewer excuses they have for poor performance, the more committed to success they are likely to be, and the more value they feel that they offer the organization.

Global Strategy and Centralization

The choice between centralization and decentralization is not absolute.[8] Frequently it makes sense to centralize some decisions and to decentralize others, depending on the type of decision and the firm's strategy. Decisions regarding overall firm strategy, major financial expenditures, financial objectives, and legal issues are typically centralized at the firm's headquarters and by the C-suite executives. However, operating decisions, such as those relating to production, marketing, R&D, and human resource management, may or may not be centralized depending on the firm's strategy.

Consider firms pursuing a global standardization strategy.[9] They must decide how to disperse the various value creation activities around the globe so location and experience economies can be realized. The head office must make the decisions about where to locate R&D, production, marketing, and so on. In addition, the globally dispersed set of value creation activities that facilitates a global strategy must be coordinated. All of this creates pressures for centralizing some operating decisions.

In contrast, the emphasis on local responsiveness in firms pursuing a localization strategy creates strong pressures for decentralizing operating decisions to subsidiaries. Firms pursuing an international strategy also tend to maintain centralized control over their core competencies and to decentralize other decisions to foreign subsidiaries. Typically, such firms centralize control over R&D in their home country but decentralize operating decisions to foreign subsidiaries. For example, Microsoft Corporation, which fits the international mode, centralizes its product development activities at its Redmond, Washington, headquarters and decentralizes marketing activities to various foreign subsidiaries. While products are developed at home, managers in the various foreign subsidiaries have significant latitude for formulating strategies to market those products in their particular settings.[10]

The situation in firms pursuing a transnational strategy is more complex. The need to realize location and experience curve economies requires some degree of centralized control over global production centers. However, the need for local responsiveness dictates the decentralization of many operating decisions, particularly for marketing, to foreign subsidiaries. Thus, in firms pursuing a transnational strategy, some operating decisions are relatively centralized, while others are relatively decentralized. In addition, global learning based on the multi-directional transfer of knowledge and skills between subsidiaries, and between subsidiaries and headquarters, is a central feature of a firm pursuing a transnational strategy. The concept of global learning is predicated on the notion that subsidiaries within a multinational firm have significant freedom to develop their own knowledge and skills. Only then can these skills be leveraged to benefit other parts of the organization. A substantial degree of decentralization is required if subsidiaries are going to have the freedom to do this. For this reason too, the pursuit of a transnational strategy requires a high degree of decentralization.[11]

HORIZONTAL DIFFERENTIATION

Horizontal differentiation is concerned with how the firm decides to divide itself into subunits.[12] The decision is normally made on the basis of function, type of business, or geographic area. In many firms, just one of these predominates, but more complex

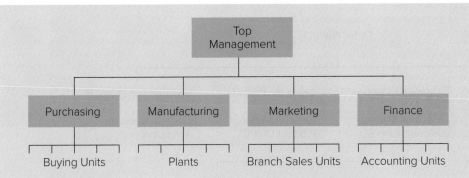

FIGURE 14.2

A typical functional structure.

solutions are adopted in others. This is particularly likely in the case of multinational firms, where the conflicting demands to organize the company around different products (to realize location and experience curve economies) and different national markets (to remain locally responsive) must be reconciled.

The Structure of Domestic Firms

Most firms begin with no formal structure and are run by a single entrepreneur or a small team of individuals. As they grow, the demands of management become too great for one individual or a small team to handle. At this point, the organization is split into functions reflecting the firm's value creation activities (e.g., production, marketing, R&D, sales). These functions are typically coordinated and controlled by top management (see Figure 14.2). Decision making in this functional structure tends to be centralized.

Further horizontal differentiation may be required if the firm significantly diversifies its product offering, which takes the firm into different business areas. For example, Dutch multinational Philips Electronics NV began as a lighting company, but diversification took the company into consumer electronics (e.g., visual and audio equipment), industrial electronics (integrated circuits and other electronic components), and medical systems (MRI scanners and ultrasound systems). In such circumstances, a functional structure can be too clumsy. Problems of coordination and control arise when different business areas are managed within the framework of a functional structure.[13] For one thing, it becomes difficult to identify the profitability of each distinct business area. For another, it is difficult to run a functional department, such as production or marketing, if it is supervising the value creation activities of several business areas.

To solve the problems of coordination and control, at this stage most firms switch to a product divisional structure (see Figure 14.3). With a product divisional structure, each division is responsible for a distinct product line (business area). Thus, Philips created

FIGURE 14.3

A typical product divisional structure.

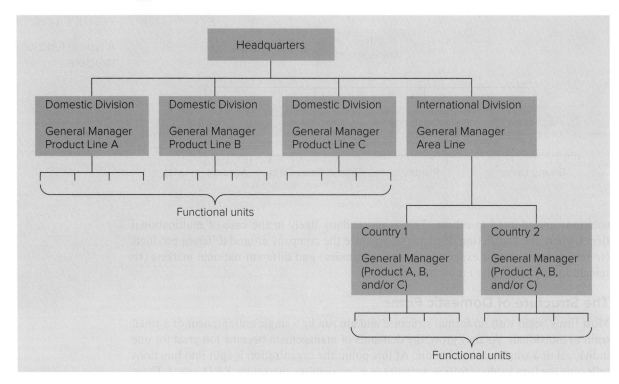

FIGURE 14.4

One company's international division structure.

divisions for lighting, consumer electronics, industrial electronics, and medical systems. Each product division is set up as a self-contained, largely autonomous entity with its own functions. The responsibility for operating decisions is typically decentralized to product divisions, which are then held accountable for their performance. Headquarters is responsible for the overall strategic development of the firm and for the financial control of the various divisions.

The International Division

When firms initially expand abroad, they often group all their international activities into an **international division**. This has tended to be the case for firms organized on the basis of functions and for firms organized on the basis of product divisions. Regardless of the firm's domestic structure, its international division tends to be organized on geography. Figure 14.4 illustrates this for a firm whose domestic organization is based on product divisions.

Many manufacturing firms expanded internationally by exporting the product manufactured at home to foreign subsidiaries to sell. Thus, in the firm illustrated in Figure 14.4, the subsidiaries in countries 1 and 2 would sell the products manufactured by divisions A, B, and C. In time, however, it might prove viable to manufacture the product in each country, and so production facilities would be added on a country-by-country basis. For firms with a functional structure at home, this might mean replicating the functional structure in every country in which the firm does business. For firms with a divisional structure, this might mean replicating the divisional structure in every country in which the firm does business.

This structure has been widely used; according to a Harvard study, 60 percent of all firms that have expanded internationally have initially adopted it. A good example of a company that uses this structure is Walmart, which created an international division in 1993 to manage its global expansion. Despite its popularity, an international division

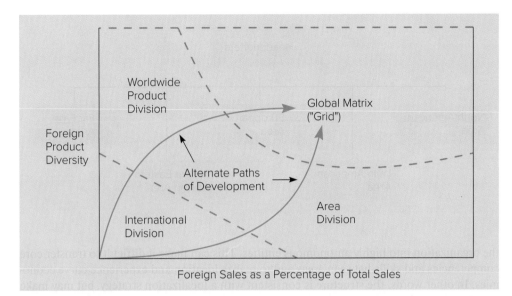

FIGURE 14.5

The international
structural stages model.

Source: M. J. Stopford and L. T.
Wells, *Strategy and Structure of
the Multinational Enterprise*
(New York: Basic Books, 1972).

structure can give rise to problems.[14] The dual structure it creates contains inherent potential for conflict and coordination problems between domestic and foreign operations. One problem with the structure is that the heads of foreign subsidiaries are not given as much voice in the organization as the heads of domestic functions (in the case of functional firms) or divisions (in the case of divisional firms). Rather, the head of the international division is presumed to be able to represent the interests of all countries to headquarters. This effectively relegates each country's manager to the second tier of the firm's hierarchy, which is inconsistent with a strategy of trying to expand internationally and build a true multinational organization.

Another problem is the implied lack of coordination between domestic operations and foreign operations, which are isolated from each other in separate parts of the structural hierarchy. This can inhibit the worldwide introduction of new products, the transfer of core competencies between domestic and foreign operations, and the consolidation of global production at key locations so as to realize location and experience curve economies.

As a result of such problems, many firms that continue to expand internationally abandon this structure and adopt one of the worldwide structures discussed next. The two initial choices are a worldwide product divisional structure, which tends to be adopted by diversified firms that have domestic product divisions, and a worldwide area structure, which tends to be adopted by undiversified firms whose domestic structures are based on functions. These two alternative paths of development are illustrated in Figure 14.5. The model in the figure is referred to as the international structural stages model and was developed by John Stopford and Louis Wells.[15]

Worldwide Area Structure

A **worldwide area structure** tends to be favored by firms with a low degree of diversification and a domestic structure based on functions (see Figure 14.6). Under this structure, the world is divided into geographic areas. An area may be a country (if the market is large enough) or a group of countries. Each area tends to be a self-contained, largely autonomous entity with its own set of value creation activities (e.g., its own production, marketing, R&D, human resources, and finance functions). Operations authority and strategic decisions relating to each of these activities are typically decentralized to each area, with headquarters retaining authority for the overall strategic direction of the firm and financial control.

This structure facilitates local responsiveness. Because decision-making responsibilities are decentralized, each area can customize product offerings, marketing strategy, and business strategy to the local conditions. However, this structure encourages fragmentation of

FIGURE 14.6

A worldwide area
structure.

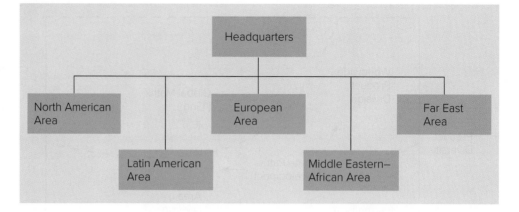

the organization into highly autonomous entities. This can make it difficult to transfer core competencies and skills between areas and to realize location and experience curve economies. In other words, the structure is consistent with a localization strategy, but may make it difficult to realize gains associated with global standardization. Firms structured on this basis may encounter significant problems if local responsiveness is less critical than reducing costs or transferring core competencies for establishing a competitive advantage.

Worldwide Product Divisional Structure

A **worldwide product division structure** tends to be adopted by firms that are reasonably diversified and, accordingly, originally had domestic structures based on product divisions. As with the domestic product divisional structure, each division is a self-contained, largely autonomous entity with full responsibility for its own value creation activities. The headquarters retains responsibility for the overall strategic development and financial control of the firm (see Figure 14.7).

Underpinning the organization is a belief that the value creation activities of each product division should be coordinated by that division worldwide. Thus, the worldwide product divisional structure is designed to help overcome the coordination problems that arise with the international division and worldwide area structures. This structure provides an organizational context that enhances the consolidation of value creation activities at key locations necessary for realizing location and experience curve economies. It also facilitates the transfer of core competencies within a division's worldwide operations and the

FIGURE 14.7

A worldwide product
divisional structure.

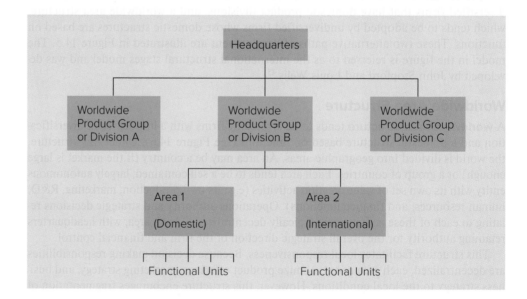

simultaneous worldwide introduction of new products. The main problem with the structure is the limited voice it gives to area or country managers since they are seen as subservient to product division managers. The result can be a lack of local responsiveness, which, as Chapter 13 showed, can lead to performance problems.

Global Matrix Structure

Both the worldwide area structure and the worldwide product divisional structure have strengths and weaknesses. The worldwide area structure facilitates local responsiveness, but it can inhibit the realization of location and experience curve economies and the transfer of core competencies between areas. The worldwide product division structure provides a better framework for pursuing location and experience curve economies and for transferring core competencies, but it is weak in local responsiveness. Other things being equal, this suggests that a worldwide area structure is more appropriate if the firm is pursuing a localization strategy, while a worldwide product divisional structure is more appropriate for firms pursuing global standardization or international strategies. However, as Bartlett and Ghoshal have argued, to survive in some industries, firms must adopt a transnational strategy. They must focus simultaneously on the following: realizing location and experience curve economies, local responsiveness, and the internal transfer of core competencies.[16]

Some firms have attempted to cope with the conflicting demands of a transnational strategy by using a matrix structure. In the classic **global matrix structure**, horizontal differentiation proceeds along two dimensions: product division and geographic area (see Figure 14.8). The philosophy is that responsibility for operating decisions pertaining to a particular product should be shared by the product division and the various areas of the firm. Thus, the nature of the product offering, the marketing strategy, and the business strategy to be pursued in area 1 for the products produced by division A are determined by conciliation between division A and area 1 management. It is believed that this dual decision-making responsibility should enable the firm to simultaneously achieve its particular objectives. In a classic matrix structure, giving product divisions and geographic areas equal status within the organization reinforces the idea of dual responsibility. Individual managers thus belong to two hierarchies (a divisional hierarchy and an area hierarchy) and have two bosses (a divisional boss and an area boss).

ABB (Asea Brown Boveri), a large multinational corporation operating in robotics and the power and automation technology areas, was one of the initial "global matrix"

FIGURE 14.8

A global matrix structure.

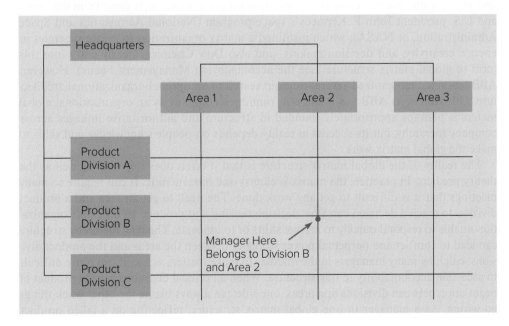

Dow—(Failed) Early Global Matrix Adopter

A select few companies are major players globally in the chemical industry. These companies include Dow Chemical, BASF, Bayer, DuPont, ExxonMobil, Formosa, Mitsubishi, and Shell. It is an industry that often takes heavy investment, knowledge, and skills. At the same time, the barriers to the free flow of chemical products between nations largely disappeared several decades ago. This along with the commodity nature of most bulk chemicals has ushered in a prolonged period of intense price competition among the companies in the industry. In such a competitive environment, the company that wins the competitive race is the one with the lowest costs. The Dow Chemical Company, usually referred to as just Dow (which is the same as its stock symbol), was long among the cost leaders.

For years, Dow's managers insisted that part of the credit should be placed at the feet of its "matrix" organization. Dow's organizational matrix had three interacting elements: functions (e.g., R&D, manufacturing, marketing), businesses (e.g., ethylene, plastics, pharmaceuticals), and geography (e.g., Spain, Germany, Brazil). Managers' job titles incorporated all three elements—for example, plastics marketing manager for Spain—and most managers reported to at least two bosses. The plastics marketing manager in Spain might report to both the head of the worldwide plastics business and the head of the Spanish operations. The intent of the matrix was to make Dow operations responsive to both local market needs and corporate objectives. Thus, the plastics business might be charged with minimizing Dow's global plastics production costs, while the Spanish operation might be charged with determining how best to sell plastics in the Spanish market.

When Dow introduced this matrix structure as one of the first large multinational corporations to do so, the results were less than promising; multiple reporting channels led to confusion and conflict. The large number of bosses made for an unwieldy bureaucracy. The overlapping responsibilities resulted in turf battles and a lack of accountability. Area managers disagreed with managers overseeing business sectors about which plants should be built and where. In short, the structure didn't work. Instead of abandoning the structure, however, Dow decided to see if it could be made more flexible. After all, Dow wanted to draw on its people's knowledge and skills in the fullest manner possible, and a matrix structure would do just that it thought.

Dow's decision to keep its matrix structure was prompted by its move into the pharmaceuticals industry. The company realized that the pharmaceuticals business is very different from the bulk chemicals business. In bulk chemicals, the big

companies. After the merger of Swedish Asea with the Swiss Brown Boveri to create ABB, the company strategically opted to create a global matrix structure to leverage synergies and to be a truly "global" company. Inspiration for the global matrix came from the 1960s and U.S. president John F. Kennedy's space program (National Aeronautics and Space Administration, or NASA), which instituted a matrix organization to create synergies in energy, creativity, and decision making, and also Dow Chemical's early entry into this form of global matrix structure (see the accompanying Management Focus). However, ABB has since reorganized several times in search of an optimal organizational architecture. Oftentimes, as ABB has found out, running a company as an organizational global matrix is perhaps appropriately founded in structure and authoritative linkages across company hierarchy, but its success in reality depends on people's knowledge and skills to make the global matrix work.

The reality of the global matrix structure is that it often does not work as well as the theory predicts. In practice, the matrix is clumsy and bureaucratic. It can require so many meetings that it is difficult to get any work done. The need to get an area and a product division to reach a decision can slow decision making and produce an inflexible organization unable to respond quickly to market shifts or to innovate. The dual-hierarchy structure can lead to conflict and perpetual power struggles between the areas and the product divisions, catching many managers in the middle. To make matters worse, it can prove difficult to ascertain accountability in this structure. When all critical decisions are the product of negotiation between divisions and areas, one side can always blame the other when things go wrong. As a manager in one global matrix structure, reflecting on a failed product returns come from achieving economies of scale in production. This dictates establishing large plants in key locations from which regional or global markets can be served. But in pharmaceuticals, regulatory and marketing requirements for drugs vary so much from country to country that local needs are far more important than reducing manufacturing costs through scale economies. A high degree of local responsiveness is essential. Dow realized its pharmaceutical business would never thrive if it were managed by the same priorities as its mainstream chemical operations.

Instead of abandoning its matrix, Dow decided to make it more flexible so it could better accommodate the different businesses, each with its own priorities, within a single management system. A small team of senior executives at headquarters helped set the priorities for each type of business. After priorities were identified for each business sector, one of the three elements of the matrix—function, business, or geographic area—was given primary authority in decision making. Which element took the lead varied according to the type of decision and the market or location in which the company was competing. Such flexibility required that all employees understand what was occurring in the rest of the matrix. Although this may seem confusing, for years Dow claimed this flexible system worked well and credited much of its success to the quality of the decisions it facilitated.

Ultimately, however, Dow refocused its business on the chemicals industry, divesting itself of its pharmaceutical activities where the company's performance had been unsatisfactory. Reflecting the change in corporate strategy, Dow decided to abandon its matrix structure in favor of a more streamlined structure based on global business divisions. The change was also driven by the realization that the matrix structure was just too complex and costly to manage in the intensely competitive global environment, particularly given the company's renewed focus on its commodity chemicals, where competitive advantage often went to the low-cost producer. As Dow's CEO put it, "We were an organization that was matrixed and depended on teamwork, but there was no one in charge. When things went well, we didn't know whom to reward; and when things went poorly, we didn't know whom to blame. So we created a global divisional structure, and cut out layers of management. There used to be 11 layers of management between me and the lowest-level employees, now there are five."[*] In short, Dow ultimately found that a matrix structure was unsuited to a company that was competing in very cost-competitive global industries, and it had to abandon its matrix to drive down operating costs.

*Quotes by Jim Fitterling, CEO of Dow Chemical Company.
Sources: Rebecca Cook, "Dow Chemical, DuPont Plan $130 Billion Merger," *Newsweek,* December 11, 2015; "Dow Draws Its Matrix Again, and Again, and Again," *The Economist,* August 5, 1989, pp. 55–56; "Dow Goes for Global Structure," *Chemical Marketing Reporter,* December 11, 1995, pp. 4–5; R. M. Hodgetts, "Dow Chemical CEO William Stavropoulos on Structure and Decision Making," *Academy of Management Executive,* November 1999, pp. 29–35.

launch, said to the author, "Had we been able to do things our way, instead of having to accommodate those guys from the product division, this would never have happened." (A manager in the product division expressed similar sentiments.) The result of such finger-pointing can be that accountability is compromised, conflict is enhanced, and headquarters loses control over the organization. (See the accompanying Management Focus on Dow Chemical for an example of the problems associated with a matrix structure.)

In light of these problems, many firms that pursue a transnational strategy have tried to build "flexible" matrix structures based more on enterprise-wide knowledge networks, as well as a shared culture and vision, than on a rigid hierarchical arrangement. Within such companies the informal structure plays a greater role than the formal structure. Clearly, companies like Uber, Lyft, Bird, Lime, Turo, and Airbnb would not be where they are today without at least some flexibility in their structures. The team of independent contractors, peer-to-peer participants, and virtual leaders can only operate effectively and efficiently within flexible matrix structures. We also continue this discussion when we consider informal integrating mechanisms in the next section.

INTEGRATING MECHANISMS

The previous section explained that firms divide themselves into subunits. One way of coordinating these subunits is through centralization. If the coordination task is complex, however, centralization may not be very effective. Higher-level managers responsible for achieving coordination can soon become overwhelmed by the volume of work required to coordinate the activities of various subunits, particularly if the subunits are large, diverse, and/or geographically dispersed. When this is the case, firms look toward integrating mechanisms, both formal and informal, to help achieve coordination. This section introduces the various integrating mechanisms that international businesses can use. But first, we explore the need for coordination in international firms and some impediments to coordination.

International Strategy and Coordination

The need for coordination between subunits varies with the international strategy of the firm.[17] The need for coordination is lowest in firms pursuing a localization strategy, is higher in international companies, higher still in global companies, and highest of all in transnational companies. Firms pursuing a localization strategy are primarily concerned with local responsiveness. Such firms are likely to operate with a worldwide area structure in which each area has considerable autonomy and its own set of value creation functions. Because each area is established as a standalone entity, the need for coordination between areas is minimized.

The need for coordination is greater in firms pursuing an international strategy and trying to profit from the transfer of core competencies and skills between units at home and abroad. Coordination is necessary to support the transfer of skills and product offerings between units. The need for coordination is also great in firms trying to profit from location and experience curve economies—that is, in firms pursuing global standardization strategies. Achieving location and experience curve economies involves dispersing value creation activities to various locations around the globe. The resulting global web of activities must be coordinated to ensure the smooth flow of inputs into the value chain, the smooth flow of semi-finished products through the value chain, and the smooth flow of finished products to markets around the world.

The need for coordination is greatest in transnational firms, which simultaneously pursue location and experience curve economies, local responsiveness, and the multi-directional transfer of core competencies and skills among all the firm's subunits (referred to as global learning). As with a global standardization strategy, coordination is required to ensure the smooth flow of products through the global value chain. As with an international strategy, coordination is required for ensuring the transfer of core competencies to subunits. However, the transnational goal of achieving multi-directional transfer of competencies requires much greater coordination than in firms pursuing an international strategy. In addition, a transnational strategy requires coordination between foreign subunits and the firm's globally dispersed value creation activities (e.g., production, R&D, marketing) to ensure that any product offering and marketing strategy is sufficiently customized to local conditions.

Impediments to Coordination

Managers of the various subunits have different orientations, partly because they have different tasks. For example, production managers are typically concerned with production issues such as capacity utilization, cost control, and quality control, whereas marketing managers are concerned with marketing issues such as pricing, promotions, distribution, and market share. These differences can inhibit communication between the managers. Quite simply, these managers often do not even "speak the same language." There may also be a lack of respect between subunits (e.g., marketing managers "looking down on" production managers, and vice versa), which further inhibits the communication required to achieve cooperation and coordination.

Differences in subunits' orientations also arise from their differing goals. For example, worldwide product divisions of a multinational firm may be committed to cost goals that require global production of a standardized product, whereas a foreign subsidiary may be committed to increasing its market share in its country, which will require a nonstandard product. These different goals can lead to conflict.

FIGURE 14.9

Formal integrating
mechanisms.

Such impediments to coordination are not unusual in any firm, but they can be particularly problematic in the multinational enterprise with its profusion of subunits at home and abroad. Differences in subunit orientation are often reinforced in multinationals by the separations of time zone, distance, and nationality between managers of the subunits.

Formal Integrating Mechanisms

The formal mechanisms used to integrate subunits vary in complexity from simple direct contact and liaison roles, to teams, to a matrix structure (see Figure 14.9). In general, the greater the need for coordination, the more complex the formal integrating mechanisms need to be.[18]

Direct contact between subunit managers is the simplest integrating mechanism. By this "mechanism," managers of the various subunits simply contact each other whenever they have a common concern. Direct contact may not be effective if the managers have differing orientations that act to impede coordination, as pointed out in the previous subsection.

Liaison roles are a bit more complex. When the volume of contacts between subunits increases, coordination can be improved by giving a person in each subunit responsibility for coordinating with another subunit on a regular basis. Through these roles, the people involved establish a permanent relationship. This helps attenuate the impediments to coordination discussed in the previous subsection.

When the need for coordination is greater still, firms tend to use temporary or permanent teams composed of individuals from the subunits that need to achieve coordination. They typically coordinate product development and introduction, but they are useful when any aspect of operations or strategy requires the cooperation of two or more subunits. Product development and introduction teams are typically composed of personnel from R&D, production, and marketing. The resulting coordination aids the development of products that are tailored to consumer needs and that can be produced at a reasonable cost (design for manufacturing).

When the need for integration is very high, firms may institute a matrix structure, in which all roles are viewed as integrating roles. The structure is designed to facilitate maximum integration among subunits. The most common matrix in multinational firms is based on geographic areas and worldwide product divisions. This achieves a high level of integration between the product divisions and the areas so that, in theory, the firm can pay close attention to both local responsiveness and the pursuit of location and experience curve economies.

In some multinationals, the matrix is more complex still, structuring the firm into geographic areas, worldwide product divisions, and functions, all of which report directly to headquarters. Thus, within a company such as Dow before it abandoned its matrix in the mid-1990s (see the Management Focus), each manager belonged to three hierarchies. For example, a plastics marketing manager in Spain was a member of the Spanish subsidiary, the plastics product division, and the marketing function. In addition to facilitating local responsiveness and location and experience curve economies, such a matrix fosters the transfer of core competencies within the organization. This occurs because core competencies tend to reside in functions (e.g., R&D, marketing). A structure such as this in theory facilitates the transfer of competencies existing in functions from division to division and from area to area.

However, as discussed earlier, such matrix solutions to coordination problems in multinational enterprises can quickly become bogged down in a bureaucratic tangle that creates as many problems as it solves. Matrix structures tend to be bureaucratic, inflexible, and characterized by conflict rather than the hoped-for cooperation. For such a structure to work, it needs to be flexible and to be supported by informal integrating mechanisms.[19] The knowledge and skills of people are typically more important than the structural reporting lines in the global matrix hierarchy. Integration and coordination via a matrix organization structure should not override the flexibility to make decisions based on people's knowledge and skills.

Informal Integrating Mechanism: Knowledge Networks

In attempting to alleviate or avoid the problems associated with formal integrating mechanisms in general, and matrix structures in particular, firms with a high need for integration have been experimenting with an informal integrating mechanism: knowledge networks that are supported by an organizational culture that values teamwork and cross-unit cooperation.[20] A **knowledge network** is a network for transmitting information within an organization that is based not on formal organizational structure, but on informal contacts between managers within an enterprise and on distributed information systems.[21] The great strength of such a network is that it can be used as a non-bureaucratic conduit for knowledge flows within a multinational enterprise.[22] For a network to exist, managers at different locations within the organization must be linked to each other at least indirectly. For example, Figure 14.10 shows the simple network relationships between seven managers within a multinational firm. Managers A, B, and C all know each other personally, as do managers D, E, and F. Although manager B does not know manager F personally, they are linked through common acquaintances (managers C and D). Thus, we can say that managers A through F are all part of the network and also that manager G is not.

Imagine manager B is a marketing manager in Spain and needs to know the solution to a technical problem to better serve an important European customer. Manager F, an R&D manager in the United States, has the solution to manager B's problem. Manager B mentions her problem to all of her contacts, including manager C, and asks if they know of anyone who might be able to provide a solution. Manager C asks manager D, who tells

FIGURE 14.10

A simple management network.

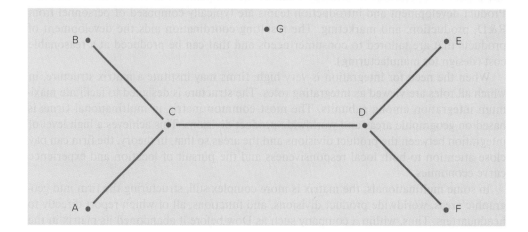

manager F, who then calls manager B with the solution. In this way, coordination is achieved informally through the network, rather than by formal integrating mechanisms such as teams or a matrix structure.

For such a network to function effectively, however, it must embrace as many managers as possible. For example, if manager G had a problem similar to manager B's, he would not be able to utilize the informal network to find a solution; he would have to resort to more formal mechanisms. Establishing company-wide knowledge networks is difficult, and although network enthusiasts speak of networks as the "glue" that binds multinational companies together, it is far from clear how successful firms have been at building company-wide networks. Two techniques being used to establish networks are information systems and management development policies.

Firms are using their distributed computer and telecommunications information systems to provide the foundation for informal knowledge networks.[23] Integrated data systems and web-based communication platforms (e.g., Skype) make it much easier for managers scattered over the globe to get to know each other, to identify contacts that might help solve a particular problem, and to publicize and share best practices within the organization. Walmart, for example, uses its intranet system to communicate ideas about merchandising strategy between stores located in different countries.

Firms are also using their management development programs to build informal networks. Tactics include rotating managers through various foreign subunits on a regular basis so they build their own informal network. Executive management education programs are used to also bring managers of foreign subunits together in a single location so they can become acquainted. These strategic get-togethers on an annual or biennial basis function well, allow for networking, and usually help both motivate the team and achieve better company-wide results.

Knowledge networks by themselves may not be sufficient to achieve coordination if subunit managers persist in pursuing sub-goals that are at variance with company-wide goals.[24] For a knowledge network to function properly—and for a formal matrix structure to work also—managers must share a strong commitment to the same goals. To appreciate the nature of the problem, consider again the case of manager B and manager F. As before, manager F hears about manager B's problem through the network. However, solving manager B's problem would require manager F to devote considerable time to the task. Insofar as this would divert manager F away from his own regular tasks—and the pursuit of subgoals that differ from those of manager B—he may be unwilling to do it. Thus, manager F may not call manager B, and the informal network would fail to provide a solution to manager B's problem.

To eliminate this flaw, the organization's managers must adhere to a common set of cultural norms and values that override differing subunit orientations.[25] In other words, the firm must have a strong organizational culture that promotes teamwork and cooperation at the corporate level and across all subunits. When this is the case, managers are willing to set aside the interests of their own subunits when it benefits the overall firm. If manager B and manager F are committed to the same norms and value systems, and if these organizational norms and values place the interests of the firm as a whole above the interests of any individual subunit, manager F should be willing to cooperate with manager B on solving his or her subunit's problems.

Integrating Mechanisms Summary

The message contained in this section on integrating mechanisms is crucial to understanding the problems of managing a multinational corporation. Multinationals need integration—particularly if they are pursuing global standardization, international, or transnational strategies—but it can be difficult to achieve due to the impediments to coordination discussed. Firms traditionally have tried to achieve coordination by adopting formal integrating mechanisms. These do not always work, however, since they tend to be bureaucratic and do not necessarily address the problems that arise from differing subunit orientations. This is particularly likely with a complex matrix structure, and yet, a complex matrix structure is required for simultaneously achieving location and experience curve economies,

TEST PREP

Use SmartBook to help retain what you have learned. Access your instructor's Connect course to check out SmartBook or go to **learnsmartadvantage.com** for help.

local responsiveness, and the multidirectional transfer of core competencies within the organization. The solution to this dilemma seems twofold. First, the firm must try to establish an informal knowledge network that can do much of the work previously undertaken by a formal matrix structure. Second, the firm must build a common culture. Neither of these partial solutions, however, is easy to achieve.[26]

Control Systems and Incentives

A major task of a firm's top leadership and managers is to control the various subunits of the firm—whether they are defined on the basis of function, product division, or geographic area—to ensure their actions are consistent with the firm's overall strategic and financial objectives. Firms achieve this with various control and incentive systems. In this section, we first review the various types of control systems firms use. We then discuss incentive systems. After that, we look at how the appropriate control and incentive systems vary according to the strategy of the multinational enterprise.

TYPES OF CONTROL SYSTEMS

Four main types of control systems are used in multinational firms: personal controls, bureaucratic controls, output controls, and cultural controls. In many firms, all four are used to some degree, but their emphasis varies with the strategy of the firm.

Personal Controls

Personal control is control achieved by personal contact with subordinates and co-workers. This type of control tends to be most widely used in small firms, where it is seen in the direct supervision of subordinates' actions. However, it also structures the relationships between managers at different levels in multinational enterprises. For example, the CEO may use a great deal of personal control to influence the behavior of his or her immediate subordinates, such as the heads of worldwide product divisions or major geographic areas. In turn, these heads may use personal control to influence the behavior of their subordinates, and so on down through the organization. Jack Welch, the legendary CEO of General Electric who retired in 2001, had regular one-on-one meetings with the heads of all of GE's major businesses (most of which are international).[27] He used these meetings to probe the managers about the strategy, structure, and financial performance of their operations. In doing so, he essentially exercised personal control over these managers and, undoubtedly, over the strategies that they favored.

Bureaucratic Controls

Bureaucratic control is control achieved through a system of rules and procedures that directs the actions of subunits. The most important bureaucratic controls in subunits within multinational firms are budgets and capital spending rules. Budgets are essentially a set of rules for allocating a firm's financial resources. A subunit's budget specifies with some precision how much the subunit may spend. Headquarters uses budgets to influence the behavior of subunits. For example, the R&D budget normally specifies how much cash the R&D unit may spend on product development. R&D managers know that if they spend too much on one project, they will have less to spend on other projects, so they modify their behavior to stay within the budget. Most budgets are set by negotiation between headquarters management and subunit management. Headquarters management can encourage the growth of certain subunits and restrict the growth of others by manipulating their budgets.

Capital spending rules require headquarters management to approve any capital expenditure by a subunit that exceeds a certain amount. A budget allows headquarters to specify the amount a subunit can spend in a given year, and capital spending rules give headquarters additional control over how the money is spent. Headquarters can be expected to deny approval for capital spending requests that are at variance with overall firm objectives and to approve those that are congruent with firm objectives.

Output Controls

Output control involves setting goals for subunits to achieve and expressing those goals in terms of relatively objective performance metrics such as profitability, productivity, growth, market share, and quality. The performance of subunit managers is then judged by their ability to achieve the goals.[28] If goals are met or exceeded, subunit managers will be rewarded. If goals are not met, top management will normally intervene to find out why and take appropriate corrective action. Thus, control is achieved by comparing actual performance against targets and intervening selectively to take corrective action. Subunits' goals depend on their role in the firm. Self-contained product divisions or national subsidiaries are typically given goals for profitability, sales growth, and market share. Functions are more likely to be given goals related to their particular activity. Thus, R&D will be given product development goals, production will be given productivity and quality goals, marketing will be given market share goals, and so on.

As with budgets, goals are normally established through negotiation between subunits and headquarters. Generally, headquarters tries to set goals that are challenging but realistic, so subunit managers are forced to look for ways to improve their operations but are not so pressured that they will resort to dysfunctional activities to do so (such as short-run profit maximization). Output controls foster a system of "management by exception," in that so long as subunits meet their goals, they are left alone. If a subunit fails to attain its goals, however, headquarters managers are likely to ask some tough questions. If they don't get satisfactory answers, they are likely to intervene proactively in a subunit, replacing top management and looking for ways to improve efficiency.

Cultural Controls

Cultural control exists when employees "buy into" the norms and value systems of the firm. When this occurs, employees tend to control their own behavior, which reduces the need for direct supervision. In a firm with a strong culture, self-control can reduce the need for other control systems. We discuss organizational culture later, but as an example, McDonald's actively promotes organizational norms and values, referring to its franchisees and suppliers as partners and emphasizing its long-term commitment to them. This commitment is not just a public relations exercise; it is backed by actions, including a willingness to help suppliers and franchisees improve their operations by providing capital and/or management assistance when needed. In response, McDonald's franchisees and suppliers are integrated into the firm's culture and thus become committed to helping McDonald's succeed. One result is that McDonald's can devote less time than would otherwise be necessary to controlling its franchisees and suppliers.

INCENTIVE SYSTEMS

Incentives refer to the devices used to reward appropriate employee behavior. Many employees receive incentives in the form of annual bonus pay. Incentives are usually closely tied to the performance metrics used for output controls. For example, setting targets linked to profitability might be used to measure the performance of a subunit, such as a global product division. To create positive incentives for employees to work hard to exceed those targets, they may be given a share of any profits above those targeted. If a subunit has set a goal of attaining a 15 percent return on investment and it actually attains a 20 percent return, unit employees may be given a share in the profits generated in excess of the 15 percent target in the form of bonus pay.

We return to the topic of incentive systems in Chapter 19 when we discuss human resource strategy in the multinational firm. For now, however, several important points can be made. First, the type of incentive used often varies depending on the employees and their tasks. Incentives for employees working on the factory floor may be very different from the incentives used for senior managers. The incentives used must be matched to the type of work being performed. The employees on the factory floor of a manufacturing plant may be broken into teams of 20 to 30 individuals, and they may have their bonus pay tied to the ability of their team to hit or exceed targets for output and product quality. In contrast, the senior managers of the plant may be rewarded according to metrics linked to the output of the entire operation. The basic principle is to make sure the incentive scheme for an individual employee is linked to an output target that he or she has some control over and can influence. The individual employees on the factory floor may not be able to exercise much influence over the performance of the entire operation, but they can influence the performance of their team, so incentive pay is tied to output at this level.

Second, the successful execution of strategy in the multinational firm often requires significant cooperation between managers in different subunits. For example, as noted earlier, some multinational firms operate with matrix structures where a country subsidiary might be responsible for marketing and sales in a nation, while a global product division might be responsible for manufacturing and product development. The managers of these different units need to cooperate closely with each other if the firm is to be successful. One way of encouraging the managers to cooperate is to link incentives to performance at a higher level in the organization. Thus, the senior managers of the country subsidiaries and global product divisions might be rewarded according to the profitability of the entire firm. The thinking here is that boosting the profitability of the entire firm requires managers in the country subsidiaries and product divisions to cooperate with each other on strategy implementation, and linking incentive systems to the next level up in the hierarchy encourages this. Most firms use a formula for incentives that links a portion of incentive pay to the performance of the subunit in which a manager or employee works and a portion to the performance of the entire firm, or some other higher-level organizational unit. The goal is to encourage employees to improve the efficiency of their unit and to cooperate with other units in the organization.

Third, the incentive systems used within a multinational enterprise often have to be adjusted to account for national differences in institutions and culture. Incentive systems that work in the United States might not work, or even be allowed, in other countries. For example, Lincoln Electric, a leader in the manufacture of arc welding equipment, has used an incentive system for its employees based on piecework rates in its American factories (under a piecework system, employees are paid according to the amount they produce). While this system has worked very well in the United States, Lincoln has found that the system is difficult to introduce in other countries. In some countries, such as Germany, piecework systems are illegal, while in others the prevailing national culture is antagonistic to a system where performance is so closely tied to individual effort.

Finally, it is important for managers to recognize that incentive systems can have unintended consequences. Managers need to carefully think through exactly what behavior certain incentives encourage. For example, if employees in a factory are rewarded solely on the basis of how many units of output they produce, with no attention paid to the quality of that output, they may produce as many units as possible to boost their incentive pay, but the quality of those units may be poor.

CONTROL SYSTEMS AND INCENTIVES

The key to understanding the relationship among international strategy, control systems, and incentive systems is the concept of performance ambiguity.

Performance Ambiguity

Performance ambiguity exists when the causes of a subunit's poor performance are not clear.[29] This is not uncommon when a subunit's performance is partly dependent on the performance of other subunits—that is, when there is a high degree of interdependence among subunits within the organization. Consider the case of a French subsidiary of a U.S. firm that depends on another subsidiary, a manufacturer based in Italy, for the products it sells. The French subsidiary is failing to achieve its sales goals, and the U.S. management asks the managers to explain. They reply that they are receiving poor-quality goods from the Italian subsidiary. The U.S. management asks the managers of the Italian operation what the problem is. They reply that their product quality is excellent—the best in the industry, in fact—and that the French simply don't know how to sell a good product. Who is right, the French or the Italians? Without more information, top management cannot tell. Because they are dependent on the Italians for their product, the French have an alibi for poor performance. U.S. management needs to have more information to determine who is correct. Collecting this information is expensive and time-consuming and will divert attention away from other issues. In other words, performance ambiguity raises the costs of control.

Consider how different things would be if the French operation were self-contained, with its own manufacturing, marketing, and R&D facilities. The French operation would lack a convenient alibi for its poor performance; the French managers would stand or fall on their own merits. They could not blame the Italians for their poor sales. The level of performance ambiguity, therefore, is a function of the interdependence of subunits in an organization.

Strategy, Interdependence, and Ambiguity

Now let us consider the relationships among strategy, interdependence, and performance ambiguity. In firms pursuing a localization strategy, each national operation is a stand-alone entity and can be judged on its own merits. The level of performance ambiguity is low. In an international firm, the level of interdependence is somewhat higher. Integration is required to facilitate the transfer of core competencies and skills. Since the success of a foreign operation is partly dependent on the quality of the competency transferred from the home country, performance ambiguity can exist.

In firms pursuing a global standardization strategy, the situation is still more complex. Recall that in a pure global firm the pursuit of location and experience curve economies leads to the development of a global web of value creation activities. Many of the activities in a global firm are interdependent. A French subsidiary's ability to sell a product does depend on how well other operations in other countries perform their value creation activities. Thus, the levels of interdependence and performance ambiguity are high in global companies.

The level of performance ambiguity is highest of all in transnational firms. Transnational firms suffer from the same performance ambiguity problems that global firms do. In addition, because they emphasize the multi-directional transfer of core competencies, they also suffer from the problems characteristic of firms pursuing an international strategy. The extremely high level of integration within transnational firms implies a high degree of joint decision making, and the resulting interdependencies create plenty of alibis for poor performance. There is lots of room for finger-pointing in transnational firms.

Implications for Control and Incentives

The arguments of the previous section, along with the implications for the costs of control, are summarized in Table 14.1. The costs of control can be defined as the amount of time top management must devote to monitoring and evaluating subunits' performance. This is greater when the amount of performance ambiguity is greater. When performance ambiguity is low, management can use output controls and a system of management by exception;

Strategy	Interdependence	Performance Ambiguity	Costs of Control
Localization	Low	Low	Low
International	Moderate	Moderate	Moderate
Global	High	High	High
Transnational	Very high	Very high	Very high

TABLE 14.1

Interdependence, Performance Ambiguity, and the Costs of Control for the Four International Business Strategies when it is high, managers have no such luxury. Output controls do not provide totally unambiguous signals of a subunit's efficiency when the performance of that subunit is dependent on the performance of another subunit within the organization. Thus, management must devote time to resolving the problems that arise from performance ambiguity, with a corresponding rise in the costs of control.

Table 14.1 reveals a paradox. We saw in Chapter 13 that a transnational strategy is desirable because it gives a firm more ways to profit from international expansion than do localization, international, and global standardization strategies. But now we see that due to the high level of interdependence, the costs of controlling transnational firms are higher than the costs of controlling firms that pursue other strategies. Unless there is some way of reducing these costs, the higher profitability associated with a transnational strategy could be canceled out by the higher costs of control. The same point, although to a lesser extent, can be made with regard to firms pursuing a global standardization strategy. Although firms pursuing a global standardization strategy can reap the cost benefits of location and experience curve economies, they must cope with a higher level of performance ambiguity, and this raises the costs of control (in comparison with firms pursuing an international or localization strategy).

This is where control systems and incentives come in. When we survey the systems that corporations use to control their subunits, we find that irrespective of their strategy, multinational firms all use output and bureaucratic controls. However, in firms pursuing either global or transnational strategies, the usefulness of output controls is limited by substantial performance ambiguities. As a result, these firms place greater emphasis on cultural controls. Cultural control—by encouraging managers to want to assume the organization's norms and value systems—gives managers of interdependent subunits an incentive to look for ways to work out problems that arise between them. The result is a reduction in finger-pointing and, accordingly, in the costs of control. The development of cultural controls may be a precondition for the successful pursuit of a transnational strategy and perhaps of a global strategy as well.[30] As for incentives, the material discussed earlier suggests that the conflict between different subunits can be reduced and the potential for cooperation enhanced if incentive systems are tied in some way to a higher level in the hierarchy. When performance ambiguity makes it difficult to judge the performance of subunits as stand-alone entities, linking the incentive pay of senior managers to the entity to which both subunits belong can reduce the resulting problems.

Processes

Processes, defined as the manner in which decisions are made and work is performed within the organization, can be found at many different levels within an organization.[31] There are processes for formulating strategy, processes for allocating resources, processes for evaluating new-product ideas, processes for handling customer inquiries and complaints, processes for improving product quality, processes for evaluating employee performance, and so on. Often, the core competencies or valuable skills of a firm are embedded in its processes. Efficient and effective processes can lower the costs of value creation and add additional value to a product. For example, the global success of many Japanese manufacturing enterprises is based in part on their processes for improving product quality and operating efficiency. Today, the competitive success of 3M, for example, can in part be attributed to a number of processes that have been widely promoted within the company. These include the company's Six Sigma process for quality improvement.

An organization's processes can be summarized by means of a flowchart, which illustrates the various steps and decision points involved in performing work. Many processes cut across functions, or divisions, and require cooperation between individuals in different subunits. For example, product development processes require employees from R&D,

manufacturing, and marketing to work together in a cooperative manner to make sure new products are developed with market needs in mind and designed in such a way that they can be manufactured at a low cost. Because they cut across organizational boundaries, performing processes effectively often requires the establishment of formal integrating mechanisms and incentives for cross-unit cooperation.

A detailed consideration of the nature of processes and strategies for process improvement and reengineering is beyond the scope of this text. However, it is important to make two basic remarks about managing processes, particularly in the context of international business.[32] The first is that in a multinational enterprise, many processes cut not only across organizational boundaries, embracing several different subunits, but also across national boundaries. Designing a new product may require the cooperation of R&D personnel located in California; production people located in Taiwan; and marketing located in Europe, America, and Asia. The chances of pulling this off are greatly enhanced if the processes are embedded in an organizational culture that promotes cooperation among individuals from different subunits and nations; if the incentive systems of the organization explicitly reward such cooperation; and if formal and informal integrating mechanisms are used to facilitate coordination among subunits.

Second, it is particularly important for a multinational enterprise to recognize that valuable new processes that might lead to a competitive advantage can be developed anywhere within the organization's global network of operations.[33] New processes may be developed by a local operating subsidiary in response to conditions pertaining to its market. Those processes might then have value to other parts of the multinational enterprise. The ability to create valuable processes matters, but it is also important to leverage those processes. This requires both formal and informal integrating mechanisms such as knowledge networks.

TEST PREP

Use SmartBook to help retain what you have learned. Access your instructor's Connect course to check out SmartBook or go to **learnsmartadvantage.com** for help.

Organizational Culture

Chapter 4 applied the concept of culture to countries. Culture, however, is also a social construct ascribed to societies, including organizations.[34] Thus, we can speak of organizational culture and subcultures. The basic definition of culture remains the same, whether we are applying it to a macro (large) society such as a country, or subcultures within countries, or a micro (small) society such as an organization or one of its subunits. *Culture* refers to a system of values and norms that are shared among people. *Values* are abstract ideas about what a group believes to be good, right, and desirable. *Norms* mean the social rules and guidelines that prescribe appropriate behavior in particular situations.

Values and norms express themselves as the behavior patterns or style of an organization that new employees are automatically encouraged to follow by their fellow employees. Although an organization's culture is rarely static, it tends to change relatively slowly. Cultural changes often come from doing something or behaving a certain way over time. Seldom do we adopt a cultural change, and then behaviors ensue without having ever been done before. Instead, repeated behaviors lead to revised values and norms, which, in turn, emphasize the new cultural makeup (whether it be at the country or organizational level).

CREATING AND MAINTAINING ORGANIZATIONAL CULTURE

An organization's culture comes from several sources. First, there seems to be wide agreement that founders or important leaders can have a profound impact on an organization's culture, often imprinting their own values on the culture.[35] A famous example of a strong founder effect concerns the Japanese firm Matsushita. Konosuke Matsushita's almost Zen-like personal business philosophy was codified in the "Seven Spiritual Values" of Matsushita that all new employees still learn today. These values are (1) national service through industry, (2) fairness, (3) harmony and cooperation, (4) struggle for betterment, (5) courtesy and humility, (6) adjustment and assimilation, and (7) gratitude. A leader does not have to be the founder to have a profound influence on organizational culture. Jack Welch is widely credited with having changed the culture of GE when he first became CEO, primarily by emphasizing a counter-cultural set of values, such as risk taking, entrepreneurship, stewardship, and boundary-less behavior. It is more difficult for a leader, however forceful, to change an established organizational culture than it is to create one from scratch in a new venture. A blank slate on culture allows for the establishment of desired values and norms, while an existing culture and any change desired often results from implemented behaviors over time.

Another important influence on organizational culture is the broader social culture of the nation where the firm was founded and/or has significant operations. In the United States, for example, the competitive ethic of individualism looms large, and there is enormous social stress on producing winners. Many American firms find ways of rewarding and motivating individuals so that they see themselves as winners.[36] The values of American firms often reflect the values of American culture. Similarly, the cooperative values found in many Japanese firms have been argued to reflect the values of traditional Japanese society, with its emphasis on group cooperation, reciprocal obligations, and harmony.[37] Thus, although it may be a generalization, there may be something to the argument that organizational culture is influenced by national culture. This influence is particularly tricky in countries that are by design going through significant culture change (e.g., many eastern European countries and some African and Latin American countries). For example, China is more and more moving toward a market-based economy, while still having significant influence from the communist system; such an economy can create inconsistent cultural makeups for companies, especially foreign companies trying to operate in China.

A third influence on organizational culture is the history of the enterprise, which over time may come to shape the values of the organization. In the language of historians, organizational culture is the path-dependent product of where the organization has been through time. For example, Koninklijke Philips Electronics NV, the Dutch multinational, long operated with a culture that placed a high value on the independence of national operating companies. This culture was shaped by the history of the company. During World War II, the Netherlands was occupied by the Germans. With the head office in occupied territories, power was devolved by default to various foreign operating companies, such as Philips' subsidiaries in the United States and United Kingdom. After the war ended, these subsidiaries continued to operate in a highly autonomous fashion. A belief that this was the right thing to do became a core value of the company.

Decisions that subsequently result in high performance tend to become institutionalized in the values of a firm. In the 1920s, 3M was primarily a manufacturer of sandpaper. Richard Drew, who was a young laboratory assistant at the time, came up with what he thought would be a great new product—a glue-covered strip of paper, which he called "sticky tape." Drew saw applications for the product in the automobile industry, where it could be used to mask parts of a vehicle during painting. He presented the idea to the company's president, William McKnight. An unimpressed McKnight suggested that Drew drop the research. Drew didn't; instead he developed the "sticky tape" and then went out and got endorsements from potential customers in the auto industry. Armed with this information, he approached McKnight again. A chastened McKnight reversed his position and gave Drew the go-ahead to start developing what was to become one of 3M's main product lines—sticky tape—a business it dominates to this day.[38] From then on, McKnight emphasized the importance of giving researchers at 3M free rein to explore their own ideas and experiment with product offerings. This soon became a core value at 3M and was enshrined in the company's famous "15 percent rule," which stated that researchers could

Some of the products produced by 3M's innovative culture.

spend 15 percent of the company time working on ideas of their own choosing. Today, new employees are often told the Drew story, which is used to illustrate the value of allowing individuals to explore their own ideas. The company also has a 3M Innovation Center to make sure that innovation is front and center in the company's culture.

Culture is maintained by a variety of mechanisms. These include (1) hiring and promotional practices of the organization, (2) reward strategies, (3) socialization processes, and (4) communication strategy. The goal is to recruit people whose values are consistent with those of the company. To further reinforce values, a company may promote individuals whose behavior is consistent with the core values of the organization. Merit review processes may also be linked to a company's values, which further reinforces cultural norms.

Socialization can be formal, such as training programs that educate employees in the core values of the organization. Informal socialization may be friendly advice from peers or bosses or may be implicit in the actions of peers and superiors toward new employees. As for communication strategy, many companies with strong cultures devote a lot of attention to framing their key values in corporate mission statements, communicating them often to employees, and using them to guide difficult decisions. Stories and symbols are often used to reinforce important values (e.g., the Drew and McKnight story at 3M).

ORGANIZATIONAL CULTURE AND PERFORMANCE

Management authors often talk about "strong cultures."[39] In a strong culture, almost all managers share a relatively consistent set of values and norms that have a clear impact on the way work is performed. New employees adopt these values very quickly, and employees who do not fit in with the core values tend to leave. In such a culture, a new executive is just as likely to be corrected by his subordinates as by his superiors if he violates the values and norms of the organizational culture. Firms with a strong culture are normally seen by outsiders as having a certain style or way of doing things. Lincoln Electric, featured in the accompanying Management Focus, is an example of a firm with a strong culture.

Strong does not necessarily mean good. A culture can be strong but bad. The culture of the Nazi Party in Germany was certainly strong, but it was most definitely not good. Nor does it follow that a strong culture leads to high performance. One study found that, some time ago, General Motors had a "strong culture," but it was a strong culture that discouraged lower-level employees from demonstrating initiative and taking risks, which the authors argued was dysfunctional and led to low performance at GM.[40] Also, a strong culture might be beneficial at one point, leading to high performance, but inappropriate at another time. The appropriateness of the culture depends on the context. When IBM was performing very well some years ago, several management authors sang the praises of its strong culture, which among other things placed a high value on consensus-based decision making.[41] These authors argued that such a decision-making process was appropriate given the substantial financial investments that IBM routinely made in new technology. However, in the fast-moving computer industry, this process eventually turned out to be a weakness in the evolution of IBM. Consensus-based decision making was slow, bureaucratic, and not particularly conducive to corporate risk taking. While this was fine early on, IBM needed rapid decision making and entrepreneurial risk taking to keep up with the competition, but its culture discouraged such behavior.

One study concluded that firms that exhibited high performance over a prolonged period tended to have strong but adaptive cultures. In an adaptive culture, most managers care deeply about and value customers, stockholders, and employees. They also strongly value people and processes that create useful change in a firm.[42] While this is interesting, it does reduce the issue to a very high level of abstraction; after all, what company would say that it doesn't care deeply about customers, stockholders, and employees? A somewhat different perspective is to argue that the culture of the firm must match the rest of the architecture of the organization, the firm's strategy, and the demands of the competitive environment for superior performance to be attained. All these elements must be consistent with each other.

Lincoln Electric provides another useful example (see the Management Focus). Lincoln competes in a business that is very competitive, where cost minimization is a key source of

Lincoln Electric and Culture

Lincoln Electric is one of the leading global manufacturers of welding products, arc welding equipment, welding consumables, plasma and oxy-fuel cutting equipment, and robotic welding systems. Lincoln's success has been based on extremely high levels of employee productivity. The company attributes its productivity to a strong organizational culture and an incentive scheme based on piecework. Lincoln's organizational culture dates back to James Lincoln, who in 1907 joined the company that his brother had established a few years earlier. Lincoln had a strong respect for the ability of the individual and believed that, correctly motivated, ordinary people could achieve extraordinary performance. He emphasized that Lincoln should be a meritocracy where people were rewarded for their individual effort. Strongly egalitarian, Lincoln removed barriers to communication between "workers" and "managers," practicing an open-door policy. He made sure that all who worked for the company were treated equally; for example, everyone ate in the same cafeteria, there were no reserved parking places for "managers," and so on. Lincoln also believed that any gains in productivity should be shared with consumers in the form of lower prices, with employees in the form of higher pay, and with shareholders in the form of higher dividends.

The organizational culture that grew out of James Lincoln's beliefs was reinforced by the company's incentive system. Production workers receive no base salary but are paid according to the number of pieces they produce. The piecework rates at the company enable an employee working at a normal pace to earn an income equivalent to the average wage for manufacturing workers in the area where a factory is based. Workers have responsibility for the quality of their output and must repair any defects spotted by quality inspectors before the pieces are included in the piecework calculation. Since 1934, production workers have been awarded a semiannual bonus based on merit ratings. These ratings are based on objective criteria (such as an employee's level and quality of output) and subjective criteria (such as an employee's attitudes toward cooperation and his or her dependability). These systems give Lincoln's employees an incentive to work hard and to generate innovations that boost productivity, for doing so influences their level of pay. Lincoln's factory workers have been able to earn a base pay that often exceeds the average manufacturing wage in the area by more than 50 percent and receive a bonus on top of this that in good years could double their base pay. Despite high employee compensation, the workers are so productive that Lincoln has a lower cost structure than its competitors.

While this organizational culture and set of incentives works well in the United States, where it is compatible with the individualistic culture of the country, it did not translate easily into foreign operations. Early on, Lincoln expanded aggressively into Europe and Latin America, acquiring a number of local arc welding manufacturers. Lincoln left local managers in place, believing that they knew local conditions better than Americans. However, the local managers had little working knowledge of Lincoln's strong organizational culture and were unable or unwilling to impose that culture on their units, which had their own long-established organizational cultures. Nevertheless, Lincoln told local managers to introduce its incentive systems in acquired companies. They frequently ran into legal and cultural roadblocks.

In many countries, piecework is viewed as an exploitive compensation system that forces employees to work ever harder. In Germany, where Lincoln made an acquisition, it is illegal. In Brazil, a bonus paid for more than two years becomes a legal entitlement! In many other countries, both managers and workers were opposed to the idea of piecework. Lincoln found that many European workers valued extra leisure more highly than extra income and were not prepared to work as hard as their American counterparts. Many of the acquired companies were also unionized, and the local unions vigorously opposed the introduction of piecework. As a result, Lincoln was not able to replicate the high level of employee productivity that it had achieved in the United States, and its expansion pulled down the performance of the entire company.

Sources: Jill Jusko, "Lincoln Electric CEO: Meeting the Skills Gap Challenge," *IndustryWeek*, October 9, 2014; J. O'Connell, "Lincoln Electric: Venturing Abroad," *Harvard Business School* Case No. 9-398-095, April 1998, www.lincolnelectric.com.

competitive advantage. Lincoln's culture and incentive systems both encourage employees to strive for high levels of productivity, which translates into the low costs that are critical for Lincoln's success. The Lincoln example also demonstrates another important point for international businesses. A culture that leads to high performance in the firm's home nation may not be easy to impose on foreign subsidiaries! Lincoln's culture has clearly helped the firm achieve superior performance in the U.S. market, but this same culture is very "American" in its form and difficult to implement in other countries. The managers and employees of several of Lincoln's European subsidiaries found the culture to be alien to their own values and were reluctant to adopt it. The result was that Lincoln found it very difficult to replicate in foreign markets the success it has had in the United States. Lincoln compounded the problem by acquiring established enterprises that already had their own organizational culture. Thus, in trying to impose its culture on foreign operating subsidiaries, Lincoln had to deal with two problems: how to change the established organizational culture of those units, and how to introduce an organizational culture whose key values might be alien to the values held by members of that society. These problems are not unique to Lincoln; many international businesses have to deal with exactly the same problems.

The solution Lincoln has adopted is to establish new subsidiaries, rather than acquiring and trying to transform an enterprise with its own culture. It is much easier to establish a set of values in a new enterprise than it is to change the values of an established enterprise. A second solution is to devote a lot of time and attention to transmitting the firm's organizational culture to its foreign operations. This was something Lincoln originally omitted. Other firms make this an important part of their strategy for internationalization.

The need for a common organizational culture that is the same across a multinational's global network of subsidiaries probably varies with the strategy of the firm. Shared norms and values can facilitate coordination and cooperation between individuals from different subunits.[43] A strong common culture may lead to goal congruence and can attenuate the problems that arise from interdependence, performance ambiguities, and conflict among managers from different subsidiaries. As noted earlier, a shared culture may help informal integrating mechanisms such as knowledge networks to operate more effectively. As such, a common culture may be of greater value in a multinational that is pursuing a strategy that requires cooperation and coordination between globally dispersed subsidiaries. This suggests that it is more important to have a common culture in firms employing a transnational strategy than a localization strategy, with global and international strategies falling between these two extremes.

TEST PREP

Use SmartBook to help retain what you have learned. Access your instructor's Connect course to check out SmartBook or go to **learnsmartadvantage.com** for help.

Synthesis: Strategy and Architecture

Chapter 13 identified four basic strategies that multinational firms pursue: localization, international, global, and transnational. So far in this chapter, we have looked at several aspects of organizational architecture, and we have discussed the interrelationships between these dimensions and strategies. Now it is time to synthesize this material.

LO14-3

Explain how the organizational architecture can be matched to global strategy to improve performance.

LOCALIZATION STRATEGY

Firms pursuing a localization strategy focus on local responsiveness. Table 14.2 shows that such firms tend to operate with worldwide area structures, within which operating decisions are decentralized to functionally self-contained country subsidiaries. The need for coordination between subunits (areas and country subsidiaries) is low. This suggests that firms pursuing a localization strategy do not have a high need for integrating mechanisms, either formal or informal, to knit together different national operations. The lack of interdependence implies that the level of performance ambiguity in such enterprises is low, as (by extension) are the costs of control. Thus, headquarters can manage foreign operations

Structure and Controls	Strategy			
	Localization	International	Global Standardization	Transnational
Vertical differentiation	Decentralized	Core competency; more centralized, rest decentralized	Some centralization	Mixed centralization and decentralization
Horizontal differentiation	Worldwide area structure	Worldwide product divisions	Worldwide product divisions	Informal matrix
Need for coordination	Low	Moderate	High	Very high
Integrating mechanisms	None	Few	Many	Very many
Performance ambiguity	Low	Moderate	High	Very high
Need for cultural controls	Low	Moderate	High	Very high

TABLE 14.2

A Synthesis of Strategy, Structure, and Control Systems

by relying primarily on output and bureaucratic controls and a policy of management by exception. Incentives can be linked to performance metrics at the level of country subsidiaries. Since the need for integration and coordination is low, the need for common processes and organizational culture is also quite low. Were it not for the fact that these firms are unable to profit from the realization of location and experience curve economies, or from the transfer of core competencies, their organizational simplicity would make this an attractive strategy.

INTERNATIONAL STRATEGY

Firms pursuing an international strategy attempt to create value by transferring core competencies from home to foreign subsidiaries. If they are diverse, as most of them are, these firms operate with a worldwide product division structure. Headquarters normally maintains centralized control over the source of the firm's core competency, which is most typically found in the R&D and/or marketing functions of the firm. All other operating decisions are decentralized within the firm to subsidiary operations in each country (which in diverse firms report to worldwide product divisions).

The need for coordination is moderate in such firms, reflecting the need to transfer core competencies. Thus, although such firms operate with some integrating mechanisms, they are not that extensive. The relatively low level of interdependence that results translates into a relatively low level of performance ambiguity. These firms can generally get by with output and bureaucratic controls and with incentives that are focused on performance metrics at the level of country subsidiaries. The need for a common organizational culture and common processes is not that great. An important exception to this is when the core skills or competencies of the firm are embedded in processes and culture, in which case the firm needs to pay close attention to transferring those processes and associated culture from the corporate center to country subsidiaries. Overall, although the organization required for an international strategy is more complex than that of firms pursuing a localization strategy, the increase in the level of complexity is not that great.

GLOBAL STANDARDIZATION STRATEGY

Firms pursuing a global standardization strategy focus on the realization of location and experience curve economies. If they are diversified, as many of them are, these firms operate with a worldwide product division structure. To coordinate the firm's globally dispersed web of value creation activities, headquarters typically maintains ultimate control over most operating decisions. In general, such firms are more centralized than enterprises pursuing a localization or international strategy. Reflecting the need for coordination of the various stages of the firms' globally dispersed value chains, the need for integration in these firms also is high. Thus, these firms tend to operate with an array of formal and informal integrating mechanisms. The resulting interdependencies can lead to significant performance ambiguities. As a result, in addition to output and bureaucratic controls, firms pursuing a global standardization strategy tend to stress the need to build a strong organizational culture that can facilitate coordination and cooperation. They also tend to use incentive systems that are linked to performance metrics at the corporate level, giving the managers of different operations a strong incentive to cooperate with each other to increase the performance of the entire corporation. On average, the organization of such firms is more complex than that of firms pursuing a localization or international strategy.

TRANSNATIONAL STRATEGY

Firms pursuing a transnational strategy focus on the simultaneous attainment of location and experience curve economies, local responsiveness, and global learning (the multidirectional transfer of core competencies or skills). These firms may operate with matrix-type structures in which both product divisions and geographic areas have significant influence. The need to coordinate a globally dispersed value chain and to transfer core competencies creates pressures for centralizing some operating decisions (particularly production and R&D). At the same time, the need to be locally responsive creates pressures for decentralizing other operating decisions to national operations (particularly marketing). Consequently, these firms tend to mix relatively high degrees of centralization for some operating decisions with relatively high degrees of decentralization for other operating decisions.

The need for coordination is high in transnational firms. This is reflected in the use of an array of formal and informal integrating mechanisms, including formal matrix structures and informal management networks. The high level of interdependence of subunits implied by such integration can result in significant performance ambiguities, which raise the costs of control. To reduce these, in addition to output and bureaucratic controls, firms pursuing a transnational strategy need to cultivate a strong culture and to establish incentives that promote cooperation between subunits.

ENVIRONMENT, STRATEGY, ARCHITECTURE, AND PERFORMANCE

Underlying the scheme outlined in Table 14.2 is the notion that a "fit" between strategy and architecture is necessary for a firm to achieve high performance. For a firm to succeed, two conditions must be fulfilled. First, the firm's strategy must be consistent with the environment in which the firm operates. We discussed this issue in Chapter 13 and noted that in some industries a global standardization strategy is most viable, in others an international or transnational strategy may be most viable, and in still others, a localization strategy may be most viable. Second, the firm's organizational architecture must be consistent with its strategy.

If the strategy does not fit the environment, the firm is likely to experience significant performance problems. If the architecture does not fit the strategy, the firm is also likely to experience performance problems. Therefore, to survive, a firm must strive to achieve a fit of its environment, its strategy, and its organizational architecture. For example, consider Koninklijke Philips NV. For reasons rooted in the history of the firm, Philips operated until recently with an organization typical of an enterprise pursuing localization; operating decisions were decentralized to largely autonomous foreign subsidiaries. Historically, electronics markets were segmented from each other by high trade barriers, so an organization consistent with a localization strategy made sense. However, the industry in which Philips competed was revolutionized by declining trade barriers, technological change, and the emergence of low-cost Japanese competitors that utilized a global strategy.

To survive, Philips needed to adopt a global standardization strategy itself. The firm recognized this and tried to adopt a global posture, but it did little to change its organizational architecture. The firm nominally adopted a matrix structure based on worldwide product divisions and national areas. In reality, however, the national areas continued to dominate the organization, and the product divisions had little more than an advisory role. As a result, Philips' architecture did not fit the strategy, and by the 1990s, Philips was losing money. It was only after four years of wrenching change and large losses that Philips was finally able to tilt the balance of power in its matrix toward the product divisions. By the 2000s, the fruits of this effort to realign the company's strategy and architecture with the demands of its operating environment finally showed up in improved financial performance.[44]

LO14-4

Discuss what is required for an international business to change its organizational architecture so that it better matches its global strategy.

Organizational Change

Multinational firms periodically have to alter their architecture so that it conforms to the changes in the environment in which they are competing and the strategy they are pursuing. To be profitable, Philips had to alter its strategy and architecture so that both matched the demands of the competitive environment in the electronics industry, which had shifted from localization toward a global industry. While a detailed consideration of organizational change is beyond the scope of this book, a few comments are warranted regarding the sources of organization inertia and the strategies and tactics for implementing organizational change.

ORGANIZATIONAL INERTIA

Organizations are difficult to change. Within most organizations are strong inertia forces. These forces come from a number of sources. One source of inertia is the existing distribution of power and influence within an organization.[45] The power and influence enjoyed by individual managers are, in part, a function of their role in the organizational hierarchy, as defined by structural position. By definition, most substantive changes in an organization require a change in structure and, by extension, a change in the distribution of power and influence within the organization. Some individuals will see their power and influence increase as a result of the organizational change, and some will see the converse. For example, Philips decided to increase the roles and responsibilities of its global product divisions and decrease the roles and responsibilities of its foreign subsidiary companies to combat organizational inertia. This meant the managers running the global product divisions saw their power and influence increase, while the managers running the foreign subsidiary companies saw their power and influence decline. As might be expected, some managers of foreign subsidiary companies did not like this change and resisted it, which slowed the pace of change. Those whose power and influence are reduced as a consequence of organizational change can be expected to resist it, primarily by arguing that the change might not work. To the extent that they are successful, this constitutes a source of organizational inertia that might slow or stop change.

Another source of organizational inertia is the existing culture, as expressed in norms and value systems. Value systems reflect deeply held beliefs, and as such, they can be very hard to change. If the formal and informal socialization mechanisms within an organization have been emphasizing a consistent set of values for a prolonged period, and if hiring, promotion, and incentive systems have all reinforced these values, then suddenly announcing that those values are no longer appropriate and need to be changed can produce resistance and dissonance among employees. For example, Philips historically placed a very high value on local autonomy. The changes the company decided to make implied a reduction in the autonomy enjoyed by foreign subsidiaries, which was counter to the established values of the company and thus resisted.

Organizational inertia might also derive from senior managers' preconceptions about the appropriate business model or paradigm. When a given paradigm has worked well in the past, managers might have trouble accepting that it is no longer appropriate. At Philips, granting considerable autonomy to foreign subsidiaries had worked very well in the past, allowing local managers to tailor product and business strategy to the conditions prevailing in a given country. Since this paradigm had worked so well, it was difficult for many managers to understand why it no longer applied. Consequently, they had difficulty accepting a new business model and tended to fall back on their established paradigm and ways of doing things. This change required managers to let go of long-held assumptions about what worked and what didn't work, which was something many of them couldn't do.

Institutional constraints might also act as a source of inertia. National regulations, including local content rules and policies pertaining to layoffs, might make it difficult for a multinational to alter its global value chain. A multinational might wish to take control for manufacturing away from local subsidiaries, transfer that control to global product divisions, and consolidate manufacturing at a few choice locations. However, if local content rules (see Chapter 7) require some degree of local production and if regulations regarding layoffs make it difficult or expensive for a multinational to close operations in a country, a multinational may find that these constraints make it very difficult to adopt the most effective strategy and architecture.

IMPLEMENTING ORGANIZATIONAL CHANGE

Although all organizations suffer from inertia, the complexity and global spread of many multinationals might make it particularly difficult for them to change their strategy and architecture to match new organizational realities. Yet at the same time, the trend toward globalization in many industries has made it more critical than ever that many multinationals do just that. In industry after industry, declining barriers to cross-border trade and investment have led to a change in the nature of the competitive environment, although some of those declining barriers have been tested in recent years with more and more countries adopting nationalistic measures and mindsets.

Even with barriers in place, cost pressures have increased, requiring multinationals to respond by streamlining their operations to realize economic benefits associated with location and experience curve economies and with the transfer of competencies and skills within the organization. Local responsiveness remains an important source of differentiation as well. To survive in this emerging competitive environment, multinationals must change not only their strategy but also their architecture so that it matches strategy in discriminating ways. The basic principles for successful organizational change can be summarized as follows: (1) unfreeze the organization through shock therapy, (2) move the organization to a new state through proactive change in the architecture, and (3) refreeze the organization in its new state.

Unfreezing the Organization

Because of inertia forces, incremental change is often no change. Those whose power is threatened by change can too easily resist incremental change. This leads to the big bang theory of change, which maintains that effective change requires taking bold action early to "unfreeze" the established culture of an organization and to change the distribution of power and influence. Shock therapy to unfreeze the organization might include the closure of plants deemed uneconomic or the announcement of a dramatic structural reorganization. It is also important to realize that change will not occur unless senior managers are committed to it. Senior managers must clearly articulate the need for change so

Jack Welch, legendary former chairman and chief executive officer of General Electric Corporation, attending a press conference in New York.

Erik Freeland/Corbis Saba/Getty Images

employees understand both why it is being pursued and the benefits that will flow from successful change. Senior managers must also practice what they preach and take the necessary bold steps. If employees see senior managers preaching the need for change but not changing their own behavior or making substantive changes in the organization, they will soon lose faith in the change effort, which then will flounder.

Moving to the New State

Once an organization has been unfrozen, it must be moved to its new state. Movement requires taking action—closing operations; reorganizing the structure; reassigning responsibilities; changing control, incentive, and reward systems; redesigning processes; and letting people go who are seen as an impediment to change. In other words, movement requires a substantial change in the form of a multinational's organizational architecture so that it matches the desired new strategic posture. For movement to be successful, it must be done with sufficient speed. Involving employees in the change effort is an excellent way to get them to appreciate and buy into the needs for change and to help with rapid movement. For example, a firm might delegate substantial responsibility for designing operating processes to lower-level employees. If enough of their recommendations are then acted on, the employees will see the consequences of their efforts and consequently buy into the notion that change is really occurring.

Refreezing the Organization

Refreezing the organization takes longer. It may require that a new culture be established while the old one is being dismantled. Thus, refreezing requires that employees be socialized into the new way of doing things. Companies will often use management education programs to achieve this. At General Electric, where longtime CEO Jack Welch instituted a major change in the culture of the company, management education programs were used as a proactive tool to communicate new values to organization members. On their own, however, management education programs are not enough. Hiring policies must be changed to reflect the new realities, with an emphasis on hiring individuals whose own values are consistent with that of the new culture the firm is trying to build. Similarly, control and incentive systems must be consistent with the new realities of the organization, or change will never take. Senior management must recognize that changing culture takes a long time. Any letup in the pressure to change may allow the old culture to reemerge as employees fall back into familiar ways of doing things. The communication task facing senior managers, therefore, is a long-term endeavor that requires managers to be relentless and persistent in their pursuit of change. One striking feature of Jack Welch's two-decade tenure at GE, for example, is that he never stopped pushing his change agenda. It was a consistent theme of his tenure. He was always thinking up new programs and initiatives to keep pushing the culture of the organization along the desired trajectory.

TEST PREP

Use SmartBook to help retain what you have learned. Access your instructor's Connect course to check out SmartBook or go to learnsmartadvantage.com for help.

Key Terms

sharing economy, p. 404
organizational architecture, p. 404
organizational structure, p. 405
control systems, p. 405
incentives, p. 406
processes, p. 406
organizational culture, p. 406
people, p. 406

vertical differentiation, p. 406
horizontal differentiation, p. 406
integrating mechanisms, p. 406
international division, p. 410
worldwide area structure, p. 411
worldwide product division
    structure, p. 412
global matrix structure, p. 413

knowledge network, p. 418
personal control, p. 420
bureaucratic control, p. 420
output controls, p. 421
cultural controls, p. 421
performance ambiguity, p. 422

SUMMARY

This chapter identified the organizational architecture that can be used by multinational enterprises to manage and direct their global operations. A central theme of the chapter was that different strategies require different architectures; strategy is implemented through architecture. To succeed, a firm must match its architecture to its strategy in discriminating ways. Firms whose architecture does not fit their strategic requirements will experience performance problems. It is also necessary for the different components of architecture to be consistent with each other. The chapter made the following points:

1. Organizational architecture refers to the totality of a firm's organization, including formal organizational structure, control systems and incentives, processes, organizational culture, and people.

2. Superior enterprise profitability requires three conditions to be fulfilled: the different elements of a firm's organizational architecture must be internally consistent, the organizational architecture must fit the strategy of the firm, and the strategy and architecture of the firm must be consistent with competitive conditions prevailing in the firm's markets.

3. Organizational structure means three things: the formal division of the organization into subunits (horizontal differentiation), the location of decision-making responsibilities within that structure (vertical differentiation), and the establishment of integrating mechanisms.

4. Control systems are the metrics used to measure the performance of subunits and make judgments about how well managers are running those subunits.

5. Incentives refer to the devices used to reward appropriate employee behavior. Many employees receive incentives in the form of annual bonus pay. Incentives are usually closely tied to the performance metrics used for output controls.

6. Processes refer to the manner in which decisions are made and work is performed within the organization. Processes can be found at many different levels within an organization. The core competencies or valuable skills of a firm are often embedded in its processes. Efficient and effective processes can help lower the costs of value creation and add additional value to a product.

7. Organizational culture refers to a system of values and norms that is shared among employees. Values and norms express themselves as the behavior patterns or style of an organization that new employees are automatically encouraged to follow by their fellow employees.

8. Firms pursuing different strategies must adopt a different architecture to implement those strategies successfully. Firms pursuing localization, global, international, and transnational strategies all must adopt an organizational architecture that matches their strategy.

9. While all organizations suffer from inertia, the complexity and global spread of many multinationals might make it particularly difficult for them to change their strategy and architecture to match new organizational realities. At the same time, the trend toward globalization in many industries has made it more critical than ever that many multinationals do just that.

Critical Thinking and Discussion Questions

1. "The choice of strategy for a multinational firm must depend on a comparison of the benefits of that strategy (in terms of value creation) with the costs of implementing it (as defined by organizational architecture necessary for implementation). On this basis, it may be logical for some firms to pursue a localization strategy, others a global or international strategy, and still others a transnational strategy." Is this statement correct?

2. Discuss this statement: "An understanding of the causes and consequences of performance

ambiguity is central to the issue of organizational design in multinational firms."

3. Describe the organizational architecture that a transnational firm might adopt to reduce the costs of control.

4. What is the most appropriate organizational architecture for a firm that is competing in an industry where a global strategy is most appropriate?

5. If a firm is changing its strategy from an international to a transnational strategy, what are the

most important challenges it is likely to face in implementing this change? How can the firm overcome these challenges?

6. Reread the Management Focus on Dow Chemical; then answer the following questions:

    a. Why did Dow first adopt a matrix structure? What were the problems with this structure? Do you think these problems are typical of matrix structures?

    b. What drove the shift away from the matrix structure for companies such as Dow and ABB? Does Dow's structure now make sense given the nature of its businesses and the competitive environment it competes in?

7. Reread the Management Focus on Lincoln Electric; then answer the following questions:

    a. To what extent is the organizational culture of Lincoln Electric aligned with the firm's strategy?

    b. How was the culture at Lincoln Electric created and nurtured over time?

    c. Why did Lincoln Electric's culture and incentive systems work well in the United States? Why did it not take in other nations?

globalEDGE research task globaledge.msu.edu

Use the globalEDGE™ website (**globaledge.msu.edu**) to complete the following exercises:

1. *Fortune* conducts an annual survey and publishes the rankings of the *world's most admired companies*. Locate the most recent ranking available, and focus on the factors used to determine which companies are most admired. Prepare an executive summary of the strategic and organizational success factors for a company of your choice.

2. You work at a European-based pharmaceutical company that is planning to expand operations to other parts of the world. To design the structure of the organization as it expands internationally, management has requested additional information on the pharmaceutical sector worldwide. Use the *Industry Profiles* section on the globalEDGE site to prepare a risk assessment of the food and beverage industry that can help management gain a better understanding of the external environment in foreign markets.

CLOSING CASE

Walmart International

When Walmart started to expand internationally in the early 1990s, the company set up an international division to oversee the process. The international division was based in Bentonville, Arkansas, at the company headquarters. Today, the international division oversees operations for Walmart as the largest global retailer in the world, with 11,695 stores under 63 banners in 28 countries that collectively generate almost $500 billion in sales. Some 2.2 million Walmart employees ("associates") work in these international positions to serve more than 100 million customers weekly. Forty percent of the customers are outside the United States.

In terms of reporting structure, the international division is divided into three regions—Europe, Asia, and the Americas—with the CEO of each region reporting to the CEO of the international division, who in turn reports to the CEO of Walmart. Initially, the senior management of the international division exerted tight centralized control over merchandising strategy and operations in different countries. The reasoning was straightforward: Walmart's managers wanted to make sure that international stores copied the format for stores, merchandising, and operations that had served the company so well in the United States. They believed, naively perhaps, that centralized control over merchandising strategy and operations was the way to make sure this was the case.

By the late 1990s, with the international division approaching $20 billion in sales, Walmart's managers concluded this centralized approach was not serving them well. Country managers had to get permission from their superiors in Bentonville before changing strategy and operations, and this was slowing decision making. Centralization also produced information overload at the headquarters and led to some poor decisions. Walmart found that managers in Bentonville were not necessarily the best ones to decide on store layouts in Mexico, merchandising strategies in Argentina, or compensation policies in the United Kingdom. The need to adapt merchandising strategies and operations to local conditions was a strong argument for greater decentralization.

The pivotal event that led to a change in policy at Walmart was the company's acquisition of Britain's ASDA supermarket chain. The ASDA acquisition added a mature and successful $14 billion operation to Walmart's international division. The company realized that it was not appropriate for managers in Bentonville to be making all-important decisions for ASDA. Accordingly, the number of staff members located in Bentonville who were devoted to international operations was reduced by 50 percent. Country leaders were given greater responsibility, especially in the area of merchandising and operations. At that stage, Walmart was at the point where it was time to break away a little bit. Company representatives said that "You can't run the world from one place. The countries have to drive the business."

Although Walmart has now decentralized decisions within the international division, it is still struggling to find the right formula for managing global sourcing. Ideally, the company would like to centralize sourcing in Bentonville, so it can use its enormous purchasing power to bargain down the prices it pays suppliers. As a practical matter, however, this has not been easy to attain, given that the product mix in Walmart stores has to be tailored to conditions prevailing in the local market. Currently, significant responsibility for sourcing remains at the country and regional level. However, Walmart would like to have a better and more efficient global sourcing strategy, such that it can negotiate on a global basis with key suppliers and can simultaneously introduce new merchandise into its stores around the world.

As merchandising and operating decisions have been decentralized, the international division has increasingly taken on a new role—that of identifying best practices and transferring them between countries. For example, the division has developed a knowledge management system whereby stores in one country—let's say, Argentina—can quickly communicate pictures of items, sales data, and ideas on how to market and promote products to stores in another country—such as Japan.

The division is also starting to move personnel between stores in different countries as a way of facilitating the flow of best practices across national borders. The division is continuously trying to be innovative and move Walmart away from its U.S.-centric mentality by leveraging ideas implemented in foreign operations to improve the efficiency and effectiveness of Walmart's operations. This is stressed by Walmart International's president and CEO, Judith McKenna, who made the point (as did her predecessor David Cheesewright) that international business is a growth engine for Walmart, and to succeed, the company must focus on being in good businesses and running them well.

Sources: Abha Bhattaral, "Walmart Is Asking Employees to Deliver Packages on Their Way Home from Work," *The Washington Post*, June 1, 2017; M. Troy, "Wal-Mart Braces for International Growth with Personnel Moves," *DSN Retailing Today*, February 9, 2004, pp. 5–7; "Division Heads Let Numbers Do the Talking," *DSN Retailing Today*, June 21, 2004, pp. 26–28; "The Division That Defines the Future," *DSN Retailing Today*, June 2001, pp. 4–7.

Case Discussion Questions

1. As one of the largest companies in the world, Walmart has a reasonably limited international exposure—only 28 countries. What do you think Walmart can do to have a broader platform in more of the world's 195 countries?

2. Walmart operates via a number of brands around the world (e.g., Asda in the United Kingdom). Many companies are becoming more and more standardized in their operations and have adopted organizational structures to support such standardization. Can Walmart adopt a more effective global strategy and, if so, what type of organizational structure should the company create to best serve its operations in the global marketplace?

3. Walmart Stores Chief Operating Officer Judith McKenna was named president and CEO of the company's international unit effective February 1, 2018. The role is seen as a stepping stone to the top job at the world's largest retailer, with current CEO Doug McMillon and his predecessor Mike Duke having run the international unit previously. If international is such an important part of the company, what can Walmart do, should do, or must do to leverage its position as the largest retailer in the world?

Endnotes

1. This has long been a central theme of the strategic management literature. See, for example, C. W. L. Hill and R. E. Hoskisson, "Strategy and Structure in the Multiproduct Firm," *Academy of Management Review,* 1987, pp. 331–41. Also see J. Wolf and W. G. Egelhoff, "A Reexamination and Extension of International Strategy Structure Theory," *Strategic Management Journal* 23 (2002), pp. 181–90.

2. Eric M. Olson, Stanley F. Slater, and G. Tomas M. Hult, "The Performance Implications of Fit among Business Strategy, Marketing Organization Structure, and Strategic Behavior," *Journal of Marketing* 69 (July 2005), pp. 49–65.

3. D. Naidler, M. Gerstein, and R. Shaw, *Organization Architecture* (San Francisco: Jossey-Bass, 1992).

4. Tomas Hult, David Closs, and David Frayer, *Global Supply Chain Management: Leveraging Processes, Measurements, and Tools for Strategic Corporate Advantage* (New York: McGraw-Hill Professional, 2014).

5. G. Morgan, *Images of Organization* (Beverly Hills, CA: Sage, 1986).

6. "Unilever: A Networked Organization," *Harvard Business Review,* November–December 1996, p. 138.

7. The material in this section draws on John Child, *Organizations* (London: Harper & Row, 1984).

8. See, for example, Mark F. Peterson, Mikael Søndergaard, and Aycan Kara, "Traversing Cultural Boundaries in IB: The Complex Relationships between Explicit Country and Implicit Cultural Group Boundaries at Multiple Levels," *Journal of International Business Studies,* 2017 (doi:10.1057/s41267-017-0082-z).

9. George S. Yip and G. Tomas M. Hult (2012), *Total Global Strategy* (Boston: Pearson, 2012).

10. Allan Cane, "Microsoft Reorganizes to Meet Market Challenges," *Financial Times,* March 16, 1994, p. 1. Interviews by Charles Hill.

11. For research evidence that is related to this issue, see J. Birkinshaw, "Entrepreneurship in the Multinational Corporation: The Characteristics of Subsidiary Initiatives," *Strategic Management Journal* 18 (1997), pp. 207–29; J. Birkinshaw, N. Hood, and S. Jonsson, "Building Firm Specific Advantages in Multinational Corporations: The Role of Subsidiary Initiatives," *Strategic Management Journal* 19 (1998), pp. 221–41; I. Bjorkman, W. Barner-Rasussen, and L. Li, "Managing Knowledge Transfer in MNCs: The Impact of Headquarters Control Mechanisms," *Journal of International Business* 35 (2004), pp. 443–60.

12. For more detail, see S. M. Davis, "Managing and Organizing Multinational Corporations," in C. A. Bartlett and S. Ghoshal, *Transnational Management* (Homewood, IL: Richard D. Irwin, 1992). Also see Wolf and Egelhoff, "A Reexamination and Extension of International Strategy Structure Theory."

13. A. D. Chandler, *Strategy and Structure: Chapters in the History of the Industrial Enterprise* (Cambridge, MA: MIT Press, 1962).

14. Davis, "Managing and Organizing Multinational Corporations."

15. J. M. Stopford and L. T. Wells, *Strategy and Structure of the Multinational Enterprise* (New York: Basic Books, 1972).

16. C. A. Bartlett and S. Ghoshal, *Managing across Borders* (Boston: Harvard Business School Press, 1989).

17. Bartlett and Ghoshal, *Managing across Borders*; A. McDonnell, P. Gunnigle, and J. Lavelle, "Learning Transfer in Multinational Companies," *Human Resource Management Journal,* 2010, pp. 23–43; George S. Yip and G. Tomas M. Hult, *Total Global Strategy* (Boston, MA: Pearson, 2012).

18. See J. R. Galbraith, *Designing Complex Organizations* (Reading, MA: Addison-Wesley, 1977).

19. M. Goold and A. Campbell, "Structured Networks: Towards the Well Designed Matrix," *Long Range Planning,* October 2003, pp. 427–60.

20. Bartlett and Ghoshal, *Managing across Borders;* F. V. Guterl, "Goodbye, Old Matrix," *Business Month,* February 1989, pp. 32–38; Bjorkman et al., "Managing Knowledge Transfer in MNCs"; M. T. Hansen and B. Lovas, "How Do Multinational Companies Leverage Technological Competencies?" *Strategic Management Journal,* 2004, pp. 801–22.

21. M. S. Granovetter, "The Strength of Weak Ties," *American Journal of Sociology* 78 (1973), pp. 1360–80.

22. A. K. Gupta and V. J. Govindarajan, "Knowledge Flows within Multinational Corporations," *Strategic Management Journal* 21, no. 4 (2000), pp. 473–96; V. J. Govindarajan and A. K. Gupta, *The Quest for Global Dominance.* (San Francisco: Jossey-Bass, 2001); U. Andersson, M. Forsgren, and U. Holm, "The Strategic Impact of External Networks: Subsidiary Performance and Competence Development in the Multinational Corporation," *Strategic Management Journal* 23 (2002), pp. 979–96.

23. For examples, see W. H. Davidow and M. S. Malone, *The Virtual Corporation* (New York: HarperCollins, 1992).

24. Erkan Ozkaya, Cornelia Droge, G. Tomas M. Hult, Roger Calantone, and Elif Ozkaya, "Market Orientation, Knowledge Competence, and Innovation," *International Journal of Research in Marketing* 32, no. 3 (2015), pp. 309–18.

25. W. G. Ouchi, "Markets, Bureaucracies, and Clans," *Administrative Science Quarterly* 25 (1980), pp. 129–44.

26. For some empirical work that addresses this issue, see T. P. Murtha, S. A. Lenway, and R. P. Bagozzi, "Global Mind Sets and Cognitive Shift in a Complex Multinational Corporation," *Strategic Management Journal* 19 (1998), pp. 97–114.

27. J. Welch and J. Byrne, *Jack: Straight from the Gut* (Warner Books: New York, 2001).

28. C. W. L. Hill, M. E. Hitt, and R. E. Hoskisson, "Cooperative versus Competitive Structures in Related and Unrelated Diversified Firms," *Organization Science* 3 (1992), pp. 501-21.

29. Constantine S. Katskieas, Neil A. Morgan, Leonidas C. Leonidou, and G. Tomas M. Hult (2016), "Assessing Performance Outcomes in Marketing," *Journal of Marketing* 80, no. 2 (2016), pp. 1-20.

30. Murtha et al., "Global Mind Sets."

31. M. Hammer and J. Champy, *Reengineering the Corporation* (New York: Harper Business, 1993); Tomas Hult, David Closs, and David Frayer (2014), *Global Supply Chain Management: Leveraging Processes, Measurements, and Tools for Strategic Corporate Advantage* (New York: McGraw-Hill Professional, 2014); George S. Yip and G. Tomas M. Hult, *Total Global Strategy* (Boston: Pearson, 2012).

32. T. Kostova, "Transnational Transfer of Strategic Organizational Practices: A Contextual Perspective," *Academy of Management Review* 24, no. 2 (1999), pp. 308-24.

33. Andersson et al., "The Strategic Impact of External Networks."

34. E. H. Schein, "What Is Culture?" in P. J. Frost et al., *Reframing Organizational Culture* (Newbury Park, CA: Sage, 1991).

35. E. H. Schein, *Organizational Culture and Leadership,* 2nd ed. (San Francisco: Jossey-Bass, 1992).

36. G. Morgan, *Images of Organization* (Beverly Hills, CA: Sage, 1986).

37. R. Dore, *British Factory, Japanese Factory* (London: Allen & Unwin, 1973).

38. M. Dickson, "Back to the Future," *Financial Times,* May 30, 1994, p. 7.

39. See J. P. Kotter and J. L. Heskett, *Corporate Culture and Performance* (New York: Free Press, 1992); M. L. Tushman and C. A. O'Reilly, *Winning through Innovation* (Boston: Harvard Business School Press, 1997).

40. Kotter and Heskett, *Corporate Culture and Performance.*

41. The classic song of praise was produced by T. Peters and R. H. Waterman, *In Search of Excellence* (New York: Harper & Row, 1982). Ironically, IBM's decline began shortly after Peters and Waterman's book was published.

42. Kotter and Heskett, *Corporate Culture and Performance.*

43. Bartlett and Ghoshal, *Managing across Borders.*

44. See F. J. Aguilar and M. Y. Yoshino, "The Philips Group: 1987," Howard Business School Case No. 388-050, 1987; "Philips Fights Flab," *The Economist,* April 7, 1990, pp. 73-74; R. Van de Krol, "Philips Wins Back Old Friends," *Financial Times,* July 14, 1995, p. 14.

45. J. Pfeffer, *Managing with Power: Politics and Influence within Organizations* (Boston: Harvard Business School Press, 1992).

Entering Developed and Emerging Markets

15

LEARNING OBJECTIVES

After reading this chapter, you will be able to:

LO15-1 Explain the three basic decisions firms must make when they decide on foreign expansion: which markets to enter, when to enter those markets, and on what scale.

LO15-2 Compare the different modes firms use to enter foreign markets.

LO15-3 Identify the factors that influence a firm's choice of entry mode.

LO15-4 Recognize the pros and cons of acquisitions versus greenfield ventures as an international market entry strategy.

LO15-5 Evaluate the pros and cons of entering into strategic alliances when going international.

Zhang Ailin/Xinhua/Getty Images

Volkswagen, Toyota, and GM in China

OPENING CASE

Global automobile manufacturers have come to rely on China as a go-to and very sizable emerging country market for new car sales during the last three decades. Since 1990, the Chinese market has seen increased auto sales annually—that is, until 2018 when Chinese auto sales fell by 2.8 percent to 28.08 million units (passenger car sales fell by 4.1 percent, while commercial vehicle sales increased by 5.1 percent). Globally, China leads in both supply and demand in the auto sector. It is the largest auto market for sales of new vehicles, and also the largest auto market for manufacturing of vehicles. The country produces roughly the same number of vehicles that customers in the market buy annually (China's 28.08 million new vehicle sales are about 36 percent of the worldwide market of 78.7 million vehicles sold). Toyota, Volkswagen, and General Motors have been among the largest auto manufacturers for some time, and China is each of those companies' largest country market.

Toyota entered China before World War II when the company built plants in Tianjin and Shanghai and carried out local assembly in China. Toyota's initial foray into China was via the exporting of four G1 trucks to the northeastern part of the country in 1936. From the early 1970s, after China's return to the United Nations, Toyota also transferred technology, worked to develop the auto parts industry in the country, and actively trained Chinese personnel in order to contribute to the development of the Chinese automobile industry. Since 2000, Toyota has full-scale auto production and sales in China. For example, Toyota has engaged in a joint venture called Tianjin Automobile Xiali Corp, received approval for manufacturing operations from The Chinese Ministry of Foreign Trade and Economic Cooperation, and has established nine local production companies and four distributors in the country. Toyota sold 1.47 million vehicles in China last year, and the forecast is for year-on-year increases of 8 percent.

Volkswagen entered China in 1978, and did so via a joint venture with a state-owned partner as required by the Chinese government. The assembly contract signed in 1982 with the Shanghai Tractor and Automobile Corporation, the largest Chinese vehicle manufacturer at the time, was also an important early-on milestone. In the subsequent 10 years, riding a continual boom in the automotive industry, the sales of Volkswagen models in China increased tenfold. But Volkswagen also had to increasingly defend its strong market position against Japanese and U.S. carmakers who had significantly expanded their manufacturing capacity after China joined the World Trade Organization in 2004. Despite fiercer competition, China continued to grow into the largest single market for the Volkswagen brands, and last year VW sold 4.2 million vehicles in the country. This made VW overwhelmingly the top auto seller in China. Importantly, China today sets the automotive trend of the future, and VW has promised to deliver 40 new locally produced plug-in hybrids and electric vehicles by 2025 in the country, in addition to gas-driven vehicles.

General Motors has 11 joint ventures, two wholly owned foreign enterprises, and more than 58,000 employees in China. GM, along with its joint ventures, offers the broadest lineup of vehicles and brands among auto manufacturers in China. The company's products are sold under the Buick, Cadillac, Chevrolet, Baojun, and Wuling nameplates. But GM does not rest on its laurels. GM introduced more than 20 new and refreshed vehicles last year in China alone to maintain its growth momentum in the world's largest vehicle market and tap emerging opportunities in new energy vehicles. "China's vehicle market has entered a new era of high-quality development, in which product and service excellence will be the key to sustained growth," said Matt Tsien, GM executive vice president and president of GM China. "GM will continue to optimize our product mix, backed by our industry-leading technologies and adjacent services, and explore more opportunities in electrification and autonomous driving."* China has been GM's largest market since 2012, and last year the company and its joint ventures sold more than 3.64 million vehicles in China.

*Matt Tsien, General Motors China, 2019.

Sources: Daniel Shane, "Toyota Is Growing in China as Its Global Rivals Stumble," *CNN Business*, February 8, 2019; "Carmakers Scramble to Prepare for a Chilly Future," *The Economist*, January 19, 2019; "VW Predicts Rising China Sales, Bucking a Shrinking Market," *Bloomberg News*, January 7, 2019; "Carmakers to Face More Pain as Sales in China Keep Sliding," *Bloomberg News*, February 17, 2019; "GM Set for a Record of Over 20 Launches in China in 2019," GM Corporate Newsroom, January 17, 2019.

Introduction

This chapter is concerned with three closely related topics: (1) the decision of which foreign markets to enter, when to enter them, and on what scale; (2) the choice of entry mode; and (3) the role of strategic alliances. Any firm contemplating foreign expansion must first decide on which foreign market or markets to enter and the timing and scale of entry. Oftentimes, small and medium-sized companies decide to enter one international market at a time, while larger companies choose strategically one or more markets to enter. For example, a large company could decide to enter all five Scandinavian countries (Denmark, Finland, Iceland, Norway, and Sweden), or a subset of them, because those countries are similar in customers' needs and wants. Most small and medium-sized enterprises (SMEs) would not undertake such an expansion due to cost constraints, supply chain challenges, and market entry barriers.

For both large and SME companies, the choice of which international markets to enter should be driven by an assessment of the relative long-run growth and profit potential. Some companies have assumed that growth and profit potential meant that they needed to enter China, India, and other markets with large populations. However, the entry decision is much deeper and should be thought out more strategically, with a focus on long-run growth and profit potential. There are 195 countries in the international marketplace and some 7.7 billion people. Small, medium, and large companies have opportunities in a number of countries, but those opportunities need to be identified and targeted strategically and appropriately.

The choice of mode for entering a foreign market is another major issue with which international businesses must wrestle. The various modes for serving foreign markets include exporting, licensing, or franchising to host-country firms; establishing joint ventures with a host-country firm; setting up a new wholly owned subsidiary in a host country to serve its market; and acquiring an established enterprise in the host nation to serve that market. Each of these options has advantages and disadvantages. The magnitude of the advantages and disadvantages associated with each entry mode is determined by a number of factors, including logistics costs, trade barriers, political risks, economic risks, business risks, costs, and firm strategy. The optimal entry mode varies by situation, depending on these factors. Thus, whereas some firms may best serve a given market by exporting, other firms may better serve the same market by setting up a new wholly owned subsidiary or by acquiring an established enterprise.

The final topic of this chapter is strategic alliances. **Strategic alliances** are cooperative agreements between potential or actual competitors, as it applies to international business and this chapter. The term is often used to embrace a variety of agreements between actual or potential competitors including cross-shareholding deals, licensing arrangements, formal joint ventures, and informal cooperative arrangements. The motives for entering strategic alliances are varied, but they often include market access, hence the overlap with the topic of entry mode in this chapter.

The three auto manufacturers in the opening case—Volkswagen, Toyota, and General Motors—have strategically put together a mixture of subsidiaries, joint ventures, and strategic alliances to engage in the global marketplace. In particular, all three companies had to enter into joint ventures with Chinese partners due to the constraints placed on foreign companies in the Chinese market. For example, Toyota has engaged in a joint venture called Tianjin Automobile Xiali Corp. Likewise, Volkswagen entered into a joint partnership agreement with a state-owned partner, and GM has 11 similar joint venture partnerships in China. It is unlikely that Volkswagen, Toyota, and General Motors would have signed these joint venture agreements with state-owned Chinese partners without this being required by the Chinese government. However, the benefits outweigh the constraints. After all, the China market accounts for 36 percent of the worldwide market of 78.7 million vehicles sold.

globalEDGE INTERACTIVE RANKINGS

Entering foreign markets is the focus of this chapter. The selection of country markets to choose from is getting larger for many product categories as more countries see their populations' growing purchasing power. With more than 200 countries in the world, the data are overwhelming, and even the starting point for analysis is not always an easy decision. The Interactive Rankings on globalEDGE can serve as a great pictorial view of the world on some 50 important variables in categories covering the economy, energy, government, health, infrastructure, labor, people, and trade and investment (**globaledge.msu.edu/tools-and-data/ interactive-rankings**). Active data maps such as the Interactive Rankings maps are a good starting point for analysis to evaluate data for a specific country, as well as the countries in a region. This allows for a focus on entry into one market now and a strategy for expansion later on to nearby countries with similar characteristics. Which are the top three countries for internet users?

Basic Entry Decisions

A firm that is thinking about expanding in foreign markets must make three basic decisions: which markets to enter, when to enter those markets, and on what scale.[1]

WHICH FOREIGN MARKETS?

The world's 7.7 million people are located in 195 countries, 61 dependent areas (e.g., Hong Kong, Puerto Rico), and 6 disputed territories (e.g., Northern Cyprus, Taiwan). But, these people do not hold the same profit potential for a firm contemplating foreign expansion.[2] Practically, not all people in the world are likely to be current or potential customers, certainly not of every product or service that is sold by the many multinational corporations that exist. So, for a firm, the entry choice must be based on an assessment of a market's long-run profit potential (or perhaps a large-scale opportunity that has a shorter life cycle).

The long-run potential is a function of several factors, many of which we have studied in earlier chapters. Chapters 2 and 3 looked in detail at the economic and political factors that influence the potential attractiveness of a foreign market. The attractiveness of a country as a potential market for an international business depends on balancing the benefits, costs, and risks associated with doing business in that country. In many cases, the combination of product or service readiness for a market, coupled with the firm's readiness to take on that foreign market, are the two critical overarching factors in making a market entry decision.

Chapters 2 and 3 also noted that the long-run economic benefits of doing business in a country are a function of factors such as the size of the market (in terms of demographics); the present wealth (purchasing power) of consumers in that market; and the likely future wealth of consumers, which depends on economic growth rates. While some markets are very large when measured by the number of consumers (the top seven countries—all with more than 200 million people—are China, India, the United States, Indonesia, Brazil, Pakistan, and Nigeria), one must also look at living standards and economic growth. On this basis, China and India, while relatively poor, are growing so rapidly that they are attractive targets for inward investment. Alternatively, weak growth in Indonesia implies that this populous nation is a far less attractive target for inward investment. And, while the economy of Pakistan is the 25th largest in the world for purchasing power parity,

LO15-1

Explain the three basic decisions firms must make when they decide on foreign expansion: which markets to enter, when to enter those markets, and on what scale.

Tesco's International Growth Strategy

Tesco, founded in 1919 by Jack Cohen, is a British multinational grocery and merchandise retailer. It is the largest grocery retailer in the United Kingdom, with a 28 percent share of the local market, and the second-largest retailer in the world after Walmart measured by revenue. Last year, Tesco had sales of more than $70 billion, employed more than 480,000 workers, and operated 6,553 stores in 13 countries.

In its home market of the United Kingdom (with a headquarters in Chestnut, Hertfordshire, England), the company's strengths are reputed to come from strong competencies in marketing and store site selection, logistics and inventory management, and its own label product offerings. By the early 1990s, these competencies had already given the company a leading position in the United Kingdom. Tesco was generating strong free cash flows, and senior managers had to decide how to use that cash. One strategy they settled on was overseas expansion.

As managers looked at international markets, they soon concluded the best opportunities were not in established markets, such as those in North America and western Europe, where strong local competitors already existed, but in the emerging markets of eastern Europe and Asia, where there were few capable competitors but strong underlying growth trends. Tesco's first international foray was into Hungary in 1995, when it acquired an

Checkout section of a large Tesco supermarket in Malaysia.
Rob Walls/Alamy Stock Photo

initial 51 percent stake in Global, a 43-store, state-owned grocery chain. By 2017, Tesco was the market leader in Hungary, with more than 200 stores and additional openings planned, accounting for 1 percent of the whole economy of Hungary!

A year after the Hungary expansion, Tesco acquired 31 stores in Poland from Stavia. The following year, in 1996, Tesco added 13 stores that the company purchased from Kmart in the Czech Republic and Slovakia; and the following year it entered the Republic of Ireland. Tesco now has

many companies stay away from Pakistan due to the political instability and risks. Similar risk-arguments can be made for Nigeria.

As we saw in Chapters 2 and 3, likely future economic growth rates appear to be a function of a free market system and a country's capacity for growth (which may be greater in less developed nations). Also, the costs and risks associated with doing business in a foreign country are typically lower in economically advanced and politically stable democratic nations, and they are greater in less developed and politically unstable nations. That said, the long-term stability in many developed European countries also means that they have limited growth potential compared with higher-risk emerging countries. These issues provide a confluence of factors that should be taken into account when deciding on which foreign markets to enter.

The discussion in Chapters 2 and 3 suggests that, other things being equal, the benefit–cost–risk trade-off is likely to be most favorable in politically stable developed and developing nations that have free market systems, and where there is not a dramatic upsurge in either inflation rates or private-sector debt. The trade-off is likely to be least favorable in politically unstable developing nations that operate with a mixed or command economy or in developing nations where speculative financial bubbles have led to excess borrowing. Less developed nations and base-of-the-pyramid citizen segments in the global marketplace also warrant careful evaluation and global strategy development for revenue (and profit) potential.

more than 450 stores in Poland, some 80 stores in the Czech Republic, more than 120 stores in Slovakia, and more than 100 stores in Ireland.

Tesco's Asian expansion began in 1998 in Thailand when it purchased 75 percent of Lotus, a local food retailer with 13 stores. Building on that base, Tesco had more than 380 stores in Thailand by 2017. In 1999, the company entered South Korea when it partnered with Samsung to develop a chain of hypermarkets. This was followed by entry into Taiwan in 2000, Malaysia in 2002, Japan in 2003, and China in 2004. The move into China came after three years of careful research and discussions with potential partners. Like many other Western companies, Tesco was attracted to the Chinese market by its large size and rapid growth. In the end, Tesco settled on a 50–50 joint venture with Hymall, a hypermarket chain that is controlled by Ting Hsin, a Taiwanese group, which had been operating in China for six years. In 2014, Tesco combined its 131 stores in China in a joint venture with the state-run China Resources Enterprise (CRE) and its nearly 3,000 stores. Tesco owns 20 percent of the joint venture.

As a result of these moves, last year Tesco generated sales of about $21 billion outside the United Kingdom (its UK annual revenues were roughly $41 billion). The addition of international stores has helped make Tesco the second-largest company in the global grocery market behind only Walmart (Tesco is also behind Carrefour of France if profits are used). Of the three, however, Tesco may be the most successful internationally. All its foreign ventures are making money.

In explaining the company's success, Tesco's managers have detailed a number of important factors. First, the company devotes considerable attention to transferring its core capabilities in retailing to its new ventures. At the same time, it does not send in an army of expatriate managers to run local operations, preferring to hire local managers and support them with a few operational experts from the United Kingdom. Second, the company believes that its partnering strategy in Asia has been a great asset. Tesco has teamed up with good companies that have a deep understanding of the markets in which they are participating but that lack Tesco's financial strength and retailing capabilities. Consequently, both Tesco and its partners have brought useful assets to the venture, increasing the probability of success. As the venture becomes established, Tesco has typically increased its ownership stake in its partner. For example, Tesco owns 100 percent of Homeplus, its South Korean hypermarket chain, but when the venture was established Tesco owned 51 percent. Third, the company has focused on markets with good growth potential but that lack strong indigenous competitors, which provides Tesco with ripe ground for expansion.

Sources: Angela Monaghan, "Tesco Boss's Bonus Cut Despite First Sales Growth in Seven Years," *The Guardian*, May 12, 2017; P. N. Child, "Taking Tesco Global," *The McKenzie Quarterly* 3 (2002); H. Keers, "Global Tesco Sets Out Its Stall in China," *The Daily Telegraph*, July 15, 2004, p. 31; K. Burgess, "Tesco Spends Pounds £140m on Chinese Partnership," *Financial Times*, July 15, 2004, p. 22; J. McTaggart, "Industry Awaits Tesco Invasion," *Progressive Grocer*, March 1, 2006, pp. 8–10; Tesco's annual reports, archived at www.tesco.com; "Tesco Set to Push Ahead in the United States," *The Wall Street Journal*, October 6, 2010, p. 19.

Another important factor is the value an international business can create in a foreign market. This depends on the suitability of its products to that market and the nature of indigenous competition.[3] If the international business can offer a product that has not been widely available in a market and that satisfies an unmet need, the value of that product to consumers is likely to be much greater than if the international business simply offers the same type of product that indigenous competitors and other foreign entrants are already offering. Greater value translates into an ability to charge higher prices and/or to build sales volume more rapidly. By considering such factors, a firm can rank countries in terms of their attractiveness and long-run profit potential. Preference is then given to entering markets that rank highly. For example, Tesco, the large British grocery chain, has been aggressively expanding its foreign operations, primarily by focusing on emerging markets that lack strong indigenous competitors (see the accompanying Management Focus).

TIMING OF ENTRY

Once attractive markets have been identified, it is important to consider the **timing of entry**. Entry is considered to be early when an international business enters a foreign market before other foreign firms and late when it enters after other international businesses have already established themselves in a market. The advantages frequently associated with entering a market early are commonly known as **first-mover advantages**.[4] One first-mover advantage is the ability to preempt rivals and capture demand by establishing a strong brand name and customer satisfaction. This desire has driven the rapid expansion by Tesco into developing nations. A second advantage is the ability to build sales volume in that country and ride down the experience curve ahead of rivals, giving the early entrant a cost advantage over later entrants. This cost advantage may enable the early entrant to cut prices below that of later entrants, thereby driving them out of the market. A third advantage is the ability of early entrants to create switching costs that tie customers into their products or services. Such switching costs make it difficult for later entrants to win business.

There can also be disadvantages associated with entering a foreign market before other international businesses. These are often referred to as **first-mover disadvantages**.[5] These disadvantages may give rise to **pioneering costs**, costs that an early entrant has to bear that a later entrant can avoid. Pioneering costs arise when the business system in a foreign country is so different from that in a firm's home market that the enterprise has to devote considerable effort, time, and expense to learning the rules of the game. Pioneering costs include the costs of business failure if the firm, due to its ignorance of the foreign environment, makes major mistakes. A certain liability is associated with being a foreigner, and this liability is greater for foreign firms that enter a national market early.[6] Research seems to confirm that the probability of survival increases if an international business enters a national market after several other foreign firms have already done so.[7] The late entrant may benefit by observing and learning from the mistakes made by early entrants.

Pioneering costs also include the costs of promoting and establishing a product offering, including the costs of educating customers. These can be significant when the product being promoted is unfamiliar to local consumers. In contrast, later entrants may be able to ride on an early entrant's investments in learning and customer education by watching how the early entrant proceeded in the market, by avoiding costly mistakes made by the early entrant, and by exploiting the market potential created by the early entrant's investments in customer education. For example, KFC introduced the Chinese to American-style fast food, but a later entrant, McDonald's, has capitalized on the market in China. Similarly, FedEx had permits to operate in China some 10 years before it actually could convince Chinese customers its service was valuable relative to the shipping operations already available to them at that time.

An early entrant may be put at a severe disadvantage, relative to a later entrant, if regulations change in a way that diminishes the value of an early entrant's investments. This is a serious risk in many developing nations where the rules that govern business practices are still evolving. Early entrants can find themselves at a disadvantage if a subsequent change in regulations invalidates prior assumptions about the best business model for operating in that country. Another potential disadvantage of being a pioneer in a country is the need to educate customers about your company's products, especially if those products have not been available in that marketplace before (e.g., FedEx in China had no natural competitor before UPS, DHL, and others joined the marketplace).

SCALE OF ENTRY AND STRATEGIC COMMITMENTS

Another issue that an international business needs to consider when contemplating market entry is the scale of entry. Entering a market on a large scale involves the commitment of significant resources and implies rapid entry. Consider the entry of the Dutch insurance company ING into the U.S. insurance market. ING had to spend several billion dollars to acquire its U.S. operations. Not all firms have the resources necessary to enter on a large scale, and even some large firms prefer to enter foreign markets on a small scale and then build slowly as they become more familiar with the market.

The consequences of entering on a significant scale—entering rapidly—are associated with the value of the resulting strategic commitments.[8] A strategic commitment has a long-term impact and is difficult to reverse. Deciding to enter a foreign market on a significant scale is a major strategic commitment. Strategic commitments, such as rapid large-scale market entry, can have an important influence on the nature of competition in a market. For example, by entering the U.S. financial services market on a significant scale, ING signaled its commitment to the market. This will have several effects. On the positive side, it will make it easier for the company to attract customers and distributors (such as insurance agents). The scale of entry gives both customers and distributors reasons for believing that ING will remain in the market for the long run. The scale of entry may also give other foreign institutions considering entry into the United States pause; now they will have to compete not only against indigenous institutions in the United States but also against an aggressive and successful European institution. On the negative side, by committing itself heavily to one country, the United States, ING may have fewer resources available to support expansion in other desirable markets, such as Japan. The commitment to the United States limits the company's strategic flexibility.

As suggested by the ING example, significant strategic commitments are neither unambiguously good nor bad. Rather, they tend to change the competitive playing field and unleash a number of changes, some of which may be desirable and some of which will not be. It is important for a firm to think through the implications of large-scale entry into a market and act accordingly. Of particular relevance is trying to identify how actual and potential competitors might react to large-scale entry into a market. Also, the large-scale entrant is more likely than the small-scale entrant to be able to capture first-mover advantages associated with demand preemption, scale economies, and switching costs.

The value of the commitments that flow from rapid large-scale entry into a foreign market must be balanced against the resulting risks and lack of flexibility associated with significant commitments. But strategic inflexibility can also have value. A famous example from military history illustrates the value of inflexibility. When Hernán Cortés landed in Mexico, he ordered his men to burn all but one of his ships. Cortés reasoned that by eliminating their only method of retreat, his men had no choice but to fight hard to win against the Aztecs—and ultimately they did.[9]

Balanced against the value and risks of the commitments associated with large-scale entry are the benefits of a small-scale entry. Small-scale entry allows a firm to learn about a foreign market while limiting the firm's exposure to that market. Small-scale entry is a way to gather information about a foreign market before deciding whether to enter on a significant scale and how best to enter. By giving the firm time to collect information, small-scale entry reduces the risks associated with a subsequent large-scale entry. But the lack of commitment associated with small-scale entry may make it more difficult for the small-scale entrant to build market share and to capture first-mover or early-mover advantages. The risk-averse firm that enters a foreign market on a small scale may limit its potential losses, but it may also miss the chance to capture first-mover advantages.

MARKET ENTRY SUMMARY

There are no "right" decisions here, just decisions that are associated with different levels of risk and reward. Entering a large developing nation such as China or India before most other international businesses in the firm's industry, and entering on a large scale, will be associated with high levels of risk. In such cases, the liability of being foreign is increased by the absence of prior foreign entrants whose experience can be a useful guide. At the same time, the potential long-term rewards associated with such a strategy are great. The early large-scale entrant into a major developing nation may be able to capture significant first-mover advantages that will bolster its long-run position in that market.[10] In contrast, entering developed nations such as Australia or Canada after other international businesses in the firm's industry, and entering on a small scale to first learn more about those markets, will be associated with much lower levels of risk. However, the potential long-term rewards are also likely to be lower because the firm is essentially forgoing the opportunity to capture first-mover advantages and because the lack of commitment signaled by small-scale entry may limit its future growth potential.

This section has been written largely from the perspective of a business based in a developed country considering entry into foreign markets (see the Management Focus section on Starbucks as an example). Christopher Bartlett and Sumantra Ghoshal have pointed out the ability that businesses based in developing nations have to enter foreign markets and become global players.[11] Although such firms tend to be late entrants into foreign markets, and although their resources may be limited, Bartlett and Ghoshal argue that such late movers can still succeed against well-established global competitors by pursuing appropriate strategies. In particular, Bartlett and Ghoshal argue that companies based in developing nations should use the entry of foreign multinationals as an opportunity to learn from these competitors by benchmarking their operations and performance against them. Furthermore, they suggest the local company may be able to find ways to differentiate itself from a foreign multinational, for example, by focusing on market niches that the multinational ignores or is unable to serve effectively if it has a standardized global product offering. Having improved its performance through learning and differentiated its product offering, the firm from a developing nation may then be able to pursue its own international expansion strategy.

TEST PREP

Use SmartBook to help retain what you have learned. Access your instructor's Connect course to check out SmartBook or go to **learnsmartadvantage.com** for help.

LO15-2

Compare the different modes firms use to enter foreign markets.

Entry Modes

Once a firm decides to enter a foreign market, the question arises as to the best mode of entry. Firms can use six different modes to enter foreign markets: exporting, turnkey projects, licensing, franchising, establishing joint ventures with a host-country firm, or setting up a new wholly owned subsidiary in the host country. Each entry mode has advantages and disadvantages. Managers need to consider these carefully when deciding which to use.[12]

EXPORTING

Many manufacturing firms begin their global expansion as exporters and only later switch to another mode for serving a foreign market. We take a close look at the mechanics of exporting in Chapter 16. Here we focus on the advantages and disadvantages of exporting as an entry mode.

Advantages

Exporting has two distinct advantages. First, it avoids the often substantial costs of establishing manufacturing or more deeply ingrained operations in the host country. Basically, exporting is a low-level commitment and low-level involvement for the firm in the global marketplace. Second, exporting may help a firm achieve experience curve and location economies (see Chapter 13). By manufacturing the product in a centralized location and exporting it to other markets, a firm can realize substantial scale economies from its global sales volume. This is how many small and medium-sized enterprises (SMEs) make inroads into various country markets.

Disadvantages

Exporting has a number of drawbacks. First, exporting from the firm's home base may not be appropriate if lower-cost locations for manufacturing the product can be found (i.e., if the firm can realize location economies by moving production to a foreign location). For firms pursuing global or transnational strategies, it may be preferable to manufacture where the mix of factor conditions is most favorable from a value creation perspective and to export to the rest of the world from that location. This is not so much an argument against exporting as an argument against exporting from the firm's home country. Many U.S. electronics firms have moved some of their manufacturing to the Far East because of the availability of low-cost, highly skilled labor. They then export from that location to the rest of the world, including the United States.

A second drawback to exporting is that high supply chain costs can make exporting uneconomical, particularly for bulk products. One way of getting around this is to manufacture bulk products regionally in the area where such products will be sold. This strategy enables the firm to realize some economies from large-scale production and at the same time limit its supply chain costs. For example, many multinational chemical firms manufacture their products regionally, serving several countries from one facility. An argument can be made that the world should be viewed as a set of separate regions and that globalization is a focus that is too costly at this time.

A third drawback is that tariff barriers can make exporting uneconomical. Similarly, the threat of tariff barriers by the host-country government can make it very risky. In the world we now live in, many countries are becoming more and more nationalistic, which means that they are increasing trade barriers (e.g., the United States) or renegotiating their partnerships (e.g., the United Kingdom). The largely unknown standing of international trade barriers in some countries—due to nationalistic, political strategies—can be a detriment to exporting across country borders.

A fourth drawback to exporting arises when a firm delegates its marketing, sales, and service in each country where it does business to another company. This is a common approach for manufacturing firms that are just beginning to expand internationally. The other company may be a local agent, or it may be another multinational with extensive international distribution operations. Local agents often carry the products of competing firms and so have divided loyalties. In such cases, the local agent may not do as good a job as the firm would if it managed its marketing itself. Similar problems can occur when another multinational takes on distribution. The way around such problems is to set up wholly owned subsidiaries in foreign nations to handle local marketing, sales, and service. By doing this, the firm can exercise tight control over marketing and sales in the country while reaping the cost advantages of manufacturing the product in a single location or a few choice locations.

TURNKEY PROJECTS

Firms that specialize in the design, construction, and start-up of turnkey plants are common in some industries. In a **turnkey project**, the contractor agrees to handle every detail of the project for a foreign client, including the training of operating personnel. At completion of the contract, the foreign client is handed the "key" to a plant that is ready for full operation—hence, the term *turnkey*. This is a means of exporting process technology to other countries. Turnkey projects are most common in the chemical, pharmaceutical, petroleum-refining, and metal-refining industries, all of which use complex, expensive production technologies.

Advantages

The know-how required to assemble and run a technologically complex process, such as refining petroleum or steel, is a valuable asset. Turnkey projects are a way of earning great economic returns from that asset. The strategy is particularly useful where foreign direct investment (FDI) is limited by host-government regulations. For example, the governments of many oil-rich countries have set out to build their own petroleum-refining industries, so they restrict FDI in their oil-refining sectors. But because many of these countries lack petroleum-refining technology, they gain it by entering into turnkey projects with foreign firms that have the technology. Such deals are often attractive to the selling firm because without them, they would have no way to earn a return on their valuable know-how in that country. A turnkey strategy can also be less risky than conventional FDI. In a country with unstable political and economic environments, a longer-term investment might expose the firm to unacceptable political and/or economic risks (e.g., the risk of nationalization or of economic collapse).

Disadvantages

Three main drawbacks are associated with a turnkey strategy. First, the firm that enters into a turnkey deal will have no long-term interest in the foreign country. This can be a disadvantage if that country subsequently proves to be a major market for the output of the process that has been exported. One way around this is to take a minority equity interest in the operation. Second, the firm that enters into a turnkey project with a foreign enterprise may inadvertently create a competitor. For example, many of the Western companies that sold oil-refining technology to firms in Saudi Arabia, Kuwait, and other Gulf states now find themselves competing with these firms in the global oil market. Third, if the firm's process technology is a source of competitive advantage, then selling this technology through a turnkey project is also selling competitive advantage to potential and/or actual competitors.

LICENSING

A **licensing agreement** is an arrangement whereby a licensor grants the rights to intangible property to another entity (the licensee) for a specified period, and in return, the licensor receives a royalty fee from the licensee.[13] Intangible property includes patents, inventions, formulas, processes, designs, copyrights, and trademarks. For example, to enter the Japanese market, Xerox, inventor of the photocopier, established a joint venture with Fuji Photo that is known as Fuji Xerox. Xerox then licensed its xerographic know-how to Fuji Xerox. In return, Fuji Xerox paid Xerox a royalty fee equal to 5 percent of the net sales revenue that Fuji Xerox earned from the sales of photocopiers based on Xerox's patented know-how. In the Fuji Xerox case, the license was originally granted for 10 years, and it has been renegotiated and extended several times. The licensing agreement between Xerox and Fuji Xerox also limited Fuji Xerox's direct sales to the Asian Pacific region (although Fuji Xerox does supply Xerox with photocopiers that are sold in North America under the Xerox label).[14]

Advantages

In the typical international licensing deal, the licensee puts up most of the capital necessary to get the overseas operation going. Thus, a primary advantage of licensing is that the firm does not have to bear the development costs and risks associated with a foreign market. Licensing is very attractive for firms lacking the capital to develop operations overseas. In addition, licensing can be attractive when a firm is unwilling to commit substantial financial resources to an unfamiliar or politically volatile foreign market. Licensing is also often used when a firm wishes to participate in a foreign market but is prohibited from doing so by barriers to investment. This was one of the original reasons for the formation of the Fuji Xerox joint venture. Xerox wanted to participate in the Japanese market but was prohibited from setting up a wholly owned subsidiary by the Japanese government. So Xerox set up the joint venture with Fuji and then licensed its know-how to the joint venture.

Licensing is also frequently used when a firm possesses some intangible property that might have business applications, but it does not want to develop those applications itself. For example, Bell Laboratories at AT&T originally invented the transistor circuit in the 1950s, but AT&T decided it did not want to produce transistors, so it licensed the technology to a number of other companies, such as Texas Instruments. Similarly, Coca-Cola has licensed its famous trademark to clothing manufacturers, which have incorporated the design into clothing. Harley-Davidson licenses its brand to Wolverine World Wide to make footwear that embodies the spirit of the open road, which Harley-Davidson is so known to emphasize in its advertisements and product positioning.

Disadvantages

Licensing has three serious drawbacks. First, it does not give a firm tight control over manufacturing, marketing, and strategy that is required for realizing experience curve and location economies. Licensing typically involves each licensee setting up its own production operations. This severely limits the firm's ability to realize experience curve and location economies by producing its product in a centralized location. When these economies are important, licensing may not be the best way to expand overseas.

Second, competing in a global market may require a firm to coordinate strategic moves across countries by using profits earned in one country to support competitive attacks in another. By its very nature, licensing limits a firm's ability to do this. A licensee is unlikely to allow a multinational firm to use its profits (beyond those due in the form of royalty payments) to support a different licensee operating in another country.

A third problem with licensing is one that we encountered in Chapter 8 when we reviewed the economic theory of foreign direct investment (FDI). This is the risk associated with licensing technological know-how to foreign companies. Technological know-how constitutes the basis of many multinational firms' competitive advantage. Most firms wish to maintain control over how their know-how is used, and a firm can lose control over its technology by licensing it. Many firms have made the mistake of thinking they could maintain control over their know-how in a licensing agreement. RCA Corporation, for example, once licensed its color TV technology to Japanese firms, including Matsushita and Sony. The Japanese firms quickly assimilated the technology, improved on it, and used it to enter the U.S. market, taking substantial market share away from RCA until it became defunct in 1986.

There are ways of reducing this risk. One way is by entering into a cross-licensing agreement with a foreign firm. Under a cross-licensing agreement, a firm might license some valuable intangible property to a foreign partner, but in addition to a royalty payment, the firm might also request that the foreign partner license some of its valuable know-how to the firm. Such agreements are believed to reduce the risks associated with licensing technological know-how, since the licensee realizes that if it violates the licensing contract (by using the knowledge obtained to compete directly with the licensor), the licensor can do the same to it. Cross-licensing agreements enable firms to hold each other hostage, which reduces the probability that they will behave opportunistically toward each other.[15] Such cross-licensing agreements are increasingly common in high-technology industries.

Another way of reducing the risk associated with licensing is to follow the Fuji Xerox model and link an agreement to license know-how with the formation of a joint venture in which the licensor and licensee take important equity stakes. Such an approach aligns the interests of licensor and licensee, because both have a stake in ensuring that the venture is successful. Thus, the risk that Fuji Photo might appropriate Xerox's technological know-how, and then compete directly against Xerox in the global photocopier market, was reduced by the establishment of a joint venture in which both Xerox and Fuji Photo had an important stake.

FRANCHISING

Franchising is similar to licensing, although franchising tends to involve longer-term commitments than licensing. **Franchising** is basically a specialized form of licensing in which the franchiser not only sells intangible property (normally a trademark) to the franchisee, but also insists that the franchisee agree to abide by strict rules as to how it does business. The franchiser will also often assist the franchisee to run the business on an ongoing basis. As with licensing, the franchiser typically receives a royalty payment, which amounts to some percentage of the franchisee's revenues. Whereas licensing is pursued primarily by manufacturing firms, franchising is employed primarily by service firms.[16] McDonald's and Subway—the two largest franchise systems in the world—are good examples of firms that have grown by using a franchising strategy. McDonald's strict rules as to how franchisees should operate a restaurant extend to control over the menu, cooking methods, staffing policies, and design and location. McDonald's also organizes the supply chain for its franchisees and provides management training and financial assistance.[17]

Advantages

The advantages of franchising as an entry mode are very similar to those of licensing. The firm is relieved of many of the costs and risks of opening a foreign market on its own. Instead, the franchisee typically assumes those costs and risks. This creates a good incentive for the franchisee to build a profitable operation as quickly as possible. Thus, using a franchising strategy, a service firm can build a global presence quickly and at a relatively low cost and risk, as McDonald's has.

Disadvantages

The disadvantages are less pronounced than in the case of licensing. Since franchising is often used by service companies, there is no reason to consider the need for coordination of manufacturing to achieve experience curve and location economies. But franchising may inhibit the firm's ability to take profits out of one country to support competitive attacks in another. A more significant disadvantage of franchising is quality control. The foundation of franchising arrangements is that the firm's brand name conveys a message to consumers about the quality of the firm's product. Thus, a business traveler checking in at a Four Seasons hotel in Hong Kong can reasonably expect the same quality of room, food, and service that she would receive in New York. The Four Seasons name is supposed to guarantee consistent product quality.

However, such quality standards across the globe may present a problem in that foreign franchisees may not be as concerned about quality as they are supposed to be. If that is the case, the result of poor quality received in one country can extend beyond lost sales in that foreign market to a decline in the firm's worldwide reputation and lost sales in other countries. For example, if the business traveler has a bad experience at the Four Seasons in Hong Kong, he or she may never go to another Four Seasons hotel and may urge colleagues to do likewise. The geographic distance of the firm from its foreign franchisees can make poor quality difficult to detect. In addition, the sheer numbers of franchisees—in the case of McDonald's, tens of thousands—can make quality control difficult. Due to these factors, quality problems may persist.

One way around this disadvantage is to set up a subsidiary in each country in which the firm expands. The subsidiary might be wholly owned by the company or a joint venture with a foreign company. The subsidiary assumes the rights and obligations to establish franchises throughout the particular country or region. McDonald's, for example, establishes a master franchisee in many countries. Typically, this master franchisee is a joint venture between McDonald's and a local firm. The proximity and the smaller number of franchises to oversee reduce the quality control challenge. In addition, because the subsidiary (or master franchisee) is at least partly owned by the firm, the firm can place its own managers in the subsidiary to help ensure that it is doing a good job of monitoring the franchises. This organizational arrangement has proven very satisfactory for McDonald's, Subway, KFC, and others.

JOINT VENTURES

A **joint venture** entails establishing a firm that is jointly owned by two or more otherwise independent firms. Fuji Xerox, for example, was set up as a joint venture between Xerox and Fuji Photo. Establishing a joint venture with a foreign firm has long been a popular mode for entering a new market. The most typical joint venture is a 50-50 venture, in which there are two parties, each of which holding a 50 percent ownership stake and contributing a team of managers to share operating control. This was the case with the Fuji-Xerox joint venture until 2001; it is now a 25-75 venture, with Xerox holding 25 percent. The GM SAIC venture in China was a 50-50 venture until 2010, when it became a 51-49 venture, with SAIC holding the 51 percent stake. Some firms, however, have sought joint ventures in which they have a majority share from the beginning, and thus tighter control.[18]

Advantages

Joint ventures have a number of advantages. First, a firm benefits from a local partner's knowledge of the host country's competitive conditions, culture, language, political systems, and business. Thus, for many U.S. firms, joint ventures have involved the U.S. company providing technological know-how and products and the local partner providing the marketing expertise and the local knowledge necessary for competing in that country. Second, when the development costs and/or risks of opening a foreign market are high, a firm might gain by sharing these costs and or risks with a local partner. Third, in many countries, political considerations make joint ventures the only feasible entry mode.

Research suggests that joint ventures with local partners face a low risk of being subject to nationalization or other forms of adverse government interference.[19] This appears to be because local equity partners, who may have some influence on host-government policy, have a vested interest in speaking out against nationalization or government interference. Governments seldom want to hurt their local businesses and that helps foreign partners in a joint venture.

Disadvantages

Despite these advantages, there are major disadvantages with joint ventures. First, as with licensing, a firm that enters into a joint venture risks giving control of its technology to its partner. Thus, a proposed joint venture between Boeing and Mitsubishi Heavy Industries to build a new wide-body jet (the 787) raised fears that Boeing might unwittingly give away its commercial airline technology to the Japanese. However, joint-venture agreements can be constructed to minimize this risk. One option is to hold majority ownership in the venture. This allows the dominant partner to exercise greater control over its technology. But it can be difficult to find a foreign partner who is willing to settle for minority ownership. Another option is to "wall off" from a partner technology that is central to the core competence of the firm, while sharing other technology.

A second disadvantage is that a joint venture does not give a firm the tight control over subsidiaries that it might need to realize experience curve or location economies. Nor does it give a firm the tight control over a foreign subsidiary that it might need for engaging in coordinated global attacks against its rivals. Consider the entry of Texas Instruments (TI) into the Japanese semiconductor market. When TI established semiconductor facilities in Japan, it did so for the dual purpose of checking Japanese manufacturers' market share and limiting their cash available for invading TI's global market. In other words, TI was engaging in global strategic coordination. To implement this strategy, TI's subsidiary in Japan had to be prepared to take instructions from corporate headquarters regarding competitive strategy. The strategy also required the Japanese subsidiary to run at a loss if necessary. Few if any potential joint-venture partners would have been willing to accept such conditions, since it would have necessitated a willingness to accept a negative return on investment. Indeed, many joint ventures establish a degree of autonomy that would make such direct control over strategic decisions all but impossible to establish.[20] Thus, to implement this strategy, TI set up a wholly owned subsidiary in Japan.

A third disadvantage with joint ventures is that the shared ownership arrangement can lead to conflicts and battles for control between the investing firms if their goals and objectives change or if they take different views as to what the strategy should be. This was apparently not a problem with the Fuji Xerox joint venture. According to Yotaro Kobayashi, the former chair of Fuji Xerox, a primary reason is that both Xerox and Fuji Photo adopted an arm's-length relationship with Fuji Xerox, giving the venture's management considerable freedom to determine its own strategy.[21] However, much research indicates that conflicts of interest over strategy and goals often arise in joint ventures. These conflicts tend to be greater when the venture is between firms of different nationalities, and they often end in the dissolution of the venture.[22] Such conflicts tend to be triggered by shifts in the relative bargaining power of venture partners. For example, in the case of ventures between a foreign firm and a local firm, as a foreign partner's knowledge about local market conditions increases, it depends less on the expertise of a local partner. This increases the bargaining power of the foreign partner and ultimately leads to conflicts over control of the venture's strategy and goals.[23] Some firms have sought to limit such problems by entering into joint ventures in which one partner has a controlling interest.

WHOLLY OWNED SUBSIDIARIES

In a **wholly owned subsidiary**, the firm owns 100 percent of the subsidiary. Establishing a wholly owned subsidiary in a foreign market can be done in two ways. The firm can either set up a new operation in that country, often referred to as a greenfield venture, or it can acquire an established firm in that host nation and use that firm to promote its products.[24] For example, ING's strategy for entering the U.S. insurance market was to acquire established U.S. enterprises, rather than build an operation from scratch.

Advantages

There are several clear advantages of wholly owned subsidiaries. First, when a firm's competitive advantage is based on technological competence, a wholly owned subsidiary will often be the preferred entry mode because it reduces the risk of losing control over that competence. (See Chapter 8 for more details.) Many high-tech firms prefer this entry mode for overseas expansion (e.g., firms in the electronics and pharmaceutical industries). Second, a wholly owned subsidiary gives a firm tight control over operations in different countries. This is necessary for engaging in global strategic coordination (i.e., using profits from one country to support competitive attacks in another).

Third, a wholly owned subsidiary may be required if a firm is trying to realize location and experience curve economies (as firms pursuing global and transnational strategies try to do). As we saw in Chapter 11, when cost pressures are intense, it may pay a firm to configure its value chain in such a way that the value added at each stage is maximized. Thus, a national subsidiary may specialize in manufacturing only part of the product line or certain components of the end product, exchanging parts and products with other subsidiaries in the firm's global system. Establishing such a global production system requires a high degree of control over the operations of each affiliate. The various operations must be prepared to accept centrally determined decisions as to how they will produce, how much they will produce, and how their output will be priced for transfer to the next operation. Because licensees or joint-venture partners are unlikely to accept such a subservient role, establishing wholly owned subsidiaries may be necessary. Finally, establishing a wholly owned subsidiary gives the firm a 100 percent share in the profits generated in a foreign market.

Disadvantage

Establishing a wholly owned subsidiary is generally the most costly method of serving a foreign market from a capital investment standpoint. Firms doing this must bear the full capital costs and risks of setting up overseas operations. The risks associated with learning to do business in a new culture are less if the firm acquires an established host-country enterprise. However, acquisitions raise additional problems, including those associated with trying to marry divergent corporate cultures. These problems may more than offset any benefits derived by acquiring an established operation. Because the choice between greenfield ventures and acquisitions is such an important one, we discuss it in more detail later in the chapter.

 TEST PREP

Use SmartBook to help retain what you have learned. Access your instructor's Connect course to check out SmartBook or go to **learnsmartadvantage.com** for help.

LO15-3

Identify the factors that influence a firm's choice of entry mode.

Selecting an Entry Mode

As the preceding discussion demonstrated, all the entry modes have advantages and disadvantages, as summarized in Table 15.1. Thus, trade-offs are inevitable when selecting an entry mode. For example, when considering entry into an unfamiliar country with a track record for discriminating against foreign-owned enterprises when awarding government contracts, a firm might favor a joint venture with a local enterprise. Its rationale might be that the local partner will help it establish operations in an unfamiliar environment and will help the company win government contracts. However, if the firm's core competence is based on proprietary technology, entering a joint venture might risk losing control of that technology to the joint-venture partner, in which case the strategy may seem unattractive. Despite the existence of such trade-offs, it is possible to make some generalizations about the optimal choice of entry mode.[25]

CORE COMPETENCIES AND ENTRY MODE

We saw in Chapter 13 that firms often expand internationally to earn greater returns from their core competencies, transferring the skills and products derived from their core

TABLE 15.1

Advantages and
Disadvantages of Entry
Modes

Entry Mode	Advantages	Disadvantages
Exporting	Ability to realize location and experience curve economies Increased speed and flexibility of engaging target markets	High transport costs Trade barriers Problems with local marketing agents
Turnkey contracts	Ability to earn returns from process technology skills in countries where FDI is restricted	Creation of efficient competitors Lack of long-term market presence
Licensing	Low development costs and risks Moderate involvement and commitment	Lack of control over technology Inability to realize location and experience curve economies Inability to engage in global strategic coordination
Franchising	Low development costs and risks Possible circumvention of import barriers Strong sales potential	Lack of control over quality Inability to engage in global strategic coordination
Joint ventures	Access to local partner's knowledge Shared development costs and risks Politically acceptable Typically no ownership restrictions	Lack of control over technology Inability to engage in global strategic coordination Inability to realize location and experience economies
Wholly owned subsidiaries	Protection of technology Ability to engage in global strategic coordination Ability to realize location and experience economies	High costs and risks Need for more human and nonhuman resources; interaction and integration with local employees

competencies to foreign markets where indigenous competitors lack those skills. The optimal entry mode for these firms depends to some degree on the nature of their core competencies. A distinction can be drawn between firms whose core competency is in technological know-how and those whose core competency is in management know-how.

Technological Know-How

As was observed in Chapter 8, if a firm's competitive advantage (its core competence) is based on control over proprietary technological know-how, licensing and joint-venture arrangements should be avoided if possible to minimize the risk of losing control over that technology. Thus, if a high-tech firm sets up operations in a foreign country to profit from a core competency in technological know-how, it will probably do so through a wholly owned subsidiary. This rule should not be viewed as hard and fast, however. Sometimes a licensing or joint-venture arrangement can be structured to reduce the risk of licensees or joint-venture partners expropriating technological know-how.

Another exception exists when a firm perceives its technological advantage to be only transitory when it expects rapid imitation of its core technology by competitors. In such cases, the firm might want to license its technology as rapidly as possible to foreign firms to gain global acceptance for its technology before the imitation occurs.[26] Such a strategy has some advantages. By licensing its technology to competitors, the firm may deter them from developing their own, possibly superior, technology. Further, by licensing its technology, the firm may establish its technology as the dominant design in the industry. This may ensure a steady stream of royalty payments. However, the attractions of licensing are frequently outweighed by the risks of losing control over technology, and if this is a risk, licensing should be avoided.

Management Know-How

The competitive advantage of many service firms is based on management know-how (e.g., KFC, McDonald's, Starbucks, Subway). For such firms, the risk of losing control over the management skills to franchisees or joint-venture partners is not that great. These firms' valuable asset is their brand name, and brand names are generally well protected by international laws pertaining to trademarks. Given this, many of the issues arising in the case of technological know-how are of less concern here. As a result, many service firms favor a combination of franchising and master subsidiaries to control the franchises within particular countries or regions. The master subsidiaries may be wholly owned or joint ventures, but most service firms have found that joint ventures with local partners work best for the master controlling subsidiaries. A joint venture is often politically more acceptable and brings a degree of local knowledge to the subsidiary.

PRESSURES FOR COST REDUCTIONS AND ENTRY MODE

The greater the pressures for cost reductions, the more likely a firm will want to pursue some combination of exporting and wholly owned subsidiaries. By manufacturing in those locations where factor conditions are optimal and then exporting to the rest of the world, a firm may be able to realize substantial location and experience curve economies. The firm might then want to export the finished product to marketing subsidiaries based in various countries. These subsidiaries will typically be wholly owned and have the responsibility for overseeing distribution in their particular countries. Setting up wholly owned marketing subsidiaries is preferable to joint-venture arrangements and to using foreign marketing agents because it gives the firm tight control that might be required for coordinating a globally dispersed value chain. It also gives the firm the ability to use the profits generated in one market to improve its competitive position in another market. In other words, firms pursuing global standardization or transnational strategies tend to prefer establishing wholly owned subsidiaries.

TEST PREP

Use SmartBook to help retain what you have learned. Access your instructor's Connect course to check out SmartBook or go to **learnsmartadvantage.com** for help.

LO15-4

Recognize the pros and cons of acquisitions versus greenfield ventures as an international market entry strategy.

Greenfield Venture or Acquisition?

A firm can establish a wholly owned subsidiary in a country by building a subsidiary from the ground up, the so-called Greenfield strategy, or by acquiring an enterprise in the target market.[27] The volume of cross-border acquisitions has been growing at a rapid rate for two decades. Over most of the past decades, between 40 and 80 percent of all foreign direct investment (FDI) inflows have been in the form of mergers and acquisitions.[28]

PROS AND CONS OF ACQUISITIONS

Acquisitions have three major points in their favor. First, they are quick to execute. By acquiring an established enterprise, a firm can rapidly build its presence in the target foreign market. When the German automobile company Daimler-Benz decided it needed a bigger presence in the U.S. automobile market, it did not increase that presence by building new factories to serve the United States, a process that would have taken years. Instead, it acquired the third-largest U.S. automobile company, Chrysler, and merged the two operations to form DaimlerChrysler (Daimler then spun off Chrysler into a private equity firm). When the Spanish telecommunications service provider Telefónica wanted to build a service presence in Latin America, it did so through a series of acquisitions, purchasing telecommunications companies in Brazil and Argentina. In these cases, the firms made acquisitions because they knew that was the quickest way to establish a sizable presence in the target market.

Second, in many cases firms make acquisitions to preempt their competitors. The need for preemption is particularly great in markets that are rapidly globalizing, such as telecommunications, where a combination of deregulation within nations and liberalization of regulations governing cross-border foreign direct investment has made it much easier for enterprises to enter foreign markets through acquisitions. Such markets may see concentrated waves of acquisitions as firms race each other to attain a global scale. In the telecommunications industry, for example, regulatory changes triggered what can be called a feeding frenzy, with firms entering each other's markets via acquisitions to establish a global presence. These included the $56 billion acquisition of AirTouch Communications in the United States by the British company Vodafone, which was the largest acquisition ever at that time; the $13 billion acquisition of One 2 One in Britain by the German company Deutsche Telekom; and the $6.4 billion acquisition of Excel Communications in the United States by Teleglobe of Canada.[29] A similar wave of cross-border acquisitions occurred in the global automobile industry, with Daimler acquiring Chrysler, Ford acquiring Volvo (and then selling Volvo as well), and Renault acquiring Nissan.

Third, managers may believe acquisitions to be less risky than greenfield ventures. When a firm makes an acquisition, it buys a set of assets that are producing a known revenue and profit stream. In contrast, the revenue and profit stream that a greenfield venture might generate is uncertain because it does not yet exist. When a firm makes an acquisition in a foreign market, it not only acquires a set of tangible assets, such as factories, logistics systems, and customer service systems, it also acquires valuable intangible assets, including a local brand name and managers' knowledge of the business environment in that nation. Such knowledge can reduce the risk of mistakes caused by ignorance of the national culture.

Despite the arguments for engaging in acquisitions, many acquisitions often produce disappointing results.[30] For example, a study by Mercer Management Consulting looked at 150 acquisitions worth more than $500 million each.[31] The Mercer study concluded that 50 percent of these acquisitions eroded shareholder value, while another 33 percent created only marginal returns. Only 17 percent were judged to be successful. Similarly, a study by KPMG, an accounting and management consulting company, looked at 700 large acquisitions. The study found that while some 30 percent of these actually created value for the acquiring company, 31 percent destroyed value, and the remainder had little impact.[32] A similar study by McKinsey & Company estimated that some 70 percent of mergers and acquisitions failed to achieve expected revenue synergies.[33] In a seminal study of the post-acquisition performance of acquired companies, David Ravenscraft and Mike Scherer concluded that, on average, the profits and market shares of acquired companies declined following acquisition.[34] They also noted that a smaller but substantial subset of those companies experienced traumatic difficulties, which ultimately led to their being sold by the acquiring company. Ravenscraft and Scherer's evidence suggests that many acquisitions destroy rather than create value. While most research has looked at domestic acquisitions, the findings probably also apply to cross-border acquisitions.[35]

Why Do Acquisitions Fail?

Acquisitions fail for several reasons. First, acquiring firms often overpay for the assets of the acquired firm. The price of the target firm can get bid up if more than one firm is interested in its purchase, as is often the case. In addition, the management of the acquiring firm is often too optimistic about the value that can be created via acquisition and is thus willing to pay a significant premium over a target firm's market capitalization. This is called the "hubris hypothesis" of why acquisitions fail. The hubris hypothesis postulates that top managers typically overestimate their ability to create value from an acquisition, primarily because rising to the top of a corporation has given them an exaggerated sense of their own capabilities.[36]

For example, Daimler acquired Chrysler in 1998 for $40 billion, a premium of 40 percent over the market value of Chrysler before the takeover bid. Daimler paid this much because it thought it could use Chrysler to help it grow market share in the United States. At the time, Daimler's management issued bold announcements about the "synergies" that would be created from combining the operations of the two companies. However, within a year of the acquisition, Daimler's German management was faced with a crisis at Chrysler, which was suddenly losing money due to weak sales in the United States. In retrospect, Daimler's management had been far too optimistic about the potential for future demand in the U.S. auto market and about the opportunities for creating value from "synergies."

Daimler acquired Chrysler at the end of a multiyear boom in U.S. auto sales and paid a large premium over Chrysler's market value just before demand slumped (and in 2007, in an admission of failure, Daimler sold its Chrysler unit to a private equity firm).[37]

Second, many acquisitions fail because there is a clash between the cultures of the acquiring and acquired firms. After an acquisition, many acquired companies experience high management turnover, possibly because their employees do not like the acquiring company's way of doing things.[38] This happened at DaimlerChrysler; many senior managers left Chrysler in the first year after the merger. Apparently, Chrysler executives disliked the dominance in decision making by Daimler's German managers, while the Germans resented that Chrysler's American managers were paid two to three times as much as their German counterparts. These cultural differences created tensions, which ultimately exhibited themselves in high management turnover at Chrysler.[39] The loss of management talent and expertise can materially harm the performance of the acquired unit.[40] This may be particularly problematic in an international business, where management of the acquired unit may have valuable local knowledge that can be difficult to replace.

Third, many acquisitions fail because attempts to realize gains by integrating the operations of the acquired and acquiring entities often run into roadblocks and take much longer than forecast. Differences in management philosophy and company culture can slow the integration of operations. Differences in national culture may exacerbate these problems. Bureaucratic haggling between managers also complicates the process. Again, this reportedly occurred at DaimlerChrysler, where grand plans to integrate the operations of the two companies were bogged down by endless committee meetings and by simple logistical considerations such as the six-hour time difference between Detroit and Germany. By the time an integration plan had been worked out, Chrysler was losing money, and Daimler's German managers suddenly had a crisis on their hands.

Finally, many acquisitions fail due to inadequate pre-acquisition screening.[41] Many firms decide to acquire other firms without thoroughly analyzing the potential benefits and costs. They often move with undue haste to execute the acquisition, perhaps because they fear another competitor may preempt them. After the acquisition, however, many acquiring firms discover that instead of buying a well-run business, they have purchased a troubled organization. This may be a particular problem in cross-border acquisitions because the acquiring firm may not fully understand the target firm's national culture and business system.

Reducing the Risks of Failure

These problems can all be overcome if the firm is careful about its acquisition strategy.[42] Screening of the foreign enterprise to be acquired—including a detailed auditing of operations, financial position, and management culture—can help to make sure the firm (1) does not pay too much for the acquired unit, (2) does not uncover any nasty surprises after the acquisition, and (3) acquires a firm whose organization culture is not antagonistic to that of the acquiring enterprise. It is also important for the acquirer to allay any concerns that management in the acquired enterprise might have. The objective should be to reduce unwanted management attrition after the acquisition. Finally, managers must move rapidly after an acquisition to put an integration plan in place and to act on that plan. Some people in both the acquiring and acquired units will try to slow or stop any integration efforts, particularly when losses of employment or management power are involved, and managers should have a plan for dealing with such impediments before they arise.

PROS AND CONS OF GREENFIELD VENTURES

The big advantage of establishing a greenfield venture in a foreign country is that it gives the firm a much greater ability to build the kind of subsidiary company that it wants. For example, it is much easier to build an organizational culture from scratch than it is to change the culture of an acquired unit. Similarly, it is much easier to establish a set of operating routines in a new subsidiary than it is to convert the operating routines of an acquired unit. This is a very important advantage for many international businesses, where transferring products, competencies, skills, and know-how from the established operations of the firm to the new subsidiary are principal ways of creating value. For example, when Lincoln Electric, the U.S. manufacturer of arc welding equipment, first ventured overseas, it did so by acquisitions, purchasing arc welding equipment companies in Europe. However, Lincoln's competitive advantage in the United States was based on a strong organizational culture and a unique set of incentives that encouraged its employees to do everything possible to increase productivity. Lincoln found through bitter experience that it was almost impossible to transfer its organizational culture and incentives to acquired firms, which had their own distinct organizational cultures and incentives. As a result, the firm switched its entry strategy and began to enter foreign countries by establishing greenfield ventures, building operations from the ground up. While this strategy takes more time to execute, Lincoln has found that it yields greater long-run returns than the acquisition strategy.

Set against this significant advantage are the disadvantages of establishing a greenfield venture. Greenfield ventures are slower to establish. They are also risky. As with any new venture, a degree of uncertainty is associated with future revenue and profit prospects. However, if the firm has already been successful in other foreign markets and understands what it takes to do business in other countries, these risks may not be that great. For example, having already gained great knowledge about operating internationally, the risk to McDonald's or Subway of entering yet another country is probably not that great. Also, Greenfield ventures are less risky than acquisitions in the sense that there is less potential for unpleasant surprises. A final disadvantage is the possibility of being preempted by more aggressive global competitors who enter via acquisitions and build a big market presence that limits the market potential for the greenfield venture.

WHICH CHOICE?

The choice between acquisitions and greenfield ventures is not an easy one. Both modes have their advantages and disadvantages. In general, the choice will depend on the circumstances confronting the firm. If the firm is seeking to enter a market where there are already well-established incumbent enterprises, and where global competitors are also interested in establishing a presence, it may pay the firm to enter via an acquisition. In such circumstances, a greenfield venture may be too slow to establish a sizable presence. However, if the firm is going to make an acquisition, its management should be cognizant of the risks associated with acquisitions that were discussed earlier and consider these when determining which firms to purchase. It may be better to enter by the slower route of a greenfield venture than to make a bad acquisition.

If the firm is considering entering a country where there are no incumbent competitors to be acquired, then a greenfield venture may be the only mode. Even when incumbents exist, if the competitive advantage of the firm is based on the transfer of organizationally embedded competencies, skills, routines, and culture, it may still be preferable to enter via a greenfield venture. Things such as skills and organizational culture, which are based on significant knowledge that is difficult to articulate and codify, are much easier to embed in a new venture than they are in an acquired entity, where the firm may have to overcome the established routines and culture of the acquired firm. Thus, as our earlier examples suggest, firms such as McDonald's and Lincoln Electric prefer to enter foreign markets by establishing greenfield ventures.

Strategic Alliances

Strategic alliances refer to cooperative agreements between potential or actual competitors. In this section, we are concerned specifically with strategic alliances between firms from different countries. Strategic alliances run the range from formal joint ventures, in which two or more firms have equity stakes (e.g., Fuji Xerox), to short-term contractual agreements, in which two companies agree to cooperate on a particular task (such as developing a new product). Collaboration between competitors is fashionable; recent decades have seen an explosion in the number of strategic alliances.

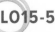 **TEST PREP**

Use SmartBook to help retain what you have learned. Access your instructor's Connect course to check out SmartBook or go to **learnsmartadvantage.com** for help.

LO15-5

Evaluate the pros and cons of entering into strategic alliances when going international.

ADVANTAGES OF STRATEGIC ALLIANCES

Firms ally themselves with actual or potential competitors for various strategic purposes.[43] First, strategic alliances may facilitate entry into a foreign market. For example, many firms believe that if they are to successfully enter the Chinese market, they need a local partner who understands business conditions and who has good connections (or *guanxi*—see Chapter 4). Thus, Warner Brothers entered into a joint venture with two Chinese partners to produce and distribute films in China. As a foreign film company, Warner found that if it wanted to produce films on its own for the Chinese market, it had to go through a complex approval process for every film, and it had to farm out distribution to a local company, which made doing business in China very difficult. Due to the participation of Chinese firms, however, the joint-venture films will go through a streamlined approval process, and the venture will be able to distribute any films it produces. Also, the joint venture will be able to produce films for Chinese TV, something that foreign firms are not allowed to do.[44]

Second, strategic alliances also allow firms to share the fixed costs (and associated risks) of developing new products or processes. An alliance between Boeing and a number of Japanese companies to build Boeing's commercial jetliner, the 787, was motivated by Boeing's desire to share the estimated $8 billion investment required to develop the aircraft. The Management Focus on Gazprom highlights how Gazprom leveraged strategic alliances in a number of ways.

Third, an alliance is a way to bring together complementary skills and assets that neither company could easily develop on its own.[45] For example, Microsoft and Toshiba established an alliance aimed at developing embedded microprocessors (essentially tiny computers) that can perform a variety of entertainment functions in an automobile (e.g., run a backseat DVD player or a wireless internet connection). The processors run a version of Microsoft's Windows operating system. Microsoft brought its software engineering skills to the alliance and Toshiba its skills in developing microprocessors.[46] The alliance between Cisco and Fujitsu was also formed to share know-how.

Fourth, it can make sense to form an alliance that will help the firm establish technological standards for the industry that will benefit the firm. For example, in 2011, Nokia, one of the leading makers of smartphones at the time, entered into an alliance with Microsoft under which Nokia agreed to license and use Microsoft's Windows Mobile operating system in Nokia's phones. The motivation for the alliance was in part to help establish Windows Mobile as the industry standard for smartphones as opposed to the rival operating systems such as Apple's iPhone and Google's Android. Unfortunately for Microsoft, the Nokia's Windows phones failed to gain sufficient market share. In 2013, Microsoft decided to acquire Nokia's mobile phone business and bring it in house so that it could ensure a continued aggressive push into the smartphone hardware business. Unfortunately, the Nokia and Microsoft deal ultimately resulted in a huge loss for Microsoft, which wrote off some $7.6 billion and cut 7,800 jobs in 2015—a short four years after the initial alliance—due to the failed purchase of Nokia.[47]

DISADVANTAGES OF STRATEGIC ALLIANCES

Some professionals have criticized strategic alliances on the grounds that they give competitors a low-cost route to new technology and markets.[48] For example, some argued that many strategic alliances between U.S. and Japanese firms are part of an implicit Japanese strategy to keep high-paying, high-value-added jobs in Japan while gaining the project engineering and production process skills that underlie the competitive success of many U.S. companies.[49] They argued that Japanese success in the machine tool and semiconductor industries was built on U.S. technology acquired through strategic alliances. And they argued that U.S. managers were aiding the Japanese by entering alliances that channel new inventions to Japan and provide a U.S. sales and distribution network for the resulting products. Although such deals may generate short-term profits, so the argument goes, in the long run the result is to "hollow out" U.S. firms, leaving them with no competitive advantage in the global marketplace.

Gazprom and Global Strategic Alliances

Gazprom (**gazprom.com**) is a Russian company headquartered in Moscow. It was founded in 1989 and is focused on the business of extraction, production, and sale of petroleum, natural gas, and other petrochemicals. The company name is a combination of the Russian words *gazovaya promyshlennost* (in the Russian alphabet: газовая промышленность, meaning "gas industry"). Gazprom has more than 400,000 employees, annual sales of 5.59 trillion rubles (roughly US$110 billion), and is owned by the Russian government. However, Gazprom also has 55 subsidiaries in which it has 100 percent ownership, 32 ventures with more than 50 percent ownership, and 21 strategic alliances where its share is less than 50 percent.

One of the strategic alliances that Gazprom has engaged in is with Royal Dutch Shell—the US$235 billion company headquartered in The Hague, Netherlands, but incorporated in the United Kingdom. From the vantage point of Gazprom, the strategic alliance with Shell allows the Russian gas giant to penetrate new markets. Additionally, the Gazprom–Shell agreement makes the expansion of the firms' joint $20 billion liquefied natural gas plant on the eastern island of Sakhalin (a Russian island in the Pacific Ocean, north of Japan) possible.

Gazprom is also involved in an alliance with Dow Chemical Company—the $60 billion American multinational chemical corporation headquartered in Midland, Michigan, in the U.S. The alliance between Gazprom and Dow is to expand trading in carbon dioxide emission credits, which is intended to slow climate change. Gazprom agreed to look at opportunities where Dow's technologies could potentially be involved in helping to reduce carbon emissions. The outcome would be that Dow could then use some of the carbon emissions credits to offset industrial activities, while Gazprom's trading arm in the United Kingdom could market any excess credits.

Gazprom has also engaged in a strategic "arctic" alliance with Lukoil, another Russian company. Lukoil is one of Russia's largest oil companies, with about US$150 billion in annual sales. This alliance is more narrowly defined than many others in that the two companies intend to support each other in bids for offshore projects and, by collaborating, counter the power of Rosneft. (Rosneft is a US$92 billion oil company that is also majority owned by the government of Russia.) A key part of this cooperation will unfold in the Barents Sea (a sea of the Arctic Ocean, located off the northern coasts of Norway and Russia).

Gazprom has also entered into alliances with other countries, such as China. The Chinese alliance came about as the Kremlin intensified efforts to focus more on East Asia to offset some of the constraints imposed on the company by Europe as a function of the Ukrainian crisis, as well as its continued conflict with Turkey. Consequently, Gazprom and China National Petroleum Corp (CNPC) signed an agreement on the cross-border section of the Power of Siberia gas pipeline, including the subwater link across the Amur River. The deal also involves the "Eastern" gas pipeline route.

Sources: "Gazprom and Shell Committed to Broader Cooperation in LNG Sector," June 16, 2016, gazprom.com/press/news/2016/june/article276698; Andrew E. Kramer, "Gazprom and Dow Chemical Expand Emissions Alliance," *The New York Times*, June 18, 2009; Atle Staalesen, "Gazprom, Lukoil in Arctic Alliance," *Barents Observer*, May 20, 2015; Sergei Blagov, "Russia Seeks to Strengthen Energy Alliance with China," *Asia Times*, December 18, 2015.

These critics have a point; alliances have risks. Unless a firm is careful, it can give away more than it receives. But there are so many examples of apparently successful alliances between firms—including alliances between U.S. and Japanese firms—that the critics' position seems extreme. It is difficult to see how the Microsoft–Toshiba alliance, the Boeing–Mitsubishi alliance for the 787, and the Fuji–Xerox alliance fit the critics' thesis. In these cases, both partners seem to have gained from the alliances. Why do some alliances benefit both firms while others benefit one firm and hurt the other? The next section provides an answer to this question.

MAKING ALLIANCES WORK

The failure rate for international strategic alliances seems to be high. One study of 49 international strategic alliances found that two-thirds run into serious managerial and financial troubles within two years of their formation, and that although many of these problems are solved, 33 percent are ultimately rated as failures by the parties involved.[50] The success of an alliance seems to be a function of three main factors: partner selection, alliance structure, and the manner in which the alliance is managed.

Partner Selection

One key to making a strategic alliance work is to select the right ally. A good ally, or partner, has three characteristics. First, a good partner helps the firm achieve its strategic goals, whether they are market access, sharing the costs and risks of product development, or gaining access to critical core competencies. The partner must have capabilities that the firm lacks and that it values. Second, a good partner shares the firm's vision for the purpose of the alliance. If two firms approach an alliance with radically different agendas, the chances are great that the relationship will not be harmonious, will not flourish, and will end in divorce. Third, a good partner is unlikely to try to opportunistically exploit the alliance for its own ends, that is, to expropriate the firm's technological know-how while giving away little in return. In this respect, firms with reputations for "fair play" probably make the best allies. For example, companies such as General Electric are involved in so many strategic alliances that it would not pay the company to trample over individual alliance partners.[51] This would tarnish GE's reputation of being a good ally and would make it more difficult for GE to attract alliance partners.

To select a partner with these three characteristics, a firm needs to conduct comprehensive research on potential alliance candidates. To increase the probability of selecting a good partner, the firm should

1. Collect as much pertinent, publicly available information on potential allies as possible. Today's social media world facilitates data collection and a better understanding of potential partners.
2. Gather data from informed third parties. These include firms that have had alliances with the potential partners, investment bankers that have had dealings with them, and former employees.
3. Get to know the potential partner as well as possible before committing to an alliance. This should include face-to-face meetings between senior managers (and perhaps middle-level managers) to ensure that the chemistry is right.

Alliance Structure

A partner having been selected, the alliance should be structured so that the firm's risks of giving too much away to the partner are reduced to an acceptable level. First, alliances can be designed to make it difficult (if not impossible) to transfer technology not meant to be transferred. The design, development, manufacture, and service of a product manufactured by an alliance can be structured so as to wall off sensitive technologies to prevent their leakage to the other participant. In a long-standing alliance between General Electric and Snecma to build commercial aircraft engines for single-aisle commercial jet aircraft, for example, GE reduced the risk of excess transfer by walling off certain sections of the production process. The modularization effectively cut off the transfer of what GE regarded as key competitive technology, while permitting Snecma access to final assembly.[52]

Second, contractual safeguards can be written into an alliance agreement to guard against the risk of opportunism by a partner (opportunism includes the theft of technology and/or markets). For example, TRW Automotive has three strategic alliances with large Japanese auto component suppliers to produce seat belts, engine valves, and steering gears for sale to Japanese-owned auto assembly plants in the United States. TRW has clauses in each of its alliance contracts that bar the Japanese firms from competing with TRW to supply U.S.-owned auto companies with component parts. By doing this, TRW protects itself against the possibility that the Japanese companies are entering into the alliances merely to gain access to the North American market to compete with TRW in its home market.

Third, both parties to an alliance can agree in advance to swap skills and technologies that the other covets, thereby ensuring a chance for equitable gain. Cross-licensing agreements are one way to achieve this goal. Fourth, the risk of opportunism by an alliance partner can be reduced if the firm extracts a significant credible commitment from its partner in advance. The long-term alliance between Xerox and Fuji to build photocopiers for the Asian market perhaps best illustrates this. Rather than enter into an informal agreement or a licensing arrangement (which Fuji Photo initially wanted), Xerox insisted that Fuji invest in a 50–50 joint venture to serve Japan and East Asia. This venture constituted such a significant investment in people, equipment, and facilities that Fuji Photo was committed from the outset to making the alliance work in order to earn a return on its investment. By agreeing to the joint venture, Fuji essentially made a credible commitment to the alliance. Given this, Xerox felt secure in transferring its photocopier technology to Fuji.[53]

Managing the Alliance

Once a partner has been selected and an appropriate alliance structure has been agreed on, the task facing the firm is to maximize its benefits from the alliance. As in all international business deals, an important factor is sensitivity to cultural differences (see Chapter 4). Many differences in management style are attributable to cultural differences, and managers need to make allowances for these in dealing with their partner. Beyond this, maximizing the benefits from an alliance seems to involve building trust between partners and learning from partners.[54]

Managing an alliance successfully requires building interpersonal relationships between the firms' managers, or what is sometimes referred to as *relational capital*.[55] This is one lesson that can be drawn from a successful strategic alliance between Ford and Mazda. Ford and Mazda set up a framework of meetings within which their managers not only discuss matters pertaining to the alliance, but also have time to get to know each other better. The belief is that the resulting friendships help build trust and facilitate harmonious relations between the two firms. Personal relationships also foster an informal management network between the firms. This network can then be used to help solve problems arising in more formal contexts (such as in joint committee meetings between personnel from the two firms).

Academics have argued that a major determinant of how much knowledge a company gains from an alliance is its ability to learn from its alliance partner.[56] For example, in a five-year study of 15 strategic alliances between major multinationals, Gary Hamel, Yves Doz, and C. K. Prahalad focused on a number of alliances between Japanese companies and Western (European or American) partners.[57] In every case in which a Japanese company emerged from an alliance stronger than its Western partner, the Japanese company had made a greater effort to learn. Few Western companies studied seemed to want to learn from their Japanese partners. They tended to regard the alliance purely as a cost-sharing or risk-sharing device, rather than as an opportunity to learn how a potential competitor does business.

To maximize the learning benefits of an alliance, a firm must try to learn from its partner and then apply the knowledge within its own organization. It has been suggested that all operating employees should be well briefed on the partner's strengths and weaknesses and should understand how acquiring particular skills will bolster their firm's competitive position. Hamel and colleagues note that this is already standard practice among Japanese companies. They made this observation:

> We accompanied a Japanese development engineer on a tour through a partner's factory. This engineer dutifully took notes on plant layout, the number of production stages, the rate at which the line was running, and the number of employees. He recorded all this despite the fact that he had no manufacturing responsibility in his own company, and that the alliance did not encompass joint manufacturing. Such dedication greatly enhances learning.[58]

For such learning to be of value, it must be diffused throughout the organization. To achieve this, the managers involved in the alliance should educate their colleagues about the skills of the alliance partner.

✔ **TEST PREP**

Use SmartBook to help retain what you have learned. Access your instructor's Connect course to check out SmartBook or go to **learnsmartadvantage.com** for help.

Key Terms

SUMMARY

The chapter made the following points:

1. Basic entry decisions include identifying which markets to enter, when to enter those markets, and on what scale.

2. The most attractive foreign markets tend to be found in politically stable developed and developing nations that have free market systems and where there is not a dramatic upsurge in either inflation rates or private-sector debt.

3. There are several advantages associated with entering a national market early, before other international businesses have established themselves. These advantages must be balanced against the pioneering costs that early entrants often have to bear, including the greater risk of business failure.

4. Large-scale entry into a national market constitutes a major strategic commitment that is likely to change the nature of competition in that market and limit the entrant's future strategic flexibility. Although making major strategic commitments can yield many benefits, there are also risks associated with such a strategy.

5. There are six modes of entering a foreign market: exporting, creating turnkey projects, licensing, franchising, establishing joint ventures, and setting up a wholly owned subsidiary.

6. Exporting has the advantages of facilitating the realization of experience curve economies and of avoiding the costs of setting up manufacturing operations in another country. Disadvantages include high transport costs, trade barriers, and problems with local marketing agents.

7. Turnkey projects allow firms to export their process know-how to countries where foreign direct investment (FDI) might be prohibited, thereby enabling the firm to earn a greater return from this asset. The disadvantage is that the firm may inadvertently create efficient global competitors in the process.

8. The main advantage of licensing is that the licensee bears the costs and risks of opening a foreign market. Disadvantages include the risk of losing technological know-how to the licensee and a lack of tight control over licensees.

9. The main advantage of franchising is that the franchisee bears the costs and risks of opening a foreign market. Disadvantages center on problems of quality control of distant franchisees.

10. Joint ventures have the advantages of sharing the costs and risks of opening a foreign market and of gaining local knowledge and political influence. Disadvantages include the risk of losing control over technology and a lack of tight control.

11. The advantages of wholly owned subsidiaries include tight control over technological know-how. The main disadvantage is that the firm must bear all the costs and risks of opening a foreign market.

12. The optimal choice of entry mode depends on the firm's strategy. When technological know-how constitutes a firm's core competence, wholly owned subsidiaries are preferred, because they best control technology. When management know-how constitutes a firm's core competence, foreign franchises controlled by joint ventures seem to be optimal. When the firm is pursuing a global standardization or transnational strategy, the need for tight control over operations to realize location and experience curve economies suggests wholly owned subsidiaries are the best entry mode.

13. When establishing a wholly owned subsidiary in a country, a firm must decide whether to do so by a greenfield venture strategy or by acquiring an established enterprise in the target market.

14. Acquisitions are quick to execute, may enable a firm to preempt its global competitors, and involve buying a known revenue and profit stream. Acquisitions may fail when the acquiring firm

overpays for the target, when the cultures of the acquiring and acquired firms clash, when there is a high level of management attrition after the acquisition, and when there is a failure to integrate the operations of the acquiring and acquired firm.

15. The advantage of a greenfield venture in a foreign country is that it gives the firm a much greater ability to build the kind of subsidiary company that it wants. For example, it is much easier to build an organizational culture from scratch than it is to change the culture of an acquired unit.

16. Strategic alliances are cooperative agreements between actual or potential competitors. The advantage of alliances is that they facilitate entry into foreign markets, enable partners to share the fixed costs and risks associated with new

products and processes, facilitate the transfer of complementary skills between companies, and help firms establish technical standards.

17. The disadvantage of a strategic alliance is that the firm risks giving away technological know-how and market access to its alliance partner.

18. The disadvantages associated with alliances can be reduced if the firm selects partners carefully, paying close attention to the firm's reputation and the structure of the alliance to avoid unintended transfers of know-how.

19. Two keys to making alliances work seem to be building trust and informal communications networks between partners and taking proactive steps to learn from alliance partners.

Critical Thinking and Discussion Questions

1. Review the Management Focus on Tesco, and then answer the following questions:

   a. Why did Tesco's initial international expansion strategy focus on developing nations?

   b. How does Tesco create value in its international operations?

   c. In Asia, Tesco has a history of entering into joint-venture agreements with local partners. What are the benefits of doing this for Tesco? What are the risks? How are those risks mitigated?

   d. Tesco's entry into the United States represented a departure from its historic strategy of focusing on developing nations. Why do you think Tesco made this decision? How is the U.S. market different from other markets that Tesco has entered?

2. Licensing proprietary technology to foreign competitors is the best way to give up a firm's competitive advantage. Discuss.

3. Discuss how the need for control over foreign operations varies with firms' strategies and core

competencies. What are the implications for the choice of entry mode?

4. A small Canadian firm that has developed valuable new medical products using its unique biotechnology know-how is trying to decide how best to serve the European Union market. Its choices are given below. The cost of investment in manufacturing facilities will be a major one for the Canadian firm, but it is not outside its reach. If these are the firm's only options, which one would you advise it to choose? Why?

   a. Manufacture the products at home, and let foreign sales agents handle marketing.

   b. Manufacture the products at home, and set up a wholly owned subsidiary in Europe to handle marketing.

   c. Enter into an alliance with a large European pharmaceutical firm. The products would be manufactured in Europe by the 50–50 joint venture and marketed by the European firm.

globalEDGE research task   globaledge.msu.edu

Use the globalEDGE™ website (**globaledge.msu.edu**) to complete the following exercises:

1. *Entrepreneur* magazine annually publishes a ranking of the *top global franchises*. Provide a list of the top 25 companies that pursue franchising as their preferred mode of international

expansion. Study one of these companies in detail, and describe its business model, its international expansion pattern, desirable qualifications in possible franchisees, and the support and training the company typically provides.

2. The U.S. Commercial Service prepares reports known as the *Country Commercial Guide* for countries of interest to U.S. investors. Utilize the *Country Commercial Guide* for Russia to gather information on this country's energy and mining industry. Considering that your company has plans to enter Russia in the foreseeable future, select the most appropriate entry method. Be sure to support your decision with the information collected.

CLOSING CASE

IKEA Entering India, Finally!

The Swedish home-furnishings giant IKEA finally entered India in 2018 after more than five years of preparation (the final two years spent building stores). Nevertheless, the question lingers: Can IKEA adapt to the aesthetic wants and needs of Indian customers, and can the company motivate Indian customers to buy into the do-it-yourself bug that is a symbol of the IKEA brand? After all, many customers around the world think that IKEA's success was built on the "L-shaped" metal IKEA tool used to put together virtually all of IKEA's furniture after you get the pieces out of the box. And no one knows what to call that L-shaped tool, incidentally—however, there is an official IKEA emoji for it for smartphones, even a keyboard app for iOS and Android phones that uses IKEA emoticons. (The meatball plate with a Swedish flag at the top looks interesting!) But is this a style, emoji, emoticons, and lifestyle that will work in India? And how is it working so far?

India became the 51st country that IKEA, the largest furniture company in the world, entered since its founding in 1943. Over the decades, IKEA has become a $43 billion company in sales annually, which has been the envy of the furniture industry and the benchmarking model for companies across several industries around the world. The flat packaging, high quality for the price you pay (i.e., great value), and global supply chains make IKEA a superbly efficient company with a very effective business model. Amazingly, the business model has been in place ever since Ingvar Kamprad founded IKEA, with only minimal changes made to that model so it could work on a much larger scale, and IKEA has seen rapid growth almost every year.

The IKEA business model and the company's assortment of products are now set to take over India, as they have in other countries. After all, IKEA's market entry into China in 1998 went reasonably well. IKEA now has 3 stores in Shanghai, 2 in Beijing, 2 in Chengdu, and 1 store each in Tianjin, Guangzhou, Shenzhen, Nanjing, Dalian, and Shenyang, as well as 11 more stores across smaller cities in China. For India, IKEA initially plans to open 25 stores, and the company is looking at 49 Indian cities where they may build an IKEA store in the future. The 25-store plans call for an investment of about $2 billion over 15 to 20 years. As we said in the opening, IKEA began its India market entry planning in 2013, and started building in 2016. The first construction took place in Hyderabad—a 400,000 square-foot store—at a cost of $110 million.

To prepare its Indian customers' mindsets before IKEA opened the store in 2018, the company unwrapped its first experiential center, IKEA Hej (Hello) Home, close to the IT hub of Hyderabad, as a way to coax Hyderabad customers into the IKEA model. The Hej Home small-scale store provides some insight into IKEA products and solutions, offering items to Indian customers that they could buy before the store opened in Hyderabad. This also eased the market entry into India and helped point out glaring problems that IKEA management could tackle before opening the actual large-scale IKEA store. The Hej Home, designed and built over a six-month period, highlights what IKEA stands for and what to expect. IKEA Hej Home reflects IKEA's understanding of life at home in India, and offers unique home-furnishing solutions for Indian homes. It showcases the IKEA food and room settings based on its understanding of "life at home" for Hyderabadi families.

The preparation to get to the IKEA Hej Home concept, and ultimately to the first large-scale store opening in Hyderabad, was a long research-oriented endeavor. The Swedish home furnishings giant, with a reputation for being very Swedish in almost everything it does, sent one of its top design executives, Marie Lundström, to India on a mission to understand the Indian mindset and aesthetic. IKEA had decided that it needed to learn everything it possibly could about its Indian customers by studying a variety of Indian homes, places, and settings. IKEA's entry into China in 1998 went well, but it was done before the era of global social media that we now live in. The company knew that they could not afford to go wrong in India; their brand depended on it.

Marie Lundström didn't leave a single stone unturned, to use a common cliché! She visited a couple hundred Indian homes across the vast landscape of India, and spent countless hours interacting with Indian family members. IKEA also handed out typical customer surveys to a large cross-section of potential customers. In all, under Lundström's leadership, IKEA found some important characteristics of Indian customers that could be effectively used by the company to make sure their market entry in 2018 was as successful as it could possibly be. For example, some of the findings indicated that Indians love color. Also, Indians' family lives center around the couch. They watch TV while eating, similar to the lifestyles of Americans and that of other nationalities. Still, this finding was helpful in understanding India, the country's customers, and their characteristics. Unfortunately, customers in India are not big fans of the IKEA trademark of "do-it-yourself."

Taking all of this into account, IKEA could now plan accordingly. The company went about meticulously arranging its large-scale store design and product selection for one of the largest economies in the world, with one of the largest potential customer populations. In some ways, it is remarkable that it took IKEA only five years to accomplish all this, from initial conception to opening its first store in Hyderabad. It has been a fascinating journey for IKEA, and a significant deviation from the normal practices of a company that prides itself on being Swedish in its processes, product names, and the food served in its restaurants! To date, IKEA has about 400 employees in India, with plans to increase that number to 15,000 workers by 2025, half of them being women.

Sources: Rathna Bhushan, "Ikea Betting on New Markets; Will Open Stores in India Next Year," *The Economic Times*, April 27, 2017; Ashish Gupta, "Is India Ready for IKEA?" *Fortune India*, March 24, 2017; Natasha Lomas, "IKEA Does Emoji," *Tech Crunch*, February 11, 2015; V. Rishi Kumar, "IKEA Opens First Hej Home in India At Hyderabad," *Business Line*, November 22, 2017. Saurabh Singh, "IKEA's India Plan: To Hire 15,000 Co-Workers with Equal Representation from Women," *EnTrackr*, December 7, 2017.

Case Discussion Questions

1. Did IKEA enter India too late in its evolution? The company started in 1943 and was already in 50 countries. Should operations in India have started sooner? If you could decide for them, what other country markets would you have IKEA enter, and why?

2. To prepare Indian customers' mindsets before IKEA opened its first store in 2018, the company unwrapped its first experiential center IKEA Hej (Hello) Home close to the IT hub of Hyderabad as a way to ingratiate Hyderabad customers into the IKEA model. How can this experiential model be used in other countries?

3. Entry into India has been a fascinating journey for IKEA, and a deviation from its normal Swedish-aligned business practices. Should IKEA become less Swedish when entering new international markets, as they did in India, or should IKEA stay Swedish as much as possible?

Endnotes

1. For interesting empirical studies that deal with the issues of timing and resource commitments, see T. Isobe, S. Makino, and D. B. Montgomery, "Resource Commitment, Entry Timing, and Market Performance of Foreign Direct Investments in Emerging Economies," *Academy of Management Journal* 43, no. 3 (2000), pp. 468–84; Y. Pan and P. S. K. Chi, "Financial Performance and Survival of Multinational Corporations in China," *Strategic Management Journal* 20, no. 4 (1999), pp. 359–74. A complementary theoretical perspective on this issue can be found in V. Govindarjan and A. K. Gupta, *The Quest for Global Dominance* (San Francisco: Jossey-Bass, 2001).

Also see F. Vermeulen and H. Barkeme, "Pace, Rhythm and Scope: Process Dependence in Building a Profitable Multinational Corporation," *Strategic Management Journal* 23 (2002), pp. 637–54.

2. Infoplease, www.infoplease.com/world/world-statistics/how-many-countries, accessed June 3, 2017.

3. This can be reconceptualized as the resource base of the entrant, relative to indigenous competitors. For work that focuses on this issue, see W. C. Bogner, H. Thomas, and J. McGee, "A Longitudinal Study of the Competitive Positions and Entry Paths of European Firms in the U.S. Pharmaceutical Market,"

Strategic Management Journal 17 (1996), pp. 85–107; D. Collis, "A Resource-Based Analysis of Global Competition," *Strategic Management Journal* 12 (1991), pp. 49–68; S. Tallman, "Strategic Management Models and Resource-Based Strategies among MNEs in a Host Market," *Strategic Management Journal* 12 (1991), pp. 69–82.

4. For a discussion of first-mover advantages, see M. Lieberman and D. Montgomery, "First-Mover Advantages," *Strategic Management Journal* 9 (Summer Special Issue, 1988), pp. 41–58.

5. J. M. Shaver, W. Mitchell, and B. Yeung, "The Effect of Own Firm and Other Firm Experience on Foreign Direct Investment Survival in the United States, 1987–92," *Strategic Management Journal* 18 (1997), pp. 811–24.

6. S. Zaheer and E. Mosakowski, "The Dynamics of the Liability of Foreignness: A Global Study of Survival in the Financial Services Industry," *Strategic Management Journal* 18 (1997), pp. 439–64.

7. Shaver et al., "The Effect of Own Firm and Other Firm Experience."

8. P. Ghemawat, *Commitment: The Dynamics of Strategy* (New York: Free Press, 1991).

9. R. Luecke, *Scuttle Your Ships before Advancing* (Oxford: Oxford University Press, 1994).

10. Isobe et al., "Resource Commitment, Entry Timing, and Market Performance"; Pan and Chi, "Financial Performance and Survival of Multinational Corporations in China"; Govindarjan and Gupta, *The Quest for Global Dominance.*

11. Christopher Bartlett and Sumantra Ghoshal, "Going Global: Lessons from Late Movers," *Harvard Business Review*, March–April 2000, pp. 132–45.

12. This section draws on numerous studies, including C. W. L. Hill, P. Hwang, and W. C. Kim, "An Eclectic Theory of the Choice of International Entry Mode," *Strategic Management Journal* 11 (1990), pp. 117–28; C. W. L. Hill and W. C. Kim, "Searching for a Dynamic Theory of the Multinational Enterprise: A Transaction Cost Model," *Strategic Management Journal* 9 (Special Issue on Strategy Content, 1988), pp. 93–104; E. Anderson and H. Gatignon, "Modes of Foreign Entry: A Transaction Cost Analysis and Propositions," *Journal of International Business Studies* 17 (1986), pp. 1–26; F. R. Root, *Entry Strategies for International Markets* (Lexington, MA: D. C. Heath, 1980); A. Madhok, "Cost, Value and Foreign Market Entry: The Transaction and the Firm," *Strategic Management Journal* 18 (1997), pp. 39–61; K. D. Brouthers and L. B. Brouthers, "Acquisition or Greenfield Start-Up?" *Strategic Management Journal* 21, no. 1 (2000), pp. 89–97; X. Martin and R. Salmon, "Knowledge Transfer Capacity and Its Implications for the Theory of the Multinational Enterprise," *Journal of International Business Studies*, July 2003, p. 356; A. Verbeke, "The Evolutionary View of the MNE and the Future of Internalization Theory," *Journal of International Business Studies*, November 2003, pp. 498–515.

13. For a general discussion of licensing, see F. J. Contractor, "The Role of Licensing in International Strategy," *Columbia Journal of World Business*, Winter 1982, pp. 73–83.

14. See E. Terazono and C. Lorenz, "An Angry Young Warrior," *Financial Times*, September 19, 1994, p. 11; K. McQuade and B. Gomes-Casseres, "Xerox and FujiXerox," Harvard Business School Case No. 9-391-156.

15. O. E. Williamson, *The Economic Institutions of Capitalism* (New York: Free Press, 1985).

16. J. H. Dunning and M. McQueen, "The Eclectic Theory of International Production: A Case Study of the International Hotel Industry," *Managerial and Decision Economics* 2 (1981), pp. 197–210.

17. Andrew E. Serwer, "McDonald's Conquers the World," *Fortune*, October 17, 1994, pp. 103–16.

18. For an excellent review of the basic theoretical literature of joint ventures, see B. Kogut, "Joint Ventures: Theoretical and Empirical Perspectives," *Strategic Management Journal* 9 (1988), pp. 319–32. More recent studies include T. Chi, "Option to Acquire or Divest a Joint Venture," *Strategic Management Journal* 21, no. 6 (2000), pp. 665–88; H. Merchant and D. Schendel, "How Do International Joint Ventures Create Shareholder Value?" *Strategic Management Journal* 21, no. 7 (2000), pp. 723–37; H. K. Steensma and M. A. Lyles, "Explaining IJV Survival in a Transitional Economy through Social Exchange and Knowledge Based Perspectives," *Strategic Management Journal* 21, no. 8 (2000), pp. 831–51; J. F. Hennart and M. Zeng, "Cross-Cultural Differences and Joint Venture Longevity," *Journal of International Business Studies*, December 2002, pp. 699–717.

19. D. G. Bradley, "Managing against Expropriation," *Harvard Business Review*, July–August 1977, pp. 78–90.

20. J. A. Robins, S. Tallman, and K. Fladmoe-Lindquist, "Autonomy and Dependence of International Cooperative Ventures," *Strategic Management Journal*, October 2002, pp. 881–902.

21. Speech given by Tony Kobayashi at the University of Washington Business School, October 1992.

22. A. C. Inkpen and P. W. Beamish, "Knowledge, Bargaining Power, and the Instability of International Joint Ventures," *Academy of Management Review* 22 (1997), pp. 177–202; S. H. Park and G. R. Ungson, "The Effect of National Culture, Organizational Complementarity, and Economic Motivation on Joint Venture Dissolution," *Academy of Management Journal* 40 (1997), pp. 279–307.

23. Inkpen and Beamish, "Knowledge, Bargaining Power, and the Instability of International Joint Ventures."

24. See Brouthers and Brouthers, "Acquisition or Greenfield Start-Up?"; J. F. Hennart and Y. R. Park, "Greenfield versus Acquisition: The Strategy of Japanese Investors in the United States," *Management Science*, 1993, pp. 1054–70.

25. This section draws on Hill et al., "An Eclectic Theory of the Choice of International Entry Mode."

26. C. W. L. Hill, "Strategies for Exploiting Technological Innovations: When and When Not to License," *Organization Science* 3 (1992), pp. 428–41.

27. See Brouthers and Brouthers, "Acquisition or Greenfield Start-Up?"; J. Anand and A. Delios, "Absolute and Relative Resources as Determinants of International Acquisitions," *Strategic Management Journal*, February 2002, pp. 119–34.

28. United Nations, *World Investment Report, 2010* (New York and Geneva: United Nations, 2010).

29. United Nations, *World Investment Report, 2010.*

30. For evidence on acquisitions and performance, see R. E. Caves, "Mergers, Takeovers, and Economic Efficiency," *International*

Journal of Industrial Organization 7 (1989), pp. 151–74; M. C. Jensen and R. S. Ruback, "The Market for Corporate Control: The Scientific Evidence," *Journal of Financial Economics* 11 (1983), pp. 5–50; R. Roll, "Empirical Evidence on Takeover Activity and Shareholder Wealth," in *Knights, Raiders and Targets*, ed. J. C. Coffee, L. Lowenstein, and S. Rose (Oxford: Oxford University Press, 1989); A. Schleifer and R. W. Vishny, "Takeovers in the 60s and 80s: Evidence and Implications," *Strategic Management Journal* 12 (Winter 1991 Special Issue), pp. 51–60; T. H. Brush, "Predicted Changes in Operational Synergy and Post-acquisition Performance of Acquired Businesses," *Strategic Management Journal* 17 (1996), pp. 1–24; A. Seth, K. P. Song, and R. R. Pettit, "Value Creation and Destruction in Cross-Border Acquisitions," *Strategic Management Journal* 23 (October 2002), pp. 921–40.

31. J. Warner, J. Templeman, and R. Horn, "The Case against Mergers," *BusinessWeek*, October 30, 1995, pp. 122–34.

32. "Few Takeovers Pay Off for Big Buyers," *Investor's Business Daily*, May 25, 2001, p. 1.

33. S. A. Christofferson, R. S. McNish, and D. L. Sias, "Where Mergers Go Wrong," *The McKinsey Quarterly* 2 (2004), pp. 92–110.

34. D. J. Ravenscraft and F. M. Scherer, *Mergers, Selloffs, and Economic Efficiency* (Washington, DC: Brookings Institution, 1987).

35. See P. Ghemawat and F. Ghadar, "The Dubious Logic of Global Mega-Mergers," *Harvard Business Review*, July–August 2000, pp. 65–72.

36. R. Roll, "The Hubris Hypothesis of Corporate Takeovers," *Journal of Business* 59 (1986), pp. 197–216.

37. "Marital Problems," *The Economist*, October 14, 2000.

38. See J. P. Walsh, "Top Management Turnover Following Mergers and Acquisitions," *Strategic Management Journal* 9 (1988), pp. 173–83.

39. B. Vlasic and B. A. Stertz, *Taken for a Ride: How Daimler-Benz Drove Off with Chrysler* (New York: HarperCollins, 2000).

40. See A. A. Cannella and D. C. Hambrick, "Executive Departure and Acquisition Performance," *Strategic Management Journal* 14 (1993), pp. 137–52.

41. P. Haspeslagh and D. Jemison, *Managing Acquisitions* (New York: Free Press, 1991).

42. Haspeslagh and Jemison, *Managing Acquisitions*.

43. See K. Ohmae, "The Global Logic of Strategic Alliances," *Harvard Business Review*, March–April 1989, pp. 143–54; G. Hamel, Y. L. Doz, and C. K. Prahalad, "Collaborate with Your Competitors and Win!" *Harvard Business Review*, January–February 1989, pp. 133–39; W. Burgers, C. W. L. Hill, and W. C. Kim, "Alliances in the Global Auto Industry," *Strategic Management Journal* 14 (1993), pp. 419–32; P. Kale, H. Singh, and H. Perlmutter, "Learning and Protection of Proprietary Assets in Strategic Alliances: Building Relational Capital," *Strategic Management Journal* 21 (2000), pp. 217–37.

44. L. T. Chang, "China Eases Foreign Film Rules," *The Wall Street Journal*, October 15, 2004, p. B2.

45. B. L. Simonin, "Transfer of Marketing Know-How in International Strategic Alliances," *Journal of International Business Studies*, 1999, pp. 463–91; J. W. Spencer, "Firms' Knowledge Sharing Strategies in the Global Innovation System," *Strategic Management Journal* 24 (2003), pp. 217–33.

46. C. Souza, "Microsoft Teams with MIPS, Toshiba," *EBN*, February 10, 2003, p. 4.

47. Tom Warren, "Microsoft Writes Off $7.6 Billion from Nokia Deal, Announces 7,800 Job Cuts," *The Verge*, July 8, 2015.

48. Kale et al., "Learning and Protection of Proprietary Assets."

49. R. B. Reich and E. D. Mankin, "Joint Ventures with Japan Give Away Our Future," *Harvard Business Review*, March–April 1986, pp. 78–90.

50. J. Bleeke and D. Ernst, "The Way to Win in Cross-Border Alliances," *Harvard Business Review*, November–December 1991, pp. 127–35.

51. C. H. Deutsch, "The Venturesome Giant," *The New York Times*, October 5, 2007, pp. C1, C8.

52. "Odd Couple: Jet Engines," *The Economist*, May 5, 2007, pp. 79–80.

53. McQuade and Gomes-Casseres, "Xerox and FujiXerox."

54. See T. Khanna, R. Gulati, and N. Nohria, "The Dynamics of Learning Alliances: Competition, Cooperation, and Relative Scope," *Strategic Management Journal* 19 (1998), pp. 193–210; Kale et al., "Learning and Protection of Proprietary Assets."

55. Kale et al., "Learning and Protection of Proprietary Assets."

56. Hamel et al., "Collaborate with Your Competitors"; Khanna et al., "The Dynamics of Learning Alliances"; E. W. K. Tang, "Acquiring Knowledge by Foreign Partners from International Joint Ventures in a Transition Economy: Learning by Doing and Learning Myopia," *Strategic Management Journal* 23 (2002), pp. 835–54.

57. Hamel et al., "Collaborate with Your Competitors."

58. G. Hamel, Y. L. Doz, and C. K. Prahalad, "Collaborate with Your Competitors and Win!" *Harvard Business Review*, January–February 1989, pp. 133–39.

Exporting, Importing, and Countertrade

16

LEARNING OBJECTIVES

After reading this chapter, you will be able to:

LO16-1 Explain the promises and risks associated with exporting.

LO16-2 Identify the steps managers can take to improve their firm's export performance.

LO16-3 Recognize the basic steps involved in export financing.

LO16-4 Identify information sources and government programs that exist to help exporters.

LO16-5 Describe how countertrade can be used to facilitate exports.

vectorikart/123RF

Higher-Education Exporting and International Competitiveness*

OPENING CASE

Higher education in the United States has been the envy of the world for decades. For years, more foreign students have received their college and university education in the U.S. than in any other country. Even considering the additional out-of-state and out-of-country costs, foreign students find American education much more valuable than their home-country options.

For its own citizens, the American education system has also produced a workforce that is always among the leaders in competitiveness, entrepreneurship, and innovation. This has resulted in the U.S. economy being the largest in the world since 1871.

Yes, China has experienced exponential growth over the past few decades, but in nominal GDP, the U.S. is far ahead. Perhaps that is why China sends so many students annually to participate in the U.S. education system.

The duality of exporting higher education and developing the U.S. workforce to be internationally competitive is important for the country. In support, the U.S., unlike many other countries, has a specific International and Foreign Language Education (IFLE) office within the U.S. Department of Education. IFLE's focus is on the country's international competitiveness.

But how important is the American education export? The answer is that some 1.1 million foreign students contribute $42 billion in export revenues to U.S. colleges and universities (e.g., tuition, fees, room and board). Foreign students make up 5.2 percent of all higher-education students in the country. Last year, some 330,000 students came from China and 170,000 from India, but over the years, students have come from virtually all of the world's 260 countries and territories. The remaining countries combined hosted 3.5 million foreign students, with the United Kingdom (506,000), China (489,000), Australia (372,000), and Canada (370,000) in the top five.

For the U.S., this means an education trade surplus of $34.2 billion, because fewer U.S. students take part in studies abroad (U.S. Bureau of Economic Analysis). The impact on the United States has been powerful—foreign students helped sustain 455,000 U.S. jobs in the last year (NAFSA).

But the practical numbers are even more impressive. The value of the education exports alone ($42 billion) is almost double the revenue from America's top agricultural export, soybeans ($21.6 billion). However, when other student spending is factored in (e.g., about $10 billion for food, cars, clothes, and discretionary items), education's total export value rivals that of U.S. pharmaceuticals ($51 billion) and automobiles ($53.6 billion; although the auto sector contributes $159 billion in trade when suppliers and parts are included).

What is troublesome, though, is that many U.S. policy makers have little awareness or interest in education exports. Some say that education helps drive U.S. international competitiveness, but many politicians continue to explore nationalistic measures that would likely result in a significant decline of foreign students in the United States.

The beauty of the duality of exporting higher education and making the U.S. workforce more internationally competitive is that there is synergy between the two. Many universities have students from more than 100 countries on campus. Such a "global campus fabric" brings in education-export dollars and creates a dynamic global education environment.

The U.S. will not be able to educate its workforce to be as internationally competitive without foreign students on campuses. And the country's trade balance would be worse off with a decline in foreign students.

Yet, nationalistic tendencies, trade barriers, and political uncertainty appear to be the new normal (the United Kingdom is facing similar education uncertainty with Brexit). And that scares off potential education-export participants. Some 1.1 million students come to the U.S. each year, but only 332,000 Americans study abroad. While the U.S. is near its peak in foreign student enrollment, new student enrollment has dropped since 2016.

This is a trend that spells trouble for U.S. higher education and the education-related trade balance. So, what happens when the current foreign-student enrollees graduate in the next couple of years? Is the country and its political leaders strategically planning for a solution? Or is that left to university administrators?

The factors to overcome to stop the new foreign-student decline are not easy to tackle. Some of these include rising costs of U.S. higher education, but more importantly, student visa delays and denials, as well as a political environment that draws on nationalistic rhetoric, makes life riskier and more difficult for foreign students. The duality premise means that this foreign-student decline will likely also result in a decline in the country's international competitiveness.

Note: This opening case was published by Tomas Hult as an op-ed article in *The Hill*, April 19, 2019, with a title of "Foreign Students Boost Our Economy in Myriad Ways" (https://thehill.com/opinion/finance/439715-foreign-students-boost-our-economy-in-myriad-ways).

*Tomas Hult, "Foreign Students Boost Our Economy in Myriad Ways," Capitol Hill Publishing Corp, April 19, 2019, https://thehill.com/opinion/finance/439715-foreign-students-boost-our-economy-in-myriad-ways.

Sources: Brook Larmer, "One of America's Most Vital Exports, Education, Never Goes Abroad, but It Still Faces Threats," *The New York Times*, January 3, 2019; "Number of International Students in the United States Reaches New High of 1.09 Million," Institute of International Education, November 13, 2018; Jie Zong and Jeanne Batalova, "International Students in the United States," Migration Policy Institute, May 9, 2018.

Introduction

Chapter 13 reviewed exporting from a strategic perspective as a part of the chapter's focus on entering foreign markets. We considered exporting as just one of a range of strategic options for profiting from international expansion. This chapter is more concerned with the nuts and bolts of exporting, along with tackling importing and countertrade. In some way, we can say that importing is exporting in reverse because the importing country and its companies buy from companies in other countries that are exporting. Unfortunately, the rules and regulations for importing and exporting are not always the same and, in fact, are often different in even the same country.

Exporting is a tremendously important mode of foreign market entry, preferred by more than 90 percent of all companies engaging in the global marketplace. The reason exporting is preferred by such a large portion of companies engaging in the global marketplace is that most small- and medium-sized enterprises (SMEs) prefer exporting as a relatively low commitment to getting their products or services out globally. Importantly, these SMEs also make up more than 80 percent of companies going international from almost every country in the world.

The volume of export activity in the world economy has increased as exporting has become easier from a large number of countries. Even countries now export themselves, such as France with its award-winning "Calling France" number. In a positive move for international trade, the gradual decline in trade barriers under the umbrella of the World Trade Organization (see Chapter 7), along with regional economic agreements such as the European Union (EU) and the North American Free Trade Agreement (NAFTA) (see Chapter 9), has significantly increased export opportunities. Presumably, the new NAFTA—the United States-Mexico-Canada Agreement, or USMCA—if and when implemented fully will continue the increase in export opportunities in the region as well.

At the same time, modern communication and transportation technologies have alleviated the logistical problems associated with exporting. Over the last two decades, firms have increasingly used e-commerce and international air services to reduce the costs, distance, and cycle time associated with exporting. Still, more than 90 percent of products and component parts still logistically get shipped via large ships around the world. Consequently, it is not unusual to find thriving exporters among small companies. In fact, of U.S. companies that trade internationally, some 85 percent of them are SMEs, and they generally do so via exporting. Nevertheless, exporting remains a challenge for many firms. Take the United States as an example. Fewer than 1 percent of all U.S. firms trade across their country borders to other countries, and those companies that do engage in trade do so with typically only one other country (about 60 percent of all U.S. companies that export trade only with one other country). This means that knowledge, data, and experience often are lacking, and smaller enterprises, in particular, can find the exporting process intimidating.

Companies wishing to export must identify foreign market opportunities, avoid a host of unanticipated problems that are often associated with doing business in a foreign market, familiarize themselves with the mechanics of export and import financing, learn where they can get financing and export credit insurance, and learn how they should deal with foreign exchange risk. The process can be made more problematic by currencies that are not freely convertible. Arranging payment for exports to countries with weak currencies can be a problem. This is where countertrade comes in as a potential solution, and why we have made countertrade a focus in this chapter. Countertrade allows payment for exports to be made through goods and services rather than money. This chapter discusses all these issues, with the exception of foreign exchange risk, which was covered in Chapter 10.

In Chapter 13, we dealt with the scale of market entry and strategic commitments in going international. Essentially, our focus was on involvement and commitment when engaging in the international marketplace. What we find is that the first international level for both involvement and commitment was the exporting (outbound international activity) and importing (inbound international activity) options. The remaining options for

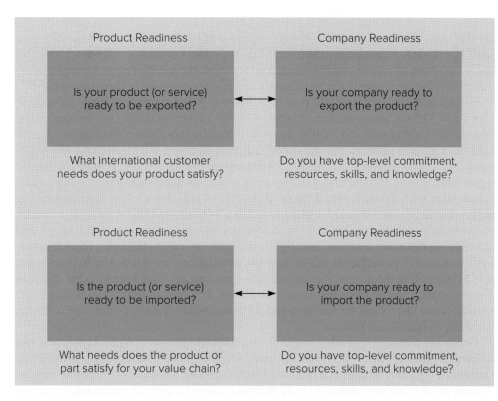

FIGURE 16.1

Product readiness and company readiness to export or import.

Source: Adapted from David Closs, David Frayer, and G. Tomas M. Hult, *Global Supply Chain Management: Leveraging Processes, Measurements, and Tools for Strategic Corporate Advantage* (New York: McGraw-Hill, 2014).

involvement and commitment, although they overlapped in some areas, were a bit different (Chapter 13 discusses turnkey projects, licensing, franchising, joint ventures, and wholly owned subsidiaries—the latter also a production facility focus in Chapter 15). That places a lot of emphasis on exporting and importing as modes of operations for many companies, and we think that this area deserves more coverage; thus, this chapter is devoted to digging deeper into the knowledge of operations ("nuts and bolts") of exporting and importing as well as the unique case of countertrade. This is, after all, the lowest level of involvement and the lowest level of commitment a company can make when going international: selling to foreign markets (exporting) or purchasing raw materials, component parts, or finished goods for operations (importing).

The bottom line is that as the global marketplace becomes more viable for many companies over time, companies must also adapt to this opportunity by strategically engaging in exporting (see Chapter 13) and operationally go about seeking opportunities globally. This could mean using suppliers from developing nations, importing products from new sources, or exporting products to new markets. Companies that have traditionally operated within national or regional trading groups may feel ill equipped to extend their market horizon. This may be as simple as feeling unable to select and manage a foreign supplier or not knowing how to sell products in a new country. But keep in mind that, by some accounts, 90 percent of the products and services that are needed locally are not produced locally; they are shipped in from somewhere else. And so, market opportunities are globally available everywhere and exporting and importing fill these voids.[1]

The chapter opens in the next section by considering the promise and pitfalls of exporting. The logic for both exporting and importing is very similar. Readiness to export and/or import is a large part of the story, as illustrated in Figure 16.1.[2]

The Promise and Pitfalls of Exporting

LO16-1

Explain the promises and risks associated with exporting.

The great promise of exporting is that large revenue and profit opportunities are to be found in foreign markets for most firms in most industries. This was true for American universities in the opening case and for both Spotify and SoundCloud in the closing case later in this chapter. The international market is normally so much larger than the firm's domestic market that exporting is nearly always a way to increase the revenue and profit base of a company. For the U.S. higher-education system—where in-state tuition is usually much lower for college students attending publicly funded universities—the out-of-state and out-of-country tuition that foreign students pay significantly increase the revenues of these universities.

For example, in-state, resident tuition and fees at Michigan State University are currently $14,522 for two semesters, but $41,328 for foreign students (for undergraduate education), a difference of $26,806. To make the math easy for this illustrative example only, let's assume all students are undergraduates. Because Michigan State University has 6,243 foreign students enrolled (12.4 percent of the total students enrolled according to MSU's official numbers), the university makes an additional $167.5 million. This is compared with if they enrolled the same number of students who are so-called in-state students, residing in the state of Michigan. Keep in mind that there are differences between undergraduate and graduate student costs and deductions for scholarships and stipends, so the exact numbers are slightly different in reality. However, the education-exporting case is powerful no matter how the calculations are done. The bottom line is that by expanding the size of the market, exporting can enable a firm to achieve economies of scale, thereby lowering its unit costs. For U.S higher education, it may mean slightly larger class sizes for teachers and students, which does not affect the costs but can bring in significant revenue.

Firms that do not export often lose out on significant opportunities for growth and cost efficiencies per unit sold.[3] Consider the case of Marlin Steel Wire Products, a Baltimore manufacturer of wire baskets and fabricated metal items with revenues of about $8 million. Among its products are baskets to hold dedicated parts for aircraft engines and automobiles. Its engineers design custom wire baskets for the assembly lines of companies such as Boeing and Toyota. It has a reputation for producing high-quality products for these niche markets. Like many small businesses, Marlin did not have a history of exporting. However, Marlin decided to engage globally in the export market, shipping small numbers of products to Mexico and Canada.

globalEDGE EXPORT TUTORIALS

Exporting, importing, and countertrade are the focus areas of Chapter 14. The exporting entry mode choice, also discussed in Chapter 13, is the most often used way to conduct cross-border trade for companies. The vast majority of small- and medium-sized enterprises, for example, use exporting as their way to expand to international markets. But that begs the question of whether the company is ready to export and whether the product the company plans to export is ready to be exported. The "Export Tutorials" section of globalEDGE™ (**globaledge.msu.edu/reference-desk/export-tutorials**) includes CORE as a diagnostic tool to assess "company readiness to export." The "Export Tutorials" section also has a lengthy set of questions and answers to the most common exporting-related questions in the categories of government regulations, financial considerations, sales and marketing, and logistics. For example, one question deals with whether a company needs a license to export. Assume you are based in the United States. How can you identify the relevant commodity jurisdiction for a product?

Marlin's president and CEO, Drew Greenblatt, soon realized that export sales could be the key to growth. In 2008, when the global financial crisis hit and America slid into a serious recession, Marlin was exporting only 5 percent of its orders to foreign markets. Greenblatt's strategy for dealing with weak demand in the United States was to aggressively expand international sales. Marlin Steel has been exporting since they made the critical decision to do so in 2008, with sales made to more than 20 countries. About one-third of the company's 45 employees are employed as a direct result of its export success. Now, exports account for some 40 percent of sales, and the company set a goal of exporting half its output.

Despite examples such as Marlin Steel Wire Products, studies have shown that while many large firms tend to be proactive about seeking opportunities for profitable exporting—systematically scanning foreign markets to see where the opportunities lie for leveraging their technology, products, and marketing skills in foreign countries—many medium-sized and small firms are very reactive.[4] Typically, such reactive firms do not even consider exporting until their domestic market is saturated and the emergence of excess productive capacity at home forces them to look for growth opportunities in foreign markets.

Many small- and medium-sized firms tend to wait for the world to come to them, rather than going out into the world to seek opportunities. Even when the world does come to them, they may not respond. An example is MMO Music Group, which makes sing-along tapes for karaoke machines. Foreign sales accounted for about 15 percent of MMO's revenues of $8 million, but the firm's CEO admits this figure would probably have been much higher had he paid attention to building international sales. Unanswered e-mails and phone messages from Asia and Europe often piled up while he was trying to manage the burgeoning domestic side of the business. By the time MMO did turn its attention to foreign markets, competitors had stepped into the breach, and MMO found it tough going to build export volume.[5]

MMO's experience is common, and it suggests a need for firms to become more proactive about seeking export opportunities. One reason more firms are not proactive is that they are unfamiliar with foreign market opportunities; they simply do not know how big the opportunities actually are or where they might lie. Simple ignorance of the potential opportunities is a huge barrier to exporting.[6] Also, many would-be exporters, particularly smaller firms, are often intimidated by the complexities and mechanics of exporting to countries where business practices, language, culture, legal systems, and currency are very different from those in the home market.[7] This combination of unfamiliarity and intimidation probably explains why exporters still account for only a tiny percentage of U.S. firms, less than 5 percent of firms with fewer than 500 employees, according to the Small Business Administration.[8]

To make matters worse, many neophyte exporters run into significant problems when first trying to do business abroad, and this sours them on future exporting ventures. Common pitfalls include poor market analysis, a poor understanding of competitive conditions in the foreign market, a failure to customize the product offering to the needs of foreign customers, a lack of an effective distribution program, a poorly executed promotional campaign, and problems securing financing.[9] Novice exporters tend to underestimate the time and expertise needed to cultivate business in foreign countries.[10] Few realize the amount of management resources that have to be dedicated to this activity. Many foreign customers require face-to-face negotiations on their home turf. An exporter may have to spend months learning about a country's trade regulations, business practices, and more before a deal can be closed. The accompanying Management Focus, which documents the experience of Embraer, illustrates cultural barriers that sometimes can hinder both exporting and importing.

Exporters often face voluminous paperwork, complex formalities, and many potential delays and errors. Exporting to Brazil is a unique experience in and of itself that still to this day often requires more than just following the rules and regulations stipulated by the country. According to a United Nations report on trade and development, a typical international trade transaction may involve 30 parties, 60 original documents, and 360 document copies—all of which have to be checked, transmitted, reentered into various information systems, processed, and filed. The UN has calculated that the time involved in preparing documentation, along with the costs of common errors in paperwork, often amounts to 10 percent of the final value of goods exported.[11]

TEST PREP

Use SmartBook to help retain what you have learned. Access your instructor's Connect course to check out SmartBook or go to **learnsmartadvantage.com** for help.

Embraer and Brazilian Importing

Embraer is a Brazilian company that manufactures commercial, military, executive, and agricultural aircraft and provides aeronautical services. It is headquartered in São José dos Campos, São Paulo State in Brazil. Importantly, Embraer is the fourth-largest airplane manufacturer in the world, and its imports of various raw material and component parts to Brazil to make its airplanes constitute up slightly more than 1 percent of the Brazilian trade balance with all other countries, which is a relatively large portion of the Brazilian economy for just one importer.

Embraer has consistently been one of the top importers in Brazil since its founding in 1969. Today, the company has about 20,000 employees from 20 countries, revenue of more than R$20 billion (Brazilian Real, BRL) or about $6 billion, and more than $300 million in net income. The company consists of three primary divisions: Embraer Defense and Security, Embraer Commercial Aviation, and Embraer Executive Jets. Across these divisions, the output is impressive. Embraer has served more than 90 airlines in more than 60 countries and delivered more than 5,000 aircraft to this clientele.

To be able to produce that many aircraft and achieve a top four position in its industry, Embraer has to import a lot of raw materials and component parts to Brazil to build the aircraft at the company's main locations at its headquarters in São José dos Campos as well as its other core plants in Brazil in Botucatu, Eugênio de Melo, and Gavião Peixoto. Some of these component parts are in reality finished products that are then inserted into the planes in a certain position, such as the PurePower Geared Turbofan engines from Pratt & Whitney to power its E-Jets. Embraer also collaborates with some of its competitors in the industry, such as Boeing, in building its stretch civilian model of the KC-390 military transport/aerial refueler.

The list of suppliers to Embraer's operations is lengthy, with partnerships with Honeywell, Saab, UTC Aerospace, SNC, Flight Safety International, Goodrich, Eaton, Thales, Sierra, and Air France Industries, to mention some of the company's top suppliers. But the complete list of suppliers needed for Embraer planes is incredibly lengthy—even lengthier than most car manufacturers, which have a reputation for using a lot of suppliers (some 50,000 in the case of General Motors, for example). Though the number of suppliers for Embraer—or any aircraft manufacturer is somewhat fluid—we can certainly put the number of parts used at more than 300,000. This places incredible pressure on operating an efficient and effective global supply chain system and, most importantly, a well-structured importing operation into Brazil.

Importing into Brazil, some would say, is a difficult task for most companies and product categories. At the consumer product level, it was almost impossible to find imported products in Brazil before 1990. The Brazilian government used a number of protectionist measures and high taxes to discourage the importing of products. Bribing of officials that can facilitate the importing process is normal. Adding to the importing difficulty, the World Bank considers Brazil to be one of the most difficult places to start a business. Brazil's tax system has also been ranked as one of the most complex worldwide by analysts at PwC.

Sources: Jon Ostrower, "You Wait Ages for a New Airplane and Then Two Come Along," *CNN Money*, March 7, 2017; Dimitra DeFotis, "Embraer Flies Higher on Earnings," *Barron's*, March 9, 2017; Asif Suria, "Embraer: An Impressive Brazilian Jet Producer," *Seeking Alpha*, August 8, 2007; and Russ Mitchell, "The Little Aircraft Company That Could," *Fortune*, November 14, 2005.

LO16-2

Identify the steps managers can take to improve their firm's export performance.

Improving Export Performance

Inexperienced exporters have a number of ways to gain information about foreign market opportunities and avoid common pitfalls that tend to discourage and frustrate novice exporters.[12] In this section, we look at information sources for exporters to increase their knowledge of foreign market opportunities, we consider a number of service providers, we review various exporting strategies that can increase the probability of successful exporting, and we illustrate the globalEDGE™ Diagnostic Tool called Company Readiness to Export (CORE) that can help exporters. We begin, however, with a look at how several nations try to help domestic firms export.

INTERNATIONAL COMPARISONS

One big impediment to exporting is the simple lack of knowledge of the opportunities available. Often, there are many markets for a firm's product, but because they are in countries separated from the firm's home base by culture, language, distance, and time, the firm does not know of them. Identifying export opportunities is made even more complex because almost 195 countries with widely differing cultures compose the world of potential opportunities. Faced with such complexity and diversity, firms sometimes hesitate to seek export opportunities.

The way to overcome ignorance is to collect information. In Germany—one of the world's most successful exporting nations—trade associations, government agencies, and commercial banks gather information, helping small firms identify export opportunities. A similar function is provided by the Japanese Ministry of International Trade and Industry (**MITI**), which is always on the lookout for export opportunities. In addition, many Japanese firms are affiliated in some way with the *sogo shosha*, Japan's great trading houses. The *sogo shosha* have offices all over the world, and they proactively, continuously seek export opportunities for their affiliated companies large and small.[13]

German and Japanese firms can draw on the large reservoirs of experience, skills, information, and other resources of their respective export-oriented institutions. Unlike their German and Japanese competitors, many U.S. firms are relatively blind when they seek export opportunities; they are information-disadvantaged. In part, this reflects historical differences. Both Germany and Japan have long made their living as trading nations, whereas until recently, the United States has been a relatively self-contained continental economy in which international trade played a minor role. This is changing; both imports and exports now play a greater role in the U.S. economy than they did 20 years ago. However, the United States has not yet created an institutional structure for promoting exports similar to that of Germany or Japan.

INFORMATION SOURCES

Despite institutional disadvantages, U.S. firms can increase their awareness of export opportunities. The most comprehensive source of information is the U.S. Department of Commerce and its district offices all over the country (U.S. Export Assistance Centers, USEAC). Within that department are two organizations dedicated to providing businesses with intelligence and assistance for attacking foreign markets: U.S. and Foreign Commercial Service and International Trade Administration (ITA). ITA regularly publishes *A Guide to Exporting*. This is the United States' "Official Government Resource for Small and Medium-Sized Businesses" in their exporting quest.

The U.S. and Foreign Commercial Service and International Trade Administration are governmental agencies that provide the potential exporter with a "best prospects" list, which gives the names and addresses of potential distributors in foreign markets along with businesses they are in, the products they handle, and their contact person. In addition, the Department of Commerce has assembled a "comparison shopping service" for countries that are major markets for U.S. exports. For a small fee, a firm can receive a customized market research survey on a product of its choice. This survey provides information on marketability, the competition, comparative prices, distribution channels, and names of potential sales representatives. Each study is conducted on site by an officer of the Department of Commerce.

The Department of Commerce also organizes trade events that help potential exporters make foreign contacts and explore export opportunities. The department organizes exhibitions at international trade fairs, which are held regularly in major cities worldwide. The department also has a matchmaker program, in which department representatives accompany groups of U.S. businesspeople abroad to meet with qualified agents, distributors, and customers. Affiliated with the U.S. Department of Commerce and its USEAC offices is a set of District Export Councils (DECs; connected also via the National District Export Council). DECs are composed of some 1,500 volunteers

MANAGEMENT FOCUS

Exporting Desserts by a Hispanic Entrepreneur

Taking basic ingredients and creating a myriad of flavors has led to worldwide exporting success for Lulu's Foods Inc. (lulus-foods.com). Started in 1982 in a 700-square-foot storefront in Torrance, California, followed by exporting to Mexico in 1992, the company is a gelatin dessert business with core customer target markets in the United States and Mexico but with exporting to several countries worldwide. Lulu is the nickname of the founder, Maria de Lourdes Sobrino.

Lulu thought of the idea of ready-to-eat flavored gelatin desserts when she was looking for the popular dessert in local stores. At the time, she was living in the United States, but originally she came from Mexico. The ready-to-eat flavored gelatin desserts were a staple in her native Mexico, but the concept was a novelty when she introduced it to American grocers. Today, Lulu's Foods Inc. can be found in a variety of well-known stores (e.g., Albertsons, Safeway, Walmart).

Back in the early 1980s, Lulu identified and recognized a need for gelatin desserts, filled it with what has now become 45 ready-to-eat products of different sizes and flavors, and transformed the food industry by creating the first ready-to-eat gelatin category based largely on her mother's recipes. The business concept has become quite a "spoon spectacular" since Lulu first began, with a catch line for the company of "More fun for your spoon.©"

The party started out very small with just Lulu making her mother's gelatin recipe desserts, with an initial production of 300 cups of gelatin per day. Ultimately, the party grew so big that Lulu could not handle it by herself and had to negotiate help from established markets and wholesale distributors. Lulu wanted everyone within reach to enjoy her festival of flavors. In going international, Lulu spent some 10 years trying to gain international sales but continued to run into all kinds of problems and issues. After the trial-and-error decade, she found assistance from the U.S. Export-Import Bank services and now has deeper confidence in her abilities to export products worldwide.

Over the years, Lulu has kept making more and more varieties of her gelatin desserts. A carnival of colors of three-layer gelatins, fruit parfaits, and festive containers of wild new colors and flavors have become identifying marks. This exporting innovation led Bill Hopkins of *USA Today* to call Maria de Lourdes Sobrino "the queen of ready-to-eat gelatins and a force in the surging number of Hispanic Entrepreneurs." Hal Lancaster of *The Wall Street Journal* also recognized her as an innovator and very successful entrepreneur in "getting out and selling customers your dream."

Today, with its exporting worldwide, but especially to Mexico, and sales across the United States, Lulu's Foods Inc.'s core focus is on gelatin cups, with flavors that include such exotic descriptors as Fruit Fantasia, Orange Blast, Creamy Vanilla with Cinnamon, and Sugar Free-De-Light.

Sources: D. Barry, "Maria de Lourdes Sobrino, Founder, LuLu's Dessert," *Exporters: The Wit and Wisdom of Small Businesspeople Who Sell Globally* (Washington, DC: U.S. Commerce Department, 2013); J. Hopkins, "Bad Times Spawn Great Start-Ups," *USA Today*, December 18, 2001; and Lulu's Foods Inc., www.lulus-foods.com.

appointed by the U.S. Secretary of Commerce to help U.S. business be more competitive internationally.

Another governmental organization, the Small Business Administration (SBA), can help potential exporters (see the accompanying Management Focus on exporting desserts for an example of the SBA's work). The SBA employs 76 district international trade officers and 10 regional international trade officers throughout the United States, as well as a 10-person international trade staff in Washington, DC. Among the SBA's no-fee services are Small Business Development Centers (SBDCs), the Service Corps of Retired Executives (SCORE), and the Export Legal Assistance Network (ELAN). The SBDCs around the country provide a full range of export assistance to business, particularly small companies new to exporting. Through SCORE, the SBA oversees some 11,500 volunteers with international trade experience to provide one-on-one counseling to active and new-to-export businesses. The SBA also coordinates ELAN, a nationwide group of international trade attorneys who provide free initial consultations to small businesses on export-related matters.

The United States has also established a set of 15 Centers for International Business Education and Research (CIBERs), which assist with exporting needs. The CIBERs were created by the U.S. Congress under the Omnibus Trade and Competitiveness Act of 1988 to increase and promote the nation's capacity for international understanding and competitiveness. Administered by the U.S. Department of Education, the CIBER network links the human resource and technological needs of the U.S. business community with the international education, language training, and research capacities of universities across the country. The 15 CIBERs, including the University of Washington where the author of this text is a professor (**www2.ed.gov/programs/iegpscibe**), serve as regional and national resources to businesspeople, students, and teachers at all levels. Many countries around the world are trying to replicate the U.S. CIBER initiative (e.g., the European Union).

Additionally, the vast majority of U.S. states, regions, and many large cities maintain active trade commissions whose purpose is to promote exports. Most of these provide business counseling, information gathering, technical assistance, and financing. Unfortunately, many have fallen victim to budget cuts or to turf battles for political and financial support with other export agencies.

A number of private organizations are also beginning to provide more assistance to would-be exporters. Commercial banks and major accounting firms are more willing to assist small firms in starting export operations than they were a decade ago. In addition, large multinationals that have been successful in the global arena are typically willing to discuss opportunities overseas with the owners or managers of small firms.[14]

SERVICE PROVIDERS

Most companies that engage in international trade enlist the help of export–import service providers, but there are many choices. Let's look at the main ones: freight forwarders, export management companies, export trading companies, export packaging companies, customs brokers, confirming houses, export agents and merchants, piggyback marketing, and economic processing zones.

Freight forwarders are mainly in business to orchestrate transportation for companies that are shipping internationally. Their primary task is to combine smaller shipments into a single large shipment to minimize the shipping cost. Freight forwarders also provide other services that are beneficial to the exporting firm, such as documentation, payment, and carrier selection.

An **export management company (EMC)** offers services to companies that have not previously exported products. EMCs offer a full menu of services to handle all aspects of exporting, similar to having an internal exporting department within your own firm. For example, EMCs deal with export documents and operate as the firm's agent and distributor; this may include selling the products directly or operating a sales unit to process sales orders.

Export trading companies export products for companies that contract with them. They identify and work with companies in foreign countries that will market and sell the products. They provide comprehensive exporting services, including export documentation, logistics, and transportation.

Export packaging companies, or export packers for short, provide services to companies that are unfamiliar with exporting. For example, some countries require packages to meet certain specifications, and the export packaging firm's knowledge of these requirements is invaluable to new exporters in particular. The export packer can also advise companies on appropriate design and materials for the packaging of their items. Export packers can assist companies in minimizing packaging to maximize the number of items to be shipped.

Customs brokers can help companies avoid the pitfalls involved in customs regulations. The customs requirements of many countries can be difficult for new or infrequent exporters to understand, and the knowledge and experience of the customs broker can be very important. For example, many countries have certain laws and documentation regulations concerning imported items that are not always obvious to the exporter. Customs brokers can offer a firm a complete package of services that are essential when a firm is exporting to a large number of countries.

Confirming houses, sometimes called buying agents, represent foreign companies that want to buy your products. Typically, they try to get the products they want at the lowest prices and are paid a commission by their foreign clients. A good place to find these potential exporting linkages is via government embassies.

Export agents, merchants, and remarketers buy products directly from the manufacturer and package and label the products in accordance with their own wishes and specifications. They then sell the products internationally through their own contacts under their own names and assume all risks. The effort it takes for you to market the product internationally is very small, but you also lose any control over the marketing, promotion, and positioning of your product.

Piggyback marketing is an arrangement whereby one firm distributes another firm's products. For example, a firm may have a contract to provide an assortment of products to an overseas client, but it does not have all the products requested. In such cases, another firm can piggyback its products to fill the contract's requirements. Successful piggybacking usually requires complementary products and the same target market of customers.

There are now more than 600 export processing zones (EPZs) in the world, and they exist in more than 100 countries. The EPZs include foreign trade zones (FTZs), special economic zones, bonded warehouses, free ports, and customs zones. Many companies use EPZs to receive shipments of products that are then reshipped in smaller lots to customers throughout the surrounding areas. Founded in 1978 by the United Nations, the World Economic Processing Zones Association (wepza.org) is a private nonprofit organization dedicated to the improvement of the efficiency of all EPZs.

EXPORT STRATEGY

In addition to using export service providers, a firm can reduce the risks associated with exporting if it is careful about its choice of export strategy.[15] A few guidelines can help firms improve their odds of success. For example, one of the most successful exporting firms in the world, 3M (originally, Minnesota Mining & Manufacturing Company), has built its export success on three main principles: enter on a small scale to reduce risks, add additional product lines once the exporting operations start to become successful, and hire locals to promote the firm's products. Another company—Two Men and a Truck (profiled in the accompanying Management Focus)—has had global success with a franchising approach.

The probability of exporting successfully can be increased dramatically by taking a handful of simple strategic steps. First, particularly for the novice exporter, it helps to hire an EMC or at least an experienced export consultant to identify opportunities and navigate the paperwork and regulations so often involved in exporting. Second, it often makes sense to initially focus on one market or a handful of markets. Learn what is required to succeed in those markets before moving to other markets. The firm that enters many markets at once runs the risk of spreading its limited management resources too thin. The result of such a shotgun approach to exporting may be a failure to become established in any one market.

Third, as with Two Men and a Truck, it often makes sense to enter a foreign market on a small scale to reduce the costs of any subsequent failure. Most important, entering on a small scale provides the time and opportunity to learn about the foreign country before making significant capital commitments to that market. Fourth, the exporter needs to recognize the time and managerial commitment involved in building export sales and should hire additional personnel to oversee this activity. Fifth, in many countries, it is important to devote a lot of attention to building strong and enduring relationships with local distributors and/or customers. Sixth, as 3M often does, it is important to hire local personnel to help the firm establish itself in a foreign market. Local people

Two Men and a Truck

By some accounts, moving is ranked as the third-most-stressful event a person can experience, after death of a relative and divorce. Two Men and a Truck (**https://twomenandatruck.com**) started as an after-school business for two high school boys in Lansing, Michigan. As a small business focused on local moving services, the company began in 1985 with $350, a hand-drawn logo, and an advertisement in a local community newspaper.

In 1989, Melanie Bergeron, the daughter of founder Mary Ellen Sheets, opened the first franchised office of Two Men and a Truck in her hometown of Atlanta, Georgia. Melanie is now board chair, with Brig Sorber as the chief executive officer and Jon Sorber as executive vice president. Randy Shacka, who joined the company as an intern in 2001, was promoted in 2012 to president. This is the first president of the company who did not come from the family.

Two Men and a Truck is no longer "two men and a truck." The company has grown both domestically and internationally to most of the United States and some 380 locations worldwide. Two Men and a Truck is the fastest-growing franchised moving company in the United States (with more than 100 consecutive months of growth), with more than $300 million in sales, 2,800 moving trucks, and some 6,000 workers. The average franchise grosses about $1.5 million annually. Bergeron said that "we never imagined being in the moving business—that is, until my mom and my brothers Brig and Jon scraped together some money to buy a truck to help raise extra cash for college."

Two Men and a Truck has remained branded as "Two Men and a Truck" in all parts of the world in which it operates franchises (e.g., Canada, Ireland, the United Kingdom). Names such as "Two Blokes and a Lorry" do not appeal to them! The company has decided to stick to the core American brand name because "that's what master franchisers and their investors want," said Bergeron. "The customers are less interested in whether it's a U.S. brand . . . the appeal is the opposite . . . it's a local [franchise] company that will be available when I need them. . . . They want the U.S. brand power and mystique."*

In going international to new markets, Two Men and a Truck's primary factors to evaluate are the size of the middle class in a country and the population's mobility. They use software tools to help pinpoint income levels by neighborhood and whether the housing market is primarily based on single- or multifamily units. The market for Two Men and a Truck is best where there is a good mix of both. In addition, Bergeron said that two other key areas in determining locations in which to operate include obtaining accurate market research and identifying potential master franchisees.

In the case of Two Men and a Truck going international, the industry itself also represented a challenge. There are plenty of moving businesses worldwide; why should franchisees represent Two Men and a Truck? The company's answer to this market differentiation problem is its exceptional focus on customer service and a sophisticated web-based tracking system. Quality control, labor costs, and cycle time to complete a move are core performance metrics in the system. In fact, the company has become known in its industry for faster and better analytics to run the business. It has installed a private cloud system to make its business operations more efficient, using business analytics to capture and identify growth opportunities worldwide.

*Doug Barry, ed., *Exporters! The Wit and Wisdom of Small Business Owners Who Sell Globally* (Washington: U.S. Commerce Department, 2013).

Sources: D. Barry, "Melanie Bergeron, Chair of the Board of Two Men and a Truck," *Exporters: The Wit and Wisdom of Small Businesspeople Who Sell Globally* (Washington, DC: U.S. Commerce Department, 2013); C. Boulton, "Moving Company Gets a Lift from Faster Analytics," *The Wall Street Journal*, August 20, 2013; and A. Wittrock, "Two Men and a Truck Wins State Grant, Plans $4 Million Expansion of Lansing-Area Headquarters," *MLive.com*, February 27, 2013.

are likely to have a much greater sense of how to do business in a given country than a manager from an exporting firm who has previously never set foot in that country. Seventh, several studies have suggested the firm needs to be proactive about seeking export opportunities.[16] Armchair exporting does not work! The world will not normally beat a pathway to your door.

Finally, it is important for the exporter to retain the option of local production. Once exports reach a sufficient volume to justify cost-efficient local production, the exporting

FIGURE 16.2

Company readiness
to export.

Source: Charles W. L. Hill and
G. Tomas M. Hult, *International
Business: Competing in the Global
Marketplace* (New York:
McGraw-Hill, 2019).

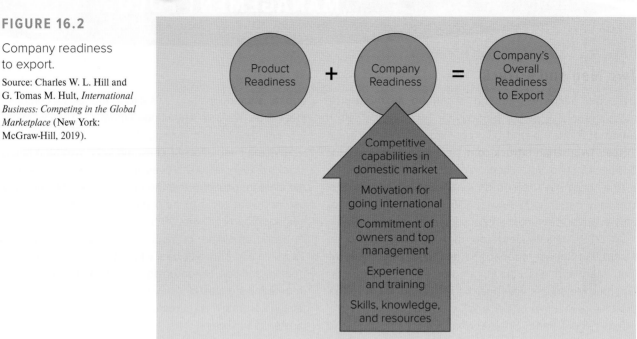

firm should consider establishing production facilities in the foreign market. Such localization helps foster good relations with the foreign country and can lead to greater market acceptance. Exporting is often not an end in itself but merely a step on the road toward establishment of foreign production (again, 3M provides an example of this philosophy).

THE GLOBALEDGE™ EXPORTING TOOL

In Chapter 1, we introduced the globalEDGE™ website (**globaledge.msu.edu**), a product of the International Business Center in the Broad College of Business at Michigan State University. globalEDGE™ has been the top-ranked website in the world for "international business resources" on Google since 2004. Some 10 million people now use globalEDGE™, with about 2 million active users. The site is free, including the "Diagnostic Tools" section. In that section of the site, the Company Readiness to Export (CORE) tool has become a frequently used option by a variety of small, medium, and large firms to assess (1) a company's readiness to export a product and (2) the product's readiness to be exported.

CORE (Company Readiness to Export) assists firms in self-assessment of their exporting proficiency, evaluates both the firm's and the intended product's readiness to be taken internationally, and systematically identifies the firm's strengths and weaknesses within the context of exporting (see Figure 16.2). The CORE tool also serves as a tutorial in exporting and has been used by the U.S. Department of Commerce, U.S. District Export Councils, and other exporting facilitators to help companies succeed with their exporting.

Figure 16.3 shows the online interface of the CORE Results Report. The overall report includes a prediction by respondents of where they think their company is in terms of readiness to export, as well as the actual readiness (organizational and product) based on the 70-question CORE diagnostic tool assessment. The users also receive scores on all questions and various strengths and weaknesses associated with their exporting capabilities and capacities.

TEST PREP

Use SmartBook to help retain what you have learned. Access your instructor's Connect course to check out SmartBook or go to **learnsmartadvantage.com** for help.

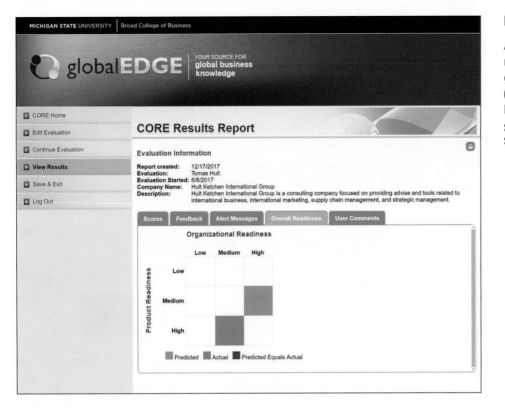

FIGURE 16.3

A screenshot of select results from the globalEDGE CORE (Company Readiness to Export) diagnostic tool.

Source: globalEDGE, Michigan State University.

Export and Import Financing

Mechanisms for financing exports and imports have evolved over the centuries in response to a problem that can be particularly acute in international trade: the lack of trust that exists when one must put faith in a stranger. In this section, we examine the financial devices that have evolved to cope with this problem in the context of international trade: the letter of credit, the draft (or bill of exchange), and the bill of lading. Then we trace the 14 steps of a typical export–import transaction.[17]

LO16-3

Recognize the basic steps involved in export financing.

LACK OF TRUST

Firms engaged in international trade have to trust someone they may have never seen, who lives in a different country, who speaks a different language, who abides by (or does not abide by) a different legal system, and who could be very difficult to track down if he or she defaults on an obligation. Consider a U.S. firm exporting to a distributor in France. The U.S. businessperson might be concerned that if he ships the products to France before he receives payment from the French businessperson, she might take delivery of the products and not pay him. Conversely, the French importer might worry that if she pays for the products before they are shipped, the U.S. firm might keep the money and never ship the products or might ship defective products. Neither party to the exchange completely trusts the other. This lack of trust is exacerbated by the distance between the two parties—in space, language, and culture—and by the problems of using an underdeveloped international legal system to enforce contractual obligations.

Due to the (quite reasonable) lack of trust between the two parties, each has his or her own preferences as to how the transaction should be configured. To make sure he is paid, the manager of the U.S. firm would prefer the French distributor to pay for the products before he ships them (see Figure 16.4). Alternatively, to ensure she receives the products, the French distributor would prefer not to pay for them until they arrive (see Figure 16.5).

FIGURE 16.4

Preference of the U.S. exporter.

Source: Charles W. L. Hill and G. Tomas M. Hult, *International Business: Competing in the Global Marketplace* (New York: McGraw-Hill, 2019).

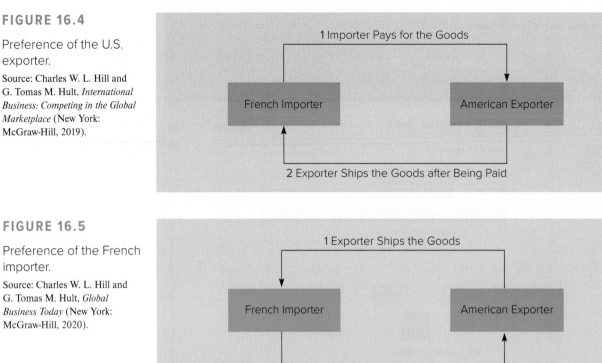

FIGURE 16.5

Preference of the French importer.

Source: Charles W. L. Hill and G. Tomas M. Hult, *Global Business Today* (New York: McGraw-Hill, 2020).

Thus, each party has a different set of preferences. Unless there is some way of establishing trust between the parties, the transaction might never occur.

The problem is solved by using a third party trusted by both—normally a reputable bank—to act as an intermediary. What happens can be summarized as follows (see Figure 16.6). First, the French importer obtains the bank's promise to pay on her behalf, knowing the U.S. exporter will trust the bank. This promise is known as a letter of credit. Having seen the letter of credit, the U.S. exporter now ships the products to France. Title to the products is given to the bank in the form of a document called a bill of lading. In return, the U.S. exporter tells the bank to pay for the products, which the bank does. The document for requesting this payment is referred to as a draft. The bank, having paid for the products, now passes the title on to the French importer, whom the bank trusts. At that time or later, depending on their agreement, the importer reimburses the bank. In the remainder of this section, we examine how this system works in more detail.

FIGURE 16.6

The use of a third party.

Source: Charles W. L. Hill and G. Tomas M. Hult, *Global Business Today* (New York: McGraw-Hill, 2018).

LETTER OF CREDIT

A letter of credit, abbreviated as L/C, stands at the center of international commercial transactions. Issued by a bank at the request of an importer, the **letter of credit** states that the bank will pay a specified sum of money to a beneficiary, normally the exporter, on presentation of particular, specified documents.

Consider again the example of the U.S. exporter and the French importer. The French importer applies to her local bank, say, the Bank of Paris, for the issuance of a letter of credit. The Bank of Paris then undertakes a credit check of the importer. If the Bank of Paris is satisfied with her creditworthiness, it will issue a letter of credit. However, the Bank of Paris might require a cash deposit or some other form of collateral from her first. In addition, the Bank of Paris will charge the importer a fee for this service. Typically, this amounts to between 0.5 and 2 percent of the value of the letter of credit, depending on the importer's creditworthiness and the size of the transaction. (As a rule, the larger the transaction, the lower the percentage.)

Assume the Bank of Paris is satisfied with the French importer's creditworthiness and agrees to issue a letter of credit. The letter states that the Bank of Paris will pay the U.S. exporter for the merchandise as long as it is shipped in accordance with specified instructions and conditions. At this point, the letter of credit becomes a financial contract between the Bank of Paris and the U.S. exporter. The Bank of Paris then sends the letter of credit to the U.S. exporter's bank, say, the Bank of New York. The Bank of New York tells the exporter that it has received a letter of credit and that he can ship the merchandise. After the exporter has shipped the merchandise, he draws a draft against the Bank of Paris in accordance with the terms of the letter of credit, attaches the required documents, and presents the draft to his own bank, the Bank of New York, for payment. The Bank of New York then forwards the letter of credit and associated documents to the Bank of Paris. If all the terms and conditions contained in the letter of credit have been complied with, the Bank of Paris will honor the draft and will send payment to the Bank of New York. When the Bank of New York receives the funds, it will pay the U.S. exporter.

As for the Bank of Paris, once it has transferred the funds to the Bank of New York, it will collect payment from the French importer. Alternatively, the Bank of Paris may allow the importer some time to resell the merchandise before requiring payment. This is not unusual, particularly when the importer is a distributor and not the final consumer of the merchandise because it helps the importer's cash flow. The Bank of Paris will treat such an extension of the payment period as a loan to the importer and will charge an appropriate rate of interest.

The great advantage of this system is that both the French importer and the U.S. exporter are likely to trust reputable banks, even if they do not trust each other. Once the U.S. exporter has seen a letter of credit, he knows that he is guaranteed payment and will ship the merchandise. Also, an exporter may find that having a letter of credit will facilitate obtaining pre-export financing. For example, having seen the letter of credit, the Bank of New York might be willing to lend the exporter funds to process and prepare the merchandise for shipping to France. This loan may not have to be repaid until the exporter has received his payment for the merchandise. As for the French importer, she does not have to pay for the merchandise until the documents have arrived and unless all conditions stated in the letter of credit have been satisfied. The drawback for the importer is the fee she must pay the Bank of Paris for the letter of credit. In addition, because the letter of credit is a financial liability against her, it may reduce her ability to borrow funds for other purposes.

DRAFT

A draft, sometimes referred to as a **bill of exchange**, is the instrument normally used in international commerce to effect payment. A **draft** is simply an order written by an exporter instructing an importer, or an importer's agent, to pay a specified amount of money at a specified time. In the example of the U.S. exporter and the French importer, the exporter writes a draft that instructs the Bank of Paris, the French importer's agent, to pay for the merchandise shipped to France. The person or business initiating the draft is known as the maker (in this case, the U.S. exporter). The party to whom the draft is presented is known as the drawee (in this case, the Bank of Paris).

International practice is to use drafts to settle trade transactions. This differs from domestic practice in which a seller usually ships merchandise on an open account, followed by a commercial invoice that specifies the amount due and the terms of payment. In domestic transactions, the buyer can often obtain possession of the merchandise without signing a formal document acknowledging his or her obligation to pay. In contrast, due to the lack of trust in international transactions, payment or a formal promise to pay is required before the buyer can obtain the merchandise.

Drafts fall into two categories: sight drafts and time drafts. A **sight draft** is payable on presentation to the drawee. A **time draft** allows for a delay in payment—normally 30, 60, 90, or 120 days. It is presented to the drawee, who signifies acceptance of it by writing or stamping a notice of acceptance on its face. Once accepted, the time draft becomes a promise to pay by the accepting party. When a time draft is drawn on and accepted by a bank, it is called a *banker's acceptance*. When it is drawn on and accepted by a business firm, it is called a *trade acceptance*.

Time drafts are negotiable instruments—that is, once the draft is stamped with acceptance, the maker can sell the draft to an investor at a discount from its face value. Imagine that the agreement between the U.S. exporter and the French importer calls for the exporter to present the Bank of Paris (through the Bank of New York) with a time draft requiring payment 120 days after presentation. The Bank of Paris stamps the time draft with an acceptance. Imagine further that the draft is for $100,000.

The exporter can either hold onto the accepted time draft and receive $100,000 in 120 days or sell it to an investor, say, the Bank of New York, for a discount from the face value. If the prevailing discount rate is 7 percent, the exporter could receive $97,700 by selling it immediately (7 percent per year discount rate for 120 days for $100,000 equals $2,300, and $100,000 − $2,300 = $97,700). The Bank of New York would then collect the full $100,000 from the Bank of Paris in 120 days. The exporter might sell the accepted time draft immediately if he needed the funds to finance merchandise in transit and/or to cover cash flow shortfalls.

BILL OF LADING

The third key document for financing international trade is the bill of lading. The **bill of lading** is issued to the exporter by the common carrier transporting the merchandise. It serves three purposes: It is a receipt, a contract, and a document of title. As a receipt, the bill of lading indicates that the carrier has received the merchandise described on the face of the document. As a contract, it specifies that the carrier is obligated to provide transportation service in return for a certain charge. As a document of title, it can be used to obtain payment or a written promise of payment before the merchandise is released to the importer. The bill of lading can also function as collateral against which funds may be advanced to the exporter by its local bank before or during shipment and before final payment by the importer.

A TYPICAL INTERNATIONAL TRADE TRANSACTION

Now that we have reviewed the elements of an international trade transaction, let us see how the process works in a typical case, sticking with the example of the U.S. exporter and the French importer. The typical transaction involves 14 steps (see Figure 16.7).

1. The French importer places an order with the U.S. exporter and asks the American if he would be willing to ship under a letter of credit.
2. The U.S. exporter agrees to ship under a letter of credit and specifies relevant information such as prices and delivery terms.
3. The French importer applies to the Bank of Paris for a letter of credit to be issued in favor of the U.S. exporter for the merchandise the importer wishes to buy.

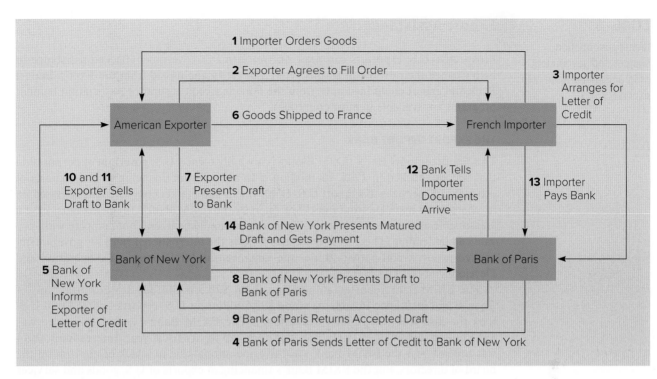

FIGURE 16.7

A typical international trade transaction.

Source: Charles W. L. Hill and G. Tomas M. Hult, *Global Business Today* (New York: McGraw-Hill, 2018).

4. The Bank of Paris issues a letter of credit in the French importer's favor and sends it to the U.S. exporter's bank, the Bank of New York.

5. The Bank of New York advises the exporter of the opening of a letter of credit in his favor.

6. The U.S. exporter ships the goods to the French importer on a common carrier. An official of the carrier gives the exporter a bill of lading.

7. The U.S. exporter presents a 90-day time draft drawn on the Bank of Paris in accordance with its letter of credit and the bill of lading to the Bank of New York. The exporter endorses the bill of lading so title to the goods is transferred to the Bank of New York.

8. The Bank of New York sends the draft and bill of lading to the Bank of Paris. The Bank of Paris accepts the draft, taking possession of the documents and promising to pay the now-accepted draft in 90 days.

9. The Bank of Paris returns the accepted draft to the Bank of New York.

10. The Bank of New York tells the U.S. exporter that it has received the accepted bank draft, which is payable in 90 days.

11. The exporter sells the draft to the Bank of New York at a discount from its face value and receives the discounted cash value of the draft in return.

12. The Bank of Paris notifies the French importer of the arrival of the documents. She agrees to pay the Bank of Paris in 90 days. The Bank of Paris releases the documents so the importer can take possession of the shipment.

13. In 90 days, the Bank of Paris receives the importer's payment, so it has funds to pay the maturing draft.

14. In 90 days, the holder of the matured acceptance (in this case, the Bank of New York) presents it to the Bank of Paris for payment. The Bank of Paris pays.

✓ **TEST PREP**

Use SmartBook to help retain what you have learned. Access your instructor's Connect course to check out SmartBook or go to **learnsmartadvantage.com** for help.

LO16-4

Identify information sources and government programs that exist to help exporters.

Export Assistance

Prospective U.S. exporters can draw on two forms of government-backed assistance to help finance their export programs. They can get financing aid from the Export-Import Bank and export credit insurance from the Foreign Credit Insurance Association (similar programs are available in most countries).

THE EXPORT-IMPORT BANK

The Export-Import Bank (EXIM Bank) is a wholly owned U.S. government corporation that was established in 1934. Its mission is to assist in the financing of U.S. exports of products and services to support U.S. employment and market competitiveness. Based on its charter and mandate from the U.S. Congress, the EXIM Bank's financing must have a "reasonable assurance of repayment" and should supplement, and not compete with, private capital lending. The EXIM Bank also follows the international rules for government-backed export credit activity under the Organisation for Economic Co-operation and Development (OECD).

The EXIM Bank reported authorizing about $20.5 billion for 3,746 transactions of finance and insurance to support some $27.5 billion in U.S. exports and 164,000 U.S. jobs the last year it was fully operational. The EXIM Bank's overall exposure was $112 billion, below the $140 billion statutory cap for its fiscal year. Interestingly, 2014 was the last year the EXIM Bank was fully operational due to a lack of quorum on the board of directors. But the EXIM Bank's financing of exports of U.S. goods and services still supported more than 50,000 jobs in the last year completed (2018), even with a smaller operation. As an example, when the author revised this textbook, the EXIM Bank had in its pipeline almost $40 billion of pending transactions that are estimated to support nearly 240,000 American jobs.

Overall, the EXIM Bank pursues its mission with various loan and loan-guarantee programs. The agency guarantees repayment of medium- and long-term loans that U.S. commercial banks make to foreign borrowers for purchasing U.S. exports. The EXIM Bank guarantee makes the commercial banks more willing to lend cash to foreign enterprises. This facilitates cross-border trade by U.S. companies. About 85 percent of the banks' transactions support small businesses (under 500 employees).

Export-Import Bank of the United States headquarters - Washington, DC USA

B Christopher/Alamy Stock Photo

The EXIM Bank also has a direct lending operation under which it lends dollars to foreign borrowers for use in purchasing U.S. exports. In some cases, it grants loans that commercial banks would not if it sees a potential benefit to the United States in doing so. The foreign borrowers use the loans to pay U.S. suppliers and repay the loan to the EXIM Bank with interest. Using the structure of the U.S. EXIM Bank, many countries now have their own export-import banks to facilitate cross-border trade (e.g., China, India).

EXPORT CREDIT INSURANCE

For reasons outlined earlier, exporters clearly prefer to get letters of credit from importers. However, sometimes an exporter who insists on a letter of credit will lose an order to one who does not require a letter of credit. Thus, when the importer is in a strong bargaining position and able to play competing suppliers against each other, an exporter may have to forgo a letter of credit.[18] The lack of a letter of credit exposes the exporter to the risk that the foreign importer will default on payment. The exporter can insure against this possibility by buying export credit insurance. If the customer defaults, the insurance firm will cover a major portion of the loss.

In the United States, export credit insurance is provided by the Foreign Credit Insurance Association (FCIA), an association of private commercial institutions operating under the guidance of the Export-Import Bank. The FCIA provides coverage against commercial risks and political risks. Losses due to commercial risk result from the buyer's insolvency or payment default. Political losses arise from actions of governments that are beyond the control of either buyer or seller. Marlin, the small Baltimore manufacturer of wire baskets discussed earlier, credits export credit insurance with giving the company the confidence to push ahead with export sales. For a premium of roughly half a percentage of the price of a sale, Marlin has been able to insure itself against the possibility of nonpayment by a foreign buyer.[19]

Countertrade

Countertrade is an alternative means of structuring an international sale when conventional means of payment are difficult, costly, or nonexistent. We first encountered countertrade in Chapter 10's discussion of currency convertibility. A government may restrict the convertibility of its currency to preserve its foreign exchange reserves so they can be used to service international debt commitments and purchase crucial imports.[20] This is problematic for exporters. Nonconvertibility implies that the exporter may not be paid in his or her home currency, and few exporters would desire payment in a currency that is not convertible. Countertrade is a common solution.[21] **Countertrade** denotes a range of barter-like agreements; its principle is to trade goods and services for other goods and services when they cannot be traded for money. Some examples of countertrade are

- An Italian company that manufactures power-generating equipment, ABB SAE Sadelmi SpA, was awarded a 720 million baht ($17.7 million) contract by the Electricity Generating Authority of Thailand. The contract specified that the company had to accept 218 million baht ($5.4 million) of Thai farm products as part of the payment.

- Saudi Arabia agreed to buy ten 747 jets from Boeing with payment in crude oil, discounted at 10 percent below posted world oil prices.

- General Electric won a contract for a $150 million electric generator project in Romania by agreeing to market $150 million of Romanian products in markets to which Romania did not have access.

- The Venezuelan government negotiated a contract with Caterpillar under which Venezuela would trade 350,000 tons of iron ore for Caterpillar earthmoving equipment.

TEST PREP

Use SmartBook to help retain what you have learned. Access your instructor's Connect course to check out SmartBook or go to **learnsmartadvantage.com** for help.

LO16-5

Describe how countertrade can be used to facilitate exports.

- Albania offered such items as spring water, tomato juice, and chrome ore in exchange for a $60 million fertilizer and methanol complex.
- Philip Morris shipped cigarettes to Russia, for which it received chemicals that can be used to make fertilizer. Philip Morris shipped the chemicals to China, and in return, China shipped glassware to North America for retail sale by Philip Morris.[22]

THE POPULARITY OF COUNTERTRADE

Countertrade emerged in the 1960s as a way for the old Soviet Union and the then-communist states of eastern Europe, whose currencies were generally nonconvertible, to purchase imports. The technique has grown in popularity among many developing nations that lack the foreign exchange reserves required to purchase necessary imports. Also, reflecting their own shortages of foreign exchange reserves, some successor states to the former Soviet Union and the eastern European communist nations periodically engage in countertrade to purchase their imports. Estimates of the percentage of world trade covered by some sort of countertrade agreement grew from 2 to 10 percent about a decade ago to, by most estimates, some 20 to 25 percent today.[23] The precise figure is unknown, but it is probably at the very low end of these estimates, given the increasing liquidity of international financial markets and wider currency convertibility. However, a short-term spike in the volume of countertrade can follow periodic financial crises (e.g., 1997, 2008). For example, countertrade activity increased notably after the Asian financial crisis of 1997. That crisis left many Asian nations with little hard currency to finance international trade. In the tight monetary regime that followed the crisis in 1997, many Asian firms found it very difficult to get access to export credit to finance their own international trade. Thus, they turned to the only option available to them—countertrade.

Given that countertrade is a means of financing international trade, albeit a minor one, prospective exporters may have to engage in this technique from time to time to gain access to certain international markets. The governments of developing nations sometimes insist on a certain amount of countertrade.[24]

TYPES OF COUNTERTRADE

With its roots in the simple trading of goods and services for other goods and services, countertrade has evolved into a diverse set of activities that can be categorized as five distinct types of trading arrangements: barter, counterpurchase, offset, switch trading, and compensation or buyback.[25] Many countertrade deals involve not just one arrangement but elements of two or more.

Barter

Barter is the direct exchange of goods and/or services between two parties without a cash transaction. Although barter is the simplest arrangement, it is not common. Its problems are twofold. First, if goods are not exchanged simultaneously, one party ends up financing the other for a period. Second, firms engaged in barter run the risk of having to accept goods they do not want, cannot use, or have difficulty reselling at a reasonable price. For these reasons, barter is viewed as the most restrictive countertrade arrangement. It is primarily used for one-time-only deals in transactions with trading partners who are not creditworthy or trustworthy.

Counterpurchase

Counterpurchase is a reciprocal buying agreement. It occurs when a firm agrees to purchase a certain amount of materials back from a country to which a sale is made. Suppose a U.S. firm sells some products to China. China pays the U.S. firm in dollars, but in exchange, the U.S. firm agrees to spend some of its proceeds from the sale on textiles produced by China. Thus, although China must draw on its foreign exchange reserves to pay the U.S. firm, it knows it will receive some of those dollars back because of the counterpurchase agreement. In one counterpurchase agreement, Rolls-Royce sold jet parts to Finland. As part of the deal, Rolls-Royce agreed to use some of the proceeds from the sale to purchase Finnish-manufactured TV sets that it would then sell in Great Britain.

Offset

An **offset** is similar to a counterpurchase insofar as one party agrees to purchase goods and services with a specified percentage of the proceeds from the original sale. The difference is that this party can fulfill the obligation with any firm in the country to which the sale is being made. From an exporter's perspective, this is more attractive than a straight counterpurchase agreement because it gives the exporter greater flexibility to choose the goods that it wishes to purchase.

Switch Trading

The term **switch trading** refers to the use of a specialized third-party trading house in a countertrade arrangement. When a firm enters a counterpurchase or offset agreement with a country, it often ends up with what are called counterpurchase credits, which can be used to purchase goods from that country. Switch trading occurs when a third-party trading house buys the firm's counterpurchase credits and sells them to another firm that can better use them. For example, a U.S. firm concludes a counterpurchase agreement with Poland for which it receives some number of counterpurchase credits for purchasing Polish goods. The U.S. firm cannot use and does not want any Polish goods, however, so it sells the credits to a third-party trading house at a discount. The trading house finds a firm that can use the credits and sells them at a profit.

In one example of switch trading, Poland and Greece had a counterpurchase agreement that called for Poland to buy the same U.S.-dollar value of goods from Greece that it sold to Greece. However, Poland could not find enough Greek goods that it required, so it ended up with a dollar-denominated counterpurchase balance in Greece that it was unwilling to use. A switch trader bought the right to 250,000 counterpurchase dollars from Poland for $225,000 and sold them to a European sultana (grape) merchant for $235,000, who used them to purchase sultanas from Greece.

Compensation or Buybacks

A **buyback** occurs when a firm builds a plant in a country—or supplies technology, equipment, training, or other services to the country—and agrees to take a certain percentage of the plant's output as partial payment for the contract. For example, Occidental Petroleum negotiated a deal with Russia under which Occidental would build several ammonia plants in Russia and as partial payment receive ammonia over a 20-year period.

PROS AND CONS OF COUNTERTRADE

Countertrade's main attraction is that it can give a firm a way to finance an export deal when other means are not available. Given the problems that many developing nations have in raising the foreign exchange necessary to pay for imports, countertrade may be the only option available when doing business in these countries. Even when countertrade is not the only option for structuring an export transaction, many countries prefer countertrade to cash deals. Thus, if a firm is unwilling to enter a countertrade agreement, it may lose an export opportunity to a competitor that is willing to make a countertrade agreement.

In addition, a countertrade agreement may be required by the government of a country to which a firm is exporting goods or services. Boeing often has to accept counterpurchase agreements to capture orders for its commercial jet aircraft. For example, in exchange for gaining an order from Air India, Boeing may be

A subsea oil and gas tree is lowered into a testing pool at the General Electric Co. manufacturing plant in Montrose, United Kingdom.

Simon Dawson/Bloomberg/Getty Images

required to purchase certain component parts, such as aircraft doors, from an Indian company. Taking this one step further, Boeing can use its willingness to enter into a counterpurchase agreement as a way of winning orders in the face of intense competition from its global rival, Airbus. Thus, countertrade can become a strategic marketing weapon.

However, the drawbacks of countertrade agreements are substantial. Other things being equal, firms would normally prefer to be paid in hard currency. Countertrade contracts may involve the exchange of unusable or poor-quality goods that the firm cannot dispose of profitably. For example, a few years ago, one U.S. firm got burned when 50 percent of the television sets it received in a countertrade agreement with Hungary were defective and could not be sold. In addition, even if the goods it receives are of high quality, the firm still needs to dispose of them profitably. To do this, countertrade requires the firm to invest in an in-house trading department dedicated to arranging and managing countertrade deals. This can be expensive and time-consuming.

Given these drawbacks, countertrade is most attractive to large, diverse multinational enterprises that can use their worldwide network of contacts to dispose of goods acquired in countertrading. The masters of countertrade are Japan's giant trading firms, the *sogo shosha*, which use their vast networks of affiliated companies to profitably dispose of goods acquired through countertrade agreements. The trading firm of Mitsui & Company, for example, has about 120 affiliated companies in almost every sector of the manufacturing and service industries. If one of Mitsui's affiliates receives goods in a countertrade agreement that it cannot consume, Mitsui & Company will normally be able to find another affiliate that can profitably use them. Firms affiliated with one of Japan's *sogo shosha* often have a competitive advantage in countries where countertrade agreements are preferred.

Western firms that are large, diverse, and have a global reach (e.g., General Electric, Philip Morris, and 3M) have similar profit advantages from countertrade agreements. Indeed, 3M has established its own trading company—3M Global Trading Inc.—to develop and manage the company's international countertrade programs. Unless there is no alternative, small and medium-sized exporters should probably try to avoid countertrade deals because they lack the worldwide network of operations that may be required to profitably utilize or dispose of goods acquired through them.[26]

TEST PREP

Use SmartBook to help retain what you have learned. Access your instructor's Connect course to check out SmartBook or go to **learnsmartadvantage.com** for help.

Key Terms

MITI, p. 477
sogo shosha, p. 477
export management company
   (EMC), p. 479
letter of credit, p. 485
bill of exchange, p. 485

draft, p. 485
sight draft, p. 486
time draft, p. 486
bill of lading, p. 486
The Export-Import Bank
   (EXIM Bank), p. 488

countertrade, p. 489
barter, p. 490
counterpurchase, p. 490
offset, p. 491
switch trading, p. 491
buyback, p. 491

SUMMARY

This chapter examined the steps that firms must take to establish themselves as exporters. The chapter made the following points:

1. One big impediment to exporting is ignorance of foreign market opportunities.

2. Neophyte exporters often become discouraged or frustrated with the exporting process because they encounter many problems, delays, and pitfalls.

3. The way to overcome ignorance is to gather information. In the United States, a number of institutions, the most important of which is the U.S. Department of Commerce, can help firms gather information in the matchmaking process. Export management companies can also help identify export opportunities.

4. Many of the pitfalls associated with exporting can be avoided if a company hires an experienced

export service provider (e.g., export management company) and if it adopts the appropriate export strategy.

5. Firms engaged in international trade must do business with people they cannot trust and people who may be difficult to track down if they default on an obligation. Due to the lack of trust, each party to an international transaction has a different set of preferences regarding the configuration of the transaction.

6. The problems arising from lack of trust between exporters and importers can be solved by using a third party that is trusted by both, normally a reputable bank.

7. A letter of credit is issued by a bank at the request of an importer. It states that the bank promises to pay a beneficiary, normally the exporter, on presentation of documents specified in the letter.

8. A draft is an instrument normally used in international commerce to effect payment. It is an order written by an exporter instructing an importer or an importer's agent to pay a specified amount of money at a specified time.

9. Drafts are either sight drafts or time drafts. Time drafts are negotiable instruments.

10. A bill of lading is issued to the exporter by the common carrier transporting the merchandise. It serves as a receipt, a contract, and a document of title.

11. U.S. exporters can draw on two types of government-backed assistance to help finance their exports: loans from the Export-Import Bank and export credit insurance from the Foreign Credit Insurance Association.

12. Countertrade includes a range of barter-like agreements. It is primarily used when a firm exports to a country whose currency is not freely convertible and may lack the foreign exchange reserves required to purchase the imports.

13. The main attraction of countertrade is that it gives a firm a way to finance an export deal when other means are not available. A firm that insists on being paid in hard currency may be at a competitive disadvantage vis-à-vis one that is willing to engage in countertrade.

14. The main disadvantage of countertrade is that the firm may receive unusable or poor-quality goods that cannot be disposed of profitably.

Critical Thinking and Discussion Questions

1. A firm based in California wants to export a shipload of finished lumber to the Philippines. The would-be importer cannot get sufficient credit from domestic sources to pay for the shipment but insists that the finished lumber can quickly be resold in the Philippines for a profit. Outline the steps the exporter should take to effect this export to the Philippines.

2. You are the assistant to the CEO of a small technology firm that manufactures quality, premium-priced, stylish clothing. The CEO has decided to see what the opportunities are for exporting and has asked you for advice as to the steps the company should take. What advice would you give the CEO?

3. An alternative to using a letter of credit is export credit insurance. What are the advantages and disadvantages of using export credit insurance rather than a letter of credit for exporting (a) a luxury yacht from California to Canada and (b) machine tools from New York to Ukraine?

4. How do you explain the use of countertrade? Under what scenarios might its use increase further by 2025? Under what scenarios might its use decline?

5. How might a company make strategic use of countertrade schemes as a marketing weapon to generate export revenues? What are the risks associated with pursuing such a strategy?

globalEDGE research task globaledge.msu.edu

Use the globalEDGE™ website (**globaledge.msu.edu**) to complete the following exercises:

1. One way that exporters analyze conditions in emerging markets is through the use of macroeconomic indicators. The Market Potential Index (MPI) is a yearly study conducted by

Michigan State University's International Business Center to compare the market potential of country markets for U.S. exporters. Provide a description of the dimensions used in the index. Which of the dimensions would have greater importance for a company that markets wireless devices? What about a company that sells clothing?

2. You work in the sales department of a company that manufactures and sells medical implants. A Brazilian company contacted your department and expressed interest in purchasing a large quantity of your products. The Brazilian company requested an FOB price quote. One of your colleagues mentioned to you that FOB is part of a collection of international shipping terms called "Incoterms," but that was all he knew. Find the *Export Tutorials* on the globalEDGE™ site, and find a more detailed explanation of Incoterms. For an FOB quote, what line items will you need to include in your price quote, in addition to the price your company will charge for the products?

CLOSING CASE

Spotify and SoundCloud

Numerous online music platforms exist today, with Apple Music, Google Play Music, Pandora, Spotify, Sound-Cloud, and YouTube as perhaps the most common ways people listen to music online around the world. What's popular, of course, can change rapidly. Numerous other music platforms exist or have existed (e.g., 8tracks, AccuRadio, Dash Radio, Deezer, Grooveshark, iHeart-Radio, Incus Tunes, Jango, last.fm, Mixloud, MusixHub, MySpace, RDIO, Slacker Radio, TuneIn Radio, The Sixty One, Xbox Music), and some of these will overtake the top platforms of today, some will be gone soon, and some already have very few users remaining. In this fierce competitive technology environment, Swedish entrepreneurs have made an incredible mark on the music industry.

It all begins, really, with the countless start-ups that Sweden has produced. The focus of this case is Spotify and SoundCloud. However, to better understand the creation of companies and brands such as these, it's important to know how a tiny country like Sweden with a population of 10 million people and pretty high government spending can be so innovative and entrepreneurial. Given its size, it should come as no surprise that companies from Sweden rely on exports for much of their sales. And the start-ups have become a cultural phenomenon in Sweden that have helped the economy grow in unimaginable ways from just a couple of decades ago.

Stockholm, the capital city of Sweden, produces the second-highest number of billion-dollar tech companies per capita, after Silicon Valley. The change happened in the 1990s when Sweden needed a boost to its economy. The country used to be heavily regulated and public monopolies dominated the market, but regulations have been eased since that time. Interestingly, while Sweden was making it harder for monopolies to dominate the market, the regulatory landscape in the U.S. was changed to favor big companies and established firms. Despite the global fascination with start-ups, only 8 percent of all firms in the U.S. meet that definition today, a remarkable drop from a few decades ago.

In Sweden, the trend has been reversed. The pace of new-business creation start-ups has been accelerating. Countries like Brazil, India, Romania, Germany, and Singapore have also seen an increasing trend of start-ups in recent years. These start-ups are critical to a country's economy. They create jobs, spur innovation, and foster the entrepreneurial spirit that drives economic growth. For example, in the United States, small- and medium-sized enterprises account for 98 percent of the country's exporters, and start-ups fall into this SME category (often as so-called "born globals"—companies that start selling internationally early on after inception). Spotify and SoundCloud fit all of these categories as start-ups—they were initially small, went international early on, and helped drive exporting numbers.

Spotify is a Swedish entertainment company founded in 2008 by Daniel Ek and Martin Lorentzon that specializes in music, podcast, and video streaming. Spotify Technology SA is headquartered in Stockholm and listed on the New York Stock Exchange as SPOT. The company has more than 3,000 employees, 200 million users, and revenue of about $5 billion. Spotify is available in most of Europe, the Americas, Oceania, and parts of Asia. Spotify gives users access to more than 30 million songs and has some 140 million active monthly users, with more than 70 million paying subscribers.

SoundCloud was founded in 2007 in Stockholm, Sweden, by Alexander Ljung and Eric Wahlforss, who almost immediately developed a headquarters for the company in Berlin, Germany. In effect, Alexander Ljung and Eric Wahlforss used the great infrastructure for start-ups in both Sweden and Germany to launch SoundCloud and build it into what it has now become—a company with 300 employees, 40 million registered users, and 175 million monthly listeners. With a different focus than Spotify, SoundCloud positioned itself as an online audio distribution platform that enables users to upload, record, promote, and share their originally created sounds.

Both Spotify and SoundCloud are service businesses that have entered into the global marketplace with music platforms that customers find valuable. Service exports are an important and increasing trend in global trade. Take, for example, the developed countries in the world, most of whose economies—around 75 percent—are service-based. If these economies, like Sweden and Germany, did not find an opportunity to export their services, they would likely fall behind in the trade balance (imports versus exports). Interestingly, the U.S. has a relatively large trade surplus in services, but a massive trade deficit in manufactured goods. If the U.S. could reduce the deficit in products to have a neutral import–export ratio, the country's service economy would automatically create a trade surplus—which the country has not seen for some 50 years. Given that a service export is really any service provided by a resident in one country to people or organizations in another country, we know many countries can be successful, or at least have the opportunity to export more services, such as what Sweden and Germany are doing with Spotify and SoundCloud.

Sources: Stacy Fisher, "The Top 14 Places to Listen to Free Music Online," *The Balance Every Day*, April 3, 2018; Namrata Ahuja, "Spotify vs. Soundcloud: What Is the Best Platform for Music Lovers?" *Odyssey*, June 1, 2016; Alana Semuels, "Why Does Sweden Have So Many Start-Ups?" *The Atlantic*, September 28, 2018; "Spotify Makes Its Stock Market Debut," *The Economist*, April 4, 2018; "Having Rescued Recorded Music, Spotify May Upend the Industry Again," *The Economist*, January 11, 2018; and "SoundCloud Streaming Hones In On Creator Uploaded Content: CEO," *BusinessWeek*, April 23, 2018.

Case Discussion Questions

1. Numerous online music platforms exist today, with Apple Music, Google Play Music, Pandora, Spotify, SoundCloud, and YouTube as perhaps the most common ways people listen to music online around the world. Which one(s) do you use and why? Which one(s) do you think will no longer be in operation in 10 years and why?

2. Based on what you can read in this case and what you are able to glean from researching Sweden, why do you think Stockholm, the capital city of Sweden, produces the second-highest number of billion-dollar tech companies per capita, after Silicon Valley?

3. What are the strengths and weaknesses of Spotify and SoundCloud, respectively? Do you think their business models will last, or will other innovative ideas overtake the market power that Spotify and SoundCloud have in the international marketplace?

Design elements: Modern textured halftone: ©VIPRESIONA/ Shutterstock; globalEDGE icon: ©globalEDGE; All others: ©McGraw-Hill Education

Endnotes

1. T. Hult, D. Closs, and D. Frayer, *Global Supply Chain Management: Leveraging Processes, Measurements, and Tools for Strategic Corporate Advantage* (New York: McGraw-Hill, 2014).

2. T. Hult, D. Closs, and D. Frayer, *Global Supply Chain Management: Leveraging Processes, Measurements, and Tools for Strategic Corporate Advantage* (New York: McGraw-Hill, 2014).

3. R. A. Pope, "Why Small Firms Export: Another Look," *Journal of Small Business Management* 40 (2002), pp. 17–26.

4. S. T. Cavusgil, "Global Dimensions of Marketing," in *Marketing*, ed. P. E. Murphy and B. M. Enis (Glenview, IL: Scott, Foresman, 1985), pp. 577–99.

5. S. M. Mehta, "Enterprise: Small Companies Look to Cultivate Foreign Business," *The Wall Street Journal*, July 7, 1994, p. B2.

6. P. A. Julien and C. Ramagelahy, "Competitive Strategy and Performance of Exporting SMEs," *Entrepreneurship Theory and Practice* (2003), pp. 227–94.

7. W. J. Burpitt and D. A. Rondinelli, "Small Firms' Motivations for Exporting: To Earn and Learn?" *Journal of Small Business Management* 38 (2000), pp. 1–14; and J. D. Mittelstaedt, G. N. Harben, and W. A. Ward, "How Small Is Too Small?" *Journal of Small Business Management* 41 (2003), pp. 68–85.

8. https://www.sba.gov/business-guide/grow-your-business/ export-products, accessed April 14, 2019.

9. A. O. Ogbuehi and T. A. Longfellow, "Perceptions of U.S. Manufacturing Companies Concerning Exporting," *Journal of Small Business Management* 32 (1994), pp. 37–59; and U.S. Department of Commerce, "A Basic Guide to Exporting,"

https://2016.export.gov/missouri/build/groups/public/@eg_us_mo/documents/webcontent/eg_us_mo_097311.pdf.

10. R. W. Haigh, "Thinking of Exporting?" *Columbia Journal of World Business* 29 (December 1994), pp. 66–86.

11. F. Williams, "The Quest for More Efficient Commerce," *Financial Times*, October 13, 1994, p. 7.

12. See Burpitt and Rondinelli, "Small Firms' Motivations for Exporting"; and C. S. Katsikeas, L. C. Leonidou, and N. A. Morgan, "Firm Level Export Performance Assessment," *Academy of Marketing Science* 28 (2000), pp. 493–511.

13. M. Y. Yoshino and T. B. Lifson, *The Invisible Link* (Cambridge, MA: MIT Press, 1986).

14. L. W. Tuller, *Going Global* (Homewood, IL: Business One-Irwin, 1991).

15. M. A. Raymond, J. Kim, and A. T. Shao. "Export Strategy and Performance," *Journal of Global Marketing* 15 (2001), pp. 5–29; P. S. Aulakh, M. Kotabe, and H. Teegen, "Export Strategies and Performance of Firms from Emerging Economies," *Academy of Management Journal* 43 (2000), pp. 342–61.

16. J. Francis and C. Collins-Dodd, "The Impact of Firms' Export Orientation on the Export Performance of High-Tech Small and Medium Sized Enterprises," *Journal of International Marketing* 8 (2000), pp. 84–103.

17. J. Koch, "Integration of U.S. Small Businesses into the Export Trade Sector Using Available Financial Tools and Resources," *Business Credit* 109, no. 10 (2007), pp. 64–68.

18. For a review of the conditions under which a buyer has power over a supplier, see M. E. Porter, *Competitive Strategy* (New York: Free Press, 1980).

19. M. C. White, "Marlin Steel Wire Products: How a Small Factory Survives and Thrives, Thanks to Overseas Sales," *Slate*, November 10, 2009.

20. *Exchange Agreements and Exchange Restrictions* (Washington, DC: International Monetary Fund, 1989).

21. It's also sometimes argued that countertrade is a way of reducing the risks inherent in a traditional money-for-goods transaction, particularly with entities from emerging economies. See C. J. Choi, S. H. Lee, and J. B. Kim, "A Note of Countertrade: Contractual Uncertainty and Transactional Governance in Emerging Economies," *Journal of International Business Studies* 30, no. 1 (1999), pp. 189–202.

22. J. R. Carter and J. Gagne, "The Do's and Don'ts of International Countertrade," *Sloan Management Review*, Spring 1988, pp. 31–37; and W. Maneerungsee, "Countertrade: Farm Goods Swapped for Italian Electricity," *Bangkok Post*, July 23, 1998.

23. Estimate from the Global Offset and Countertrade Association (G.O.C.A.) at www.globaloffset.org. See also D. West, "Countertrade," *Business Credit* 104, no. 4 (2001), pp. 64–67; and B. Meyer, "The Original Meaning of Trade Meets the Future of Barter," *World Trade* 13 (January 2000), pp. 46–50.

24. Carter and Gagne, "The Do's and Don'ts of International Countertrade."

25. For details, see Carter and Gagne, "The Do's and Don'ts of International Countertrade"; J. F. Hennart, "Some Empirical Dimensions of Countertrade," *Journal of International Business Studies* 21, no. 2 (1990), pp. 240–60; and West, "Countertrade."

26. D. J. Lecraw, "The Management of Countertrade: Factors Influencing Success," *Journal of International Business Studies*, Spring 1989, pp. 41–59.

Global Production and Supply Chain Management

17

LEARNING OBJECTIVES

After reading this chapter, you will be able to:

LO17-1 Explain why global production and supply chain management decisions are of central importance to many global companies.

LO17-2 Explain how country differences, production technology, and production factors all affect the choice of where to locate production activities.

LO17-3 Recognize how the role of foreign subsidiaries in production can be enhanced over time as they accumulate knowledge.

LO17-4 Identify the factors that influence a firm's decision of whether to source supplies from within the company or from foreign suppliers.

LO17-5 Understand the functions of logistics and purchasing (sourcing) within global supply chains.

LO17-6 Describe what is required to efficiently manage a global supply chain.

Blockchain Technology and Global Supply Chains

OPENING CASE

Global production and supply chain management are by design complex and geographically disjointed, especially in a multinational corporation's network of global supply chains. Each supply chain involves multiple companies, multiple links in the chain, and lots of resource ties between these entities and links. Given such a dynamic and multifaceted setup, the nature of globalization with trade barriers, varied policies worldwide, diverse cultural and environmental issues, and people from business and nonbusiness functions make it difficult to have a good handle on information that flows in global supply chains. It also makes it difficult to manage risk, security, and value-added aspects of the chain. Every company wants just-in-time information at their disposal, but not every organization in a global supply chain is willing or able to supply such information easily.

Meanwhile, many supply chain executives and corporate strategists make a compelling case that information flows in global supply chains are perhaps more critical than even the flow of products, component parts, and raw materials. Timing in production relies on information flows. In particular, traceability is becoming an urgent requirement and a fundamental differentiator in many supply chains (e.g., agri-food sector, pharmaceutical and medical products, high-value goods). Lack of information transparency in these chains prevents organizations and customers from verifying and validating the true value of the product, component part, or even raw materials. The cost involved in managing chain intermediaries, their reliability, and performance further complicate traceability in the chain. In fact, both strategic and operational issues arise from these risks and lack of transparency.

To solve some of these supply chain issues, nearly all of the world's leading companies use sophisticated enterprise resource planning (ERP) and supply chain software. Some of the systems include connected manufacturing equipment to digital shipping notices and RFID scanning. Most multinational corporations track the earliest origins of a shipment, often all the way to the recycling bin, if needed. However, even with such tracking, most large companies have only limited information on where all their shipment is at any given moment in the global supply chain even after investing heavily in their digital infrastructure. One of the core reasons for this limited information is that even as supply chains are becoming more efficient, corporations often do not have an up-to-date technology infrastructure to manage the chains. Then again, even if possible, not every organization in a global supply chain is willing or able to supply such information easily.

Enter blockchain technology! Blockchains make it possible for ecosystems of supply chain partners (or any business partners) to share and agree upon key pieces of information. Importantly, the partners can agree on the information without having to deal with all the complex negotiations and power plays that come with setting the rules before handing over really critical business information. Blockchains synchronize all data and transactions across the global network, and each supply chain partner can verify the work and calculations of others. Such redundancy and crosschecking are why financial solutions like bitcoins and blockchain technology are secure and reliable, even as they synchronize millions of transactions across thousands of network nodes weekly (blockchain is the technology that underlies bitcoin).

Within supply chains, the core logic of blockchains means that no piece of inventory (e.g., raw material, work-in-process, component parts, finished goods) can exist in the same place twice. If a product is moved from finished goods to in-transit, the transaction status will be updated for everyone, everywhere, within minutes, with full traceability back to the point of origin. Such traceability is important for a number of reasons. For example, if a company wants to negotiate procurement deals based on total volume that the company and its subsidiaries and partners buy, a blockchain-based solution can facilitate the calculations of the exact volume discount based on total purchasing. And in a trusting and transparent way, the companies involved can mathematically prove that the calculation is correct because of the blockchain technology. Plus, the calculations can be done while preserving the privacy of each company's individual volumes.

Through blockchains companies gain a live, real-time digital ledger of all transactions and supply chain movements for all participants in their supply chain network. While seemingly simplistic as a concept, the real-time feature involving a company and companies in that company's network would not have been a simplistic feature to implement without blockchains, given transparency, trust, ability, and willingness problems. But with blockchain technology, companies can negotiate sourcing discounts based on the total number of purchases they do: purchases done on their behalf by others, purchases done by business partners, and purchases made by everyone else in the supply chain network. With a constantly refreshed digital ledger that incorporates data from all relevant partners, a company can see the total volume regardless of who directed the purchase activity without each user having to share its operational data with others. The efficiencies are real as well. Without blockchain's "distributed ledger technology," companies would enlist lots of people to audit their orders to try to capture as much of these volume benefits as possible, but would seldom be successful in capturing all aspects of the supply chain network.

Despite the many positives of blockchain technology, everything is not as optimistic as what the blockchain appears to be, not yet at least. Investment, infrastructure, and implementation are concerns, especially on a worldwide scale. In a Deloitte survey reported in *The Wall Street Journal*, a majority of organizations see a compelling case for the use of blockchain technology, but only one-third of the business executives who participated in the study said that their companies had initiated implementation of the technology. One issue is that large companies have legacy concerns with their current technology. Fitting blockchain technology into existing systems around the globe is difficult, costly, and not as efficient as possible to reap the short-term, immediate advantages that blockchain technology offers companies. Plus, worldwide, not all companies have the same opportunities to invest in blockchain (due to costs, software compatibility, infrastructure, etc.), which means companies in any given supply chain network may still not reap all the advantages expected by implementing blockchain technology.

Sources: "The Meaning of the Blockchain," *The Economist*, January 8, 2019; Paul Brody, "How Blockchain Revolutionizes Supply Chain Management," *Digitalist Magazine*, August 23, 2017; "The Promise of the Blockchain Technology," *The Economist*, August 30, 2018; Olga Kharif and Matthew Leising, "Bitcoin and Blockchain," *Bloomberg BusinessWeek*, November 2, 2018; Olga Kharif, "Blockchain, Once Seen as a Corporate Cure-All, Suffers Slowdown," *Bloomberg BusinessWeek*, July 31, 2018; Christopher Mims, "Why Blockchain Will Survive, Even If Bitcoin Doesn't," *The Wall Street Journal*, March 11, 2018.

Introduction

As trade barriers fall and global markets develop, many firms increasingly confront a set of interrelated issues. First, where in the world should production activities be located? Should they be concentrated in a single country, or should they be dispersed around the globe, matching the type of activity with country differences in factor costs, tariff barriers, political risks, and the like to minimize costs and maximize value added? Single-country strategies may be efficient operationally but often become ineffective strategically. For example, what if the company focused all of its attention on one country for production and that country became politically or economically unstable? Some redundancy is usually the best approach in both global production and supply chain management practices, and such redundancy often demands that a company spreads its production and supply chains across countries.

Second, what should be the long-term strategic role of foreign production sites? Should the firm abandon a foreign site if factor costs change, moving production to another more favorable location, or is there value to maintaining operations at a given location even if underlying economic conditions change? Value can come from cost inefficiencies. Moving factory locations from one country to another solely due to cost considerations is usually not a strategic move. Successful companies typically evaluate cost considerations along with quality, flexibility, and time issues. At the same time, the cost is one of the most important considerations and serves as the starting point for discussion of making a strategic move from one country to a more advantageous production home.

Third, should the firm own foreign production activities, or is it better to outsource those activities to independent vendors? Outsourcing means less control, but it can be cost-efficient. Fourth, how should a globally dispersed supply chain be managed, and what is the role of information technology in the management of global logistics, purchasing (sourcing), and operations? Fifth, similar to issues of production, should the company manage global supply chains itself, or should it outsource the management to enterprises that specialize in this activity? There are myriad options for supply chain management by third parties. Few companies want to manage the full supply chain from raw material to delivering the product to the end-customer. The question, though, is which portion of the supply chain should be managed by third parties, and which portion should be managed by the company itself.

In addition, managing supply chains in general and the chains that are global in scope in particular is the key critical aspect of realizing efficiencies in operations: Global supply chains connect global production with global customers. As noted in the opening case, global production and supply chain management are, by design, complex and geographically disjointed, especially in a multinational corporation's network of global supply chains. Enter blockchain technology to help! Blockchains make it possible for ecosystems of supply chain partners (or any business partners) to share and agree upon key pieces of information. The strategic supply-chain partners can also agree on the information without having to deal with all the complex negotiations and power plays that come with setting the rules before handing over really critical business information. Through blockchains, companies gain a live, real-time digital ledger of all transactions and supply chain movements for all participants in their supply chain network, offsetting issues concerning transparency, trust, ability, and willingness problems that prevented such sharing before.

This chapter also includes illustrations of some of the best-operating global supply chain networks in the world. Take a look at each and see what they do that is similar and different, and where they obtain both efficiencies and effectiveness in their supply chains (e.g., P&G in the closing case; Alibaba in the end-of-the-book integrated case related to Chapter 17; and IKEA and Amazon in the Management Focus features in the chapter text). One important aspect of how these companies run their global supply chains is that they constantly think about the *total costs* of their chains. A total cost focus of a global supply chain ensures that the goal is not necessarily to strive for the lowest cost possible at each stage of the supply chain (each node in the chain), but to instead strive for the lowest total cost to the customer—and, by extension, the greatest value—at the end of the product supply chain. This means that all aspects of cost—including integration and coordination of companies in the supply chain—have been incorporated in addition to the cost of raw material, component parts, and assembly worldwide. And these cost issues, as they relate to global logistics and global purchasing—both considered supply chains functions in a company—have been strategically and tactically addressed.

Strategy, Production, and Supply Chain Management

LO17-1

Explain why global production and supply chain management decisions are of central importance to many global companies.

Chapter 13 introduced the concept of the value chain and discussed a number of value creation activities, including production, marketing, logistics, R&D, human resources, and information systems. This chapter focuses on two of these value creation activities—**production** and **supply chain management**—and attempts to clarify how they might be performed internationally to (1) lower the costs of value creation and (2) add value by better serving customer needs. Production is sometimes also referred to as manufacturing or operations when discussed in relation to global supply chains. We also discuss the contributions of information technology to these activities, which has become particularly important in a globally integrated world. The remaining chapters in this text look at other value creation activities in the international context (marketing, R&D, and human resource management).

In Chapter 13, we stated that production is concerned with the creation of a good or service. We used the term *production* to denote both service and manufacturing activities because either a service or a physical product can be produced. Although in this chapter we focus more on the production of physical goods, we should not forget that the term can also be applied to services. This has become more evident in recent years, with the continued pattern among U.S. firms to outsource the "production" of certain service activities to developing nations where labor costs are lower (e.g., the trend among many U.S. companies to outsource customer care services to places such as India, where English is widely spoken and labor costs are much lower). Supply chain management is the integration and coordination of logistics, purchasing, operations, and market channel activities from raw material to the end-customer. Production and supply chain management are closely linked because a firm's ability to perform its production activities efficiently depends on a timely supply of high-quality material and information inputs, for which **purchasing** and **logistics** are critical functions. Purchasing represents the part of the supply chain that involves worldwide buying of raw material, component parts, and products used in manufacturing of the company's products and services. Logistics is the part of the supply chain that plans, implements, and controls the effective flows and inventory of raw material, component parts, and products used in manufacturing.

The production and supply chain management functions (purchasing, logistics) of an international firm have a number of important strategic objectives.[1] One is to ensure that the total cost of moving from raw materials to finished goods is as low as possible for the value provided to the end-customer. Dispersing production activities to various locations around the globe where each activity can be performed most efficiently can lower the total costs. Costs can also be cut by managing the global supply chain efficiently to better match supply and demand. This involves both coordination and integration of the supply chain functions *inside* a global company (e.g., purchasing, logistics, production and operations management) and *across* the independent organizations (e.g., suppliers) involved in the chain. For example, efficient logistics practices reduce the amount of inventory in the system, increase inventory turnover, and facilitate the appropriate transportation modes being used. Maximizing purchasing operations enhances the order fulfillment and delivery, outsourcing initiatives, and supplier selections. Efficient operations ensure that the right location of production is made, establishes which production priorities should be stressed, and facilitates a high-quality outcome of the supply chain.

Another strategic objective shared by production and supply chain management is to increase product (or service) quality by establishing process-based quality standards and eliminating defective raw material, component parts, and products from the manufacturing process and the supply chain.[2] In this context, *quality* means *reliability*, implying that ultimately the finished product has no defects and performs well. These quality assurances should be embedded in both the **upstream** and **downstream** portions of the global supply chain. The upstream supply chain includes all of the organizations (e.g., suppliers) and resources that are involved in the portion of the supply chain from raw materials to the production facility (this is sometimes also called the inbound supply chain). The downstream supply chain includes all of the organizations (e.g., wholesaler, retailer) that are involved in the portion of the supply chain from the production facility to the end-customer (this is also sometimes called the outbound supply chain). Through the upstream and downstream chains, the objectives of reducing costs and increasing quality are not independent of each other. As illustrated in Figure 17.1, the firm that improves its quality control will also reduce its costs of value creation. Improved quality control reduces costs by

- Increasing productivity because time is not wasted producing poor-quality products that cannot be sold, leading to a direct reduction in unit costs.
- Lowering rework and scrap costs associated with defective products.
- Reducing the warranty costs and time associated with fixing defective products.

The effect is to lower the total costs of value creation by reducing both production and after-sales service costs. This creates an increased overall reliability in global production and supply chain management.

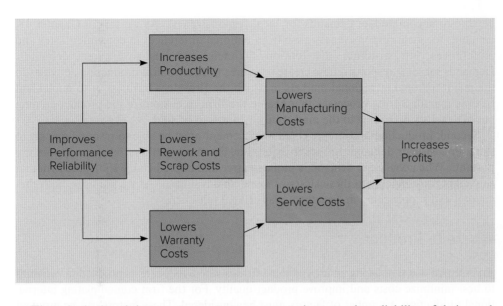

FIGURE 17.1

The relationship between quality and costs.

Source: A. David Garvin, "What Does 'Product Quality' Really Mean?" *MIT Sloan Management Review*, Fall 1984, http://sloanreview.mit.edu/article/what-does-product-quality-really-mean/.

The principal tool that most managers now use to increase the reliability of their product offering is the Six Sigma quality improvement methodology. Six Sigma is a direct descendant of the **total quality management (TQM)** philosophy that was widely adopted, first by Japanese companies and then American companies, during the 1980s and early 1990s.[3] The TQM philosophy was developed by a number of American consultants such as W. Edwards Deming, Joseph Juran, and A. V. Feigenbaum.[4] Deming identified a number of steps that should be part of any TQM program. He argued that management should embrace the philosophy that mistakes, defects, and poor-quality materials are not acceptable and should be eliminated. Deming suggested that the quality of supervision should be improved by allowing more time for supervisors to work with employees and by providing them with the tools they need to do the job. Deming also recommended that management should create an environment in which employees will not fear reporting problems or recommending improvements. He believed that work standards should not only be defined as numbers or quotas, but also include some notion of quality to promote the production of defect-free output. Deming argued that management has the responsibility to train employees in new skills to keep pace with changes in the workplace. In addition, he believed that achieving better quality requires the commitment of everyone in the company.

Six Sigma, the modern successor to TQM, is a statistically based philosophy that aims to reduce defects, boost productivity, eliminate waste, and cut costs throughout a company. Six Sigma programs have been adopted by several major corporations, such as Motorola, General Electric, and Honeywell. Sigma comes from the Greek letter that statisticians use to represent a standard deviation from a mean; the higher the number of "sigmas," the smaller the number of errors. At six sigmas, a production process would be 99.99966 percent accurate, creating just 3.4 defects per million units. While it is almost impossible for a company to achieve such perfection, Six Sigma quality is a goal to strive toward. The Six Sigma program is particularly informative in structuring global processes that multinational corporations can follow in quality and productivity initiatives. As such, increasingly companies are adopting Six Sigma programs to try to boost their product quality and productivity.[5]

The growth of international standards has also focused greater attention on the importance of product quality. In Europe, for example, the European Union requires that the quality of a firm's manufacturing processes and products be certified under a quality standard known as **ISO 9000** before the firm is allowed access to the EU marketplace. Although the ISO 9000 certification process has proved to be somewhat bureaucratic and costly for many firms, it does focus management attention on the need to improve the quality of products and processes.[6]

In addition to lowering costs and improving quality, two other objectives have particular importance in international businesses. First, production and supply chain functions must be able to accommodate demands for local responsiveness. As we saw in Chapter 13, demands for local responsiveness arise from national differences in consumer tastes and preferences, infrastructure, distribution channels, and host-government demands. Demands for local responsiveness create pressures to decentralize production activities to the major national or regional markets in which the firm does business or to implement flexible manufacturing processes that enable the firm to customize the product coming out of a factory according to the market in which it is to be sold.

Second, production and supply chain management must be able to respond quickly to shifts in customer demand. In recent years, time-based competition has grown more important.[7] When consumer demand is prone to large and unpredictable shifts, the firm that can adapt most quickly to these shifts will gain an advantage.[8] As we shall see, both production and supply chain management play critical roles here.

TEST PREP

Use SmartBook to help retain what you have learned. Access your Instructor's Connect course to check out SmartBook or go to **learnsmartadvantage.com** for help.

LO17-2

Explain how country differences, production technology, and production factors all affect the choice of where to locate production activities.

Where to Produce

An essential decision facing an international firm is where to locate its production activities to best minimize costs and improve product quality. For the firm contemplating international production, a number of factors must be considered. These factors can be grouped under three broad headings: country factors, technological factors, and production factors.[9]

COUNTRY FACTORS

We reviewed country-specific factors in some detail earlier in the book. Political and economic systems, culture, and relative factor costs differ from country to country. In Chapter 6, we saw that due to differences in factor costs, some countries have a comparative advantage for producing certain products. In Chapters 2, 3, and 4, we saw how differences in political and economic systems—and national culture—influence the benefits, costs, and risks of doing business in a country. Other things being equal, a firm should locate its various manufacturing activities where the economic, political, and cultural conditions—including relative factor costs—are conducive to the performance of those activities (for an example, see the accompanying Management Focus, which looks at the IKEA production in China). In Chapter 13, we referred to the benefits derived from such a strategy as location economies. We argued that one result of the strategy is the creation of a global web of value creation activities.

Also important in some industries is the presence of global concentrations of activities at certain locations. In Chapter 8, we discussed the role of location externalities in influencing foreign direct investment decisions. Externalities include the presence of an appropriately skilled labor pool and supporting industries.[10] Such externalities can play an important role in deciding where to locate production activities. For example, because of a cluster of semiconductor manufacturing plants in Taiwan, a pool of labor with experience in the semiconductor business has developed. In addition, the plants have attracted a number of supporting industries, such as the manufacturers of semiconductor capital equipment and silicon, which have established facilities in Taiwan to be near their customers. This implies that there are real benefits to locating in Taiwan, as opposed to another location that lacks such externalities. Other things being equal, the externalities make Taiwan an attractive location for semiconductor manufacturing facilities. The same process is now under way in two Indian cities, Hyderabad and Bangalore, where both Western and Indian information technology companies have established operations. For example, locals refer to a section of Hyderabad as "Cyberabad," where Microsoft, IBM, Infosys, and Qualcomm (among others) have major facilities.

Of course, other things are not equal. Differences in relative factor costs, political economy, culture, and location externalities are important, but other factors also loom large. Formal and informal trade barriers obviously influence location decisions (see Chapter 7), as do transportation costs and rules and regulations regarding foreign direct investment (see Chapter 8). For example, although relative factor costs may make a country look attractive as a location for performing a manufacturing activity, regulations prohibiting

IKEA Production in China

Founded in Sweden in 1943 by 17-year-old Ingvar Kamprad, IKEA is the largest furniture retailer in the world. We covered some of the global strategy of IKEA in the opening case to Chapter 13. As mentioned, the IKEA name comes from its founder, Ingvar Kamprad—an acronym of the founder's initials from his first and last names (**I**ngvar **K**amprad) along with the first initials of the farm where he grew up (**E**lmtaryd) and his hometown in Sweden (**A**gunnaryd).

Beyond its founding in Sweden and its current headquarters in Delft, The Netherlands, IKEA presents an amazing global supply chain story and production apparatus. IKEA is a multinational corporation where most of the company's operations, management of the more than 350 stores in 46 countries, and design and manufacturing of furniture are run by a trust, INGKA Holding. It is the trust that is headquartered in Delft, Holland. Most of the furniture designs of IKEA products are still made in Sweden, but the manufacturing of that furniture—or, really, the pieces that customers buy to put together into furniture—has been outsourced to China and other Asian countries.

Considering that IKEA produces an assortment of some 12,000 furniture and related products, production capabilities and capacities are at a premium for IKEA to sustain its market leadership in the world. To start, IKEA has a clear vision for the products that it designs and produces. The company's idea is to provide well-designed, functional home furnishings at prices so low that as many people around the world as possible will be able to afford them. Importantly, the critical functions to make this happen, such as global supply chains and global inventory management, work in concert to support IKEA's distinctive value proposition.

The Sweden-based home furnishing giant opened its first wholly owned manufacturing facility in China on August 28, 2013. In a local move, the factory supports the rapid expansion in Asia and, especially, in China (the facility is located in Nantong, Jiangsu province). As the largest sourcing country for IKEA, China accounts for more than 20 percent of its global procurement, with about 300 local Chinese suppliers. The factory is also not far from IKEA's two biggest warehouses, which are located in Shanghai.

Sources: Lindsey Rupp, "Ikea, Dollar General CEOs Lobby Republicans in Tax Showdown," *Bloomberg Businessweek*, March 7, 2017; D. L. Yohn, "How IKEA Designs Its Brand Success," *Forbes*, June 10, 2015; J. Kane, "The 21 Emotional Stages of Shopping at IKEA, From Optimism to Total Defeat," *The Huffington Post*, May 6, 2015; J. Leland, "How the Disposable Sofa Conquered America," *The New York Times Magazine*, October 5, 2005, p. 45; "The Secret of IKEA's Success," *The Economist*, February 24, 2011; B. Torekull, *Leading by Design: The IKEA Story* (New York: HarperCollins, 1998); and P. M. Miller, "IKEA with Chinese Characteristics," *Chinese Business Review*, July–August 2004, pp. 36–69.

foreign direct investment may eliminate this option. Similarly, consideration of factor costs might suggest that a firm should source production of a certain component from a particular country, but trade barriers could make this uneconomical.

Another important country factor is the expected future movements in its exchange rate (see Chapters 10 and 11). Adverse changes in exchange rates can quickly alter a country's attractiveness as a manufacturing base. Currency appreciation can transform a low-cost location into a high-cost location. Many Japanese corporations had to grapple with this problem during the 1990s and early 2000s. The relatively low value of the yen on foreign exchange markets between 1950 and 1980 helped strengthen Japan's position as a low-cost location for manufacturing. More recently, however, the yen's steady appreciation against the dollar increased the dollar cost of products exported from Japan, making Japan less attractive as a manufacturing location. In response, many Japanese firms moved their manufacturing offshore to lower-cost locations in East Asia.

TECHNOLOGICAL FACTORS

The type of technology a firm uses to perform specific manufacturing activities can be pivotal in location decisions. For example, because of technological constraints, in some cases it is necessary to perform certain manufacturing activities in only one location and serve the world market from there. In other cases, technology may make it feasible to perform an activity in multiple locations. Three characteristics of manufacturing technology are of interest here: the level of fixed costs, the minimum efficient scale, and the flexibility of the technology.

Fixed Costs

As noted in Chapter 13, in some cases the fixed costs of setting up a production plant are so high that a firm must serve the world market from a single location or from very few locations. For example, it now costs up to $5 billion to set up a state-of-the-art plant to manufacture semiconductor chips. Given this, other things being equal, serving the world market from a single plant sited at a single (optimal) location can make sense.

Conversely, a relatively low level of fixed costs can make it economical to perform a particular activity in several locations at once. This allows the firm to better accommodate demands for local responsiveness. Manufacturing in multiple locations may also help the firm avoid becoming too dependent on one location. Being too dependent on one location is particularly risky in a world of floating exchange rates. Many firms disperse their manufacturing plants to different locations as a "real hedge" against potentially adverse moves in currencies.

Minimum Efficient Scale

The concept of economies of scale tells us that as plant output expands, unit costs decrease. The reasons include the greater utilization of capital equipment and the productivity gains that come with specialization of employees within the plant.[11] However, beyond a certain level of output, few additional scale economies are available. Thus, the "unit cost curve" declines with output until a certain output level is reached, at which point further increases in output realize little reduction in unit costs. The level of output at which most plant-level scale economies are exhausted is referred to as the **minimum efficient scale** of output. This is the scale of output a plant must operate to realize all major plant-level scale economies (see Figure 17.2).

The implications of this concept are as follows: The larger the minimum efficient scale of a plant relative to total global demand, the greater the argument for centralizing production in a single location or a limited number of locations. Alternatively, when the minimum efficient scale of production is low relative to global demand, it may be economical to manufacture a product at several locations. For example, the minimum efficient scale for a plant to manufacture personal computers is about 250,000 units a year, while the total global demand exceeds 35 million units a year. The low level of minimum efficient scale in relation to total global demand makes it economically feasible for companies such as Dell and Lenovo to assemble PCs in multiple locations.

As in the case of low fixed costs, the advantages of a low minimum efficient scale include allowing the firm to accommodate demands for local responsiveness or to hedge against currency risk by manufacturing the same product in several locations.

FIGURE 17.2

Typical unit cost curve.

Source: Charles W. L. Hill and G. Tomas M. Hult, *Global Business Today* (New York: McGraw-Hill, 2020).

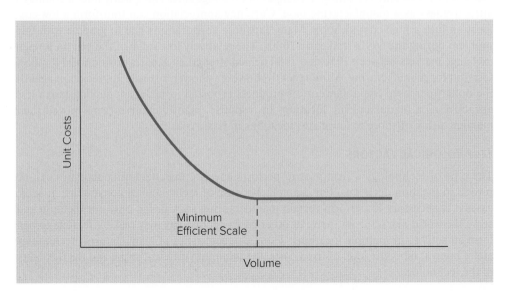

Flexible Manufacturing and Mass Customization

Central to the concept of economies of scale is the idea that the best way to achieve high efficiency, and hence low unit costs, is through the mass production of a standardized output. The trade-off implicit in this idea is between unit costs and product variety. Producing greater product variety from a factory implies shorter production runs, which in turn implies an inability to realize economies of scale. That is, wide product variety makes it difficult for a company to increase its production efficiency and thus reduce its unit costs. According to this logic, the way to increase efficiency and drive down unit costs is to limit product variety and produce a standardized product in large volumes.

This view of production efficiency has been challenged by the rise of flexible manufacturing technologies. The term **flexible manufacturing technology**—or **lean production**, as it is often called—covers a range of manufacturing technologies designed to (1) reduce setup times for complex equipment, (2) increase the utilization of individual machines through better scheduling, and (3) improve quality control at all stages of the manufacturing process.[12] Flexible manufacturing technologies allow the company to produce a wider variety of end products at a unit cost that at one time could be achieved only through the mass production of a standardized output. Research suggests the adoption of flexible manufacturing technologies may actually increase efficiency and lower unit costs relative to what can be achieved by the mass production of a standardized output while enabling the company to customize its product offering to a much greater extent than was once thought possible. The term **mass customization** has been coined to describe the ability of companies to use flexible manufacturing technology to reconcile two goals that were once thought to be incompatible: low cost and product customization.[13] Flexible manufacturing technologies vary in their sophistication and complexity.

One of the most famous examples of flexible manufacturing technology, Toyota's production system, has been credited with making Toyota the most efficient auto company in the world. Toyota's flexible manufacturing system was developed by one of the company's engineers, Taiichi Ohno. After working at Toyota for five years and visiting Ford's U.S. plants, Ohno became convinced that the mass production philosophy for making cars was flawed. He saw numerous problems with mass production.

First, long production runs created massive inventories that had to be stored in large warehouses. This was expensive, both because of the cost of warehousing and because inventories tied up capital in unproductive uses. Second, if the initial machine settings were wrong, long production runs resulted in the production of a large number of defects (i.e., waste). Third, the mass production system was unable to accommodate consumer preferences for product diversity.

In response, Ohno looked for ways to make shorter production runs economically. He developed a number of techniques designed to reduce setup times for production equipment (a major source of fixed costs). By using a system of levers and pulleys, he reduced the time required to change dies on stamping equipment from a full day to three minutes. This made small production runs economical, which allowed Toyota to respond better to consumer demands for product diversity. Small production runs also eliminated the need to hold large inventories, thereby reducing warehousing costs. Plus, small product runs and the lack of inventory meant that defective parts were produced only in small numbers and entered the assembly process immediately. This reduced waste and helped trace defects back to their source to fix the problem. In sum, these innovations enabled Toyota to produce a more diverse product range at a lower unit cost than was possible with conventional mass production.[14]

Flexible machine cells are another common flexible manufacturing technology. A flexible machine cell is a grouping of various types of machinery, a common materials handler, and a centralized cell controller. Each cell normally contains four to six machines capable of performing a variety of operations. The typical cell is dedicated to the production of a family of parts or products. The settings on machines are computer controlled, which allows each cell to switch quickly between the production of different parts or products.

Improved capacity utilization and reductions in work in progress (i.e., stockpiles of partly finished products) and in waste are major efficiency benefits of flexible machine cells.

Improved capacity utilization arises from the reduction in setup times and from the computer-controlled coordination of production flow between machines, which eliminates bottlenecks. The tight coordination between machines also reduces work-in-progress inventory. Reductions in waste are due to the ability of computer-controlled machinery to identify ways to transform inputs into outputs while producing a minimum of unusable waste material. While freestanding machines might be in use 50 percent of the time, the same machines when grouped into a cell can be used more than 90 percent of the time and produce the same end product with half the waste. This increases efficiency and results in lower costs.

The effects of installing flexible manufacturing technology on a company's cost structure can be dramatic. The Ford Motor Company has been introducing flexible manufacturing technologies into its automotive plants around the world. These new technologies allow Ford to produce multiple models from the same line and to switch production from one model to another much more quickly than in the past, allowing Ford to take $2 billion out of its cost structure.[15]

Besides improving efficiency and lowering costs, flexible manufacturing technologies enable companies to customize products to the demands of small consumer groups—at a cost that at one time could be achieved only by mass-producing a standardized output. Thus, the technologies help a company achieve mass customization, which increases its customer responsiveness. Most important for international business, flexible manufacturing technologies can help a firm customize products for different national markets. The importance of this advantage cannot be overstated. When flexible manufacturing technologies are available, a firm can manufacture products customized to various national markets at a single factory sited at the optimal location. And it can do this without absorbing a significant cost penalty. Thus, firms no longer need to establish manufacturing facilities in each major national market to provide products that satisfy specific consumer tastes and preferences, part of the rationale for a localization strategy (Chapter 13).

PRODUCTION FACTORS

Several production factors feature prominently into the reasons why production facilities are located and used in a certain way worldwide. They include (1) product features, (2) locating production facilities, and (3) strategic roles for production facilities.

Product Features

Two product features affect location decisions. The first is the product's *value-to-weight* ratio because of its influence on transportation costs. Many electronic components and pharmaceuticals have high value-to-weight ratios; they are expensive, and they do not weigh very much. Thus, even if they are shipped halfway around the world, their transportation costs account for a very small percentage of total costs. Given this, other things being equal, there is great pressure to produce these products in the optimal location and to serve the world market from there. The opposite holds for products with low value-to-weight ratios. Refined sugar, certain bulk chemicals, paint, and petroleum products all have low value-to-weight ratios; they are relatively inexpensive products that weigh a lot. Accordingly, when they are shipped long distances, transportation costs account for a large percentage of total costs. Thus, other things being equal, there is great pressure to make these products in multiple locations close to major markets to reduce transportation costs.

The other product feature that can influence location decisions is whether the product serves universal needs, needs that are the same all over the world. Examples include many industrial products (e.g., industrial electronics, steel, bulk chemicals) and modern consumer products (e.g., Apple's iPhone or iPad, Amazon's Kindle, Lenovo's ThinkPad, Sony's Cyber-shot camera, Microsoft's Xbox). Because there are few national differences in consumer taste and preference for such products, the need for local responsiveness is reduced. This increases the attractiveness of concentrating production at an optimal location.

Locating Production Facilities

LO17-3

Recognize how the role of foreign subsidiaries in production can be enhanced over time as they accumulate knowledge.

There are two basic strategies for locating production facilities: (1) concentrating them in a centralized location and serving the world market from there or (2) decentralizing them in various regional or national locations that are close to major markets. The appropriate strategic choice is determined by the various country-specific, technological, and product factors discussed in this section and summarized in Table 17.1.

As can be seen, the concentration of production makes most sense when

- Differences among countries in factor costs, political economy, and culture have a substantial impact on the costs of manufacturing in various countries.
- Trade barriers are low.
- Externalities arising from the concentration of like enterprises favor certain locations.
- Important exchange rates are expected to remain relatively stable.
- The production technology has high fixed costs and high minimum efficient scale relative to global demand or flexible manufacturing technology exists.
- The product's value-to-weight ratio is high.
- The product serves universal needs.

Alternatively, decentralization of production is appropriate when

- Differences among countries in factor costs, political economy, and culture do not have a substantial impact on the costs of manufacturing in various countries.
- Trade barriers are high.
- Location externalities are not important.
- Volatility in important exchange rates is expected.
- The production technology has low fixed costs and low minimum efficient scale, and flexible manufacturing technology is not available.
- The product's value-to-weight ratio is low.
- The product does not serve universal needs (i.e., significant differences in consumer tastes and preferences exist among nations).

	Concentrated Production Favored	Decentralized Production Favored
Country Factors		
Differences in political economy	Substantial	Few
Differences in culture	Substantial	Few
Differences in factor costs	Substantial	Few
Trade barriers	Few	Substantial
Location externalities	Important in industry	Not important in industry
Exchange rates	Stable	Volatile
Technological Factors		
Fixed costs	High	Low
Minimum efficient scale	High	Low
Flexible manufacturing technology	Available	Not available
Product Factors		
Value-to-weight ratio	High	Low
Serves universal needs	Yes	No

TABLE 17.1

Location Strategy and Production

In practice, location decisions are seldom clear-cut. For example, it is not unusual for differences in factor costs, technological factors, and product factors to point toward concentrated production, while a combination of trade barriers and volatile exchange rates points toward decentralized production. This seems to be the case in the world automobile industry. Although the availability of flexible manufacturing and cars' relatively high value-to-weight ratios suggest concentrated manufacturing, the combination of formal and informal trade barriers and the uncertainties of the world's current floating exchange rate regime (see Chapter 10) have inhibited firms' ability to pursue this strategy. For these reasons, several automobile companies have established "top-to-bottom" manufacturing operations in three major regional markets: Asia, North America, and Western Europe.

Strategic Roles for Production Facilities

The growth of global production among multinational companies has been tremendous over the past two decades, outdoing the growth of home country production by more than 10-fold.[16] In essence, since the early 1990s, multinationals have opted to set up production facilities outside their home country 10 times for every 1 time they have opted to create such facilities at home. There is a clear strategic rationale for this; multinationals are trying to capture the gains associated with a dispersed global production system. This trend is expected to continue going forward. Thus, managers need to be ready to make the decision to open up a new production facility outside of their home base and decide where to locate the facility.

When making these decisions, managers need to think about the strategic role assigned to a foreign factory. A major consideration here is the importance of **global learning**—the idea that valuable knowledge does not reside just in a firm's domestic operations; it may also be found in its foreign subsidiaries. Foreign factories that upgrade their capabilities over time are creating valuable knowledge that might benefit the whole corporation. Foreign factories can have one of a number of strategic roles or designations, including (1) offshore factory, (2) source factory, (3) server factory, (4) contributor factory, (5) outpost factory, and (6) lead factory.[17]

An **offshore factory** is one that is developed and set up mainly for producing component parts or finished goods at a lower cost than producing them at home or in any other market. At an offshore factory, investments in technology and managerial resources should ideally be kept to a minimum to achieve greater cost-efficiencies. Basically, the best offshore factory should involve minimal everything—from engineering to development to engaging with suppliers to negotiating prices to any form of strategic decisions being made at that facility. In reality, we expect at least some strategic decisions to include input from the offshore factory personnel.

The primary purpose of a **source factory** is also to drive down costs in the global supply chain. The main difference between a source factory and an offshore factory is the strategic role of the factory, which is more significant for a source factory than for an offshore factory. Managers of a source factory have more of a say in certain decisions, such as purchasing raw materials and component parts used in the production at the source factory. They also have a strategic input into production planning, process changes, logistics issues, product customization, and implementation of newer designs when needed. Centrally, a source factory is at the top of the standards in the global supply chain, and these factories are used and treated just like any factory in the global firm's home country. This also means that source factories should be located where production costs are low, where infrastructure is well developed, and where it is relatively easy to find a knowledgeable and skilled workforce to make the products.

A **server factory** is linked into the global supply chain for a global firm to supply specific country or regional markets around the globe. This type of factory—often with the same standards as the top factories in the global firm's system—is set up to overcome intangible and tangible barriers in the global marketplace. For example, a server factory may be intended to overcome tariff barriers, reduce taxes, and reinvest money made in the region. Another obvious reason for a server factory is to reduce or eliminate costly global supply chain operations that would be needed if the factory were located much farther away from the end customers. Managers at a server factory typically have more authority to make minor customizations to please their customers, but they still do not have much more input than managers in an offshore factory relative to the home country factories of the same global firm.

A **contributor factory** also serves a specific country or world region. The main difference between a contributor factory and a server factory is that a contributor factory has responsibilities for product and process engineering and development. This type of factory also has much more of a choice in terms of which suppliers to use for raw materials and component parts. In fact, a contributor factory often competes with the global firm's home factories for testing new ideas and products. A contributor factory has its own infrastructure when it comes to development, engineering, and production. This means that a contributor factory is very much stand-alone in terms of what it can do and how it contributes to the global firm's supply chain efforts.

An **outpost factory** can be viewed as an intelligence-gathering unit. This means that an outpost factory is often placed near a competitor's headquarters or main operations, near the most demanding customers, or near key suppliers of unique and critically important parts. An outpost factory also has a function to fill in production; it often operates as a server and/or offshore factory as well. The outpost factory can be very much connected to the idea of selecting countries for operations based on the countries' strategic importance rather than on the production logic of a location. Maintaining and potentially even enhancing the position of the global firm in strategic countries is sometimes viewed as a practical factor. For example, the fact that Nokia has its headquarters in Finland may result in another mobile phone manufacturer locating some operations in Finland, even though the country market is rather small (about 5.5 million people).

A **lead factory** is intended to create new processes, products, and technologies that can be used throughout the global firm in all parts of the world. This is where cutting-edge production should take place or at least be tested for implementation in other parts of the firm's production network. Given the lead factory's prominent role in setting a high bar for how the global firm wants to provide products to customers, we also expect that it will be located in an area where highly skilled employees can be found (or where they want to locate). A lead factory scenario also implies that managers and employees at the site have a direct connection to and say in which suppliers to use, what designs to implement, and other issues that are of critical importance to the core competencies of the global firm.

THE HIDDEN COSTS OF FOREIGN LOCATIONS

There may be some "hidden costs" to basing production in a foreign location. Numerous anecdotes suggest that high employee turnover, shoddy workmanship, poor product quality, and low productivity are significant issues in some outsourcing locations.[18]

Microsoft, for example, established a major facility in Hyderabad, India, for four very good reasons: (1) The wage rate of software programmers in India is one-third of that in the United States; (2) India has an excellent higher education system that graduates many computer science majors every year; (3) there was already a high concentration of information technology companies and workers in Hyderabad; and (4) many of Microsoft's highly skilled Indian employees, after spending years in the United States, wanted to return home, and Microsoft saw the Hyderabad facility as a way of holding on to this valuable human capital.

However, the company found that the turnover rate among its Indian employees is higher than in the United States. Demand for software programmers in India is high, and many employees are prone to switch jobs to get better pay. Although Microsoft has tried to limit turnover by offering good benefits and long-term incentive pay, such as stock grants to high performers who stay with the company, many of the Indians who were hired locally apparently place little value on long-term incentives and prefer higher current pay. High employee turnover, of course, has a negative impact on productivity. One Microsoft manager in India noted that 40 percent of his core team had left within the past 12 months, making it very difficult to stay on track with development projects.[19]

Amazon's Global Supply Chains

Amazon.com Inc.—typically referred to as just Amazon—has ranked among the top companies for years in the "Gartner Global Supply Chain Top 25" ranking. Other regular entries among the companies with the best global supply chains include Unilever, McDonald's, and Intel. Amazon is passing through about $200 billion in sales via its global supply chains and partnerships annually, a staggering amount given that the company seldom takes possession in any true sense of the products that it channels to customers from various companies.

Amazon is based in Seattle, Washington. It has now become the largest online retailer in the United States, surpassing Walmart as the most valuable retailer by market capitalization (but Walmart's revenue is still gigantic at about $500 billion annually). Amazon started in 1994 as an online bookstore but has diversified to a variety of products, including music downloads, furniture, food, and almost all consumer electronics. These days, customers can seemingly buy anything they need via the Amazon platform. In the United States alone, roughly 150 million customers per month visit Amazon.com. But this massive availability of products also puts a strain on Amazon's global supply chains.

As customers, we have come to expect that Amazon will deliver whatever we buy in the shortest cycle time possible, often no more than two days, especially if a customer is signed up for Amazon Prime. The Amazon Prime service includes free two-day shipping (on many products), video streaming, music, photos, and the Kindle lending library for an annual fee (currently $99 per year or $12.99 per month). All these services are welcomed by customers, but the free two-day shipping is really what drives the Amazon Prime service.

The free two-day shipping (and myriad other shipping alternatives for a fee) requires Amazon to leverage its inventory management practices, global supply chains, and technology to cost-effectively reach customers. Delivery speed and efficiency require Amazon to have strategically located fulfillment centers worldwide that can be used by select vendors on the Amazon platform. This includes strict requirements for packaging, labeling, and shipment. Amazon stores these vendors' products in bulk or in individual "pickable" locations.

So far, in addition to the United States, Amazon has retail websites for Australia, Brazil, Canada, China, France, Germany, India, Italy, Japan, Mexico, the Netherlands, Spain, the United Kingdom, and Ireland. And, the Amazon Prime service places great strain on Amazon's supply chains where it is available in its worldwide locations (e.g., Canada, France, Germany, Italy, Japan, and the United Kingdom).

In addition, Amazon's customer service centers span some 15 countries worldwide. Plus, the company operates retail websites for international brands such as Sears Canada, Bebe Stores, Marks & Spencer, Mothercare, and Lacoste. This means that Amazon is benefiting from both its global supply chains for delivery of vendors' products and its service as a technology supply chain vendor to businesses.

Another interesting development—or, at least, idea at this stage—is the speculation that Amazon is thinking about launching a global shipping and logistics operation that can compete with United Parcel Service (UPS) and FedEx. Of course, Chief Financial Officer (CFO) Brian Olsavsky downplayed Amazon's ambitions on this front. He said that Amazon was just looking to supplement its delivery partners—not replace them—during the very busy peak periods like the holiday seasons.

Sources: Todd Bishop, "Amazon Sales Rises 22% to $43.7B, Profit Beats Expectations But Stock Slips on Revenue Miss," *GeekWire*, February 2, 2017; Spencer Soper, "Amazon Building Global Delivery Business to Take On Alibaba," *Bloomberg Technology*, February 9, 2016; V. Walt, "How Jeff Bezos Aims to Conquer the Next Trillion-dollar Market," *Fortune*, January 1, 2016; B. Stone, "The Secrets of Bezos: How Amazon Became the Everything Store," *Bloomberg Business*, October 10, 2013; and A. Cuthbertson, "Amazon Buries Zombie Apocalypse Clause in Terms of Service," *Newsweek*, February 11, 2016.

✓ **TEST PREP**

Use SmartBook to help retain what you have learned. Access your Instructor's Connect course to check out SmartBook or go to **learnsmartadvantage.com** for help.

Microsoft is not alone in experiencing this problem. The manager of an electronics company that outsourced the manufacture of wireless headsets to China noted that after four years of frustrations with late deliveries and poor quality, his company decided to move production *back* to the United States. In his words: "On the face of it, labor costs seemed so much lower in China that the decision to move production there was a very easy one. In retrospect, I wish we had looked much closer at productivity and workmanship. We have actually lost market share because of this decision."[20] Another example of efficiency and effectiveness issues is highlighted in the accompanying Management Focus, which looks at Amazon and its world-leading global supply chains.

Make-or-Buy Decisions

LO17-4

Identify the factors that influence a firm's decision of whether to source supplies from within the company or from foreign suppliers.

The **make-or-buy decision** for a global firm is the strategic decision concerning whether to produce an item in-house ("make") or purchase it from an outside supplier ("buy"). Make-or-buy decisions are made at both the strategic and operational levels, with the strategic level being focused on the long term and the operational level being more focused on the short term. In some ways, the make-or-buy decision is also the starting point for operations' influence on global supply chains. That is, someone in the chain—within one firm—has to take the lead in deciding whether the global firm should make the product in-house or buy it from an external supplier. If the decision is to make it in-house, there are certain implications for that firm's global supply chains (e.g., where to purchase raw materials and component parts). If the decision is to buy the product, that decision also has certain implications (e.g., quality control and competitive priorities management).

A number of things are involved in determining which decision is the correct one for a particular global firm in a particular situation. At a broad level, issues of product success, specialized knowledge, and strategic fit can lead to the make (produce) decision. For example, if the item or part is critical to the success of the product, including perceptions among primary stakeholders, such a scenario skews the decision in favor of make. Another reason for a make decision is that the item or part requires specialized design or production skills and/or equipment and reliable alternatives are very scarce. Strategic fit is also important. If the item or part strategically fits within the firm's current and/or planned core competencies, then it should be a make decision for the global firm.

However, these are strategic decisions at a general level. In reality, the make-or-buy decision is often based largely on two critical factors: cost and production capacity. Cost issues include such things as acquiring raw materials, component parts, and any other inputs into the process, along with the costs of finishing the product. The production capacity is really presented as an opportunity cost. That is, does the firm have the capacity to produce the product at a cost that is at least no higher than the cost of buying it from an external supplier? And if the product is made in-house, what opportunity cost would be incurred as a result (e.g., what product or item was the firm unable to produce because of limited production capacity)? Unfortunately, many, and perhaps most, global companies think that cost and production capacity are the only factors playing into the make-or-buy decision. This is simply not true!

Cost and production capacity are just the two main drivers behind make-or-buy choices made by global companies when they engage in global supply chains. The decision of whether to buy or make a product is a much more complex and research-intensive process than the typical global firm may expect. For example, how many times have we heard, "Let's move our production to China because we can get the same quality for a dime-on-the-dollar cost, and that will free up production capacity that we can use to focus on other products"? Of course, dime-on-the-dollar cost is not the sole relevant factor because we have to take into account the costs of quality control measures that have to be instituted, raw materials that have to be purchased far away from home, foreign entry requirements, multiple-party contracts, management responsibilities for the outsourced production operations, and so on. Ultimately, we are unlikely to end up with a dime-on-the-dollar cost. But where do we end up and how do we get there? In other words, what are the core elements that we should be evaluating when we are determining whether the correct decision is to make or to buy?

To facilitate your understanding of the make-or-buy decision, we have captured the dynamics of this choice in two graphics that illustrate either operationally favoring a make decision or operationally favoring a buy decision (see Figures 17.3 and 17.4). As shown in the figures, the core elements in both cases are cost and production capacity. However, the other elements differ for each of the decisions and influence the choice differently. This means that we need to evaluate each decision separately, not jointly. In fact, through this process, we may end up thinking that both a make decision and a buy decision would be acceptable and strategically logical for our firm. Keep in mind that this simply means that we have a choice; if both choices seem positive for your firm, choose the best one—the one that is the best strategic fit with the least opportunity cost.

FIGURE 17.3

Operationally favoring a make decision.

Source: Charles W. L. Hill and G. Tomas M. Hult, *Global Business Today* (New York: McGraw-Hill, 2020).

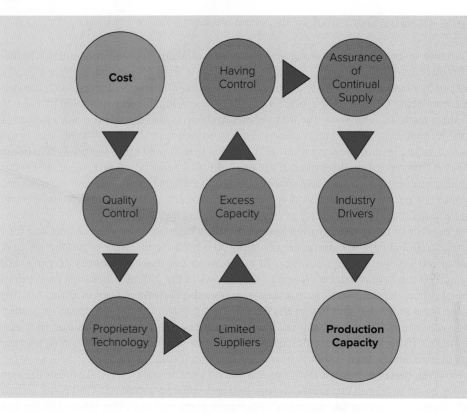

FIGURE 17.4

Operationally favoring a buy decision.

Source: Charles W. L. Hill and G. Tomas M. Hult, *Global Business Today* (New York: McGraw-Hill, 2020).

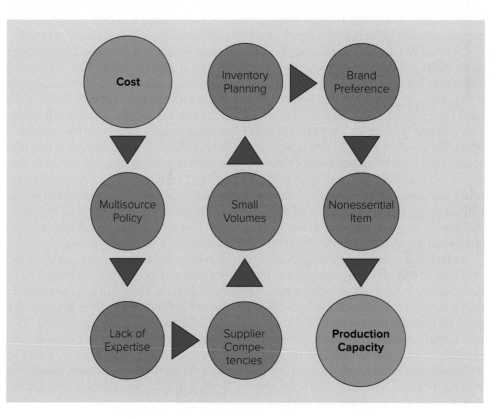

The elements that favor a make decision—beyond the core elements of cost and production capacity—include quality control, proprietary technology, having control, excess capacity, limited suppliers, assurance of continual supply, and industry drivers (see Figure 17.3). So, the starting point is lower (or at least no greater) cost than what we can expect when we outsource the production to an external party in another country (or another external party in general). The limitation is that we must have excess production capacity or capacity that is best used by our firm for making the product in-house.

After the cost and production capacity decisions have been explored and made (really, after the cost and production hurdles have been overcome), the next set of decisions follows logically from the path in Figure 17.3. For example, if quality control is important to the global firm, cannot be relied on fully if the part is outsourced, and is at the center of the strategic core that customers expect from the firm, then the quality control issue favors a make decision. If there is proprietary technology involved in making the product that cannot or should not be shared with outsourcing parties, then the decision has to be to make.

The idea that limited suppliers may influence the make-or-buy choice in the direction of the make selection is important as well. Specifically, it could be that some suppliers do not want to work with certain companies in certain parts of the world. It could also be that a supplier cannot, because of various restrictions on production or location or because of international barriers, follow the production of your firm's products to wherever you see fit to locate your production lines.

Naturally, if the firm has excess capacity that otherwise would not be productively used, the decision should favor a make choice to allow that excess capacity to be used for the benefit of the firm in the global marketplace. Some companies also simply want to have control over certain elements of their production processes. This affects the make-or-buy decision in favor of the make choice.

A make decision is also favored if there is any chance that supply cannot be guaranteed if the firm moves its production overseas. And, finally, the industry globalization drivers may dictate that a make decision should be the choice for various trust and commitment reasons involving your industry and the marketplace that you engage with in order to find success.

Now, some of these elements that favor make can probably influence a buy decision as well. Naturally, if one of the make elements is not in favor of the make decision (e.g., if there is no excess capacity), this would suggest that the global firm should think more seriously about a buy decision. However, again, the buy decision also involves a number of other elements that are not necessarily factors in the make decision (see Figure 17.4). As with the make decision, after the cost and production capacity decisions have been considered and made, the next set of decisions for the buy choice follow logically from the path in Figure 17.4. For example, if the global firm has minimal restrictions on which firms or companies it can source raw materials and component parts from, then a buy decision is more likely because outsourcing production also increases the likelihood that other and/or more suppliers in those parts of the world will be used.

Another good reason to choose a buy scenario is if the firm lacks the needed expertise to make a product or component part and the supplier or outsourced production choice has that expertise. Supplier competencies can affect the decision in favor of a buy choice as well, especially if those competencies reside closer to the production facility that you buy from than the ones that will be available if you make the product. Small volumes would also be a reason favoring a buy decision; cost-efficiencies can seldom be achieved when only small volumes are produced.

Inventory planning is also of critical importance. Even if your firm can make the product equally well in terms of quality and expectations set, perhaps a better choice is to buy simply in order to strategically manage inventory (which is a cost center in the global supply chain). In certain cases, even brand preference is a reason to go with a buy decision; for example, many computer users favor Intel microchips in their computers, so many of the large computer manufacturers opt to buy chips from Intel instead of making them in-house for that reason. And, of course, if the item to be made is a so-called nonessential item that has little effect on the firm's core competencies and what the customers expect in terms of uniqueness, this is a factor in favor of a buy decision.

LO17-5

Understand the functions of logistics and purchasing (sourcing) within global supply chains.

Global Supply Chain Functions

To this point in the chapter, we have emphasized global production, a component of the operations management of a supply chain. Issues such as where to produce, the strategic role of a foreign production site, and the make-or-buy decisions are the core aspects of global production. In addition to global production, three additional supply chain functions need to be developed in concert with global production. They are logistics, purchasing (sourcing), and the company's distribution strategy (i.e., marketing channels). The latter—distribution strategy—is addressed in Chapter 18, where we discuss marketing and R&D. Here we address logistics and purchasing. From earlier in this chapter, we know that production and supply chain management are closely linked because a firm's ability to perform its production activities depends on information inputs and the timely supply of high-quality material (raw material, component parts, and even finished products that are used in the manufacturing of new products). Logistics and purchasing are critical functions in ensuring that materials are ordered and delivered and that an appropriate level of inventory is managed.

GLOBAL LOGISTICS

From earlier in this chapter, we know that logistics is the part of the supply chain that plans, implements, and controls the effective flows and inventory of raw material, component parts, and products used in manufacturing. The core activities performed in logistics are (1) global distribution center management, (2) inventory management, (3) packaging and materials handling, (4) transportation, and (5) reverse logistics. Each of these core logistics is described in the next paragraphs.

A **global distribution center** (or warehouse) is a facility that positions and allows customization of products for delivery to worldwide wholesalers or retailers or directly to consumers anywhere in the world. Distribution centers (DCs) are used by manufacturers, importers, exporters, wholesalers, retailers, transportation companies, and customs agencies to store products and provide a location where customization can be facilitated. When warehousing shifted from passive storage of products to strategic assortments and processing, the term *distribution center* became more widely used to capture this strategic and dynamic aspect of not only storing, but adding value to products that are being warehoused or staged. A DC is at the center of the global supply chain; specifically, the order-processing part of the order-fulfillment process. DCs are the foundation of a global supply network because they allow either a single location or satellite warehouses to store quantities and assortments of products and allow for value-added customization. They should be located strategically in the global marketplace, considering the aggregate total labor and transportation cost of moving products from plants or suppliers through the distribution center and then delivering them to customers.

Global inventory management can be viewed as the decision-making process regarding the raw materials, work-in-process (component parts), and finished goods inventory for a multinational corporation. The decisions include how much inventory to hold, in what form to hold it, and where to locate it in the supply chain. Examining the largest 20,910 global companies with headquarters in 105 countries, we find that these companies, on average across all industries, carry 14.41 percent of their total assets in some form of inventory.[21] These companies have 32 percent of their inventory in raw materials, 18 percent of their inventory in work-in-process, and 50 percent of their inventory in finished goods.[22] At the company level, Toyota (**www.toyota.com**) from Japan, one of the largest automobile firms in the world, has 8.71 percent of its total assets in inventory, with a mix of 26, 14, and 60 percent in raw materials, work-in-process, and finished vehicles, respectively. Another example is Sinopec (**www.sinopec.com**), a petroleum firm and the largest firm in

China. Sinopec has 21 percent of its total assets in inventory, with a mix of 37, 43, and 20 percent in raw materials and component parts, work-in-process, and finished goods, respectively. Note that Sinopec maintains a much higher percentage of its inventories in work-in-process and a much lower percentage in finished goods than Toyota does. This suggests that petroleum firms want more flexibility in deciding exactly how to formulate the finished product. The company's global inventory strategy must effectively trade off the service and economic benefits of making products in large quantities and positioning them near customers against the risk of having too much stock or the wrong items.

Packaging comes in all shapes, sizes, forms, and uses. It can be divided into three different types: primary, secondary, and transit. *Primary packaging* holds the product itself. These are the packages brought home from the store, usually a retailer, by the end-consumer. *Secondary packaging* (sometimes called case-lot packaging) is designed to contain several primary packages. Bulk buying or warehouse store customers may take secondary packages home (e.g., from Sam's Club), but this is not the typical mode for retailers. Retailers can also use secondary packaging as an aid when stocking shelves in the store. *Transit packaging* comes into use when a number of primary and secondary packages are assembled on a pallet or unit load for transportation. Unit-load packaging—through palletizing, shrink-wrapping, or containerization—is the outer packaging envelope that allows for easier handling or product transfer among international suppliers, manufacturers, distribution centers, retailers, and any other intermediaries in the global supply chain.

Regardless of where the product is in the global supply chain, the packaging is intended to achieve a set of multilayered functions. These can be grouped into (1) perform, (2) protect, and (3) inform.[23] *Perform* refers to (1) the ability of the product in the package to handle being transported between nodes in the global supply chain, (2) the ability of the product to be stored for typical lengths of time for a particular product category, and (3) the package providing the convenience expected by both the supply chain partners and the end-customers. *Protect* refers to the package's ability to (1) contain the products properly, (2) preserve the products to maintain their freshness or newness, and (3) provide the necessary security and safety to ensure that the products reach their end destination in their intended shape. *Inform* refers to the package's inclusion of (1) logical and sufficient instructions for the use of the products inside the package, including specific requirements to satisfy local regulations; (2) a statement of a compelling product guarantee; and (3) information about service for the product if and when it is needed.

Transportation refers to the movement of raw material, component parts, and finished goods throughout the global supply chain. It typically represents the largest percentage of any logistics budget and an even greater percentage for global companies because of the distances involved. Global supply chains are directly or indirectly responsible for transporting raw materials from their suppliers to the production facilities, work-in-process, and finished goods inventories between plants and distribution centers, and finished goods from distribution centers to customers. The primary drivers of transportation rates and the resulting aggregate cost are distance, transport mode (ocean, air, or land), size of the load, load characteristics, and oil prices. As would be expected, longer distances require more fuel and more time from vehicle operators, so transport rates increase with distance. Transport mode influences rates because of the different technologies involved. The ocean is the least expensive because of the size of the vehicles used and the low friction of water. Land is the next least expensive, with rail being less expensive than motor carriers. Air is the most expensive because there is a substantial charge for defying gravity. Transportation rates are heavily influenced by economies of scale, so larger shipments are typically relatively less expensive than smaller shipments. The characteristics of the shipment also influence transportation rates through such factors as product density, value, perishability, the potential for damage, and other such factors. Finally, oil prices have a major impact on transportation rates because anywhere from 10 to 40 percent of most carrier costs, depending on the mode, are related to fuel.

Reverse logistics is the process of planning, implementing, and controlling the efficient, cost-effective flow of raw materials, in-process inventory, finished goods, and related information from the point of consumption to the point of origin for the purpose of recapturing value or proper disposal. The ultimate goal is to optimize the after-market activity or make it more efficient, thus saving money and environmental resources. Reverse logistics is critically important in global supply chains. For example, product returns cost manufacturers and retailers more than $100 billion per year in the United States, or an average of 3.8 percent in lost profits.[24] Overall, manufacturers spend about 9 to 14 percent of their sales revenue on returns. Even more staggering, each year, consumers in America return more than the GDP of two-thirds of the nations in the world. Just these sample numbers suggest that reverse logistics is an incredibly important part of the global supply chain.

GLOBAL PURCHASING

As we defined it earlier in this chapter, purchasing represents the part of the supply chain that involves worldwide buying of raw material, component parts, and products used in the manufacturing of the company's products and services. The core activities performed in purchasing include the development of an appropriate strategy for global purchasing and selecting the type of purchasing strategy best suited for the company.

There are five strategic levels—from domestic to international to global—that can be undertaken by a global company.[25] Level I is simply companies engaging in domestic purchasing activities only. Often, these companies stay close to their home base in their domestic market when purchasing raw materials, component parts, and the like for their operations (e.g., a Michigan firm purchasing raw materials, such as cherries, from another Michigan firm). Levels II and III are both considered "international purchasing," but of various degrees and forms. Companies that are at level II engage in international purchasing activities only as needed. This means that their approach to international purchasing is often reactive and uncoordinated among the buying locations within the firm and/or across the various units that make up the firm, such as strategic business units and functional units. Companies at level III engage in international purchasing activities as part of the firm's overall supply chain management strategy. At the level III stage, companies begin to recognize that a well-formulated and well-executed worldwide international purchasing strategy can be very effective in elevating the firm's competitive edge in the marketplace. Levels IV and V both involve "global purchasing" to various degrees. Level IV refers to global purchasing activities that are integrated across worldwide locations. This involves integration and coordination of purchasing strategies across the firm's buying locations worldwide. With level IV, we are now dealing with a sophisticated form of worldwide purchasing. Level V involves engaging in global purchasing activities that are integrated across worldwide locations and functional groups. Broadly, this means that the firm integrates and coordinates the purchasing of common items, purchasing processes, and supplier selection efforts globally, for example.

Beyond the domestic, international, and global purchasing strategies in levels I through V, purchasing includes a number of basic choices that companies make in deciding how to engage with markets.[26] The starting point is a choice of internal purchasing versus external purchasing—in other words, "how to purchase." We find that roughly 35 percent of the purchasing in global companies today is internal (i.e., from sources within their own company), with 65 percent being classified as external (i.e., from sources outside their company). The next decision, in both internal and external purchasing, is to figure out "where to purchase" (domestically or globally). This takes us ultimately to the "types of purchasing" (where and how) and the four choices for purchasing strategy: domestic internal purchasing, global internal purchasing, domestic external purchasing, and global external purchasing.

The types of purchasing activities and strategies just discussed come with a set of generic options for the "international arena." But we all know that outsourcing and offshoring, along with many by-products and other similar yet quite different options, exist in the purchasing world today. At this stage of the text, we feel it is important to go over the outsourcing-related terms and options that companies have, especially the following terms that are often confusing to understand, develop strategy around, and implement: outsourcing, insourcing, offshoring, offshore outsourcing, nearshoring, and co-sourcing (see Table 17.2).

TEST PREP

Use SmartBook to help retain what you have learned. Access your Instructor's Connect course to check out SmartBook or go to **learnsmartadvantage.com** for help.

TABLE 17.2

Outsourcing Terms
and Options

Outsourcing	A multinational corporation buys products or services from one of its suppliers that produces them somewhere else, whether domestically or globally. In that sense, it also refers to external purchasing in relation to purchasing strategy.
Insourcing	A multinational corporation decides to stop outsourcing products or services and instead starts to produce them internally; insourcing is the opposite of outsourcing. Thus, it refers to internal purchasing in the context of purchasing strategy.
Offshoring	A multinational corporation buys products or services from one of its suppliers that produces them somewhere globally (outside the MNCs home country). Offshoring is thus a form of global external purchasing in terms of purchasing strategy.
Offshore outsourcing	A multinational corporation buys products or services from one of its suppliers in a country other than the one in which the product is manufactured or the service is developed. This again is a form of global external purchasing in terms of purchasing strategy.
Nearshoring	A multinational corporation transfers business or information technology processes to suppliers in a nearby country, often one that shares a border with the firm's own country. While nearshoring is not a purchasing activity per se, it involves facilitating global external purchasing.
Co-sourcing	A multinational corporation uses both its own employees from inside the firm and an external supplier to perform certain tasks, often in concert with each other. This applies to all four forms of purchasing strategy. It implies that the relationship between the firm and its supplier is rather strategic in nature—often, this involves the top suppliers in a particular product or component category.

Managing a Global Supply Chain

LO17-6

Describe what is required to efficiently manage a global supply chain.

The potential for reducing costs through more efficient supply chain management is enormous. For the typical manufacturing enterprise, material costs account for between 50 and 70 percent of revenues, depending on the industry. Even a small reduction in these costs can have a substantial impact on profitability. According to one estimate, for a firm with revenues of $1 million, a return on investment rate of 5 percent, and materials costs that are 50 percent of sales revenues, a $15,000 increase in total profits could be achieved either by increasing sales revenues 30 percent or by reducing materials costs by 3 percent.[27] In a saturated market, it would be much easier to reduce materials costs by 3 percent than to increase sales revenues by 30 percent. Thus, managing global supply chains is one of the strategically most important areas for a global company. Four main areas are of concern in managing a global supply chain, including the role of just-in-time inventory, the role of information technology, coordination in global supply chains, and interorganizational relationships in global supply chains.

ROLE OF JUST-IN-TIME INVENTORY

Pioneered by Japanese firms during that country's remarkable economic transformation during the 1960s and 1970s, just-in-time inventory systems now play a major role in most manufacturing firms. The basic philosophy behind **just-in-time (JIT)** inventory systems is to economize on inventory holding costs by having materials arrive at a manufacturing plant just in time to enter the production process and not before. The major cost savings comes from speeding up inventory turnover. This reduces inventory holding costs, such as warehousing and storage costs. It means the company can reduce the amount of working capital it needs to finance inventory, freeing capital for other uses and/or lowering the total capital requirements of the enterprise. Other things being equal, this will boost the company's profitability as measured by return on capital invested. It also means the company is less likely to have excess unsold inventory that it has to write off against earnings or price low to sell.

In addition to the cost benefits, JIT systems can also help firms improve product quality. Under a JIT system, parts enter the manufacturing process immediately; they are not warehoused. This allows defective inputs to be spotted right away. The problem can then be traced to the supply source and fixed before more defective parts are produced. Under a more traditional system, warehousing parts for weeks before they are used allows many defective parts to be produced before a problem is recognized.

The drawback of a JIT system is that it leaves a firm without a buffer stock of inventory. Although buffer stocks are expensive to store, they can help a firm respond quickly to increases in demand and tide a firm over shortages brought about by disruption among suppliers. Such a disruption occurred after the September 11, 2001, attacks on the World Trade Center and Pentagon, when the subsequent shutdown of international air travel and shipping left many firms that relied on globally dispersed suppliers and tightly managed "just-in-time" supply chains without a buffer stock of inventory. A less pronounced but similar situation occurred again in April 2003, when the outbreak of the pneumonia-like severe acute respiratory syndrome (SARS) virus in China resulted in the temporary shutdown of several plants operated by foreign companies and disrupted their global supply chains. Similarly, in late 2004, record imports into the United States left several major West Coast shipping ports clogged with too many ships from Asia that could not be unloaded fast enough, which disrupted the finely tuned supply chains of several major U.S. enterprises.[28]

There are ways of reducing the risks associated with a global supply chain that operates using just-in-time principles. To reduce the risks associated with depending on one supplier for an important input, some firms source these inputs from several suppliers located in different countries. While this may not help in the case of an event with global ramifications—such as September 11, 2001, in the United States, or the Tōhoku earthquake and tsunami on March 11, 2011, in Japan—it does help manage country-specific supply disruptions, which are more common. Strategically, all global companies need to build in some degree of redundancy in supply chains by having multiple options for suppliers.

ROLE OF INFORMATION TECHNOLOGY

Web and cloud-based information systems play a crucial role in modern global supply chains. For example, by tracking component parts as they make their way across the globe toward an assembly plant, information systems enable a firm to optimize its production scheduling according to when components are expected to arrive. By locating component parts in the supply chain precisely, good information systems allow the firm to accelerate production when needed by pulling key components out of the regular supply chain and having them flown to the manufacturing plant.

Firms now typically use some form of a supply chain information system to coordinate the flow of materials into manufacturing, through manufacturing, and out to customers. There are a variety of options for global supply chains. Electronic data interchange (EDI) refers to the electronic interchange of data between two or more companies. Enterprise resource planning (ERP) is a wide-ranging business planning and control system that includes supply chain-related subsystems (e.g., materials requirements planning, or MRP). Collaborative planning, forecasting, and replenishment (CPFR) was developed to fill the inter-organizational connections that ERP cannot fill. Vendor management of inventory (VMI) allows for a holistic overview of the supply chain with a single point of control for all inventory management. A warehouse management system (WMS) often operates in concert with ERP systems; for example, an ERP system defines material requirements, and these are transmitted to a distribution center for a WMS.

Before the emergence of the internet as a major communication medium, firms and their suppliers normally had to purchase expensive proprietary software solutions to implement EDI systems. The ubiquity of the internet and the availability of web- and cloud-based applications have made most of these proprietary solutions obsolete. Less expensive systems that are much easier to install and manage now dominate the market for global supply chain management software. These systems have transformed the management of globally dispersed supply chains, allowing even small firms to achieve a much better balance between supply and demand, thereby reducing the inventory in their systems and reaping the associated economic benefits. Importantly, with most firms now using these systems, those that do not will find themselves at a competitive disadvantage. This has implications for small and medium-sized companies that may not always have the resources to implement the most sophisticated supply chain information systems.

Having at least some form of a supply chain information system to coordinate the flow of materials into manufacturing, through manufacturing, and out to customers is paramount to be part of the global supply chain networks that exist today. Now, enter blockchain technology as an additional layer in the systems! As we saw in the opening case, blockchains make it possible for ecosystems of supply chain partners (or any business partners) to share and agree upon key pieces of information. Importantly, the partners can agree on the information without having to deal with all the complex negotiations and power plays that come with setting the rules before handing over really critical business information. Blockchains synchronize all data and transactions across the global network. Through blockchains, companies gain a live, real-time digital ledger of all transactions and supply chain movements for all participants in their supply chain network. However, the added coordination-value that companies can achieve via blockchain technology has at least, for now, short-term concerns as well. For example, fitting blockchain technology into existing systems around the globe is difficult, costly, and not as efficient as possible to reap the short-term, immediate advantages that blockchain technology offers companies. That said, coordination in global supply chains and networks is critically important for a well-functioning system.

COORDINATION IN GLOBAL SUPPLY CHAINS

Consider how to turn an aircraft, and think in terms of coordination and leverage points. Traditionally, aircraft were typically steered using an integrated system of ailerons on the wings and the rudder at the tail of the aircraft. In comparison to the aircraft, the ailerons and rudder seem very small. However, leverage allows the coordinated effort of the ailerons and the rudder to turn the aircraft. In other words, putting the right combination of a little leverage in the right places together with a coordinated effort leads to incredible maneuvering ability for the plane. Global supply chains are the same. Integration and coordination are critically important. **Global supply chain coordination** refers to shared decision-making opportunities and operational collaboration of key global supply chain activities.

Shared decision making—such as joint consideration of replenishment, inventory holding costs, collaborative planning, costs of different processes, the frequency of orders, batch size, and product development—creates a more integrated, coherent, efficient, and effective global supply chain. This includes shared decision making by supply chain members both inside an organization (e.g., logistics, purchasing, operations, and marketing channels employees) and across organizations (e.g., raw materials producers, transportation companies, manufacturers, wholesalers, retailers). *Shared* decision making is not *joint* decision making; it is decision making involving joint considerations. Shared decision making helps in resolving potential conflicts among global supply chain members and fosters a culture of coordination and integration. In most supply chains, certain parties are more influential, and shared decision making, at a minimum, should include the critically important chain members.

To achieve operational integration and collaboration within a global supply chain, six operational objectives should be addressed: responsiveness, variance reduction, inventory reduction, shipment consolidation, quality, and life-cycle support.[29] *Responsiveness* refers to a global firm's ability to satisfy customers' requirements across global supply chain functions in a timely manner. *Variance reduction* refers to integrating a control system across global supply chain functions to eliminate global supply chain disruptions. *Inventory reduction* refers to integrating an inventory system, controlling asset commitment, and turning velocity across global supply chain functions. *Shipment consolidation* refers to using various programs to combine small shipments and provide timely, consolidated movement. This includes multi-unit coordination across global supply chain functions. *Quality* refers to integrating a system so it achieves zero defects throughout global supply chains. Finally, *lifecycle support* refers to integrating the activities of reverse logistics, recycling, after-market service, product recall, and product disposal across global supply chain functions.

INTERORGANIZATIONAL RELATIONSHIPS

Interorganizational relationships have been studied and talked about in various contexts for decades. The two keys are trust and commitment. If we always had 100 percent trust in relationships and 100 percent commitment to them, most global supply chains would ultimately be efficient and effective. But we don't! However, by looking at the building blocks for global supply chains, we would also assume that not all relationships are equally valuable and that they should not be treated as if they were. Two examples centered on upstream/inbound and downstream/outbound supply chain activities can effectively be used to illustrate this point. Figure 17.5 focuses on the upstream (or inbound) supply chain relationships, and Figure 17.6 focuses on the downstream (or outbound) supply chain relationships.

For the upstream/inbound portion of the global supply chain, the three logical scenarios of interacting organizations are labeled as vendors, suppliers, and partners. Each scenario is based on the degree of coordination, integration, and transactional versus relationship emphasis that the firm should adopt in partnering with other entities in the global supply chain. For instance, a firm uses vendors to obtain raw materials and component parts through a transactional relationship that can change easily. A given firm may use suppliers to obtain raw materials and parts and maintain a relationship with those suppliers based on experience and performance. Another firm may engage with partners to obtain raw materials and parts, maintaining a relationship based on trust and commitment.

For the downstream/outbound portion of the global supply chain, the three logical scenarios of interacting organizations are labeled as buyers, customers, and clients. As with the upstream/inbound examples, each downstream/outbound scenario is based on the

FIGURE 17.5

Upstream/inbound relationships.

Source: Charles W. L. Hill and G. Tomas M. Hult, *Global Business Today* (New York: McGraw-Hill, 2020).

FIGURE 17.6

Downstream/outbound relationships.

Source: Charles W. L. Hill and G. Tomas M. Hult, *Global Business Today* (New York: McGraw-Hill, 2020).

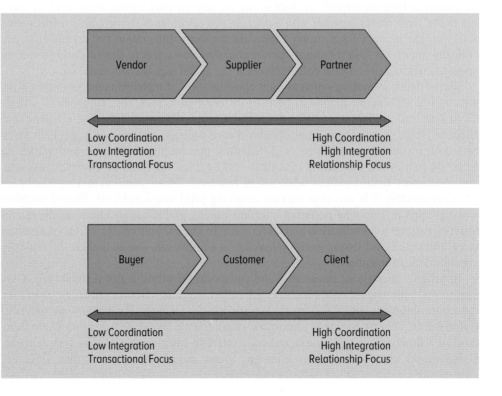

degree of coordination, integration, and transactional versus relationship focus that the firm should adopt in partnering with other entities in the global supply chain. One firm may sell products and parts to buyers through a transactional relationship that can change easily. Another firm may sell products and parts to customers and maintain a relationship that is based on experience and performance. Yet another firm may sell products and parts to clients and maintain a relationship that is based on trust and commitment.

Having reviewed the three scenarios for the upstream/inbound and downstream/outbound portions of the global supply chain, let's look at the emphasis a global company should place on the relationships with each entity: the benefits to be expected, favorable points of distinction, and resonating focus in the relationship.[30] First, however, some basics on value are appropriate. The value between nodes and actors in global supply chains is a function of the cost (money and nonmoney resources) given up in return for the quality (products, services, information, trust, and commitment) received. Basically, greater value is achieved if the quality is greater while the cost remains the same or is reduced or when the cost is reduced and the quality remains constant.

A global company should allocate 20 percent of its efforts to the vendor category, 30 percent to the supplier category, and 50 percent to the partner category in the upstream/inbound portion of the global supply chain. Likewise, a global company should allocate 20 percent of its efforts to the buyer category, 30 percent to the customer category, and 50 percent to the client category in the downstream/outbound portion of the chain. In the vendor (upstream) and buyer (downstream) portions of the supply chain, the benefits that can be expected include those typical of a transactional exchange (costs equal to quality for the goods bought but not necessarily the best goods in the marketplace). In the supplier (upstream) and customer (downstream) stages, the expectation is that the firm will receive all the favorable points that the raw materials, component parts, and/or products have relative to the next best alternative in the global marketplace. This takes into account the ideas that the costs are equal to quality for the goods bought and that the goods are among the best goods in the marketplace. Finally, in the partner (upstream) and client (downstream) portions of the supply chain, the benefits that the firm can expect to receive include the one or two points of difference for the raw materials, component parts, and/or products whose improvements will deliver the greatest value to the customer for the foreseeable future (quality greater than cost).

> **✓ TEST PREP**
>
> Use SmartBook to help retain what you have learned. Access your Instructor's Connect course to check out SmartBook or go to **learnsmartadvantage.com** for help.

Key Terms

production, p. 501
supply chain management, p. 501
purchasing, p. 501
logistics, p. 501
upstream supply chain, p. 502
downstream supply chain, p. 502
total quality management
    (TQM), p. 503
Six Sigma, p. 503
ISO 9000, p. 503
minimum efficient scale, p. 506

flexible manufacturing
    technology, p. 507
lean production, p. 507
mass customization, p. 507
flexible machine cells, p. 507
global learning, p. 510
offshore factory, p. 510
source factory, p. 510
server factory, p. 510
contributor factory, p. 511
outpost factory, p. 511

lead factory, p. 511
make-or-buy decision, p. 513
global distribution center, p. 516
global inventory
    management, p. 516
packaging, p. 517
transportation, p. 517
reverse logistics, p. 517
just in time (JIT), p. 519
global supply chain
    coordination, p. 521

 SUMMARY

This chapter explained how global production and supply chain management can improve the competitive position of an international business by lowering the total costs of value creation and by performing value creation activities in such ways that customer

service is enhanced and value added is maximized. We looked closely at five issues central to global production and supply chain management: where to produce, the strategic role of foreign production sites, what to make and what to buy, global supply chain functions, and managing a global supply chain. The chapter made the following points:

1. The choice of an optimal production location must consider country factors, technological factors, and production factors.

2. Country factors include the influence of factor costs, political economy, and national culture on production costs, along with the presence of location externalities.

3. Technological factors include the fixed costs of setting up production facilities, the minimum efficient scale of production, and the availability of flexible manufacturing technologies that allow for mass customization.

4. Production factors include product features, locating production facilities, and strategic roles for production facilities.

5. Location strategies either concentrate or decentralize manufacturing. The choice should be made in light of country, technological, and production factors. All location decisions involve trade-offs.

6. Foreign factories can improve their capabilities over time, and this can be of immense strategic benefit to the firm. Managers need to view foreign factories as potential centers of excellence and encourage and foster attempts by local managers to upgrade factory capabilities.

7. An essential issue in many international businesses is determining which component parts should be manufactured in-house and which should be outsourced to independent suppliers. Both making and buying component parts are primarily based on cost considerations and production capacity constraints, but each decision (make or buy) is also influenced by several different factors.

8. The core global supply chain functions are logistics, purchasing (sourcing), production (and operations management), and marketing channels.

9. Logistics is the part of the supply chain that plans, implements, and controls the effective flows and inventory of raw material, component parts, and products used in manufacturing. The core activities performed in logistics are to manage global distribution centers, inventory management, packaging and materials handling, transportation, and reverse logistics.

10. Purchasing represents the part of the supply chain that involves worldwide buying of raw material, component parts, and products used in manufacturing of the company's products and services. The core activities performed in purchasing include development of an appropriate strategy for global purchasing and selecting the type of purchasing strategy best suited for the company.

11. Managing a supply chain involves orchestrating effective just-in-time inventory systems, using information technology, coordination among functions and entities in the chain, and developing interorganizational relationships.

12. Just-in-time systems generate major cost savings by reducing warehousing and inventory holding costs and by reducing the need to write off excess inventory. In addition, JIT systems help the firm spot defective parts and remove them from the manufacturing process quickly, thereby improving product quality.

13. Information technology, particularly internet-based electronic data interchange, plays a major role in materials management. EDI facilitates the tracking of inputs, allows the firm to optimize its production schedule, lets the firm and its suppliers communicate in real time, and eliminates the flow of paperwork between a firm and its suppliers.

14. Global supply chain coordination refers to shared decision-making opportunities and operational collaboration of key global supply chain activities.

15. The depth and involvement in interorganizational relationships in global supply chains should be based on the degree of coordination, integration, and transactional versus relationship emphasis that the firm should adopt in partnering with other entities in the global supply chain.

Critical Thinking and Discussion Questions

1. An electronics firm is considering how best to supply the world market for microprocessors used in consumer and industrial electronic products. A manufacturing plant costs about $500 million to construct and requires a highly skilled workforce. The total value of the world market for this product over the next 10 years is estimated to be between $10 billion and $15 billion. The tariffs prevailing in this industry are currently low. What kind of location(s) should the firm favor for its plant(s)?

2. A chemical firm is considering how best to supply the world market for sulfuric acid. A manufacturing plant costs about $20 million to construct and requires a moderately skilled workforce. The total value of the world market for this product over the next 10 years is estimated to be between $20 billion and $30 billion.

The tariffs prevailing in this industry are moderate. What kind of location(s) should the firm seek for its plant(s)?

3. A firm must decide whether to make a component part in-house or to contract it out to an independent supplier. Manufacturing the part requires a nonrecoverable investment in specialized assets. The most efficient suppliers are located in countries with currencies that many foreign exchange analysts expect to appreciate substantially over the next decade. What are the pros and cons of (a) manufacturing the component in-house and (b) outsourcing manufacturing to an independent supplier? Which option would you recommend? Why?

4. Reread the Management Focus "IKEA Production in China," and then answer the following questions:

a. What are the benefits to IKEA of shifting so much of its global production to China?

b. What are the risks associated with a heavy concentration of manufacturing assets in China?

c. What strategies might IKEA adopt to maximize the benefits and mitigate the risks associated with moving so much product?

5. Explain how the global supply chain functions of (a) logistics and (b) purchasing can be used to strategically leverage the global supply chains for a manufacturing company producing mobile phones.

6. What type of interorganizational relationship should a global company consider in the (a) inbound portion of its supply chains if the goal is to buy commodity-oriented component parts for its own production and (b) outbound portion of its supply chains if the goal is to establish a strong partnership in reaching end-customers?

globalEDGE research task globaledge.msu.edu

Use the globalEDGE™ website (**globaledge.msu.edu**) to complete the following exercises:

1. The globalization of production makes many people aware of the differences in manufacturing costs worldwide. The U.S. Department of Labor's Bureau of International Labor Affairs publishes the *Chartbook of International Labor Comparisons*. Locate the latest edition of this report, and identify the hourly compensation costs for manufacturing workers in China, Brazil, Mexico, Turkey, Germany, and the United States.

2. The World Bank's Logistics Performance Index (LPI) assesses the trade logistics environment and performance of countries. Locate the most recent LPI ranking. What components for each country are examined to construct the index? Identify the top 10 logistics performers. Prepare an executive summary highlighting the key findings from the LPI. How are these findings helpful for companies trying to build a competitive supply chain network?

CLOSING CASE

Procter & Gamble Remakes Its Global Supply Chains

Procter & Gamble (P&G) is the world's leading manufacturer of consumer products. P&G, founded in 1837 by British American William Procter and Irish American James Gamble, is headquartered in Cincinnati in the United States, and the company has now been built into a $67 billion conglomerate. Within its portfolio, P&G has 21 billion-dollar brands (e.g., Bounty, Crest, Tide), operates 130 plants staffed by 95,000 people, has some 70,000 suppliers around the world, and sells its products in more than 180 countries. By all accounts, P&G has been a giant multinational corporation for more than a century and will continue to be highly influential in consumer products for years to come.

At the same time, very few industries are as competitive as consumer packaged goods. Just think about the options you now have compared with five years ago. In most cases, we as customers have many more options in every consumer packaged-goods category than we did then. The global marketplace has a lot to do with this competitive environment. Fragmentation and specialization in consumer products from more companies have resulted in more products and more places from which to buy. The infrastructure for developing products, entering markets, and maintaining customer relationships is more robust than ever, resulting in small- and medium-sized enterprises (SMEs) being competitive with companies like P&G (which they could not have competed with just a few years ago).

This market competitiveness has led companies like P&G to constantly assess the efficiencies and effectiveness of their production, operations, and global supply chains. For a long-standing industry titan like P&G, this increasingly competitive global environment—see the figures in Chapter 1 that show the drastically increased international trade in the last 20 years—has led to a newfound sense of urgency for P&G to get closer to both its customers and suppliers to maximize diminishing margins while selling products at a competitive price. This is not an easy task, because margins in the consumer packaged goods market are already very tight. That led P&G to evaluate and ultimately remake their global supply chains.

P&G's goal is to replenish at least 80 percent of the retail orders the company receives in less than a day. To be able to do this, P&G redesigned its distribution network. The company has improved transparency throughout the end-to-end supply chain, developed even stronger partnerships with its suppliers, and focused on maximizing synergy throughout the production cycle. Given this focus on synergy and supplier partnerships, P&G now develops global strategic supply chain plans jointly with (at least) its core suppliers. This is not to say that all 70,000 suppliers working with P&G are involved, but the so-called "strategic suppliers" are very much entrenched in working together with P&G.

P&G's 70,000 suppliers include chemical companies (e.g., Dow Chemicals, DuPont) that supply raw materials for cleaning supplies; packaging companies (e.g., Diamond Packaging, Van Genechten Packaging) that supply packaging materials for the company's products; and indirect providers (e.g., Jones Lang Lasalle) that deliver services such as warehouse maintenance and janitorial services. With the number and breadth of suppliers, P&G continuously focuses on maintaining a strong supplier relations program. Guiding its supplier relations program, P&G has a set of core principles: (1) Best Total Value, (2) Honest, Ethical, and Fair Dealings, (3) Externally Linked Supply Solutions, (4) Competition and Collaboration, and (5) Supplier Incumbency.

P&G appears to be in the forefront of continually evaluating and, when needed, remaking its global supply chains to maintain the titan position in the consumer packaged goods industry. Despite this success at being able to remake itself so far, one can wonder if P&G, at some point, will run into difficulties competing with companies like Alibaba and Amazon. Or, will Alibaba and Amazon simply continue to sell P&G's products (instead of starting to market their own). Alternatively, will companies like P&G be able to use their sophisticated global supply chains to expand into new territories similar to what Alibaba and Amazon did not too long ago?

Sources: "Technology Has Upended the World's Advertising Giants," *The Economist*, March 28, 2018; Demitrios Kalogeropoulo, "Will 2018 Be Procter & Gamble's Best Year Yet?" *The Motley Fool*, November 12, 2017; and Matt Gunn, "How Supply Chain Transformation Saved P&G $1.2 Billion," *GT Nexus Commerce Network*, April 29, 2015.

Case Discussion Questions

1. P&G is the world's leading manufacturer of consumer products, but most customers do not really know the P&G brand. Does that matter, or should P&G brand more of their products under the P&G brand (instead of Bounty, Crest, Tide, and so on)?

2. Considering P&G's massive product portfolio and the company's enormous size, what global supply chain efficiencies do you think P&G has that other companies cannot match given the size and scope of P&G?

3. Given P&G's focus on synergy and supplier partnerships, how many of P&G's suppliers do you think should be labeled strategic, and how many should be considered just transactional relationships, and why?

Endnotes

1. T. Hult, D. Closs, and D. Frayer, *Global Supply Chain Management: Leveraging Processes, Measurements, and Tools for Strategic Corporate Advantage* (New York: McGraw-Hill Professional, 2014).

2. D. A. Garvin, "What Does Product Quality Really Mean," *Sloan Management Review* 26 (Fall 1984), pp. 25–44.

3. See the articles published in the special issue of the *Academy of Management Review on Total Quality Management* 19, no. 3

(1994). The following article provides a good overview of many of the issues involved from an academic perspective: J. W. Dean and D. E. Bowen, "Management Theory and Total Quality," *Academy of Management Review* 19 (1994), pp. 392–418. Also see T. C. Powell, "Total Quality Management as Competitive Advantage," *Strategic Management Journal* 16 (1995), pp. 15–37; and S. B. Han et al., "The Impact of ISO 9000 on TQM and Business Performance," *Journal of Business and Economic Studies* 13, no. 2 (2007), pp. 1–25.

4. For general background information, see "How to Build Quality," *The Economist*, September 23, 1989, pp. 91–92; A. Gabor, *The Man Who Discovered Quality* (New York: Penguin, 1990); P. B. Crosby, *Quality Is Free* (New York: Mentor, 1980); and M. Elliot et al., "A Quality World, a Quality Life," *Industrial Engineer*, January 2003, pp. 26–33.

5. G. T. Lucier and S. Seshadri, "GE Takes Six Sigma Beyond the Bottom Line," *Strategic Finance*, May 2001, pp. 40–46; and U. D. Kumar et al., "On the Optimal Selection of Process Alternatives in a Six Sigma Implementation," *International Journal of Production Economics* 111, no. 2 (2008), pp. 456–70.

6. M. Saunders, "U.S. Firms Doing Business in Europe Have Options in Registering for ISO 9000 Quality Standards," *Business America,* June 14, 1993, p. 7; Han et al., "The Impact of ISO 9000."

7. G. Stalk and T. M. Hout, *Competing against Time* (New York: Free Press, 1990).

8. N. Tokatli, "Global Sourcing: Insights from the Global Clothing Industry—The Case of Zara, a Fast Fashion Retailer," *Journal of Economic Geography* 8, no. 1 (2008), pp. 21–39.

9. Diana Farrell, "Beyond Offshoring," *Harvard Business Review*, December 2004, pp. 1–8; and M. A. Cohen and H. L. Lee, "Resource Deployment Analysis of Global Manufacturing and Distribution Networks," *Journal of Manufacturing and Operations Management* 2 (1989), pp. 81–104.

10. P. Krugman, "Increasing Returns and Economic Geography," *Journal of Political Economy* 99, no. 3 (1991), pp. 483–99; J. M. Shaver and F. Flyer, "Agglomeration Economies, Firm Heterogeneity, and Foreign Direct Investment in the United States," *Strategic Management Journal* 21 (2000), pp. 1175–93; and R. E. Baldwin and T. Okubo, "Heterogeneous Firms, Agglomeration Economies, and Economic Geography," *Journal of Economic Geography* 6, no. 3 (2006), pp. 323–50.

11. For a review of the technical arguments, see D. A. Hay and D. J. Morris, *Industrial Economics: Theory and Evidence* (Oxford, UK: Oxford University Press, 1979). See also C. W. L. Hill and G. R. Jones, *Strategic Management: An Integrated Approach* (Boston: Houghton Mifflin, 2004).

12. See P. Nemetz and L. Fry, "Flexible Manufacturing Organizations: Implications for Strategy Formulation," *Academy of Management Review* 13 (1988), pp. 627–38; N. Greenwood, *Implementing Flexible Manufacturing Systems* (New York: Halstead Press, 1986); J. P. Womack, D. T. Jones, and D. Roos, *The Machine That Changed the World* (New York: Rawson Associates, 1990); R. Parthasarthy and S. P. Seith, "The Impact of Flexible Automation on Business Strategy and Organizational Structure," *Academy of Management Review* 17 (1992), pp. 86–111.

13. B. J. Pine, *Mass Customization: The New Frontier in Business Competition* (Boston: Harvard Business School Press, 1993); S. Kotha, "Mass Customization: Implementing the Emerging Paradigm for Competitive Advantage," *Strategic Management Journal* 16 (1995), pp. 21–42; J. H. Gilmore and B. J. Pine II, "The Four Faces of Mass Customization," *Harvard Business Review,* January–February 1997, pp. 91–101; M. Zerenler and D. Ozilhan, "Mass Customization Manufacturing: The Drivers and Concepts," *Journal of American Academy of Business* 12, no. 1 (2007), pp. 230–62.

14. M. A. Cusumano, *The Japanese Automobile Industry* (Cambridge, MA: Harvard University Press, 1989); and T. Ohno, *Toyota Production System* (Cambridge, MA: Productivity Press, 1990); Womack et al., *The Machine That Changed the World*.

15. P. Waurzyniak, "Ford's Flexible Push," *Manufacturing Engineering*, September 2003, pp. 47–50.

16. Hult et al., *Global Supply Chain Management*.

17. F. Kasra, "Making the Most of Foreign Factories," in *World View*, ed. J. E. Garten (Boston: Harvard Business School Press, 2000).

18. "The Boomerang Effect," *The Economist*, April 21, 2012; and Charles Fishman, "The Insourcing Boom," *The Atlantic*, December 2012.

19. This anecdote was told to one of the authors by a Microsoft manager while the author was visiting Microsoft facilities in Hyderabad, India.

20. Interview by one of the authors. The manager was a former executive MBA student of the author.

21. Hult et al., *Global Supply Chain Management*.

22. Hult et al., *Global Supply Chain Management*.

23. D. A. Beeton, *Technology Roadmapping in the Packaging Sector* (Cambridge, UK: Institute for Manufacturing, University of Cambridge, 2004).

24. J. A. Peterson and V. Kumar, "Can Product Returns Make You Money?" *MIT Sloan Management Review* 51, no. 3 (2013), pp. 85–89.

25. Hult et al., *Global Supply Chain Management*; and R. J. Trent and R. M. Monczka, "Achieving Excellence in Global Sourcing," *MIT Sloan Management Review* 47, no. 1 (2005), pp. 24–32.

26. M. Kotabe and K. Helsen, *Global Marketing Management* (Hoboken, NJ: Wiley, 2010).

27. H. F. Busch, "Integrated Materials Management," *IJPD & MM* 18 (1990), pp. 28–39.

28. T. Aeppel, "Manufacturers Cope with the Costs of Strained Global Supply Lines," *The Wall Street Journal*, December 8, 2004, p. A1.

29. D. J. Bowersox, D. J. Closs, M. B. Cooper, and J. C. Bowersox, *Supply Chain Logistics Management* (New York: McGraw-Hill Companies, 2012).

30. J. C. Anderson, J. A. Narus, and W. van Rossum, "Customer Value Propositions in Business Markets," *Harvard Business Review*, March 2006, pp. 1–10.

Global Marketing and Business Analytics

18

LEARNING OBJECTIVES

After reading this chapter, you will be able to:

LO18-1   Understand the importance of business analytics and international market research.

LO18-2   Explain why it might make sense to vary the attributes of a product from country to country.

LO18-3   Recognize why and how a firm's distribution strategy might vary among countries.

LO18-4   Identify why and how advertising and promotional strategies might vary among countries.

LO18-5   Explain why and how a firm's pricing strategy might vary among countries.

LO18-6   Understand how to configure the marketing mix globally.

LO18-7   Describe how globalization is affecting product development.

Sarah Stier/Stringer/Getty Images

Marketing Sneakers

OPENING CASE

"Zion Williamson is about to get paid," read the headline in an article on April 1, 2019, on the ESPN website. Zion Williamson averaged 22.6 points, 8.9 rebounds, 2.1 assists, and made 68 percent of his field goals in his one year of American college basketball, playing for coach Mike Krzyzewski at Duke University during the 2018–2019 season. Williamson is 6'7" and 285 lbs (2.01 meters and 129 kg), had the best Player Efficiency Rating (PER) in college basketball in at least a decade (42.55), and was the top pick in the NBA draft in 2019. Before even being drafted to play in the National Basketball Association's league, it was well-known that, behind-the-scenes, Williamson had received several $100-million offers to sign a sneaker contract with Adidas, Anta, New Balance, Nike, Puma, or Under Armour.

And who can blame these companies for going after what is perhaps the best player to be drafted into the NBA since Shaquille O'Neal went to the Orlando Magic out of Louisiana State University in 1992, or since Kobe Bryant made the leap from Lower Merion High School in 1996 to the Los Angeles Lakers. Williamson is expected to have a once-in-a-generation NBA career. Because he entered the NBA at 18 years of age (his season started October 2019) and will likely play until his mid-30s, NBA and sneaker-company executives are drooling over the sales prospects. At the same time, Michael Jordan—arguably the best basketball player ever—retired from the NBA in 2003, and yet is still helping Nike sell some $3 billion in sneakers annually. The Jordan brand, a subsidiary of Nike since 1997, has been a Nike property since 1984 (when Jordan left the University of North Carolina after three seasons to play NBA basketball).

It is clear that the sneaker competition is fierce in the international marketplace. The Zion Williamson and Michael Jordan stories—albeit incredible—are only part of the global landscape of athlete-driven sales. In tennis, Roger Federer, Serena Williams, and Novak Djokovic, to mention only a few players, make millions in endorsements. So do Cristiano Ronaldo, Lionel Messi, and Neymar in the global sport of football (soccer), as well as Tiger Woods and Phil Michelson, among many others, in golf. There are many more examples, say, with Usain Bolt in track, or even Mahendra Singh Dhoni in cricket—although not having a widespread fanbase in the United States (unlike NBA basketball), cricket is still an international game, and Mahendra Singh Dhoni is the highest-paid batsman in the sport and a social media juggernaut, serving as brand ambassador for PepsiCo, for example.

In this unique international marketplace populated by sports superstars, it is fascinating to see companies like Adidas, Anta, New Balance, Nike, Puma, and Under Armour compete for players, particularly when it comes to the sneaker sector of the industry. It clearly goes way beyond Zion Williamson, Michael Jordan, and the NBA. And given that the world of sports and the different types of sneakers used are so different around the world and are dependent on which sport is being played or followed, these companies have strategic decisions to make each year regarding every sport they engage in worldwide—such as which superstars to use for their brands, how many, and in what way.

Mahendra Singh Dhoni's name and image do not sell many shoes in the United States, but they clearly do in the cricket-playing world. When it comes to Michael Jordan, he helps sell shoes everywhere, and that is the hope regarding Zion Williamson. Football (or "soccer," as it's known in the U.S.) is the world's largest sport, with 4 billion fans. But can a soccer mega-star like Cristiano Ronaldo or Lionel Messi carry a brand as successfully as Michael Jordan can? Serena Williams clearly helps sell sports items in the U.S., but what about Novak Djokovic? Roger Federer may be the most famous tennis player in recent memory, and is quite a valuable commodity, but how do international tennis stars like Caroline Wozniacki (Denmark) and Maria Sharapova (Russia) stack up next to him when it comes to selling power? They may not have his star wattage, but they too have won Grand Slam tournaments.

Multinational corporations use a mix of marketing research and business analytics to evaluate the potential impact of players like Zion Williamson. Research has shown that there is a positive payoff on signing athletic stars to endorsement deals to brand a company's products. The right endorsement increases sales in general, as well as relative to a product's competitors. If the athlete then also achieves success, in addition to their fame, the brand benefits immediately. However, returns will diminish over time if the athlete's success lessens. Very few athletes transcend the success of their time in the sport. Michael Jordan is clearly one such basketball player, as is Shaquille O'Neal, but on a more limited scale. Other retired athletes, such as Jack Nicklaus (golf), David Beckham (football/soccer), and Wayne Gretzky (hockey), carry brands as well. Can Zion Williamson follow in their footsteps while active, and once retired?

Sources: John Gotty, "Where Does Jordan Brand Go in 2019?" *Complex*, January 10, 2019; Megan Armstrong, "Michael Jordan, LeBron James and 10 of the Biggest Sports Endorsement Deals," *MSN Sports*, February 15, 2017; "The Highest-Paid Retired Athletes," *Forbes*, April 15, 2019; Joe Boozzell, "Is Zion Williamson Having the Best Individual College Basketball Season of the last 20 Years?" *NCAA*, January 21, 2019.

Introduction

Chapter 17 looked at the roles of global production and supply chain management in international business. This chapter continues our focus on specific business functions by examining the roles of global marketing, business analytics, and research and development (R&D). Specifically, we focus on how marketing, analytics, and R&D can be performed so they will reduce the costs of value creation, as well as add value to companies and customers by better serving customers' needs in the global marketplace. This includes distribution strategy (sometimes called marketing channels or place), which is also a part of global supply chains that we discussed in Chapter 17.

globalEDGE   GET INSIGHTS BY INDUSTRY

When conducting research and development (R&D) and creating international marketing campaigns, the vast majority of global companies focus on the customers' needs in a particular industry. Industries worldwide are classified according to the Harmonized Commodity Description and Coding System, or simply HS Codes, which are maintained by the World Customs Organization. The HS Codes are divided into about 20 sections for its roughly 5,000 commodity groups. The "Get Insights by Industry" section on globalEDGE™ (**globaledge.msu.edu/global-insights/by/industry**) is a great source for international business–related resources, statistics, risk assessments, regulatory agencies, corporations, and events for these 20 industry sectors. An interesting aspect of each industry section on globalEDGE™ is the rating provided of the industry's level of fragmentation. Highly concentrated industries are dominated by many large firms that are capable of shaping the industry's direction and price levels. Highly fragmented industries have many companies involved, with none of them really large enough to be able to influence the industry's direction or price levels. Which do you think is more fragmented: consumer products or technology? Check out the industry section on globalEDGE™ for an answer.

In Chapter 13, we spoke of the tension that exists in most international businesses between the need to reduce costs and, at the same time, respond to local conditions, which tends to raise costs. This tension continues to be a theme in this chapter. Basically, the world is becoming more globalized in some respects but remains different in others. A global marketing strategy that views the world's consumers as similar in their tastes and preferences is consistent with the mass production of a standardized output. By mass-producing a standardized output—whether it be soap, semiconductor chips, or high-end apparel—the firm can realize substantial unit cost reductions from experience curve effects and other economies of scale.

At the same time, ignoring country differences in consumer tastes and preferences can lead to failure. Some industries are more ripe for globalization than others; check out the globalEDGE™ "Get Insights by Industry" section for comparisons. Strategically, the global marketing function of a company needs to determine when product standardization is appropriate, how standardized it can be, and when it is not in the business's best interest to standardize a product too much. And, even if product standardization is appropriate, the way in which a product is positioned in a market, and the promotions and messaging used to sell that product, may still have to be customized so they resonate with local consumers.

Thankfully, we are now in a time when homogenization of customers' needs and wants, especially of younger populations across developed and emerging nations, help marketing professionals sell products globally. To some degree, the globalization of product and service needs is age-dependent. Younger people want more similar products worldwide and actually expect to be able to buy any products anywhere and get them immediately. Globalization is also industry-dependent in that some industries are more likely to be able to standardize their products and value proposition (e.g., electronics) than other industries (e.g., furniture), at least not to the same degree, based on customers' desires. This chapter is exciting as a learning experience because globalization has increased the pressure on marketing to deliver on product quality, customer satisfaction, and availability in a far-spanning way worldwide—by using effective distribution strategies, appropriate communication strategies, and competitive pricing strategies.

We consider marketing, business analytics, and R&D within the same chapter in this international business textbook because of their close relationships. The opening case also illustrates the close connections between marketing, business analytics, and R&D in understanding how to tackle the diverse marketplace for athletic gear and sneakers. In particular, a critical aspect of the marketing function is identifying gaps in the market so that the firm can develop new products to fill those gaps. Developing new products requires R&D and analytics—thus the linkage between marketing, analytics, and R&D. A firm should develop new products with market needs in mind, and marketing is best suited to define those needs for R&D personnel, given, among many things, its closeness to the market via front-line customer service personnel. Also, marketing personnel are well suited to communicate with R&D personnel whether to produce globally standardized or locally customized products. Additionally, the reason marketing is so well positioned to communicate with R&D about (1) customer needs and wants and (2) degree of product standardization or customization needed is that the marketing function is responsible for the international marketing research that is conducted by the global company. Business analytics then enhances international marketing research and creates a better understanding of data and potential customer needs and wants.[1]

In this chapter, we begin by reviewing the debate on the globalization of markets. Then we discuss the issue of market segmentation. Next, we look at four elements that constitute a firm's marketing mix: product attributes, distribution strategy, communication strategy, and pricing strategy (these are sometimes called the 4 Ps for *product*, *place*, *promotion*, and *price* in many basic marketing texts). The **marketing mix** is the set of choices the firm offers to its targeted markets. Many firms vary their marketing mix from country to country, depending on differences in national culture, economic development, product standards, distribution channels, and so on. The best way to think about the marketing mix is that it represents the tactical activities and behaviors that are implemented by a global company based on its international marketing strategy to offer the best possible "mix" of product, distribution, communication, and price to a specific target market in a country or region.

Given the importance of the marketing mix and having the right products, we include three sections on those topics here, after a detailed discussion of the marketing mix elements. First, there is a section on configuring an appropriate marketing mix for each unique international market segment. This includes a set of sample questions to ask for each of the marketing mix elements (product, distribution, communication, and price) to gauge how standardized or customized a marketing mix should be for a certain international market segment. Next, we discuss business analytics and international market research as a way to better understand how to configure the marketing mix for international market segments. Third, we focus on product development issues, with a particular emphasis on new product development. In that section, we integrate R&D, marketing, and production issues, along with management issues such as cross-functional teams.

Globalization of Markets and Brands

In a now-classic *Harvard Business Review* article in 1983, Theodore Levitt wrote lyrically about the globalization of world markets. Levitt's arguments have become something of a lightning rod in the debate about the extent of globalization. According to Levitt,

> A powerful force drives the world toward a converging commonality, and that force is technology. It has proletarianized communication, transport, and travel. The result is a new commercial reality—the emergence of global markets for standardized consumer products on a previously unimagined scale of magnitude.

Gone are accustomed differences in national or regional preferences. The globalization of markets is at hand. With that, the multinational commercial world nears its end, and so does the multinational corporation. The multinational corporation operates in a number of countries and adjusts its products and practices to each—at high relative costs. The global corporation operates with resolute consistency—at low relative cost—as if the entire world were a single entity; it sells the same thing in the same way everywhere.

Commercially, nothing confirms this as much as the success of McDonald's from the Champs Élysées to the Ginza, of Coca-Cola in Bahrain and Pepsi-Cola in Moscow, and of rock music, Greek salad, Hollywood movies, Revlon cosmetics, Sony television, and Levi's jeans everywhere.

Ancient differences in national tastes or modes of doing business disappear. The commonalty of preference leads inescapably to the standardization of products, manufacturing, and the institutions of trade and commerce.[2]

This is eloquent and evocative writing, but is Levitt correct? Was he correct in 1983, and is he correct today? The rise of social media and the ability of such media to shape a global culture would seem to lend weight to Levitt's argument. If Levitt is correct, his argument has major implications for the marketing strategies pursued by international businesses. However, many academics feel that Levitt overstates his case.[3] Although he may have a point when it comes to many basic industrial products, such as steel, bulk chemicals, and semiconductors, globalization in the sense used by Levitt seems to be the exception rather than the rule in many consumer goods markets and industrial markets. Even a firm such as McDonald's, which Levitt holds up as the archetypal example of a consumer products firm that sells a standardized product worldwide, modifies its menu from country to country in light of local consumer preferences. In select Arab countries and Pakistan, for example, McDonald's sells the McArabia, a chicken sandwich on Arabian-style bread, and in France, the Croque McDo, a hot ham-and-cheese sandwich.[4]

On the other hand, Levitt is probably correct to assert that technologies are facilitating a convergence of certain tastes and preferences among consumers in the more advanced countries of the world, and this has become even more prevalent since he wrote his article. Technological and other forces are clearly leading us closer to global consumer culture. However, the continuing persistence of unique cultural and economic differences between nations acts as a brake on many trends toward the standardization of consumer tastes and preferences. While we clearly see more homogenization and standardization of needs and wants among younger people, typically 40 years and younger, there are still wide gaps in tastes among older people. What will be interesting to find out is if this increased homogenization among younger people will remain when they become older. Some indications exist that standardization of needs and wants stays with people when they become older, but, at least anecdotally, we also see people adopt more culturally specific needs as they grow older.

So, we may never see a world where globalization is fully spread across its 260 countries and territories (see **globaledge.msu.edu** for a comparison of information and data on the world's countries). Some writers have argued that the rise of global culture does not mean that consumers share the same tastes and preferences.[5] Rather, people in different nations, often with conflicting viewpoints, are increasingly participating in a shared "global" conversation, drawing on shared symbols that include global brands from Nike and Dove to Coca-Cola and Sony but also Toyota and Volkswagen, as the world's largest automobile makers.[6] But the way in which these brands are perceived, promoted, and used still varies from country to country, depending on local differences in tastes and preferences.

Another reason it appears that globalization is spreading is that certain products simply exist everywhere—but that does not mean consumers prefer those products if local product alternatives exist. Better technology, production processes, and innovation may lead to better local product alternatives in the future that can compete with global products. Today, global products win in many local markets today due to cost efficiencies and effective supply chains, not necessarily because of a customer's preference. If so, international marketing is going to be even more critical than it already is for global and local companies.[7] Furthermore, trade barriers and differences in product and technical standards also constrain a firm's ability to sell a standardized product to a global market using a standardized marketing strategy. We discuss the sources of these differences when we look at how products must be altered from country to country.

Market Segmentation

Market segmentation refers to identifying distinct groups of consumers whose needs, wants, and purchasing behavior differ from others in important ways. Markets can be segmented in numerous ways: by geography, demography (e.g., gender, age, income, race, education level), sociocultural factors (e.g., social class, values, religion, lifestyle choices), and psychological factors (e.g., personality). Because different segments exhibit different needs, wants, and patterns of purchasing behavior, firms often adjust their marketing mix from segment to segment. Thus, the precise design of a product, the pricing strategy, the distribution channels used, and the choice of communication strategy may all be varied from segment to segment. The goal is to optimize the fit between the purchasing behavior of consumers in a given segment and the marketing mix, thereby maximizing sales to that segment. Automobile companies, for example, use a different marketing mix to sell cars to different socioeconomic segments. Thus, Toyota uses its Lexus division to sell high-priced luxury cars to high-income consumers while selling its entry-level models, such as the Toyota Corolla, to lower-income consumers. Similarly, computer manufacturers will offer different computer models, embodying different combinations of product attributes and price points, to appeal to consumers from different market segments (e.g., business users and home users).

When managers in an international business consider market segmentation in foreign countries, they need to be cognizant of two main issues: the differences between countries in the structure of market segments and the existence of segments that transcend national borders. For example, some companies opt to target a country with a number of different product options based on the multiple unique market segments in a country. Other companies opt to target one unique market segment in a country that also has parallels in other countries. A segment that spans multiple countries, transcending national borders, is often called an **intermarket segment**. Strategically, marketing managers have marketing mix options with these two choices. Targeting one country and its multiple potential market segments with multiple marketing mixes allows a company to focus on the cultural characteristics of one country (or the characteristics of a manageable set of countries). Targeting many countries and the intermarket segment that has characteristics that are largely the same across countries allows a company to focus on the cultural characteristics that are universal for certain customers across countries.

These are important choices because the structure of the many potential market segments may differ significantly from country to country as well as within countries. In fact, an important market segment in a foreign country may have no parallel in the firm's home country, and vice versa. In such a case, the focus cannot be on an intermarket segment, at least not one involving the home-country market. The firm may have to develop a unique marketing mix to appeal to the needs, wants, and purchasing behavior of a certain segment in a given country. An example of such a market segment is given in the accompanying Management Focus, where Marvel Studios targets certain audiences with its various superhero movies—one of the most recent being the Black Panther, which has reached Marvel's most diverse audience ever.

In another example, a segment of consumers in China in the 65-to-80 age range has few parallels in other countries.[8] This group came of age during China's Cultural Revolution (1966 to 1976). The group's values have been shaped by their members' experiences during the Cultural Revolution. They tend to be highly sensitive to price and respond negatively to new products and most forms of marketing. Thus, firms doing business in China may need to customize their marketing mix to address the unique values and purchasing

✓ TEST PREP

Use SmartBook to help retain what you have learned. Access your Instructor's Connect course to check out SmartBook or go to **learnsmartadvantage.com** for help.

Global Branding, Marvel Studios, and the Walt Disney Company

Marvel Studios is an American TV and motion picture studio that is part of Marvel Entertainment, a wholly owned subsidiary of the Walt Disney Company. As a part of the Walt Disney Empire, Marvel Studios operates jointly with Walt Disney Studios on the distribution and marketing of Marvel's films, such as the incredibly successful Iron Man and Avengers series. Other high-profile projects of Marvel Studios have included the X-Men, Spider-Man, and Captain America franchises. As might be expected, anything embedded in the global branding of the Walt Disney Company has tremendous potential, reach, and longevity.

Walter Elias ("Walt") Disney was an American business mogul, as well as an animator, cartoonist, director, philanthropist, producer, screenwriter, and voice actor, who lived from 1901 to 1966. An international icon, he started Disney Brothers Cartoon Studio with his brother, Roy O. Disney, in 1923. The current name of the Walt Disney Company has been around since 1986. Disney has one of the largest and most well-known studios in the world. It also operates numerous related businesses, such as the ABC broadcast TV network, cable TV networks (e.g., Disney Channel, ESPN), publishing, merchandising, theater divisions, theme parks (e.g., Disney World, Disneyland), and much more. Mickey Mouse is the primary symbol of the Walt Disney Company, and one of the most globally recognized brands ever!

Global branding is a staple at Walt Disney, and this branding prowess transfers well into its Marvel Studios projects. In a global branding move, the post-credits to the original *Iron Man* movie had S.H.I.E.L.D. director Nick Fury visit Tony Stark's home. In the scene, Fury tells Stark that Iron Man is not "the only superhero in the world," and says he wants to discuss the "Avenger's Initiative." This started the ball rolling in 2008, and has led to 22 films in the "Avengers" portfolio, with 2019's *Avengers: Endgame* intended as an epic grand finale to the Marvel cinematic universe!

The Avengers and Iron Man movie franchises have made billions of dollars for Marvel Studios. They have also contributed heavily to making Robert Downey, Jr. one of the highest-paid actors in Hollywood. Robert Downey, Jr. was born in 1965 in the United States, and made his movie debut at the age of five when he appeared in his father's movie, *Pound*. The "up-and-down-and-up" career of Downey is also a fascinating global brand story. He is riding high with three incredible multi-sequel franchises—Iron Man, The Avengers, and Sherlock Holmes. He has also portrayed Tony Stark—his Iron Man and Avengers

behaviors of the group. The existence of such a segment constrains the ability of firms to standardize their global marketing strategy.

In contrast, the existence of market segments that transcend national borders clearly enhances the ability of an international business to view the global marketplace as a single entity and pursue a global strategy—selling a standardized product worldwide and using the same basic marketing mix to help position and sell that product in a variety of national markets. For a segment to transcend national borders, consumers in that segment must have some compelling similarities along important dimensions—such as age, values, lifestyle choices—and those similarities must translate into similar needs, wants, and purchasing behavior. If this is true, the company can globalize its marketing mix efforts by adopting the so-called intermarket segment to target customers' needs, wants, and purchasing behavior. Although such segments clearly exist in certain industrial markets, they have historically been rarer in consumer markets.

The forecast, however, is that these intermarket segments will become more and more common with the increased globalization among younger consumers (40 years and younger) in the developed- and emerging-country markets. For example, one emerging global segment that is attracting the attention of international marketers of consumer goods is the global teenage segment. Global media are paving the way for a global youth segment. Evidence that such a segment exists comes from a study of the cultural attitudes and purchasing behavior of more than 6,500 teenagers in 26 countries.[9] The findings suggest that teens and young adults around the world are increasingly living parallel lives that share many common values. It follows that they are likely to purchase the same kind of consumer goods and for the same reasons.

 TEST PREP

Use SmartBook to help retain what you have learned. Access your Instructor's Connect course to check out SmartBook or go to **learnsmartadvantage.com** for help.

character—in several other related Marvel Studios projects (e.g., *The Incredible Hulk*, *Captain America: Civil War*, *Spider-Man: Homecoming*) and coming sequels.

Iron Man premiered April 30, 2008, in international markets, and a few days later in the United States. Amazingly, the movie had been in development since 1990 at Universal Pictures, 20th Century Fox, and New Line Cinema. Marvel Studios reacquired the rights to the movie in 2006. The basic plot has playboy, philanthropist, and genius Tony Stark (played by Downey) as the "superhero." Iron Man is a fictional character that first appeared in the Marvel Comics, Tales of Suspense, in 1963. The character itself was created by Stan Lee. *Iron Man 2* was released in 2010, and *Iron Man 3* was released in 2013, with plans for additional sequels after more Avengers movies.

The Avengers premiered on April 11, 2012. The film's development began in 2005, is based on the Marvel Comics superhero team with the same name, and was written and directed by Joss Whedon. The Avengers are a superhero team with familiar heroes such as Iron Man, Captain America, Hulk, Thor, Black Widow, Hawkeye, and so on. The second movie in the Avengers franchise came out in 2015 (*Avengers: Age of Ultron*), the third debuted in 2018 (*Avengers: Infinity War*), and the fourth in 2019 (*Avengers: Endgame*), with likely more to come using various character configurations.

While the movie character Iron Man is heavily connected to Downey, he also plays an integral part as Tony Stark in The Avengers. In doing so, the actor has been part of various Marvel Studios productions that have brought in more than $1.5 billion (*The Avengers*) and $1.2 billion (*Iron Man 3*). *Iron Man 1* and *Iron Man 2*, respectively, made more than $600 million each as well. In total, Downey has starred in six films that have made more than $500 million each at the box office worldwide, as well as numerous other successful movies that were part of the Marvel Studios lineup.

Marvel Comics has drawn from more than 100 characters for its Avengers superheroes since 1963, but Iron Man was one of its original heroes (along with Ant-Man, the Wasp, Thor, and the Hulk). The global branding success of Downey's Tony Stark across these two brands is also very advantageous for Marvel Studios' global branding. But with a new focus on characters such as Black Panther, the Black Widow, Doctor Strange, Shang-Chi, and The Eternals, Marvel Studios is set for a string of successful runs—and nothing less would be expected of the Walt Disney Company.

Sources: Megan Peters, "The MCU Will Be Very Different After Avengers 4," Comic Book, April 23, 2017; K. Buchanan and J. Wolk, "How Vulture Ranked Its 2013 Most Valuable Stars List," www.vulture.com, October 22, 2013; T. Culpan, "HTC Said to Hire Robert Downey Jr. for $12 Million Ad Campaign," *Bloomberg Businessweek*, June 20, 2013; C. Isidore, "Avengers Set to Rescue Disney and Hollywood," *CNNMoney*, May 7, 2012; "Iron Man 3: Clank Clank Bang Bang," *The Wall Street Journal*, May 2, 2013; Bryan Alexander, "One for the Ages: First 'Avengers: Endgame' Social Media Reactions Hail Marvel Epic," *USA Today*, April 23, 2019.

Business Analytics

LO18-1

Understand the importance of business analytics and international market research.

In the context of companies focusing on the global marketplace as their current or potential market to target customers, **business analytics** can be defined as the knowledge, skills, and technology that allow for the exploration as well as deeper investigation of a company's international business strategies and activities to gain insight and drive future strategy development and implementation. The extension of this definition is that business analytics has become the preferred terminology when we talk about understanding data and help companies develop and maintain a particular customer strategy.

Broadly, the process of using business analytics begins with a dataset that has been collected to address a specific international business issue. The knowledge and skills that the business analyst's previous experiences and education have resulted in serve as the guide for the type of data collected. After the data have been collected or compiled, technologies such as computer clouds, data warehousing, or traditional office computers can store data. If the database includes smaller datasets (e.g., a few hundred cases and dozens of variables), then storage can be done on almost any technological device (e.g., secured office computer). If the data is larger—"**big data**"—where the data include a massive volume of both structured and unstructured data that are so large they may be difficult to process using traditional database and software techniques, then the data would often be stored on large-scale servers (e.g., computer clouds, data warehousing).

Business analytics can be focused on one of three core applications: descriptive, predictive, and prescriptive. Descriptive analytics refers to the use of relatively simple statistical techniques to describe what is contained in a dataset. For example, the descriptive statistics can be an age bar chart that is used to depict Starbucks customers in Uppsala, Sweden (a medium-sized university town in the middle of Sweden). This would give the Starbucks franchise owner a basic understanding of the clientele he or she has developed and, perhaps, a better understanding of the type of bakery items to offer in the store. The purpose of descriptive analytics is to get a rough picture of what the data look like in the most general sense.

Predictive analytics can be defined as the use of advanced statistical techniques (and software) to identify and build predictive models that can help to identify trends and relationships not readily observed in descriptive analyses. Oftentimes, we talk about the use of longitudinal data that can help show cause-and-effect relationships (i.e., an increase in social media exposure for Starbucks in Uppsala, Sweden leads to an increase in number of cups of coffee sold at the local Uppsala, Sweden Starbucks location within two weeks of the increased social media coverage).

Prescriptive analytics can be defined as the use of management science methodologies (i.e., applied mathematical techniques) to guide a company in its endeavors to best use allocable resources. For example, the Starbucks store in Uppsala, Sweden has a limited budget to allocate to advertising to target customers (which is often the case for franchise owners for their specific store). In such a case, management science tools (e.g., linear programming) can be used to optimally allocate advertising spending to various advertising opportunities (e.g., social media interactions driven by the local Starbucks store, advertising in the newspaper or on the local radio station, or messaging via Snapchat, Instagram, and similar vehicles). The goal then is to allocate the Starbucks store's limited resources optimally and to include the best possible trends or future opportunities.

Whether we talk about "small data" or "big data," business analytics can be used to better understand a company's current products and services in the global marketplace and future business opportunities. To effectively configure the marketing mix (which we will discuss later in this chapter) and answer questions such as those in Table 18.1, global companies use the toolkit offered within business analytics and conduct international marketing research.

INTERNATIONAL MARKETING RESEARCH

To effectively segment the global marketplace, companies conduct international marketing research. **International market research** is defined as the systematic collection, recording, analysis, and interpretation of data to provide knowledge that is useful for decision making in a global company. Compared with market research that is domestic only, international market research involves additional issues such as (1) translation of questionnaires and reports into appropriate foreign languages and (2) accounting for cultural and environmental differences in data collection. In this section, some of the more prominent international market research companies are highlighted; the basic steps and issues in conducting international market research are then discussed.

International market research is one of the most critical aspects of understanding the global marketplace. Given this importance, global companies often have their own in-house marketing research department to continually assess customers' needs, wants, and purchasing behavior.[10] In addition, global companies also typically undertake ongoing data collection to assess customers' satisfaction with products and services offered.[11] J.D. Power (**www.jdpower.com**) and the American Customer Satisfaction Index (ACSI) (**www.theacsi.org**) are two of the most prominent companies that measure customer satisfaction of a cross-section of the industries globally. In addition, for large-scale projects such as better understanding a new country market, global companies often work with outside marketing research firms for input. A sample of prominent international market research firms includes Nielsen, Kantar, Ipsos, and the NPD Group.

- Nielsen (**www.nielsen.com**) is an international market research company with headquarters in New York in the United States and Diemen in the Netherlands. The company was founded in 1923, is active in more than 100 countries, employs

Mix Element	Sample Questions to Address
Product Strategy	
Product core	Do the customers have similar product needs across international market segments?
Product adoption	How is the product bought by customers in the international market segments targeted?
Product management	How are established products versus new products managed for customers in the international market segments?
Product branding	What is the perception of the product brand by customers in the international market segments?
Distribution Strategy	
Distribution channels	Where is the product typically bought by customers in the international market segments?
Wholesale distribution	What is the role of wholesalers for the international market segments targeted?
Retail distribution	What is the availability of different types of retail stores in the international markets for the customer segments targeted?
Communication Strategy	
Advertising	How is product awareness created for a product to reach customers in the international market segments targeted?
Publicity	What role does publicity (e.g., public relations) play among customers in the international market segments targeted?
Mass media	What role do various media (e.g., TV, radio, newspapers, magazines, billboards) have in reaching customers in the international market segments targeted?
Social media	What role do various social media (e.g., Facebook, Twitter, blogs, virtual communities), mainly focused on user-generated content, have in communicating with customers in the international market segments targeted?
Sales promotion	Are rebates, coupons, and other sale offers a widespread activity to motivate customers in the international market segments targeted to buy a company's products?
Pricing Strategy	
Value	Is the price of a product critical to the customer's understanding (or perception) of the value of the product itself among customers in the international market segments?
Demand	Is the demand for the product among customers in the international market segments targeted similar to domestic demands?
Costs	Are the fixed and variable costs of the product the same when targeting customers in the international market segments (e.g., are there variable costs that change significantly when going international)?
Retail price	Are there trade tariffs, nontariff barriers, and/or other regulatory influences on price that will influence the pricing equation used to determine the retail price to customers in the international market segments?

TABLE 18.1

Questions to Address to Configure the Marketing Mix

about 40,000 people, and has revenue of about $6 billion annually.[12] Nielsen says on its website that "Whether you're eyeing markets in the next town or across continents, we understand the importance of knowing what consumers watch and buy."[13]

- Kantar (**www.kantar.com**) is an international market research company based in London. The company was founded in 1993 as the market research, insight, and consultancy division of WPP (an advertising and public relations firm). It operates in more than 100 countries, employs some 28,000 people, and has revenues of about \$4 billion annually. As a conglomerate of research companies, Kantar works with more than half of the *Fortune* 500 companies (a *kantar* is a measure for cotton that is still used in the ports of Egypt today).

- Ipsos (**www.ipsos.com**) is an international market research company based in Paris, France. The company was founded in 1975, has offices in some 90 countries, employs about 15,000 people, and has revenue of about \$2 billion annually. Ipsos is now the only major international market research firm that is controlled and operated by market researchers; it focuses on a mantra of BQC ("better, quicker, cheaper") as a way to be competitive in the global marketplace.

- NPD Group (**www.npd.com**) is an international market research firm based in Port Washington, New York.[14] The company was founded in 1967, has 25 worldwide offices, employs about 5,000 people, and is a privately held company (estimated to have revenues of about \$500 million annually). NPD Group is known for its retail tracking services and market size and trends analysis. Today, it tracks businesses that represent more than \$1 trillion in sales worldwide.

Nielsen, Kantar, Ipsos, and the NPD Group, along with many other market research firms, follow a similar process when conducting international market research. The basic data that companies want collected in international market research include (1) data on the country and potential market segments (geography, demography, sociocultural factors, and psychological factors), (2) data to forecast customer demands within specific country or world region (social, economic, consumer, and industry trends), and (3) data to make marketing mix decisions (product, distribution, communication, and price). The data collection needed to address these three areas always entails give-and-take in terms of time, cost, and available data collection techniques. The process, however, is somewhat universal across both domestic and international settings and includes (1) defining the research objectives, (2) determining the data sources, (3) assessing the costs and benefits of the research, (4) collecting the data, (5) analyzing and interpreting the research, and (6) reporting the research findings.[15] Each step is discussed in more detail in the following paragraphs (see Figure 18.1).

Defining the research objectives includes both (1) defining the research problem and (2) setting objectives for the international market research. At the outset of any international market research project, one of the problem areas is to have a baseline understanding of a country market or target segment that is sufficient enough to properly capture what should be done and what can be accomplished with the research. Oftentimes, the research starts with a relatively vague idea of the research problem and the objectives, subsequently refined when a better understanding of country markets and potential customer segments has been reached and more data have been collected.[16] One of the most critical aspects of the early stages of international market research is a willingness to refine the research problem and objectives throughout the process; not doing so may lead to unwanted conclusions. For example, not understanding the scope of the research problem (i.e., children turning to more electronic devices and video games) and accompanying objectives led Mattel Inc., the world's largest toy maker by sales, to suffer dismal holiday season sales. While the NPD Group reported that U.S. toy sales dropped just 1 percent, Mattel's CEO, Bryan G. Stockton, concluded that "our product innovations and our marketing programs were not strong enough."[17]

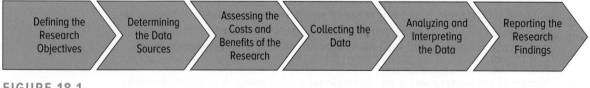

FIGURE 18.1

International market research steps.

Source: Charles W. L. Hill and G. Tomas M. Hult, *Global Business Today* (New York: McGraw-Hill, 2020).

Determining the data sources that will address specific research problems and ultimately achieve the objectives is often not an easy task, especially if the international market research spans more than one country market. In market research, we talk about two forms of data that can be used: primary and secondary data.[18] Primary data refers to data collected by the global company and/or its recruited international market research agency for the purpose of addressing the research problem and objectives defined by the company. Given the costs of collecting international data, most companies try to avoid duplicating similar data that have been collected previously. However, for more than half of the world's countries, so-called secondary data that can be helpful can be tough to come by, are often unreliable, and typically do not address what global companies require to better understand the needs, wants, and purchasing behaviors of targeted customers. Secondary data refers to data that have been collected previously by organizations, people, or agencies for purposes other than specifically addressing the research problem and objectives at hand. Overall, the data used in international market research should be evaluated based on (1) availability, (2) comparability across countries and potential market segments, (3) reliability (whether the research produces consistent results), and (4) validity (whether the research measures what it set out to measure). globalEDGE.msu.edu is a great starting point for secondary data on countries and industries, among many data categories, and the research firms mentioned earlier (i.e., Nielsen, Kantar, Ipsos, and the NPD Group) are great organizations used by many global companies for primary data collection worldwide.

Assessing the costs and benefits of the research often relates to the cost of collecting primary data that can address the research problem and objectives directly versus using available secondary data. If secondary data are available, such data are typically available as a less costly alternative to collecting primary data. The costs that drive up the spending in primary data collections broadly include survey development and sampling frame issues. For the survey, the questions have to be developed so that they clearly communicate the attitudes, attributes, or characteristics about a product or customer issue in such a way that the respondent recognizes the value. This also means overcoming any barriers or differences in language, answer choices, and cultural values and beliefs. For example, the most common way of converting a survey question into another language is to have the question translated into the foreign language (e.g., from English to Spanish) and then back-translated into English again by another person. The two English versions are then compared to ensure similarity in the back-translated version with the original. For the sampling frame, one of the core issues internationally is to make sure that comparable samples can be drawn in the countries in which international market research is conducted. This includes identifying reliable lists or groups of potential people to survey and cultivating potential people to respond to the survey.[19]

Collecting the data simply refers to gathering data via primary or secondary methods that address the research problem and objectives that the global company has established. The two mechanisms to collect data are quantitative and qualitative data collection. Quantitative methods include experiments, clinical trials, observing and recording events, and administering surveys with closed-end questions. The goal of quantitative methods is to systematically gain an understanding of customers' needs, wants, and purchase behavior via numerical data and computational techniques. A popular way of collecting quantitative data today is to use online surveys and consumer mail panels. Most large international market research firms have access to global customer mail panels and potential sampling frames that target both business-to-business customers and end-customers. Qualitative methods include in-depth interviews, observation methods, and document reviews. Here, the focus is broad-based questions aimed at gaining an in-depth understanding of customers' needs, wants, and purchase behaviors.

Analyzing and interpreting the research begins when the data have been collected. Assuming the survey is reliable and valid, whether the data come from primary or secondary data collection methods, analyzing and interpreting the data is an important step in the international market research process. It takes a fairly high degree of knowledge—both statistically and culturally—to analyze and interpret international market research. First, statistically the goal should be to use the technique that best addresses the research problem—often stated in the form of research questions or hypothesis (a specified relationship between study variables). There is a plethora of quantitative and qualitative methods of analyzing data, often taught in sophisticated marketing research programs around the world.[20] In these programs, software such as SAS, SPSS, LISREL, and Smart-PLS[21] are used for quantitative analysis, and ATLAS.ti and MAXQDA are used for qualitative methods. Second, the researcher interpreting the findings must be in tune culturally with the values, beliefs, norms, and artifacts that affect a respondent's answers in a certain world region, country, and/or subculture. If possible, it is always advisable to include at least one native of the country being researched to add to the understanding of the research findings, social customs, semantics, attitudes, and business customs. For example, some societies have a tendency to not provide extreme answers (e.g., strongly agree or strongly disagree) to questions but instead answer by using middle-of-the-scale choices (e.g., Japan), while other countries use more of the extreme answer choices (e.g., the United States).

Reporting the research findings is a way to communicate the overall results of the international market research project. Such reports often include information about customers, competitors, countries, the industry, and the environment that affect how the global company develops an appropriate marketing mix for the targeted international market segment. Ultimately, the focus will be on how best to reach customers by addressing their needs, wants, and purchasing behavior in a way that is competitive vis-à-vis existing competitors and potential new entrants into the market. Ideally, top executives who receive the report should have been part of the formulation of the research problem and objectives earlier on in the international market research process. Preferably, they should also take part in some of the fieldwork to collect the data to better understand the voices of customers. If critical employee levels of the global company—from front-line service employees to market researchers to top executives—are insiders of the culture in which the customers are targeted, a lot of misunderstanding and faulty market research can be prevented. The worst-case scenario would be if customers misunderstand the questions and managers misunderstand the answers! One such example was the case of the Toyota accelerator debacle. Toyota had issues with accelerator pedals that could get stuck, causing vehicles to speed unintentionally.[22] Toyota was slow to correct the problems with the accelerator due to a disconnect between identifying the problem (i.e., it did not know why the accelerator pedals got stuck), analyzing the damage, and reporting it to senior management for rectification. Culturally, Japan prides itself on quality products, which means that disclosing poor quality, assuming responsibility, communicating with senior management, and fixing the problem are very difficult tasks within a Japanese firm.

✅ **TEST PREP**

Use SmartBook to help retain what you have learned. Access your Instructor's Connect course to check out SmartBook or go to **learnsmartadvantage.com** for help.

LO18-2

Explain why it might make sense to vary the attributes of a product from country to country.

Product Attributes

A product can be viewed as a bundle of attributes.[23] For example, the attributes that make up a car include power, design, quality, performance, fuel consumption, and comfort; the attributes of a hamburger include taste, texture, and size; a hotel's attributes include atmosphere, quality, comfort, and service. Products sell well when their attributes match consumer needs (and when their prices are appropriate). BMW cars sell well to people who have high needs for luxury, quality, and performance precisely because BMW builds those attributes into its cars. If consumer needs were the same the world over, a firm could simply sell the same product worldwide. However, consumer needs vary from country to country, depending on culture and the level of economic development. A firm's ability to sell the same product worldwide is further constrained by countries' differing product standards. This section reviews each of these issues and discusses how they influence product attributes.

CULTURAL DIFFERENCES

We discussed countries' cultural differences in Chapter 4. Countries differ along a whole range of dimensions, including social structure, language, religion, and education.[24] These differences have important implications for marketing strategy.[25] For example, "hamburgers" do not sell well in Islamic countries, where the consumption of ham is forbidden by Islamic law (thus, the sandwich's name is changed). The most important aspect of cultural differences is probably the impact of tradition. Tradition is particularly important in foodstuffs and beverages. For example, reflecting differences in traditional eating habits, the Findus frozen food division of Nestlé, the Swiss food giant, markets fish cakes and fish fingers in Great Britain, but beef bourguignon and coq au vin in France and vitéllo con funghi and braviola in Italy. In addition to its normal range of products, Coca-Cola in Japan markets Georgia, a cold coffee in a can, and Aquarius, a tonic drink, both of which appeal to traditional Japanese tastes.

Takayama vending machine coffee in Japan.
Phillip Augustavo/Alamy Stock Photo

For historical and idiosyncratic reasons, a range of other cultural differences exist among countries. For example, scent preferences differ from one country to another. SC Johnson, a manufacturer of waxes and polishes, encountered resistance to its lemon-scented Pledge furniture polish among older consumers in Japan. Careful market research revealed the polish smelled similar to a latrine disinfectant used widely in Japan. Sales rose sharply after the scent was adjusted.[26]

There is some evidence of the trends Levitt talked about. Tastes and preferences are becoming more cosmopolitan. Coffee is gaining ground against tea in Japan and the United Kingdom, while American-style frozen dinners have become popular in Europe (with some fine-tuning to local tastes). Taking advantage of these trends, Nestlé has found that it can market its instant coffee, spaghetti bolognese, and Lean Cuisine frozen dinners in essentially the same manner in both North America and Western Europe. However, there is no market for Lean Cuisine dinners in most of the rest of the world, and there may not be for years or decades. Although some cultural convergence has occurred, particularly among the advanced industrial nations of North America and Western Europe, Levitt's global culture characterized by standardized tastes and preferences is still a long way off.

ECONOMIC DEVELOPMENT

Just as important as differences in culture are differences in the level of economic development. We discussed the extent of country differences in economic development in Chapter 3. Consumer behavior is influenced by the level of economic development of a country. Firms based in highly developed countries such as the United States tend to build a lot of extra performance attributes into their products. These extra attributes are not usually demanded by consumers in less developed nations, where the preference is for more basic products. Thus, cars sold in less developed nations typically lack many of the features found in developed nations, such as air-conditioning, power steering, power windows, radios, and CD players. For most consumer durables, product reliability may be a more important attribute in less developed nations, where such a purchase may account for a major proportion of a consumer's income than it is in advanced nations.

Contrary to Levitt's suggestions, consumers in the most developed countries are often not willing to sacrifice their preferred attributes for lower prices. Consumers in the most advanced countries often shun globally standardized products that have been developed with the lowest common denominator in mind. They are willing to pay more for products that have additional features and attributes customized to their tastes and preferences. For example, demand for top-of-the-line four-wheel-drive sport-utility vehicles—such as Chrysler's Jeep, Ford's Explorer, and Toyota's Land Cruiser—has been largely restricted to the United States. This is due to a combination of factors, including the high income level of U.S. consumers, the country's vast distances, the relatively low cost of gasoline, and the culturally grounded "outdoor" theme of American life.

PRODUCT AND TECHNICAL STANDARDS

Even with the forces that are creating some convergence of consumer tastes and preferences among advanced, industrialized nations, Levitt's vision of global markets may still be a long way off because of national differences in product and technological standards.[27] However, if anything, the increased development, and implementation of regional trade agreements, often taking into account technical standards setting, may influence certain regional markets to become more globalized, as Levitt suggested.

For now, differing government-mandated product standards can often result in companies ruling out mass production and marketing of a fully global and standardized product. Differences in technical standards also constrain the globalization of markets. Some of these differences result from idiosyncratic decisions made long ago, rather than from government actions, but their long-term effects are profound. For example, DVD equipment manufactured for sale in the United States will not play DVDs recorded on equipment manufactured for sale in Great Britain, Germany, and France (and vice versa). Thankfully, most songs and movies are now streamed and, thus, can be played in a compatible way almost anywhere in the world.[28]

LO18-3

Recognize why and how a firm's distribution strategy might vary among countries.

Distribution Strategy

A critical element of a firm's marketing mix is its distribution strategy: the means it chooses for delivering the product to the consumer.[29] The way the product is delivered is determined by the firm's entry strategy, discussed in Chapter 13. This section examines a typical distribution system, discusses how its structure varies between countries and looks at how appropriate distribution strategies vary from country to country.

Figure 18.2 illustrates a typical distribution system consisting of a channel that includes a wholesale distributor and a retailer. If the firm manufactures its product in a particular country, it can sell directly to the consumer, to the retailer, or to the wholesaler. The same options are available to a firm that manufactures outside the country. Plus, this firm may decide to sell to an import agent, which then deals with the wholesale distributor, the retailer, or the consumer. Later in the chapter, we consider the factors that determine the firm's choice of channel.

DIFFERENCES BETWEEN COUNTRIES

The four main differences between distribution systems worldwide are retail concentration, channel length, channel exclusivity, and channel quality.

Retail Concentration

In some countries, the retail system is very concentrated, but it is fragmented in others. In a **concentrated retail system**, a few retailers supply most of the market. A **fragmented**

FIGURE 18.2

A typical distribution system.

Source: Charles W. L. Hill and G. Tomas M. Hult, *Global Business Today* (New York: McGraw-Hill, 2020).

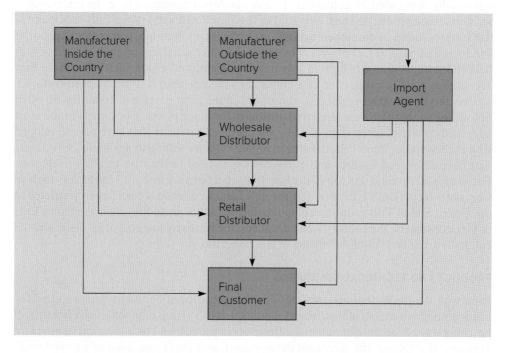

retail system is one in which there are many retailers, none of which has a major share of the market. Many of the differences in concentration are rooted in history and tradition. In the United States, the importance of the automobile and the relative youth of many urban areas have resulted in a retail system centered on large stores or shopping malls to which people can drive. This has facilitated system concentration. Japan, with a much greater population density and a large number of urban centers that grew up before the automobile, has a more fragmented retail system, with many small stores serving local neighborhoods and to which people frequently walk. In addition, the Japanese legal system protects small retailers. Small retailers can try to block the establishment of a large retail outlet by petitioning their local government.

There is a tendency for greater retail concentration in developed countries. Three factors that contribute to this are the increases in car ownership, the number of households with refrigerators and freezers, and the number of two-income households. All these factors have changed shopping habits and facilitated the growth of large retail establishments sited away from traditional shopping areas. The last decade has seen consolidation in the global retail industry, with companies such as Walmart and Carrefour attempting to become global retailers by acquiring retailers in different countries. This has increased retail concentration.

In contrast, retail systems are very fragmented in many developing countries, which can make for interesting distribution challenges. In rural China, large areas of the country can be reached only by traveling rutted dirt roads. In India, Unilever has to sell to retailers in 600,000 rural villages, many of which cannot be accessed via paved roads, which means products can reach their destination only by bullock, bicycle, or cart. In neighboring Nepal, the terrain is so rugged that even bicycles and carts are not practical, and businesses rely on yak trains and the human back to deliver products to thousands of small retailers.

Channel Length

Channel length refers to the number of intermediaries between the producer (or manufacturer) and the consumer. If the producer sells directly to the consumer, the channel is very short. If the producer sells through an import agent, a wholesaler, and a retailer, a long channel exists. The choice of a short or long channel is, in part, a strategic decision for the producing firm. However, some countries have longer distribution channels than others. The most important determinant of channel length is the degree to which the retail system is fragmented. Fragmented retail systems tend to promote the growth of wholesalers to serve retailers, which lengthens channels.

The more fragmented the retail system, the more expensive it is for a firm to make contact with each individual retailer. Imagine a firm that sells toothpaste in a country where there are more than a million small retailers, as in rural India. To sell directly to the retailers, the firm would have to build a huge sales force. This would be very expensive, particularly because each sales call would yield a very small order. But suppose a few hundred wholesalers in the country supply retailers not only with toothpaste but also with all other personal care and household products. Because these wholesalers carry a wide range of products, they get bigger orders with each sales call, making it worthwhile for them to deal directly with the retailers. Accordingly, it makes economic sense for the firm to sell to the wholesalers and the wholesalers to deal with the retailers.

Because of such factors, countries with fragmented retail systems also tend to have long channels of distribution, sometimes with multiple layers. The classic example is Japan, where there are often two or three layers of wholesalers between the firm and retail outlets. In countries such as Great Britain, Germany, and the United States, where the retail systems are far more concentrated, channels are much shorter. When the retail sector is very concentrated, it makes sense for the firm to deal directly with retailers, cutting out wholesalers. A relatively small sales force is required to deal with a concentrated retail sector, and the orders generated from each sales call can be large. Such circumstances tend to prevail in the United States, where large food companies may sell directly to supermarkets rather than going through wholesale distributors.

Another factor that is shortening channel length in some countries is the entry of large discount superstores, such as Carrefour, Walmart, and Tesco. The business model of these retailers is, in part, based on the idea that in an attempt to lower prices, they cut out wholesalers and instead deal directly with manufacturers. Thus, when Walmart entered Mexico, its policy of dealing directly with manufacturers, instead of buying merchandise through wholesalers, helped shorten distribution channels in that nation. Similarly, Japan's historically long distribution channels are now being shortened by the rise of large retailers, some of them foreign-owned, such as Walmart, and some of them indigenous enterprises that are imitating the American model, all of which are progressively cutting out wholesalers and dealing directly with manufacturers.

Channel Exclusivity

An **exclusive distribution channel** is one that is difficult for outsiders to access. For example, it is often difficult for a new firm to get access to shelf space in supermarkets. This occurs because retailers tend to prefer to carry the products of established manufacturers of foodstuffs with national reputations rather than gamble on the products of unknown firms. The exclusivity of a distribution system varies among countries. Japan's system is often held up as an example of a very exclusive system. In Japan, relationships among manufacturers, wholesalers, and retailers often go back decades. Many of these relationships are based on the understanding that distributors will not carry the products of competing firms. In return, the distributors are guaranteed an attractive markup by the manufacturer. As many U.S. and European manufacturers have learned, the close ties that result from this arrangement can make access to the Japanese market difficult. However, it is possible to break into the Japanese market with a new consumer product. Procter & Gamble did with its Joy brand of dish soap. P&G was able to overcome a tradition of exclusivity for two reasons. First, after two decades of lackluster economic performance, Japan is changing. In their search for profits, retailers are far more willing than they have been historically to violate the old norms of exclusivity. Second, P&G has been in Japan long enough and has a broad enough portfolio of consumer products to give it considerable leverage with distributors, enabling it to push new products out through the distribution channel.

Channel Quality

Channel quality refers to the expertise, competencies, and skills of established retailers in a nation and their ability to sell and support the products of international businesses. Although the quality of retailers is good in most developed nations, in emerging markets and less developed nations from Russia to Indonesia, channel quality is variable at best. The lack of a high-quality channel may impede market entry, particularly in the case of new or sophisticated products that require significant point-of-sale assistance and after-sales services and support. When channel quality is poor, an international business may have to devote considerable attention to upgrading the channel, for example, by providing extensive education and support to existing retailers and, in extreme cases, by establishing its own channel. Thus, after pioneering its Apple retail store concept in the United States, Apple opened retail stores in several nations—including the United Kingdom, France, Germany, Japan, and China—to provide point-of-sales education, service, and support for its popular iPhone, iPad, and MacBook products. Apple believes that this strategy will help it gain market share in these nations.

CHOOSING A DISTRIBUTION STRATEGY

A choice of distribution strategy determines which channel the firm will use to reach potential consumers. Should the firm try to sell directly to the consumer? Or should it go through retailers, go through a wholesaler, use an import agent, or invest in establishing its own channel? The optimal strategy is determined by the relative costs and benefits of each alternative, which vary from country to country, depending on the four factors we have just discussed: retail concentration, channel length, channel exclusivity, and channel quality.

Because each intermediary in a channel adds its own markup to the products, there is generally a critical link among channel length, the final selling price, and the firm's profit margin. The longer a channel, the greater the aggregate markup, and the higher the price that consumers are charged for the final product. To ensure that prices do not get too high as a result of markups by multiple intermediaries, a firm might be forced to operate with lower profit margins. Thus, if price is an important competitive weapon, and if the firm does not want to see its profit margins squeezed, other things being equal, the firm would prefer to use a shorter channel.

However, the benefits of using a longer channel may outweigh these drawbacks. As we have seen, one benefit of a longer channel is that it cuts selling costs when the retail sector is very fragmented. Thus, it makes sense for an international business to use longer channels in countries where the retail sector is fragmented and shorter channels in countries where the retail sector is concentrated. Another benefit of using a longer channel is market access—the ability to enter an exclusive channel. Import agents may have long-term relationships with wholesalers, retailers, or important consumers and thus be better able to win orders and get access to a distribution system. Similarly, wholesalers may have long-standing relationships with retailers and be better able to persuade them to carry the firm's product than the firm itself would.

Import agents are not limited to independent trading houses; any firm with a strong local reputation could serve as well. For example, to break down channel exclusivity and gain greater access to the Japanese market, when Apple Computer originally entered Japan, it signed distribution agreements with five large Japanese firms, including business equipment giant Brother Industries, stationery leader Kokuyo, Mitsubishi, Sharp, and Minolta. These firms use their own long-established distribution relationships with consumers, retailers, and wholesalers to push Apple computers through the Japanese distribution system. Today, Apple has supplemented this strategy with its own stores in the country.

If such an arrangement is not possible, the firm might want to consider other, less traditional alternatives to gaining market access. Frustrated by channel exclusivity in Japan, some foreign manufacturers of consumer goods have attempted to sell directly to Japanese consumers using direct mail and catalogs. Finally, if channel quality is poor, a firm should consider what steps it could take to upgrade the quality of the channel, including establishing its own distribution channel.

Communication Strategy

Another critical element in the marketing mix is communicating the attributes of the product to prospective customers. A number of communication channels are available to a firm, including **social media** (a technology that facilitates the sharing of information and the building of virtual global networks and communities), direct selling, sales promotion, and various forms of advertising. A firm's communication strategy is partly defined by its choice of channel. Unfortunately, the number of channels available today has also resulted in companies having less control over the messaging that they try to do regarding their products and services.

Traditionally, some firms have relied on direct selling, others on point-of-sale promotions, and others on mass advertising; still others have used several channels simultaneously to communicate their message to prospective customers. Prior to social media, firms were able to "signal" what type of product or service they offered in the global marketplace. Today, that messaging is collectively done by customers and the companies. Consequently, multinational corporations need to have active, interactive social media platforms to go along with the more traditional direct selling, sales promotion, and various forms of advertising that they use.

This section on communications strategy looks first at the barriers to these types of international communications. Keep in mind that the approach to communicating with and among customers (e.g., social media, direct selling, sales promotion, and various forms of advertising) is one aspect of the global company's communication strategy. The other is the potential barriers to communication and forms of advertising that can be used. Operating within these constraints and opportunities, the accompanying Management Focus illustrates nicely how an old-fashioned brand such as Burberry used social media marketing to resurrect and reinvent its high-profile luxurious brand.

✓ TEST PREP

Use SmartBook to help retain what you have learned. Access your Instructor's Connect course to check out SmartBook or go to **learnsmartadvantage.com** for help.

LO18-4

Identify why and how advertising and promotional strategies might vary among countries.

Burberry's Social Media Marketing

Burberry, the icon British luxury apparel retailer founded in 1856 by Thomas Burberry and famed for its trench coats and plaid-patterned accessories, has been on a roll in recent years. In the late 1990s, one critic described Burberry as "an outdated business with a fashion cache of almost zero." But by 2019, Burberry has become widely recognized as one of the world's premier luxury brands with a strong presence in many of the world's richest cities, some 500 retail stores, about 10,800 employees, and revenues in excess of $3.6 billion. The reason is that Burberry used social media to become a digital marketing icon and one of the top social media brands.

Two successive American CEOs were behind Burberry's transformation, and it started before the current revolution of the digital marketplace. The first, Rose Marie Bravo, joined the company in 1997 from Saks Fifth Avenue. Bravo saw immense hidden value in the Burberry brand. One of her first moves was to hire world-class designers to re-energize the brand. The company also shifted its orientation toward a younger, hipper demographic, perhaps best exemplified by the ads featuring supermodel Kate Moss that helped to reposition the brand. By the time Bravo retired in 2006, she had transformed Burberry into what one commentator called an "achingly hip," high-end fashion brand whose raincoats, clothes, handbags, and other accessories were must-have items for younger, well-heeled, fashion-conscious consumers worldwide.

Bravo was succeeded by Angela Ahrendts, whose career had taken her from a small town in Indiana and a degree at Ball State University, through Warnaco and LizClaiborne, to become the CEO of Burberry at age 46. Ahrendts realized that for all of Bravo's success, Burberry still faced significant problems. The company had long pursued a licensing strategy, allowing partners in other countries to design and sell their own offerings under the Burberry label. This lack of control over the offering was hurting its brand equity. The Spanish partner, for example, was selling casual wear that bore no relationship to what was being designed in London. So long as this state of affairs continued, Burberry would struggle to build a unified global brand.

Ahrendts's solution was to start acquiring partners and/or buying back licensing rights in order to regain control over the brand. Hand in hand with this, she pushed for an aggressive expansion of the company's retail store strategy. The company's core demographics under Ahrendts remained the well-heeled, younger, fashion-conscious set. To reach this demographic, Burberry has focused on 25 of the world's wealthier cities. Key markets include New York, London, and Beijing, which according to Burberry account for more than half the global luxury fashion trade. As a result of this strategy, the number of retail stores increased from 211 in 2007 to 556 today.

An important aspect of Burberry's strategy has been to embrace digital marketing tools to reach its tech-savvy customer base. Indeed, there are few luxury brand companies that have utilized digital technology as aggressively as Burberry. Burberry has simulcast its runway shows in 3-D in New York, Los Angeles, Dubai, Paris, and Tokyo. Viewers at home can stream the shows over the internet and post comments in real time. Outerwear and bags are made available through "click and buy" technology with delivery several months before they reach the stores. Burberry had more than 17 million Facebook fans as of 2018. At "The Art of the Trench," a company-run social media site, people can submit photos of themselves in the company's iconic rainwear.

The global marketing strategy seems to be working. Between 2007 and today, revenues at Burberry increased from some $1.3 billion to $3.6 billion. In April 2014, Angela Ahrendts was replaced as CEO by Christopher Bailey (Ahrendts took a position as senior vice president of retail and online at Apple, Inc.). Bailey, with a heritage from Halifax, United Kingdom, first started with Burberry in May 2001 as a creative director. One of the branding decisions that happened on his creative director watch was to remove the Burberry brand's iconic check pattern from virtually all Burberry products, leaving only 10 percent of the products with the famous check pattern. He also masterminded the design of Burberry's largest store, 121 Regent Street in London, United Kingdom, which opened as a bricks-and-mortar incarnation of the brand's website.

Sources: S. Davis, "Burberry's Blurred Lines: The Integrated Customer Experience," *Forbes*, March 27, 2014; A. Ahrendts, "Burberry's CEO on Turning an Aging British Icon into a Global Luxury Brand," *Harvard Business Review*, January-February 2013; Nancy Hass, "Earning Her Stripes," *The Wall Street Journal*, September 9, 2010; "Burberry Shines as Aquascutum Fades," *The Wall Street Journal*, April 17, 2010; Peter Evans, "Burberry Sales Ease from Blistering Pace," *The Wall Street Journal*, April 17, 2010; and "Burberry Case Study," Market Line, http://marketline.com.

BARRIERS TO INTERNATIONAL COMMUNICATION

International communication occurs whenever a firm uses a marketing message to sell its products in another country. The effectiveness of a firm's international communication can be jeopardized by three potentially critical variables: cultural barriers, source effects, and noise levels.

Cultural Barriers

Cultural barriers can make it difficult to communicate messages across cultures. We discussed some sources and consequences of cultural differences between nations in Chapter 4 and in the previous section of this chapter. Because of cultural differences, a message that means one thing in one country may mean something quite different in another. Benetton, the Italian clothing manufacturer and retailer, ran into cultural problems with its advertising. The company launched a worldwide advertising campaign with the theme "United Colors of Benetton" that had won awards in France. One of its ads featured a black woman breastfeeding a white baby, and another one showed a black man and a white man handcuffed together. Benetton was surprised when the ads were attacked by U.S. civil rights groups for promoting white racial domination. Benetton withdrew its ads and fired its advertising agency, Eldorado of France.

The best way for a firm to overcome cultural barriers is to develop cross-cultural literacy (see Chapter 4). In addition, it should use local input, such as a local advertising agency, in developing its marketing message. If the firm uses direct selling rather than advertising to communicate its message, it should develop a local sales force whenever possible. Cultural differences limit a firm's ability to use the same marketing message and selling approach worldwide. What works well in one country may be offensive in another.

Source and Country of Origin Effects

Source effects occur when the receiver of the message (the potential consumer in this case) evaluates the message on the basis of status or image of the sender. Source effects can be damaging for an international business when potential consumers in a target country have a bias against foreign firms. For example, a wave of "Japan bashing" swept the United States in the early 1990s. Worried that U.S. consumers might view its products negatively, Honda responded by creating ads that emphasized the U.S. content of its cars to show how "American" the company had become.

Many international businesses try to counter negative source effects by deemphasizing their foreign origins. When the French antiglobalization protester José Bové was hailed as a hero by some in France for razing a partly built McDonald's, the French franchisees of McDonald's responded with an ad depicting a fat, ignorant American who could not understand why McDonald's France used locally produced food that wasn't genetically modified. The edgy ad worked, and McDonald's French operations are now among the most robust in the company's global network.[30]

A subset of source effects is referred to as **country of origin effects**, or the extent to which the place of manufacturing influences product evaluations. Research suggests that the consumer may use country of origin as a cue when evaluating a product, particularly if he or she lacks more detailed knowledge of the product. For example, one study found that Japanese consumers tended to rate Japanese products more favorably than U.S. products across multiple dimensions, even when independent analysis showed that they were actually inferior.[31] When a negative country of origin effect exists, an international business may have to work hard to counteract this effect by, for example, using promotional messages that stress the positive performance attributes of its product.

Source effects and country of origin effects are not always negative. French wine, Italian clothes, and German luxury cars benefit from nearly universal positive source effects. In such cases, it may pay a firm to emphasize its foreign origins.

Noise Levels

Noise tends to reduce the probability of effective communication. **Noise** refers to the number of other messages competing for a potential consumer's attention, and this too varies across countries. In highly developed countries such as the United States, noise is extremely high. Fewer firms vie for the attention of prospective customers in developing countries; thus, the noise level is lower.

PUSH VERSUS PULL STRATEGIES

The main decision with regard to communications strategy is the choice between a push strategy and a pull strategy. A **push strategy** emphasizes personal selling rather than mass media advertising in the promotional mix. Although effective as a promotional tool, personal selling requires intensive use of a sales force and is relatively costly. A **pull strategy** depends more on mass media advertising to communicate the marketing message to potential consumers.

Although some firms employ only a pull strategy and others only a push strategy, still other firms combine direct selling with mass advertising to maximize communication effectiveness. Factors that determine the relative attractiveness of push and pull strategies include product type relative to consumer sophistication, channel length, and media availability.

Product Type and Consumer Sophistication

Firms in consumer goods industries that are trying to sell to a large segment of the market generally favor a pull strategy. Mass communication has cost advantages for such firms; thus, they rarely use direct selling. Exceptions can be found in poorer nations with low literacy levels, where direct selling may be the only way to reach consumers. Firms that sell industrial products or other complex products favor a push strategy. Direct selling allows the firm to educate potential consumers about the features of the product. This may not be necessary in advanced nations where a complex product has been in use for some time, where the product's attributes are well understood, where consumers are sophisticated, and where high-quality channels exist that can provide point-of-sale assistance. However, customer education may be important when consumers have less sophistication toward the product, which can be the case in developing nations or in advanced nations when a new complex product is being introduced, or where high-quality channels are absent or scarce.

Channel Length

The longer the distribution channel, the more intermediaries there are that must be persuaded to carry the product for it to reach the consumer. This can lead to inertia in the channel, which can make entry difficult. Using direct selling to push a product through many layers of a distribution channel can be expensive. In such circumstances, a firm may try to pull its product through the channels by using mass advertising to create consumer demand; once demand is created, intermediaries will feel obliged to carry the product.

In Japan, products often pass through two, three, or even four wholesalers before they reach the final retail outlet. This can make it difficult for foreign firms to break into the Japanese market. Not only must the foreign firm persuade a Japanese retailer to carry its product, but it may also have to persuade every intermediary in the chain to carry the product. Mass advertising may be one way to break down channel resistance in such circumstances. However, in countries such as India, which has a very long distribution channel to serve its massive rural population, mass advertising may not work because of low literacy levels, in which case the firm may need to fall back on direct selling or rely on the goodwill of distributors.

Media Availability

A pull strategy relies on access to advertising media. Around the world, especially the relatively developed world that includes some 80 countries, a large number of media are available, including print media (newspapers and magazines), broadcasting media (television and radio), and various forms of social media. These media options have facilitated extremely focused advertising (e.g., MTV for teens and young adults, Lifetime for women, ESPN for sports enthusiasts, and Google-targeted advertising). However, in some developing nations, the situation is more restrictive because mass media of all types are typically more limited. Consequently, a firm's ability to use a pull strategy is limited in some countries by media availability. In such circumstances, a push strategy is more attractive. For example, Unilever uses a push strategy to sell consumer products in rural India, where few mass media are available.

Media availability is limited by law in some cases. Few countries allow advertisements for tobacco and alcohol products on television and radio, though they are usually permitted in print media. When the leading Japanese whiskey distiller, Suntory, entered the U.S. market, it had to do so without television, its preferred medium. The firm spends about $50 million annually on television advertising in Japan. Similarly, while advertising pharmaceutical products directly to consumers is allowed in the United States, it is prohibited in many other advanced nations. In such cases, pharmaceutical firms must rely heavily on advertising and direct-sales efforts focused explicitly at doctors to get their products prescribed.

The Push-Pull Mix

The optimal mix between push and pull strategies depends on product type and consumer sophistication, channel length, and media sophistication. Push strategies tend to be emphasized

- For industrial products or complex new products.
- When distribution channels are short.
- When few print or social media are available.

Pull strategies tend to be emphasized

- For consumer goods.
- When distribution channels are long.
- When sufficient print and social media are available to carry the marketing message.

GLOBAL ADVERTISING

In recent years, largely inspired by the work of visionaries such as Theodore Levitt, there has been much discussion about the pros and cons of standardizing advertising worldwide.[32] One of the most successful standardized campaigns in history was Philip Morris's promotion of Marlboro cigarettes. When the brand was repositioned, the idea was to ensure smokers that Marlboro cigarettes would maintain the customary flavor. The campaign theme of "Come to where the flavor is: Come to Marlboro country" was a worldwide success some time ago. Marlboro built on this when it introduced "the Marlboro man," a rugged cowboy smoking his Marlboro while riding his horse through the great outdoors. This ad proved successful in almost every major market around the world, and it helped propel Marlboro to the top of the world market. These days, traditional cigarettes are less popular after the introduction of vaping and electronic cigarettes worldwide.

For Standardized Advertising

The support for global advertising is threefold. First, it has significant economic advantages. Standardized advertising lowers the costs of value creation by spreading the fixed costs of developing the advertisements over many countries. For example, McCann Erickson, claims to have saved Coca-Cola more than $100 million over 20 years by using certain elements of its campaigns globally.

Second, there is the concern that creative talent is scarce, so one large effort to develop a campaign will produce better results than 40 or 50 smaller efforts. A third justification for a standardized approach is that many brand names are global. With the substantial amount of international travel today and the considerable overlap in media across national borders, many international firms want to project a single brand image to avoid confusion caused by local campaigns. This is particularly important in regions such as Western Europe, where travel across borders is almost as common as travel across state lines in the United States.

Against Standardized Advertising

There are two main arguments against globally standardized advertising. First, as we have seen repeatedly in this chapter and in Chapter 4, cultural differences among nations are such that a message that works in one nation can fail miserably in another. Cultural diversity makes it extremely difficult to develop a single advertising theme that is effective worldwide. Messages directed at the culture of a given country may be more effective than global messages.

Second, advertising regulations may block implementation of standardized advertising. For example, Kellogg could not use a television commercial it produced in Great Britain to promote its cornflakes in many other European countries. A reference to the iron and vitamin content of its cornflakes was not permissible in the Netherlands, where claims relating to health and medical benefits are outlawed. A child wearing a Kellogg T-shirt had to be edited out of the commercial before it could be used in France because French law forbids the use of children in product endorsements. The key line "Kellogg's makes their cornflakes the best they have ever been" was disallowed in Germany because of a prohibition against competitive claims.[33]

Dealing with Country Differences

Some firms are experimenting with capturing some benefits of global standardization while recognizing differences in countries' cultural and legal environments. A firm may select some features to include in all its advertising campaigns and localize other features. By doing so, it may be able to save on some costs and build international brand recognition and yet customize its advertisements to different cultures.

Nokia tried to do this. Historically, Nokia had used a different advertising campaign in different markets. In 2004, however, when Nokia was still a Finnish company (Nokia was later bought by Microsoft in 2013, but for practical purposes dissolved the Nokia unit in 2016), the company launched a global advertising campaign that used the slogan "1001 reasons to have a Nokia imaging phone." Nokia did this to reduce advertising costs, capture some economies of scale, and establish a consistent global brand image. At the same time, Nokia tweaked the advertisements for different cultures. The campaign used actors from the region where the ad ran to reflect the local population, though they said the same lines. Perhaps Nokia's strategy should have been even more culturally sensitive, because it got bought up and dissolved by Microsoft, and was supplanted by the likes of Apple's iPhone and Samsung's Galaxy. Local settings were also modified when showcasing the phones by, for example, using a marketplace when advertising in Italy, or a bazaar when advertising in the Middle East.[34]

✓ TEST PREP

Use SmartBook to help retain what you have learned. Access your Instructor's Connect course to check out SmartBook or go to **learnsmartadvantage.com** for help.

LO18-5

Explain why and how a firm's pricing strategy might vary among countries.

Pricing Strategy

International pricing strategy is an important component of the overall international marketing mix.[35] This section looks at three aspects of international pricing strategy. First, we examine the case for pursuing price discrimination, charging different prices for the same product in different countries. Second, we look at what might be called strategic pricing. Third, we review regulatory factors, such as government-mandated price controls and antidumping regulations that limit a firm's ability to charge the prices it would prefer in a country.

PRICE DISCRIMINATION

Price discrimination exists whenever consumers in different countries are charged different prices for the same product or for slightly different variations of the product.[36]

Price discrimination involves charging whatever the market will bear; in a competitive market, prices may have to be lower than in a market where the firm has a monopoly. Price discrimination can help a company maximize its profits. It makes economic sense to charge different prices in different countries.

Two conditions are necessary for profitable price discrimination. First, the firm must be able to keep its national markets separate. If it cannot do this, individuals or businesses may undercut their attempt at price discrimination by engaging in arbitrage. Arbitrage occurs when an individual or business capitalizes on a price differential for a firm's product between two countries by purchasing the product in the country where prices are lower and reselling it in the country where prices are higher. For example, many automobile firms have long practiced price discrimination in Europe. A Ford Escort once cost $2,000 more in Germany than it did in Belgium. This policy broke down when car dealers bought Escorts in Belgium and drove them to Germany, where they sold them at a profit for slightly less than Ford was selling Escorts in Germany. To protect the market share of its German auto dealers, Ford had to bring its German prices into line with those being charged in Belgium. Ford could not keep these markets separate, unlike in Britain where the need for right-hand-drive cars keeps the market separate from the rest of Europe.

The second necessary condition for profitable price discrimination is different price elasticities of demand in different countries. The **price elasticity of demand** is a measure of the responsiveness of demand for a product to change in price. Demand is said to be **elastic** when a small change in price produces a large change in demand; it is said to be **inelastic** when a large change in price produces only a small change in demand. Figure 18.3 illustrates elastic and inelastic demand curves. Generally, a firm can charge a higher price in a country where demand is inelastic.

The elasticity of demand for a product in a given country is determined by a number of factors, of which income level and competitive conditions are the two most important. Price elasticity tends to be greater in countries with low income levels. Consumers with limited incomes tend to be very price conscious; they have less to spend, so they look much more closely at price. Thus, price elasticity for products such as computers is greater in countries such as India, where a computer is still a luxury item for a large portion of the population, compared to the United States, where it is now considered a necessity. The same is true of the software that resides on those computers; thus, to sell more software in India, Microsoft has had to introduce low-priced versions of its products into that market, such as Windows Starter Edition.

In general, the more competitors there are, the greater consumers' bargaining power will be and the more likely consumers will be to buy from the firm that charges the lowest

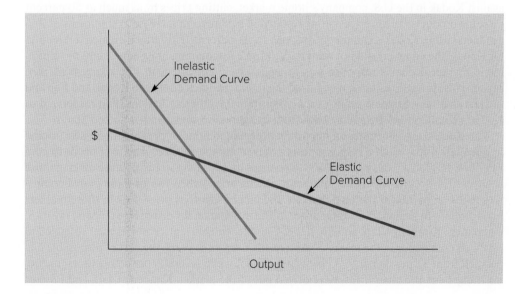

FIGURE 18.3

Elastic and inelastic demand curves.

Source: Charles W. L. Hill and G. Tomas M. Hult, *Global Business Today* (New York: McGraw-Hill, 2020).

price. Thus, many competitors cause high elasticity of demand. In such circumstances, if a firm raises its prices above those of its competitors, consumers will switch to the competitors' products. The opposite is true when a firm faces few competitors. When competitors are limited, consumers' bargaining power is weaker, and price is less important as a competitive weapon. Thus, a firm may charge a higher price for its product in a country where competition is limited than in one where competition is intense.

STRATEGIC PRICING

The concept of strategic pricing has three aspects, which we refer to as predatory pricing, multipoint pricing, and experience curve pricing. Both predatory pricing and experience curve pricing may violate antidumping regulations. After we review predatory and experience curve pricing, we will look at anti-dumping rules and other regulatory policies.

Predatory Pricing

Predatory pricing is the use of price as a competitive weapon to drive weaker competitors out of a national market. Once the competitors have left the market, the firm can raise prices and enjoy high profits. For such a pricing strategy to work, the firm must normally have a profitable position in another national market, which it can use to subsidize aggressive pricing in the market it is trying to monopolize. Historically, many Japanese firms were accused of pursuing such a policy. The argument ran like this: Because the Japanese market was protected from foreign competition by high informal trade barriers, Japanese firms could charge high prices and earn high profits at home. They then used these profits to subsidize aggressive pricing overseas, with the goal of driving competitors out of those markets. Once this had occurred, so it is claimed, the Japanese firms then raised prices. Matsushita was accused of using this strategy to enter the U.S. TV market. As one of the major TV producers in Japan, Matsushita earned high profits at home. It then used these profits to subsidize the losses it made in the United States during its early years there, when it priced low to increase its market penetration. Ultimately, Matsushita became the world's largest manufacturer of TVs.[37]

Multipoint Pricing Strategy

Multipoint pricing becomes an issue when two or more international businesses compete against each other in two or more national markets. Multipoint pricing refers to the fact that a firm's pricing strategy in one market may have an impact on its rivals' pricing strategy in another market. Aggressive pricing in one market may elicit a competitive response from a rival in another market. For example, Fuji launched an aggressive competitive attack against Kodak in the U.S. company's home market, cutting prices by as much as 50 percent on some products.[38] This price cutting resulted in a 28 percent increase in shipments of Fuji products, while Kodak's shipments dropped by 11 percent. This attack created a dilemma for Kodak: the company did not want to start price discounting in its largest and most profitable market. Kodak's response was to aggressively cut prices in Fuji's largest market, Japan. This strategic response recognized the interdependence between Kodak and Fuji and the fact that they compete against each other in many different nations. Fuji responded to Kodak's counterattack by pulling back from its aggressive stance in the United States.

The Kodak story illustrates an important aspect of multipoint pricing: Aggressive pricing in one market may elicit a response from rivals in another market. The firm needs to consider how its global rivals will respond to changes in its pricing strategy before making those changes. The second aspect of multipoint pricing arises when two or more global companies focus on particular national markets and launch vigorous price wars in those markets in an attempt to gain market dominance. In Brazil's market for disposable diapers, two U.S. companies, Kimberly-Clark and Procter & Gamble, entered a price war as each struggled to establish dominance in the market.[39] As a result, over three years, the cost of disposable diapers fell from $1 per diaper to 33 cents per diaper, while several other competitors, including indigenous Brazilian firms, were driven out of the market. Kimberly-Clark and Procter

& Gamble are engaged in a global struggle for market share and dominance, and Brazil is one of their battlegrounds. Both companies can afford to engage in this behavior, even though it reduces their profits in Brazil because they have profitable operations elsewhere in the world that can subsidize these losses.

Pricing decisions around the world need to be centrally monitored. It is tempting to delegate full responsibility for pricing decisions to the managers of various national subsidiaries, thereby reaping the benefits of decentralization. However, because pricing strategy in one part of the world can elicit a competitive response in another, central management needs to at least monitor and approve pricing decisions in a given national market, and local managers need to recognize that their actions can affect competitive conditions in other countries.

Experience Curve Pricing

We first encountered the experience curve in Chapter 17. As a firm builds its accumulated production volume over time, unit costs fall due to experience effects. Learning effects and economies of scale underlie the experience curve. Price comes into the picture because aggressive pricing (along with aggressive promotion and advertising) can build accumulated sales volume rapidly and thus move production down the experience curve. Firms farther down the experience curve have a cost advantage vis-à-vis those farther up the curve.

Many firms pursuing an experience curve pricing strategy on an international scale will price low worldwide in attempting to build global sales volume as rapidly as possible, even if this means taking large losses initially. Such a firm believes that, in several years when it has moved down the experience curve, it will be making substantial profits and have a cost advantage over its less aggressive competitors.

REGULATORY INFLUENCES ON PRICES

The ability to engage in either price discrimination or strategic pricing may be limited by national or international regulations. Most importantly, a firm's freedom to set its own prices is constrained by antidumping regulations and competition policy.

Antidumping Regulations

Both predatory pricing and experience curve pricing can run afoul of antidumping regulations. Dumping occurs whenever a firm sells a product for a price that is less than the cost of producing it. Most regulations, however, define dumping more vaguely. For example, a country is allowed to bring antidumping actions against an importer under Article 6 of GATT, as long as two criteria are met: sales at "less than fair value" and "material injury to a domestic industry." The problem with this terminology is that it does not indicate what a fair value is. The ambiguity has led some to argue that selling abroad at prices below those in the country of origin, as opposed to below cost, is dumping.

Antidumping rules set a floor under export prices and limit firms' ability to pursue strategic pricing. The rather vague terminology used in most antidumping actions suggests that a firm's ability to engage in price discrimination also may be challenged under antidumping legislation.

Competition Policy

Most developed nations have regulations designed to promote competition and to restrict monopoly practices. These regulations can be used to limit the prices a firm can charge in a given country. For example, at one time, the Swiss pharmaceutical manufacturer, Hoffmann-La Roche, had a monopoly on the supply of Valium and Librium tranquilizers. The company was investigated by the British Monopolies and Mergers Commission, which is responsible for promoting fair competition in Great Britain. The commission found that Hoffmann-La Roche was overcharging for its tranquilizers and ordered the company to reduce its prices 50 to 60 percent and repay excess profit of $30 million. Hoffmann-La Roche maintained unsuccessfully that it was merely engaging in price discrimination. Similar actions were later brought against Hoffmann-La Roche by the German cartel office and by the Dutch and Danish governments.[40]

Configuring the Marketing Mix

A firm might vary aspects of its marketing mix from country to country to consider local differences in culture, economic conditions, competitive conditions, product and technical standards, distribution systems, government regulations, and the like. Such differences may require variation in product attributes, distribution strategy, communication strategy, and pricing strategy.

The cumulative effect of these factors made it rare that a firm would adopt the same marketing mix worldwide just a few years ago, and it holds true in many cases still. But we are also seeing a new generation of customers—younger customers—worldwide who appear more and more willing to engage in a "global" way in what they want, need, and use in their daily lives.

The movie industry and the financial services industry are often thought of as industries in which global standardization of the marketing mix is the norm. A financial services company such as American Express sells the same basic charge card service worldwide, utilizes the same basic fee structure for that product, and adopts the same basic global advertising message ("Don't leave home without it"). That said, Amex also runs into differences in national regulations, which means that it still has to vary aspects of its communication strategy from country to country.

Similarly, while McDonald's is often thought of as the quintessential example of a firm that sells the same basic standardized product worldwide, in reality, it varies one important aspect of its marketing mix—its menu—from country to country. McDonald's also varies its distribution strategy. In Canada and the United States, most McDonald's are located in areas that are easily accessible by car, whereas in more densely populated and less automobile-reliant societies of the world, such as Japan and Great Britain, location decisions are driven by the accessibility of a restaurant to pedestrian traffic. Because countries typically still differ along one or more of the dimensions discussed earlier, some customization of the marketing mix is normal.

Basically, there are significant opportunities for standardization along one or more elements of the marketing mix.[41] Firms may find that it is possible and desirable to standardize their global advertising message or core product attributes to realize substantial cost economies. They may find it desirable to customize their distribution and pricing strategy to take advantage of local differences. In reality, the "customization versus standardization" debate is not an all-or-nothing issue; it frequently makes sense to standardize some aspects of the marketing mix and customize others, depending on conditions in various national marketplaces.

Table 18.1 illustrates issues that should be evaluated to assess how standardized or customized the marketing mix needs to be for various international market segments. Keep in mind that a truly "globalized" product—a product that is 100 percent standardized across worldwide markets—is generally an illusion, but companies can come close by leveraging certain marketing mix attributes and customizing others.

✓ **TEST PREP**

Use SmartBook to help retain what you have learned. Access your Instructor's Connect course to check out SmartBook or go to **learnsmartadvantage.com** for help.

Product Development and R&D

So far in this chapter, we have discussed several issues related to globalization of markets and brands, business analytics and international market research, characteristics of the marketing mix (product attributes, distribution strategy, communication strategy, and pricing strategy), and configuring the marketing mix. These issues represent the core of this chapter's discussion of international marketing and R&D. However, firms that successfully develop and market new products can earn enormous returns, and this final section of the chapter addresses the interplay among international marketing, R&D, and manufacturing.

Examples of firms that have been very successful at mastering the interplay among international marketing, R&D, and manufacturing include DuPont, which has produced a steady stream of successful innovations such as cellophane, nylon, Freon, and Teflon (non-stick coating); Sony, whose successes include PlayStation and Blu-ray; Pfizer, the drug company that developed Viagra; 3M, which has applied its core competency in tapes and adhesives to developing a wide range of new products; Intel, which has consistently managed to lead in the development of innovative microprocessors to run personal computers; and Apple, with its string of hits, including the iPod, iPhone, and iPad. These and other success stories warrant a specific focus. We draw on the material up to this point in the chapter and combine it with the global production material in Chapter 17 to illustrate this interplay of marketing, R&D, and manufacturing.

In today's world, competition is as much about technological innovation as anything else. The pace of technological change has accelerated since the Industrial Revolution in the eighteenth century, and it continues to do so today. The result has been a dramatic shortening of product life cycles. Technological innovation is both creative and destructive.[42] An innovation can make established products obsolete overnight. But an innovation can also make a host of new products possible. Witness changes in the electronics industry. For 40 years before the early 1950s, vacuum tubes were a major component in radios and then in record players and early computers. The advent of transistors destroyed the market for vacuum tubes, but at the same time, it created new opportunities connected with transistors. Transistors took up far less space than vacuum tubes, creating a trend toward miniaturization that continues today. The transistor held its position as the major component in the electronics industry for just a decade. Microprocessors were developed in the 1970s, and the market for transistors declined rapidly. The microprocessor created yet another set of new-product opportunities: handheld calculators (which destroyed the market for slide rules), compact disc players (which destroyed the market for analog record players), personal computers (which destroyed the market for typewriters), and smartphones (which are making landline phones and some computer gadgets obsolete).

This "creative destruction" unleashed by technological change makes it critical that a firm stays on the leading edge of technology, lest it lose out to a competitor's innovations. As explained next, this not only creates a need for the firm to invest in R&D, but also requires the firm to establish R&D activities at those locations where expertise is concentrated. As we shall see, leading-edge technology on its own is not enough to guarantee a firm's survival. The firm must also apply that technology to developing products that satisfy consumer needs, and it must design the product so that it can be manufactured in a cost-effective manner. To do that, the firm needs to build close links among R&D, marketing, and manufacturing. This is difficult enough for the domestic firm, but it is even more problematic for the international business competing in an industry where consumer tastes and preferences differ from country to country.[43] With all of this in mind, we move on to examine locating R&D activities and building links among R&D, marketing, and manufacturing.

THE LOCATION OF R&D

Ideas for new products are stimulated by the interactions of scientific research, demand conditions, and competitive conditions. Other things being equal, the rate of new-product development seems to be greater in countries where

- More money is spent on basic and applied research and development.
- Underlying demand is strong.
- Consumers are affluent.
- Competition is intense.[44]

Basic and applied research and development discovers new technologies and then commercializes them. Strong demand and affluent consumers create a potential market for new products. Intense competition among firms stimulates innovation as the firms try to beat their competitors and reap potentially enormous first-mover advantages that result from successful innovation.

For most of the post–World War II period, the country that ranked highest on these criteria was the United States. The United States devoted a greater proportion of its gross domestic product to R&D than any other country did. Its scientific establishment was the largest and most active in the world. U.S. consumers were the most affluent, the market was large, and competition among U.S. firms was brisk. Due to these factors, the United States was the market where most new products were developed and introduced. Accordingly, it was the best location for R&D activities; it was where the action was.

Over the past 25 years, things have been changing quickly. The U.S. monopoly on new-product development has weakened considerably. Although U.S. firms are still at the leading edge of many new technologies, Asian and European firms are also strong players. Companies such as Sony, Sharp, Samsung, Ericsson, Nokia, and Philips have often driven product innovation in their respective industries. In addition, Japan, the European Union, and increasingly parts of China and other developing nations are large, affluent markets, and the wealth gap between them and the United States is closing.

As a result, it is often no longer appropriate to consider the United States as the lead market. In video games, for example, Japan is often the lead market, with companies such as Sony and Nintendo introducing their latest video-game players in Japan some six months before they introduce them in the United States. However, it often is questionable whether any developed nation can be considered the lead market. To succeed in today's high-technology industries, it is often necessary to simultaneously introduce new products in all major industrialized markets. When Intel introduces a new microprocessor, for example, it does not first introduce it in the United States and then roll it out in Europe a year later. It introduces it simultaneously around the world. The same is true of Microsoft with new versions of its Windows operating system or Samsung with a new smartphone.

Because leading-edge research is now carried out in many locations around the world, the argument for centralizing R&D activity in the United States is not as strong as it was three decades ago. (It used to be argued that centralized R&D eliminated duplication.) Much leading-edge research is now occurring in Asia and Europe. Dispersing R&D activities to those locations allows a firm to stay close to the center of leading-edge activity to gather scientific and competitive information and to draw on local scientific resources.[45] This may result in some duplication of R&D activities, but the cost disadvantages of duplication are outweighed by the advantages of dispersion.

For example, to expose themselves to the research and new-product development work being done in Japan, many U.S. firms have set up satellite R&D centers in Japan. U.S. firms that have established R&D facilities in Japan include Corning, IBM, Procter & Gamble, Pfizer, DuPont, Monsanto, and Microsoft.[46] The National Science Foundation (NSF) has documented a sharp increase in the proportion of total R&D spending by U.S. firms that is now done abroad.[47] For example, Bristol-Myers Squibb has 12 facilities in five countries. At the same time, to internationalize their own research and gain access to U.S. talent, many European and Asian firms are investing in U.S.-based research facilities, according to the NSF.

INTEGRATING R&D, MARKETING, AND PRODUCTION

Although a firm that is successful at developing new products may earn enormous returns, new-product development has a high failure rate. One study of product development in 16 companies in the chemical, drug, petroleum, and electronics industries suggested that only about 20 percent of R&D projects result in commercially successful products or processes.[48] Another in-depth case study of product development in three companies (one in chemicals and two in drugs) reported that about 60 percent of R&D projects reached technical completion, 30 percent were commercialized, and only 12 percent earned an economic profit that exceeded the company's cost of capital.[49] Along the same lines, another study concluded that one in nine major R&D projects, or about 11 percent, produced commercially successful products.[50] In sum, the evidence suggests that only 10 to 20 percent of major R&D projects give rise to commercially successful products.

The reasons for such high failure rates are various and include development of a technology for which demand is limited, failure to adequately commercialize promising technology, and inability to manufacture a new product cost effectively. Firms can reduce the probability of making such mistakes by insisting on tight cross-functional coordination and integration among three core functions involved in the development of new products: R&D, marketing, and production.[51] Tight cross-functional integration among R&D, production, and marketing can help a company ensure that

1. Product development projects are driven by customer needs.
2. New products are designed for ease of manufacture.
3. Development costs are kept in check.
4. Time to market is minimized.

Close integration between R&D and marketing is required to ensure that product development projects are driven by the needs of customers. A company's customers can be a primary source of new-product ideas. Identification of customer needs, particularly unmet needs, can set the context within which successful product innovation occurs. As the point of contact with customers, the marketing function of a company can provide valuable information in this regard. Integration of R&D and marketing is crucial if a new product is to be properly commercialized. Without integration of R&D and marketing, a company runs the risk of developing products for which there is little or no demand.

Integration between R&D and production can help a company design products with manufacturing requirements in mind. Designing for manufacturing can lower costs and increase product quality. Integrating R&D and production can also help lower development costs and speed products to market. If a new product is not designed with manufacturing capabilities in mind, it may prove too difficult to build. Then the product will have to be redesigned, and both overall development costs and the time it takes to bring the product to market may increase significantly. Making design changes during product planning could increase overall development costs by 50 percent and add 25 percent to the time it takes to bring the product to market.[52] Many quantum product innovations require new processes to manufacture them, which makes it all the more important to achieve close integration between R&D and production. Minimizing time to market and development costs may require the simultaneous development of new products and new processes.[53]

CROSS-FUNCTIONAL TEAMS

One way to achieve cross-functional integration is to establish cross-functional product development teams composed of representatives from R&D, marketing, and production.[54] Because these functions may be located in different countries, the team will sometimes have a multinational membership. The objective of a team should be to take a product development project from the initial concept development to market introduction. A number of attributes seem to be important for a product development team to function effectively and meet all its development milestones.[55]

First, the team should be led by a "heavyweight" project manager who has high status within the organization and who has the power and authority required to get the financial and human resources the team needs to succeed. The leader should be dedicated primarily, if not entirely, to the project. He or she should be someone who believes in the project (a champion) and who is skilled at integrating the perspectives of different functions and at helping personnel from different functions and countries work together for a common goal. The leader should also be able to act as an advocate of the team to senior management.

Second, the team should be composed of at least one member from each key function. The team members should have a number of attributes, including an ability to contribute functional expertise, high standing within their function, a willingness to share responsibility for team results, and an ability to put functional and national advocacy aside. It is generally preferable if core team members are 100 percent dedicated to the project for its duration. This ensures their focus on the project, not on the ongoing work of their function.

Third, the team members should physically be in one location if possible to create a sense of camaraderie and to facilitate communication. This presents problems if the team members are drawn from facilities in different nations. One solution is to transfer key individuals to one location for the duration of a product development project.

Fourth, the team should have a clear plan and clear goals, particularly with regard to critical development milestones and development budgets. The team should have incentives to attain those goals, such as receiving pay bonuses when major development milestones are hit.

Fifth, each team needs to develop its own processes for communication and conflict resolution. For example, one product development team at Quantum Corporation, a California-based manufacturer of hard drives for personal computers, instituted a rule that all major decisions would be made and conflicts resolved at meetings that were held every Monday afternoon. This simple rule helped the team meet its development goals. In this case, it was also common for team members to fly in from Japan, where the product was to be manufactured, to the U.S. development center for the Monday morning meetings.[56]

BUILDING GLOBAL R&D CAPABILITIES

The need to integrate R&D and marketing to adequately commercialize new technologies poses special problems in the international business because commercialization may require different versions of a new product to be produced for various countries.[57] To do this, the firm must build close links between its R&D centers and its various country operations. A similar argument applies to the need to integrate R&D and production, particularly in those international businesses that have dispersed production activities to different locations around the globe in consideration of relative factor costs and the like.

Integrating R&D, marketing, and production in an international business may require R&D centers in North America, Asia, and Europe that are linked by formal and informal integrating mechanisms with marketing operations in each country in their regions and with the various manufacturing facilities. In addition, the international business may have to establish cross-functional teams whose members are dispersed around the globe. This complex endeavor requires the company to utilize formal and informal integrating mechanisms to knit its far-flung operations together so they can produce new products in an effective and timely manner.

While there is no one best model for allocating product development responsibilities to various centers, one solution adopted by many international businesses involves establishing a global network of R&D centers. Within this model, fundamental research is undertaken at basic research centers around the globe. These centers are normally located in regions or cities where valuable scientific knowledge is being created and where there is a pool of skilled research talent (e.g., Silicon Valley in the United States, Cambridge in England, Kobe in Japan, Singapore). These centers are the innovation engines of the firm. Their job is to develop the basic technologies that become new products.

These technologies are picked up by R&D units attached to global product divisions and are used to generate new products to serve the global marketplace. At this level, commercialization of the technology and design for manufacturing are emphasized. If further customization is needed so the product appeals to the tastes and preferences of consumers in individual markets, such redesign work will be done by an R&D group based in a subsidiary in that country or at a regional center that customizes products for several countries in the region.

Hewlett-Packard has seven basic research centers located in Palo Alto, California; Bristol, England; Haifa, Israel; Beijing, China; Singapore; Bangalore, India; and St. Petersburg, Russia.[58] These labs are the seedbed for technologies that ultimately become new products and businesses. They are the company's innovation engines. The Palo Alto center, for

John Maltabes, research engineer at Hewlett-Packard, takes out a thin flexible electronic display that has etched resistors and uses self-aligned imprint lithography technology for testing at Hewlett-Packard Laboratories.

Tony Avelar/The Christian Science Monitor/Getty Images

example, pioneered HP's thermal ink-jet technology. The products are developed by R&D centers associated with HP's global product divisions. Thus, HP's Consumer Products Group, which has its worldwide headquarters in San Diego, California, designs, develops, and manufactures a range of imaging products using HP-pioneered thermal ink-jet technology. Subsidiaries might then customize the product so that it best matches the needs of important national markets. HP's subsidiary in Singapore, for example, is responsible for the design and production of thermal ink-jet printers for Japan and other Asian markets. This subsidiary takes products originally developed in San Diego and redesigns them for the Asian market. In addition, the Singapore subsidiary has taken the lead from San Diego in the design and development of certain portable thermal ink-jet printers. HP delegated this responsibility to Singapore because this subsidiary has acquired important competencies in the design and production of thermal ink-jet products, so it has become the best place in the world to undertake this activity.

 TEST PREP

Use SmartBook to help retain what you have learned. Access your Instructor's Connect course to check out SmartBook or go to **learnsmartadvantage.com** for help.

Key Terms

marketing mix, p. 531
market segmentation, p. 533
intermarket segment, p. 533
business analytics, p. 535
big data, p. 535
international market
    research, p. 536
concentrated retail system, p. 542
fragmented retail system, p. 542

channel length, p. 543
exclusive distribution
    channel, p. 544
channel quality, p. 544
social media, p. 545
source effects, p. 547
country of origin effects, p. 547
noise, p. 548
push strategy, p. 548

pull strategy, p. 548
price elasticity of demand, p. 551
elastic, p. 551
inelastic, p. 551
strategic pricing, p. 552
predatory pricing, p. 552
multipoint pricing, p. 552
experience curve pricing, p. 553

SUMMARY

This chapter discussed the marketing, business analytics, and R&D functions in international business. A persistent theme of the chapter is the tension that exists between the need to reduce costs and the need to be responsive to local conditions, which raises costs. The chapter made the following points:

1. Theodore Levitt argued that due to the advent of modern communications and transport technologies, consumer tastes and preferences are becoming global, which is creating global markets for standardized consumer products. However, this position is regarded as extreme by many experts, who argue that substantial differences still exist between customers from different countries and cultures.

2. Market segmentation refers to the process of identifying distinct groups of consumers whose needs, wants, and purchasing behavior differs from each other in important ways. Managers in an international business need to be aware of two main issues relating to segmentation: the extent to which there are differences between countries in the structure of market segments and the existence of segments that transcend national borders (i.e., intermarket segments).

3. In the context of companies focusing on the global marketplace as their current or potential market to target customers, business analytics can be defined as the knowledge, skills, and technology that allow for the exploration as well as deeper investigation of a company's international business strategies and activities to gain insight and drive future strategy development and implementation.

4. A product can be viewed as a bundle of attributes. Product attributes often need to be varied from country to country to satisfy different consumer tastes and preferences.

5. Country differences in consumer tastes and preferences are due to differences in culture and economic development. In addition, differences in product and technical standards may require the firm to customize product attributes from country to country.

6. A distribution strategy decision is an attempt to define the optimal channel for delivering a product to the consumer. In the global supply chain, the marketing channel is a part of the downstream (also called outbound) portion of the supply chain (refer to Chapter 15).

7. Significant country differences exist in distribution systems. In some countries, the retail system is concentrated; in others, it is fragmented. In some countries, channel length is short; in others, it is long. Access to distribution channels is difficult to achieve in some countries, and the quality of the channel may be poor, especially in less developed nations.

8. A critical element in the marketing mix is communication strategy, which defines the process the firm will use in communicating the attributes of its product to prospective customers.

9. Barriers to international communication include cultural differences, source effects, and noise levels.

10. A communication strategy is either a push strategy or a pull strategy. A push strategy emphasizes personal selling, and a pull strategy emphasizes mass media advertising. Whether a push strategy or a pull strategy is optimal depends on the type of product, consumer sophistication, channel length, and media availability.

11. A globally standardized advertising campaign, which uses the same marketing message all over the world, has economic advantages, but it fails to account for differences in culture and advertising regulations.

12. Price discrimination exists when consumers in different countries are charged different prices for the same product. Price discrimination can help a firm maximize its profits. For price discrimination to be effective, the national markets must be separate and their price elasticities of demand must differ.

13. Predatory pricing is the use of profit gained in one market to support aggressive pricing in another market to drive competitors out of that market.

14. Multipoint pricing refers to the fact that a firm's pricing strategy in one market may affect rivals' pricing strategies in another market. Aggressive pricing in one market may elicit a competitive response from a rival in another market that is important to the firm.

15. Experience curve pricing is the use of aggressive pricing to build accumulated volume as rapidly as possible to quickly move the firm down the experience curve.

16. International market research involves (*a*) defining the research objectives, (*b*) determining the

data sources, (c) assessing the costs and benefits of the research, (d) collecting the data, (e) analyzing and interpreting the research, and (f) reporting the research findings.

17. New-product development is a high-risk, potentially high-return activity. To build competency in new-product development, an international

business must do two things: disperse R&D activities to those countries where new products are being pioneered and integrate R&D with marketing and manufacturing.

18. Achieving tight integration among R&D, marketing, and manufacturing requires the use of cross-functional teams.

Critical Thinking and Discussion Questions

1. Imagine that you are the marketing manager for a U.S. manufacturer of disposable diapers. Your firm is considering entering the Brazilian market. Your CEO believes the advertising message that has been effective in the United States will suffice in Brazil. Outline some possible objections to this. Your CEO also believes that the pricing decisions in Brazil can be delegated to local managers. Why might she be wrong?

2. Within 20 years, we will have seen the emergence of enormous global markets for standardized consumer products. Do you agree with this statement? Justify your answer.

3. You are the marketing manager of a food products company that is considering entering the Indian market. The retail system in India tends to be very fragmented. Also, retailers and wholesalers tend to have long-term ties with Indian food companies; these ties make access to distribution channels difficult. What distribution strategy would you advise the company to pursue? Why?

4. Price discrimination is indistinguishable from dumping. Discuss the accuracy of this statement.

5. You work for a company that designs and manufactures personal computers. Your company's R&D center is in Michigan. The computers are manufactured under contract in Taiwan. Marketing strategy is delegated to the heads of three regional groups: a North American group (based in Chicago), a European group (based in Paris), and an Asian group (based in Singapore). Each regional group develops the marketing approach within its region. In order of importance, the largest markets for your products are North America, Germany, Great Britain, China, and Australia. Your company is experiencing problems in its product development and commercialization process. Products are late to market, the manufacturing quality is poor, costs are higher than projected, and market acceptance of new products is less than hoped for. What might be the source of these problems? How would you fix them?

globalEDGE research task   globaledge.msu.edu

Use the globalEDGE™ website (**globaledge.msu.edu**) to complete the following exercises:

1. The consumer purchase of specific brands is an indication of the relationship that develops over time between a company and its customers. Locate and retrieve the most current ranking of *best global brands*. Identify the criteria used. Which countries appear to dominate the top 100 global brands list? Why do you think this is the case? Now, look at which sectors appear to dominate the list, and try to identify the reasons. Prepare a short report identifying the countries that possess global brands and the potential reasons for success.

2. Part of developing a long-term R&D strategy is to locate facilities in countries that are widely known to be competitive. Your company seeks to develop R&D facilities in Asia to counter recent competitor responses. A publication that evaluates economies based on their competitiveness is the *Global Competitiveness Report*. Locate this report, and develop a presentation for the top management team that presents the benefits and drawbacks for the top five Asian economies listed.

CLOSING CASE

Fake News and Alternative Facts

Advertising is an important part of marketing, but mass advertising, which is generally despised by many people around the world, is more and more becoming an ancient way of doing business. Today, with big data, business analytics, and much more sophisticated international marketing research, customization of advertisements in line with a company's marketing mix is becoming a must for most multinational corporations. That is not to say that you will not get the customary phone call about supporting some cause you are not interested in, or that an advertisement during a prime-time TV show will be for a product you want. Some level of mass marketing will most likely always exist as a form of spreading the word and building buzz in the marketplace, engaging people who have not been identified (yet) as within the company's prime target market, or simply trying to sell more products via the old adage that advertising leads to sales.

But we as customers expect more: The least that companies can do is understand our wants and needs and gear advertisements toward us appropriately. In such cases, these are also not really advertisements—they are a form of messaging that informs us of opportunities we had not yet considered. This is one of the strategic elements of Facebook, for example. Today, more than two billion people use Facebook on a monthly basis. Companies around the world can target just the right segment of those two billion Facebook users with advertisements in people's newsfeeds based on interests and characteristics that are likely to be important and/or similar to existing or potential customers (e.g., demographics, interests, and behaviors). This is targeted global messaging with a much higher probability of customer action than traditional advertising.

While targeted, customized ads seem like they should be preferred over mass advertisements that often annoy people, these customized ads by Facebook and Google, as heavyweights in this space, also annoy customers! Interestingly, Mark Zuckerberg's former pollster at Facebook, Tavis McGinn, concluded based on a survey that Facebook is having a negative impact on the global society. In effect, customers want companies marketing to them to know who they are and what they may potentially want and need, but they don't want companies to be too intrusive into their personal life. This is a gigantic challenge that has put Facebook in a negative light. As the founder of Facebook, Zuckerberg clearly set out to collect "big data" on everyone interacting in some way with Facebook and even those who are nonusers.

Amazingly, Facebook with all its sophisticated technology and user tracking got caught off guard in the rollout of the fake news and alternative facts debacle that became pronounced in the 2016 U.S. presidential election and also in the mid-term elections in 2018. Organizations—in particular, political action organizations—used Facebook for fake news distribution about political competitors (e.g., Donald Trump vs. Hillary Clinton) and political referendums (e.g., the United Kingdom leaving the European Union—i.e., Brexit). Facebook's solution apparently is to reduce the visual prominence of feed stories that are fact-checked as false by third-party fact-checkers instead of editorializing those stories by removing them from the Facebook newsfeeds. Clearly, the editorializing/removal would constitute a form of censoring, but if the information is deemed to be inaccurate, what obligation should Facebook have to mark such postings as false and/or remove them altogether?

That people and organizations are using alternative facts when they don't like or agree with real news based on real data and information is surely problematic. Proponents of "alternative facts" say that it is a way to provide additional facts and information, while opponents, of course, say that alternative facts are simply lies and inaccurate information. Most people would argue that information and data should be presented in an accurate, trustworthy, and correct manner, and there is really no middle ground. Interestingly, that is not the crux of the debate. The focus is instead on interpreting the truth of the data and information—the key word being "interpretation." Apparently, everything is open to interpretation. If there is even a tiny sliver of a chance that a piece of data or information is not trustworthy and accurate, a portion of the populace will interpret the data or information as inaccurate if they dislike it (97 percent of the world's climate scientists agree that global warming is real, but people still cannot totally agree that it is!).

The prevalence of "fake news" and "alternative facts," whatever your opinion of them, creates a conundrum for global marketing professionals and companies marketing globally. For now, what is real news or not is in the eye of the beholder. What is promotional or trustworthy for one customer may be viewed as an opinionated viewpoint or a downright false claim by another in this overheated atmosphere, where general mistrust prevails. Clearly, fake news is not new and did not start in 2016, even though the term was popularized at that time. Companies can leverage big data, business analytics, and international marketing research today in sophisticated ways that potentially should be good for society and useful to the consumer. But the temptation to make fake news is a troublesome development abetted by technology—at least as long as (some) people believe the storyline.

Sources: Rani Molla and Kurt Wagner, "Many Believe Facebook Is Having a Negative Impact on Society around the World," *Recode*, April 12, 2018; Thuy Ong, "Facebook Is Shrinking Fake News Posts in the News Feed," *The Verge*, April 30, 2018; "Scientists Agree: Global Warming is Happening and Humans Are the Primary Cause," Union of Concerned Scientists, January 9, 2018; "Demand for Lies and Misinformation Encourages Media Organizations to Provide Them," *The Economist*, April 5, 2018; and "Fake News: You Ain't Seen Nothing Yet," *The Economist*, July 1, 2017.

Case Discussion Questions

1. Should it be the responsibility of news media and social media organizations like Facebook, Twitter, Instagram, and LinkedIn to monitor fake news, or should it be up to consumers to interpret the messages?

2. Most people would argue that information and data should be presented in an accurate, trustworthy, and correct manner. The focus is instead on interpreting the truth of the data and information. Can we trust people to correctly interpret the information flowing on social media and in media in general? Why or why not?

3. If we do not trust people to interpret the messaging and information on social media, who should be monitoring that information and whether it is true or not? Can we develop a system to monitor fake news? What about alternative facts? If 97 percent of the world's climate scientists say global warming is real, is that a high enough percentage to say that global warming is real?

Design elements: Modern textured halftone: ©VIPRESIONA/ Shutterstock; globalEDGE icon: ©globalEDGE; All others: ©McGraw-Hill Education

Endnotes

1. See R. W. Ruekert and O. C. Walker, "Interactions between Marketing and R&D Departments in Implementing Different Business-Level Strategies," *Strategic Management Journal* 8 (1987), pp. 233–48; and K. B. Clark and S. C. Wheelwright, *Managing New Product and Process Development* (New York: Free Press, 1993).

2. Levitt, Theodore. "The Globalization of Markets." *Harvard Business Review* (May–June 1983): 92-102. https://hbr.org/1983/05/the-globalization-of-markets.

3. For example, see S. P. Douglas and Y. Wind, "The Myth of Globalization," *Columbia Journal of World Business*, Winter 1987, pp. 19-29; C. A. Bartlett and S. Ghoshal, *Managing across Borders: The Transnational Solution* (Boston: Harvard Business School Press, 1989); V. J. Govindarajan and A. K. Gupta, *The Quest for Global Dominance* (San Francisco: Jossey-Bass, 2001); J. Quelch, "The Return of the Global Brand," *Harvard Business Review*, August 2003, pp. 1-3; and P. J. Ghemawat, *Redefining Global Strategy* (Boston: Harvard Business School Press, 2007).

4. J. Tagliabue, "U.S. Brands Are Feeling Global Tension," *The New York Times*, March 15, 2003, p. C3.

5. D. B. Holt, J. A. Quelch, and E. L. Taylor, "How Global Brands Compete," *Harvard Business Review*, September 2004.

6. Bertel Schmitt, "It's Official: Volkswagen Is World's Largest Automaker In 2016. Or Maybe Toyota," *Forbes*, January 30, 2017.

7. Brian R. Chabowski, Samiee Saeed, and G. Tomas M. Hult "A Bibliometric Analysis of the Global Branding Literature and a Research Agenda," *Journal of International Business Studies* 44, no. 6(2013), pp. 622-34.

8. J. T. Landry, "Emerging Markets: Are Chinese Consumers Coming of Age?" *Harvard Business Review*, May–June 1998, pp. 17-20.

9. C. Miller, "Teens Seen as the First Truly Global Consumers," *Marketing News*, March 27, 1995, p. 9.

10. Michael Giebelhausen, Helen Chun HaeEun J. Joseph Cronin Jr., and G. Tomas M. Hult, "Adjusting the Warm Glow Thermostat: How Incentivizing Participation in Voluntary Green Programs Moderates Their Impact on Service Satisfaction," *Journal of Marketing* 80, no. 4 (2016), pp. 56-71.

11. Claes Fornell, Forrest V. Morgeson III, and G. Tomas M. Hult, "Stock Returns on Customer Satisfaction Do Beat the Market: Gauging the Effect of a Marketing Intangible" *Journal of Marketing* 80, no. 5 (2016), pp. 92-107.

12. Austen Hufford, "Nielsen Revenue Up, But Profit Slips," *The Wall Street Journal*, February 9, 2017.

13. About Us. The Nielsen Company (US), LLC. www.nielsen.com.

14. For full disclosure, G. Tomas M. Hult, who is an author on this text, holds the John William Byington Endowed Chair in Global Marketing. J. W. Byington was a former president of the NPD Group Worldwide Inc.

15. We summarized the basic steps in the international market research process. Detailed discussions of similar processes can be found in P. Cateora, M. Gilly, and J. Graham, *International Marketing* (New York: McGraw-Hill, 2013); V. Kumar, *International Marketing Research* (Upper Saddle River, NJ: Pearson Prentice Hall, 2000); and C. S. Craig and S. P. Douglas, *International Marketing Research* (West Sussex, UK: Wiley, 2005).

16. B. Pedersen, T. Pedersen, and M. Lyles, "Closing the Knowledge Gaps in Foreign Markets," *Journal of International Business Studies* 39 (2008), pp. 1097-13.

17. Quoted in P. Ziobro, "Mattel Takes a Hit as Barbie Sales Slump," *The Wall Street Journal*, January 31, 2014.

18. Kumar, *International Marketing Research*; and Craig and Douglas, *International Marketing Research*.

19. A-W. Harzing, "Response Rates in International Mail Surveys: Results of a 22-Country Study," *International Business Review* 6 (1997), pp. 641-65.

20. Kumar, *International Marketing Research*; Craig and Douglas, *International Marketing Research*; J. Hair, W. Black, B. Babin, and R. Anderson, *Multivariate Data Analysis* (Upper Saddle River, NJ: Pearson Prentice Hall, 2010); andJ. Hair, T. Hult, C. Ringle, and M. Sarstedt, *A Primer on Partial Least Squares Structural Equation Modeling (PLS-SEM)* (Los Angeles, CA: Sage, 2014).

21. Joseph F. Hair Jr., G. Tomas M. Hult, Christian Ringle, and Marko Sarstedt, *A Primer on Partial Least Squares Structural Equation Modeling (PLS-SEM)*, 2nd ed. (Newbury Park, CA: Sage, 2017).

22. N. Bunkley, "Toyota Issues a 2nd Recall," *The New York Times*, January 21, 2010.

23. This approach was originally developed in K. Lancaster, "A New Approach to Demand Theory," *Journal of Political Economy* 74 (1965), pp. 132-57.

24. Vassiliki Bamiatzi, Konstantinos Bozos, S. Tamer Cavusgil, and G. Tomas M. Hult, "Revisiting the Firm, Industry and Country Effects on Profitability under Recessionary and Expansion Periods: A Multi-Level Analysis," *Strategic Management Journal* 37, no. 7 (2016), pp. 1448-71.

25. Tatiana Kostova and G. Tomas M. Hult, "Meyer and Peng's 2005 Article as a Foundation for an Expanded and Refined International Business Research Agenda: Context, Organizations, and Theories," *Journal of International Business Studies* 47, no. 1 (2016), pp. 23-32.

26. V. R. Alden, "Who Says You Can't Crack Japanese Markets?" *Harvard Business Review*, January–February 1987, pp. 52-56.

27. G. Tomas M. Hult, Forrest V. Morgeson III, Neil A. Morgan, Sunil Mithas, and Claes Fornell, "Do Firms Know What Their Customers Think and Why?" *Journal of the Academy of Marketing Science* 45, no. 1 (2017), pp. 37-54.

28. Amelia Josephson, "The Economics of Video Streaming Services," *Smart Asset*, January 8, 2016.

29. Tomas Hult, David Closs, and David Frayer, *Global Supply Chain Management: Leveraging Processes, Measurements, and Tools for Strategic Corporate Advantage* (New York: McGraw-Hill Professional, 2014).

30. C. Matlack and P. Gogoi, "What's This? The French Love McDonald's?" *BusinessWeek*, January 13, 2003, pp. 50-51.

31. Z. Gurhan-Cvanli and D. Maheswaran, "Cultural Variation in Country of Origin Effects," *Journal of Marketing Research*, August 2000, pp. 309-17.

32. See M. Laroche, V. H. Kirpalani, F. Pons, and L. Zhou, "A Model of Advertising Standardization in Multinational Corporations," *Journal of International Business Studies* 32 (2001), pp. 249-66; and D. A. Aaker and E. Joachimsthaler, "The Lure of Global Branding," *Harvard Business Review*, November–December 1999, pp. 137-44.

33. "Advertising in a Single Market," *The Economist*, March 24, 1990, p. 64.

34. R. G. Matthews and D. Pringle, "Nokia Bets One Global Message Will Ring True in Many Markets," *The Wall Street Journal*, September 27, 2004, p. B6.

35. R. J. Dolan and H. Simon, *Power Pricing* (New York: Free Press, 1999).

36. B. Stottinger, "Strategic Export Pricing: A Long Winding Road," *Journal of International Marketing* 9 (2001), pp. 40-63; S. Gil-Pareja, "Export Process Discrimination in Europe and Exchange Rates," *Review of International Economics*, May 2002, pp. 299-312; and G. Corsetti and L. Dedola, "A Macro Economic Model of International Price Discrimination," *Journal of International Economics*, September 2005, pp. 129-40.

37. These allegations were made on a PBS *Frontline* documentary telecast in the United States in May 1992.

38. G. Smith and B. Wolverton, "A Dark Moment for Kodak," *BusinessWeek*, August 4, 1997, pp. 30-31.

39. R. Narisette and J. Friedland, "Disposable Income: Diaper Wars of P&G and Kimberly-Clark Now Heat Up in Brazil," *The Wall Street Journal*, June 4, 1997, p. A1.

40. J. F. Pickering, *Industrial Structure and Market Conduct* (London: Martin Robertson, 1974).

41. S. P. Douglas, C. Samuel Craig, and E. J. Nijissen, "Integrating Branding Strategy across Markets," *Journal of International Marketing* 9, no. 2 (2001), pp. 97-114.

42. The phrase was first used by economist Joseph Schumpeter in *Capitalism, Socialism, and Democracy* (New York: Harper Brothers, 1942).

43. S. Kotabe, S. Srinivasan, and P. S. Aulakh. "Multinationality and Firm Performance: The Moderating Role of R&D and Marketing," *Journal of International Business Studies* 33 (2002), pp. 79-97.

44. D. C. Mowery and N. Rosenberg, *Technology and the Pursuit of Economic Growth* (Cambridge, UK: Cambridge University Press, 1989); and M. E. Porter, *The Competitive Advantage of Nations* (New York: Free Press, 1990).

45. W. Kuemmerle, "Building Effective R&D Capabilities Abroad," *Harvard Business Review*, March–April 1997, pp. 61-70; and C. Le Bas and C. Sierra, "Location versus Home Country Advantages in R&D Activities," *Research Policy* 31 (2002), pp. 589-609.

46. "When the Corporate Lab Goes to Japan," *The New York Times*, April 28, 1991, sec. 3, p. 1.

47. D. Shapley, "Globalization Prompts Exodus," *Financial Times*, March 17, 1994, p. 10.

48. E. Mansfield, "How Economists See R&D," *Harvard Business Review*, November-December 1981, pp. 98-106.

49. E. Mansfield, "How Economists See R&D."

50. G. A. Stevens and J. Burley, "Piloting the Rocket of Radical Innovation," *Research Technology Management* 46 (2003), pp. 16-26.

51. K. B. Clark and S. C. Wheelwright, *Managing New Product and Process Development* (New York: Free Press, 1993); and M. A. Shilling and C. W. L. Hill, "Managing the New Product Development Process," *Academy of Management Executive* 12, no. 3 (1998), pp. 67-81.

52. O. Port, "Moving Past the Assembly Line," *BusinessWeek Special Issue: Reinventing America*, 1992, pp. 177-80.

53. K. B. Clark and T. Fujimoto, "The Power of Product Integrity," *Harvard Business Review*, November-December 1990, pp. 107-18; Clark and Wheelwright, *Managing New Product and Process*

Development; S. L. Brown and K. M. Eisenhardt, "Product Development: Past Research, Present Findings, and Future Directions," *Academy of Management Review* 20 (1995), pp. 348-78; and G. Stalk and T. M. Hout, *Competing against Time* (New York: Free Press, 1990).

54. G. Tomas M. Hult, *Boundary-Spanning Marketing Organization: A Theory and Insights from 31 Organization Theories* (Springer, 2012).

55. Shilling and Hill, "Managing the New Product Development Process."

56. C. Christensen, "Quantum Corporation—Business and Product Teams," Harvard Business School case no. 9-692-023.

57. R. Nobel and J. Birkinshaw, "Innovation in Multinational Corporations: Control and Communication Patterns in International R&D Operations," *Strategic Management Journal* 19 (1998), pp. 479-96.

58. Information comes from the company's website; also see K. Ferdows, "Making the Most of Foreign Factories," *Harvard Business Review*, March–April 1997, pp. 73-88.

Global Human Resource Management

19

LEARNING OBJECTIVES

After reading this chapter, you will be able to:

LO19-1 Summarize the strategic role of human resource management in international business.

LO19-2 Identify the pros and cons of different approaches to staffing policy in international business.

LO19-3 Explain why managers may fail to thrive in foreign postings.

LO19-4 Recognize how management development and training programs can increase the value of human capital in an international business firm.

LO19-5 Explain how and why performance appraisal systems might vary across nations.

LO19-6 Understand how and why compensation systems might vary across nations.

LO19-7 Understand how organized labor can influence strategic choices in international business firms.

Scott Olson/Getty Images News/Getty Images

Evolution of the Kraft Heinz Company

OPENING CASE

The Kraft Heinz Company is a food company formed by the merger of Kraft Foods and H.J. Heinz that is based in Chicago, Illinois, and Pittsburgh, Pennsylvania. Kraft Heinz is the third-largest food and beverage company in North America and the fifth-largest in the world, with about $26 billion in annual sales. The company has more than 200 brands that are sold in some 200 countries and territories. The portfolio includes eight brands with annual revenue of more than $1 billion in retail and foodservice sales (e.g., Heinz, Kraft, Lunchables, Maxwell House, Oscar Mayer, Philadelphia, Velveeta). Plus, five brands have sales between $500 million and $1 billion, and some 25 brands around the world have sales between $100 million and $500 million.

This is where we are today. Tracing the Kraft Heinz 150-year story is much tougher, involves numerous mergers and acquisitions, and human resource issues. However, using the two core examples that are embedded in what is now called the Kraft Heinz Company can serve as a nice illustration of the complexities of brands and global human resource management. We will first focus on Heinz and trace its history. Then, we turn our attention to Kraft and trace its history. Both brands ultimately became part of the Kraft Heinz Company, albeit with some spinoffs along the way (e.g., Kraft Foods Inc. into Mondelēz International, Inc.). The merger was agreed on by the Board of Directors of both companies, with approval by the companies' shareholders and regulatory authorities, on March 25, 2015.

Originally, Heinz was founded in 1869 by German-American entrepreneur Henry J. Heinz and L. Clarence Noble. Heinz was born in the United States to German immigrants (John Henry Heinz of Kallstadt and Anna Margaretha Schmidt of Kruspis). Henry Heinz was a second cousin to Frederick Trump, who emigrated to the United States in 1885. Trump was the immigrant ancestor and paternal grandfather of Donald Trump, the forty-fifth President of the United States. Interestingly, in 1991, Tereza Heinz, then spouse of U.S. Senator John Heinz, a Republican, became the owner of Heinz but subsequently sold her controlling shares as a part of Warren Buffett's Berkshire Hathaway and Brazilian 3G Capital acquiring Heinz in 2013. Tereza Heinz is now the spouse of 2004 Democratic nominee for U.S. President, John Kerry.

Heinz evolved a lot in its initial three decades. This included several early partners being bought out, going bankrupt in 1875, and then re-emerging in 1888 as the H. J. Heinz Company, which was incorporated in 1905. In 2015, Heinz shareholders received a 51 percent ownership stake while Kraft shareholders took 49 percent (Kraft shareholders also received an aggregate $10 billion cash dividend, or $16.50 per share) when the companies merged to become the Kraft Heinz Company. It was the food industry's largest ever merger (or acquisition, depending on how the 51/49 split is counted). In between those early days in 1875 and 2015, the company developed its famous Heinz Tomato Ketchup in 1876 (which still has 50 percent of the U.S. market share), acquired several companies and brands, and integrated employees from 40 countries into its organization.

Switching to Kraft, which grew out of a wholesale cheese–delivery business established in Chicago in 1903 by James L. Kraft, takes us down a different but also very complex path, with enormous human resource issues and organizational integration. A few steps later, three of James' brothers had joined the firm, and in 1909 it was incorporated as J.L. Kraft Bros. & Company. The brothers patented a spoil-resistant processed cheese, which was sold in great quantities to the U.S. Army during World War I.

Then, a rapid succession of M&A (mergers and acquisitions) involving Kraft started. In 1930, J.L. Kraft Bros. & Company was acquired by the National Dairy Products Corporation (which had been founded in 1923), and adopted the names Kraftco Corporation in 1969 and Kraft, Inc., in 1976. In 1980, Kraft, Inc. merged with Dart Industries, Inc., a diversified company. Kraft, Inc., split off in 1986, and was then acquired in 1988 by tobacco giant Philip Morris Companies, which had purchased General Foods in 1985 and went on to buy Nabisco Holdings in 2000. For a number of reasons, Philip Morris Companies rebranded and a new holding company, Altria, emerged in 2003 (but still has several Philip Morris companies in its portfolio).

General Foods' and Nabisco's operations, human resources, and core competencies were integrated into Kraft General Foods, Inc. In 2001, with a partial stock offering, Philip Morris began to sell off its stake in Kraft, and in 2007 Kraft Foods Inc. became an independent, publicly traded corporation. With the new independence, in 2007 Kraft purchased the biscuit division of Groupe Danone, a French company, for some $7 billion, and in 2010, after lengthy negotiations, Kraft acquired Cadbury, a British candy company, for more than $19 billion. About two years later, in 2012, another reorganization took place and the company split into two separate companies, one selling grocery products in North America (Kraft) and the other snack products worldwide (Mondelēz International). And so we are back to where we started when, in 2015, Kraft's parent company merged with the H.J. Heinz Holding Corporation. Kraft Foods became a brand and division within the newly formed conglomerate.

2015 was not the end to all the M&A involving the Kraft Heinz Company, of course. In 2017, the company tried to complete what many considered a hostile takeover of Unilever, a $62 billion-in-revenue British-Dutch transnational consumer goods company that was founded in 1929 (by a merger of Dutch Margarine Unie and British soap maker Lever Brothers). Unilever has 169,000 employees, and a global footprint in 190 countries. Kraft Heinz offered $143 billion in cash and stocks. Ultimately, Kraft Heinz withdrew its offer and blamed the somewhat forced withdrawal on early deal leaks, which the company said thwarted efforts to negotiate a merger or acquisition on a friendly basis. The deal was likely too large to be logical anyway.

How do you melt together the human resources of a $26-billion company (Kraft Heinz) with a $62-billion company (Unilever) in a $143-billion deal in a seamless, synergistic way that leverages the great human resources in both companies? As it turns out, Kraft and Heinz have not truly melded together with great human-resource synergy either. Much of Kraft Heinz's management team is from 3G Capital, rather than being food industry veterans, and they have not impressed Wall Street with their ability to manage such a large food conglomerate. The fear is that Kraft Heinz has been focused too much on cost-cutting instead of building its brands. Brand equity goes nicely with human-resource development, but cost-cutting negatively affects both in most companies. This seems to be the case for the Kraft Heinz Company.

Sources: Lauren Hirsch, "Kraft Heinz Backer 3G Capital Faces Reality: Brutal Cost-Cutting Isn't Enough," *CNBC*, February 22, 2019; Paul R. La Monica, "What Went Wrong at Kraft Heinz," *CNN Business*, February 22, 2019; "3G Capital Discovers the Limits of Cost-Cutting and Debt," *The Economist*, March 2, 2019; Antoine Gara, "Kraft Heinz Withdraws Its $143 Billion Bid For Unilever," *Forbes*, February 19, 2017; Dana Cimilluca, Dana Mattioli, and Chelsey Dulaney, "Kraft, Heinz to Merge, Forming Food Giant," *The Wall Street Journal*, March 25, 2015.

Introduction

This chapter continues our focus on business functions within a company engaged in a global marketplace of some 7.7 billion people by looking at global human resource management. **Human resource management (HRM)** refers to the activities an organization carries out to use its human resources effectively.[1] These activities include determining the firm's human resource strategy, staffing, performance evaluation, management development, compensation, and labor relations. Taken together, these activities determine how an international business builds and manages its global workforce in the global marketplace, including local, regional, global, and expatriate human resources.

None of these global HRM activities is performed in a vacuum; all are related to the global strategy of the firm. As we will see in this chapter, HRM has an important strategic component.[2] Through its influence on the character, development, quality, and productivity of the firm's human resources, the HRM function can help the firm achieve its primary strategic goals of reducing the costs of value creation and adding value by better serving customers.

An interesting example of how human resources need to be integrated is shown in this chapter's opening case about the evolution of the Kraft Heinz Company. The duality of Kraft and Heinz—as previously separate companies—have gone through so many mergers and acquisitions (M&A) that it is difficult to follow their collective evolution. What we do know, however, is that each time a merger or acquisition takes place, human resource positions are the first to be (1) cut, (2) integrated, or (3) reassigned to new roles.

Another good example of human resource issues is given in the closing case, which looks at how Shell uses its human resources around the world. At any one time, some 7 percent of Shell's employees are working outside of their home country, many for extended periods. The benefits of this include transferring valuable managerial and technical skills to local operations, developing leaders who know what it is like to do business in different countries (a major issue in a multinational such as Shell, which has operations in 70 nations), and ensuring management oversight of local operations.

Irrespective of the desire of managers in multinational companies, such as Kraft Heinz and Shell, to build a truly global enterprise with a global workforce, the reality is that HRM practices oftentimes have to be modified to national contexts. The strategic role of HRM is complex enough in a purely domestic firm, but it is more complex in an international business, where staffing, management development, performance evaluation, and compensation activities are complicated by profound differences between countries in labor markets, culture, legal systems, economic systems, and the like (see Chapters 2, 3, and 4). For example,

- Compensation practices may vary depending on countries' customs.
- Labor laws may prohibit unions in one country and mandate it in another.
- Equal employment legislation may be pursued in one country and not in another.
- Ethnic and cultural realities may require some modification of company policies.

If it is to build a cadre of managers capable of managing a multinational enterprise, the HRM function must deal with a host of issues. It must decide how to staff key management posts in the company, how to develop managers so that they are familiar with the nuances of doing business in different countries, how to compensate people in different nations, and how to evaluate the performance of managers based in different countries. HRM must also deal with a myriad of issues related to expatriate managers. (An **expatriate manager** is a citizen of one country who is working abroad in one of the firm's subsidiaries.) It must decide when to use expatriates, determine whom to send on expatriate postings, be clear about the reasons why, compensate expatriates appropriately, and make sure that they are adequately debriefed and reoriented once they return home.

This chapter looks closely at the role of HRM in an international business. It begins by briefly discussing the strategic role of HRM. Then we turn our attention to four major tasks of the HRM function: staffing policy, management training and development, performance appraisal, and compensation policy. We point out the strategic implications of each task. We then look at how firms can build a globally diverse workforce, and why this can benefit the enterprise, resulting in higher financial performance. The chapter closes with a look at international labor relations and the relationship between the firm's management of labor relations and its overall strategy.

Strategic Role of Global HRM: Managing a Global Workforce

LO19-1

Summarize the strategic role of human resource management in international business.

A large and expanding body of academic research suggests that a strong fit between human-resource practices and a company's strategy is required for high profitability.[3] You will recall from Chapter 13 that superior performance requires not only the right strategy, but that the strategy be supported by the right organizational architecture. Strategy is implemented through the organization, which we discussed in Chapter 14. As shown in Figure 19.1, people are the linchpin of a firm's organizational architecture. For a firm to outperform its rivals in the global marketplace, it must have the right people in the right postings. Those people must be trained appropriately so that they have the skill sets required to perform their jobs effectively and so that they behave in a manner that is congruent with the desired culture of the firm. Their compensation packages must create incentives for them to take actions that are consistent with the strategy of the firm, and the performance appraisal system that the firm uses must measure the behavior that the firm wants to encourage to achieve superior performance.

FIGURE 19.1

The role of human resources in shaping organizational architecture.

As indicated in Figure 19.1, the HRM function, through its staffing, training, compensation, and performance appraisal policies, has a critical impact on the people, culture, incentive, and control system elements of the firm's organizational architecture (performance appraisal systems are part of the control systems in an enterprise). Thus, HRM professionals have a critically important strategic role. It is incumbent on them to shape these elements of a firm's organizational architecture in a manner that is consistent with the strategy of the enterprise so that the firm can effectively implement its strategy.

globalEDGE INTERNATIONAL INTERNSHIP DIRECTORY

People are what make value chains "valuable," and global human resource management, which is the focus of Chapter 17, is a critical part of operating worldwide. The obvious HR issue to me as an author is YOU—the student and reader of this text! My goal is to provide information and data and infuse my knowledge to each student using the text. globalEDGE™ can help take this knowledge to another level with its International Internship Directory (**globaledge.msu.edu/international-internships**). The directory is a reference guide for students and others (e.g., faculty, staff, and administrators) to help match students with international internship opportunities offered by universities, governmental agencies, nonprofit groups, private organizations, and corporations. To search for an internship, you can select a type of organization, country, or subject of study (e.g., international business). Check it out. What opportunities can you find based on your interests?

In short, superior human resource management can be a sustained source of high productivity and competitive advantage in the global economy. At the same time, research suggests that many international businesses have room for improving the effectiveness of their HRM function. In one study of competitiveness among 326 large multinationals, the author found that human resource management was one of the weakest capabilities in most firms, suggesting that improving the effectiveness of international HRM practices might have substantial performance benefits.[4]

In Chapter 13, we examined four strategies pursued by international businesses: localization strategy, global standardization strategy, transnational strategy, and international strategy. In this chapter, we will see that success also requires HRM policies to be congruent with the firm's strategy. For example, a transnational strategy imposes different requirements for staffing, management development, and compensation practices from a localization strategy. Firms pursuing a transnational strategy need to build a strong corporate culture and an informal management network for transmitting information and knowledge within the organization. Through its employee selection, management development, performance appraisal, and compensation policies, the HRM function can help develop these things. Thus, as we have noted, HRM has a critical role to play in implementing strategy. In each section that follows, we review the strategic role of HRM in some detail.

✓ TEST PREP

Use SmartBook to help retain what you have learned. Access your Instructor's Connect course to check out SmartBook or go to **learnsmartadvantage.com** for help.

LO19-2

Identify the pros and cons of different approaches to staffing policy in international business.

Staffing Policy

Staffing policy is concerned with the selection of employees for particular jobs. At one level, this involves selecting individuals who have the skills required to do particular jobs. At another level, staffing policy can be a tool for developing and promoting the desired corporate culture of the firm.[5] By **corporate culture**, we mean the organization's norms and value systems. A strong corporate culture can help a firm implement its strategy.

General Electric, for example, is not just concerned with hiring people who have the skills required for performing particular jobs; it wants to hire individuals whose behavioral styles, beliefs, and value systems are consistent with those of GE. This is true whether an American is being hired, or a Brit, or a German, or a Swede, and whether the hiring is for a U.S. operation or a foreign operation. The belief is that if employees are predisposed toward the organization's norms and value systems by their personality type, the firm will be able to attain higher performance.

TYPES OF STAFFING POLICIES

Research has identified three types of staffing policies in international businesses: the ethnocentric approach, the polycentric approach, and the geocentric approach.[6] We review each policy and link it to the strategy pursued by the firm. The most attractive staffing policy is probably the geocentric approach, although there are several impediments to adopting it.

The Ethnocentric Approach

An **ethnocentric staffing policy** is one in which all key management positions are filled by parent-country nationals. This practice was widespread at one time. Firms such as Procter & Gamble, Philips, and Matsushita (now called Panasonic) originally followed it. In the Dutch firm Philips, for example, all important positions in most foreign subsidiaries were at one time held by Dutch nationals, who were referred to by their non-Dutch colleagues as the Dutch Mafia. Historically, in many Japanese and South Korean firms, such as Toyota, Matsushita, and Samsung, key positions in international operations have often been held by home-country nationals. For example, according to the Japanese Overseas Enterprise Association, only 29 percent of foreign subsidiaries of Japanese companies had presidents who were not Japanese. In contrast, 66 percent of the Japanese subsidiaries of foreign companies had Japanese presidents.[7] Today, there is evidence that as Chinese enterprises are expanding internationally, they too are using an ethnocentric staffing policy in their foreign operations.[8]

Firms pursue an ethnocentric staffing policy for three reasons. First, the firm may believe the host country lacks qualified individuals to fill senior management positions. This argument is heard most often when the firm has operations in less developed countries. Second, the firm may see an ethnocentric staffing policy as the best way to maintain a unified corporate culture. Many Japanese firms, for example, have traditionally preferred their foreign operations to be headed by expatriate Japanese managers because these managers will have been socialized into the firm's culture while employed in Japan.[9] Procter & Gamble until fairly recently preferred to staff important management positions in its foreign subsidiaries with U.S. nationals who had been socialized into P&G's corporate culture by years of employment in its U.S. operations. Such reasoning tends to predominate when a firm places a high value on its corporate culture.

Third, if the firm is trying to create value by transferring core competencies to a foreign operation, as firms pursuing an international strategy are, it may believe that the best way to do this is to transfer parent-country nationals who have knowledge of that competency to the foreign operation. Imagine what might occur if a firm tried to transfer a core competency in marketing to a foreign subsidiary without a corresponding transfer of home-country marketing personnel. The transfer would probably fail to produce the anticipated benefits because the knowledge underlying a core competency cannot easily be articulated and written down. Such knowledge often has a significant tacit dimension; it is acquired through experience. Just like the great tennis player who cannot instruct others how to become great tennis players simply by writing a handbook, the firm that has a core competency in marketing, or anything else, cannot just write a handbook that tells a foreign subsidiary how to build the firm's core competency anew in a foreign setting. It must also transfer management personnel to the foreign operation to show foreign managers how to become good marketers, for example. The need to transfer managers overseas arises because the knowledge that underlies the firm's core competency resides in the heads of its domestic managers and was acquired through years of experience, not by reading a handbook. Thus, if a firm is to transfer a core competency to a foreign subsidiary, it must also transfer the appropriate managers.

Despite this rationale for pursuing an ethnocentric staffing policy, the policy is now on the wane in most international businesses for two reasons. First, an ethnocentric staffing policy limits advancement opportunities for host-country nationals. This can lead to resentment, lower productivity, and increased turnover among that group. Resentment can be greater still if, as often occurs, expatriate managers are paid significantly more than home-country nationals.

Second, an ethnocentric policy can lead to *cultural myopia*—the firm's failure to understand host-country cultural differences that require different approaches to marketing and management. The adaptation of expatriate managers can take a long time, during which they may make major mistakes. For example, expatriate managers may fail to appreciate how product attributes, distribution strategy, communications strategy, and pricing strategy should be adapted to host-country conditions. The result may be costly blunders. They may also make decisions that are ethically suspect simply because they do not understand the culture in which they are managing.[10] In one highly publicized case in the United States, Mitsubishi Motors was sued by the federal Equal Employment Opportunity Commission for tolerating extensive and systematic sexual harassment in a plant in Illinois. The plant's top management, all Japanese expatriates, denied the charges. The Japanese managers may have failed to realize that behavior viewed as acceptable in Japan was not acceptable in the United States.[11]

The Polycentric Approach

A **polycentric staffing policy** requires host-country nationals to be recruited to manage subsidiaries, while parent-country nationals occupy key positions at corporate headquarters. In many respects, a polycentric approach is a response to the shortcomings of an ethnocentric approach. One advantage of adopting a polycentric approach is that the firm is less likely to suffer from cultural myopia. Host-country managers are unlikely to make the mistakes arising from cultural misunderstandings to which expatriate managers are vulnerable. A second advantage is that a polycentric approach may be less expensive to implement, reducing the costs of value creation. Expatriate managers can be expensive to maintain.

A polycentric approach has its drawbacks. Host-country nationals have limited opportunities to gain experience outside their own country and thus cannot progress beyond senior positions in their own subsidiary. As in the case of an ethnocentric policy, this may cause resentment. Perhaps the major drawback with a polycentric approach, however, is the gap that can form between host-country managers and parent-country managers. Language barriers, national loyalties, and a range of cultural differences may isolate the corporate headquarters staff from the various foreign subsidiaries. The lack of management transfers from home to host countries and vice versa can exacerbate this isolation and lead to a lack of integration between corporate headquarters and foreign subsidiaries. The result can be a "federation" of largely independent national units with only nominal links to the corporate headquarters. Within such a federation, the coordination required to transfer core competencies or to pursue experience curve and location economies may be difficult to achieve. Thus, although a polycentric approach may be effective for firms pursuing a localization strategy, it is inappropriate for other strategies.

The federation that may result from a polycentric approach can also be a force for inertia within the firm. After decades of pursuing a polycentric staffing policy, food and detergents giant Unilever found that shifting from a strategic posture that emphasized localization to a transnational posture was very difficult. Unilever's foreign subsidiaries had evolved into quasi-autonomous operations, each with its own strong national identity. These "little kingdoms" objected strenuously to corporate headquarters' attempts to limit their autonomy and to rationalize global manufacturing.[12]

The Geocentric Approach

A **geocentric staffing policy** seeks the best people for key jobs throughout the organization, regardless of nationality. This policy has a number of advantages. First, it enables the firm to make the best use of its human resources. Second, and perhaps more important, a geocentric policy enables the firm to build a cadre of international executives who feel at home working in a number of cultures. Creation of such a cadre may be a critical first step toward building a strong unifying corporate culture and an informal management network, both of which are required for global standardization and transnational strategies.[13] Firms pursuing a geocentric staffing policy may be better able to create value from the pursuit of experience curve and location economies and from the multidirectional transfer of core competencies than firms pursuing other staffing policies. In addition, the multinational composition of the management team that results from geocentric staffing tends to reduce cultural myopia and to enhance local responsiveness.

In sum, other things being equal, a geocentric staffing policy seems the most attractive. Indeed, in recent years there has been a sharp shift toward adoption of a geocentric staffing policy by many multinationals. For example, India's Tata Group, now more than a $100 billion global conglomerate, runs several of its companies with American and British executives. Japan's Sony Corporation broke 60 years of tradition in 2005 when it installed its first non-Japanese chair and CEO, Howard Stringer, a former CBS president and a U.S. citizen who was born and raised in Wales. American companies increasingly draw their managerial talent from overseas. In 2014, for example, Microsoft appointed Satya Nadella, a native of India, to its CEO position. One study found that by the mid-2000s, 24 percent of the managers among the top 100 to 250 people in U.S. companies were from outside the United States. For European companies, the average was 40 percent.[14]

However, a number of problems limit the firm's ability to pursue a geocentric policy. Many countries want foreign subsidiaries to employ their citizens. To achieve this goal, they use immigration laws to require the employment of host-country nationals if they are available in adequate numbers and have the necessary skills. Most countries, including the United States, require firms to provide extensive documentation if they wish to hire a foreign national instead of a local national. This documentation can be time-consuming, expensive, and at times futile. A geocentric staffing policy also can be expensive to implement. Training and relocation costs increase when transferring managers from country to country. The company may also need a compensation structure with a standardized international base pay level higher than national levels in many countries. In addition, the higher pay enjoyed by managers placed on an international fast track may be a source of resentment within a firm.

Types of Staffing Policies Summary

The advantages and disadvantages of the three approaches to staffing policy are summarized in Table 19.1. Broadly speaking, an ethnocentric approach is compatible with an international strategy, a polycentric approach is compatible with a localization strategy, and a geocentric approach is compatible with both global standardization and transnational strategies. (See Chapter 13 for details of the strategies.)

While the staffing policies described here are well known and widely used among both practitioners and scholars of international businesses, some critics have claimed that the typology is too simplistic and that it obscures the internal differentiation of management practices within international businesses. The critics claim that within some international businesses, staffing policies vary significantly from national subsidiary to national subsidiary; while some are managed on an ethnocentric basis, others are managed in a polycentric or geocentric manner.[15] Other critics note that the staffing policy adopted by a firm is primarily driven by its geographic scope, as opposed to its strategic orientation. Firms that have a broad geographic scope are the most likely to have a geocentric mindset.[16]

Staffing Approach	Strategic Appropriateness	Advantages	Disadvantages
Ethnocentric	International	Overcomes lack of qualified managers in host nation Unifies culture Helps transfer core competencies	Produces resentment in host country Can lead to cultural myopia
Polycentric	Localization	Alleviates cultural myopia Inexpensive to implement	Limits career mobility Isolates headquarters from foreign subsidiaries
Geocentric	Global standardization and transnational	Uses human resources efficiently Helps build strong culture and informal management networks	National immigration policies may limit implementation Expensive

LO19-3

Explain why managers may fail to thrive in foreign postings.

EXPATRIATE MANAGERS

Two of the three staffing policies we have discussed—the ethnocentric and the geocentric—rely on extensive use of expatriate managers. As defined earlier, expatriates are citizens of one country who are working in another country. Sometimes the term *inpatriates* is used to identify a subset of expatriates who are citizens of a foreign country working in the home country of their multinational employer.[17] Thus, a citizen of Japan who moves to the United States to work at Microsoft would be classified as an inpatriate (Microsoft has large numbers of inpatriates working at its main U.S. location, near Seattle). With an ethnocentric policy, the expatriates are all home-country nationals who are transferred abroad. With a geocentric approach, the expatriates need not be home-country nationals; the firm does not base transfer decisions on nationality. A prominent issue in the international staffing literature is **expatriate failure**—the premature return of an expatriate manager to his or her home country.[18] Here, we briefly review the evidence on expatriate failure before discussing a number of ways to minimize the failure rate.

Expatriate Failure Rates

Expatriate failure represents a failure of the firm's selection policies to identify individuals who will not thrive abroad.[19] The consequences include premature return from a foreign posting and high resignation rates, with expatriates leaving their company at about twice the rate of domestic managers.[20] The costs of expatriate failure are high. One estimate is that the average cost per failure to the parent firm can be as high as three times the expatriate's annual domestic salary plus the cost of relocation (which is affected by currency exchange rates and location of assignment). Estimates of the costs of each failure run between $40,000 and $1 million.[21] In addition, approximately 30 to 50 percent of American expatriates, whose average annual compensation package runs to $250,000, stay at their international assignments but are considered ineffective or marginally effective by their firms.[22] In a seminal study, Rosalie Tung surveyed a number of U.S., European, and Japanese multinationals.[23] Her results, summarized in Table 19.2, show that 76 percent of U.S. multinationals experienced expatriate failure rates of 10 percent or more, and 7 percent experienced a failure rate of more than 20 percent. Tung's work also suggests that U.S.-based multinationals experience a much higher expatriate failure rate than either European or Japanese multinationals. However, more recent work suggests that Tung's widely quoted estimates may no longer hold. For example, a more recent study of 136 large

Recall Rate Percentage	Percentage of Companies
U.S. multinationals	
20–40%	7%
10–20	69
<10	24
European multinationals	
11–15%	3%
6–10	38
<5	59
Japanese multinationals	
11–19%	14%
6–10	10
<5	76

TABLE 19.2

Expatriate Failure Rates

Source: R. L. Tung, "Selection and Training Procedures of U.S., European, and Japanese Multinationals," *California Management Review* 25, no. 1 (1982): 51–71.

multinationals from four different countries found that the rate of premature return of expatriate managers had dropped to 6.3 percent and that there was little difference between multinationals from different nations. The authors of this study suggest that multinationals have gotten much better at the selection and training of expatriates since Tung's study.[24]

Tung asked her sample of multinational managers to indicate reasons for expatriate failure. For U.S. multinationals, the reasons, in order of importance, were

1. Inability of spouse to adjust.
2. Manager's inability to adjust.
3. Other family problems.
4. Manager's personal or emotional maturity.
5. Inability to cope with larger overseas responsibilities.

Managers of European firms gave only one reason consistently to explain expatriate failure: the inability of the manager's spouse to adjust to a new environment. For the Japanese firms, the reasons for failure were

1. Inability to cope with larger overseas responsibilities.
2. Difficulties with new environment.
3. Personal or emotional problems.
4. Lack of technical competence.
5. Inability of spouse to adjust.

The most striking difference between these lists is that "inability of spouse to adjust" was the top reason for expatriate failure among U.S. and European multinationals but only the fifth reason among Japanese multinationals. Tung comments that this difference was not surprising, given the role and status to which Japanese society traditionally relegates the wife and the fact that most of the Japanese expatriate managers in the study were men.

Since Tung's study, a number of other studies have consistently confirmed that the inability of a spouse to adjust, the inability of the manager to adjust, or other family problems remain major reasons for continuing high levels of expatriate failure.[25] One study by International Orientation Resources, an HRM consulting firm, found that 60 percent of expatriate failures occur due to these three reasons.[26] Another study found that the most common reason for assignment failure is lack of partner (spouse) satisfaction, which was listed by 27 percent of respondents.[27] The inability of expatriate managers to adjust to foreign postings seems to be caused by a lack of cultural skills on the part of the manager being transferred. According to one HRM consulting firm, this is because the expatriate selection process at many firms is fundamentally flawed: "Expatriate assignments rarely fail because the person cannot accommodate to the technical demands of the job. Typically, the expatriate selections are made by line managers based on technical competence. They fail because of family and personal issues and lack of cultural skills that haven't been part of the selection process."[28]

The failure of spouses to adjust to a foreign posting seems to be related to a number of factors. Often, spouses find themselves in a foreign country without the familiar network of family and friends. Language differences make it difficult for them to make new friends. While this may not be a problem for the manager, who can make friends at work, it can be difficult for the spouse, who might feel trapped at home. The problem is often exacerbated by immigration regulations prohibiting the spouse from taking employment. With the recent rise of two-career families in many developed nations, this issue has become much more important. One survey found that 69 percent of expatriates are married, with spouses accompanying them 77 percent of the time. Of those spouses, half were employed before an assignment and only 12 percent were employed during an assignment.[29] Research suggests that the main reason managers now turn down international assignments is concern over the impact such an assignment might have on their spouse's career.[30] For an example of the kind of program that might be used, see the accompanying Management Focus that looks at international postings and repatriation at AstraZeneca.

Expatriate Selection

One way to reduce expatriate failure rates is by improving selection procedures to screen out inappropriate candidates. In a review of the research on this issue, Mendenhall and Oddou state that a major problem in many firms is that HRM managers tend to equate domestic performance with overseas performance potential.[31] Domestic performance and overseas performance potential are *not* the same thing. An executive who performs well in a domestic setting may not be able to adapt to managing in a different cultural setting. From their review of the research, Mendenhall and Oddou identified four dimensions that seem to predict success in a foreign posting: self-orientation, others-orientation, perceptual ability, and cultural toughness.

1. *Self-orientation.* The attributes of this dimension strengthen the expatriate's self-esteem, self-confidence, and mental well-being. Expatriates with high self-esteem, self-confidence, and mental well-being were more likely to succeed in foreign postings. Mendenhall and Oddou concluded that such individuals were able to adapt their interests in food, sport, and music; had interests outside of work that could be pursued (e.g., hobbies); and were technically competent.

2. *Others-orientation.* The attributes of this dimension enhance the expatriate's ability to interact effectively with host-country nationals. The more effectively the expatriate interacts with host-country nationals, the more likely he or she is to succeed. Two factors seem to be particularly important here: relationship development and willingness to communicate. Relationship development refers to the ability to develop long-lasting friendships with host-country nationals. Willingness to communicate refers to the expatriate's willingness to use the host-country language. Although language fluency helps, an expatriate need not be fluent to show willingness to communicate. Making the effort to use the language is what is important. Such gestures tend to be rewarded with greater cooperation by host-country nationals.

3. *Perceptual ability.* This is the ability to understand why people of other countries behave the way they do—that is, the ability to empathize. This dimension seems critical for managing host-country nationals. Expatriate managers who lack this ability tend to treat foreign nationals as if they were home-country nationals. As a result, they may experience significant management problems and considerable frustration. As one expatriate executive from Hewlett-Packard observed, as reported by in the Mendenhall and Oddou study: "It took me six months to

AstraZeneca and Global Staffing Policy

AstraZeneca is one of the world's largest pharmaceutical companies. Headquartered in London, UK, the company has 61,000 employees around the world. Some 22 percent are in the United States, 33 percent in Europe (including at the headquarters), 18 percent in China, and the remaining 27 percent of its employees are spread across the globe. AstraZeneca is active in more than 100 countries and had sales in excess of $22 billion last year, with profits of about $2 billion. A key strategic imperative for this multinational is to build a talented global workforce, led by managers who have a global perspective and are comfortable moving around the world, interacting with people from other cultures, and doing business in different nations.

To help build international bench strength, the company moves managers to another country for up to three years. Such assignments are not cheap for the company, nor easy for the employees and their families. AstraZeneca estimates it can cost two to four times an employee's salary to cover expenses when they are on assignment in a foreign country (to offset cost-of-living differences). Expenses can include a child's school tuition, tax equalization, cultural training, and subsidized housing. Because of these expenses, AstraZeneca focuses its international assignments only on the most promising, "high-potential" employees—those employees who are strategically in line for scheduled advancement and leadership positions within the company.

In every case of an international assignment, the human resources staff at AstraZeneca assesses whether the investment in the employee is worth making, relative to the person's potential in the company. Simply posting an employee to a foreign country is not enough. To get promoted, employees must also learn to work in international teams and to manage across borders. If a person is judged to lack capability or interest to do this, he or she will not get the foreign posting. And if an employee fails in his or her foreign assignment, advancement prospects will be reduced.

To ease the transition to a new country, AstraZeneca offers employees and their spouses help with moving, locating schools for their children, learning a language, and understanding cultural differences. The company also offers repatriation training for employees coming back home after extended posts abroad. AstraZeneca does this because experience has shown that many expatriates and their families have problems readjusting to their old life after an extended time in a different country.

Another problem that the human resource function at AstraZeneca has to grapple with is how to raise the talent base of employees in emerging markets where AstraZeneca has been making big investments in recent years. An example is China, where until recently there was very little in the way of professional management education (this is now changing rapidly). In 2003, the company had a little more than 1,000 employees in China. By 2020, there were more than 10,000 employees in China. AstraZeneca has been trying to raise the skill level of key Chinese employees as fast as possible.

With regard to key Chinese managerial talent, the company has been sending them abroad to get exposure to other cultures and to acculturate them into the way in which AstraZeneca does business. It wants these employees to understand what it is like to be part of a global business. Each expatriate will have a host-country line manager assigned to him or her, as well as a home-country line manager who monitors the expatriate's progress. After a period, the majority of them return to China, where the most successful are targeted for future leadership positions within the Chinese subsidiary. The most talented, however, may go beyond this and, ultimately, move into senior management positions at the corporate level.

AstraZeneca has also been working hard to increase the diversity of its global workforce. The company believes that diversity fuels innovation, emphasizing that teams need people who don't all think the same, and who approach challenges differently. Women comprise half of the company's global workforce, comprise 30 percent of the board of directors, and occupy 43 percent of all senior roles in the company. For several years, the company has run a European Women as Leaders program to support the accelerated development of high-potential women. AstraZeneca is also trying to ensure that employees from fast-growing emerging markets are promoted into leadership positions. Some 15 percent of managers who reported to the senior leadership team had a country of origin that was an emerging market or they came from Japan.

Sources: John Lauerman, "AstraZeneca Departures Continue as Medical Chief Bohen Exits," *Bloomberg BusinessWeek*, January 14, 2019; "AstraZeneca Says China Drug Plan Opens Up Room for New Medicine," *Bloomberg Law*, March 13, 2019; "AstraZeneca Announces Organizational Changes," *AstraZeneca.com*, January 7, 2019; "AstraZeneca Global Policy," *AstraZeneca.com*, April 15, 2019.

FIGURE 19.2

The global mindset of Americans.

This question deals with your own **global mindset** in general, as it is today and what you expect (or hope) it would be 5 years from now, 10 years from now, and 20 years from now (with 100 percent indicating a complete global mindset, meaning that you act and behave as a global citizen in everything you do).

How strong is your global mindset today?	47
How strong do you think your global mindset will be in 5 years?	54
How strong do you think your global mindset will be in 10 years?	60
How strong do you think your global mindset will be in 20 years?	65

accept the fact that my staff meetings would start 30 minutes late, and that it would bother no one but me."* According to Mendenhall and Oddou, well-adjusted expatriates tend to be nonjudgmental and nonevaluative in interpreting the behavior of host-country nationals and willing to be flexible in their management style, adjusting it as cultural conditions warrant.

4. *Cultural toughness.* This dimension refers to the relationship between the country of assignment and how well an expatriate adjusts to a particular posting. Some countries are much tougher postings than others because their cultures are more unfamiliar and uncomfortable. For example, many Americans regard Great Britain as a relatively easy foreign posting and for good reason—the two cultures have much in common. But many Americans find postings in non-Western cultures, such as India, Southeast Asia, and the Middle East, to be much tougher.[32] The reasons are many, including poor health care and housing standards, inhospitable climate, lack of Western entertainment, and language difficulties. Also, many cultures are extremely male-dominated and may be particularly difficult postings for female Western managers.

GLOBAL MINDSET

Some researchers suggest that a global mindset, one characterized by cognitive complexity and a cosmopolitan outlook, is the fundamental attribute of a global manager. Such managers can deal with high levels of complexity and ambiguity, and are open to the world. In a study of 615 people in the United States (done for this textbook), the global mindset of the test group was assessed as it is today and what each person hopes or predicts it will be in the next 20 years (the margin of error = 3.89 percent). Figure 19.2 illustrates the findings, indicating that people act and behave like global citizens in less than half of what

*Mendenhall, Mark E., and Gary Oddou. "The Dimensions of Expatriate Acculturation: A Review." *The Academy of Management Review* 10, no. 1 (January 1985): 39–47. DOI: 10.2307/258210.

they do today, but that the expectation is that people's global mindset will improve significantly in the next 20 years.

Given that people are expected to become more globally minded over time, how do you develop these attributes (high levels of complexity, ambiguity, and openness to the world)? Often they are gained in early life from a family that is bicultural, lives in foreign countries, or learns foreign languages as a regular part of family life. Mendenhall and Oddou note that standard psychological tests can be used to assess the first three of these dimensions, whereas a comparison of cultures can give managers a feeling for the fourth dimension.

Mendenhall and Oddou contend that these four dimensions, in addition to domestic performance, should be considered when selecting a manager for foreign posting. However, practice does not often conform to the authors' recommendations. Tung's research, for example, showed that only 5 percent of the firms in her sample used formal procedures and psychological tests to assess the personality traits and relational abilities of potential expatriates.[33] Research by International Orientation Resources suggests that when selecting employees for foreign assignments, only 10 percent of the 50 *Fortune* 500 firms surveyed tested for important psychological traits such as cultural sensitivity, interpersonal skills, adaptability, and flexibility. Instead, 90 percent of the time employees were selected on the basis of their technical expertise, not their cross-cultural fluency.[34]

Mendenhall and Oddou do not address the problem of expatriate failure due to a spouse's inability to adjust. According to a number of other researchers, a review of the family situation should be part of the expatriate selection process (see the closing case on Royal Dutch Shell for an example).[35] A survey by Windam International, another international HRM consulting firm, found that spouses were included in preselection interviews for foreign postings only 21 percent of the time and that only half of them received any cross-cultural training. The rise of dual-career families has added an additional and difficult dimension to this long-standing problem.[36] Increasingly, spouses wonder why they should have to sacrifice their own career to further that of their partner.[37]

TEST PREP

Use SmartBook to help retain what you have learned. Access your Instructor's Connect course to check out SmartBook or go to **learnsmartadvantage.com** for help.

Training and Management Development

LO19-4

Recognize how management development and training programs can increase the value of human capital in the international business firm.

Selection is just the first step in matching a manager with a job. The next step is training the manager to do the specific job. For example, an intensive training program might be used to give expatriate managers the skills required for success in a foreign posting. However, management development is a much broader concept. It is intended to develop the manager's skills over his or her career with the firm. Thus, as part of a management development program, a manager might be sent on several foreign postings over a number of years to build his or her cross-cultural sensitivity and experience. At the same time, along with other managers in the firm, the person might attend management education programs at regular intervals. The thinking behind job transfers is that broad international experience will enhance the management and leadership skills of executives. Research suggests this may be the case.[38]

Historically, most international businesses have been more concerned with training than with management development. Plus, they tended to focus their training efforts on preparing home-country nationals for foreign postings. Recently, however, the shift toward greater global competition and the rise of transnational firms have changed this. It is increasingly common for firms to provide general management development programs in addition to training for particular posts. In many international businesses, the explicit purpose of these management development programs is strategic. Management development is seen as a tool to help the firm achieve its strategic goals, not only by giving managers the required skill set but also by helping reinforce the desired culture of the firm and by facilitating the creation of an informal network for sharing knowledge within the multinational enterprise.

With this distinction between training and management development in mind, we first examine the types of training managers receive for foreign postings. Then we discuss the connection between management development and strategy in the international business.

TRAINING FOR EXPATRIATE MANAGERS

Earlier in the chapter, we saw that the two most common reasons for expatriate failure were the inability of a manager's spouse to adjust to a foreign environment and the manager's own inability to adjust to a foreign environment. Training can help the manager and spouse cope with both these problems. Cultural training, language training, and practical training all seem to reduce expatriate failure. We discuss each of these kinds of training here.[39] Despite the usefulness of the training, evidence suggests that many managers receive no training before they are sent on foreign postings. One study found that only about 30 percent of managers sent on one- to five-year expatriate assignments received training before their departure.[40]

Cultural Training

Cultural training seeks to foster an appreciation for the host country's culture. The belief is that understanding a host country's culture will help the manager empathize with the culture, which will enhance his or her effectiveness in dealing with host-country nationals. It has been suggested that expatriates should receive training in the host country's culture, history, politics, economy, religion, and social and business practices.[41] If possible, it is also advisable to arrange for a familiarization trip to the host country before the formal transfer, because this seems to ease culture shock. Given the problems related to spouse adaptation, it is important that the spouse, and perhaps the whole family, be included in cultural training programs.

Language Training

English is the language of world business; it is quite possible to conduct business all over the world using only English. Notwithstanding the prevalence of English, however, an exclusive reliance on English diminishes an expatriate manager's ability to interact with host-country nationals. As noted earlier, a willingness to communicate in the language of the host country, even if the expatriate is far from fluent, can help build rapport with local employees and improve the manager's effectiveness. Despite this, one study of 74 executives of U.S. multinationals found that only 23 believed knowledge of foreign languages was necessary for conducting business abroad.[42] Those firms that did offer foreign language training for expatriates believed it improved their employees' effectiveness and enabled them to relate more easily to a foreign culture, which fostered a better image of the firm in the host country.

Chairman of China's Lenovo Group Ltd., Yang Yuanqing (left), shakes hands with CEO Steve Ward (right), as the nonexecutive director, Li Chuanzhi (center), smiles after a press conference in Hong Kong.

Vincent Yu/AP Images

Practical Training

Practical training is aimed at helping the expatriate manager and family ease themselves into day-to-day life in the host country. The sooner a routine is established, the better are the prospects that the expatriate and his or her family will adapt successfully. One critical need is for a support network of friends for the expatriate. Where an expatriate community exists, firms often devote considerable effort to ensuring the new expatriate family is quickly integrated into that group. The expatriate community can be a useful source of support and information and can be invaluable in helping the family adapt to a foreign culture.

REPATRIATION OF EXPATRIATES

A largely overlooked but critically important issue in the training and development of expatriate managers is to prepare them for reentry into their home-country organization.[43] Repatriation should be seen as the final link in an integrated, circular process that connects good selection and cross-cultural training of expatriate managers with completion of their term abroad and reintegration into their national organization. However, instead of coming home to share their knowledge and encourage other high-performing managers to take the same international career track, expatriates too often face a different scenario.[44]

Often when they return home after a stint abroad—where they have typically been autonomous, well compensated, and celebrated as a big fish in a little pond—they face an organization that doesn't know what they have done for the past few years, doesn't know how to use their new knowledge, and doesn't particularly care. In the worst cases, reentering employees have to scrounge for jobs, or firms will create standby positions that don't use the expatriate's skills and capabilities and fail to make the most of the business investment the firm has made in that individual.

Research illustrates the extent of this problem. According to one study of repatriated employees, 60 to 70 percent didn't know what their position would be when they returned home. Also, 60 percent said their organizations were vague about repatriation, about their new roles, and about their future career progression within the company; 77 percent of those surveyed took jobs at a lower level in their home organization than in their international assignments.[45] Not surprisingly, 15 percent of returning expatriates leave their firms within a year of arriving home, and 40 percent leave within three years.[46]

The key to solving this problem is good human resource planning. Just as the HRM function needs to develop good selection and training programs for its expatriates, it also needs to develop good programs for reintegrating expatriates back into work life within their home-country organization, for preparing them for changes in their physical and professional landscape, and for utilizing the knowledge they acquired while abroad. For an example of the kind of program that might be used, see the accompanying Management Focus that looks at the repatriation program developed by Monsanto.

MANAGEMENT DEVELOPMENT AND STRATEGY

Management development programs are designed to increase the overall skill levels of managers through a mix of ongoing management education and rotations of managers through a number of jobs within the firm to give them varied experiences. They are attempts to improve the overall productivity and quality of the firm's management resources.

International businesses are increasingly using management development as a strategic tool. This is particularly true in firms pursuing a transnational strategy, as increasing numbers are. Such firms need a strong unifying corporate culture and informal management networks to assist in coordination and control. In addition, transnational firm managers need to be able to detect pressures for local responsiveness—and that requires them to understand the culture of a host country.

Management development programs help build a unifying corporate culture by socializing new managers into the norms and value systems of the firm. In-house company training programs and intense interaction during offsite training can foster esprit de corps—shared experiences, informal networks, perhaps a company language or jargon—as well as develop technical competencies. These training events often include songs, picnics, and sporting events that promote feelings of togetherness. These rites of integration may include "initiation rites" wherein personal culture is stripped, company uniforms are donned (e.g., T-shirts bearing the company logo), and humiliation is inflicted (e.g., a pie in the face). All these activities aim to strengthen a manager's identification with the company.[47]

Bringing managers together in one location for extended periods and rotating them through different jobs in several countries help the firm build an informal management network. Such a network can then be used as a conduit for exchanging valuable performance-enhancing knowledge within the organization.[48] Consider the Swedish telecommunications company Ericsson. Interunit cooperation is extremely important at Ericsson, particularly for transferring know-how and core competencies from the parent to foreign subsidiaries, from foreign subsidiaries to the parent, and between foreign subsidiaries. To facilitate cooperation, Ericsson transfers large numbers of people back and forth between headquarters and subsidiaries. Ericsson sends a team of 50 to 100 engineers and managers

TEST PREP

Use SmartBook to help retain what you have learned. Access your Instructor's Connect course to check out SmartBook or go to **learnsmartadvantage.com** for help.

Monsanto's Repatriation Program

Monsanto is a global provider of agricultural products with some 22,000 employees and about $15 billion in sales. At any one time, the company will have 100 mid- and higher-level managers on extended postings abroad. Two-thirds of these are Americans posted overseas; the remainder are foreign nationals employed in the United States. At Monsanto, managing expatriates and their repatriation begins with a rigorous selection process and intensive cross-cultural training, both for the managers and for their families. As is the case at many other global companies, the idea is to build an internationally minded cadre of highly capable managers who will lead the organization in the future.

One of the strongest features of this program is that employees and their sending and receiving managers, or sponsors, develop an agreement about how this assignment will fit into the firm's business objectives. The focus is on why employees are going abroad to do the job and what their contribution to Monsanto will be when they return. Sponsoring managers are expected to be explicit about the kind of job opportunities the expatriates will have once they return home.

Once they arrive back in their home country, expatriate managers meet with cross-cultural trainers during debriefing sessions. They are also given the opportunity to showcase their experiences to their peers, subordinates, and superiors in special information exchanges.

However, Monsanto's repatriation program focuses on more than just business; it also attends to the family's reentry. Monsanto has found that difficulties with repatriation often have more to do with personal and family-related issues

than with work-related issues. But the personal matters obviously affect an employee's on-the-job performance, so it is important for the company to pay attention to such issues.

This is why Monsanto offers returning employees an opportunity to work through personal difficulties. About three months after they return home, expatriates meet for three hours at work with several colleagues of their choice. The debriefing session is a conversation aided by a trained facilitator who has an outline to help the expatriate cover all the important aspects of the repatriation. The debriefing allows the employee to share important experiences and to enlighten managers, colleagues, and friends about his or her expertise so others within the organization can use some of the global knowledge. According to one participant, "It sounds silly, but it's such a hectic time in the family's life, you don't have time to sit down and take stock of what's happening. You're going through the move, transitioning to a new job, a new house, and the children may be going to a new school. This is a kind of oasis; a time to talk and put your feelings on the table."* Apparently it works; since the program was introduced, the attrition rate among returning expatriates has dropped sharply.

*C. M. Solomon, "Repatriation: Up, Down, or Out?" *Personnel Journal* 74, no. 1 (January 1995): 28–34.

Sources: A. Walton, "Who Says Monsanto Roundup Ingredient Is 'Probably Carcinogenic.' Are They Right?" *Forbes*, March 21, 2015; C. M. Solomon, "Repatriation: Up, Down, or Out?" *Personnel Journal*, January 1995, pp. 28–34; and J. Schaefer, E. Hannibal, and J. O'Neill, "How Strategy, Culture and Improved Service Delivery Reshape Monsanto's International Assignment Program," *Journal of Organizational Excellence* 22, no. 3 (2003), pp. 35–40.

from one unit to another for a year or two. This establishes a network of interpersonal contacts. This policy is effective for both solidifying a common culture in the company and coordinating the company's globally dispersed operations.[49]

LO19-5

Explain how and why performance appraisal systems might vary across nations.

Performance Appraisal

Performance appraisal systems are used to evaluate the performance of managers against some criteria that the firm judges to be important for the implementation of strategy and the attainment of competitive advantage globally. A firm's performance appraisal systems are an important element of its control systems, and control systems are a central component of organizational architecture. A particularly thorny issue in many international businesses is how best to evaluate the performance of expatriate managers.[50] This section of the textbook looks at performance evaluation and considers guidelines for appraising expatriate performance.

PERFORMANCE APPRAISAL PROBLEMS

Unintentional bias makes it difficult to evaluate the performance of expatriate managers objectively. In many cases, two groups evaluate the performance of expatriate managers—host-nation managers and home-office managers—and both are subject to bias. The host-nation managers may be biased by their own cultural frame of reference and expectations. For example, Oddou and Mendenhall report the case of a U.S. manager who introduced participative decision making while working in an Indian subsidiary.[51] The manager subsequently received a negative evaluation from host-country managers because in India, the strong social stratification means managers are seen as experts who should not have to ask subordinates for help. The local employees apparently viewed the U.S. manager's attempt at participatory management as an indication that he was incompetent and did not know his job.

Home-country managers' appraisals may be biased by distance and by their own lack of experience working abroad. Home-office managers are often not aware of what is going on in a foreign operation. Accordingly, they tend to rely on hard data in evaluating an expatriate's performance, such as the subunit's productivity, profitability, or market share. Such criteria may reflect factors outside the expatriate manager's control (e.g., adverse changes in exchange rates, economic downturns). Also, hard data do not take into account many less visible soft variables that are also important, such as an expatriate's ability to develop cross-cultural awareness and to work productively with local managers. Due to such biases, many expatriate managers believe that headquarters management evaluates them unfairly and does not fully appreciate the value of their skills and experience. This could be one reason many expatriates believe a foreign posting does not benefit their careers. In one study of personnel managers in U.S. multinationals, 56 percent of the managers surveyed stated that a foreign assignment is either detrimental or immaterial to one's career.[52]

GUIDELINES FOR PERFORMANCE APPRAISAL

Several things can reduce bias in the performance appraisal process.[53] First, most expatriates believe more weight should be given to an onsite manager's appraisal than to an offsite manager's appraisal. Due to proximity, an onsite manager is more likely to evaluate the soft variables that are important aspects of an expatriate's performance. The evaluation may be especially valid when the onsite manager is of the same nationality as the expatriate because cultural bias should be alleviated. In practice, home-office managers often write performance evaluations after receiving input from onsite managers. When this is the case, most experts recommend that a former expatriate who served in the same location should be involved in the appraisal to help reduce bias. Finally, when the policy is for foreign onsite managers to write performance evaluations, home-office managers should be consulted before an onsite manager completes a formal termination evaluation. This gives the home-office manager the opportunity to balance what could be a very hostile evaluation based on a cultural misunderstanding.

Compensation

Two issues are raised in every discussion of compensation practices in an international business. One is how compensation should be adjusted to reflect national differences in economic circumstances and compensation practices (see Shell in the closing case of this chapter). The other issue is how expatriate managers should be paid. From a strategic perspective, the important point is that whatever compensation system is used, it should reward managers for taking actions that are consistent with the strategy of the enterprise.

NATIONAL DIFFERENCES IN COMPENSATION

Differences exist in the compensation of executives at the same level in various countries. The results of a survey undertaken by Towers Watson, for example, suggest that U.S. CEOs earn, on average, roughly double the pay of non-U.S. CEOs.[54]

National differences in compensation raise a perplexing question for an international business: Should the firm pay executives in different countries according to the prevailing

TEST PREP

Use SmartBook to help retain what you have learned. Access your Instructor's Connect course to check out SmartBook or go to **learnsmartadvantage.com** for help.

LO19-6

Understand how and why compensation systems might vary across nations.

standards in each country, or should it equalize pay on a global basis? The problem does not arise in firms pursuing ethnocentric or polycentric staffing policies. In ethnocentric firms, the issue can be reduced to that of how much home-country expatriates should be paid (which we consider later). As for polycentric firms, the lack of managers' mobility among national operations implies that pay can and should be kept country-specific. There would seem to be no point in paying executives in Great Britain the same as U.S. executives if they never work side by side.

However, this problem is very real in firms with geocentric staffing policies. A geocentric staffing policy is consistent with a transnational strategy. One aspect of this policy is the need for a cadre of international managers that may include many different nationalities. Should all members of such a cadre be paid the same salary and the same incentive pay? For a U.S.-based firm, this would mean raising the compensation of foreign nationals to U.S. levels, which could be expensive. If the firm does not equalize pay, it could cause considerable resentment among foreign nationals who are members of the international cadre and work with U.S. nationals. If a firm is serious about building an international cadre, it may have to pay its international executives the same basic salary irrespective of their country of origin or assignment. Currently, however, this practice is not widespread.

Over the past decade, many firms have moved toward a compensation structure that is based on consistent global standards, with employees being evaluated by the same grading system and having access to the same bonus pay and benefits structure irrespective of where they work. Some 85 percent of the companies in a survey by Mercer Management Consulting stated they now have a global compensation strategy in place.[55] McDonald's, which is featured in the accompanying Management Focus, is one such enterprise. Another survey found that two-thirds of multinationals now exercise central control over the benefit plans offered in different nations.[56] However, except for a relatively small cadre of internationally mobile executives, base pay in most firms is set with regard to local market conditions.

EXPATRIATE PAY

The most common approach to expatriate pay is the balance sheet approach. According to Organizational Resources Counselors, some 80 percent of the 781 companies it surveyed used this approach.[57] This approach equalizes purchasing power across countries so employees can enjoy the same living standard in their foreign posting that they enjoyed at home. In addition, the approach provides financial incentives to offset qualitative differences between assignment locations.[58] Figure 19.3 shows a typical balance sheet. Note that home-country outlays for the employee are designated as income taxes, housing expenses,

FIGURE 19.3

The balance sheet approach to expatriate pay.

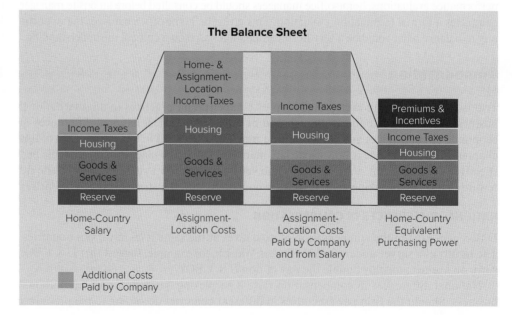

McDonald's Global Compensation Practices

With more than 400,000 managers and senior staff employees in 118 countries around the world, by the early 2000s McDonald's realized it had to develop a consistent global compensation and performance appraisal strategy. As with many companies that have expanded to many corners of the world, McDonald's found itself with a decentralized and inconsistent compensation program. Many reasons existed for this new global HR compensation strategy. Foremost among them was that McDonald's executive of worldwide human resources, Rich Floersch, pointed to a need to have a consistent global HR strategy to attract and retain better people. After months of consultation with global managers to ensure that any new system was formed via a collaborative approach, McDonald's began to roll out its new global compensation program.

One important element of this program calls for the corporate head office to provide local-country managers with a menu of business principles to focus on in the coming year. These principles include areas such as customer service, marketing, and restaurant re-imaging. Each country manager then picks three to five areas to focus on for success in the local market. For example, if France is introducing a new menu item, it might create business targets around that for the year. Human resource managers then submit their business cases and targets to senior executives at headquarters for approval. At the end of the year, the country's annual incentive pool is based on how the region met its targets, as well as on the business unit's

operating income. A portion of an individual employee's annual bonus is based on that mix.

The other portion of an employee's annual incentive is based on individual performance. McDonald's has always had a performance rating system, but within its new HR management strategy, the company has now introduced global guidelines that suggest 20 percent of employees receive the highest rating, 70 percent the middle, and 10 percent the bottom. By giving guidelines rather than forced ranking, McDonald's hopes to encourage differentiation of performance while allowing for some local flexibility. Also, by providing principles and guidance, and yet allowing local-country managers to customize their compensation programs to meet local market demands, McDonald's also claims it has seen a reduction in turnover. The company's own internal surveys suggest more employees now believe that their compensation is fair and reflects local market conditions. Overall, "McDonald's benefits and compensation program is designed to attract, retain and engage talented people who will deliver strong performance and help McDonald's achieve our business goals and objectives."*

*"McDonald's Corporate Careers," http://careers.mcdonalds.com/corporate/benefits.jsp, accessed May 9, 2018.

Sources: J. Marquez, "McDonald's Rewards Program Leaves Room for Some Local Flavor," *Workforce Management*, April 10, 2006, 26; C. Zillman, "McDonald's Loses Big on Labor Ruling," *Forbes*, July 29, 2014; "McDonald's Corporate Careers," http://careers.mcdonalds.com/corporate/benefits.jsp, accessed May 9, 2018; and V. Black, "How I Got Here: Rich Floersch of McDonald's," *Bloomberg Business*, August 14, 2012.

expenditures for goods and services (food, clothing, entertainment, etc.), and reserves (savings, pension contributions, etc.). The balance sheet approach attempts to provide expatriates with the same standard of living in their host countries as they enjoy at home plus a financial inducement (i.e., premium, incentive) for accepting an overseas assignment.

The components of the typical expatriate compensation package are a base salary, a foreign service premium, allowances of various types, tax differentials, and benefits. We briefly review each of these components.[59] An expatriate's total compensation package may amount to three times what he or she would cost the firm in a home-country posting. Because of the high cost of expatriates, many firms have reduced their use of them. However, a firm's ability to reduce its use of expatriates may be limited, particularly if it is pursuing an ethnocentric or geocentric staffing policy.

Base Salary

An expatriate's base salary should normally be in the same range as the base salary for a similar position in the home country. At the same time, while an expatriate may have a base salary that he or she would have in their home country, foreign nationals in these expatriate locations do not necessarily get the same salary levels. Oftentimes, developed nations (e.g., Germany, the United States) offer higher base salaries than comparable jobs and positions in the company in other, developing or less developed, countries. The base salary is normally paid in either the home-country currency or in the local currency.

Foreign Service Premium

A foreign service premium is an extra pay which the expatriate receives for working outside his or her country of origin. It is offered as an inducement to accept foreign postings. It compensates the expatriate for having to live in an unfamiliar country isolated from family and friends, having to deal with a new culture and language, and having to adapt to new work habits and practices. Many firms pay foreign service premiums as a percentage of base salary, ranging from 10 to 30 percent after tax, with 16 percent being the average premium.[60]

Allowances

Four types of allowances are often included in an expatriate's compensation package: hardship, housing, cost of living, and education. A hardship allowance is paid when the expatriate is being sent to a difficult location, usually defined as one where such basic amenities as health care, schools, and retail stores are grossly deficient by the standards of the expatriate's home country. A housing allowance is normally given to ensure that the expatriate can afford the same quality of housing in the foreign country as at home. In locations where housing is expensive (e.g., London, Tokyo), this allowance can be substantial—as much as 10 to 30 percent of the expatriate's total compensation package. A cost-of-living allowance ensures that the expatriate will enjoy the same standard of living in the foreign posting as at home. An education allowance ensures that an expatriate's children receive adequate schooling (by home-country standards). Host-country public schools are sometimes not suitable for an expatriate's children, in which case they must attend a private school.

Taxation

Unless a host country has a reciprocal tax treaty with the expatriate's home country, the expatriate may have to pay income tax to both the home- and host-country governments. When a reciprocal tax treaty is not in force, the firm typically pays the expatriate's income tax in the host country. In addition, firms normally make up the difference when a higher income tax rate in a host country reduces an expatriate's take-home pay.

Benefits

Many firms also ensure that their expatriates receive the same level of medical and pension benefits abroad that they received at home. This can be costly for the firm, because many benefits that are tax-deductible for the firm in the home country (e.g., medical and pension benefits) may not be deductible out of the country.

TEST PREP

Use SmartBook to help retain what you have learned. Access your Instructor's Connect course to check out SmartBook or go to **learnsmartadvantage.com** for help.

Building a Diverse Global Workforce

A diverse global workforce can be a source of competitive advantage. A diverse workforce is one that has a significant mix of both genders and in which cultural and ethnic minorities are well represented. Workforce diversity has been linked to superior financial performance. One study by McKinsey and Company found that companies in the top quartile of gender and ethnic diversity were 35 percent more likely to have financial returns above their national industry median. Another study concluded that companies with the strongest record of promoting women to the executive suite outperformed their industry norms, with a return on assets 18 percent higher.[61]

There are a number of reasons for thinking that a diverse workforce will improve performance.[62] First, diverse talents bring insights into the needs of a diverse customer base that (for example) a homogenous management group composed exclusively of white males cannot. Due to their different perspective and life experiences, women and minorities may see things that white males don't. People with different lifestyles and different backgrounds challenge each other more, which can lead to creative insights. This can result in improved problem solving, better product design and delivery, more effective marketing, and better sales promotions.

Second, an enterprise with a homogenous employee base is underutilizing the talent to be found among women and minorities. Its human capital will not be a strong as it could be, and performance will suffer as a result.

Third, when the customer set is diverse (as is often the case for many global businesses), those customers may appreciate interacting with an enterprise whose employees look like them, and therefore, have a better understanding of their needs, tastes, and preference.

Fourth, a diverse workforce may improve the brand image of an enterprise, setting up a virtuous circle where it does better among its customer set and is more able to attract top talent from among women and minorities.

Fifth, there is evidence that diversity increases employee satisfaction, which results in higher productivity, so long as the workforce is diverse enough.[63] For minority workers, the boost in satisfaction kicks in when representation exceeds 15 percent of the workforce. In contrast, when diversity recruitment is a token effort, psychological outcomes are poorer.

The available evidence suggests that many companies still have a long way to go when it comes to promoting diversity. For example, the consulting company Mercer looked at gender diversity among 164 companies from 28 different countries.[64] It found that women continue to be underrepresented at all levels in the labor force worldwide. Fewer women participate in the global labor force, and women make up a small percentage of senior management positions in most organizations. For example, the study found that only 24 percent of senior executives in North America were women, 18 percent in Europe, and just 12 percent in Latin America. The imbalance between men and women also tends to get larger the higher up in an organization one goes. For the average global organization, Mercer found that while 36 percent of lower-level managers were women, only 26 percent of senior managers and 19 percent of company executives were women.

Building a diverse workforce is not easy—particularly for an international business—since the definition of what constitutes a cultural and ethnic minority may vary across nations, as may the acceptance of women in the workplace. If the numbers are any guide, acceptance of women as senior managers is lower in Latin America than in North America, probably for cultural reasons. Similarly, relative to North America, it is unlikely that there will be many women in senior management positions in Japan or the Middle East, where traditional values are emphasized.

This being said, there are a number of steps that international businesses can take to promote workforce diversity.[65] It is important to understand that diversity efforts represent a type of organizational change. As with all change efforts, it must be driven from the top but also incorporate all levels of the organization. Top managers must create a clear value proposition that identifies the benefits of building a diverse and inclusive culture. They must also set clear goals (not quotas) for what they would like to achieve, identify the gap between the current situation and the desired state, and measure performance improvements over time. It is also important to hold managers accountable for attaining global diversity goals and reward those who hit or exceed goals. Senior management must also lead by example, hiring and promoting people from diverse backgrounds.

Diversity workshops can be used to educate employees at all levels about the value of building a more inclusive and diverse workforce. A key task here is to overcome the subconscious biases and stereotyping of the majority that may lead to discrimination against minority employees. Techniques include (1) role-playing, where members of the majority get to experience bias personally; (2) reminding people about biases at key moments, such as just before performance reviews; and (3) helping people to focus on differences to reduce stereotyping. In one experiment, French students discriminated against potential employees who were Arabs but stopped doing so if asked to describe the differences between photos. The act of articulating differences made the students aware of their own subconscious biases.

Outreach to women and minorities can help to increase recruitment from these demographics. Adjusting work policies can help to foster a more diverse workforce (e.g., having childcare facilities on site can make a company more attractive to women). Several companies have also found that it helps to create employee reference groups where minorities can help each other through networking, advice, and mutual support.

LO19-7

Understand how organized labor can influence strategic choices in international business firms.

International Labor Relations

The HRM function of an international business is typically responsible for international labor relations. From a strategic perspective, the key issue in international labor relations is the degree to which organized labor can limit the choices of an international business. A firm's ability to integrate and consolidate its global operations to realize experience curve and location economies can be limited by organized labor, constraining the pursuit of a transnational or global standardization strategy. Prahalad and Doz cite the example of General Motors, which gained peace with labor unions in Germany by agreeing not to integrate and consolidate operations in the most efficient manner.[66] General Motors made substantial investments in Germany—matching its investments in Austria and Spain—at the demand of the German metalworkers' unions.

One task of the HRM function is to foster harmony and minimize conflict between the firm and organized labor. With this in mind, this section is divided into three parts. First, we review organized labor's concerns about multinational enterprises. Second, we look at how organized labor has tried to deal with these concerns. And third, we look at how international businesses manage their labor relations to minimize labor disputes.

THE CONCERNS OF ORGANIZED LABOR

Labor unions generally try to get better pay, greater job security, and better working conditions for their members through collective bargaining with management. Unions' bargaining power is derived largely from their ability to threaten to disrupt production, either by a strike or some other form of work protest (e.g., refusing to work overtime). This threat is credible, however, only insofar as management has no alternative but to employ union labor.

A principal concern of domestic unions about multinational firms is that the company can counter its bargaining power with the power to move production to another country. Ford, for example, clearly threatened British unions with a plan to move manufacturing to continental Europe unless British workers abandoned work rules that limited productivity, showed restraint in negotiating for wage increases, and curtailed strikes and other work disruptions.[67]

Employees work on the chassis of an Adam Opel AG car at a GM factory in Eisenach, Germany.

Martin Leissl/Bloomberg/Getty Images

Another concern of organized labor is that an international business will keep highly skilled tasks in its home country and farm out only low-skilled tasks to foreign plants. Such a practice makes it relatively easy for an international business to switch production from one location to another as economic conditions warrant. Consequently, the bargaining power of organized labor is once more reduced.

A final union concern arises when an international business attempts to import employment practices and contractual agreements from its home country. When these practices are alien to the host country, organized labor fears the change will reduce their influence and power. This concern has surfaced in response to Japanese multinationals that have been trying to export their style of labor relations to other countries. For example, much to the annoyance of the United Auto Workers, many Japanese auto plants in the United States are not unionized. As a result, union influence in the auto industry is declining.

THE STRATEGY OF ORGANIZED LABOR

Organized labor has responded to the increased bargaining power of multinational corporations by taking three actions: (1) trying to establish international labor organizations, (2) lobbying for national legislation to restrict multinationals, and (3) trying to achieve international regulations on multinationals through such organizations as the United Nations. These efforts have not been very successful.

In the 1960s, organized labor began to establish international trade secretariats (ITSs) to provide worldwide links for national unions in particular industries. The long-term goal was to be able to bargain transnationally with multinational firms. Organized labor believed that by coordinating union action across countries through an ITS, it could counter the power of a multinational corporation by threatening to disrupt production on an international scale. For example, Ford's threat to move production from Great Britain to other European locations would not have been credible if the unions in various European countries had united to oppose it.

However, the ITSs have had virtually no real success. Although national unions may want to cooperate, they also compete with each other to attract investment from international businesses and hence jobs for their members. For example, in attempting to gain new jobs for their members, national unions in the auto industry often court auto firms that are seeking locations for new plants. One reason Nissan chose to build its European production facilities in Great Britain rather than Spain was that the British unions agreed to greater concessions than the Spanish unions did. As a result of such competition between national unions, cooperation is difficult to establish.

A further impediment to cooperation has been the wide variation in union structure. Trade unions developed independently in each country. As a result, the structure and ideology of unions tend to vary significantly from country to country, as does the nature of collective bargaining. For example, in Great Britain, France, and Italy, many unions are controlled by left-wing socialists, who view collective bargaining through the lens of "class conflict." In contrast, most union leaders in Germany, the Netherlands, Scandinavia, and Switzerland are far more moderate politically. The ideological gap between union leaders in different countries has made cooperation difficult. Divergent ideologies are reflected in radically different views about the role of a union in society and the stance unions should take toward multinationals.

Organized labor has also met with only limited success in its efforts to get national and international bodies to regulate multinationals. Such international organizations as the International Labour Organization and the Organisation for Economic Co-operation and Development have adopted codes of conduct for multinational firms to follow in labor relations. However, these guidelines are not as far-reaching as many unions would like. They also do not provide any enforcement mechanisms. Many researchers report that such guidelines are of only limited effectiveness.[68]

APPROACHES TO LABOR RELATIONS

International businesses differ markedly in their approaches to international labor relations. The main difference is the degree to which labor relations activities are centralized or decentralized. Historically, most international businesses have decentralized international labor relations activities to their foreign subsidiaries because labor laws, union power, and the nature of collective bargaining varied so much from country to country. It made sense to decentralize the labor relations function to local managers. The belief was that there was no way central management could effectively handle the complexity of simultaneously managing labor relations in a number of different environments.

Although this logic still holds, the trend is toward greater centralized control. This trend reflects international firms' attempts to rationalize their global operations. The general rise in competitive pressure in industry after industry has made it more important for firms to control their costs. Because labor costs account for such a large percentage of total costs, some firms are now using the threat to move production to another country in their negotiations with unions to change work rules and limit wage increases (as Ford did in Europe). Because such a move would involve major new investments and plant closures, this bargaining tactic requires the input of headquarters management. Thus, the level of centralized input into labor relations is increasing.

In addition, the realization is growing that the way work is organized within a plant can be a major source of competitive advantage. Much of the competitive advantage of Japanese automakers, for example, has been attributed to the use of self-managing teams, job rotation, cross-training, and the like in their Japanese plants.[69] To replicate their domestic performance in foreign plants, the Japanese firms have tried to replicate their work practices there. This often brings them into direct conflict with traditional work practices in those countries, as sanctioned by the local labor unions, so the Japanese firms have often made their foreign investments contingent on the local union accepting a radical change in work practices. To achieve this, the headquarters of many Japanese firms bargains directly with local unions to get union agreement to changes in work rules before committing to an investment. For example, before Nissan decided to invest in northern England, it got a commitment from British unions to agree to a change in traditional work practices. By its very nature, pursuing such a strategy requires centralized control over the labor relations function.

TEST PREP

Use SmartBook to help retain what you have learned. Access your Instructor's Connect course to check out SmartBook or go to **learnsmartadvantage.com** for help.

Key Terms

human resource management (HRM), p. 568	staffing policy, p. 570	polycentric staffing policy, p. 572
expatriate manager, p. 569	corporate culture, p. 570	geocentric staffing policy, p. 573
	ethnocentric staffing policy, p. 571	expatriate failure, p. 574

SUMMARY

This chapter focused on human resource management in international businesses. HRM activities include human resource strategy, staffing, performance evaluation, management development, compensation, and labor relations. None of these activities is performed in a vacuum; all must be appropriate to the firm's strategy. The chapter made the following points:

1. Firm success requires HRM policies to be congruent with the firm's strategy and with its formal and informal structure and controls.

2. Staffing policy is concerned with selecting employees who have the skills required to perform particular jobs. Staffing policy can be a tool for developing and promoting a corporate culture.

3. An ethnocentric approach to staffing policy fills all key management positions in an international business with parent-country nationals. The policy is congruent with an international strategy. A drawback is that ethnocentric staffing can result in cultural myopia.

4. A polycentric staffing policy uses host-country nationals to manage foreign subsidiaries and parent-country nationals for the key positions at corporate headquarters. This approach can minimize the dangers of cultural myopia, but

it can create a gap between home- and host-country operations. The policy is best suited to a localization strategy.

5. A geocentric staffing policy seeks the best people for key jobs throughout the organization, regardless of their nationality. This approach is consistent with building a strong, unifying culture and informal management network and is well suited to both global standardization and transnational strategies. Immigration policies of national governments may limit a firm's ability to pursue this policy.

6. A prominent issue in the international staffing literature is expatriate failure, defined as the premature return of an expatriate manager to his or her home country. The costs of expatriate failure can be substantial.

7. Expatriate failure can be reduced by selection procedures that screen out inappropriate candidates. The most successful expatriates seem to be those who have high self-esteem and self-confidence, can get along well with others, are willing to attempt to communicate in a foreign language, and can empathize with people of other cultures.

8. Training can lower the probability of expatriate failure. It should include cultural training, language training, and practical training, and it should be provided to both the expatriate manager and the spouse.

9. Management development programs attempt to increase the overall skill levels of managers through a mix of ongoing management education and rotation of managers through different jobs within the firm to give them varied experiences. Management development is often used as a strategic tool to build a strong unifying culture and informal management network, both of which support transnational and global standardization strategies.

10. It can be difficult to evaluate the performance of expatriate managers objectively because of unintentional bias. A firm can take a number of steps to reduce this bias.

11. Country differences in compensation practices raise a difficult question for an international business: Should the firm pay executives in different countries according to the standards in each country or equalize pay on a global basis?

12. The most common approach to expatriate pay is the balance sheet approach. This approach aims to equalize purchasing power so employees can enjoy the same living standard in their foreign posting that they had at home.

13. A diverse global workforce can be a source of competitive advantage. A diverse workforce is one that has a significant mix of both genders, and in which cultural and ethnic minorities are well represented. Workforce diversity has been linked to superior financial performance.

14. A key issue in international labor relations is the degree to which organized labor can limit the choices available to an international business. A firm's ability to pursue a transnational or global standardization strategy can be significantly constrained by the actions of labor unions.

15. A principal concern of organized labor is that the multinational can counter union bargaining power with threats to move production to another country. Organized labor has tried to counter the bargaining power of multinationals by forming international labor organizations. In general, these efforts have not been effective.

Critical Thinking and Discussion Questions

1. What are the main advantages and disadvantages of the ethnocentric, polycentric, and geocentric approaches to staffing policy? When is each approach appropriate?

2. Research suggests that many expatriate employees encounter problems that limit both their effectiveness in a foreign posting and their contribution to the company when they return home. What are the main causes and consequences of these problems, and how might a firm reduce the occurrence of such problems?

3. What is the link between an international business's strategy and its human resource management policies, particularly with regard to the use of expatriate employees and their pay scale?

4. In what ways can organized labor constrain the strategic choices of an international business? How can an international business limit these constraints?

5. Reread the Management Focus "McDonald's Global Compensation Practices." How does McDonald's approach help the company take into account local differences when reviewing the performance of different country managers and awarding bonus pay?

6. Why is diversity good for an international business? What actions can a company take to foster greater diversity?

globalEDGE research task   globaledge.msu.edu

Use the globalEDGE™ website (**globaledge.msu.edu**) to complete the following exercises:

1. You work in the human resource department at the headquarters of a multinational corporation. Your company is about to send a number of managers overseas as expatriates to France and New Zealand. You need to create an executive summary evaluating, comparing, and contrasting the possible issues expats may encounter in these two countries. Your manager tells you that a tool called *Expat Explorer* created by HSBC can assist you in your task.

CLOSING CASE

Global Mobility At Shell

Royal Dutch Shell is a British-Dutch multinational oil and gas company, founded in 1907, that is headquartered in the Netherlands and incorporated in the United Kingdom. The company is one of the world's largest oil producers with revenues of about $388 billion (profit of $24 billion) and operations in more than 70 countries. The company has some 82,000 employees, of which about 7,000 employees are at any one time on expatriate assignments outside their home country. A crucial task for Shell is to manage this extensive population of expatriate workers in order to meet its commercial goals and transfer valuable technical and managerial knowledge across operations located in different nations. It's no easy task.

Shell's long-term goal is to develop local talent wherever possible, thereby leveraging local employees' networks, market knowledge, and language skills, while also minimizing costs. However, there are many cases where deploying foreign nationals makes the most commercial sense. First, there is often a shortage of skills in certain locations. Shell has found this to be a vital issue in the Middle East and North Africa, where the company often works with local joint-venture partners or third parties. Moving Shell employees from other countries to work with partners and transfer expertise is often a key part of the company's strategy. Second, Shell recognizes that the skills of staff and senior leadership are improved by significant exposure to overseas markets. In other words, in a multinational like Shell, high-potential employees need to understand what it is like to live and work in other countries—to get a sense of the conditions on the ground. Third, in many instances, senior Shell employees need to be on the management boards of local subsidiaries in order to effectively monitor and control those operations and keep the head office informed of developments.

As Shell has found, however, moving employees to other countries raises a number of important challenges. It's not always easy to recruit skilled personnel to work in different locations. A survey of expatriate personnel at Shell found that five issues had the greatest impact on the willingness of an employee to accept an international assignment. In order of importance, these were (1) separation from children during their secondary education, (2) harm done to a spouse's career and employment, (3) failure to recognize and involve a spouse in the relocation decision, (4) failure to provide adequate information and assistance regarding

relocation, and (5) health issues. The underlying message was that the family is the basic unit of expatriation, not the individual, and Shell needed to do more to recognize this.

To deal with these issues, Shell implemented a number of programs designed to address some of these problems. To help with the education of children, Shell built elementary schools for Shell employees where there was a heavy concentration of expatriates. As for secondary school education, Shell worked with local schools (e.g., often providing grants) to help them upgrade their educational offerings. It also offered an education supplement to help expatriates send their children to private schools in the host country.

Helping spouses with their careers is a more vexing problem. According to the survey data, half the spouses accompanying Shell staff on assignment were employed until the transfer. When expatriated, only 12 percent were able to secure employment, while a further 33 percent wished to be employed. Shell set up a spouse employment center to address the problem. The center provides career counseling and assistance in locating employment opportunities both during and immediately after an international assignment. The company also agreed to reimburse up to 80 percent of the costs of vocational training, further education, or reaccreditation.

Shell set up a global information and advice network known as "The Outpost" to provide support for families facing the challenges of global mobility. The Outpost has its headquarters in The Hague with about 50 local offices around the world. The center recommends schools and medical facilities and provides housing advice and up-to-date information on employment, study, self-employment, and volunteer work.

Finally, there are also important issues with expatriate pay. An expatriate's basic salary and bonus are linked to what they would receive in their home country. Additional pay is given to expatriates moving to more expensive locations so they can maintain their standard of living. Shell also recognizes that employees often need additional financial incentives to persuade them to leave family and friends and location "premiums" to persuade them to move to less popular expatriate destinations, such as Kuwait and Iraq. Shell also uses tax equalization as part of its expatriate pay approach. Specifically, home country taxes are deducted from an expatriate's pay, while the host country taxes are paid by the company. Of course, all of these added factors make expatriates an expensive resource that can cost up to three times as much as a local employee.

Sources: Aysha Binbraik, "International Mobility at Shell," *Mercer Management Consulting*, 2016; J. DeGraff, "Single System Expatriate Compensation," *Cornell HR Review*, April 7, 2010; J. Barbian, "Return to Sender," *Training*, January 2002, 40–43; and J. Mainwaring, "Shell Schools: Supporting Expat Families," *Rigzone*, June 21, 2012.

Case Discussion Questions

1. Royal Dutch Shell is one of the largest companies in the world and has been for years. With sales approaching $400 billion and 82,000 employees worldwide, including some 7,000 employees on expatriate assignments, the company is large, complex, and powerful. Compared with retail or consumer companies, Shell is much more narrowly focused and much more technical in orientation. How do you think this narrower focus and technical orientation affects global human resource management at Shell?

2. Shell's long-term goal is to develop local talent wherever possible, thereby leveraging local employees' networks, market knowledge, and language skills, while also minimizing costs. Moving Shell employees from other countries to work with partners and transfer expertise is often a key part of the company's strategy. Can this be done effectively in all world regions (e.g., Middle East and North Africa), where potential local employees do not have the educational background in many cases? How would you solve the education, skill, and knowledge gaps if you were a Shell C-suite leader?

3. Spending significant time (e.g., three years) on an expatriate assignment has significant family and professional implications, as can be seen in the Shell survey that was mentioned in the case. How would you feel if you were given an expatriate assignment today? How would you feel about it if you were 25 years old? 35? 50?

Endnotes

1. P. J. Dowling and R. S. Schuler, *International Dimensions of Human Resource Management* (Boston: PSW-Kent, 1990).

2. J. Millman, M. A. von Glinow, and M. Nathan, "Organizational Life Cycles and Strategic International Human Resource Management in Multinational Companies," *Academy of Management Review* 16 (1991), pp. 318–39; A. Bird and S. Beechler, "Links between Business Strategy and Human Resource Management," *Journal of International Business Studies* 26 (1995), pp. 23–47; B. A. Colbert, "The Complex Resource-Based View: Implications for Theory and Practice of Strategic Human Resource Management," *Academy of Management Review* 29 (2004), pp. 341–60; and C. J. Collins and K. D. Clark, "Strategic Human Resource Practices, Top Management Team Social Networks, and Firm Performance," *Academy of Management Journal* 46 (2003), pp. 740–60.

3. See Peter Bamberger and Ilan Meshoulam, *Human Resource Strategy: Formulation, Implementation, and Impact* (Thousand Oaks, CA: Sage, 2000); P. M. Wright and S. Snell, "Towards a Unifying Framework for Exploring Fit and Flexibility in Human Resource Management," *Academy of Management Review* 23 (October 1998), pp. 756–72; Colbert, "The Complex Resource-Based View"; R. S. Schuler and S. E. Jackson, "A Quarter Century Review of Human Resource Management in the US: The Growth in Importance of the International Perspective," *Management Review* 16 (2005), pp. 1–25.

4. R. Colman, "HR Management Lags behind at World Class Firms," *CMA Management*, July–August 2002, p. 9.

5. E. H. Schein, *Organizational Culture and Leadership* (San Francisco: Jossey-Bass, 1985).

6. H. V. Perlmutter, "The Tortuous Evolution of the Multinational Corporation," *Columbia Journal of World Business* 4 (1969), pp. 9–18; D. A. Heenan and H. V. Perlmutter, *Multinational Organizational Development* (Reading, MA: Addison-Wesley, 1979); D. A. Ondrack, "International Human Resources Management in European and North American Firms," *International Studies of Management and Organization* 15 (1985), pp. 6–32; and T. Jackson, "The Management of People across Cultures: Valuing People Differently," *Human Resource Management* 41 (2002), pp. 455–75.

7. V. Reitman and M. Schuman, "Men's Club: Japanese and Korean Companies Rarely Look Outside for People to Run Their Overseas Operations," *The Wall Street Journal*, September 26, 1996, p. 17.

8. E. Wong, "China's Export of Labor Faces Growing Scorn," *The New York Times*, December 21, 2009, p. A1.

9. S. Beechler and J. Z. Yang, "The Transfer of Japanese-Style Management to American Subsidiaries," *Journal of International Business Studies* 25 (1994), pp. 467–91. See also R. Konopaske, S. Warner, and K. E. Neupert, "Entry Mode Strategy and

Performance: The Role of FDI Staffing," *Journal of Business Research*, September 2002, pp. 759–70.

10. M. Banai and L. M. Sama, "Ethical Dilemma in MNCs' International Staffing Policies," *Journal of Business Ethics*, June 2000, pp. 221–35.

11. Reitman and Schuman, "Men's Club."

12. C. A. Bartlett and S. Ghoshal, *Managing across Borders: The Transnational Solution* (Boston: Harvard Business School Press, 1989).

13. S. J. Kobrin, "Geocentric Mindset and Multinational Strategy," *Journal of International Business Studies* 25 (1994), pp. 493–511.

14. F. Hansen, "International Business Machine," *Workforce Management*, July 2005, pp. 36–44.

15. P. M. Rosenzweig and N. Nohria, "Influences on Human Resource Management Practices in Multinational Corporations," *Journal of International Business Studies* 25 (1994), pp. 229–51.

16. Kobrin, "Geocentric Mindset and Multinational Strategy."

17. M. Harvey and H. Fung, "Inpatriate Managers: The Need for Realistic Relocation Reviews," *International Journal of Management* 17 (2000), pp. 151–59.

18. S. Black, M. Mendenhall, and G. Oddou, "Toward a Comprehensive Model of International Adjustment," *Academy of Management Review* 16 (1991), pp. 291–317; J. Shay and T. J. Bruce, "Expatriate Managers," *Cornell Hotel & Restaurant Administration Quarterly*, February 1997, pp. 30–40; and Y. Baruch and Y. Altman, "Expatriation and Repatriation in MNCs—A Taxonomy," *Human Resource Management* 41 (2002), pp. 239–59.

19. M. G. Harvey, "The Multinational Corporation's Expatriate Problem: An Application of Murphy's Law," *Business Horizons* 26 (1983), pp. 71–78.

20. J. Barbian, "Return to Sender," *Training*, January 2002, pp. 40–43.

21. Barbian, "Return to Sender"; K. Yeaton and N. Hall, "Expatriates: Reducing Failure Rates," *Journal of Corporate Accounting and Finance*, March–April 2008, pp. 75–78.

22. Black et al., "Toward a Comprehensive Model of International Adjustment."

23. R. L. Tung, "Selection and Training Procedures of U.S., European, and Japanese Multinationals," *California Management Review* 25 (1982), pp. 57–71.

24. T. Zsuzzanna and M. Pieperl, "Expatriate Practices in German, Japanese, U.K., and U.S. Multinational Companies: A Comparative Survey of Changes," *Human Resource Management*, January–February 2009, pp. 153–71.

25. H. W. Lee, "Factors That Influence Expatriate Failure," *International Journal of Management* 24 (2007), pp. 403–15.

26. C. M. Solomon, "Success Abroad Depends upon More Than Job Skills," *Personnel Journal*, April 1994, pp. 51–58.

27. C. M. Solomon, "Unhappy Trails," *Workforce*, August 2000, pp. 36–41.

28. Solomon, Charlene. "Success Abroad Depends upon More Than Job Skills." *Personnel Journal* 73, no. 4 (April 1994): 56–60.

29. Solomon, "Unhappy Trails."

30. M. Harvey, "Addressing the Dual-Career Expatriation Dilemma," *Human Resource Planning* 19, no. 4 (1996), pp. 18–32.

31. M. Mendenhall and G. Oddou, "The Dimensions of Expatriate Acculturation: A Review," *Academy of Management Review* 10 (1985), pp. 39–47.

32. I. Torbiorin, *Living Abroad: Personal Adjustment and Personnel Policy in the Overseas Setting* (New York: Wiley, 1982).

33. R. L. Tung, "Selection and Training of Personnel for Overseas Assignments," *Columbia Journal of World Business* 16 (1981), pp. 68–78.

34. Solomon, "Success Abroad."

35. S. Ronen, "Training and International Assignee," in *Training and Career Development*, ed. I. Goldstein (San Francisco: Jossey-Bass, 1985); and Tung, "Selection and Training of Personnel for Overseas Assignments."

36. Solomon, "Success Abroad."

37. Harvey, "Addressing the Dual-Career Expatriation Dilemma"; and J. W. Hunt, "The Perils of Foreign Postings for Two," *Financial Times*, May 6, 1998, p. 22.

38. C. M. Daily, S. T. Certo, and D. R. Dalton, "International Experience in the Executive Suite: A Path to Prosperity?" *Strategic Management Journal* 21 (2000), pp. 515–23.

39. Dowling and Schuler, *International Dimensions*.

40. Dowling and Schuler, *International Dimensions*.

41. G. Baliga and J. C. Baker, "Multinational Corporate Policies for Expatriate Managers: Selection, Training, and Evaluation," *Advanced Management Journal*, Autumn 1985, pp. 31–38.

42. J. C. Baker, "Foreign Language and Departure Training in U.S. Multinational Firms," *Personnel Administrator*, July 1984, pp. 68–70.

43. A 1997 study by the Conference Board looked at this in depth. For a summary, see L. Grant, "That Overseas Job Could Derail Your Career," *Fortune*, April 14, 1997, p. 166. Also see J. S. Black and H. Gregersen, "The Right Way to Manage Expatriates," *Harvard Business Review*, March–April 1999, pp. 52–63.

44. J. S. Black and M. E. Mendenhall, *Global Assignments: Successfully Expatriating and Repatriating International Managers* (San Francisco: Jossey-Bass, 1992); and K. Vermond, "Expatriates Come Home," *CMA Management*, October 2001, pp. 30–33.

45. Black and Mendenhall, *Global Assignments*; and Vermond, "Expatriates Come Home."

46. Figures from the Conference Board study. For a summary, see Grant, "That Overseas Job Could Derail Your Career."

47. S. C. Schneider, "National vs. Corporate Culture: Implications for Human Resource Management," *Human Resource Management* 27 (Summer 1988), pp. 231–46.

48. I. M. Manve and W. B. Stevenson, "Nationality, Cultural Distance and Expatriate Status," *Journal of International Business Studies* 32 (2001), pp. 285–303; and D. Minbaeva et al., "MNC Knowledge Transfer, Subsidiary Absorptive Capacity, and HRM," *Journal of International Business Studies* 34, no. 6 (2003), pp. 586–604.

49. Bartlett and Ghoshal, *Managing across Borders*.

50. See G. Oddou and M. Mendenhall, "Expatriate Performance Appraisal: Problems and Solutions," in *International Human Resource Management*, ed. M. Mendenhall and G. Oddou (Boston: PWS-Kent, 1991); Dowling and Schuler, *International*

Dimensions; R. S. Schuler and G.W. Florkowski, "International Human Resource Management," in *Handbook for International Management Research*, ed. B. J. Punnett and O. Shenkar (Oxford: Blackwell, 1996); and K. Roth and S. O'Donnell, "Foreign Subsidiary Compensation Strategy: An Agency Theory Perspective," *Academy of Management Journal* 39, no. 3 (1996), pp. 678–703.

51. Oddou and Mendenhall, "Expatriate Performance Appraisal."

52. "Expatriates Often See Little Benefit to Careers in Foreign Stints, Indifference at Home," *The Wall Street Journal*, December 11, 1989, p. B1.

53. Oddou and Mendenhall, "Expatriate Performance Appraisal"; and Schuler and Florkowski, "International Human Resource Management."

54. Towers Perrin, *Towers Perrin Worldwide Total Remuneration Study, 2005-2006*, www.towerswatson.com. Not all researchers agree with this conclusion; see, for example, N. Fernandes et al., "Are US CEOs Paid More? New International Evidence," *The Review of Financial Studies* 26, no. 2 (2013), pp. 323–67.

55. J. Cummings and L. Brannen, "The New World of Compensation," *Business Finance*, June 2005, p. 8.

56. "Multinationals Tighten Control of Benefit Plans," *Workforce Management*, May 2005, p. 5.

57. Organizational Resource Counselors, *2002 Survey of International Assignment Policies and Practices*, March 2003.

58. C. Reynolds, "Compensation of Overseas Personnel," in *Handbook of Human Resource Administration*, ed. J. J. Famularo (New York: McGraw-Hill, 1986).

59. M. Helms, "International Executive Compensation Practices," in *International Human Resource Management*, ed. M. Mendenhall and G. Oddou (Boston: PWS-Kent, 1991).

60. G. W. Latta, "Expatriate Incentives," *HR Focus* 75, no. 3 (March 1998), p. S3.

61. Vivian Hunt, Dennis Layton, and Sara Prince, *Diversity Matters*, McKinsey & Co, February 2, 2015; Roy D. Adler, "Profit Thy Name Is Woman," *Pacific Standard*, February 27, 2009.

62. Hunt et al., Diversity Matters; Boris Groysberg and Katherine Connolly, "Great Leaders Who Make the Mix Work," *Harvard Business Review*, September 2013, pp. 68–76.

63. Groysberg and Connolly, "Great Leaders Who Make the Mix Work."

64. Mercer Consulting, *When Women Thrive, Businesses Thrive*, Mercer LLC, 2014.

65. Hunt et al., *Diversity Matters*.

66. C. K. Prahalad and Y. L. Doz, *The Multinational Mission* (New York: Free Press, 1987).

67. C. K. Prahalad and Y. L. Doz, *The Multinational Mission* (New York: Free Press, 1987).

68. Schuler and Florkowski, "International Human Resource Management."

69. See J. P. Womack, D. T. Jones, and D. Roos, *The Machine That Changed the World* (New York: Rawson Associates, 1990).

Accounting and Finance in International Business

20

LEARNING OBJECTIVES

After reading this chapter, you will be able to:

LO20-1 Discuss the national differences in accounting standards.

LO20-2 Explain the implications of the rise of international accounting standards.

LO20-3 Explain how accounting systems affect control systems within the multinational enterprise.

LO20-4 Discuss how operating in different nations affects investment decisions within the multinational enterprise.

LO20-5 Discuss the different financing options available to the foreign subsidiary of a multinational enterprise.

LO20-6 Understand how money management in the international business can be used to minimize cash balances, transaction costs, and taxation.

LO20-7 Understand the basic techniques for global money management.

PAUL J. RICHARDS/Getty Images

Pfizer, Novartis, Bayer, and GlaxoSmithKline

OPENING CASE

Pfizer from the United States, Novartis from Switzerland, Bayer from Germany, and GlaxoSmithKline from the United Kingdom are four of the largest pharmaceutical companies in the world. Johnson & Johnson (United States) and Roche (Switzerland) are technically larger companies focused on pharmaceuticals, but they also have more diversified lines of business that contribute to their total revenues (e.g., Johnson & Johnson has medical devices and consumer packaged goods divisions; Roche focuses on diagnostics). Merck & Co. (United States), Sanofi (France), AbbVie (United States), and Abbot Laboratories (United States) are also pharmaceutical companies, with revenues greater than $30 billion.

Few other industries (e.g., automotive, oil and gas, electronics) can financially compare to the pharmaceutical industry's collection of heavy-revenue, top-10 companies like Pfizer, Novartis, Bayer, and GlaxoSmithKline. These companies are large, old, and financially resourceful. Pfizer, founded in 1849, has $54 billion in annual revenue and $159 billion in assets. Novartis, tracing its history to 1859, has $53 billion in annual revenue and $146 billion in assets. Bayer, founded in 1863, has $45 billion in annual revenue and $142 billion in assets. And, Glaxo-SmithKline, founded in 1849, has $39 billion in annual revenue and $77 billion in assets. These companies also employ a lot of people (between 92,000 and 125,000 employees each), who work and serve a worldwide customer base (with customers in at least 155 of the world's 195 countries).

Are these companies too big, too powerful, and make too much money? For so long now, there have been political and financial debates worldwide about the nature of health care and prescription drugs. Should health care be a public good paid for by taxes, or should it be an opt-in service paid for by individuals? Most countries fall somewhere in between those extremes. The answer, though, is important for the financial well-being of individuals and countries' economies. Spending on prescription drugs in the United States, in particular, is on the rise and is projected to outpace growth in other parts of the health care sector (and the overall economy). Will individuals be able to keep up with these increases and will the country be able to maintain its international competitiveness in the face of increased health-care costs?

With a benchmark spending of $404 billion on retail prescription drugs in 2020 and an expected increase of 6.3 percent annually until (at least) 2025, the United States will see its spending on prescription drugs go from 2 percent of the country's GDP to about 2.5 percent by 2025 ($548 billion). Prescription drug prices are outpacing GDP growth (forecast at around 2.5 percent). In comparison, prescription drugs represent about 10 percent of all health-care expenditures (which also means that health care is forecast to make up a quarter of the GDP of the United States by 2025). As a comparison, other industrialized (OECD) nations will spend, on average, 9.5 percent of GDP on health care in 2020, with an expected growth of 2.5 percent annually. At the current 20 percent, the United States spends the most on health care of all countries, followed by Switzerland (13 percent) and France (12 percent).

A different way to look at the health care financials is that products made in Switzerland include a health-care fee of 13 percent on the cost-of-good-sold. Meanwhile, collectively for the country, U.S. companies have to build in a 20 percent cost—meaning U.S. companies from the start have to be 7 percentage points better than Swiss companies to be equally competitive. Now, the math is not that simplistic due to influences from a variety of other sources (e.g., a number of the factors we have discussed in Chapters 2 through 12). Also, the business environment in the United States is usually favorable in most of these factors, but why is it that the U.S. has such high health-care costs? In either case, the simplicity of the 20 versus 13 percent argument for the United States versus Switzerland portrays a dilemma for many U.S. companies that affects their international competitiveness (we could also compare this with OECD countries such as Mexico and Turkey that spend only between 4.2 and 5.4 percent of their GDP on health care).

Thankfully, the world has become more standardized in terms of at least accounting for cost-related factors. The International Accounting Standards Board (IASB) has emerged as a major proponent of standardization, although compliance is still voluntary. Clearly, we cannot standardize the costs of health care and prescription drugs around the world as we are trying to do with accounting standards. So, how can the United States effectively and efficiently tackle rising health care costs, while still providing patient service at the level and quality the country and its citizens have been accustomed to for decades? The argument on the macro side is that making health care a public good paid for by taxes (i.e., universal health care) would save the country some $600 billion annually. The argument on the micro side is that the quality, provider choice, and timeliness of care are superior in a privatized, insurance-based and individual-payer system.

As always, being on one end of the two extremes (universal health care versus fully privatized health care) is likely not an optimal solution, but this is as much a political question as it is a financial (individual) and economic (country) topic. This case was written to go along with this chapter and its subject of accounting and finance in international business. As such, the cost-related issues in the case fit within the context of companies' international competitiveness and strategic planning. The political aspects are interesting, dynamic, and important —and do affect the cost issues—but companies can usually only deal with the macro issues they face in their environment (e.g., United States versus

Switzerland) and the industry they are in (e.g., pharmaceuticals, health care). So, politics aside, what are the accounting and, perhaps more importantly, financial implications of the prescription drug and health-care costs worldwide?

Sources: "Health Expenditure," OECD, April 17, 2019; "Universal Health Care Would Save Americans $600 Billion a Year," *Sanigest Internacional*, April 17, 2019; Robert Pear, "Drug Makers Try to Justify Prescription Prices to Senators at Hearing," *The New York Times*, February 26, 2019; Ben Hirschler, "How the U.S. Pays 3 Times More for Drugs," *Scientific American*, April 17, 2019.

Introduction

This chapter deals with two related topics: international accounting and international finance. By those topics, we focus on accounting and finance, respectively, as they apply as functions within an international business, such as a multinational corporation or small and medium-sized enterprise (SME). The goal of this chapter is to provide you with a nontechnical overview of some of the main issues in international accounting and international finance that confront managers in, for example, a multinational corporation. As such, similar to the other chapters on the various international business functions (exporting, importing, and countertrade in Chapter 16; global production and supply chain management in Chapter 17; global marketing and R&D in Chapter 18; and global HRM in Chapter 19), this chapter on accounting and finance in international business integrates core materials into the course on international business.

Uniquely connected to this chapter, though, is the set of chapters on global trade and the investment environment (with topics such as international trade theory in Chapter 6; government policy and international trade in Chapter 7; FDI in Chapter 8; and regional economic integration in Chapter 9) and the chapters on the global monetary system (the foreign exchange market in Chapter 10; the international monetary system in Chapter 11; and the global capital market in Chapter 12). The topics covered in these seven chapters in the text provide a foundation for what many multinational corporations can do regarding their international finance strategies and tactics, as well as how they structure many of their international accounting operations. As such, we encourage you to look back at some of these "macro" topics as they apply to the material and learning in this chapter on the accounting and finance functions of the company.

Accounting has often been referred to as "the language of business."[1] This language finds expression in profit and loss statements, balance sheets, budgets, investment analysis, and tax analysis. Accounting information is the means by which firms communicate their financial position to the providers of capital, enabling them to assess the value of their investments and make decisions about future resource allocations. Accounting information is also the means by which firms report their income to the government, so the government can assess how much tax the firm owes. It is also the means by which the firm can evaluate its performance, control its internal expenditures, and plan for future expenditures and income. Thus, a good accounting function is critical to the smooth running of the firm and to a nation's financial system. In this regard, international businesses face a number of accounting problems that do not confront purely domestic businesses—most notably, the lack of consistency in the accounting standards of the more than 200 countries and territories in the world.

Financial management in an international business includes three sets of related decisions: (1) investment decisions, decisions about what activities to finance; (2) financing decisions, decisions about how to finance those activities; and (3) money management decisions, decisions about how to manage the firm's financial resources most efficiently. In an international business, investment, financing, and money management decisions are complicated by the fact that countries have different currencies, different tax regimes, different regulations concerning the flow of capital across their borders, different norms regarding the financing of business activities, different levels of economic and political risk, and so on. Financial managers must consider all these factors when deciding which activities to finance, how best to finance those activities, how best to manage the firm's financial resources, and how best to protect the firm from political and economic risks (including foreign exchange risk).

As we shall see, one of the money management goals that financial managers try to achieve in an international business is to minimize global tax liability. The closing case looks at Shoprite and its product assortment as a hedge against financial downturns and nurturing repeat business as a financial strategy to build the company. Much of this is done by focusing on being the lowest price retailer in most of its markets. These somewhat simplistic strategies have allowed The Shoprite Group to have tremendous financial success in what many other companies consider a weak buying power market while also helping to socially develop the local African communities. The opening case might be a bit more controversial because it also includes political issues, but the cost factors associated with health care and prescription drugs are becoming an important part of the financial calculations for companies (and countries) and, as such, provide a unique scenario to discuss and debate accounting and finance in an international business. My goal, as always, is to try to stay neutral on topics as an author of this textbook, so I will leave the nuanced debate and interpretation to you!

Instead, as a road map, this chapter begins by looking at country differences in accounting standards and attempts aimed at harmonizing accounting standards across nations. Next, we discuss the issues that can arise when managers in a multinational corporation or international SME use accounting systems to control foreign subsidiaries. Then we move on to look at investment decisions in an international business. We discuss how such factors as political and economic risk complicate investment decisions. This is followed by a review of financing decisions in an international business. Finally, we examine money management decisions in an international business, including decisions aimed at reducing tax liabilities.

National Differences in Accounting Standards

LO20-1

Discuss the national differences in accounting standards.

Accounting is shaped by the environment in which it operates. Just as different countries have different political systems, economic systems, and cultures, historically they have also had different accounting systems.[2] These differences had a number of sources. For example, in countries where well-developed capital markets exist, such as the United States and the United Kingdom, firms typically raised capital by issuing stock or bonds to investors. Investors in these countries demanded detailed accounting disclosures so that they could better assess the risk and likely return on their investments. The accounting system evolved to accommodate these requests.

In contrast, in Germany and Switzerland, the banks emerged as the main providers of capital to enterprises. Bank officers often sat on the boards of these companies and were privy to detailed information about their operations and financial position. As a consequence, there were fewer demands for detailed accounting disclosures, and public accounts tended to reveal less information. Another important influence has been the political or economic ties between nations. U.S.-style accounting systems were adopted in the Philippines, which was once a U.S. protectorate. Similarly, the vast majority of former colonies of the British Empire have accounting practices modeled after Great Britain's, while former French colonies followed the French system.

Diverse accounting practices were enshrined in national accounting and auditing standards. **Accounting standards** are rules for preparing financial statements; they define what is useful accounting information. **Auditing standards** specify the rules for performing an audit—the technical process by which an independent person (the auditor) gathers evidence for determining if financial accounts conform to required accounting standards and if they are also reliable.

One result of national differences in accounting and auditing standards was a general lack of comparability of financial reports from one country to another (something that is now changing). For example, (1) Dutch standards favored the use of current values for replacement assets, and Japanese law generally prohibited revaluation and prescribed historic cost; (2) capitalization of financial leases was required practice in Great Britain, but not practiced in France; (3) research and development costs must be written off in the year they are incurred in the United States, but in Spain they could be deferred as an asset and need not be amortized as long as benefits that will cover them are expected to arise in the future; and (4) German accountants treated depreciation as a liability, whereas British companies deducted it from assets.

Such differences would not matter much if there were little need for a firm head-quartered in one country to report its financial results to citizens of another country. However, one striking development of the past two decades has been the development of global capital markets. We have seen the growth of both transnational financing and transnational investment. Transnational financing occurs when a firm based in one country enters another country's capital market to raise capital from the sale of stocks or bonds. Transnational investment occurs when an investor based in one country enters the capital market of another nation to invest in the stocks or bonds of a firm based in that country.

The rapid expansion of transnational financing and investment has been accompanied by a corresponding growth in transnational financial reporting. However, the lack of comparability between accounting standards in different nations caused some confusion. For example, the German firm that issued two sets of financial reports, one set prepared under German standards and the other under U.S. standards, may have found that its financial position looked significantly different in the two reports, and its investors may have had difficulty identifying the firm's true worth.

In an example of the confusion that can arise from different accounting standards, British Airways reported a loss under British accounting rules of £21 million, but under U.S. rules, its loss was £412 million. Most of the difference could be attributed to adjustments for a number of relatively small items such as depreciation and amortization, pensions, and deferred taxation. The largest adjustment was due to a reduction in revenue reported in the U.S. accounts of £136 million. This reduced revenue was related to frequent flyer miles, which under U.S. rules have to be deferred until the miles are redeemed. But, this is not the case under British rules.

In addition to the problems lack of comparability gives investors, it can give the firm major headaches. The firm has to explain to its investors why its financial position looks so different in the two accounting reports. Also, an international business may find it difficult to assess the financial positions of important foreign customers, suppliers, and competitors.

TEST PREP

Use SmartBook to help retain what you have learned. Access your instructor's Connect course to check out SmartBook or go to **learnsmartadvantage.com** for help.

LO20-2

Explain the implications of the rise of international accounting standards.

International Accounting Standards

Substantial efforts have been made in recent years to harmonize accounting standards across countries.[3] The rise of global capital markets during the past three decades has added urgency to this endeavor. Today, many companies raise money from providers of capital outside their national borders. Those providers are demanding consistency in the way financial results are reported so they can make more informed investment decisions. Also, there is a realization that the adoption of common accounting standards will facilitate the development of global capital markets because more investors will be willing to invest across borders, and the end result will be to lower the cost of capital and stimulate economic growth. It is increasingly accepted that the standardization of accounting practices across national borders is in the best interests of all participants in the world economy.

The International Accounting Standards Board (IASB) has emerged as a major proponent of standardization. The IASB was formed in March 2001 to replace the International Accounting Standards Committee (IASC), which had been established in 1973. IASB is responsible for developing International Financial Reporting Standards (IFRS). These were previously previously known as the International Accounting Standards (IAS). IASB also promotes the use and application of these standards globally.

The IASB has 16 members who are responsible for the formulation of new international financial reporting standards. To issue a new standard, 75 percent of the 16 members of the board must agree. It can be difficult to get the three-quarters agreement, particularly since members come from different cultures and legal systems. To get around this problem, most IASB statements provide two acceptable alternatives. As Arthur Wyatt, former IASB

Chinese Accounting

Over time, more and more Chinese companies are tapping global capital markets, and more and more foreigners are investing in Chinese companies. These investments also come with certain strings and need for transparency. Basically, foreign investors want to be assured that the financial picture they are getting of Chinese enterprises is reliable. That has not always been the case and, many argue, is still oftentimes not the case.

If we go back only a few years to 2003, for example, China Life Insurance successfully listed its stock on the Hong Kong and New York stock exchanges, raising some $3.4 billion. However, in 2004, the head of China's National Audit Office let it slip that a routine audit of China Life's state-owned parent company had uncovered $652 million in financial irregularities. The stock immediately fell, and China Life found itself the target of a class action lawsuit on behalf of investors claiming financial fraud. Soon afterward, plans to list China Minsheng Banking Corp., China's largest private bank, on the New York Stock Exchange were put on hold after the company admitted it had faked a shareholder meeting. The stock of another successful Chinese offering in New York, Semiconductor Manufacturing International, slid when its chief financial officer made statements that contradicted those contained in filings with the U.S. Securities and Exchange Commission.

The core of the problem is that accounting rules in China are not consistent with international standards, making it difficult for investors to accurately value Chinese companies. Accounting in China has traditionally been rooted in information gathering and compliance reporting designed to measure the government's production and tax goals. The Chinese system was based on the old Soviet system, which had little to do with profit. Although the system has been changing rapidly, many problems associated with the old order still remain. Indeed, it is often said, only half in jest, that Chinese firms keep several sets of books—one for the government, one for company records, one for foreigners, and one to report what is actually going on.

To bring its rules into closer alignment with international standards, China has signaled that it will move toward adopting standards developed by the International Accounting Standards Board (IASB). China has already adopted a regulation, called the Accounting System for Business Enterprises, that was largely based on IASB standards. The system is now used to regulate both local and foreign companies operating in China. Encouragingly, the Chinese have also decided to take it one step further. The largest 1,200 firms listed on the Shanghai and Shenzhen exchanges have to adopt a broad set of accounting rules that are based on, but not identical to, IASB standards. It remains to be seen whether adoption of these new rules will actually be widespread, enforced, and transparent.

At present, many large public Chinese companies are reporting results according to two sets of rules: Chinese accounting standards and IASB standards. The differences between the two are instructive. For example, China Eastern, one of the largest airlines in China, said its net profit fell 29 percent from a year earlier to 41.6 million yuan ($6.1 million) under Chinese accounting rules. Based on international standards, however, the airline incurred a net loss of 212.5 million yuan, more than five times as great!

Sources: Weining Hu, "China's Accounting Standards: Chinese GAAP vs. US GAAP and IFRS," *China Briefing*, May 31 2017; Christopher Balding, "China's Control Problem," *Bloomberg View*, April 23, 2017; E. McDonald, "Shanghai Surprise," *Forbes*, March 26, 2007, pp. 62–63; "Cultural Revolution: Chinese Accounting," *The Economist*, January 13, 2007, p. 63; S. Hong and J. Ng, "Two Chinese Airlines Post Declines in Profit," *The Wall Street Journal*, August 27, 2008, p. B9.

chair, once said, "It's not much of a standard if you have two alternatives, but it's better than having six. If you can get agreement on two alternatives, you can capture the 11 required votes and eliminate some of the less used practices."[4]

Another hindrance to the development of international accounting standards is that compliance is voluntary; the IASB has no power to enforce its standards. Despite this, support for the IASB and recognition of its standards has been growing. Increasingly, the IASB is regarded as an effective voice for defining acceptable worldwide accounting principles. Japan, for example, began requiring financial statements to be prepared on a consolidated basis after the IASB issued its initial standards on the topic. Japan has also opted for mandatory adoption of International Financial Reporting Standards (IFRS). Russia and China have stated their intention to adopt emerging international standards (see the Country Focus for a discussion of accounting practices in China). So far, more than 100 nations had either adopted the IASB standards or permitted their use to report financial results, including three-quarters of the G20 (Group of Twenty), the world's 20 largest economies.

To date, the impact of the IASB standards has probably been least noticeable in the United States because most of the standards issued by the IASB have been consistent with opinions already articulated by the U.S. Financial Accounting Standards Board (FASB). The FASB writes the generally accepted accounting principles (GAAP) by which the financial statements of U.S. firms must be prepared. Nevertheless, differences between IASB and FASB standards remain, although the IASB and FASB have a goal of convergence. The U.S. Securities and Exchange Commission has been considering whether to allow U.S. public companies to use IASB standards, rather than GAAP, to report their results, a move that some believe could ultimately spell the end of GAAP.[5]

Another body that is having a substantial influence on the harmonization of accounting standards is the European Union. In accordance with its plans for closer economic and political union, the EU has mandated harmonization of the accounting principles of its member countries. The EU does this by issuing directives that the member states are obligated to incorporate into their own national laws. Because EU directives have the power of law, the EU might have a better chance of achieving harmonization than the IASB does. The EU has required that since January 1, 2005, financial accounts issued by some 7,000 publicly listed companies in the EU were to be in accordance with IASB standards. The Europeans hope that this requirement, by making it easier to compare the financial position of companies from different EU member states, will facilitate the development of a pan-European capital market and ultimately lower the cost of capital for EU firms.

Given the harmonization in the EU, and given that countries including Japan, China, and Russia are following suit, there could soon be only two major accounting bodies with dominant influence on global reporting: FASB in the United States and IASB elsewhere. Under an agreement, these two bodies are trying to align their standards, suggesting that differences in accounting standards across countries may disappear eventually.

In a move that indicates the trend toward adoption of acceptable international accounting standards is accelerating, the IASB has developed accounting standards for firms seeking stock listings in global markets. Also, the FASB has joined forces with accounting standard setters in Canada, Mexico, and Chile to explore areas in which the four countries can harmonize their accounting standards. The SEC has also dropped many of its objections to international standards, which could accelerate their adoption.

TEST PREP

Use SmartBook to help retain what you have learned. Access your instructor's Connect course to check out SmartBook or go to **learnsmartadvantage.com** for help.

LO20-3

Explain how accounting systems affect control systems within the multinational enterprise.

Accounting Aspects of Control Systems

One role of corporate headquarters in large complex multinational enterprises is to control subunits within the organization to ensure that they achieve the best possible performance. In the typical firm, the control process is annual and involves three main steps: (1) Head office and subunit management jointly determine subunit goals for the coming year; (2) throughout the year, the head office monitors subunit performance against the agreed goals; (3) if a subunit fails to achieve its goals, the head office intervenes in the subunit to learn why the shortfall occurred, taking corrective action when appropriate.

The accounting function assumes a critical role in this process. Most of the goals for subunits are expressed in financial terms and are embodied in the subunit's budget for the coming year. The budget is the main instrument of financial control. The budget is typically prepared by the subunit, but it must be approved by headquarters management. During the approval process, headquarters and subunit managers debate the goals that should be incorporated in the budget. One function of headquarters management is to ensure a subunit's budget contains challenging but realistic performance goals. Once a budget is agreed to, accounting information systems are used to collect data throughout the year so a subunit's performance can be evaluated against the goals contained in its budget.

In most international businesses, many of the firm's subunits are foreign subsidiaries. The performance goals for the coming year are thus set by negotiation between corporate management and the managers of foreign subsidiaries. According to one survey of control practices within multinational enterprises, the most important criterion for evaluating the performance of a foreign subsidiary is the subsidiary's actual profits compared to budgeted profits.[6] This is closely followed by a subsidiary's actual sales compared to budgeted sales and its return on investment. The same criteria are also useful in evaluating the performance of the subsidiary managers. We discuss this point later in this section. First, however, we examine two factors that can complicate the control process in an international business: exchange rate changes and transfer pricing practices.

EXCHANGE RATE CHANGES AND CONTROL SYSTEMS

Most international businesses require all budgets and performance data within the firm to be expressed in the "corporate currency," which is normally the home currency. Thus, the Malaysian subsidiary of a U.S. multinational would probably submit a budget prepared in U.S. dollars, rather than Malaysian ringgit, and performance data throughout the year would be reported to headquarters in U.S. dollars. This facilitates comparisons between subsidiaries in different countries, and it makes things easier for headquarters management. However, it also allows exchange rate changes during the year to introduce substantial distortions. For example, the Malaysian subsidiary may fail to achieve profit goals not because of any performance problems, but merely because of a decline in the value of the ringgit against the dollar. The opposite can occur, also, making a foreign subsidiary's performance look better than it actually is.

The Lessard–Lorange Model

According to research by Donald Lessard and Peter Lorange, a number of methods are available to international businesses for dealing with this problem.[7] Lessard and Lorange point out three exchange rates that can be used to translate foreign currencies into the corporate currency in setting budgets and in the subsequent tracking of performance:

- The initial rate, the spot exchange rate when the budget is adopted.

- The projected rate, the spot exchange rate forecast for the end of the budget period (i.e., the forward rate).

- The ending rate, the spot exchange rate when the budget and performance are being compared.

These three exchange rates imply nine possible combinations (see Figure 20.1). Lessard and Lorange ruled out four of the nine combinations as illogical and unreasonable;

FIGURE 20.1

Possible combinations of exchange rates in the control process.

		Rate Used to Translate Actual Performance for Comparison with Budget		
		Initial (I)	Projected (P)	Ending (E)
Rate Used for Translating Budget	Initial (I)	**(II)** Budget at Initial Actual at Initial	Budget at Initial Actual at Projected	**(IE)** Budget at Initial Actual at Ending
	Projected (P)	Budget at Projected Actual at Initial	**(PP)** Budget at Projected Actual at Projected	**(PE)** Budget at Projected Actual at Ending
	Ending (E)	Budget at Ending Actual at Initial	Budget at Ending Actual at Projected	**(EE)** Budget at Ending Actual at Ending

Figure 20.1 shows the four in color. For example, it would make no sense to use the ending rate to translate the budget and the initial rate to translate actual performance data. Any of the remaining five combinations might be used for setting budgets and evaluating performance.

With three of these five combinations—II, PP, and EE—the same exchange rate is used for translating both budget figures and performance figures into the corporate currency. All three combinations have the advantage that a change in the exchange rate during the year does not distort the control process. This is not true for the other two combinations, IE and PE. In those cases, exchange rate changes can introduce distortions. The potential for distortion is greater with IE; the ending spot exchange rate used to evaluate performance against the budget may be quite different from the initial spot exchange rate used to translate the budget. The distortion is less serious in the case of PE because the projected exchange rate considers future exchange rate movements.

Of the five combinations, Lessard and Lorange recommend that firms use the projected spot exchange rate to translate both the budget and performance figures into the corporate currency, combination PP. The projected rate in such cases will typically be the forward exchange rate as determined by the foreign exchange market (see Chapter 10 for the definition of *forward rate*) or some company-generated forecast of future spot rates, which Lessard and Lorange refer to as the **internal forward rate**. The internal forward rate may differ from the forward rate quoted by the foreign exchange market if the firm wishes to bias its business in favor of, or against, the particular foreign currency.

TRANSFER PRICING AND CONTROL SYSTEMS

Chapter 13 reviewed the various strategies that international businesses pursue. Two of these strategies, the global strategy and the transnational strategy, give rise to a globally dispersed web of productive activities. Firms pursuing these strategies disperse each value creation activity to its optimal location in the world. Thus, a product might be designed in one country, some of its components manufactured in a second country, other components manufactured in a third country, all assembled in a fourth country, and then sold worldwide.

The volume of intrafirm transactions in such firms is very high. The firms are continually shipping component parts and finished goods between subsidiaries in different countries. This poses a very important question: How should goods and services transfer between subsidiary companies in a multinational firm be priced? The price at which such goods and services are transferred is referred to as the *transfer price*.

The choice of transfer price can critically affect the performance of two subsidiaries that exchange goods or services. Consider this example: A French manufacturing subsidiary of a U.S. multinational imports a major component from Brazil. It incorporates this part into a product that it sells in France for the equivalent of $230 per unit. The product costs $200 to manufacture, of which $100 goes to the Brazilian subsidiary to pay for the component part. The remaining $100 covers costs incurred in France. Thus, the French subsidiary earns $30 profit per unit.

	Before Change in Transfer Price	After 20 Percent Increase in Transfer Price
Revenues per unit	$230	$230
Cost of component per unit	100	120
Other costs per unit	100	100
Profit per unit	$ 30	$ 10

See what happens if corporate headquarters decides to increase transfer prices by 20 percent ($20 per unit). The French subsidiary's profits will fall by two-thirds from $30 per unit to $10 per unit. Thus, the performance of the French subsidiary depends on the transfer price for the component part imported from Brazil, and the transfer price is controlled by corporate headquarters. When setting budgets and reviewing a subsidiary's performance, corporate headquarters must keep in mind the distorting effect of transfer prices.

How should transfer prices be determined? We discuss this issue in detail later in the chapter. International businesses often manipulate transfer prices to minimize their worldwide tax liability, minimize import duties, and avoid government restrictions on capital flows. For now, however, it is enough to note that the transfer price must be considered when setting budgets and evaluating a subsidiary's performance.

SEPARATION OF SUBSIDIARY AND MANAGER PERFORMANCE

In many international businesses, the same quantitative criteria are used to assess the performance of both a foreign subsidiary and its managers. Many accountants, however, argue that although it is legitimate to compare subsidiaries against each other on the basis of return on investment (ROI) or other indicators of profitability, it may not be appropriate to use these for comparing and evaluating the managers of different subsidiaries. Foreign subsidiaries do not operate in uniform environments; their environments have widely different economic, political, and social conditions, all of which influence the costs of doing business in a country and hence the subsidiaries' profitability. Thus, the manager of a subsidiary in an adverse environment that has an ROI of 5 percent may be doing a better job than the manager of a subsidiary in a benign environment that has an ROI of 20 percent. Although the firm might want to pull out of a country where its ROI is only 5 percent, it may also want to recognize the manager's achievement.

Accordingly, it has been suggested that the evaluation of a subsidiary should be kept separate from the evaluation of its manager.[8] The manager's evaluation should consider how hostile or benign the country's environment is for that business. Further, managers should be evaluated in local currency terms after making allowances for those items over which they have no control (e.g., interest rates, tax rates, inflation rates, transfer prices, exchange rates).

TEST PREP

Use SmartBook to help retain what you have learned. Access your instructor's Connect course to check out SmartBook or go to **learnsmartadvantage.com** for help.

---

globalEDGE   INSIGHTS BY ECONOMIC CLASSIFICATION

This chapter deals with international accounting and international finance. These are functions performed by an international business organization. What companies can do often depends on what country they are headquartered in, decide to operate in, or market to around the world. The globalEDGE Insights by Economic Classification focuses on market types (e.g., emerging markets, frontier markets). Emerging markets, for example, are countries that have some characteristics of a developed market, like the United States and Sweden, but are not yet a fully developed market. A wealth of information and data on emerging markets can be found at **globaledge.msu.edu/global-insights/by/econ-class**. Did you know that a key difference between emerging markets and emerging economies is that emerging markets are not fully described by, or constrained to, geography or economic strength whereas emerging economies are constrained by political and geographic boundaries?

TEST PREP

Use SmartBook to help retain what you have learned. Access your instructor's Connect course to check out SmartBook or go to **learnsmartadvantage.com** for help.

Financial Management: The Investment Decision

LO20-4

Discuss how operating in different nations affects investment decisions within the multinational enterprise.

One role of the financial manager in an international business is to try to quantify the various benefits, costs, and risks that are likely to flow from an investment in a given location. A decision to invest in activities in a given country must consider many economic, political, cultural, and strategic variables. We have been discussing this issue throughout much of this book. Chapters 2, 3, and 4 touched on it when we discussed how the political, economic, legal, and cultural environment of a country can influence the benefits, costs, and risks of doing business there and thus its attractiveness as an investment site. We returned to the issue in Chapter 8 with a discussion of the economic theory of foreign direct investment. We identified a number of factors that determine the economic attractiveness of a foreign investment opportunity. We also looked at the political economy of foreign direct investment in Chapter 7, and we considered the role that government intervention can play in foreign investment. In Chapter 13, we pulled much of this material together when we considered how a firm can reduce its costs of value creation and/or increase its value added by investing in productive activities in other countries. We returned to the issue again in Chapter 15 when we considered the various modes for entering foreign markets.

CAPITAL BUDGETING

Capital budgeting is the technique financial managers use to try to quantify the benefits, costs, and risks of an investment. This enables top managers to compare, in a reasonably objective fashion, different investment alternatives within and across countries so they can make informed choices about where the firm should invest its scarce financial resources. Capital budgeting for a foreign project uses the same theoretical framework that domestic capital budgeting uses; that is, the firm must first estimate the cash flows associated with the project over time. In most cases, the cash flows will be negative at first, because the firm will be investing heavily in production facilities. After some initial period, however, the cash flows will become positive as investment costs decline and revenues grow. Once the cash flows have been estimated, they must be discounted to determine their net present value using an appropriate discount rate. The most commonly used discount rate is either the firm's cost of capital or some other required rate of return. If the net present value of the discounted cash flows is greater than zero, the firm should go ahead with the project.[9]

Although this might sound quite straightforward, capital budgeting is in practice a very complex and imperfect process. Among the factors complicating the process for an international business are these:

1. A distinction must be made between cash flows to the project and cash flows to the parent company.
2. Political and economic risks, including foreign exchange risk, can significantly change the value of foreign investment.
3. The connection between cash flows to the parent and the source of financing must be recognized.

We look at the first two of these issues in this section. Discussion of the connection between cash flows and the source of financing is postponed until the next section, where we discuss the source of financing.

PROJECT AND PARENT CASH FLOWS

A theoretical argument exists for analyzing any foreign project from the perspective of the parent company because cash flows to the project are not necessarily the same thing as cash flows to the parent company. The project may not be able to remit all its cash flows to the parent for a number of reasons. For example, cash flows may be blocked from repatriation by the host-country government, they may be taxed at an unfavorable rate, or the host government may require that a certain percentage of the cash flows generated from the project be reinvested within the host nation. While these restrictions don't affect the net present value of the project itself, they do affect the net present value of the project to the parent company because they limit the cash flows that can be remitted to it from the project.

When evaluating a foreign investment opportunity, the parent should be interested in the cash flows it will receive—as opposed to those the project generates—because those are the basis for dividends to stockholders, investments elsewhere in the world, repayment of worldwide corporate debt, and so on. Stockholders will not perceive blocked earnings as

Black Sea Oil and Gas Ltd.

Black Sea Oil and Gas Ltd., of Calgary, Canada, formed a 50–50 joint venture with the Tyumen Oil Company, Russia's sixth-largest integrated oil company. The objective of the venture, known as the Tura Petroleum Company, was to explore the Tura oil field in western Siberia. Tyumen was 90 percent owned by the Russian government; consequently Black Sea negotiated directly with representatives of the Russian government when establishing the joint venture. The agreement called for both parties to contribute more than $40 million to the formation of the venture, Black Sea in the form of cash, technology, and expertise, and Tyumen in the form of infrastructure and the licenses for oil exploration and production that it held in the region.

From an operational perspective, the venture proved to be a success. Following the injection of cash and technology from Black Sea, production at the Tura field went from 4,000 barrels a day to nearly 12,000. However, Black Sea did not capture any of the economic profits flowing from this investment. Consequently, the Moscow-based Alfa Group, one of Russia's largest private companies, purchased a controlling stake in Tyumen from the Russian government. The new owners of Tyumen quickly concluded that the Tura

joint venture was not fair to them, and they wanted it canceled. Their argument was that the value of the assets contributed by Tyumen to the joint venture was far in excess of $40 million, while the value of the technology and expertise contributed by Black Sea was significantly less than $40 million. The new owners also found some conflicting legislation that seemed to indicate the licenses held by Tura were owned by Tyumen and that Black Sea therefore had no right to the resulting production.

Tyumen took the issue to court in Russia and won, despite the fact that the original deal had been negotiated by the Russian government. Black Sea had little choice but to walk away from the deal. According to Black Sea, by legal maneuvering, Tyumen expropriated Black Sea's investment in the Tura venture. In contrast, the management of Tyumen claimed it had behaved in a perfectly legal manner.

Sources: S. Block, "Integrating Traditional Capital Budgeting Concepts into an International Decision-Making Environment," *The Engineering Economist* 45 (2000), pp. 309–25; J. C. Backer and L. J. Beardsley, "Multinational Companies' Use of Risk Evaluation and Profit Measurement for Capital Budgeting Decisions," *Journal of Business Finance,* Spring 1973, pp. 34–43.

contributing to the value of the firm, and creditors will not count them when calculating the parent's ability to service its debt. The Management Focus on Black Sea Oil and Gas Ltd. illustrates the risks associated with a project.

But the problem of blocked earnings is not as serious as it once was. The worldwide move toward greater acceptance of free-market economics (discussed in Chapter 2 and 3) has reduced the number of countries in which governments are likely to prohibit the affiliates of foreign multinationals from remitting cash flows to their parent companies. In addition, as explained later in the chapter, firms have a number of options for circumventing host-government attempts to block the free flow of funds from an affiliate.

ADJUSTING FOR POLITICAL AND ECONOMIC RISK

When analyzing a foreign investment opportunity, the company must consider the political and economic risks that stem from the foreign location.[10] We discuss these before looking at how capital budgeting methods can be adjusted to take risks into account.

Political Risk

The concept of political risk was introduced in Chapter 2. There we defined it as the likelihood that political forces will cause drastic changes in a country's business environment that hurt the profit and other goals of a business enterprise. Political risk tends to be greater in countries experiencing social unrest or disorder and in countries where the underlying nature of the society makes the likelihood of social unrest high. When the political risk is high, there is a high probability that a change will occur in the country's political environment that will endanger foreign firms there.

In extreme cases, political change may result in the expropriation of foreign firms' assets. This occurred to U.S. firms after the Iranian revolution of 1979. In more recent decades, the risk of outright expropriations has become almost zero. However, a lack of consistent legislation and proper law enforcement and no willingness on the part of the government to enforce contracts and protect private property rights can result in the de facto expropriation of the assets of a foreign multinational.

Political and social unrest may also result in economic collapse, which can render worthless a firm's assets. In less extreme cases, political changes may result in increased tax rates, the imposition of exchange controls that limit or block a subsidiary's ability to remit earnings to its parent company, the imposition of price controls, and government interference in existing contracts. The likelihood of any of these events impairs the attractiveness of a foreign investment opportunity.

Many firms devote considerable attention to political risk analysis and to quantifying political risk. globalEDGE™ reports on a series of indices by country (**globaledge.msu. edu/global-insights/by/country**) that address various country risk factors such as corruption, ease of doing business, employment protection, global competitiveness, global enabling trade, global manufacturing competitiveness, economic freedom, property rights, open budget, paying taxes, and several more. However, the problem with virtually all attempts to forecast political risk is that they try to predict a future that can only be guessed at—and, in many cases, the guesses are wrong. Few people foresaw the Iranian revolution, the collapse of communism in eastern Europe, the dramatic breakup of the Soviet Union, the terrorist attack on the World Trade Center, Great Britain's proposed exit ("Brexit") from the European Union, or the election of Donald Trump as the 45th president of the United States; yet all these events had a profound impact on the business environments of many countries. This is not to say that political risk assessment is without value, but it is more art than science.

Economic Risk

The concept of economic risk was also introduced in Chapter 3. It was defined as the likelihood that economic mismanagement will cause drastic changes in a country's business environment that hurt the profit and other goals of a business enterprise. In practice, the biggest problem arising from economic mismanagement has been inflation. Historically, many governments have expanded their domestic money supply in misguided attempts to stimulate economic activity. The result has often been too much money chasing too few goods, resulting in price inflation. As we saw in Chapter 10, price inflation is reflected in a drop in the value of a country's currency on the foreign exchange market. This can be a serious problem for a foreign firm with assets in that country because the value of the cash flows it receives from those assets will fall as the country's currency depreciates on the foreign exchange market. The likelihood of this occurring decreases the attractiveness of foreign investment in that country.

There have been many attempts to quantify countries' economic risk and long-term movements in their exchange rates. (e.g., *Euromoney*'s annual country risk rating incorporates an assessment of economic risk in its calculation of each country's overall level of risk). As we saw in Chapter 11, there have been extensive empirical studies of the relationship between countries' inflation rates and their currencies' exchange rates. These studies show there is a long-run relationship between a country's relative inflation rates and changes in exchange rates. However, the relationship is not as close as theory would predict; it is not reliable in the short run and is not totally reliable in the long run. So as with political risk, any attempts to quantify economic risk must be tempered with some healthy skepticism.

RISK AND CAPITAL BUDGETING

In analyzing a foreign investment opportunity, the additional risk that stems from its location can be handled in at least two ways. The first method is to treat all risk as a single problem by increasing the discount rate applicable to foreign projects in countries where political and economic risks are perceived as high. Thus, for example, a firm might apply a 6 percent discount rate to potential investments in Great Britain, the United States, and Germany, reflecting those countries' economic and political stability, and it might use a 12 percent discount rate for potential investments in Russia, reflecting the greater perceived political and economic risks in that country. The higher the discount rate, the higher the projected net cash flows must be for an investment to have a positive net present value.

Adjusting discount rates to reflect a location's riskiness seems to be fairly widely practiced. For example, several studies of large U.S. multinationals have found that many of them routinely add a premium percentage for risk to the discount rate they used in evaluating potential foreign investment projects.[11] However, critics of this method argue that it penalizes early cash flows too heavily and does not penalize distant cash flows enough.[12] They point out that if political or economic collapse were expected in the near future, the investment would not occur anyway. So for any investment decisions, the political and economic risk being assessed is not of immediate possibilities but at some distance in the future. Accordingly, it can be argued that rather than using a higher discount rate to evaluate such risky projects, which penalizes early cash flows too heavily, it is better to revise future cash flows from the project downward to reflect the possibility of adverse political or economic changes sometime in the future. Surveys of actual practice within multinationals suggest that the practice of revising future cash flows downward is almost as popular as that of revising the discount rate upward.[13]

Financial Management: The Financing Decision

When considering its options for financing, an international business must consider how foreign investment will be financed. If external financing is required, the firm must decide whether to tap the global capital market for funds or borrow from sources in the host country. If the firm is going to seek external financing for a project, it will want to borrow funds from the lowest-cost source of capital available. As we saw in Chapter 12, firms increasingly are turning to the global capital market to finance their investments. The cost of capital is typically lower in the global capital market, by virtue of its size and liquidity, than in many domestic capital markets, particularly those that are small and relatively illiquid. Thus, for example, a U.S. firm making an investment in Denmark may finance the investment by borrowing through the London-based Eurobond market rather than the Danish capital market.

However, despite the trends toward deregulation of financial services, in some cases, host-country government restrictions may rule out this option. The governments of some countries require, or at least prefer, foreign multinationals to finance projects in their country by local debt financing or local sales of equity. In countries where liquidity is limited, this raises the cost of capital used to finance a project. Thus, in capital budgeting decisions, the discount rate must be adjusted upward to reflect this. However, this is not the only possibility. In Chapter 8, we saw that some governments court foreign investment by offering foreign firms low-interest loans, lowering the cost of capital. Accordingly, in capital budgeting decisions, the discount rate should be revised downward in such cases.

In addition to the impact of host-government policies on the cost of capital and financing decisions, the firm may wish to consider local debt financing for investments in countries where the local currency is expected to depreciate on the foreign exchange market. The amount of local currency required to meet interest payments and retire principal on local debt obligations is not affected when a country's currency depreciates. However, if foreign debt obligations must be served, the amount of local currency required to do this will increase as the currency depreciates, and this effectively raises the cost of capital. Thus, although the initial cost of capital may be greater with local borrowing, it may be better to borrow locally if the local currency is expected to depreciate on the foreign exchange market.

TEST PREP

Use SmartBook to help retain what you have learned. Access your instructor's Connect course to check out SmartBook or go to **learnsmartadvantage.com** for help.

LO20-5

Discuss the different financing options available to the foreign subsidiary of a multinational enterprise.

TEST PREP

Use SmartBook to help retain what you have learned. Access your instructor's Connect course to check out SmartBook or go to **learnsmartadvantage.com** for help.

Financial Management: Global Money Management

Money management decisions attempt to manage the firm's global cash resources—its working capital—most efficiently. This involves minimizing cash balances, reducing transaction costs, and minimizing the corporate tax burden.

LO20-6

Understand how money management in the international business can be used to minimize cash balances, transaction costs, and taxation.

MINIMIZING CASH BALANCES

Every business needs to hold some cash balances for servicing accounts that must be paid and for insuring against unanticipated negative variation from its projected cash flows. The critical issue for an international business is whether each foreign subsidiary should hold its own cash balances or whether cash balances should be held at a centralized depository. In general, firms prefer to hold cash balances at a centralized depository for three reasons.

First, by pooling cash reserves centrally, the firm can deposit larger amounts. Cash balances are typically deposited in liquid accounts, such as overnight money market accounts. Because interest rates on such deposits normally increase with the size of the deposit, by pooling cash centrally, the firm should be able to earn a higher interest rate than it would if each subsidiary managed its own cash balances.

Second, if the centralized depository is located in a major financial center (e.g., London, New York, or Tokyo), it should have access to information about good short-term investment opportunities that the typical foreign subsidiary would lack. Also, the financial experts at a centralized depository should be able to develop investment skills and know-how that managers in the typical foreign subsidiary would lack. Thus, the firm should make better investment decisions if it pools its cash reserves at a centralized depository.

Third, by pooling its cash reserves, the firm can reduce the total size of the cash pool it must hold in highly liquid accounts, which enables the firm to invest a larger amount of cash reserves in longer-term, less liquid financial instruments that earn a higher interest rate. For example, a U.S. firm has three foreign subsidiaries—one in Korea, one in China, and one in Japan. Each subsidiary maintains a cash balance that includes an amount for dealing with its day-to-day needs plus a precautionary amount for dealing with unanticipated cash demands. The firm's policy is that the total required cash balance is equal to three standard deviations of the expected day-to-day needs amount. The three-standard-deviation requirement reflects the firm's estimate that, in practice, there is a 99.87 percent probability that the subsidiary will have sufficient cash to deal with both day-to-day and unanticipated cash demands. Cash needs are assumed to be normally distributed in each country and independent of each other (e.g., cash needs in Japan do not affect cash needs in China).

The individual subsidiaries' day-to-day cash needs and the precautionary cash balances they should hold are as follows (in millions of dollars):

	Day-to-Day Cash Needs (A)	One Standard Deviation (B)	Required Cash Balance (A + 3 × B)
Korea	$10	$ 1	$13
China	6	2	12
Japan	12	3	21
Total	$28	$ 6	$46

Thus, the Korean subsidiary estimates that it must hold $10 million to serve its day-to-day needs. The standard deviation of this is $1 million, so it is to hold an additional $3 million as a precautionary amount. This gives a total required cash balance of $13 million. The total of the required cash balances for all three subsidiaries is $46 million.

Now consider what might occur if the firm decided to maintain all three cash balances at a centralized depository in Tokyo. Because variances are additive when probability distributions are independent of each other, the standard deviation of the combined precautionary account would be

$$\text{Standard derivation} = \sqrt{\$1,000,000^2 + \$2,000,000^2 + \$3,000,000^2}$$
$$= \sqrt{\$14,000,000}$$
$$= \$3,741,657$$

Therefore, if the firm used a centralized depository, it would need to hold $28 million for day-to-day needs plus (3 × $3,741,657) as a precautionary amount, or a total cash balance of $39,224,971. In other words, the firm's total required cash balance would be reduced from $46 million to $39,224,971, a saving of $6,775,029. This is cash that could be invested in less liquid, higher-interest accounts or in tangible assets. The saving arises simply due to the statistical effects of summing the three independent, normal probability distributions.

However, a firm's ability to establish a centralized depository that can serve short-term cash needs might be limited by government-imposed restrictions on capital flows across borders (e.g., controls put in place to protect a country's foreign exchange reserves). Also, the transaction costs of moving money into and out of different currencies can limit the advantages of such a system. Despite this, many firms hold at least their subsidiaries' precautionary cash reserves at a centralized depository, having each subsidiary hold its own cash balance for day-to-day needs. The globalization of the world capital market and the general removal of barriers to the free flow of cash across borders (particularly among advanced industrialized countries) are two trends likely to increase the use of centralized depositories.

REDUCING TRANSACTION COSTS

Transaction costs are the cost of exchange. Every time a firm changes cash from one currency into another currency it must bear a transaction cost—the commission fee it pays to foreign exchange dealers for performing the transaction. Most banks also charge a transfer fee for moving cash from one location to another; this is another transaction cost. The commission and transfer fees arising from intrafirm transactions can be substantial; according to the United Nations, 40 percent of international trade involves transactions between the different national subsidiaries of transnational corporations. The volume of such transactions is likely to be particularly high in a firm that has a globally dispersed web of interdependent value creation activities. Multilateral netting allows a multinational firm to reduce the transaction costs that arise when many transactions occur between its subsidiaries by reducing the number of transactions.

Multilateral netting is an extension of bilateral netting. Under bilateral netting, if a French subsidiary owes a Mexican subsidiary $6 million and the Mexican subsidiary simultaneously owes the French subsidiary $4 million, a bilateral settlement will be made with a single payment of $2 million from the French subsidiary to the Mexican subsidiary, the remaining debt being canceled.

Under multilateral netting, this simple concept is extended to the transactions between multiple subsidiaries within an international business. Consider a firm that wants to establish multilateral netting among four Asian subsidiaries based in Korea, China, Japan, and Taiwan. These subsidiaries all trade with each other, so at the end of each month, a large volume of cash transactions must be settled. Figure 20.2 shows how the payment schedule might look at the end of a given month. Figure 20.3 is a payment matrix that summarizes the obligations among the subsidiaries. Note that $43 million needs to flow among the subsidiaries. If the transaction costs (foreign exchange commissions plus transfer fees) amount to 1 percent of the total funds to be transferred, this will cost the parent firm $430,000. However, this amount can be reduced by multilateral netting. Using the payment matrix (Figure 20.3), the firm can determine the payments that need to be made among its subsidiaries to settle these obligations. Figure 20.4 shows the results. By multilateral netting, the transactions depicted in Figure 20.2 are reduced to just three; the

FIGURE 20.2

Cash flows before
multilateral netting.

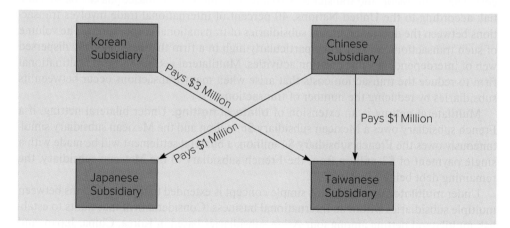

Receiving Subsidiary	Paying Subsidiary				Total Receipts	Net Receipts (payments)
	Korea	China	Japan	Taiwan		
Korean	—	$ 3	$4	$5	$12	($3)
Chinese	$ 4	—	2	3	9	(2)
Japanese	5	3	—	1	9	1
Taiwanese	6	5	2	—	13	4
Total payments	$15	$11	$8	$9	$43	$5

FIGURE 20.3

Calculation of net receipts (all amounts in millions).

FIGURE 20.4

Cash flows after
multilateral netting.

Korean subsidiary pays $3 million to the Taiwanese subsidiary, and the Chinese subsidiary pays $1 million to the Japanese subsidiary and $1 million to the Taiwanese subsidiary. The total funds that flow among the subsidiaries are reduced from $43 million to just $5 million, and the transaction costs are reduced from $430,000 to $50,000, a savings of $380,000 achieved through multilateral netting.

MANAGING THE TAX BURDEN

Different countries have different tax regimes. For example, among developed nations the top rates for corporate income tax varies from a high of 35 percent in several countries to a low of 12.5 percent in Ireland. In Germany and Japan, the tax rate is lower on income distributed to stockholders as dividends (36 and 35 percent, respectively), whereas in France the tax on profits distributed to stockholders is higher (42 percent). In the United States, the rate varies from state to state. The federal top rate is 21 percent (which went into effect in 2018, after having been 35 percent), but states also tax corporate income, with state and local taxes ranging from 0 percent to 12 percent.

Many nations follow the worldwide principle that they have the right to tax income earned outside their boundaries by entities based in their country.[14] Thus, the U.S. government can tax the earnings of the German subsidiary of an enterprise incorporated in the United States. Double taxation occurs when the income of a foreign subsidiary is taxed both by the host-country government and by the parent company's home government. However, double taxation is mitigated by tax credits, tax treaties, and the deferral principle.

A **tax credit** allows an entity to reduce the taxes paid to the home government by the amount of taxes paid to the foreign government. A **tax treaty** between two countries is an agreement specifying which items of income will be taxed by the authorities of the country where the income is earned. For example, a tax treaty between the United States and Germany may specify that a U.S. firm need not pay tax in Germany on any earnings from its German subsidiary that are remitted to the United States in the form of dividends. A **deferral principle** specifies that parent companies are not taxed on foreign source income until they actually receive a dividend.

For the international business with activities in many countries, the various tax regimes and the tax treaties have important implications for how the firm should structure its internal payments system among the foreign subsidiaries and the parent company. As we will see in the next section, the firm can use transfer prices and fronting loans to minimize its global tax liability. In addition, the form in which income is remitted from a foreign subsidiary to the parent company (e.g., royalty payments versus dividend payments) can be structured to minimize the firm's global tax liability.

Some firms use **tax havens** such as the Bahamas and Bermuda to minimize their tax liability. A tax haven is a country with an exceptionally low, or even no, income tax. International businesses avoid or defer income taxes by establishing a wholly owned, nonoperating subsidiary in the tax haven. The tax haven subsidiary owns the common stock of the operating foreign subsidiaries. This allows all transfers of funds from foreign operating subsidiaries to the parent company to be funneled through the tax haven subsidiary. The tax levied on foreign source income by a firm's home government, which might normally be paid when a dividend is declared by a foreign subsidiary, can be deferred under the deferral principle until the tax haven subsidiary pays the dividend to the parent. This dividend payment can be postponed indefinitely if foreign operations continue to grow and require new internal financing from the tax haven affiliate.

Many U.S. multinationals maintain large tax balances in foreign tax havens because they do not want to pay U.S. corporate taxes when those earnings are repatriated to the United States. Estimates suggest that American multinationals have more than $2 trillion in accumulated foreign earnings parked in foreign tax havens. Companies with large cash holdings in tax-sheltered subsidiaries include Apple, Cisco Systems, Microsoft, and Google. Apple alone has roughly 70 percent of its short-term securities on its balance sheet held overseas. As seen in the Management Focus, Microsoft has about 90 percent of its "cash" held in subsidiaries located in tax havens or at foreign locations.[15]

Some argue that holding such cash balances overseas to avoid tax is counterproductive and that shareholders would benefit more if the cash was repatriated to the United States, tax paid on it, and the remaining funds returned to shareholders in the form of dividend payouts and stock buybacks. Due to tax credits, for example, Microsoft would probably pay a U.S. corporate tax rate close to the maximum of 21 percent on the money held overseas if it decided to send it back to the United States. But the argument is that lots of cash would be remaining after the taxes are paid that should be distributed to shareholders.

MANAGEMENT FOCUS

Microsoft and Its Foreign Cash Holdings

When Microsoft announced it would be purchasing the internet communications company Skype for $8.5 billion, less than a decade after Skype's founding, people in the technology industry took notice. When the deal was announced as an all-cash deal, shareholders and taxpayers in the United States also started wondering. Why would Microsoft buy Skype using all cash, and where does Microsoft have such large cash reserves?

But, let's backtrack: Skype was founded in 2003 by two Scandinavians: Janus Friis from Denmark and Niklas Zennström from Sweden. The Skype software was created by Estonians Ahti Heinla, Priit Kasesalu, and Jaan Tallinn. At this time, Skype is an instant messaging app that can manage both text messages and video chat services. Users may transmit both text and video messages, and they can exchange digital documents such as images, text, and video via the Skype software on a computer or app via various gadgets (e.g., smartphones). Skype also allows video conference calls.

After the sale, Skype was incorporated as a division of Microsoft. The acquisition was the largest in Microsoft's history at that time (2011). Skype had been purchased by eBay in 2005 for $3.1 billion, but eBay took a $1.4 billion accounting charge in 2007 after the acquisition failed to realize hoped-for synergies. In 2009, eBay sold a 70 percent

stake in Skype to a group of investors led by the U.S. private equity firm Silver Lake Partners. The sale to Silver Lake valued Skype at $2.75 billion. Many observers were surprised that only 18 months later, Microsoft was prepared to pay $8.5 billion. Microsoft's stated goal was to integrate Skype's voice and video communication offerings into Microsoft's suite of products in order to bolster sales of those products and make Microsoft more relevant in the age of digital devices, mobile communication, and cloud computing.

Perhaps the most eye-opening aspects of the sale of Skype to Microsoft was that the company used cash held overseas in foreign subsidiaries. These are subsidiaries located in countries with very low corporate tax rates, such as Ireland, Singapore, and Bermuda. Microsoft stated in its annual report that it had more than $30 billion in "permanently reinvested earnings" outside the United States. As an example, in a report to the U.S. Senate, Microsoft Corp explained that it does 85 percent of its R&D in the United States. In fact, 36,000 of Microsoft's 94,000 employees are in product R&D. Last year, the company reported income of $23.2 billion but paid only $3.11 billion in federal tax (13.4 percent). That $3.11 billion—as much as it sounds—is much lower than the corporate tax rate of 21 percent (it was 35 percent

---

LO20-7

Understand the basic techniques for global money management.

MOVING MONEY ACROSS BORDERS

Pursuing the objectives of utilizing the firm's cash resources most efficiently and minimizing the firm's global tax liability requires the firm to be able to transfer funds from one location to another around the globe. International businesses use a number of techniques to transfer liquid funds across borders. These include dividend remittances, royalty payments and fees, transfer prices, and fronting loans. Some firms rely on more than one of these techniques to transfer funds across borders—a practice known as *unbundling*. By using a mix of techniques to transfer liquid funds from a foreign subsidiary to the parent company, unbundling allows an international business to recover funds from its foreign subsidiaries without piquing host-country sensitivities with large "dividend drains."

A firm's ability to select a particular policy is severely limited when a foreign subsidiary is part-owned either by a local joint-venture partner or by local stockholders. Serving the legitimate demands of the local co-owners of a foreign subsidiary may limit the firm's ability to impose the kind of dividend policy, royalty payment schedule, or transfer pricing policy that would be optimal for the parent company.

Dividend Remittances

Payment of dividends is the most common method by which firms transfer funds from foreign subsidiaries to the parent company. The dividend policy typically varies with each for a long time in the United States before being lowered to 21 percent in 2018).

Now, Microsoft is no exception to holding foreign cash and monetary instruments. It is estimated that American corporations stash more than $2 trillion in untaxed profits outside the country. Interestingly, as divided as the United States is politically, there appears to be growing political consensus that a change in the tax rules should be made to encourage repatriation of the vast troves of multinational corporations' earnings held outside the country. However, companies, American taxpayers, and investors often have conflicting stakes in the outcome, so it remains to be seen what economic climate the United States will be in moving forward. What we do know is that the corporate tax rate in the United States has ranged from a low of 15 percent to a high of 50 percent in the last half a century (corporate taxes in the U.S. effectively began in 1909), and that even at the rate of 21 percent, the U.S. has a relatively high corporate tax rate.

What we also know is that the $2 trillion in untaxed profits residing collectively with numerous U.S. multinationals in various subsidiaries outside the country can be used for spending splurges like Microsoft buying Skype. In Microsoft's case, foreign cash represents the accumulated net proceeds from foreign sales. Under U.S. law, Microsoft does not pay taxes on those earnings until they are repatriated to the United States. In theory, at least, they can be held indefinitely overseas. Microsoft stated that by using foreign cash to acquire Skype, it was being tax-efficient.

Microsoft wasn't the only company involved in the acquisition that reaped tax benefits. Skype itself was incorporated in Luxembourg, a country with a corporate income tax rate of just 0.4 percent. At the time of the acquisition, the U.S. private equity firm Silver Lake owned 39 percent of Skype. Two of the three Silver Lake entities that owned shares in Skype were based in the Caribbean tax haven of George Town, Cayman Islands, suggesting that Silver Lake would not be paying much in the way of U.S. capital gains tax on the profits made from its investments in Skype. In addition, 30 percent of Skype was owned by eBay. Despite being an American company, eBay's Skype shareholding was held by eBay International AG, which is based in Switzerland, where corporate tax rates are between 13 and 25 percent.

Despite paying $8.5 billion for Skype, Microsoft's foreign cash hoard has continued to grow. Microsoft holds more than $100 billion in cash in foreign subsidiaries, representing more than 90 percent of all of the company's cash holdings. In its regulatory filings, the company noted that this cash would be subject to material repatriation tax effects if returned to the United States.

Sources: Jeff Sommer, "A Stranded $2 Trillion Overseas Stash Gets Closer to Coming Home," *The New York Times*, November 4, 2016; David Kocieniewski, "Why Microsoft, with $100 Billion, Wants a Loan for LinkedIn," *Bloomberg Technology*, June 13, 2016; S. Murray-Morris, "Apple and Microsoft Have Bigger Cash Holdings Than UK," *The Telegraph*, April 11, 2014; R. Jilani, "Microsoft Structured Acquisition of Skype to Avoid US Taxes," *Think Progress*, May 13, 2011; N. Wingfield, "Microsoft Dials Up Change," *The Wall Street Journal*, May 11, 2011.

subsidiary depending on such factors as tax regulations, foreign exchange risk, the age of the subsidiary, and the extent of local equity participation. For example, the higher the rate of tax levied on dividends by the host-country government, the less attractive this option becomes relative to other options for transferring liquid funds. With regard to foreign exchange risk, firms sometimes require foreign subsidiaries based in "high-risk" countries to speed up the transfer of funds to the parent through accelerated dividend payments. This moves corporate funds out of a country whose currency is expected to depreciate significantly. The age of a foreign subsidiary influences dividend policy in that older subsidiaries tend to remit a higher proportion of their earnings in dividends to the parent, presumably because a subsidiary has fewer capital investment needs as it matures. Local equity participation is a factor because local co-owners' demands for dividends must be recognized.

Royalty Payments and Fees

Royalties represent the remuneration paid to the owners of technology, patents, or trade names for the use of that technology or the right to manufacture and/or sell products under those patents or trade names. It is common for a parent company to charge its foreign subsidiaries royalties for the technology, patents, or trade names it has transferred to them. Royalties may be levied as a fixed monetary amount per unit of the product the subsidiary sells or as a percentage of a subsidiary's gross revenues.

A fee is a compensation for professional services or expertise supplied to a foreign subsidiary by the parent company or another subsidiary. Fees are sometimes differentiated into "management fees" for general expertise and advice and "technical assistance fees" for guidance in technical matters. Fees are usually levied as fixed charges for the particular services provided.

Royalties and fees have certain tax advantages over dividends, particularly when the corporate tax rate is higher in the host country than in the parent's home country. Royalties and fees are often tax-deductible locally (because they are viewed as an expense), so arranging for payment in royalties and fees will reduce the foreign subsidiary's tax liability. If the foreign subsidiary compensates the parent company by dividend payments, local income taxes must be paid before the dividend distribution, and withholding taxes must be paid on the dividend itself. Although the parent can often take a tax credit for the local withholding and income taxes it has paid, part of the benefit can be lost if the subsidiary's combined tax rate is higher than the parent's.

Transfer Prices

Any international business normally involves a large number of transfers of goods and services between the parent company and foreign subsidiaries and between foreign subsidiaries. This is particularly likely in firms pursuing global and transnational strategies because these firms are likely to have dispersed their value creation activities to various "optimal" locations around the globe (see Chapter 13). As noted earlier, the price at which goods and services are transferred between entities within the firm is referred to as the transfer price.[16]

Transfer prices can be used to position funds within an international business. For example, funds can be moved out of a particular country by setting high transfer prices for goods and services supplied to a subsidiary in that country and by setting low transfer prices for the goods and services sourced from that subsidiary. Conversely, funds can be positioned in a country by the opposite policy: setting low transfer prices for goods and services supplied to a subsidiary in that country and setting high transfer prices for the goods and services sourced from that subsidiary. This movement of funds can be between the firm's subsidiaries or between the parent company and a subsidiary.

At least four gains can be derived by adjusting transfer prices:

1. The firm can reduce its tax liabilities by using transfer prices to shift earnings from a high-tax country to a low-tax one.

2. The firm can use transfer prices to move funds out of a country where a significant currency devaluation is expected, thereby reducing its exposure to foreign exchange risk.

3. The firm can use transfer prices to move funds from a subsidiary to the parent company (or a tax haven) when financial transfers in the form of dividends are restricted or blocked by host-country government policies.

4. The firm can use transfer prices to reduce the import duties it must pay when an ad valorem tariff is in force—a tariff assessed as a percentage of value. In this case, low transfer prices on goods or services being imported into the country are required. Since this lowers the value of the goods or services, it lowers the tariff.

However, significant problems are associated with pursuing a transfer pricing policy.[17] Few governments like it.[18] When transfer prices are used to reduce a firm's tax liabilities or import duties, most governments feel they are being cheated of their legitimate income. Similarly, when transfer prices are manipulated to circumvent government restrictions on capital flows (e.g., dividend remittances), governments perceive this as breaking the spirit—if not the letter—of the law. Many governments now limit international businesses' ability to manipulate transfer prices in the manner described. The United States has strict regulations governing transfer pricing practices. According to Section 482 of the Internal Revenue Code, the Internal Revenue Service (IRS) can reallocate gross income, deductions, credits, or allowances between related corporations to prevent tax evasion or to reflect more clearly a proper allocation of income. Under the IRS guidelines and subsequent judicial interpretation, the burden of proof is on the taxpayer to show that the IRS has been arbitrary or unreasonable in reallocating income. The correct transfer price, according to the IRS guidelines, is an arm's-length price—the price that would prevail between unrelated firms in a market setting. Such a strict interpretation of what is a correct transfer price theoretically limits a firm's ability to manipulate transfer prices to achieve the benefits we have discussed. Many other countries have followed the U.S. lead in emphasizing that transfer prices should be set on an arm's-length basis.

Another problem associated with transfer pricing is related to management incentives and performance evaluation.[19] Transfer pricing is inconsistent with a policy of treating each subsidiary in the firm as a profit center. When transfer prices are manipulated by the firm and deviate significantly from the arm's-length price, the subsidiary's performance may depend as much on transfer prices as it does on other pertinent factors, such as management effort. A subsidiary told to charge a high transfer price for a good supplied to another subsidiary will appear to be doing better than it actually is, while the subsidiary purchasing the goodwill appear to be doing worse. Unless this is recognized when performance is being evaluated, serious distortions in management incentive systems can occur. For example, managers in the selling subsidiary may be able to use high transfer prices to mask inefficiencies, while managers in the purchasing subsidiary may become disheartened by the effect of high transfer prices on their subsidiary's profitability.

Despite these problems, research suggests that not all international businesses use arm's-length pricing but instead use some cost-based system for pricing transfers among their subunits (typically cost plus some standard markup). A survey of 164 U.S. multinational firms found that 35 percent of the firms used market-based prices, 15 percent used negotiated prices, and 65 percent used a cost-based pricing method. (The figures add up to more than 100 percent because some companies use more than one method.)[20] Only market and negotiated prices could reasonably be interpreted as arm's-length prices. The opportunity for price manipulation is much greater with cost-based transfer pricing. Other more sophisticated research has uncovered indirect evidence that many corporations do manipulate transfer prices in order to reduce global tax liabilities.[21]

Although a firm may be able to manipulate transfer prices to avoid tax liabilities or circumvent government restrictions on capital flows across borders, this does not mean the firm should do so. Since the practice often violates at least the spirit of the law in many countries, the ethics of engaging in transfer pricing are dubious at best. Also, there are clear signs that tax authorities in many countries are increasing their scrutiny of this practice in order to stamp out abuses. A survey of some 600 multinationals undertaken by accountants at Ernst & Young found that 75 percent of them believed they would be the subject of a transfer pricing audit by tax authorities in the next two years.[22] Some 61 percent of the multinationals in the survey stated that transfer pricing was the top tax issue that they faced.

Fronting Loans

A fronting loan is a loan between a parent and its subsidiary channeled through a financial intermediary, usually a large international bank. In a direct intrafirm loan, the parent company lends cash directly to the foreign subsidiary, and the subsidiary repays it later. In a fronting loan, the parent company deposits funds in an international bank, and the bank then lends the same amount to the foreign subsidiary. Thus, a U.S. firm might deposit $100,000 in a London bank. The London bank might then lend that $100,000 to an Indian subsidiary of the firm. From the bank's point of view, the loan is risk-free because it has 100 percent collateral in the form of the parent's deposit. The bank "fronts" for the parent, hence the name. The bank makes a profit by paying the

FIGURE 20.5

An example of the tax aspects of a fronting loan.

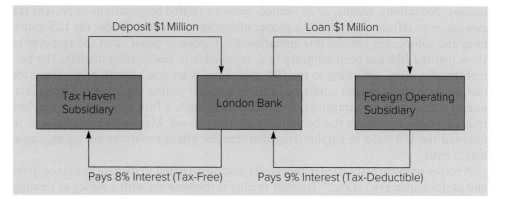

parent company a slightly lower interest rate on its deposit than it charges the foreign subsidiary on the borrowed funds.

Firms use fronting loans for two reasons. First, fronting loans can circumvent host-country restrictions on the remittance of funds from a foreign subsidiary to the parent company. A host government might restrict a foreign subsidiary from repaying a loan to its parent in order to preserve the country's foreign exchange reserves, but it is less likely to restrict a subsidiary's ability to repay a loan to a large international bank. To stop payment to an international bank would hurt the country's credit image, whereas halting payment to the parent company would probably have a minimal impact on its image. Consequently, international businesses sometimes use fronting loans when they want to lend funds to a subsidiary based in a country with a fairly high probability of political turmoil that might lead to restrictions on capital flows (i.e., where the level of political risk is high).

A fronting loan can also provide tax advantages. For example, a tax haven (Bermuda) subsidiary that is 100 percent owned by the parent company deposits $1 million in a London-based international bank at 8 percent interest. The bank lends the $1 million to a foreign operating subsidiary at 9 percent interest. The country where the foreign operating subsidiary is based taxes corporate income at 50 percent (see Figure 20.5).

Under this arrangement, interest payments net of income tax will be as follows:

1. The foreign operating subsidiary pays $90,000 interest to the London bank. Deducting these interest payments from its taxable income results in a net after-tax cost of $45,000 to the foreign operating subsidiary.

2. The London bank receives the $90,000. It retains $10,000 for its services and pays $80,000 interest on the deposit to the Bermuda subsidiary.

3. The Bermuda subsidiary receives $80,000 interest on its deposit tax-free.

The net result is that $80,000 in cash has been moved from the foreign operating subsidiary to the tax haven subsidiary. Because the foreign operating subsidiary's after-tax cost of borrowing is only $45,000, the parent company has moved an additional $35,000 out of the country by using this arrangement. If the tax haven subsidiary had made a direct loan to the foreign operating subsidiary, the host government may have disallowed the interest charge as a tax-deductible expense by ruling that it was a dividend to the parent disguised as an interest payment.

TEST PREP

Use SmartBook to help retain what you have learned. Access your instructor's Connect course to check out SmartBook or go to **learnsmartadvantage.com** for help.

Key Terms

○ SUMMARY

This chapter focused on accounting and financial management in the international business. It explained why accounting practices and standards differ from country to country and surveyed the efforts under way to harmonize countries' accounting practices. We reviewed several issues related to the use of accounting-based control systems within international businesses. We discussed how investment decisions, financing decisions, and money management decisions are complicated by the fact that different countries have different currencies, different tax regimes, different levels of political and economic risk, and so on. This chapter made the following points:

1. Each country's accounting system evolved in response to the local demands for accounting information. National differences in accounting and auditing standards resulted in a general lack of comparability in countries' financial reports.

2. This lack of comparability has become a problem as transnational financing and transnational investment have grown rapidly in recent decades (a consequence of the globalization of capital markets). Due to the lack of comparability, a firm may have to explain to investors why its financial position looks very different on financial reports that are based on different accounting practices.

3. The most significant push for harmonization of accounting standards across countries has come from the International Accounting Standards Board (IASB).

4. In most international businesses, the annual budget is the main instrument by which headquarters controls foreign subsidiaries. Throughout the year, headquarters compares a subsidiary's performance against the financial goals incorporated in its budget, intervening selectively in its operations when shortfalls occur.

5. Most international businesses require all budgets and performance data within the firm to be expressed in the corporate currency. This enhances comparability, but it distorts the control process if the relevant exchange rates change between the time a foreign subsidiary's budget is set and the time its performance is evaluated. According to the Lessard–Lorange model, the best way to deal with this problem is to use a projected spot exchange rate to translate both budget figures and performance figures into the corporate currency.

6. Transfer prices can introduce significant distortions into the control process and thus must be considered when setting budgets and evaluating a subsidiary's performance.

7. When using capital budgeting techniques to evaluate a potential foreign project, the firm needs to recognize the specific risks arising from its foreign location. These include political risks and economic risks (including foreign exchange risk). Political and economic risks can be incorporated into the capital budgeting process by using a higher discount rate to evaluate risky projects or by forecasting lower cash flows for such projects.

8. The cost of capital is lower in the global capital market than in domestic markets. Consequently, other things being equal, firms prefer to finance their investments by borrowing from the global capital market.

9. Borrowing from the global capital market may be restricted by host-government regulations or demands. In such cases, the discount rate used in capital budgeting must be revised upward to reflect this.

10. The firm may want to consider local debt financing for investments in countries where the local currency is expected to depreciate.

11. The principal objectives of global money management are to utilize the firm's cash resources in the most efficient manner and to minimize the firm's global tax liabilities.

12. By holding cash at a centralized depository, the firm may be able to invest its cash reserves more efficiently. It can reduce the total size of the cash pool that it needs to hold in highly liquid accounts, thereby freeing cash for investment in higher-interest-bearing (less liquid) accounts or in tangible assets.

13. Firms use a number of techniques to transfer funds across borders, including dividend remittances, royalty payments and fees, transfer prices, and fronting loans. Dividend remittances are the most common method used for transferring funds across borders, but royalty payments and fees have certain tax advantages over dividend remittances.

14. The manipulation of transfer prices may be used by firms to move funds out of a country to minimize tax liabilities, hedge against foreign exchange risk, circumvent government restrictions on capital flows, and reduce tariff payments. However, manipulating transfer prices in this manner runs counter to government regulations in many countries, it may distort incentive systems within the firm, and it has ethically dubious foundations.

15. Fronting loans involves channeling funds from a parent company to a foreign subsidiary through a third party, normally an international bank. Fronting loans can circumvent host-government restrictions on the remittance of funds and provide certain tax advantages.

Critical Thinking and Discussion Questions

1. Why do the accounting systems of different countries differ? Why do these differences matter?

2. Why might an accounting-based control system provide headquarters management with biased information about the performance of a foreign subsidiary? How can these biases best be corrected?

3. You are the CFO of a U.S. firm whose wholly owned subsidiary in Mexico manufactures component parts for your U.S. assembly operations. The subsidiary has been financed by bank borrowings in the United States. One of your analysts told you that the Mexican peso is expected to depreciate by 30 percent against the dollar on the foreign exchange markets over the next year. What actions, if any, should you take?

4. You are the CFO of a Canadian firm that is considering building a $10 million factory in Russia to produce milk. The investment is expected to produce net cash flows of $3 million each year for the next 10 years, after which the investment will have to close because of technological obsolescence. Scrap values will be zero. The cost of capital will be 6 percent if financing is arranged through the Eurobond market. However, you have an option to finance the project by borrowing funds from a Russian bank at 12 percent. Analysts tell you that due to high inflation in Russia, the Russian ruble is expected to depreciate against the Canadian dollar. Analysts also rate the probability of violent revolution occurring in Russia within the next 10 years as high. How would you incorporate these factors into your evaluation of the investment opportunity? What would you recommend the firm do?

globalEDGE research task globaledge.msu.edu

Use the globalEDGE™ website (**globaledge.msu.edu**) to complete the following exercises:

1. The inflation rate of a country can affect financial planning in multinational corporations since the value of receivables in each country can face significant devaluation if the inflation rates are high. Your company has operations in the following countries: Belarus, Costa Rica, Finland, Iceland, Paraguay, Thailand, and Zimbabwe. Use the *Country Comparator* on the globalEDGE site to rank the risk of devaluation of your company's receivables from highest to lowest, based on the most recent data available for each country. What precautions can your company take in the countries at the top of this list to minimize the risk?

2. The top management of your company has requested information on the tax policies of Argentina. Using the country guide for Argentina on *Deloitte International Tax and Business Guides*—a resource that provides information on the investment climate, operating conditions, and tax systems of major trading countries—prepare a short report summarizing your findings on business taxation in Argentina.

CLOSING CASE

Shoprite: The Financial Success of a Food Retailer in Africa

The Shoprite Group is Africa's largest food retailer, operating more than 2,300 stores in 15 countries across Africa and the Indian Ocean Islands. The company began in 1979, has 143,000 employees, has revenue of about $11 billion, and is headquartered in the Western Cape province of South Africa. Shoprite has expanded rapidly since the company's founding by making a number of financial acquisitions, including Checkers in 1991, Sentra in 1995, OK Bazaars in 1997, Madagascar in 2002, Foodworld in 2005, and Computicket in 2005.

This expansion has led to Deloitte's Global Powers of Retailing ranking The Shoprite Group as the 94th largest retailer in the world and the largest in Africa. Some 76 percent of South Africa's adult population shops at one of Shoprite's supermarket brands.

Shoprite views the combination of controlling its own supply chain, investing in employee skills, investing in infrastructure, and incorporating value-added services to compliment the shopping experience as the recipe for financial success. And the company measures its financial success via a large set of traditional and nontraditional statistics. Some of the nontraditional outcome measures include serving a billion customers in a single year, donating food worth R109 million (about $9 million U.S. dollars), and 4.5 million free meals of soup and bread served by mobile kitchens.

The more traditional, expected outcomes include 108 new corporate stores opened in the last year, 4,833 new jobs created, sales growth of 14.4 percent, a profit increase of 15.0 percent, and an increase in return-on-shareholders' equity of 19.2 percent. But Shoprite also counts the 1.8 million training hours invested in employees as a positive performance metric that has long-term financial implications.

Building on these financial and nonfinancial metrics, The Shoprite Group's primary business is food retailing, but the Group's financial success also depends on offering a broad range of products and services. For example, these include household products, furniture, pharmaceuticals, and financial services. In all endeavors, Shoprite has an unwavering dedication to providing the lowest prices to customers of all income levels across the 15 countries it serves in Africa and the Indian Ocean Islands.

Its financial success depends as much on repeat customers as it does on pursuing efficiency in everything that the company does. Shoprite's advanced distribution centers and sophisticated supply chain infrastructure provide greater control over operations. This empowers Shoprite to overcome eventual economic challenges without compromising on quality. By setting the conditions for enduring success, Shoprite can provide affordable food to all communities, invest in social initiatives that help the communities in which they operate, and contribute to the African economy—all while creating value for all stakeholders. The Shoprite Group of companies have created tremendous financial success in what many other companies consider a weak buying power market, while also helping to socially develop local African communities.

Sources: Shoprite Holdings Ltd., March 27, 2017, shopriteholdings.co.za; "Global Powers of Retailing 2017," March 27, 2017, deloitte.com/za/en/pages/consumer-industrial-products/articles/global-powers-of-retailing-2017.html; "Supermarkets in Africa: The Grocers Great Trek," *The Economist*, September 21, 2013; "Is It Worth It?" *The Economist*, April 14, 2016; Liezel Hill, "Shoprite Jumps Most Since 1997 as African Sales Growth Rises," *Bloomberg Businessweek*, July 20, 2016; Memory Mataranyika, "Shoprite Expands into West Africa as Urbanization Gathers Pace," FIN 24, November 25, 2016; Janice Kew, "Christo Wiese Says He'll Learn from Failed Merger Talks," FIN 24, February 21, 2017.

Case Discussion Questions

1. Some 76 percent of South Africa's adult population shops at one of Shoprite's supermarket brands, and the Shoprite Group is the 94th largest retailer in the world and the largest in Africa. Yet, Shoprite is only in Africa and the Indian Ocean Islands. Should the company expand its global footprint? Can it be more financially successful worldwide with the same business model it operates in Africa?

2. Shoprite measures its financial success via a large set of traditional and nontraditional statistics. If you worked for Shoprite, how would you feel about being evaluated on the nontraditional statistics?

3. Shoprite has an unwavering dedication to providing the lowest prices to customers of all income levels across the 15 countries it serves in Africa and the Indian Ocean Islands. Usually low-cost firms get sidestepped at some point in the future by another company that can offer even lower

costs. How can Shoprite ensure that the company is viable in the long-term with its low-cost approach?

4. The financial success of Shoprite depends as much on repeat customers as it does on pursuing efficiency in everything that the company does. Shoprite's advanced distribution centers and

sophisticated supply chain infrastructure provide greater control over operations. How can the supply chain infrastructure be leveraged to excel in financial performance?

Design elements: Modern textured halftone: ©VIPRESIONA/ Shutterstock; globalEDGE icon: ©globalEDGE; All others: ©McGraw-Hill Education

Endnotes

1. G. G. Mueller, H. Gernon, and G. Meek, *Accounting: An International Perspective* (Burr Ridge, IL: Richard D. Irwin, 1991).

2. S. J. Gary, "Towards a Theory of Cultural Influence on the Development of Accounting Systems Internationally," *Abacus* 3 (1988), pp. 1–15; R. S. Wallace, O. Gernon, and H. Gernon, "Frameworks for International Comparative Financial Accounting," *Journal of Accounting Literature* 10 (1991), pp. 209–64.

3. R. G. Barker, "Global Accounting Is Coming," *Harvard Business Review,* April 2003, pp. 2–3.

4. Fleming, P. D. "The Growing Importance of International Accounting Standards." *Journal of Accountancy* (September 1991): 100–06.

5. D. Reilly, "SEC to Consider Letting Companies Use International Accounting Rules," *The Wall Street Journal,* April 25, 2007, p. C3.

6. F. Choi and I. Czechowicz, "Assessing Foreign Subsidiary Performance: A Multinational Comparison," *Management International Review* 4, 1983, pp. 14–25.

7. D. Lessard and P. Lorange, "Currency Changes and Management Control: Resolving the Centralization/Decentralization Dilemma," *Accounting Review,* July 1977, pp. 628–37.

8. Mueller et al., *Accounting: An International Perspective.*

9. For details of capital budgeting techniques, see R. A. Brealey and S. C. Myers, *Principles of Corporate Finance* (New York: McGraw-Hill, 1988).

10. D. J. Feils and F. M. Sabac, "The Impact of Political Risk on the Foreign Direct Investment Decision: A Capital Budgeting Analysis," *The Engineering Economist* 45 (2000), pp. 129–34.

11. See S. Block, "Integrating Traditional Capital Budgeting Concepts into an International Decision-Making Environment,"

The Engineering Economist 45 (2000), pp. 309–25; J. C. Backer and L. J. Beardsley, "Multinational Companies' Use of Risk Evaluation and Profit Measurement for Capital Budgeting Decisions," *Journal of Business Finance,* Spring 1973, pp. 34–43.

12. For example, see D. K. Eiteman, A. I. Stonehill, and M. H. Moffett, *Multinational Business Finance* (Reading, MA: Addison-Wesley, 1992).

13. M. Stanley and S. Block, "An Empirical Study of Management and Financial Variables Influencing Capital Budgeting Decisions for Multinational Corporations in the 1980s," *Management International Review* 23 (1983), pp. 61–71.

14. "Taxing Questions," *The Economist,* May 22, 1993, p. 73.

15. J. Sommer, "How to Unlock That Stashed Foreign Cash," *The New York Times,* March 23, 2013.

16. S. Crow and E. Sauls, "Setting the Right Transfer Price," *Management Accounting,* December 1994, pp. 41–47.

17. V. H. Miesel, H. H. Higinbotham, and C. W. Yi, "International Transfer Pricing: Practical Solutions for Inter-company Pricing," *International Tax Journal* 28 (Fall 2002), pp. 1–22.

18. J. Kelly, "Administrators Prepare for a More Efficient Future," *Financial Times Survey: World Taxation,* February 24, 1995, p. 9.

19. Crow and Sauls, "Setting the Right Transfer Price."

20. M. F. Al-Eryani, P. Alam, and S. Akhter, "Transfer Pricing Determinants of U.S. Multinationals," *Journal of International Business Studies,* September 1990, pp. 409–25.

21. D. L. Swenson. "Tax Reforms and Evidence of Transfer Pricing," *National Tax Journal,* March 2001, pp. 7–25.

22. "Transfer Pricing Survey Shows Multinationals Face Greater Scrutiny," *The CPA Journal,* March 2000, p. 10.

Integrative Cases

For *International Business*, 13e, we have again included a set of 20 cases as value-added materials at the end of the text, in addition to the 40 cases—opening and closing cases—that appear in the 20 chapters. We started this practice of including integrative cases in the eleventh edition to provide instructors and students with a better platform for learning across chapters.

The end-of-the-book cases fill strategically aligned objectives for the core features of *International Business*, 13e. Specifically, we are able to build on and enhance the worldwide market leadership of our text and its focus on current, application-rich,

Case	Primary	Secondary	Part One Introduction and Overview	Part Two National Differences	Part Three The Global Trade and Investment Environment	Part Four The Global Monetary System	Part Five The Strategy and Structure of International Business	Part Six International Business Functions
Globalization of BMW, Rolls-Royce, and the MINI	1	13	X	X	X		X	
The Decline of Zimbabwe	2	3, 6		X	X			
Economic Development in Bangladesh	3	6, 7		X	X			
The Swatch Group and Cultural Uniqueness	4	7, 8	X	X	X			
Woolworths' Corporate Responsibility Strategy	5	4, 13	X	X	X			
The Trans Pacific Partnership (TPP) Is Dead: Long Live the CPTPP	6	7, 8, 9	X		X			
Boeing and Airbus Are in a Dogfight over Illegal Subsidies	7	6, 13			X			
FDI in the Indian Retail Sector	8	2, 3, 13, 15	X	X	X	X	X	
Free Trade in Africa	9	6,7	X		X			
The Mexican Peso, the Japanese Yen, and Pokémon Go	10	11				X		
Egypt and the IMF	11	3, 12		X		X		
Alibaba's Record-Setting IPO	12	13	X			X		
Sony Corporation: Still a Leader Globally?	13	14, 17	X				X	X
Organizational Architecture at P&G	14	13	X				X	
Cutco Corporation—Sharpening Your Market Entry	15	13, 14	X				X	
Tata Motors and Exporting	16	15	X				X	X
Alibaba and Global Supply Chains	17	13, 14, 15	X				X	X
Best Buy Doing a Turnaround Again	18	16, 17	X				X	X
Sodexo: Building a Diverse Global Workforce	19	14	X				X	X
Tesla, Inc.—Subsidizing Tesla Automobiles Globally	20	12, 14, 15	X			X	X	X

relevant, and comprehensive materials by including a set of cases that both (1) tackle chapter-relevant topics and (2) serve as integrated learning vehicles covering materials across chapters.

Several of these cases focus on company and country scenarios related to dozens of companies and countries. Importantly, we do cover scenarios that focus on small, medium-sized, and large companies in these integrative cases. This breadth and dept of focus allow us to include cases that can be used as a complement to the opening and closing cases of each chapter by teachers who prefer a case-oriented and practically focused teaching method. The integrative cases also allow for a holistic and strategic take on the content across chapter topics for those teachers who prefer to delve into a more comprehensive set of issues in international business.

To understand the positioning of each end-of-the-book case, we have included a matrix that outlines which chapters are the most heavily covered in the case ("primary chapters"), which chapters have supplementary coverage in the case ("secondary chapters"), and which textbook "parts" are covered by a case (i.e., Introduction and Overview; National Differences; The Global Trade and Investment Environment; The Global Monetary System; The Strategy and Structure of International Business; and International Business Functions).

The end-of-the-book cases have been composed to be similar in length to the opening and closing cases (800 to 1,500 words). For the International Business course—whether it be at the undergraduate or graduate level—cases at the 800-to-1,500-word length have been shown to resonate with both students and teachers. These cases motivate students to learn the material in a chapter and provide an application-rich connection to relevant practice, while also comprehensively covering important topics. Each case has a particular focus—as highlighted in the matrix—but we have also written each case to be possibly used in a deeper discussion around the company, country, and/or issue highlighted, for those teachers who prefer to dig deeper into a case scenario.

Globalization of BMW, Rolls-Royce, and the MINI

Bayerische Motoren Werke, which is German for Bavarian Motor Works, is better known globally for its acronym BMW (**bmwgroup.com**). BMW was created as a combination of three German manufacturing companies: Rapp Motorenwerke and Bayerische Flugzeugwerke in Bavaria and Fahrzeugfabrik Eisenach in Thuringia. Aircraft engine manufacturer Rapp Motorenwerke became Bayerische Motorenwerke in 1916, and the company added motorcycles to its product repertoire in 1923. BMW expanded to automobiles in 1929 when it purchased Fahrzeugfabrik Eisenach, which built Austin 7 cars under a license from Dixi. Fittingly, the first BMW car was called the BMW Dixi.

Globally, BMW is known for streamlined design, incredible luxury, and top-notch performance. The company has more than 125,000 employees, delivers about 2.4 million vehicles annually, and has a revenue of €95 billion (about $103 billion in U.S. dollars). Its leadership spans products in automobiles, motorcycles, and aircraft engines. Innovation is one of the main success factors for the BMW Group, and innovation is infused into all of BMW's product lines. The company claims that focusing on the future is an important part of BMW's identity and day-to-day work, and the reason for its global success. In addition to the well-known BMW brand, BMW also owns the iconic Rolls-Royce brand and the distinctive MINI automobiles.

BMW and "driving pleasure" are synonymous, even by people not owning a BMW! BMW creates driving pleasure from the perfect combination of dynamic, sporty performance; ground-breaking innovations; and breath-taking design. With a range of car models, a unique feature of BMW is its "M" designation models that takes the "driving pleasure" to another level. BMW "M" (for Motorsport) was initially created to facilitate BMW's racing program, but has since become a supplement to BMW's vehicles portfolio with specially modified higher-trim features. BMW M is part of an outstanding motorsports heritage and stands for high performance out of passion, with the latest addition to the line being the BMW M760. It's the evolutionary link that connects BMW and Rolls-Royce, bridging the gap between the 7 Series and the entry-level Rolls-Royce Ghost.

Rolls-Royce is considered the most exclusive luxury automobile brand in the world, and the company delivers on its promise of effortless power, luxury, quality, and perfect sanctuary. This reputation is rooted in the brand's long history and rich tradition. The entry-level Rolls-Royce Ghost carries a price tag of around $250,000, and the models' cost increase from there. Rolls-Royce has, from its early days of daring experimentation, created a vision for luxury that is rooted in constantly chasing perfection. This perfection drives the supreme quality, exquisite hand craftsmanship, and attention to the finest detail to maintain its global position as the pinnacle luxury automobile manufacturer in the world. Like Rolls-Royce, the MINI also traces its roots to the United Kingdom.

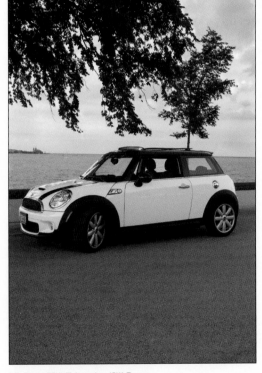

McGraw-Hill Education/Jill Braaten

MINI is a car brand owned by BMW that specializes in small cars. The full platform of MINI cars is small, with the idea of maximizing the experience and concentrating on the essential. A long-standing attention to clever solutions with distinctive designs unlocks urban driving and caters to customers' individual needs. The most iconic is the MINI Cooper, named after British racing legend John Cooper. The MINI Cooper product line has a uniquely sporty blend of classic British mini-car heritage and appeal, and precise German engineering and construction. According to the MINI team, they are targeting affluent urban dwellers in their 20s and 30s who enjoy the fun, freedom, and individuality that the MINI cars offer—or perhaps we should just say they target newly graduated college students living in cities!

To help with its targeting of affluent urban dwellers for the MINI or the even more affluent clientele for the BMW or Rolls-Royce, the BMW Group's leaders have studied brands outside of the automobile industry to create the company's future retail strategy. Enter the "product genius." BMW's product genius is a noncommissioned car expert who will spend whatever time is needed to educate customers about their car choices, options, and any issue that the customer wants to get more information on. This shifts the "performance" from closing the sale of a car to making the customer satisfied, which lessens the typical pressure most customers feel when walking into a car dealership (and likewise lessens the pressure on the salesperson to sell a car to get a commission).

Sources

Jonathan M. Gitlin, "The 2017 BMW M760i Is a Hell of a Car, but Is It an M?" *ARS Technica*, February 8, 2017; "BMW at 100: Bavarian Rhapsody," *The Economist*, March 12, 2016; Carmine Gallo, "BMW Radically Rethinks the Car Buying Experience," *Forbes*, April 18, 2014; "How German Cars Beat British Motors—and Kept Going," *BBC News*, August 2, 2013; and Hannah Elliott, "The Best Luxury Sedan Is Still a BMW," *Bloomberg BusinessWeek*, June 6, 2016.

Case Discussion Questions

1. How do you think BMW integrates its various unique brands into a global effort that works for them (BMW, Rolls-Royce, and the MINI) across the world's many global markets?

2. What is your reaction to the global brand of BMW when you hear its name, think of the brand, and see BMW vehicles on the road?

3. Rolls-Royce's chase of perfection drives the supreme quality, exquisite hand craftsmanship, and attention to the finest detail to maintain its global position as the pinnacle luxury automobile manufacturer in the world. How do you think the Rolls-Royce brand helps, or hurts, other BMW brands globally (i.e., BMW, the MINI)?

4. The MINI is a unique car offering in the BMW portfolio. It has long-engaged in clever solutions and distinctive designs that have enabled terrific urban driving and have catered to customers' individual needs. Do you agree that this is the focus for the MINI, and do you think it is working as advertised globally?

The Decline of Zimbabwe

In 1980, the southern African state of Zimbabwe gained independence from its colonial master, Great Britain. Speaking at the time, the late Tanzanian President, Julius Nyerere, described Zimbabwe as "the jewel of Africa." It was a country that boasted a strong economy, abundant natural resources, and a vibrant agricultural sector. As part of the independence process, the British bequeathed Zimbabwe a number of democratic political institutions.

Zimbabwe's birth as an independent nation was a difficult one. In 1965, the minority white rulers of what was then known as Rhodesia unilaterally declared independence from Britain, setting up an apartheid state where blacks were excluded from power. The British government wanted majority rule, stated that the declaration of independence was an illegal rebellion, and imposed sanctions on Rhodesia. Other nations that followed suit included the United States. An armed conflict ensued, with two guerrilla movements waging war against Rhodesia's white government. One of those guerrilla movements, the Zimbabwe African National Union (ZANU) was headed by Robert Mugabe, who aligned himself and his movement with the Maoist version of communism. A combination of international sanctions and guerrilla activity eventually forced the white minority rulers of Rhodesia to end their rebellion. In 1979, Rhodesia reverted to British colonial status.

The following year, Zimbabwe gained legal independence. Robert Mugabe was elected as the country's first prime minister. Thirty-seven years later, Mugabe was still in power, now as President. His ZANU-PF party had won every election since independence. Once a largely ceremonial position, Mugabe had systematically consolidated power in the Presidency and restricted his political opponents. He was re-elected as President in 2013 in a general election that, like many in the Mugabe era, was widely seen as rigged. The country has also been beset by endemic corruption. Corruption watchdog Transparency International recently ranked Zimbabwe as one of the most corrupt nations in the world.

Zimbabwe's economic performance in recent years ranks among the worst in the world. Although the economy maintained a positive economic growth rate through the 1980s and 1990s, it has deteriorated rapidly since 2000. Between 1999 and 2009, Zimbabwe saw the lowest economic growth rate ever recorded, with an annual decline of 6.1 percent in GDP.

The decline occurred after Mugabe launched a "fast-track" land reform program that encouraged seizure by the state without compensation of land owned by white farmers. At the time, some 4,000 white farmers were the backbone of the country's strong agricultural sector. The land was given to members of the ZANU-PF party and other supporters of Mugabe, who lacked experience with

McGraw-Hill Education

modern agricultural practices and had never farmed at all. In the wake of the land reform program, agricultural productivity slumped and the country is now a net importer of food.

Another drag on the country's growth was the 2008 Indigenisation and Economic Empowerment Act, which required that enterprises doing business in Zimbabwe have at least 51 percent local ownership. In practice, this often meant high-ranking ZANU-PF party members. After the act was passed, a number of foreign corporations doing business in the country pulled out.

The country's mining sector remains potentially lucrative, with large platinum and diamond deposits mined by private enterprises, but almost all of the licensing revenues due to the state have reportedly disappeared into the hands of army officers and ZANU-PF politicians. Taxes and tariffs are high for private enterprises, which discourages private business formation, while state-owned enterprises are strongly subsidized. Tourism, once a big revenue earner, has declined as Zimbabwe's wildlife has been decimated by poaching and deforestation. As economic activity slumped, the country's formal unemployment rate reached a staggering 80 percent.

To complicate matters, Zimbabwe was devastated by the AIDS epidemic, with HIV infection rates hitting a high of 40 percent of the population in 1998. Due to AIDS and other public health problems, life expectancy fell to just 43.1 years in 2003, down from 61.6 years in 1986. By 2014, with HIV prevalence down to 15 percent, life expectancy had risen back to 54 years.

With tax revenues collapsing, Mugabe funded government programs by printing money. Inflation quickly spiraled out of control, reaching 231,000,000 percent in 2008 and requiring the Central Bank to introduce a 100 trillion Zimbabwe dollar note! In April 2009, the Zimbabwe dollar was suspended (at the time the trillion dollar note was worth around $0.40 USD). Zimbabwe allowed trade to be conducted using other currencies, particularly the U.S. dollar, the South Africa Rand, the euro, and the British pound.

Despite the country's economic implosion, the World Bank still believes that Zimbabwe has enormous potential for sustained economic growth given its generous endowment of natural resources, its existing stock of public infrastructure, and comparatively skilled human resources. Attaining that potential will require a change in leadership and policies.

Mugabe showed no signs of giving up the reins of power. In February 2017, he held a lavish 93rd birthday party for himself and stated that he wanted to stand for another five-year term as president in 2018. However, much to the surprise of many observers, in November 2017, Mugabe was forced to resign from office after his own party started impeachment proceedings against him. He was quickly replaced by his former vice president, Emmerson Mnangagwa, whom Mugabe had fired on November 6 in an action that precipitated the impeachment hearings. Mnangagwa has stated that he will get rid of Mugabe's more ruinous policies in an effort to improve Zimbabwe's battered economy. Mugabe himself passed away in September of 2019, although the country still struggles with his legacy.

Sources

"Will Emmerson Mnangagwa Be Better than Robert Mugabe?" *The Economist*, November 30, 2017; "How Robert Mugabe Ruined Zimbabwe," *The Economist*, February 26, 2017; Irwin Chifera, "What Happened to Zimbabwe, Once Known as the Jewel of Africa?" *VoaZimbabwe*, April 17, 2015; "The Real Balancing Rocks on Every Zimbabwe Dollar," *Slate*, January 23, 2017; "Diamonds in the Rough," *Human Rights Watch Report*, June 26, 2009; "Zimbabwe," The World Bank, **http://www. worldbank.org/en/country/zimbabwe/overview**.

Case Discussion Questions

1. Why has Zimbabwe's economic performance been so poor?

2. Do you think Zimbabwe's economic performance would have been better under a different system of government? Which one? Explain your reasoning.

3. What steps need to be taken now to improve the economic outlook for Zimbabwe?

Economic Development in Bangladesh

When Bangladesh gained independence from Pakistan in 1971 after a brutal civil war that may have left as many as 3 million dead, the U.S. National Security Adviser, Henry Kissinger, referred to the country as a "basket case." Kissinger's assessment was accurate enough. At the time, Bangladesh was one of the world's poorest nations. Although most of the country is dominated by the fertile Ganges-Brahmaputra delta, a lack of other natural resources, coupled with poor infrastructure, political instability, and high levels of corruption, long held the country back. To compound matters, Bangladesh is prone to natural disasters. Most of Bangladesh is less than 12 meters above sea level. The extensive low-lying areas are vulnerable to tropical cyclones, floods, and tidal bores.

Beginning in the mid-1990s, however, Bangladesh began to climb the ladder of economic progress. From the early 2000s onward, the country grew its economy at around 6 percent per annum compounded. Today, this Muslim majority country of 160 million people has joined the ranks of lower-middle-income nations. Poverty reduction has been dramatic, with the percentage of the population living in poverty falling from 44.2 percent in 1991 to 18.5 percent in 2010, an achievement that raised 20.5 million people out of abject poverty. Today, the country ranks 64th out of the 154 countries included in the World Bank's global poverty database. It has a considerable way to go, but it is no longer one of the world's poorest countries.

Several reasons underlie Bangladesh's relative economic success. In its initial post-independence period, Bangladesh adopted socialist policies, nationalizing many companies and subsidizing the costs of agricultural production and basic food products. These policies failed to deliver the anticipated gains. Policy reforms in the 1980s were directed toward the withdrawal of food and agricultural subsidies, the privatization of state-owned companies, financial liberalization, and the withdrawal of some import restrictions. Further reforms aimed at liberalizing the economy were launched in the 1990s. These included making the currency convertible (which led to a floating exchange rate in 2003), reducing import duties to much lower levels, and removing most of the controls on the movement of foreign private capital (which allowed for more foreign direct investment). The reforms of the 1990s coincided with the transition to a parliamentary democracy from semi-autocratic rule.

Bangladesh's private sector has expanded rapidly since then. Leading the growth has been the country's vibrant textile sector, which is now the second-largest exporter of ready-made garments in the world after China. Textiles account for 80 percent of Bangladesh's exports. The development of the textile industry has been helped by the availability of low-cost labor, managerial skills, favorable trade agreements, and government policies that eliminated import duties on inputs for the textile business, such as raw materials. The Bangladesh economy has also benefited from its productive agricultural sector and remittances from more than 10 million Bangladesh citizens who work in other nations. Bangladesh is also the home of the microfinance movement, which has enabled entrepreneurs with no prior access to the banking system to borrow small amounts of capital to start businesses.

This being said, the country still faces considerable impediments to sustaining its growth. Infrastructure remains poor; corruption continues to be a major problem; and the political system is, at best, an imperfect democracy where opposition is stifled. The country is too dependent upon its booming textile sector and needs to diversify its industrial base. Bangladesh is also one of the countries most prone to the adverse affects of climate change. A one-meter rise in sea level would leave an estimated 10 percent of the country under water and increase the potential for damaging floods in much of the remainder. Nevertheless, according to the U.S. investment bank Goldman Sachs, Bangladesh is one of the 11 lower-middle-income nations poised for sustained growth.

Sources

W. Mahmud, S. Ahmed, and S. Mahajan, "Economic Reforms, Growth, and Governance: The Political Economy Aspects of Bangladesh's Development Surprise," World Bank Commission on Development and Growth, 2008; "Freedom in the World 2016," *Freedom House*; "Tiger in the Night," *The Economist*, October 15, 2016; Sanjay Kathuria, "How Will Bangladesh Reach High Levels of Prosperity?" *World Bank blog*, January 5, 2017; and Qimiao Fan, "Bangladesh: Setting a Global Standard in Ending Poverty," *World Bank blog*, October 5, 2016.

Case Discussion Questions

1. What were the principal reasons for the economic stagnation of Bangladesh after its war for independence?

2. Explain how the liberalization program in the 1990s enabled Bangladesh to start climbing the ladder of economic progress. What are the main lessons here that can be applied to economic development in other nations?

3. Bangladesh is dependent for its prosperity upon agriculture and textile exports. What are the risks here? How might Bangladesh diversify its industrial and commercial base?

The Swatch Group and Cultural Uniqueness

The Swatch Group (**swatchgroup.com**) with its headquarters in Biel, Switzerland, is a world-renowned manufacturer of watches and jewelry. The company was founded in 1983 by Lebanese-born Nicolas Hayek from the merging of Allgemeine Gesellschaft der Schweizerischen Uhrenindustrie and Société Suisse pour l'Industrie Horlogère. Nicolas's daughter, Nayla Hayek, has been chair of the board since her father's death in 2010. She is also CEO of the luxury jeweler Harry Winston Inc., which was acquired by the Swatch Group in 2013. Georges Nicolas "Nick" Hayek Jr. has been the CEO and president of the Swatch Group since 2003. Overall, the Hayek family controls nearly 40 percent of the Swatch Group.

Brand X Pictures/Getty Images

Swatch Group is a diversified multinational holding company active in the manufacturing and sale of finished watches, jewelry, watch movements, and watch components. It is the world's largest watchmaking group. To stay true to its cultural ideals, the company supplies nearly all the components required for the watches sold by its eighteen individual brands. The Group's production companies supply movements and watch components to third-party watchmakers in Switzerland and all around the world. This makes the Group a key player in the manufacturing of electronic systems used in watchmaking. It is also a leader in the field of sports event timing.

The company has been built into a large and complex organization in its roughly four decades in existence. Swatch and its 37 global subsidiaries employ about 37,000 people, and the company's revenue is about $9 billion. The company's headquarters in Biel sits on the language border between French- and German-speaking parts of Switzerland and is, by design, bilingual and culturally diverse. In fact, everything that Swatch engages in is based on diversity and culture. This cultural diversity is embedded in its overall brand and global strategizing. For example, many of the Swatch brands have become cultural icons among a strong core of customers. Some even talk about the "Swatch Revolution" that began when Nicolas Hayek founded the company. It was the combination of legendary Swiss watch making and the unexpected appearance of an affordable plastic watch that turned the watch world upside down.

Suddenly, a watch was more than a way to measure time. It was a new individualized culture, a new language, and a way to speak from the heart without words. By definition, "swatch" means a sample of material or color, oftentimes referring to a small piece of fabric. It is remarkable how Swatch has been able to develop culturally unique watches while also building the fabric for a globally integrated world by its watch making. The Swatch Group's brands go far beyond the iconic Swatch watches, though. They also include top global brands like Blancpain, Breguet, and Omega, along with unique and classic products such as Balmain, Calvin Klein watches and jewelry, Certina, Flik Flak, Glashütte, Hamilton, Harry Winston, Jaquet Droz, Léon Hatot, Longines, Mido, Original, Rado, Tissot, Tourbillon, and Union Glashütte. These brands form the "art" of Swatch—a focus that is almost always emphasized upfront in the company's annual report and something the Swatch Group nurtures in various ways.

On Swatch's Instagram (**instagram.com/swatch**), the storyline is clear. Swatch wants you to create your own unique way of accessorizing through the use of a Swatch watch. A person can showcase his or her individualized Swatch use by tagging #MySwatch. The new line of "Skin" watches also helps users "dance with the unknown," break down barriers, and make #YourMove with Skin. The product is minimalist in style, yet unique, stylish, and culturally diverse— much similar to how Swatch has created its cultural uniqueness for decades in the global marketplace. Swatch's own description of its brand captures this cultural uniqueness:

> Everyone knows a Swatch when they see one. There's clearly something that makes Swatch different from every other watch brand. What is it? The look, the colors, the plastic? The design, perhaps, or the fact that it's Swiss made and versatile enough to be worn with almost anything. There are Swatch watches for people of all ages, and a Swatch for every occasion. But there's more to Swatch than market coverage. Swatch is an attitude, an approach to life, a way of seeing. The sight of a Swatch excites emotion. Wearing one is a way to communicate, to speak without speaking. Heart to heart.

The Swatch Group is not just about being culturally diverse, or a company marketing products globally to customers of different cultures. In many respects, the company is actually creating the values, beliefs, norms, and artifacts that form a globally unique culture worldwide.

Swatch's large-scale production of watches and jewelry is used to help create individually and culturally based customer uniqueness. These watches are fashion items and are not simply focused on being timepieces. They are culturally interesting, different, and unique to each person's taste and characteristics. Seldom will you run into someone who has exactly the same Swatch.

Sources

"The Swiss Invent a Novel Watch Spring," *The Economist*, November 15, 2018; Corinne Gretler, "Swatch CEO Nick Hayek Sees Swiss Watch Turnaround in 2017," *BusinessWeek*, February 2, 2017; Silke Koltrowitz, "Swatch Group Seeing Strong Demand So Far in 2017," *Reuters*, March 16, 2017; "The Amazing Adventures of the Second Watch," Swatch History 2017 (**www.swatch.com/en_us/explore/history**); "Swatch Is Challenging Google and Apple with Its Own Operating System," *Fortune*, March 16, 2017; **https://www.swatch.com/en_us/explore/swatch-chronology**.

Case Discussion Questions

1. With the Hayek family controlling nearly 40 percent of The Swatch Group, how do you think the family's influence impacts the corporate culture in the company? What about the company's international culture being impacted by the Hayek family?

2. Many of the Swatch brands have become cultural icons among a strong core following of customers in the global marketplace. Some even talk about the "Swatch Revolution" that began when Nicolas Hayek founded the company. Why do you think Swatch has such a strong cultural following?

3. As mentioned, Swatch wants you to create your own unique way of accessorizing through its Swatch watch. Is a watch a way to show who a person is culturally? Does a watch get embedded into a person's culture? Can a watch create a cultural image?

Woolworths' Corporate Responsibility Strategy

The Woolworths Group (**woolworthsgroup.com.au**) is an Australian conglomerate founded in 1924. The company's headquarters is in Bella Vista in New South Wales, a southeastern Australian state. Colloquially known as "Woolies" there, the company has extensive retail interests in the Oceania region, particularly in Australia and New Zealand, but it also has a substantial foothold in India. The Woolworths Group consists of three core businesses (Woolworths Food Group, Endeavour Drinks, and Portfolio Businesses), which altogether employ more than 205,000 people, and have a combined revenue of about $46 billion USD. Woolworths has 13 subsidiaries across the three businesses.

Integrating these 13 subsidiaries into a corporate social responsibility program is a challenge for a company with so many employees and diverse interests. To accomplish its objective, Woolworths Group's Corporate Responsibility Strategy identifies 20 corporate responsibility and sustainability goals. These goals cover a broad range of Woolworths' stakeholders (e.g., customers, team members, suppliers, and local communities in which Woolworths operates). In particular, the indirect employees—in various supply chain partners—create a challenge when Woolworths designs and implements CSR initiatives. Woolworths' Corporate Responsibility Strategy is based on a framework of People, Planet, and Prosperity. Here, we will take a look at these "three P" areas, where Woolworths thinks it can make a difference.

The primary focus on *People* in Woolworths' CSR approach is about encouraging diversity: "We value diversity across Woolworths. Our customers should see in Woolworths' people a reflection of themselves and their communities. In this strategy we embrace targets that support diversity and, hand in hand with this aim, tolerance and respect." The target goals include striving for gender equity by targeting at least 40 percent of executive and senior manager positions to be held by women. Woolworths is also setting a goal of no salary wage gap between male and female employees of equivalent positions at all levels of the company. And being rooted in Australian business, the company is embracing diversity by increasing the number of indigenous employees so it is in line with the company's stated commitments under the Australian Federal Government's Employment Parity Initiative.

The focus on the *Planet* in Woolworths' CSR approach is innovating: "We recognize the environmental impact we have across our value chain and will work with our suppliers, service providers and operations to innovate for a healthy planet. We will move to a circular economy, source environmentally sustainable commodities and respond to climate change." Woolworths is working toward zero food waste going to landfills. According to the U.S. Environmental Protection Agency, 20 percent of

Shutterstock/haireena

what goes into municipal landfills is food. Woolworths is also trying to reduce its carbon emissions by 10 percent. Many of our daily activities (e.g., using electricity, driving a car, or disposing of waste) cause greenhouse gas emissions. A *carbon footprint* is defined as the set of greenhouse gas emissions caused by an individual, event, organization, or product, and it is expressed as a carbon dioxide equivalent. Emissions trap heat in the atmosphere, which according to most scientists contributes to disruptive climate change.

The focus on *Prosperity* in Woolworths' CSR approach is founded on trusted relationships: "We will focus on positive relationships with suppliers, give back to the communities in which we operate, and rebuild trust with our customers."[1] Woolworths' targets are to achieve a top quartile ranking in how the business engages fairly and equitably with its suppliers, as measured by independent supplier surveys. Inspiration is also built into prosperity in the form of the company implementing activities to inspire customers to consume all of Woolworths' products in a healthy, sustainable way. The most transparent Prosperity initiative, though, is to invest the equivalent of 1 percent of total earnings in community partnerships and programs.

Woolworths' People-Planet-Prosperity strategies drive how the company does business. The strategies outline that Woolworths is committed to hard work and that its integrity is resolute. The foundation is a down-to-earth culture with family friendly values. Every aspect of Woolworths' business exists for the purpose of making customers' lives simpler, easier, and better. Underpinning Woolworths' operations is a working relationship built on mutual trust with suppliers. More than 80 percent of the company's suppliers have been strategic partners with Woolworths for a decade or longer.

[1]"Woolworths Group's Corporate Responsibility Strategy 2020." Woolworths Group, 2020. **https://www.woolworthsgroup.com.au/icms_docs/ 186036_woolworths-group-corporate-responsibility-strategy-2020.pdf.**

Sources

Dimitri Sotiropoulos, "Woolworths Sets Sights on Sustainability," *Inside Retail* (Australia), February 14, 2017; Justin Smith, "How Woolworths Is Building Resilience in Its Food Supply Chain," *Sustainable Brands*, April 11, 2016; Jason LaChappelle, "Woolworths Sees Benefits of Working with Sustainability Standards," *Iseal Alliance*, September 19, 2014; "Woolworths Group's Corporate Responsibility Strategy 2020," **https:// woolworthsgroup.com.au/page/community-and-responsibility/ group-responsibility**.

Case Discussion Questions

1. What challenges do you think a company like Woolworths Group is facing when developing and implementing a companywide corporate social responsibility strategy that considers more than 205,000 employees, diverse interests, and stakeholders?

2. As mentioned, the focus on *People* is about encouraging diversity. The idea is to increase the number of indigenous employees so as to be in line with the company's stated commitments under the Australian Federal Government's Employment Parity Initiative. Does such a diversity approach enhance the company's sustainability strategy, or no? How?

3. Woolworths Group is trying to reduce its carbon emissions or footprint by 10 percent. Based on where we are as a world, is 10 percent enough of a reduction? Perhaps global warming is not real, albeit the vast majority of scientists clearly suggest it is; what do you think?

4. Woolworths' targets are to achieve a top quartile ranking in how the business engages fairly and equitably with its suppliers. How do supplier relationships and the fairness in dealing with suppliers relate to sustainability and "doing good" for society (and the company)?

The Trans Pacific Partnership (TPP) Is Dead: Long Live the CPTPP!

On February 4, 2016, ministers from 12 governments signed off on the Trans Pacific Partnership (TPP), a free trade deal among 12 countries, including the United States, Japan, Australia, New Zealand, Chile, Canada, Mexico, and Vietnam. China was not part of the deal. Together, these countries accounted for 36 percent of the world's GDP and 26 percent of world trade. In the United States, critics of the deal were quick to register their opposition. Donald Trump, now president of the United States, said that the "TPP is a terrible deal." Bernie Sanders, one of the leading Democratic contenders, called it "disastrous" and "a victory for Wall Street and other big corporations." Many other politicians, wary of the fact that 2016 was a general election year in the United States, were also quick to criticize the deal. In contrast, the administration of Barack Obama heralded the TPP as a historic deal of major importance. Editorials in influential publications such as *The Wall Street Journal* and *The Economist* urged the U.S. Congress to ratify the deal.

The TPP planned to eliminate or reduce about 18,000 tariffs, taxes, and nontariff barriers such as quotas on trade between and among the member countries. By expanding market access and lowering prices for consumers, economists claimed that the deal would boost economic growth rates among TPP countries and add about $285 billion to global GDP by 2025. Because the United States already has very low tariff barriers, most of the tariff reductions would occur in other countries.

U.S. agriculture would have been a big beneficiary. The TPP would eliminate import tariffs as high as 40 percent on U.S. poultry products and fruit and 35 percent on soybeans—all products where the United States has a comparative advantage in production. Cargill Inc., a giant U.S. grain exporter and meat producer, urged lawmakers to support the pact. A number of large, efficient U.S. manufacturers also came out in support of the deal, which would eliminate import tariffs as high as 59 percent on U.S. machinery exports to TPP countries. Boeing, the country's largest exporter, said that the deal would help it compete overseas, where it gets 70 percent of its revenue. Several technology companies, including Intel, voiced support for the deal, pointing out that it would eliminate import taxes as high as 35 percent on the sale

Shuttestock/creativetan

of information and communication technology to some other TPP countries.

Some U.S. companies urged Congress to vote against the deal. Ford opposed the deal because it would phase out a 2.5 percent tariff on imports of Japanese cars into the United States and a 25 percent tariff on imports of light trucks—even though under the agreement, those tariffs would be phased down over 30 years. Labor unions opposed the deal, arguing that it would result in further losses of U.S. manufacturing jobs and lead to lower wages. The tobacco company Philip Morris opposed the deal because it would prevent tobacco companies from suing foreign governments over antismoking measures that restrict tobacco companies from using their logos and brands to market tobacco products. Several big drug companies also opposed the deal because it only protected new biotechnology products from generic competition for 5 years, rather than the 12 years they had before.

Data supporting these various claims and counterclaims were offered by a number of independent studies, including those from the World Bank, the Institute of International Economics (IIE), and Tufts University. Both the World Bank and the IIE concluded that by creating more overseas demand for American goods and services, by 2030 the TPP would raise U.S. wages slightly above what they would have been without the deal. The IIE study estimated that the TPP would increase annual U.S. exports by $357 billion, or 9 percent, by 2030. The IIE study also calculated that overall, there would be no job losses in the United States. Although some sectors would see job losses, the IIE suggested that these would be offset by job gains elsewhere. The study from Tufts University was the most pessimistic, estimating that the deal would result in the loss of 450,000 jobs in the United States over 10 years. To put this in context, between 2010 and 2015, the U.S. economy created 13 million new jobs, so the worst-case estimate of losses amounted to no more than two months of job growth during the 2010–2015 period.

Just three days into his administration, President Donald Trump withdrew the United States from the TPP, calling it a "ridiculous trade deal." Many predicted that without the United States, the deal would quickly collapse—but that did not happen. Instead, led by Japan, the remaining 11 nations pressed ahead with a revamped deal. Renamed the Comprehensive and Progressive Trans Pacific Partnership (CPTPP)—or TPP for short—the deal signed in Chile on March 8, 2018, will dramatically lower tariffs and other trade barriers between the 11 nations. The revised agreement, which still excludes China, covers 500 million people in nations that produce more than 13 percent of global gross domestic product.

According to David Parker, New Zealand's Trade Minister: "I think this agreement serves as an antidote to the protectionist trend we're seeing in the world. I think the CPTPP is more important than it was a year ago. This rise of protectionism is worrisome. . . . Countries that are in the agreement have got a different route where they can club together in a friendly manner, and facilitate the growth of their own economies for the benefit of their people."[2]

Although the United States is no longer party to this deal, several leaders of the signatory nations have indicated that they would welcome the U.S. back into the fold, although this seems unlikely to happen so long as Donald Trump is president. There are also indications that a post-Brexit Britain might seek to join the CPTPP.

Sources

Caitlin McGee, "Controversial TPP Pact Signed amid New Zealand Protests," *Aljazeera*, February 4, 2016; Catherine Ho,

---

[2]"The New TPP Trade Deal: Going Ahead without Trump." *Al Jazeera News*, March 24, 2018. **https://www.aljazeera.com/programmes/talktojazeera/2018/03/tpp-trade-deal-trump-180323073314104.html.**

"Fact Checking the Campaigns for and against the TPP Trade Deal," *The Washington Post*, February 11, 2016; Tripp Mickle and Theo Francis, "Trade Pact Sealed," *The Wall Street Journal*, October 6, 2015; Peter Petri, and Michael Plummer, "The Economic Effects of the Trans Pacific Partnership: New Estimates," Peterson Institute for International Economics, working paper 16-2, January 1, 2016; "China Picks Up the U.S. Trade Fumble," *The Wall Street Journal*, November 17, 2016; "The New TPP Trade Deal: Going Ahead without Trump," *Aljazeera News*, March 24, 2018; and "Japan Approves Bill to Ratify Successor to TPP Free Trade Pact," *Japan Times*, March 24, 2018.

Case Discussion Questions

1. What were the proposed benefits of the TPP?

2. What were the potential drawbacks of the U.S. entering the TPP? What would be the drawbacks to other nations?

3. Why do you think Donald Trump was so adamantly opposed to the TPP?

4. Why do you think the 11 remaining signatories went ahead with a revised deal after the United States withdrew?

5. Is the CPTTP a threat to American economic interests?

6. What is the opportunity cost to the United States of withdrawing from the TPP?

7. If you were in a position to advise Donald Trump regarding future American relations with the CPTPP, what would you tell him?

Boeing and Airbus Are in a Dogfight over Illegal Subsidies

Boeing and Airbus are the dominant players in the global market for large commercial jet aircraft of 100 seats or more. The two companies are locked in a relentless battle for market share, and for decades have been accusing each other of benefiting from government subsidies. In its early years, Airbus received 100 percent of the funds it needed to develop new aircraft from the governments of four European countries where Airbus' operations were based: Germany, France, Spain, and the United Kingdom. These funds were provided in the form of loans at below-market interest rates. For its part, Airbus claimed that Boeing has long been the recipient of R&D grants from the U.S. Department of Defense and NASA, which amount to indirect subsidies. The two companies reached an agreement on phasing out subsidies back in 1992, but Boeing walked away from that deal in 2004, claiming that Airbus was still benefiting from billions in illegal development subsidies.

In 2006, the U.S. government filed a case with the World Trade Organization (WTO) alleging that Airbus had received $25 billion in illegal subsidies, mostly in the form of launch aid for developing new aircraft. In 2010, the WTO ruled that Airbus had benefited from $18 billion in illegal government subsidies, including $15 billion in launch aid. The WTO gave the European governments until December 2011 to remove the harmful effects of the subsidies.

In September 2016, the WTO issued another ruling criticizing the Europeans for failing to comply with its 2010 ruling and, moreover, for giving another $5 billion to Airbus in the form of noncommercial loans to help develop its latest aircraft, the A350. In this latest ruling, the WTO stated that "it is apparent that the A350 could not have been launched and brought to market in the absence of launch aid."[3] In total, the WTO calculated that Boeing had lost 104 wide-bodied jet orders and 271 narrow-bodied jet orders as a result of Airbus launch subsidies. This latest ruling opens the door for the United States to apply retaliatory trade sanctions against non-compliant European governments.

However, it seems unlikely that the United States will apply retaliatory sanctions any time soon. Part of the reason is the the United States itself has been countersued by the EU through the WTO for providing illegal subsidies to Boeing. In November 2016, the WTO ruled that

Boeing would receive around $5.7 billion in illegal tax breaks from Washington State, where Boeing's main production facilities are located. The state of Washington had promised to give Boeing these tax breaks between 2020 and 2040 on the condition that the company kept the production of the wings for the wide-bodied 777X aircraft in the state. According to Airbus, these tax breaks give the 777X an unfair advantage against its rival aircraft, an assessment that the WTO seems to agree with.

It remains to be seen what the final outcome will be. The WTO has yet to rule on how much damage Boeing's tax breaks might impose upon Airbus. For its part, Boeing claims that the benefits from the subsidies to the 777X program only amount to $50 million a year, an assessment that Airbus vigorously disagrees with. The EU appealed this decision.

Sources

Dominic Gates, "Airbus Scoffs, Boeing Crows as WTO Slams EU for Failing to Address Illegal Subsidies," *Seattle Times*, September 22, 2016; "Boeing Illegally Given $5.7 Billion in Tax Breaks by Washington State, WTO Rules," *Associated Press*, November 28, 2016; Robert Wall and Doug Cameron, "EU Failed to Cut Off Illegal Subsidies to Airbus, WTO Rules," *The Wall Street Journal*, September 22, 2016.

Case Discussion Questions

1. Are there circumstances under which the subsidies that Airbus received in its early years might be justified?

2. Do you think that Boeing benefited from subsidies when it developed the 707 back in the 1960s? If they did, could they be justified?

3. Boeing and Airbus have allegedly been receiving subsidies for decades. How might these ongoing subsidies distort the market for large commercial jet aircraft?

4. Who benefits from government subsidies to Boeing and Airbus? Who loses?

5. Under what circumstances, if any, should national governments subsidize the development of new technology?

6. What would be the optimal outcome (in terms of global economic welfare) of the ongoing trade dispute between the EU and the U.S. over subsidies in the market for large commercial jet aircraft? How might such an agreement be enforced?

---

[3]Gates, Dominic. "Airbus Scoffs, Boeing Crows as WTO Slams EU for Failing to Address Illegal Subsidies." *Seattle Times*, September 22, 2016. https://www.seattletimes.com/business/boeing-aerospace/wto-slams-eu-for-failing-to-remedy-harm-to-boeing-from-illegal-airbus-subsidies/.

FDI in the Indian Retail Sector

Historically, the structure of retailing in India was very fragmented, with a large number of very small stores serving most of the market. Supply chains were also very poorly developed and fragmented. As recently as 2010, larger format big box stores, chain stores, and supermarkets only accounted for 4 percent of retail sales in the country (compared to 85 percent in the United States). This might sound like an ideal opportunity for efficient foreign retailers such as Walmart, IKEA, Tesco, and Carrefour. In theory, these multinational enterprises could enter the market and transform India's retail space, making it more efficient and bringing modern retail formats, technology, and supply chains to the country. This would benefit consumers and producers, from farmers to manufacturers. For example, it has been estimated that up to 40 percent of the food produced by Indian farmers is currently wasted because chronically underdeveloped supply chains mean that food rots before it reaches the market.

In practice, small-store owners in India have a long history of using their political power to lobby the government to impose restrictions on direct investment by foreigners in the retail space. Like incumbents everywhere, their goal has been to limit competition and protect their businesses and jobs. Until 2011, foreign multi-brand retailers such as Costco, Tesco, and Walmart were forbidden from owning retail outlets in the country. Even single-brand retailers such as IKEA and Nike had to partner with a local retailer, were limited to a 51 percent ownership stake, and had to go through a lengthy bureaucratic approval process.

By 2011, the Indian federal government had come to the conclusion that foreign investment in retailing was needed to improve India's supply chain, increase consumer choice, and help farmers bring their products to market. This view was supported by much of Indian industry, which saw the modernization of the retailing sector as an important condition for continued economic development. Clearly, the government believed that greater foreign capital and technology would help India grow its economy.

In late 2011, the Indian government announced a plan to reform foreign direct investment regulations. The plan was to allow foreign multi-brand retailers such as Walmart and Tesco to open retail stores, although they would be limited to a 51 percent ownership stake. At the same time, the government stated its intention to allow single-brand retailers to set up wholly owned stores, although anything over a 49 percent foreign ownership stake would still require formal government approval. These plans were greeted with strong opposition from small retailers and rival political parties, and the government was forced to temporarily shelve them.

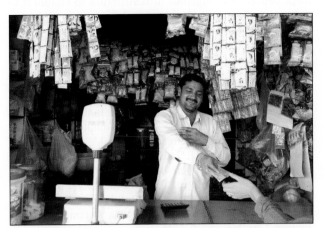

SIBSA Digital Pvt. Ltd./Alamy Stock Photo

In early 2012, the Indian government managed to secure approval for plans to allow foreign single-brand retailers to open wholly owned stores, but imposed the requirement that a single-brand retailer had to source 30 percent of its inventory from India. One of the first retailers to respond to these changes was IKEA, which announced it would invest $1.9 billion and set up 25 stores in the country. More generally though, many analysts viewed the 30 percent sourcing requirement as a major impediment to entering India. Both Apple and Nike, for example, would have to establish significant production facilities in the country in order to meet that requirement and set up their own brand stores.

In early 2018, the government modified the 30 percent requirement, giving single-brand retailers five years after their initial entry to reach the 30 percent figure. The government also allowed single-brand retailers to establish wholly owned subsidiaries without having to go through the cumbersome government approval process.

In late 2012, the federal Indian government allowed foreign investors to open multi-brand retail stores in India, but limited ownership to 51 percent. Moreover, in a nod to the strength of the political opposition, the federal government made this requirement subject to approval by individual states within the country, allowing some to opt out. Several states have done so, which reduces the attractiveness of India as a market for foreign retailers.

At the same time, India has allowed 100 percent ownership of online retail marketplaces in India. Amazon took advantage of this to enter the country in 2014 and has committed to invest $5 billion in India. Unlike in the United States, however, Amazon does not sell goods it has taken ownership of because that would classify the company as a multi-brand retailer, limit its ownership stake in Indian operation to 51 percent, and require it to take an Indian partner. Instead, Amazon only sells goods offered through its marketplace platform by third

parties. However, Amazon is investing heavily in fulfillment centers and logistics infrastructure to enable it to
deliver goods efficiently to Indian customers. Its investment may help to boost the efficiency of supply chains
in the country.

Sources

Greg Bensinger, "Amazon Plans $3 Billion Indian Investment,"
The Wall Street Journal, June 7, 2016; Vibhuto Agarwal and
Megha Bahree, "India Retreats on Retail," *The Wall Street
Journal*, December 8, 2011; "India Online," *The Economist*, May 5,
2016; Newley Purnell, "Jeff Bezos Invests Billions to Make
Amazon a Top E-Commerce Player in India," *The Wall Street
Journal*, November 19, 2016; and K.R. Srivats, "Cabinet Okays
100% FDI in Single Brand Retailing via Automatic Route,"
Business Line, January 10, 2018.

Case Discussion Questions

1. What explains the fragmented nature of India's
   retail sector? What are the benefits of this system?
   What are the costs?

2. How might investment by foreign retailers change
   retailing in India? What are the potential benefits
   of such FDI?

3. Who stands to lose from FDI into India's retail
   sector? Who stands to gain?

4. Why has India been so slow to change its laws
   regarding foreign ownership of retailers? What,
   if anything, can foreign retailers do to influence
   the laws in a way that benefits entry?

5. Given the political and economic realities in India,
   what is the best entry strategy for a foreign retailer?

Free Trade in Africa

On June 10, 2015, representatives from 26 African nations signed an agreement pledging to work together to establish a free trade area that would remove or reduce many tariffs and eliminate time-consuming customs procedures between them. Known as the Tripartite Free Trade Area (TFTA), this common market would encompass more than 630 million people and link together three existing regional trading blocks in Southern and Eastern Africa with a combined gross domestic product of $1.2 trillion and more than $102 billion in trade between member states.

The existing regional trading blocks are the East African Community, created in 2000; the Southern African Development Community, created in 1980; and an overlapping Common Market for Eastern and Southern Africa, which also took shape in the 1980s. The East Africa Community has made some progress fostering trade between its member countries, which include Kenya, Tanzania, and Uganda. Countries in the Southern African Development Community have a common set of external tariffs, and several member states use the South African rand, the most liquid and widely traded currency on the continent.

However, the existing patchwork of African trading blocks—there are some 17 in all, with many countries being members of more than one—has made it difficult to realize the gains from trade that could flow from an expanded single market. An African firm selling goods on the continent still faces an average tariff of 8.7 percent, compared with a 2.5 percent tariff on goods sold overseas. Other costs of intra-African trade include often-lengthy stops at borders for customs inspection, excessive customs-related bureaucracy and red tape, and a lack of adequate physical infrastructure, including roads and railways. As a consequence of such factors, it can take three weeks for a shipping container to travel the 700 miles from the Kenyan port of Mombasa to

Shutterstock/Matthias G. Ziegler

Kampala, the capital of Uganda. There are also some vexing local content requirements. The South African Development Community, for example, requires that clothes traded within the region are both manufactured and sourced there to qualify for lower tariffs. However, because few textiles are produced in the region, the rules have stifled trade in garments.

For all these reasons, African countries are more likely to trade with Europe and America than they are with each other. Only 19 percent of Africa's $930 billion in trade is with other countries on the continent. By comparison, some 60 percent of Europe's trade is within its own continent, as is 40 percent of North American trade. Other factors contributing to the lack of intra-African trade include low industrialization levels, restricted movement of labor, poor infrastructure, and a high dependence on exporting unprocessed commodities in many countries.

The thinking behind the TFTA is that harmonizing rules, reducing tariffs, and streamlining or removing customs procedures will allow African firms to sell more goods and services to their neighbors, enabling them to achieve greater economies of scale and lower costs, which would benefit all parties to the agreement. On the other hand, such agreements may prove difficult to reach and, if the past is any guide, even more difficult to implement, given political realities on the ground. Some observers think that the TFTA is too ambitious an undertaking and that focusing effort on improving the three existing regional groups would yield more gains. It's easier, they argue, to reach an agreement between five adjacent member states, as in the case of the East African Community, than 26 very different countries scattered over the entire continent.

Despite the skepticism surrounding TFTA, Africa nations have even bigger ambitions. In 2016, African leaders committed themselves to establishing a Continental Free Trade Area (CFTA) that encompasses all African countries. Two years later, in March 2018, 44 of those nations signed an agreement to create a CFTA. The pact will eliminate tariffs on 90 percent of products, liberalize services, and reduce nontariff barriers. A second phase of negotiations, to begin later this year, will focus on investment, competition, and intellectual property rights. Proponents of the deal believe that it will merge Africa's fragmented markets into one large continental market, ignite industrialization, boost economic growth, and create jobs. However, 11 African nations have yet to sign onto the deal, including Nigeria and South Africa, the two largest African economies. While both countries seem to agree with the pact in principle, they view the pact as incomplete. They point out that countries have not yet decided which goods will be excluded from the tariff reductions. Nor have they finalized key annexes to the text. For example, the chapter on "rules of origin" is incomplete, raising the possibility that goods from outside Africa could be imported, have African labels placed on them, and then be traded within the bloc as African goods. There is also strong opposition to the pact from labor unions within Nigeria, who have called the trade deal a "radioactive neoliberal policy initiative."

Sources

"Intra-African Trade: The Road Less Travelled," *The Economist*, April 17, 2013; Martin Stevis and Patrick McGroarty, "African Leaders Pledge to Create a Free Trade Zone," *The Wall Street Journal*, June 10, 2015; "Trade Within Africa: Tear Down These Walls," *The Economist*, February 27, 2016; John Aglionby, "Africa Looks to Boost Growth and Jobs with Free Trade Area," *Financial Times*, December 1, 2016; "Why Africa's Two Biggest Economies Did Not Sign Its Landmark Trade Deal," *The Economist*, March 29, 2018.

Case Discussion Questions

1. Why are African countries more likely to trade with Europe and America than they are with each other?

2. What are the likely gains from trade to be had from TFTA if it is fully implemented as a common market?

3. Why do you think free trade areas established so far in Africa have not lived up to their expectations?

4. What will African countries need to do to make the TFTA a success? What are the likely impediments to doing this?

5. What could the impact of CFTA be on Africa?

The Mexican Peso, the Japanese Yen, and *Pokémon Go*

Nintendo's hit game *Pokémon Go* is a lot less lucrative in Mexico than the Japanese company originally thought it would be. This is because Mexicans purchase the "Pokécoins" they need to navigate the game in Mexican pesos, and the peso has been falling in value against the Japanese yen. Back in early 2015, 1 Mexican peso bought 8 Japanese yen. By September 2016, 1 peso was only worth about 5.1 Japanese yen. This meant that when pesos spent on *Pokémon Go* were translated back into Japanese yen, they were worth less in yen, which negatively affected Nintendo's profits from Mexico.

The diverging values on the yen and peso are a function of their exchange rates against the U.S. dollar. Most trades between the yen and the peso are converted through the U.S. dollar, rather than traded directly. This is because the U.S. dollar is the world's most widely traded and liquid currency. It's easier to trade dollars for yen, and dollars for pesos, than it is to trade yen for pesos. For much of 2016, the yen gained against the dollar, while the Mexican peso fell, leading to a fall in the peso/yen exchange rate.

The strength of the yen reflected the belief that Japan is a safe haven in which to park cash. Although the Japanese economy has been stagnant for decades, inflation is low and the yen has been a strong currency. The Mexican peso is the most liquid emerging market currency, which makes it an easy one to sell when investors worry about the economic strength of developing economies, which they did in 2015 and 2016. To compound matters, worries about the health of the Mexican economy following the election of Donald Trump to the U.S. presidency put further pressure on the peso. Trump threatened to pull the United States out of NAFTA—the regional trade deal that has been a major boon for Mexico. The Mexican peso hit a record low against the U.S. dollar following the election of Mr. Trump.

In addition to Nintendo, the fall in the value of the peso against the yen has created problems for other Japanese firms. Japanese automakers have significant assembly operations in Mexico. Companies such as Toyota and Mazda import a large number of specialty electronic components from suppliers in Japan. The price of these components has gone up when translated into pesos, raising costs for their Mexican operations and making them less profitable.

On the other hand, the weak peso has boosted demand for some Mexican products in Japan. For example, Japan imports a large quantity of frozen Mexican pork. The price has fallen when translated into yen, and demand has surged. Mexico dices up the pork and exports it to Japanese convenience stores, where it is sold in bento boxes. The dicing process is labor intensive—and one less step they have to perform in Japan. Mexico can do it cheaper, and the currency moves have only added to the cost savings, which is good for Japanese consumers.

Sources

Julie Wernau, "Pokéman Go Illustrates a Currency Problem," *The Wall Street Journal*, August 11, 2016; Elena Holodny and Portia Crowe, "Mexican Peso Crashes to Record Low," *Business Insider*, November 8, 2016; and "Peso Falls to Session Lows after Meeting between US and Mexico Presidents Falls Through," *Reuters*, January 26, 2017.

Case Discussion Questions

1. Why are most trades between the Japanese yen and the Mexican peso made through U.S. dollars?

2. Explain why the peso fell in value against the Japanese yen during 2016. How predictable was this fall?

3. What were the benefits of the fall in the value of the peso against the yen for Mexican companies? What were the costs?

4. What were the benefits of the fall in the value of the peso against the yen for Japanese companies? What were the costs?

5. Should Japanese companies, such as Nintendo and Toyota, with business in Mexico have hedged against adverse changes in the peso/yen exchange rate? How might they have done that?

Egypt and the IMF

When President Abdel Fatah al-Sissi came to power in a 2013 military coup, he promised to fix Egypt's mounting economic problems. Three years later, those problems had only intensified. The country was struggling with low economic growth; 13 percent unemployment; a 12 percent inflation rate; a large trade deficit, amounting to 7 percent of GDP; a persistent budget deficit of around 12 percent of GDP; and public debt, which by 2016 stood at 92 percent of GDP. The tourism trade, a major source of foreign currency, had collapsed in the wake of concerns about terrorism, which included an Islamic State–linked insurgency in the Sinai Peninsula that claimed the bombing of a Russian passenger jet in 2016. Foreign direct investment, another source of foreign currency, had also slumped in the wake of Egypt's economic and political problems.

One major issue was a lack of foreign currency in the country, which made it difficult to pay for imports and resulted in shortages of key commodities. For example, Egypt imports one-third of its sugar. By mid-2016, this commodity was in short supply due to the inability of Egyptian traders to get the foreign currency required to pay for imported sugar. Historically, in times of trouble, the oil-rich Arab states of the Persian Gulf had loaned foreign currency to Egypt at low interest rates, but a collapse in oil prices had left those states financially strained, and loans were not forthcoming. In an indication of the depth of Egypt's problems, while the official exchange rate of the Egyptian pound was pegged at 9 pounds to the U.S. dollar, the black market rate had soared to 18 pounds to the dollar.

In mid-2016, with its foreign exchange reserves being rapidly depleted, the Egyptian government applied to the IMF for a loan. The IMF agreed to loan Egypt up to $12 billion, but only if the government undertook a number of economic reforms. These included liberalizing the exchange rate, letting the Egyptian pound float against other currencies. The thinking was that the pound would immediately depreciate against major currencies such as the U.S. dollar and the euro, making Egyptian exports cheaper and its imports more expensive. This should help the country to improve its trade deficit and earn more foreign currency. At the same time, the IMF required the Egyptian government to implement an austerity program that included an immediate end to energy subsidies, which had kept energy prices artificially low; reforms to public enterprises to make them more efficient; a tighter monetary policy to rein in inflation; and the imposition of a value-added tax to raise government revenues.

In November 2016, Egypt let the pound float freely. It immediately lost 50 percent of its value against the U.S. dollar, trading at around 13 pounds to the dollar. The depreciation continued into the new year, with the pound falling to 19 pounds to the dollar by mid-January 2017, bringing the official exchange rate and the black-market rate into equality. Egypt also moved rapidly to impose the value-added tax. In return, the IMF released the first $2.75 billion of its loan to Egypt. Further tranches of the loan will be released as Egypt makes progress on the economic reforms advocated by the IMF.

Only time will tell if these policies will work. In addition to a fall in the value of the pound, the immediate impact included a surge in the annual inflation rate to around 20 percent. The IMF envisages the inflation rate falling to 7 percent within three years, while there should be sharp improvements in both the trade deficit and the budget deficit. However, the planned austerity measures carry significant political risks for the Egyptian government. If protests materialize over short-term hardships, the government might cave in to political pressure and pull back from the IMF-mandated reforms. If that happens, the IMF might withhold further installments under the loan program, and the Egyptian economy could continue to deteriorate.

Sources

Heba Mahfouz and Paul Schemm, "Struggling Egypt Devalues Currency by Almost 50% Ahead of IMF Loan," *The Washington Post*, November 3, 2016; Lin Noueihed and Ahmed Aboulenein, "Egypt on Track to Receive IMF Loan's Second Tranche," *Reuters*, January 18, 2017; "State of Denial," *The Economist*, August 6, 2016; and *CIA World Fact Book*, Egypt, accessed February 2017.

Case Discussion Questions

1. What was the root cause of Egypt's economic problems?

2. Was it appropriate for Egypt to bring in the IMF? What other alternatives did they have?

3. Do you think the policy measures required by the IMF are appropriate? What are these policy measures designed to do? What might be the unintended consequences of these measures?

4. As a potential foreign investor, at what point would you be willing to invest in the Egyptian economy? To what extent would policies imposed by the IMF influence your decision?

Alibaba's Record-Setting IPO

In 2013, senior managers at Alibaba, China's largest e-commerce enterprise, decided it was time to take the company public and offer its shares for sale to retail and institutional investors. Alibaba was founded in 1999 by a former English teacher, Jack Ma, with just $60,000 in capital. Often described as a fusion of Amazon and eBay, by 2013 Alibaba was already the world's largest online e-commerce company. In 2012, transactions at its online sites totaled $248 billion, more than those of Amazon and eBay combined. Driven by rapid growth in China's online shopping market, projections called for the company to reach online sales of $713 billion by 2017.

Ma and his colleagues had several motives for the IPO. First, they wanted to raise capital to finance the infrastructure investment required at a company that was growing at breakneck speed. Second, publicly traded shares would give Alibaba a currency that it could use to acquire other enterprises (by offering its shares in exchange for the shares of an acquired company). Third, a public market in Alibaba shares would be a major liquidity event for the large number of Alibaba employees who held stock in the enterprise. It would enable them to more easily sell shares in order to raise cash for other purchases.

Initially, Alibaba considered doing an IPO in Hong Kong. The choice made sense. Hong Kong has a large and liquid stock market that attracts investors from all over the world. However, while Hong Kong is part of China, it retains its own legal system. Hong Kong's stock exchange has a "one share one vote" requirement. Ma and his colleagues were opposed to this. Even though they would hold only a minority of shares after the IPO, they wanted to retain the ability to nominate more than half of the company's board of directors, ensuring that they maintained control over the management of the enterprise.

Alibaba entered into negotiations with the Hong Kong Stock Exchange to see if the rules could be changed, but to no avail. As it became increasingly apparent that the Hong Kong exchange was unwilling to change its rules in a timely manner, Alibaba made inquiries to the New York Stock Exchange (NYSE) and the U.S. Securities and Exchange Commission (SEC). The NYSE and SEC indicated they would have no problem with Alibaba's partners retaining control over more than half of all board seats.

Alibaba realized that an offering on the NYSE would have other advantages beyond retaining control of the board. The NYSE is the largest and most liquid exchange in the world. The recent successful IPO of Facebook and

Twitter had demonstrated that U.S. investors had an appetite for internet offerings. Demand for Alibaba shares was expected to be high, raising the possibility that Alibaba might have a record-setting IPO. Moreover, if its shares were listed on the NYSE, this might make it easier for Alibaba to subsequently use those shares to acquire U.S. and other foreign enterprises, giving Alibaba a bigger global footprint.

The biggest obstacle standing in the way of a U.S. listing was the Chinese government–imposed limits on foreign ownership of Chinese technology businesses. Alibaba was able to circumvent these limits by establishing a complex corporate structure in which investors would actually own shares in a Cayman Island entity, Alibaba Group Holdings, which has contractual rights to all of the earnings of Alibaba China, but no ownership interest in the Chinese entity, which would continue to be owned by Ma and his partners.

The IPO took place on the NYSE on September 18, 2014. The initial offering price was $68 a share, but demand was so strong that Alibaba's shares opened at $92.70. Alibaba sold 368 million shares in the offering, or about 15 percent of the company. The IPO raised $25 billion for Alibaba, $6 billion more than originally estimated, and valued the company at $231 billion, making it the largest IPO in history.

Sources

S. D. Solomon, "Alibaba Investors Will Buy a Risky Corporate Structure," *The New York Times*, May 6, 2014; T. Demos and J. Osawa, "Alibaba Debut Makes a Splash," *The Wall Street Journal*, September 19, 2014; D. Thomas and E. Barreto, "Alibaba's Choice of US IPO Spurred by Rivals, Hong Kong Impass," *Reuters*, March 19, 2014.

Case Discussion Questions

1. Why did Jack Ma decide it was time to take Alibaba public?

2. Why do you think the management of Alibaba decided against doing the IPO in China's main stock market in Shanghai? Why did they ultimately decide against Hong Kong?

3. What were the legal, financial, and strategic advantages to Alibaba of undertaking its IPO in New York?

4. Because the IPO was undertaken in New York, does this make Alibaba an American enterprise?

Sony Corporation: Still a Leader Globally?

Sony Corporation (**sony.com**) is one of the most well-known companies in the world. With a heritage from Japan as a multinational conglomerate that was founded in 1946, the company is headquartered in Tokyo. Sony has annual sales of more than $76 billion, 125,000 employees, and some 100 global subsidiaries and affiliates. It has been recognized as an innovator in its industries of electronics, semiconductors, computers, video games, and telecommunications equipment—both for its research and development (R&D) and for its business strategy to constantly be competitive in the international marketplace.

Strategically, Sony's products and services can be classified into 12 core business segments: TV and video, audio, digital camera, professional products and solutions, medical, semiconductors, smartphones and internet, game and network services, pictures, music, and financial services. To integrate these 12 segments, Sony has a vision of "using our unlimited passion for technology, content, and services to deliver ground-breaking new excitement and entertainment." The mission is even clearer. Sony is "a company that inspires and fulfills your curiosity." But is that mission too broad to signal to the marketplace and global customers what the company can do for them?

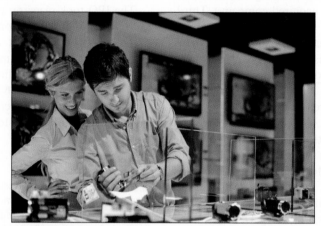

Shutterstock/ESB Professional

For the company, this strategic curiosity, innovativeness, and passion for technology have served Sony well as a global innovation leader for more than seven decades. Most customers expect Sony to offer cutting-edge products—at least at or near the top of the innovation scale—and manufacture high-quality goods that are priced at a fair level. For example, Sony launched the world's first direct-view portable transistor TV in 1960, and the company developed the world's first transistor-based videotape recorder in 1961. The strategy for the future is through what Sony sees as the stunning reality of visuals that can be created by big-screen TVs and dynamic sound. Sony plans to transform the viewing experience from "watching" to "feeling."

Behind the scenes, Sony has also spent more than 50 years honing its technological excellence in the field of broadcasting and in professional products. The company's products are widely used in the production of movies and television shows, as well as in live sporting events.

This has resulted in a high global market share for Sony in the business-to-business arena as well as the company receiving a number of Emmy Awards. Moving forward, Sony is placing a strategic emphasis on providing new value through end-to-end solutions that meet the needs of various customers by incorporating technologies enhanced in the area of content creation. One can wonder, though, will Sony's future depend on end-customers at the people level or its B2B customers (e.g., movie and TV production companies)?

Beyond the 12 core segments that have served Sony well strategically for decades, the company is embarking on global initiatives to create new business opportunities. They are accelerating R&D to bring about innovations that can, if successful, become new strategic business segments serving customers' needs and wants. To strategically evaluate and nurture potential opportunities, Sony divides these into new business ventures (Life Space UX, Seed Acceleration Program, and Sports Entertainment) and R&D opportunities (Future Lab Program and Sony Computer Science Laboratories Inc.). Through these ventures, the regular, individual customer is front and center, meaning Sony places its focus on its traditional customer base.

On the business venture side, Life Space UX is a concept that is defined by delivering unique experiences and facilitating new ways to transform a person's living space. The Seed Acceleration Program's goal is to gather and nurture new business ideas from beyond the boundaries of existing Sony organizations (which is very similar to many organizations' strategies that are innovatively new and outside-the-box of what the company normally does). Additionally, with its range of products and services designed to enrich various everyday life situations, Sony is focused on the new business venture of providing discoveries and experiences in sports. The "watching" to "feeling" transformation of what the company wants to achieve can help provide discoveries and experiences in sports and other areas.

The Future Lab Program is a part of Sony's heavy investment in R&D. Sony embraces an approach to technological R&D that emphasizes an open creative environment and direct lines of communication with society, with the end goal being to co-create new lifestyles and customer value. At Sony Computer Science Laboratories Inc.—often abbreviated as Sony CSL—value is assessed based on achievements that can contribute to humanity and society, to new science and technology, to industrial progress, and to product development. While an open creative environment and direct lines of communication with society appear to be a new direction for Sony's previously guarded R&D efforts, creating new lifestyles and customer value in today's international marketplace is very much about co-creation (i.e., working with customers to address their needs and wants jointly).

Sources

Anousha Sakoui and Yuji Nakamura, "Sony CEO Heads to Hollywood in Push to Revive Movie Studio," *Bloomberg Businessweek*, January 31, 2017; "New Business and R&D," March 22, 2017 (**sony.net/SonyInfo/CorporateInfo/newbusiness**); "Here's Sony's New Business Strategy," *The Economist*, February 21, 2015; "Sony Global Corporate Strategy," June 29, 2016 (**sony.net/SonyInfo/IR/strategy**).

Case Discussion Questions

1. Do you see Sony as an innovator in its industries of electronics, semiconductors, computers, video games, and telecommunications equipment? Why or why not?

2. Sony has a vision of "using our unlimited passion for technology, content, and services to deliver groundbreaking new excitement and entertainment." The mission is even clearer. Sony is "a company that inspires and fulfills your curiosity." Does Sony inspire and fulfill *your* curiosity? Why or why not?

3. Sony has 12 core segments in its business. Is this too many or not enough? Are today's companies diversified like they used to be a few decades ago? Can Sony's 12-segment business model be sustainable?

4. The Future Lab Program, which is part of Sony's investment in R&D, embraces an approach to technological R&D that emphasizes an open creative environment and direct lines of communication with society, with the end goal being to co-create new lifestyles and customer value. Does Sony create significant customer value? Do you think Sony creates new lifestyles?

Organizational Architecture at P&G

The Procter & Gamble Company (P&G) is a force in the global marketplace. It is the biggest U.S. advertiser at some $5 billion annually, and spends a staggering $9 billion annually worldwide on advertising. Beyond ad spending, P&G is also the world's largest maker of household products, with more than $80 billion in annual sales and a net worth (sometimes referred to as "market capitalization") greater than the gross domestic product (GDP) of most countries. P&G markets products in more than 180 countries. Geographically, these 180 countries are divided into the following core markets: Asia; Europe; India, the Middle East, and Africa; Latin America; and North America. The company sells products to about 5 billion of the world's 7 billion people.

P&G organizes its many products into four industry-based sectors: (1) Baby, Feminine and Family Care; (2) Beauty, Hair and Personal Care; (3) Fabric and Home Care; and (4) Health and Grooming. In fact, P&G states that "we have made P&G's organization structure an important part of our capability to grow . . . it combines global scale benefits with a local focus to win with consumers and retail customers in each country where P&G products are sold."[4]

To best serve the global markets, P&G decided it would cut around 100 brands from its portfolio and focus on its core remaining 80 brands, which generated 95 percent of the company's profits. Alan "A.G." Lafley, then the company's board chair, president, and CEO, said, "This will be a much simpler, much less complex company of leading brands that's easier to manage and operate." Additionally, P&G cut its marketing and advertising agency roster by 50 percent over the previous three years, from around 6,000 to 3,000 companies, in a bid to increase its marketing productivity.

With the organizational size and product line breadth come both industry responsibility and business opportunity (see Chapter 5 on ethics, corporate social responsibility, and sustainability for a discussion of combining industry and business opportunities). P&G says that "our responsibility is to be an ethical corporate citizen" and the company articulates this in its Purpose Statement: "We will provide branded products and services of superior quality and value that improve the lives of the world's consumers, now and for generations to come. As a result, consumers will reward us with leadership sales, profit and value creation, allowing our people, our shareholders and the communities in which we live and work to prosper."[5]

As P&G continues to streamline its product assortment, it focuses heavily on its Selling and Market Operations (SMOs) as a mechanism to reach global customers in all four of its industry-based sectors. P&G views the SMOs as more of a name change from its old Market Development Organizations to a structure that supports each of the four industry sectors with "superior, effective and efficient selling, distribution, shelving, pricing execution and merchandising—every day, every week—in every store." The SMOs are staffed with employees representing 140 different nationalities. At the same time, fewer than 1 percent of job applicants actually get a job offer from P&G. There is strength in architecture (structure, people, incentives and control, culture, processes) at P&G.

Sources

Antoine Gara, "Reckitt Benckiser Is Building a 21st Century Procter & Gamble," *Forbes*, February 10, 2017; Leonie Roderick, "P&G On How It Cut Agencies by Almost 50% to Optimize Its Marketing Spend," *Marketing Week*, November 21, 2016; "Global Structure and Governance," **www.pg.com**, accessed March 29, 2017; J. Neff, "Biggest Ad Spender P&G Has New North America Media Chief," *Advertising Age*, January 15, 2015; "Around 100 Brands to Be Dropped by Procter and Gamble to Boost Sales," *CincinnatiNews.net*, August 1, 2014; S. Ng, "P&G CEO Lafley Lays Groundwork for Exit," *The Wall Street Journal*, April 13, 2015.

Case Discussion Questions

1. Advertising is important for most companies, especially companies such as P&G that sells mostly to end customers. But most people already know about P&G products such as Charmin bathroom tissue and moist towelettes, Crest toothpaste, and so on. Does P&G really need to constantly put money into advertising when its products already have a stronghold in the global marketplace?

2. P&G cut its marketing and advertising agency roster by 50 percent over the past three years from around 6,000 to 3,000 companies in a bid to increase its marketing productivity, efficiency, and effectiveness. Given that it spends $9 billion worldwide on advertising, should P&G have more or fewer marketing and advertising agencies doing its advertising?

3. By consolidating and cutting 100 brands from its consumer portfolio of brands, does P&G run the risk of ultimately losing out on global market opportunities?

---

[4]"Corporate Structure." Procter & Gamble, 2019. **https://www.pg.com/en_balkans/company/global_structure_operations/corporate_structure.shtml.**

[5]"Our Purpose, Values and Principles." Procter & Gamble, 2019. **https://www.pg.com/translations/pvp_pdf/english_PVP.pdf.**

Cutco Corporation—Sharpening Your Market Entry

The name Cutco comes from "Cooking UTensils COmpany," a name once owned by Alcoa. Alcoa is a U.S. company that now concentrates on work with lightweight metals and advanced manufacturing techniques. Together with W.R. Case & Sons Cutlery Company, Alcoa created the joint venture Alcas Corporation in 1949, which subsequently became Cutco Corporation in 2009.

Cutco Corporation includes the wholly owned subsidiaries of Vector Marketing Corporation, which it acquired in 1985, and Cutco Cutlery Corporation. Vector Marketing is the U.S.-based sales arm of Cutco Corporation, which is headquartered in Olean, New York. More than 700 manufacturing and administrative employees work at the Olean location.

Cutco is now the largest manufacturer of high-quality kitchen cutlery in the United States and Canada. The product line includes kitchen knives and utensils, shears, flatware, cookware, and sporting knives. Look around your house and your friends' houses—you are likely to see one of their well-known blocks of knives in the kitchen! The price for one of the blocks with a dozen or so knives ranges from about $100 to upward of a few thousand dollars. Some 16 million people have bought Cutco knives.

Originally, Cutco was created as a product for Wear-Ever Aluminum (a company focused on cookware), which at the time was a division of Alcoa. Cutco evolved from there, eventually adding its signature Wedge-Lock handle and Double-D recessed edge on some of its knives. Two things that have never changed are Cutco's commitment to fine craftsmanship and the Forever Guarantee. The guarantee means what it implies—that Cutco stands behind its knives' performance and sharpness forever. They also have a forever guarantee of replacing their knives for any misuse or abuse at half the cost.

Cutco, as it operates today, was formed in 1982 following a management buyout that took the company private. As with any employee or manager buyout, it was a leap of faith for the team that bought the company. But, based on the company's story, it was also the moment that secured Cutco's future for generations to come. In this process, in 1985, Vector Marketing Corporation became the exclusive marketer of Cutco products directly to consumers via sales representatives located throughout the United States and Canada. Cutco International Inc. is responsible for international marketing.

Annual sales for Cutco now stand at about $200 million worldwide, but mainly in the United States and Canada. The product line includes more than 100 choices under the Cutco name alone. The extended line includes kitchen utensils, gadgets and flatware, sporting and pocket knives, and garden tools. For the Cutco line, the products are marketed via what is called "direct selling"

McGraw-Hill Education

(marketing of products directly to the consumer away from a fixed retail location). Internationally, outside North America, Cutco has independent office arrangements in Australia, Costa Rica, Germany, South Korea, and the United Kingdom. Puerto Rico also has independently run sales locations.

In the United States and Canada, Vector Marketing Corporation typically employs college students in the 18-to-24 age range part-time during the school year, as well as full-time during the summers, to be part of their direct sales force. The sales pitch to students is good pay, flexible schedules, personal growth, no experience needed, great training, and engagement with quality products. In fact, 85 percent of the sales force at Cutco is college-aged individuals.

This sales force is a drastic change from the early days of the company. Early on, Cutco had hundreds of small independent sellers of the company's knives and other products. Vector Marketing became one of these sellers in 1981 and stayed in this role until 1984. In 1985, Cutco bought out Vector Marketing, and Vector became the sole channel for sales across the United States. As a core member of the Direct Selling Association, Vector Marketing Corporation drives Cutco sales using college-aged students who they pay $12 to $20 per hour in a direct-to-customer business model. But internationally, Cutco products are still sold via myriad independent sellers in Australia, Costa Rica, Germany, South Korea, and the United Kingdom.

Sources

Cutco website, **http://www.cutco.com**; Vector Marketing Corporation, **http://vectormarketing.com**; "Company Overview of Cutco Corporation," *Bloomberg Business*, March 24, 2016; J. Berghoff, *Cutting Edge Sales: Confessions of Success, Influence*

& *Self-Fulfillment from the World's Finest Knife Dealers* (Morgan James Publishing, New York, 2009); "Bringing Help to Haiti: Vector Marketing Sales Record Holder Michael Arrieta," *PRweb*, September 15, 2015.

Case Discussion Questions

1. The Cutco brand is affiliated with Cutco Corporation, Vector Marketing Corporation, and Cutco Cutlery Corporation. It seems overly cumbersome for customers to understand that Vector Marketing Corporation is selling Cutco knives! Meanwhile, Cutco is now the largest manufacturer of high-quality kitchen cutlery in the United States and Canada. How would you structure Cutco's branding if you entered a new international market?

2. Is Cutco's Forever Guarantee a viable international strategy when considering entering the vastly diverse markets that exist globally?

3. As mentioned, Vector Marketing Corporation is the exclusive marketer of Cutco products directly to consumers via sales representatives located throughout the U.S. and Canada, and Cutco International Inc. is responsible for international marketing. Do you think that the direct sales model will work as a market entry strategy internationally? Where might it work and where might it not potentially work?

4. Given that Cutco's product line includes more than 100 choices under the Cutco name alone, is it realistic to think that Cutco can enter global markets with all of its products, for each market, every time it considers a new market entry?

Tata Motors and Exporting

Tata Motors Limited (**tatamotors.com**) was formerly called TELCO, an abbreviation for Tata Engineering and Locomotive Company. Today, Tata Motors is an Indian multinational automotive company headquartered in Mumbai and a core member of the very successful Tata Group. The Tata Group was founded in 1868 and has annual sales of more than 105 billion USD, of which Tata Motors makes up about INR (Indian rupees) 262,796 crores, or about 42 billion USD. Tata Motors has more than 60,000 employees, was founded in 1945, and serves a worldwide clientele with Tata Motors Cars, Jaguar Land Rover, Tata Daewoo, and Tata Hispano. The company entered the passenger vehicle market in 1991 with the launch of the model Tata Sierra (a three-door sport utility vehicle).

Tata Motors thrives in exporting, strategically using it as a global vector to sell cars worldwide, as well as to help offset cyclical tendencies in sales in its home market of India. Tata Motors exported about 55,000 commercial vehicles last year and plans to export 100,000 commercial units within the next two years. The target for the increase in exporting is everywhere worldwide, except in Europe and North America. The global strategy for Tata Motors specifically includes making deeper inroads into the Middle East, Africa, and Latin America.

As the fourth-largest bus manufacturer globally, Tata Motors provides innovatively designed and technologically sophisticated buses for the smart cities of tomorrow. The buses personify safety and comfort, reliability, and profitability. Designed using the most advanced technology, Tata Motors' bus chassis are a benchmark in terms of performance and reliability in the bus industry. Fully finished, built buses from Tata Motors are often viewed as a hallmark of excellence, and these buses have been designed with the utmost quality standards in mind.

Tata Motors exports buses and trucks to nearly 47 countries, including Russia, 18 countries in Africa, four markets in Latin America, and various countries in Europe, the Middle East, and the Asia Pacific region. Some of the popular vehicles exported include the company's globally benchmarked range of Prima and Ultra autos. These brands have been developed with modern design and global markets in mind. Tata Motors also exports a variety of premium buses and coaches, from luxurious intercity travel vehicles to safe choices for the transportation of elementary school children. The buses come in 12 seaters to 67 seaters. Additionally, in the pickup and small commercial vehicle (SCV) segments,

Xenon XT and Super Ace have been popular choices in many countries.

Future exporting activities for Tata Motors are mainly planned to target an increased presence in emerging countries (e.g., Africa, Asia Pacific, Middle Eastern, and Latin America). The company is placing its global bets on world-class products like the Xenon, Super Ace, Prima, and Ultra range of trucks. The overall exporting goal is to continue entering new markets and to keep expanding the global footprint of Tata Motors.

Sources

Shally Seth Mohile, "Tata Motors Plans to Double Export of Commercial Vehicles in Two Years," *Live Mint*, September 16, 2016; "Tata Motors Exports Up 12% in December at 5,119 Units," *Indian Information Online* (IIFL), January 2, 2017; and "Tata Motors Expect 30% Growth in Exports," *Business Standard*, October 23, 2015.

Case Discussion Questions

1. How can Tata Motors use their core competencies in doing well in India as a way to also do well in exporting?

2. Jaguar Land Rover Automotive PLC is the holding company of Jaguar Land Rover Limited, a British automotive company which has its headquarters in the United Kingdom. It is also subsidiary of Indian automotive company Tata Motors. How can Tata Motors leverage Jaguar Land Rover in its exporting? How can Jaguar Land Rover leverage Tata Motors in its exporting?

3. The Volvo Group is a manufacturer of trucks, buses, and construction equipment, which is owned by Swedish interests. Volvo Car Corporation or Volvo Cars, on the other hand, is owned by the Zhejiang Geely Holding Group (it was formerly owned by Ford Motor Company). Because they are already successful in much of the world market, should Tata Motors use this Volvo Group example and focus more, or even exclusively on, buses and trucks in its exporting?

4. Tata Motors is primarily targeting emerging countries (e.g., Africa, Asia Pacific, Middle Eastern, and Latin America) for its future export growth. Is this a viable and logical export strategy?

Alibaba and Global Supply Chains

Alibaba Group Holding Limited (**alibaba.com**) was founded in 1999 by Jack Ma as an e-commerce company to facilitate sales among companies that provide consumer-to-consumer, business-to-consumer, and business-to-business products sold via the internet. As the world's largest e-commerce platform, Alibaba is on a path to realizing its vision of facilitating $1 trillion in product sales annually, while it also pursues a goal of reaching 2 billion consumers. The company is headquartered in Hangzhou, China, has a revenue of more than $23 billion (primarily via advertisements on its sites), and employs about 51,000 people.

Alibaba's global supply chains are strained tremendously on "Singles Day" or Guanggun Jie, a Chinese holiday celebrated on November 11 (the solitary 1s of the date—11/11—suggesting "bare branches," the common slang for singles in China). On this day alone, more than $20 billion in sales (more than 300 million orders) takes place on Alibaba's internet platforms (e.g., Tmall, Taobao). When global retailers think of mega-sales online, they generally think of Black Friday or Cyber Monday, but they ought to be watching 11/11 closely as well, especially because 11/11 amounts to double the combined sales of both of those U.S. e-commerce holidays.

Each year, Alibaba handles more than 80 percent of China's e-commerce business. The company also now operates in 190 countries. Moving forward, the vision for Alibaba is simple: Bring in non-Chinese brands to the Chinese market and expand products to customers outside of China's borders. So far, the impact is clear. Beyond its own employees, Jack Ma claims that Alibaba has created more than 30 million jobs in China related to companies that sell their products on the Alibaba e-commerce platforms. Ma has also committed to creating 1 million new jobs in the U.S. With such large ambitions, Alibaba's global supply chains must be top-notch, innovative, and always pushing the boundaries for what can be done to deliver products from manufacturers to consumers.

Alibaba does this by focusing on a differentiation strategy, partner connections, buyer protection, mobile technology, and large-scale product selections. Its differentiation strategy entails operating as an intermediary, connecting buyers and sellers, while largely avoiding the need for maintaining capital-intensive warehouses and depots. Partnering with Alibaba enables small manufacturers and suppliers to reach thousands, and likely tens of thousands, of new customers. Importantly, in these buyer–seller exchanges, Alibaba emphasizes buyer protection. That is, if a customer is not satisfied for any reason, he or she can request a refund. This consumer focus also carries over into how customers interact with the company. Alibaba has seamlessly adapted its e-commerce sites to mobile platforms, an important part of its strategy given that more than 80 percent of its sales is done via mobile devices. The large-scale product selection on Alibaba's platforms has resulted in some 15 billion products sold annually and 15 million packages shipped daily (compared with 5 billion items sold on Amazon and 3 million packages shipped per day).

Sources

"How to Cut Supply Chain Costs: 6 Lessons From Alibaba," *UNA Purchasing Solutions*, March 26, 2017; Frank Lavin, "Alibaba's Singles' Day: What We Know about the World's Biggest Shopping Event," *Forbes*, November 6, 2016; Bob Bryan, "Alibaba Just Proved It's More Than Just Some Chinese Company," *Business Insider*, November 15, 2015; Catherine Cadell, "Alibaba Posts Record Singles Day Sales, But Growth Slows," *Technology News*, November 11, 2016; Jake Novak, "Here's the Really Brilliant Thing about Trump's Meeting with Alibaba's Jack Ma," *CNBC*, January 10, 2017; Brian Deagon, "Alibaba's Audacious Goal to Reach $1 Trillion in Merchandise Sales," *Investor's Business Daily*, May 6, 2016; Catherine Clifford, "By the Numbers: Amazon vs. Alibaba," *Entrepreneur*, July 13, 2015; Nick Wells, "A Tale of Two Companies: Matching Up Alibaba vs. Amazon," *CNBC*, May 5, 2016.

Case Discussion Questions

1. According to Alibaba's promotional efforts and strategic initiatives, Alibaba is on a path to realizing its vision of facilitating $1 trillion in product sales annually as it also pursues a goal of reaching 2 billion consumers. It is already the world's largest e-commerce platform. Can one company really achieve $1 trillion in sales and reach 2 billion of the world's 7 billion people?

2. Each year, Alibaba handles more than 80 percent of China's e-commerce business, and now operates in 190 countries (only 196 countries and 61 territories exist in the world). Moving forward, the vision for Alibaba sounds simple: Bring in non-Chinese brands to the Chinese market and expand products to customers outside of China's borders. Do you think this global strategy is viable?

3. As mentioned, Alibaba's immense number of sales and shipments puts tremendous pressure on its global supply chains. Do you think its supply chains can continuously facilitate the increased demand that its customers place on the global supply chain systems? Why or why not?

Best Buy Doing a Turnaround Again

Best Buy Co., Inc. is an American multinational consumer electronics retailer headquartered in Richfield, Minnesota. The company was founded by Richard Schulze and James Wheeler in 1966 as an audio specialty store called Sound of Music. In 1983, Sound of Music was rebranded to Best Buy after having achieved $10 million in sales in its seven stores to place more emphasis on consumer electronics. From 1983 to about 2012, Best Buy was an American success story, achieving $1 billion in sales in 1992 in a short period of time and entering its first international location in Canada in 2001 by acquiring Future Shop Ltd. More sales followed after entries into China, Puerto Rico, United Kingdom, Mexico, and Turkey.

In this period (2001 to 2009), Best Buy was named "Company of the Year" by *Forbes* magazine in 2004, "Specialty Retailer of the Decade" by *Discount Store News* in 2001, ranked in the Top 10 of "America's Most Generous Corporations" by *Forbes* in 2005, and made *Fortune* magazine's list of "Most Admired Companies" in 2006. The retail model that Best Buy had created seemed to be on the upswing, and customers flocked to the stores to check out new gadgets and purchase products. Then, Best Buy's expansion, business model, and interest among customers declined in just a few years.

A katz/Shutterstock

As a result, Best Buy closed its operations in the United Kingdom, China, and Europe between 2010 and 2012, and appointed Hubert Joly as its CEO in September 2012. Best Buy had annual revenues of about $29 billion in 2012, but Joly turned around the company in such a way that its 2013 saw $45 billion in revenue, an amazing increase of 55 percent in just one year. Joly did this, in part, by quickly issuing a five-point manifesto to revamp the Best Buy brand, known as "Renew Blue."

- Reinvigorate the customer experience
- Attract "transformational leaders" and energize employees
- Work with vendors to innovate and drive value
- Increase the company's ROIC by growing revenue and efficiency
- Make the world a better place through recycling efforts and giving people access to technology

In addition to immediately selling its European stores, Joly trimmed staff and promised to revive sales by using "omnichannel" retailing. The simple but powerful idea in omnichannel is to reach customers wherever they are—in a store, online, or via their smartphones—and use technology to turn costly stores into an advantage. For example, Joly added a "Store Pickup" button to Best Buy's online shop because many shoppers like to browse and pay online, but prefer to pick their consumer electronics in person. They just had no way of doing that before. The omnichannel became the turnaround strategy for Best Buy in 2012–2013.

Fast forward to 2018, and Best Buy has just closed 250 brick-and-mortar stores in the United States. These days, the international exposure of Best Buy is only in Canada and Mexico; all other international engagements have been divested or closed. At the peak, Best Buy's international operations accounted for about 17 percent of its revenues. So, while companies such as Walmart see their international operations as a key growth driver, especially in emerging markets, Best Buy strategically decided to concentrate on only the North America region for now (Canada, Mexico, and the United States).

With these measures in place, after declining revenues for several years, Best Buy saw an upswing in 2018 that the company hopes will continue. Also, Best Buy was ranked as "The Most Sustainable Company in the United States" by Barron's in 2019. In addition, the company ranked among the Top 100 in the *Fortune* 500 list of the largest corporations in the United States by total revenue. Some of it has to do with the omnichannel carryover effect carrying over from when the 2012 turnaround measures were implemented. One idea was even to use its existing store infrastructure as distribution centers, in addition to being retail stores.

Joly stayed on as CEO until 2019 to see through much of the downturn and turnaround for Best Buy in the 2017–2018 period. On June 11, 2019, Corie Barry took over as CEO, after having previously served as Chief Financial Officer and Strategic Information Officer of Best Buy. Mike Mohan was elevated to President at the same time, keeping his previous title of Chief Operating Officer as well. This leadership change came after Best Buy launched a new growth strategy in which Joly shifted Best Buy's focus from short-term problem solutions to long-term investments that would help the company compete more effectively with Amazon and other rivals.

In the process, Joly—at the time on his way to becoming Chair of the Board at Best Buy—said that "Stores are a great asset." In making the Joly-to-Barry move, Best Buy announced it was doing so to "provide leadership continuity as the company continues to execute its strategic growth initiatives." "I am so proud of the strategic, financial and cultural transformation we have achieved," Joly said in a statement, "and with Best Buy well positioned for continued growth well into the future, now is the right time to begin a leadership transition." "Today's technology and consumer landscape creates tremendous opportunities for Best Buy to further expand and deepen relationships with our customers and employees, while continuing to deliver shareholder value,"[6] Barry said when the CEO change was announced.

Sources

David Trainer, "Best Buy Rising from Ashes to Lead New Retail Paradigm," *Forbes*, June 7, 2018; Michael Fitzgerald, "Best Buy Battles Back Online," *MIT Technology Review*, November 20, 2013; Sharon Bailey, "Best Buy Reconsiders Its International Operations," *Market Realist*, January 21, 2015; Khadeeja Safdar, "Best Buy Sets Five-Year Plan for Sales and Cost-Cutting," *The*

---

[6]Press Release. Best Buy Co., Inc., 2019.

Wall Street Journal, September 17, 2017; Ben Tobin, "Best Buy Names Corie Barry as New CEO, Will Replace Hubert Joly," *USA Today*, April 15, 2019.

Case Discussion Questions

1. Best Buy has had an interesting evolution in an industry (technology and consumer electronics) that has seen drastic changes in the last few decades. Based on this case writeup, how do you expect Best Buy to perform in the next 10 years?

2. The omnichannel approach that Best Buy implemented in 2012 proved to be a winner at the time, and is something all companies these days have to be mindful of. The goal is to reach customers wherever they are: in a store, online, or via their smartphones. Given the omnichannel environment we live in, how would you market Best Buy in the future?

3. In the process of switching CEOs from Hubert Joly to Corie Barry, Joly said that "Stores are a great asset." Joly also said that Best Buy is "well positioned for continued growth well into the future." Do you agree or not? Why?

4. As a starting point before she even took over as CEO, Corie Barry stated that "Today's technology and consumer landscape creates tremendous opportunities for Best Buy to further expand and deepen relationships with our customers and employees, while continuing to deliver shareholder value." What do you read into this statement, and her thinking about what Best Buy needs to do to be successful?

Sodexo: Building a Diverse Global Workforce

Founded in 1966 by Pierre Bellon in France, Sodexo (**sodexo.com**) is the worldwide leader in providing a range of "quality of life" services, including workplace design, onsite food provision, facilities management, cleaning, health care, prisoner rehabilitation, employee benefits and rewards, and personal and home services. The company has 425,000 employees in 80 countries, serves 75 million customers every day, and generates more than $23 billion in revenues annually. Headquartered in France, 43 percent of its revenues are generated in North America; 11 percent in the United Kingdom; 30 percent in continental Europe, including France; and 16 percent in the rest of the world.

Sodexo is well known for its commitment to building a globally diverse workforce and was ranked number 6 in the world in *Diversity Inc*'s 2017 list of the top 50 companies for workforce diversity (although the company dropped out in 2018). Sodexo's commitment to workforce diversity derives from a deeply held belief that there is a relationship between workforce diversity and company performance. This belief has been confirmed in a recent study by McKinsey and Company that found that companies in the top quartile of gender and ethnic diversity were 35 percent more likely to have financial returns above their national industry median. Sodexo sees diversity as a marketplace differentiator that is important for many of its clients, who are themselves diverse. Diversity initiatives can also be used to attract top talent. Moreover, bringing a diverse perspective to bear on problems can improve decision making and result in innovative solutions for clients and customers.

Sodexo focuses on five key areas of diversity: generations, sexual orientation, disabilities, culture and origins, and gender. Globally, Sodexo's board of directors is 50 percent female, and 31 percent of its global executive team are women, as are 30 percent of its top 1,400 senior leaders. CEO Michel Landel would like 40 percent of all senior leaders to be women by 2025. Some 60 percent of managers at Sodexo are also people of color.

Sodexo translates its commitment to building a diverse workforce and management team into practice through a number of mechanisms. It starts at the top with CEO Denis Machuel, who also chairs the company's Diversity Leadership Council, which sets companywide diversity priorities and oversees corporate staffing and diversity training programs. The company then decentralizes authority to develop and fine-tune programs and implement them to managers in each country. Each country reports to a regional Diversity Leadership Council (North America, Europe, South America, etc.) that is chaired by the CEO for that region. The company allows each country to establish its own local diversity initiatives while also requiring them to participate in some corporate initiatives, such as diversity training.

This decentralized approach can result in varying progress throughout the company, reflecting different national conditions. As the company's chief diversity office in the United States explained, "Even though we're more advanced in the U.S. around diversity efforts, we're really not able to necessarily use the successes to engage the rest of the organization, because everything happens from the ground up. For each of the 25 countries [in Europe], we have . . . to start from the ground and build the diversity efforts so they have more ownership of it. Each country feels that . . . if it's not made here [locally] it's rejected."[7] At the same time, Sodexo has put a Cross Market Diversity Council in place to make sure good ideas can be shared across the company.

To drive home the importance of diversity, Sodexo measures the performance of individual managers against a diversity scorecard that includes quantitative and qualitative metrics and can be varied by country to account for different cultural contexts. Twenty-five percent of the annual bonus of executive team members and 10 to 15 percent of the bonuses for senior and mid-level managers are connected to how they perform on the diversity scorecard metrics.

Sources

"The 2017 DiversityInc Top 50 Companies for Diversity," Diversity Inc, **www.diversityinc.com/sodexo-2017**; "Leaders in Diversity and Inclusion," Aperian Global, **www.aperianglobal. com/leaders-diversity-inclusion-5-lessons-top-global-companies**; "Driving Global Diversity: Selected Examples of Global Diversity Efforts," *Diversity Best Practice*, May 2013; V. Hunt, D. Layton, and S. Prince, "Diversity Matters," McKinsey & Co, February 2, 2015; and Betsy Silva, "Diversity and Inclusion: A Strategic Imperative—The Sodexo Story," Commission on Economic Inclusion, Greater Cleveland Partnership Change Management Conference, July 17, 2011.

Case Discussion Questions

1. How might building a more diverse global workforce help Sodexo achieve high performance?

2. What barriers do companies like Sodexo face when trying to increase workforce diversity in their global operations?

3. How does Sodexo implement its policy of increasing the diversity of its global workforce?

4. Evaluate Sodexo's diversity policy. Is the company doing the right thing? Are the right policies in place? Are there other things the company might do?

5. Sodexo's strategy is to decentralize authority to develop and fine-tune programs and implement them to managers in each country. What are the benefits of this approach? What are the potential drawbacks?

---

[7]"Driving Global Diversity: Selected Examples of Global Diversity Efforts." *Diversity Best Practice*, May, 2013. **https://www.diversitybestpractices.com/ news-articles/driving-global-diversity-selected-examples-global-diversity-efforts.**

Tesla, Inc.—Subsidizing Tesla Automobiles Globally

Tesla Inc. (**tesla.com**) is an American automobile manufacturer, energy storage producer, and solar panel manufacturer headquartered in Palo Alto, California. It specializes in electric cars, lithium-ion batteries, and residential solar panels via its subsidiary SolarCity. Most people, however, know the company as the maker of electric cars, often still referring to the old name of Tesla Motors. Tesla Inc. was founded as Tesla Motors in 2003 by Martin Eberhard and Marc Tarpenning. However, both the company and the general public also consider Elon Musk, J. B. Straubel, and Ian Wright as its co-founders. Today, the company has sales of over $7 billion, assets of some $25 billion, and more than 30,000 employees.

Tesla became a well-known entity following its production of the Tesla Roadster in 2008, the world's first electric sports car. The second vehicle, an electric luxury sedan labeled Model S, hit the market in 2012. More than 150,000 cars of Model S type have been sold. This ranks Model S as the world's second best-selling plug-in after the Nissan Leaf. After Model S, Tesla went to market with Model X in 2015, a crossover SUV, and Model 3 in 2017 (code name "Tesla BlueStar" in the original business plan). Model 3 was unveiled in 2016, but was introduced into the market in the latter part of 2017 at a base price of $35,000 before any government incentives.

Government incentives are really the subject of this Tesla case. Normally, our focus in a case related to Chapter 20 would be on the financing of a company or accounting practices globally (as in the scenarios played out in the opening case on the Kraft Heinz Company and the closing case on Shoprite). However, financing and accounting practices worldwide come in many forms, and companies like Tesla have taken advantage of tremendous governments subsidies in various countries to sell their products in the global marketplace and be competitive with traditional car manufacturers such as Volkswagen, Toyota, and General Motors, to mention just a few of the top automobile makers in 2017. As such, the Tesla scenario is a perfect integrated case for this book: It relates to Chapter 20 on finance and accounting, but also serves multiple purposes in understanding the economics of the global marketplace.

For example, according to recent data from the European Automobile Manufacturers Association (ACEA), sales of electric cars (including plug-in hybrids) in 2017 were brisk across much of Europe. Sales of these kinds of cars rose by 80 percent compared with last year in eco-friendly Sweden, 78 percent in Germany, and 40 percent in Belgium. Across all European Union countries, electrical car sales grew by roughly 30 percent. However, the major exception was in Denmark, where sales went down by more than 60 percent. There was one simple reason for this drop: The Danish government phased out taxpayer subsidies to buy electric cars. Basically, the take on it from the Danish experience is that clean-energy vehicles are not attractive enough to (at least) the Danish customers to compete with more established traditional car brands without some form of taxpayer-backed subsidy.

This may set the tone for how to market electric cars in the future. If it can't be done in Denmark, can these cars really be marketed globally? Denmark is one of the more progressive countries in the world when it comes to clean air, clean energy, and clean everything! Add to that, Denmark's infatuation with "green" electrical automobiles is globally well known. The country's bicycle-loving population bought more than 5,000 of these electrical cars last year, more than double the number sold in Italy, and Italy is about 10 times the size of Denmark. Perhaps these amazing sales were more due to the customers being spared the hefty 180 percent that the Danish government applies on vehicles fueled by a traditional combustion engine than the electrical vehicles actually being a preference of customers. So, losing the government subsidy also meant a loss of electric car sales in the country in favor of more traditional cars.

Sources

Tyler Durden, "It's Confirmed: Without Government Subsidies, Tesla Sales Implode," *Zero Hedge*, June 12, 2017; "Overview of Tax Incentives for Electric Vehicles in the EU," European Automobile Manufacturers Association, accessed June 20, 2017; Peter Levring, "Denmark Is Killing Tesla (and Other Electric Cars)," *Bloomberg Markets*, June 2, 2017; "Tesla Increases Deliveries of Electric Cars," *The Economist*, April 6, 2017; "Electric Cars Are Set to Arrive Far More Speedily Than Anticipated," *The Economist*, February 18, 2017.

VDWI Automotive/Alamy Stock Photo

Case Discussion Questions

1. Should companies like Tesla rely on government subsidies in selling their cars because they are better for the environment than traditional cars based on the old technology of traditional combustion engines? Basically, should the environmental issues be built into the competitiveness of the car pricing of electrical cars, or should supply and demand be the driver of the electrical cars' prices?

2. Some governments are more likely to subsidize electric cars (and many other products) than other governments. Denmark took a stand to not subsidize (for now) electric cars. Should such subsidies be up to each country or region in a country (e.g., California in the United States), or should there be a world standard enforced perhaps via the World Trade Organization, United Nations, or a similar organization?

3. Tesla had remarkable sales growth: from a startup (albeit with great financing) to $7 billion in sales with some $25 billion in assets. Does this mean that the Tesla business model was good, and the market reacted positively, government subsidies were generous, and the market favored the car brand because of it, or was it a combination of these factors, and if the latter, which factors?

4. If all government subsidies to electric cars went away worldwide, do you think Tesla would be as successful five years from now as it is today? (Given this idea, do you think Tesla would even exist in 10 years?)

GLOSSARY

A

absolute advantage   A country has an absolute advantage in the production of a product when it is more efficient than any other country at producing it.

accounting standards   Rules for preparing financial statements.

ad valorem tariff   A tariff levied as a proportion of the value of an imported good.

administrative trade policies   Administrative policies, typically adopted by government bureaucracies, that can be used to restrict imports or boost exports.

Andean Community   A 1969 agreement among Bolivia, Chile, Ecuador, Colombia, and Peru to establish a customs union.

antidumping policies   Designed to punish foreign firms that engage in dumping and thus protect domestic producers from unfair foreign competition.

arbitrage   The purchase of securities in one market for immediate resale in another to profit from a price discrepancy.

Association of Southeast Asian Nations (ASEAN)   Formed in 1967, an attempt to establish a free trade area among Brunei, Cambodia, Indonesia, Laos, Malaysia, Myanmar, the Philippines, Singapore, Vietnam, and Thailand.

B

balance-of-payments accounts   National accounts that track both payments to and receipts from foreigners.

balance-of-trade equilibrium   Reached when the income a nation's residents earn from exports equals money paid for imports.

bandwagon effect   Movement of traders like a herd, all in the same direction and at the same time, in response to each other's perceived actions.

banking crisis   A loss of confidence in the banking system that leads to a run on banks, as individuals and companies withdraw their deposits.

barter   The direct exchange of goods or services between two parties without a cash transaction.

big data   A massive volume of structured and/or unstructured data that are so large they may be difficult to process using traditional database and software techniques.

bill of exchange   An order written by an exporter instructing an importer, or an importer's agent, to pay a specified amount of money at a specified time.

bill of lading   A document issued to an exporter by a common carrier transporting merchandise. It serves as a receipt, a contract, and a document of title.

business analytics   The knowledge, skills, and technology that allow for the exploration as well as deeper investigation of a company's international business strategies and activities to gain insight and drive future strategy development and implementation.

business ethics   The accepted principles of right and wrong governing the conduct of businesspeople.

buyback   Agreement to accept a percentage of a plant's output as payment for contract to build a plant.

C

capital account   In the balance of payments, records transactions involving one-time changes in the stock of assets.

capital flight   Converting domestic currency into a foreign currency.

Caribbean Single Market and Economy (CSME)   The six CARICOM members that agreed to lower trade barriers and harmonize macroeconomic and monetary policies.

CARICOM   An association of English-speaking Caribbean states that are attempting to establish a customs union.

carry trade   A kind of speculation that involves borrowing in one currency where interest rates are low and then using the proceeds to invest in another currency where interest rates are high.

caste system   A system of social stratification in which social position is determined by the family into which a person is born, and change in that position is usually not possible during an individual's lifetime.

Central America Free Trade Agreement (CAFTA)   The agreement of the member states of the Central American Common Market joined by the Dominican Republic to trade freely with the United States.

Central American Common Market   A trade pact among Costa Rica, El Salvador, Guatemala, Honduras, and Nicaragua, which began in the early 1960s but collapsed in 1969 due to war.

channel length   The number of intermediaries that a product has to go through before it reaches the final consumer.

channel quality   The expertise, competencies, and skills of established retailers in a nation and their ability to sell and support the products of international businesses.

civil law system   A system of law based on a very detailed set of written laws and codes.

class consciousness   A tendency for individuals to perceive themselves in terms of their class background.

class system   A system of social stratification in which social status is determined by the family into which a person is born and by subsequent socioeconomic achievements; mobility between classes is possible.

code of ethics   A business's formal statement of ethical priorities.

collectivism   A political system that emphasizes collective goals as opposed to individual goals.

command economy   An economic system where the allocation of resources, including determination of what goods and services should be produced, and in what quantity, is planned by the government.

common law   A system of law based on tradition, precedent, and custom; when law courts interpret common law, they do so with regard to these characteristics.

common market   A group of countries committed to (1) removing all barriers to the free flow of goods, services, and factors of production between each other and (2) the pursuit of a common external trade policy.

communist totalitarianism   A version of collectivism advocating that socialism can be achieved only through a totalitarian dictatorship.

communists   Those who believe socialism can be achieved only through revolution and totalitarian dictatorship.

concentrated retail system   A retail system in which a few retailers supply most of the market.

constant returns to specialization   The units of resources required to produce a good are assumed to remain constant no matter where one is on a country's production possibility frontier.

contract   A document that specifies the conditions under which an exchange is to occur and details the rights and obligations of the parties involved.

contract law   The body of law that governs contract enforcement.

contributor factory   A factory that serves a specific country or world region.

controls   The metrics used to measure the performance of subunits and make judgments about how well managers are running those subunits.

Convention on Combating Bribery of Foreign Public Officials in International Business Transactions   An OECD convention that establishes legally binding standards to criminalize bribery of foreign public officials in international business transactions and provides for a host of related measures that make this effective.

copyrights   The exclusive legal rights of authors, composers, playwrights, artists, and publishers to publish and disperse their work as they see fit.

core competence   Firm skills that competitors cannot easily match or imitate.

corporate culture   The organization's norms and value systems.

corporate social responsibility (CSR)   Refers to the idea that businesspeople should consider the social consequences of economic actions when making business decisions and that there should be a presumption in favor of decisions that have both good economic and social consequences.

counterpurchase   A reciprocal buying agreement.

countertrade   The trade of goods and services for other goods and services.

countervailing duties   Antidumping duties.

country of origin effects   A subset of source effects, the extent to which the place of manufacturing influences product evaluations.

Court of Justice   Supreme appeals court for EU law.

cross-cultural literacy   Understanding how the culture of a country affects the way business is practiced.

cultural relativism   The belief that ethics are culturally determined and that firms should adopt the ethics of the cultures in which they operate.

culture   A system of values and norms that are shared among a group of people and that when taken together constitute a design for living.

currency board   Means of controlling a country's currency.

currency crisis   Occurs when a speculative attack on the exchange value of a currency results in a sharp depreciation in the value of the currency or forces authorities to expend large volumes of international currency reserves and sharply increase interest rates to defend the prevailing exchange rate.

currency speculation   Involves short-term movement of funds from one currency to another in hopes of profiting from shifts in exchange rates.

currency swap   Simultaneous purchase and sale of a given amount of foreign exchange for two different value dates.

current account   In the balance of payments, records transactions involving the export or import of goods and services.

current account deficit   The current account of the balance of payments is in deficit when a country imports more goods, services, and income than it exports.

current account surplus   The current account of the balance of payments is in surplus when a country exports more goods, services, and income than it imports.

customs union   A group of countries committed to (1) removing all barriers to the free flow of goods and services between each other and (2) the pursuit of a common external trade policy.

D

democracy   Political system in which government is by the people, exercised either directly or through elected representatives.

deregulation   Removal of government restrictions concerning the conduct of a business.

dirty-float system   A system under which a country's currency is nominally allowed to float freely against other currencies but in which the government will intervene, buying and selling currency, if it believes that the currency has deviated too far from its fair value.

dollarization   The process of aligning a country's currency with the U.S. dollar.

downstream supply chain   The portion of the supply chain from the production facility to the end-customer.

draft   An order written by an exporter telling an importer what and when to pay.

dumping   Selling goods in a foreign market for less than their cost of production or below their "fair" market value.

E

eclectic paradigm   Argument that combining location-specific assets or resource endowments and the firm's own unique assets often requires FDI; it requires the firm to establish production facilities where those foreign assets or resource endowments are located.

economic exposure   The extent to which a firm's future international earning power is affected by changes in exchange rates.

economic risk   The likelihood that events, including economic mismanagement, will cause drastic changes in a country's business environment that adversely affect the profit and other goals of a particular business enterprise.

economic union   A group of countries committed to (1) removing all barriers to the free flow of goods, services, and factors of production between each other; (2) the adoption of a common currency; (3) the harmonization of tax rates; and (4) the pursuit of a common external trade policy.

economies of scale   Cost advantages associated with large-scale production.

efficient market   A market where prices reflect all available information.

elastic   A small change in price produces a large change in demand.

entrepreneurs   Those who first commercialize innovations.

ethical dilemma   A situation in which there is no ethically acceptable solution.

ethical strategy   A course of action that does not violate a company's business ethics.

ethical system   A set of moral principles, or values, that is used to guide and shape behavior.

ethnocentric staffing policy   A staffing approach within the multinational enterprise in which all key management positions are filled by parent-country nationals.

ethnocentrism   Behavior that is based on the belief in the superiority of one's own ethnic group or culture; often shows disregard or contempt for the culture of other countries.

European Commission   Responsible for proposing EU legislation, implementing it, and monitoring compliance.

European Council   The heads of state of EU members and the president of the European Commission.

European Free Trade Association (EFTA)   A free trade association including Norway, Iceland, Liechtenstein, and Switzerland.

European Monetary System (EMS)   EU system designed to create a zone of monetary stability in Europe, control inflation, and coordinate exchange rate policies of EU countries.

European Parliament   Elected EU body that provides consultation on issues proposed by the European Commission.

European Union (EU)   An economic and political union of 28 countries (2017) that are located in Europe.

exchange rate   The rate at which one currency is converted into another.

exclusive distribution channel   A distribution channel that outsiders find difficult to access.

expatriate failure   The premature return of an expatriate manager to the home country.

expatriate manager   A national of one country appointed to a management position in another country.

experience curve   Systematic production cost reductions that occur over the life of a product.

experience curve pricing   Aggressive pricing designed to increase volume and help the firm realize experience curve economies.

export ban   A policy that partially or entirely restricts the export of a good.

export management company (EMC)   Export specialist that acts as an export marketing department for client firms.

export tariff   A tax placed on the export of a good.

Export-Import Bank (Ex-Im Bank)   Agency of the U.S. government whose mission is to provide aid in financing and facilitate exports and imports.

exporting   Sale of products produced in one country to residents of another country.

external stakeholders   Individuals or groups that have some claim on a firm such as customers, suppliers, and unions.

externalities   Knowledge spillovers.

externally convertible currency   Limitations on the ability of residents to convert domestic currency, though nonresidents can convert their holdings of domestic currency into foreign currency.

F

factor endowments   A country's endowment with resources such as land, labor, and capital.

factors of production   Inputs into the productive process of a firm, including labor, management, land, capital, and technological know-how.

financial account   In the balance of payments, transactions that involve the purchase or sale of assets.

first-mover advantages   Advantages accruing to the first to enter a market.

first-mover disadvantages   Disadvantages associated with entering a foreign market before other international businesses.

Fisher effect   Nominal interest rates (i) in each country equal the required real rate of interest (r) and the expected rate of inflation over the period of time for which the funds are to be lent (I). That is, $i = r + I$.

fixed exchange rate   A system under which the exchange rate for converting one currency into another is fixed.

flexible machine cells   Flexible manufacturing technology in which a grouping of various machine types, a common materials handler, and a centralized cell controller produce a family of products.

flexible manufacturing technology   Manufacturing technology designed to improve job scheduling, reduce setup time, and improve quality control.

floating exchange rate   A system under which the exchange rate for converting one currency into another is continuously adjusted depending on the laws of supply and demand.

flow of FDI   The amount of foreign direct investment undertaken over a given time period (normally one year).

folkways   Routine conventions of everyday life.

Foreign Corrupt Practices Act (FCPA)   U.S. law regulating behavior regarding the conduct of international business in the taking of bribes and other unethical actions.

foreign debt crisis   Situation in which a country cannot service its foreign debt obligations, whether private-sector or government debt.

foreign direct investment (FDI)   Direct investment in business operations in a foreign country.

foreign exchange market   A market for converting the currency of one country into that of another country.

foreign exchange risk   The risk that changes in exchange rates will hurt the profitability of a business deal.

forward exchange   When two parties agree to exchange currency and execute a deal at some specific date in the future.

forward exchange rate   The exchange rate governing a forward exchange transaction.

fragmented retail system   A retail system in which there are many retailers, none of which has a major share of the market.

franchising   A specialized form of licensing in which the franchiser sells intangible property to the franchisee and insists on rules to conduct the business.

free trade   The absence of barriers to the free flow of goods and services between countries.

free trade area   A group of countries committed to removing all barriers to the free flow of goods and services between each other but pursuing independent external trade policies.

freely convertible currency   A country's currency is freely convertible when the government of that country allows both residents and nonresidents to purchase unlimited amounts of foreign currency with the domestic currency.

G

General Agreement on Tariffs and Trade (GATT)   International treaty that committed signatories to lowering barriers to the free flow of goods across national borders and led to the WTO.

geocentric staffing policy   A staffing policy where the best people are sought for key jobs throughout a multinational enterprise, regardless of nationality.

global distribution center   A facility that positions and allows customization of products for delivery to worldwide wholesalers or retailers or directly to consumers anywhere in the world; also called a global distribution warehouse.

global inventory management   The decision-making process regarding the raw materials, work-in-process (component parts), and finished goods inventory for a multinational corporation.

global learning   The flow of skills and product offerings from foreign subsidiary to home country and from foreign subsidiary to foreign subsidiary.

global standardization strategy   A firm focuses on increasing profitability and profit growth by reaping the cost reductions that come from economies of scale, learning effects, and location economies.

global supply chain coordination   The shared decision-making opportunities and operational collaboration of key global supply chain activities.

global web When different stages of value chain are dispersed to those locations around the globe where value added is maximized or where costs of value creation are minimized.

globalization Trend away from distinct national economic units and toward one huge global market.

globalization of markets Moving away from an economic system in which national markets are distinct entities, isolated by trade barriers and barriers of distance, time, and culture, and toward a system in which national markets are merging into one global market.

globalization of production Trend by individual firms to disperse parts of their productive processes to different locations around the globe to take advantage of differences in cost and quality of factors of production.

gold par value The amount of currency needed to purchase one ounce of gold.

gold standard The practice of pegging currencies to gold and guaranteeing convertibility.

greenfield investment Establishing a new operation in a foreign country.

gross national income (GNI) Measures the total annual income received by residents of a nation.

group An association of two or more individuals who have a shared sense of identity and who interact with each other in structured ways on the basis of a common set of expectations about each other's behavior.

Group of Twenty (G20) Established in 1999, the G20 comprises the finance ministers and central bank governors of the 19 largest economies in the world, plus representatives from the European Union and the European Central Bank.

H

Human Development Index (HDI) An attempt by the United Nations to assess the impact of a number of factors on the quality of human life in a country.

human resource management (HRM) Activities an organization conducts to use its human resources effectively.

I

import quota A direct restriction on the quantity of a good that can be imported into a country.

incentives The devices used to reward appropriate managerial behavior.

individualism An emphasis on the importance of guaranteeing individual freedom and self-expression.

individualism versus collectivism Theory focusing on the relationship between the individual and his or her fellows; in individualistic societies, the ties between individuals are loose and individual achievement is highly valued; in societies where collectivism is emphasized, ties between individuals are tight, people are born into collectives, such as extended families, and everyone is supposed to look after the interests of his or her collective.

inefficient market One in which prices do not reflect all available information.

inelastic When a large change in price produces only a small change in demand.

infant industry argument New industries in developing countries must be temporarily protected from international competition to help them reach a position where they can compete on world markets with the firms of developed nations.

inflows of FDI Flow of foreign direct investment into a country.

innovation Development of new products, processes, organizations, management practices, and strategies.

intellectual property Products of the mind, ideas (e.g., books, music, computer software, designs, technological know-how); intellectual property can be protected by patents, copyrights, and trademarks.

intermarket segment A segment of customers that spans multiple countries, transcending national borders.

internal stakeholders People who work for or own the business such as employees, directors, and stockholders.

internalization theory Marketing imperfection approach to foreign direct investment.

international division Division responsible for a firm's international activities.

International Fisher Effect (IFE) For any two countries, the spot exchange rate should change in an equal amount but in the opposite direction to the difference in nominal interest rates between countries.

international market research The systematic collection, recording, analysis, and interpretation of data to provide knowledge that is useful for decision making in a global company.

International Monetary Fund (IMF) International institution set up to maintain order in the international monetary system.

international monetary system Institutional arrangements countries adopt to govern exchange rates.

international strategy Trying to create value by transferring core competencies to foreign markets where indigenous competitors lack those competencies.

international trade Occurs when a firm exports goods or services to consumers in another country.

ISO 9000 Certification process that requires certain quality standards that must be met.

J

joint venture   A cooperative undertaking between two or more firms.

just distribution   A distribution of goods and services that is considered fair and equitable.

just in time (JIT)   Inventory logistics system designed to deliver parts to a production process as they are needed, not before.

K

Kantian ethics   The belief that people should be treated as ends and never as means to the ends of others.

L

lag strategy   Delaying the collection of foreign currency receivables if that currency is expected to appreciate and delaying payables if that currency is expected to depreciate.

late-mover disadvantages   Handicaps experienced by being a late entrant in a market.

law of one price   In competitive markets free of transportation costs and barriers to trade, identical products sold in different countries must sell for the same price when their price is expressed in the same currency.

lead factory   A factory that is intended to create new processes, products, and technologies that can be used throughout the global firm in all parts of the world.

lead strategy   Collecting foreign currency receivables early when a foreign currency is expected to depreciate and paying foreign currency payables before they are due when a currency is expected to appreciate.

lean production   *See* flexible manufacturing technology.

learning effects   Cost savings from learning by doing.

legal risk   The likelihood that a trading partner will opportunistically break a contract or expropriate intellectual property rights.

legal system   System of rules that regulate behavior and the processes by which the laws of a country are enforced and through which redress of grievances is obtained.

letter of credit   Issued by a bank, indicating that the bank will make payments under specific circumstances.

licensing   Occurs when a firm (the licensor) licenses the right to produce its product, use its production processes, or use its brand name or trademark to another firm (the licensee). In return for giving the licensee these rights, the licensor collects a royalty fee on every unit the licensee sells.

licensing agreement   Arrangement in which a licensor grants the rights to intangible property to a licensee for a specified period and receives a royalty fee in return.

local content requirement (LCR)   A requirement that some specific fraction of a good be produced domestically.

localization strategy   Increasing profitability by customizing the firm's goods and services so that they provide a good match to tastes and preferences in different national markets.

location economies   Cost advantages from performing a value creation activity at the optimal location for that activity.

location-specific advantages   Advantages that arise from using resource endowments or assets that are tied to a particular foreign location and that a firm finds valuable to combine with its own unique assets (such as the firm's technological, marketing, or management know-how).

logistics   The part of the supply chain that plans, implements, and controls the effective flows and inventory of raw material, component parts, and products used in manufacturing.

long-term versus short-term orientation   The theory of the extent to which a culture programs its citizens to accept delayed gratification of their material, social, and emotional needs. It captures attitudes toward time, persistence, ordering by status, protection of face, respect for tradition, and reciprocation of gifts and favors.

M

Maastricht Treaty   Treaty agreed to in 1992, but not ratified until January 1, 1994, that committed the 12 member states of the European Community to a closer economic and political union.

make-or-buy decision   The strategic decision concerning whether to produce an item in-house ("make") or purchase it from an outside supplier ("buy").

managed-float system   System under which some currencies are allowed to float freely, but the majority are either managed by government intervention or pegged to another currency.

market economy   An economic system in which the interaction of supply and demand determines the quantity in which goods and services are produced.

market imperfections   Imperfections in the operation of the market mechanism.

market segmentation   Identifying groups of consumers whose purchasing behavior differs from others in important ways.

marketing mix   Choices about product attributes, distribution strategy, communication strategy, and pricing strategy that a firm offers its targeted markets.

masculinity versus femininity   Theory of the relationship between gender and work roles. In masculine cultures, sex roles are sharply differentiated and traditional "masculine values" such as achievement and the effective exercise of power determine cultural ideals; in feminine cultures, sex roles are less sharply distinguished, and little differentiation is made between men and women in the same job.

mass customization The production of a variety of end products at a unit cost that could once be achieved only through mass production of a standardized output.

mercantilism An economic philosophy advocating that countries should simultaneously encourage exports and discourage imports.

Mercosur Pact among Argentina, Brazil, Paraguay, and Uruguay to establish a free trade area.

minimum efficient scale The level of output at which most plant-level scale economies are exhausted.

MITI Japan's Ministry of International Trade and Industry.

Moore's law The power of microprocessor technology doubles and its costs of production fall in half every 18 months.

moral hazard Arises when people behave recklessly because they know they will be saved if things go wrong.

mores Norms seen as central to the functioning of a society and to its social life.

multilateral or bilateral trade agreements Reciprocal trade agreements between two or more partners.

multinational enterprise (MNE) A firm that owns business operations in more than one country.

multipoint competition Arises when two or more enterprises encounter each other in different regional markets, national markets, or industries.

multipoint pricing Occurs when a pricing strategy in one market may have an impact on a rival's pricing strategy in another market.

N

naive immoralist One who asserts that if a manager of a multinational sees that firms from other nations are not following ethical norms in a host nation, that manager should not either.

new trade theory The observed pattern of trade in the world economy may be due in part to the ability of firms in a given market to capture first-mover advantages.

noise The number of other messages competing for a potential consumer's attention.

nonconvertible currency A currency is not convertible when both residents and nonresidents are prohibited from converting their holdings of that currency into another currency.

norms Social rules and guidelines that prescribe appropriate behavior in particular situations.

North American Free Trade Agreement (NAFTA) Free trade area among Canada, Mexico, and the United States.

O

offset Agreement to purchase goods and services with a specified percentage of proceeds from an original sale in that country from any firm in the country.

offshore factory A factory that is developed and set up mainly for producing component parts or finished goods at a lower cost than producing them at home or in any other market.

offshore production FDI undertaken to serve the home market.

oligopoly An industry composed of a limited number of large firms.

operations The various value creation activities a firm undertakes.

optimal currency area Region in which similarities in economic activity make a single currency and exchange rate feasible instruments of macroeconomic policy.

organizational architecture Totality of a firm's organization.

organizational culture The values and norms shared among an organization's employees.

organizational structure The three-part structure of an organization, including its formal division into subunits such as product divisions, its location of decision-making responsibilities within that structure, and the establishment of integrating mechanisms to coordinate the activities of all subunits.

outflows of FDI Flow of foreign direct investment out of a country.

outpost factory A factory that can be viewed as an intelligence-gathering unit.

P

packaging The container that holds the product itself. It can be divided into primary, secondary, and transit packaging.

Paris Convention for the Protection of Industrial Property International agreement to protect intellectual property.

patent Grants the inventor of a new product or process exclusive rights to the manufacture, use, or sale of that invention.

pegged exchange rate Currency value is fixed relative to a reference currency.

people The employees of the organization, the strategy used to recruit, compensate, and retain those individuals, and the type of people that they are in terms of their skills, values, and orientation.

pioneering costs   Costs an early entrant bears that later entrants avoid, such as the time and effort in learning the rules, failure due to ignorance, and the liability of being a foreigner.

political economy   The political, economic, and legal systems of a country.

political risk   The likelihood that political forces will cause drastic changes in a country's business environment that will adversely affect the profit and other goals of a particular business enterprise.

political system   System of government in a nation.

political union   A central political apparatus coordinates economic, social, and foreign policy.

polycentric staffing policy   A staffing policy in a multinational enterprise in which host-country nationals are recruited to manage subsidiaries in their own country, while parent-country nationals occupy key positions at corporate headquarters.

power distance   Theory of how a society deals with the fact that people are unequal in physical and intellectual capabilities. High power distance cultures are found in countries that let inequalities grow over time into inequalities of power and wealth; low power distance cultures are found in societies that try to play down such inequalities as much as possible.

predatory pricing   Reducing prices below fair market value as a competitive weapon to drive weaker competitors out of the market ("fair" being cost plus some reasonable profit margin).

price elasticity of demand   A measure of how responsive demand for a product is to changes in price.

private action   Violation of property rights through theft, piracy, blackmail, and the like by private individuals or groups.

privatization   The sale of state-owned enterprises to private investors.

processes   The manner in which decisions are made and work is performed within any organization.

product liability   Involves holding a firm and its officers responsible when a product causes injury, death, or damage.

product safety laws   Set certain safety standards to which a product must adhere.

production   Activities involved in creating a product.

profit growth   The percentage increase in net profits over time.

profitability   A ration or rate of return concept.

property rights   Bundle of legal rights over the use to which a resource is put and over the use made of any income that may be derived from that resource.

public action   The extortion of income or resources of property holders by public officials, such as politicians and government bureaucrats.

pull strategy   A marketing strategy emphasizing mass media advertising as opposed to personal selling.

purchasing   The part of the supply chain that includes the worldwide buying of raw material, component parts, and products used in manufacturing of the company's products and services.

purchasing power parity (PPP)   An adjustment in gross domestic product per capita to reflect differences in the cost of living.

push strategy   A marketing strategy emphasizing personal selling rather than mass media advertising.

Q

quota rent   Extra profit producers make when supply is artificially limited by an import quota.

R

regional economic integration   Agreements among countries in a geographic region to reduce and ultimately remove tariff and nontariff barriers to the free flow of goods, services, and factors of production between each other.

religion   A system of shared beliefs and rituals concerned with the realm of the sacred.

representative democracy   A political system in which citizens periodically elect individuals to represent them in government.

reverse logistics   The process of moving inventory from the point of consumption to the point of origin in supply chains for the purpose of recapturing value or proper disposal.

right-wing totalitarianism   A political system in which political power is monopolized by a party, group, or individual that generally permits individual economic freedom but restricts individual political freedom, including free speech, often on the grounds that it would lead to the rise of communism.

righteous moralist   One who claims that a multinational's home-country standards of ethics are the appropriate ones for companies to follow in foreign countries.

rights theories   Twentieth-century theories that recognize that human beings have fundamental rights and privileges that transcend national boundaries and cultures.

S

server factory   A factory linked into the global supply chain for a global firm to supply specific country or regional markets around the globe.

sight draft   A draft payable on presentation to the drawee.

Six Sigma   Statistically based methodology for improving product quality.

Smoot–Hawley Act　Enacted in 1930 by the U.S. Congress, this act erected a wall of tariff barriers against imports into the United States.

social democrats　Those committed to achieving socialism by democratic means.

social media　A technology that facilitates the sharing of information and the building of virtual global networks and communities.

social mobility　The extent to which individuals can move out of the social strata into which they are born.

social strata　Hierarchical social categories often based on family background, occupation, and income.

social structure　The basic social organization of a society.

socialists　Those who believe in public ownership of the means of production for the common good of society.

society　Group of people who share a common set of values and norms.

sogo shosha　Japanese trading companies; a key part of the keiretsu, the large Japanese industrial groups.

source effects　Effects that occur when the receiver of the message (i.e., a potential consumer) evaluates the message on the basis of status or image of the sender.

source factory　A factory whose primary purpose is also to drive down costs in the global supply chain.

specific tariff　Tariff levied as a fixed charge for each unit of good imported.

spot exchange rate　The exchange rate at which a foreign exchange dealer will convert one currency into another that particular day.

staffing policy　Strategy concerned with selecting employees for particular jobs.

stakeholders　The individuals or groups that have an interest, stake, or claim in the actions and overall performance of a company.

stock of FDI　The total accumulated value of foreign-owned assets at a given time.

strategic alliances　Cooperative agreements between potential or actual competitors.

strategic pricing　The concept containing the three aspects: predatory pricing, multipoint pricing, and experience curve pricing.

strategic trade policy　Government policy aimed at improving the competitive position of a domestic industry and/or domestic firm in the world market.

strategy　Actions managers take to attain the firm's goals.

subsidy　Government financial assistance to a domestic producer.

supply chain management　The integration and coordination of logistics, purchasing, operations, and market channel activities from raw material to the end-customer.

sustainable strategies　Strategies that not only help the multinational firm make good profits but that do so without harming the environment, while simultaneously ensuring that the corporation acts in a socially responsible manner with regard to its multiple stakeholders.

switch trading　Use of a specialized third-party trading house in a countertrade arrangement.

T

tariff　A tax levied on imports.

tariff rate quota　Lower tariff rates applied to imports within the quota than those over the quota.

theocratic law system　A system of law based on religious teachings.

theocratic totalitarianism　A political system in which political power is monopolized by a party, group, or individual that governs according to religious principles.

time draft　A promise to pay by the accepting party at some future date.

timing of entry　Entry is early when a firm enters a foreign market before other foreign firms and late when a firm enters after other international businesses have established themselves.

total quality management (TQM)　Management philosophy that takes as its central focus the need to improve the quality of a company's products and services.

totalitarianism　Form of government in which one person or political party exercises absolute control over all spheres of human life and opposing political parties are prohibited.

trade creation　Trade created due to regional economic integration; occurs when high-cost domestic producers are replaced by low-cost foreign producers within a free trade area.

trade diversion　Trade diverted due to regional economic integration; occurs when low-cost foreign suppliers outside a free trade area are replaced by higher-cost suppliers within a free trade area.

trademarks　The designs and names, often officially registered, by which merchants or manufacturers designate and differentiate their products.

transaction exposure　The extent to which income from individual transactions is affected by fluctuations in foreign exchange values.

translation exposure　The extent to which the reported consolidated results and balance sheets of a corporation are affected by fluctuations in foreign exchange values.

transnational strategy   Attempt to simultaneously achieve low costs through location economies, economies of scale, and learning effects while also differentiating product offerings across geographic markets to account for local differences and fostering multidirectional flows of skills between different subsidiaries in the firm's global network of operations.

transportation   The movement of inventory through the supply chain.

Treaty of Lisbon   A European Union–sanctioned treaty that will allow the European Parliament to become the co-equal legislator for almost all European laws.

Treaty of Rome   The 1957 treaty that established the European Community.

tribal totalitarianism   A political system in which a party, group, or individual that represents the interests of a particular tribe (ethnic group) monopolizes political power.

turnkey project   A project in which a firm agrees to set up an operating plant for a foreign client and hand over the "key" when the plant is fully operational.

U

uncertainty avoidance   Extent to which cultures socialize members to accept ambiguous situations and to tolerate uncertainty.

United Nations (UN)   An international organization made up of 193 countries headquartered in New York City, formed in 1945 to promote peace, security, and cooperation.

United Nations Convention on Contracts for the International Sale of Goods (CISG)   A set of rules governing certain aspects of the making and performance of commercial contracts between sellers and buyers who have their places of businesses in different nations.

Universal Declaration of Human Rights   A United Nations document that lays down the basic principles of human rights that should be adhered to.

universal needs   Needs that are the same all over the world, such as steel, bulk chemicals, and industrial electronics.

upstream supply chain   The portion of the supply chain from raw materials to the production facility.

utilitarian approaches to ethics   These hold that the moral worth of actions or practices is determined by their consequences.

V

value creation   Performing activities that increase the value of goods or services to consumers.

values   Abstract ideas about what a society believes to be good, right, and desirable.

voluntary export restraint (VER)   A quota on trade imposed from the exporting country's side, instead of the importer's; usually imposed at the request of the importing country's government.

W

wholly owned subsidiary   A subsidiary in which the firm owns 100 percent of the stock.

World Bank   International institution set up to promote general economic development in the world's poorer nations.

World Intellectual Property Organization   An international organization whose members sign treaties to agree to protect intellectual property.

World Trade Organization (WTO)   The organization that succeeded the General Agreement on Tariffs and Trade (GATT) as a result of the successful completion of the Uruguay Round of GATT negotiations.

Z

zero-sum game   A situation in which an economic gain by one country results in an economic loss by another.

ORGANIZATION INDEX

NAME INDEX

SUBJECT INDEX